GO!

with Microsoft®

Office 2007

Introductory
Second Edition

Shelley Gaskin, Robert L. Ferrett, Alicia Vargas, and Suzanne Marks

PEARSON

Prentice Hall

Upper Saddle River, New Jersey

This book is dedicated to my students, who inspire me every day, and to my husband, Fred Gaskin.
—Shelley Gaskin

I dedicate this book to my granddaughters, who bring me great joy and happiness: Clara and Siena.
—Robert L. Ferrett

This book is dedicated with all my love to my husband Vic, who makes everything possible;
and to my children Victor, Phil, and Emmy, who are an unending source of inspiration
and who make everything worthwhile.
—Alicia Vargas

This book is dedicated with much love to my husband Phil, who is my everything; and to my children
Jeff and Laura, who are the center of my universe.
—Suzanne Marks

Library of Congress Cataloging-in-Publication Data

Go! with Microsoft Office 2007 / Shelley Gaskin ... [et al.]. -- 2nd ed.
   p. cm.
Includes index.
ISBN 0-13-241887-8
1. Microsoft Office. 2. Business--Computer programs. I. Gaskin, Shelley.
HF5548.4.M525G6245 2007
005.5--dc22

2007040821

Vice President and Publisher: Natalie E. Anderson
Associate VP/Executive Acquisitions Editor,
  Print: Stephanie Wall
Executive Acquisitions Editor, Media: Richard Keaveny
Product Development Manager: Eileen Bien Calabro
Editorial Project Manager: Sarah Parker McCabe
Development Editor: Ginny Munroe
Editorial Assistant: Terenia McHenry
Executive Producer: Lisa Strite
Content Development Manager: Cathi Profitko
Media Project Manager: Alana Coles
Production Media Project Manager: Lorena Cerisano
Director of Marketing: Margaret Waples
Senior Marketing Manager: Tori Olson-Alves
Marketing Assistants: Angela Frey, Kathryn Ferranti

Senior Sales Associate: Rebecca Scott
Senior Managing Editor: Cynthia Zonneveld
Associate Managing Editor: Camille Trentacoste
Production Project Manager: Mike Lackey
Production Editor: GGS Book Services
Photo Researcher: GGS Book Services
Operations Specialist: Natacha Moore
Senior Art Director: Jonathan Boylan
Cover Photo: Courtesy of Getty Images, Inc./Marvin
  Mattelson
Composition: GGS Book Services
Project Management: GGS Book Services
Cover Printer: Phoenix Color
Printer/Binder: RR Donnelley/Willard

Microsoft, Windows, Word, PowerPoint, Outlook, FrontPage, Visual Basic, MSN, The Microsoft Network, and/or other Microsoft products referenced herein are either trademarks or registered trademarks of Microsoft Corporation in the U.S.A. and other countries. Screen shots and icons reprinted with permission from the Microsoft Corporation. This book is not sponsored or endorsed by or affiliated with Microsoft Corporation.

Credits and acknowledgments borrowed from other sources and reproduced, with permission, in this textbook are as follows or on the appropriate page within the text.

Pages 2: Getty Images, Inc. – Taxi; pages 86, 332, and 444: iStockphoto.com; page 174: PhotoEdit, Inc.; page 260 Omni-Photo Communications, Inc.; page 528: Dorling Kindersley Media Library; page 610: Index Stock Imagery, Inc.; page 816: Getty Images, Inc. – Liaison; page 916: Rough Guides Dorling Kindersley; page 992: AGE Fotostock America, Inc.; and page 1076: The Stock Connection.

10 9 8 7 6 5 4 3
ISBN 10: 0-13-241887-8
ISBN 13: 978-0-13-241887-4

Contents in Brief

Table of Contents

Excel 2007

Chapter 9 Creating a Worksheet and Charting Data 333

PowerPoint 2007

Chapter 15 Getting Started with Microsoft PowerPoint 2007 915

Chapter 16 Designing a PowerPoint Presentation 993

Letter from the Editor

Dear Instructors and Students,

The primary goal of the *GO!* Series is two-fold. The first goal is to help instructors teach the course they want in less time. The second goal is to provide students with the skills to solve business problems using the computer as a tool, for both themselves and the organization for which they might be employed.

The *GO!* Series was originally created by Series Editor Shelley Gaskin and published with the release of Microsoft Office 2003. Her ideas came from years of using textbooks that didn't meet all the needs of today's diverse classroom and that were too confusing for students. Shelley continues to enhance the series by ensuring we stay true to our vision of developing quality instruction and useful classroom tools.

But we also need your input and ideas.

Over time, the *GO!* Series has evolved based on direct feedback from instructors and students using the series. *We are the publisher that listens.* To publish a textbook that works for you, it's critical that we continue to listen to this feedback. It's important to me to talk with you and hear your stories about using *GO!* Your voice can make a difference.

My hope is that this letter will inspire you to write me an e-mail and share your thoughts on using the *GO!* Series.

Stephanie Wall
Executive Editor, *GO!* Series
stephanie_wall@prenhall.com

GO! System Contributors

We thank the following people for their hard work and support in making the *GO!* System all that it is!

Additional Author Support

Bell, Susan	Mendocino College
Coyle, Diane	Montgomery County Community College
Fry, Susan	Boise State
Townsend, Kris	Spokane Falls Community College
Stroup, Tracey	Amgen Corporation

Instructor Resource Authors

Amer, Beverly	Northern Arizona University	Paterson, Jim	Paradise Valley Community College
Boito, Nancy	Harrisburg Area Community College	Prince, Lisa	Missouri State
Coyle, Diane	Montgomery County Community College	Rodgers, Gwen	Southern Nazarene University
Dawson, Tamara	Southern Nazarene University	Ruymann, Amy	Burlington Community College
Driskel, Loretta	Niagara County Community College	Ryan, Bob	Montgomery County Community
Elliott, Melissa	Odessa College		College
Fry, Susan	Boise State	Smith, Diane	Henry Ford Community College
Geoghan, Debra	Bucks County Community College	Spangler, Candice	Columbus State Community College
Hearn, Barbara	Community College of Philadelphia	Thompson, Joyce	Lehigh Carbon Community College
Jones, Stephanie	South Plains College	Tiffany, Janine	Reading Area Community College
Madsen, Donna	Kirkwood Community College	Watt, Adrienne	Douglas College
Meck, Kari	Harrisburg Area Community College	Weaver, Paul	Bossier Parish Community College
Miller, Cindy	Ivy Tech	Weber, Sandy	Gateway Technical College
Nowakowski, Tony	Buffalo State	Wood, Dawn	
Pace, Phyllis	Queensborough Community College	Weissman, Jonathan	Finger Lakes Community College

Super Reviewers

Brotherton, Cathy	Riverside Community College	Maurer, Trina	Odessa College
Cates, Wally	Central New Mexico Community	Meck, Kari	Harrisburg Area Community College
	College	Miller, Cindy	Ivy Tech Community College
Cone, Bill	Northern Arizona University	Nielson, Phil	Salt Lake Community College
Coverdale, John	Riverside Community College	Rodgers, Gwen	Southern Nazarene University
Foster, Nancy	Baker College	Smolenski, Robert	Delaware Community College
Helfand, Terri	Chaffey College	Spangler, Candice	Columbus State Community College
Hibbert, Marilyn	Salt Lake Community College	Thompson, Joyce	Lehigh Carbon Community College
Holliday, Mardi	Community College of Philadelphia	Weber, Sandy	Gateway Technical College
Jerry, Gina	Santa Monica College	Wells, Lorna	Salt Lake Community College
Martin, Carol	Harrisburg Area Community College	Zaboski, Maureen	University of Scranton

Technical Editors

Janice Snyder
Joyce Nielsen
Colette Eisele
Janet Pickard
Mara Zebest
Lindsey Allen
William Daley
LeeAnn Bates

Student Reviewers

Allen, John	Asheville-Buncombe Tech	Erickson, Mike	Ball State University
	Community College	Gadomski, Amanda	Northern Michigan University
Alexander, Steven	St. Johns River Community College	Gyselinck, Craig	Central Washington University
Alexander, Melissa	Tulsa Community College	Harrison, Margo	Central Washington University
Bolz, Stephanie	Northern Michigan University	Heacox, Kate	Central Washington University
Berner, Ashley	Central Washington University	Hill, Cheretta	Northwestern State University
Boomer, Michelle	Northern Michigan University	Innis, Tim	Tulsa Community College
Busse, Brennan	Northern Michigan University	Jarboe, Aaron	Central Washington University
Butkey, Maura	Central Washington University	Klein, Colleen	Northern Michigan University
Christensen, Kaylie	Northern Michigan University	Moeller, Jeffrey	Northern Michigan University
Connally, Brianna	Central Washington University	Nicholson, Regina	Athens Tech College
Davis, Brandon	Northern Michigan University	Niehaus, Kristina	Northern Michigan University
Davis, Christen	Central Washington University	Nisa, Zaibun	Santa Rosa Community College
Den Boer, Lance	Central Washington University	Nunez, Nohelia	Santa Rosa Community College
Dix, Jessica	Central Washington University	Oak, Samantha	Central Washington University
Moeller, Jeffrey	Northern Michigan University	Oertii, Monica	Central Washington University
Downs, Elizabeth	Central Washington University	Palenshus, Juliet	Central Washington University

Pohl, Amanda	Northern Michigan University	Shanahan, Megan	Northern Michigan University
Presnell, Randy	Central Washington University	Teska, Erika	Hawaii Pacific University
Ritner, April	Northern Michigan University	Traub, Amy	Northern Michigan University
Rodriguez, Flavia	Northwestern State University	Underwood, Katie	Central Washington University
Roberts, Corey	Tulsa Community College	Walters, Kim	Central Washington University
Rossi, Jessica Ann	Central Washington University	Wilson, Kelsie	Central Washington University
Shafapay, Natasha	Central Washington University	Wilson, Amanda	Green River Community College

Series Reviewers

Abraham, Reni	Houston Community College
Agatston, Ann	Agatston Consulting Technical College
Alexander, Melody	Ball Sate University
Alejandro, Manuel	Southwest Texas Junior College
Ali, Farha	Lander University
Amici, Penny	Harrisburg Area Community College
Anderson, Patty A.	Lake City Community College
Andrews, Wilma	Virginia Commonwealth College, Nebraska University
Anik, Mazhar	Tiffin University
Armstrong, Gary	Shippensburg University
Atkins, Bonnie	Delaware Technical Community College
Bachand, LaDonna	Santa Rosa Community College
Bagui, Sikha	University of West Florida
Beecroft, Anita	Kwantlen University College
Bell, Paula	Lock Haven College
Belton, Linda	Springfield Tech. Community College
Bennett, Judith	Sam Houston State University
Bhatia, Sai	Riverside Community College
Bishop, Frances	DeVry Institute—Alpharetta (ATL)
Blaszkiewicz, Holly	Ivy Tech Community College/Region 1
Branigan, Dave	DeVry University
Bray, Patricia	Allegany College of Maryland
Brotherton, Cathy	Riverside Community College
Buehler, Lesley	Ohlone College
Buell, C	Central Oregon Community College
Byars, Pat	Brookhaven College
Byrd, Lynn	Delta State University, Cleveland, Mississippi
Cacace, Richard N.	Pensacola Junior College
Cadenhead, Charles	Brookhaven College
Calhoun, Ric	Gordon College
Cameron, Eric	Passaic Community College
Carriker, Sandra	North Shore Community College
Cannamore, Madie	Kennedy King
Carreon, Cleda	Indiana University—Purdue University, Indianapolis
Chaffin, Catherine	Shawnee State University
Chauvin, Marg	Palm Beach Community College, Boca Raton
Challa, Chandrashekar	Virginia State University
Chamlou, Afsaneh	NOVA Alexandria
Chapman, Pam	Wabaunsee Community College
Christensen, Dan	Iowa Western Community College
Clay, Betty	Southeastern Oklahoma State University
Collins, Linda D.	Mesa Community College
Conroy-Link, Janet	Holy Family College
Cosgrove, Janet	Northwestern CT Community
Courtney, Kevin	Hillsborough Community College
Cox, Rollie	Madison Area Technical College
Crawford, Hiram	Olive Harvey College
Crawford, Thomasina	Miami-Dade College, Kendall Campus
Credico, Grace	Lethbridge Community College
Crenshaw, Richard	Miami Dade Community College, North
Crespo, Beverly	Mt. San Antonio College
Crossley, Connie	Cincinnati State Technical Community College
Curik, Mary	Central New Mexico Community College
De Arazoza, Ralph	Miami Dade Community College
Danno, John	DeVry University/Keller Graduate School
Davis, Phillip	Del Mar College
DeHerrera, Laurie	Pikes Peak Community College
Delk, Dr. K. Kay	Seminole Community College
Doroshow, Mike	Eastfield College
Douglas, Gretchen	SUNYCortland
Dove, Carol	Community College of Allegheny
Driskel, Loretta	Niagara Community College
Duckwiler, Carol	Wabaunsee Community College
Duncan, Mimi	University of Missouri-St. Louis
Duthie, Judy	Green River Community College
Duvall, Annette	Central New Mexico Community College
Ecklund, Paula	Duke University
Eng, Bernice	Brookdale Community College
Evans, Billie	Vance-Granville Community College
Feuerbach, Lisa	Ivy Tech East Chicago
Fisher, Fred	Florida State University
Foster, Penny L.	Anne Arundel Community College
Foszcz, Russ	McHenry County College
Fry, Susan	Boise State University
Fustos, Janos	Metro State
Gallup, Jeanette	Blinn College
Gelb, Janet	Grossmont College
Gentry, Barb	Parkland College
Gerace, Karin	St. Angela Merici School
Gerace, Tom	Tulane University
Ghajar, Homa	Oklahoma State University
Gifford, Steve	Northwest Iowa Community College
Glazer, Ellen	Broward Community College
Gordon, Robert	Hofstra University
Gramlich, Steven	Pasco-Hernando Community College
Graviett, Nancy M.	St. Charles Community College, St. Peters, Missouri
Greene, Rich	Community College of Allegheny County
Gregoryk, Kerry	Virginia Commonwealth State
Griggs, Debra	Bellevue Community College
Grimm, Carol	Palm Beach Community College
Hahn, Norm	Thomas Nelson Community College
Hammerschlag, Dr. Bill	Brookhaven College
Hansen, Michelle	Davenport University
Hayden, Nancy	Indiana University—Purdue University, Indianapolis

Hayes, Theresa	Broward Community College
Helfand, Terri	Chaffey College
Helms, Liz	Columbus State Community College
Hernandez, Leticia	TCI College of Technology
Hibbert, Marilyn	Salt Lake Community College
Hoffman, Joan	Milwaukee Area Technical College
Hogan, Pat	Cape Fear Community College
Holland, Susan	Southeast Community College
Hopson, Bonnie	Athens Technical College
Horvath, Carrie	Albertus Magnus College
Horwitz, Steve	Community College of Philadelphia
Hotta, Barbara	Leeward Community College
Howard, Bunny	St. Johns River Community
Howard, Chris	DeVry University
Huckabay, Jamie	Austin Community College
Hudgins, Susan	East Central University
Hulett, Michelle J.	Missouri State University
Hunt, Darla A.	Morehead State University, Morehead, Kentucky
Hunt, Laura	Tulsa Community College
Jacob, Sherry	Jefferson Community College
Jacobs, Duane	Salt Lake Community College
Jauken, Barb	Southeastern Community
Johnson, Kathy	Wright College
Johnson, Mary	Kingwood College
Johnson, Mary	Mt. San Antonio College
Jones, Stacey	Benedict College
Jones, Warren	University of Alabama, Birmingham
Jordan, Cheryl	San Juan College
Kapoor, Bhushan	California State University, Fullerton
Kasai, Susumu	Salt Lake Community College
Kates, Hazel	Miami Dade Community College, Kendall
Keen, Debby	University of Kentucky
Keeter, Sandy	Seminole Community College
Kern-Blystone, Dorothy Jean	Bowling Green State
Keskin, Ilknur	The University of South Dakota
Kirk, Colleen	Mercy College
Kleckner, Michelle	Elon University
Kliston, Linda	Broward Community College, North Campus
Kochis, Dennis	Suffolk County Community College
Kramer, Ed	Northern Virginia Community College
Laird, Jeff	Northeast State Community College
Lamoureaux, Jackie	Central New Mexico Community College
Lange, David	Grand Valley State
LaPointe, Deb	Central New Mexico Community College
Larson, Donna	Louisville Technical Institute
Laspina, Kathy	Vance-Granville Community College
Le Grand, Dr. Kate	Broward Community College
Lenhart, Sheryl	Terra Community College
Letavec, Chris	University of Cincinnati
Liefert, Jane	Everett Community College
Lindaman, Linda	Black Hawk Community College
Lindberg, Martha	Minnesota State University
Lightner, Renee	Broward Community College
Lindberg, Martha	Minnesota State University
Linge, Richard	Arizona Western College
Logan, Mary G.	Delgado Community College
Loizeaux, Barbara	Westchester Community College
Lopez, Don	Clovis-State Center Community College District

Lord, Alexandria	Asheville Buncombe Tech
Lowe, Rita	Harold Washington College
Low, Willy Hui	Joliet Junior College
Lucas, Vickie	Broward Community College
Lynam, Linda	Central Missouri State University
Lyon, Lynne	Durham College
Lyon, Pat Rajski	Tomball College
MacKinnon, Ruth	Georgia Southern University
Macon, Lisa	Valencia Community College, West Campus
Machuca, Wayne	College of the Sequoias
Madison, Dana	Clarion University
Maguire, Trish	Eastern New Mexico University
Malkan, Rajiv	Montgomery College
Manning, David	Northern Kentucky University
Marcus, Jacquie	Niagara Community College
Marghitu, Daniela	Auburn University
Marks, Suzanne	Bellevue Community College
Marquez, Juanita	El Centro College
Marquez, Juan	Mesa Community College
Martyn, Margie	Baldwin-Wallace College
Marucco, Toni	Lincoln Land Community College
Mason, Lynn	Lubbock Christian University
Matutis, Audrone	Houston Community College
Matkin, Marie	University of Lethbridge
McCain, Evelynn	Boise State University
McCannon, Melinda	Gordon College
McCarthy, Marguerite	Northwestern Business College
McCaskill, Matt L.	Brevard Community College
McClellan, Carolyn	Tidewater Community College
McClure, Darlean	College of Sequoias
McCrory, Sue A.	Missouri State University
McCue, Stacy	Harrisburg Area Community College
McEntire-Orbach, Teresa	Middlesex County College
McLeod, Todd	Fresno City College
McManus, Illyana	Grossmont College
McPherson, Dori	Schoolcraft College
Meiklejohn, Nancy	Pikes Peak Community College
Menking, Rick	Hardin-Simmons University
Meredith, Mary	University of Louisiana at Lafayette
Mermelstein, Lisa	Baruch College
Metos, Linda	Salt Lake Community College
Meurer, Daniel	University of Cincinnati
Meyer, Marian	Central New Mexico Community College
Miller, Cindy	Ivy Tech Community College, Lafayette, Indiana
Mitchell, Susan	Davenport University
Mohle, Dennis	Fresno Community College
Monk, Ellen	University of Delaware
Moore, Rodney	Holland College
Morris, Mike	Southeastern Oklahoma State University
Morris, Nancy	Hudson Valley Community College
Moseler, Dan	Harrisburg Area Community College
Nabors, Brent	Reedley College, Clovis Center
Nadas, Erika	Wright College
Nadelman, Cindi	New England College
Nademlynsky, Lisa	Johnson & Wales University
Ncube, Cathy	University of West Florida
Nagengast, Joseph	Florida Career College
Newsome, Eloise	Northern Virginia Community College Woodbridge
Nicholls, Doreen	Mohawk Valley Community College
Nunan, Karen	Northeast State Technical Community College

Contributors xix

Odegard, Teri — Edmonds Community College
Ogle, Gregory — North Community College
Orr, Dr. Claudia — Northern Michigan University South
Otieno, Derek — DeVry University
Otton, Diana Hill — Chesapeake College
Oxendale, Lucia — West Virginia Institute of Technology

Paiano, Frank — Southwestern College
Patrick, Tanya — Clackamas Community College
Peairs, Deb — Clark State Community College
Prince, Lisa — Missouri State University-Springfield Campus
Proietti, Kathleen — Northern Essex Community College
Pusins, Delores — HCCC
Raghuraman, Ram — Joliet Junior College
Reasoner, Ted Allen — Indiana University—Purdue
Reeves, Karen — High Point University
Remillard, Debbie — New Hampshire Technical Institute
Rhue, Shelly — DeVry University
Richards, Karen — Maplewoods Community College
Richardson, Mary — Albany Technical College
Rodgers, Gwen — Southern Nazarene University
Roselli, Diane — Harrisburg Area Community College
Ross, Dianne — University of Louisiana in Lafayette
Rousseau, Mary — Broward Community College, South
Samson, Dolly — Hawaii Pacific University
Sams, Todd — University of Cincinnati
Sandoval, Everett — Reedley College
Sardone, Nancy — Seton Hall University
Scafide, Jean — Mississippi Gulf Coast Community College
Scheeren, Judy — Westmoreland County Community College
Schneider, Sol — Sam Houston State University
Scroggins, Michael — Southwest Missouri State University
Sever, Suzanne — Northwest Arkansas Community College
Sheridan, Rick — California State University-Chico
Silvers, Pamela — Asheville Buncombe Tech
Singer, Steven A. — University of Hawai'i, Kapi'olani Community College
Sinha, Atin — Albany State University
Skolnick, Martin — Florida Atlantic University
Smith, T. Michael — Austin Community College
Smith, Tammy — Tompkins Cortland Community Collge
Smolenski, Bob — Delaware County Community College
Spangler, Candice — Columbus State
Stedham, Vicki — St. Petersburg College, Clearwater
Stefanelli, Greg — Carroll Community College
Steiner, Ester — New Mexico State University
Stenlund, Neal — Northern Virginia Community College, Alexandria
St. John, Steve — Tulsa Community College

Sterling, Janet — Houston Community College
Stoughton, Catherine — Laramie County Community College
Sullivan, Angela — Joliet Junior College
Szurek, Joseph — University of Pittsburgh at Greensburg
Tarver, Mary Beth — Northwestern State University
Taylor, Michael — Seattle Central Community College
Thangiah, Sam — Slippery Rock University
Thompson-Sellers, Ingrid — Georgia Perimeter College
Tomasi, Erik — Baruch College
Toreson, Karen — Shoreline Community College
Trifiletti, John J. — Florida Community College at Jacksonville
Trivedi, Charulata — Quinsigamond Community College, Woodbridge
Tucker, William — Austin Community College
Turgeon, Cheryl — Asnuntuck Community College
Turpen, Linda — Central New Mexico Community College
Upshaw, Susan — Del Mar College
Unruh, Angela — Central Washington University
Vanderhoof, Dr. Glenna — Missouri State University-Springfield Campus
Vargas, Tony — El Paso Community College
Vicars, Mitzi — Hampton University
Villarreal, Kathleen — Fresno
Vitrano, Mary Ellen — Palm Beach Community College
Volker, Bonita — Tidewater Community College
Wahila, Lori (Mindy) — Tompkins Cortland Community College
Waswick, Kim — Southeast Community College, Nebraska
Wavle, Sharon — Tompkins Cortland Community College
Webb, Nancy — City College of San Francisco
Wells, Barbara E. — Central Carolina Technical College
Wells, Lorna — Salt Lake Community College
Welsh, Jean — Lansing Community College Nebraska
White, Bruce — Quinnipiac University
Willer, Ann — Solano Community College
Williams, Mark — Lane Community College
Wilson, Kit — Red River College
Wilson, Roger — Fairmont State University
Wimberly, Leanne — International Academy of Design and Technology
Worthington, Paula — Northern Virginia Community College
Yauney, Annette — Herkimer County Community College
Yip, Thomas — Passaic Community College
Zavala, Ben — Webster Tech
Zlotow, Mary Ann — College of DuPage
Zudeck, Steve — Broward Community College, North

About the Authors

Shelley Gaskin, Series Editor, is a professor of business and computer technology at Pasadena City College in Pasadena, California. She holds a master's degree in business education from Northern Illinois University and a doctorate in adult and community education from Ball State University. Dr. Gaskin has 15 years of experience in the computer industry with several Fortune 500 companies and has developed and written training materials for custom systems applications in both the public and private sector. She is also the author of books on Microsoft Outlook and word processing.

Robert L. Ferrett recently retired as the director of the Center for Instructional Computing at Eastern Michigan University, where he provided computer training and support to faculty. He has authored or co-authored more than 70 books on Access, PowerPoint, Excel, Publisher, WordPerfect, and Word. Before writing for the GO! Series, Bob was a series editor and author for the Learn Series. He has a bachelor's degree in psychology, a master's degree in geography, and a master's degree in interdisciplinary technology from Eastern Michigan University. Bob's doctoral studies were in instructional technology at Wayne State University. For fun, Bob teaches a four-week computers and genealogy class and has written genealogy and local history books.

Alicia Vargas is a faculty member in Business Information Technology at Pasadena City College. She holds a master's and a bachelor's degree in business education from California State University, Los Angeles, and has authored several textbooks and training manuals on Microsoft Word, Microsoft Excel, and Microsoft PowerPoint.

Suzanne Marks is a faculty member in Business Technology Systems at Bellevue Community College, Bellevue, Washington. She holds a bachelor's degree in business education from Washington State University, and was project manager for the first IT Skills Standards in the United States.

Visual Walk-Through of the *GO!* System

The *GO!* System is designed for ease of implementation on the instructor side and ease of understanding on the student. It has been completely developed based on professor and student feedback.

The *GO!* System is divided into three categories that reflect how you might organize your course— **Prepare**, **Teach**, and **Assess**.

Prepare

NEW

Transition Guide

New to *GO!*–We've made it quick and easy to plan the format and activities for your class.

GO!

Because the GO! System was designed and written by instructors like yourself, it includes the tools that allow you to Prepare, Teach, and Assess in your course. We have organized the GO! System into these three categories that match how you work through your course and thus, it's even easier for you to implement.

To help you get started, here is an outline of the first activities you may want to do in order to conduct your course.

There are several other tools not listed here that are available in the GO! System so please refer to your GO! Guide for a complete listing of all the tools.

Prepare
1. Prepare the course syllabus
2. Plan the course assignments
3. Organize the student resources

Teach
4. Conduct demonstrations and lectures

Assess
5. Assign and grade assignments, quizzes, tests, and assessments

PREPARE

1. Prepare the course syllabus

A syllabus template is provided on the IRCD in the **go07_syllabus_template** folder of the main directory. It includes a course calendar planner for 8-week, 12-week, and 16-week formats. Depending on your term (summer or regular semester) you can modify one of these according to your course plan, and then add information pertinent to your course and institution.

2. Plan course assignments

For each chapter, an Assignment Sheet listing every in-chapter and end-of-chapter project is located on the IRCD within the **go01_gooffice2007intro_instructor_resources_by_chapter** folder. From there, navigate to the specific chapter folder. These sheets are Word tables, so you can delete rows for the projects that you choose not to assign or add rows for your own assignments—if any. There is a column to add the number of points you want to assign to each project depending on your grading scheme. At the top of the sheet, you can fill in the course information.

Transitioning to GO! Office 2007   Page 1 of 1

Syllabus Template

Includes course calendar planner for 8-,12-, and 16-week formats.

GO! with Microsoft Office 2007 Introductory
SAMPLE SYLLABUS (16 weeks)

I. COURSE INFORMATION

Course No.:   Semester:
Course Title: Credits:
Course Hours:

Instructor: Office:
Office Hours:
Email: Phone:

II. TEXT AND MATERIALS

Before starting the course, you will need the following:

> GO! with Microsoft Office 2007 Introductory by Shelley Gaskin, Robert L. Ferrett, Alicia Vargas, Suzanne Marks ©2007, published by Pearson Prentice Hall. ISBN 0-13-167990-6

> Storage device for saving files (any of the following: multiple diskettes, CD-RW, flash drive, etc.)

III. WHAT YOU WILL LEARN IN THIS COURSE

This is a hands-on course where you will learn to use a computer to practice the most commonly used Microsoft programs including the Windows operating system, Internet Explorer for navigating the Internet, Outlook for managing your personal information and the four most popular programs within the Microsoft Office Suite (Word, Excel, PowerPoint and Access). You will also practice the basics of using a computer, mouse and keyboard. You will learn to be an intermediate level user of the Microsoft Office Suite.

Within the Microsoft Office Suite, you will use Word, Excel, PowerPoint, and Access. Microsoft Word is a word processing program with which you can create common business and personal documents. Microsoft Excel is a spreadsheet program that organizes and calculates accounting-type information. Microsoft PowerPoint is a presentation graphics program with which you can develop slides to accompany an oral presentation. Finally, Microsoft Access is a database program that organizes large amounts of information in a useful manner.

Assignment Sheet

One per chapter. Lists all possible assignments; add to and delete from this simple Word table according to your course plan.

Assignment Sheet for GO! with Microsoft Office 2007 Introductory — Chapter 5

GO! with Microsoft Office 2007 Introductory

**Assignment Sheet for GO! with Microsoft Office 2007 Introductory
Chapter 5**

Instructor Name: _____
Course Information: _____

Do This (✔ when done)	Then Hand in This Check each Project for the elements listed on the Assignment Tag. Attach the Tag to your Project.	Submit Printed Formulas	By This Date	Possible Points	Your Points
Study the text and perform the steps for Activities 5.1 – 5.11	Project 5A Application Letter				
Study the text and perform the steps for Activities 5.12 – 5.23	Project 5B Company Overview				
End-of-Chapter Assessments					
Complete the Matching and Fill-in-the-Blank questions	As directed by your instructor				
Complete Project 5C	Project 5C Receipt Letter				
Complete Project 5D	Project 5D Marketing				
Complete Project 5E	Project 5E School Tour				
Complete Project 5F	Project 5F Scouting Trip				
Complete Project 5G	Project 5G Contract				
Complete Project 5H	Project 5H Invitation				
Complete Project 5I	Project 5I Fax Cover				
Complete Project 5J	Project 5J Business Running Case				
Complete Project 5K	Project 5K Services				
Complete Project 5L	Project 5L Survey Form				
Complete Project 5M	Project 5M Press Release				

Copyright © 2008 Pearson Prentice Hall   Page 1 of 1

File Guide to the *GO!* Supplements

Tabular listing of all supplements and their file names.

Assignment Planning Guide

Description of *GO!* assignments with recommendations based on class size, delivery mode, and student needs. Includes examples from fellow instructors.

GO! with Microsoft Office 2007 Introductory Assignment Planning Guide

Planning the Course Assignments

For each chapter in GO!, an Assignment Sheet listing every in-chapter and end-of-chapter project is located on the IRCD. These sheets are Word tables, so you can delete rows for the projects that you will not assign, and then add rows for any of your own assignments that you may have developed. There is a column to add the number of points you want to assign to each project—depending on your grading scheme. At the top of the sheet, you can fill in your course information.

Additionally, for each chapter, student Assignment Tags are provided for every project (including Problem Solving projects)—also located on the IRCD. These are small scoring checklists on which you can check off errors made by the student, and with which the student can verify that all project elements are complete. For campus classes, the student can attach the tags to his or her paper submissions. For online classes, many GO! instructors have the student include these with the electronic submission.

Deciding What to Assign

Front Portion of the Chapter—Instructional Projects: The projects in the front portion of the chapter, which are listed on the first page of each chapter, are the instructional projects. Most instructors assign all of these projects, because this is where the student receives the instruction and engages in the active learning.

End-of-Chapter—Practice and Critical Thinking Projects: In the back portion of the chapter (the gray pages), you can assign on a prescriptive basis; that is, for students who were challenged by the instructional projects, you might assign one or more projects from the two *Skills Reviews*, which provide maximum prompting and a thorough review of the entire chapter. For students who have previous software knowledge and who completed the instructional projects easily, you might assign only the *Mastery Projects*.

You can also assign prescriptively by Objective, because each end-of-chapter project indicates the Objectives covered. So you might assign, on a student-by-student basis, only the projects that cover the Objectives with which the student seemed to have difficulty in the instructional projects.

The five Problem Solving projects and the You and GO! project are the authentic assessments that pull together the student's learning. Here the student is presented with a "messy real-life situation" and then uses his or her knowledge and skill to solve a problem, produce a product, give a presentation, or demonstrate a procedure. You might assign one or more of the Problem

GO! Assignment Planning Guide   Page 1 of 1

Student Data Files

Music School Records discovers, launches, and and develops the careers of young artists in classical, jazz, and contemporary music. Our philosophy is to not only shape, distribute, and sell a music product, but to help artists create a career that can lats a lifetime. too often in the music industry, artists are forced to fit their music to a trend that is short-lived. Music School Records doesn't just follow trends, we take a long-term view of the music industry and help our artists develop a style and repertiore that is fluid and flexible and that will appeal to audiences for years and even decades.

The music industry is constantly changing, but over the last decade the changes have been enormous. New forms of entertainment such as DVDs, video games, and the Internet mean there are more competition for the leisure dollar in the market. New technologies give consomers more options for buying and listening to music, and they are demaning high quality recordings. Young consomers are comfortable with technology and want the music they love when and where they want it, no matter where they are or what they are doing.

Music School Records embraces new technologies and the sophisticated market of young music lovers. We believe that providing high quality recordings of truly talented artists make for more discerning listeners who will cherish the gift of music for the rest of their lives. The expertise of Music School Records includes:

- Insight into our target market and the ability to reach the desired audience
- The ability to access all current sources of music income
- A management team with years of experience in music commerce
- Innovative business strategies and artist development plans
- Investment in technology infrastructure for high quality recordings and business services
- Initiative and proactive management of artist careers

Online Study Guide for Students

Interactive objective-style questions based on chapter content.

PowerPoint Slides

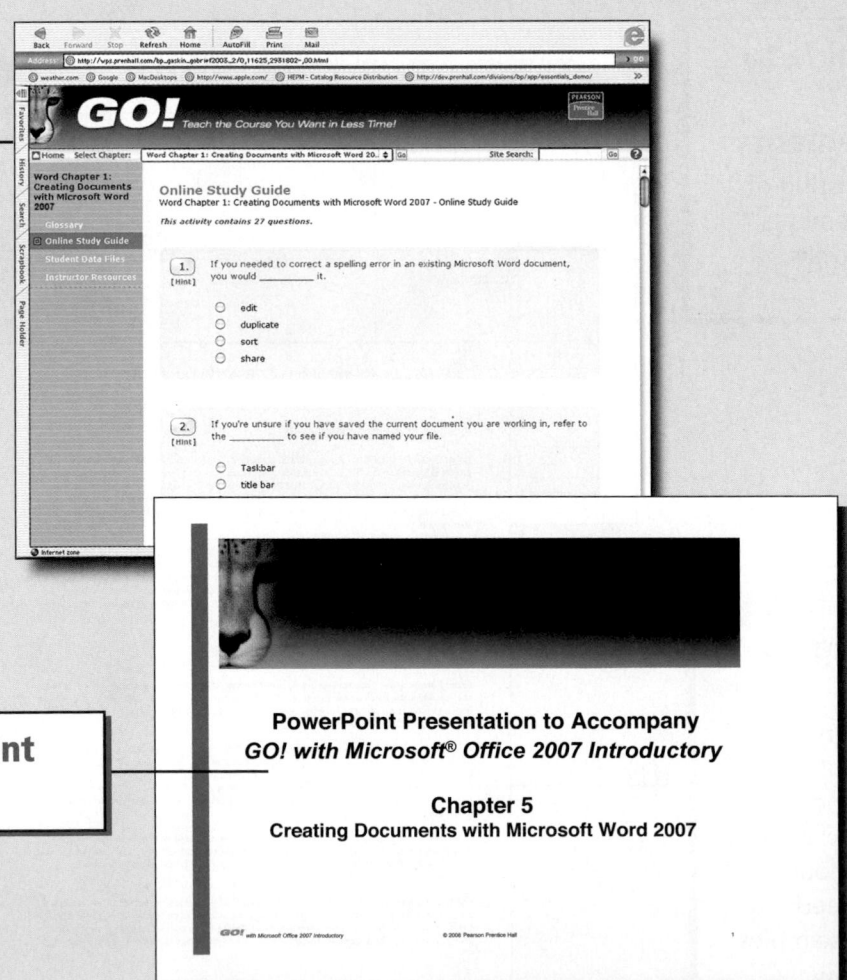

Teach

Student Textbook

Learning Objectives and Student Outcomes

Objectives are clustered around projects that result in student outcomes. They help students learn how to solve problems, not just learn software features.

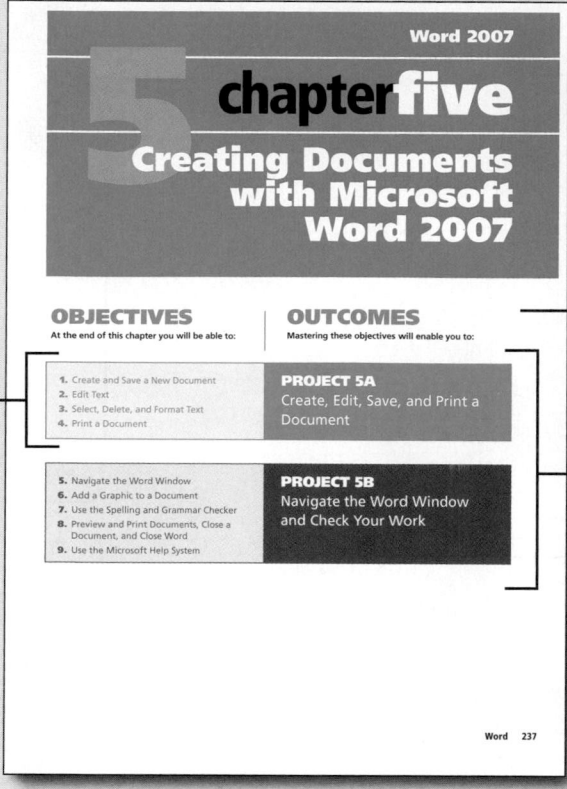

Project-Based Instruction

Students do not practice features of the application; they create real projects that they will need in the real world. Projects are color coded for easy reference and are named to reflect skills the students will be practicing.

A and B Projects

Each chapter contains two instructional projects—A and B.

Each chapter opens with a story that sets the stage for the projects the student will create; the instruction does not force the student to pretend to be someone or make up a scenario.

Each chapter has an introductory paragraph that briefs students on what is important.

Visual Summary

Shows students upfront what their projects will look like when they are done.

Project Summary

Stated clearly and quickly in one paragraph.

NEW

File Guide

Clearly shows students which files are needed for the project and the names they will use to save their documents.

Objective

The skills the student will learn are clearly stated at the beginning of each project and color coded to match projects listed on the chapter opener page.

Teachable Moment

Expository text is woven into the steps—at the moment students need to know it—not chunked together in a block of text that will go unread.

NEW

Screen Shots

Larger screen shots.

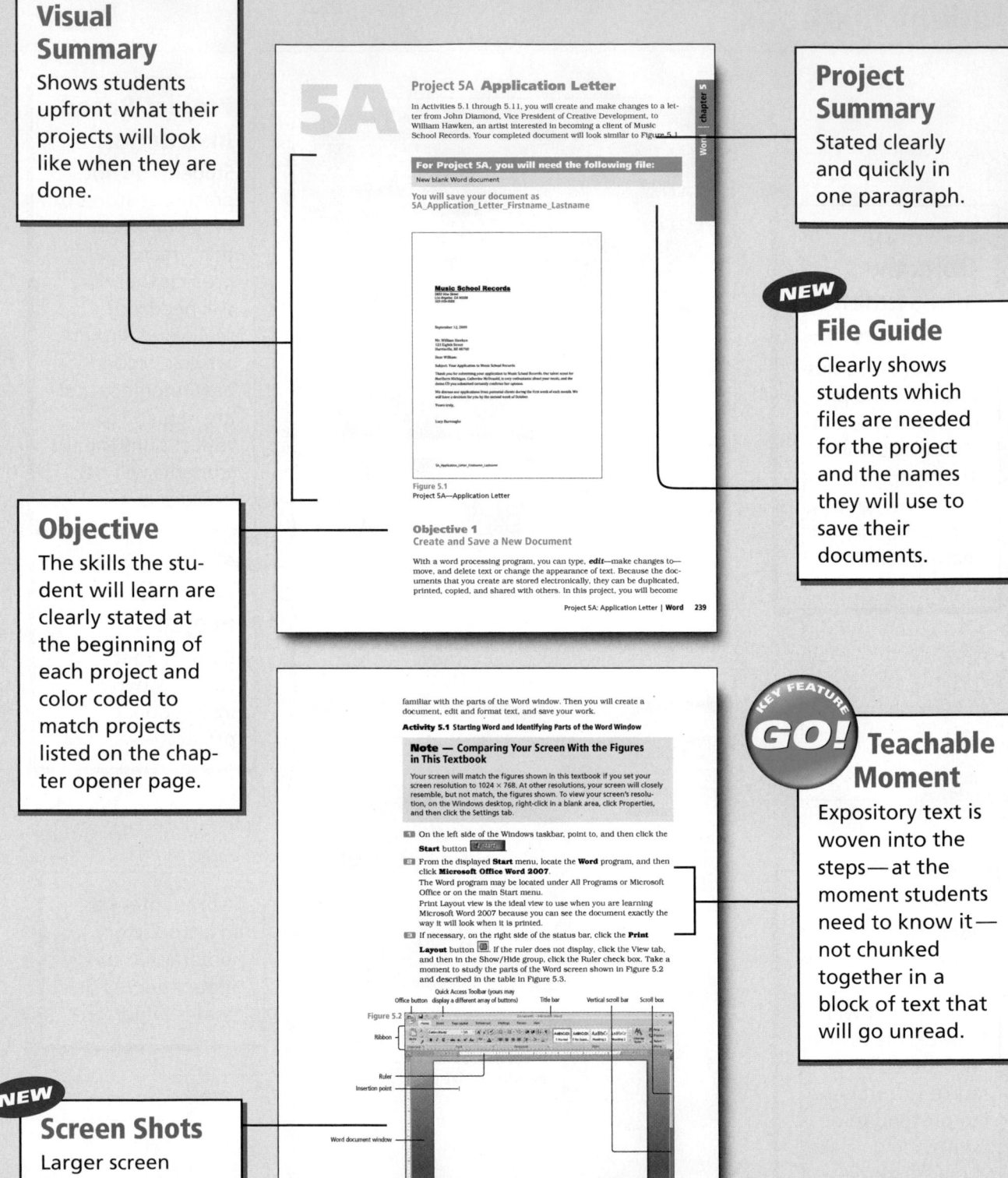

Steps

Color coded to the current project, easy to read, and not too many to confuse the student or too few to be meaningless.

KEY FEATURE GO! Sequential Pagination

No more confusing letters and abbreviations.

KEY FEATURE GO! Microsoft Procedural Syntax

All steps are written in Microsoft Procedural Syntax to put the student in the right place at the right time.

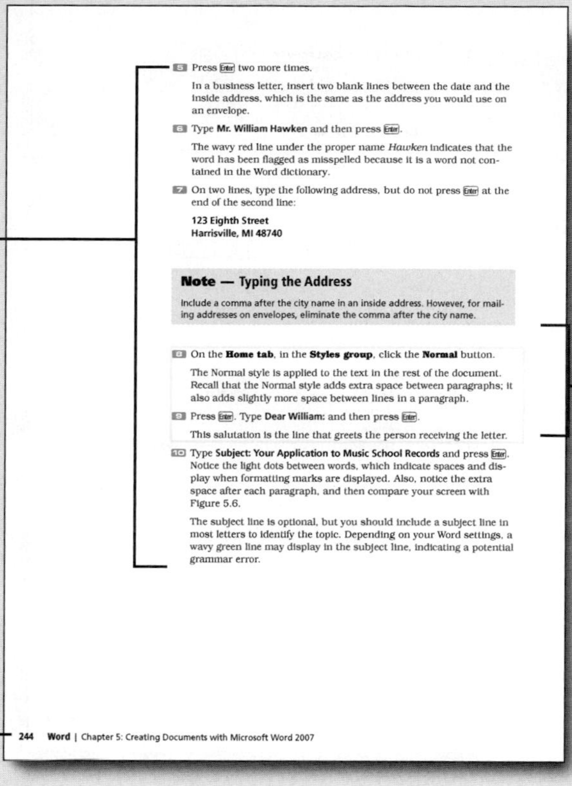

5 Press Enter two more times.

In a business letter, insert two blank lines between the date and the inside address, which is the same as the address you would use on an envelope.

6 Type **Mr. William Hawken** and then press Enter.

The wavy red line under the proper name *Hawken* indicates that the word has been flagged as misspelled because it is a word not contained in the Word dictionary.

7 On two lines, type the following address, but do not press Enter at the end of the second line:

123 Eighth Street
Harrisville, MI 48740

Note — Typing the Address

Include a comma after the city name in an inside address. However, for mailing addresses on envelopes, eliminate the comma after the city name.

8 On the **Home tab**, in the **Styles group**, click the **Normal** button.

The Normal style is applied to the text in the rest of the document. Recall that the Normal style adds extra space between paragraphs; it also adds slightly more space between lines in a paragraph.

9 Press Enter. Type **Dear William:** and then press Enter.

This salutation is the line that greets the person receiving the letter.

10 Type **Subject: Your Application to Music School Records** and press Enter. Notice the light dots between words, which indicate spaces and display when formatting marks are displayed. Also, notice the extra space after each paragraph, and then compare your screen with Figure 5.6.

The subject line is optional, but you should include a subject line in most letters to identify the topic. Depending on your Word settings, a wavy green line may display in the subject line, indicating a potential grammar error.

244 **Word** | Chapter 5: Creating Documents with Microsoft Word 2007

End-of-Project Icon

All projects in the *GO! Series* have clearly identifiable end points, useful in self-paced or online environments.

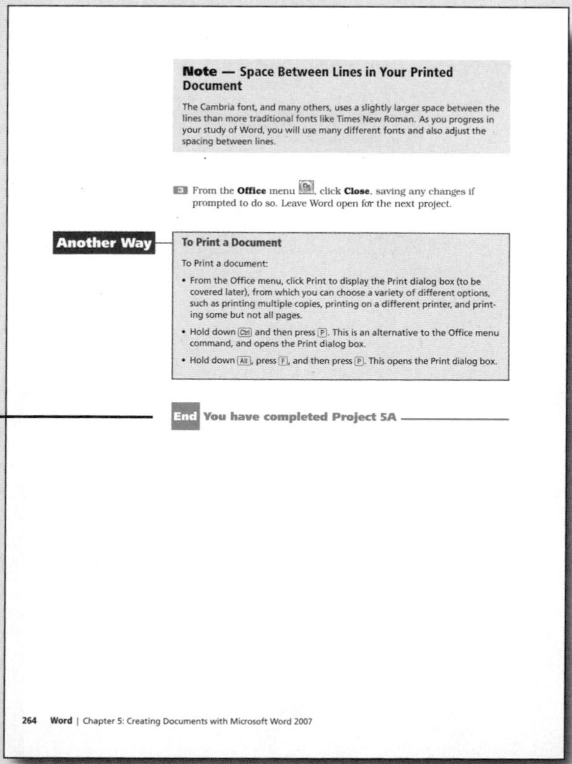

Note — Space Between Lines in Your Printed Document

The Cambria font, and many others, uses a slightly larger space between the lines than more traditional fonts like Times New Roman. As you progress in your study of Word, you will use many different fonts and also adjust the spacing between lines.

3 From the **Office** menu, click **Close**, saving any changes if prompted to do so. Leave Word open for the next project.

Another Way

To Print a Document

To Print a document:

- From the Office menu, click Print to display the Print dialog box (to be covered later), from which you can choose a variety of different options, such as printing multiple copies, printing on a different printer, and printing some but not all pages.
- Hold down Ctrl and then press P. This is an alternative to the Office menu command, and opens the Print dialog box.
- Hold down Alt, press F, and then press P. This opens the Print dialog box.

End You have completed Project 5A

264 **Word** | Chapter 5: Creating Documents with Microsoft Word 2007

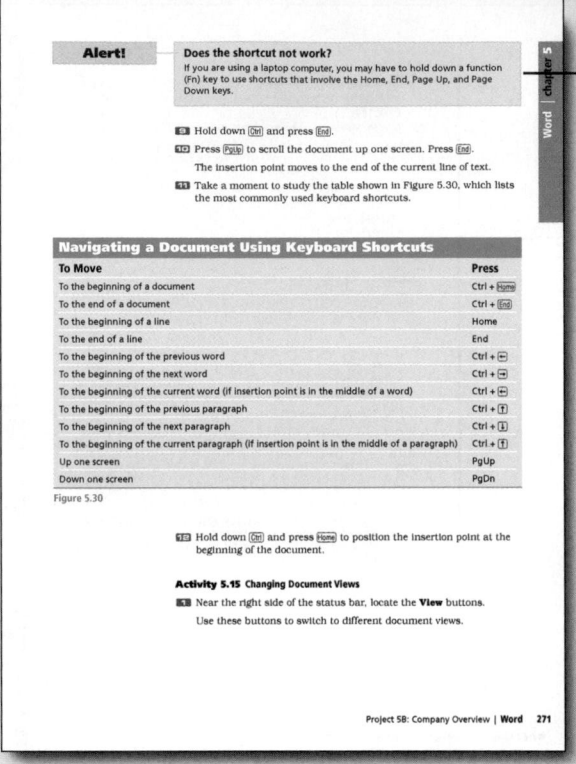

Alert box
Draws students' attention to make sure they aren't getting too far off course.

Another Way box
Shows students other ways of doing tasks.

More Knowledge box
Expands on a topic by going deeper into the material.

Note box
Points out important items to remember.

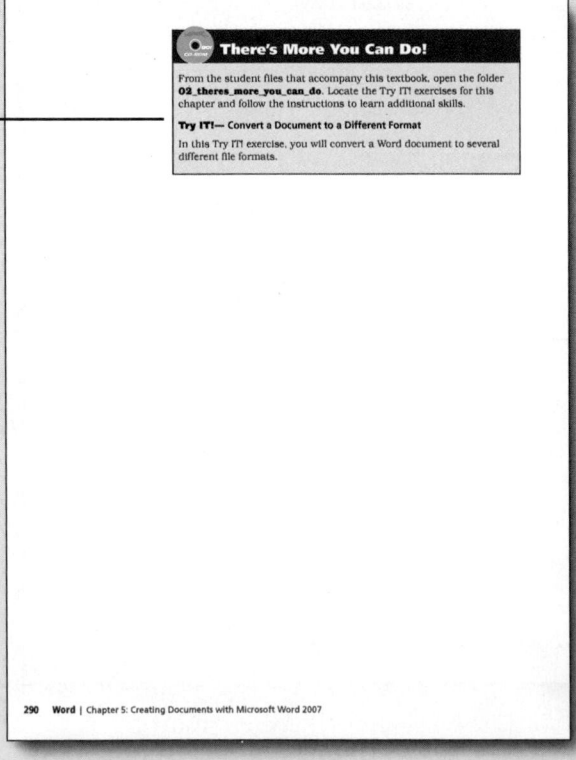

NEW

There's More You Can Do!
Try IT! exercises that teach students additional skills.

Teach (continued)

End-of-Chapter Material

Take your pick! Content-based or Outcomes-based projects to choose from. Below is a table outlining the various types of projects that fit into these two categories.

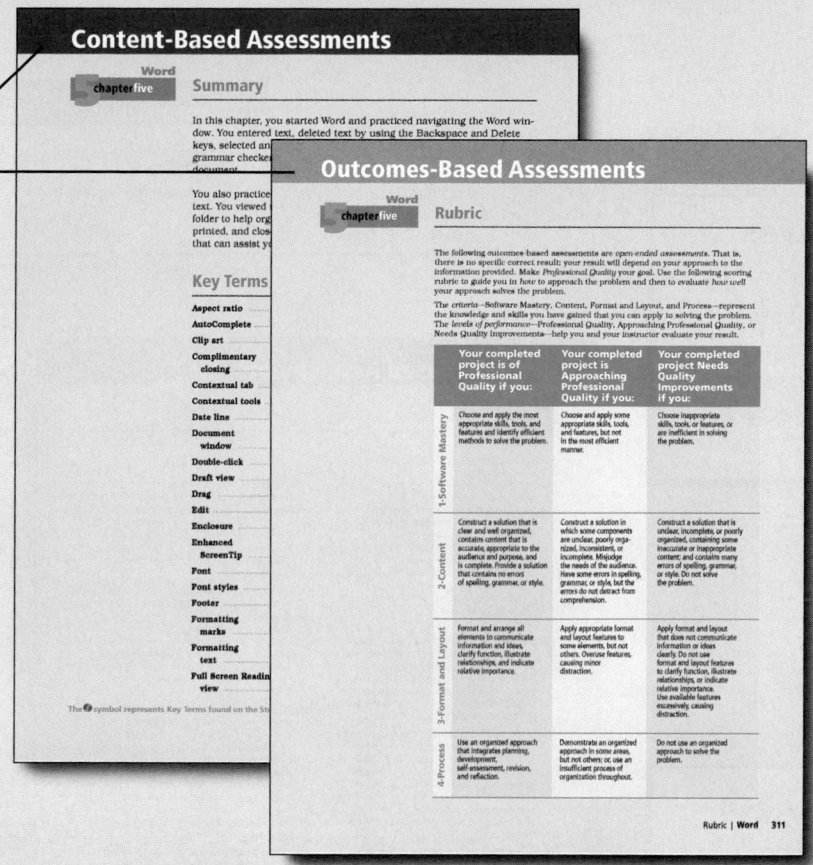

Content-Based Assessments
(Defined solutions with solution files provided for grading)

Project Letter	Name	Objectives Covered
N/A	Summary and Key Terms	
N/A	Multiple Choice	
N/A	Fill-in-the-blank	
C	Skills Review	Covers A Objectives
D	Skills Review	Covers B Objectives
E	Mastering Excel	Covers A Objectives
F	Mastering Excel	Covers B Objectives
G	Mastering Excel	Covers any combination of A and B Objectives
H	Mastering Excel	Covers any combination of A and B Objectives
I	Mastering Excel	Covers all A and B Objectives
J	Business Running Case	Covers all A and B Objectives

Outcomes-Based Assessments
(Open solutions that require a rubric for grading)

Project Letter	Name	Objectives Covered
N/A	Rubric	
K	Problem Solving	Covers as many Objectives from A and B as possible
L	Problem Solving	Covers as many Objectives from A and B as possible.
M	Problem Solving	Covers as many Objectives from A and B as possible.
N	Problem Solving	Covers as many Objectives from A and B as possible.
O	Problem Solving	Covers as many Objectives from A and B as possible.
P	You and GO!	Covers as many Objectives from A and B as possible
Q	GO! Help	Not tied to specific objectives
R	* Group Business Running Case	Covers A and B Objectives

* This project is provided only with the *GO! with Microsoft Office 2007 Introductory* book.

Objectives List

Most projects in the end-of-chapter section begin with a list of the objectives covered.

End of Each Project Clearly Marked

Clearly identified end points help separate the end-of-chapter projects.

Content-Based Assessments

Word
chapter five   Skills Review

Project 5C — Receipt Letter

In this project, you will apply the skills you practiced from the Objectives in Project 5A.

Objectives: 1. Create and Save a New Document; **2.** Edit Text; **3.** Select, Delete, and Format Text; **4.** Print a Document.

In the following Skills Review, you will create and edit a follow-up letter from Jamal Anderssen, a production manager for Music School Records, to William Hawken, a recording artist who has submitted a demo CD with his application. Your completed letter will look similar to the one 5.49.

5C, you will need the following file:
ocument

our document as
ter_Firstname_Lastname

ol Records

ot Letter continues on the next page)

osoft Word 2007

Content-Based Assessments

Word
chapter five   Skills Review

(Project 5C–Receipt Letter continued)

14. Save the changes you have made to your document. Press Ctrl + A to select the entire document. On the **Home tab**, in the **Font group**, click the **Font button arrow**. Scroll as necessary, and watch Live Preview change the document font as you point to different font names. Click to choose **Tahoma**. Recall that you can type *T* in the Font box to move quickly to the fonts beginning with that letter. Click anywhere in the document to cancel the selection.

15. Select the entire first line of text—*Music School Records*. On the Mini toolbar, click the **Font button arrow**, and then click **Arial Black**. With the Mini toolbar still displayed, click the **Font Size button arrow**, and then click **20**. With the Mini toolbar still displayed, click the **Bold** button.

16. Select the second, third, and fourth lines of text, beginning with *2620 Vine Street* and ending with the telephone number. On the Mini toolbar, click the **Font button arrow**, and then click **Arial**. With the Mini toolbar still displayed, click the **Font Size button arrow**, and then click **10**. With the Mini toolbar still displayed, click the **Italic** button.

17. In the paragraph beginning *Your demonstration*, select the text *Music School Records*. On the Mini toolbar, click the **Italic** button, and then click anywhere to deselect the text.

18. Click the **Insert tab**. In the **Header & Footer group**, click the **Footer** button,

and then click **Edit Footer**. On the **Design tab**, in the **Insert group**, click the **Quick Parts** button, and then click **Field**. In the **Field** dialog box, under **Field names**, scroll down and click to choose **FileName**, and then click **OK**. Double-click anywhere in the document to leave the footer area.

19. Click the **Page Layout tab**. In the **Page Setup group**, click the **Margins** button to display the Margins gallery. At the bottom of the **Margins gallery**, click **Custom Margins** to display the **Page Setup** dialog box. Near the top of the **Page Setup** dialog box, click the **Layout tab**. Under **Page**, click the **Vertical alignment arrow**, click **Center**, and then click **OK**.

20. From the **Office** menu, point to the **Print arrow**, and then click **Print Preview** to make a final check of your letter. Follow your instructor's directions for submitting this file. Check your *Chapter Assignment Sheet* or *Course Syllabus* or consult your instructor to determine if you are to submit your assignments on paper or electronically. To submit electronically, go to Step 22, and then follow the instructions provided by your instructor.

21. On the **Print Preview tab**, in the **Print group**, click the **Print** button. Collect your printout from the printer and submit it as directed.

22. From the **Office** menu, click **Exit Word**, saving any changes if prompted to do so.

End You have completed Project 5C —

Content-Based Assessments

Excel
chapter five   Mastering Excel

Project 5K — GO! Fix It

In this project, you will construct a solution by applying any combination of the skills you practiced from the Objectives in Projects 5A and 5B.

For Project 5K, you will need the following file:

e05_fixit_Accessories

You will save your workbook as
5K_Accessories_Firstname_Lastname

From the student files that accompany this textbook, open the folder **05_go_fix_it**. Locate and open the file **w05_fixit_Accessories**, and then save the file in your chapter folder as **5K_Accessories_Firstname_Lastname**

In this project, you will edit the first draft of an Excel workbook that contains information about sales of automotive electronic accessories. The workbook was prepared for Arthur Potempa, Retail Accessories Manager of Rio Rancho Auto Gallery.

This workbook contains **ten errors** that you must find and correct. Read and examine the document, and then edit to correct the errors that you find. Types of errors could include:

- Spelling, grammar, and punctuation errors in cells, charts, worksheet tabs, or file names.
- Errors in data entry and workbook layout. Formatting errors in text, numbers, alignment, indents and spacing, tabs, wrapping, merge and center, text direction and orientation, fonts, borders, patterns, protection, AutoFormat, conditional formatting, data sort, filter, and validation.
- Formula and function errors such as incorrect and missing formulas, error indicators and values, relative vs. absolute cell referencing, What-If Analysis, Paste Special, function arguments, and Goal Seek.
- Errors in object design, layout, and formatting, for example chart type, location, data source, elements, size, scale, positioning, pictures, and hyperlinks.
- Row and column formatting errors such as height, width, and AutoFit.
- Worksheet, tab design, and formatting errors such as missing or blank worksheets, worksheet tab colors, and locations.
- Page setup errors such as page orientation and scaling, margins and centering, headers and footers, sheet gridlines, and row and column headings.

(Project 5K–GO! Fix It continues on the next page)

434 **Excel** | Chapter 5: Creating a Worksheet and Charting Data

---

NEW

GO! Fix It

Students will apply the skills they have learned to practice debugging and correcting preexisting files.

NEW

Rubric
A matrix that states the criteria and standards for grading student work. Used to grade open-ended assessments.

GO! with Help
Students practice using the Help feature of the Office application.

NEW

You and *GO!*
A project in which students use information from their own lives and apply the skills from the chapter to a personal task.

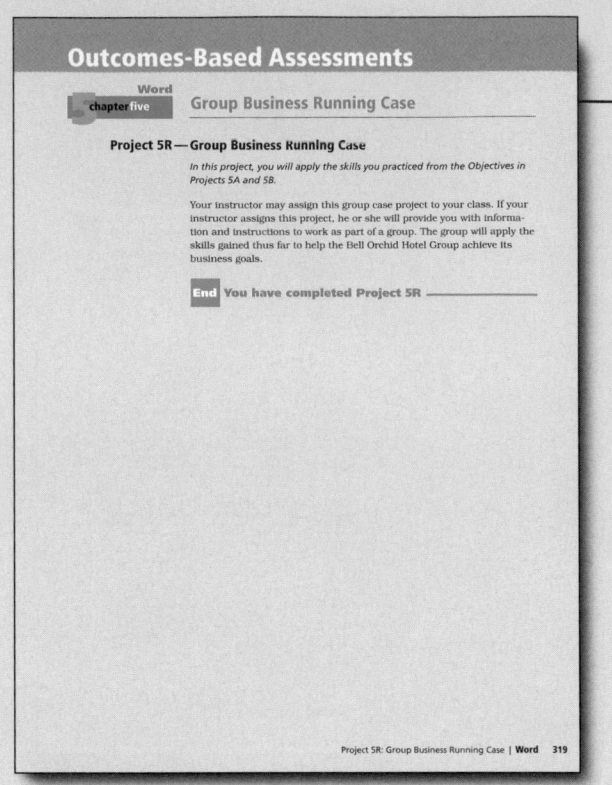

NEW

Group Business Running Case

A continuing project developed for groups that spans the chapters within each application.

Student CD includes:

- Student Data Files
- There's More You Can Do!
- Business Running Case
- You and *GO!*

Companion Web site

An interactive Web site to further student leaning.

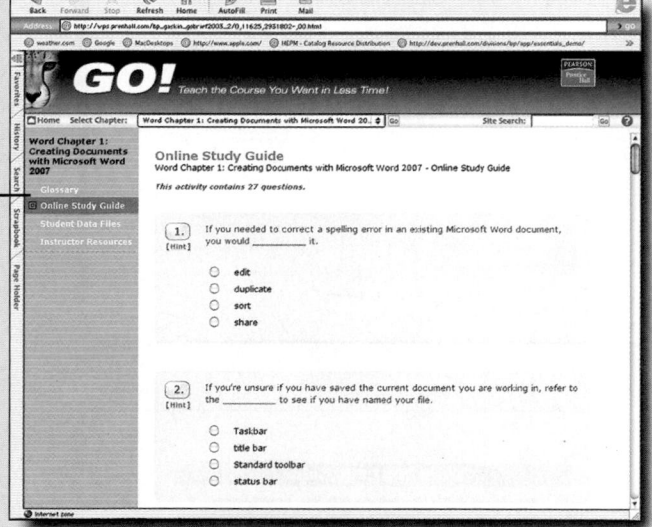

Online Study Guide

Interactive objective-style questions to help students study.

NEW

Podcasts

Videos that reinforce some of the more difficult topics in Microsoft Office 2007.

Annotated Instructor Edition

The Annotated Instructor Edition contains a full version of the student textbook that includes tips, supplement references, and pointers on teaching with the *GO!* instructional system.

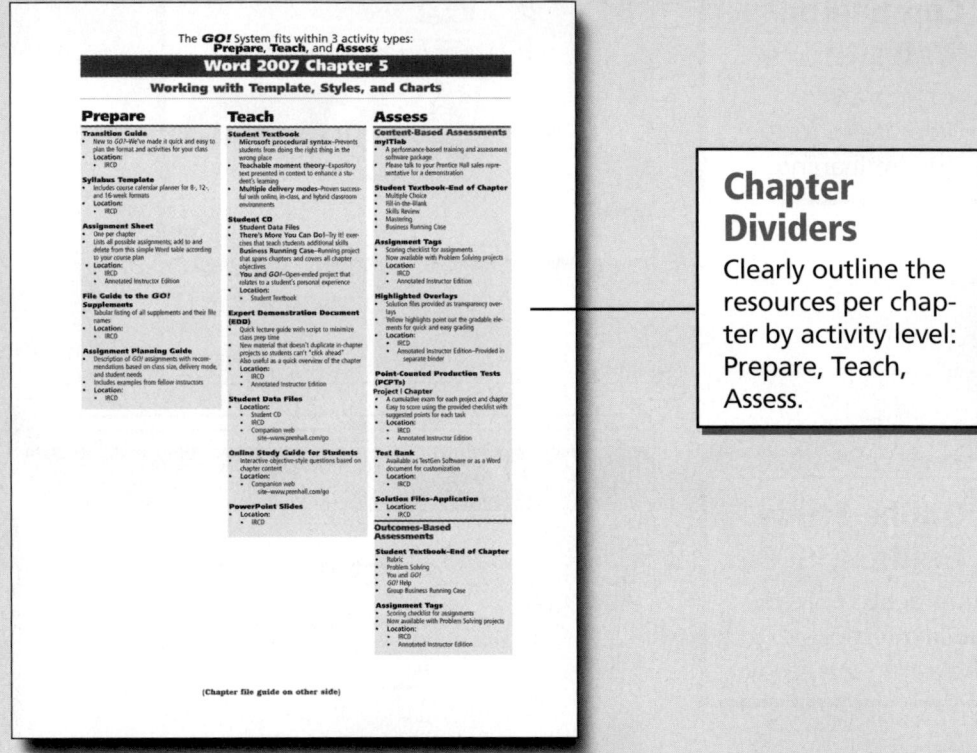

Chapter Dividers

Clearly outline the resources per chapter by activity level: Prepare, Teach, Assess.

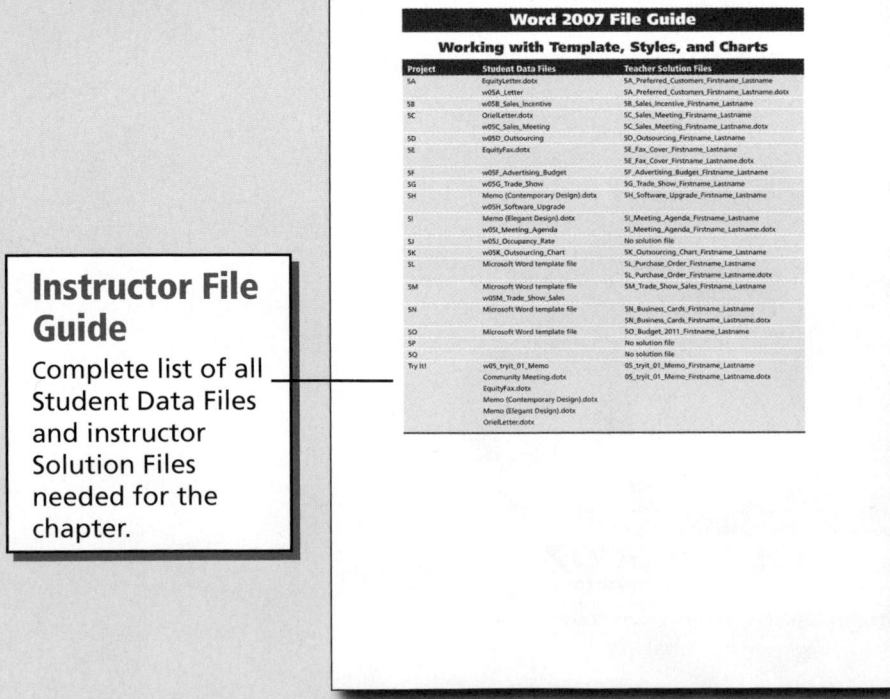

Instructor File Guide

Complete list of all Student Data Files and instructor Solution Files needed for the chapter.

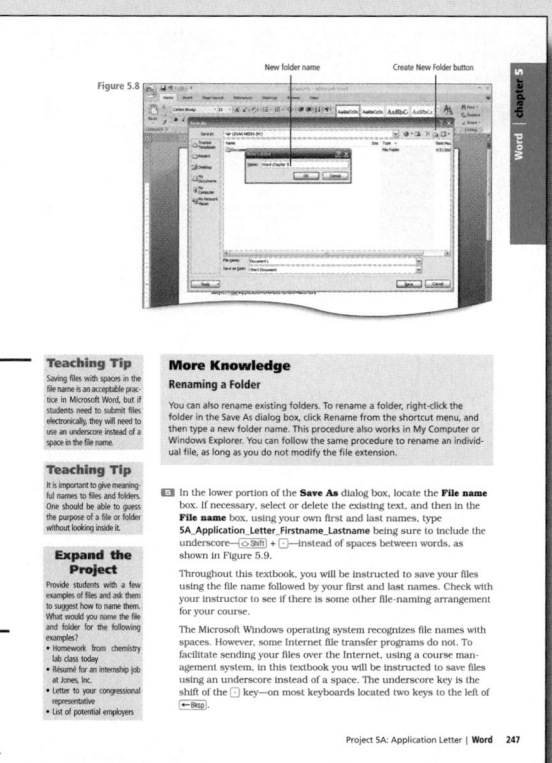

Helpful Hints, Teaching Tips, Expand the Project

References correspond to what is being taught in the student textbook.

NEW

Full-Size Textbook Pages

An instructor copy of the textbook with traditional Instructor Manual content incorporated.

End-of-Chapter Concepts Assessments contain the answers for quick reference.

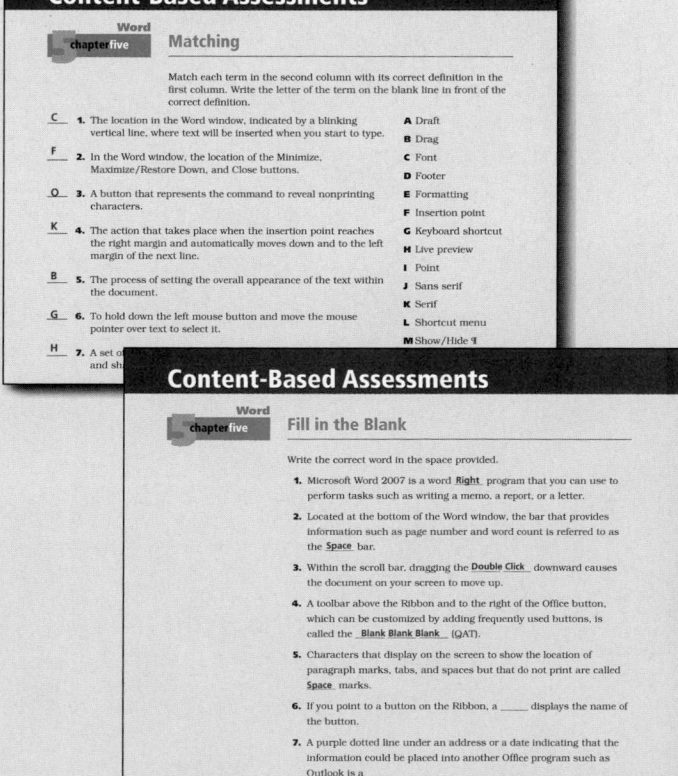

URL

Rubric

A matrix to guide the student on how they will be assessed is reprinted in the Annotated Instructor Edition with suggested weights for each of the criteria and levels of performance. Instructors can mod-

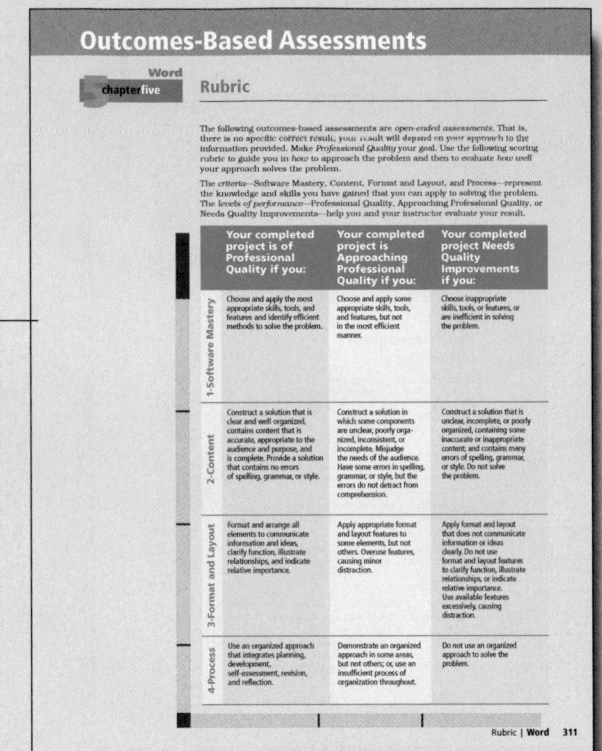

Assignment Tags

Scoring checklist for assignments. **NEW** Now also available for Problem-Solving projects.

GO! with Microsoft® Office 2007

Assignment Tags for GO! with Office 2007
Word Chapter 5

Name:	Project:	5A
Professor:	Course:	

Task	Points	Your Score
Center text vertically on page	2	
Delete the word "really"	1	
Delete the words "try to"	1	
Replace "last" with "first"	1	
Insert the word "potential"	1	
Replace "John W. Diamond" with "Lucy Burrows"	2	
Change entire document to the Cambria font	2	
Change the first line of text to Arial Black 20 pt. font	2	
Bold the first line of text	2	
Change the 2nd through 4th lines to Arial 10 pt.	2	
Italicize the 2nd through 4th lines of text	2	
Correct/Add footer as instructed	2	
Circled information is incorrect or formatted incorrectly		
Total Points	**20**	**0**

Name:	Project:	5B
Professor:	Course:	

Task	Points	Your Score
Insert the file w05B_Music_School_Records	4	
Insert the Music Logo	4	
Remove duplicate "and"	2	
Change spelling and grammar errors (4)	8	
Correct/Add footer as instructed	2	
Circled information is incorrect or formatted incorrectly		
Total Points	**20**	**0**

Name:	Project:	5C
Professor:	Course:	

Task	Points	Your Score
Add four line letterhead	2	
Insert today's date	1	
Add address block, subject line, and greeting	2	
Add two-paragraph body of letter	2	
Add closing, name, and title	2	
In subject line, capitalize "receipt"	1	
Change "standards" to "guidelines"	1	
Insert "quite"	1	
Insert "all"	1	
Change the first line of text to Arial Black 20 pt. font	2	
Bold the first line of text	1	
Change the 2nd through 4th lines to Arial 10 pt.	1	
Italicize the 2nd through 4th lines of text	1	
Correct/add footer as instructed	2	
Circled information is incorrect or formatted incorrectly		
Total Points	**20**	**0**

Name:	Project:	5D
Professor:	Course:	

Task	Points	Your Score
Insert the file w05D_Marketing	4	
Bold the first two title lines	2	
Correct spelling of "Marketting"	2	
Correct spelling of "geners"	2	
Correct all misspellings of "already"	2	
Correct grammar error "are" to "is"	2	
Insert the Piano image	4	
Correct/add footer as instructed	2	
Circled information is incorrect or formatted incorrectly		
Total Points	**20**	**0**

Highlighted Overlays

Solution files provided as transparency overlays. Yellow highlights point out the gradable elements for quick and easy grading.

Music School Records

2620 Vine Street
Los Angeles, CA 90028
323-555-0028

[20 point Arial Black, bold and underline]

[10 point Arial, italic]

[Text vertically centered on page]

[Body of document changed to Cambria font, 11 point]

September 12, 2009

Mr. William Hawken
123 Eighth Street
Harrisville, MI 48740

Dear William:

Subject: Your Application to Music School Records

Thank you for submitting your application to Music School Records. Our talent scout for Northern Michigan, Catherine McDonald, is very enthusiastic about your music, and the demo CD you submitted certainly confirms her opinion.

[Word "really" deleted]

We discuss our applications from potential clients during the first week of each month. We will have a decision for you by the second week of October.

[Words "try to" deleted]

Yours Truly,

Lucy Burroughs

Point-Counted Production Tests (PCPTs)

A cumulative exam for each **project**, **chapter**, and **application**. Easy to score using the provided checklist with suggested points for each task.

GO! with Microsoft® Office 2007 Introductory

Point-Counted Production Test—Project for GO! with Microsoft® Office 2007 Introductory Project 5A

Instructor Name: _____
Course Information: _____

1. Start Word 2007 to begin a new blank document. Save your document as 5A_Cover_Letter_Firstname_Lastname Remember to save your file frequently as you work.

2. If necessary, display the formatting marks. With the insertion point blinking in the upper left corner of the document to the left of the default first paragraph mark, type the current date (you can use AutoComplete).

3. Press Enter three times and type the inside address:

   Music School Records
   2620 Vine Street
   Los Angeles, CA 90028

4. Press Enter three times, and type Dear Ms. Burroughs:

   Press Enter twice, and type Subject: Application to Music School Records

   Press Enter twice, and type the following text (skipping one line between paragraphs):

   I read about Music School Records in Con Brio magazine and I would like to inquire about the possibility of being represented by your company.

   I am very interested in a career in jazz and am planning to relocate to the Los Angeles area in the very near future. I would be interested in learning more about the company and about available opportunities.

   I was a member of my high school jazz band for three years. In addition, I have been playing in the local coffee shop for the last two years. My demo CD, which is enclosed, contains three of my most requested songs.

   I would appreciate the opportunity to speak with you. Thank you for your time and consideration. I look forward to speaking with you about this exciting opportunity.

5. Press Enter three times, and type the closing Sincerely, Press enter four times, and type your name.

6. Insert a footer that contains the file name.

7. Delete the first instance of the word *very* in the second body paragraph, and insert the word modern in front of *jazz*.

Copyright © 2008 Pearson Prentice Hall   Page 1 of 1

Test Bank

Available as TestGen Software or as a Word document for customization.

Chapter 5: Creating Documents with Microsoft Word 2007

Multiple Choice:

1. With word processing programs, how are documents stored?

   A. On a network

   B. On the computer

   C. Electronically

   D. On the floppy disk

   Answer: C   **Reference:** Objective 1: Create and Save a New Document   **Difficulty:** Moderate

2. Because you will see the document as it will print, _____ view is the ideal view to use when learning Microsoft Word 2007.

   A. Reading

   B. Normal

   C. Print Layout

   D. Outline

   Answer: C   **Reference:** Objective 1: Create and Save a New Document   **Difficulty:** Moderate

3. The blinking vertical line where text or graphics will be inserted is called the:

   A. cursor.

   B. insertion point.

   C. blinking line.

   D. I-beam.

   Answer: B   **Reference:** Objective 1: Create and Save a New Document   **Difficulty:** Easy

**Solution Files–
Application
and PDF
format**

Music School Records

Music School Records discovers, launches, and develops the careers of young artists in classical, jazz, and contemporary music. Our philosophy is to not only shape, distribute, and sell a music product, but to help artists create a career that can last a lifetime. Too often in the music industry, artists are forced to fit their music to a trend that is short-lived. Music School Records does not just follow trends, we take a long-term view of the music industry and help our artists develop a style and repertoire that is fluid and flexible and that will appeal to audiences for years and even decades.

The music industry is constantly changing, but over the last decade, the changes have been enormous. New forms of entertainment such as DVDs, video games, and the Internet mean there is more competition for the leisure dollar in the market. New technologies give consumers more options for buying and listening to music, and they are demanding high quality recordings. Young consumers are comfortable with technology and want the music they love when and where they want it, no matter where they are or what they are doing.

Music School Records embraces new technologies and the sophisticated market of young music lovers. We believe that providing high quality recordings of truly talented artists make for more discerning listeners who will cherish the gift of music for the rest of their lives. The expertise of Music School Records includes:

- Insight into our target market and the ability to reach the desired audience
- The ability to access all current sources of music income
- A management team with years of experience in music commerce
- Innovative business strategies and artist development plans
- Investment in technology infrastructure for high quality recordings and business services

pagexxxix_top.docx

Online Assessment and Training

myitlab is Prentice Hall's new performance-based solution that allows you to easily deliver outcomes-based courses on Microsoft Office 2007, with customized training and defensible assessment. Key features of myitlab include:

A _true_ "system" approach: myitlab content is the same as in your textbook.
Project-based _and_ skills-based: Students complete real-life assignments.
Advanced reporting _and_ gradebook: These include student click stream data.
_No_ installation required: myitlab is completely Web-based. You just need an Internet connection, small plug-in, and Adobe Flash Player.

Ask your Prentice Hall sales representative for a demonstration or visit:

www.prenhall.com/myitlab

Students and Instructors – To better meet your needs, we have removed Chapters 1–4 (identified below) from this textbook and have made them available as individual textbooks.

For this reason, this textbook starts with Chapter 5.

GO! with Windows Vista™ Getting Started
978-0-13-614097-9

GO! with Microsoft® Outlook 2007 Getting Started
978-0-13-225617-9

GO! with Internet Explorer® 7.0 Getting Started
978-0-13-157244-7

GO! with Basic Computer Concepts Getting Started
978-0-13-232793-0

5 chapterfive

Creating Documents with Microsoft Word 2007

OBJECTIVES

At the end of this chapter you will be able to:

1. Create and Save a New Document
2. Edit Text
3. Select, Delete, and Format Text
4. Print a Document

OUTCOMES

Mastering these objectives will enable you to:

PROJECT 5A
Create, Edit, Save, and Print a Document

5. Navigate the Word Window
6. Add a Graphic to a Document
7. Use the Spelling and Grammar Checker
8. Preview and Print Documents, Close a Document, and Close Word
9. Use the Microsoft Help System

PROJECT 5B
Navigate the Word Window and Check Your Work

Music School Records

Music School Records was created to launch young musical artists with undiscovered talent in jazz, classical, and contemporary music. The creative management team searches internationally for talented young people, and has a reputation for mentoring and developing the skills of its artists. The company's music is tailored to an audience that is young, knowledgeable about music, and demands the highest quality recordings. Music School Records releases are available in CD format as well as digital downloads.

Getting Started with Microsoft Office Word 2007

A word processor is the most common program found on personal computers and one that almost everyone has a reason to use. When you learn word processing you are also learning skills and techniques that you need to work efficiently on a personal computer. You can use Microsoft Word to perform basic word processing tasks such as writing a memo, a report, or a letter. You can also use Word to complete complex word processing tasks, such as those that include sophisticated tables, embedded graphics, and links to other documents and the Internet. Word is a program that you can learn gradually, and then add more advanced skills one at a time.

Project 5A **Application Letter**

In Activities 5.01 through 5.11, you will create and make changes to a letter from John Diamond, Vice President of Creative Development, to William Hawken, an artist interested in becoming a client of Music School Records. Your completed document will look similar to Figure 5.1.

For Project 5A, you will need the following file:

New blank Word document

You will save your document as
5A_Application_Letter_Firstname_Lastname

Music School Records
2620 Vine Street
Los Angeles, CA 90028
323-555-0028

September 12, 2009

Mr. William Hawken
123 Eighth Street
Harrisville, MI 48740

Dear William:

Subject: Your Application to Music School Records

Thank you for submitting your application to Music School Records. Our talent scout for Northern Michigan, Catherine McDonald, is very enthusiastic about your music, and the demo CD you submitted certainly confirms her opinion.

We discuss our applications from potential clients during the first week of each month. We will have a decision for you by the second week of October.

Yours truly,

Lucy Burroughs

5A_Application_Letter_Firstname_Lastname

Figure 5.1
Project 5A—Application Letter

Objective 1
Create and Save a New Document

With a word processing program, you can type, ***edit***—make changes to—move, and delete text or change the appearance of text. Because the documents that you create are stored electronically, they can be duplicated, printed, copied, and shared with others. In this project, you will become familiar with the parts of the Word window. Then you will create a document, edit and format text, and save your work.

Activity 5.01 Starting Word and Identifying Parts of the Word Window

> ### Note — Comparing Your Screen With the Figures in This Textbook
>
> Your screen will match the figures shown in this textbook if you set your screen resolution to 1024 × 768. At other resolutions, your screen will closely resemble, but not match, the figures shown. To view your screen's resolution, on the Windows desktop, right-click in a blank area, click Personalize, and then click Display Settings.

1 On the left side of the Windows taskbar, point to, and then click the **Start** button.

2 From the displayed **Start** menu, locate the **Word** program, and then click **Microsoft Office Word 2007**.

The Word program may be located under All Programs or Microsoft Office or on the main Start menu.

Print Layout view is the ideal view to use when you are learning Microsoft Word 2007 because you can see the document exactly the way it will look when it is printed.

3 If necessary, on the right side of the status bar, click the **Print Layout** button. If the ruler does not display, click the View tab, and then in the Show/Hide group, click the Ruler check box. Take a moment to study the parts of the Word screen shown in Figure 5.2 and described in the table in Figure 5.3.

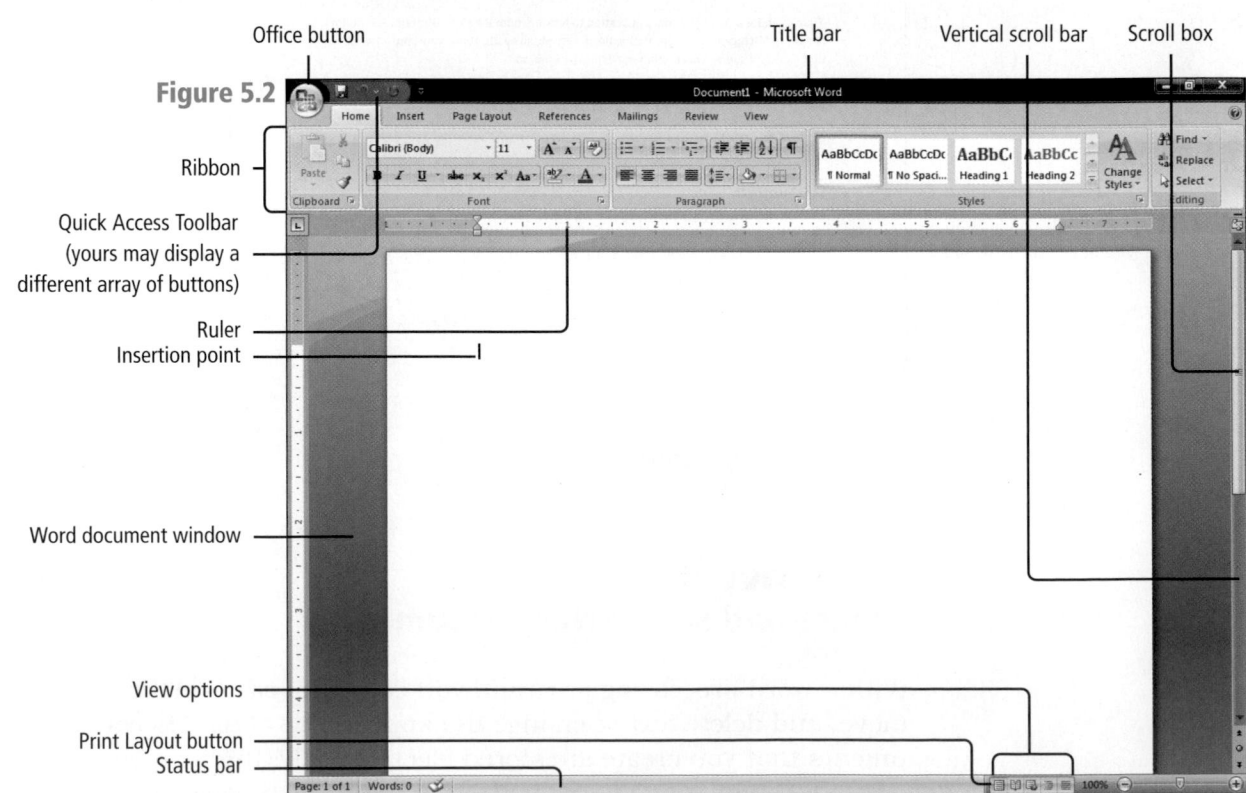

Figure 5.2

Office button · Title bar · Vertical scroll bar · Scroll box

Ribbon

Quick Access Toolbar (yours may display a different array of buttons)

Ruler
Insertion point

Word document window

View options
Print Layout button
Status bar

Microsoft Word Screen Elements

Screen Element	Description
Insertion point	Indicates, with a blinking vertical line, where text or graphics will be inserted.
Office button	Displays a list of commands related to things you can do *with* a document, such as opening, saving, printing, or sharing.
Quick Access Toolbar (QAT)	Displays buttons to perform frequently used commands with a single click. Frequently used commands in Word include Save, Undo, and Redo. For commands that *you* use frequently, you can add additional buttons to the Quick Access Toolbar.
Ribbon	Organizes commands on tabs, and then groups the commands by topic for performing related document tasks.
Ruler	Displays the location of margins, indents, columns, and tab stops for the selected paragraph(s).
Scroll box	Provides a visual indication of your location in a document. It can also be used with the mouse to drag a document up and down to reposition the document.
Status bar	Displays, on the left side, the page number, word count, and the Proof button. On the right side, displays buttons to control the look of the window. The status bar can be customized to include other information.
Title bar	Displays the name of the document and the name of the program. The Minimize, Maximize/Restore Down, and Close buttons are grouped on the right side of the title bar.
Vertical scroll bar	Enables you to move up and down in a document to display text that is not visible.
View options	Contains buttons for viewing the document in Print Layout, Full Screen Reading, Web Layout, Outline, or Draft views, and also displays controls to Zoom Out and Zoom In.
Word document window	Displays the active document.

Figure 5.3

Alert!

Does your screen differ?

The appearance of the screen can vary, depending on various settings that were established when Office 2007 was installed. Additionally, the Quick Access Toolbar can display any combination of buttons.

Activity 5.02 Beginning a New Document and Displaying Formatting Marks

When you start the Word program, you need only start typing to create a new document. As you work on a document, save your changes frequently—the Save button is always available on the Quick Access Toolbar.

1 On the title bar, notice that *Document1* displays.

Word displays the file name of a document in both the title bar at the top of the screen and on a button in the Windows taskbar at the lower edge of the screen—including new unsaved documents. The new unsaved document displays *Document* followed by a number; the number depends on how many times you have started a new document during your current Word session.

2 In the displayed blank document, determine if a paragraph symbol (¶) displays in the upper left corner of the document, as shown in Figure 5.4. If you do *not* see the paragraph symbol, on the Ribbon, on the **Home tab**, in the **Paragraph group**, click the **Show/Hide ¶** button ![¶] to display the formatting marks.

When you press Enter, Spacebar, or Tab on your keyboard, characters display in your document to represent these keystrokes. These characters do not print and are referred to as **formatting marks** or **nonprinting characters**. Because formatting marks guide your eye in a document—like a map and road signs guide you along a high-way—these marks will display throughout this instruction.

Default document name   No Spacing style button

Figure 5.4

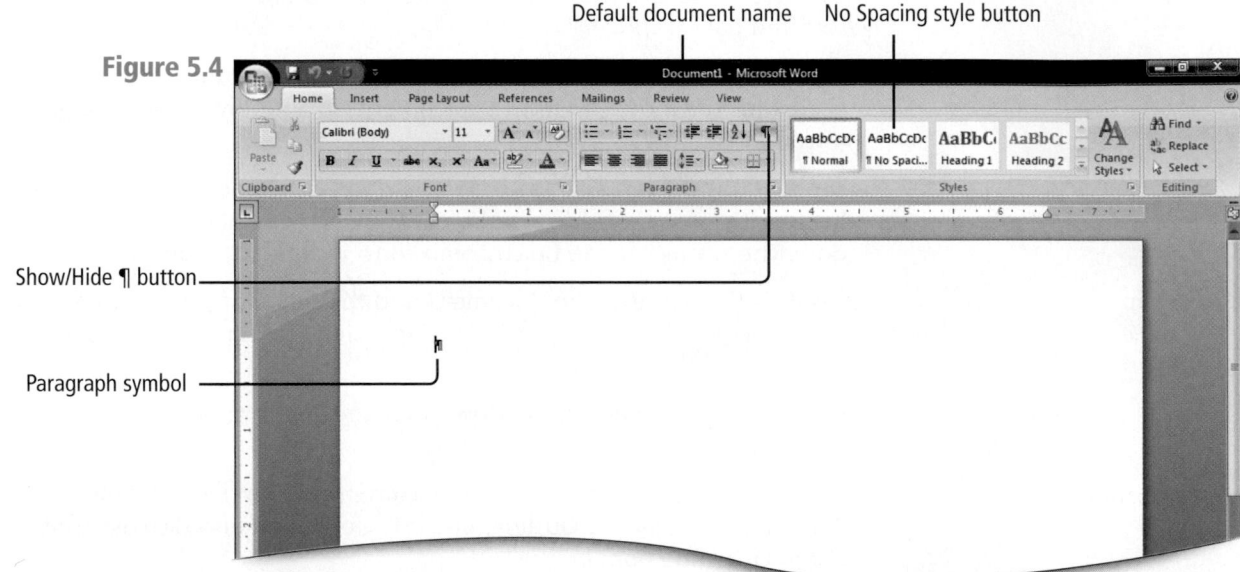

Show/Hide ¶ button

Paragraph symbol

3 Click the **Show/Hide ¶** button ![¶] to turn off the display of nonprinting characters. Then, click the **Show/Hide ¶** button ![¶] one more time to turn it on again.

The Show/Hide ¶ button is referred to as a **toggle button**—you can click the button one time to turn it on and click it again to turn it off.

4 On the **Home tab**, in the **Styles group**, click the **No Spacing** style button.

By default, Word adds spacing after each paragraph. In a business letter, the address block should be single-spaced, with no spacing after each paragraph. The No Spacing button applies a style to the text that removes extra spacing. A **style** is a set of formatting characteristics—such as line spacing, space after paragraphs, font, and font style—that can be applied to text, paragraphs, tables, or lists.

Activity 5.03 Entering Text and Inserting Blank Lines

Business letters follow a standard format and contain the following parts: the current date—the **date line**; the name and address of the person receiving the letter—the **inside address**; a greeting—the **salutation**; an optional subject—the **subject line**; the body of the letter; a closing line—the **complimentary closing**; and the **writer's identification**, which includes the name or job title (or both) of the writer. Some letters also include the initials of the person who typed the letter, and a list of **enclosures**—documents included with the letter. In this activity, you will begin to enter the text of a business letter.

1 With the insertion point blinking in the upper left corner of the document to the left of the default first paragraph mark, type **Music School Records** and then press Enter.

The first paragraph is complete and the insertion point is positioned at the beginning of the next line. A paragraph is created when you press Enter. Thus, a paragraph can be a single line or a blank line.

2 Type the following text, and then press Enter after each line:

2620 Vine Street
Los Angeles, CA 90028
323-555-0028

3 Press Enter five more times, type **Sept** and then compare your screen with Figure 5.5.

A **ScreenTip** displays *September (Press ENTER to Insert)*. This feature, called **AutoComplete**, assists you in typing. After you type the first few characters, AutoComplete suggests commonly used words and phrases to enter. A ScreenTip is a small note, activated by holding the pointer over a button or other screen object, which displays information about a screen element.

Figure 5.5

ScreenTip

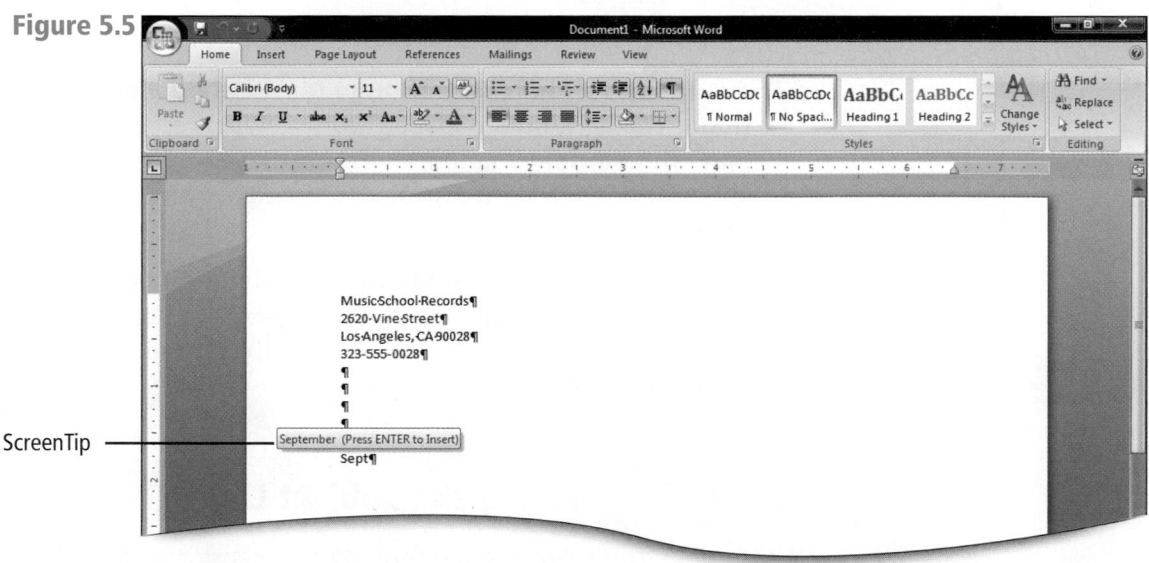

4 To finish the word *September*, press Enter. Press Spacebar, type **12, 2009** and then press Enter. If you are completing this activity during the month of September, AutoComplete may offer to fill in the current date. To ignore the suggestion, type as indicated.

5 Press [Enter] two more times.

In a business letter, insert two blank lines between the date and the inside address, which is the same as the address you would use on an envelope.

6 Type **Mr. William Hawken** and then press [Enter].

The wavy red line under the proper name *Hawken* indicates that the word has been flagged as misspelled because it is a word not contained in the Word dictionary.

7 On two lines, type the following address, but do not press [Enter] at the end of the second line:

123 Eighth Street
Harrisville, MI 48740

Note — Typing the Address

Include a comma after the city name in an inside address. However, for mailing addresses on envelopes, eliminate the comma after the city name.

8 On the **Home tab**, in the **Styles group**, click the **Normal** button.

The Normal style is applied to the text in the rest of the document. Recall that the Normal style adds extra space between paragraphs; it also adds slightly more space between lines in a paragraph.

9 Press [Enter]. Type **Dear William:** and then press [Enter].

This salutation is the line that greets the person receiving the letter.

10 Type **Subject: Your Application to Music School Records** and press [Enter]. Notice the light dots between words, which indicate spaces and display when formatting marks are displayed. Also, notice the extra space after each paragraph, and then compare your screen with Figure 5.6.

The subject line is optional, but you should include a subject line in most letters to identify the topic. Depending on your Word settings, a wavy green line may display in the subject line, indicating a potential grammar error.

Note — Locating the Subject Line

According to *The Gregg Reference Manual*, Tenth Edition (William A. Sabin, 2005), the subject line is placed between the salutation and the body of the letter. In *Business Communication Process and Product, Fourth Edition* (Mary Ellen Guffey, 2003), "Although experts suggest placing the subject line 1 blank line below the salutation, many businesses actually place it above the salutation. Use whatever style your organization prefers."

Light dots indicate spaces resulting
from pressing the space bar on your keyboard

Figure 5.6

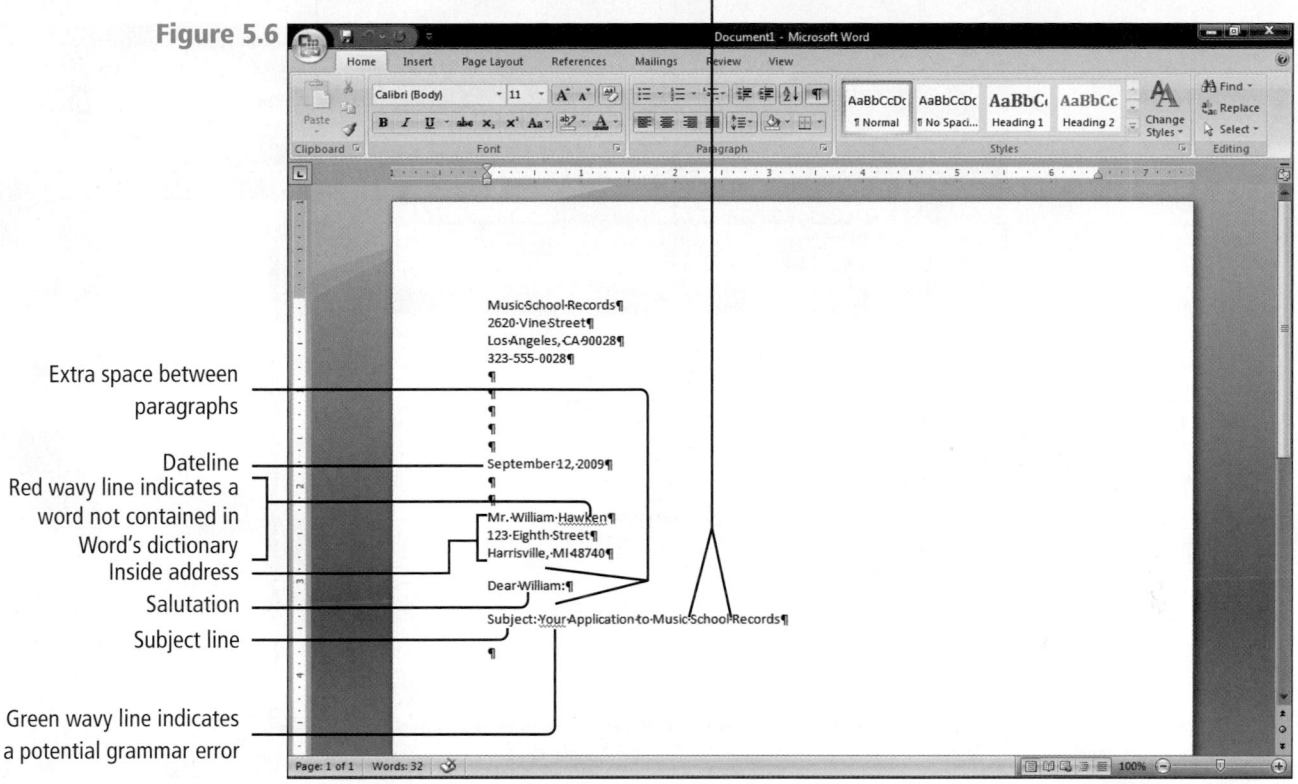

Extra space between
paragraphs

Dateline

Red wavy line indicates a
word not contained in
Word's dictionary

Inside address

Salutation

Subject line

Green wavy line indicates
a potential grammar error

Activity 5.04 Creating Folders for Document Storage and Saving a Document

In the same way that you use file folders to organize your paper documents, Windows uses a hierarchy of electronic folders to keep your electronic files organized. When you save a document file, the Windows operating system stores your document permanently on a storage medium. Changes that you make to existing documents, such as changing text or typing in new text, are not permanently saved until you perform a Save operation.

1 In the upper left corner of your screen, click the **Office** button ,
and from the displayed menu, point to the words **Save As**—not the
Save As arrow—and click.

2 In the displayed **Save As** dialog box, in the **Navigation** pane, click
Computer to view a list of the drives available to you, as shown in
Figure 5.7. If you are saving your files on your hard drive, in the
Navigation pane, click Documents.

Figure 5.7

New Folder button

Your list of available
drives will differ

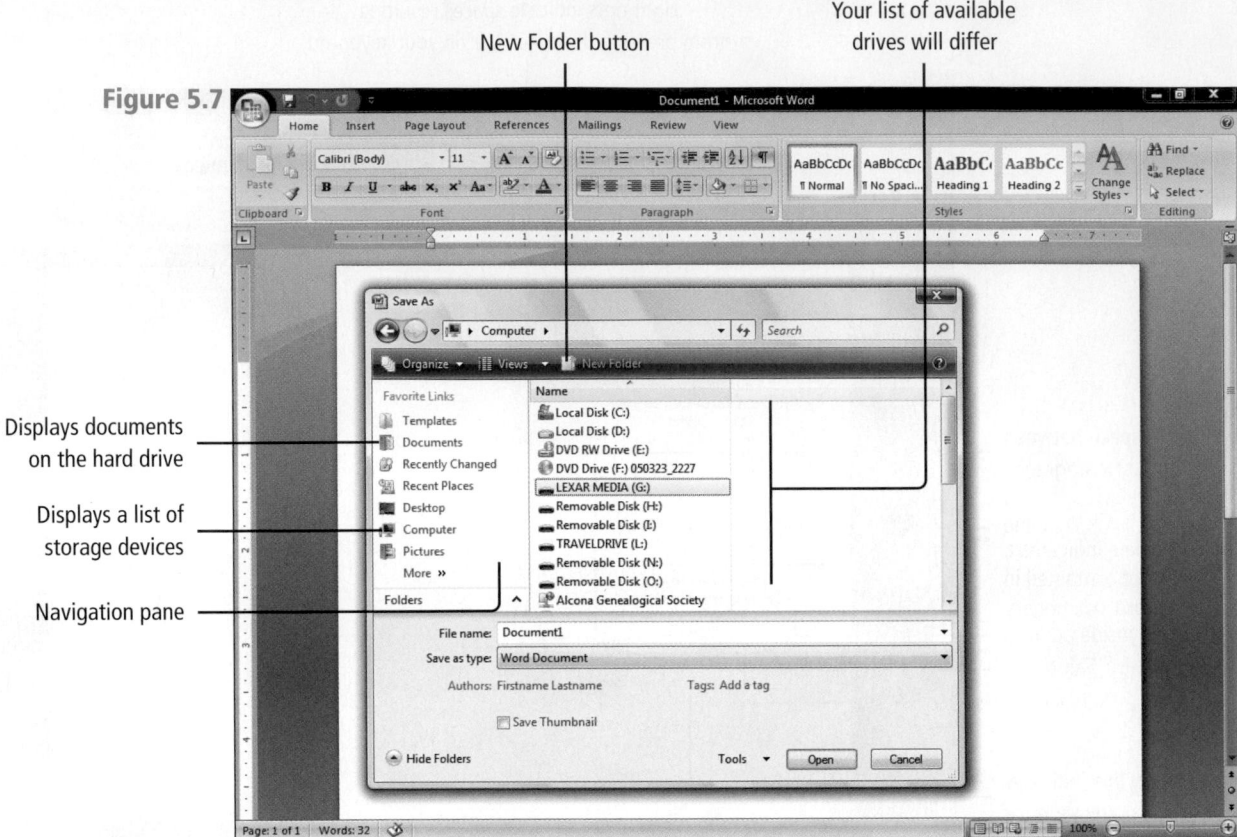

Displays documents
on the hard drive

Displays a list of
storage devices

Navigation pane

3 Navigate to the location in which you will be storing your folders and projects for this chapter—for example, a USB flash drive that you have connected, a shared drive on a network, the Documents folder on your computer's hard drive, or the drive designated by your instructor or lab coordinator.

4 In the **Save As** dialog box, on the toolbar, click the **New Folder** button. With the **New Folder** in edit mode, type **Word Chapter 5**, as shown in Figure 5.8, and then press Enter. If the new folder is not displayed in edit mode, right-click the words New Folder, and then from the displayed shortcut menu, click Rename and type the new folder name.

The new folder name displays in the Address bar, indicating that the folder is open and ready to store your document. The folder is currently empty.

Figure 5.8

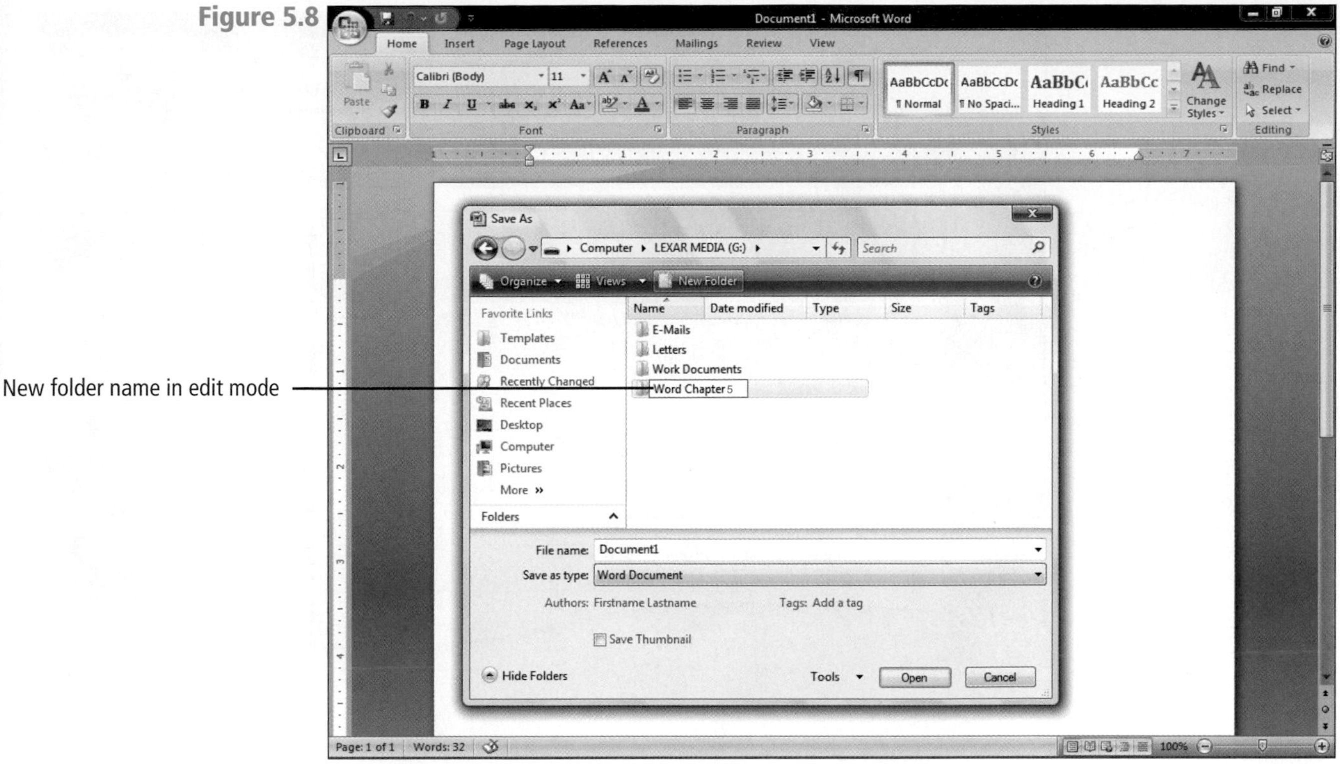

New folder name in edit mode ————

More Knowledge

Renaming a Folder

You can also rename existing folders. To rename a folder, right-click the folder in the Save As dialog box, click Rename from the shortcut menu, and then type a new folder name. This procedure also works in Computer or Windows Explorer. You can follow the same procedure to rename an individual file, as long as you do not modify the file extension.

5 In the lower portion of the **Save As** dialog box, locate the **File name** box. If necessary, select or delete the existing text, and then in the **File name** box, using your own first and last names, type **5A_Application_Letter_Firstname_Lastname** being sure to include the underscore—[⇧ Shift] + [-]—instead of spaces between words, as shown in Figure 5.9.

Throughout this textbook, you will be instructed to save your files using the file name followed by your first and last names. Check with your instructor to see if there is some other file-naming arrangement for your course.

The Microsoft Windows operating system recognizes file names with spaces. However, some Internet file transfer programs do not. To facilitate sending your files over the Internet, using a course management system, in this textbook you will be instructed to save files using an underscore instead of a space.

Figure 5.9

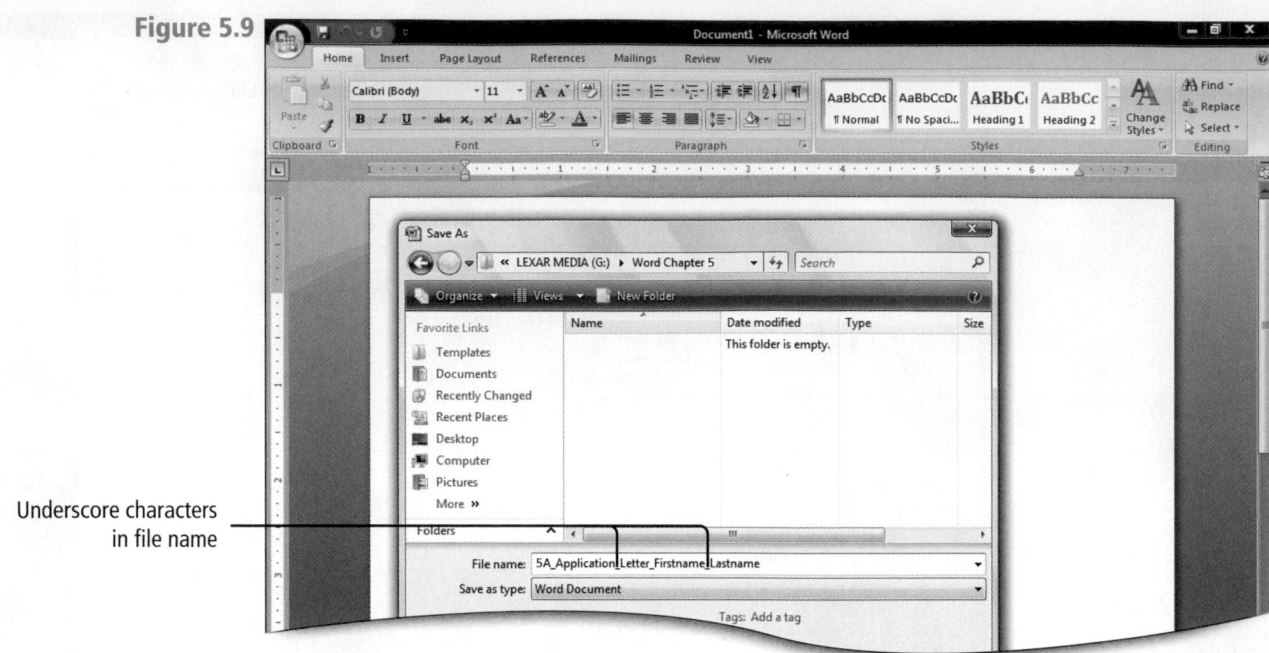

Underscore characters in file name

6 In the lower portion of the **Save As** dialog box, click the **Save** button, or press Enter. The file extension *.docx* may or may not display, depending on your Word settings.

Your file is saved on the storage device that you selected, and it is contained in the *Word Chapter 5* folder with the new file name. The new file name also displays in the title bar.

7 As you type the following text, press the Spacebar only one time at the end of a sentence: **Thank you for submitting your application to Music School Records. Our talent scout for Northern Michigan, Catherine McDonald, is really very enthusiastic about your music, and the demo CD you submitted certainly confirms her opinion.** Press Enter.

As you type, the insertion point moves to the right, and when it approaches the right margin, Word determines whether or not the next word in the line will fit within the established right margin. If the word does not fit, Word will move the whole word down to the next line. This feature is called *wordwrap*, and means that you do not press Enter until you reach the end of a paragraph.

Note — Spacing Between Sentences

Although you may have learned to press Spacebar two times at the end of a sentence, it is common practice now to space only one time between sentences.

8 Type **We discuss our applications from clients during the last week of each month. We will try to have a decision for you by the second week of October.**

9 Press Enter. Type **Yours truly,** and then press Enter.

10 Press Enter again, and then type **John W. Diamond** and then compare your screen with Figure 5.10.

As you reach the bottom of the screen, the page scrolls up to enable you to read what you are typing.

One space between sentences

Figure 5.10

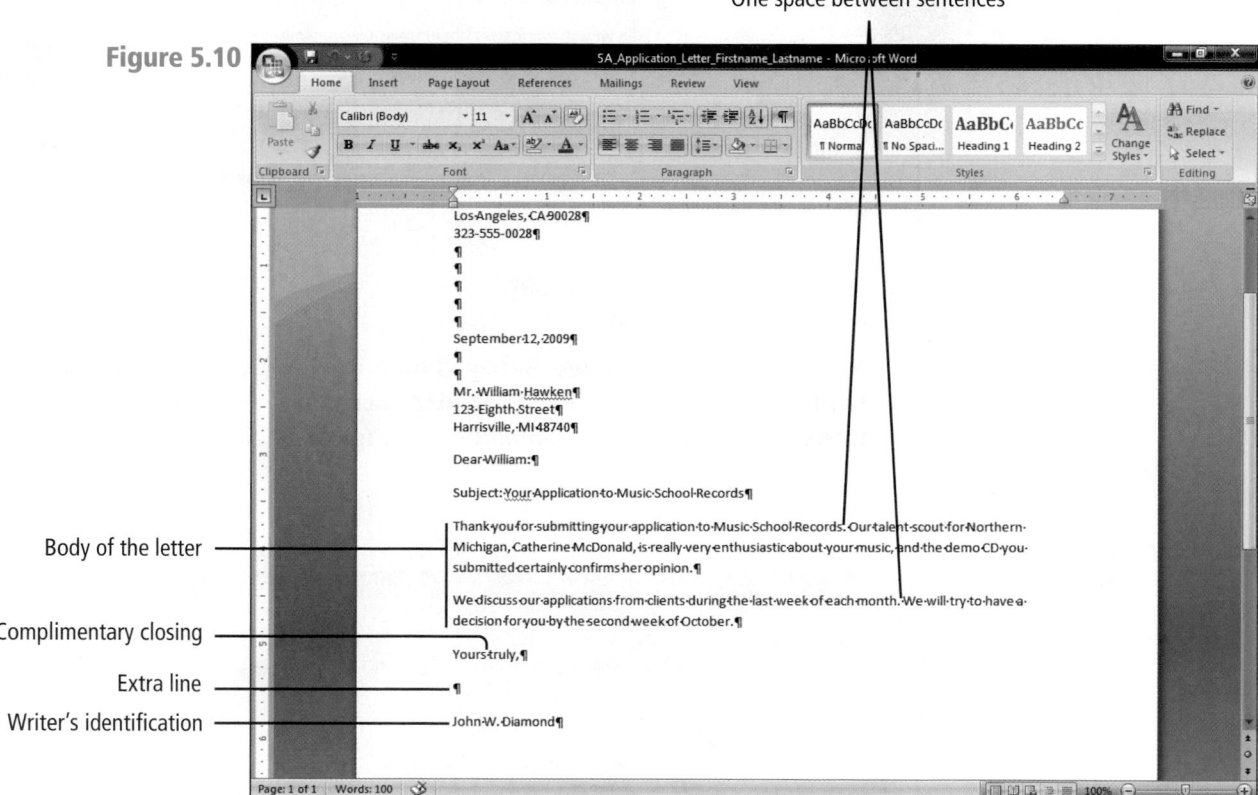

Body of the letter

Complimentary closing

Extra line

Writer's identification

11 On the Ribbon, click the **Page Layout tab**. In the **Page Setup group**, click the **Margins** button to display the **Margins gallery**, as shown in Figure 5.11.

A *gallery* displays a list of potential results.

Figure 5.11

Margins button

Margins gallery

Custom Margins

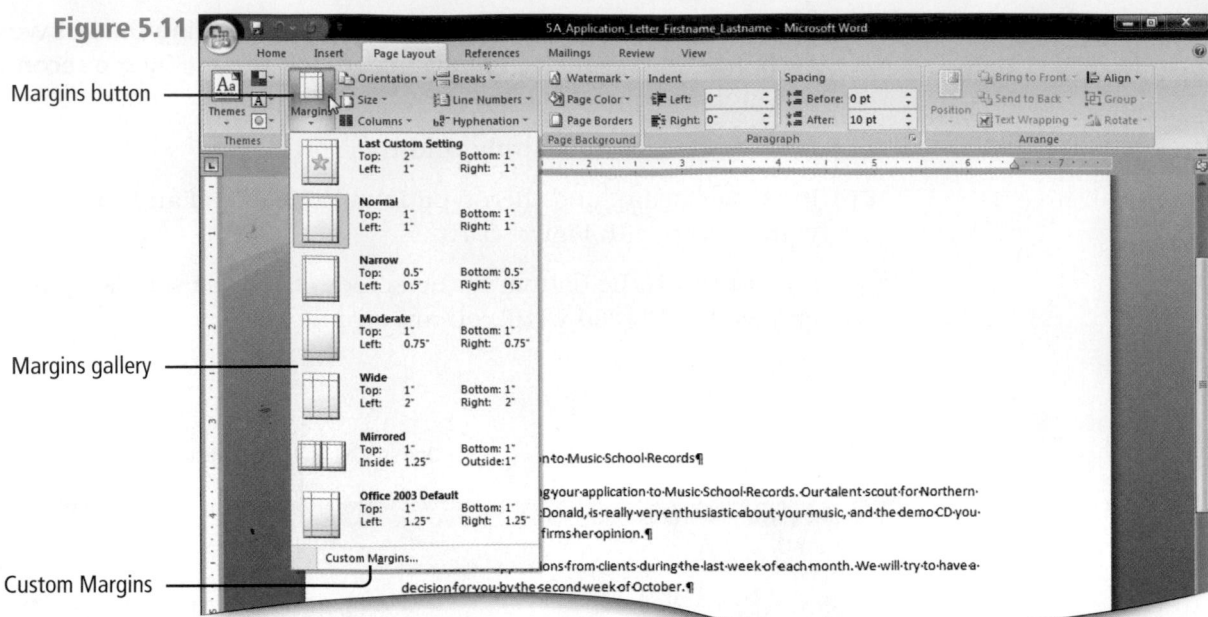

12 At the bottom of the **Margins gallery**, click **Custom Margins** to display the **Page Setup** dialog box.

13 Near the top of the **Page Setup** dialog box, click the **Layout tab**. Under **Page**, click the **Vertical alignment arrow**, and then click **Center**. Compare your dialog box to Figure 5.12.

Layout tab

Figure 5.12

Center

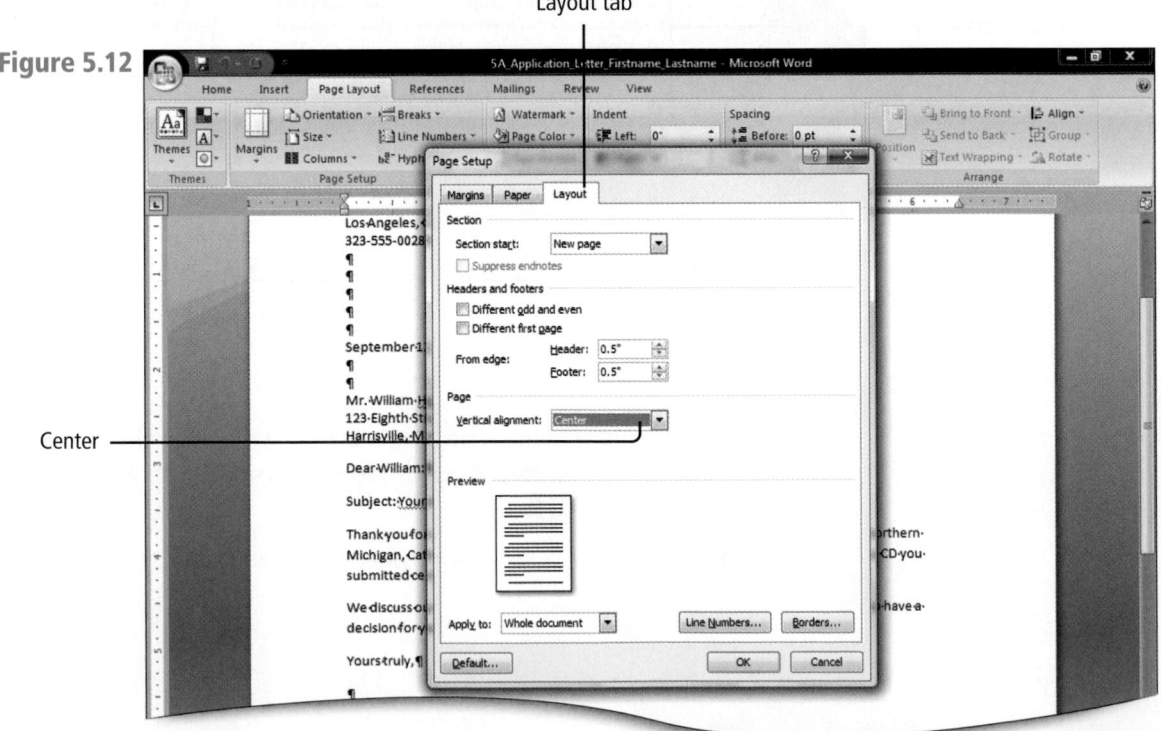

14 In the lower right corner of the **Page Setup** dialog box, click **OK**.

The text is centered vertically on the page. This makes the letter more visually appealing.

15 On the **Quick Access Toolbar**, click the **Save** button ▣ to save the changes you have made to the letter since your last save operation.

More Knowledge

Letter Placement

According to *The Gregg Reference Manual*, Tenth Edition (Sabin, 2005), a one-page letter typed on blank stationery may be centered vertically in this manner. If you are using letterhead stationery, leave at least a 0.5-inch space between the letterhead and the first element typed. Always consult trusted references when deciding on the proper formats for your personal and professional documents.

Objective 2
Edit Text

When you change text or formatting in a document, you are editing the text. Two commonly used editing tools are the Delete key and the Backspace key. The Backspace and Delete keys on your keyboard are used to remove text from the screen one character at a time. Backspace removes a character to the left of the insertion point; Delete removes a character to the right of the insertion point. You can also insert characters in the middle of existing text.

Activity 5.05 Editing Text with the Delete and Backspace Keys

1 Using the vertical scroll bar, scroll as necessary to view the paragraph beginning *Thank you.* In the middle of the second line of the paragraph, click to position your insertion point to the left of the *v* in the word *very* and then press ←Bksp. Compare your screen with Figure 5.13.

The space between the words *really* and *very* is removed.

Insertion point

Figure 5.13

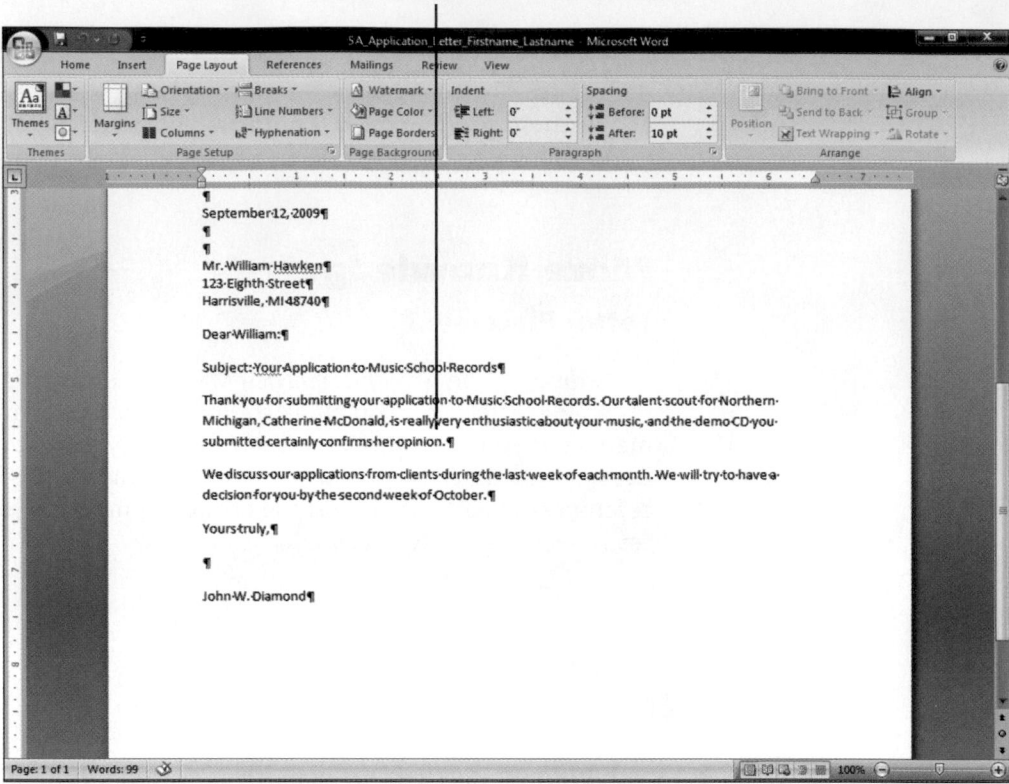

2 With the insertion point between the two words, press ⌫Bksp six times.

The word *really* is removed. Be sure there is only one dot—recall that dots are the formatting marks that indicate spaces—between *is* and *very*. You can see that when editing text, it is useful to display formatting marks.

3 In the paragraph beginning *We discuss*, in the first line, locate the phrase *try to* and then click to position the insertion point to the left of the word *to*.

4 Press ⌫Bksp four times to remove the word *try* and the extra space. Press Delete three times, and then compare your screen with Figure 5.14.

The word *to* at the right of the insertion point is removed, along with the space following the word. Be sure there is only one dot (space) between *will* and *have*.

Figure 5.14

One space

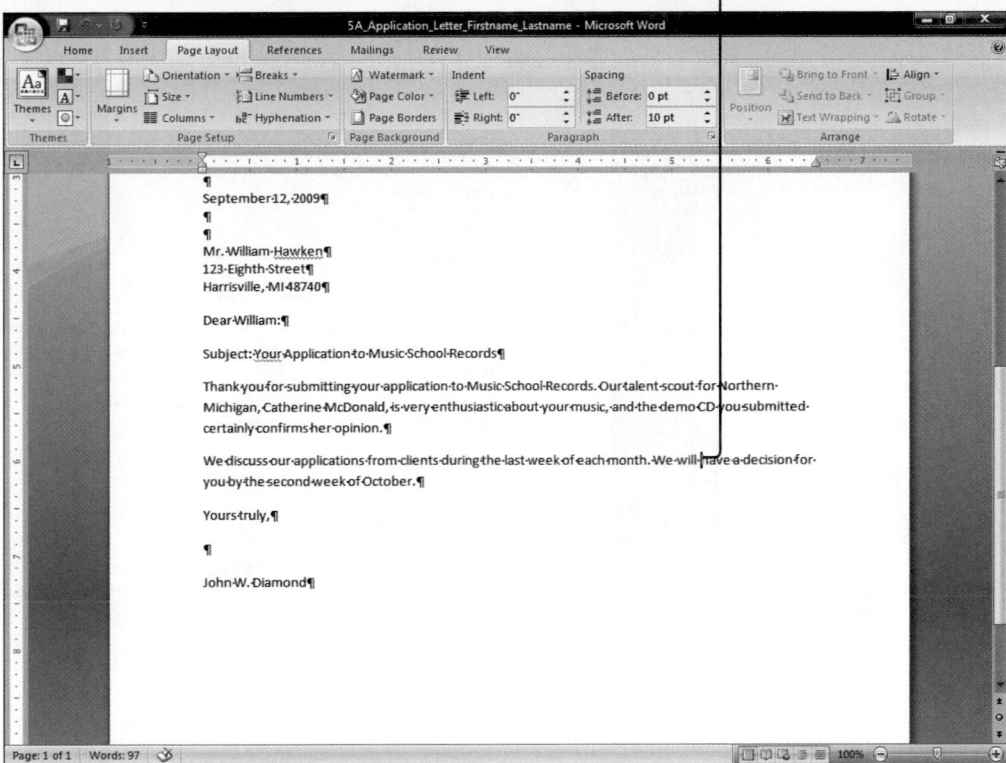

⑤ On the **Quick Access Toolbar**, click the **Save** button 🔲 to save the changes you have made to the letter since your last save operation.

Activity 5.06 Inserting New Text

When you place the insertion point in the middle of a word or sentence and start typing, the existing text moves to the right to make space for your new keystrokes. This is called **insert mode** and is the default setting in Word.

1 In the paragraph beginning *We discuss*, in the first line, click to place the insertion point to the left of the letter *c* in the word *clients*.

2 Type **potential** and then press [Spacebar].

As you type, the existing text moves to the right to make space for your new keystrokes.

3 In the last line of the document, click to place the insertion point to the left of *John W. Diamond*.

4 Type **Lucy Burroughs** and then press [Delete] until the name *John W. Diamond* is removed.

5 Compare your screen with Figure 5.15.

Figure 5.15

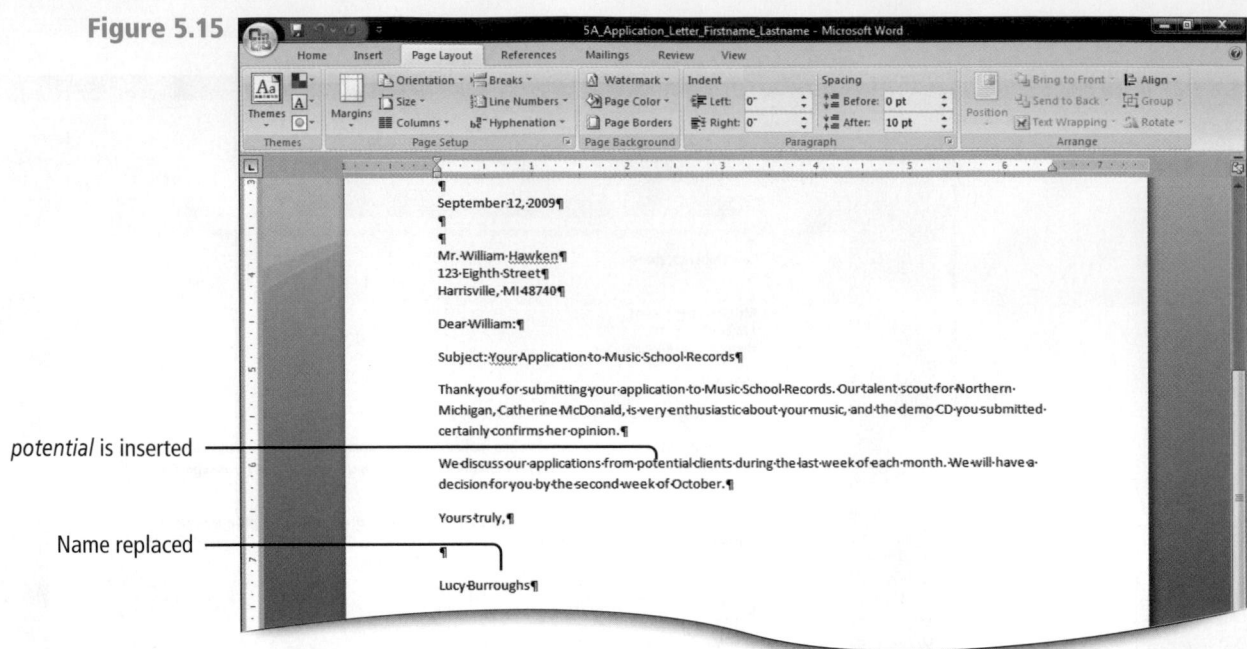

potential is inserted ——————

Name replaced ——————

6 **Save** 💾 the changes you have made to your document.

Objective 3
Select, Delete, and Format Text

Selecting text refers to highlighting, by dragging with your mouse, areas of text so that the text can be edited, formatted, copied, or moved. Word recognizes a selected area of text as one unit, to which you can make changes. **Formatting text** is the process of setting the overall appearance of the text within the document by changing the layout, color, shading, emphasis, or font characteristics of text.

Activity 5.07 Selecting and Deleting Text

1 In the paragraph beginning *Thank you*, position the [I] pointer to the left of *Thank*, hold down the left mouse button, and then drag to the right to select the first sentence including the ending period and its following space, as shown in Figure 5.16. Release the mouse button.

The first sentence of the paragraph is selected, and a **Mini toolbar** displays above and to the right of the selected text. **Dragging** is the technique of holding down the left mouse button and moving over an area of text. Selected text is indicated when the background changes to a light blue or gray. The Mini toolbar displays buttons that are commonly used with the selected object. When you move the pointer away from the Mini toolbar, it fades from view. Selecting text may require some practice. If you are not satisfied with your result, click anywhere in the document and begin again.

Figure 5.16

Mini toolbar

Period and space included
in the selection

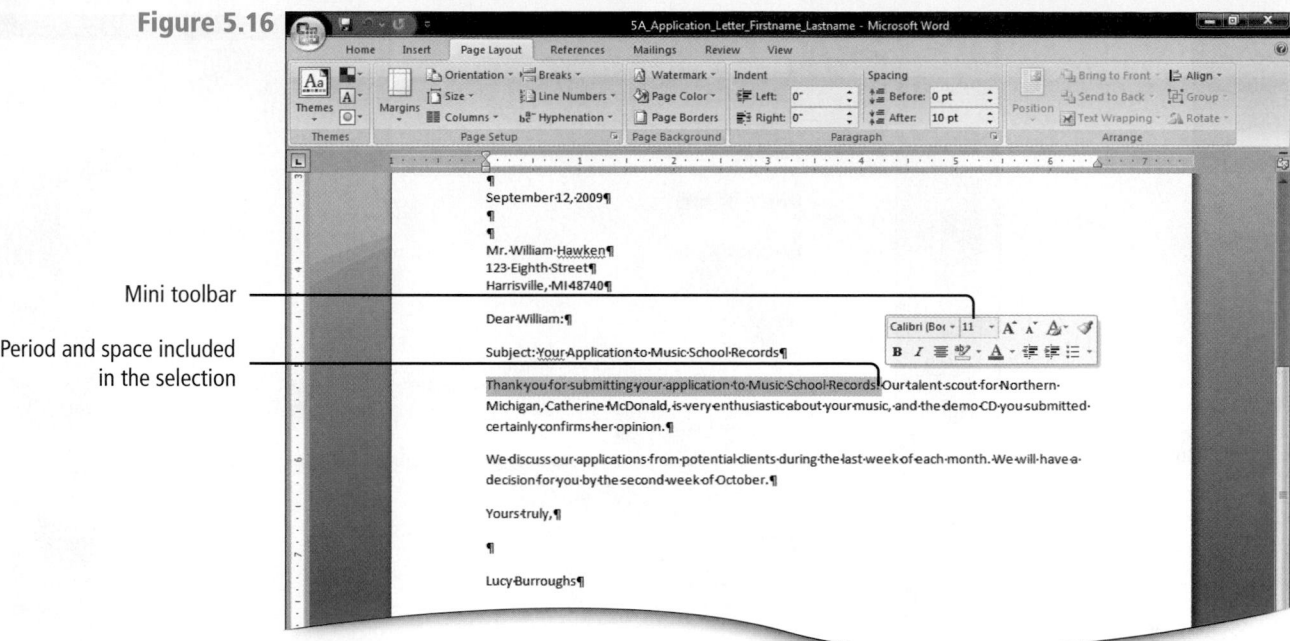

② Click anywhere in the document to deselect the sentence. Then, in the same sentence, move the pointer over the word *Music* and **double-click**—click the left mouse button two times in rapid succession.

The entire word is selected and the Mini toolbar displays. Double-clicking takes a steady hand. The speed of the two clicks is not difficult (although you only have about a second between clicks), but you must hold the mouse perfectly still between the two clicks. If you are not satisfied with your result, try again.

③ Click anywhere in the document to deselect the word *Music*. Then, in the paragraph that begins *We discuss*, move the pointer over the word *last* and double-click. Type **first** and notice that when you type the first letter, the selected word is deleted.

④ In the paragraph beginning *Thank you*, move the pointer over the word *Music* and triple-click the left mouse button.

The entire paragraph is selected. You can triple-click anywhere in a paragraph to select the entire paragraph; keeping the mouse perfectly still between the clicks will guarantee the desired result.

⑤ Hold down ⟨Ctrl⟩ and press ⟨A⟩ to select the entire document, as shown in Figure 5.17.

Holding down ⟨Ctrl⟩ and typing a letter to perform a command is called a **keyboard shortcut**. There are many keyboard shortcuts for selecting text. Take a moment to study the shortcuts shown in the table in Figure 5.18.

Figure 5.17

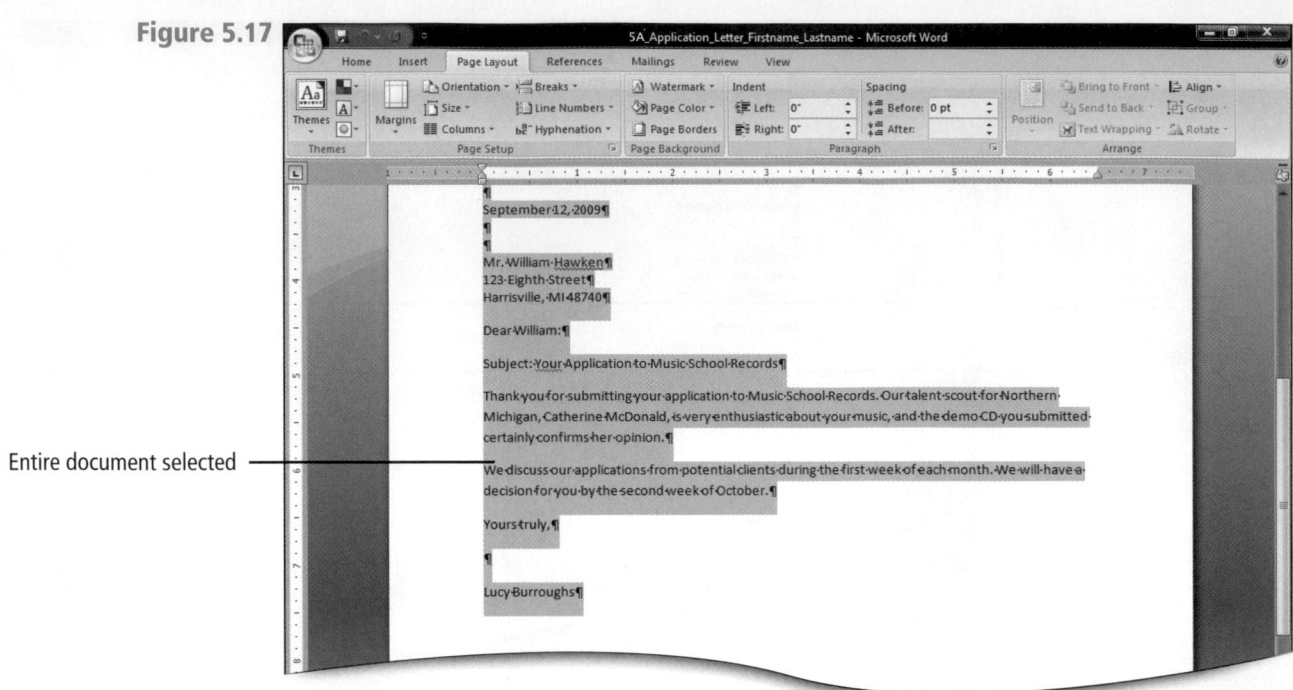

Entire document selected

Selecting Text in a Document

To Select	Do This
A portion of text	Click to position the insertion point at the beginning of the text you want to select, hold down ⟨⇧ Shift⟩, and then click at the end of the text you want to select. Alternatively, hold down the left mouse button and drag from the beginning to the end of the text you want to select.
A word	Double-click the word.
A sentence	Hold down ⟨Ctrl⟩ and click anywhere in the sentence.
A paragraph	Triple-click anywhere in the paragraph; or, move the pointer to the left of the line, into the margin area. When the ⟨⤢⟩ pointer displays, double-click.
A line	Move the pointer to the left of the line. When the ⟨⤢⟩ pointer displays, click one time.
One character at a time	Position the insertion point to the left of the first character, hold down ⟨⇧ Shift⟩, and press → or ← as many times as desired.
A string of words	Position the insertion point to the left of the first word, hold down ⟨⇧ Shift⟩ and ⟨Ctrl⟩, and then press → or ← as many times as desired.
Consecutive lines	Position the insertion point to the left of the first word, hold down ⟨⇧ Shift⟩ and press ↑ or ↓.
Consecutive paragraphs	Position the insertion point to the left of the first word, hold down ⟨⇧ Shift⟩ and ⟨Ctrl⟩ and press ↑ or ↓.
The entire document	Hold down ⟨Ctrl⟩ and press ⟨A⟩ or move the pointer to the left of any line in the document. When the ⟨⤢⟩ pointer displays, triple-click.

Figure 5.18

6 Click anywhere in the document to cancel the text selection. **Save** 💾 your work.

Activity 5.08 Changing Font and Font Size

A **font** is a set of characters with the same design and shape. There are two basic types of fonts—serif and sans serif. **Serif fonts** contain extensions or lines on the ends of the characters. Examples of serif fonts include Cambria, Times New Roman, and Garamond. **Sans serif fonts** do not have lines on the ends of characters. Examples of sans serif fonts include Calibri, Arial, and Comic Sans MS. The table in Figure 5.19 shows examples of serif and sans serif fonts.

Examples of Serif and Sans Serif Fonts

Serif Fonts	Sans Serif Fonts
Cambria	Calibri
Times New Roman	Arial
Garamond	Comic Sans MS

Figure 5.19

1 Hold down Ctrl and press A to select the entire document.

2 With the document selected, click the **Home tab**, and then in the **Font group**, click the **Font button arrow** Cambria ▾. At the top of the **Font** gallery, under **Theme Fonts**, point to—but do not click—**Cambria**. Notice that the font in the document changes to a preview of the Cambria font, as shown in Figure 5.20.

This is an example of **Live Preview**—a technology that shows the results of applying an editing or formatting change as you move the pointer over the results presented in a gallery or list. Here, Live Preview changes the selected text to the Cambria font, even though you did not click the font name.

A **theme** is a predefined set of colors, fonts, lines, and fill effects that look good together and that can be applied to your entire document or to specific items—for example, to a paragraph or table. As you progress in your study of Word, you will use more theme features.

Font button arrow   List of fonts   Live Preview displays the document in the chosen font

Figure 5.20

Theme Fonts

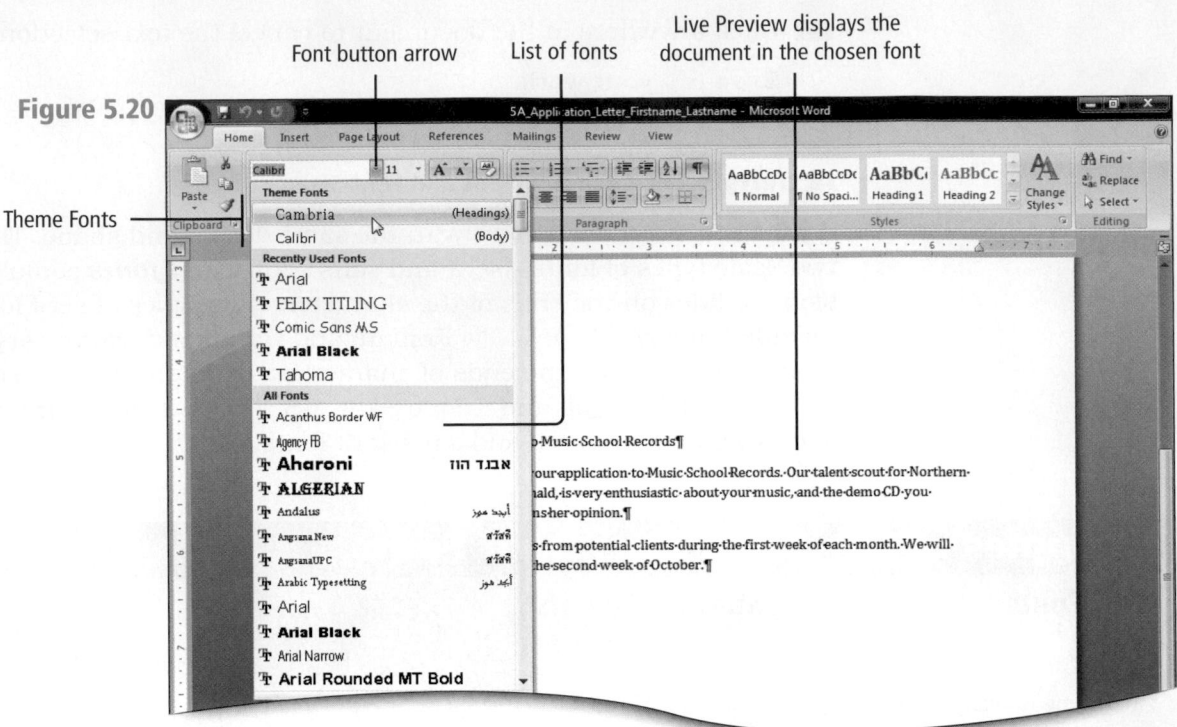

3 Click **Cambria** to apply the font to the entire document. On the Ribbon, in the **Font group**, click the **Font Size button arrow** 12 ▾, click **12**, and then click anywhere to cancel the selection. Scroll up, and then move the pointer into the left margin area, slightly to the left of the first line of the document—*Music School Records*. When the ⟨pointer⟩ pointer displays, click one time to select the entire first line of text.

Fonts are measured in ***points***, with one point equal to 1/72 of an inch. A higher point size indicates a larger font size. For large amounts of text, font sizes between 10 point and 12 point are good choices. Headings and titles are often formatted by using a larger font size. The word *point* is abbreviated as ***pt***.

4 On the Mini toolbar, click the **Font button arrow** Cambria ▾, scroll down if necessary, and then click **Arial Black**.

5 With the Mini toolbar still displayed, click the **Font Size button arrow** 12 ▾, and then click **20**.

6 Position the ⟨pointer⟩ pointer to the left of the second line of the document—*2620 Vine Street*. Drag down to select the second, third, and fourth lines of the document, ending with the telephone number.

7 On the Mini toolbar, click the **Font button arrow** Cambria ▾, and then click **Arial**. With the Mini toolbar still displayed, click the **Font Size button arrow** 12 ▾, and then click **10**. Click anywhere to cancel the selection and close the Mini toolbar, and then compare your screen with Figure 5.21.

Figure 5.21

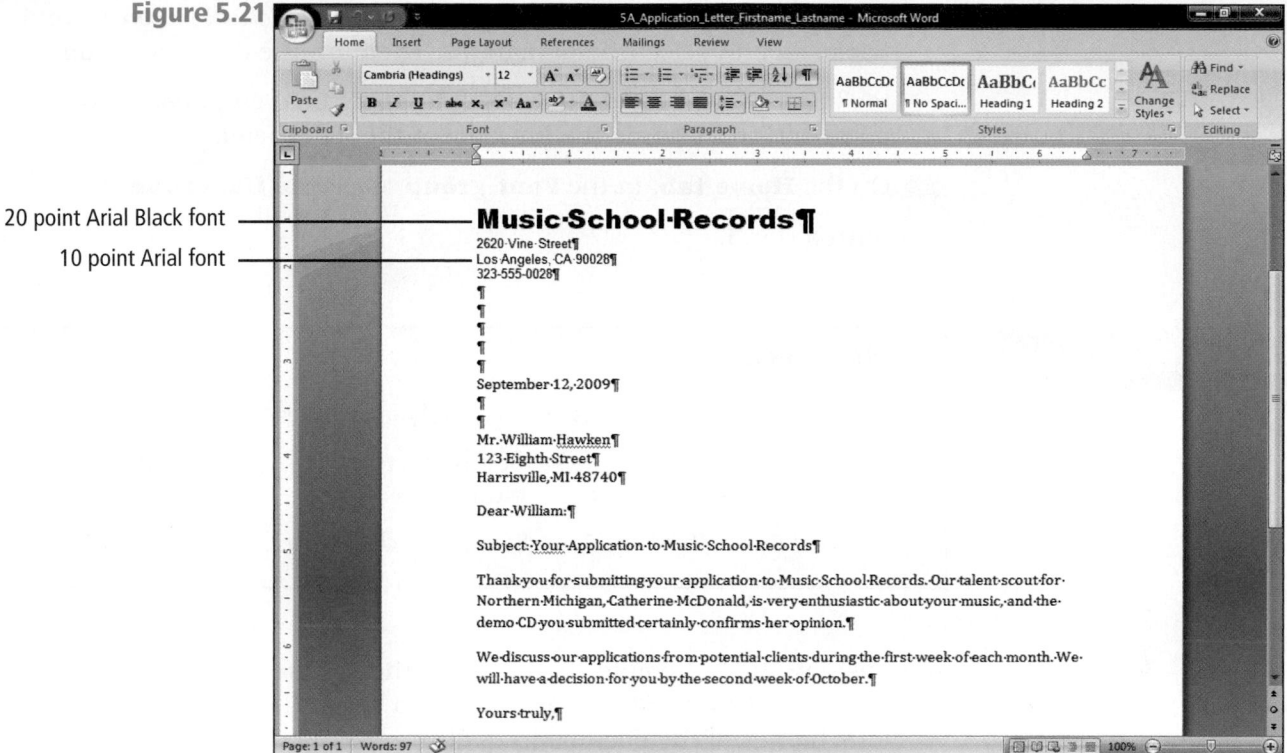

20 point Arial Black font
10 point Arial font

Note — Moving Quickly in a Long List

The list of available fonts is frequently very long. You can move quickly to any font by typing the first (or even first and second) letter of the font after you click the Font button arrow.

8 **Save** 💾 the changes you have made to your document.

Activity 5.09 Adding Emphasis to Text

Font styles emphasize text and are a visual cue to draw the reader's eye to important text. Font styles include bold, italic, and underline, although underline is not commonly used for emphasis. You can add emphasis to existing text, or you can turn the emphasis on before you start typing the word or phrase, and then turn it off.

1 Point anywhere in the first line of text—*Music School Records*—and triple-click to select the paragraph. Then, on the displayed Mini toolbar, click the **Bold** button **B** to apply bold emphasis to the paragraph that forms the first line of the letterhead.

2 On the **Home tab**, in the **Font group**, click the **Underline** button **U ▾**.

Another Way ── **To Apply Font Styles**

There are two other methods used to apply font styles:

- From the keyboard, use the keyboard shortcuts of Ctrl + B for bold, Ctrl + I for italic, or Ctrl + U for underline.
- From the Font tab of the Font dialog box, click the desired font styles.

3 Position the ⬚ pointer to the left of the second line of the document—*2620 Vine Street*. Drag down to select the second, third, and fourth lines of the document, ending with the telephone number.

4 On the displayed Mini toolbar, click the **Italic** button **I** to apply italic emphasis to the paragraph that forms the remainder of the letterhead. Click anywhere to cancel the selection.

5 From the **Office** menu ⬚ , point to **Print**, and then click **Print Preview**. Alternatively, press Ctrl + F2 to display Print Preview. Compare your screen with Figure 5.22.

The Ribbon displays the Print Preview *program tab*, which replaces the standard set of tabs when you switch to certain authoring modes or views, including Print Preview. Print Preview displays the entire page and enables you to see what the document will look like when printed.

Note — Viewing Keyboard Shortcuts

The key combinations for Ctrl keyboard shortcuts are identified in the ScreenTip for each button. The Alt keyboard shortcuts are displayed by pressing and then releasing the Alt key.

Figure 5.22

Print Preview
program tab

Close Print Preview
button

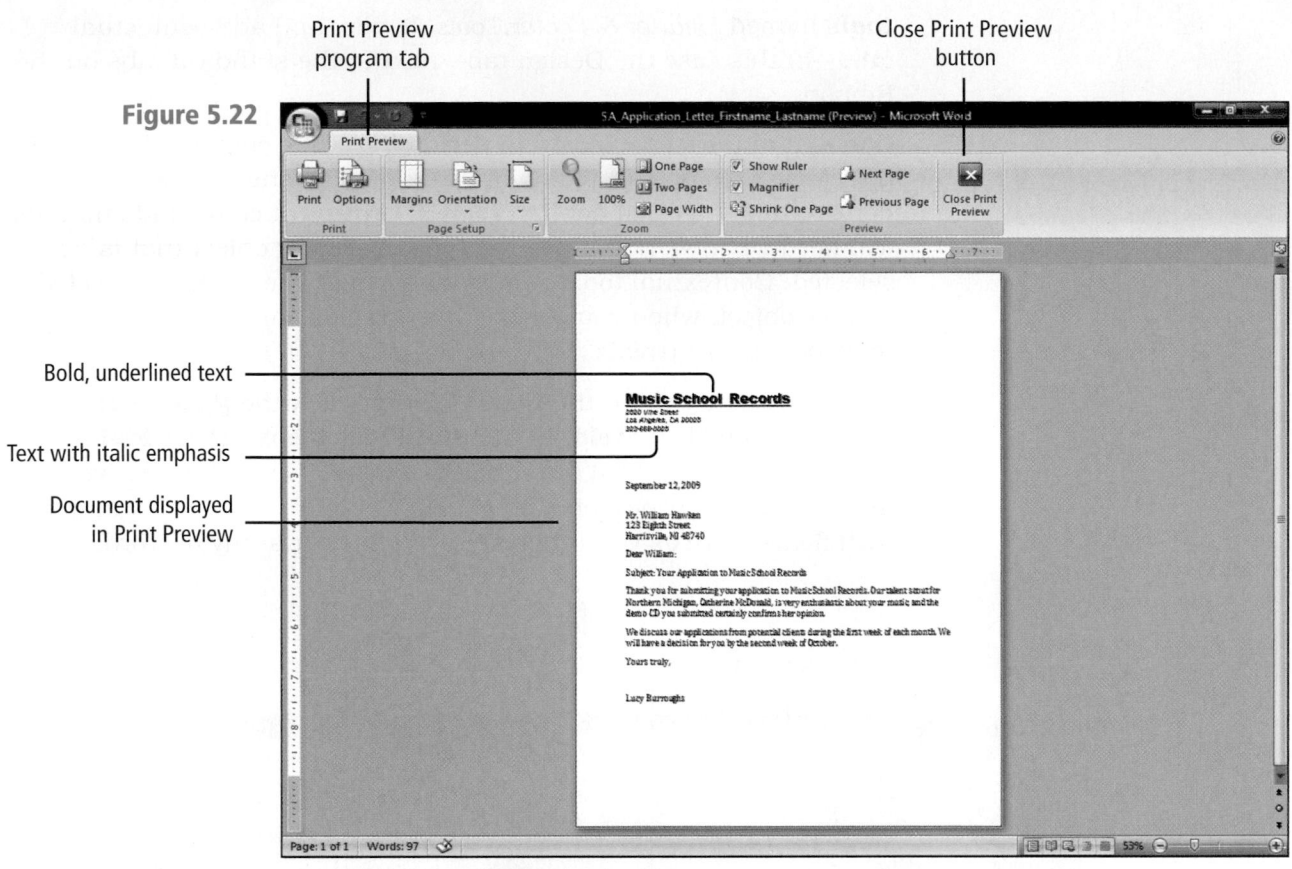

Bold, underlined text

Text with italic emphasis

Document displayed
in Print Preview

6 On the **Print Preview tab**, in the **Preview group**, click the **Close Print Preview** button, and then **Save** 💾 your changes.

Objective 4
Print a Document

Information in headers and footers helps identify a document when it is printed. A **header** is information that prints at the top of every page, and a **footer** is information that prints at the bottom of every page.

Activity 5.10 Accessing Headers and Footers

1 Click the **Insert tab**, and then, in the **Header & Footer group**, click the **Footer** button.

Another Way — **To Open a Footer**

Scroll to the bottom of the page, right-click near the bottom edge of the page, and then click Edit Footer to open the footer area.

2 At the bottom of the **Footer gallery**, click **Edit Footer**.

The footer area displays with the insertion point blinking at the left edge of the footer area. Because the footer area is active, **contextual**

tools named *Header & Footer Tools* display and add contextual tabs—in this case the Design tab—next to the standard tabs on the Ribbon.

Contextual tools enable you to perform specific commands related to the active area or selected object, and display one or more **contextual tabs** that contain related **groups** of commands that you will need when working with the type of area or object that is selected. Contextual tools display only when needed for a selected area or object; when you deselect the area or object, the contextual tools no longer display.

3 On the **Design tab**, in the **Insert group**, click the **Quick Parts** button, and then click **Field**. In the **Field** dialog box, under **Field names**, use the vertical scroll bar to examine the items that you can insert in a header or footer, as shown in Figure 5.23. You will work with fields more as you progress through your study of Word.

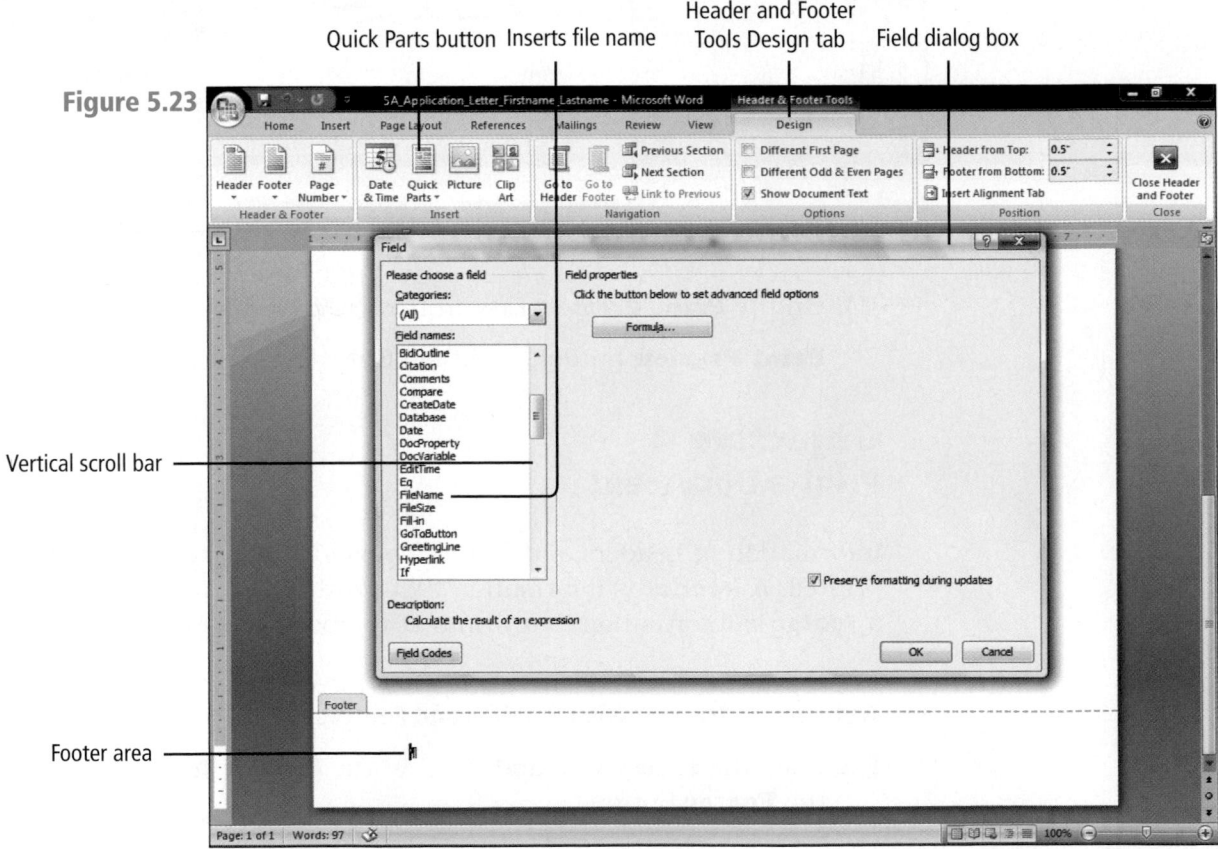

Figure 5.23

Quick Parts button   Inserts file name   Header and Footer Tools Design tab   Field dialog box

Vertical scroll bar

Footer area

4 In the **Field names** list, scroll as necessary to locate and click **FileName**, and then click **OK**.

The file name displays in the Footer area. The file extension *.docx* may or may not display, depending on your Windows settings.

5 Double-click anywhere in the document to leave the footer area. Alternatively, in the Close group, click the Close Header and Footer button. Scroll down until you can see the footer, and then compare your screen with Figure 5.24.

The footer displays in gray. Because it is a proper name and is likely not in Word's dictionary, your name in the footer may display with wavy red lines.

Figure 5.24

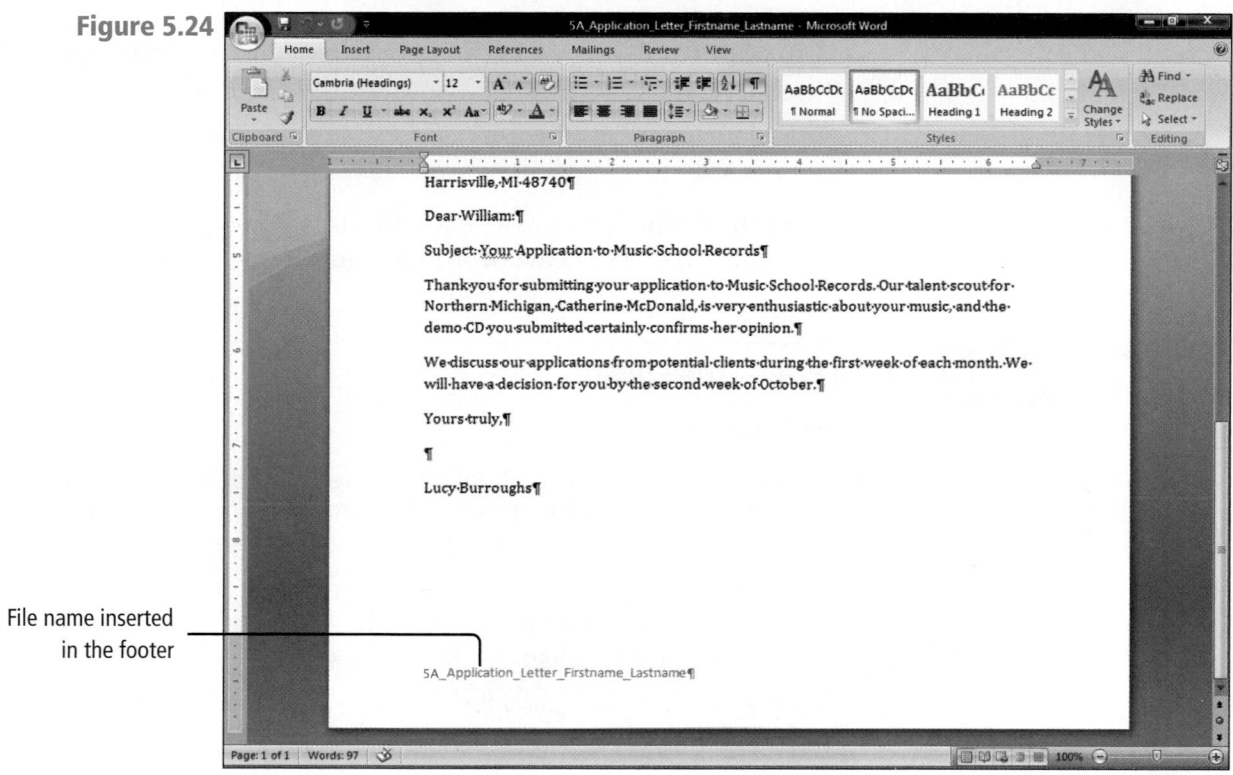

File name inserted
in the footer
5A_Application_Letter_Firstname_Lastname¶

6 Save your changes.

More Knowledge

Moving to the Header or Footer

To quickly edit an existing header or footer, double-click in the header or footer area. This will display the Header & Footer contextual tools and place the insertion point at the beginning of the header or footer. The file name field that you inserted will display with a gray background.

Activity 5.11 Printing a Document

1 Check your *Chapter Assignment Sheet* or *Course Syllabus*, or consult your instructor, to determine if you are to submit your assignments on paper or electronically, using your college's course information management system. To submit electronically, go to Step 3, and then follow the instructions provided by your instructor.

2 Click the **Office** button , point to the **Print arrow**, and then click **Quick Print**.

One copy of your document prints on the default printer connected to your system. The formatting marks that indicate spaces and paragraphs do not print.

Note — Space Between Lines in Your Printed Document

The Cambria font, and many others, uses a slightly larger space between the lines than more traditional fonts like Times New Roman. As you progress in your study of Word, you will use many different fonts and also adjust the spacing between lines.

3 From the **Office** menu 🔘 , click **Close**, saving any changes if prompted to do so. Leave Word open for the next project.

Another Way

To Print a Document

To print a document:

• From the Office menu, click Print to display the Print dialog box (to be covered later), from which you can choose a variety of different options, such as printing multiple copies, printing on a different printer, and printing some but not all pages.

• Hold down Ctrl, and then press P. This is an alternative to the Office menu command, and opens the Print dialog box.

• Hold down Alt, press F, and then press P. This opens the Print dialog box.

End **You have completed Project 5A** ————————————

Project 5B **Company Overview**

In Activities 5.12 through 5.23, you will create a document that describes the mission of Music School Records. You will add a graphic image to the document, and insert text from another document. Your completed document will look similar to Figure 5.25.

For Project 5B, you will need the following files:

w05B_Music_School_Records
w05B_Music_Logo

You will save your document as
5B_Company_Overview_Firstname_Lastname

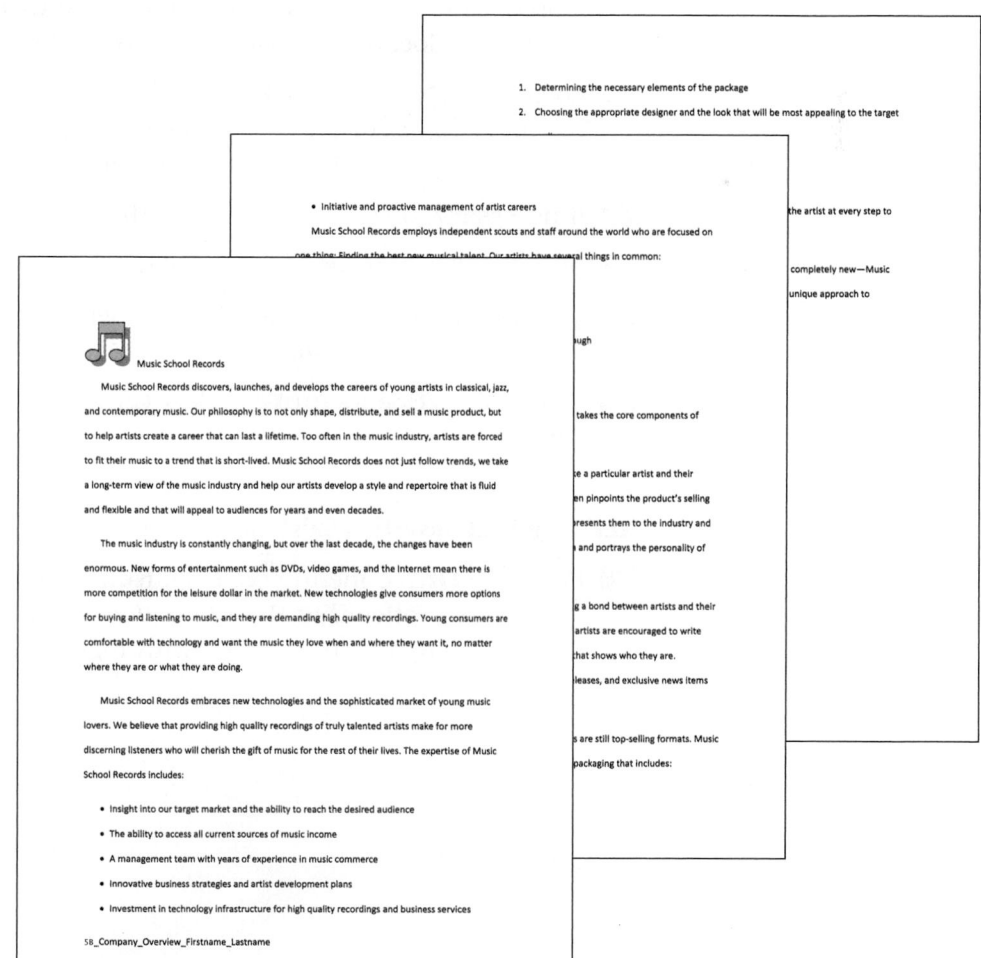

Figure 5.25
Project 5B—Company Overview

Objective 5
Navigate the Word Window

Most Word documents are longer than the Word window—some are wider than the window. Use the scroll bars to *navigate*—move around in—a document. Keyboard shortcuts provide additional navigation techniques that you cannot accomplish with scroll bars. For example, using keyboard shortcuts, you can move the insertion point to the beginning or end of a word, line, paragraph, or document.

Activity 5.12 Opening and Closing an Existing Document

1 If necessary, **Start** Word. From the **Office** menu, click **Open**.

2 Navigate to the location where the student files for this textbook are stored, which may be on a CD that came with your textbook or in some other location designated by your instructor.

3 Locate **w05B_Music_School_Records** and click to select it. Then, in the lower right corner of the **Open** dialog box, click the **Open** button. Alternatively, double-click the file name.

4 If necessary, on the Home tab, in the Paragraph group, click the Show/Hide ¶ button ¶ to display the nonprinting characters.

The document displays in the Word window. This text will be inserted into a new document in Activity 5.13.

5 From the **Office** menu, click **Close** to close the document and leave Word open.

Activity 5.13 Inserting Existing Text into a New Document

1 From the **Office** menu, click **New** to display the **New Document** dialog box. Notice that the *Blank document* button is selected by default. Compare your screen with Figure 5.26.

Blank document button

Figure 5.26

New Document dialog box

Create button

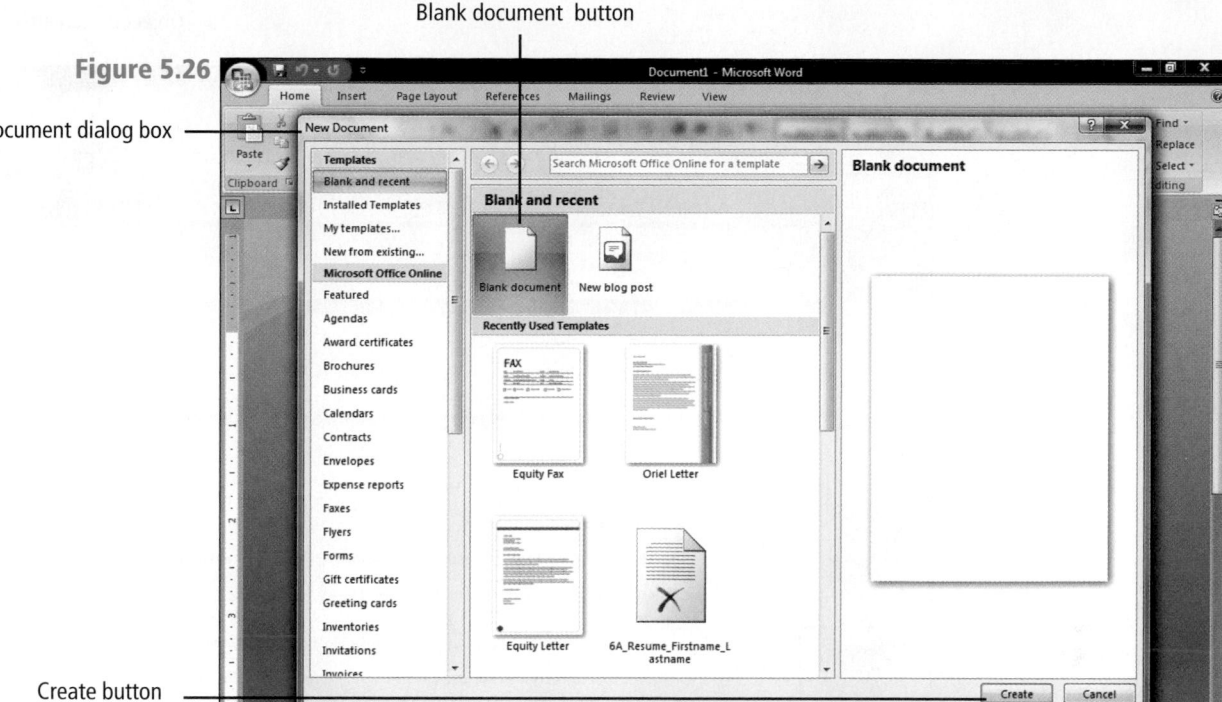

2 In the lower right corner of the **New Document** dialog box, click **Create** to create a new document. Type **Music School Records** and then press Enter.

3 On the Ribbon, click the **Insert tab**. In the **Text group**, click the **Object button arrow**, and then click **Text from File**.

Alert!

Did the Object dialog box display?

If the Object dialog box displays, then you clicked the Object button instead of the Object button arrow. Close the Object dialog box, and then in the Text group, click the Object button arrow, as shown in Figure 5.27. Click Text from File, and then continue with Step 4.

4 In the displayed **Insert File** dialog box, navigate to the location where the student files for this textbook are stored. Locate **w05B_Music_School_Records**, click to select it, and then in the lower right corner, click the **Insert** button. Compare your screen with Figure 5.27.

A copy of the text from the w05B_Music_School_Records document is inserted into the blank document, the last page of the three-page document displays, and the insertion point displays at the end of the inserted text. The original w05B_Music_School_Records document remains intact and undisturbed. The page number, total number of pages in the document, and number of words in the document display in the status bar.

Object button arrow

Figure 5.27

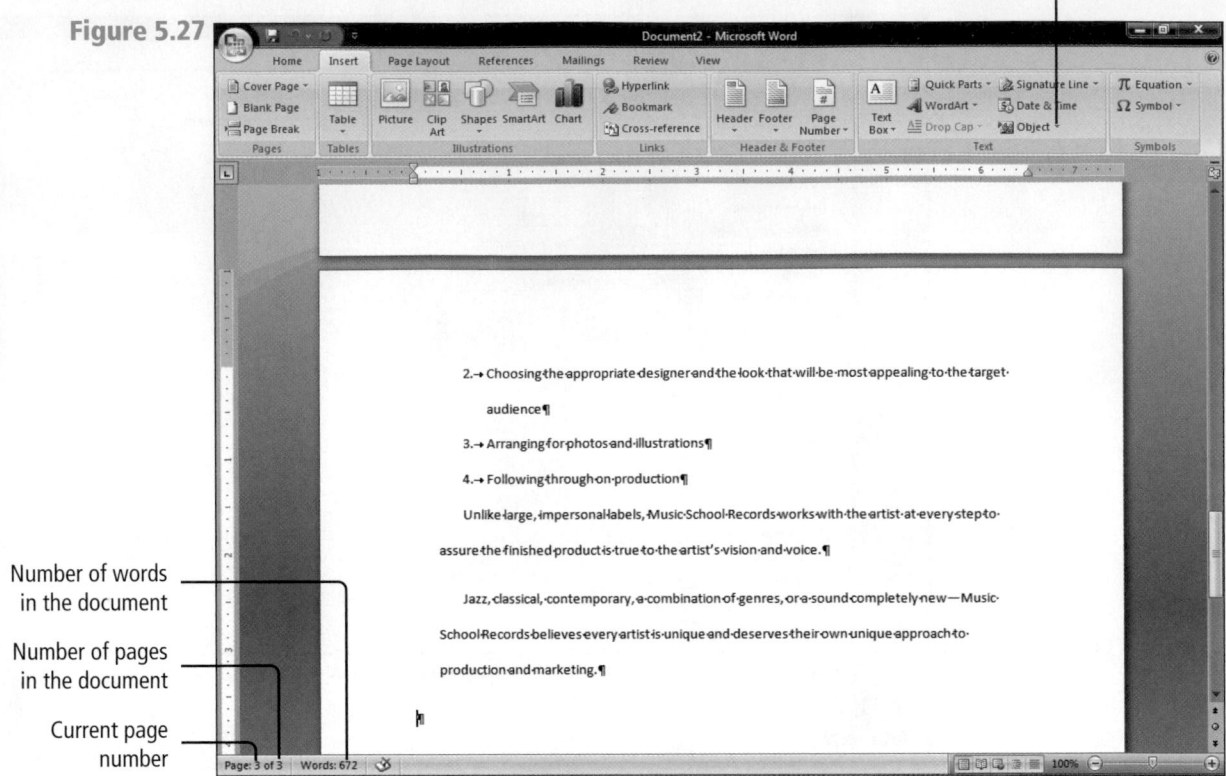

Number of words in the document

Number of pages in the document

Current page number

5 Press ←Bksp to delete the blank line at the end of the document. On the **Quick Access Toolbar**, click the **Save** button. In the displayed **Save As** dialog box, navigate to your **Word Chapter 5** folder.

Recall that because this is a new unnamed document—*Document2* or some other number displays in the title bar—the *Save As* dialog box displays so that you can name and designate a storage location for the document. The first line of text in the document displays in the *File name* box.

6 In the **File name** box, delete any existing text, and then using your own first and last names, type **5B_Company_Overview_Firstname_Lastname** and then click **Save**.

7 On the **Insert tab**, in the **Header & Footer group**, click the **Footer** button. At the bottom of the displayed **Footer gallery**, click **Edit Footer**. Alternatively, right-click near the bottom edge of the page, and then from the shortcut menu, click Edit Footer.

A *shortcut menu* is a context-sensitive menu that displays commands relevant to the selected object.

8 On the **Design tab**, in the **Insert group**, click the **Quick Parts** button, and then click **Field**. In the **Field** dialog box, under **Field names**, locate and click **FileName**, and then click **OK**.

9 Double-click anywhere in the document to leave the footer area. Alternatively, in the Close group, click the Close Header and Footer button. **Save** your document.

Activity 5.14 Navigating a Document

1 At the right of your screen, in the vertical scroll bar, locate the **up scroll arrow** at the top of the scroll bar as shown in Figure 5.28. Then, click the **up scroll arrow** five times. Notice that the document scrolls up one line at a time. Also, notice that the scroll box is near the bottom of the vertical scroll bar.

Up scroll arrow

Figure 5.28

Scroll box

Down scroll arrow

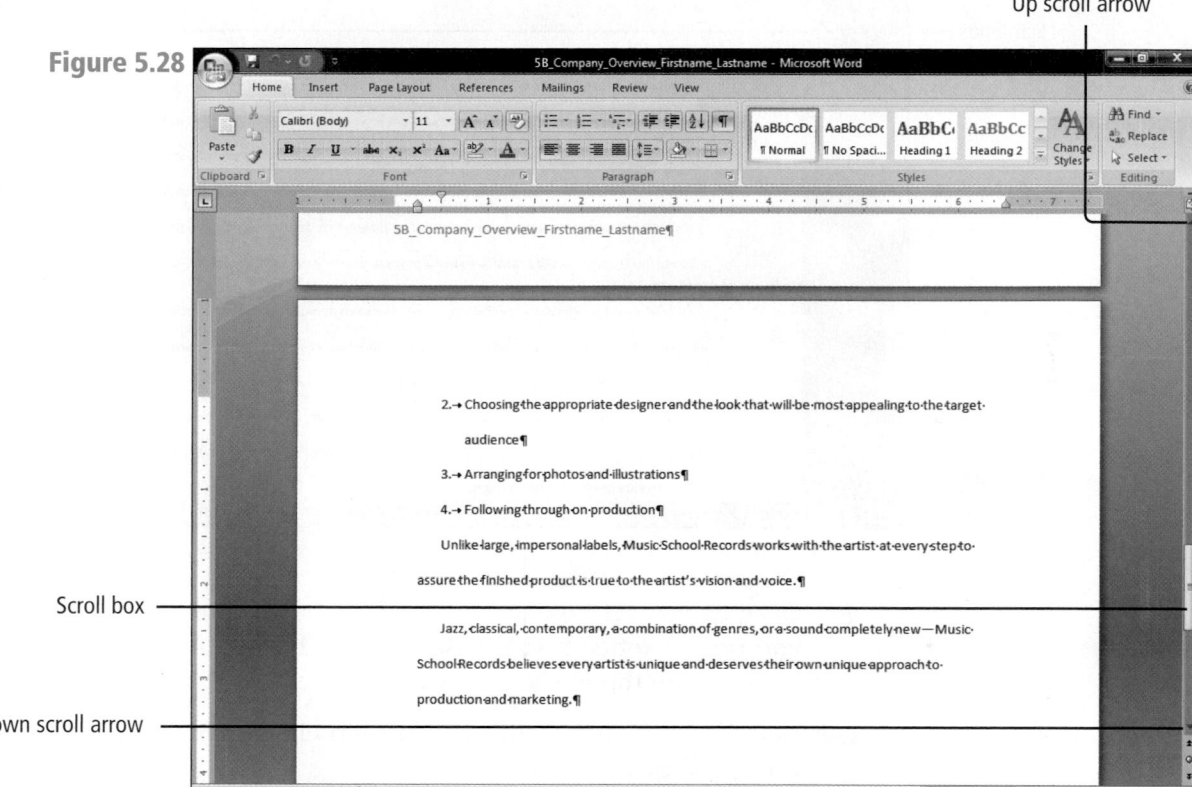

2 Point to the **up scroll arrow** again. Click and hold down the mouse button for several seconds.

The document text scrolls up continuously, one line at a time.

3 At the top of the vertical scroll bar, point to the **up scroll arrow**, and then click and hold down the mouse button until you have scrolled to the beginning of the document. As you do so, notice that the scroll box moves up in the scroll bar—like an elevator going to the top floor.

4 Near the top of the vertical scroll bar, point to the **scroll box**, and then press and hold down the left mouse button. Compare your screen with Figure 5.29.

A ScreenTip displays, indicating the page number. The page number and total number of pages in the document are displayed in the status bar—in this case, page 1 of 3 pages.

Figure 5.29

ScreenTip

Scroll box

Page 1 of 3 pages

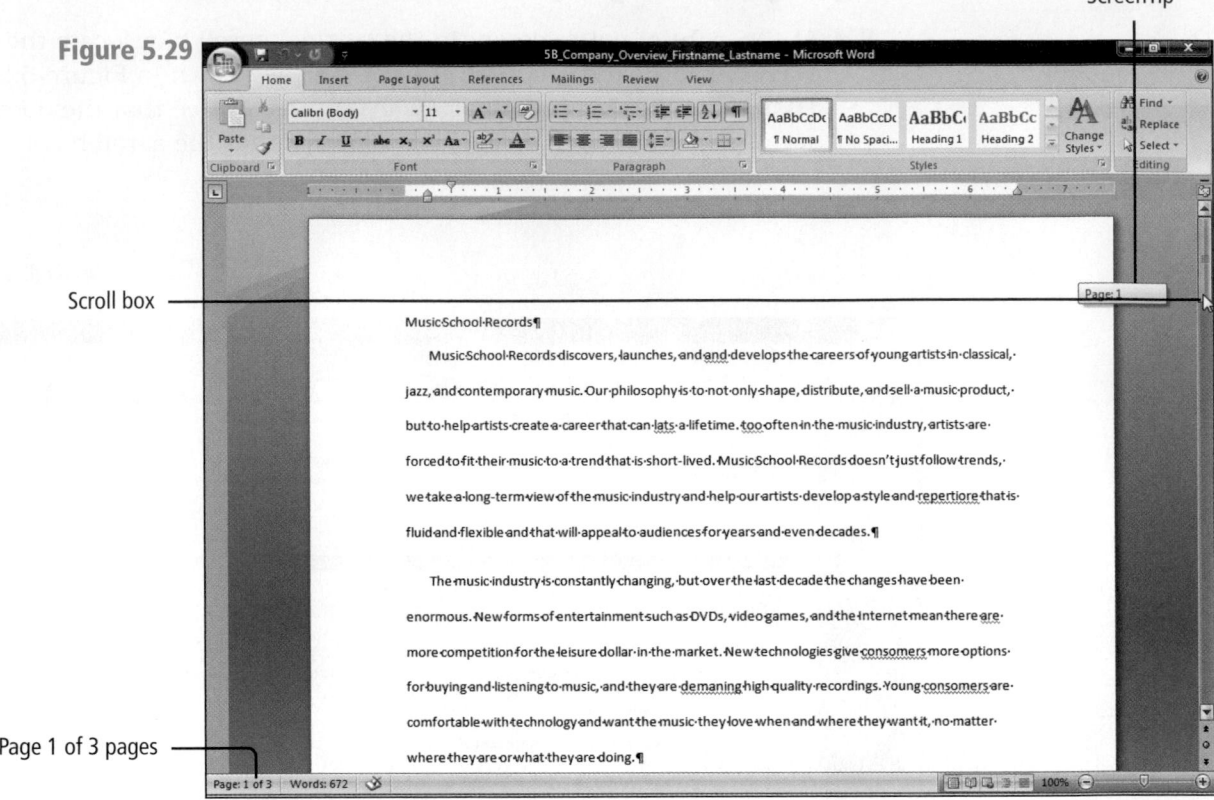

5 Drag the **scroll box** slowly down to the bottom of the scroll bar. As you do so, notice that the ScreenTip changes as each new page reaches the top of the screen.

6 Release the mouse button, and then click in the dark area just above the scroll box.

The document scrolls up one screen. This is a quick way to scan a document.

7 Practice clicking in the area above and below the scroll box.

Another Way — To Scroll Through a Document

If your mouse has a small wheel button between the left and right mouse buttons, you can scroll up and down in the document by rotating the wheel.

8 On your keyboard, hold down Ctrl and press Home.

The beginning of the document displays, and the insertion point moves to the left of the first word in the document. In this document, Word has flagged some spelling, grammar, and contextual errors (red, green, and blue wavy lines), which you will correct in Activity 5.19.

Alert!

Does the shortcut not work?

If you are using a laptop computer, you may have to hold down a function `Fn` key to use shortcuts that involve the `Home`, `End`, `PgUp`, and `PageDown` keys.

9 Hold down `Ctrl` and press `End`.

10 Press `PgUp` to scroll the document up one screen. Press `End`.

The insertion point moves to the end of the current line of text.

11 Take a moment to study the table shown in Figure 5.30, which lists the most commonly used keyboard shortcuts.

Navigating a Document Using Keyboard Shortcuts

To Move	Press
To the beginning of a document	`Ctrl` + `Home`
To the end of a document	`Ctrl` + `End`
To the beginning of a line	`Home`
To the end of a line	`End`
To the beginning of the previous word	`Ctrl` + `←`
To the beginning of the next word	`Ctrl` + `→`
To the beginning of the current word (if insertion point is in the middle of a word)	`Ctrl` + `←`
To the beginning of the previous paragraph	`Ctrl` + `↑`
To the beginning of the next paragraph	`Ctrl` + `↓`
To the beginning of the current paragraph (if insertion point is in the middle of a paragraph)	`Ctrl` + `↑`
Up one screen	`PgUp`
Down one screen	`PageDown`

Figure 5.30

12 Hold down `Ctrl` and press `Home` to position the insertion point at the beginning of the document.

Activity 5.15 Changing Document Views

1 Near the right side of the status bar, locate the **View** buttons.

Use these buttons to switch to different document views.

To View Documents

There are five ways to view your document on the screen. Each view is useful in different situations.

- Print Layout view displays the page borders, margins, text, and graphics as they will look when you print the document. Most Word users prefer this view for most tasks, and it is the default view.

- Full Screen Reading view creates easy-to-read pages that fit on the screen to increase legibility. This view does not represent the pages as they would print. Each screen page is labeled with a screen number, rather than a page number.

- Web Layout view shows how the document will look when saved as a Web page and viewed in a Web browser.

- Outline view shows the organizational structure of your document by headings and subheadings and can be collapsed and expanded to look at individual sections of a document.

- Draft view simplifies the page layout for quick typing, and shows a little more text on the screen than the Print Layout view. Graphics, headers, and footers do not display.

2 Click the **Draft** button, and then examine the way the document is displayed.

3 Click the **Full Screen Reading** button.

Text displays in a side-by-side format, and can be read like a book.

4 Near the upper right corner of the screen, click the **Close** button to display the document in Print Layout view.

In this view, you can see all of the elements that will display on paper when you print the document. The instructions in this textbook will use Print Layout view for most documents.

Activity 5.16 Using the Zoom Slider

To *zoom* means to increase or decrease the viewing area of the screen. You can zoom in to look closely at a particular section of a document, and then zoom out to see a whole page on the screen. You can also zoom to view multiple pages on the screen.

1 On the right side of the status bar, just to the right of the View buttons, drag the **Zoom slider** to the right until you have zoomed to approximately 150%, as shown in Figure 5.31.

Figure 5.31

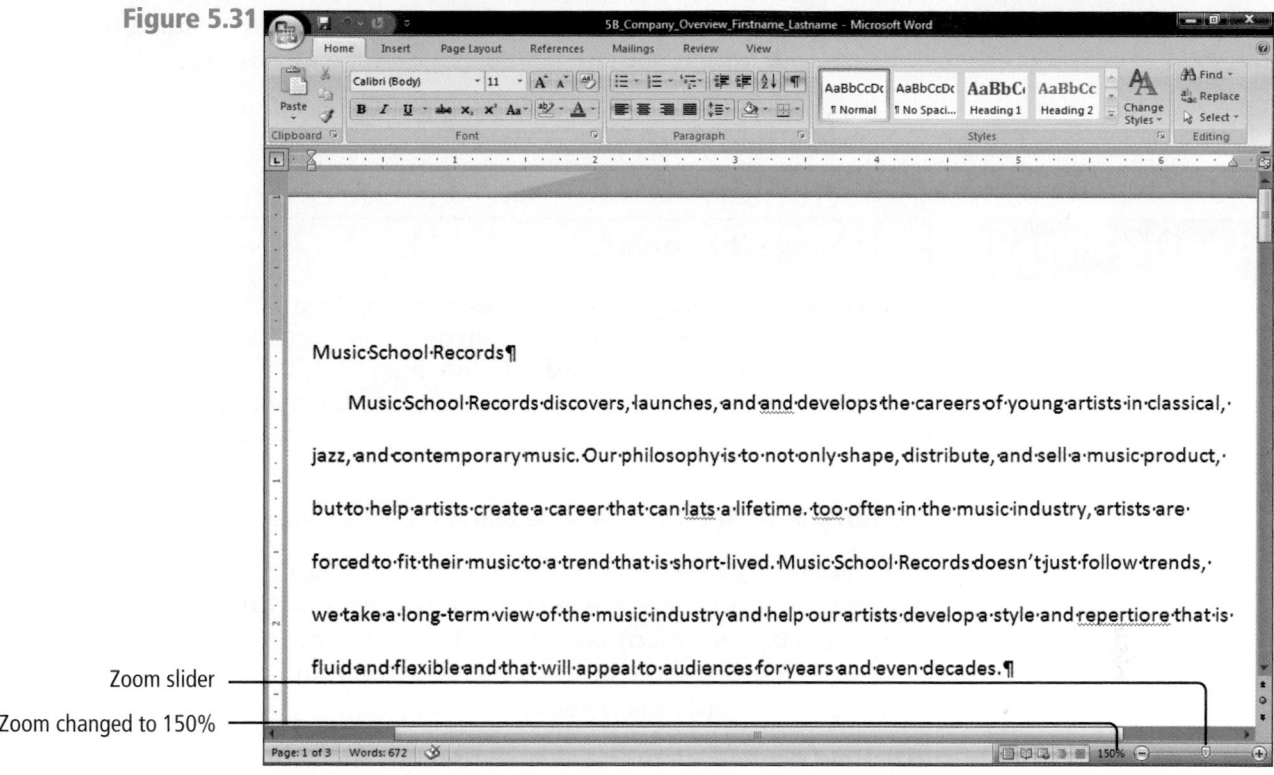

Zoom slider

Zoom changed to 150%

2 Drag the **Zoom slider** to the left until you have zoomed to approximately 40%, as shown in Figure 5.32. Notice that as the pages get smaller, multiple pages display.

Figure 5.32

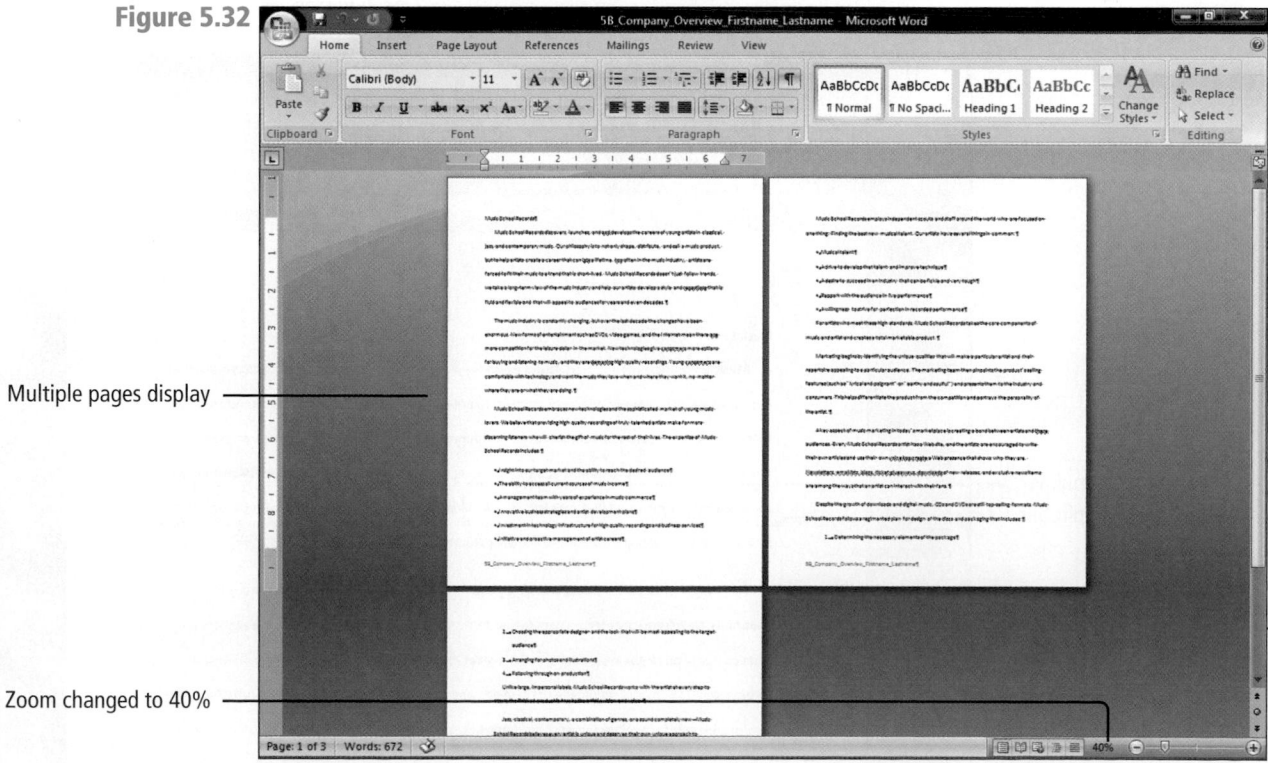

Multiple pages display

Zoom changed to 40%

3 Drag the **Zoom slider** to the right until you have zoomed to a page size with which you are comfortable—typically 100%.

As you work on various documents, you can adjust the zoom to best display the document.

Activity 5.17 Splitting Windows and Arranging Panes

Word enables you to split the screen, which enables you to look at two different parts of the same document at the same time. In a long document, this is convenient for viewing both the first page and the last page at the same time. You can also view two different documents side by side and make comparisons between the two.

1 Hold down Ctrl and press Home to move the insertion point to the beginning of the document. On the Ribbon, click the **View tab**, and then, in the **Window group**, click the **Split** button. Notice that a *split bar* displays near the middle of the document area, with a move pointer ⊞ on the bar. The split bar indicates the location of the border between the windows. Compare your screen to Figure 5.33.

Figure 5.33

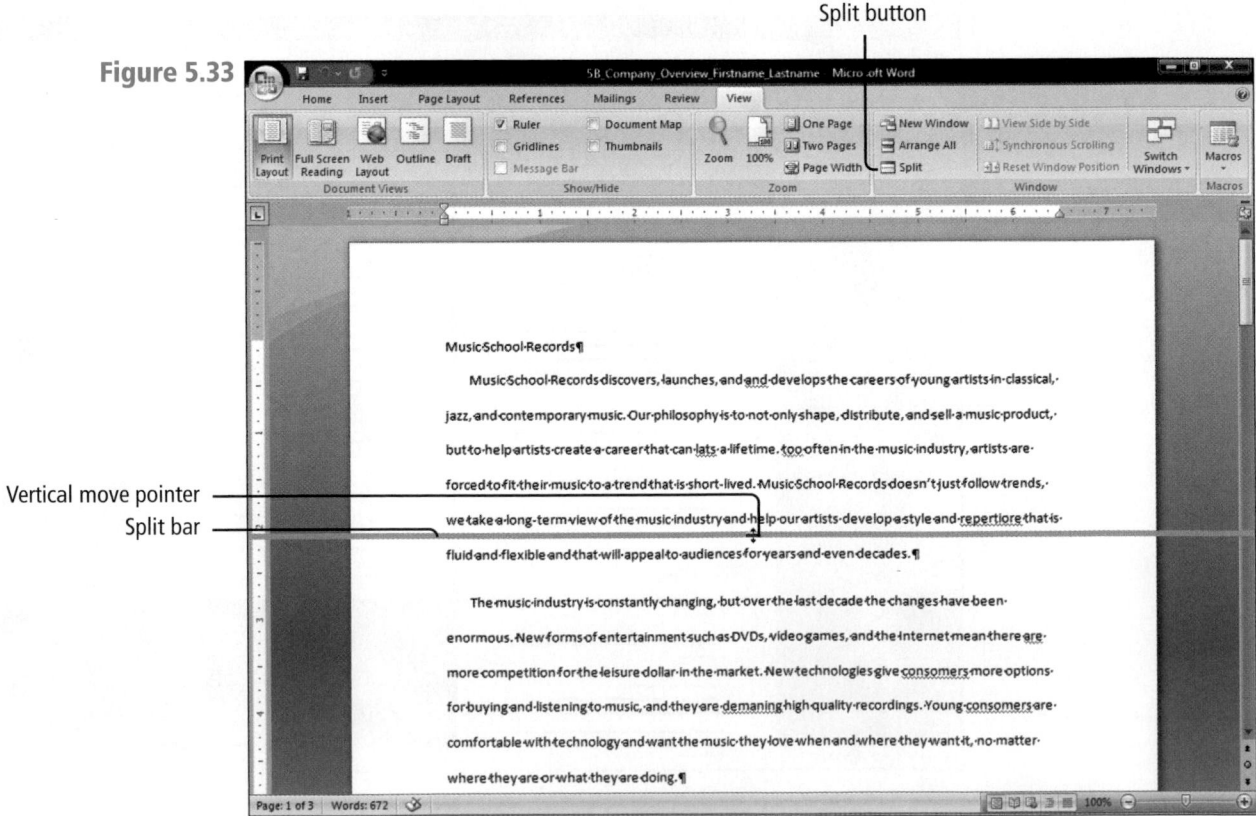

2 Drag the split bar to just below the fifth line of text—including the title—that contains the phrase *that is short lived*, and then click to position the split bar. Notice that both the top and bottom halves of the screen display rulers, and two different parts of the same document display in the two document windows, as shown in Figure 5.34. If you don't see the rulers, on the **View** tab, in the **Show/Hide** group, select the **Ruler** check box.

Different areas of the same document

Figure 5.34

Split bar extends across the screen

Two document windows

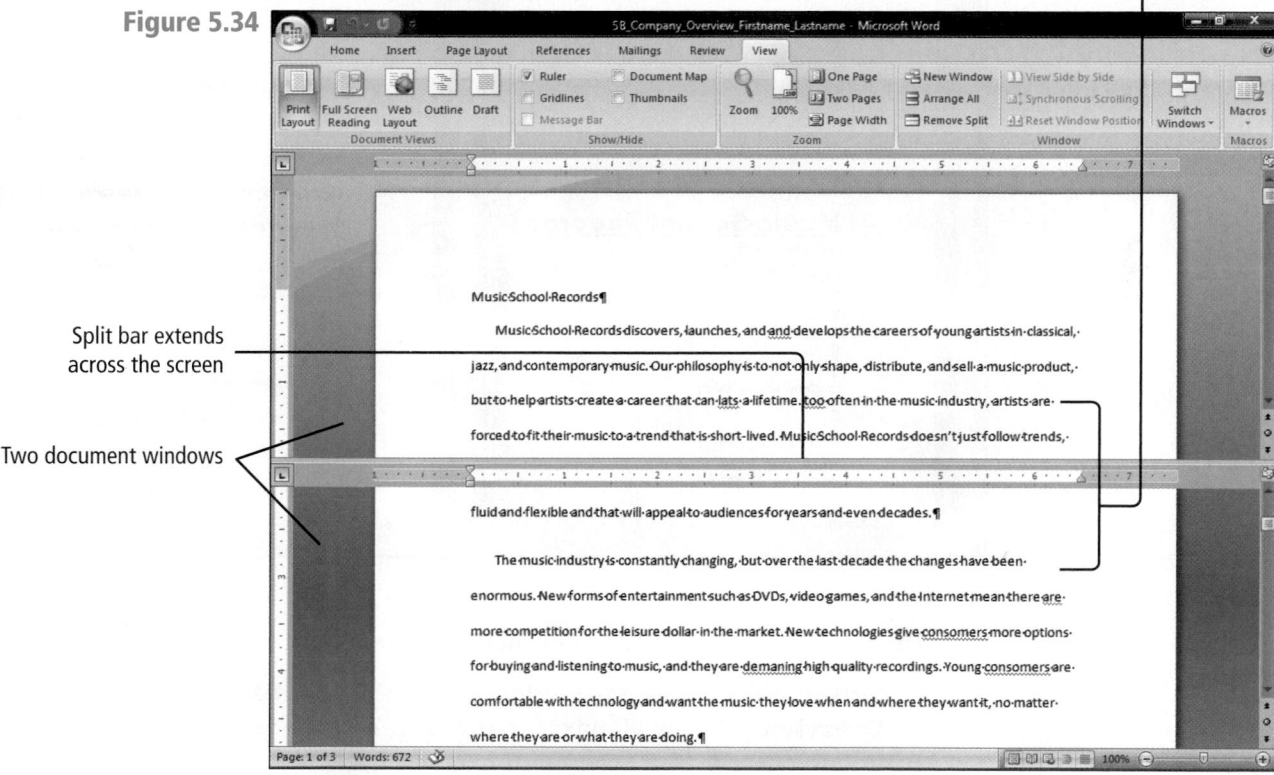

3 Using the top vertical scroll bar, scroll down and up in the top window. Notice that the portion of the document displayed in the top window moves independently from the portion of the document displayed in the bottom window.

4 Using the bottom vertical scroll bar, scroll up and down in the bottom window.

5 On the **View tab**, in the **Window group**, click the **Remove Split** button to return to a single document window.

6 From the **Office** menu, click **Open**. Locate and open the **5A_Application_Letter** document that you created in Project 5A.

7 Click the **View tab**, and then in the **Window group**, click the **View Side by Side** button to display both documents at the same time, as shown in Figure 5.35. Alternatively, in the Window group, you can click the Arrange All button to arrange the two documents in horizontal windows that look similar to the two document windows you created by using the split button.

With two documents open, you can edit both at the same time, or move text or objects between the documents.

Different documents   View tab

Figure 5.35

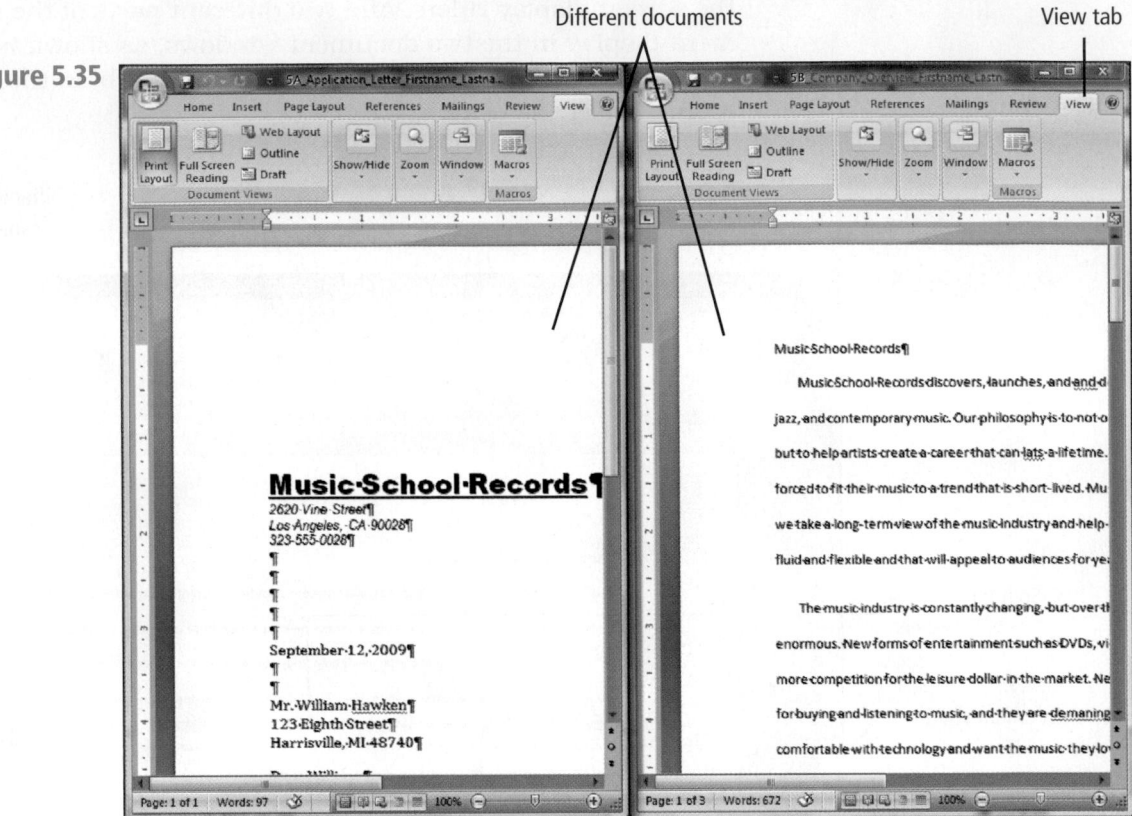

8 On the title bar of the document on the left, click the **Close**
button ![X] to close the letter. Notice that the **5B_Company_Overview** window is maximized when the other window is closed.

Objective 6
Add a Graphic to a Document

Graphics can be inserted into a document from many sources. *Clip art* images—predefined graphics included with Microsoft Office or down-loaded from the Web—can make your document more interesting and visually appealing.

Activity 5.18 Inserting Clip Art

1 Press Ctrl + Home to move the insertion point to the beginning of the document. Press Spacebar three times, and then press ← three times to move the insertion point back to the beginning of the line.

2 Click the **Insert tab**, and then in the **Illustrations group**, click the **Clip Art** button.

3 In the displayed **Clip Art** task pane, in the **Search for** box, type **Music** and then in the **Search in** box, be sure **All collections** is selected. Click the **Results should be arrow**, and then clear all the check boxes except **Clip Art**. Click **Go**, and then compare your screen with Figure 5.36. If necessary, scroll up to view the first displayed music images.

Figure 5.36

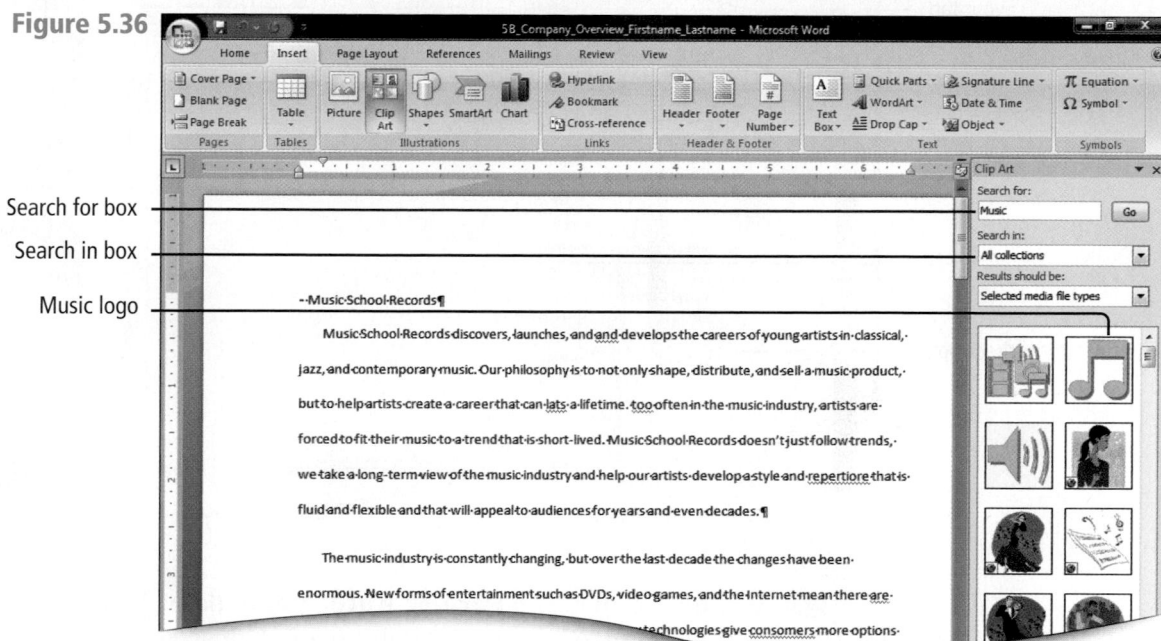

Search for box
Search in box
Music logo

4 Click the **music logo** clip art image. Notice that the image displays over the text.

Alert! ——— **Can't find the right image?**

Some minimum installations of Microsoft Word contain very few clip art images. If the music logo image does not display in the Clip Art task pane, close the task pane. Then, from the Illustrations group, click the Picture button. Navigate to the location where your student files for this textbook are stored, click the w05B_Music_Logo file, and then click Insert. If you use the student file, the image will not need to be formatted. Go to step 8.

5 Right-click the image, and then from the displayed shortcut menu, click **Format AutoShape**. In the displayed **Format AutoShape** dialog box, on the **Layout tab**, under **Wrapping style**, click **In line with text**, which will treat the clip art image as a text character.

6 In the **Format AutoShape** dialog box, click the **Size tab**. Under **Scale**, click the **Lock aspect ratio** check box. In the **Height** box, select the current value, and then type **30** to reduce the image to 30% of its original size. Compare your dialog box to Figure 5.37.

The ***aspect ratio*** of an object is the relationship of its height to its width. If you lock the aspect ratio, changing either the height or width of an object will resize the object proportionally.

Figure 5.37

Layout tab

Size tab

New size of object

Lock aspect ratio check box

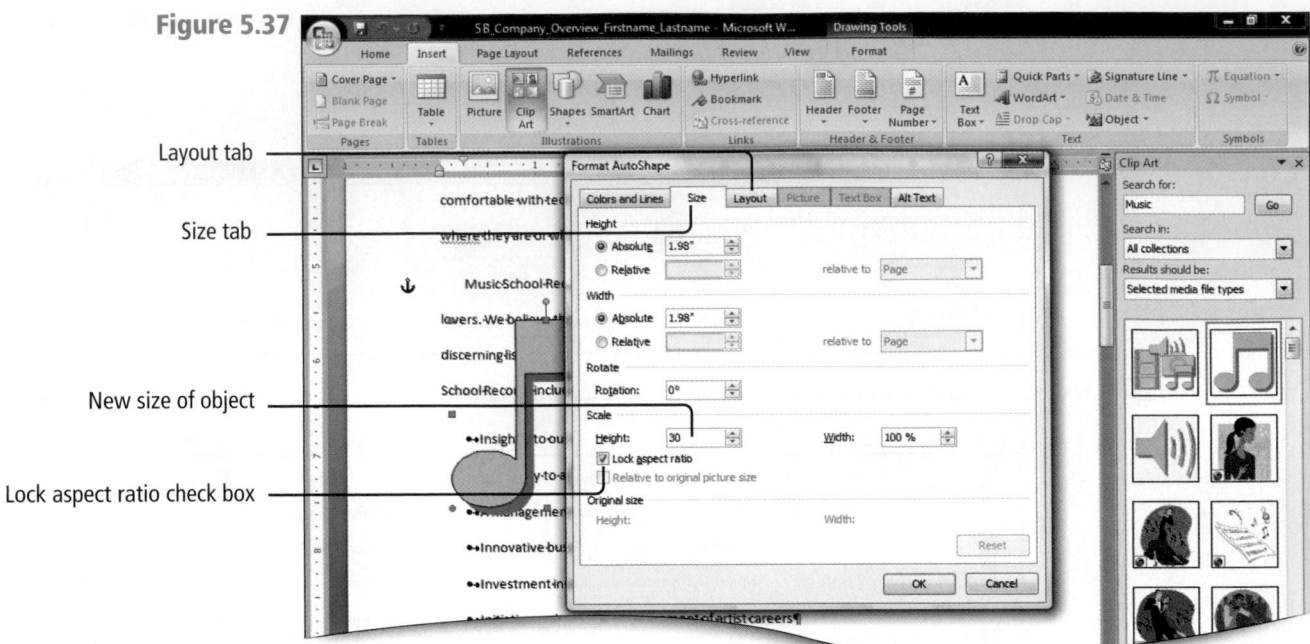

7 At the bottom of the **Format AutoShape** dialog box, click **OK**, and then click anywhere in the document to deselect the image. Compare your screen with Figure 5.38.

Figure 5.38

Task pane Close button

Inserted clip art image

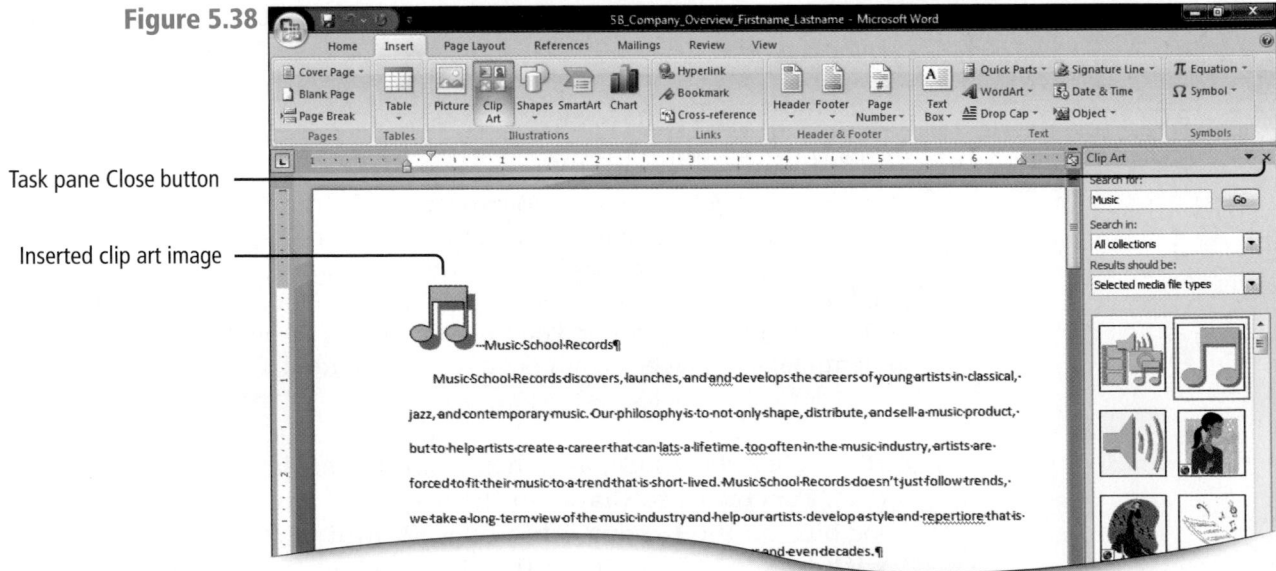

8 **Close** the **Clip Art** task pane, and then **Save** your document.

Objective 7
Use the Spelling and Grammar Checker

As you type, Word compares your words to those in the Word dictionary and compares your phrases and punctuation to a list of grammar rules. Words that are not in the Word dictionary are marked with a wavy red underline. Phrases and punctuation that differ from the grammar rules are marked with a wavy green underline. Because a list of grammar rules applied by a computer program can never be exact, and because a computer dictionary cannot contain all known words and proper names, you will need to check any words flagged by Word as misspellings or grammar errors.

Word will also place a blue wavy underline under a word that is spelled correctly but used incorrectly, such as the misuse of *their*, *there*, and *they're*. However, Word will not flag the word *sign* as misspelled, even though you intended to type *sing a song* rather than *sign a song*, because both are legitimate words contained within Word's dictionary, but not variations of the same word.

Activity 5.19 Checking Individual Spelling and Grammar Errors

One way to check spelling and grammar errors flagged by Word is to right-click the flagged word or phrase, and then from the displayed shortcut menu, choose a suitable correction or instruction.

1 Scan the text on the screen to locate green, red, and blue wavy underlines.

Note — Activating Spelling and Grammar Checking

If you do not see any wavy red, green, or blue lines under words, the automatic spelling and/or grammar checking has been turned off on your system. To activate the spelling and grammar checking, display the Office menu, click Word Options, and then in the list, click Proofing. Under *When correcting spelling in Office programs*, click the first four check boxes. Under *When correcting spelling and grammar in Word*, click the first four check boxes, and then click the Writing Style arrow and click Grammar & Style. Under *Exceptions for*, clear both check boxes. To display the flagged spelling and grammar errors, click the Recheck Document button, and then close the dialog box.

2 In the first line of the paragraph that begins *Music School Records discovers*, locate the word *and* with the wavy red underline. Point to the word and **right-click**—click the right mouse button—to display a shortcut menu, as shown in Figure 5.39.

A shortcut menu displays under the Mini toolbar. Word identified a duplicate word, and provides two suggestions—*Delete Repeated Word* or *Ignore*. The second option is included because sometimes the same word will be correctly used two times in succession.

Word flagged with red wavy underline

Figure 5.39

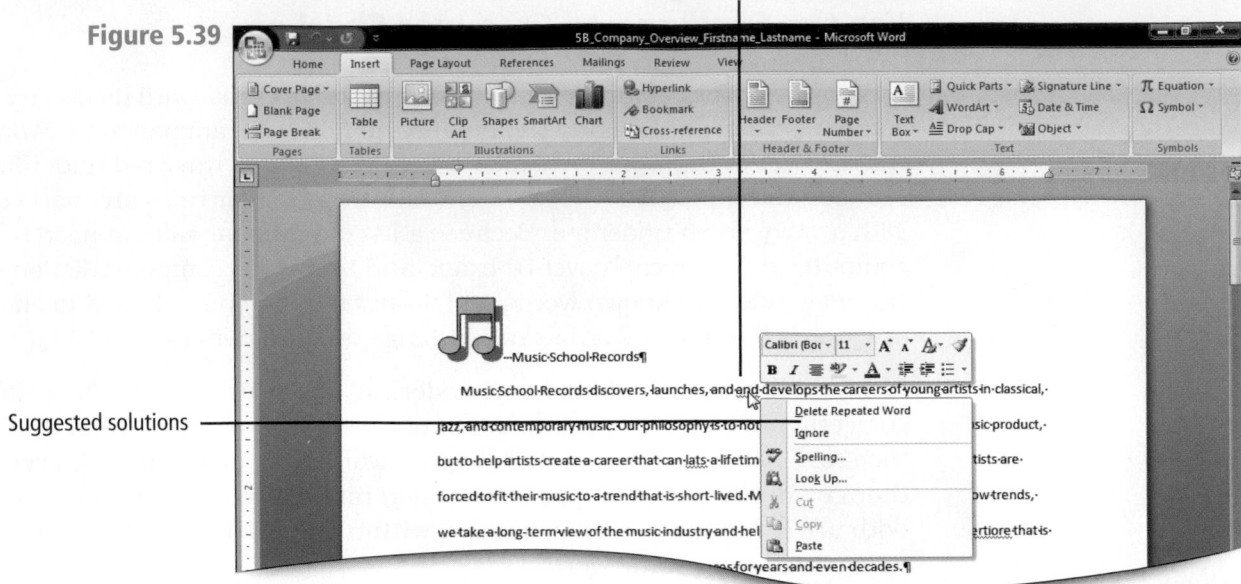

Suggested solutions

3 From the shortcut menu, click **Delete Repeated Word** to delete the duplicate word.

4 In the third line of the same paragraph, locate and right-click the misspelled word *lats*, and then compare your screen to Figure 5.40.

In this instance, Word has identified a misspelled word. Suggested replacements are shown at the top of the shortcut menu.

Figure 5.40

Suggested replacements

Word flagged with wavy red underline

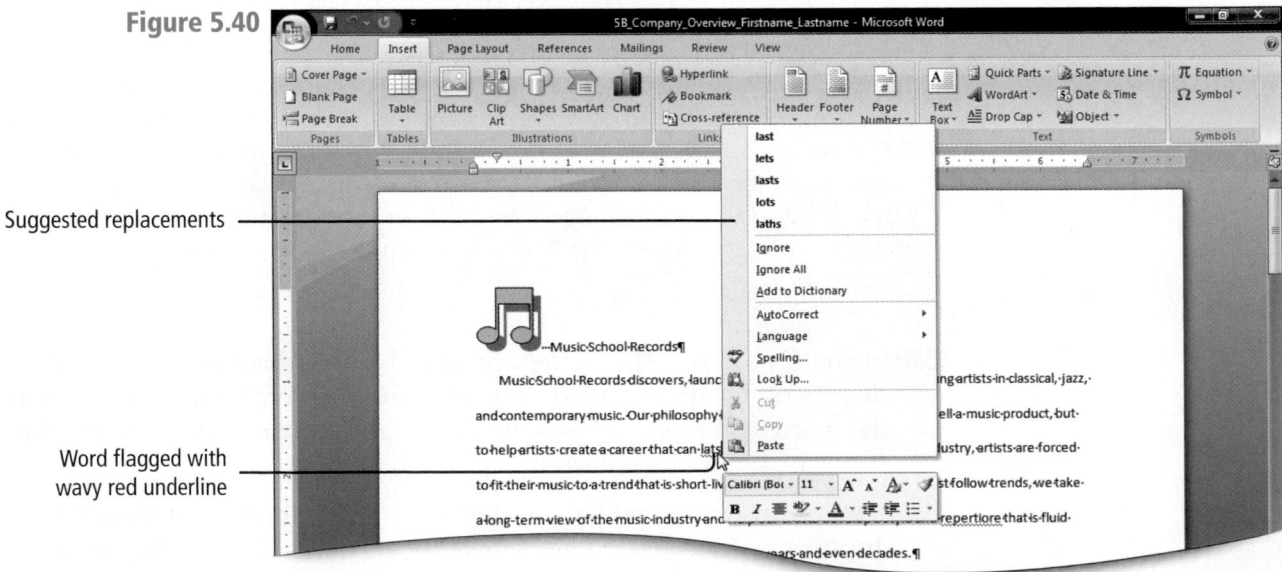

5 At the top of the shortcut menu, click **last** to replace the misspelled word.

6 In the third line of the same paragraph, locate and right-click the word *too* that has a wavy green underline.

The wavy green underline indicates a grammar error; in this case, a word at the beginning of a sentence that should be capitalized.

7 From the displayed shortcut menu, click **Too** to capitalize the word.

8 Scroll down to display the bottom of **Page 2**. In the paragraph beginning *A key aspect*, notice that two words have wavy blue underlines.

The wavy blue underline indicates a word that is recognized by the dictionary, but may be the wrong form of the word—in this case *there* is incorrectly used instead of *their*, and *too* is used instead of *to*.

9 In the paragraph beginning *A key aspect*, right-click *there*, and then from the shortcut menu, click **their**. In the same paragraph, right-click *too*, and then from the shortcut menu, click **to**.

10 **Save** the changes you have made to your document.

Activity 5.20 Checking Spelling and Grammar in an Entire Document

Initiating the spelling and grammar checking feature from the Ribbon displays the Spelling and Grammar dialog box, which provides more options than the shortcut menus.

1 Scan the document to locate red, green, and blue wavy underlines.

Notice the icon in the status bar, which indicates that the document contains flagged entries that need to be addressed.

2 Press Ctrl + Home to move the insertion point to the beginning of the document. Click the **Review tab**, and then in the **Proofing group**, click the **Spelling & Grammar** button to begin to check the document.

The first suggested error may be a potential grammar error—using a passive voice.

Alert!

Do your spelling and grammar selections differ?

The errors that are flagged by Word depend on the Proofing settings. Not all of the potential errors listed in this activity may appear in your spelling and grammar check. Your document may also display errors not noted here. If you run across flagged words or phrases that aren't included here, click the Ignore Once button to move to the next potential error.

3 If a *passive voice* error is flagged, in the **Spelling and Grammar** dialog box, click the **Ignore Once** button. If necessary, point to the title bar of the dialog box, and then drag the dialog box out of the way so you can see the misspelled word *repertiore*, which is selected. Compare your screen with Figure 5.41.

Under Not in Dictionary, the misspelled word displays in red, and under Suggestions, a suggested change is presented.

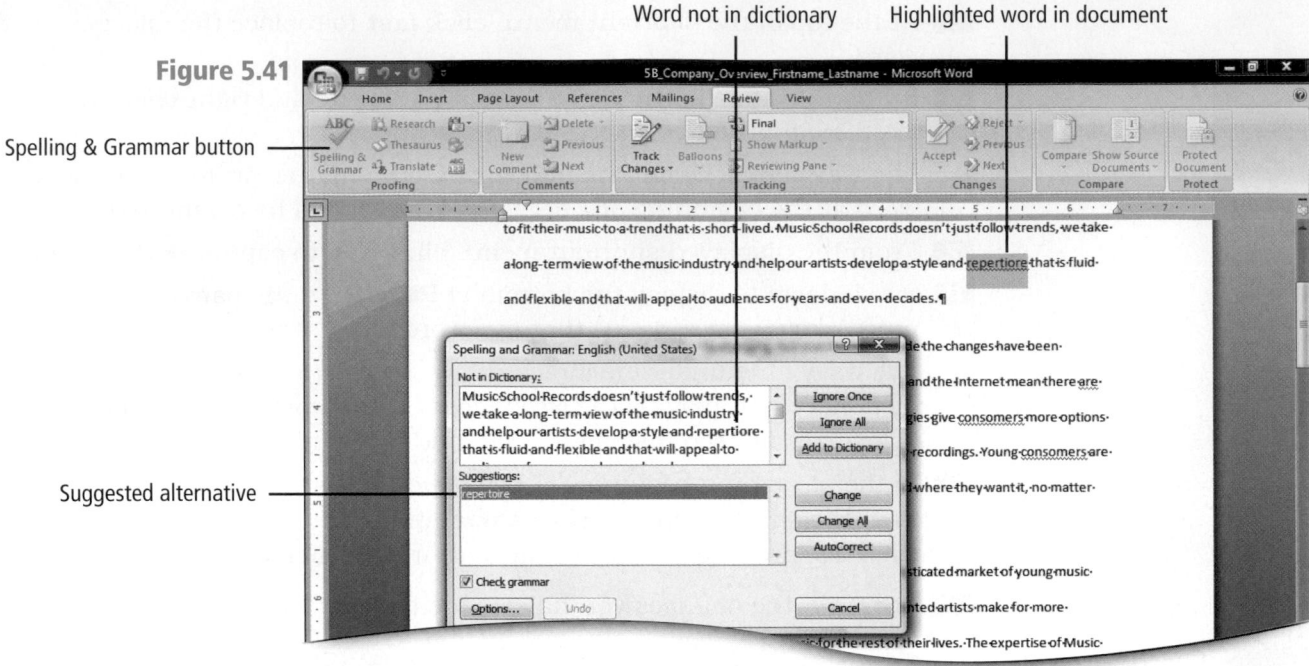

Figure 5.41

Spelling & Grammar button

Word not in dictionary

Highlighted word in document

Suggested alternative

4 Take a moment to study the spelling and grammar options available in the **Spelling and Grammar** dialog box as shown in the table in Figure 5.42.

Spelling and Grammar Dialog Box Buttons

Button	Action
Ignore Once	Ignores the identified word one time, but flags it in other locations in the document.
Ignore All	Discontinues flagging any instance of the word anywhere in the document.
Add to Dictionary	Adds the word to a custom dictionary, which can be edited. This option does not change the built-in Office dictionary.
Change	Changes the identified word to the word highlighted under Suggestions.
Change All	Changes every instance of the word in the document to the word highlighted under Suggestions.
AutoCorrect	Adds the flagged word to the AutoCorrect list, which will subsequently correct the word automatically if misspelled in any documents typed in the future.
Ignore Rule (Grammar)	Ignores the specific rule used to determine a grammar error and removes the green wavy line.
Next Sentence (Grammar)	Moves to the next identified error.
Explain (Grammar)	Displays the rule used to identify a grammar error.
Options	Displays the Proofing section of the Word Options dialog box.

Figure 5.42

5 If necessary, under **Suggestions**, select **repertoire**, and then click the **Change** button. Compare your screen with Figure 5.43.

The correction is made and the next identified error is highlighted, which is a contraction use error. Under Contraction Use, the entire sentence displays, with the contraction *doesn't* displayed in green. The suggested replacement—*does not*—displays in the Suggestions box. If you do not see a Contraction Use error, you have Grammar checking turned on, but not Style checking. When the spelling check is done, go back and make this change manually.

Alert! ⎯⎯⎯ **If the Contraction Use Error Does Not Display**

Recall that because of the settings on your computer, your spelling and grammar selections may differ.

Grammar error

Figure 5.43

Suggested replacement

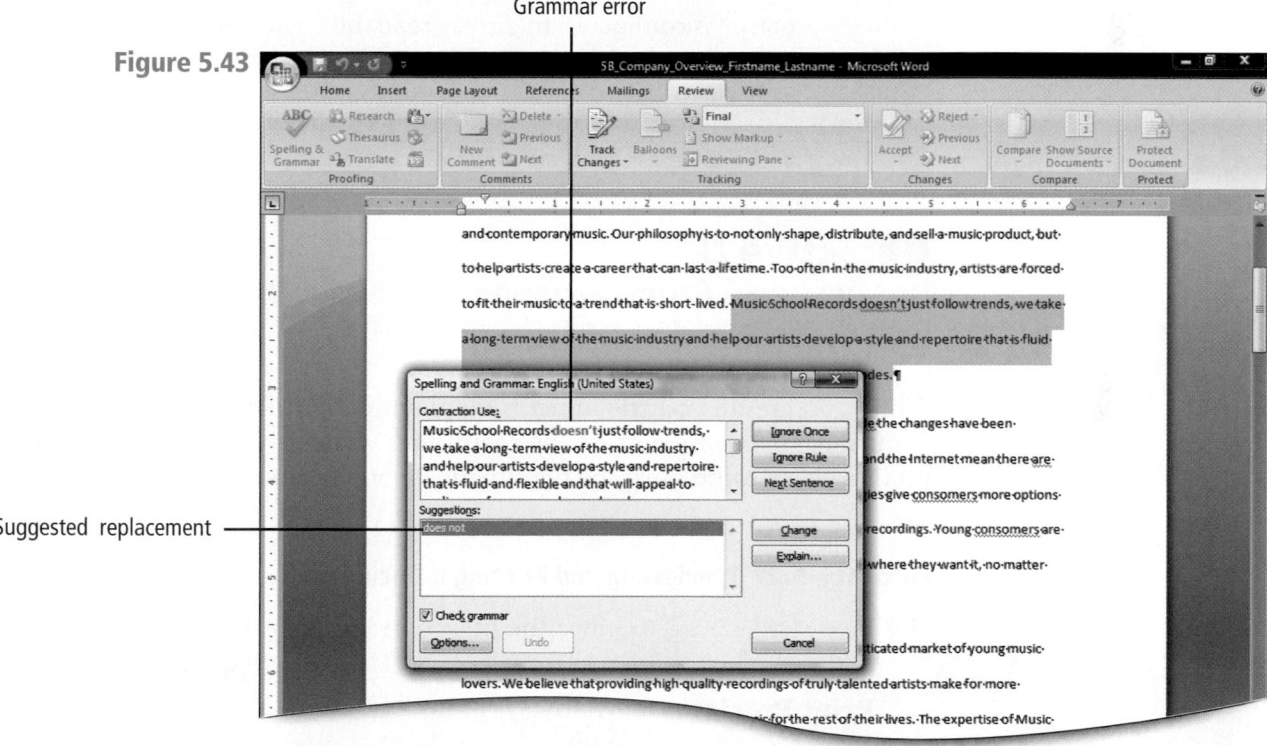

6 Under **Suggestions**, be sure **does not** is selected, and then click the **Change** button.

The correction is made and the next identified error is highlighted, which is a grammar error. Under Comma Use, the entire sentence displays. The suggested change is to add a comma.

7 Under **Suggestions**, be sure **decade,** is selected, and then click the **Change** button.

The error is corrected, and the next potential error displays, a Subject-Verb Agreement grammar error.

8 Under **Suggestions**, be sure **is** is selected, and then click the **Change** button.

The error is corrected, and the next potential error displays. The word *consomers* is misspelled in two successive sentences.

9 Under **Suggestions**, be sure **consumers** is selected, and then click the **Change All** button to change all instances of the misspelled word.

10 Continue to the end of the document. Change *demaning* to **demanding**, and then click **Ignore Once** for any other marked words or phrases.

A message indicates that the spelling and grammar check is complete.

11 Click **OK** to close the dialog box, and then **Save** 💾 your changes.

Alert!

Does the Readability Statistics box display?

If your program is configured to display readability statistics, a Readability Statistics dialog box displays. Readability statistics include character, word, paragraph, and sentence counts, along with reading level statistics. After reviewing the information, click OK to close the dialog box.

Objective 8
Preview and Print Documents, Close a Document, and Close Word

While you create your document, displaying Print Preview helps to ensure that you are getting the result you want. Before printing, make a final preview to be sure the document layout is what you intended.

Activity 5.21 Previewing and Printing a Document

1 Press Ctrl + Home to move the insertion point to the beginning of the document. From the **Office** menu 🗔 , point to **Print**, and then click **Print Preview**. Alternatively, press Ctrl + F2.

One or more pages of your document display exactly as they will print. The formatting marks, which do not print, are not displayed. The size of the preview depends on the zoom level used the last time the Print Preview window was opened.

2 In the **Print Preview** window, move the mouse pointer anywhere over the document. Notice that the pointer becomes a magnifying glass with a plus in it, indicating that you can magnify the view, as shown in Figure 5.44.

If you are viewing multiple pages, you may have to click on a page before the magnifying glass displays.

Figure 5.44

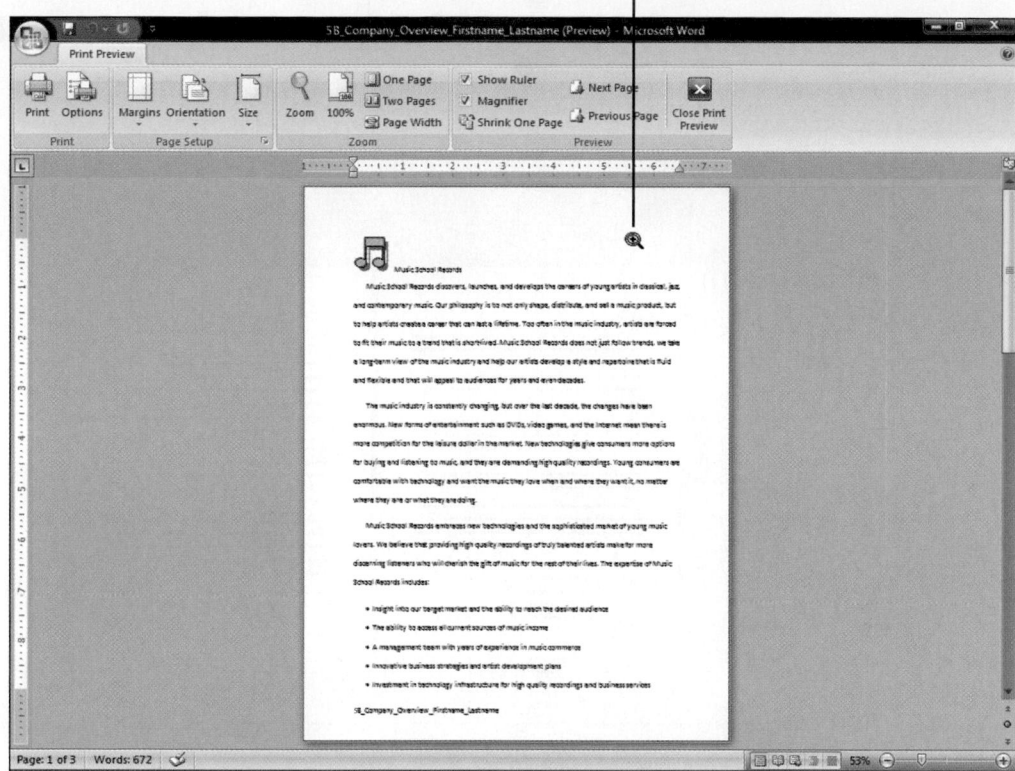

3 Move the 🔍 pointer over the upper portion of the first page of the document and click one time.

The top portion of the document is magnified, making it easier to read. The pointer changes to a magnifying glass with a minus sign.

4 Click anywhere on the document to zoom out. On the right side of the status bar, drag the **Zoom slider** to the left until you can see all three pages, as shown in Figure 5.45.

All three pages of the document display on the screen. The footers display on the bottom of each page.

One Page button

Figure 5.45

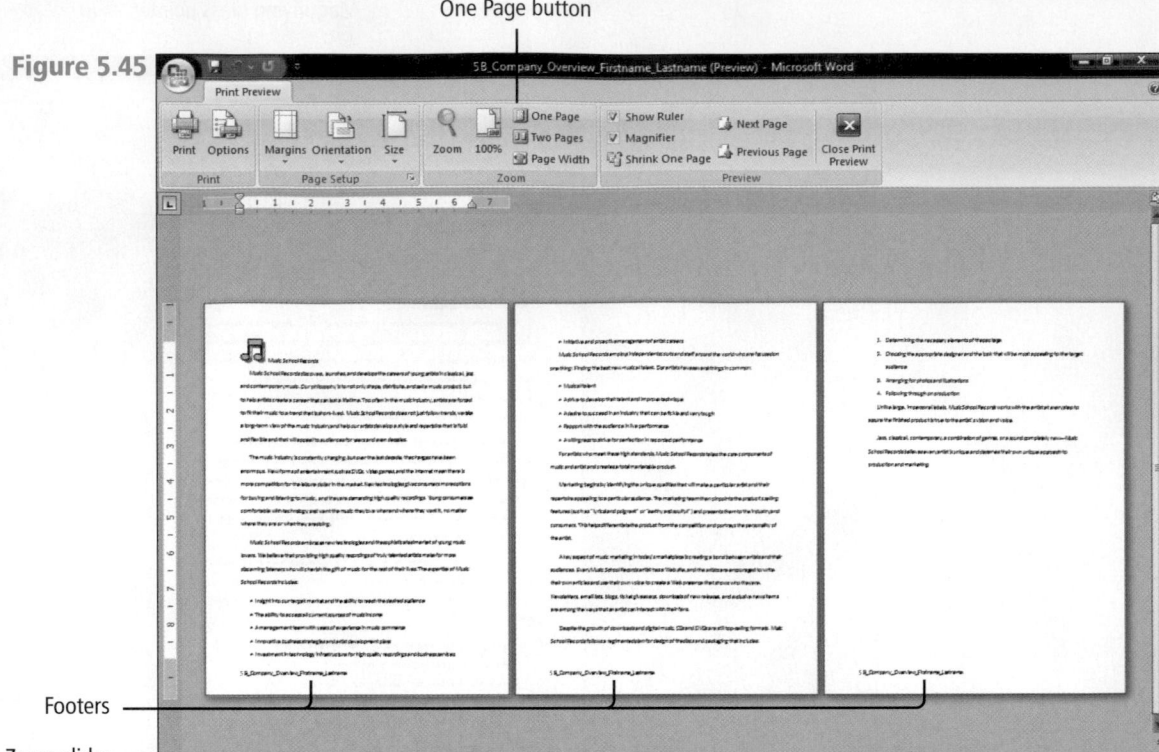

Footers

Zoom slider

5 On the **Print Preview tab**, in the **Zoom group**, click the **One Page** button to display a single page of the document.

6 In the **Preview group**, click the **Close Print Preview** button.

7 From the **Office** menu 🔘 , click **Print**, and then compare your screen with Figure 5.46.

The Print dialog box displays. Here you can specify which pages to print and how many copies you want. Additional command buttons for Options and Properties provide more printing choices. The printer that displays will be the printer that is selected for your computer.

Figure 5.46

Selected printer

Number of copies

Current page option

Pages to print

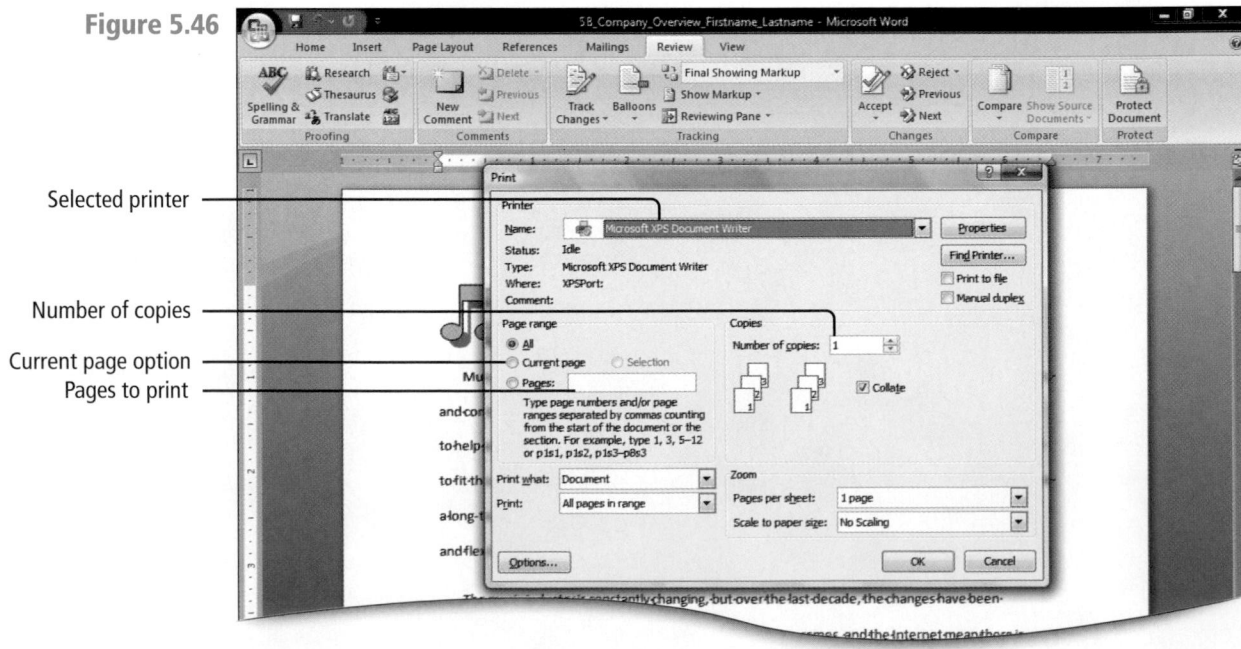

8 In the displayed **Print** dialog box, under **Copies**, change the number of copies to *2* by typing **2** in the text box, or by clicking the **spin box up arrow**.

A *spin box* is a small box with upward- and downward-pointing arrows that enables you to move—spin—through a set of values by clicking.

9 Under **Page range**, click the **Current page** option button, and then, at the bottom of the **Print** dialog box, click **OK** if you want to print two copies of the first page. If you do not want to print, click **Cancel**.

Activity 5.22 Closing a Document and Closing Word

1 Check your *Chapter Assignment Sheet* or *Course Syllabus* or consult your instructor to determine if you are to submit your assignments on paper or electronically. To submit electronically, go to Step 3, and then follow the instructions provided by your instructor.

2 From the **Office** menu , click **Print**. At the bottom of the displayed **Print** dialog box, click **OK**. Collect your printout from the printer and submit it as directed.

3 From the **Office** menu , click **Close**, saving any changes if prompted to do so.

The document closes, but the Word program remains open.

4 At the far right edge of the title bar, click the **Close** button to exit the Word program.

Objective 9
Use the Microsoft Help System

As you work with Word, you can get assistance by using the Help feature. You can type key words and phrases and Help will provide you with information and step-by-step instructions for performing tasks.

Activity 5.23 Getting Help

Word Help is available on your computer, online at the Microsoft Web site, and on your screen with enhanced ScreenTips.

1 **Start** Word. On the Ribbon, click the **Page Layout tab**, and then in the **Page Setup group**, point to—but do not click—the **Hyphenation** button.

The ScreenTip for this button has more information than just the name, including a link to the topic in the Help system. This is called an *Enhanced ScreenTip*, and is part of the Microsoft Office 2007 Help system.

2 Move your pointer to the right side of the Ribbon and click the **Microsoft Office Word Help** button 🔘. In the **Word Help** dialog box, click the **Search button arrow**, and then under **Content from this computer**, click **Word Help**.

This search for Help will be restricted to the Help installed on your computer. Depending on your Word settings, the *Table of Contents* on the left of the Word Help dialog box may not display.

3 To the left of the **Search** button, click in the **Type words to search for** box, type **save a file** and then press Enter. Notice that a list of related topics displays, as shown in Figure 5.47. Your list may differ.

Search button arrow | Search results | Help button

Figure 5.47

Type words to search for box

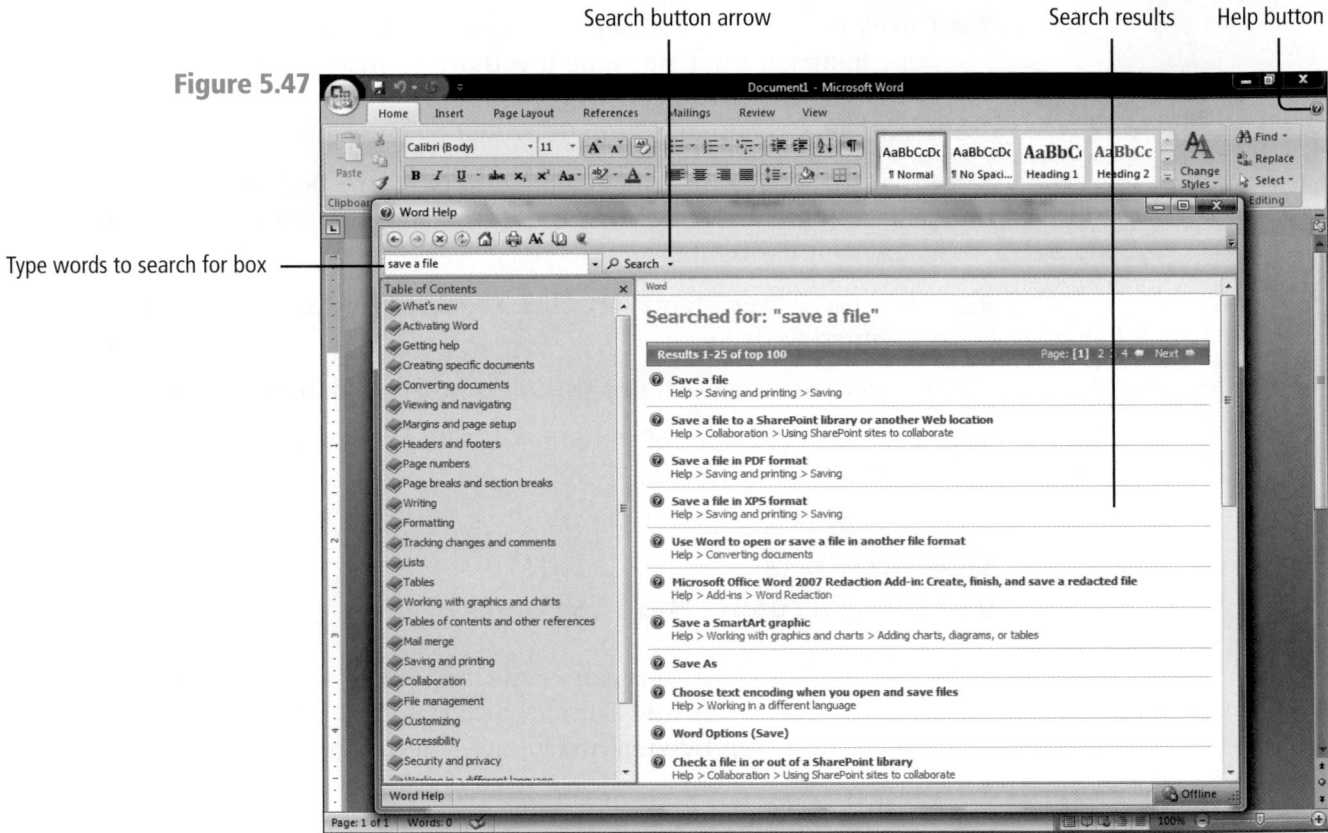

4 From the displayed list, point to, and then click **Save a file**.

5 Under **What do you want to do?** click **Save a file to another format (Save As command)**—the wording for this topic may vary. Notice that step-by-step instructions are given, as shown in Figure 5.48.

Instructions for saving a document under another format

Figure 5.48

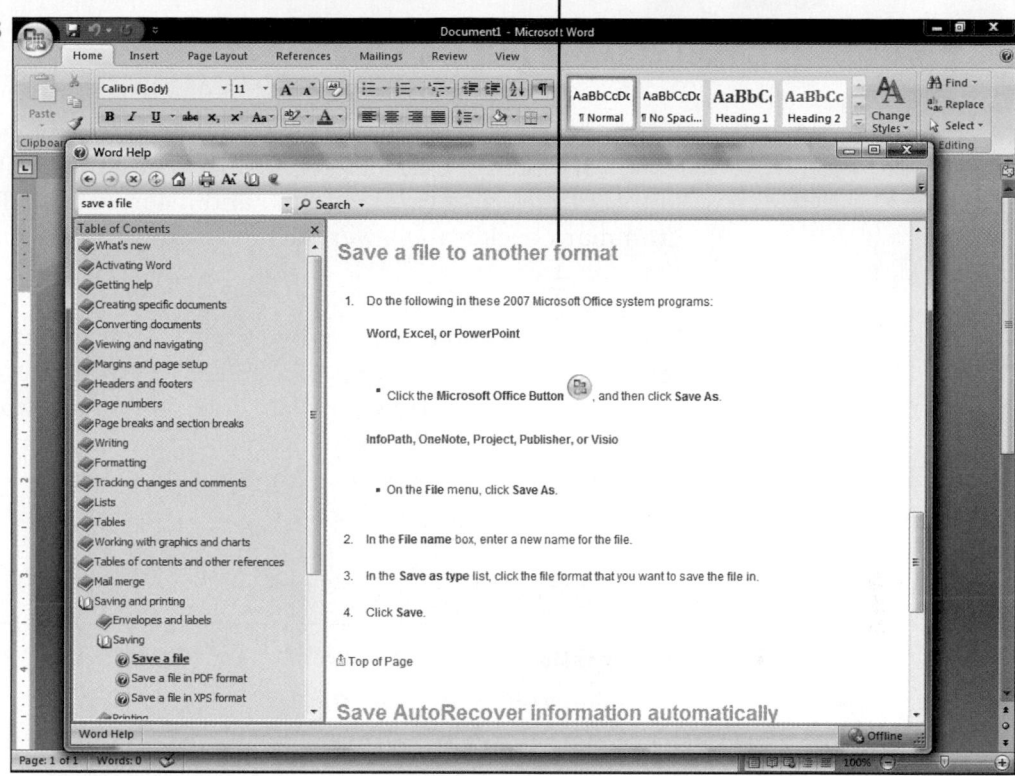

6 In the upper right corner of the Word Help window, click the **Close** button [X]. From the **Office** menu 🔘 , click **Exit Word** to close the Word program.

End | You have completed Project 5B ─────────────

🔘 GO! CD-ROM — There's More You Can Do!

Close Word and any other open windows. Display the Start menu, click Computer, and then navigate to the student files that accompany this textbook. In the folder **02_theres_more_you_can_do**, locate and open the folder for this chapter. Open and print the instructions for this project, which are provided to you in Adobe PDF format.

Try IT!—Convert a Document to a Different Format

In this Try It! exercise, you will convert a Word document to several different file formats.

Content-Based Assessments

Summary

In this chapter, you started Word and practiced navigating the Word window. You entered text, deleted text by using the Backspace and Delete keys, selected and replaced text, and inserted text. The spelling and grammar checker tools were demonstrated, and an image was added to a document.

You also practiced changing font style and size and adding emphasis to text. You viewed the header and footer areas, and created a chapter folder to help organize your files. Each document was saved, previewed, printed, and closed. Finally, the Help program was introduced as a tool that can assist you in using Word.

Key Terms

The ◉ symbol represents Key Terms found on the Student CD in the 02_theres_more_you_can_do folder for this chapter.

Content-Based Assessments

Matching

Match each term in the second column with its correct definition in the first column. Write the letter of the term on the blank line in front of the correct definition.

_____ **1.** The location in the Word window, indicated by a blinking vertical line, where text will be inserted when you start to type.

_____ **2.** In the Word window, the location of the Minimize, Maximize/Restore Down, and Close buttons.

_____ **3.** A button that represents the command to reveal nonprinting characters.

_____ **4.** The action that takes place when the insertion point reaches the right margin and automatically moves down and to the left margin of the next line.

_____ **5.** The process of setting the overall appearance of the text within the document.

_____ **6.** To hold down the left mouse button and move the mouse pointer over text to select it.

_____ **7.** A set of characters (letters and numbers) with the same design and shape.

_____ **8.** A unit of measure to describe the size of a font.

_____ **9.** A font type, such as Calibri or Arial, that does not have lines on the ends of characters.

_____ **10.** A font type, such as Cambria or Times New Roman, that has extensions or lines on the ends of the characters.

_____ **11.** The term that refers to pressing one or more keys to navigate a window or execute commands.

_____ **12.** This feature changes the selected text when the pointer points to a button or list item to display what the text will look like if the button or list item is clicked.

_____ **13.** A reserved area for text and graphics that displays at the bottom of each page in a document or section of a document.

_____ **14.** A view that simplifies the page layout for quick typing and can show more text on a smaller screen.

_____ **15.** A context-sensitive list that displays when you click the right mouse button.

A Draft

B Drag

C Font

D Footer

E Formatting

F Insertion point

G Keyboard shortcut

H Live Preview

I Point

J Sans serif

K Serif

L Shortcut menu

M Show/Hide ¶

N Title bar

O Wordwrap

Content-Based Assessments

Fill in the Blank

Write the correct word in the space provided.

1. Microsoft Word 2007 is a word _____ program that you can use to perform tasks such as writing a memo, a report, or a letter.

2. Located at the bottom of the Word window, the bar that provides information such as page number and word count is referred to as the _____ bar.

3. Within the scroll bar, dragging the _____ _____ downward causes the document on your screen to move up.

4. A toolbar above the Ribbon and to the right of the Office button, which can be customized by adding frequently used buttons, is called the _____ _____ _____ (QAT).

5. Characters that display on the screen to show the location of paragraph marks, tabs, and spaces but that do not print are called _____ marks.

6. If you point to a button on the Ribbon, a(n) _____ displays the name of the button.

7. In a business letter, the address of the recipient is called a(n) _____ address.

8. When you select text, the _____ toolbar displays buttons that are commonly used with the selected object.

9. Before text can be edited, changed, formatted, copied, or moved, it must first be _____

10. To add emphasis to text, use the _____ or _____ or _____ command, each of which has a button on the Ribbon.

11. The view that displays the page borders, margins, text, and graphics is the _____ _____ view.

12. The View buttons are located on the right side of the _____ bar.

13. To enlarge or decrease the viewing area of the document, use the _____ _____ on the status bar.

14. Graphic images, of which some are included with Word, that can be inserted in the document are called _____ art.

15. To display a shortcut menu, click the _____ mouse button.

Content-Based Assessments

Skills Review

Project 5C—Receipt Letter

In this project, you will apply the skills you practiced from the Objectives in Project 5A.

Objectives: 1. *Create and Save a New Document;* **2.** *Edit Text;* **3.** *Select, Delete, and Format Text;* **4.** *Print a Document.*

In the following Skills Review, you will create and edit a follow-up letter from Jamal Anderssen, a production manager for Music School Records, to William Hawken, a recording artist who has submitted a demo CD with his application. Your completed letter will look similar to the one shown in Figure 5.49.

For Project 5C, you will need the following file:

New blank Word document

You will save your document as
5C_Receipt_Letter_Firstname_Lastname

Figure 5.49

Music School Records
2620 Vine Street
Los Angeles, CA 90028
323-555-0028

September 22, 2009

Mr. William Hawken
123 Eighth Street
Harrisville, MI 48740

Dear Mr. Hawken:

Subject: Receipt of Your CD

I received your demo CD yesterday. Thank you for following our submission and recording guidelines so carefully. Everything is quite satisfactory, and we will be able to duplicate the CD and send it to our internal reviewers.

Your demonstration CD will not be circulated outside *Music School Records*. You retain all rights to your material until such time as a contract is finalized.

Best regards,

Jamal Anderssen
Production Manager

5C_Receipt_Letter_Firstname_Lastname

(Project 5C–Receipt Letter continues on the next page)

Content-Based Assessments

(Project 5C–Receipt Letter continued)

1. **Start** Word. If necessary, on the Ribbon, in the **Paragraph group**, click the **Show/Hide ¶** button to display the formatting marks. In the status bar, use the **Zoom slider** to adjust the page width to display both the left and right page edges.

2. On the **Home tab**, in the **Styles group**, click the **No Spacing** style. With the insertion point blinking in the upper left corner of the document to the left of the default first paragraph mark, type **Music School Records** and then press Enter. Type the following text and press Enter after each line:

   2620 Vine Street
   Los Angeles, CA 90028
   323-555-0028

3. Press Enter five more times. Begin typing today's date and let AutoComplete assist in your typing by pressing Enter when the ScreenTip displays. Press Enter four times. Type the inside address on three lines:

   Mr. William Hawken
   123 Eighth Street
   Harrisville, MI 48740

4. On the **Quick Access Toolbar**, click the **Save** button. In the **Save As** dialog box, navigate to your **Word Chapter 5** folder. In the displayed **File name** box, using your own first and last names, type **5C_Receipt_Letter_Firstname_Lastname** and then click **Save**.

5. On the **Home tab**, in the **Styles group**, click the **Normal** style. Press Enter, type the salutation **Dear Mr. Hawken:** and then press Enter.

6. Type **Subject: receipt of Your CD** and then press Enter. Then, using just one space following the periods at the end of sentences, type the following text:

I received your demo CD yesterday. Thank you for following our submission and recording standards so carefully. Everything is satisfactory, and we will be able to duplicate the CD and send it to our internal reviewers.

7. Press Enter to begin a new paragraph, and then type the following:

   Your demonstration CD will not be circulated outside Music School Records. You retain the rights to your material until such time as a contract is finalized.

8. Press Enter, type the closing **Best regards,** and then press Enter two times.

9. On the **Quick Access Toolbar**, click the **Save** button to save your changes. On the **Home tab**, in the **Styles group**, click the **No Spacing** style. Finish the letter by typing the writer's identification on two lines:

   Jamal Anderssen
   Production Manager

10. If necessary, drag the vertical scroll box to the top of the scroll bar to view the upper portion of the document. In the *Subject* line, position the insertion point to the left of *receipt*, and then press the **Delete** button. Type **R** to capitalize *Receipt*.

11. In the paragraph beginning *I received*, double-click the word **standards** to select it, and then type **guidelines**

12. In the same paragraph, position the insertion point to the left of the word *satisfactory*. Type **quite** and then press Spacebar one time.

13. In the paragraph beginning *Your demonstration*, click to position the insertion point to the left of *rights*, press the **Backspace** button four times. Type **all** and then press Spacebar to change the phrase to *retain all rights*.

(Project 5C–Receipt Letter continues on the next page)

(Project 5C–Receipt Letter continued)

14. **Save** the changes you have made to your document. Press [Ctrl] + [A] to select the entire document. On the **Home tab**, in the **Font group**, click the **Font button arrow**. Scroll as necessary, and watch Live Preview change the document font as you point to different font names. Click to choose **Tahoma**. Recall that you can type *T* in the Font box to move quickly to the fonts beginning with that letter. Click anywhere in the document to cancel the selection.

15. Select the entire first line of text—*Music School Records*. On the Mini toolbar, click the **Font button arrow**, and then click **Arial Black**. With the Mini toolbar still displayed, click the **Font Size button arrow**, and then click **20**. With the Mini toolbar still displayed, click the **Bold** button.

16. Select the second, third, and fourth lines of text, beginning with *2620 Vine Street* and ending with the telephone number. On the Mini toolbar, click the **Font button arrow**, and then click **Arial**. With the Mini toolbar still displayed, click the **Font Size button arrow**, and then click **10**. With the Mini toolbar still displayed, click the **Italic** button.

17. In the paragraph beginning *Your demonstration*, select the text *Music School Records*. On the Mini toolbar, click the **Italic** button, and then click anywhere to deselect the text.

18. Click the **Insert tab**. In the **Header & Footer group**, click the **Footer** button, and then click **Edit Footer**. On the **Design tab**, in the **Insert group**, click the **Quick Parts** button, and then click **Field**. In the **Field** dialog box, under **Field names**, scroll down and click to choose **FileName**, and then click **OK**. Double-click anywhere in the document to leave the footer area.

19. Click the **Page Layout tab**. In the **Page Setup group**, click the **Margins** button to display the Margins gallery. At the bottom of the **Margins gallery**, click **Custom Margins** to display the **Page Setup** dialog box. Near the top of the **Page Setup** dialog box, click the **Layout tab**. Under **Page**, click the **Vertical alignment arrow**, click **Center**, and then click **OK**.

20. From the **Office** menu, point to **Print**, and then click **Print Preview** to make a final check of your letter. Check your *Chapter Assignment Sheet* or *Course Syllabus* or consult your instructor to determine if you are to submit your assignments on paper or electronically. To submit electronically, go to Step 22, and then follow the instructions provided by your instructor.

21. On the **Print Preview tab**, in the **Print** group, click the **Print** button. Click **OK**, and then **Close Print Preview**. Collect your printout from the printer and submit it as directed.

22. From the **Office** menu, click **Exit Word**, saving any changes if prompted to do so.

End **You have completed Project 5C** ───────────

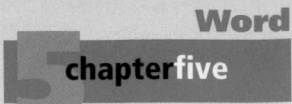

Skills Review

Project 5D — Marketing

In this project, you will apply the skills you practiced from the Objectives in Project 5B.

Objectives: 5. *Navigate the Word Window;* **6.** *Add a Graphic to a Document;* **7.** *Use the Spelling and Grammar Checker;* **8.** *Preview and Print Documents, Close a Document, and Close Word;* **9.** *Use the Microsoft Help System.*

In the following Skills Review, you will edit a document that details the marketing and promotion plan for Music School Records. Your completed document will look similar to Figure 5.50.

For Project 5D, you will need the following files:

New blank Word document
w05D_Marketing
w05D_Piano

You will save your document as
5D_Marketing_Firstname_Lastname

Figure 5.50

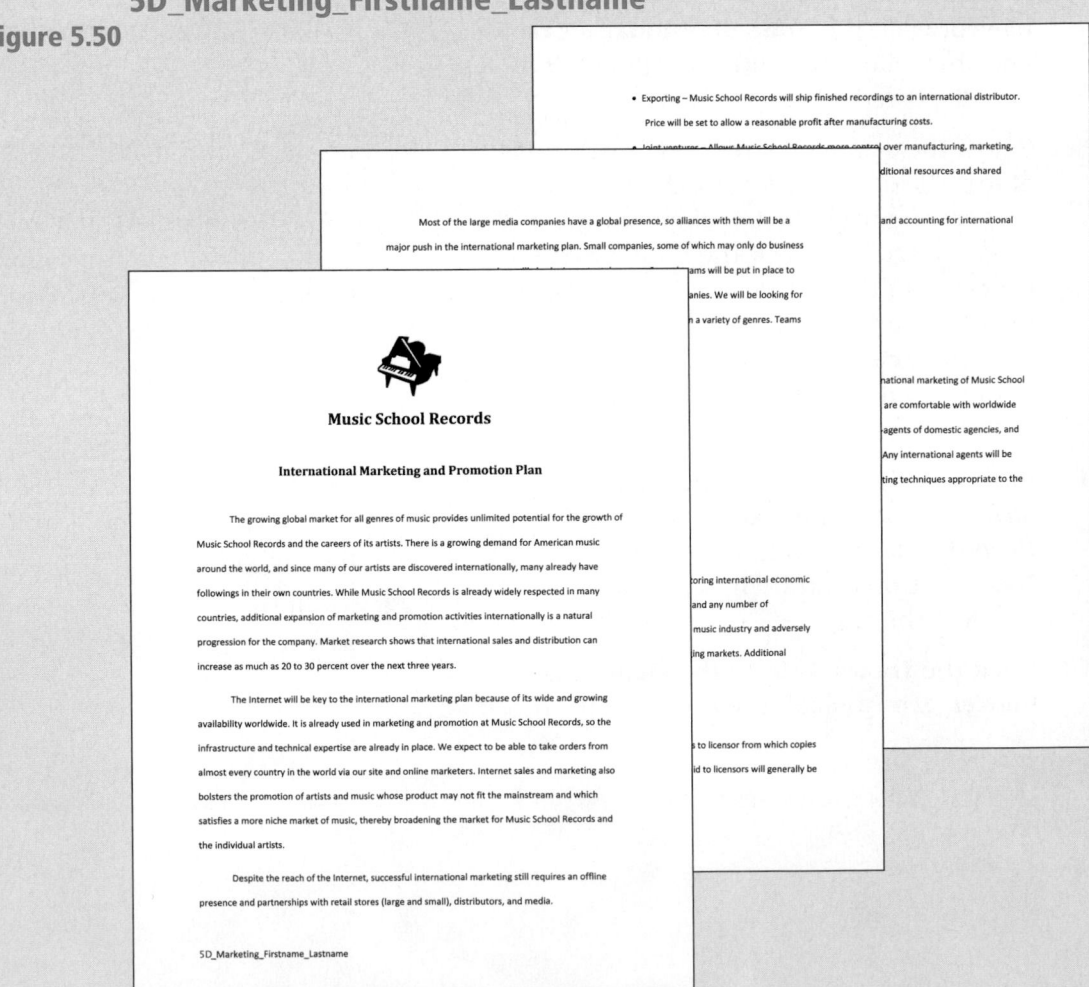

(Project 5D–Marketing continues on the next page)

Content-Based Assessments

(Project 5D–Marketing continued)

1. **Start** Word and be sure a new blank document is displayed. If necessary, on the Ribbon, in the **Paragraph group**, click the **Show/Hide ¶** button to display the formatting marks. In the status bar, use the **Zoom slider** to adjust the page width to display both the left and right page edges.

2. On the **Quick Access Toolbar**, click the **Save** button. In the **Save As** dialog box, navigate to your **Word Chapter 5** folder. In the **File name** box, using your own first and last names, type 5D_Marketing_Firstname_Lastname and then click **Save**.

3. Click the **Insert tab**. In the **Header & Footer group**, click the **Footer** button to display the Footer gallery. At the bottom of the **Footer gallery**, click **Edit Footer**. On the **Design tab**, in the **Insert group**, click the **Quick Parts** button, and then click **Field**. In the **Field** dialog box, under **Field names**, scroll down and click **FileName**, and then click **OK**. Double-click anywhere in the document to leave the footer area.

4. Click the **Insert tab**. In the **Text group**, click the **Object button arrow**, and then click **Text from File**. In the displayed **Insert File** dialog box, navigate to the location where the student files for this textbook are stored. Locate and select **w05D_Marketing**, and then click the **Insert** button to insert the text.

5. Press ←Bksp to remove the blank line at the end of the document. Use the vertical scroll bar to examine the document. When you are finished, press Ctrl + Home to move to the beginning of the document.

6. **Save** your document. Move the ⬀ pointer into the margin area to the left of the title *Music School Records* and drag down to select the title, the blank line, and the second title that begins *International*

   Marketting. Be sure to include the blank line between the two titles. On the Mini toolbar, click the **Bold** button. Click anywhere in the document to deselect the text.

7. In the second title line, notice that the word *Marketting* is marked as misspelled. Right-click *Marketting*, and from the shortcut menu, click **Marketing**. In the first line of the paragraph that begins *The growing global*, right-click *geners*, and from the shortcut menu, locate and click **genres**.

8. Click the **Review tab**, and then, in the **Proofing group**, click the **Spelling & Grammar** button to open the **Spelling and Grammar** dialog box. The first word flagged is *allready*. Notice that this word is misspelled several times in the document.

9. In the **Spelling and Grammar** dialog box, click the **Change All** button to correct all occurrences of this misspelled word. The next potential error—a subject-verb agreement problem—is highlighted. Notice that two suggested corrections are listed. If necessary, click **is a growing demand**, and then click the **Change** button.

10. If a Passive Voice error is identified next, click Ignore Once. In the paragraph that begins *The Internet will be key*, another potential grammar problem is highlighted. Click the **Ignore Once** button to leave the sentence the way it was written. Ignore other grammar errors, and then correct the spelling error for the word *Millenium*. Continue to click the **Ignore Once** button until you reach the end of the document. When a message box tells you the check is complete, click **OK**.

11. Hold down Ctrl and press Home to move to the beginning of the document, and then press Enter to add a blank line. Click to

(Project 5D–Marketing continues on the next page)

Content-Based Assessments

(Project 5D–Marketing continued)

position the insertion point in the new blank line.

12. Click the **Microsoft Office Word Help** button. In the **Word Help** dialog box, click the **Search button arrow**, and then under **Content from this computer**, click **Word Help**. In the **Type words to search for** box, type **graphic file types** and then press Enter. In the search results, click **Types of media files you can add** and examine the list of graphic file types that can be added to a Word document.

13. **Close** the **Word Help** window, and then click the **Insert tab**. In the **Illustrations group**, click the **Picture** button. In the displayed **Insert Picture** dialog box, navigate to the student files that accompany this textbook, click the **w05D_Piano** file, and then click **Insert**.

14. **Save** your changes. Check your *Chapter Assignment Sheet* or *Course Syllabus* or consult your instructor to determine if you are to submit your assignments on paper or electronically. To submit electronically, go to Step 16, and then follow the instructions provided by your instructor.

15. From the **Office** menu, point to **Print**, and then click **Print Preview** to make a final check of your document. On the **Print Preview tab**, in the **Print group**, click the **Print** button, and from the displayed **Print** dialog box, click **OK**. Then, in the **Preview group**, click the **Close Print Preview** button. Collect your printout from the printer and submit as directed.

16. From the **Office** menu, click **Close**. At the right end of the title bar, click the **Close** button to close Word.

 You have completed Project 5D ————————————————————

Content-Based Assessments

Project 5E — School Tour

In this project, you will apply the skills you practiced from the Objectives in Project 5A.

Objectives: 1. *Create and Save a New Document;* **2.** *Edit Text;* **3.** *Select, Delete, and Format Text;* **4.** *Print a Document;* **7.** *Use the Spelling and Grammar Checker.*

In the following Mastering Word project, you will write a thank-you letter to the Dean of the Music Center School of Atlanta to thank him for a tour of his school's facilities. You will leave enough room at the top of the page to print it on preprinted company letterhead stationery. Your completed document will look similar to Figure 5.51.

For Project 5E, you will need the following file:

New blank Word document

You will save your document as
5E_School_Tour_Firstname_Lastname

Figure 5.51

> September 29, 2009
>
> Dr. Adair Leake, Dean
> Music Center School of Atlanta
> 1395 Peachtree Street, Suite 1850
> Atlanta, GA 30309
>
> Dear Dr. Leake:
>
> Thank you for the tour of your school's facilities and for the opportunity to watch the jazz piano recital. I was very impressed with the methods you are using to draw new and interesting sounds from the students in the piano program. **Music School Records** intends to send a team from *Artists & Repertoire* to the school over the next few months to meet with some of these students individually to determine their next steps in their music careers.
>
> I enjoyed meeting you and the students, and I look forward to talking with you again soon. Please send my regards to the students.
>
> Sincerely,
>
>
> Lisa Ivanko
> Talent Developer
>
>
> 5E_School_Tour_Firstname_Lastname

(Project 5E–School Tour continues on the next page)

Content-Based Assessments

(Project 5E–School Tour continued)

1. **Start** Word and be sure a new blank document displays. Display formatting marks, and be sure your screen displays both the left and right document edges. Save the document in your **Word Chapter 5** folder as **5E_School_Tour_Firstname_Lastname** Open the document footer area and add the file name to the footer.

2. Use the letter formatting skills you practiced in Project 5A to create a letter. Begin with the current date. Then, on the **Home tab**, apply the **No Spacing** style. Add the appropriate number of blank lines, and then add the following inside address (at the end of the last line of the address, apply the **Normal** style).

   Dr. Adair Leake, Dean
   Music Center School of Atlanta
   1395 Peachtree Street, Suite 1850
   Atlanta, GA 30309

3. Add the salutation **Dear Dr. Leake:** and then type the following paragraphs, saving your work frequently. Be sure to space only one time following end-of-sentence punctuation:

   Thank you for the tour of your school's facilities and for the opportunity to watch the jazz piano recital. I was very impressed with the methods you are using to draw new and interesting sounds from the students in the piano program. Music School Records intends to send a team from Artists & Repertoire to the school over the next few

   months to meet with some of these students individually to determine their next steps in their music careers.

   I liked meeting you and the students, and I very much look forward to talking with you again soon. Please send my regards to the students.

4. **Save** your document. Use the appropriate spacing, add the complimentary closing **Sincerely,** and then add the following writer's identification:

   Lisa Ivanko
   Talent Developer

5. In the paragraph beginning *I liked meeting you*, use either `Delete` or `← Bksp` to change *liked* to **enjoyed** In the same paragraph, select the text *very much*, and then press `Delete` to remove this phrase.

6. In the paragraph beginning *Thank you for the tour*, in the third line, locate the text *Music School Records* and add **Bold** emphasis. In the same sentence, locate *Artists & Repertoire* and add **Italic** emphasis.

7. Select the entire document. Change the **Font** to **Arial**, and the **Font Size** to **12**. Center the letter vertically on the page.

8. Check the spelling and grammar. Preview the document, and then print it, or submit it electronically as directed. **Close** the document, and then **Close** Word.

End **You have completed Project 5E** ——————————

Content-Based Assessments

Mastering Word

Project 5F — Scouting Trip

In this project, you will apply the skills you practiced from the Objectives in Project 5B.

Objectives: 5. *Navigate the Word Window;* **6.** *Add a Graphic to a Document;* **7.** *Use the Spelling and Grammar Checker;* **8.** *Preview and Print Documents, Close a Document, and Close Word.*

In the following Mastering Word project, you will edit a memo from one of Music School Records' talent developers highlighting her third quarter accomplishments. Your completed document will look similar to Figure 5.52.

For Project 5F, you will need the following files:

w05F_Scouting_Trip
w05F_Piano

**You will save your document as
5F_Scouting_Trip_Firstname_Lastname**

Figure 5.52

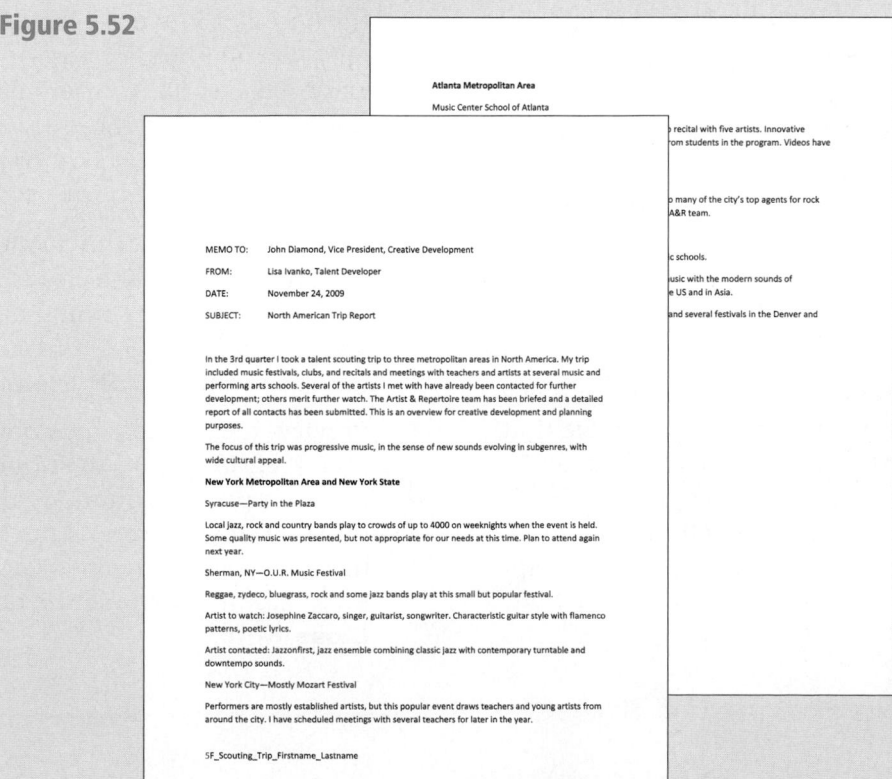

(Project 5F–Scouting Trip continues on the next page)

(Project 5F–Scouting Trip continued)

1. Locate and open the document **w05F_Scouting Trip**. Display formatting marks, display the ruler, and be sure your screen displays both the left and right document edges. **Save** the file in your **Word Chapter 5** folder as 5F_Scouting_Trip_Firstname_Lastname and add the file name to the footer.

There are numerous acceptable memo formats. This format is an example from the *Gregg Reference Manual* (Sabin, 2005). Always consult a trusted reference manual or Business Communication textbook when formatting business documents.

2. Use the vertical scroll bar to examine the document. Notice the potential spelling and grammar errors that have been flagged. Also notice that there is a heading—*Atlanta Metropolitan Area*—at the bottom of the first page that should be placed at the top of the second page.

3. On the **View tab**, in the **Window group**, click the **Split** button and drag the split bar so it is in the middle of your screen. Use the vertical scroll bars in the top and bottom windows to display the Subject line in the top window, and the last line of the first page—*Atlanta Metropolitan Area*—in the bottom window.

4. Position the insertion point at the end of the *Subject* line and press Enter. Notice that the *Atlanta Metropolitan Area* heading moves to the top of the second page. Scroll within the bottom window if necessary to view the top of page 2. Then, close the split screen. As you progress in your study of

Microsoft Word, you will discover other ways to manually end a page and move text to the next page.

5. View the document in **Full Screen Reading** view. Return to **Print Layout** view and use the **Zoom slider** to display two pages on the screen. Zoom back to a comfortable document size.

6. In the first line of the memo, the word *Creative* may be flagged as a potential grammar error. If so, use the shortcut menu to Ignore Once. In the *FROM:* line, use the shortcut menu to ignore the flagged word *Ivanko*.

7. Open the **Spelling and Grammar** dialog box to check the remainder of the potential spelling and grammar errors. Although there are a number of uncommon words and proper names that are flagged because they are not in Word's dictionary, there are only two additional errors—the misspelled word *focuss* and the grammar error *Videos has been*. Correct these errors, and ignore any other names, words, or phrases that are flagged. **Save** your work.

8. Move to the end of the document. Place the insertion point at the end of the last paragraph—the one beginning *My next trip*—and then press Enter. From your student files, insert the **w05F_Piano** image.

9. Preview the memo to see how it will print on paper. If you are to submit the document on paper, print and submit it as directed. If you are to submit the document electronically, follow your instructor's directions. **Close** the document and **Close** Word.

End **You have completed Project 5F**

Content-Based Assessments

Mastering Word

Project 5G — Contract

In this project, you will apply the skills you practiced from the Objectives in Projects 5A and 5B.

Objectives: 2. *Edit Text;* **3.** *Select, Delete, and Format Text;* **4.** *Print a Document;* **5.** *Navigate the Word Window;* **7.** *Use the Spelling and Grammar Checker;* **8.** *Preview and Print Documents, Close a Document, and Close Word.*

In the following Mastering Word project, you will edit a contract between a client and Music School Records. Your completed document will look similar to Figure 5.53.

For Project 5G, you will need the following file:

w05G_Contract

You will save your document as 5G_Contract_Firstname_Lastname

Figure 5.53

Contract for Services

PARTIES TO THE CONTRACT
The First Party's name is Music School Records, a Corporation.

The Second Party's name is **Evie Chardan**, an individual proprietor.

WHO HAS TO DO WHAT
Music School Records and **Evie Chardan** agree to the following:
Music School Records will provide the Second Party various marketing materials and recordings of **Evie Chardan** (the Artist) for the purposes of publicizing and promoting the Artist to music stores in the Chicago metropolitan area.

The materials provided by Music School Records may include printed brochures, promotional CDs, pre-loaded digital music players, advertising copy, Artist fact sheets, photographs, and press clips. Also available as requested will be low-value promotional items such as buttons, stickers, and other trinkets.

Music School Records will also provide, with proper notice and approval of venue, access to the Artist for press conferences, interviews, media appearances, and performances. All such personal appearances will be subject to Music School Records' contract with the Artist.

Music School Records is responsible for the accuracy of all printed materials. Music School Records is also

The Second Party will take all legally required actions and professionally appropriate care in protecting the copyrights of Music School Records and the Artist. The Second Party is responsible for the health and safety of the Artist while at appearances arranged by the Second Party. If the Artist is a minor, the Second Party will follow all applicable laws relating to care and work of a minor.

The Second Party will be responsible for writing/producing and releasing press clips (print, audio and video) following any promotional events. The Second Party is responsible for the accuracy of such releases and clips. Other promotional actions are expected to include, but are not limited to:

- Announcements and listings in local press entertainment calendars
- Arrangement of and public service announcements for charity events
- Mailings, faxes, and phone calls to local press, club owners, music store managers, etc.
- Any necessary local Web presence

5G_Contract_Firstname_Lastname

The Second Party is required to present an individualized promotional plan for the Artist in the Chicago Metropolitan Area. Upon approval of the plan, Music School Records will release the above-mentioned products and allow access to the Artist. The Second Party
...an implementation and sales figures to...

...e Second Party will be paid an amount
...ago Metropolitan Area during the
...e year after the contract has been

...ubject to renewal and/or revision at

...'s fees.
... Los Angeles, County of Los Angeles,

...l: _____

...l: _____

(Project 5G–Contract continues on the next page)

Content-Based Assessments

(Project 5G–Contract continued)

1. Locate and open the document **w05G_Contract**. **Save** the document in your **Word Chapter 5** folder as **5G_Contract_Firstname_Lastname** and then add the file name to the footer. Display formatting marks, display the ruler, and set the page width to a comfortable size for you.

2. If necessary, move to the beginning of the document, type **Contract for Services** and press [Enter]. Select *Contract for Services*, change the **Font Size** to **18** points, and apply **Bold** emphasis.

3. Use the **Spelling and Grammar** checker to correct the errors in the document. There are several misspellings of the word *responsibel* and a subject-verb agreement error—*are* instead of *is*. Ignore all other flagged items.

4. Locate the three headings in uppercase letters. Select each one and add **Bold** emphasis. Recall that when you select the text, the Mini toolbar displays with the Bold button on it.

5. Locate the black lines in the document that represent blanks to be filled in. In the line beginning *The Second Party's name*, select the long line, but not the comma following it. Type **Evie Chardan** and notice that as you type, your typing will be displayed in bold. On the next two long lines, use the same technique to type **Evie Chardan** again.

6. On **Page 2**, in the paragraph beginning *For services provided*, select the line and type **12** Select the line following *This agreement will be in force for*, type **2** and then delete *months/* so that the sentence reads *in force for 2 years*.

7. **Save** your changes. At the end of the contract, under *Signed*, select the text *Music School Records*, and then on the Mini toolbar, change the font size to **10** and add **Bold** emphasis. **Save** your changes. Preview the document and then print it, or submit it electronically as directed. **Close** the document, and then **Close** Word.

End **You have completed Project 5G**

Content-Based Assessments

Project 5H—Invitation

In this project, you will apply the skills you practiced from the Objectives in Projects 5A and 5B.

Objectives: 1. *Create and Save a New Document;* **2.** *Edit Text;* **3.** *Select, Delete, and Format Text;* **4.** *Print a Document;* **5.** *Navigate the Word Window;* **6.** *Add a Graphic to a Document;* **7.** *Use the Spelling and Grammar Checker;* **8.** *Preview and Print Documents, Close a Document, and Close Word.*

In the following Mastering Word project, you will create a new letter to a talent agent, and then insert and edit text from a file. Your completed document will look similar to Figure 5.54.

For Project 5H, you will need the following files:

New blank Word document
w05H_Invitation
w05H_Letterhead

You will save your document as
5H_Invitation_Firstname_Lastname

Figure 5.54

Music School Records

2620 Vine Street

Los Angeles, CA 90028

323-555-0028

Musicschoolrecords.com

September 30, 2009

Ms. Caroline Westbrook
Artists' Workshop Agency
249 Fifth Avenue #2700
New York, NY 10001

Dear Ms. Westbrook:

Thank you for the introduction to your client, Ms. Evie Chardan. Our representatives were very impressed with the quality of Ms. Chardan's music, stage presence, and obvious rapport with the young audience for which she performed. It is certainly our pleasure to invite Ms. Chardan to consider a recording contract with **Music School Records**.

Upon your approval, we will draft a standard contract for your and Ms. Chardan's attorneys' review. The contract will be subject to the laws of California and will include language outlining the term of the contract, guaranteed minimum payments per year, and obligations of the artist and **Music School Records**. As part of the standard contract, we do require a period of exclusivity regarding the artist's recording, and this period is subject to negotiation.

Please call me as soon as possible to confirm your client's agreement to draft the contract. We are looking forward to working with you again and playing a key role in the development of Ms. Chardan's career.

Sincerely,

John Diamond
Vice President, Creative Development

5H_Invitation_Firstname_Lastname

(Project 5H–Invitation continues on the next page)

Content-Based Assessments

Word

chapter **five**

Mastering Word

(Project 5H–Invitation continued)

1. **Start** Word and be sure a new blank document is displayed. Display formatting marks, display the ruler, and be sure your screen displays both the left and right document edges. **Save** the document in your **Word Chapter 5** folder as 5H_Invitation_ Firstname_Lastname Open the document footer and add the file name.

2. Locate and insert the file **w05H_ Letterhead**. Be sure the insertion point is positioned at the second blank line below the letterhead, and then type the current date. Using the skills you practiced in Project 5A, be sure the address style is set to **No Spacing**, and then add the following inside address:

   Ms. Caroline Westbrook
   Artists' Workshop Agency
   249 Fifth Avenue #2700
   New York, NY 10001

3. Change the style back to **Normal**, press Enter, and then type **Dear Ms. Westbrook:** Press Enter, and then locate and insert the file **w05H_Invitation**. Add the following paragraph at the end of the document:

   Please call me as soon as possible to confirm your client's agreement to draft the contract. We are looking forward to working with you again and playing a key role in the development of Ms. Chardan's career.

4. Using appropriate spacing, add the complimentary closing **Sincerely,** and then add the following writer's identification:

   John Diamond
   Vice President, Creative Development

5. **Save** your changes. Be sure grammar errors are flagged in the document. In the paragraph beginning *Thank you*, in the second sentence, correct the grammar error *was*, and then type **very** between *were* and *impressed*. In the third line of the same paragraph, add **certainly** between *It is* and *our pleasure*. In the last sentence of the same paragraph, change *sign* to **consider**

6. Use the **Spelling & Grammar** checker to correct the errors in the document. There is one error—the misspelled word *qualty*. Ignore all other flagged items.

7. At the end of the paragraph beginning *Thank you for the introduction*, locate the text *Music School Records* and add **Bold** emphasis. In the paragraph beginning *Upon your approval*, add **Bold** emphasis to *Music School Records*.

8. Select the entire document. Change the **Font** to **Cambria**. **Save** your changes.

9. Preview the document and then print it, or submit it electronically as directed. **Close** the file, and then **Close** Word.

End **You have completed Project 5H**

Content-Based Assessments

Project 5I — Fax Cover

In this project, you will apply the skills you practiced from the Objectives in Projects 5A and 5B.

Objectives: 1. *Create and Save a New Document;* **2.** *Edit Text;* **3.** *Select, Delete, and Format Text;* **4.** *Print a Document;* **5.** *Navigate the Word Window;* **6.** *Add a Graphic to a Document;* **7.** *Use the Spelling and Grammar Checker;* **8.** *Preview and Print Documents, Close a Document, and Close Word.*

In the following Mastering Word project, you will create a cover sheet for a facsimile (fax) transmission. When sending a fax, it is common practice to include a cover sheet with a note describing the pages that will follow. Your completed document will look similar to Figure 5.55.

For Project 5I, you will need the following files:

New blank Word document
w05I_Fax_Cover
w05I_Fax_Machine

You will save your document as
5I_Fax_Cover_Firstname_Lastname

Figure 5.55

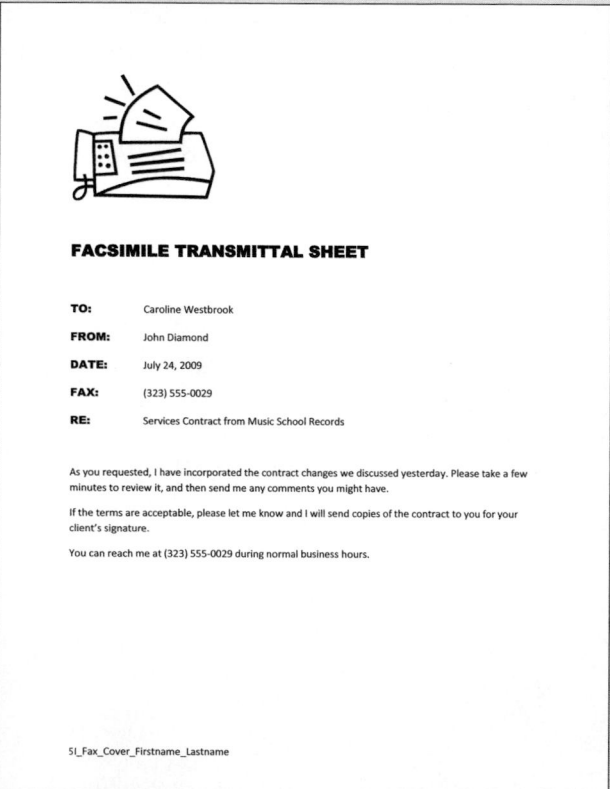

(Project 5I–Fax Cover continues on the next page)

Content-Based Assessments

(Project 5I–Fax Cover continued)

1. **Start** Word and be sure a new blank document is displayed. Display formatting marks and rulers, and be sure your screen displays both the left and right document edges. **Save** the document in your **Word Chapter 5** folder as **5I_Fax_Cover_Firstname_Lastname** Open the document footer and add the file name to the footer.

2. Move the insertion point to the top of the document. Press [Enter] two times, and then move back to the top of the document. From your student files, insert the **w05I_Fax_Machine** picture. Press [Ctrl] + [End]. Press [CapsLock], type **FACSIMILE TRANS-MITTAL SHEET** and then press [Enter] two times. Press [CapsLock] again.

3. Locate and insert the file **w05I_Fax_Cover**. Move to the blank line at the end of the document, and then type **You can reach me at (323) 555-0029 during normal business hours. Save** your work.

4. Select the text *FACSIMILE TRANSMITTAL SHEET*. Change the **Font Size** to **16**, and the **Font** to **Arial Black**. Change the font

of the line headings *TO:, FROM:, DATE:, FAX:,* and *RE:* to **Arial Black**.

5. In the paragraph that begins *As you requested*, select and delete the text *on the telephone*. In the same paragraph, replace the phrase *look it over* with **review it** and, in the same sentence, add an **s** to *comment*.

6. There are several grammar and spelling errors that need to be corrected. Use the **Spelling & Grammar** checker to correct the duplicate or misspelled words. In the paragraph beginning *If the term are*, select the **terms are** suggested change. **Save** your changes.

7. Use [Ctrl] + [Home] to navigate to the beginning of the document. Proofread the fax cover to be sure you have made all necessary corrections.

8. Preview the document. Print and submit as directed, or submit the document electronically according to your instructor's directions. **Close** the document, and **Close** Word.

 You have completed Project 5I

Content-Based Assessments

Project 5J — Business Running Case

In this project, you will apply the skills you practiced in Projects 5A and 5B.

Close Word and any other open windows. Display the Start menu, click Computer, and then navigate to the student files that accompany this textbook. In the folder **03_business_running_case**, locate and open the folder for this chapter. Open and print the instructions for this project, which are provided to you in Adobe PDF format. Follow the instructions and use the skills you have gained thus far to assist Jennifer Nelson in meeting the challenges of owning and running her business.

End You have completed Project 5J ——————————

Content-Based Assessments

Mastering Word

Project 5K — *GO!* Fix It

In this project, you will construct a solution by applying any combination of the skills you practiced from the Objectives in Projects 5A and 5B.

For Project 5K, you will need the following files:

w05_fixit_Approval_Letter
w05_fixit_Music_Logo

You will save your document as
5K_Approval_Letter_Firstname_Lastname

From the student files that accompany this textbook, open the folder **05_go_ fix_it**. Locate and open the file **w05K_fixit_Approval_Letter**, and then save the file in your chapter folder as **5K_Approval_Letter_Firstname_Lastname**

This document contains errors that you must find and correct. Read and examine the document, and then edit to correct the errors that you find. Types of errors could include:

- Spelling, grammar, punctuation, and usage errors such as text case, repeated text, subject-verb agreement, and meaning.
- Content errors such as missing or incorrect text.
- Paragraph formatting and positioning errors such as wordwrap, sentence spacing, missing text, or unnecessary text or blank lines.
- Page setup errors such as margins, orientation, layout, or alignment.

Things you should know to complete this project:

- Displaying formatting marks will assist in locating spacing errors.
- The name Hawken and the name HawkenDove are spelled correctly.
- Set the Word Proofing Options so that when correcting spelling and grammar in Word, Grammar & Style is selected.
- There are no errors in the fonts or font sizes.
- A logo graphic is missing in the letterhead. From your student files, insert the logo graphic **w05_fixit_Music_Logo** to the left of *Music School Records* followed by one space. Format the logo graphic using wrapping style **In line with text**. For the size, modify the scale height to 50% and select the lock aspect ratio.
- Spacing following the inside address should change to Normal style.

Save the changes you have made, add the file name to the footer, and then submit as directed.

End **You have completed Project 5K**

Outcomes-Based Assessments

Rubric

The following outcomes-based assessments are *open-ended assessments*. That is, there is no specific correct result; your result will depend on your approach to the information provided. Make *Professional Quality* your goal. Use the following scoring rubric to guide you in *how* to approach the problem and then to evaluate *how well* your approach solves the problem.

The *criteria*—Software Mastery, Content, Format and Layout, and Process—represent the knowledge and skills you have gained that you can apply to solving the problem. The *levels of performance*—Professional Quality, Approaching Professional Quality, or Needs Quality Improvements—help you and your instructor evaluate your result.

	Your completed project is of Professional Quality if you:	Your completed project is Approaching Professional Quality if you:	Your completed project Needs Quality Improvements if you:
1-Software Mastery	Choose and apply the most appropriate skills, tools, and features and identify efficient methods to solve the problem.	Choose and apply some appropriate skills, tools, and features, but not in the most efficient manner.	Choose inappropriate skills, tools, or features, or are inefficient in solving the problem.
2-Content	Construct a solution that is clear and well organized, contains content that is accurate, appropriate to the audience and purpose, and is complete. Provide a solution that contains no errors of spelling, grammar, or style.	Construct a solution in which some components are unclear, poorly organized, inconsistent, or incomplete. Misjudge the needs of the audience. Have some errors in spelling, grammar, or style, but the errors do not detract from comprehension.	Construct a solution that is unclear, incomplete, or poorly organized, containing some inaccurate or inappropriate content; and contains many errors of spelling, grammar, or style. Do not solve the problem.
3-Format and Layout	Format and arrange all elements to communicate information and ideas, clarify function, illustrate relationships, and indicate relative importance.	Apply appropriate format and layout features to some elements, but not others. Overuse features, causing minor distraction.	Apply format and layout that does not communicate information or ideas clearly. Do not use format and layout features to clarify function, illustrate relationships, or indicate relative importance. Use available features excessively, causing distraction.
4-Process	Use an organized approach that integrates planning, development, self-assessment, revision, and reflection.	Demonstrate an organized approach in some areas, but not others; or, use an insufficient process of organization throughout.	Do not use an organized approach to solve the problem.

Outcomes-Based Assessments

Problem Solving

Project 5L — Services

In this project, you will construct a solution by applying any combination of the skills you practiced from the Objectives in Projects 5A and 5B.

For Project 5L, you will need the following file:

New blank Word document

**You will save your document as
5L_Services_Firstname_Lastname**

Using the information provided, compose a form letter from Lucy Burroughs—founder and CEO of Music School Records—that explains the services offered by the company. Music School Records is located at 2620 Vine Street, Los Angeles, CA 90028, (323) 555-0028. The tone of the letter should be positive and sales-oriented. The letter should answer the question "Why do I need this service?" As you write the letter, use the information in Project 5B that describes the company. The letter should contain three paragraphs—an introductory paragraph, a second paragraph describing the services offered, and a closing paragraph.

The letter should include the appropriate business letter components, and should be in the proper business format. Add the file name to the footer. Check the letter for spelling or grammar errors. Save the letter as **5L_Services_Firstname_Lastname** and submit it as directed.

End **You have completed Project 5L** ————————————

Outcomes-Based Assessments

Problem Solving

Project 5M — Survey Form

In this project, you will construct a solution by applying any combination of the skills you practiced from the Objectives in Projects 5A and 5B.

For Project 5M, you will need the following file:

New blank Word document

**You will save your document as
5M_Survey_Form_Firstname_Lastname**

In Project 5M, you will create a brief survey form to be filled out by potential clients of Music School Records. The purpose of the survey form is to do a quick screening of applicants to be sure they are a match for the company before they talk to a field representative or send in a demo recording.

The target audience will be high school and college students, and young performers already working in their field. The form should include information that may be important to a screening committee, including the student's:

- Place of residence

- Current school (if any)

- Type of talent (instrument, voice)

- Genre of music

- Professional experience (if any)

- Awards and other types of public recognition

Include any other topics you feel would be helpful in a brief survey form. The form should list the topics down the left side of the page, and should leave three or four blank lines between each so the person filling out the form will have enough space to write.

Add the file name to the footer. Check the survey form for spelling or grammar errors. Save the document as **5M_Survey_Form_Firstname_Lastname** and submit it as directed.

End **You have completed Project 5M** —————————

Outcomes-Based Assessments

Problem Solving

Project 5N — Press Release

In this project, you will construct a solution by applying any combination of the skills you practiced from the Objectives in Projects 5A and 5B.

For Project 5N, you will need the following files:

New blank Word document

w05N_Music_Logo

You will save your document as
5N_Press_Release_Firstname_Lastname

In Project 5N, you will write a press release to announce the opening of an East Coast location for Music School Records. The information for the press release should be taken from the following information about the company:

Music School Records is located at 2620 Vine Street, Los Angeles, CA 90028, (323) 555-0028. The new office will be located in Manhattan at 250 5th Avenue #1460, New York, NY 10001, (212) 555-9124.

Music School Records is owned by Lucy Burroughs, who founded the company in 1994. The company was created to launch young musical artists with undiscovered talent in jazz, classical, and contemporary music. The creative management team searches internationally for talented young people, and has a reputation for mentoring and developing the skills of its artists. The company's music is tailored to an audience that is young, knowledgeable about music, and demands the highest quality recordings. Music School Records releases are available in CD format as well as digital downloads.

For artists who meet the company's high standards, Music School Records takes the core components of music and artist and creates a total marketable product. Marketing begins by identifying the unique qualities that will make a particular artist and their repertoire appealing to a particular audience. The marketing team then pinpoints the product's selling features and presents them to the industry and consumers. This helps differentiate the product from the competition and portrays the personality of the artist.

A key aspect of music marketing in today's marketplace is creating a bond between artists and audiences. Every Music School Records artist has a Web site, and the artists are encouraged to write their own articles and use their own voice to create a Web presence that shows who they are. Newsletters, email lists, blogs, ticket giveaways, downloads of new releases, and exclusive news items are among the ways that an artist can interact with their fans.

(Project 5N—Press Release continues on the next page)

Outcomes-Based Assessments

Problem Solving

(Project 5N–Press Release continued)

To complete this assignment:

- Insert a clip art image as the company logo at the top of the page. Find one of your own, or use **O5N_Music_Logo**, which is included in your student files.

- Add the contact information of the person writing the press release, which should be in either the upper-right or upper-left corner of the release. It should look similar to the address block you typed in Project 5A, but with the addition of a telephone number. Use the name of the owner and the address and telephone number from the previous information.

- Add a **For Immediate Release** line before the body of the press release, but lower on the page than the address block. Format the line so it stands out from the rest of the text.

- Create an interesting title for the press release, and place it below the *For Immediate Release* line.

- Use the preceding information to create a two- or three-paragraph press release, with a space between each paragraph.

- Save the document as **5N_Press_Release_Firstname_Lastname** and add the file name to the footer.

The press release should include the most important information first, and should be simple and straightforward. For example, the information about the new location should come in the first paragraph, and the general information about the company should be presented in the second paragraph. A quote from the owners may make an interesting highlight in the third paragraph—you will need to create an appropriate quote.

 End **You have completed Project 5N** ———————————

Outcomes-Based Assessments

Word
chapterfive

Problem Solving

Project 5O — Holidays

In this project, you will construct a solution by applying any combination of the skills you practiced from the Objectives in Projects 5A and 5B.

For Project 5O, you will need the following files:

New blank Word document
w05O_Musical_Score

You will save your document as
5O_Holidays_Firstname_Lastname

In Project 5O, you will write a memo to announce the days that Music School Records will be closed for holidays in the upcoming year. Use a memo format that you like. If you are unsure of what should be contained in the memo heading, search **memo format** on the Internet. Most memos have at least four lines at the top—Date, To, From, and Subject.

The memo should be from Mahadevan Ropa, Vice President for Business Development, to all employees at the Los Angeles office. Include an opening paragraph that mentions the reason for the memo, and then identify seven or eight holidays for which the office will be closed. Choose any typical holidays that you want to include. If you are not sure of the dates of holidays, or which ones to include, search the Web, using as search terms the year and the word *holidays*.

Add the file name to the footer. Check the memo for spelling or grammar errors. Add the **w05O_Musical_Score** image where appropriate. Save the document as **5O_Holidays_Firstname_Lastname** and submit it as directed.

End **You have completed Project 5O** _____

Outcomes-Based Assessments

Problem Solving

Project 5P—Concert

In this project, you will construct a solution by applying any combination of the skills you practiced from the Objectives in Projects 5A and 5B.

For Project 5P, you will need the following files:

New blank Word document
w05P_Singer

You will save your document as
5P_Concert_Firstname_Lastname

In Project 5P, you will write a letter inquiring about a venue for an upcoming concert featuring three new clients of Music School Records. The following information is necessary to complete the letter:

- Contact person: Jamie Buchanan, Manager, Prince Island Auditorium

- Address: 112 Forkbend Rd., Los Angeles, California, 90030

- Performer 1: Jimmie O'Farrell, trumpet

- Performer 2: Alicia Jones, singer

- Performer 3: The Sturgeon Pointers, instrumental trio

- Musical style: Jazz/Pop fusion

- Desired date: second or third week in June

- Letter from: John Diamond, VP, Creative Development, Music School Records (323-555-0028)

Use the letter format you practiced in Project 5A to create a letter to Jamie Buchanan. The letter should be an inquiry about the availability of the auditorium during the specified time. All three of the performers are from the West Coast, and have recently become clients of Music School Records. Each performer or group will be releasing debut CDs just before the anticipated concert date.

Add the **w05P_Singer** image included with your student files. Add the filename to the footer. Check the memo for spelling or grammar errors. Save the document as **5P_Concert_Firstname_Lastname** and submit it as directed.

End **You have completed Project 5P** _____

Outcomes-Based Assessments

 You and *GO!*

Project 5Q—You and *GO!*

In this project, you will construct a solution by applying any combination of the skills you practiced from the Objectives in Projects 5A and 5B.

Close Word and any other open windows. Display the Start menu, click Computer, and then navigate to the student files that accompany this textbook. In the folder **04_you_and_go**, locate and open the folder for this chapter. Open and print the instructions for this project, which are provided to you in Adobe PDF format. Follow the instructions to create a cover letter for your resume.

 End **You have completed Project 5Q** ————————————

GO! with Help

Project 5R—*GO!* with Help

The Word Help system is extensive and can help you as you work. In this chapter, you used the Quick Access Toolbar on several occasions. You can customize the Quick Access Toolbar by adding buttons that you use regularly, making them quickly available to you from any tab on the Ribbon. In this project, you will use Help to find out how to add buttons.

1 **Start** Word. At the far right end of the Ribbon, click the **Microsoft Office Word Help** button. In the **Word Help** window, click the **Search button arrow**, and then click **Word Help**.

2 In the **Type words to search fo**r box, type **Quick Access Toolbar** and then press Enter.

3 From the list of search results, click **Customize the Quick Access Toolbar**.

4 Click each of the links to find out how to add buttons from the Ribbon and from the **Options** dialog box.

5 When you are through, **Close** the Help window, and then **Close** Word.

 End **You have completed Project 5R** ————————————

Outcomes-Based Assessments

Group Business Running Case

Project 5S—Group Business Running Case

In this project, you will apply the skills you practiced from the Objectives in Projects 5A and 5B.

Your instructor may assign this group case project to your class. If your instructor assigns this project, he or she will provide you with information and instructions to work as part of a group. The group will apply the skills gained thus far to help the Bell Orchid Hotel Group achieve its business goals.

 You have completed Project 5S ————————————

chaptersix

Formatting and Organizing Text

OBJECTIVES

At the end of this chapter you will be able to:

1. Change Document and Paragraph Layout
2. Change and Reorganize Text
3. Create and Modify Lists

OUTCOMES

Mastering these objectives will enable you to:

PROJECT 6A
Format Text and Use Lists

4. Insert and Format Headers and Footers
5. Insert Frequently Used Text
6. Insert and Format References

PROJECT 6B
Create a Research Paper

GHS Law Partners

GHS Law Partners specializes in patent and intellectual property law and government contracts, serving clients in the e-commerce, computer technology, pharmaceutical, and health care fields. The firm researches and prepares patents, litigates intellectual property infringement, handles licensing disputes, and prepares appeals. In the growing area of government contracts, the firm counsels its clients regarding United States government policymaking and prepares contracts according to government procurement policies. The firm's experienced staff of attorneys includes many who have formerly worked as prosecutors, federal court law clerks, and United States patent inspectors and procurement contract attorneys.

Formatting and Organizing Text

Typing text is just the beginning of the process of creating an effective, professional looking document. Microsoft Word provides many tools for formatting paragraphs and documents. For example, there are tools to create shortcuts for entering commonly used text, and quick ways to copy, cut, and move text. Word also provides tools that enable you to create specialized formats, such as footnotes, bulleted and numbered lists, and indented paragraphs.

In this chapter, you will edit a seminar announcement, and then you will create and format a research paper.

Project 6A Seminar

In Activities 6.01 through 6.15, you will edit an announcement from GHS Law Partners about an upcoming Intellectual Property Seminar. Your completed document will look similar to Figure 6.1.

For Project 6A, you will need the following file:

w06A_Seminar

You will save your document as
6A_Seminar_Firstname_Lastname

GHS Law Partners
Intellectual Property Seminar for Business Attorneys

July 12, 2009
Atlanta, GA
Draft Announcement

GHS Law Partners will present its fifth annual Intellectual Property Seminar for Business Attorneys in Atlanta, GA, on July 12, 2009. This event is intended for attorneys who want to expand their knowledge of intellectual property in order to better serve their clients. Intellectual property law affects every kind of business and clients' rights, obligations, and strategies. GHS Law Partners believes that sharing knowledge and expertise in this area of law enhances the business climate and improves the ability of business-focused firms to serve their diverse client base.

Some states confer Continuing Legal Education credits for this seminar. Each attendee will receive a complete set of all seminar materials along with an Intellectual Property textbook written by one of our partners. Audio tapes and DVDs of selected sessions will also be available.

The three morning sessions will focus on copyrights:

1. Introduction to Copyrights
2. Copyright FAQs
3. Current Issues in Copyrights

Lunch will feature a panel discussion of GHS attorneys and other trademark experts. Among the topics discussed will be:

Use of trademarks
Trademark enforcement
Avoiding dilution of trademark

The four afternoon sessions will cover patents:

1. Patent Basics
2. Understanding Trade Secrets and Patent Protection
3. Current Issues in Patents
4. Business Considerations in Patents and Trademarks

Questions and discussion are encouraged at all sessions, and attendees are reminded that such discussions should be kept confidential to protect the wide array of clients represented by the group.

Registration will open on April 1, 2009, and is limited to 400 attendees. Discounted rates are available at several nearby hotels. A "dine-around" dinner will be arranged at several local restaurants for those who want to participate.

If you would like a brochure containing much more detailed information about the topics to be covered in the upcoming Intellectual Property Seminar, contact Melissa Rosella at (404) 555-0022. You can also register online at www.ghslaw.com/ipseminar.

6A_Seminar_Firstname_Lastname

Figure 6.1
Project 6A—Seminar

Objective 1
Change Document and Paragraph Layout

Document layout includes *margins*—the space between the text and the top, bottom, left, and right edges of the paper. Paragraph layout includes line spacing, indents, and tabs. In Word, the information about paragraph formats is stored in the paragraph mark at the end of a paragraph. When you press the Enter key, the new paragraph mark contains the formatting of the previous paragraph, unless you take steps to change it.

Activity 6.01 Setting Margins

You can change each of the four page margins—top, bottom, left, and right—independently. You can also change the margins for the entire document at one time or change the margins for only a portion of the document.

> ## Note — Comparing Your Screen With the Figures in This Textbook
>
> Your screen will match the figures shown in this textbook if you set your screen resolution to 1024 × 768. At other resolutions, your screen will closely resemble, but not match, the figures shown. To view your screen's resolution, on the Windows desktop, right-click in a blank area, click Personalize, and then click Display Settings.

1 **Start** Word. From your student files, locate and open the document **w06A_Seminar**.

2 From the **Office** menu , display the **Save As** dialog box, and then navigate to the location where you are saving your files. On the toolbar, click the **New Folder** button. Name the new folder **Word Chapter 6** and then press [Enter].

3 In the **File name** box, delete the existing text. Using your own name, type **6A_Seminar_Firstname_Lastname** and then click **Save**. If necessary, in the Paragraph group, click the Show/Hide ¶ button to display formatting marks. Set the page width to display the left and right page edges.

4 On the Ribbon, click the **Page Layout tab**. In the **Page Setup group**, click the **Margins** button, and then at the bottom of the **Margins gallery**, click **Custom Margins**.

5 In the displayed **Page Setup** dialog box, press [Tab] as necessary to select the value in the **Left** box, and then, with *1.25"* selected, type **1**

This action will change the left margin to 1 inch on all pages of the document. You do not need to type the inch (") mark.

6 Press [Tab] to select the measurement in the **Right** box, type **1** and then compare your screen with Figure 6.2. Notice that the new margins will be applied to the entire document.

Figure 6.2

New left margin   New right margin

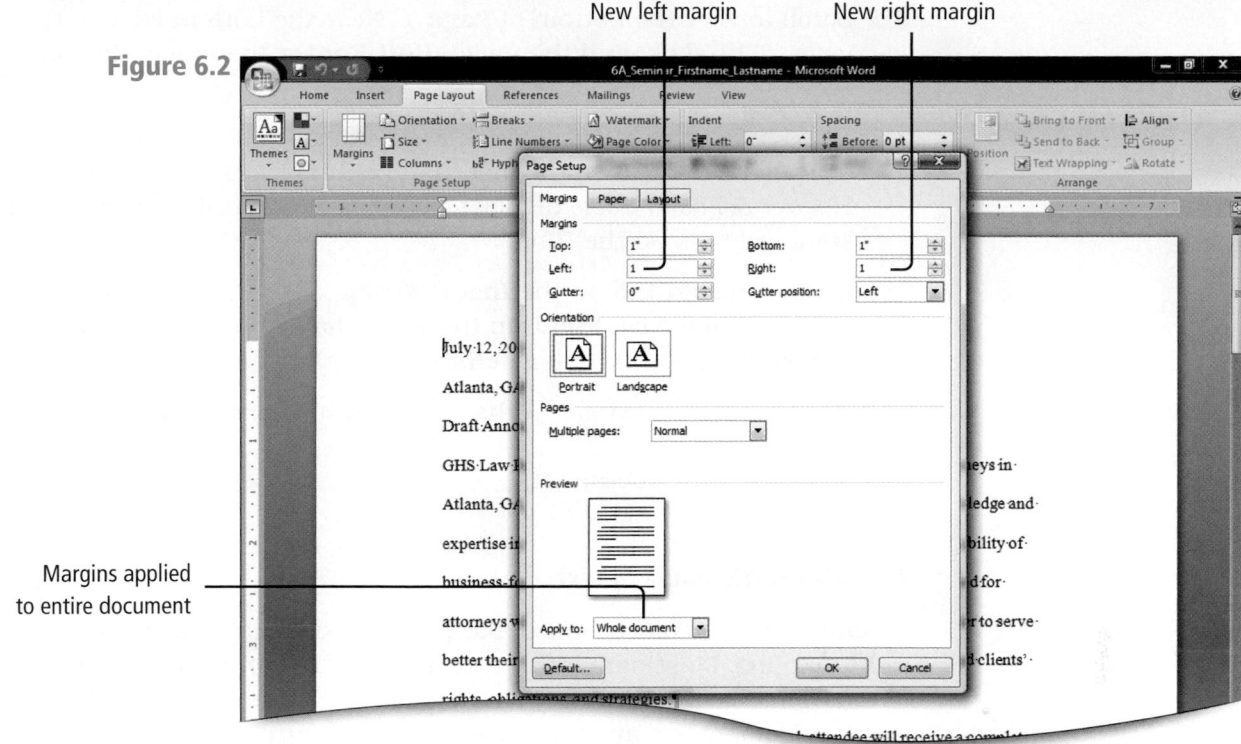

Margins applied
to entire document

7 In the lower right corner of the dialog box, click **OK** to apply the new margins and close the dialog box. If the ruler below the Ribbon is not displayed, at the top of the vertical scroll bar, click the **View Ruler** button [icon]. Compare your screen with Figure 6.3.

View Ruler button

Figure 6.3

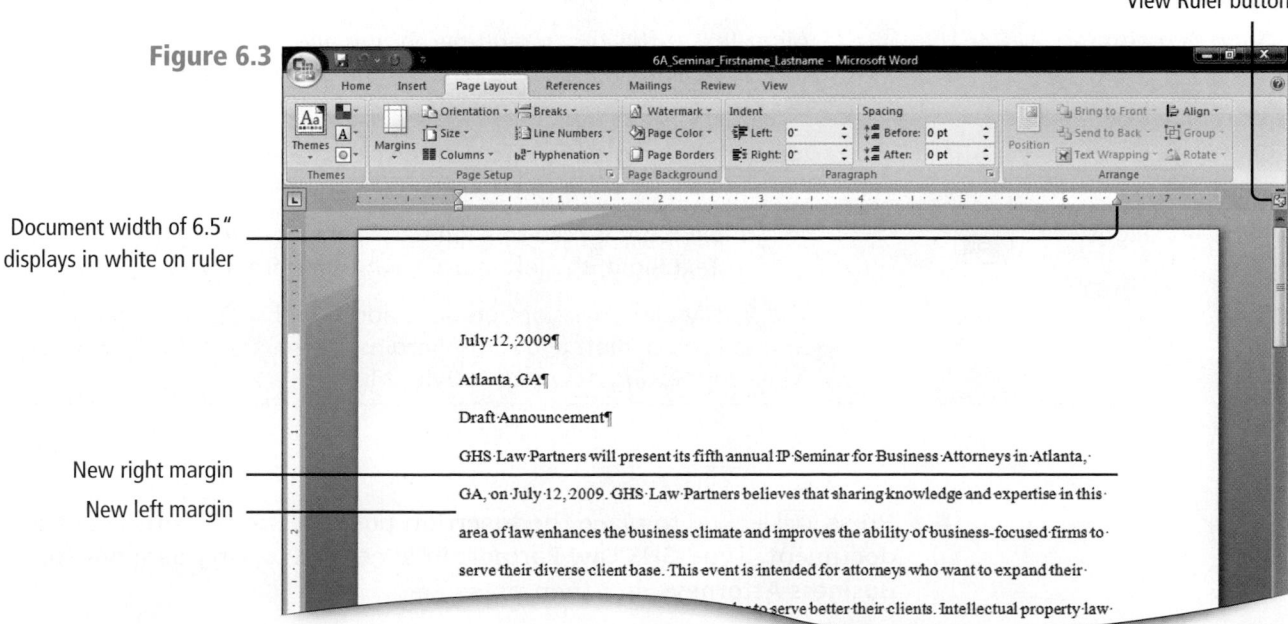

Document width of 6.5″
displays in white on ruler

New right margin
New left margin

8 Scroll to view the bottom of **Page 1**. Near the bottom edge of the page, right-click, and then click **Edit Footer** to display the footer area.

This shortcut provides a quick way to display either the footer or header area. Because the insertion point is in the footer area, *Header & Footer Tools* displays, and the Design tab is added to the standard tabs on the Ribbon.

9 On the **Design tab**, in the **Insert group**, click the **Quick Parts** button, and then click **Field**. In the **Field** dialog box, under **Field names**, locate and click **FileName**, and then click **OK**.

10 Double-click anywhere in the document to close the footer area.

Save [icon] your document.

Activity 6.02 Aligning Text

Alignment is the placement of paragraph text relative to the left and right margins. Most paragraph text uses *left alignment*—aligned at the left margin, leaving the right margin uneven. Three other types of paragraph alignment are available: *center alignment*—centered between the left and right margins; *right alignment*—aligned on the right margin; and *justified alignment*—text aligned on both the left and right margins. Examples are shown in the table in Figure 6.4.

Paragraph Alignment Options

Alignment	Button	Description and Example
Align Text Left	[icon]	Align Text Left is the default paragraph alignment in Word. Text in the paragraph aligns at the left margin, and the right margin is uneven.
Center	[icon]	Center alignment aligns text in the paragraph so that it is centered between the left and right margins.
Align Text Right	[icon]	Align Text Right is used to align text at the right margin. Using Align Text Right, the left margin, which is normally even, is uneven.
Justify	[icon]	The Justify alignment option adds additional space between words so that both the left and right margins are even. Justify is often used when formatting newspaper-style columns.

Figure 6.4

1 Press [Ctrl] + [Home] to place the insertion point at the beginning of the document. Type **GHS Law Partners Intellectual Property Seminar for Business Attorneys** and then press [Enter].

2 Click to place the insertion point anywhere in the first line of the document—the title that you just typed that begins *GHS Law Partners*. On the **Home tab**, in the **Paragraph group**, click the **Center** button [icon].

The first paragraph, which is a title, is centered. To format a paragraph, you just need to have the insertion point somewhere in the paragraph—you do not need to select all of the text in the paragraph.

3 Move the pointer into the left margin area to the left of the second line of text that begins *July 12* until the pointer displays. Drag down to select that line and the two lines following it, ending with *Draft Announcement*, and then on the Mini toolbar, click the

Center button . Compare your screen with Figure 6.5.

A paragraph consists of a paragraph mark and all the text in front of it. To format multiple paragraphs, they must all be selected.

Figure 6.5

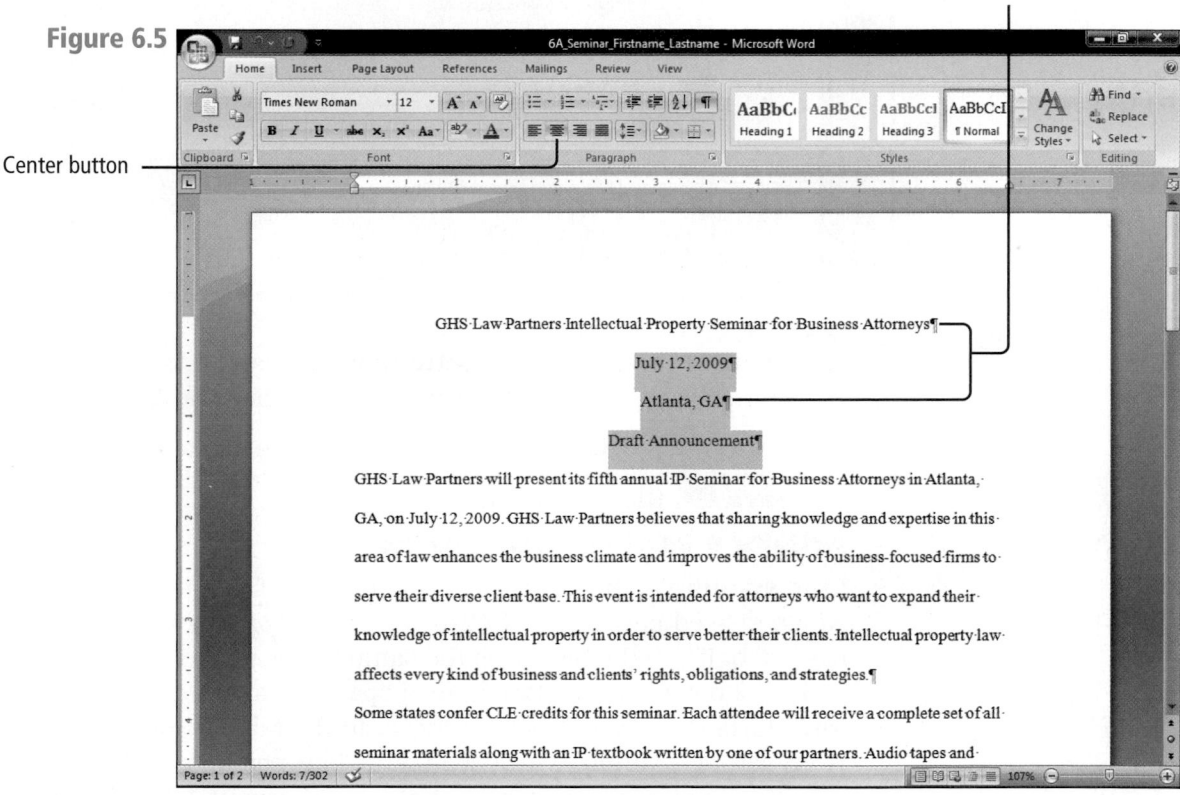

Center button

First four lines centered

4 Move the pointer into the left margin area to the left of the fifth line of text that begins *GHS Law Partners will present* until the pointer displays. Then, drag down to select this line of text and the next eight lines of text—including the line that ends *will also be available.*

5 In the **Paragraph group**, click the **Justify** button , and then compare your screen with Figure 6.6.

Both the left and right edges of the paragraphs are even. The other paragraphs are not affected.

Figure 6.6

Right edge aligned

Justify button

Left edge aligned

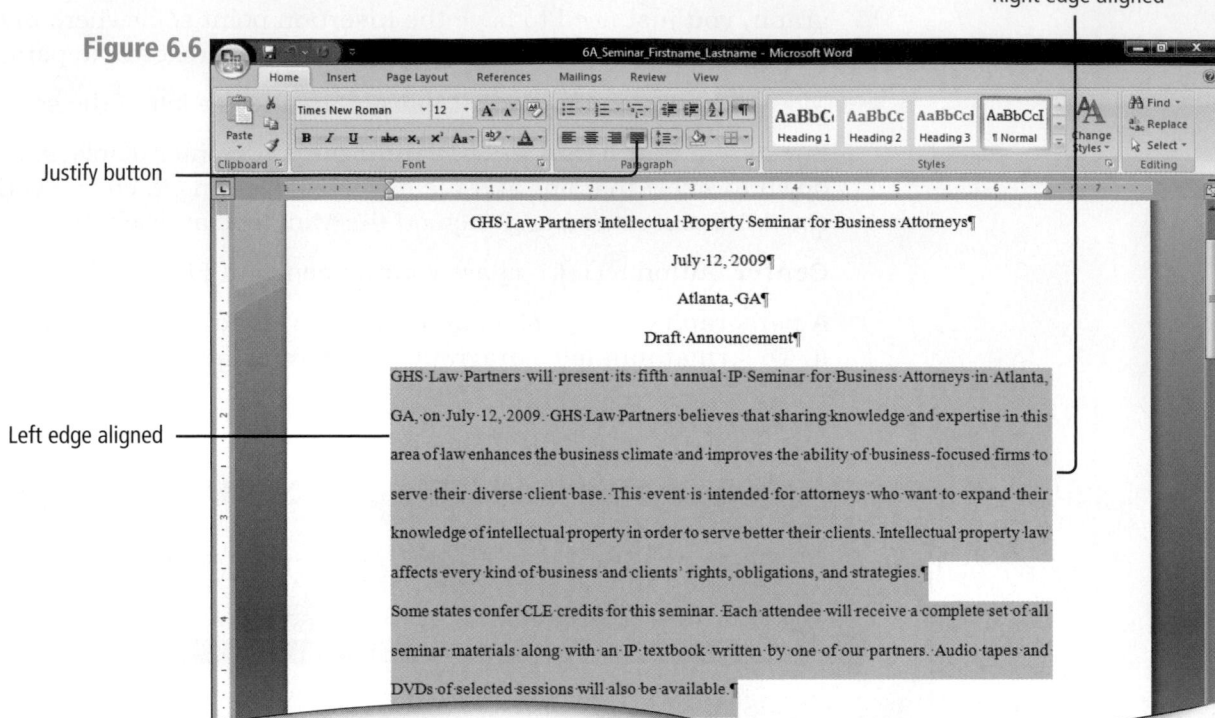

6 Because justified text is better used in narrow columns, with the text still selected, in the **Paragraph group**, click the **Align Text Left** button 📄. Click anywhere in the document to deselect the text. **Save** 💾 the document.

Activity 6.03 Changing Line Spacing

Line spacing is the distance between lines of text in a paragraph. A single-spaced paragraph of 12-point text accommodates six lines in a vertical inch. If you double-space the same text, each line will be 24 points high—12 points of text, 12 points of space—and will accommodate only three lines in a vertical inch as shown in the table in Figure 6.7. The default Word setting—Multiple—uses 14 points between lines of 12-point text resulting in single line spacing that is 1.15 (about 1 $\frac{1}{6}$) line spacing.

Paragraph Alignment Options

Spacing	Example
Single (1.0)	Most business documents are single-spaced. This means that the spacing between lines is just enough to separate the text.
Multiple with 1.15 line spacing	The default line spacing in Microsoft Word 2007 is 1.15, which is equivalent to single spacing with an extra 1/6 line added between lines.
Double (2.0)	Many college research papers and reports, and many draft documents that need space for notes, are double-spaced; there is space for a full line of text between each document line.

Figure 6.7

1 Press `Ctrl` + `Home` to place the insertion point at the beginning of the document. In the left margin area, display the 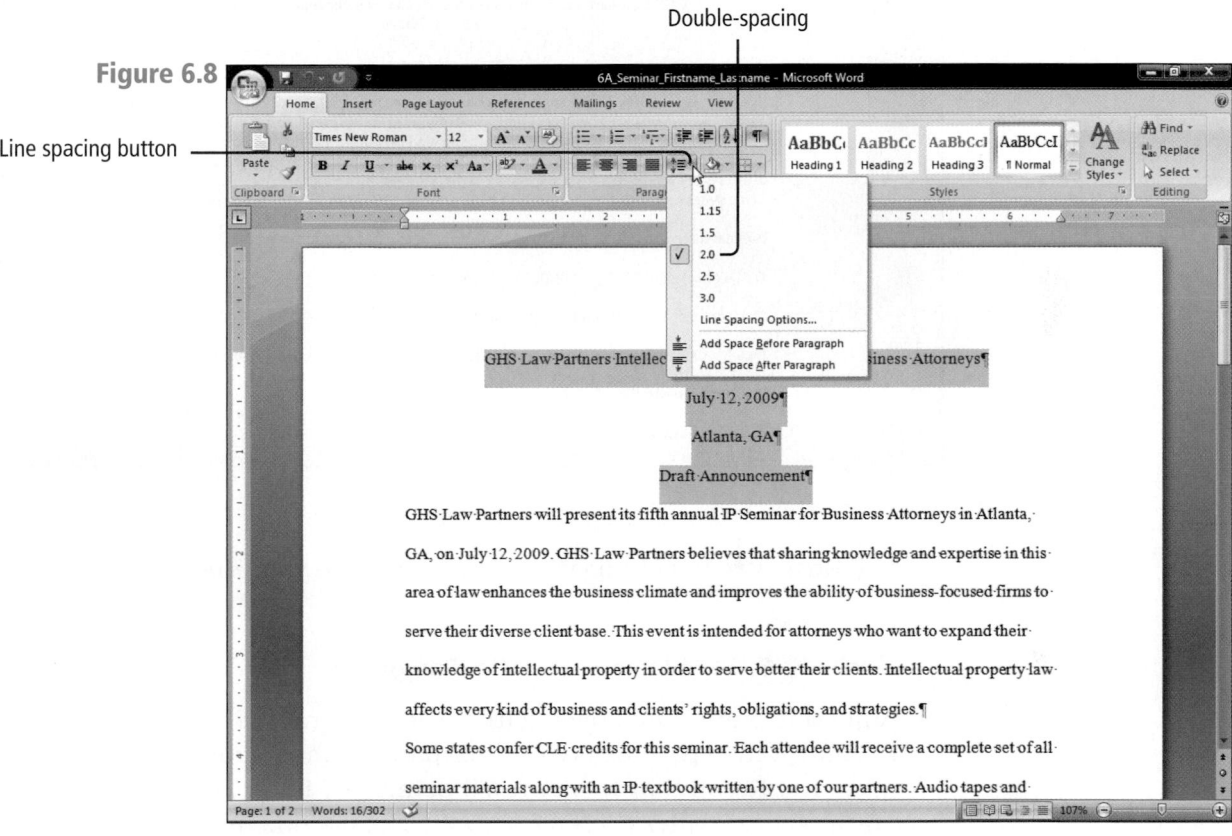 pointer and drag down to select the first four lines of text—the four centered title lines.

2 In the **Paragraph group**, click the **Line spacing** button, and then compare your screen with Figure 6.8.

A check mark next to 2.0 indicates that the selected paragraphs are double-spaced.

Double-spacing

Figure 6.8

Line spacing button

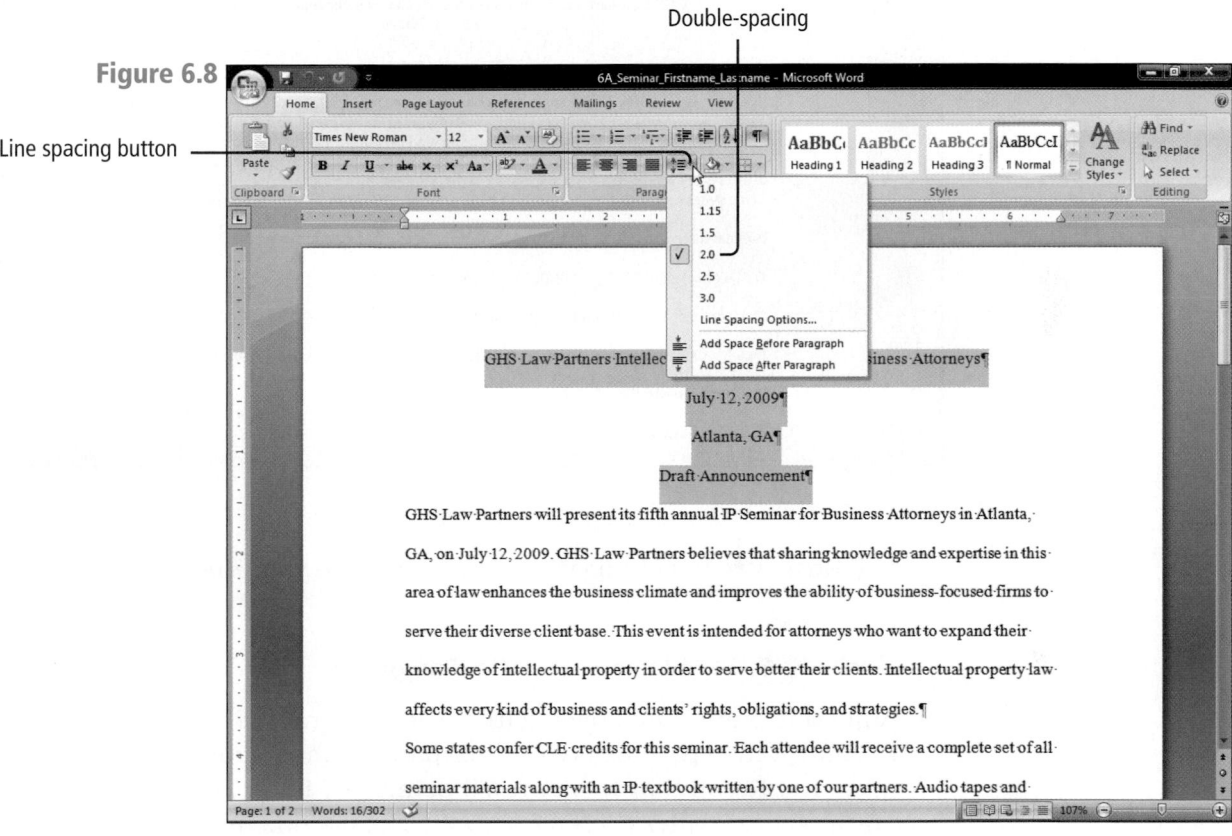

3 In the **Line spacing** list, click **1.0** to change the line spacing of the first four paragraphs.

4 Click to place the insertion point in the paragraph that begins *GHS Law Partners will present*. In the **Paragraph group**, click the **Line spacing** button, and then click **1.0**. Compare your screen with Figure 6.9.

Recall that you do not have to select the entire paragraph to change the paragraph formatting. The first five paragraphs of the document are single-spaced.

Figure 6.9

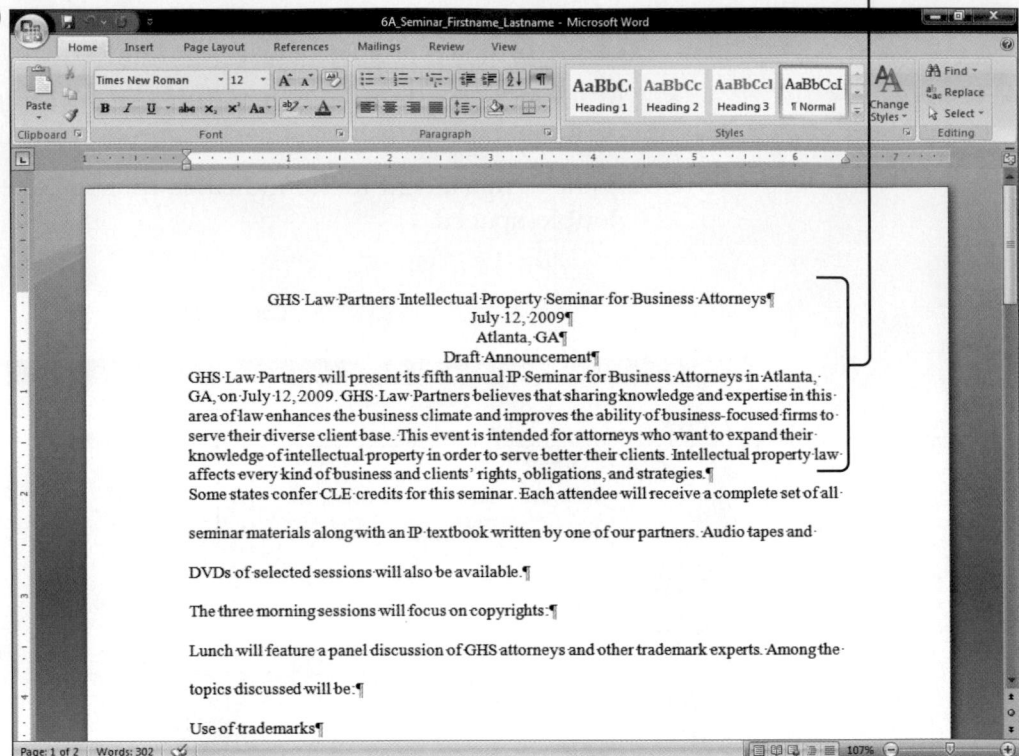

5 **Save** 🖫 the changes you have made to your document.

Activity 6.04 Adding Space After Paragraphs

Adjusting paragraph spacing from the Paragraph dialog box enables you to control the space before or after paragraphs using points as the unit of measure. Recall that there are 72 points per inch. The Word default adds 10-pt. spacing after each paragraph. The document you are working on has no extra spacing after each paragraph.

1 Press Ctrl + Home to place the insertion point at the beginning of the first line of text in the document. In the lower right corner of the **Paragraph group**, click the **Dialog Box Launcher** 🖫. Alternatively, click the Line spacing button, and then click Line Spacing Options from the displayed list.

2 In the displayed **Paragraph** dialog box, click the **Indents and Spacing tab**. Under **Spacing**, in the **After** spin box, click the **up spin arrow** two times, and then compare your screen with Figure 6.10.

The value in the box changes from 0 pt to 12 pt. A *spin box* is a small box with an upward- and downward-pointing arrow that lets you move (spin) through a set of values by clicking. The up and down arrows, called *spin box arrows*, increment the point size by six points at a time. Alternatively, type a number of your choice directly into the spin box.

Figure 6.10

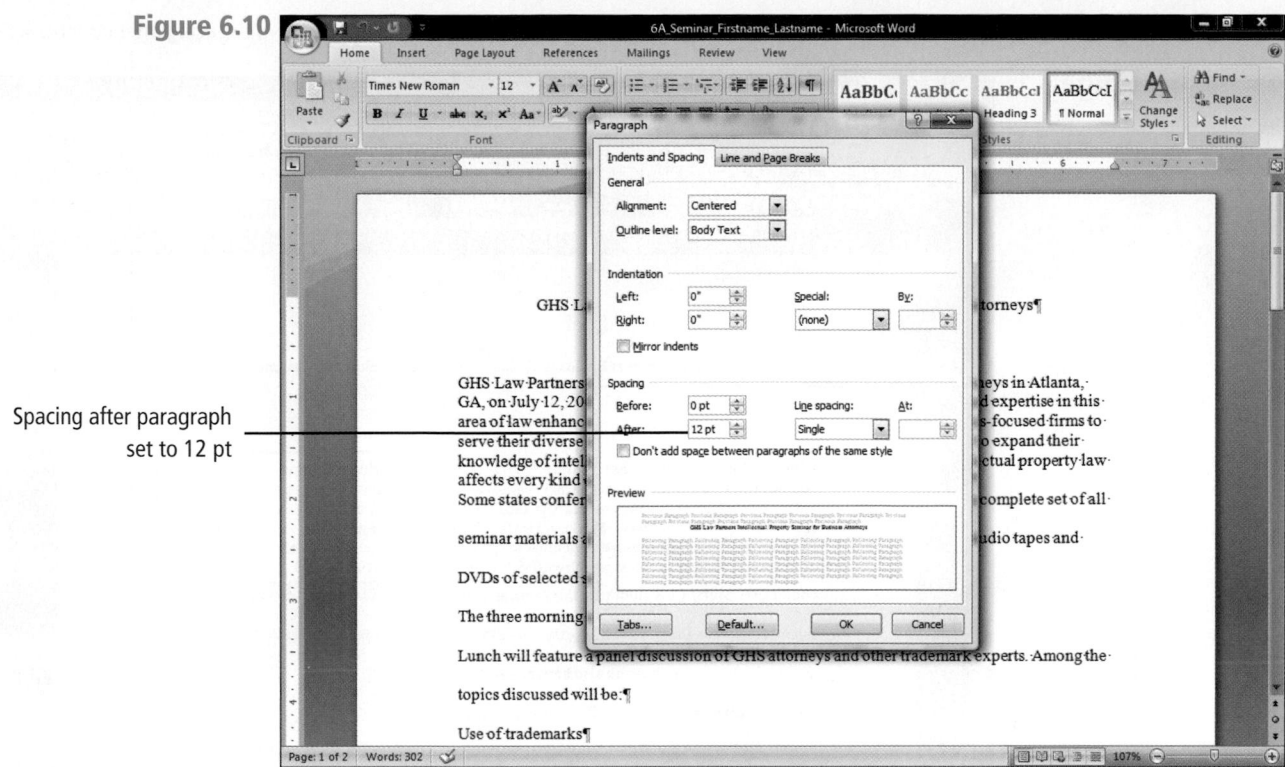

Spacing after paragraph
set to 12 pt

3 Click **OK** to add a 12-pt space after the paragraph.

4 In the *Draft Announcement* paragraph, click to position the insertion point anywhere in the paragraph. In the **Paragraph group**, click the **Dialog Box Launcher** . Under **Spacing**, in the **After** box, click the **up spin arrow** one time to change the value in the box from *0 pt* to **6 pt**. Click **OK**.

Another Way ── **To Add Spacing Before and After Paragraphs**

The Paragraph dialog box gives you a great deal of control over paragraph layout. You can also change the spacing before and after paragraphs using the Ribbon. Click the Page Layout tab, and then use the Spacing buttons in the Paragraph group.

5 In the paragraph beginning *GHS Law Partners will present*, click to position the insertion point anywhere in the paragraph. In the **Paragraph group**, display the **Paragraph** dialog box. Under **Spacing**, set **After** to **6 pt**, and then click **OK**. Compare your screen with Figure 6.11.

Figure 6.11

12-pt. spacing
after the first paragraph

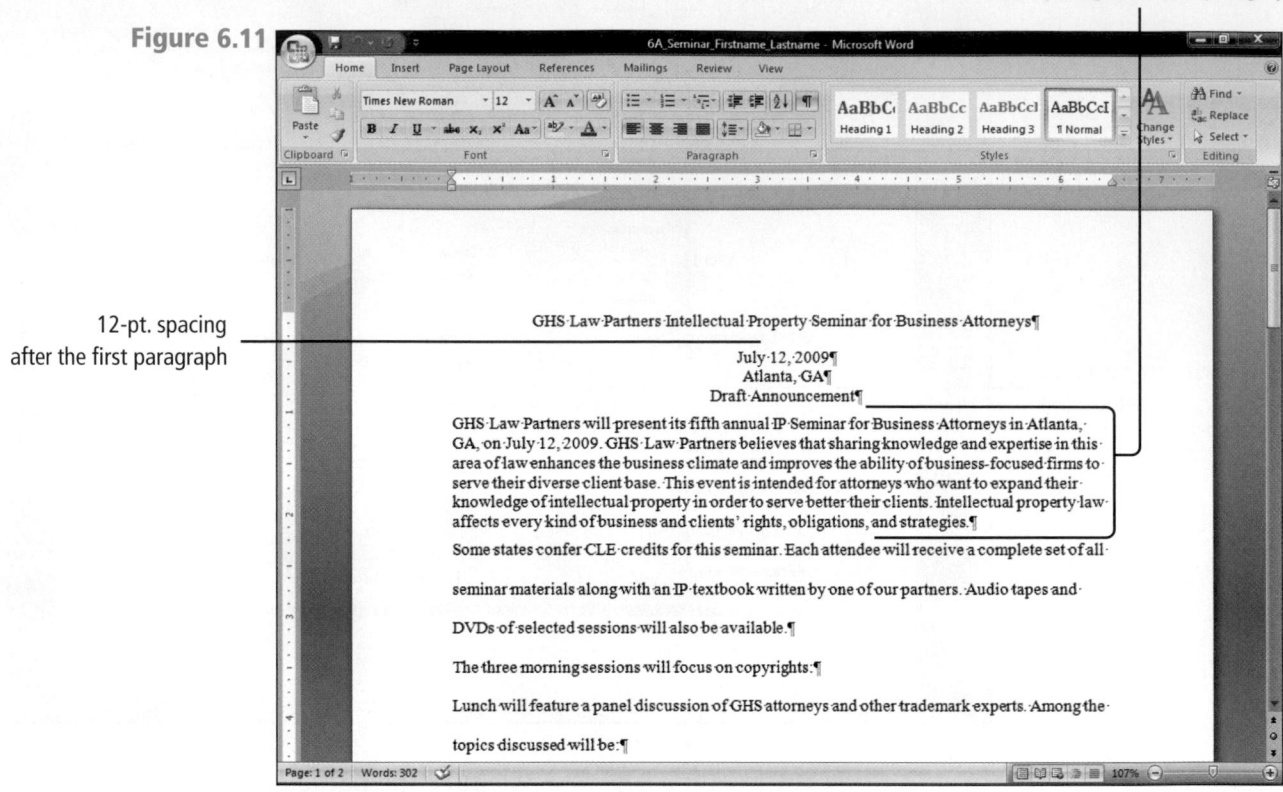

6 Save the changes you have made to your document.

Activity 6.05 Using the Format Painter

Use the ***Format Painter*** to copy the formatting of specific text or of a paragraph and then apply it in other locations in your document.

1 Click anywhere in the paragraph that begins *GHS Law Partners will present*. On the **Home tab**, in the **Clipboard group**, click the **Format Painter** button. Position the pointer anywhere in the paragraph that begins *Some states confer*, and then compare your screen with Figure 6.12.

The pointer takes the shape of a paintbrush, and contains the formatting information from the paragraph where the insertion point is positioned. Instructions on how to turn the Format Painter off display in the status bar.

Figure 6.12

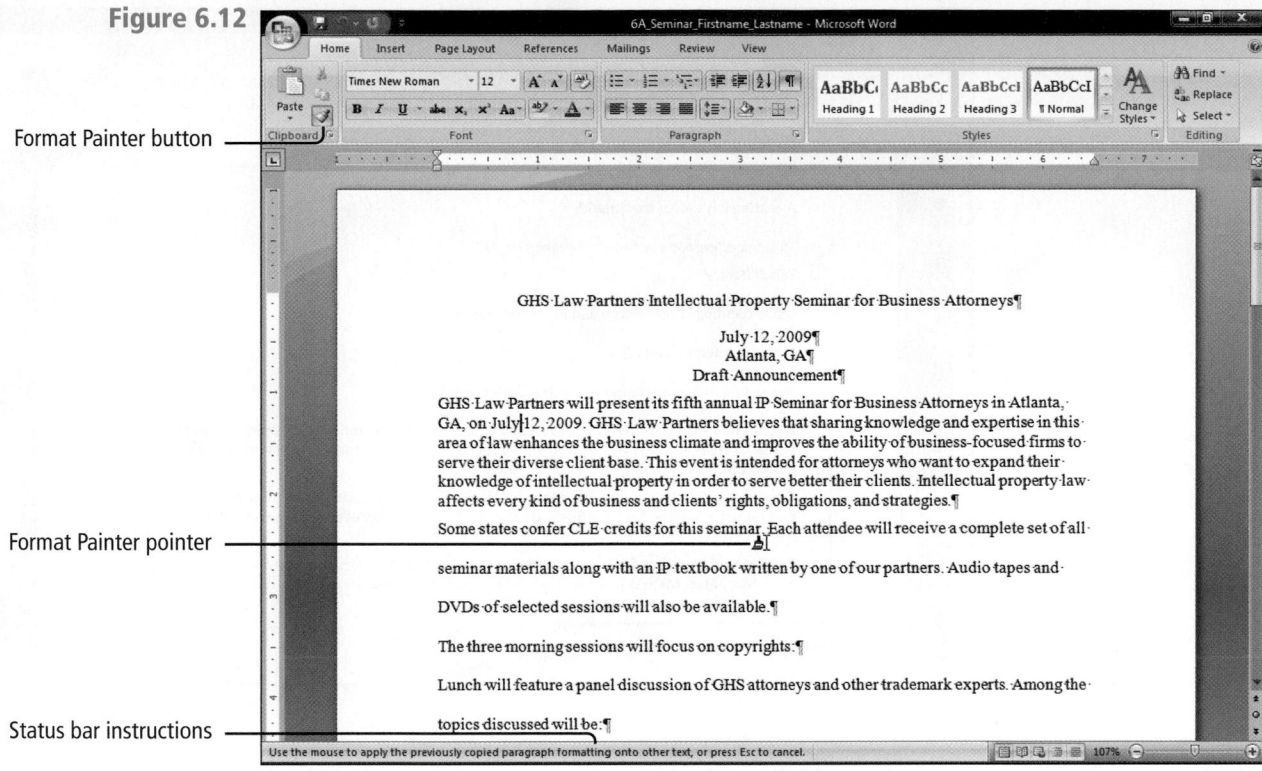

Format Painter button

Format Painter pointer

Status bar instructions

GHS Law Partners Intellectual Property Seminar for Business Attorneys¶

July 12, 2009¶
Atlanta, GA¶
Draft Announcement¶

GHS Law Partners will present its fifth annual IP Seminar for Business Attorneys in Atlanta, GA, on July 12, 2009. GHS Law Partners believes that sharing knowledge and expertise in this area of law enhances the business climate and improves the ability of business-focused firms to serve their diverse client base. This event is intended for attorneys who want to expand their knowledge of intellectual property in order to serve better their clients. Intellectual property law affects every kind of business and clients' rights, obligations, and strategies.¶

Some states confer CLE credits for this seminar. Each attendee will receive a complete set of all seminar materials along with an IP textbook written by one of our partners. Audio tapes and DVDs of selected sessions will also be available.¶

The three morning sessions will focus on copyrights:¶

Lunch will feature a panel discussion of GHS attorneys and other trademark experts. Among the topics discussed will be:¶

Use the mouse to apply the previously copied paragraph formatting onto other text, or press Esc to cancel.

---

2 Click the ▲I pointer one time.

The paragraph formatting from the original paragraph—single-spacing, 6-pt space after the paragraph—is copied to this paragraph. The Format Painter is no longer active.

3 With the insertion point in the recently formatted paragraph, double-click the **Format Painter** button to use the Format Painter multiple times.

4 Move the ▲I pointer to the paragraph that begins *The three morning sessions*, and then click one time.

The paragraph formatting from the original paragraph is copied to this paragraph, and the Format Painter remains active.

5 Move the ▲I pointer over the paragraph that begins *Lunch will feature*, and then click one time.

6 Using the down scroll arrow, locate and click in the paragraph that begins *The four afternoon sessions*. Use the Format Painter to change the formatting of the last three paragraphs, starting with the paragraph that begins *Registration will open*. Compare your screen with Figure 6.13.

Figure 6.13

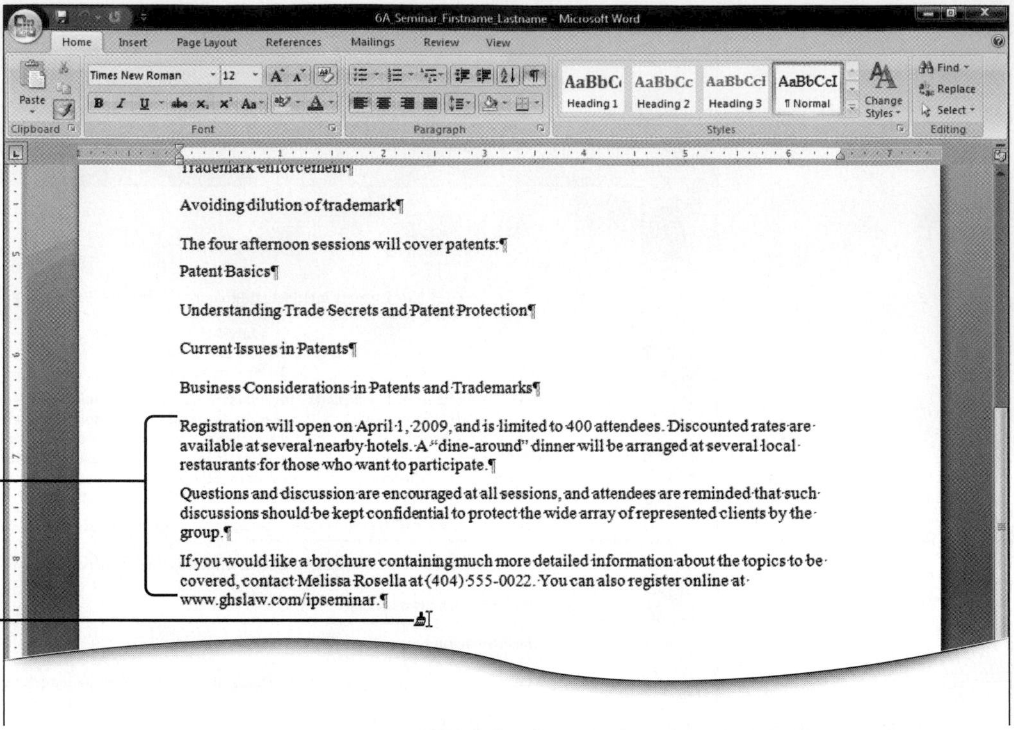

Last three paragraphs single-spaced with 6 pt spacing after

Format Painter still active

Alert!

If You Click the Wrong Paragraph

If you accidentally click in one of the other paragraphs while scrolling down, click the Undo button to undo the formatting. Clicking the Undo button turns off the Format Painter, so you will need to click in the paragraph with the desired formatting again, and then turn the Format Painter on again to format the last paragraphs.

7 In the **Clipboard group**, click the **Format Painter** button to turn the command off. Alternatively, press Esc to turn off the Format Painter feature. **Save** your document.

Objective 2
Change and Reorganize Text

Changing and reorganizing text is accomplished using Word features such as the Find and Replace dialog box and the *Office Clipboard*, a temporary storage area that holds text. You can *copy* text to the Office Clipboard, which leaves the original text in place, or *cut* text, which removes it from its original location. Then, you can ***paste***—insert—the contents of the Office Clipboard in a new location. The keyboard shortcuts for these commands are shown in the table in Figure 6.14.

Keyboard Shortcuts for Editing Text

Keyboard Shortcut	Action
Ctrl + X	Cut text or graphic and move it to the Office Clipboard.
Ctrl + C	Copy text or graphic to the Office Clipboard.
Ctrl + V	Paste the contents of the Office Clipboard.
Ctrl + Z	Undo an action.
Ctrl + Y	Redo an action.
Ctrl + F	Find text.
Ctrl + H	Find and replace text.

Figure 6.14

Activity 6.06 Finding and Replacing Text

Finding and then replacing text is a quick way to make the same change more than one time in a document. For example, if you consistently misspell someone's last name, Word can search for all instances of the name and replace it with the correct spelling.

1 Press Ctrl + Home to position the insertion point at the beginning of the document.

When you initiate a find operation or a find and replace operation, the search begins from the location of the insertion point and proceeds to the end of the document. If you begin a search in the middle of a document, Word will prompt you to return to the beginning of the document and continue the operation.

2 On the **Home tab**, in the **Editing group**, click the **Find** button. In the **Find and Replace** dialog box, in the **Find what** box, type **CLE** which is an acronym for *Continuing Legal Education*.

You can use the Find command to move quickly to a specific location in a document if you know that a word or phrase is located in the document.

3 In the **Find and Replace** dialog box, click the **Find Next** button to select the first occurrence of *CLE*.

4 In the **Find and Replace** dialog box, click **Cancel**. Press Ctrl + Home to position the insertion point at the beginning of the document.

5 In the **Editing group**, click the **Replace** button. Alternatively, in the Find and Replace dialog box, click the Replace tab.

6 If necessary, in the displayed **Find and Replace** dialog box, in the **Find what** box, type **CLE** and then in the **Replace with** box, type **Continuing Legal Education**

7 Click the **More** button to expand the dialog box, and then under **Search Options**, select the **Match case** and **Find whole words only** check boxes. Click **Find Next**, and then compare your screen with Figure 6.15.

By searching for whole words only, you will avoid changing the search text if it occurs in the middle of a word—for example, *CLEVELAND*. By matching case, you not only instruct the program to look for text in the same case, but you also instruct the program to replace text using the same case as the text in the Replace with box.

Find what box   *Replace with* box

Figure 6.15

Match case check box

Find whole words only check box

First instance of found text

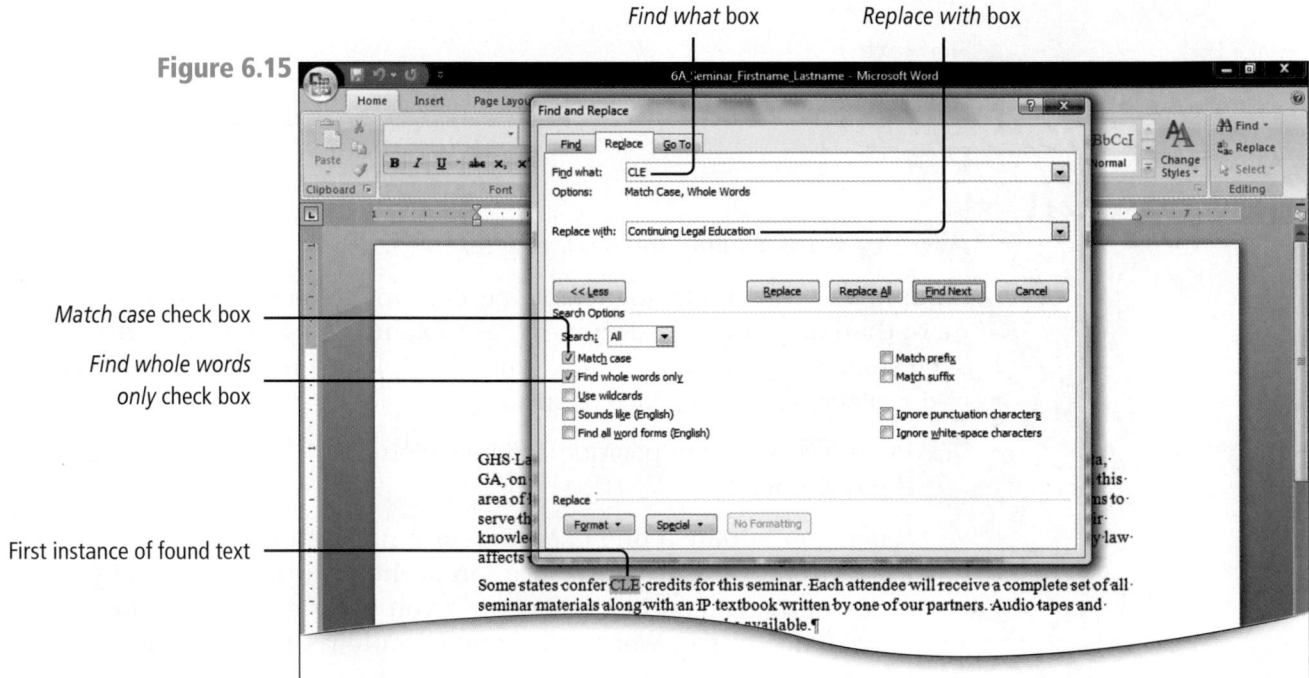

8 In the **Find and Replace** dialog box, click the **Replace** button.

The text is replaced, and a message indicates that Word has finished searching the document; no other instances of the search text were found.

9 Click **OK** to close the message box. In the **Find what** box, type **IP** and in the **Replace with** box, type **Intellectual Property**

10 Click **Replace All**.

A message displays, indicating that two replacements have been made.

11 Click **OK** to close the message box. Clear the two **Search Options** check boxes, click the **Less** button, and then click **Close** to close the Find and Replace dialog box. **Save** your document.

Activity 6.07 Cutting, Copying, and Pasting Text

You can move text from one location in a document to a different location in the same document with the Cut and Paste commands. Use the Cut command to move text out of the document to the Office Clipboard—the temporary storage location for text or graphics. Then, use the Paste command to paste the contents of the Office Clipboard to the new location. The Copy command moves a copy of selected text to the Office Clipboard, which you can then paste to another location. Unlike the Cut command, the Copy command does not remove the selected text from its original location.

1 Near the end of the document, locate the paragraph that begins *Questions and discussion*, and then double-click to select the word *represented*.

2 On the **Home tab**, in the **Clipboard group**, click the **Cut** button . Alternatively, right-click the selected text and click Cut from the shortcut menu; or, press Ctrl + X.

The selected text is removed from the document and moved to the Office Clipboard.

Note — The Difference Between Using Delete, Backspace, and Cut

When you use the Cut command to remove text, it is moved to the Office Clipboard and can be pasted into the same—or a different—document. When you use Delete or Backspace to remove text, the text is not moved to the Office Clipboard. The only way you can retrieve text removed with Delete or Backspace is by using the Undo command.

3 In the same line of text, click to position the insertion point between *clients* and *by*. In the **Clipboard group**, click the **Paste** button. Alternatively, right-click, and then click Paste from the shortcut menu; or, press Ctrl + V. Adjust the spacing before and after the word if necessary.

The text is placed at the insertion point, but also remains on the Office Clipboard. The Paste Options button displays below the pasted word. When you click the button, a list displays that lets you determine how the information is pasted into your document.

4 Point to the **Paste Options** button until its ScreenTip *Paste Options* displays, click the button, and then compare your screen with Figure 6.16.

The displayed list provides commands related specifically to the Paste command. You can determine whether you want to format the pasted text the same as the surrounding text or retain its original formatting. The available options depend on the type of content you are pasting, the program from which you are pasting, and the format of the text where you are pasting. Performing another screen action will cancel the display of the button.

Pasted text

Figure 6.16

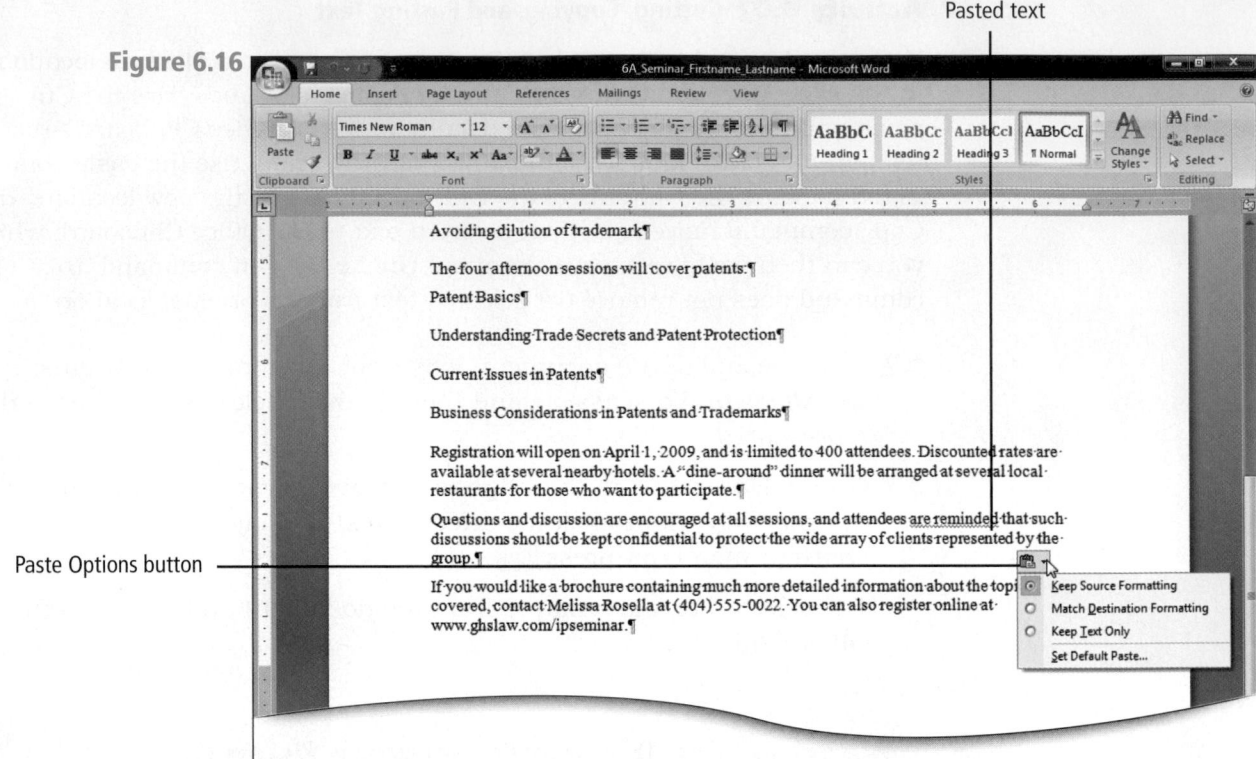

Paste Options button

5 Click anywhere in the document to close the **Paste Options** menu and retain the same formatting. Alternatively, press Esc to cancel its display.

6 Position the pointer in the paragraph that begins *Registration will open*, and then triple-click to select the entire paragraph. Alternatively, select the paragraph by dragging with your mouse, but be sure to include the paragraph mark.

7 In the **Clipboard group**, click the **Cut** button. Locate the paragraph that begins *If you would like* and position the insertion point at the beginning of that paragraph. In the **Clipboard group**, click the **Paste** button to paste the text in the new location.

Alert! | **If the Clipboard Task Pane Opens**

The Clipboard task pane may display on your screen depending on the options that have been set for the Office Clipboard on your computer. If the task pane opens, click the Close button on the task pane title bar.

8 Press Ctrl + Home. In the first title line, select *Intellectual Property Seminar*. In the **Clipboard group**, click the **Copy** button. Press Ctrl + End to move to the end of the document.

9 In the last paragraph, locate the word *covered* and position the insertion point between the word and the following comma. Press Spacebar, type **in the upcoming** and then press Spacebar. In the **Clipboard group**, click the **Paste** button, and then compare your screen with Figure 6.17.

The copied text is inserted in the new location, but is not removed from the original location. The Paste Options button displays below the pasted text.

Figure 6.17

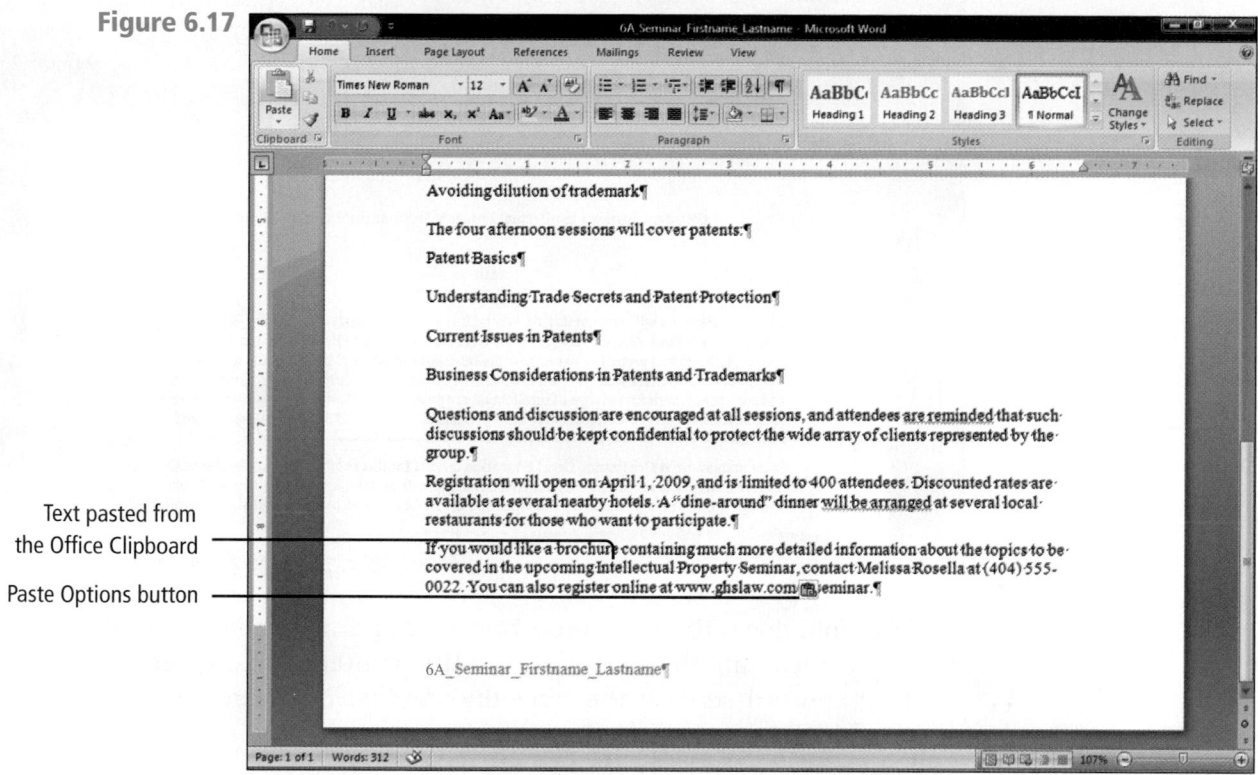

Text pasted from
the Office Clipboard

Paste Options button

10 **Save** the changes you have made to your document.

Activity 6.08 Moving Text to a New Location

Another method of moving text is the ***drag-and-drop*** technique, which uses the mouse to drag selected text from one location to another. This method is useful if the text to be moved is on the same screen as the destination location.

1 Press Ctrl + Home to position the insertion point at the beginning of the document. In the fifth line of the paragraph that begins *GHS Law Partners will present*, locate and select *better*.

2 Point to the selected word to display the ⬚ pointer as shown in Figure 6.18.

Figure 6.18

better selected

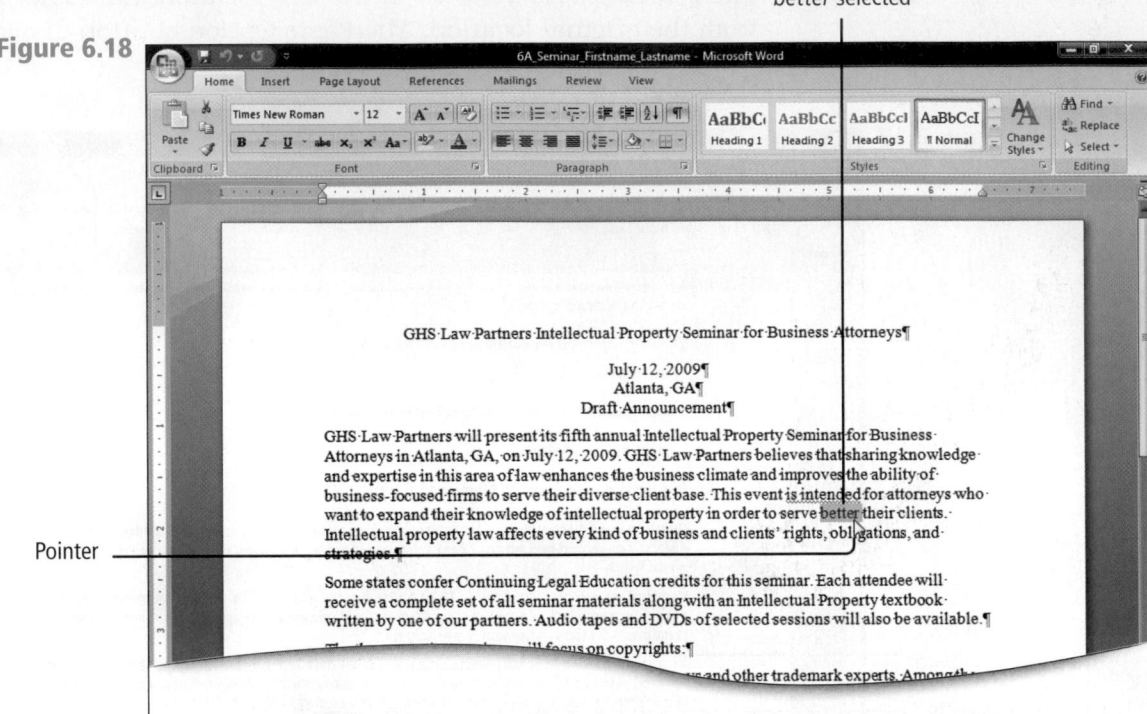

Pointer

3 Hold down the left mouse button and drag to the left until the dotted vertical line that floats next to the pointer is positioned to the left of the word *serve* in the same line, and then release the left mouse button.

4 Click anywhere to deselect the text, and then compare your screen with Figure 6.19.

The word is moved to the insertion point location. The vertical line of the pointer assists you in dropping the moved text in the place where you want it. The small box attached to the pointer indicates that there is text attached to the pointer.

Figure 6.19

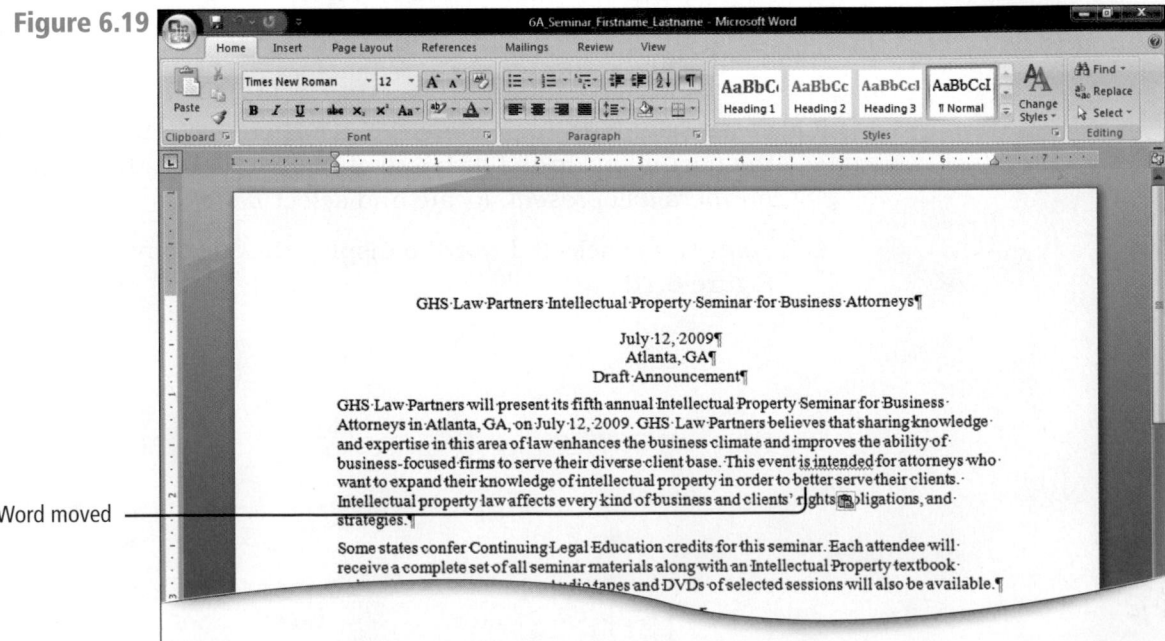

Word moved

5 In the same paragraph, point to the second sentence—the one that begins *GHS Law Partners believes*. Hold down Ctrl and click one time to select the entire sentence.

6 Point to the selected sentence to display the 🔲 pointer, and then drag down to the end of the paragraph and position the vertical line to the right of the period at the end of *obligations, and strategies*, as shown in Figure 6.20.

Figure 6.20

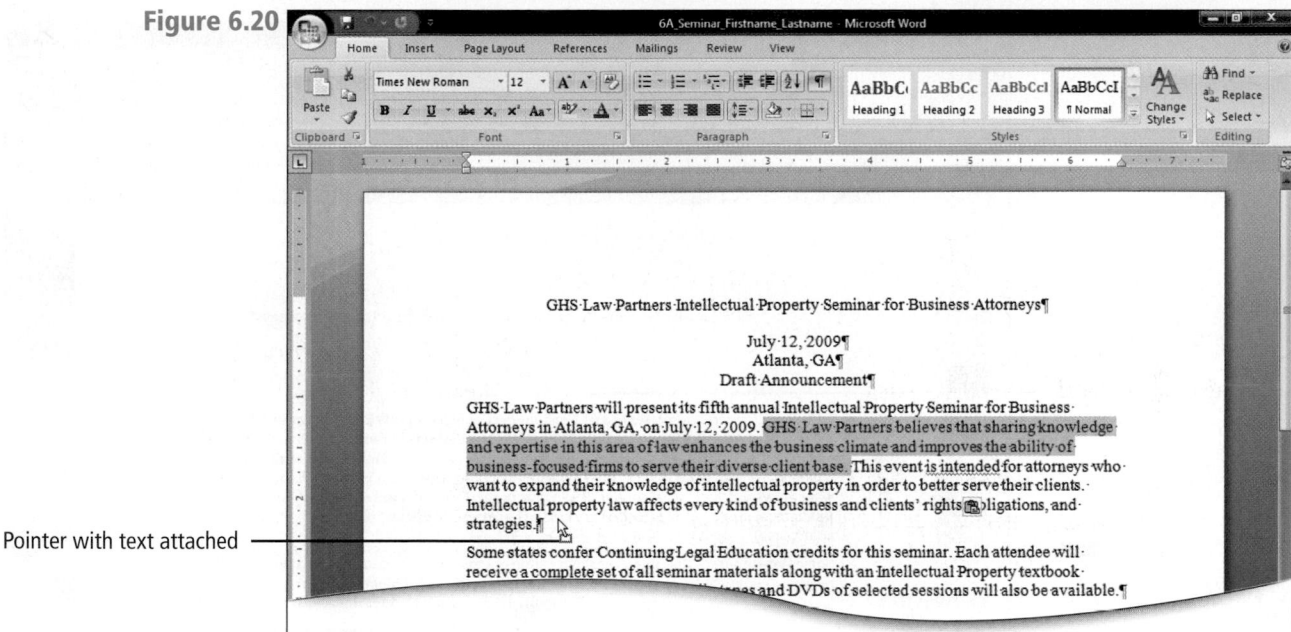

Pointer with text attached

7 Release the mouse button, and click anywhere in the document to deselect the text. The sentence you moved becomes the last sentence in the paragraph. Notice that a space was automatically added before the sentence.

8 Save 💾 the changes you have made to your document.

More Knowledge
Drag and Drop Using the Right Mouse Button

You can also drag and drop using the right mouse button. Select the text, point to the selected text and hold the right mouse button down, and then drag to a new location. A shortcut menu displays, giving you the option of moving the text to the new location, copying the text to the new location, or creating a link.

Activity 6.09 Undoing and Redoing Changes

You can undo one or more actions that you made to an active document. An Undo action can be reversed with the Redo command.

1 In the fourth paragraph, *Draft Announcement*, double-click *Draft* to select it, and then press Delete.

2 On the **Quick Access Toolbar**, click the **Undo** button 🔄.

The word you deleted returns to its original location.

3 On the **Quick Access Toolbar**, click the **Undo** button 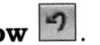 two times.

The sentence you dragged and dropped returns to its original location, and the words *serve* and *better* are switched back to their original locations, as shown in Figure 6.21.

Undo button

Figure 6.21

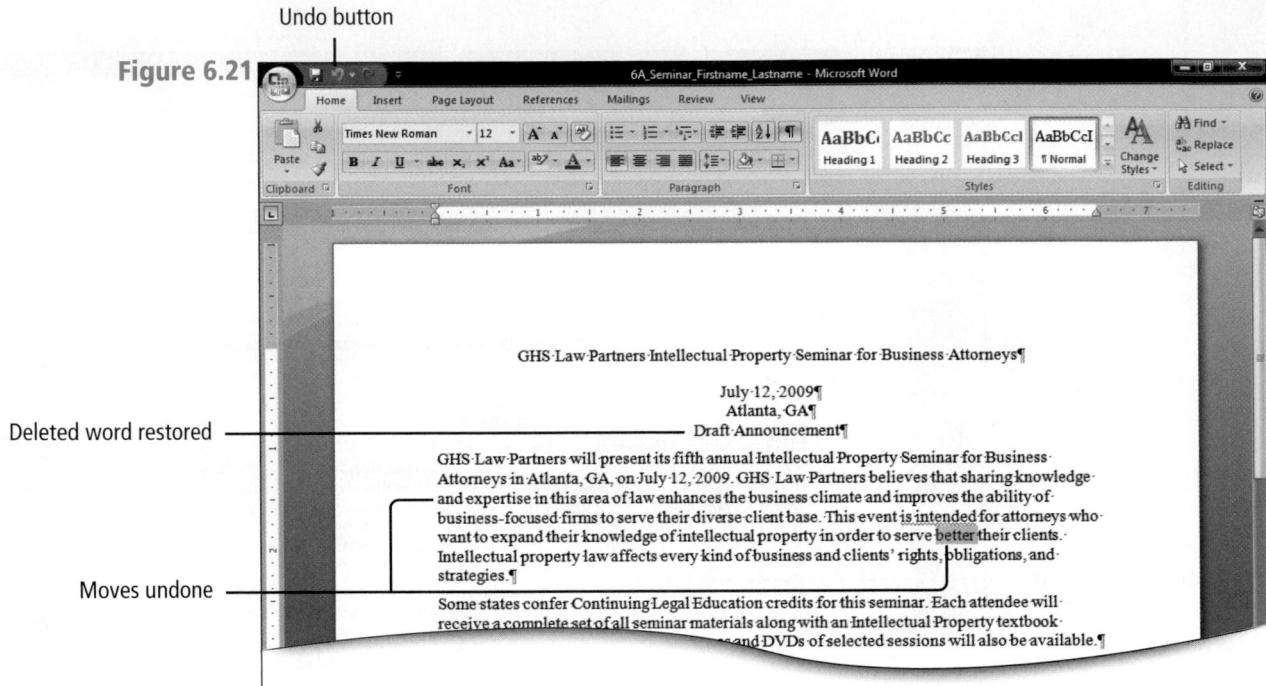

Deleted word restored

Moves undone

4 On the **Quick Access Toolbar**, click the **Redo** button two times.

The words are switched back, and the sentence moves back to the end of the paragraph. Clicking the Undo and Redo buttons changes one action at a time.

5 On the **Quick Access Toolbar**, click the **Undo button arrow**.

A list of changes displays showing all of the changes made since you last opened your document. From the displayed list, you can click any of the actions and undo it, but all of the changes above the one you select will also be undone.

6 Click anywhere in the document to close the Undo button list without undoing any other actions.

Activity 6.10 Inserting Nonbreaking Spaces and Hyphens

When you want to keep two words together regardless of where they fall in a paragraph, use a ***nonbreaking space***, which will wrap both words even if only the second word would normally wrap to the next line. For example, if the words *Mt. McKinley* fall at the end of a line so that *Mt.* is on one line and *McKinley* moves to the next, inserting a nonbreaking space will treat the two words as one so that they are not split between two lines. Similarly, you may have a hyphenated term, such as a postal code with the four-digit extension. If you want that term to be treated as one entity, use a nonbreaking hyphen.

1 Press Ctrl + End to move to the end of the document. Locate the paragraph that begins *If you would like*, and then click to position the insertion point at the end of the second line.

2 In the telephone number, delete the hyphen. While holding down both Ctrl and ⇧ Shift, press ⌷ one time. Alternatively, on the Insert tab, in the Symbols group, click Symbol, and then click More Symbols. In the displayed Symbol dialog box, click the Special Characters tab, click Nonbreaking Hyphen, and then click Close.

The hyphen is replaced with a **nonbreaking hyphen**; the telephone number will not break at the hyphen if you edit the paragraph. The nonbreaking hyphen is indicated by a slightly longer, slightly higher line than a standard hyphen, but prints as a normal hyphen.

3 At the end of the second line, after the telephone number area code, delete the space. While holding down both Ctrl and ⇧ Shift, press Spacebar one time. Compare your screen with Figure 6.22.

This combination of keys inserts a nonbreaking space. The result of inserting the nonbreaking space and nonbreaking hyphen is that the telephone number is treated as one word, so when Word applies its word-wrapping rules, the number is kept together on the same line. The nonbreaking space is indicated by an open circle rather than the dot normally used to indicate a space, but prints as a normal space.

The telephone number stays together

Figure 6.22

Nonbreaking space indicator

Nonbreaking hyphen indicator

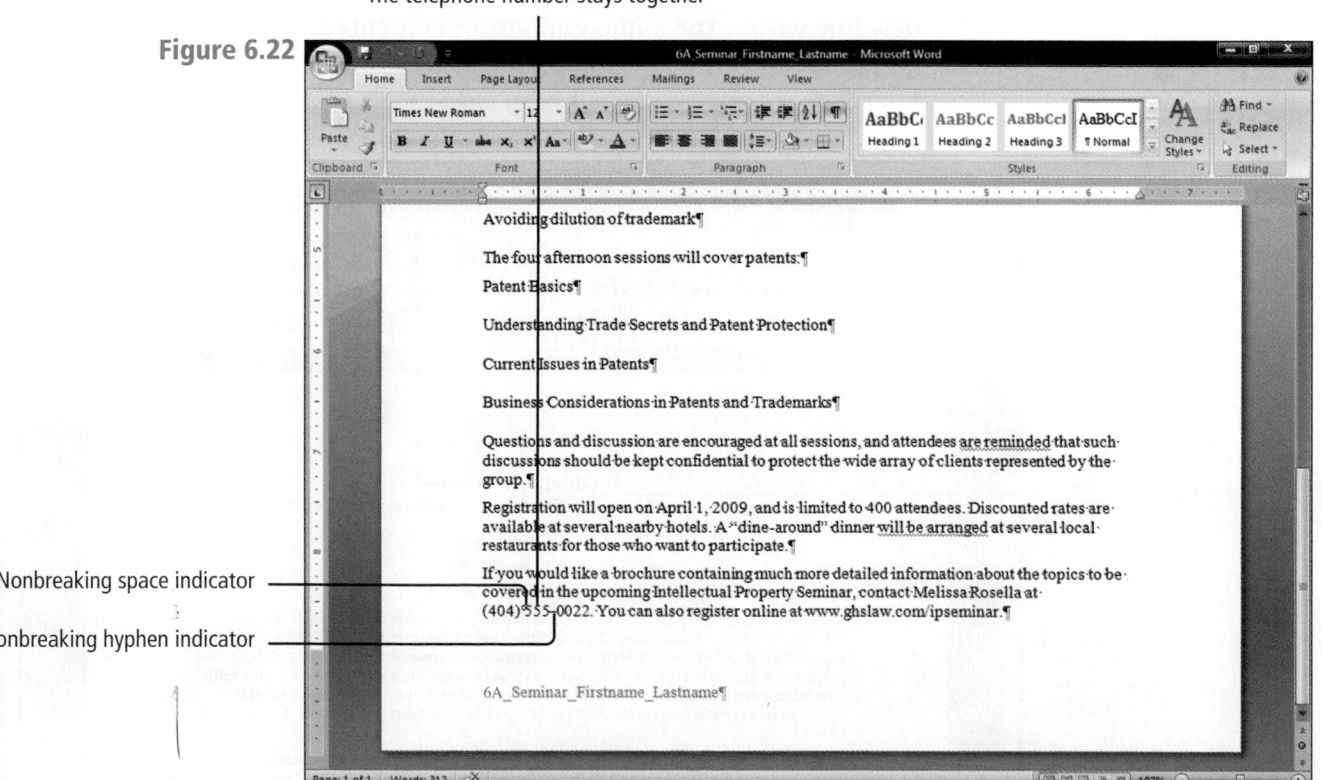

4 In the same sentence, locate and select the word *Seminar*, and then press [Delete]. Notice that the telephone number moves to the previous line as one word.

5 On the **Quick Access Toolbar**, click the **Undo** button 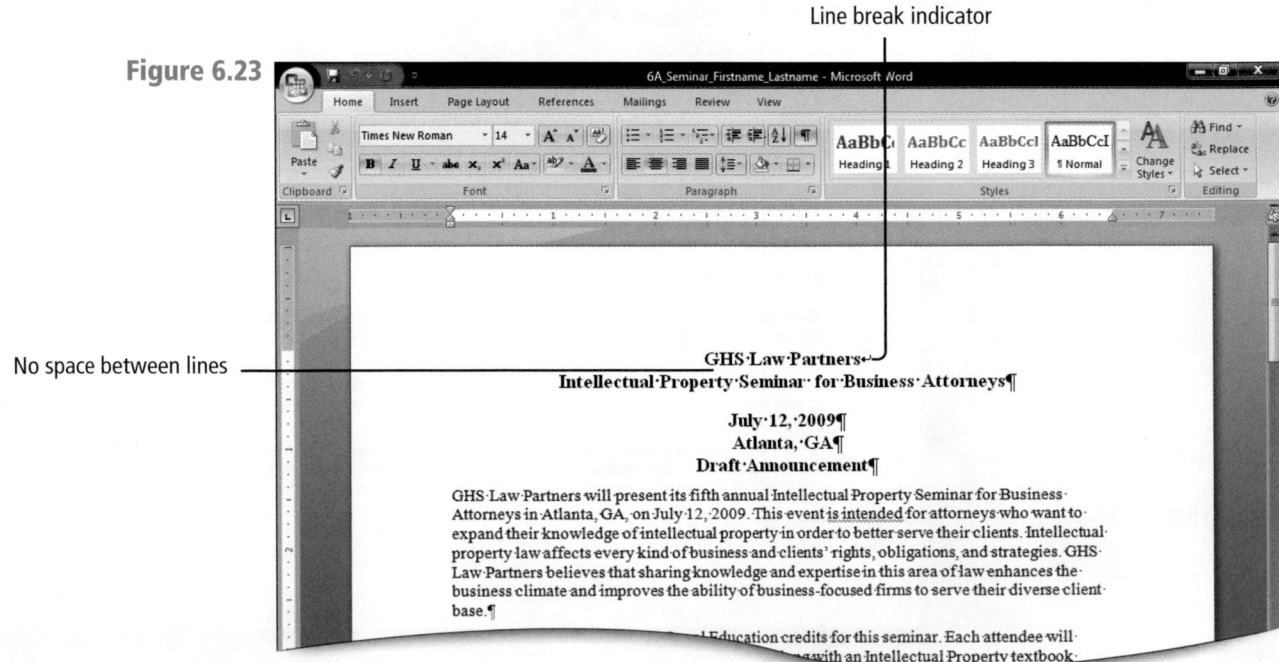 to reinsert the deleted word. **Save** your changes.

Activity 6.11 Entering a Line Break

You can end a line of text with a ***manual line break***, which moves the insertion point to the next line without creating a new paragraph. For example, if your paragraph style includes space before or after paragraphs, you may want to begin a new line without adding the additional space.

1 Press [Ctrl] + [Home] to move to the beginning of the document. Position the pointer in the left margin area, and then select the first four lines of text—the four centered title lines.

2 On the Mini toolbar, click the **Bold** button [B]. On the Mini toolbar, click the **Font Size button arrow** [12 ▼], and then click **14**.

3 In the first title line, notice the 12-point spacing after the first paragraph. Then, select the space between *Partners* and *Intellectual* and press [Delete].

4 Hold down [Shift], and then press [Enter]. Compare your screen with Figure 6.23.

By using a manual line break, the 12-pt spacing after the paragraph is not inserted because a new paragraph is not created; rather, a new line within the same paragraph is created. The bent arrow at the end of the first line indicates an inserted line break.

Line break indicator

Figure 6.23

No space between lines

5 **Save** your changes.

Objective 3
Create and Modify Lists

Word displays lists of information in two ways. A ***bulleted list*** uses ***bullets***, which are text symbols such as small circles or check marks, to introduce each piece of information. ***Numbered lists*** use consecutive numbers or letters to introduce each item in a list. Use bulleted lists when the items in the list can be displayed in any order; use numbered lists for items that have definite steps, a sequence of actions, or are in chronological order.

Activity 6.12 Creating a Bulleted List

1 Locate the *Use of trademarks* paragraph, and then move the pointer into the left margin area to display the ▨ pointer. Drag down to select this paragraph and the next two paragraphs.

2 On the Mini toolbar, click the **Bullets** button ▦ ▾. Alternatively, on the Home tab, in the Paragraph group, click the Bullets button.

The default bullet is a large, round, black dot. Your bullet symbols may differ, depending on which bullets were most recently used on your computer.

3 With the bulleted list still selected, in the **Paragraph group**, click the **Increase Indent** button ▦ one time. Click anywhere in the document to deselect the text.

The bulleted list is indented another 0.25 inch to the right.

4 Move the pointer into the left margin area to the left of the *Use of trademarks* paragraph until the ▨ pointer displays. Then, drag down to select this paragraph and the next paragraph.

5 In the **Paragraph group**, click the **Line spacing** button ▦ ▾ and notice that the items are double-spaced. Click **1.0** to single-space the selected text, click anywhere in the document to deselect the text, and then compare your screen with Figure 6.24.

6 **Save** ▦ your changes.

Figure 6.24

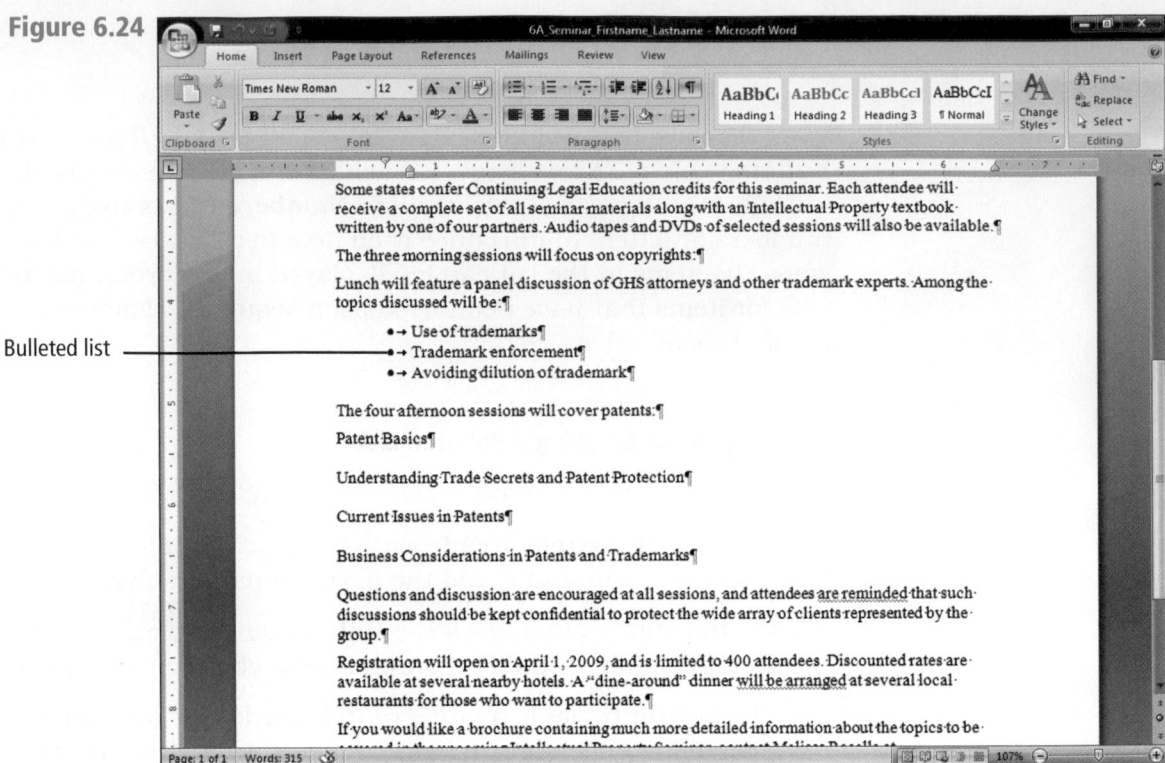

Bulleted list

Activity 6.13 Using AutoFormat to Create a Numbered List

In the previous activity, you created a list using existing text. In this activity, you will create a new list. Because the list items are the names of sessions in sequential order, you will number the items using Word's Numbering command.

1 Locate the paragraph that begins *The three morning sessions*, and then position the insertion point at the end of that paragraph. Press Enter to create a blank line.

This paragraph retains the formatting of the previous paragraph, which is stored in the paragraph mark you just created when you pressed Enter. Recall that formatting carries forward to a new paragraph mark unless you take specific steps to change the formatting for the newly created paragraph.

2 From the **Office** menu , in the lower right corner click **Word Options**. In the list on the left side of the **Word Options** dialog box, click **Proofing**. Under **AutoCorrect options**, click the **AutoCorrect Options** button.

3 In the displayed **AutoCorrect** dialog box, click the **AutoFormat As You Type tab**, and then compare your screen with Figure 6.25.

AutoFormat As You Type is a Word feature that anticipates formatting based on what you type. There are several formatting options; each can be turned on or off independently of the others.

Figure 6.25

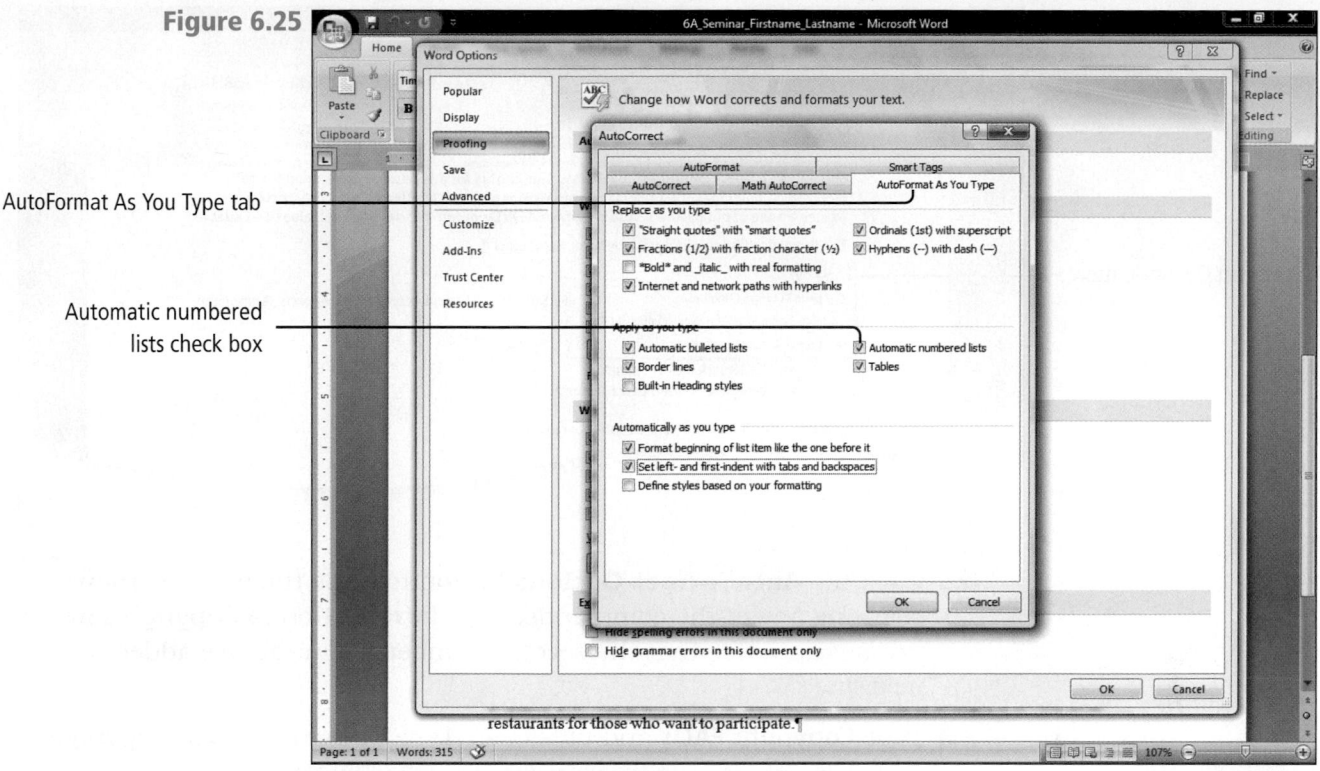

AutoFormat As You Type tab

Automatic numbered
lists check box

4 Under **Apply as you type**, if it is not selected, select the **Automatic numbered lists** check box, and then click **OK**. At the bottom of the **Word Options** dialog box, click **OK**.

5 Type **1.** and press Spacebar. Be sure to type the period after the number.

Word determines that this paragraph is the first item in a numbered list and formats the new paragraph following it accordingly. The space after the number changes to a tab, and the AutoCorrect Options button displays to the left of the list item.

6 Click the **AutoCorrect Options** button, and then compare your screen with Figure 6.26.

From the displayed list, you can remove the automatic formatting in this instance, or stop using the automatic numbered lists option in this document. You also have the option to open the AutoCorrect dialog box to *Control AutoFormat Options*.

Figure 6.26

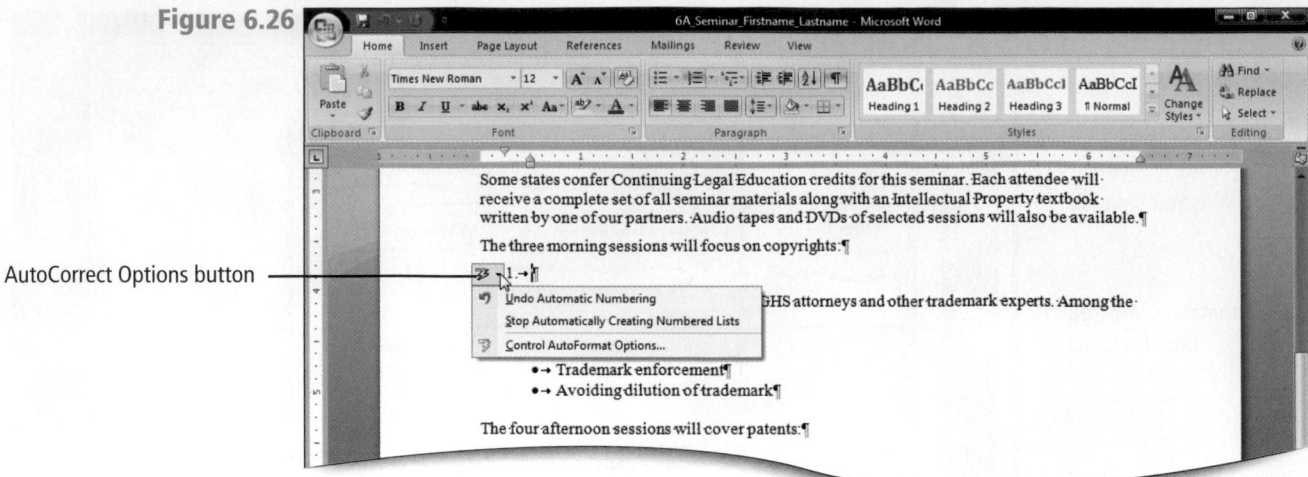

AutoCorrect Options button

7 Click the **AutoCorrect Options** button to close the menu without selecting any of the commands. Type **Introduction to Copyrights** and press Enter. Notice that the second number and a tab are added to the next line.

8 Type **Copyright FAQs** and press Enter. Type **Current Issues in Copyrights** and press Enter. Compare your screen with Figure 6.27.

Figure 6.27

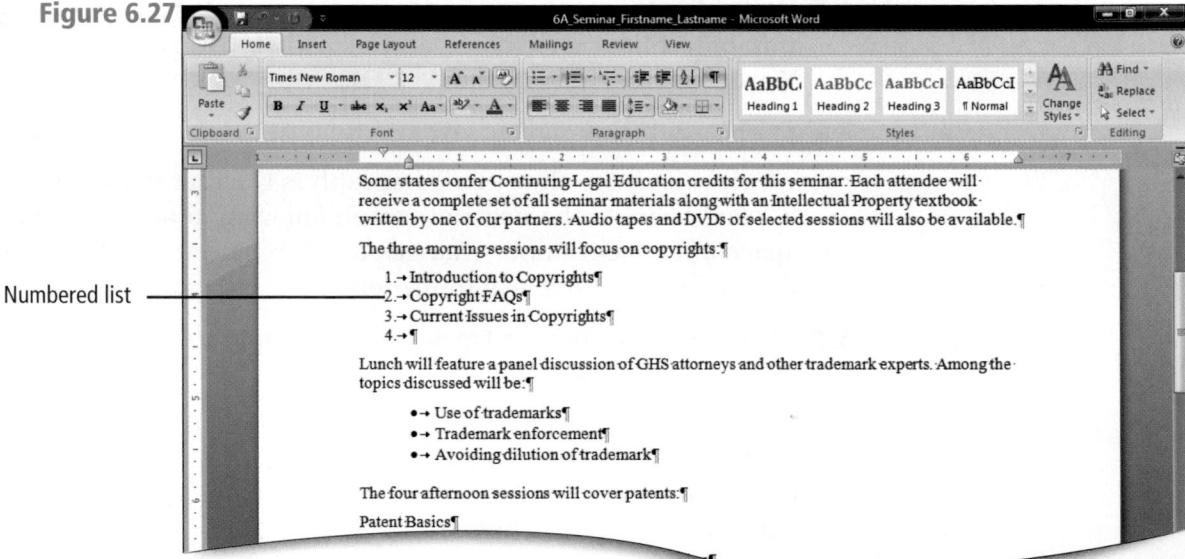

Numbered list

9 Press ←Bksp to turn off the list. Then, press ←Bksp as necessary to remove the blank line.

More Knowledge

To End a List

When you end a list and press [Enter], the next line will be formatted as a list item. To turn the list off, you can press [←Bksp], click the Numbering or Bullets button, or press [Enter] a second time. Both list buttons—Numbering and Bullets—act as *toggle buttons*; that is, clicking the button one time turns the feature on, and clicking the button again turns the feature off.

10 Select all three items in the numbered list. In the **Paragraph group**, click the **Increase Indent** button one time to move the list 0.25 inch to the right.

11 **Save** your document.

Activity 6.14 Formatting Lists

Each item in a list is a separate paragraph and can be formatted in the same way other paragraphs are formatted. The Format Painter can also be used to create lists.

1 In the bulleted list, click anywhere in the last bulleted item, which begins *Avoiding dilution*. Display the **Paragraph** dialog box. Under **Spacing**, click the **Line spacing arrow**, and then click **Single**. Under **Spacing**, in the **After** spin box, click the **up spin arrow** one time to add **6pt** spacing, and then click **OK**. Compare your screen with Figure 6.28.

The last item in the bulleted list now has the same formatting as the last item in the numbered list.

Figure 6.28

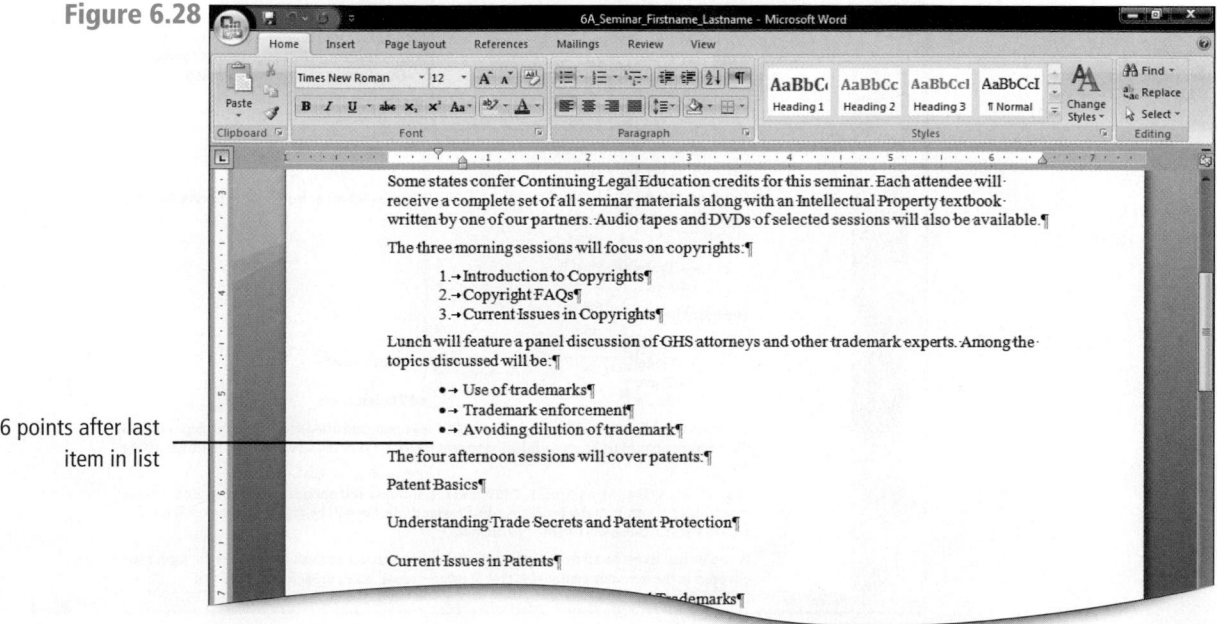

6 points after last item in list

2 In the first item of the numbered list, click anywhere to place the insertion point. In the **Clipboard group**, click the **Format Painter** button 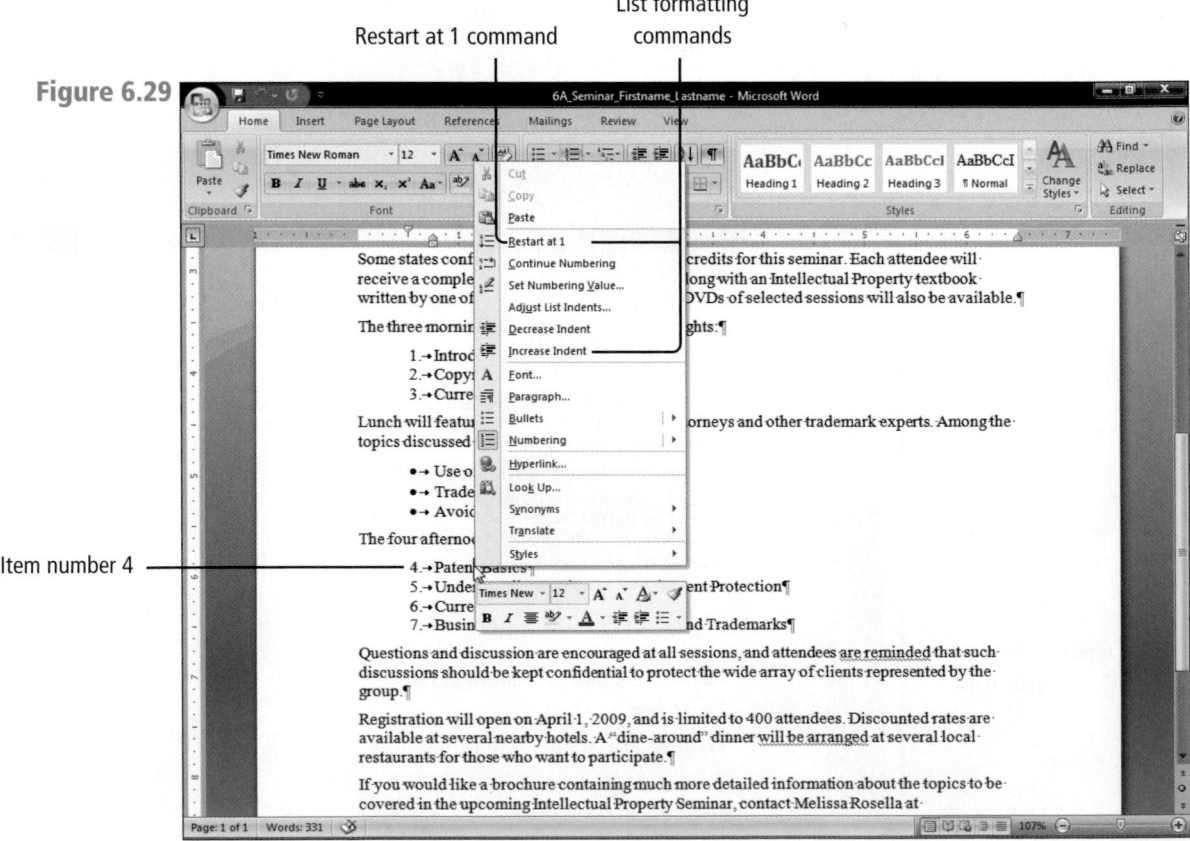.

3 Move the pointer to the *Patent Basics* one-line paragraph, and then click one time. Notice that the *Patent Basics* paragraph takes on the formatting characteristics of the first item in the numbered list, and the numbering continues with the number 4. Also notice that the Format Painter pointer no longer displays.

4 In the **Clipboard group**, double-click the **Format Painter** button.

Use the pointer to change the paragraph beginning *Understanding Trade*.

The Format Painter pointer still displays. When you double-click the Format Painter button, it remains active until you turn it off.

5 Use the pointer to change the paragraphs that begin *Current Issues* and *Business Considerations*. Then, in the **Clipboard group**, click the **Format Painter** button to turn it off. Alternatively, press [Esc] to turn off the Format Painter.

6 Move to **item number 4** in the list—*Patent Basics*—and then right-click. Notice that the displayed shortcut menu contains list-formatting commands, as shown in Figure 6.29.

Restart at 1 command   List formatting commands

Figure 6.29

Item number 4

7 From the shortcut menu, click **Restart at 1**.

The numbering is restarted for the second numbered list.

8 **Save** 💾 your document.

More Knowledge

Using Multiple Levels in a Numbered List

If your numbered list contains two levels of information, type all of the list entries using automatic numbering. When you have completed the list, select the items that are at the lower level and click the Increase Indent button. The top level will retain the *1, 2, 3* format, while the lower level will use an *a, b, c* format.

Activity 6.15 Customizing Bullets

You are not restricted to the bullet symbol that displays when you click the Bullets button. You can use any symbol from any font on your computer for your bullet character.

1 Select the three bulleted points, and then right-click anywhere in the selected text. From the shortcut menu, point to **Bullets**. Notice that a gallery displays showing recently used bullets and a library of popular bullet shapes, as shown in Figure 6.30. The bullets that display in your gallery may differ.

Bullets command   Bullets gallery

Figure 6.30

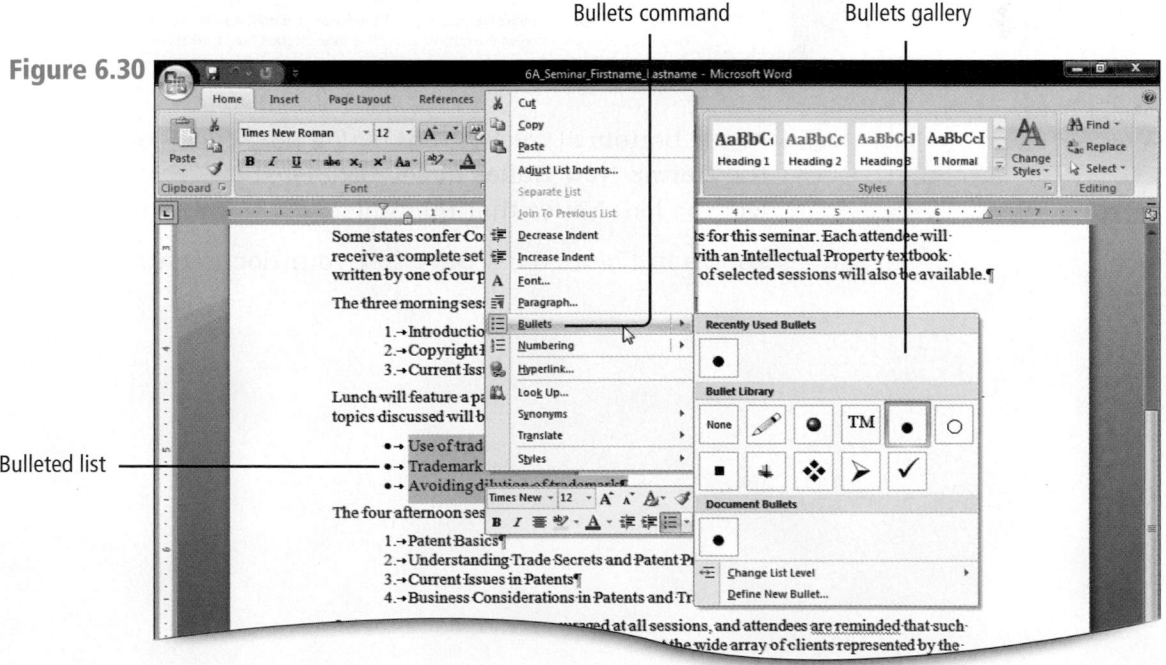

Bulleted list

2 At the bottom of the **Bullets gallery**, click **Define New Bullet**. In the **Define New Bullet** dialog box, click the **Symbol** button.

3 In the displayed **Symbol** dialog box, be sure *Symbol* displays in the **Font** box. Scroll to the bottom of the list of symbols, and then in the third row from the bottom, click the trademark (^{TM}) symbol, as shown in Figure 6.31.

Symbol font

Figure 6.31

Trademark symbol

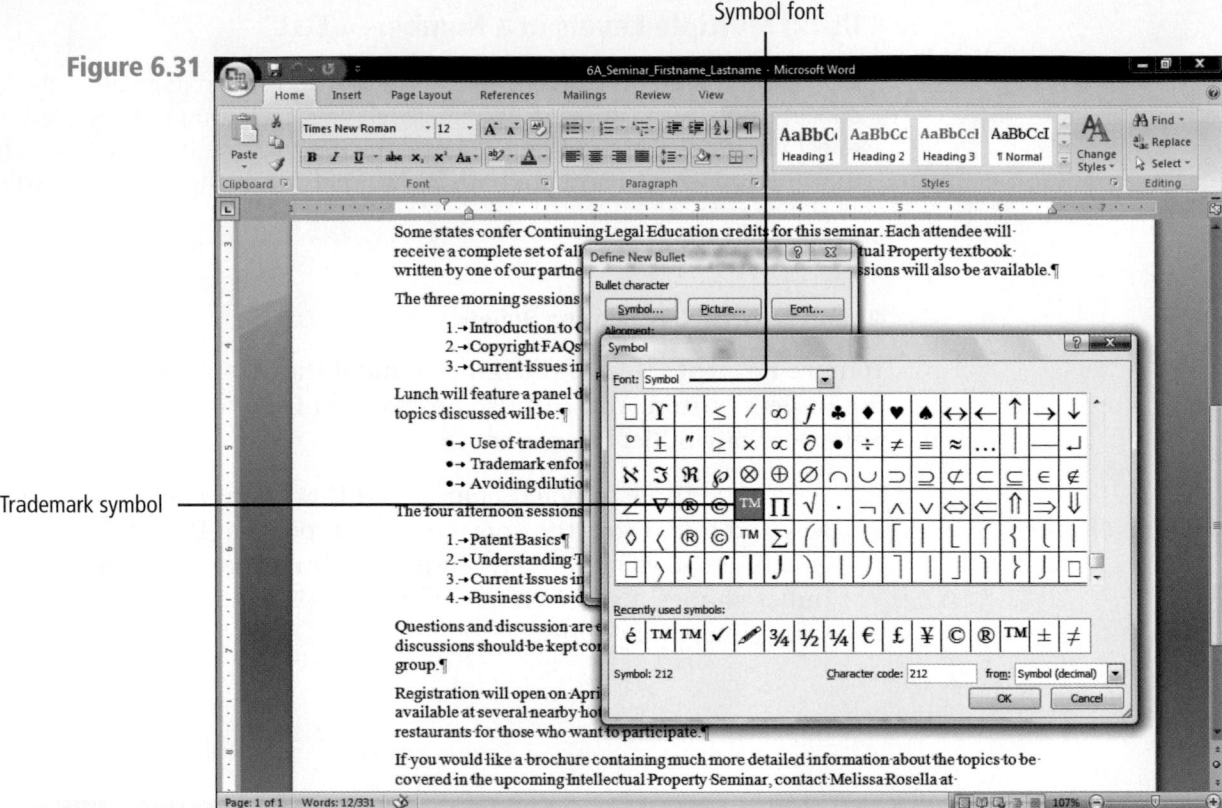

4 At the bottom of the **Symbol** dialog box, click **OK**. At the bottom of the **Define New Bullet** dialog box, click **OK**. Click anywhere to deselect the list. Notice that the bullets change to a trademark symbol, as shown in Figure 6.32. **Save** 🖫 your document.

Figure 6.32

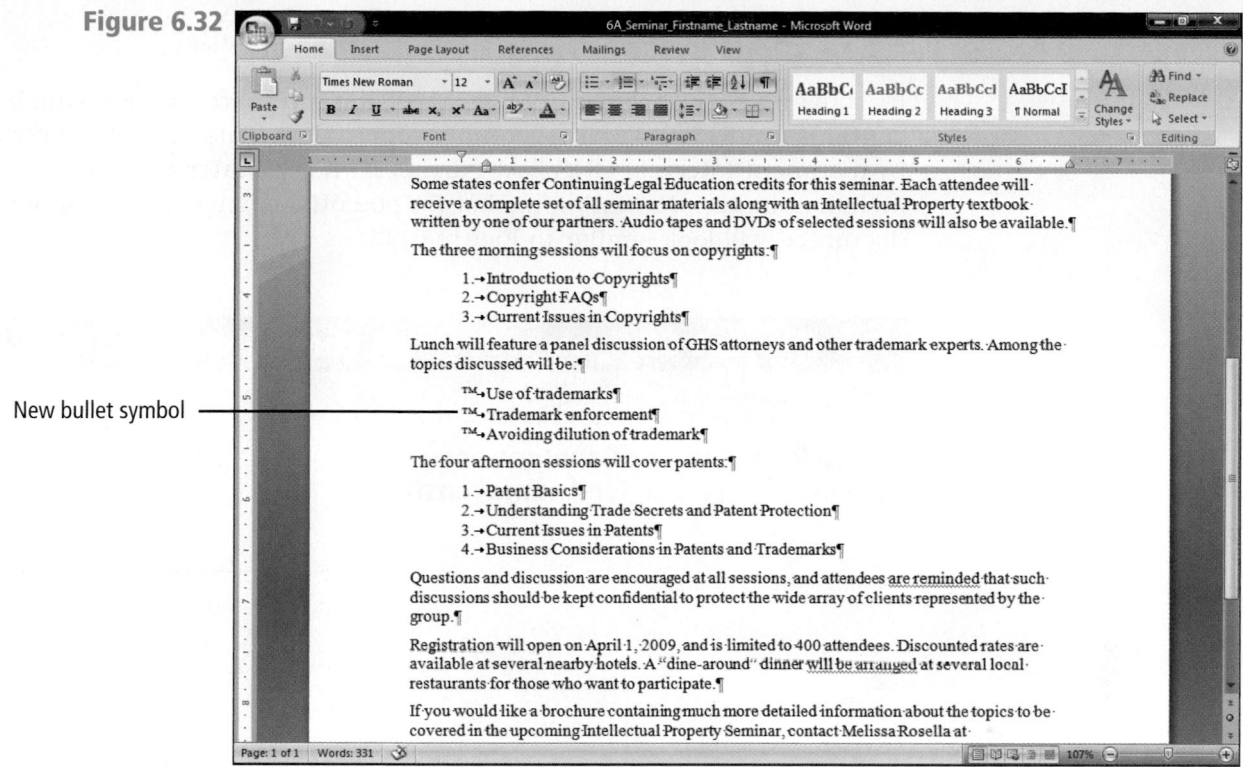

New bullet symbol ————

5 From the **Office** menu , point to the **Print arrow**, and then click **Print Preview** to make a final check of your document. Check your *Chapter Assignment Sheet* or *Course Syllabus* or consult your instructor to determine if you are to submit your assignments on paper or electronically. To submit electronically, go to Step 7, and then follow the instructions provided by your instructor.

6 On the **Print Preview tab**, in the **Print group**, click the **Print** button. Click **OK**, **Close** the **Print Preview** window and submit your printout as directed.

7 **Close** your document, and then **Close** Word.

End **You have completed Project 6A** ————————————

Project 6B Law Overview

In Activities 6.16 through 6.24, you will edit a research paper, which contains an overview of intellectual property law. This paper was created by a student intern of GHS Law Partners, and will later be modified for inclusion in an information packet for potential clients. Your completed document will look similar to Figure 6.33.

For Project 6B, you will need the following file:

w06B_Law_Overview

You will save your document as
6B_Law_Overview_Firstname_Lastname

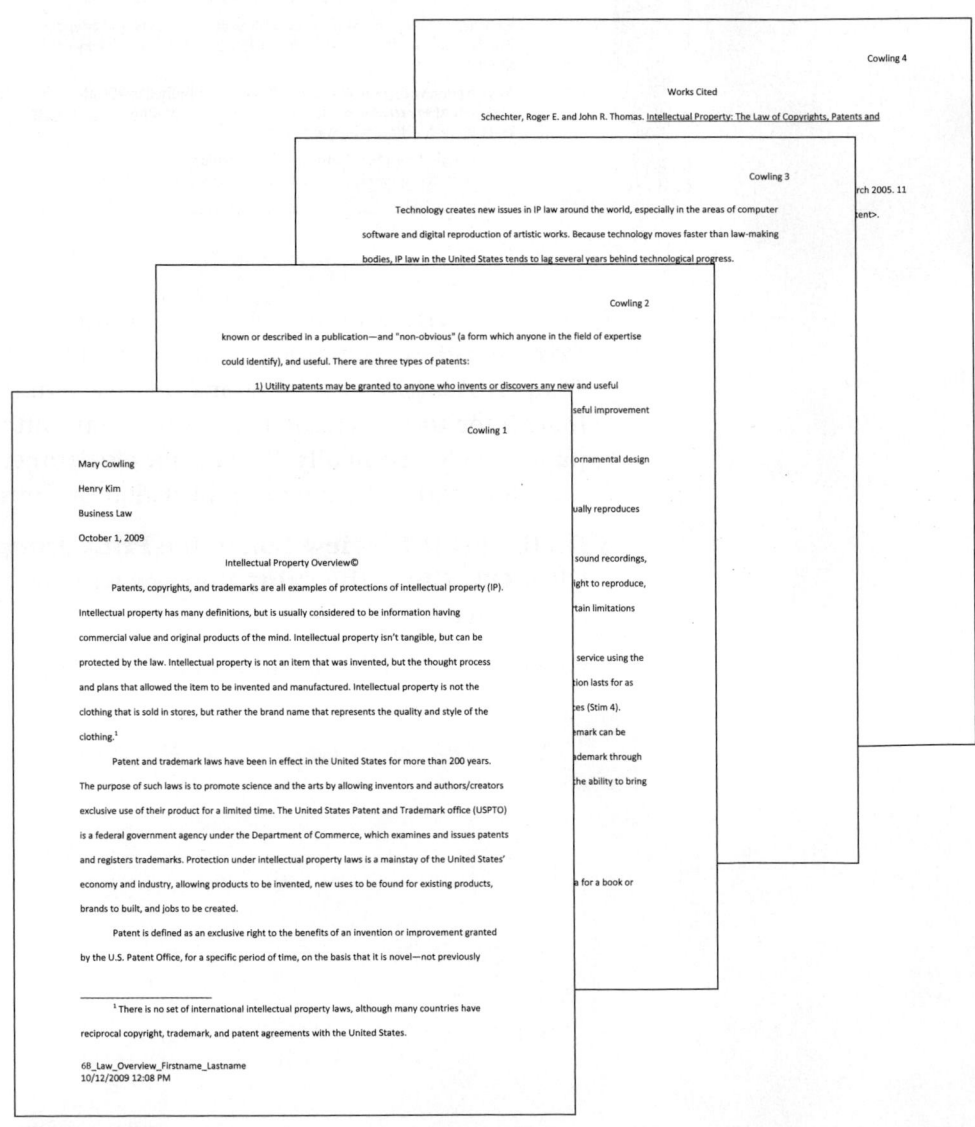

Figure 6.33
Project 6B—Law Overview

Objective 4
Insert and Format Headers and Footers

Text that you insert into a header or footer displays on every page of a document. Within a header or footer, you can add automatic page numbers, dates, times, the file name, and pictures.

Activity 6.16 Inserting and Formatting Page Numbers

1 **Start** Word. From your student files, locate and open the document **w06B_Law_Overview**. Display formatting marks, display the ruler, and set the page width to display the left and right page edges. Be sure all document margins are set to **1"**. **Save** the file in your **Word Chapter 6** folder as **6B_Law_Overview_Firstname_Lastname**

Note — Standard Styles for Research Papers

When you write a research paper or a report for college or business, you will probably be asked to follow a format prescribed by one of the standard style guides. The two most commonly used styles are those created by the *Modern Language Association (MLA)* and the *American Psychological Association (APA)*; there are several others. This project uses the MLA style.

2 Press [Ctrl] + [A] to select all of the text in the document. Right-click the selected text, and then from the shortcut menu, click **Paragraph**. In the displayed **Paragraph** dialog box, under **Spacing**, click the **After down spin arrow** two times to set the space after to **0**. Click the **Line spacing arrow**, and then click **Double**. Click **OK**.

The MLA style uses 1-inch margins and double spacing throughout the document, with no extra space between paragraphs.

3 Press [Ctrl] + [Home] to move to the beginning of the document. Type **Mary Cowling** and press [Enter], and then type **Henry Kim** and press [Enter]. Type **Business Law** and press [Enter], and then type **October 1, 2009** and press [Enter].

The first line in an MLA research paper is the name of the author; the second is the name of the person for whom the report is prepared—often the professor of a class. The third line contains the name of the class, and the fourth line contains the date.

4 Type **Intellectual Property Overview** and then press [Enter]. Press [↑] to place the insertion point in the line you just typed. In the

Paragraph group, click the **Center** button ▤, and then compare your screen with Figure 6.34.

Figure 6.34

Title centered

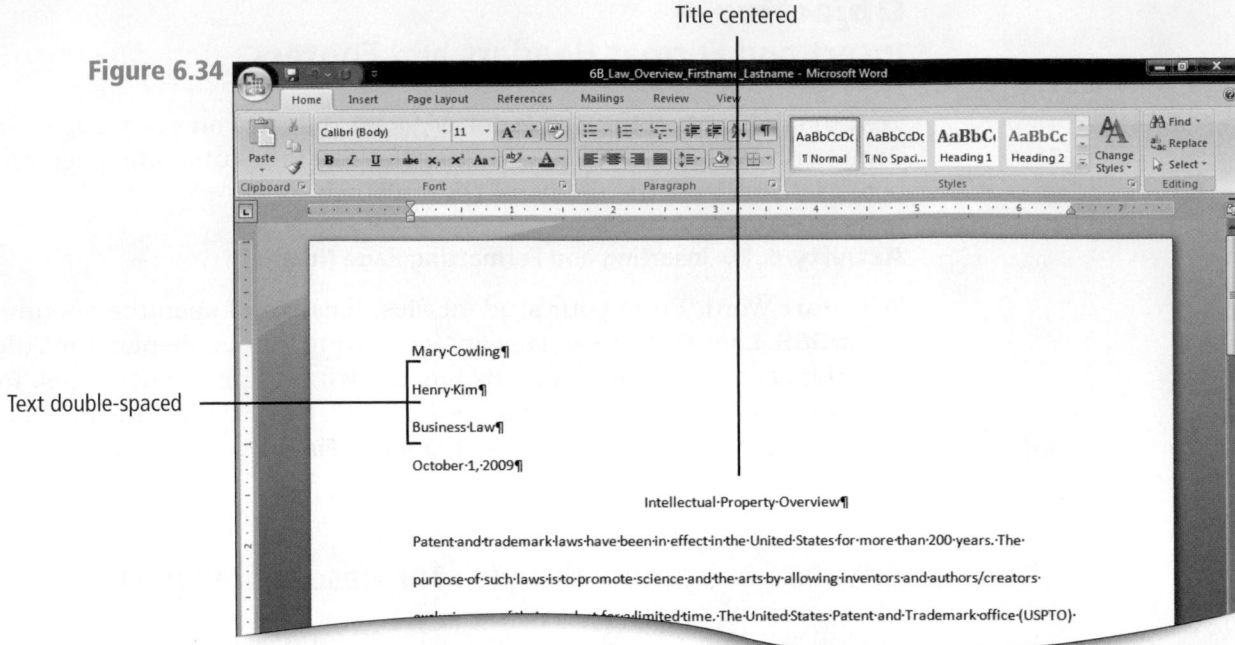

Text double-spaced

Mary·Cowling¶

Henry·Kim¶

Business·Law¶

October·1,·2009¶

Intellectual·Property·Overview¶

Patent·and·trademark·laws·have·been·in·effect·in·the·United·States·for·more·than·200·years.·The·

purpose·of·such·laws·is·to·promote·science·and·the·arts·by·allowing·inventors·and·authors/creators·

which·examines

for·a·limited·time.·The·United·States·Patent·and·Trademark·office·(USPTO)·

5 Move the pointer to the top edge of **Page 1** and right-click. Click **Edit Header**, and then in the header area, type **Cowling** and then press Spacebar.

6 On the **Design tab**, in the **Insert group**, click the **Quick Parts** button, and then click **Field**. In the **Field** dialog box, under **Field names**, locate and click **Page**. Under **Field properties**, click the first page number style—**1, 2, 3**. Compare your screen with Figure 6.35.

Page number format   Design tab

Figure 6.35

Header area

Page field

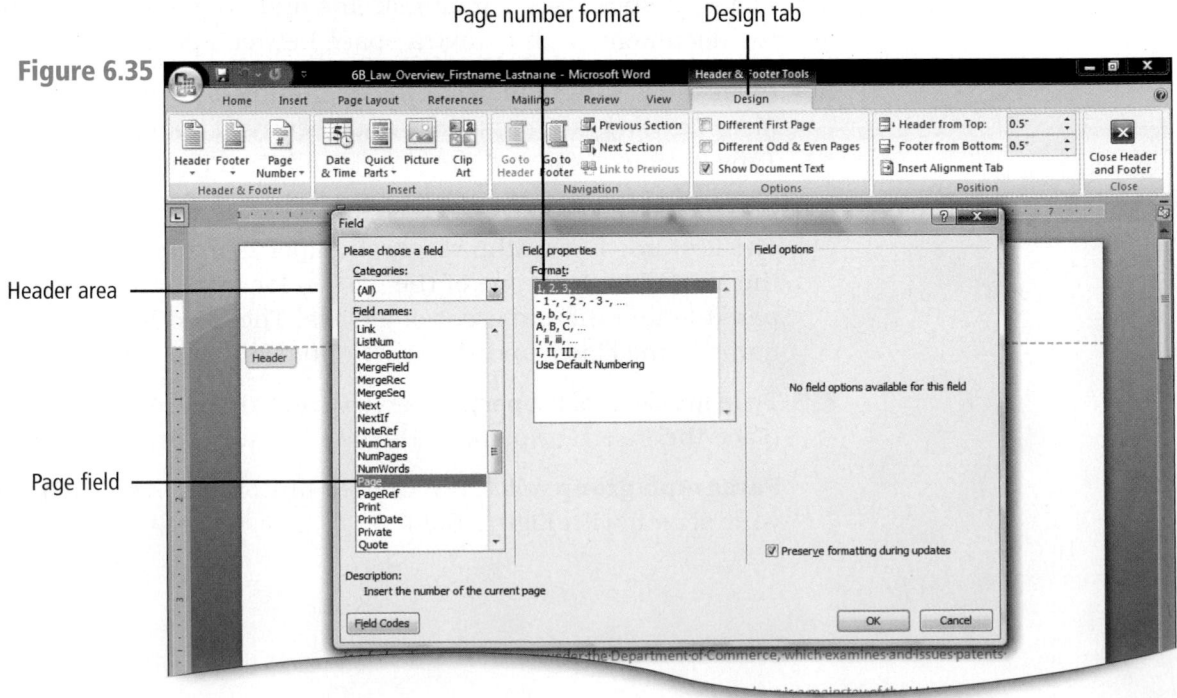

7 Click **OK** to place the page number at the insertion point location. Click the **Home tab**, and then in the **Paragraph group**, click the **Align Text Right** button . Compare your screen with Figure 6.36.

Figure 6.36

Name and page number inserted

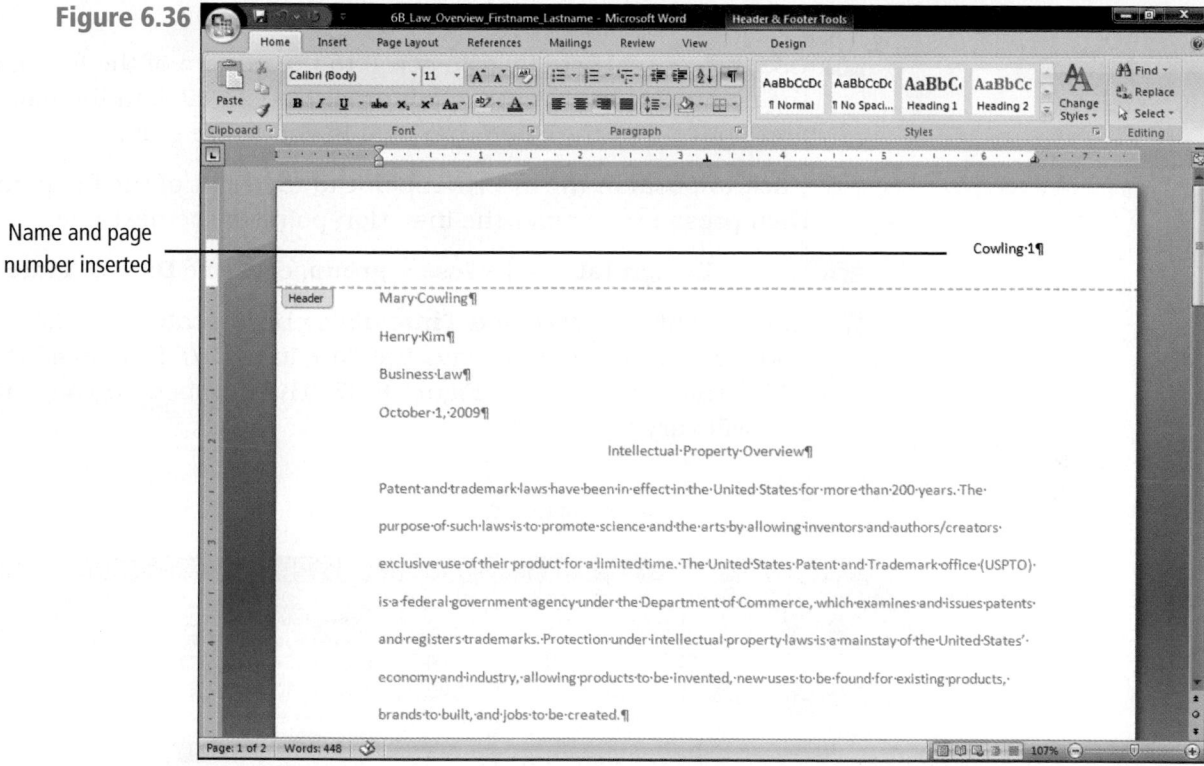

8 Click the **Design tab**, and then in the **Navigation group**, click the **Go to Footer** button. In the **Insert group**, click the **Quick Parts** button, and then click **Field**. In the **Field** dialog box, under **Field names**, locate and click **FileName**, and then click **OK**.

9 Double-click anywhere outside the footer area, and then press Ctrl + Home to move to the top of the document. **Save** your changes.

More Knowledge

Suppressing the Page Number on the First Page of a Document

Some style guidelines may require that the page number on the first page be hidden from view—suppressed. To hide the information contained in the header and footer areas on Page 1 of a document, double-click in the header or footer area. On the Design tab, in the Options group, select the Different First Page check box.

Activity 6.17 Inserting the Current Date and Time

The current date, time, or both can be inserted anywhere in a document. When you are working on a research paper, which will likely be revised several times, put the date and time in the footer to help identify the various revisions you will make. Then, remove the date and time before submitting the paper.

1 Use the vertical scroll bar to scroll to the bottom of the first page of the document to view the footer area. Double-click in the footer area, and notice that the **FileName** field is shaded in gray.

2 Click to position the insertion point to the right of the file name, and then press Enter to move the insertion point to the next line.

3 On the **Design tab**, in the **Insert group**, click the **Date & Time** button.

4 In the displayed **Date and Time** dialog box, locate and click the date and time format that displays the date in a *10/01/2009 4:43 PM* (or *AM*) format, as shown in Figure 6.37. The numbers in your dialog box will vary.

Selected format (your date and time will vary)

Figure 6.37
Date & Time button

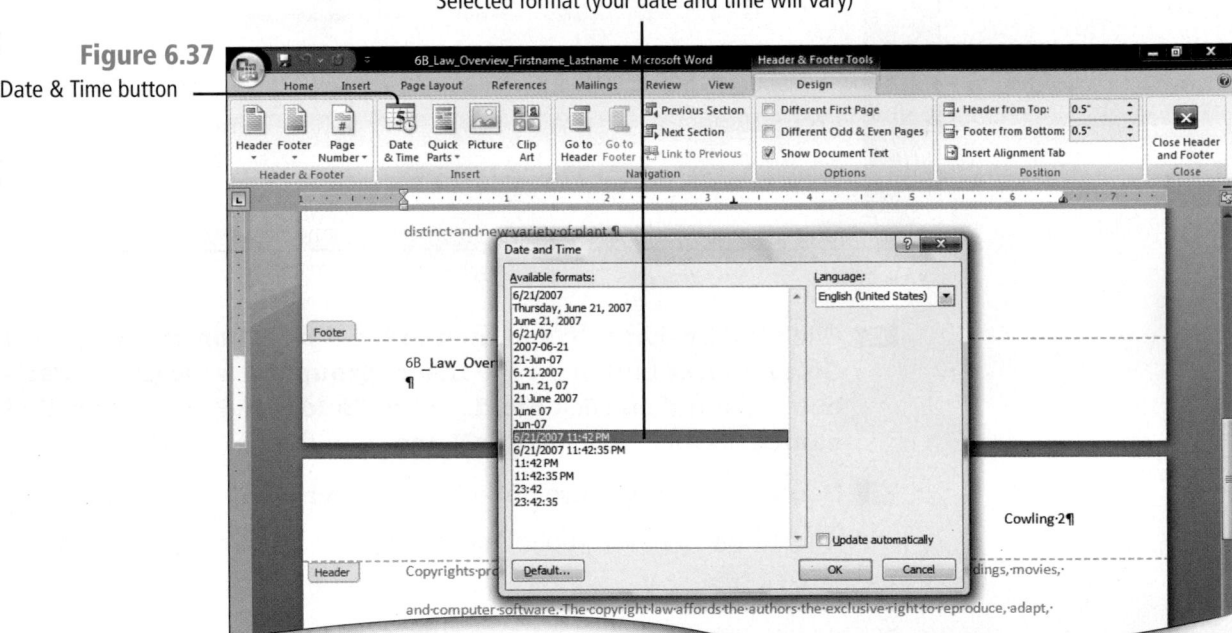

Note — Automatically Update the Date

At the bottom of the Date and Time dialog box, you can select the *Update automatically* check box to have Word update the date every time you open the document.

5 In the **Date and Time** dialog box, click **OK**. Double-click anywhere outside the footer area, and then press Ctrl + Home to move to the top of the document.

6 **Save** 🖫 your changes.

Objective 5
Insert Frequently Used Text

AutoCorrect corrects common spelling errors as you type. When you type a word incorrectly, for example *teh*, Word automatically changes it to *the*. You can add words that you frequently misspell to the AutoCorrect list. You can also add shortcuts to phrases you type often. Another type of frequently used text includes various symbols, such as the trademark symbol™ or copyright symbol ©. These are accessed from the Symbols group on the Insert tab.

Activity 6.18 Recording AutoCorrect Entries

You probably have words that you frequently misspell. You can add these to the AutoCorrect list for automatic correction.

1 From the **Office** menu 🔘, click **Word Options**. In the **Word Options** list, click **Proofing**, and then under **AutoCorrect options**, click the **AutoCorrect Options** button.

2 In the **AutoCorrect** dialog box, click the **AutoCorrect tab**. Under **Replace**, type **intellectaul** and under **With**, type **intellectual** Compare your screen with Figure 6.38.

If another student has already added this AutoCorrect entry, the Add button will change to a Replace button.

Figure 6.38

intellectaul and *intellectual* added to the AutoCorrect list

Replace or Add button displays

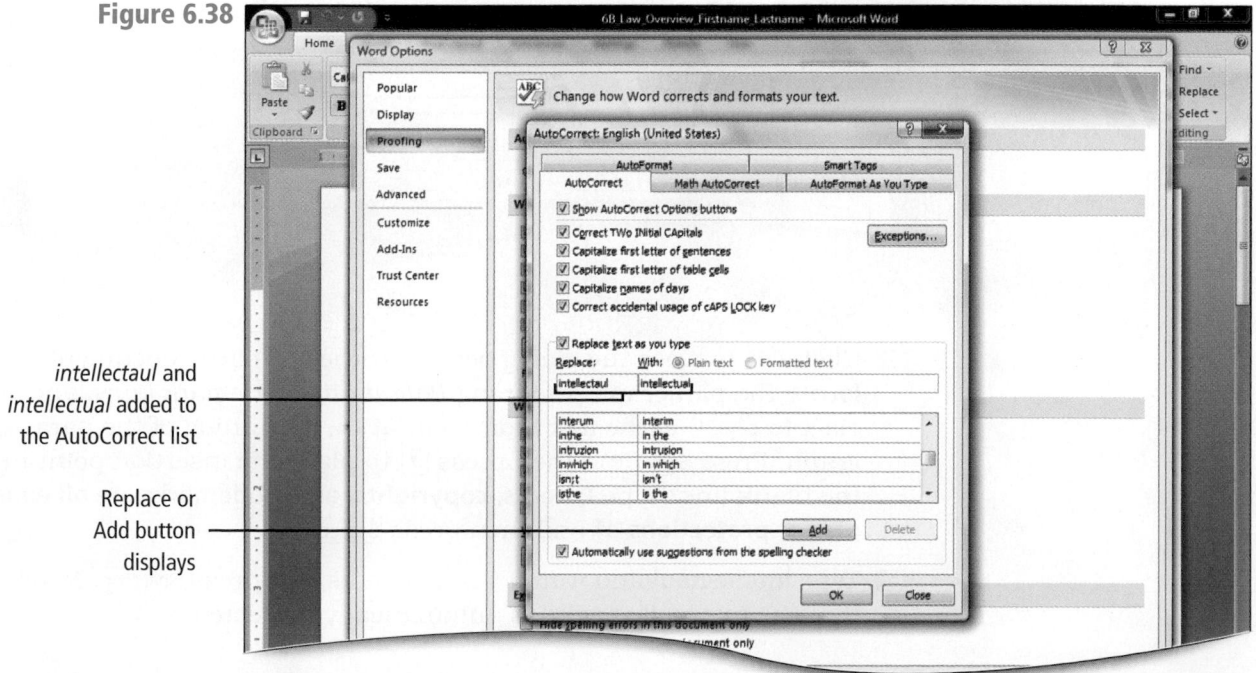

3 Click **Add**. If the entry already exists, click Replace instead, and then click Yes. Click **OK** two times to close the dialog boxes.

4 Near the top of the document, locate the paragraph beginning *Patent and trademark laws*, and then click to position the insertion point at the beginning of the paragraph. Scroll to the end of the document, hold down ⇧ Shift, and then click to the right of the last paragraph mark. Scroll up to see the top of the document. Right-click the selected text, and then from the shortcut menu, click **Paragraph**. On the **Indents and Spacing tab**, under **Indentation**, click the **Special arrow**, and then click **First line**. Under **Indentation**, in the **By** box, be sure *0.5″* displays. Compare your screen with Figure 6.39.

Indenting—moving the beginning of the first line of a paragraph to the right or left of the rest of the paragraph—provides visual cues to the reader to help break the document up and make it easier to read. The MLA style uses 0.5-inch indents at the beginning of the first line of every paragraph.

Indentation will be applied to the *First line* of the paragraph

Figure 6.39

First line will be indented 0.5 (one-half) inch

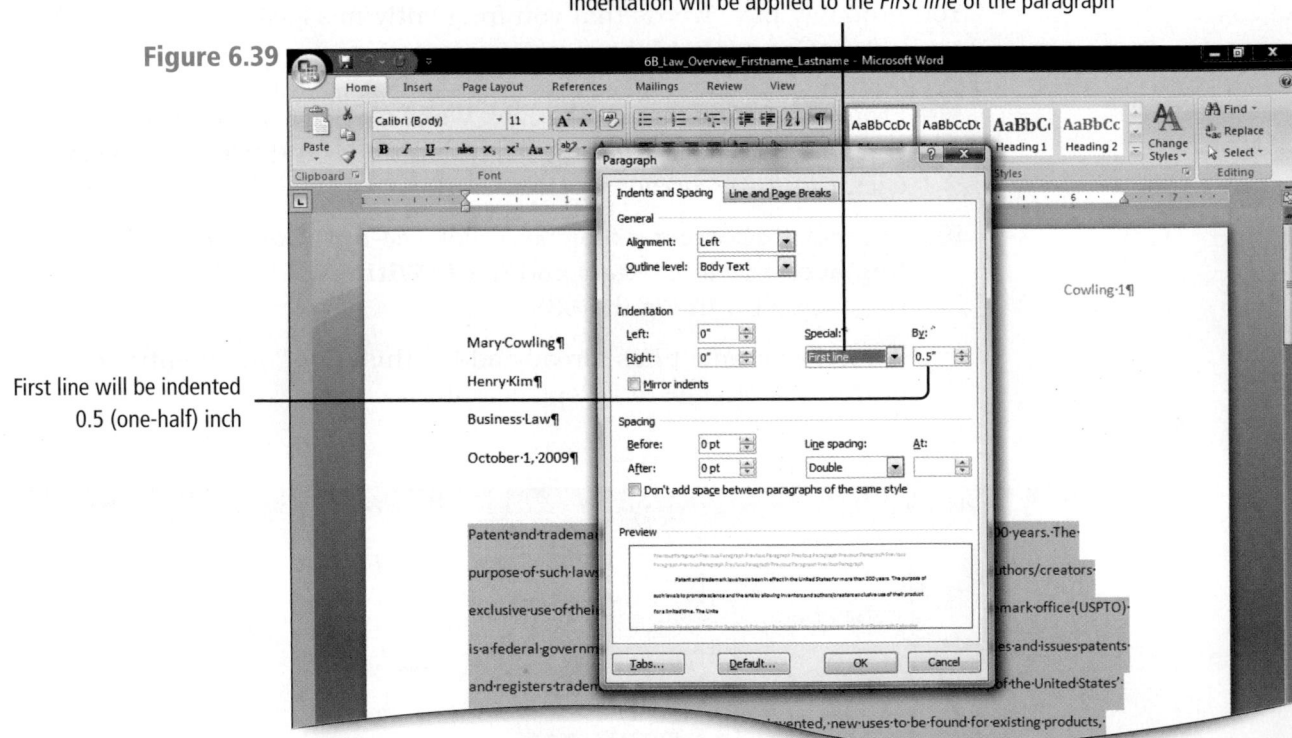

5 Click **OK** to close the dialog box. Near the top of the document, locate the paragraph beginning *Patent and trademark laws*, and then click to position the insertion point at the beginning of the paragraph. Press Enter, and then press ↑ to place the insertion point in the blank line. Type **Patents, copyrights, and trademarks are all examples of protections of** and then press Spacebar.

6 Type **intellectaul** and watch the screen as you press Spacebar. Notice that the misspelled word is automatically corrected.

7 Click in the corrected word, and then notice the blue line that displays under the word. Move the pointer over the blue line until the **AutoCorrect Options** button displays, and then click the button. Compare your screen with Figure 6.40.

Corrected word

Figure 6.40

AutoCorrect Options button ——

AutoCorrect options ——

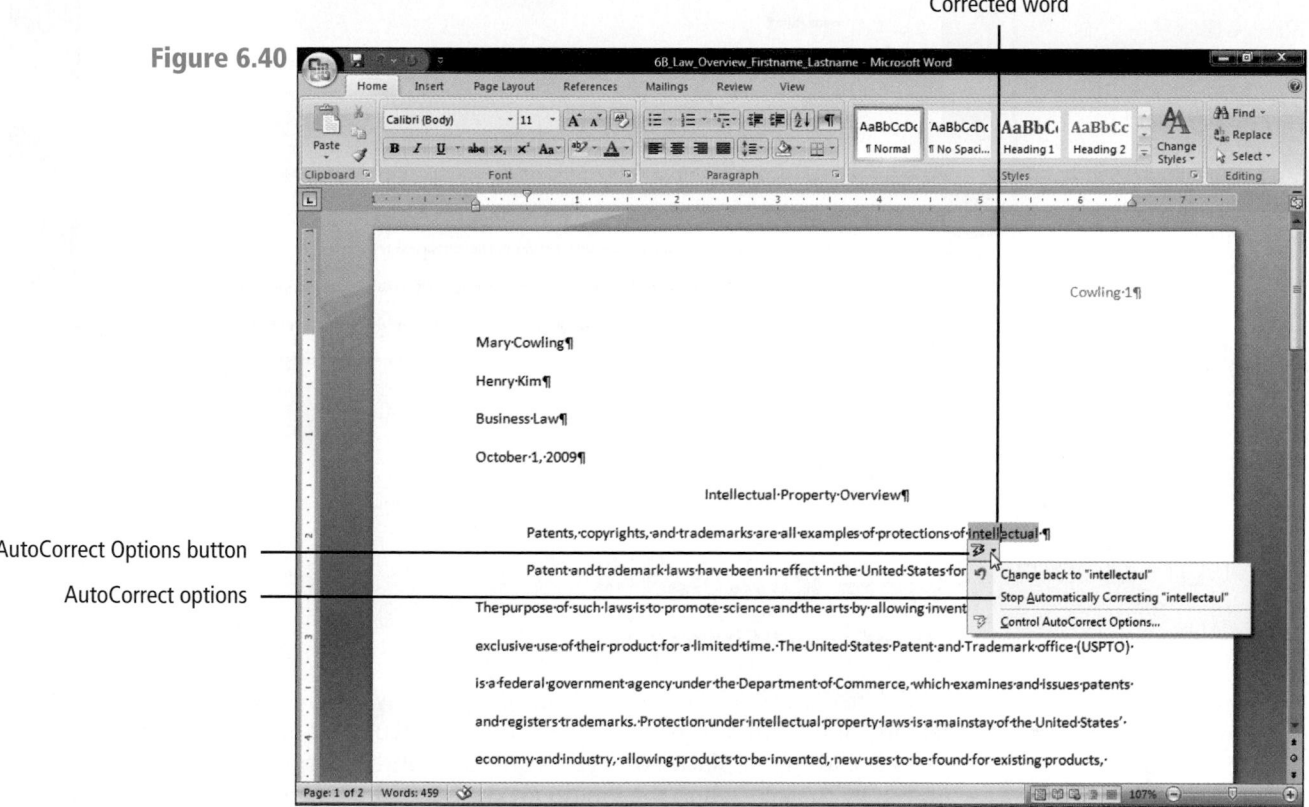

8 Click anywhere in the document to close the **AutoCorrect Options** menu without selecting a command. Locate the word *intellectual* that you just corrected and position the insertion point at the end of that line. Type **property (IP).** and then press Spacebar.

9 Type the remainder of the paragraph, and then compare your screen with Figure 6.41.

Intellectual property has many definitions, but is usually considered to be information having commercial value and original products of the mind. Intellectual property isn't tangible, but can be protected by the law. Intellectual property is not an item that was invented, but the thought process and plans that allowed the item to be invented and manufactured. Intellectual property is not the clothing that is sold in stores, but rather the brand name that represents the quality and style of the clothing.

Figure 6.41

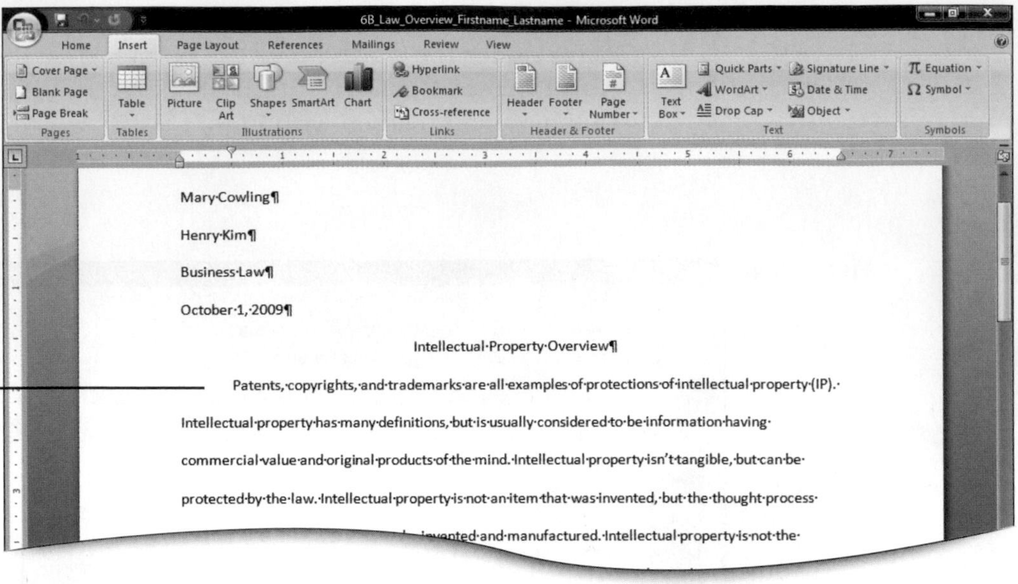

First line indented 0.5 inch

10 **Save** 💾 your changes.

More Knowledge
AutoCorrect Shortcuts

The AutoCorrect replacement is most commonly used to correct spelling errors, but it can also be used to expand shortcut text into longer words or phrases. In the Replace box, type a shortcut phrase, and type the full phrase in the With box. When setting up an AutoCorrect shortcut, it is best not to use shortcut text that is an actual word or a commonly used abbreviation. Even though you can reverse an AutoCorrect replacement by using the AutoCorrect Options shortcut menu, it is best to avoid the problem by adding a letter to the shortcut text. For example, if you type both *GHS* and *GHS Law Partners* frequently, you may want to add ghsx (or just ghx) as an AutoCorrect shortcut for the text *GHS Law Partners*.

Activity 6.19 Inserting Symbols

There are many symbols that are used occasionally, but not often enough to put on a standard keyboard. These symbols can be found on, and inserted from, the Symbols group on the Insert tab.

1 Use the vertical scroll bar to move down in the document to display the bottom half of **Page 1**. In the paragraph that begins *Patent is defined*, in the second line, locate the word *novel*, and then place the insertion point just to the right of the word. Press ⌨Delete two times to remove the space and the left parenthesis.

The phrase that follows *novel* should be separated by a dash rather than parentheses.

2 Click the **Insert tab**, and then in the **Symbols group**, click the **Symbol** button. At the bottom of the **Symbol gallery**, click **More**

Symbols. In the **Symbol** dialog box, click the **Special Characters tab**. Be sure the **Em Dash** is selected. In the lower right corner of the dialog box, click **Insert**, and then compare your screen with Figure 6.42.

An **_em dash_** is the default symbol in the list of commonly used symbols. An em dash is the word processing name for a long dash in a sentence. An em dash in a sentence marks a break in thought, similar to a comma but stronger. The keyboard shortcuts for inserting the commonly used symbols display to the right of the character name.

Figure 6.42

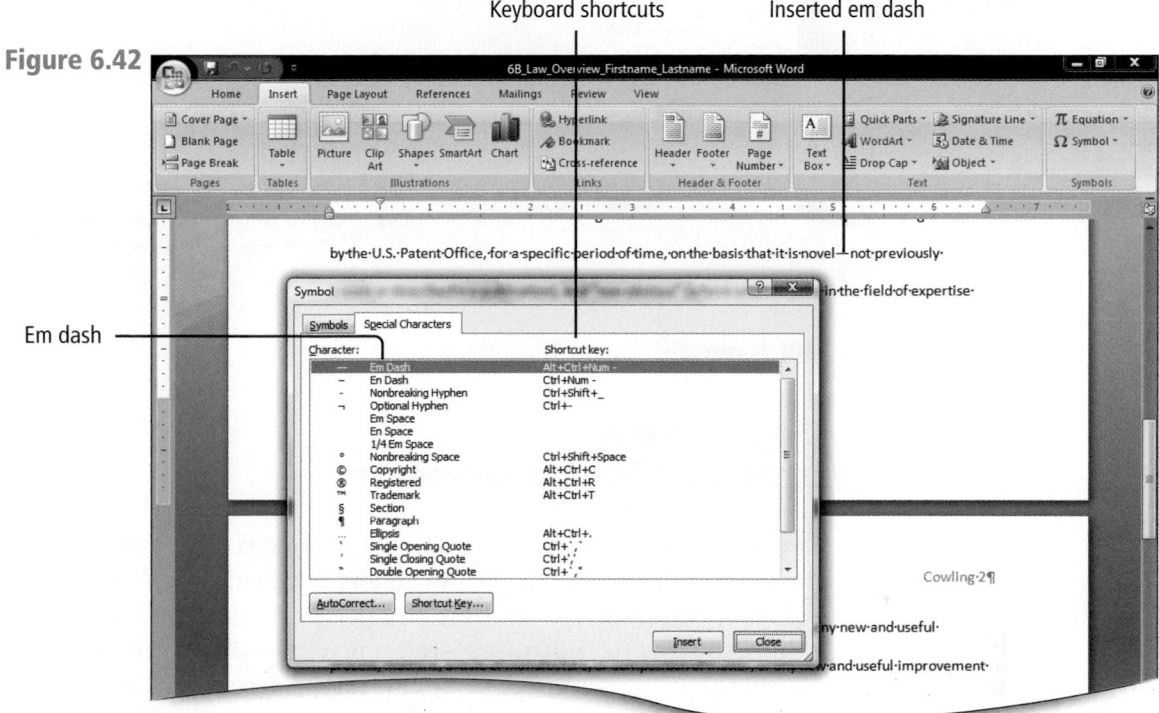

Keyboard shortcuts   Inserted em dash

Em dash

3 If necessary, click the title bar of the dialog box, and then drag the dialog box out of the way so you can see the third line of the same paragraph. With the **Symbol** dialog box still open, to the right of _in a publication_, remove the right parenthesis, the comma, and the space; and then click the **Insert** button again. At the bottom of the **Symbol** dialog box, click **Close**.

4 Press Ctrl + Home to move to the beginning of the document. Place the insertion point to the right of the title text _Intellectual Property Overview_, and then type **(c)** Alternatively, on the Insert tab, in the Symbol group, click the Symbol button, and then click the last item in the first row—the copyright symbol. Compare your document with Figure 6.43.

Your typed text _(c)_ changes to the copyright symbol ©. Although this symbol is available from the Symbol gallery, it is also included in Word's AutoCorrect list. The parentheses are necessary for AutoComplete to insert a Copyright symbol. Notice that if you point to the copyright symbol, the AutoCorrect Options button displays, which enables you to remove the copyright symbol and display _(c)_ instead.

Figure 6.43

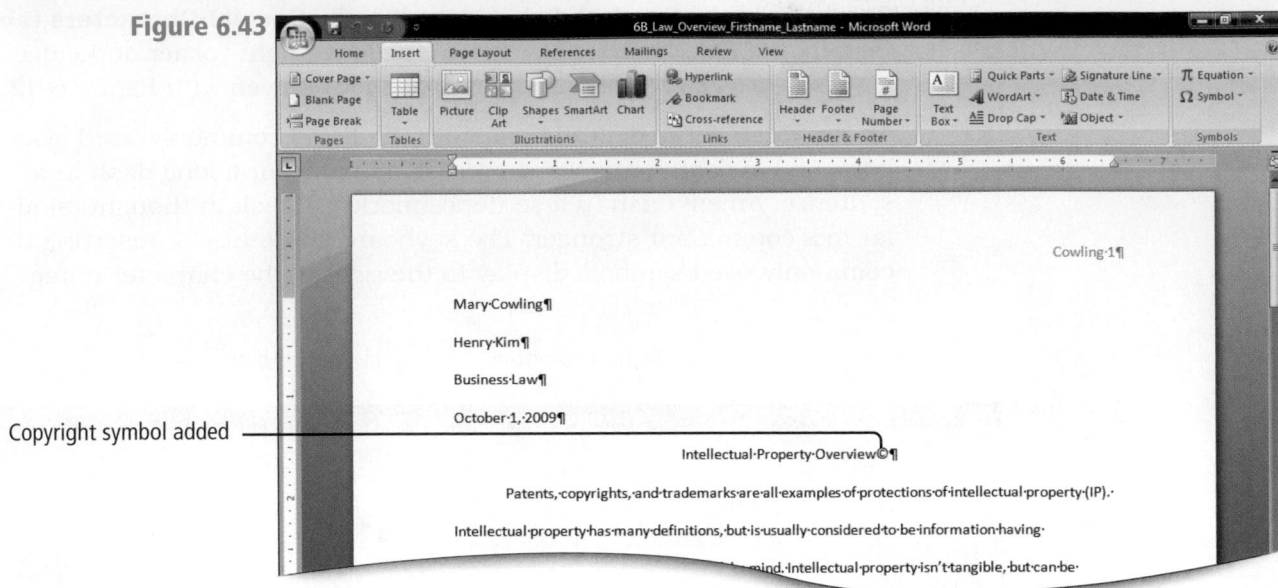

Copyright symbol added

5 **Save** 📷 your changes.

Objective 6
Insert and Format References

Reports frequently include information taken from other sources, and these must be credited. Within report text, numbers mark the location of *references*—information that has been taken from another source. The numbers refer to *footnotes*—references placed at the bottom of the page containing the reference, or *endnotes*—references placed at the end of a document or chapter.

When footnotes or endnotes are included in a report, a page listing the references is included. Such a list is commonly titled *Works Cited*, *Bibliography*, *Sources*, or References.

Activity 6.20 Inserting Footnotes

Footnotes can be added as you type the document or after the document is complete. Footnotes do not need to be entered in order, and if one footnote is removed, Word renumbers the remaining footnotes automatically.

1 Scroll to view **Page 2** and locate the paragraph that begins *Copyrights protect*. At the end of the paragraph, position the insertion point following the period.

2 Click the **References tab**, and then in the **Footnotes group**, click **Insert Footnote**.

A footnote area is created at the bottom of the page, and a footnote number is added to the text at the insertion point location. Footnote 1 is placed at the top of the footnote area, and the insertion point is moved to the right of the number. A short blank line is added just above the footnote area. You do not need to type the footnote number.

3 Type **According to the United States Copyright Office, abstractions, such as an idea for a book or movie, are not subject to copyright law.** and then compare your screen with Figure 6.44.

This is an explanatory footnote, giving additional information that does not fit well in the body of the report. The new footnote is single-spaced, even though the document text is double-spaced.

Figure 6.44

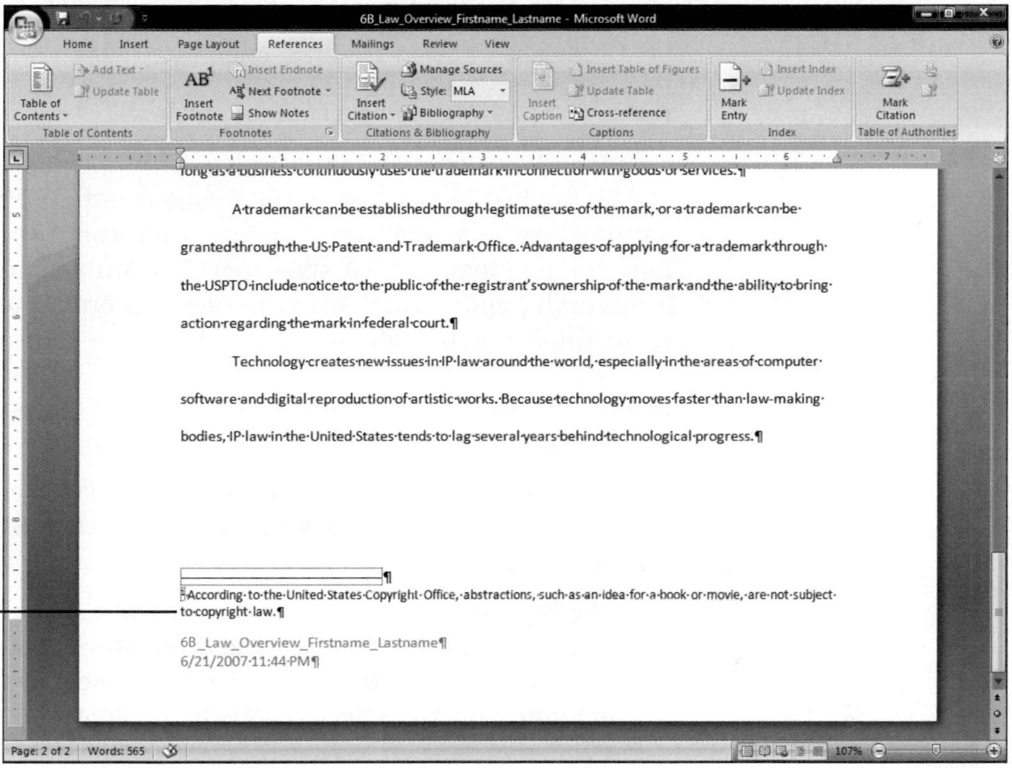

Footnote text, single- spaced

4 Press [Ctrl] + [Home] to move to the beginning of the document. Locate the paragraph that begins *Patents, copyrights*. At the end of the paragraph, position the insertion point following the period.

This sentence refers to the *protections* of intellectual property, and the report's author wants to clarify the scope of protections by adding a reference.

5 In the **Footnotes group**, click the **Insert Footnote** button. Type **There is no set of international intellectual property laws, although many countries have reciprocal copyright, trademark, and patent agreements with the United States.** Notice that the footnote you just added is the new footnote *1*, while the other footnote is renumbered as footnote *2*.

6 **Save** 🖫 your changes.

More Knowledge

Using Symbols Rather Than Numbers for Notes

Instead of using numbers to designate footnotes, you can use standard footnote symbols. The seven traditional symbols, available from the Footnote and Endnote dialog box, in order, are * (asterisk), † (dagger), ‡ (double dagger), § (section mark), || (parallels), ¶ (paragraph mark), and # (number or pound sign). This sequence can be continuous (this is the default setting), or can begin anew with each page.

Activity 6.21 Modifying a Footnote Style

Microsoft Word contains built-in paragraph formats called *styles*, which can be applied to a paragraph with one command. The default style for footnote text is a single-spaced paragraph that uses a 10-point Calibri font and no indents. MLA style specifies double-spaced text in all areas of a research paper—including footnotes. According to the MLA style, footnotes must also be indented 0.5 inch.

In this activity, you will modify the footnote style so that all of your inserted footnotes are formatted according to MLA guidelines.

1 Scroll to view the bottom of **Page 1** and right-click anywhere in the footnote text. From the shortcut menu, click **Style**. Compare your screen with Figure 6.45.

The Style dialog box displays, listing the styles currently in use in the document, in addition to some of the word processing elements that come with special built-in styles. Because you right-clicked on the footnote text, the selected style is the Footnote Text paragraph style.

Elements with
special built-in styles

Modify button

Figure 6.45

All styles selected

Footnote Text
paragraph style

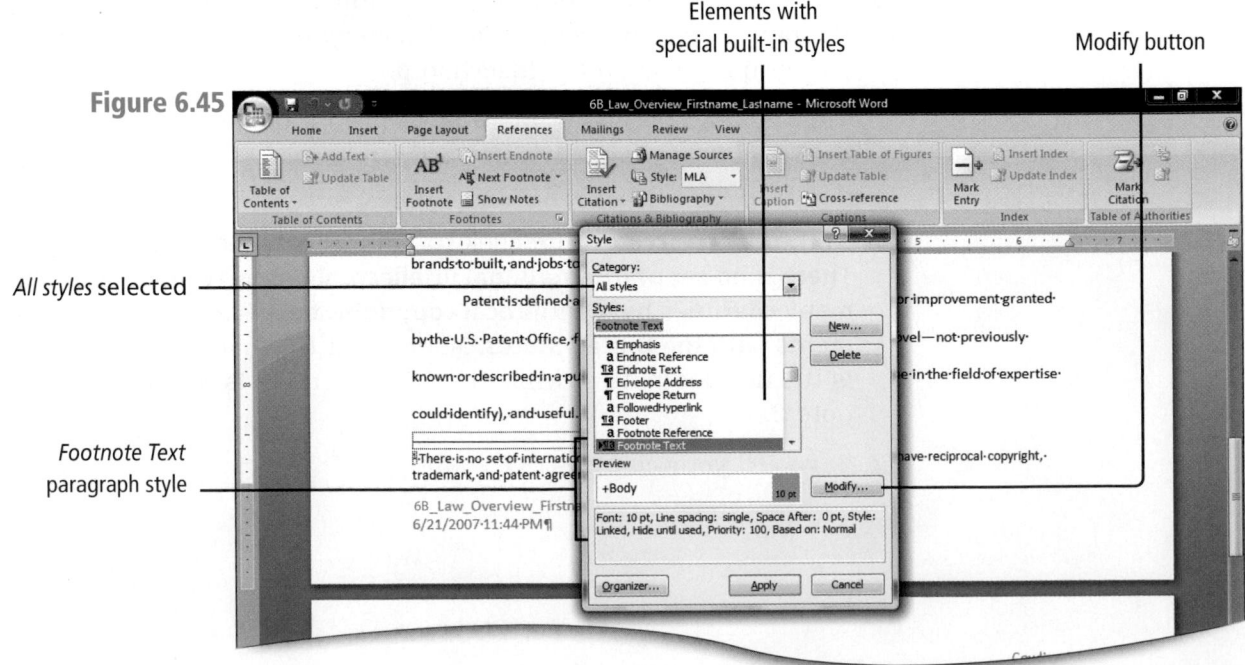

2 In the displayed **Style** dialog box, click the **Modify** button. In the **Modify Style** dialog box, locate the small Formatting toolbar in the center of the dialog box, click the **Font Size button arrow**, click **11**, and then compare your screen with Figure 6.46.

Font Size button arrow

Formatting toolbar in the Modify Style dialog box

Figure 6.46

Format button

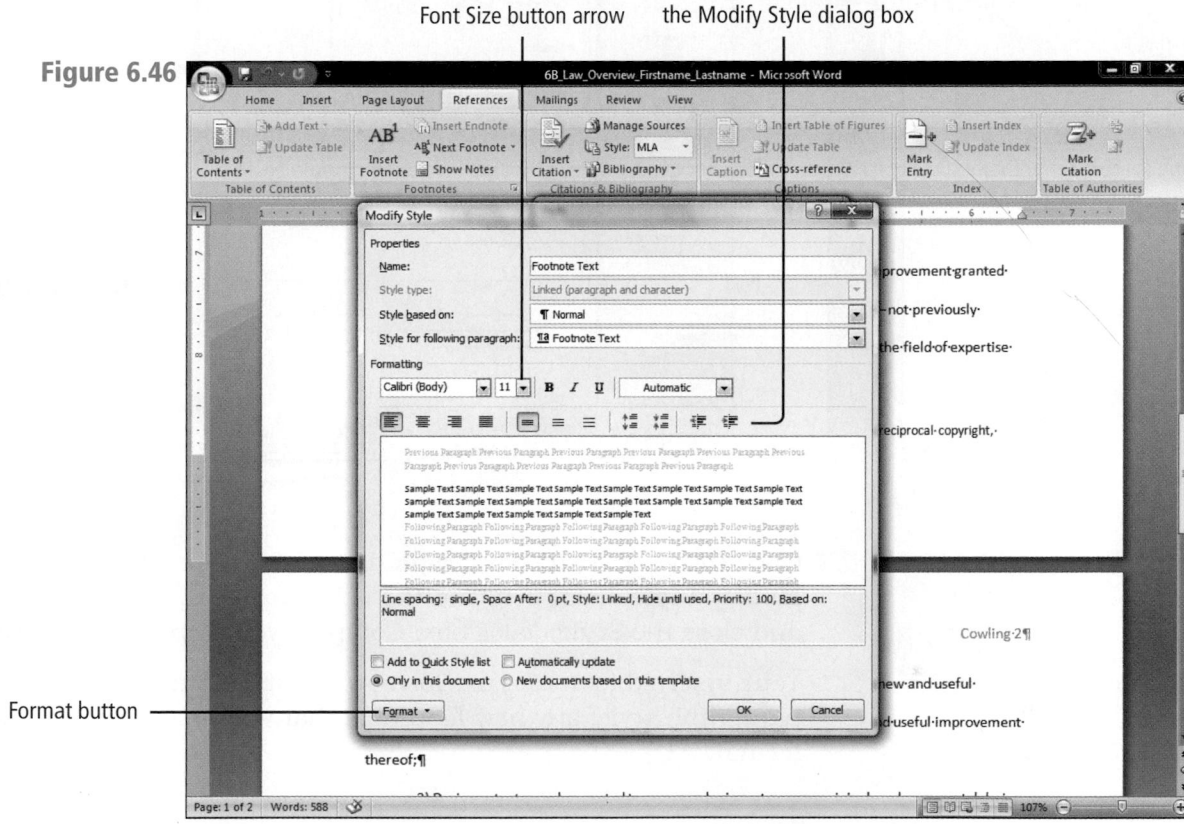

3 In the lower left corner of the dialog box, click the **Format** button, and then click **Paragraph**. In the displayed **Paragraph** dialog box, under **Indentation**, click the **Special arrow**, and then click **First line**. If necessary, change the By box to 0.5".

4 Under **Spacing**, click the **Line spacing button arrow**, and then click **Double**. Alternatively, line spacing can be adjusted using the Modify Style toolbar. Compare your dialog box with Figure 6.47.

First line indent

Figure 6.47

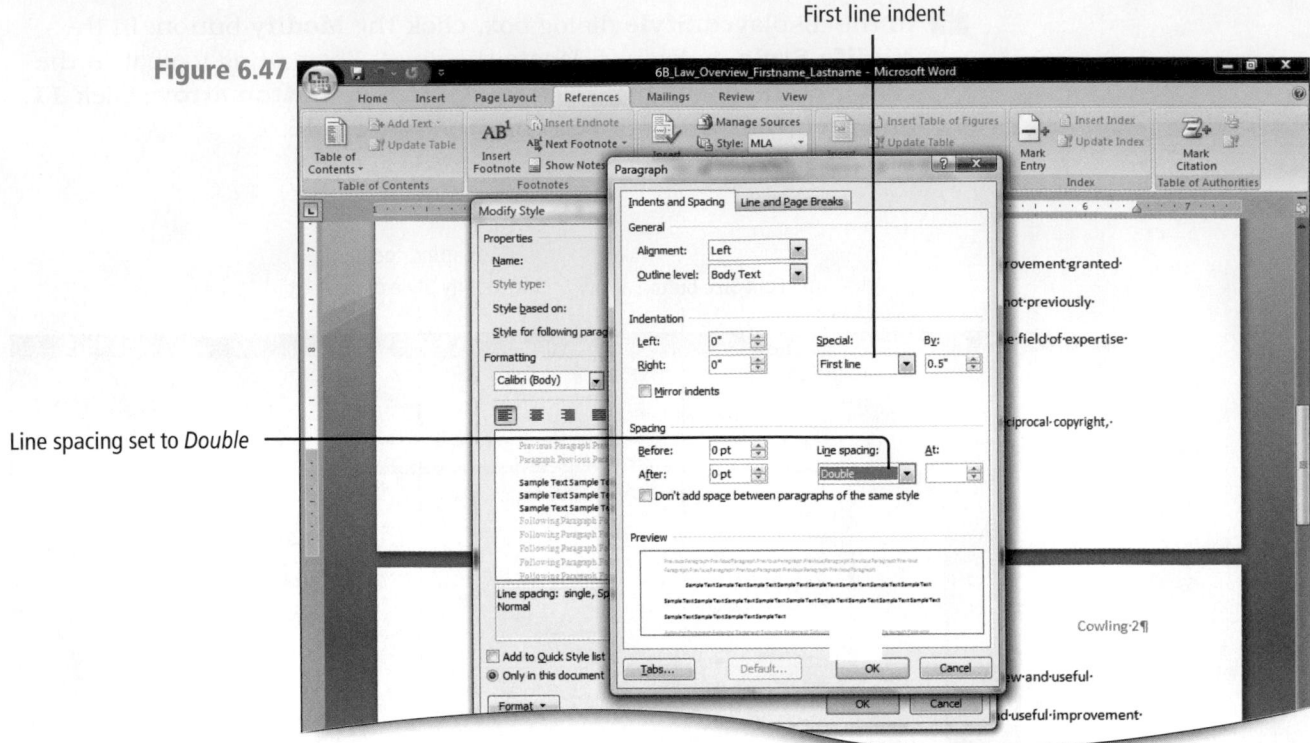

Line spacing set to *Double*

5 Click **OK** to close the **Paragraph** dialog box, click **OK** to close the **Modify Style** dialog box, and then click **Apply** to apply the new style and close the **Style** dialog box. Compare your screen with Figure 6.48.

Your inserted footnotes are formatted with the new Footnote Text paragraph style; any new footnotes that you insert will also use this format.

Footnote text double-spaced

Figure 6.48

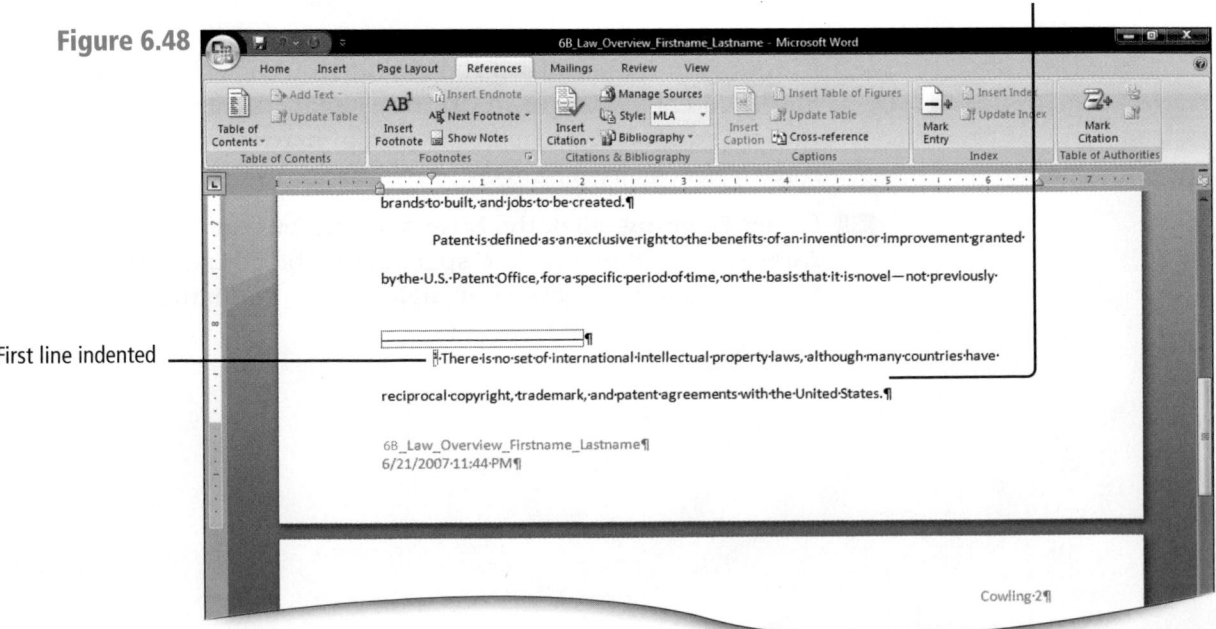

First line indented

6 Scroll to view the bottom of **Page 2** to confirm that the new format was also applied to the second footnote, and then **Save** 💾 the changes you have made to your research paper.

By modifying the formats of the existing Footnote Text style, the new formats were applied to any text in the document that had the Footnote style applied.

Activity 6.22 Adding Citations

When writing a long research paper, you will likely reference numerous books, articles, and Web sites. Some of your research sources may be referenced many times, others only one time.

References to sources within the text of your research paper are indicated in an *abbreviated* manner. However, as you enter a reference for the first time, you can also enter the *complete* information about the source. Then, when you have finished your paper, you will be able to automatically generate the list of sources that must be included at the end of your research paper.

1 On **Page 2** of the document, locate the paragraph that begins *Copyrights protect*, and then position the insertion point at the end of the paragraph, but before the period. Click the **References tab** to begin the process of inserting a citation.

A **citation** is a list of information about a source, usually including the name of the author, the full title of the work, the year of publication, and other publication information.

2 In the **Citations & Bibliography group**, click the **Style button arrow**, and then click **MLA** to insert a reference using MLA style. Click the **Insert Citation** button, and then click **Add New Source**. Be sure **Book** is selected as the **Type of Source**. Add the following information, and then compare your screen with Figure 6.49:

Author:	**Schechter, Roger E.; Thomas, John R.**
Title:	**Intellectual Property: The Law of Copyrights, Patents and Trademarks**
Year:	**2003**
City:	**St. Paul, MN**
Publisher:	**West Publishing Company**

Insert Citation button on the Ribbon

Figure 6.49

Source type

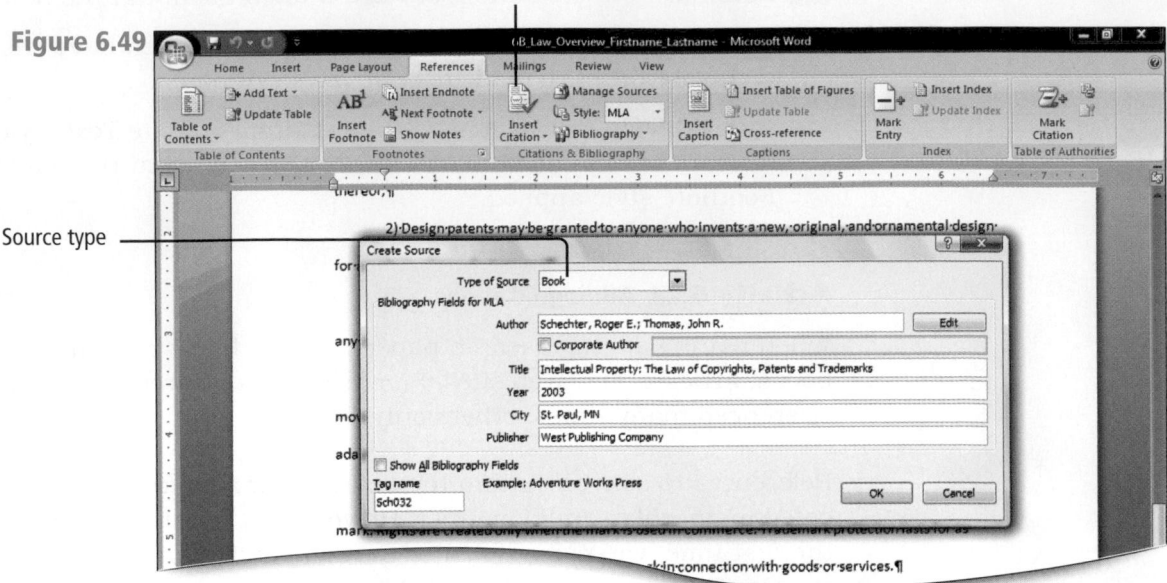

In the MLA style, references to items on the Works Cited page are placed in *parenthetical references*—references that include the last name of the author or authors and the page number in the referenced source, which you add to the reference. No year is indicated, and there is no comma between the name and the page number.

3 Click **OK** to insert the reference. Click to select the reference, and notice that a small box surrounds the reference and an arrow displays in the lower right corner of the box. Click this **Citation Options arrow**, and then from the displayed list of options, click **Edit Citation**. In the displayed **Edit Citation** dialog box, under **Add**, in the **Pages** box, type **2** to indicate that you are citing from page 2 of this source. Compare your screen with Figure 6.50. Notice that the citation wraps from one line to the next, so the citation box also wraps between lines.

Page number of the citation

Figure 6.50

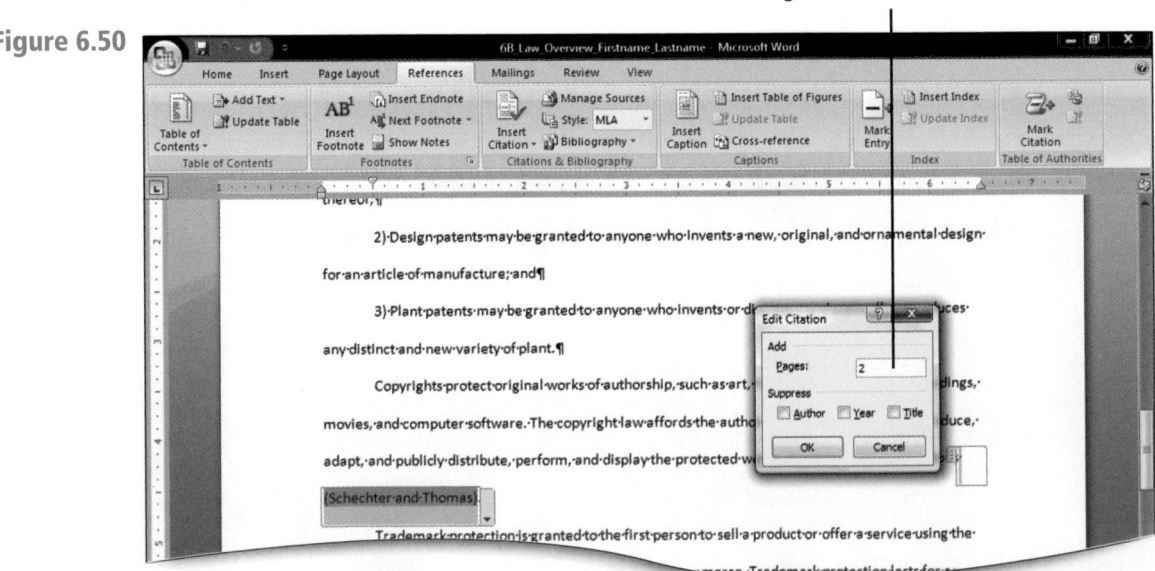

4 Click **OK** to display the page number of the citation. In the next paragraph, which begins *Trademark protection*, position the insertion point at the end of the paragraph, but before the period. In the **Citations & Bibliography group**, click the **Insert Citation** button, and then click **Add New Source**. Be sure **Book** is selected as the **Type of Source**, and then add the following information:

Author:	**Stim, Richard W.**
Title:	**Trademark Law**
Year:	**2000**
City:	**Stamford, CT**
Publisher:	**Thomson Delmar Learning**

5 Click **OK**. Click to select the reference, click the **Citation Options arrow**, and then click **Edit Citation**. In the displayed **Edit Citation** dialog box, under **Add**, in the **Pages** box, type **4** to indicate that you are citing from page 4 of this source. Click **OK**.

6 On the same page, locate the paragraph that begins *3) Plant patents*. At the end of that sentence, click to position the insertion point before the period. In the **Citations & Bibliography group**, click the **Insert Citation** button, and then click **Add New Source**. Click the **Type of Source arrow**, scroll down, and select **Web site** from the list. Under **Bibliography Fields for MLA**, click to select the **Corporate Author** check box.

When the author of a cited work is a corporation, the parenthetical reference is handled differently.

7 Type the following information:

Corporate Author:	**United States Patent and Trademark Office**
Name of Web Page:	**General Information Concerning Patents**
Year:	**2005**
Month:	**March**
Day:	**22**
Year Accessed:	**2009**
Month Accessed:	**October**
Day Accessed:	**11**
URL:	**http://www.uspto.gov/web/offices/pac/doc/ general/index.html#patent**

8 Click **OK** to insert the reference, and then compare your screen with Figure 6.51.

A parenthetical reference is added. Because the cited Web page has no page numbers, only the author name is used in the parenthetical reference.

Figure 6.51

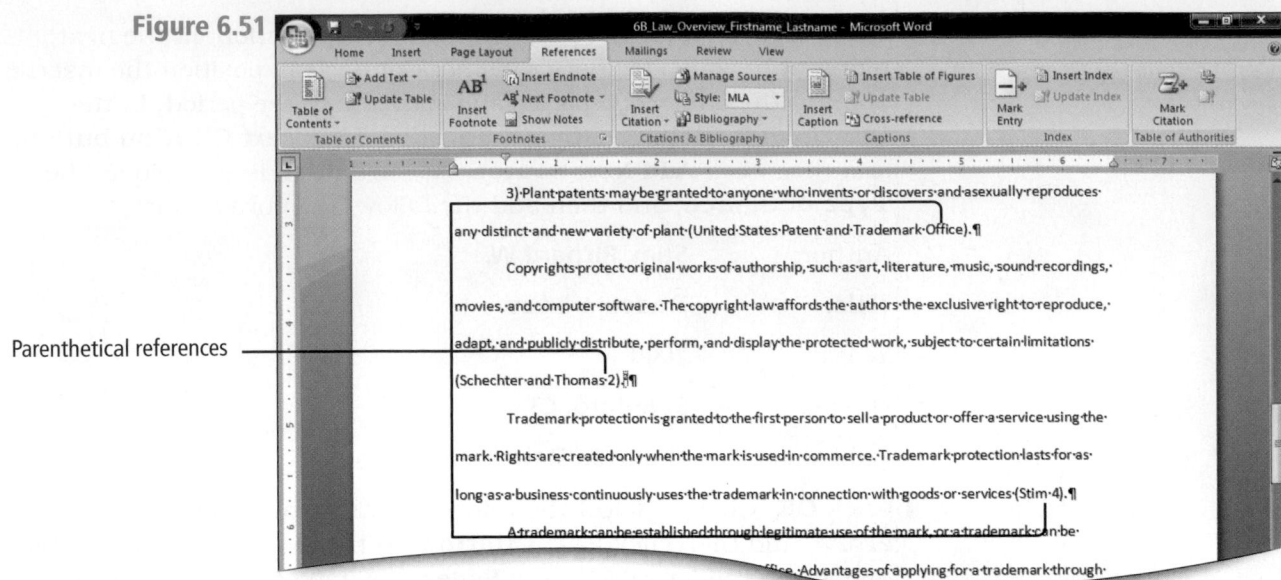

Parenthetical references

9 On the **References tab**, in the **Citations & Bibliography group**, click the **Manage Sources** button, and then compare your screen with Figure 6.52.

The Source Manager dialog box displays. You may have fewer sources, more sources, or different sources. Other citations on your computer display in the Master List box. The citations for the current document display in the Current List box. If you use the same sources regularly, you can copy sources from your Master List to the current document. You can also edit sources and preview the citations using the selected style.

Citations in the current document

Figure 6.52

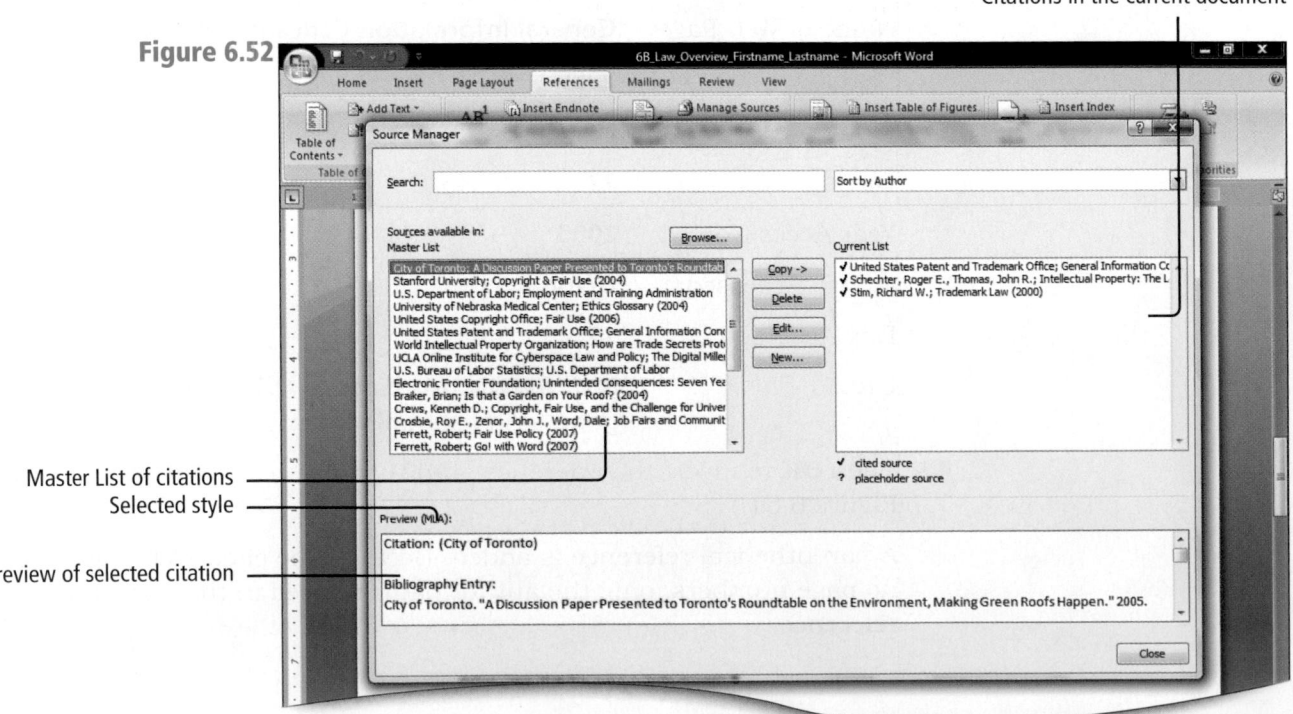

Master List of citations
Selected style

Preview of selected citation

10 At the bottom of the **Source Manager** dialog box, click **Close**. **Save** 🖫 your changes.

Activity 6.23 Creating a Reference Page

It is common to include, at the end of a report, a list of each source referenced. *Works Cited* is the reference page heading used in the MLA style guidelines. Other styles may refer to this page as a *Bibliography* (Business Style) or *References* (APA Style).

1 Press Ctrl + End to move the insertion point to the end of the document. Hold down Ctrl and then press Enter to insert a manual page break.

2 Type **Works Cited** and then press Enter. On the **References tab**, in the **Citations & Bibliography group**, be sure **MLA** displays in the **Style** box.

3 In the **Citations & Bibliography group**, click the **Bibliography** button, and then click **Insert Bibliography** to insert the citations you typed earlier.

The bibliography is inserted as a field, and the field is linked to the citations Source Manager. The references are sorted alphabetically by author name.

4 In the bibliography, move the pointer to the left of the first entry—beginning *Schechter, Roger*—to display the 🔼 pointer. Drag down to select all three references. Right-click the selected text, and then click **Paragraph**.

5 Under **Indentation**, click the **Special arrow**, and then click **Hanging**. Under **Spacing**, click the **Line spacing arrow**, and then click **Double**. Under **Spacing**, in the **After** box, type **0** and then click **OK**.

The text is double-spaced, and the first line of each entry extends 0.5 inch to the left of the remaining lines of the entry. This is called a *hanging indent*, and the lines are double-spaced according to MLA guidelines.

6 At the top of the last page, right-click the *Works Cited* title, and then click **Paragraph**. In the displayed **Paragraph** dialog box, under **General**, click the **Alignment arrow**, and then click **Centered**. Under **Indentation**, click the **Special arrow**, and then click **(none)**. Click **OK**, and then compare your screen with Figure 6.53.

In MLA style, the *Works Cited* title is aligned and centered. The first line indent of 0.5 inch was removed to center the title between the left and right margins.

Figure 6.53

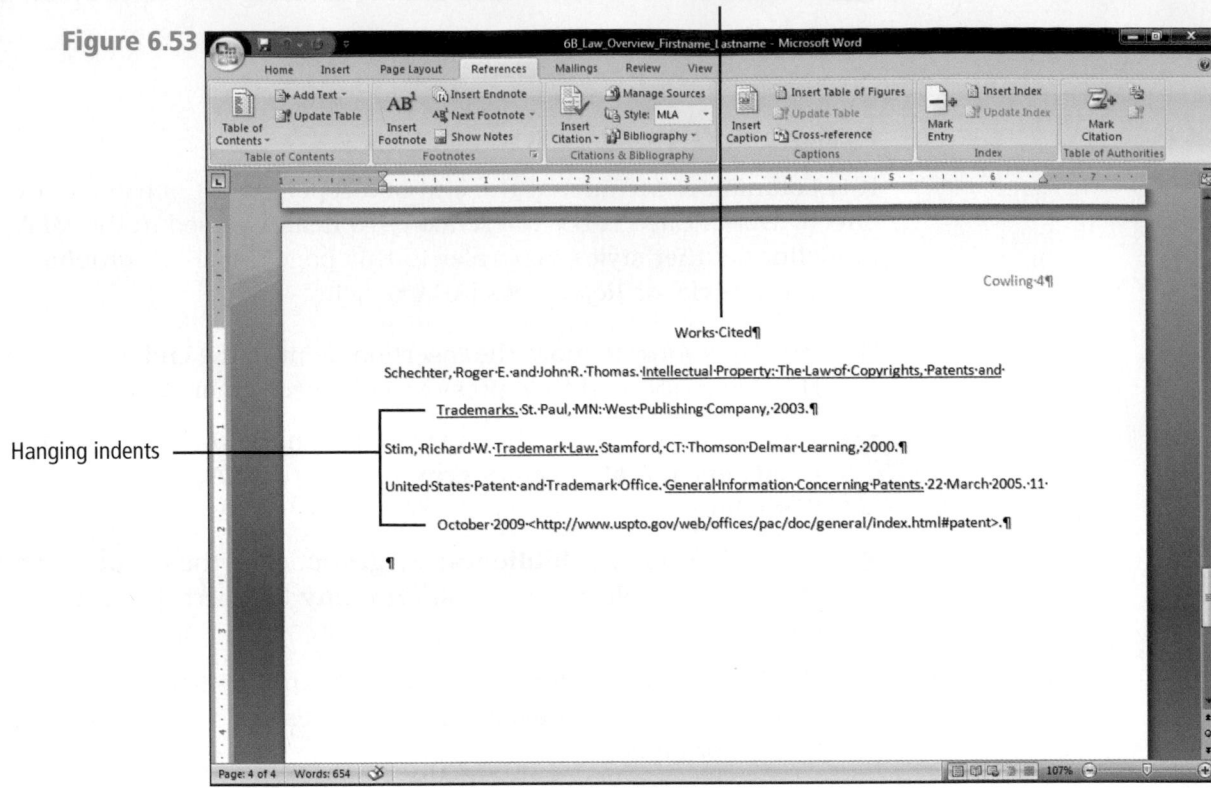

Works Cited title centered

Hanging indents

7 **Save** 💾 your document.

Activity 6.24 Managing Document Properties

Document properties refer to the detailed information about your Word document file that can help you identify or organize your electronic files. Document property information is stored in the ***Document Information Panel***, and can include the document title, the name of the author, the subject of the document, and keywords that will help you search for the document in your computer system.

1 From the **Office** menu 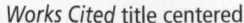, point to **Prepare**, and then click **Properties** to display the **Document Information Panel**.

2 In the **Author** box, type your name, if necessary.

3 In the **Title** box, type **Intellectual Property Law**

4 In the **Keywords** box, type **copyright, patent, trademark** and then compare your screen with Figure 6.54. Notice that not all boxes need to be filled in.

Figure 6.54

Keywords

Close button

Author

Title

Document Information Panel

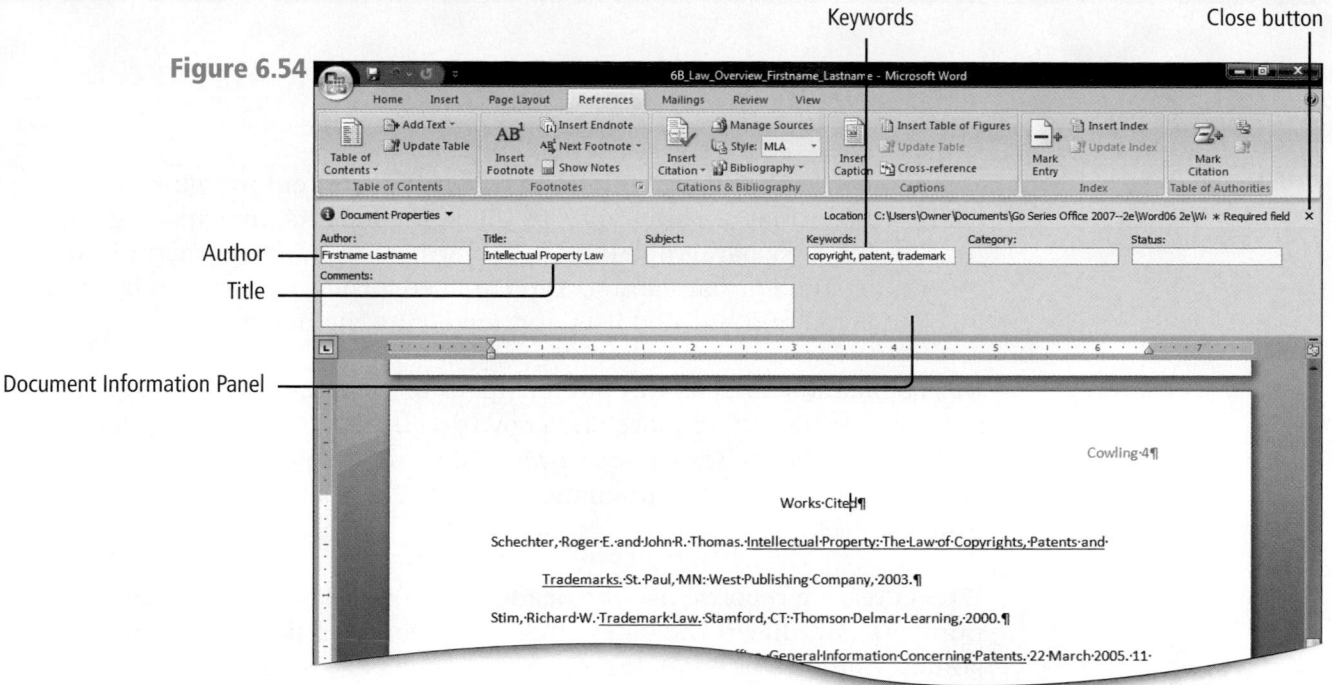

5 On the right side of the **Document Information Panel**, click the **Close** button ☒. **Save** 🖫 your document.

6 From the **Office** menu 🔘, point to the **Print arrow**, and then click **Print Preview** to make a final check of your research paper. Check your *Chapter Assignment Sheet* or your *Course Syllabus* or consult your instructor to determine if you are to submit your assignments on paper or electronically. To submit electronically, go to Step 8, and then follow the instructions provided by your instructor.

7 On the **Print Preview tab**, in the **Print group**, click the **Print** button, click **OK**, and then click **Close Print Preview**.

8 From the **Office** menu 🔘, click **Exit Word**, saving any changes if prompted to do so.

End **You have completed Project 6B** ————

There's More You Can Do!

Close Word and any other open windows. Display the Start menu, click Computer, and then navigate to the student files that accompany this textbook. In the folder **02_theres_more_you_can_do_**, locate and open the folder for this chapter. Open and print the instructions for this project, which are provided to you in Adobe PDF format.

Try IT!—Add a Custom Entry to the Quick Part Gallery

In this Try It! exercise, you will add a custom entry to the Quick Part gallery.

Content-Based Assessments

Summary

You can change the format of pages by setting different margins, and change the format of paragraphs by changing indents, line spacing, and the spacing after paragraphs. To apply formats from one paragraph to others, use the Format Painter. You can also format paragraphs by creating numbered and bulleted lists and modifying the bullets.

Use commands such as Cut and Paste, or techniques such as the drag-and-drop operation, to move and copy text. Use the Find and Replace dialog box to locate text that you want to modify. Some formatting in Word can be performed automatically using AutoCorrect and AutoComplete.

When creating reports, use the header and footer areas to add page numbers or to insert the date, time, or file name. Reports also require adding footnotes or endnotes and a reference page to list other sources of information cited within the report.

Key Terms

The 🔵 symbol represents Key Terms found on the Student CD in the 06_theres_more_you_can_do folder for this chapter.

Content-Based Assessments

Matching

Match each term in the second column with its correct definition in the first column by writing the letter of the term on the blank line in front of the correct definition.

_____ **1.** The most commonly used text alignment, where text is aligned at the left margin, leaving the right margin uneven.

_____ **2.** The alignment of text centered between the left and right margins.

_____ **3.** Text that is aligned on both the left and right margins.

_____ **4.** The distance between lines of text in a paragraph.

_____ **5.** A small box with upward- and downward-pointing arrows that let you move rapidly through a set of values.

_____ **6.** A Word tool with which you can copy the formatting of specific text, or of a paragraph, to text in another location in the document.

_____ **7.** A temporary storage area that holds text or graphics that have been cut or copied, and that can subsequently be placed in another location in the document or in another Office program.

_____ **8.** The action of removing selected text from a document and moving it to the Office Clipboard.

_____ **9.** A small button that displays beneath pasted text, and lets you determine how the information is pasted into your document.

_____ **10.** Text symbols such as small circles or check marks used to introduce items in a list.

_____ **11.** A Word feature that automatically corrects common typing and spelling errors as you type, such as changing *teh* to *the*.

_____ **12.** The word processing name for a long dash in a sentence that marks a break in thought, similar to a comma but stronger.

_____ **13.** In a report or research paper, references placed at the bottom of a report page containing the source of the reference.

_____ **14.** A term used to describe a list of referenced works placed at the end of a research paper or report when using the MLA style.

_____ **15.** An indent style in which the first line of a paragraph extends to the left of the remaining lines; this indent style is commonly used for bibliographic entries.

A AutoCorrect

B Bullets

C Center alignment

D Cutting

E Em dash

F Footnotes

G Format Painter

H Hanging indent

I Justified alignment

J Left alignment

K Line spacing

L Office Clipboard

M Paste Options

N Spin box

O Works Cited

Content-Based Assessments

Fill in the Blank

Write the correct answer in the space provided.

1. The space between the text and the top, bottom, left, and right edges of the paper is known as the _____.

2. The placement of paragraph text relative to the left and right margins is known as the _____.

3. When you paste text, the text is moved from the _____ _____ and placed where the insertion point is positioned.

4. The keyboard shortcut used to copy text is Ctrl + _____.

5. When you drag text and then drop it in another location, the text is _____ from one place to another.

6. When you click the Redo button, it reverses the action of the _____ button.

7. To keep two words together as one unit, so that Word does not split them at the end of a line, insert a(n) _____ space.

8. To move the insertion point to the next line without pressing Enter and without creating a new paragraph, insert a manual _____ _____.

9. A list of items with each item introduced by a consecutive number to indicate definite steps, a sequence of actions, or chronological order is a(n) _____ list.

10. In a report or research paper, a reference placed at the end of a report is called a(n) _____.

11. If you need to add ™ or ® or © to a document, display the _____ dialog box.

12. A set of formatting characteristics that can be applied to a paragraph with one shortcut command is known as a(n) _____.

13. In the MLA report style, references placed in parentheses within the report text that includes the last name of the author or authors and the page number in the referenced source, are called _____ _____.

14. A list of information about a reference source, usually including the name of the author, the full title of the work, the year of publication, a Web address, and other publication information, is called a(n) _____.

15. The detailed information about a document that can help you identify or organize your files, including author name, title, and keywords, is called the Document _____.

Skills Review

Project 6C—Patent Search

In this project, you will apply the skills you practiced from the Objectives in Project 6A.

Objectives: 1. *Change Document and Paragraph Layout;* **2.** *Change and Reorganize Text;* **3.** *Create and Modify Lists.*

In the following Skills Review, you will edit a document describing the patent search process performed by GHS Law Partners. Your completed document will look similar to the one shown in Figure 6.55.

For Project 6C, you will need the following file:

w06C_Patent_Search

You will save your document as
6C_Patent_Search_Firstname_Lastname

Figure 6.55

permit storage of information about large numbers of chips having complex designs.

e, CA); Hubbell; Earl (Los alo Alto, CA); Cheung; an Jose, CA)

ra, CA)

2000

to drawings and figures

of patent searches, such as infringement can reveal whether a product already in rches, conducted as part of large research recent developments in a particular area.

GHS Law Partners
Patent Search Process and Procedures

GHS Law Partners conducts patent searches on behalf of its clients. Patent searches are conducted before preparing the patent application in order to discern if a similar product or process has been patented already. If a similar patent is discovered, the client's pending patent application can be abandoned before too much time or money is invested in it; or, the information in the existing patent can be used to modify the patent application or change its focus.

Patents are grouped into numerous classifications covering all areas of technology. The search process can be time consuming and expensive, but it is valuable for clients to have a search conducted by experts before investing millions of dollars in a new product or process. The number of patents granted by the United States Patent and Trademark Office is large, and has been growing every year. According to the USPTO, in 1963, 48,971 patents were granted. In 2004, 181,302 patents were granted.

GHS Law Partners conducts three main portions of the patent search:

1. Organize the search and determine whether manual searches will be needed in addition to electronic searches. Manual searches may be needed for older technologies not available in the USPTO databases.
2. Run electronic searches and/or manually search at USPTO depository libraries or the USPTO main office in Virginia.
3. Examine the patent documents.

GHS Law Partners employs experts in many fields who will examine the patent documents for their similarity to the new product or process. Patent documents consist of:

• Reference section
• Abstract – for example:

United States Patent 6,826,296

Balaban, et al. November 30, 2004

Method and system for providing a probe array chip design database

Abstract

Systems and method for organizing information relating to the design of polymer probe array chips including oligonucleotide array chips. A database model is provided which organizes information interrelating probes on a chip, genomic items investigated by the chip, and sequence information relating to the design of the chip. The model is readily translatable into database languages such as SQL. The database model scales to

6C_Patent_Search_Firstname_Lastname

(Project 6C–Patent Search continues on the next page)

Content-Based Assessments

(Project 6C–Patent Search continued)

1. **Start** Word. Locate and open the file **w06C_Patent_Search**, and then save the file in your **Word Chapter 6** folder as **6C_Patent_Search_Firstname_Lastname** Display formatting marks and rulers, and adjust the page width to display both the left and right page edges.

2. Click the **Page Layout tab**, click the **Margins** button, and then at the bottom of the **Margins gallery**, click **Custom Margins**. In the displayed **Page Setup** dialog box, press Tab as necessary to select the value in the **Left** box. With *1.25"* selected, type **1** and then press Tab. In the **Right** box, change the value from *1.25"* to **1** and then click **OK**.

3. Click the **Insert tab**. In the **Header & Footer group**, click the **Footer** button, and then click **Edit Footer**. On the **Design tab**, in the **Insert group**, click the **Quick Parts** button, and then click **Field**. In the **Field** dialog box, under **Field names**, locate and click **FileName**, and then click **OK**. Double-click anywhere in the document to close the footer area. **Save** your document.

4. Select the first line of the document. On the Mini toolbar, click the **Center** button, and then click the **Bold** button.

5. Right-click anywhere in the paragraph beginning *GHS Law Partners conducts patent*, and then from the shortcut menu, click **Paragraph**. In the displayed **Paragraph** dialog box, under **Indentation**, click the **Special arrow**, and then click **First line**. Under **Spacing**, in the **After** box, click the **up spin arrow** to change the spacing from *10 pt* to **12 pt**. Under **Spacing**, click the **Line spacing arrow**, and then click **Single**. Click **OK** to close the Paragraph dialog box.

6. With the insertion point in the paragraph beginning *GHS Law Partners conducts patent*, in the **Clipboard group**, double-click the **Format Painter** button. Move the ⊿I pointer to the paragraph beginning *The search process* and click one time. Use the **Format Painter** to format the paragraph that begins *GHS Law Partners conducts three*, the paragraph beginning *GHS Law Partners employs*, and the last paragraph in the document, beginning *GHS Law Partners can also*. In the **Clipboard group**, click the **Format Painter** button again to turn it off.

7. **Save** your changes. Press Ctrl + Home to position the insertion point at the beginning of the document. On the right side of the **Home tab**, in the **Editing group**, click the **Replace** button. In the **Find and Replace** dialog box, in the **Find what** box, type **USPTO** and in the **Replace with** box, type **United States Patent and Trademark Office**

8. In the **Find and Replace** dialog box, click the **More** button, and then under **Search Options**, if necessary, select the **Match case** check box. Click **Find Next** to find the first instance of *USPTO*, and then click the **Replace** button. **Close** the dialog box.

9. In the fourth line of the document, double-click to select the word *already*, and then in the **Clipboard group**, click the **Cut** button. Move the pointer to the right of the next word in the sentence—*patented*—and then click the **Paste** button. In the next paragraph, beginning *The search process*, hold down Ctrl and click to select the last sentence, beginning *Patents are grouped*. In the **Clipboard group**, click the **Cut** button. Move the insertion point to the beginning of the same paragraph, and then click

(Project 6C–Patent Search continues on the next page)

Content-Based Assessments

(Project 6C–Patent Search continued)

the **Paste** button. Adjust spacing at the end of the pasted sentence as necessary.

10. In the fifth paragraph beginning *Examine the patent*, select the entire paragraph, including the paragraph mark. Drag the paragraph down to the beginning of the paragraph beginning *GHS Law Partners employs*. In the same paragraph, select *Examine* and replace it with **Study**

11. On the **Quick Access Toolbar**, click the **Undo** button to remove *Study* and replace it with *Examine*. Click the **Undo** button one more time to move the paragraph back to its original location, and then click the **Redo** button to move it back to its new location.

12. Near the top of **Page 2**, in the paragraph beginning *Appl. No.: 737838*, select the space before *2000*. Hold down Ctrl and ⇧ Shift, and then press Spacebar to add a nonbreaking space. Use the same procedure to add a nonbreaking space between *December* and *14* to keep the date together if the line is edited.

13. Press Ctrl + Home to move to the top of the document. Right-click the title, and then click **Paragraph**. Under **Spacing**, in the **After** box, click the **up spin arrow** two times to change the value in the box from *10 pt* to **18 pt**. Click the **Line spacing arrow**, and then click **Single**. Click **OK** to close the dialog box. In the title, click to the left of **Patent**, and then remove the space between *Partners* and *Patent*. Hold down ⇧ Shift and press Enter to enter a manual line break. **Save** your document.

14. In the middle of **Page 1**, point to the left of the paragraph beginning *Organize the*

search, and then drag down to select the next four lines, including the line beginning *Examine the patent*. On the **Home tab**, in the **Paragraph group**, click the **Numbering** button.

15. Below the numbered list, select the two paragraphs that begin *Reference section* and *Abstract*. In the **Paragraph group**, click the **Bullets** button. Use the same procedure to add bullets to the four paragraphs near the end of the document beginning *Field and background* and ending with *Inventor's description*.

16. On **Page 1**, below the second bulleted point, point to the left of the paragraph beginning *United States Patent*, and then drag down to select the text through the paragraph beginning *Appl. No.*—the line above the second part of the bulleted list. In the **Paragraph group**, click the **Increase Indent** button two times. **Save** your document.

17. From the **Office** menu, point to **Print**, and then click **Print Preview** to make a final check of your document. Check your *Chapter Assignment Sheet* or *Course Syllabus* or consult your instructor to determine if you are to submit your assignments on paper or electronically. To submit electronically, go to Step 19, and then follow the instructions provided by your instructor.

18. On the **Print Preview tab**, click the **Print** button, click **OK**, and then click **Close Print Preview**.

19. From the **Office** menu, click **Exit Word**, saving any changes if prompted to do so.

End **You have completed Project 6C**

Content-Based Assessments

Project 6D — Copyright Law

In this project, you will apply the skills you practiced from the Objectives in Project 6B.

Objectives: 4. *Insert and Format Headers and Footers;* **5.** *Insert Frequently Used Text;* **6.** *Insert and Format References.*

In the following Skills Review, you will edit a short research paper about the Digital Millennium Copyright Act. This paper was written by an intern at GHS Law Partners. Your completed document will look similar to Figure 6.56.

For Project 6D, you will need the following files:

New blank Word document
w06D_Copyright_Law

You will save your document as
6D_Copyright_Law_Firstname_Lastname

Figure 6.56

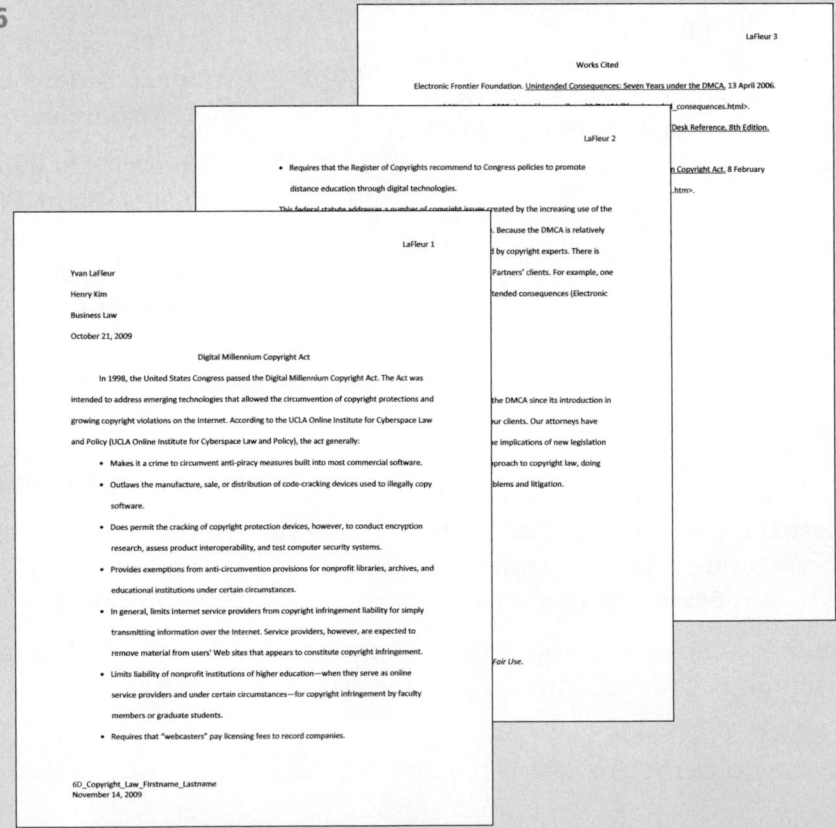

(Project 6D–Copyright Law continues on the next page)

Content-Based Assessments

(Project 6D–Copyright Law continued)

1. **Start** Word and be sure a new blank document is displayed. Display formatting marks, and display both the left and right page edges. Be sure the **Top**, **Bottom**, **Left**, and **Right** margins are set to **1** inch.

2. On the **Quick Access Toolbar**, click the **Save** button. In the **Save As** dialog box, navigate to your **Word Chapter 6** folder. Name your file **6D_Copyright_Law_Firstname_Lastname** and then click **Save**.

3. Type **Yvan LaFleur** and press Enter, and then type **Henry Kim** and press Enter. Type **Business Law** and press Enter, and then type **October 21, 2009** and press Enter. Click the **Home tab**, and then in the **Paragraph group**, click the **Center** button, type **Digital Millennium Copyright Act** and press Enter. Then, in the **Paragraph group**, click the **Align Text Left** button.

4. Click the **Insert tab**. In the **Header & Footer group**, click **Header**, and then click **Edit Header**. In the header area, type **LaFleur** and then press Spacebar. On the **Design tab**, in the **Insert group**, click the **Quick Parts** button, and then click **Field**. In the **Field** dialog box, under **Field names**, locate and click **Page**. Under **Field properties**, click the first page number style—**1, 2, 3**, and then click **OK**. Click the **Home tab**, and then in the **Paragraph group**, click the **Align Text Right** button.

5. Click the **Design tab**, and then in the **Navigation group**, click the **Go to Footer** button. In the **Insert group**, click the **Quick Parts** button, and then click **Field**. In the **Field** dialog box, under **Field names**, locate and click **FileName**, and then click **OK**. Press Enter to create a new line in the footer.

6. In the **Insert group**, click the **Date & Time** button. In the **Date and Time** dialog box, locate and click the date and time format that displays the date in a *November 14, 2009* format. Click **OK**. Recall that the date in your dialog box will vary. Double-click anywhere in the document to close the footer area. **Save** your changes.

7. Press Ctrl + End to move to the end of the document. Click the **Insert tab**. In the **Text group**, click the **Object button arrow**, and then click **Text from File**. Navigate to your student files, select **w06D_Copyright_Law**, and then click **Insert**. Press ←Bksp to remove the empty paragraph at the end of the document. Press Ctrl + A to select the entire document. On the **Home tab**, in the **Paragraph group**, click the **Line spacing** button, and then click **2.0**. Click the **Page Layout tab**, and then in the **Paragraph group**, click the **After down spin arrow** to set the space after to **0**. Click anywhere in the document to deselect the text.

8. From the **Office** menu, click **Word Options**. Click **Proofing**, and then under **AutoCorrect options**, click the **AutoCorrect Options** button. In the **AutoCorrect** dialog box, under **Replace**, type **intruzion** and under **With**, type **intrusion** and then click **OK** two times to close both dialog boxes.

9. Locate the last bulleted item near the end of the document, and then click to place the insertion point to the right of the space after *computer*. Watch the screen as you type **intruzion** and then press Spacebar to see the AutoCorrect feature work.

10. On **Page 1**, locate the bulleted item that begins *Limits liability*. In the first line,

(Project 6D–Copyright Law continues on the next page)

(Project 6D—Copyright Law continued)

select the two hyphens. On the **Insert tab**, in the **Symbols group**, click the **Symbol** button, and then click **More Symbols**. In the **Symbol** dialog box, click the **Special Characters tab**. Be sure the **Em Dash** is selected, and then click **Insert**. Repeat this procedure to replace the two hyphens in the second line of the same bulleted item with an em dash. Click **Close** to close the **Symbol** dialog box.

11. Scroll to view the middle of **Page 2**, locate the first bulleted item that begins *Jeopardizing*, and then position the insertion point following the last quotation mark. Click the **References tab**, and then in the **Footnotes group**, click the **Dialog Box Launcher**. In the **Footnote and Endnote** dialog box, under **Location**, be sure **Footnotes** is selected. Under **Format**, in the **Custom mark** box, type an asterisk (*) and then click **Insert**. Type **See GHS Law Partners internal memorandum** *The Changing Face of Fair Use.*

12. At the bottom of **Page 2**, right-click the footnote text, and then from the shortcut menu, click **Style**. In the **Style** dialog box, click **Modify**, change the **Font Size** to **11** and then click **OK**. **Close** the **Style** dialog box.

13. In the middle of **Page 2**, in the paragraph that begins *This federal statute*, at the end of the first sentence, click to place the insertion point before the period. Click the **References tab**. In the **Citations & Bibliography group**, be sure **MLA** style is selected, click the **Insert Citation** button, and then click **Add New Source**. Click the **Type of Source arrow**, and then click **Book**. Add the following book citation:

Author:	**Stim, Richard W.**
Title:	**Patent, Copyright & Trademark: An Intellectual Property Desk Reference, 8th Edition**

Year:	**2006**
City:	**Berkeley, CA**
Publisher:	**NOLO**

14. Click **OK** to insert the reference. If prompted to Update an existing reference, click Yes. Click to select the reference, click the **Citation Options arrow**, and then click **Edit Citation**. In the displayed **Edit Citation** dialog box, under **Add**, in the **Pages** box, type **227** and then click **OK** to insert the page number. **Save** your document.

15. Move to the top of the document. In the paragraph beginning *In 1998*, in the last line of the paragraph, place the insertion point after the word *Policy*, but before the comma. In the **Citations & Bibliography group**, click the **Insert Citation** button, and then click **Add New Source**. Click the **Type of Source arrow**, and then scroll down and select **Web site** from the list. Under **Bibliography Fields for MLA**, select the **Corporate Author** check box. Type the following information:

Corporate Author:	**UCLA Online Institute for Cyberspace Law and Policy**
Name of Web Page:	**The Digital Millennium Copyright Act**
Year:	**2001**
Month:	**February**
Day:	**8**
Year Accessed:	**2009**
Month Accessed:	**November**
Day Accessed:	**14**
URL:	**http://www.gseis.ucla.edu/iclp/dmca1.htm**

(Project 6D—Copyright Law continues on the next page)

(Project 6D–Copyright Law continued)

16. Click **OK** to insert the reference. If you are prompted to update an existing reference, click Yes.

17. Move to **Page 2** and locate the paragraph beginning *This federal statute*. At the end of the last sentence, after *unintended consequences*, place the insertion point before the comma. In the **Citations & Bibliography group**, click the **Insert Citation** button, and then click **Add New Source**. Under **Type of Source**, be sure **Web site** is selected. Under **Bibliography Fields for MLA**, select the **Corporate Author** check box. Type the following information:

Corporate Author:	Electronic Frontier Foundation
Name of Web Page:	Unintended Consequences: Seven Years under the DMCA
Year:	2006
Month:	April
Day:	13
Year Accessed:	2009
Month Accessed:	November
Day Accessed:	14
URL:	http://www.eff.org/IP/ DMCA/?f=unintended_ consequences.html

18. Click **OK** to insert the reference. If you are prompted to update an existing reference, click Yes.

19. **Save** your document. Hold down [Ctrl] and press [End] to move to the end of the document. Hold down [Ctrl] and press [Enter] to insert a manual page break. Type **Works Cited** and press [Enter]. On the **References tab**, in the **Citations & Bibliography**

group, be sure **MLA** displays in the **Style** box.

20. In the **Citations & Bibliography group**, click the **Bibliography** button, and then click **Insert Bibliography** to insert the citations you typed earlier. Select the three references, right-click the selected text, and then click **Paragraph**.

21. Under **Indentation**, click the **Special arrow**, and then click **Hanging**. Under **Spacing**, click the **Line spacing button arrow**, and then click **Double**. Under **Spacing**, in the **After** box, type **0** and then click **OK**.

22. Right-click the *Works Cited* title, and then click **Paragraph**. In the displayed **Paragraph** dialog box, under **General**, click the **Alignment arrow**, and then click **Centered**. Under **Indentation**, click the **Special arrow**, and then click **(none)**. Click **OK**.

23. From the **Office** menu, point to **Prepare**, and then click **Properties**. In the displayed **Document Information Panel**, in the **Author** box, type your name, and in the **Title** box, type **Digital Millennium Copyright Act** On the right side of the **Document Information Panel**, click the **Close** button.

24. From the **Office** menu, point to the **Print arrow**, and then click **Print Preview** to make a final check of your document. Check your *Chapter Assignment Sheet* or *Course Syllabus* or consult your instructor to determine if you are to submit your assignments on paper or electronically. To submit electronically, go to Step 26, and then follow the instructions provided by your instructor.

(Project 6D–Copyright Law continues on the next page)

Content-Based Assessments

(Project 6D–Copyright Law continued)

25. On the **Print Preview tab**, click the **Print** button, click **OK**, and then click **Close Print Preview**.

26. From the **Office** menu, click **Exit Word**, saving any changes if prompted to do so.

 End **You have completed Project 6D** _____

Content-Based Assessments

Mastering Word

Project 6E — New Services

In this project, you will apply the skills you practiced from the Objectives in Project 6A.

Objectives: 1. *Change Document and Paragraph Layout;* **2.** *Change and Reorganize Text;* **3.** *Create and Modify Lists.*

In the following Mastering Word project, you will edit a memo about law firm expansion from Rachel Glazer to the staff of GHS Law Partners. Your completed document will look similar to Figure 6.57.

For Project 6E, you will need the following files:

New blank Word document
w06E_New_Services

**You will save your document as
6E_New_Services_Firstname_Lastname**

Figure 6.57

TO:	GHS Law Partners Staff
FROM:	Rachel Glazer
DATE:	July 7, 2009
SUBJECT:	Service and Space Expansion

With the recent addition of three new attorneys to our firm, GHS Law Partners is in a position to begin adding to the array of services we offer our clients. Our new attorneys bring expertise in the following fields:

- Mandy Esposito specializes in privacy policies for business in general, and in terms of use and Web site audits for online businesses.
- Cliff Meyers is an acknowledged expert on digital rights management and has extensive experience litigating cases brought under the Digital Millennium Copyright Act.
- Julian Nguyen has helped clients file over 500 patents in the areas of bioinformatics and computer software for biological sciences.

Mandy will lead the firm's expansion of already existing services in domain name disputes, spam- and phishing-related fraud, and Web design agreements. In addition, she will work with existing clients to develop appropriate privacy policies and terms of use that protect both businesses and customers. The need for these services is growing, and it is expected that the firm's client base will expand through these offerings.

Cliff will serve our current and new clients that are involved in digital rights cases, including fair use and infringement issues. Cliff's practice is expected to include aspects of patent and trademark law, adding to our base of expertise in these areas as well as growing the digital rights clientele.

The fast-growing and extremely technical area of biotechnology and pharmaceutical patent law will become a much larger part of our practice under Julian's leadership. This area of practice incorporates copyrights, trademarks, patents, and trade secrets, and affects client products such as diagnostic tests, gene therapy, therapeutic proteins, bioinformatics, and computer programs.

This major expansion of our practice areas will also require expansion of our space. As this affects everyone, I will outline generally the major steps of our physical expansion:

1. We will take over the seventh floor of our current building for attorney and administrative office space.
2. We are negotiating for space in the 1440 Peachtree building next door.
3. Some offices and work areas in our current space will be redesigned for more efficiency to improve traffic flow.
4. Some of the attorneys and staff with scientific backgrounds who work with our biotechnology and pharmaceutical clients will work from the clients' laboratories and office space in order to more fully utilize their expertise.

These are big projects, but we are doing big things. All of the partners know that change and growth on this scale is difficult, but we believe in our firm and believe that working together we can continue to provide the highest quality services to our clients. We will continue to update you as our practice areas expand, and details on new and changing office space will be disseminated as soon as they are available.

Thank you for your continued dedication to the firm.

6E_New_Services_Firstname_Lastname

(Project 6E–New Services continues on the next page)

Content-Based Assessments

Mastering Word

(Project 6E–New Services continued)

1. **Start** Word and be sure a new blank document is displayed. Display formatting marks and the rulers, and be sure your screen displays both the left and right document edges. **Save** the document in your **Word Chapter 6** folder as **6E_New_Services_Firstname_Lastname** Open the document footer and add the file name to the footer.

2. As you type the following text, press ⌈Tab⌋ two times after *TO*, and *FROM*, and *DATE* and one time after *SUBJECT*. Press ⌈Enter⌋ one time after each line.

   TO: GHS Law Partners Staff

   FROM: Rachel Glazer

   DATE: July 7, 2009

   SUBJECT: Service and Space Expansion

3. In the blank line below the SUBJECT line, from your student files, insert the file **w06E_New_Services**. Delete the blank line at the end of the document. Select and single-space the inserted text. On the **Page Layout tab**, in the **Paragraph group**, change the spacing **After** to **0 pt**.

4. Near the top of the document, select the three paragraphs beginning *Mandy Esposito, Cliff Meyers,* and *Julian Nguyen.* Create a bulleted list from the selected paragraphs.

5. Near the bottom of **Page 1**, select the four paragraphs beginning *We will take over, We are negotiating, Some offices,* and *Some of the attorneys.* Create a numbered list from the selected paragraphs.

6. Move to the top of the document, and then display the **Find and Replace** dialog box. Click the **More** button and select the **Match case** and the **Find whole words only** check boxes. Replace all occurrences of **DMCA** with **Digital Millennium Copyright Act** and then clear the two check boxes you selected. **Close** the dialog box.

7. Near the middle of **Page 1**, in the paragraph beginning *The fast-growing,* use drag and drop to switch the words *pharmaceutical* and *biotechnology.*

8. Add **24-pt** spacing after the SUBJECT line.

9. Near the top of the document, locate and click in the paragraph beginning *With the recent addition,* and then add **6-pt** spacing after the paragraph. Use the **Format Painter** to apply the same formatting to all the other paragraphs in the document, *excluding* the four heading lines and the lists.

10. Add **6-pt** spacing after the last item in each list. Then, select all of the text in the document and change the **Font** to **Cambria**.

11. Near the bottom of the document, in the paragraph beginning *All of the partners,* cut the last sentence in the paragraph—beginning *These are big projects,* but not including the paragraph mark—and then move it to the beginning of the same paragraph. Adjust spacing if necessary.

12. **Save** your document. Preview the document and then print it, or submit it electronically as directed. **Close** the file, and then **Close** Word.

 You have completed Project 6E

Project 6F—Employee Agreement

In this project, you will apply the skills you practiced from the Objectives in Project 6B.

Objectives: 4. *Insert and Format Headers and Footers;* **5.** *Insert Frequently Used Text;* **6.** *Insert and Format References.*

In the following Mastering Word project, you will edit a report on employer/employee intellectual property ownership. Your completed document will look similar to Figure 6.58.

For Project 6F, you will need the following file:

w06F_Employee_Agreement

You will save your document as 6F_Employee_Agreement_Firstname_Lastname

Figure 6.58

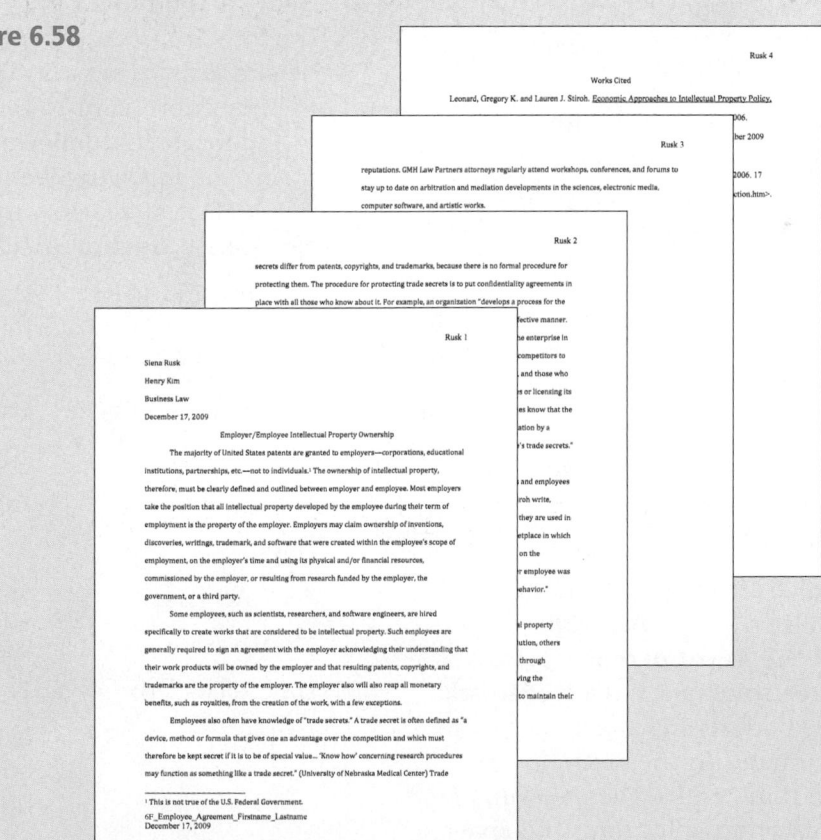

(Project 6F–Employee Agreement continues on the next page)

Content-Based Assessments

(Project 6F–Employee Agreement continued)

1. **Start** Word. Locate and open the file **w06F_Employee_Agreement**. Display formatting marks and rulers, and adjust the page width to display both the left and right page edges. Change all document margins to **1** inch.

2. Select the entire document and change the **Line spacing** to **2.0**, and the **Font Size** to **11**. **Save** your file in your **Word Chapter 6** folder as **6F_Employee_Agreement_Firstname_Lastname**

3. Move to the beginning of the document. Type the following, pressing Enter after each line:

   Siena Rusk
   Henry Kim
   Business Law
   December 17, 2009

4. Center the fifth line document title that begins *Employer/Employee*. Open the header area, type **Rusk** and then add a space and insert the **Page** field, using the **1, 2, 3** format. Right align the header text.

5. Open the footer area, and then add the **FileName** field. Press Enter, and then insert the current date field, using the *December 17, 2009* date format.

6. Select all of the document text except the first five lines. Indent the first line of each paragraph **0.5 inches**.

7. Open the **Word Options** dialog box, click **Proofing**, and then under **AutoCorrect options**, click the **AutoCorrect Options** button. **Replace tradmark With trademark** and then close both dialog boxes. Near the top of the document, in the sixth line of the paragraph that begins *The majority of*, position the insertion point after the space following *writings*, type **tradmark** and then

add a comma and a space to test the AutoCorrect entry.

8. In the first line of the same paragraph, select the two hyphens and use the **Symbol** dialog box to replace them with an **em dash**. Repeat this procedure in the second line of the same paragraph.

9. In the second line of the same paragraph, position the insertion point after the period following the word *individuals*. Insert a footnote with the text **This is not true of the U.S. Federal Government.** Right-click the footnote and display the **Style** dialog box. Modify the **Footnote Text** style **Font** to **Cambria**, and the **Font Size** to **11**.

10. Near the bottom of **Page 1**, at the end of the fourth line in the paragraph that begins *Employees also often have*, position the insertion point to the right of the quotation mark that follows *trade secret*. Insert the following **Web site** citation, using **MLA** style. Be sure to select the **Corporate Author** check box:

Corporate Author:	**University of Nebraska Medical Center**
Name of Web Page:	**Ethics Glossary**
Year:	**2004**
Month:	**February**
Day:	**3**
Year Accessed:	**2009**
Month Accessed:	**November**
Day Accessed:	**22**
URL:	**http://www.unmc. edu/ethics/words. html#T**

(Project 6F–Employee Agreement continues on the next page)

Content-Based Assessments

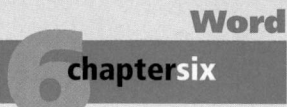
(Project 6F–Employee Agreement continued)

11. **Save** your document. At the end of the same paragraph, use the same procedure to add the following **Web site** citation:

Corporate Author: **World Intellectual Property Organization**

Name of Web Page: **How are Trade Secrets Protected?**

Year: **2006**

Month: **June**

Day: **25**

Year Accessed: **2009**

Month Accessed: **November**

Day Accessed: **17**

URL: **http://www.wipo.int/sme/en/ip_business/trade_secrets/protection.htm**

12. **Save** your document. At the end of the second-to-last paragraph of the document, beginning *Disputes regarding ownership*, position the insertion point at the end of the paragraph. Use the same procedure to add the following **Book** citation:

Author: **Leonard, Gregory K.; Stiroh, Lauren J.**

Title: **Economic Approaches to Intellectual Property Policy, Litigation, and Management**

Year: **2006**

City: **New York, NY**

Publisher: **NERA Economic Consulting**

13. Edit the citation and add the page numbers **106–7**

14. **Save** your document. Move to the end of the document and insert a manual page break. Type **Works Cited** and press Enter. Center the *Works Cited* title and remove the first line indent. Position the insertion point in the blank line below *Works Cited*.

15. On the **References tab**, click the **MLA** style, and then insert a **Bibliography**. Select the bibliography text. Display the **Paragraph** dialog box, double-space the selected text, and then apply a hanging indent.

16. **Save** your changes. Preview the document, and then print it, or submit it electronically as directed. **Close** the file, and then **Close** Word.

 End **You have completed Project 6F**

Word
chaptersix 6

Mastering Word

Project 6G — Disputes

In this project, you will apply the skills you practiced from the Objectives in Projects 6A and 6B.

Objectives: 1. *Change Document and Paragraph Layout;* **2.** *Change and Reorganize Text;* **3.** *Create and Modify Lists;* **4.** *Insert and Format Headers and Footers;* **5.** *Insert Frequently Used Text;* **6.** *Insert and Format References.*

In the following Mastering Word project, you will edit an internal document on domain name disputes for GHS Law Partners. Your completed document will look similar to Figure 6.59.

For Project 6G, you will need the following file:

w06G_Disputes

**You will save your document as
6G_Disputes_Firstname_Lastname**

Figure 6.59

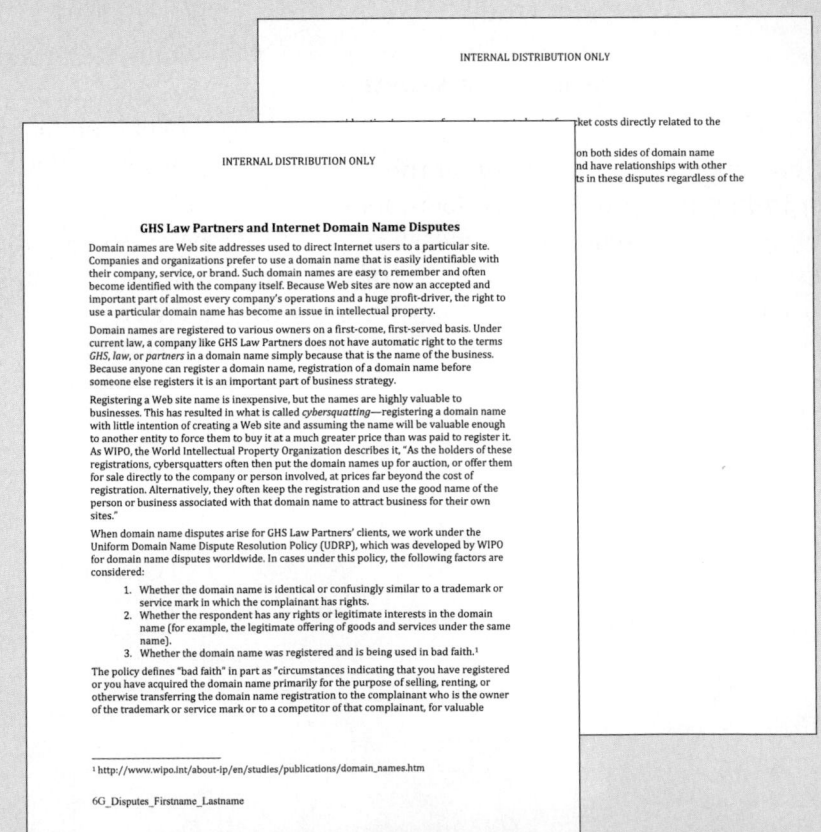

(Project 6G–Disputes continues on the next page)

Content-Based Assessments

(Project 6G–Disputes continued)

1. Locate and open the file **w06G_Disputes**. **Save** the file in your **Word Chapter 6** folder as **6G_Disputes_Firstname_Lastname** and then add the file name to the footer. Display formatting marks, and set the page width to a comfortable size for you.

2. Select the document title, increase the **Font Size** to **14** points, and add **Bold** emphasis. Select all of the text in the document, change the font to **Cambria**, change the line spacing to **1.0**, and then add **6 pt.** spacing after each paragraph.

3. Change the top margin to **1.5** inches and the other margins to **1** inch. Open the document header, type **INTERNAL DISTRIBUTION ONLY** and then **Center** the header. Change the header font to **Cambria**.

4. Near the top of the document, in the paragraph beginning *Because Web sites*, select the first sentence of the paragraph and move it to the end of the same paragraph.

5. In the paragraph that begins *Registering a Web site*, locate the two hyphens (--) after the word *cybersquatting*, and then replace the hyphens with an **em dash**.

6. **Save** your changes. Use the **Find and Replace** dialog box to locate the second occurrence of *World Intellectual Property Organization*, replace it with **WIPO** and then remove the word *the* preceding WIPO.

7. Near the bottom of **Page 1**, select the three paragraphs that begin with *Whether*. Change the selected paragraphs to a numbered list, and **Increase Indent** one time.

8. At the end of the third item in the list, after the period following *bad faith*, insert the following footnote:

http://www.wipo.int/about-ip/en/ studies/publications/domain_names.htm

9. At the bottom of **Page 1**, at the end of the paragraph beginning *The policy defines*, insert the following footnote:

http://www.icann.org/udrp/udrp-policy-24oct99.htm

10. Modify the **Footnote** style to use the **Cambria** font, and **11** point font size.

11. **Save** your changes. Preview the document, and then print it, or submit it electronically as directed. **Close** the file, and then **Close** Word.

 End **You have completed Project 6G**

Content-Based Assessments

Mastering Word

Project 6H — Trademarks

In this project, you will apply the skills you practiced from the Objectives in Projects 6A and 6B.

Objectives: 1. *Change Document and Paragraph Layout;* **2.** *Change and Reorganize Text;* **3.** *Create and Modify Lists;* **4.** *Insert and Format Headers and Footers;* **5.** *Insert Frequently Used Text;* **6.** *Insert and Format References.*

In the following Mastering Word project, you will edit a handout on trademarks and commercial identifiers prepared by GHS Law Partners. Your completed document will look similar to Figure 6.60.

For Project 6H, you will need the following files:

New blank Word document
w06H_Trademarks

**You will save your document as
6H_Trademarks_Firstname_Lastname**

Figure 6.60

(Project 6H–Trademarks continues on the next page)

Content-Based Assessments

Mastering Word

(Project 6H–Trademarks continued)

1. **Start** Word and be sure a new blank document is displayed. Display formatting marks and display both the left and right page edges. Change the top margin to **2** inches and the other margins to **1** inch.

2. Type **Trademarks and Commercial Identifiers** and press Enter. Select the title and increase the **Font Size** to **14 pt**, add **Bold** emphasis, and **Center** the title. **Save** the file in your **Word Chapter 6** folder as **6H_Trademarks_Firstname_Lastname** and then add the file name to the footer. With the footer open, insert a blank line under the **FileName** field, and then insert the **Date** field in the format *6/26/2009 5:15 PM*. Close the footer.

3. Place the insertion point in the blank line below the title. Locate and insert the file **w06H_Trademarks**. Remove the blank line at the end of the document. Select all of the text in the document—including the title—change the line spacing to **1.0**, and add **12 pt.** spacing after each paragraph.

4. Open the document header, type **GHS LAW PARTNERS** and then **Center** the header. Select the header text and change the font to **Arial Black**, **28 pt**.

5. Near the top of **Page 2**, at the end of the second line, position the insertion point after the word *generic*. Display the **Footnote and Endnote** dialog box, and then change the footnote mark from a number to an asterisk (*). Insert a footnote and type **If infringements or disputes arise, we**

handle all details from cease and desist letters (which often end the case) through litigation.

6. **Save** your changes and move to the beginning of the document. Use the **Find and Replace** dialog box to find the word **allow** and then replace it with **enable**

7. Near the top of the document, in the paragraph beginning *Trademarks, also known as*, delete the comma and space after *Trademarks* and insert an **em dash**. In the same line, after *marks*, delete the comma and space and insert an **em dash**.

8. Near the bottom of **Page 1**, select the four lines of trademarked names, beginning with *Xerox*. Change the selected paragraphs to a bulleted list, and increase the indent one time. With the bullets still selected, right-click any of the list items, display the **Define New Bullet** dialog box, and then change the bullet type to a trademark symbol (TM).

9. Near the top of **Page 1**, select the three lines beginning with *Entering the mark* and ending with *Using the mark*. Change the selected paragraphs to a bulleted list using black dots for bullets, and increase the indent one time.

10. In the bottom bulleted list, select the fourth bullet point—*Jacuzzi*—and move it up so it becomes the first bullet point.

11. **Save** your changes. Preview the document, and then print it, or submit it electronically as directed. **Close** the file, and then **Close** Word.

 You have completed Project 6H

Word

chaptersix

Mastering Word

Project 6I — Fair Use

In this project, you will apply the skills you practiced from all the Objectives in Projects 6A and 6B.

Objectives: 1. *Change Document and Paragraph Layout;* **2.** *Change and Reorganize Text;* **3.** *Create and Modify Lists;* **4.** *Insert and Format Headers and Footers;* **5.** *Insert Frequently Used Text;* **6.** *Insert and Format References.*

In the following Mastering Word project, you will edit a report on fair use of copyrighted material, created by summer intern Clara Madison for GHS Law Partners. Your completed document will look similar to Figure 6.61.

For Project 6I, you will need the following files:

New blank Word document
w06I_Fair_Use

You will save your document as 6I_Fair_Use_Firstname_Lastname

Figure 6.61

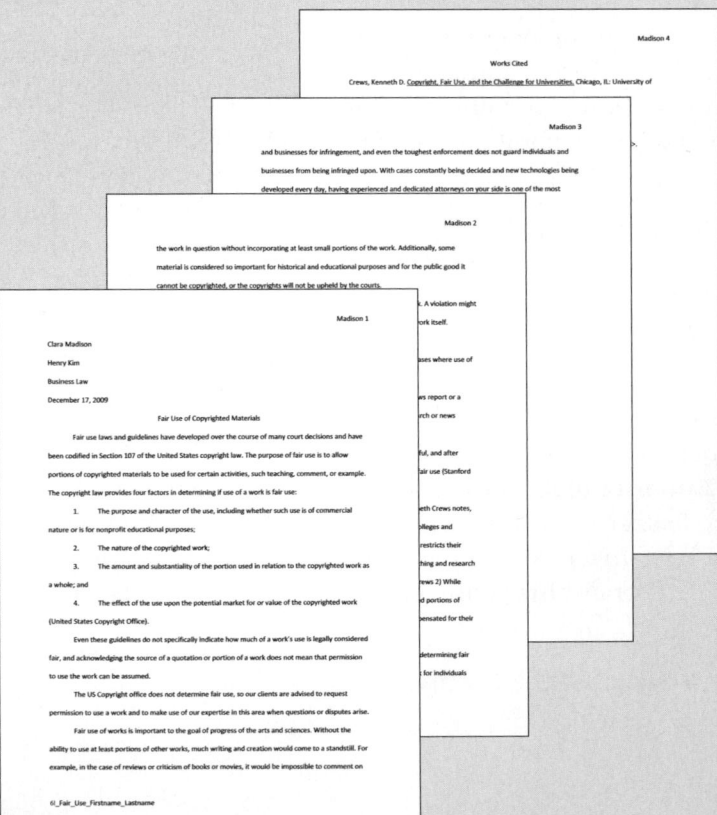

(Project 6I–Fair Use continues on the next page)

Content-Based Assessments

(Project 6I–Fair Use continued)

1. **Start** Word and be sure a new blank document is displayed. Display formatting marks and the rulers, and display the left and right document edges. If necessary, change all document margins to **1** inch. **Save** the document as **6I_Fair_Use_ Firstname_Lastname** Open the document footer and add the file name to the footer.

2. Move to the document header. In the header area, type **Madison** and then add a space and the page number, using the **1, 2, 3** format. Right align the header text.

3. Move to the beginning of the document. Type the following, pressing Enter after each line:

   **Clara Madison
   Henry Kim
   Business Law
   December 17, 2009
   Fair Use of Copyrighted Materials**

4. Center the last paragraph you typed—*Fair Use of Copyrighted Materials*. In the blank line below the centered title, insert the **w06I_Fair_Use** file. Delete the blank line at the end of the document. Select all of the document text. Set the **Line Spacing** to **2**, and the space **After** to **0**.

5. Select the inserted text, but not the five lines at the beginning of the document that you typed. Open the **Paragraph** dialog box, add a **0.5** inch first line indent.

6. Near the top of **Page 1**, select the four paragraphs, starting with the paragraph beginning *The purpose and character*. Create a numbered list from the selected paragraphs. Decrease the indent of the numbered list until it is aligned with the left margin of the document. Display the **Paragraph** dialog box, and set the **Special** indentation to **First line**. Set the **First line** indent to **0.5** inches.

7. Near the middle of **Page 2**, select the two paragraphs starting with the paragraph beginning *You use a very small excerpt*. Create a bulleted list from the selected paragraphs. Decrease the indent of the bulleted list until it is aligned with the left margin of the document. Modify the paragraph formatting using the procedure in Step 6.

8. Move to the end of the document. In the second-to-last paragraph, beginning with *Laws governing*, locate and select the three periods between *availability* and *many*. Display the **Symbol** dialog box, and from the **Special Characters tab**, insert an **Ellipsis** (…).

9. In the last paragraph of the document, move the first sentence—beginning with *With cases constantly*—to the end of the paragraph.

10. Display the **Find and Replace** dialog box, use it to replace **make the determinations into** with **determine** and then **Save** your document.

11. Near the top of **Page 1**, in the fourth item in the numbered list, position the insertion point to the left of the period. Insert the following **Web site** citation, using **MLA** style. Be sure to select the **Corporate Author** check box:

Corporate Author:	**United States Copyright Office**
Name of Web Page:	**Fair Use**
Year:	**2006**
Month:	**January**
Day:	**31**
Year Accessed:	**2009**
Month Accessed:	**June**
Day Accessed:	**6**
URL:	**http://www.copyright. gov/fls/fl102.html**

(Project 6I–Fair Use continues on the next page)

Content-Based Assessments

(Project 6I–Fair Use continued)

12. **Save** your document. On **Page 2**, at the end of the second bullet point, use the same procedure to add the following **Web site** citation:

Corporate Author: **Stanford University**

Name of Web Page: **Copyright & Fair Use**

Year: **2004**

Year Accessed: **2009**

Month Accessed: **June**

Day Accessed: **8**

URL: **http://fairuse. stanford.edu/Copyright_ and_Fair_Use_Overview/ chapter9/9-d. html**

13. **Save** your document. At the end of the second-to-last paragraph of the document, locate the long quotation, which begins *"Copyright is among,"* and position the insertion point to the right of the second quotation mark. Add the following **Book** citation:

Author: **Crews, Kenneth D.**

Title: **Copyright, Fair Use, and the Challenge for Universities**

Year: **1993**

City: **Chicago, IL**

Publisher: **University of Chicago Press**

14. Add the page number **2** to the citation.

15. **Save** your document. Move to the end of the document and insert a manual page break. Type **Works Cited** and press Enter. **Center** the *Works Cited* title and remove the first line indent. Position the insertion point in the blank line below *Works Cited*.

16. On the **References tab**, click the **MLA** style, and then insert a **Bibliography**. Select the bibliography field, and then display the **Paragraph** dialog box. Double-space the selected text, and then add a hanging indent.

17. **Save** your changes. Preview the document, and then print it, or submit it electronically as directed. **Close** the file, and then **Close** Word.

 End **You have completed Project 6I**

Content-Based Assessments

Project 6J — Business Running Case

In this project, you will apply the skills you practiced in Projects 6A and 6B.

Close Word and any other open windows. Display the Start menu, click Computer, and then navigate to the student files that accompany this textbook. In the folder **03_business_running_case**, locate and open the folder for this chapter. Open and print the instructions for this project, which are provided to you in Adobe PDF format. Follow the instructions and use the skills you have gained thus far to assist Jennifer Nelson in meeting the challenges of owning and running her business.

End You have completed Project 6J ——————————

Content-Based Assessments

Mastering Word

Project 6K — *GO!* Fix It

In this project, you will construct a solution by applying any combination of the skills you practiced from the Objectives in Projects 6A and 6B.

For Project 6K, you will need the following file:

w06K_fixit_Garageman

**You will save your document as
6K_Garageman_Firstname_Lastname**

From the student files that accompany this textbook, open the folder **05_go_fix_it**. Locate and open the file **w06_fixit_Garageman**, and then save it in your chapter folder as **6K_Garageman_Firstname_Lastname**

This short research paper, which was written for GHS Law Partners by their intern, Yvan LeFleur, contains errors that you must find and correct. Read and examine the document, and then edit to correct the errors that you find. Types of errors may include:

- Spelling, grammar, punctuation, and usage errors such as text case, repeated text, subject-verb agreement, and meaning.
- Content errors such as missing or incorrect data, text, pictures, hyperlinks, or other objects.
- Font formatting and positioning errors such as font used, style, size, color, underline style, effects, font character spacing, text effects, special characters, and styles.
- Paragraph formatting and positioning errors such as indents and spacing, tabs, line and page breaks, wordwrap, sentence spacing, missing text or unnecessary text or blank lines, or errors in footnotes or endnotes or references.
- Page setup errors such as margins, orientation, layout, or alignment.

Things you should know to complete this project:

- The research paper should conform to the MLA formatting style that was covered in Project 6A.
- The AutoFormat feature in Word may cause paragraph indents to shift position when lists are reformatted. An easy way to correct this problem is to select the text and then drag the indent marker(s) on the ruler to the correct position.
- Numbered lists are used in this project, instead of bulleted lists, to allow easier identification of individual items.
- There are no errors in the citation on the reference page.

Save the changes you have made, add the file name to the footer, and then submit it as directed.

End **You have completed Project 6K**

Outcomes-Based Assessments

Rubric

The following outcomes-based assessments are *open-ended assessments*. That is, there is no specific correct result; your result will depend on your approach to the information provided. Make *Professional Quality* your goal. Use the following scoring rubric to guide you in *how* to approach the problem and then to evaluate *how well* your approach solves the problem.

The *criteria*—Software Mastery, Content, Format and Layout, and Process—represent the knowledge and skills you have gained that you can apply to solving the problem. The *levels of performance*—Professional Quality, Approaching Professional Quality, or Needs Quality Improvements—help you and your instructor evaluate your result.

	Your completed project is of Professional Quality if you:	Your completed project is Approaching Professional Quality if you:	Your completed project Needs Quality Improvements if you:
1-Software Mastery	Choose and apply the most appropriate skills, tools, and features and identify efficient methods to solve the problem.	Choose and apply some appropriate skills, tools, and features, but not in the most efficient manner.	Choose inappropriate skills, tools, or features, or are inefficient in solving the problem.
2-Content	Construct a solution that is clear and well organized, contains content that is accurate, appropriate to the audience and purpose, and is complete. Provide a solution that contains no errors of spelling, grammar, or style.	Construct a solution in which some components are unclear, poorly organized, inconsistent, or incomplete. Misjudge the needs of the audience. Have some errors in spelling, grammar, or style, but the errors do not detract from comprehension.	Construct a solution that is unclear, incomplete, or poorly organized, containing some inaccurate or inappropriate content; and contains many errors of spelling, grammar, or style. Do not solve the problem.
3-Format and Layout	Format and arrange all elements to communicate information and ideas, clarify function, illustrate relationships, and indicate relative importance.	Apply appropriate format and layout features to some elements, but not others. Overuse features, causing minor distraction.	Apply format and layout that does not communicate information or ideas clearly. Do not use format and layout features to clarify function, illustrate relationships, or indicate relative importance. Use available features excessively, causing distraction.
4-Process	Use an organized approach that integrates planning, development, self-assessment, revision, and reflection.	Demonstrate an organized approach in some areas, but not others; or, use an insufficient process of organization throughout.	Do not use an organized approach to solve the problem.

Outcomes-Based Assessments

Word

Problem Solving

Project 6L — Seminar

In this project, you will construct a solution by applying any combination of the skills you practiced from the Objectives in Projects 6A and 6B.

For Project 6L, you will need the following file:

New blank Word document

**You will save your document as
6L_Seminar_Firstname_Lastname**

College students are often asked to write research papers and presentations that involve information gathered from many sources. GHS Law Partners has been asked by the local college to conduct a seminar for faculty members that covers the topic of how students use the intellectual property of others. In this Problem Solving project, you will create a one-page document that outlines the topic.

Your document should consist of an introduction to the law firm and the topic, followed by a list of definitions of terms, including—but not limited to—*intellectual property*, *copyright*, *fair use*, and *plagiarism*. Add a footnote indicating your source for the definitions. Then, add a list of the topics to be covered in the order in which they will be presented. You might include topics such as quotations, downloaded pictures from the Web, and how to cite sources. Add a title to the document, and format the text appropriately. You may want to do some research on the Web or in your school library on such topics as copyrights, plagiarism, and citing sources to develop your topics.

Add the file name to the footer. Check your document for spelling and grammar errors. Save the document as **6L_Seminar_Firstname_Lastname** and submit it as directed.

 You have completed Project 6L —————————————

Outcomes-Based Assessments

Problem Solving

Project 6M — Evaluation

In this project, you will construct a solution by applying any combination of the skills you practiced from the Objectives in Projects 6A and 6B.

> **For Project 6M, you will need the following file:**
>
> New blank Word document

You will save your document as
6M_Evaluation_Firstname_Lastname

In this project, you will write a letter that summarizes the categories and the criteria to be used in a job performance evaluation for summer interns. The letter should be addressed to Andrea Smith, 1884 Bullpen Dr., Black River, GA 30366, and should be from Michael Scott, the Office Manager of the law firm, GHS Law Partners.

Be sure to

- Use the letter style you practiced in Chapter 1.

- Research the topic in your library or on the Web. There are many sites that discuss the types of criteria used when rating employee performance. (Hint: Search for *employee evaluation* or *job evaluation.*)

- Divide the criteria into two or three categories. Introduce the categories, and then add a short list of criteria under each category.

- Use at least one special bullet symbol for a list.

Add the file name to the footer. Check the letter for spelling and grammar errors. Save the document as **6M_Evaluation_Firstname_Lastname** and submit it as directed.

End **You have completed Project 6M**

Word

Problem Solving

chaptersix

Project 6N—Trademarks

In this project, you will construct a solution by applying any combination of the skills you practiced from the Objectives in Projects 6A and 6B.

> ### For Project 6N, you will need the following file:
>
> New blank Word document

**You will save your document as
6N_Trademarks_Firstname_Lastname**

When a company has a very recognizable name that is used for a product, they often get protection for that name from the U.S. Patent and Trademark Office. Microsoft, for example, has a long list of trademarks, logos, and trade names, including Microsoft Windows® and MapVision™. To view the list, use a Web browser and go to *www.microsoft.com*. At the bottom of the Microsoft home page, click **Trademarks**. Notice that some of the items use the Registered® symbol, and some use the Trademark™ symbol.

Write a 400–600 word research paper (about two pages long) that identifies the similarities and differences between items that are identified as *registered* and those identified as *trademarked*. Your paper should follow MLA style guidelines, or other style guidelines as directed by your instructor. Use at least two references, and include a Works Cited page. Detailed information about writing in the MLA style can be found in your college library and also online. Include at least one list, two symbols, and one informational endnote or footnote. Save the research paper as **6N_Trademarks_Firstname_Lastname** and then create a footer that contains the file name. Submit the document as directed.

End You have completed Project 6N ———————————

Outcomes-Based Assessments

Problem Solving

Project 6O — Calendar

In this project, you will construct a solution by applying any combination of the skills you practiced from the Objectives in Projects 6A and 6B.

For Project 6O, you will need the following file:

New blank Word document

You will save your document as
6O_Calendar_Firstname_Lastname

Create a memo that contains a MEMO heading from you to the employees of GHS Law Partners listing the scheduled holidays and breaks during the upcoming calendar year. Include a date and subject header. Use the memo style you practiced in Chapter 1.

Write one or two introductory sentences indicating that this is the list of holiday and conference dates that were proposed by the GHS Personnel Committee, and agreed to by the law firm's senior partners. Consult a calendar and create a list of official holiday names and dates for next year that will be easy for the reader to scan. Add two one-week business law conferences that will be hosted by the law firm. Save the memo as **6O_Calendar_Firstname_Lastname** and then create a footer that contains the file name. Submit the document as directed.

 End **You have completed Project 6O** ———————————

Outcomes-Based Assessments

Word

chaptersix

Problem Solving

Project 6P — APA Research Paper

In this project, you will construct a solution by applying any combination of the skills you practiced from the Objectives in Projects 6A and 6B.

> **For Project 6P, you will need the following files:**
>
> w06P_APA_Research_Paper
> 6B_Law_Overview_Firstname_Lastname
>
> **You will save your document as**
> **6P_APA_Research_Paper_Firstname_Lastname**

In Project 6B, you edited a research paper and formatted it in the Modern Language Association (MLA) style. The other major style guide used for research papers is published by the American Psychological Association (APA). APA guidelines differ in several ways; for example, formats for margins, titles, headers, and references differ from the MLA style.

This research paper should conform to APA style. Information on the APA style is available on the Web in many places—search for *APA research paper guidelines* to find sites that provide assistance using the APA style. There are *two approaches* you can use to complete this project:

1. Open the **w06P_APA_Research_Paper** file, save the file as **6P_APA_Research_Paper_Firstname_Lastname** and follow the steps in Project 6B, formatting the text in APA format instead of MLA format.

OR

2. Open your **6B_Law_Overview_Firstname_Lastname** file from your Word Chapter 6 folder, save the file as **6P_APA_Research_Paper_Firstname_Lastname** and change the formatting to conform to APA guidelines.

Add the file name to the footer, and submit the document as directed.

 End **You have completed Project 6P** ⎯⎯⎯⎯⎯⎯

Outcomes-Based Assessments

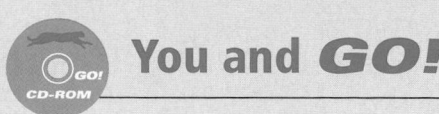
chaptersix

You and GO!

Project 6Q — You and *GO!*

In this project, you will construct a solution by applying any combination of the skills you practiced from the Objectives in Projects 6A and 6B.

Close Word and any other open windows. Display the Start menu, click Computer, and then navigate to the student files that accompany this textbook. In the folder **04_you_and_go**, locate and open the folder for this chapter. Open and print the instructions for this project, which are provided to you in Adobe PDF format. Follow the instructions to create a flyer for a family reunion.

 You have completed Project 6Q ——————————

GO! with Help

Project 6R — *GO!* with Help

When you insert a file name in a footer, or insert the date or time in a footer or in a document, you are adding a field to that document. Fields have other uses in Microsoft Word, including calculations, indexes, and reference lists. In this project, you will explore inserting and editing fields.

1 **Start** Word. Click the **Microsoft Office Word Help** button.

2 Click the **Search arrow**, and then click **All Word**. In the **Type words to search for** box, type **field** and then click **Search**.

3 In the **Word Help** window, from the **Results** list, click **Insert and format field codes in Word**. Read the introduction, and then click the links to learn more about fields, how to insert a field, and how to edit a field.

4 If you want to print a copy of the information, click the **Print** button at the top of the **Word Help** window.

5 **Close** the Help window, and then **Close** Word.

 You have completed Project 6R ——————————

Outcomes-Based Assessments

Group Business Running Case

Project 6S — Group Business Running Case

In this project, you will apply the skills you practiced from all the Objectives in Projects 6A and 6B.

Your instructor may assign this group case project to your class. If your instructor assigns this project, he or she will provide you with information and instructions to work as part of a group. The group will apply the skills gained thus far to help the Bell Orchid Hotel Group achieve its business goals.

 End **You have completed Project 6S** —————————

7 chapterseven

Using Graphics and Tables

OBJECTIVES

At the end of this chapter you will be able to:

1. Insert and Format Graphics
2. Set Tab Stops
3. Insert and Modify Text Boxes and Shapes

4. Create a Table
5. Format a Table

OUTCOMES

Mastering these objectives will enable you to:

PROJECT 7A
Insert and Modify Graphics and Set Tab Stops

PROJECT 7B
Create and Format a Table

Memories Old and New

Professional and amateur artists, photographers, students, teachers, and hobbyists have made Memories Old and New one of Chicago's fastest-growing art, photography, and scrapbooking supply stores. The store carries a wide variety of premium art supplies, such as paints, pencils, cutting and framing tools, and brushes. Local photographers are featured in the small gallery, and photo restoration services and supplies are offered. For scrapbookers, the store provides the newest and highest quality books, papers, stencils, and archival supplies. Scrapbooking classes are also offered to assist customers in adding principles of art and design to their projects.

Using Graphics and Tables

Adding graphics enhances the effectiveness of documents. Digital images, such as those obtained from a digital camera or a scanner, can be inserted into documents. You can also create your own graphic objects by using the Drawing tools.

Tab stops are useful to horizontally align text and numbers. Use the Tab key to move text to specific tab stop locations on a line. You can set and specify the alignment of your own tab locations.

Tables present data effectively and efficiently. The row and column format of a table makes information easy to find and easy to read. A table also helps the reader organize and categorize the data. The Word table feature has tools that enable you to format text, change column width and row height, and change the background for all or part of a table. You can also modify the table's borders and lines.

Project 7A **Photography Flyer**

In Activities 7.01 through 7.14, you will create a flyer for an upcoming exhibition of photographs by photographer Annie DeCesare at Memories Old and New. Your completed document will look similar to Figure 7.1.

For Project 7A, you will need the following files:

New blank Word document
w07A_Photography_Flyer
w07A_Machine
w07A_Ore_Cart

You will save your document as
7A_Photography_Flyer_Firstname_Lastname

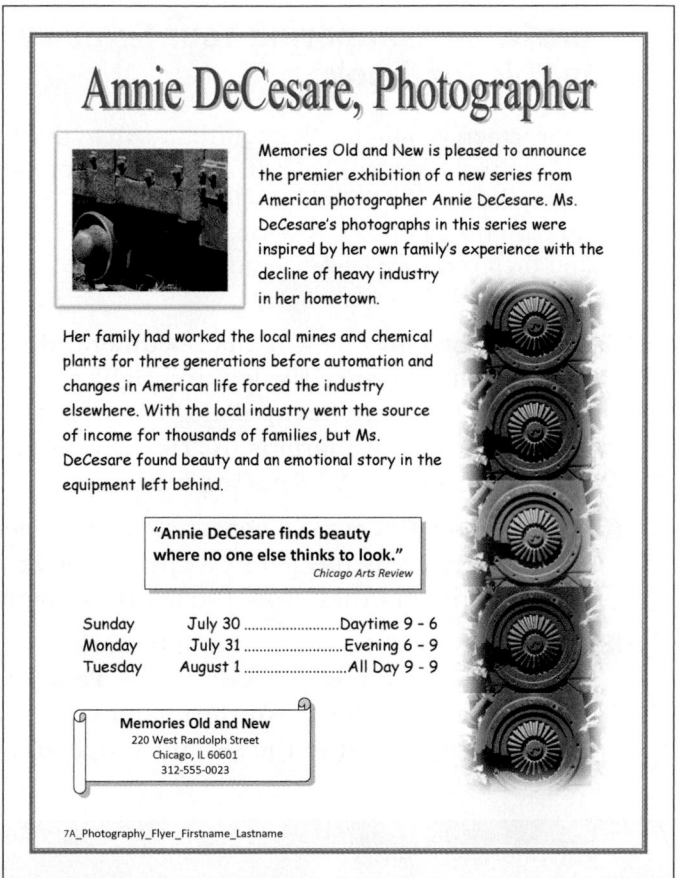

Figure 7.1
Project 7A—Photography Flyer

Objective 1
Insert and Format Graphics

Graphics include pictures, clip art, charts, and *drawing objects*—shapes, diagrams, lines, and so on. You can modify drawing objects by changing their color, pattern, border, and other characteristics.

Graphics that you insert in a document convey information in a way that plain text cannot. For additional visual interest, you can convert text to an attractive graphic format; add, resize, move and format pictures; and provide an attractive finishing touch to your document by adding a page border.

Activity 7.01 Formatting Text Using WordArt

You can insert decorative text with the *WordArt* command, and then edit and format the decorative text. WordArt is a gallery of text styles with which you can create decorative effects, such as shadowed or mirrored text.

> ## Note — Comparing Your Screen With the Figures in This Textbook
>
> Your screen will match the figures shown in this textbook if you set your screen resolution to 1024 x 768. At other resolutions, your screen will closely resemble, but not match, the figures shown. To view your screen's resolution, on the Windows desktop, right-click in a blank area, click Personalize and then click Display Settings.

1 **Start** Word. In a new blank document, display formatting marks and rulers, and be sure the left and right edges of the document display. Display the **Page Setup** dialog box, and then set the **Top**, **Bottom**, **Left**, and **Right** margins to **.75"**. On the **Home tab,** in the **Styles group**, click the **No Spacing** button.

2 Type **Annie DeCesare, Photographer** and then press Enter. Notice that the last name is flagged as a spelling error. Right-click the name *DeCesare*, and then from the shortcut menu, click **Ignore All**.

3 Without selecting the paragraph mark at the end, select the first line of text. Click the **Insert tab**. In the **Text group**, click the **WordArt** button to display the WordArt gallery, as shown in Figure 7.2. In the second row, point to the second shape and notice the ScreenTip *WordArt style 8*.

Figure 7.2

WordArt button ———

WordArt style 8 ———

Selected text ———

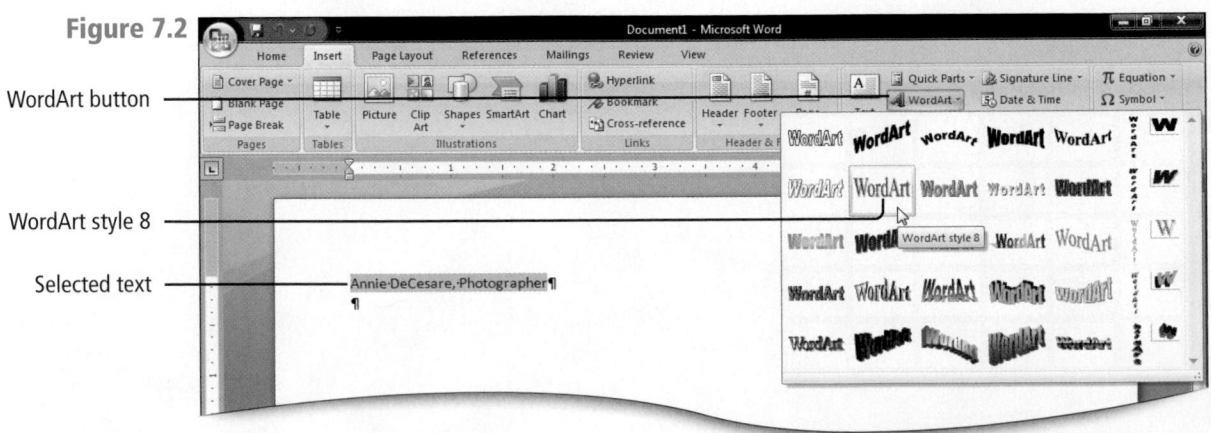

4 From the **WordArt gallery**, click **WordArt style 8**, and then compare your screen with Figure 7.3.

The Edit WordArt Text dialog box displays, and the selected text displays in the Text box. The default font size is 36 point.

Figure 7.3

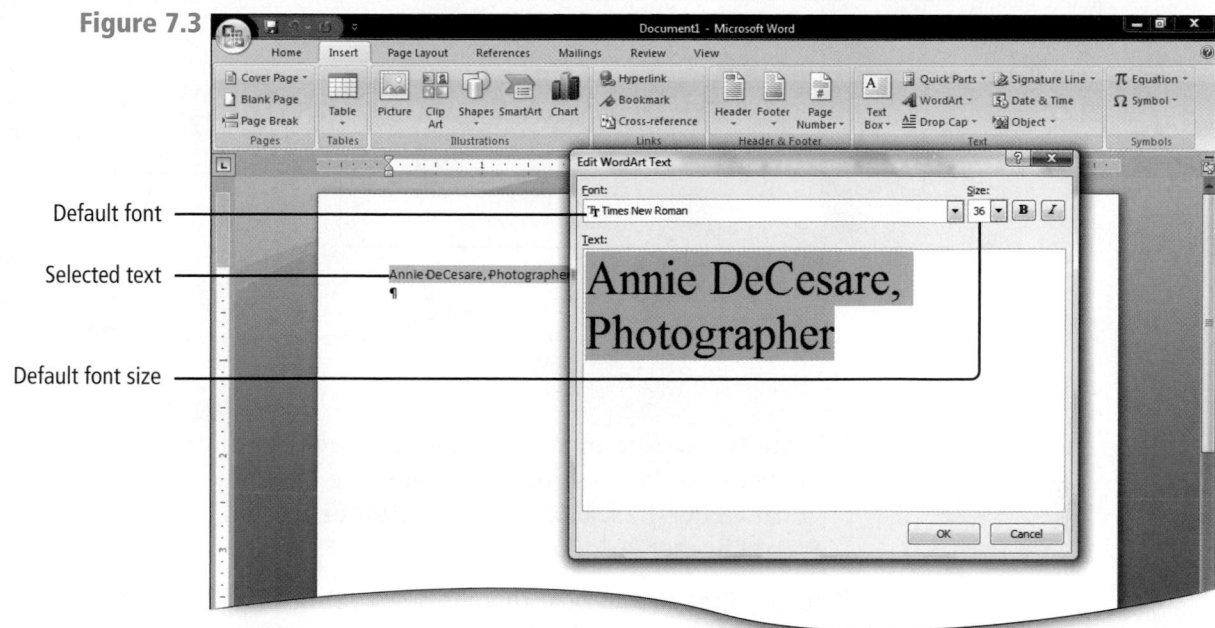

Default font

Selected text

Default font size

5 At the bottom of the **Edit WordArt Text** dialog box, click **OK**.

The WordArt contextual tools display on the Ribbon. A WordArt is a type of drawing object, and thus it displays *sizing handles*—small dark boxes with which you can manually change the size of the WordArt.

6 On the **Format tab**, in the **Size group**, click the **Shape Height button up spin arrow** as necessary to change the height of the WordArt to **0.7"**. Click the **Shape Width button up spin arrow** as necessary to change the width of the WordArt to **6.5"**.

7 In the **Arrange group**, click the **Position** button, and then under **With Text Wrapping**, in the top row of the gallery, point to the second button to display the ScreenTip *Position in Top Center with Square Text Wrapping*, and then click the button. Compare your screen with Figure 7.4.

The WordArt is centered between the left and right margins, and positioned at the top of the document. The *anchor* symbol indicates the paragraph to which the WordArt is attached and the corner sizing handles change to circles. Additionally, a *rotate handle* to rotate the WordArt and an *adjustment handle* to drag parts of the object into various positions display.

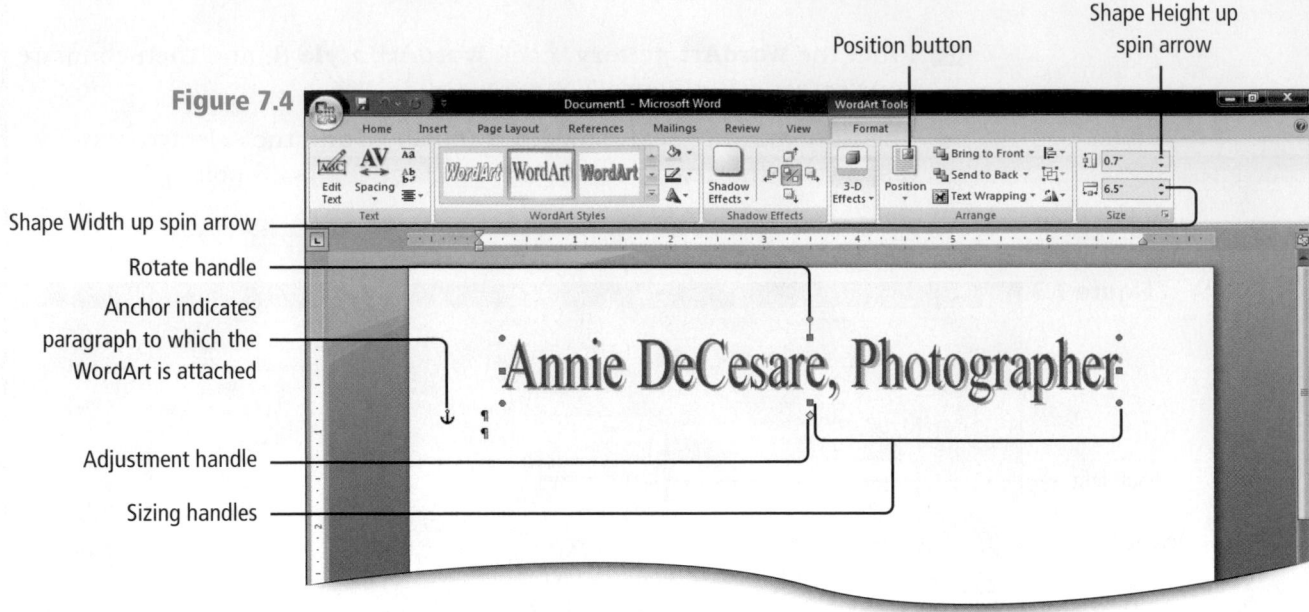

Figure 7.4

Shape Height up spin arrow

Position button

Shape Width up spin arrow

Rotate handle

Anchor indicates paragraph to which the WordArt is attached

Adjustment handle

Sizing handles

Annie DeCesare, Photographer

---

8 From the **Office** menu, display the **Save As** dialog box, and then navigate to the location where you are saving your files. Near the top of the dialog box, click the **New Folder** button. Name the new folder **Word Chapter 7** and then click **OK**.

9 In the **File name** box, delete the existing text. Using your own name, type **7A_Photography_Flyer_Firstname_Lastname** and then click **Save**.

Activity 7.02 Inserting Pictures from Files

1 Press Ctrl + End to move to the last line of the document and deselect the WordArt title. Click the **Insert tab**. In the **Text group**, click the **Object button arrow**, and then click **Text from File**. Locate and **Insert** the file **w07A_Photography_Flyer**. Delete the blank line at the end of the document.

2 If necessary, right-click any words flagged with wavy underlines and ignore all suggested corrections.

3 In the paragraph beginning *Memories Old and New*, click to position the insertion point at the beginning of the paragraph. On the **Insert tab**, in the **Illustrations group**, click the **Picture** button. From your student data files, **Insert** the file **w07A_Ore_Cart**. Compare your screen with Figure 7.5.

The Picture contextual tools display on the Ribbon. The Picture command places the picture in the document as an *inline object*; that is, the picture is positioned directly in the text at the insertion point, just like a character in a sentence.

Sizing handles display around the edges of the picture; recall that sizing handles enable you to manually resize a graphic. The corner sizing handles are round and resize the graphic proportionally. The square sizing handles in the center of each border are used to

---

resize a graphic vertically or horizontally only, which will distort the graphic. A rotate handle, with which you can rotate the graphic to any angle, displays above the top center sizing handle.

4 **Save** 📄 your document.

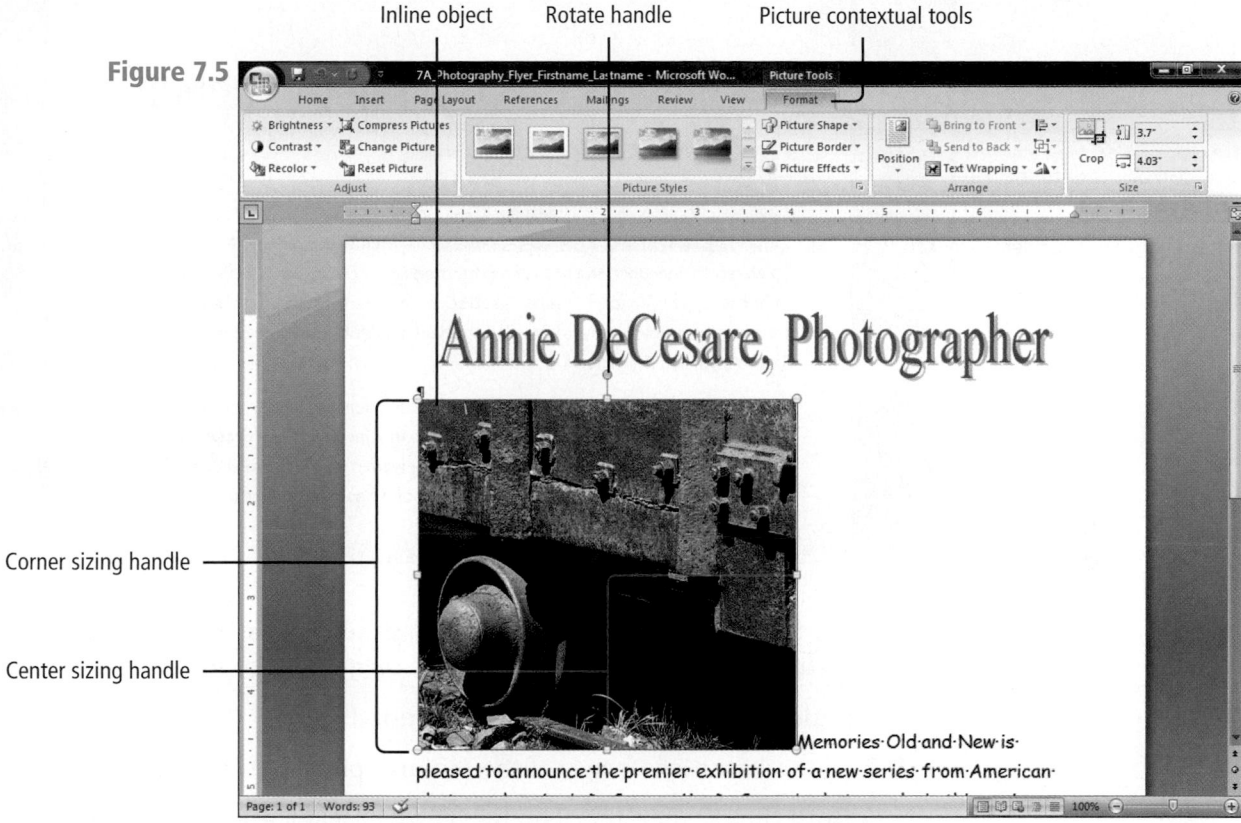

Figure 7.5

Inline object   Rotate handle   Picture contextual tools

Corner sizing handle ——

Center sizing handle ——

Activity 7.03 Resizing a Graphic

In this activity, you will adjust the size of the picture.

1 If necessary, click to select the ore cart picture.

2 On the lower edge of the picture, point to the center square sizing handle until the 🔼 pointer displays. Drag upward until the bottom of the graphic is aligned at approximately **2 inches on the vertical ruler**. Notice that the height of the graphic has been resized, but the width remains unchanged, as shown in Figure 7.6.

Figure 7.6

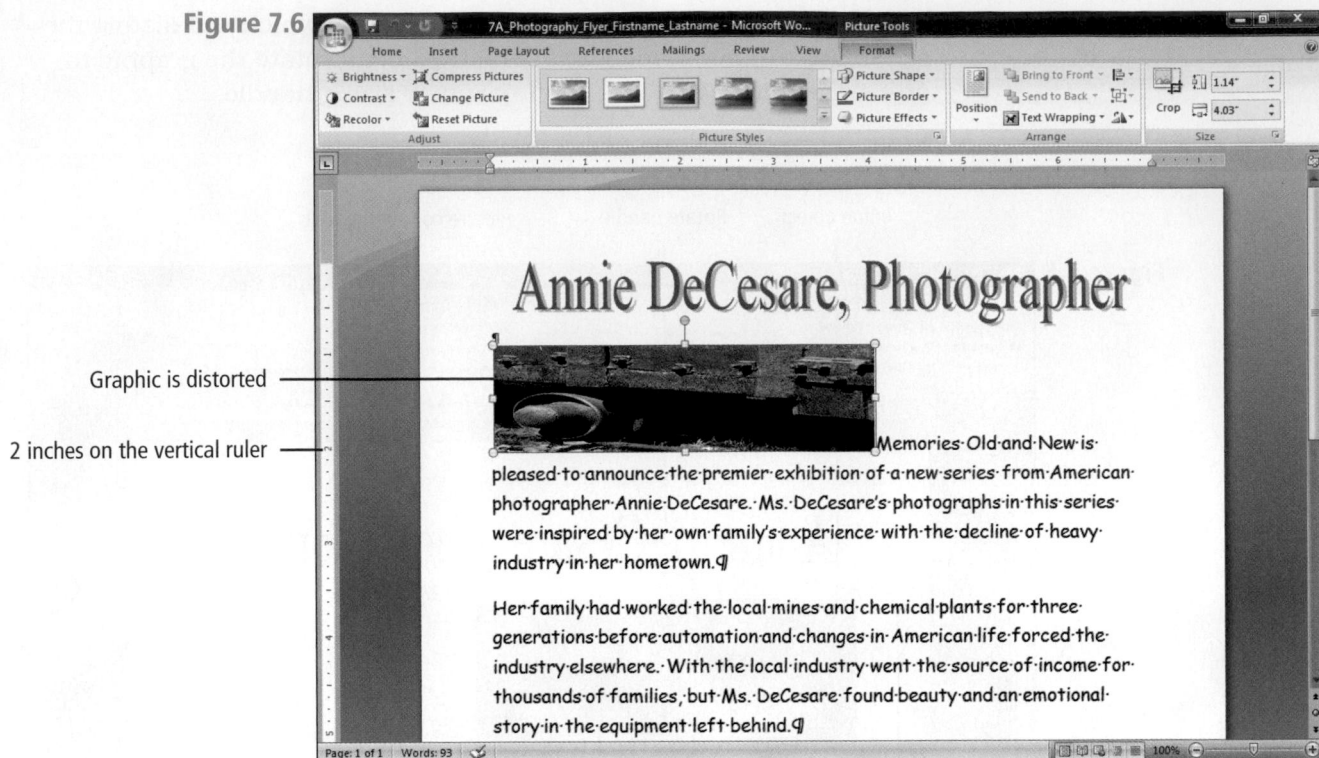

Graphic is distorted

2 inches on the vertical ruler

3 On the **Format tab**, in the **Adjust group**, click the **Reset Picture** button to return the graphic to its original size. Alternatively, on the Quick Access Toolbar, click the Undo button.

4 At the lower left corner of the picture, point to the round sizing handle until the ⬍ pointer displays. Drag upward and to the right until the bottom of the graphic is aligned at approximately **2 inches on the vertical ruler**. Notice that the graphic is resized proportionally and not distorted.

5 In the **Adjust group**, click the **Reset Picture** button.

6 On the **Format tab**, in the **Size group**, click the **Shape Height button spin box down arrow** 1.51" as necessary to change the height of the picture to **2"**. Notice that the picture resizes proportionally—the width adjusts as you change the height—as shown in Figure 7.7.

Figure 7.7

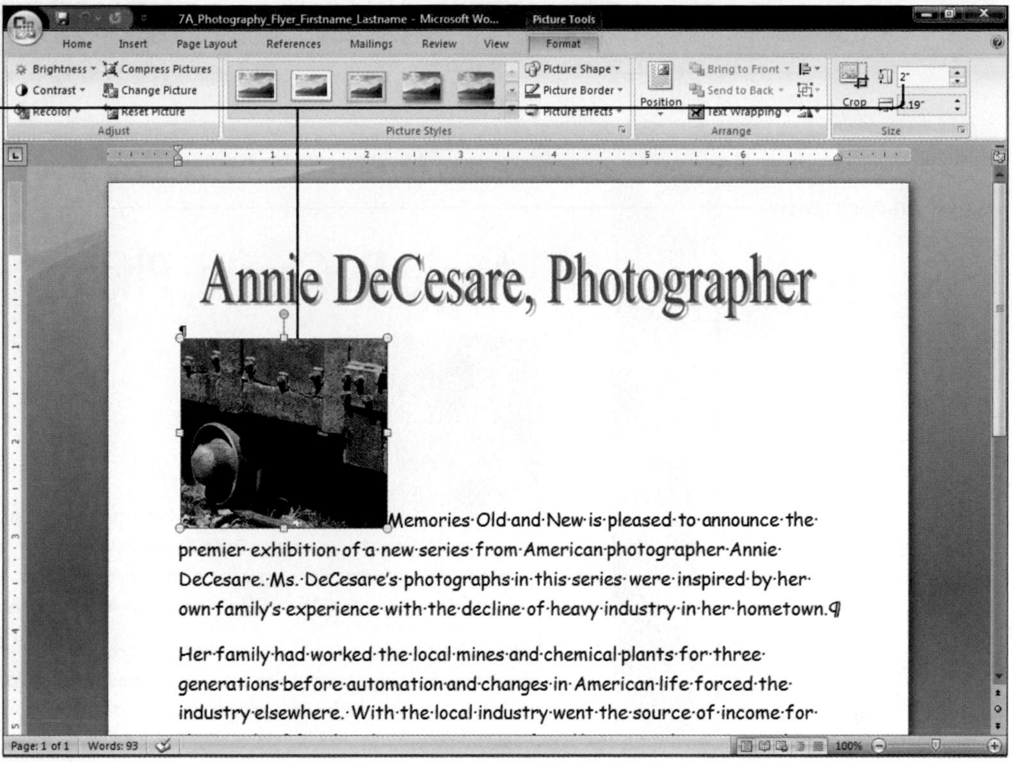

Graphic is 2 inches high
and proportionally resized

7 **Save** 🖫 your document.

Activity 7.04 Wrapping Text Around a Graphic

Graphics inserted as inline objects are treated like characters in a sentence, which can result in unattractive spacing. You can change an inline object to a *floating object*—a graphic that can be moved independently of the surrounding text characters.

1 Be sure the **ore cart** picture is still selected. On the **Format tab**, in the **Arrange group**, click the **Text Wrapping** button to display the **Text Wrapping gallery**, as shown in Figure 7.8.

Text wrapping refers to the manner in which text displays around an object.

Figure 7.8

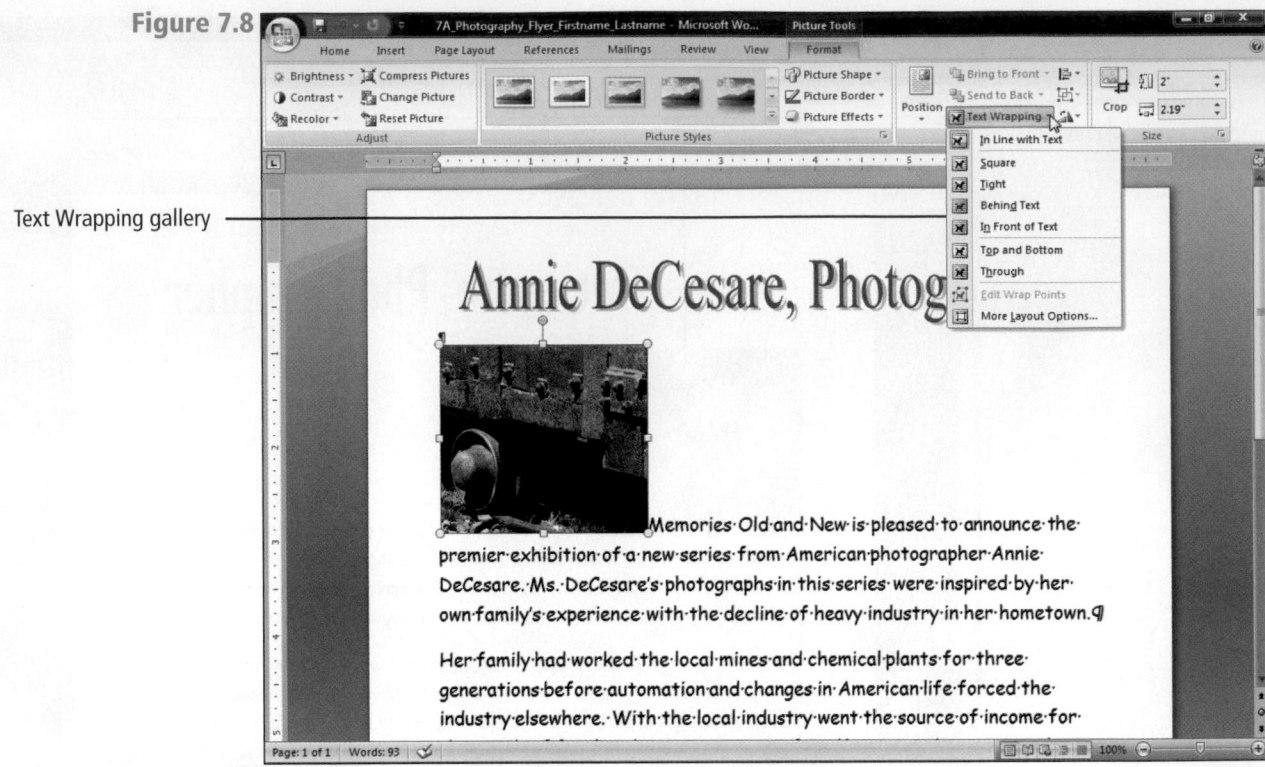

Text Wrapping gallery

2 From the **Text Wrapping gallery**, click **Square** to wrap the text around the graphic.

Square text wrapping insures that all four edges of the surrounding text will be straight. To wrap text around an irregularly shaped object use the Tight text wrap format.

3 Click to the left of *M* in the first line of the paragraph that begins *Memories Old and New* to deselect the picture. Click the **Insert tab**. In the **Illustrations group**, click the **Picture** button. Locate and **Insert** the file **w07A_Machine**.

Recall that pictures are inserted as inline objects; the inserted picture becomes the first character in the paragraph and the text is forced down in the document.

4 On the **Format tab**, in the **Arrange group**, click the **Text Wrapping** button, and then click **Square**. Compare your screen with Figure 7.9.

The text wraps around the second graphic.

Figure 7.9

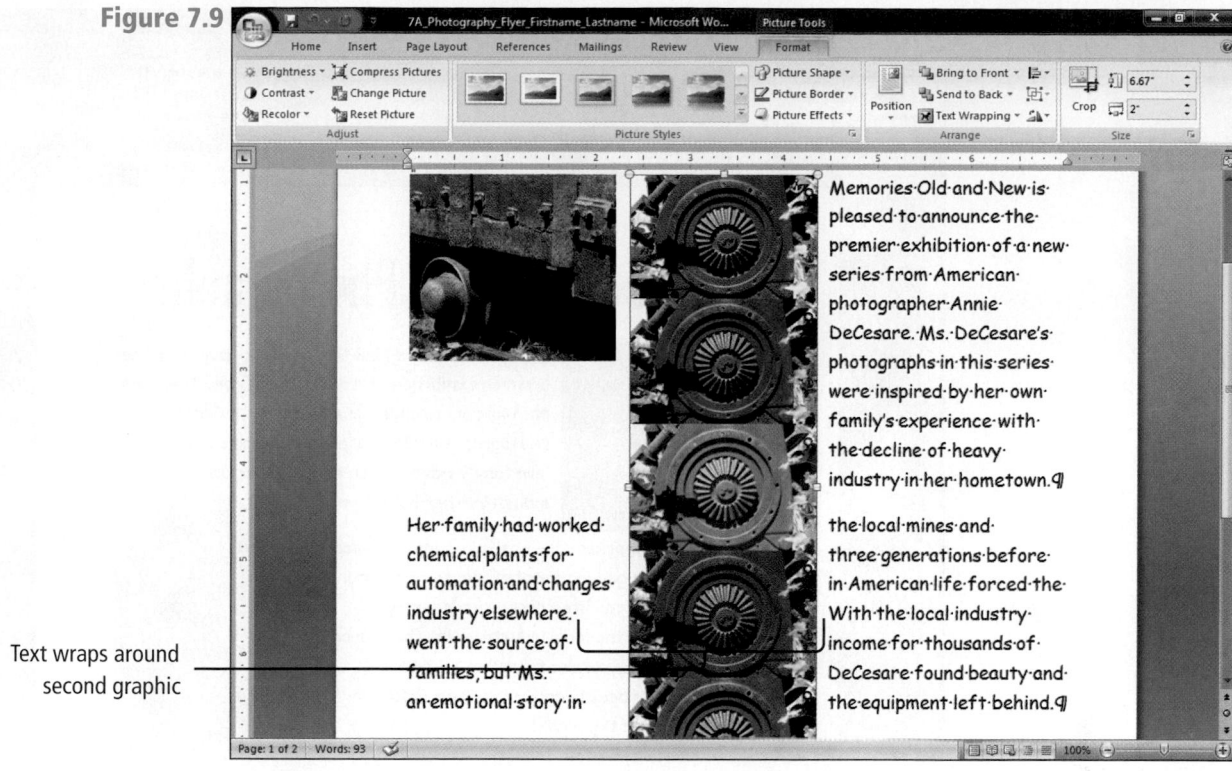

Text wraps around second graphic

---

⑤ **Save** 💾 your document.

Activity 7.05 Moving a Graphic

① Point anywhere in the **machine** picture to display the 🔧 pointer.

The Move pointer displays a four-way arrow, and enables you to move a floating object anywhere in the document.

② Drag the picture to the right until the right edge of the picture is aligned at approximately **7 inches on the horizontal ruler**, and then drag downward until the top edge of the picture is aligned at approximately **2.5 inches on the vertical ruler**. Compare your screen with Figure 7.10.

Figure 7.10

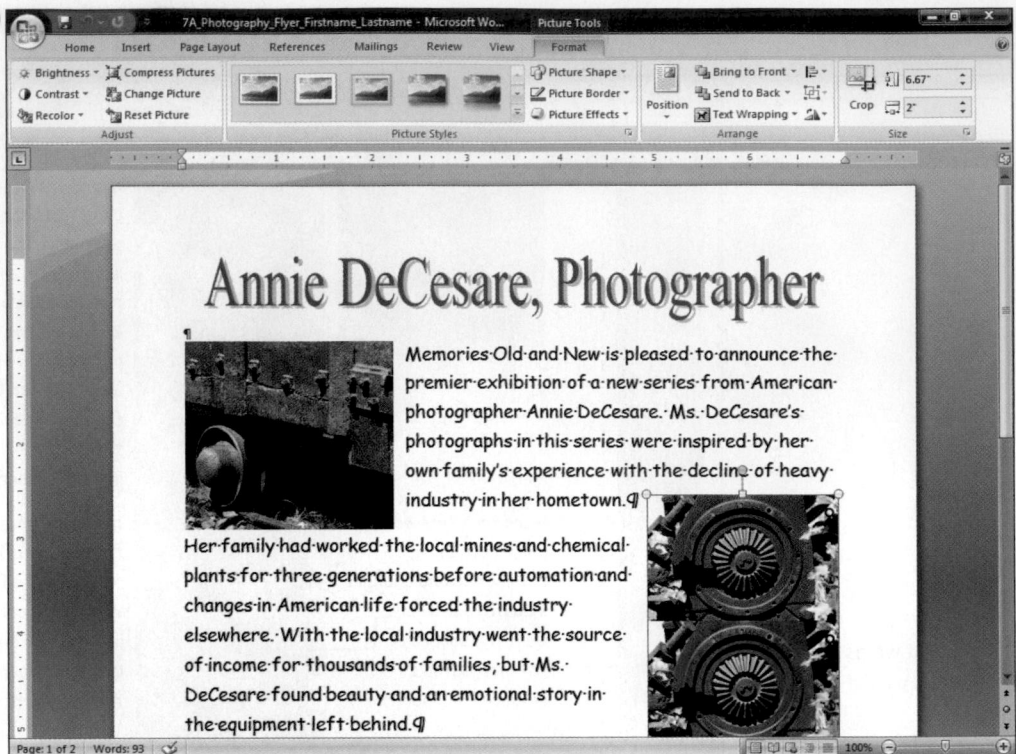

---

3 Move the graphics as necessary to align them in approximately the same position as those shown in Figure 7.10.

Recall that you can nudge an object in small increments by pressing the arrow keys.

4 **Save** 🖫 your document.

Activity 7.06 Applying Picture Styles

In this activity, you will use picture styles to add sophisticated visual features to your pictures.

1 Click to select the **ore cart** picture. Click the **Format tab**, and then in the **Picture Styles group**, point to the first picture style—**Simple Frame, White**. Notice that Live Preview displays the graphic as it would look if you clicked the *Simple Frame, White* button.

2 Point to the other picture styles to view some of the styles that are available.

3 To the right of the **Picture Styles gallery**, click the **More** button ⊽ to display more available styles. Click the **Beveled Matte, White** button—the second button in the first row. Click anywhere in the document to deselect the picture, and then compare your screen with Figure 7.11.

Figure 7.11

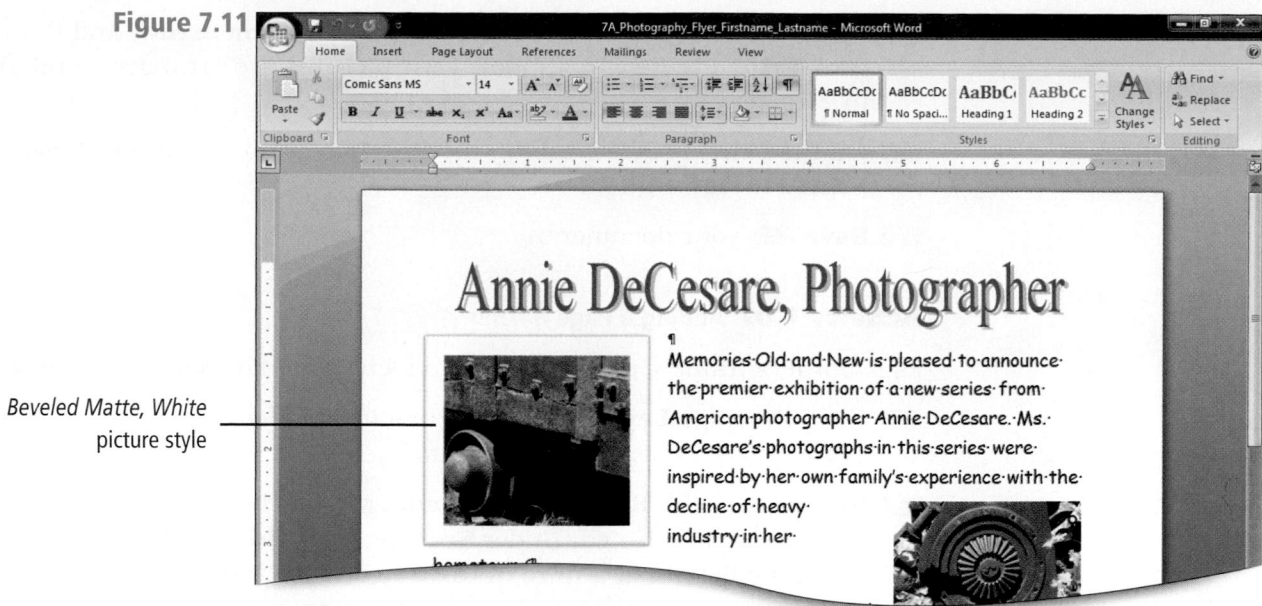

Beveled Matte, White picture style

4 Click to select the **w07A_Machine** picture. On the **Format tab**, in the **Picture Styles group**, click the **Picture Effects** button. In the **Picture Effects gallery**, point to **Soft Edges**, and then click **25 Point**. Click anywhere in the document to deselect the picture, and then compare your screen with Figure 7.12.

The Soft Edges feature fades the edges of the picture. The number of points you choose determines how far the fade goes inward from the edges of the picture. Recall that a point is 1/72 of an inch.

Figure 7.12

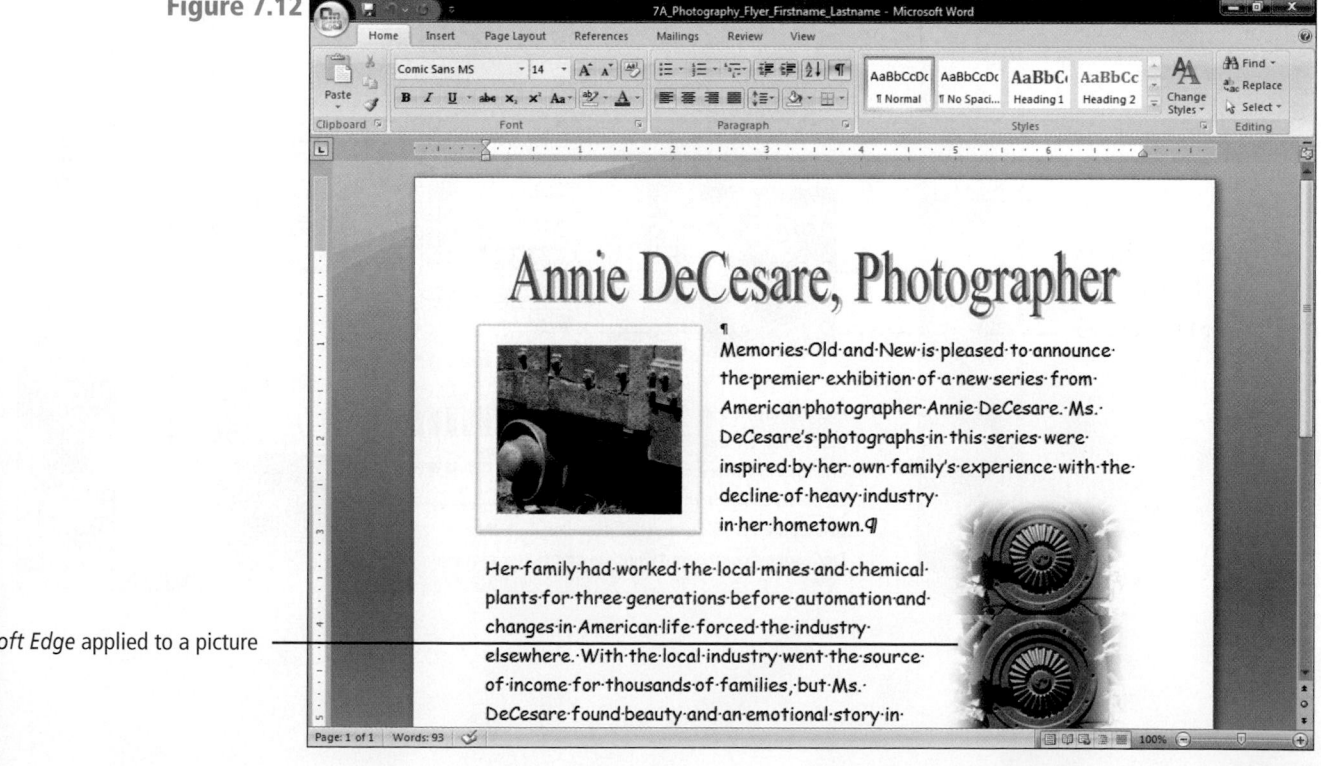

Soft Edge applied to a picture

5 From the **Office** menu, point to the **Print button arrow**, and then click **Print Preview** to see how your pictures are arranged in relation to your text.

6 On the **Print Preview tab**, in the **Preview group**, click the **Close Print Preview** button.

7 **Save** 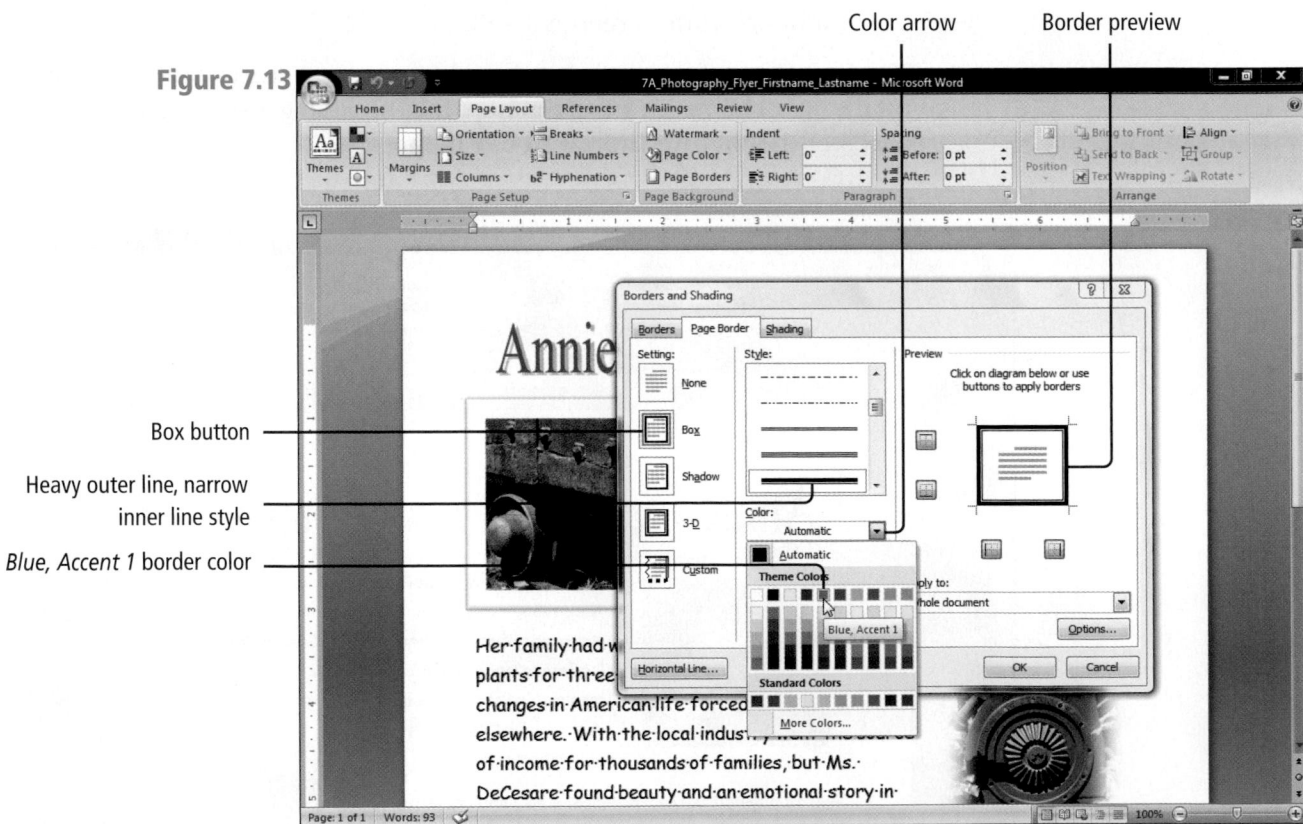 your document.

Activity 7.07 Adding a Page Border

Page borders frame a page and help to focus the information on the page.

1 Click the **Page Layout tab**, and then in the **Page Background group**, click the **Page Borders** button.

2 In the displayed **Borders and Shading** dialog box, be sure the **Page Border tab** is selected. Under **Setting**, click **Box**. Under **Style**, scroll down the list about a third of the way and click the heavy outer line with the thin inner line—check the **Preview** area to be sure the heavier line is the nearest to the edges of the page. Click the **Color arrow**, and then under **Theme Colors**, in the first row of colors, point to the fifth button—**Blue, Accent 1**. Compare your screen with Figure 7.13.

Color arrow   Border preview

Figure 7.13

Box button

Heavy outer line, narrow inner line style

Blue, Accent 1 border color

3 Click **Blue, Accent 1**, and then at the bottom of the **Borders and Shading** dialog box, click **OK**. Notice that a border is placed around the page, about 0.5 inch in from the edge of the page, as shown in Figure 7.14.

Page border

Figure 7.14

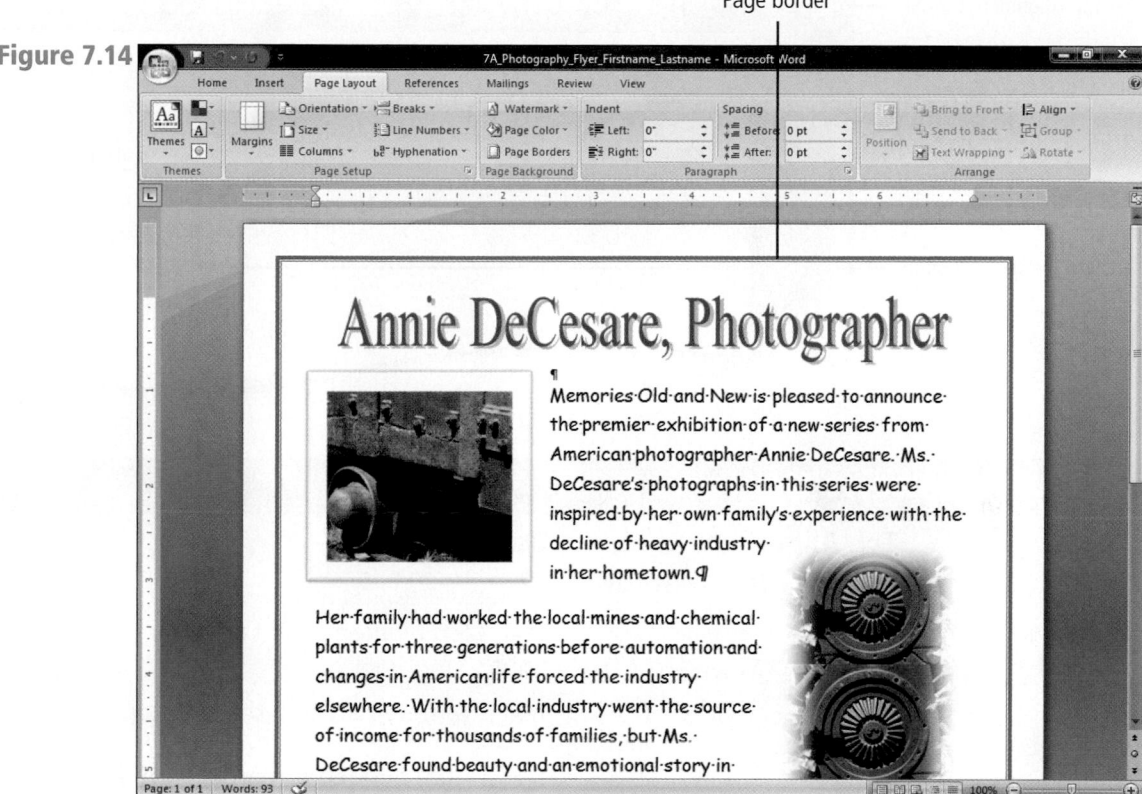

4 **Save** your document.

Objective 2
Set Tab Stops

Tab stops mark specific locations on a line of text; use tab stops to indent and align text. Press the Tab key to move to tab stops. In this activity, you will use tab stops to format a short table of dates and times that the photography exhibit will be open.

Activity 7.08 Setting Tab Stops and Using Click and Type

1 Take a moment to study the tab alignment options shown in Figure 7.15 and described in the table in Figure 7.16.

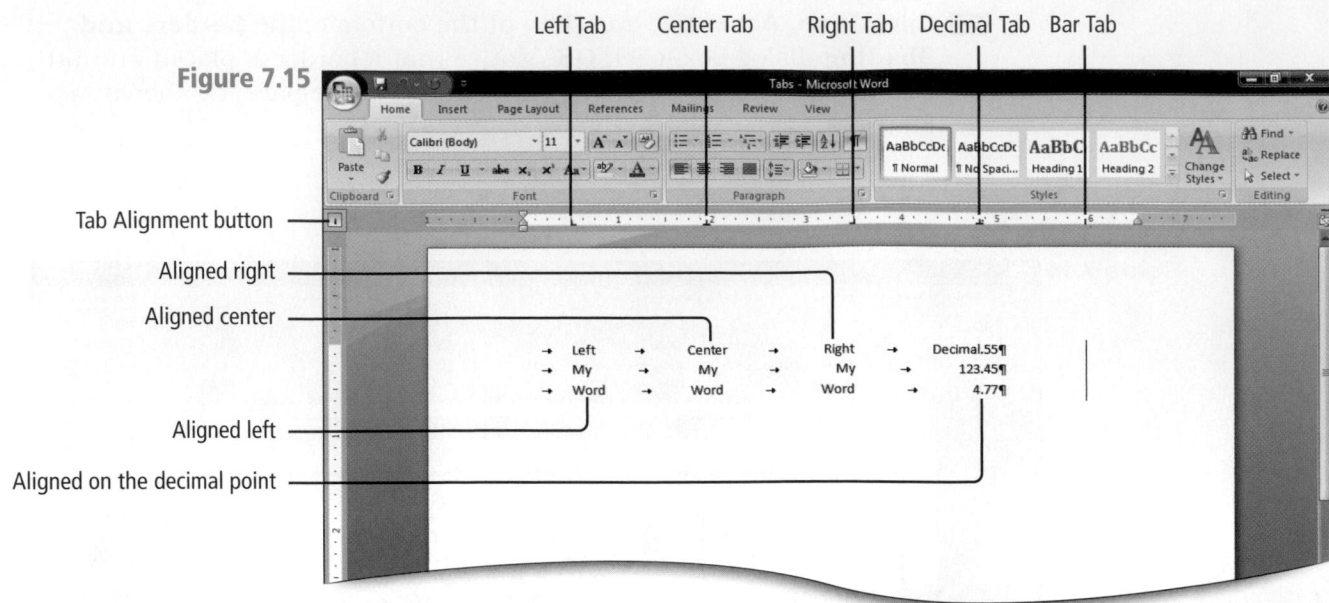

Figure 7.15

Tab Alignment Options

Type	Tab Alignment Button Displays This Marker	Description
Left	⌊	Text is left aligned at the tab stop and extends to the right.
Center	⊥	Text is centered around the tab stop.
Right	⌋	Text is right aligned at the tab stop and extends to the left.
Decimal	⊥	The decimal point aligns at the tab stop.
Bar	∣	A vertical bar is inserted in the document at the tab stop.
First Line Indent	▽	Indents the first line of a paragraph.
Hanging Indent	⊔	Indents all lines but the first in a paragraph.

Figure 7.16

2 Scroll to the bottom of the document and click anywhere in the last paragraph. Position the pointer below the text and near the left margin to display the ⌶ pointer, as shown in Figure 7.17.

This is one of several **_click and type pointers_**; a series of pointers with lines attached in various arrangements to depict alignment. In this instance, the pointer displays left aligned horizontal lines. The shape attached to the pointer indicates what type of formatting will be applied if you double-click at the pointer location on the page.

Figure 7.17

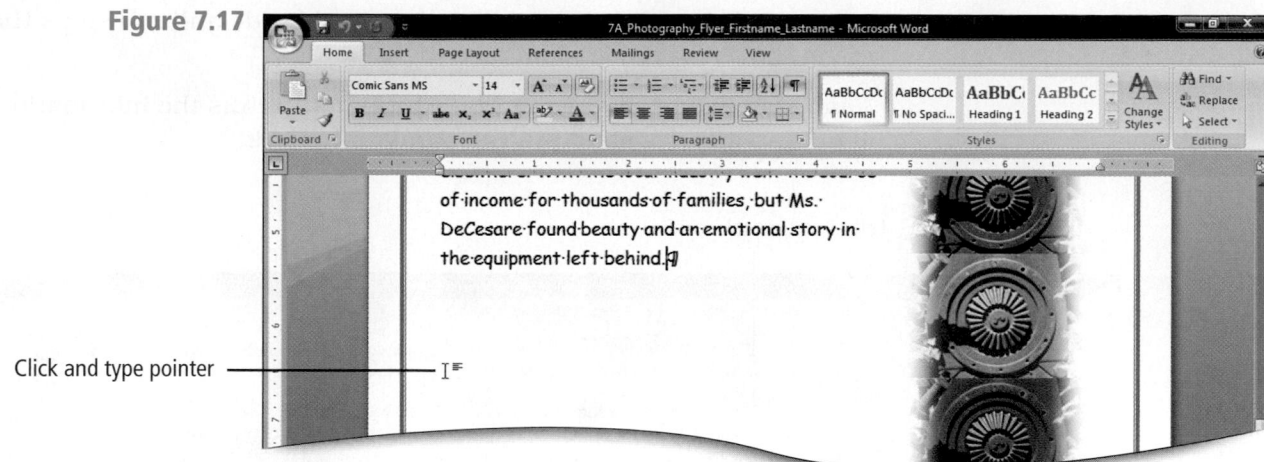

Click and type pointer ———————————— I≡

Alert!

What if the click and type pointer does not display?

If you move the pointer around the blank area of the document and do not see the click and type pointer, click the Office button, and then click Word Options. Click Advanced, and then under *Editing options,* select the *Enable click and type* check box.

3 With the ⌐I≡⌐ pointer displayed at approximately **7 inches on the vertical ruler** and at the left margin, double-click to place the insertion point.

The insertion point is positioned at the left margin. If you double-click the click and type pointer near the horizontal middle of the document, a center tab is inserted and the insertion point is positioned at the center of the line. If you double-click near the right margin, a right tab is inserted.

Because you cannot type in a blank area of a document without some type of paragraph formatting in place, click and type inserts blank lines quickly without having to press Enter numerous times—and uses the formatting of the nearest paragraph above.

4 To the left of the horizontal ruler, point to the **Tab Alignment** button and observe the *Left Tab* ScreenTip. Click the **Tab Alignment** button ⌐L⌐ one time, move the mouse pointer away, and then point to the button again to display the next ScreenTip—*Center Tab.* Repeat this process to cycle through and view the ScreenTip for each of the types of tab stops, and then stop at the **Left Tab** button ⌐L⌐.

5 Move the pointer into the horizontal ruler, click at **0.5 inch on the horizontal ruler**, and then compare your screen with Figure 7.18.

A left tab stop is inserted on the ruler for the paragraph containing the insertion point. Left tab stops are used when you want the information to align on the left. By default, tab stops are set every half inch, but they do not display on the ruler. When you customize a tab as you did here, the custom tab stop overrides default tab stops that are to the left of the custom tab.

A tab stop is part of a paragraph's format and thus the information about tab stops is stored in the paragraph mark.

Left alignment tab at 0.5 inch

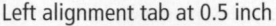

Figure 7.18

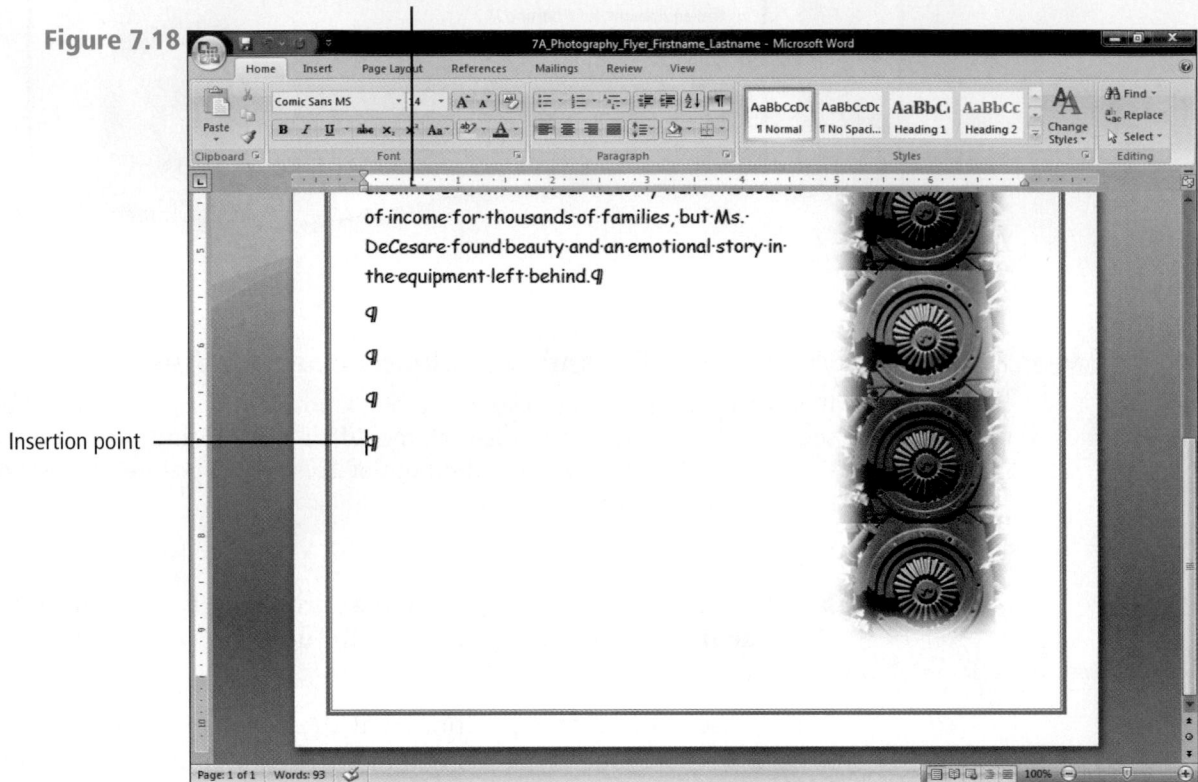

Insertion point

6 Click the **Tab Alignment** button two times to display the **Right Tab** button . Point to **2.25 inches on the horizontal ruler**, and then click one time.

A right tab stop is inserted in the ruler. Right tab stops are used to align information on the right. As you type, the text will extend to the left of the tab stop.

7 Click the **Tab Alignment** button six times to display the **Center Tab** button . Click at **3.5 inches on the horizontal ruler**, and then click again at **4.5 inches**. Compare your screen with Figure 7.19.

Two center tab stops display on the ruler. Center tab stops are used when you want to center information over a particular point.

Center alignment tabs

Figure 7.19

Right alignment tab

Tabs set only for the line in
which the insertion point
is positioned

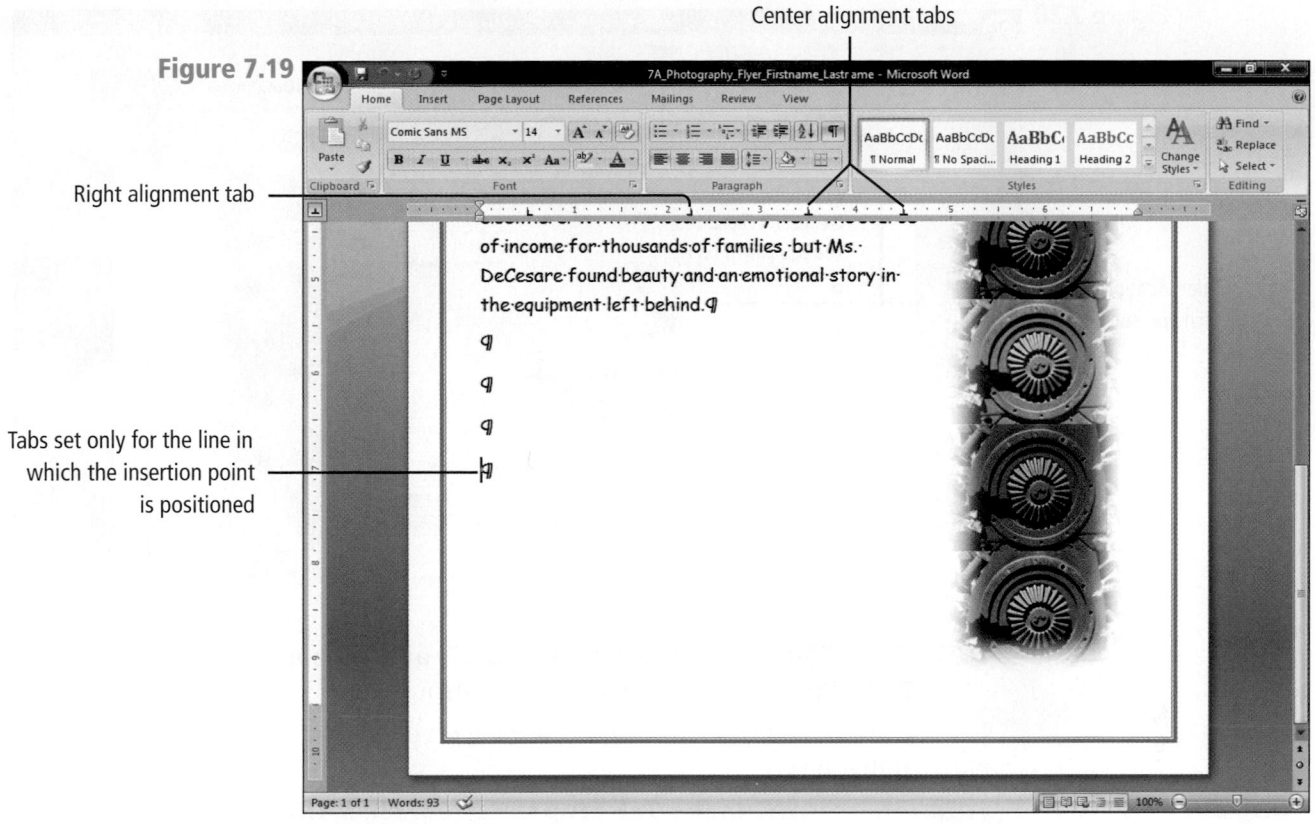

8 **Save** 💾 your document.

Activity 7.09 Formatting and Removing Tab Stops

Recall that tab stops are a form of paragraph formatting, and thus, the
information about them is stored in the paragraph mark to which they
were applied.

1 On the **Home tab**, in the **Paragraph group**, click the **Dialog Box
Launcher** 🔲. If necessary, change the spacing *After* to 0, and the
Line Spacing to Single, and then click **OK**. Move the pointer to any of
the tab markers on the ruler, double-click to display the **Tab** dialog
box, and then compare your screen with Figure 7.20.

The tabs you just added to the ruler display under *Tab stop position*.
In the Tabs dialog box, you have more flexibility in adding, removing,
and formatting tab stops.

Figure 7.20

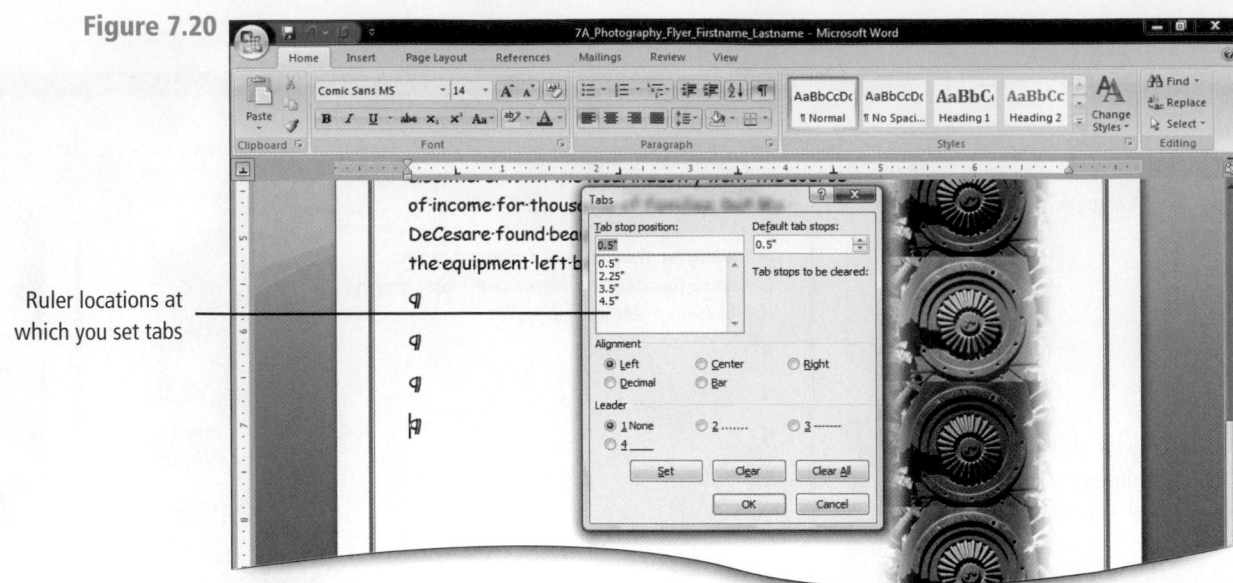

Ruler locations at
which you set tabs

Under **Tab stop position**, click **3.5"**, and then at the bottom of the **Tabs** dialog box, click the **Clear** button.

The cleared tab stop will be removed when you click OK to close the dialog box.

If necessary, under **Tab stop position**, click **4.5"**. Under **Alignment**, click the **Right** option button. Under **Leader**, click the **2** option button. Near the bottom of the **Tabs** dialog box, click **Set**, and then compare your screen with Figure 7.21.

The Set button saves the change. The tab stop at 4.5 inches is changed to a right tab, and now has a *leader character*. Leader characters create a solid, dotted, or dashed line that fills the space used by a tab character. A leader character draws the reader's eyes across the page from one item to the next. Later, when you move to this location with the Tab key, a row of dots will display. When the character used for the leader is a dot, this is commonly referred to as a *dot leader*.

Figure 7.21

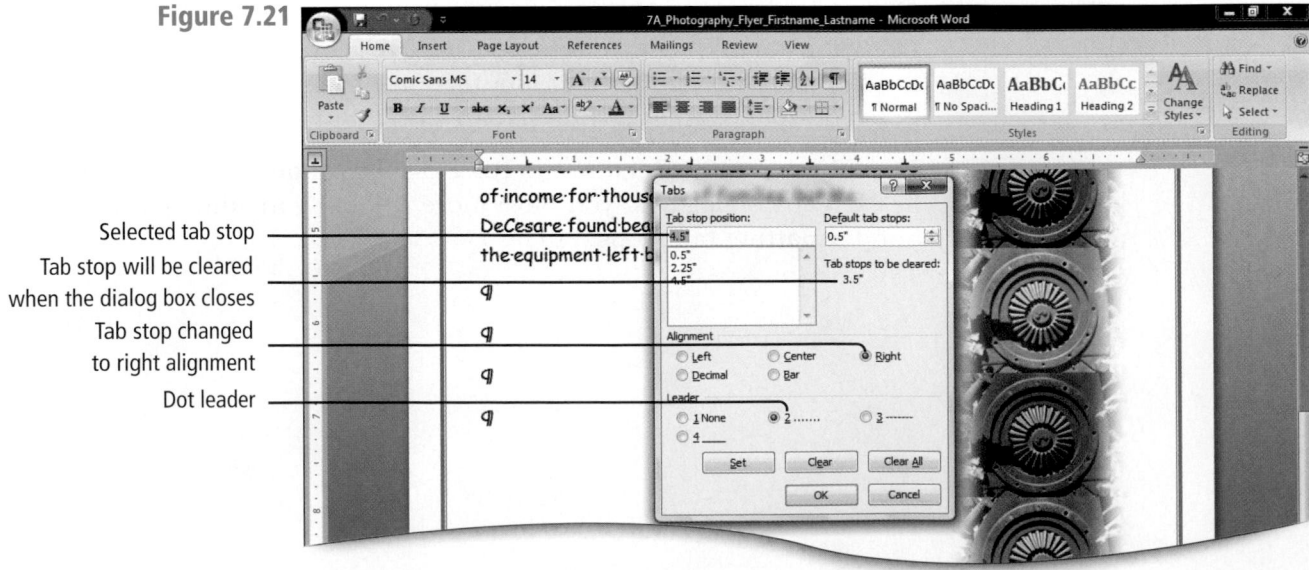

Selected tab stop

Tab stop will be cleared
when the dialog box closes

Tab stop changed
to right alignment

Dot leader

4 At the bottom of the **Tabs** dialog box, click **OK**, and notice that the changes are reflected in the ruler.

5 **Save** 🖫 your document.

Activity 7.10 Using Tab Stops to Enter Text

1 With the insertion point positioned at the beginning of the line with the new tab stops, Press Tab, and then compare your screen with Figure 7.22.

The insertion point moves to the first tab stop, which is at 0.5 inch, and the nonprinting character for a tab—a small arrow—displays.

Figure 7.22

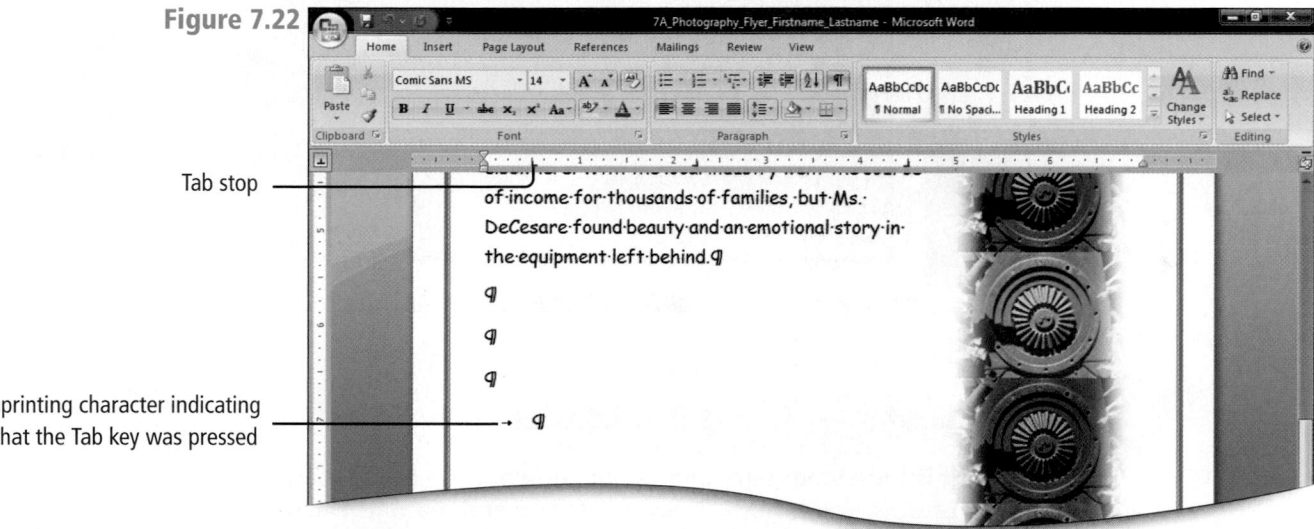

Tab stop

Nonprinting character indicating that the Tab key was pressed

2 Type **Sunday** and notice that the left edge of the text remains aligned with the tab stop. Press Tab, and then type **July 30**

The insertion point moves to the tab stop at 2.25 inches, and the text moves to the left of the right tab mark. With a right tab, the right edge of the text remains aligned with the tab mark, and the text moves to the left.

3 Press Tab, and then type **Daytime 9 - 6** and press Enter. Compare your screen with Figure 7.23. Look at the ruler, and notice that when you press Enter, the formatting of the previous paragraph, including tab stops, is copied to the new paragraph.

A dot leader is added, helping to draw your eyes across the page to the next item. Depending on your Word settings, when you type a hyphen surrounded by spaces, the hyphen may change to a longer dash.

Tab stops included in new paragraph

Figure 7.23

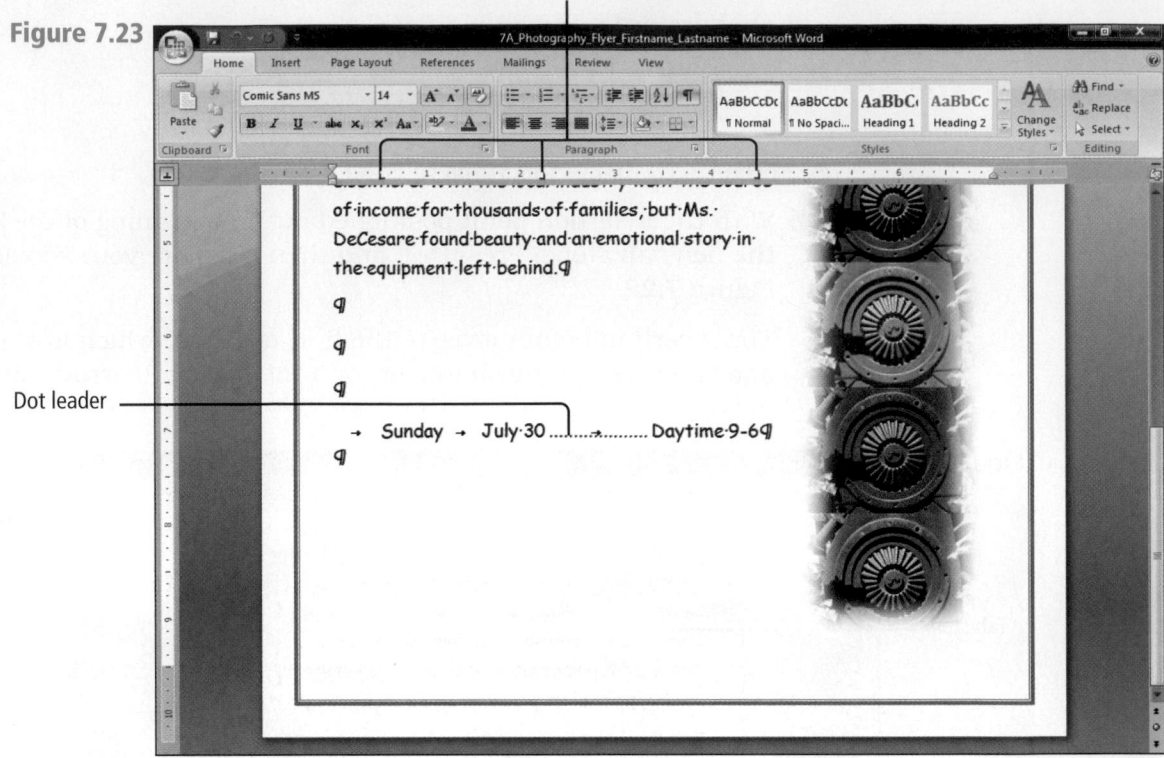

Dot leader

Note — Using Dot Leaders

It is sometimes tempting to hold down ⌐.⌐ on the keyboard to create a string of dots. This is not a good idea for several reasons. The periods, because of proportional spacing, may be spaced differently between rows. The periods will not line up, and, most importantly, the column on the right side of the string of periods may look lined up on the screen, but will be crooked when printed. If you need a string of dots, always insert a tab stop with a dot leader.

4 Type the following—first pressing Tab one time to indent each line—to complete the exhibition schedule. Click **Save**, and then compare your screen with Figure 7.24:

Monday	**July 31**	**Evening 6 - 9**
Tuesday	**August 1**	**All Day 9 - 9**

Figure 7.24

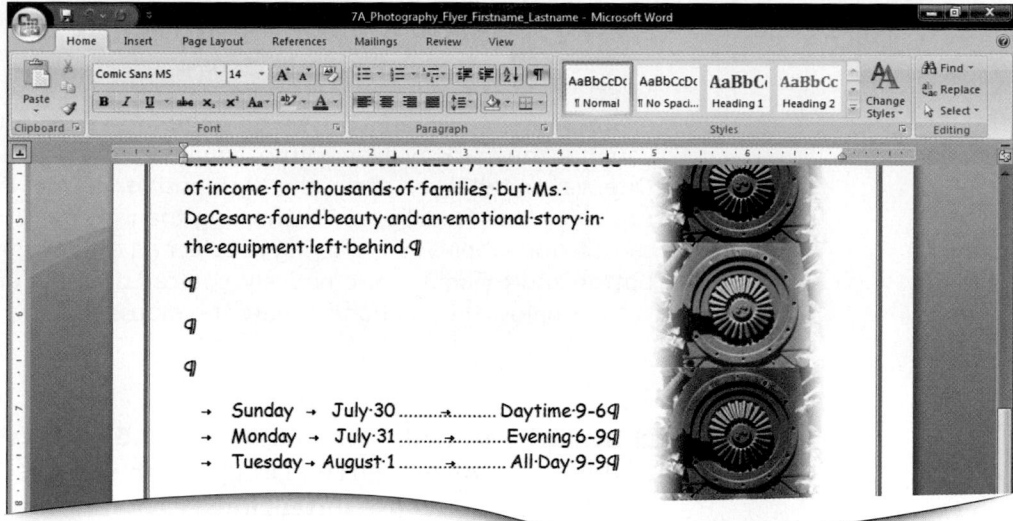

Another Way ── To Create an Indent

If the items in the first column of a list are indented the same amount using a left-aligned tab, you can save keystrokes by indenting the paragraph instead. You can do this on the Home tab by clicking the Increase Indent button in the Paragraph group, or by using the Paragraph dialog box. You can also drag the Left Indent marker from the left side of the ruler and position it at the desired location. When you are finished typing the list, you can drag the marker back to the left margin position. When you use an indent at the beginning of the paragraph for a tabbed list, you do not have to press Tab before you type the first item in the list.

Activity 7.11 Moving Tab Stops

If you are not satisfied with the arrangement of your text after setting tab stops, you can reposition the text by moving tab stops.

1 Move the pointer into the left margin area, to the left of the first line of tabbed text. When the ⬚ pointer displays, drag downward to select the three lines of tabbed text.

By selecting all of the paragraphs, changes you make to the tabs will be made to the tab stops in all three lines simultaneously.

2 With the three lines of tabbed text selected, point to the horizontal ruler and position the pointer so the tip of the pointer arrow is touching the **0.5-inch tab stop**. When you see the *Left Tab* ScreenTip, drag the tab stop mark to the left to **0.25 inch on the ruler**, and then release the mouse button.

3 In the horizontal ruler, point to the **4.5-inch tab stop** until you see the *Right Tab* ScreenTip. Drag the tab stop mark to the right to **4.75 inches on the horizontal ruler**. Compare your screen with Figure 7.25.

Tab stop at 0.25 inch   Tab stop at 4.75 inches

Figure 7.25

Selected text moved

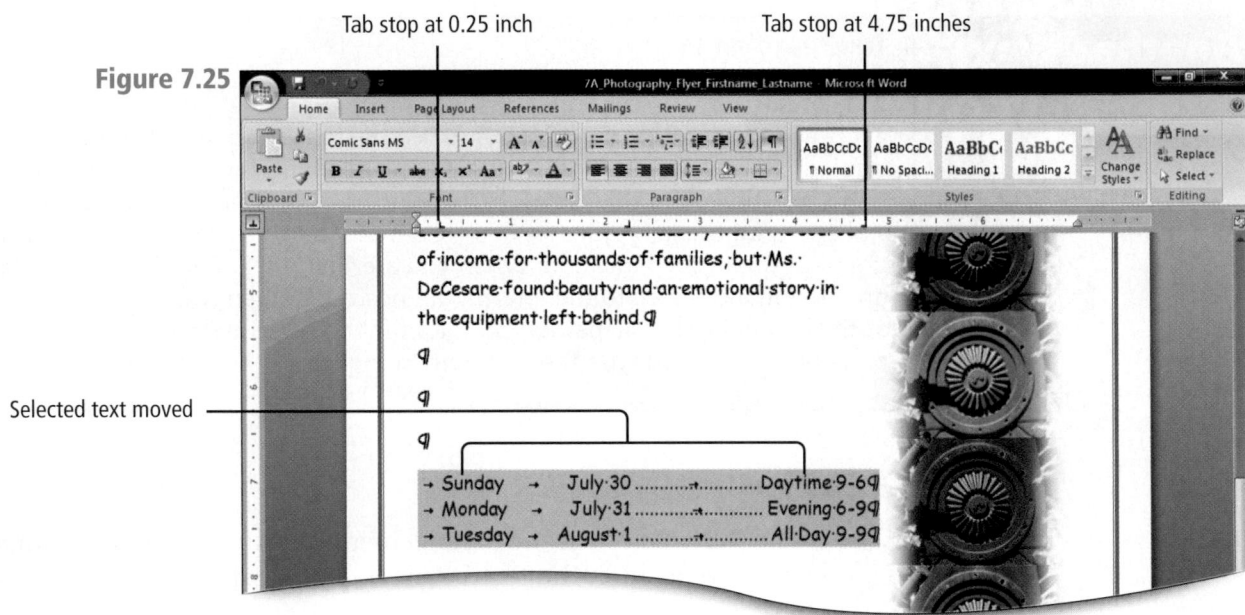

4 Click anywhere to deselect the text, and then **Save** 🖫 your document.

Objective 3
Insert and Modify Text Boxes and Shapes

In addition to graphics such as pictures and clip art you can also add predefined shapes and text boxes to documents. A ***drawing canvas*** is provided as a work area for complex drawings; however, when inserting and formatting simple drawing objects, it is more convenient to leave the drawing canvas off.

Activity 7.12 Inserting a Text Box

A **text box** is a movable, resizable container for text or graphics. A text box is useful to give text a different orientation from other text in the document because a text box can be placed anywhere in the document in the manner of a floating object. A text box can be placed outside the document margin, resized, and moved.

1 Scroll down to display the bottom edge of the document. Click the **Insert tab**, and then from the **Text group**, click the **Text Box** button. At the bottom of the **Text Box gallery**, click **Draw Text Box**.

2 Position the ⊞ pointer at the left margin and at approximately **5.5 inches on the vertical ruler**. Drag down and to the right to create a text box approximately **1.25 inches** high and **4 inches** wide. Then in the **Size group**, use the spin arrows to set the height and width precisely at **1.3** and **4** inches. Compare your screen with Figure 7.26. If you are not satisfied with your result, click the Undo button and try again.

Height of text box

Figure 7.26

Width of text box

Text box

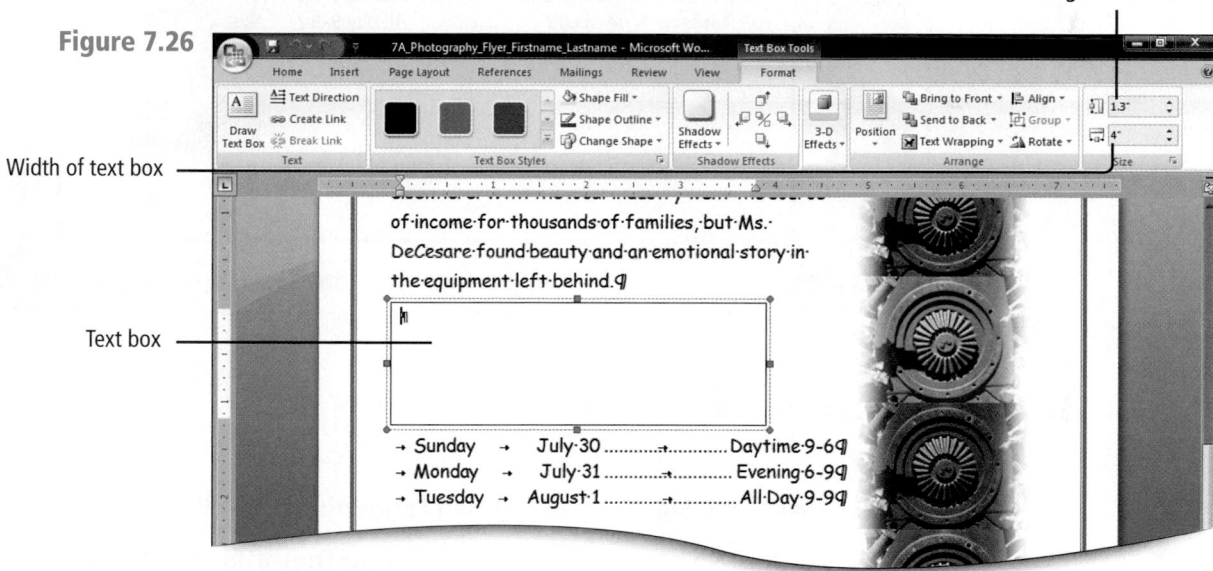

3 With the insertion point displayed in the text box, click the **Home tab**. If necessary, in the **Styles group**, click the **No Spacing** style to remove the space *After* paragraphs and change the line spacing to *Single*. Include the quotation marks as you type **"Annie DeCesare finds beauty where no one else thinks to look."** and press Enter. Type **Chicago Arts Review**

4 In the text box, select the quote, including both quotation marks and the paragraph mark. On the Mini toolbar, click the **Font Size button arrow** 12 ▼, and then click **16**. With the text still selected, on the Mini toolbar, click the **Bold** button **B**.

5 In the text box, select **Chicago Arts Review**, and then on the Mini toolbar, click the **Italic** button I . In the **Paragraph group**, click the **Align Text Right** button ▤ . Click anywhere outside the text box, and then compare your screen with Figure 7.27.

Figure 7.27

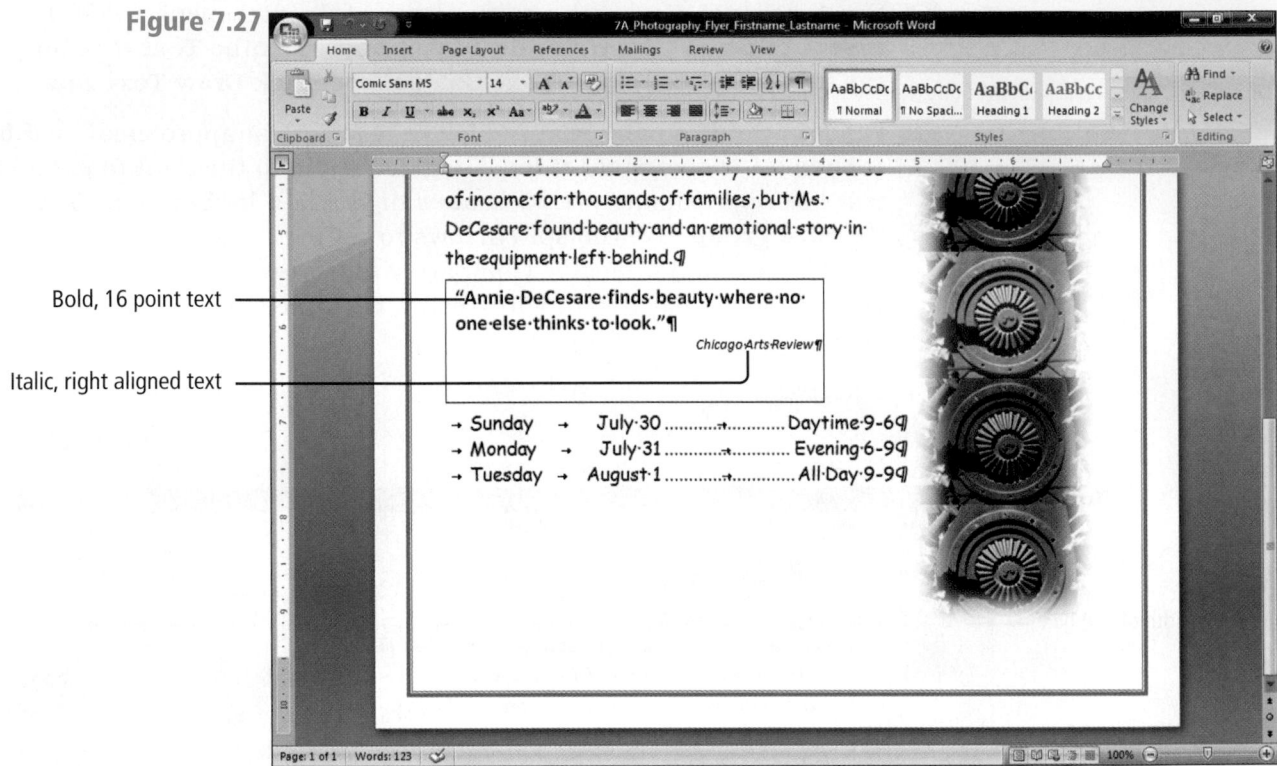

Bold, 16 point text

Italic, right aligned text

6 **Save** 🖫 your document.

Activity 7.13 Moving, Resizing, and Formatting a Text Box

1 Click anywhere inside the text box so that it is selected and the text inside is deselected. Click the **Format tab**. In the **Size group**, change the **Height** of the text box to **0.9"** and the **Width** to **3.5"**.

2 Point to one of the text box borders until the 🔁 pointer displays. Drag the text box down and to the right until it is centered in the same approximate location as the one shown in Figure 7.28. Position the right edge at approximately **4.5 inches on the horizontal ruler**, and the top edge at approximately **5.75 inches on the vertical ruler**.

Because the rulers show the size of the text box, but not the location of the document relative to the rest of the document, you will likely need to deselect the text box, check the position, and then move the box again.

Figure 7.28

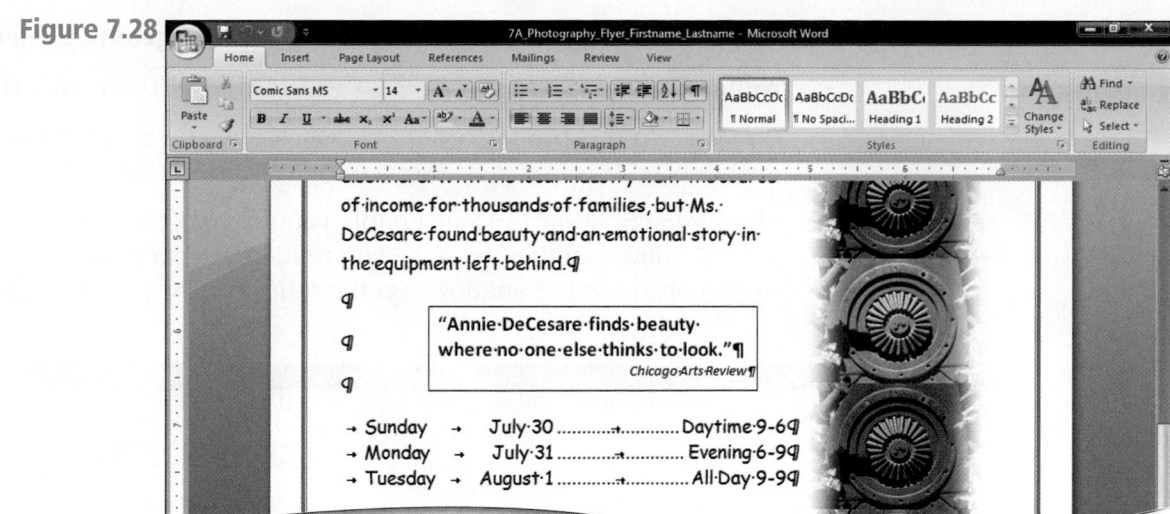

3 If necessary, select the text box. On the **Format tab**, in the **Shadow Effects group**, click the **Shadow Effects** button. In the **Shadow Effects gallery**, under **Drop Shadow**, in the first row, point to the fourth shadow—**Shadow Style 4**. Notice that Live Preview displays a shadow around the text box, as shown in Figure 7.29.

Because the default shadow on the WordArt is down and to the right, it is good design to create a text box shadow in the same direction.

Shadow Effects gallery

Figure 7.29

Shadow Style 4

Live Preview displays the shadow

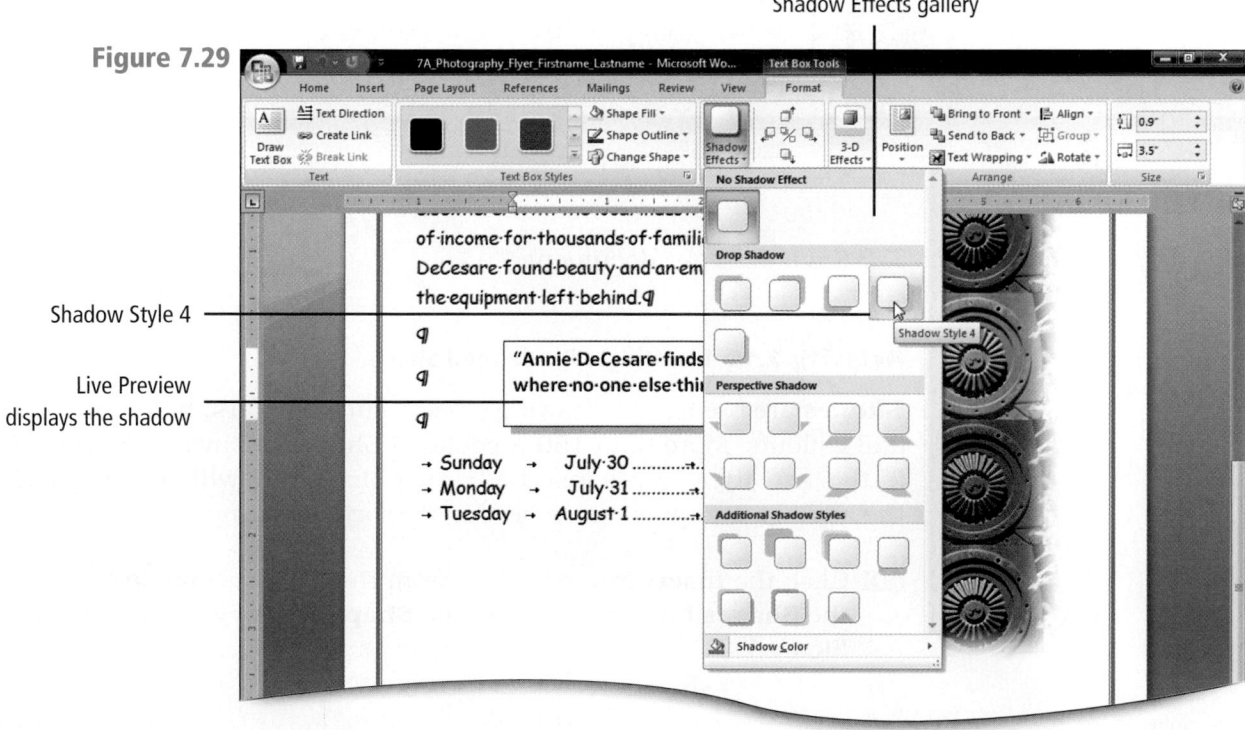

4 Click **Shadow Style 4**. In the **Shadow Effects group**, click the **Nudge Shadow Left** button two times, and then click the **Nudge Shadow Up** button two times. Click anywhere in the document to deselect the text box, and then compare your screen with Figure 7.30.

The Nudge Shadow buttons enable you to apply precision formatting to your shadows; in this instance you made the shadow more subtle and in proportion to the shadows on the other two graphics on the page.

Figure 7.30

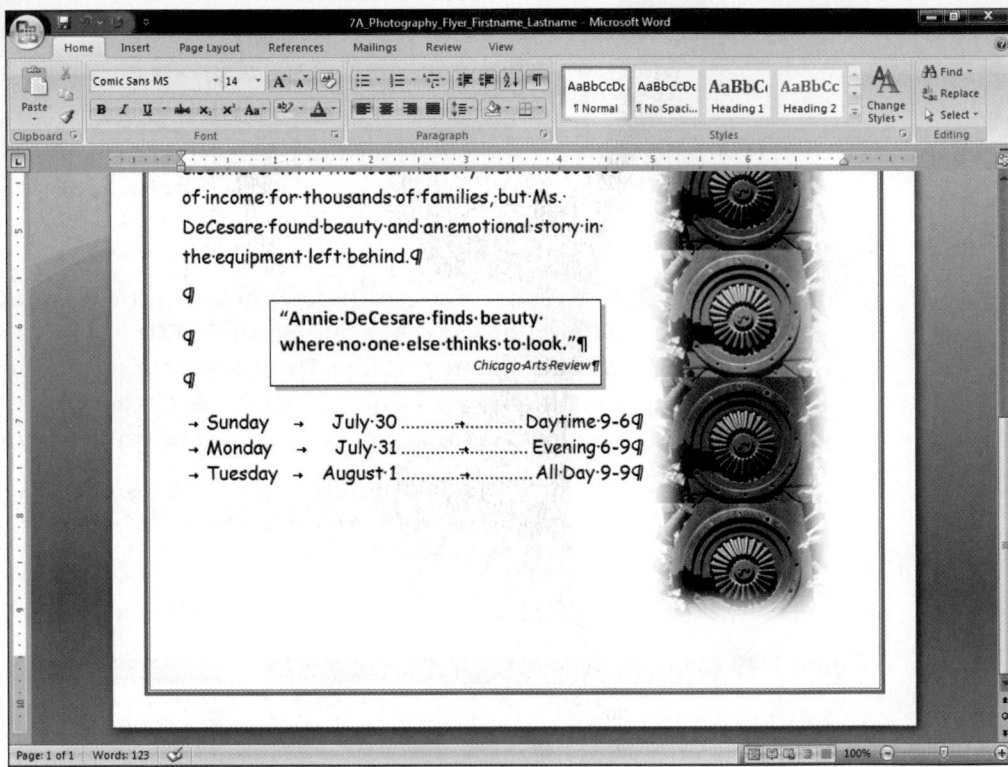

5 **Save** your document.

Activity 7.14 Inserting a Predefined Shape

Shapes are predefined drawing objects such as stars, banners, arrows, and callouts. More than 150 predefined Shapes are available with Word. In this activity, you will insert a banner shape into which you will add the address and phone number for Memories Old and New.

1 Click the **Insert tab**, and then from the **Illustrations group**, click the **Shapes** button to display the **Shapes gallery**, as shown in Figure 7.31.

Figure 7.31

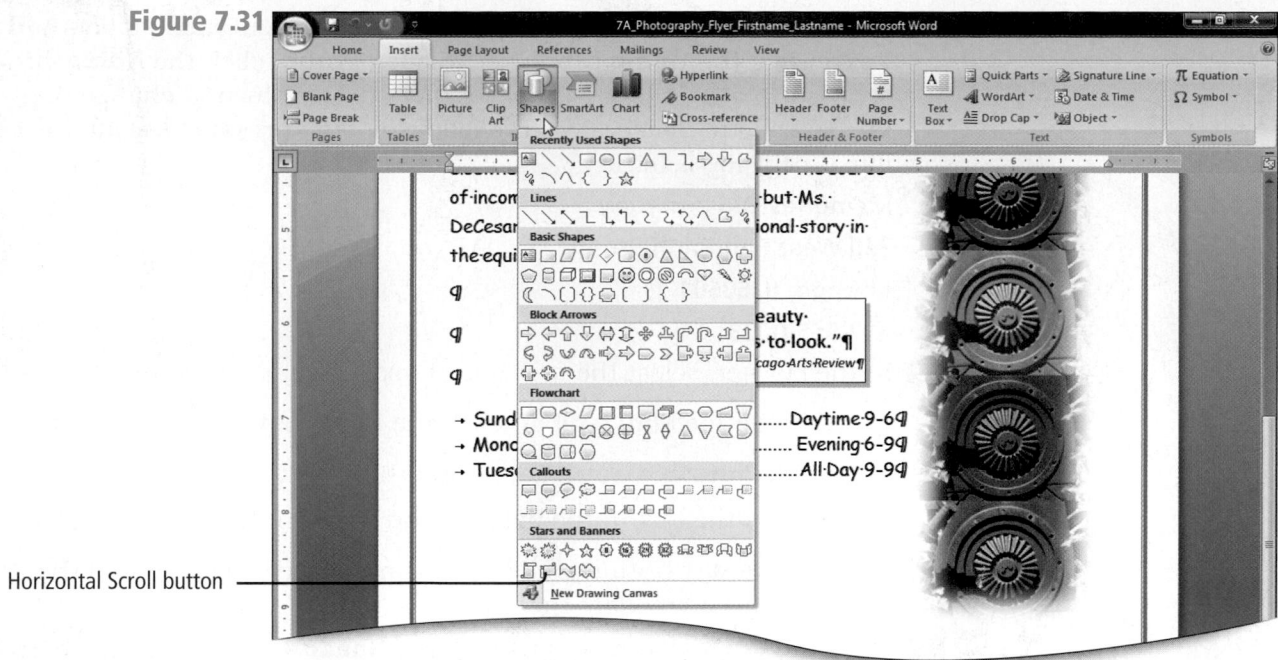

Horizontal Scroll button

2 From the displayed **Shapes gallery**, under **Stars and Banners**, in the second row, click the second shape—**Horizontal Scroll**.

3 Move the ⊞ pointer near the left margin at approximately **8 inches on the vertical ruler**. Using both the horizontal and vertical rulers as guides, drag down and to the right to create a banner approximately **1 inch** high and **3 inches** wide. Then in the **Size group**, use the **Shape Height** and **Shape Width spin box arrows** to set the **Height** precisely to **1.2"** and the **Width** to **3"**. Compare your screen with Figure 7.32. If you are not satisfied with your result, click the Undo button 🔄 and begin again.

Figure 7.32

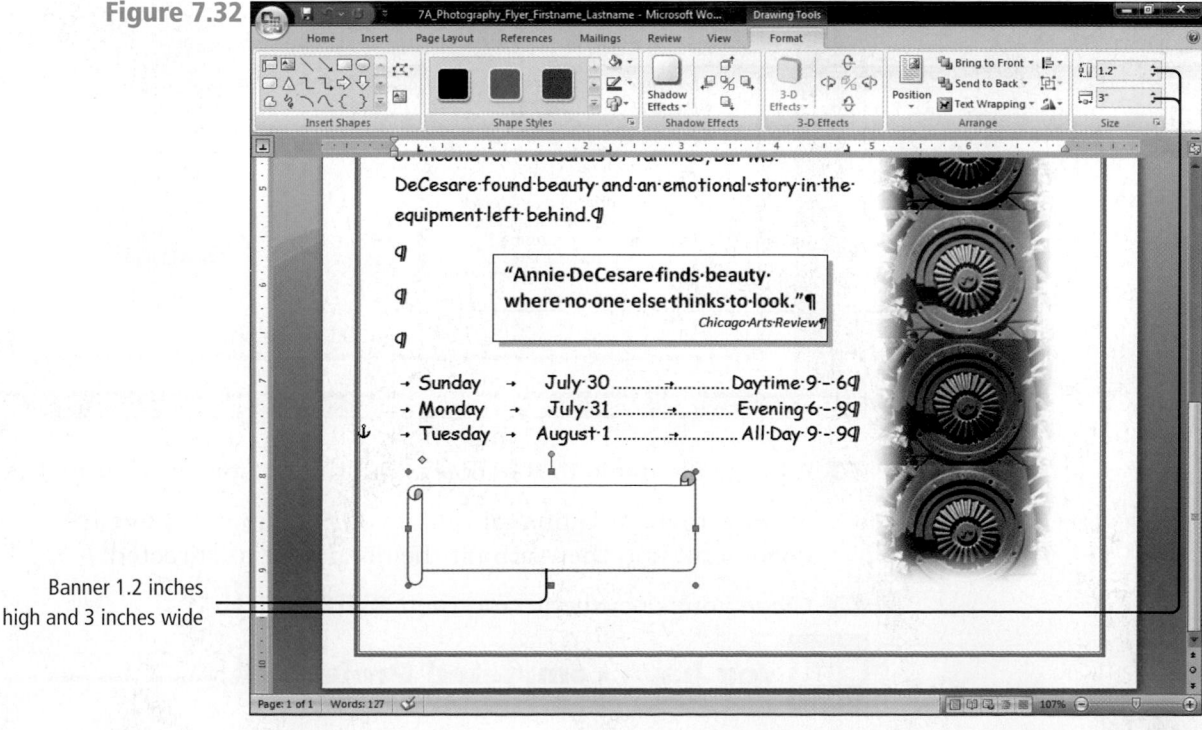

Banner 1.2 inches high and 3 inches wide

4 Right-click the banner, and then from the shortcut menu, click **Add Text**. Click the **Home tab**. In the **Styles group**, click the **No Spacing** style button to remove the space *After* paragraphs and change the line spacing to *Single*. Type the following text, pressing Enter after each line except the last line:

Memories Old and New

220 West Randolph Street

Chicago, IL 60601

312-555-0023

5 In the banner, select the first line of text—*Memories Old and New*— and then on the Mini toolbar, click the **Bold** button **B**. Click the **Font Size button arrow** 12 ▼, and then click **14**.

6 Select all of the text in the banner, and then on the Mini toolbar, click the **Center** button ☰. If necessary, adjust the height of the banner to accommodate the text.

7 Click the **Format tab**, and then in the **Shadow Effects group**, click the **Shadow Effects** button. Use the technique you practiced with the text box to apply **Shadow Style 4**. Nudge the shadow **Up** two times and to the **Left** two times. Click outside of the banner to deselect it, and then compare your screen with Figure 7.33.

Figure 7.33

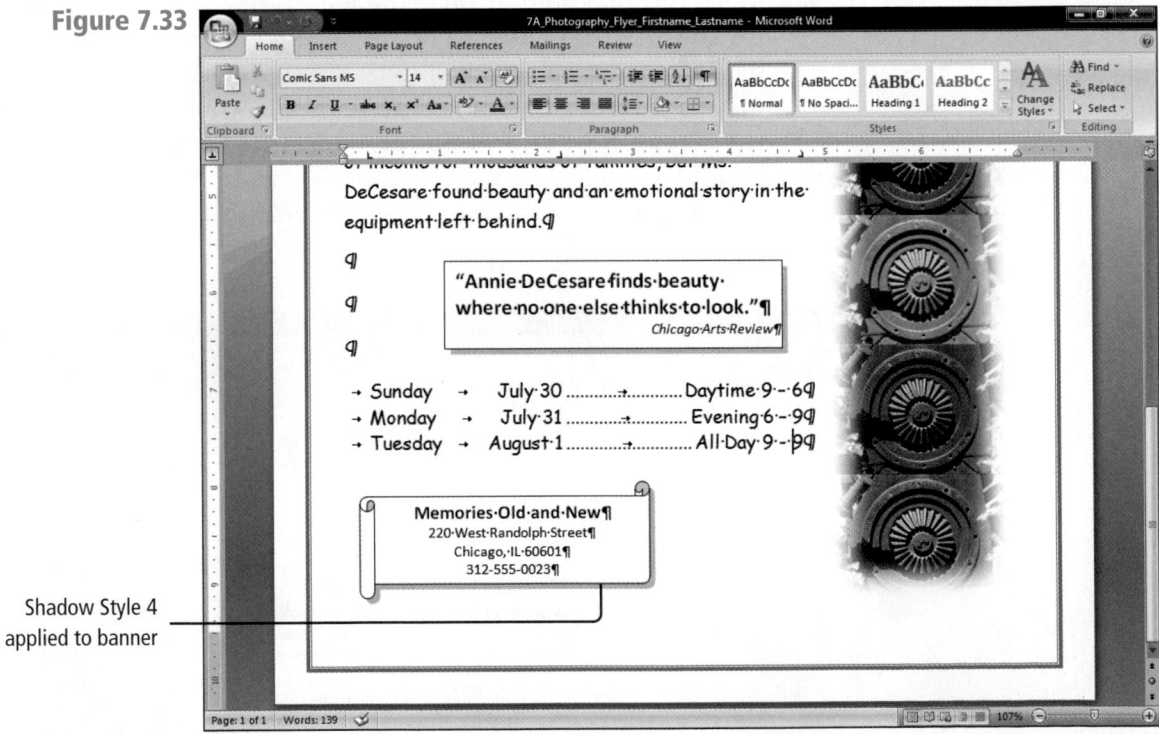

Shadow Style 4
applied to banner

8 Add the file name to the footer, and then display the **Print Preview** window to make a final check of your document. **Save** 🖫 your document, and then submit the document as directed.

9 **Close** your document, and then **Exit** Word.

End You have completed Project 7A

Project 7B Price List

In Activities 7.15 through 7.24, you will create a price list for framed and unframed prints by photographer Annie DeCesare at Memories Old and New. Your completed document will look similar to Figure 7.34.

For Project 7B, you will need the following file:

w07B_Price_List

**You will save your document as
7B_Price_List_Firstname_Lastname**

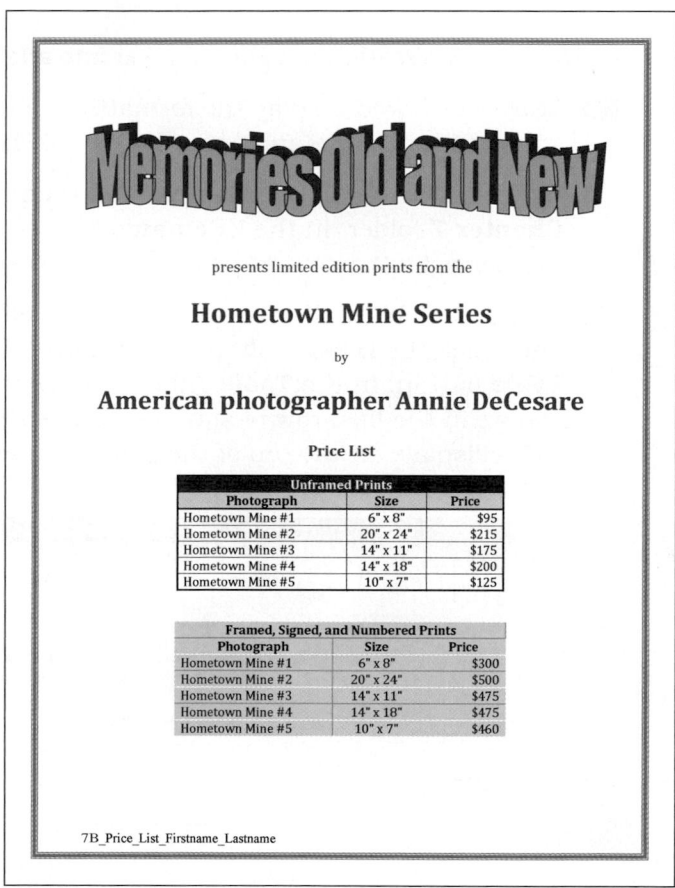

Figure 7.34
Project 7B—Price List

Objective 4
Create a Table

The table feature in Word has largely replaced the use of tabs because of its flexibility and ease of use. ***Tables*** consist of rows and columns and are used to organize data. You can create an empty table, and then fill in the ***cells***—the boxes created by the intersections of the columns and the rows. You can also convert existing text into a table if the text is properly formatted.

To adjust a table, you can add rows or columns and change the height of rows and the width of columns. You can format the text and numbers in the cells and the backgrounds and borders of cells.

Activity 7.15 Creating and Entering Text into a Table

1 **Start** Word, and display the formatting marks and rulers. From your student files, locate and open the file **w07B_Price_List**. From the **Office** menu 📎 , click **Save As**, and then navigate to your **Word Chapter 7** folder. In the **File name** box, type 7B_Price_List_ Firstname_Lastname and press ⏎.

2 In the three blank lines under *Price List*, click in the middle blank line. Click the **Insert tab**, and then in the **Tables group**, click the **Table** button. In the **Table gallery**, move the pointer to the second square in the fifth row of squares. Notice that the size of the table— 2x5—displays at the top of the gallery, as shown in Figure 7.35.

Figure 7.35

Table size

Preview of inserted table

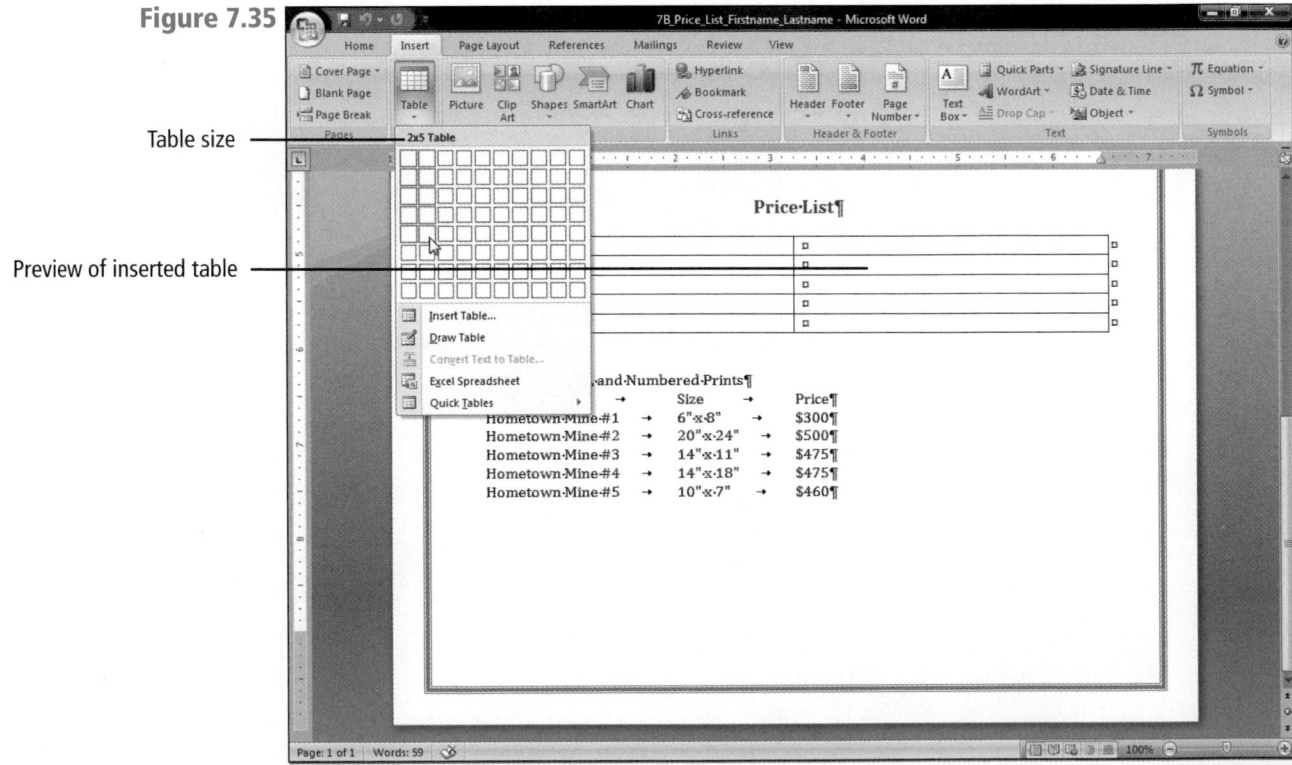

3 Click the mouse button, and then compare your screen with Figure 7.36.

A table with five rows and two columns is created at the insertion point location, and the insertion point is placed in the upper left cell. The table fills the width of the page, from the left margin to the right margin. Table Tools display on the Ribbon, and add two contextual tabs—*Design* and *Layout*.

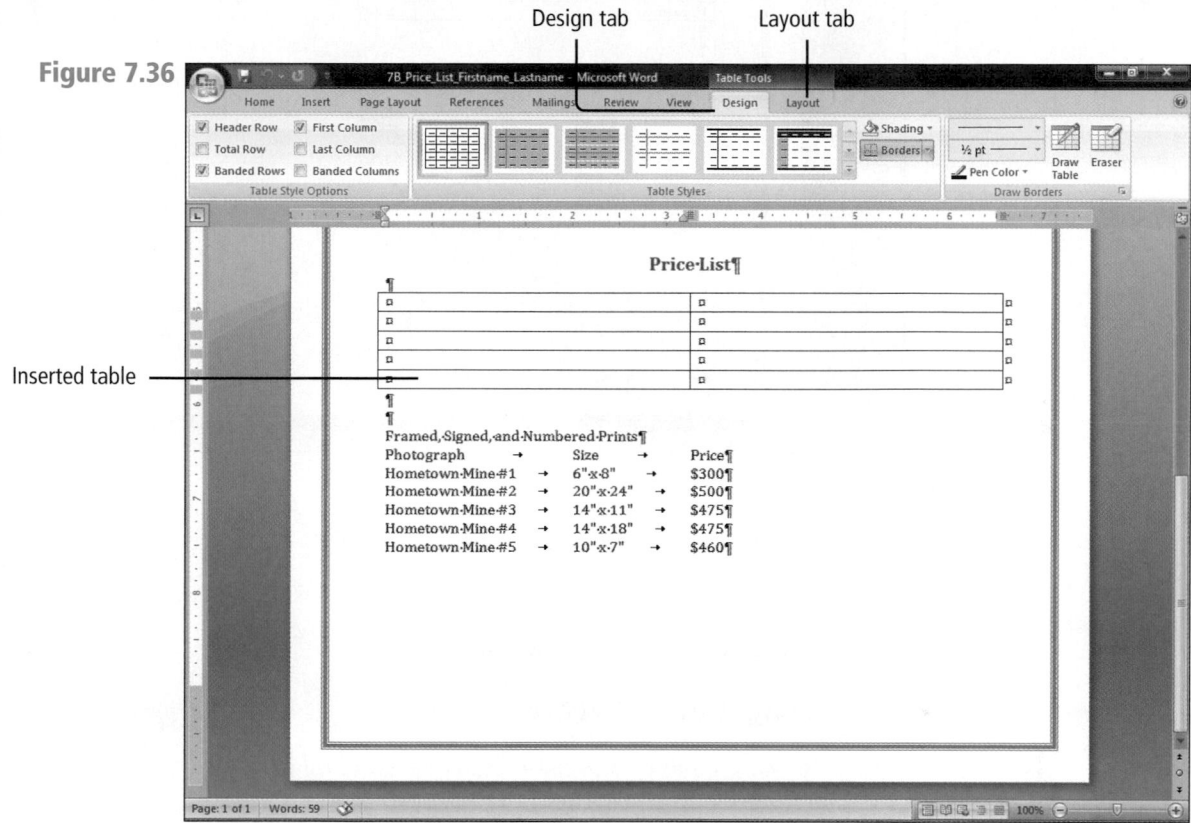

Figure 7.36

Inserted table

4 Type **Unframed Prints** and then press Tab to move to the second cell in the first row of the table.

The Tab key is used to move from cell to cell in a Word table. The natural tendency is to press Enter to move from one cell to the next. In a table, however, pressing Enter creates another line in the same cell, similar to the way you add a new line in a document. If you press Enter by mistake, you can remove the extra line by pressing ←Bksp.

5 Press Tab again to move to the first cell in the second row. Type **Hometown Mine #1** and press Tab. Type **$95** and press Tab.

6 Type the following to complete the table, but do not press Tab after the last item. Compare your screen with Figure 7.37.

Hometown Mine #2	**$215**
Hometown Mine #3	**$175**
Hometown Mine #4	**$200**

Figure 7.37

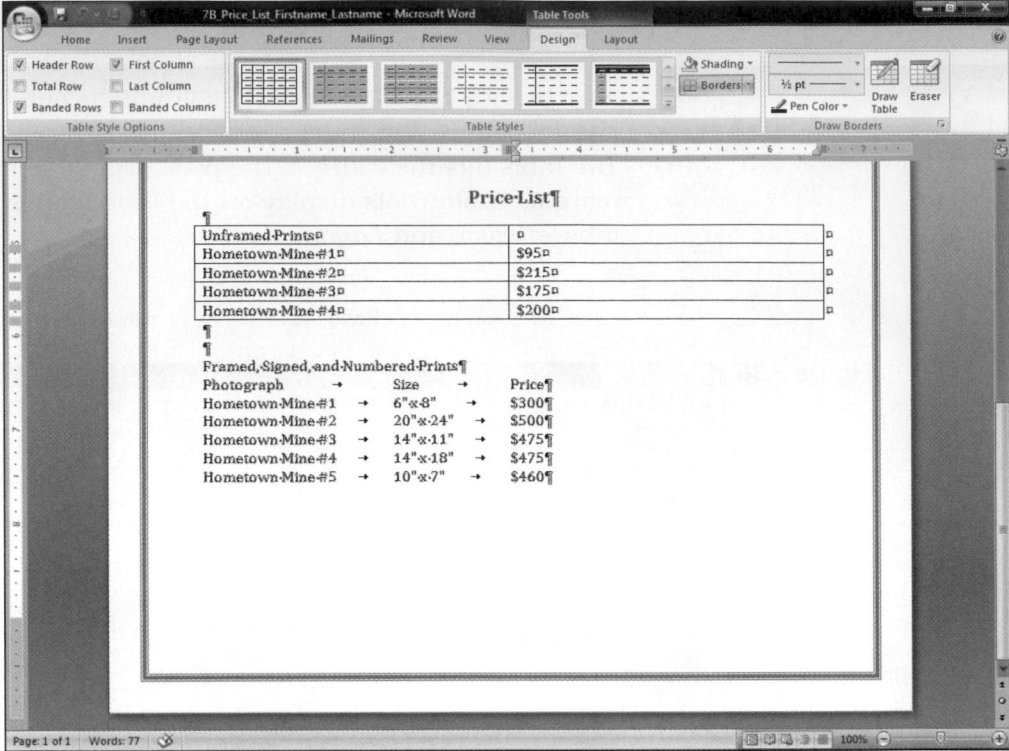

7 **Save** 💾 the document.

More Knowledge

Navigating in a Table

You can move to a previous cell in a table by pressing ⬆Shift + Tab. This action selects the contents of the previous cell. The selection moves back one cell at a time each time you press Tab while holding down ⬆Shift. You can also use the up or down arrow keys to move up or down a column. The left and right arrow keys, however, move the insertion point one character at a time within a cell.

Activity 7.16 Adding a Row to a Table

You can add rows to the beginning, middle, or end of a table.

1 With the insertion point in the last cell in the table, press Tab to add a new row to the bottom of the table. Type **Hometown Mine #5** and press Tab. Type **$125** and then, in the second row of the table, click anywhere to position the insertion point.

2 Click the **Layout tab**, and then in the **Rows & Columns group**, click the **Insert Above** button to insert a new row.

3 In the new row, type **Photograph** and press Tab.

When the entire row is selected, text that you type automatically begins in the cell on the left.

4 Type **Price** and then compare your table with Figure 7.38.

Figure 7.38

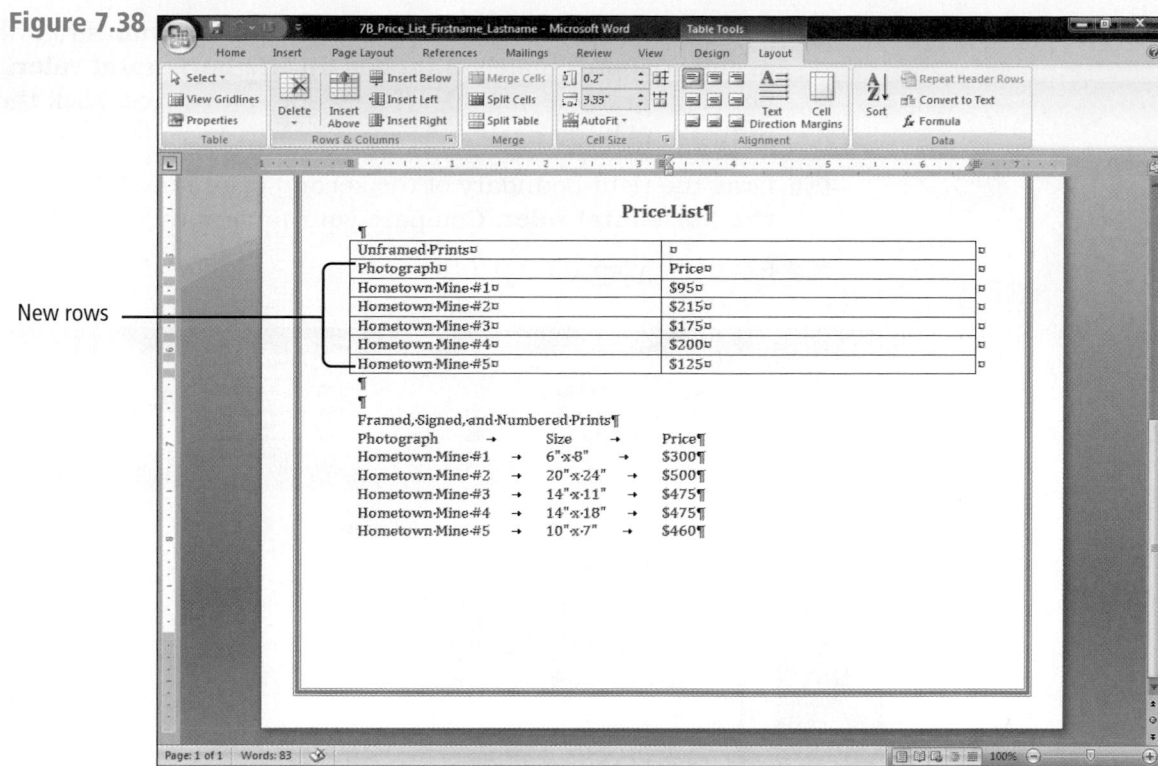

New rows

5 **Save** your document.

Activity 7.17 Changing the Width of a Table Column

1 In the first column of the table, move the pointer to the right boundary until the pointer displays, as shown in Figure 7.39.

Figure 7.39

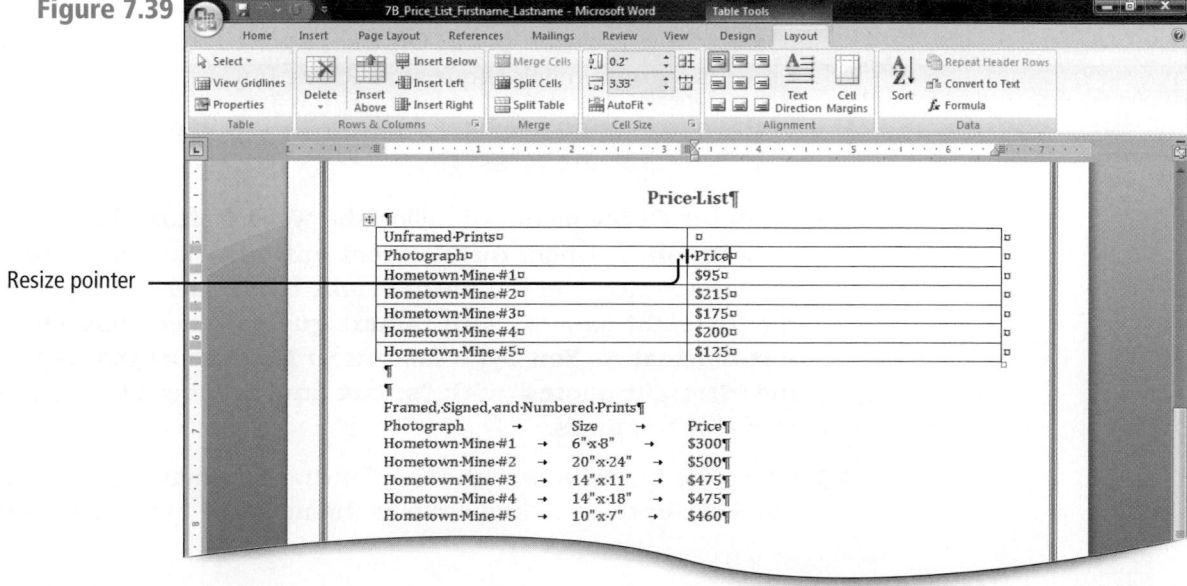

Resize pointer

2 Drag the boundary to the left until the first column's right boundary aligns at approximately **2 inches on the horizontal ruler**. Use the horizontal ruler as a guide. If only one row resizes, click the Undo button and begin again.

3 Drag the right boundary of the second column to **2.75 inches on the horizontal ruler**. Compare your table with Figure 7.40.

4 **Save** 🖫 your document.

Figure 7.40

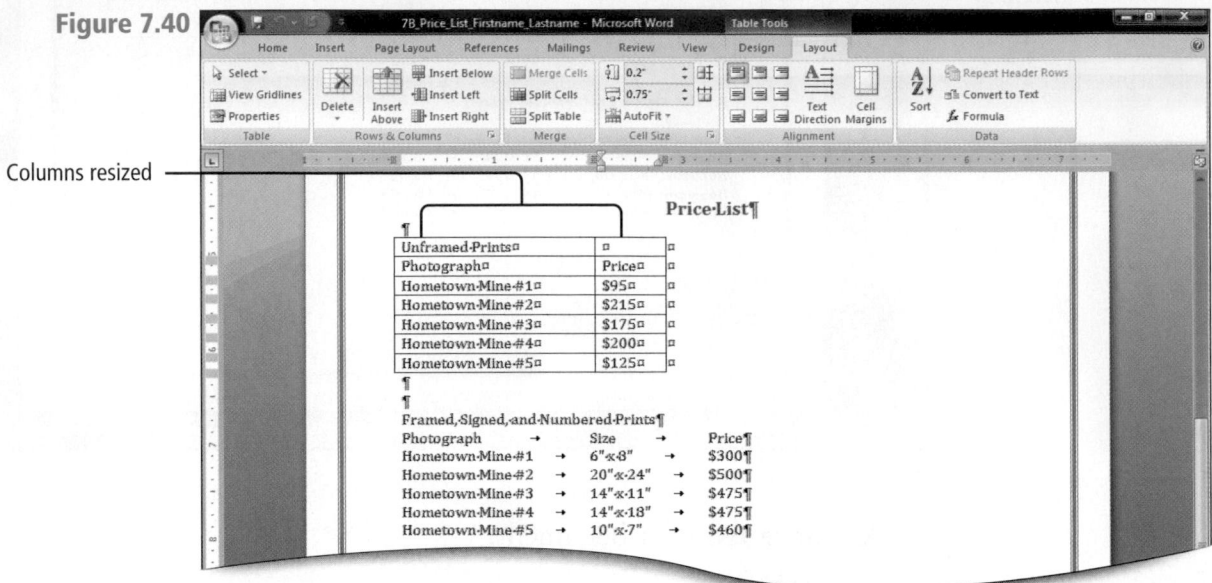

Columns resized

Activity 7.18 Adding a Column to a Table

You can add a column to a Word table in a manner similar to inserting a row.

1 In the first column of the table, click anywhere in the column to position the insertion point. On the **Layout tab**, in the **Rows & Columns group**, click the **Insert Right** button.

2 In the new column, click to place the insertion point in the second row. Type **Size** and press ↓.

3 From the **Office** menu 🏛, click the **Word Options** button, and then click **Proofing**. Under **AutoCorrect options**, click the **AutoCorrect Options** button. On the **AutoFormat tab**, under **Replace**, clear the **"Straight quotes" with "smart quotes"** check box. On the **AutoFormat As You Type tab**, under **Replace as you type**, clear the **"Straight quotes" with "smart quotes"** check box, and then click **OK** two times.

4 Complete the column with the following information. The text may be too wide for the cell, and wrap to the next line in the same cell.

6" x 8"
20" x 24"
14" x 11"
14" x 18"
10" x 7"

5 Drag the right boundary of the third column to **4 inches on the horizontal ruler**.

If you try to resize the middle column first, the right border of the table will remain fixed, thus decreasing the width of the column on the right.

6 Drag the right boundary of the second column to **3 inches on the horizontal ruler**, and then compare your screen with Figure 7.41.

Figure 7.41

New column inserted

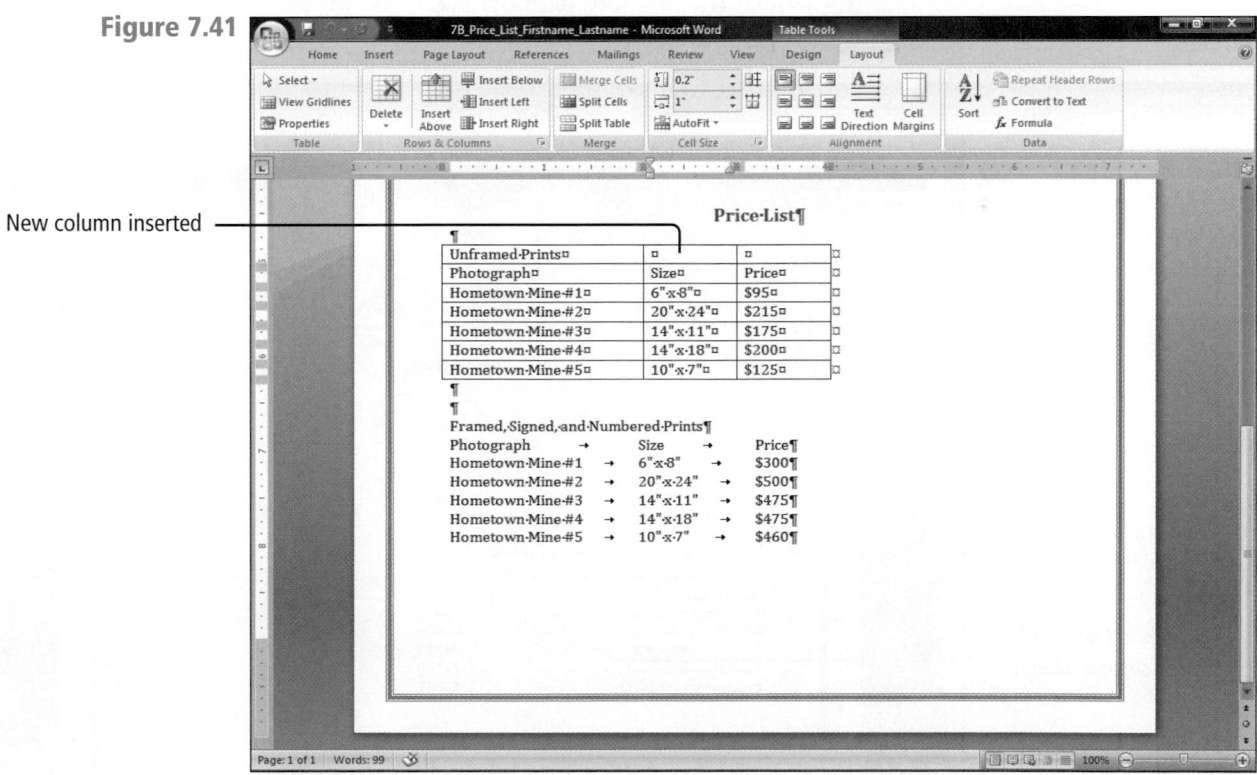

7 **Save** your document.

More Knowledge

Using Tabs in Tables

You can add tabs to a table column; doing so lets you indent items within a table cell. The easiest way to add a tab is to click on the ruler to set the location within a column. Then you can drag the tab stop indicator to change the location of the tab within the column or add the hanging indent marker so multiple lines in a list are evenly indented. To move to the tabbed location within the cell—and not to the next cell—press Ctrl + Tab.

Activity 7.19 Converting Text to Tables

The Insert Table feature is useful if you are beginning a new table, but Word also provides a tool that enables you to convert existing text into a table. The text must be marked using *separator characters*—usually tabs or commas that separate the text in each line. When you convert text to a table, you can have Word optimize the column widths at the same time. You can also add blank rows or columns, if needed.

1 Scroll as necessary to view the lower portion of the document. In the block of text at the end of the document, beginning with *Framed* and continuing to the end of the document, notice the tab marks indicating where the Tab key was pressed, as shown in Figure 7.42.

Tab marks can act as separator characters for the purpose of converting text to a table.

Figure 7.42

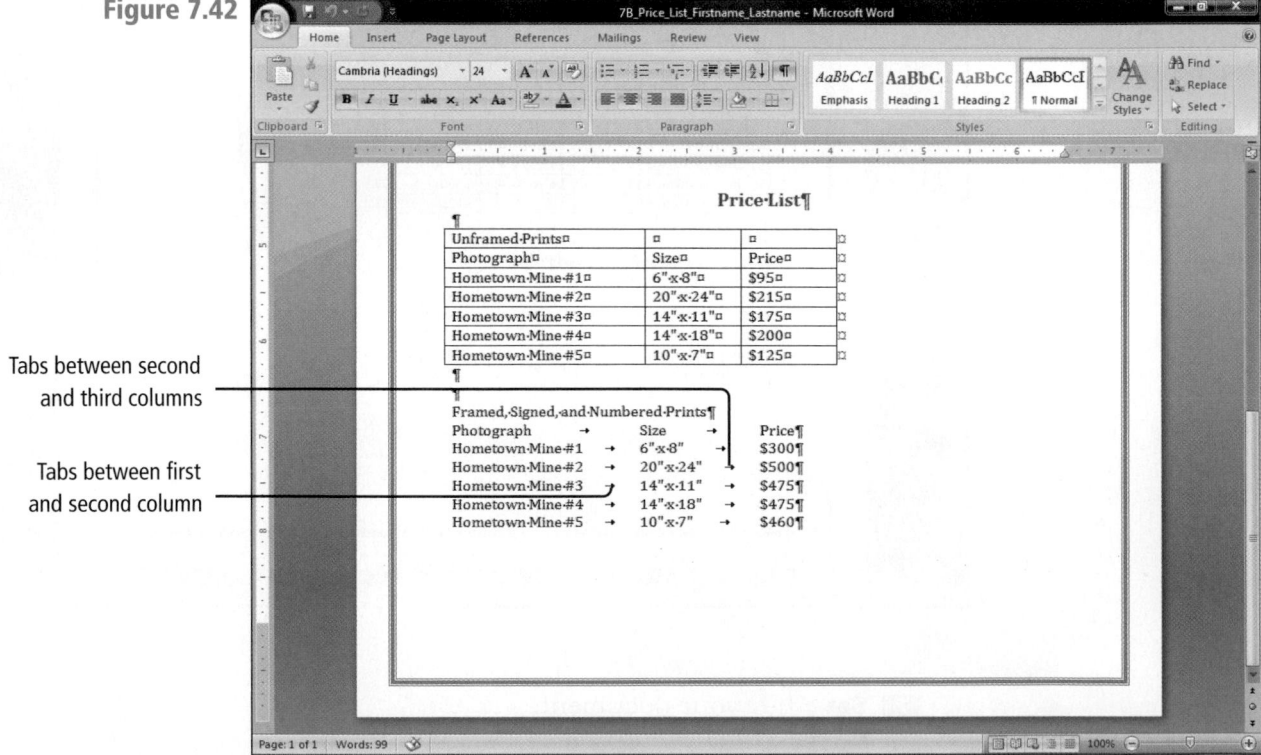

Tabs between second and third columns

Tabs between first and second column

2 Click to position the insertion point to the left of the word *Framed*, hold down ⇧ Shift, and then click at the end of the last line, after *$460*. Be sure you include the paragraph mark to the right of *$460*.

3 With the text selected, click the **Insert tab**. In the **Tables group**, click the **Table** button, and then click **Convert Text to Table**. In the displayed **Convert Text to Table** dialog box, under **Table size**, click the **Number of columns up spin arrow** to change the number of columns to **3**. Then, under **AutoFit behavior**, click the **AutoFit to contents** option button.

The AutoFit to contents option instructs Word to evaluate the contents of the columns and choose appropriate column widths for each column.

4 Under **Separate text at**, click the **Tabs** option button. Compare your dialog box with Figure 7.43.

Figure 7.43

Three columns

Column width adjusts to fit contents

Separator type

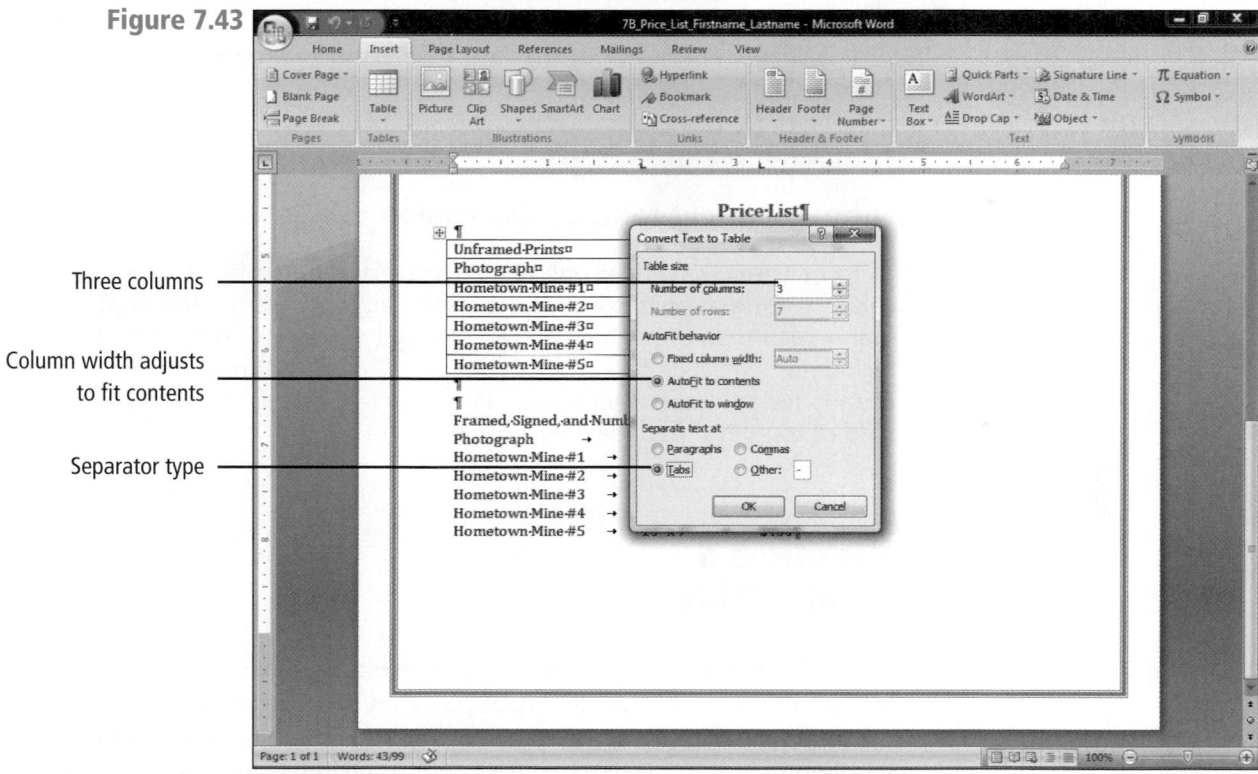

5 At the bottom of the **Convert Text to Table** dialog box, click **OK**.

Click anywhere in the document to deselect the table. **Save** 🖫 your document, and then compare your table with Figure 7.44.

The columns are set to the width of the widest item in each column.

Three columns—column widths adjust to fit contents

Figure 7.44

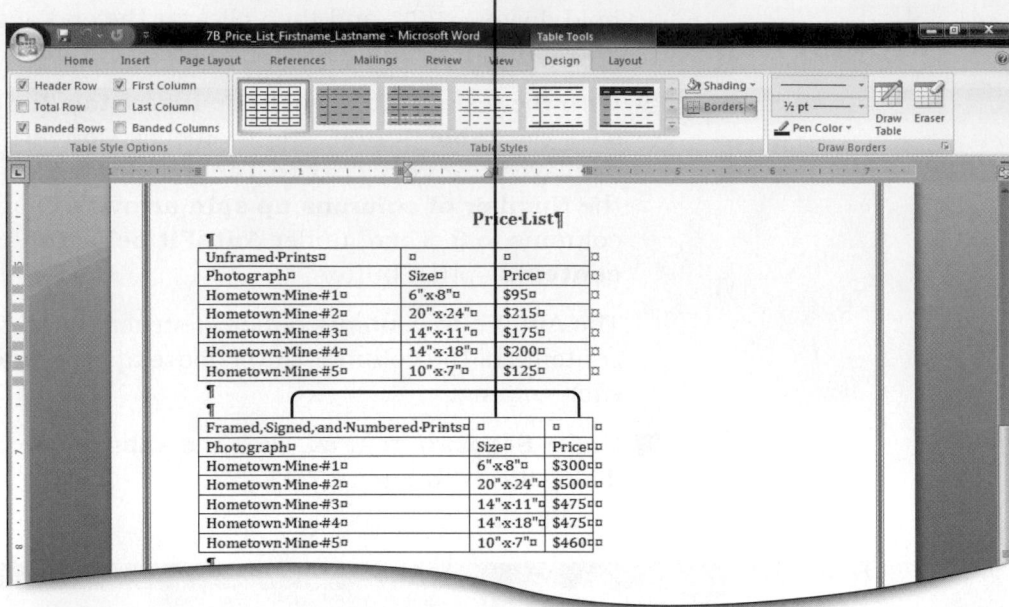

More Knowledge

Formatting Text for Easy Conversion to a Table

To format text that will eventually be converted into a table, separate the columns using a separator character. Tabs and commas are the most commonly used separators, but you can specify a number of different marks, including dashes, dollar signs, or colons. Word will not recognize a mixture of tabs and commas as separators in the same block of text. Use only one kind of separator between each column item.

Objective 5
Format a Table

You can format tables to make them more attractive and easier to read. When you type numbers, for example, they line up on the left of a column instead of on the right. With Word's formatting tools, you can shade cells, format the table borders and grid, align text, and center the table between the document margins. All of these features make a table more inviting to the reader.

Activity 7.20 Formatting Text in Cells and Shading Cells

1 In the upper table, click anywhere in the cell containing the word *Photograph*, hold down the left mouse button, and then drag to the right to select all three cells in the second row. On the Mini toolbar, click the **Bold** button **B** , and then click the **Center** button 　. Compare your screen with Figure 7.45.

Figure 7.45

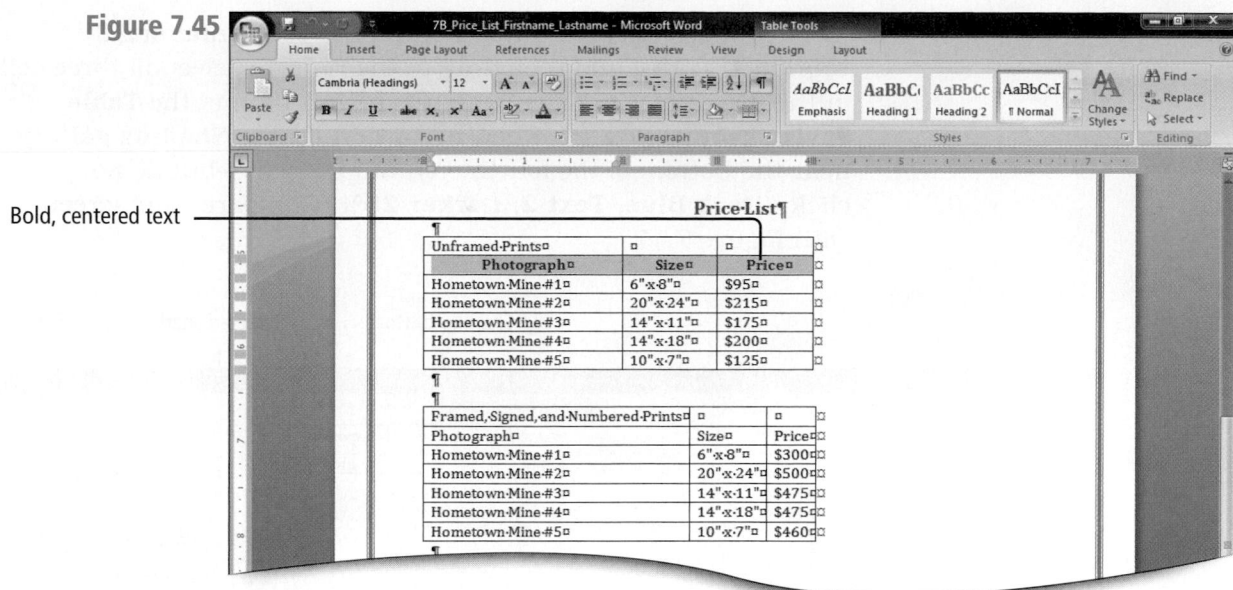

Bold, centered text ———

2 In the second column, click in the cell containing *6" × 8"* and then drag down to select the third cell through the seventh cell. On the Mini toolbar, click the **Center** button ▤.

3 In the third column, click in the cell containing *$95* and then drag down to select the third cell through the seventh cell. On the **Home tab**, in the **Paragraph group**, click the **Align Text Right** button ▤. Compare your screen with Figure 7.46.

Centered text   Right-aligned text

Figure 7.46

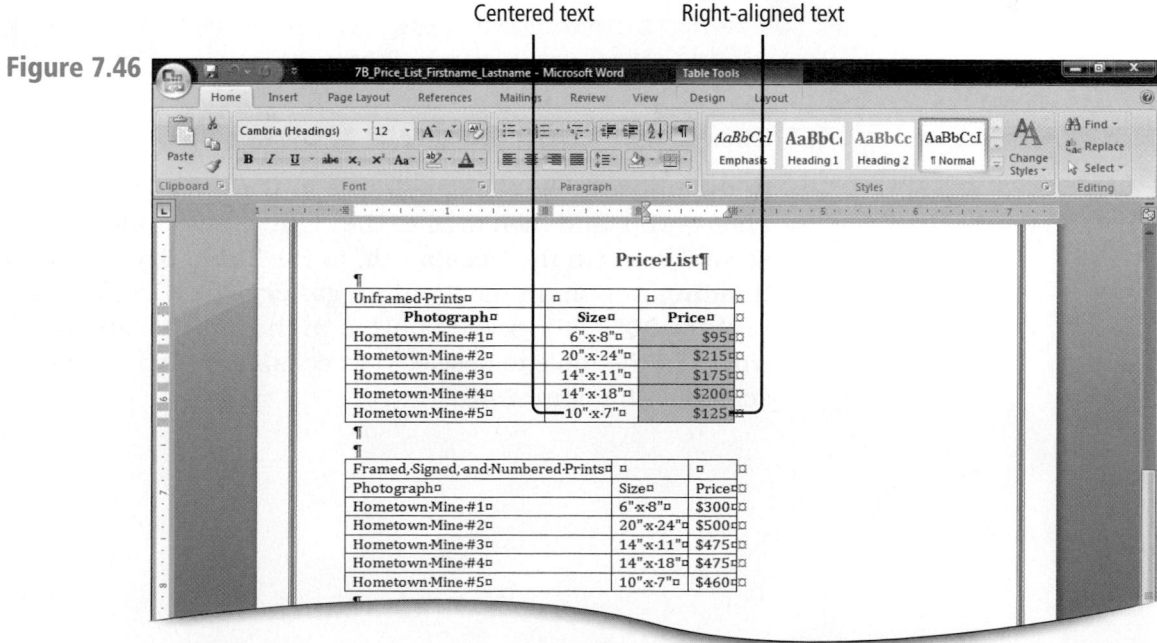

4 In the upper table, click anywhere in the cell containing the *Unframed Prints*, and then drag to the right to select all three cells in the first row. Click the **Design tab**, and then in the **Table Styles group**, click the **Shading** button. In the **Shading gallery**, near the bottom of the fourth column, point to—but do not click—**Dark Blue, Text 2, Darker 25%**. Compare your screen with Figure 7.47.

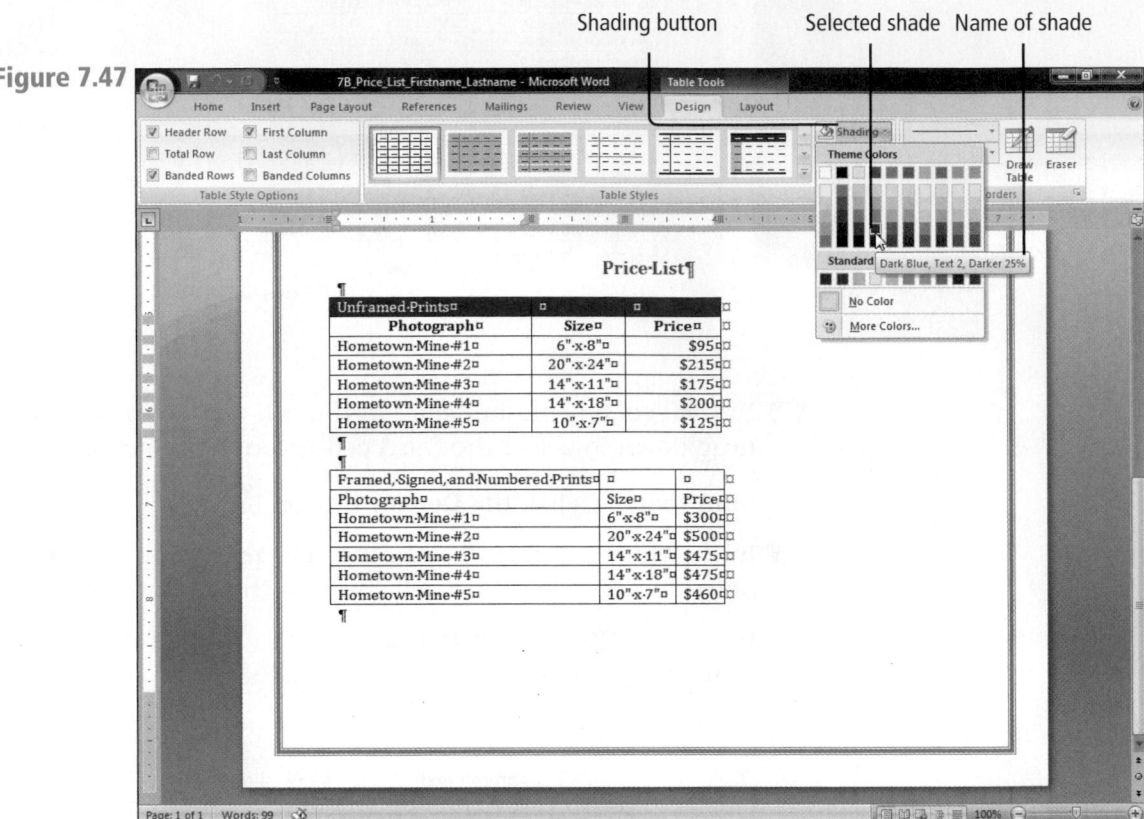

Figure 7.47

Shading button   Selected shade   Name of shade

5 Click to apply **Dark Blue, Text 2, Darker 25%**.

6 In the upper table, click anywhere in the cell containing the word *Photograph*, and then drag to the right to select all three cells in the second row. On the **Design tab**, in the **Table Styles group**, click the **Shading** button. In the **Shading gallery**, click **Dark Blue, Text 2, Lighter 80%**—the second button in the fourth column. Click anywhere in the table to deselect the cells, and then compare your screen with Figure 7.48.

Figure 7.48

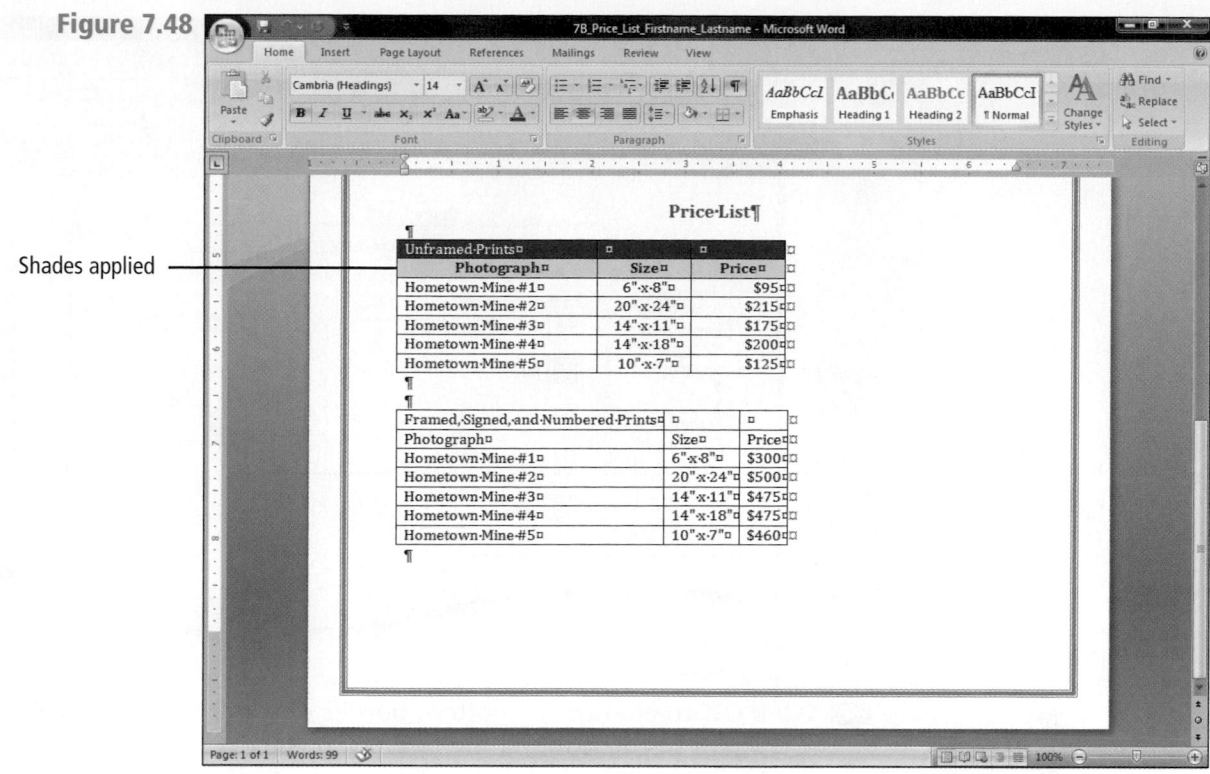

Shades applied

7 Save ![save icon] the document.

Activity 7.21 Changing the Table Border

You can modify or remove the border from an entire table, a selected cell, or individual boundaries of a cell.

1 In the upper table, click anywhere in the cell containing the word *Photograph*, and then drag to the right to select all three cells in the second row.

2 On the **Design tab**, in the **Table Styles group**, click the **Borders button arrow**, and then click **Borders and Shading**. Alternatively, right-click anywhere in the selected cells and click Borders and Shading.

3 In the displayed **Borders and Shading** dialog box, under **Setting**, click the **Custom** button. Click the **Width arrow**, and then click **1 1/2 pt**. In the **Preview** area, click the bottom border of the preview diagram. Notice that the Preview area displays a bottom border that is heavier than the side or top borders, as shown in Figure 7.49.

The Custom setting enables you to change the characteristics of individual border lines, rather than change all of the borders at one time.

Figure 7.49

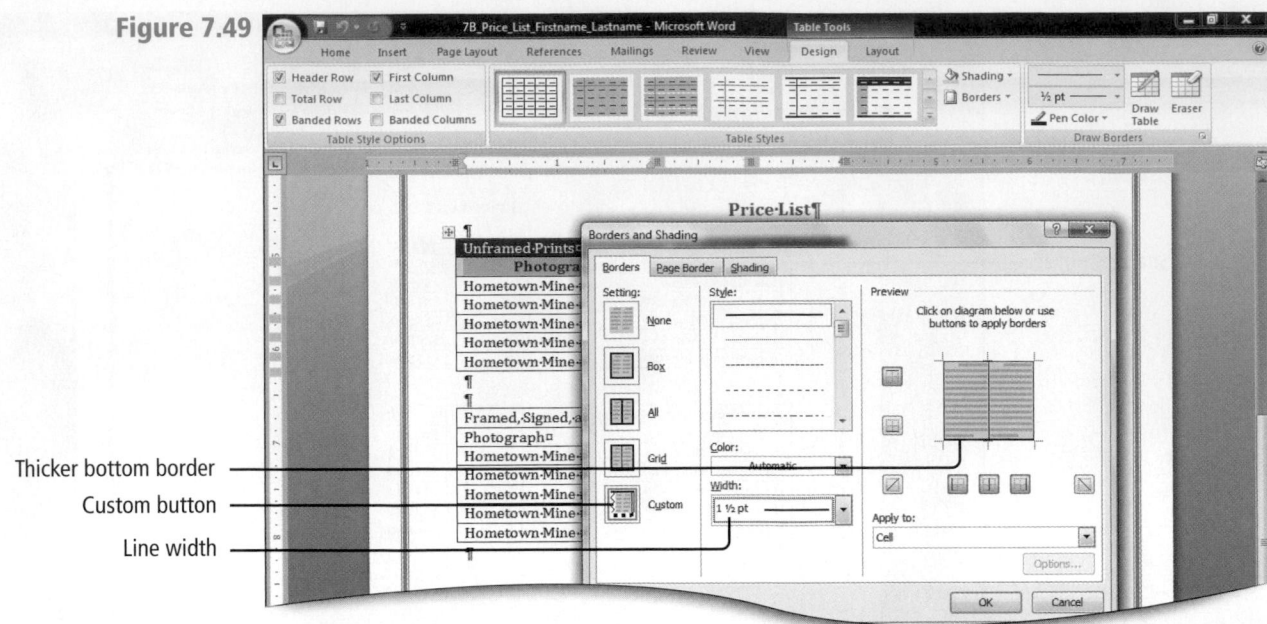

Thicker bottom border

Custom button

Line width

4 Click **OK** to change the bottom border of the selected cells. Click anywhere in the upper table, and then click the **Layout tab**. In the **Table group**, click the **Select** button, and then click **Select Table**.

5 Click the **Design tab**, and then in the **Table Styles group**, click the **Borders** button. In the displayed **Borders and Shading** dialog box, under **Setting**, click the **Custom** button, if necessary. Click the **Width arrow**, and then click **1 1/2 pt**. In the **Preview** area, click the four outside borders, and then click **OK**.

6 Click anywhere in the document to deselect the table, and then compare your screen with Figure 7.50.

Figure 7.50

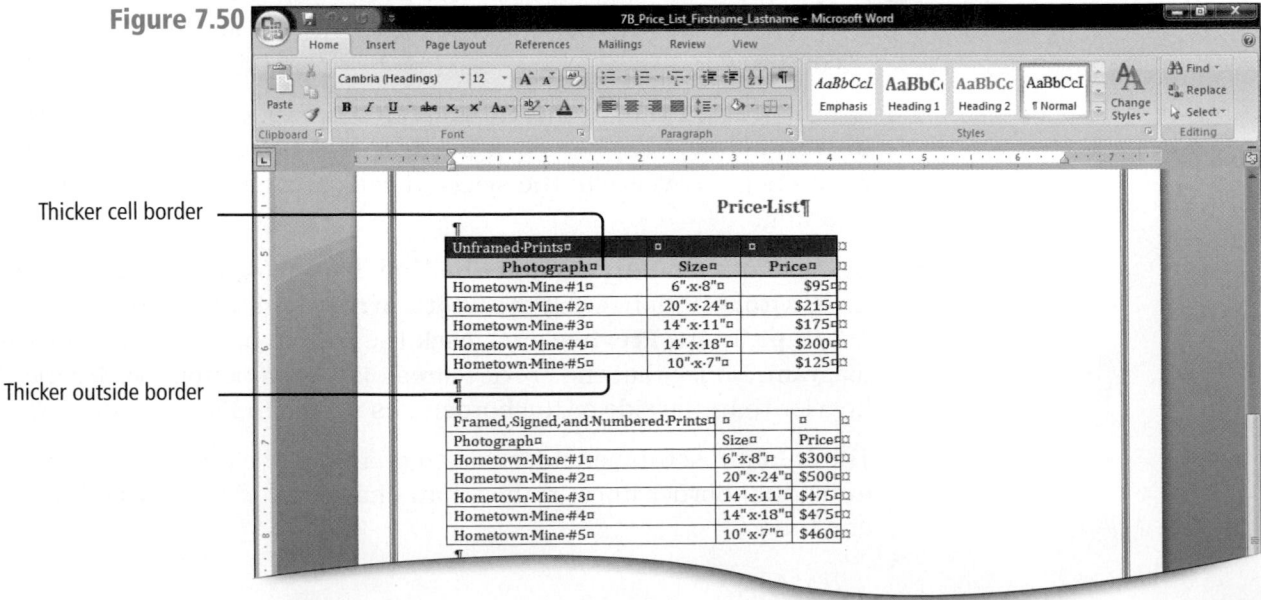

Thicker cell border

Thicker outside border

7 **Save** the document.

Activity 7.22 Centering a Table

1 Click anywhere in the upper table, and then click the **Layout tab**. In the **Table group**, click the **Select** button, and then click **Select Table**.

2 Click the **Home tab**, and then in the **Paragraph group**, click the **Center** button ▤.

Another Way

To Center a Table

You can center a table without selecting the table first. Right-click anywhere in the table, and then, from the shortcut menu, click Table Properties. In the Table Properties dialog box, on the Table tab, under Alignment, click Center. The Table Properties dialog box also enables you to wrap text around a table the way you wrap text around a graphic.

3 Click anywhere in the document to deselect the table, and then compare your screen with Figure 7.51.

Table centered horizontally on the page

Figure 7.51

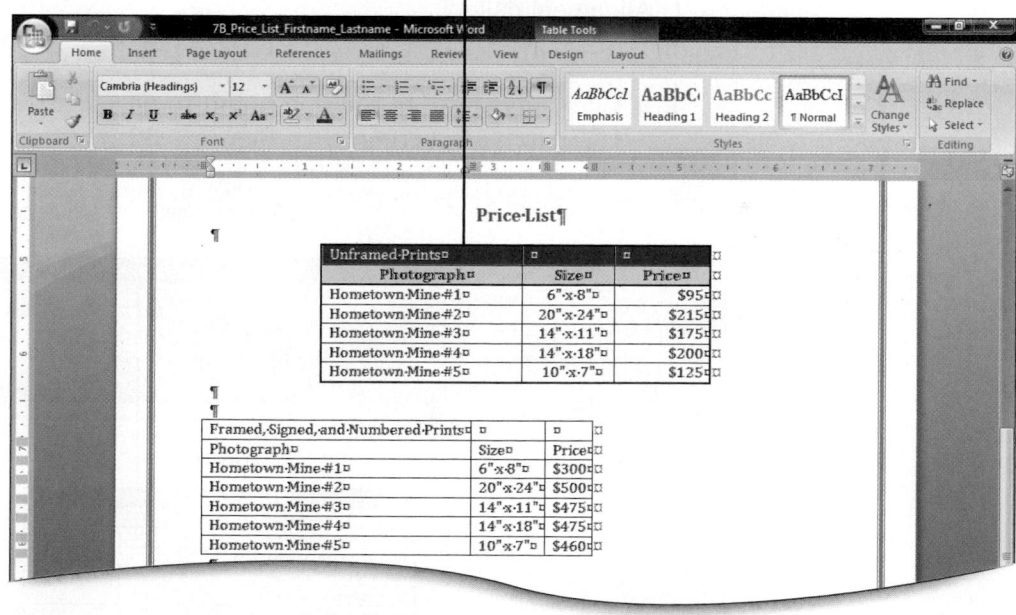

4 **Save** ▤ the document.

Activity 7.23 Merging Cells

The title of a table typically spans two or more columns. In this activity, you will merge cells so that you can position the table title across the columns.

1 In the upper table, click anywhere in the cell containing the word *Unframed Prints*, and then drag to the right to select all three cells in the first row.

2 Click the **Layout tab**, and then in the **Merge group**, click the **Merge Cells** button.

The cells are merged, and the borders between the top row of cells are removed.

3 Select the text in the top cell—**Unframed Prints**. On the Mini toolbar, click the **Bold** button ⬛, and then click the **Center** button ⬛.

Another Way — **To Align Text in a Table**

You can use shortcut menus to align text in a table. Right-click the cell, point to Cell Alignment from the shortcut menu, and then click the alignment style you want from the Cell Alignment gallery that displays. You can choose from both vertical and horizontal cell alignment options using the Cell Alignment gallery.

---

4 Click anywhere in the document to deselect the table, and then compare your screen with Figure 7.52.

Text is merged across three cells

Figure 7.52

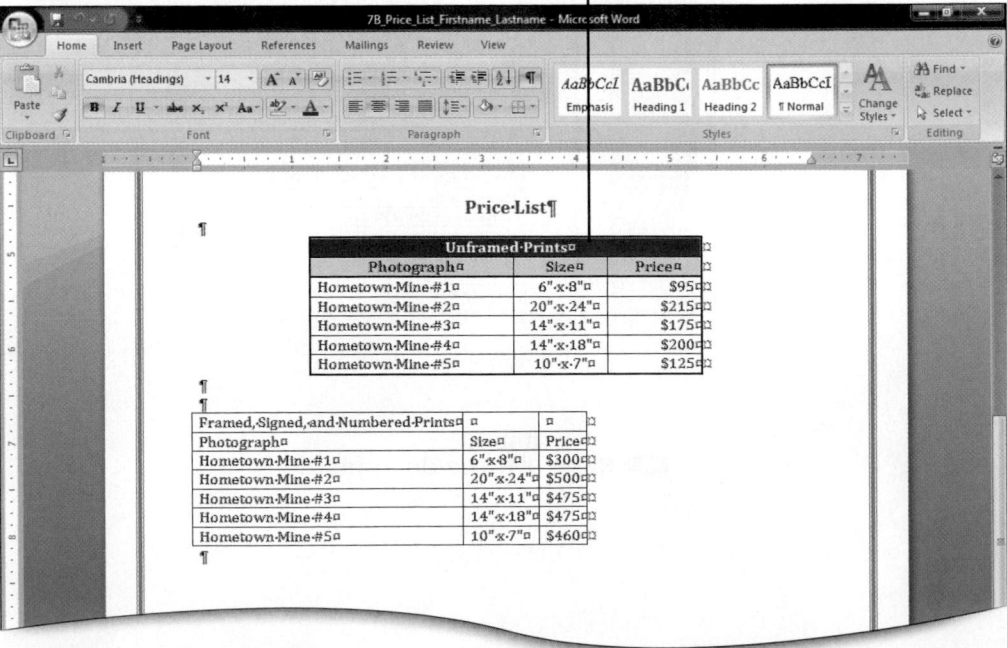

5 Save ⬛ the document.

Activity 7.24 Applying a Predefined Format to a Table

Word includes a number of built-in table formats with which you can quickly give your table a professional design. This is accomplished by applying a ***Table Style***—a predefined set of formatting characteristics, including font, alignment, and cell shading.

1 In the lower table, click anywhere to position the insertion point within the table—you need not select the entire table to use Table Styles.

2 Click the **Design tab**. In the **Table Styles group**, point to the second Table Style—**Table 3D effects 1** and notice that Live Preview displays the table the way it would look if you clicked that style, as shown in Figure 7.53.

Live Preview displays the table style   Table 3D effects 1 style

Figure 7.53

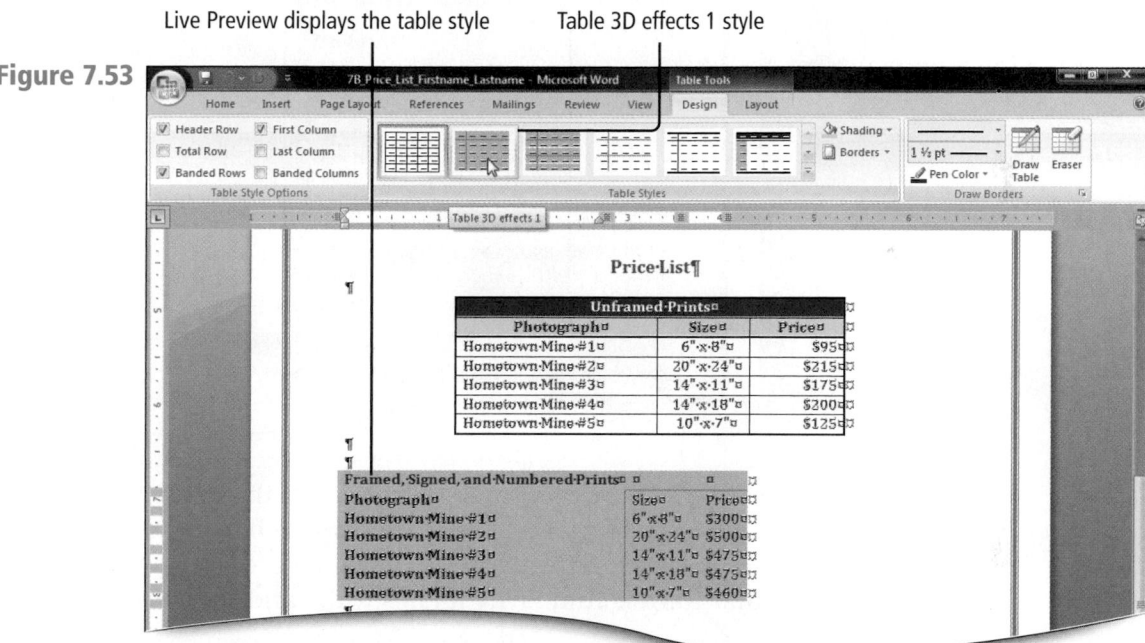

3 In the **Table Styles group**, click the **More** button . Scroll down to view the available table styles, and then point to several of the styles in the gallery. Click anywhere in the document to close the gallery.

4 In the **Table Styles group**, point to the third style—**Table 3D effects 2**—and click to apply the style. Click the **Layout tab**, and then in the **Table group**, click the **Select** button, and then click **Select Table**.

5 Click the **Design tab**. In the **Table Styles group**, click the **Shading** button, and then in the second row, click the fourth color—**Dark Blue, Text 2, Lighter 80%**.

6 Right-click the table, and then from the shortcut menu, click **Table Properties**. In the displayed **Table Properties** dialog box, on the **Table tab**, under **Alignment**, click **Center**.

7 Point to the Table Properties dialog box title bar, and then drag the dialog box up and to the right so that you can see most of the lower table. In the **Table Properties** dialog box, click the **Column tab**. Under **Size**, click the **Next Column** button to select the first column, as shown in Figure 7.54.

First column is highlighted   Next Column button

Figure 7.54

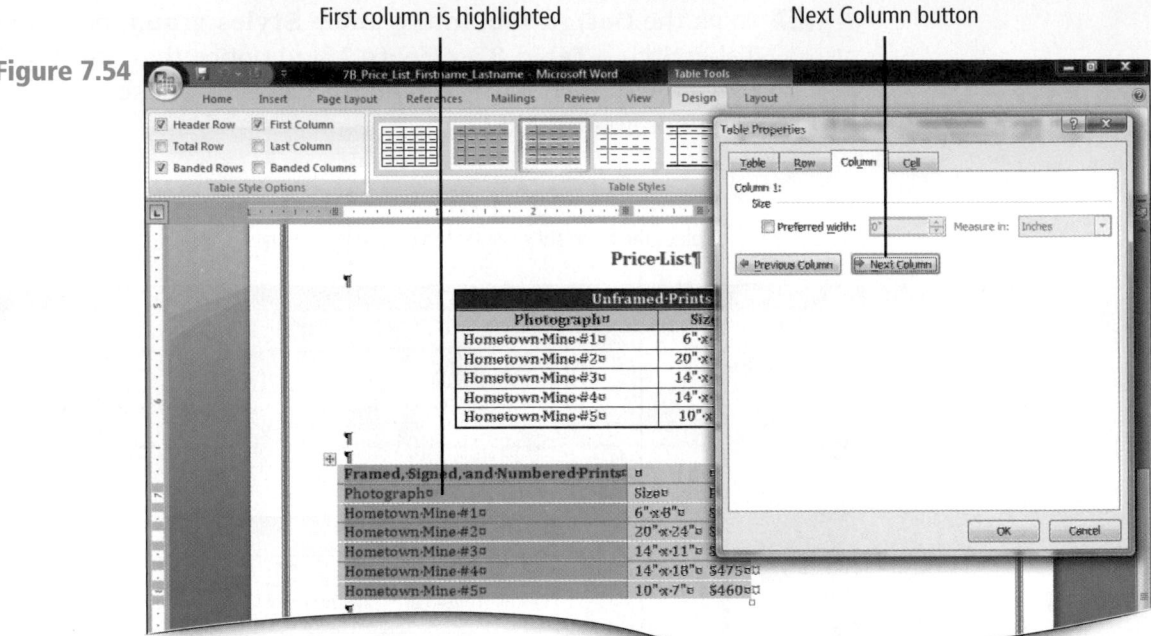

8 With the first column selected, select the **Preferred width** check box, select the text in the **Preferred width** box, type **2** and then click the **Next Column** button. Use the same procedure to make the second and third columns **1.1** inches wide, and then click **OK**.

9 Point to the first cell of the top row and drag to the right to select all three cells. Click the **Layout tab**. In the **Merge group**, click the **Merge Cells** button. In the **Alignment group**, click the **Align Center** button ⊟.

10 In the second row of the table, select all three cells, and then on the Mini toolbar, click the **Bold** button **B**, and then click the **Center** button ☰.

11 In the second column, click in the cell containing *6″ × 8″*, and then drag down to select the third cell through the seventh cell. On the Mini toolbar, click the **Center** button ☰.

12 In the third column, click in the cell containing *$300*, and then drag down to select the third cell through the seventh cell. Click the **Home tab**, and then in the **Paragraph group**, click the **Align Text Right** button ☰. Click anywhere in the document to deselect the cells, and then compare your screen with Figure 7.55.

Figure 7.55

Centered text   Right-aligned text

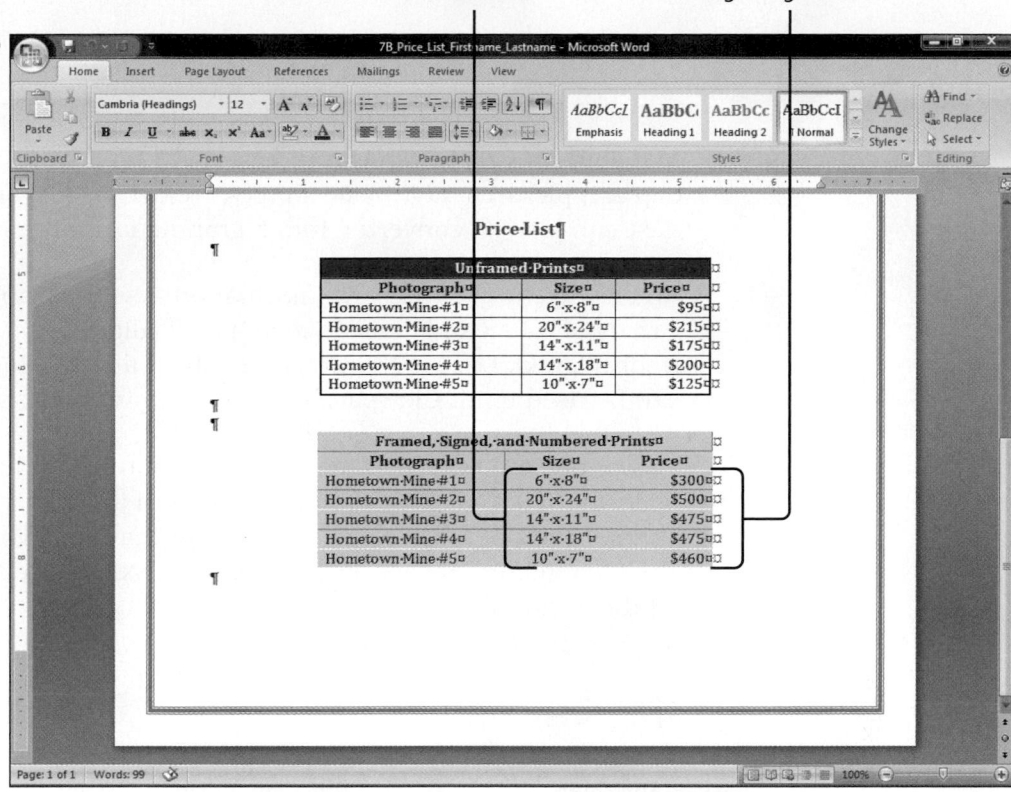

13 From the **Office** menu 🔘, click the **Word Options** button, and then click **Proofing**. Under **AutoCorrect options**, click the **AutoCorrect Options** button. On the **AutoFormat tab**, under **Replace**, select the **"Straight quotes" with "smart quotes"** check box. Repeat this procedure on the **AutoFormat As You Type tab**, and then click **OK** two times.

14 Add the file name to the footer, and then **Save** 💾 your document. Submit the document as directed.

15 **Close** your document, and then **Exit** Word.

End **You have completed Project 7B** ——————————

There's More You Can Do!

Close Word and any other open windows. Display the Start menu, click Computer, and then navigate to the student files that accompany this textbook. In the folder **02_theres_more_you_can_do**, locate and open the folder for this chapter. Open and print the instructions for this project, which are provided to you in Adobe PDF format.

Try It!—Create a Chart

In this Try It! exercise, you will insert a chart into a Word document.

Content-Based Assessments

Summary

Many graphic elements can be inserted into a Word document, including clip art, pictures, and basic shapes created with Word's drawing tools. Text can also be converted into a graphic format using WordArt.

An effective way to present information is with a tabbed list or a table. A variety of tabs can be used, such as left-aligned, decimal, centered, or right-aligned. Leader characters, such as a solid, dotted, or dashed line, can be used to fill the space created by using a tab stop.

Tables present information in a format of rows and columns. Tables can be formatted to display the information in a manner that emphasizes certain parts of the table. Text in a table can be formatted using both the Table contextual tools and Table Styles. Existing text can be converted to a table format.

Key Terms

Adjustment handle 177	**Floating object** 181	**Smart quote** 209
Anchor 177	**Graphic** 176	**Straight quote** 209
Cell 204	**Inline object** 178	**Tab stop** 187
Click and type pointer 188	**Leader character** 192	**Table** 205
Column chart .... 🌐	**Pie chart** .... 🌐	**Table Style** 219
Dot leader 192	**Rotate handle** 177	**Text box** 197
Drawing canvas 196	**Separator character** 210	**Text wrapping** 181
Drawing object 176	**Shapes** 200	**WordArt** 176
	Sizing handle 177	

The 🌐 symbol represents Key Terms found on the Student CD in the 02_theres_more_you_can_do folder for this chapter.

Content-Based Assessments

Matching

Match each term in the second column with its correct definition in the first column by writing the letter of the term on the blank line in front of the correct definition.

_____ 1. A gallery of text styles with which you can create decorative effects, such as shadowed or mirrored text.

_____ 2. An object or graphic that can be moved independently of the surrounding text.

_____ 3. An object or graphic inserted in a document that acts like a character in a sentence.

_____ 4. Small squares or circles in the corners of a selected graphic with which you can resize the graphic proportionally.

_____ 5. A movable, resizable container for text or graphics.

_____ 6. A handle on a selected graphic that can be dragged to rotate the graphic to any angle.

_____ 7. The symbol that indicates the paragraph to which an object is attached.

_____ 8. Predefined drawing shapes, such as stars, banners, arrows, and callouts, included with Microsoft Office, and that can be inserted into documents.

_____ 9. Characters that form a solid, dotted, or dashed line that fills the space used by a tab character.

_____ 10. A character used to identify column placement in text; usually a tab or a comma.

_____ 11. A mark on the ruler that indicates the location where the insertion point will be placed when you press the Tab key.

_____ 12. The text select (I-beam) pointer with various attached shapes that indicate which formatting will be applied when you double-click—such as a left-aligned, centered, or right-aligned tab stop.

_____ 13. The rectangular box in a table formed by the intersection of a row and column.

_____ 14. Rows and columns of text or numbers used to organize data and present it effectively.

_____ 15. A command that applies one of a number of built-in table formats—resulting in a table with a professional design.

A Anchor

B Cell

C Click and type pointer

D Corner sizing handles

E Floating object

F Inline object

G Leader characters

H Rotate handle

I Separator character

J Shapes

K Tab stop

L Table

M Table Style

N Text box

O WordArt

Content-Based Assessments

Fill in the Blank

Write the correct answer in the space provided.

1. A(n) _____ symbol indicates the paragraph to which an object is attached.

2. When a graphic is selected, _____ _____ display around the edge of the graphic.

3. To align text to the contours of an irregularly shaped graphic, choose _____ Text Wrapping.

4. A banner is an example of a predefined _____ that can be inserted into a document.

5. Tab stops are a form of paragraph formatting and are stored in the _____ mark.

6. The tab alignment option that centers text around a tab stop is the _____ tab.

7. A series of dots following a tab that serve to guide the reader's eyes is known as a dot _____.

8. To move text aligned with tabs, select the text and drag the _____ _____ on the ruler.

9. To move from cell to cell across a table as you enter text, press _____.

10. To create a table in Word, click the _____ button on the Insert tab.

11. When you press [Tab] with the insertion point in the last cell in a table, a new _____ is added to the table.

12. On the Table Tools Design tab, click the _____ button to add gray or color to a table cell.

13. To set the alignment of a table on a page, display the Table tab of the _____ _____ dialog box.

14. A predefined set of table formatting characteristics, including font, alignment, and cell shading is called a Table _____.

15. To combine two or more cells into one cell, use the _____ _____ button on the Layout tab.

Content-Based Assessments

Project 7C—Creative Supplies

In this project, you will apply the skills you practiced from the Objectives in Project 7A.

Objectives: 1. *Insert and Format Graphics;* **2.** *Set Tab Stops;* **3.** *Insert and Modify Text Boxes and Shapes.*

In the following Skills Review, you will create a flyer for Memories Old and New that describes the range of products available at the store. Your completed flyer will look similar to the one shown in Figure 7.56.

For Project 7C, you will need the following files:

New blank Word document
w07C_Art_Supplies
w07C_Supplies

You will save your document as
7C_Creative_Supplies_Firstname_Lastname

Figure 7.56

(Project 7C–Creative Supplies continues on the next page)

Content-Based Assessments

(Project 7C–Creative Supplies continued)

1. **Start** Word and display formatting marks and rulers. From the **Page Layout tab**, display the **Page Setup** dialog box, set the **Top** and **Bottom** margins to **1"**, the **Left** and **Right** margins to **1.25"**, and then click **OK**.

2. Type **Memories Old and New** and then press [Enter] two times. Select the text you just typed, but do not select the paragraph mark. Click the **Insert tab**. In the **Text group**, click the **WordArt** button. From the displayed **WordArt gallery**, in the second row, click the second style—**WordArt style 8**. Click **OK**.

3. On the **Format tab**, in the **Size group**, click the **Shape Height button up spin arrow** as necessary to change the height of the WordArt to **1"**. Click the **Shape Width button up spin arrow** as necessary to change the width of the WordArt to **6"**. Display the **Save As** dialog box, navigate to your **Word Chapter 7** folder, save the document as **7C_Creative_Supplies_ Firstname_Lastname** and then add the file name to the footer.

4. Close the footer area. Press [Ctrl] + [End]. Click the **Insert tab**. From the **Text group**, click the **Object button arrow**, and then click **Text from File**. Locate and insert the file **w07C_Supplies**. In the paragraph beginning *Scrapbookers*, click to position the insertion point at the beginning of the paragraph. In the **Illustrations group**, click the **Picture** button. Locate and insert **w07C_Art_Supplies**.

5. On the **Format tab**, in the **Size group**, click the **Shape Height spin box down arrow** as necessary to change the height of the picture to **1.4"**. With the graphic still selected, on the **Format tab**, in the **Arrange group**, click the **Text Wrapping** button. From the **Text Wrapping gallery**, click **Square** to wrap the text around the graphic.

6. Point anywhere in the **w07C_Art_Supplies** graphic to display the pointer, and then drag the graphic up until the top edge of the graphic is aligned with the top edge of the paragraph beginning *Memories Old and New*. Be sure the left side of the graphic is aligned with the left side of the text. With the graphic still selected, on the **Format tab**, in the **Picture Styles group**, click the third picture style—**Metal Frame**. Move the picture as necessary to match Figure 7.56.

7. Click anywhere in the document to deselect the graphic. Click the **Page Layout tab**, and then in the **Page Background group**, click the **Page Borders** button. In the displayed **Borders and Shading** dialog box, under **Setting**, click **Box**. Click the **Color arrow**, and then in the last column of colors, click the fifth button—**Orange, Accent 6, Darker 25%**. Click the **Width arrow**, click **3 pt**, and then click **OK**. **Save** your document.

8. Scroll to display the lower half of the document on your screen, and then click in the blank line at the end of the document. Move the pointer on your screen to position it at approximately **6.5 inches on the vertical ruler** and at the left margin, double-click to place the insertion point. If necessary, change the **Font** to **Cambria**, and the **Font Size** to **14**. Type **Store Hours** and press [Enter].

9. Be sure the **Tab Alignment** button displays a **Left tab**. Click on **4 inches on the horizontal ruler**. Double-click the tab stop you just added to the ruler. In the

(Project 7C–Creative Supplies continues on the next page)

Content-Based Assessments

(Project 7C–Creative Supplies continued)

displayed **Tabs** dialog box, under **Tab stop position**, click to select the lower **4"**. Under **Alignment**, click the **Right** option button. Under **Leader**, click the **2** option button to add a dot leader. Click the **Set** button, and then click **OK**.

10. Display the **Paragraph** dialog box. Under **Indentation**, click the **Left spin box up arrow** to change the left margin indent to **1"**. Under **Spacing**, click the **After down spin arrow** two times to change the spacing to **0**. Click the **Line spacing arrow**, click **Single**, and then click **OK**. Type the following text, pressing Tab after the days of the week, and Enter after the time:

Monday to Friday   9 a.m. – 9 p.m.
Saturday   9 a.m. – 6 p.m.
Sunday   10 a.m. – 4 p.m.

11. Select the text *Store Hours*. On the Mini toolbar, click the **Bold** and **Center** buttons. Click the **Font Size button arrow**, and then click **16**. Select the three lines of tabbed text. Point to the horizontal ruler and position the pointer so the tip of the pointer arrow is touching the **4-inch tab stop**. When you see the *Right Tab* ScreenTip, drag the tab stop mark to the right to **5 inches on the ruler**. Click anywhere in the document to deselect the text.

12. Click the **Insert tab**, and then from the **Text group**, click the **Text Box** button. At the bottom of the **Text Box gallery**, click **Draw Text Box**. Move the + pointer to the left margin at **5 inches on the vertical ruler**. Using both the horizontal and vertical rulers as guides, drag down and to the right to create a text box approximately **1 inch** high and **3 inches** wide—then use the spin arrows in the **Size group** to size the text box precisely. With the insertion

point displayed in the text box, type **See our schedule for in-house classes. We have just added classes on scrapbooking and archival photo storage techniques.**

13. In the text box, select all of the text. On the Mini toolbar, click the **Font Size button arrow**, and then click **14**. If necessary, click the **Font button arrow**, and then click **Calibri**. Click the **Center** button. Display the **Paragraph** dialog box. Change the spacing **After** to **0** and the **Line spacing** to **Single**. With the text box still selected, on the **Format tab**, in the **Size group**, click the **Shape Width button up spin arrow** as necessary to change the width of the text box to **4"**. Click the **Shape Height button down spin arrow** as necessary to change the height of the text box to **0.8"**.

14. Point to one of the text box borders until the pointer displays. Drag the text box down and to the right until the left edge is at approximately **1 inch on the horizontal ruler**, and the top edge is at approximately **5.5 inches on the vertical ruler**. Use Figure 7.56 as a guide. On the **Format tab**, in the **3-D Effects group**, click the **3-D Effects** button. Under **Parallel**, click the first button—**3-D Style 1**. Click anywhere in the document to deselect the text box. **Save** your document.

15. Click the **Insert tab**, and then in the **Illustrations group**, click the **Shapes** button. From the displayed **Shapes gallery**, under **Stars and Banners**, in the first row, click the last button—**Curved Down Ribbon**. Move the + pointer to the left margin at **8 inches on the vertical ruler**. Using both the horizontal and vertical rulers as guides, drag down and to the

(Project 7C–Creative Supplies continues on the next page)

(Project 7C–Creative Supplies continued)

right to create a banner approximately **0.8 inch** high and **6 inches** wide—then use the spin box arrows in the **Size group** to size the banner precisely. Center the banner between the left and right border, and between the tabbed list and the bottom border.

16. Right-click the banner. From the shortcut menu, click **Add Text**. Type **Student and Teacher Discounts Are Available** Select the banner text, and then, on the Mini toolbar, click the **Bold** button, and then click the **Center** button. Click the **Font Color button arrow**, and then in the last column, click the last button—click **Orange, Accent 6, Darker 50%**. Click the **Font**

Size button arrow, and then click **16**. On the **Home tab**, in the **Paragraph group**, click the **Line spacing button arrow**, and then click **1.0**.

17. On the **Format tab**, in the **Text Box Styles group**, click the **Shape Fill arrow**, and then in the last column, click the third button—**Orange, Accent 6, Lighter 60%**. Click to deselect the banner, and then **Save** your document.

18. Display the **Print Preview** to make a final check of your document. Submit your document as directed.

19. **Close** your document, and then **Exit** Word.

End **You have completed Project 7C**

Content-Based Assessments

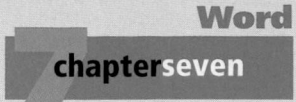
Skills Review

Project 7D—Sales Figures

In this project, you will apply the skills you practiced from the Objectives in Project 7B.

Objectives: 4. *Create a Table;* **5.** *Format a Table.*

In the following Skills Review, you will edit a memo about the recent photography exhibition at Memories Old and New. You will create and format a table, convert text to a table, and then AutoFormat the table. Your completed document will look similar to Figure 7.57.

For Project 7D, you will need the following file:

w07D_Sales_Figures

**You will save your document as
7D_Sales_Figures_Firstname_Lastname**

Figure 7.57

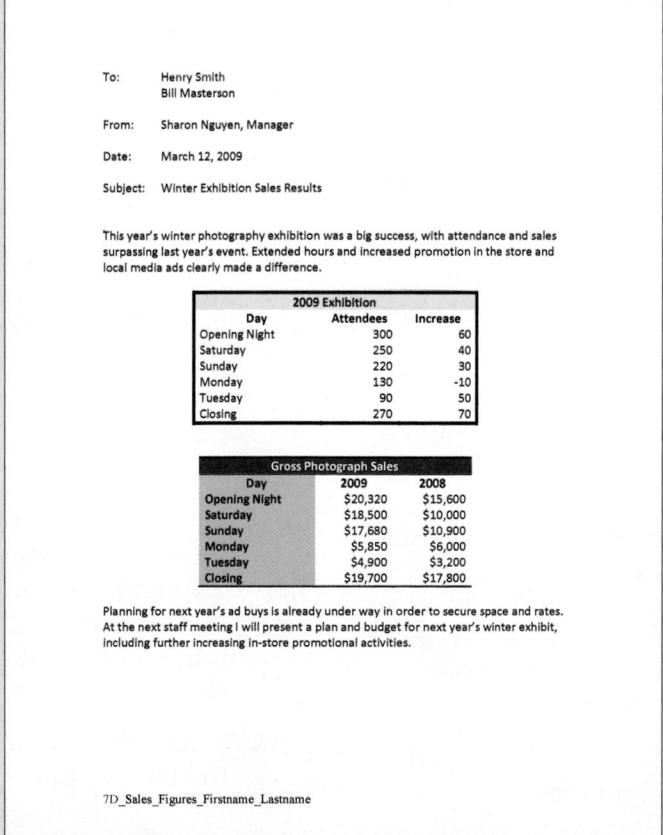

(Project 7D–Sales Figures continues on the next page)

Content-Based Assessments

(Project 7D—Sales Figures continued)

1. **Start** Word. From your student files, locate and open the document **w07D_Sales_Figures**, and display formatting marks and rulers. In the three blank lines under the paragraph beginning *This year's winter*, click in the middle blank line. Click the **Insert tab**, and then in the **Tables group**, click the **Table** button. In the **Table gallery**, in the sixth row of squares, point to the second square, and then click to insert a **2x6** table.

2. Type **2009 Exhibition** and then press ↓ to move to the first cell in the second row. Type **Opening Night** and press Tab. Type **300** and press Tab.

3. Type the following to complete the table, but do not press Tab after the last item.

Saturday	250
Sunday	220
Monday	130
Tuesday	90

4. From the **Office** menu, display the **Save As** dialog box, and then navigate to your **Word Chapter 7 folder**. In the **File name** box, type **7D_Sales_Figures_Firstname_Lastname** and press Enter. Add the file name to the footer area.

5. Position the insertion point in the last cell in the table, and then press Tab to add a new row to the bottom of the table. Type **Closing** and press Tab. Type **270** and then in the second row of the table, click anywhere to position the insertion point. Click the **Layout tab**, and then in the **Rows & Columns group**, click the **Insert Above** button to insert a new row. Type **Day** and press Tab. Type **Attendees**

6. In the first column of the table, move the pointer to the right boundary

until the ⊹ pointer displays. Drag the boundary to the left until the first column's right boundary aligns at approximately **1.5 inches on the horizontal ruler**. If only one row resizes, click the Undo button and begin again. In the second column, drag the right boundary to **2.5 inches on the horizontal ruler**. **Save** your document.

7. In the second column of the table, click anywhere in the column to position the insertion point. On the **Layout tab**, in the **Rows & Columns group**, click the **Insert Right** button. In the new column, click to place the insertion point in the second row. Type **Increase** and press ↓.

8. Complete the column with the following information:

60
40
30
-10
50
70

9. In the second row, click anywhere in the first cell, and then drag to the right to select all three cells in the second row. On the Mini toolbar, click the **Bold** and **Center** buttons.

10. In the second column, click in the cell containing *300*, and then drag down and to the right to select the third cell through the eighth cell of the second and third columns, ending with *70*. Click the **Home tab**, and then in the **Paragraph group**, click the **Align Text Right** button.

11. Select all three cells in the first row. Click the **Design tab**, and then in the **Table**

(Project 7D—Sales Figures continues on the next page)

(Project 7D–Sales Figures continued)

Styles group, click the **Shading** button. Under **Theme Colors**, click the third button in the first row—**Tan Background 2**. Click the **Layout tab**, and then in the **Merge group**, click the **Merge Cells** button. Select the text in the top cell—**2009 Exhibition**. On the Mini toolbar, click the **Bold** and **Center** buttons. **Save** the document.

12. Click anywhere in the table to deselect the cells. On the **Design tab**, in the **Table Styles group**, click the **Borders button arrow**, and then click **Borders and Shading**. In the displayed **Borders and Shading** dialog box, under **Setting**, click **Box**. Click the **Width arrow**, and then click **3 pt**. In the **Apply to** box, be sure that **Table** is indicated, and then click **OK**.

13. Click the **Layout tab**. In the **Table group**, click the **Select** button, and then click **Select Table**. Click the **Home tab**, and then in the **Paragraph group**, click the **Center** button. **Save** the document.

14. In the block of text near the end of the document, beginning with *Gross Photograph Sales*, click to position the insertion point to the left of the word *Gross*, hold down ⇧ Shift, and then click after the paragraph mark at the end of the line beginning *Closing*—after *$17,800*.

15. With the text selected, click the **Insert tab**. In the **Tables group**, click the **Table** button, and then click **Convert Text to Table**. In the **Convert Text to Table** dialog box, under **Table size**, click the **Number of columns up spin arrow** to change the number of columns to **3**. Under **AutoFit behavior**, click the **AutoFit to contents** option button. Then, under **Separate text at**, click the **Tabs** option button. At the

bottom of the **Convert Text to Table** dialog box, click **OK**.

16. Click anywhere to position the insertion point in the lower table. On the **Design tab**, in the **Table Styles group**, click the **More** button. Under **Built-In**, in the first row, click the fifth table style—**Table Classic 2**. Right-click the table, and then from the shortcut menu, click **Table Properties**. In the **Table Properties** dialog box, on the **Table tab**, under **Alignment**, click **Center**.

17. Drag the dialog box so that you can see most of the lower table. In the **Table Properties** dialog box, click the **Column tab**. Under **Size**, click the **Next Column** button until the first column of the lower table is highlighted. Select the **Preferred width** check box, and then in the box to the right, click the spin box arrows as necessary to set the **Preferred width** to **1.5"**. Click the **Next Column** button. Use the same procedure to make the second and third columns **1"** wide, and then click **OK**.

18. In the lower table, point to the first cell of the top row and drag to the right to select all three cells. Click the **Layout tab**, and then in the **Merge group**, click the **Merge Cells** button. In the **Alignment group**, click the **Align Center** button.

19. In the second row of the table, select the second and third cells, and then on the Mini toolbar, click the **Bold** and **Center** buttons. In the second row, in the first cell, select the text *Day*, and then on the Mini toolbar, click the **Center** button.

20. In the second column, click in the cell containing *$20,320*, and then drag down and to the right to select the third cell of the

(Project 7D–Sales Figures continues on the next page)

Content-Based Assessments

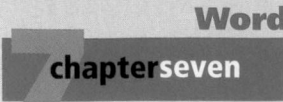
(Project 7D–Sales Figures continued)

second column through the eighth cell of the third column—*$17,800*. Click the **Home tab**, and then in the **Paragraph group**, click the **Align Text Right** button.

21. Display the **Print Preview** to make a final check of your document. **Save** your

changes, and then submit your document as directed.

22. **Close** your document, and then **Exit** Word.

 You have completed Project 7D ————————————————————

Content-Based Assessments

Project 7E—Modern Scrapbook

In this project, you will apply the skills you practiced from the Objectives in Project 7A.

Objectives: 1. *Insert and Format Graphics;* **2.** *Set Tab Stops;* **3.** *Insert and Modify Text Boxes and Shapes.*

In the following Mastering Word project, you will create a flyer describing a scrapbooking class to be offered at Memories Old and New. Your completed document will look similar to Figure 7.58.

For Project 7E, you will need the following files:

New blank Word document
w07E_Scrapbook

You will save your document as
7E_Modern_Scrapbook_Firstname_Lastname

Figure 7.58

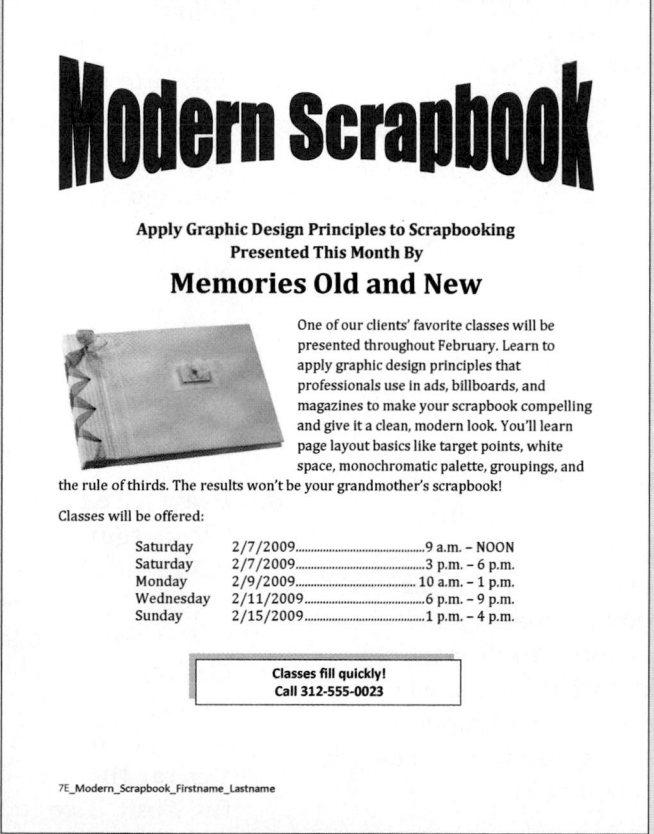

(Project 7E–Modern Scrapbook continues on the next page)

Content-Based Assessments

(Project 7E–Modern Scrapbook continued)

1. **Start** Word and be sure a new blank document is displayed. Display formatting marks and rulers. **Save** the document in your **Word Chapter 7** folder as **7E_Modern_Scrapbook_Firstname_Lastname** Open the document footer and add the file name to the footer. Change all four document margins to **0.75 inch**.

2. **Insert** a WordArt title using **WordArt style 4** and type **Modern Scrapbook** as the text. Change the **WordArt** size to **7 inches** wide and **2 inches** high. In the **WordArt Styles group**, click the **Shape Fill** button, and then under **Theme Colors**, click the fourth color in the first row **Dark Blue, Text 2**.

3. Click to the right of the WordArt title, and then press Enter. Type **Apply Graphic Design Principles to Scrapbooking** and press Enter. Type **Presented This Month By** and press Enter. Type **Memories Old and New** and press Enter. Select the three lines you just typed, change the **Font** to **Cambria**, **Center** the text and apply **Bold**. Change the **Font Size** of the first two lines to **16**, and change the space **After** the paragraphs to **0**. Change the **Font Size** of the third line to **28**.

4. Position the insertion point in the last blank line, change the **Font** to **Cambria**, change the **Font Size** to **14**, and then type the following text:

   One of our clients' favorite classes will be presented throughout February. Learn to apply graphic design principles that professionals use in ads, billboards, and magazines to make your scrapbook compelling and give it a clean, modern look. You'll learn page layout basics like target points, white space, monochromatic palette, groupings, and the rule of thirds. The results won't be your grandmother's scrapbook!

   Classes will be offered:

5. Press Enter. From your student files, insert the picture **w07E_Scrapbook**. Change the **Width** of the picture to **3"**, and apply **Square Text Wrapping**. Move the picture to the left margin, with the top edge even with the first paragraph you just typed—beginning with *One of our*.

6. Press Ctrl + End. Insert a **Left tab stop** at **2.25 inches on the horizontal ruler** and another **Left tab stop** at **6 inches**. In the horizontal ruler, double-click either of the new tab marks to open the **Tabs** dialog box. Select the tab stop at **6 inches on the horizontal ruler**, change the alignment to **Right**, and then add a **dot leader** to the tab stop. Display the **Paragraph** dialog box, and set the spacing **After** to **0**, and the **Line spacing** to **Single**. Type the following text, pressing Tab between the weekday and the date, and between the date and the times:

Saturday	2/7/2009	9 a.m. - NOON
Saturday	2/7/2009	3 p.m. - 6 p.m.
Monday	2/9/2009	10 a.m. - 1 p.m.
Wednesday	2/11/2009	6 p.m. - 9 p.m.
Sunday	2/15/2009	1 p.m. - 4 p.m.

7. Select the tabbed text, display the **Paragraph** dialog box, and then set the **Left Indentation** to **1 inch**. Click anywhere in the document to deselect the text.

8. **Draw** a **Text Box** that is aligned with the left margin, with the top edge about 0.5 inches below the tabbed text. Use the **Size** buttons to change the **Width** to **3.5"** and the **Height** to **.6"**. In the text box, type **Classes fill quickly!** and press Enter. Type **Call 312-555-0023** Select the two lines of text in the text box, and use the Mini toolbar to **Center** the text, apply **Bold**, and change the **Font Size** to **14**. Display the

(Project 7E–Modern Scrapbook continues on the next page)

Content-Based Assessments

(Project 7E–Modern Scrapbook continued)

Paragraph dialog box, and set the spacing **After** to **0**, and the **Line spacing** to **Single**. Add a **Shadow Style 1** shadow effect to the text box. On the **Format tab**, in the **Arrange group**, click the **Align** button, and then click **Align Center**.

9. Preview the document, and then print it, or submit it electronically as directed. **Save** your changes. **Close** the document, and then **Exit** Word.

 End You have completed Project 7E ————————————————

Content-Based Assessments

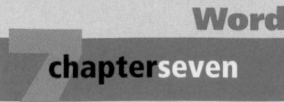

Mastering Word

Project 7F — Scrapbook Supplies

In this project, you will apply the skills you practiced from the Objectives in Project 7B.

Objectives: 4. *Create a Table;* **5.** *Format a Table.*

In the following Mastering Word project, you will edit a flyer to distribute to the scrapbooking customers of Memories Old and New. Your completed document will look similar to Figure 7.59.

For Project 7F, you will need the following file:

w07F_Scrapbook_Supplies

**You will save your document as
7F_Scrapbook_Supplies_Firstname_Lastname**

Figure 7.59

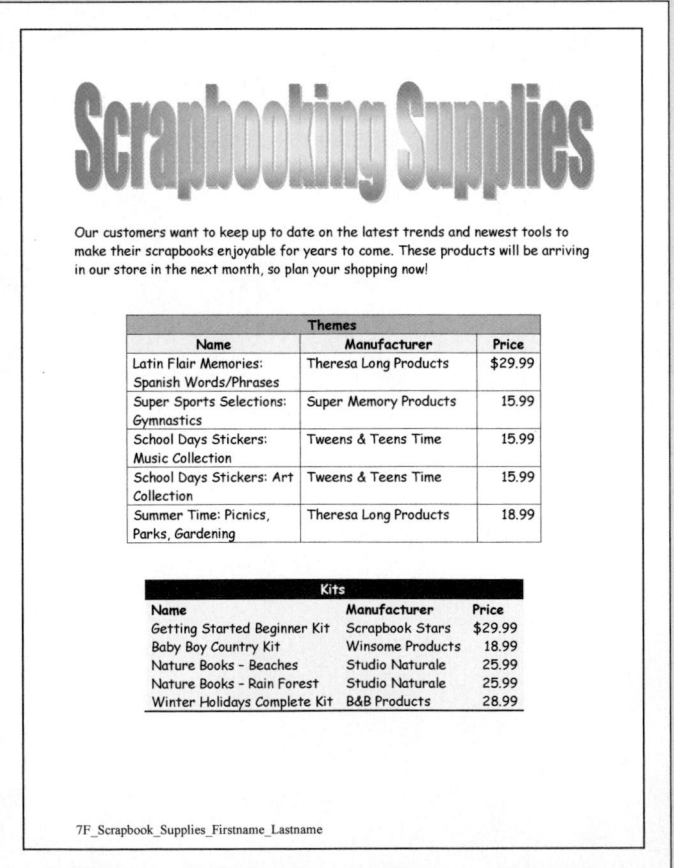

(Project 7F–Scrapbook Supplies continues on the next page)

Content-Based Assessments

(Project 7F–Scrapbook Supplies continued)

1. Locate and open the file **w07F_Scrapbook_Supplies**. Display formatting marks and rulers. **Save** the file in your **Word Chapter 7** folder as **7F_Scrapbook_Supplies_Firstname_Lastname** and add the file name to the footer. Be sure all four margins are set at **1 inch**.

2. With the insertion point at the beginning of the document, insert **WordArt** with the text **Scrapbooking Supplies** using **WordArt style 13**. Set the **Width** to **6.5 inches** and the **Height** to **1.5 inches**.

3. Move the pointer to the left of the paragraph that begins *Themes* to display the pointer, and then drag down to select all of the text through the paragraph that ends *18.99*. On the **Insert tab**, display the **Convert Text to Table** dialog box. Set the **Number of columns** to **3**, click the **AutoFit to contents** option button, and then, under **Separate text at**, choose the **Tabs** option button, and then click **OK**.

4. Display the **Table Properties** dialog box and **Center** the table. Click the **Column tab**, and then set the first two columns to **2.2 inches** wide, and set the width of the third column to **0.8 inch** wide. In the third column of the table, format all of the cells that contain numbers with the **Align Text Right** command.

5. In the first row, merge the three cells, and then apply **Center** alignment and **Bold** emphasis to the word *Themes*. **Center** and **Bold** the text in the three cells in the second row of the table. Select the first row of the table, display the **Shading gallery**, and apply **White, Background 1, Darker 25%** shading—the fourth color in the first column. Select the second row of the table, and then from the **Shading gallery**, apply **White, Background 1, Darker 5%** shading—the second color in the first column. **Save** your document.

6. Click to place the insertion point in the blank line below the table, and then press [Enter] two times. **Insert** a **3x7** table, and then add the following text:

Kits		
Name	Manufacturer	Price
Getting Started Beginner Kit	Scrapbook Stars	$29.99
Baby Boy Country Kit	Winsome Products	18.99
Nature Books - Beaches	Studio Naturale	25.99
Nature Books - Rain Forest	Studio Naturale	25.99
Winter Holidays Complete Kit	B&B Products	28.99

7. With the insertion point in the lower table, display the **Table Styles gallery**, and then under **Built-In**, in the second row, click the second style—**Table Colorful 2**. Right-click anywhere in the lower table, point to **AutoFit**, and then click **AutoFit to Contents**.

8. Select the first column of the lower table, and then click the **Italic** button to remove the italic emphasis. In the second row, select the second and third cells and apply **Bold** emphasis. In the third column, apply the **Align Text Right** command to the cells that contain numbers. In the first column, remove the **Bold** emphasis from the last five cells.

(Project 7F–Scrapbook Supplies continues on the next page)

Content-Based Assessments

(Project 7F–Scrapbook Supplies continued)

9. Select and **Center** the lower table horizontally on the page. Select all three cells in the first row of the same table and **Merge** the cells. In the same row, select and **Center** *Kits*.

10. Add a **Box** page border, using a **1 1/2 pt** line width and the default black color.

11. Preview the document, and then print it, or submit it electronically as directed. **Save** your changes. **Close** the document, and then **Exit** Word.

 End **You have completed Project 7F** ————————————————

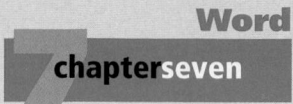

Word

chapterseven

Mastering Word

Project 7G — Photo Enhancement

In this project, you will apply the skills you practiced from the Objectives in Projects 7A and 7B.

Objectives: 1. *Insert and Format Graphics;* **3.** *Insert and Modify Text Boxes and Shapes;* **4.** *Create a Table;* **5.** *Format a Table.*

In the following Mastering Word project, you will create a handout that describes the photo enhancement services offered by Memories Old and New. Your completed document will look similar to Figure 7.60.

For Project 7G, you will need the following files:

w07G_Photo_Enhancement
w07G_Chess

**You will save your document as
7G_Photo_Enhancement_Firstname_Lastname**

Figure 7.60

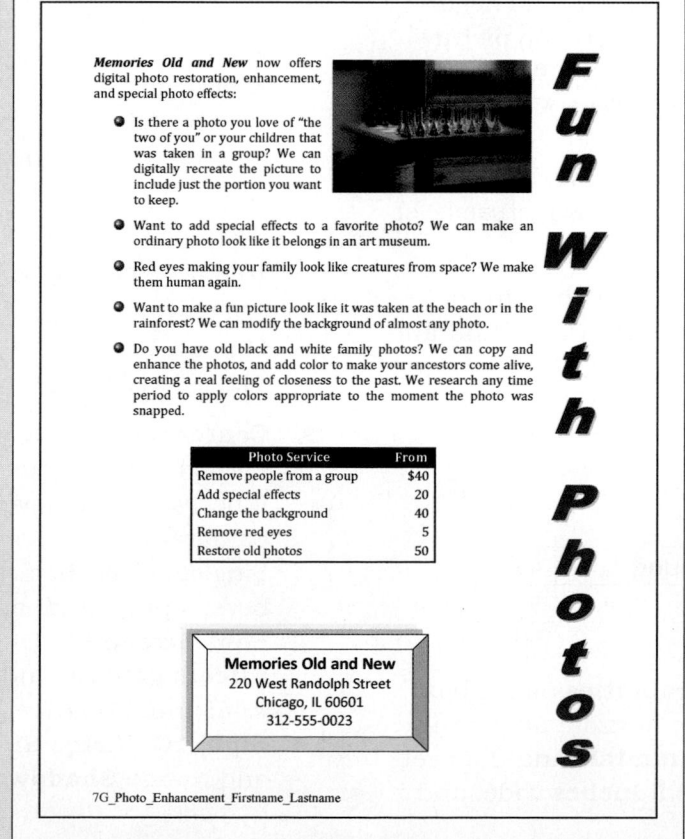

(Project 7G–Photo Enhancement continues on the next page)

Content-Based Assessments

(Project 7G–Photo Enhancement continued)

1. Locate and open the file **w07G_Photo_Enhancement**. **Save** the file in your chapter folder as 7G_Photo_Enhancement_Firstname_Lastname and then add the file name to the footer. Display formatting marks and rulers.

2. Position the insertion point at the beginning of the document. **Insert** a **Fun With Photos** vertical **WordArt** title using **WordArt style 12**—in the second row, the sixth style. Set the **Width** to **9 inches** and the **Height** to **.8 inch**. Note that with a vertical WordArt, the Width setting is actually the height. Add **Square** text wrapping, and then drag the WordArt title so that the upper right corner is at **0 inches on the vertical ruler** and **6.5 inches on the horizontal ruler**.

3. Position the insertion point at the beginning of the document. **Insert** the picture **w07G_Chess**, and change the **Width** to **2.5 inches**. Change the **Text Wrapping** to **Square**, and then position left edge of the picture at **3 inches on the horizontal ruler**, and the top edge of the picture level with the top edge of the text.

4. Click to place the insertion point in the blank line at the end of the document, and then press Enter. **Insert** a **2x6 Table**, and then add the following text:

Photo Service	From
Remove people from a group	$40
Add special effects	20
Change the background	40
Remove red eyes	5
Restore old photos	50

5. Display the **Table Properties** dialog box and **Center** the table horizontally on the page. Click the **Column tab**, and then set the first column to **2.5 inches** wide, and

set the width of the second column to **.6 inch** wide. In the second column of the table, format the cells that contain numbers with the **Align Text Right** command.

6. In the first row, apply **Center** and **Bold** to both cells. Select the first row of the table, display the **Shading gallery**, and add **Black, Text 1** shading—the second color in the first row. **Save** your work.

7. Click to place the insertion point anywhere in the table and display the **Borders and Shading** dialog box. Click **Box**, and then change the line width to **1 1/2 pt**.

8. Press Ctrl + End to move the insertion point to the end of the document. Display the **Shapes gallery**. Under **Basic Shapes**, click the **Bevel** shape—the fourth shape in the second row. Starting at **7.25 inches on the vertical ruler**, and at **1 inch on the horizontal ruler**, draw a bevel that is **3 inches** wide by **1.5 inches** high. Use the **Size** buttons to make the measurements exact. Right-click on the bevel, click **Add Text**, and type the following:

Memories Old and New
220 West Randolph Street
Chicago, IL 60601
312-555-0023

9. **Center** the bevel text, change the **Font** to **Calibri**, and increase the **Font Size** to **14**. If necessary, remove any spacing *After* the paragraphs, and set the *Line Spacing* to Single. Select the first line of text in the bevel, apply **Bold**, and then change the **Font Size** to **16**. Display the **Shadow Effects gallery**, and then under **Additional Shadow Styles**, click **Shadow Style 16**. **Nudge Shadow Left** two clicks and **Nudge Shadow Up** two clicks.

(Project 7G–Photo Enhancement continues on the next page)

Content-Based Assessments

(Project 7G–Photo Enhancement continued)

10. Move the bevel so that it is centered horizontally under the table, with the top edge at about **7.25 inches on the vertical ruler**. Add a **Box** page border to the document, using a **1 1/2 pt** line width and the default black color.

11. Preview the document, and then print it, or submit it electronically as directed. **Save** your changes. **Close** the file, and then **Exit** Word.

 End **You have completed Project 7G**

Content-Based Assessments

Project 7H — Photo Restoration

In this project, you will apply the skills you practiced from the Objectives in Projects 7A and 7B.

Objectives: 1. *Insert and Format Graphics;* **2.** *Set Tab Stops;* **3.** *Insert and Modify Text Boxes and Shapes.*

In the following Mastering Word project, you will create a handout about photograph restoration services available at Memories Old and New. Your completed document will look similar to Figure 7.61.

For Project 7H, you will need the following files:

w07H_Photo_Restoration
w07H_Original
w07H_Quick_Restore

You will save your document as
7H_Photo_Restoration_Firstname_Lastname

Figure 7.61

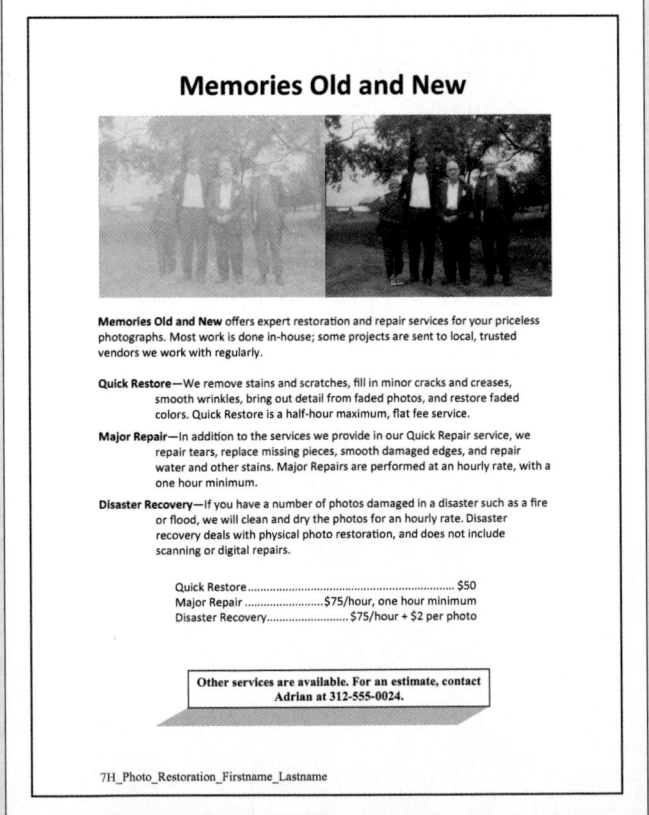

(Project 7H–Photo Restoration continues on the next page)

Content-Based Assessments

(Project 7H–Photo Restoration continued)

1. Locate and open the file **w07H_Photo_ Restoration**. **Save** the file in your chapter folder as 7H_Photo_Restoration_Firstname_ Lastname and then add the file name to the footer. Display formatting marks and rulers.

2. Position the insertion point in the blank line under the title. Locate and **Insert** the picture **w07H_Original**. Reduce the **Width** of the picture to **3 inches**, and then change the **Text Wrapping** of the picture to **Square**. Click to position the insertion point in the blank line under the title, and then **Insert** the **w07H_Quick_Restore** picture. Format this second picture in the same manner you formatted the first picture. Move the second picture to the right of (and touching) the first picture—use Figure 7.61 as a guide.

3. Press Ctrl + End. Insert a **Right tab stop** at **5 inches on the horizontal ruler**. Display the **Paragraph** dialog box and set the **Left Indentation** to **1 inch**. Display the **Tabs** dialog box. Add a **dot leader** to the tab stop at **5 inches on the horizontal ruler**. Type the following text, pressing Tab between the service and the price:

Quick Restore	$50
Major Repair	$75/hour, one hour minimum
Disaster Recovery	$75/hour + $2 per photo

4. **Save** your changes. **Draw** a **Text Box** that is aligned with the left margin, with the top edge at **8 inches on the vertical ruler**. Use the **Size** buttons to change the **Width** to **4"** and the **Height** to **.5"**. In the text box, type **Other services are available. For an estimate, contact Adrian at 312-555-0024.** Select all of the text in the text box, and use the Mini toolbar to **Center** the text and add **Bold** emphasis.

5. With the insertion point in the text box, display the **Shadow Effects gallery**. Under **Perspective Shadow**, add a **Shadow Style 8** shadow effect to the text box. Drag the text box to center it horizontally on the page, and position the top edge at about **7.75 inches on the vertical ruler**, as shown in Figure 7.61.

6. Add a **Box** page border, using a **1 1/2 pt** line width and the default black color.

7. **Save** your document. Preview the document, and then print it, or submit it electronically as directed. **Close** the file, and then **Exit** Word.

End You have completed Project 7H

Content-Based Assessments

Project 7I — Student Days

In this project, you will apply the skills you practiced from all the Objectives in Projects 7A and 7B.

Objectives: 1. *Insert and Format Graphics;* **2.** *Set Tab Stops;* **3.** *Insert and Modify Text Boxes and Shapes;* **4.** *Create a Table;* **5.** *Format a Table.*

In the following Mastering Word Assessment, you will create a flyer for the Student Days celebration at Memories Old and New. Your completed document will look similar to Figure 7.62.

For Project 7I, you will need the following files:

New blank Word document
w07I_Student_Artist

You will save your document as
7I_Student_Days_Firstname_Lastname

Figure 7.62

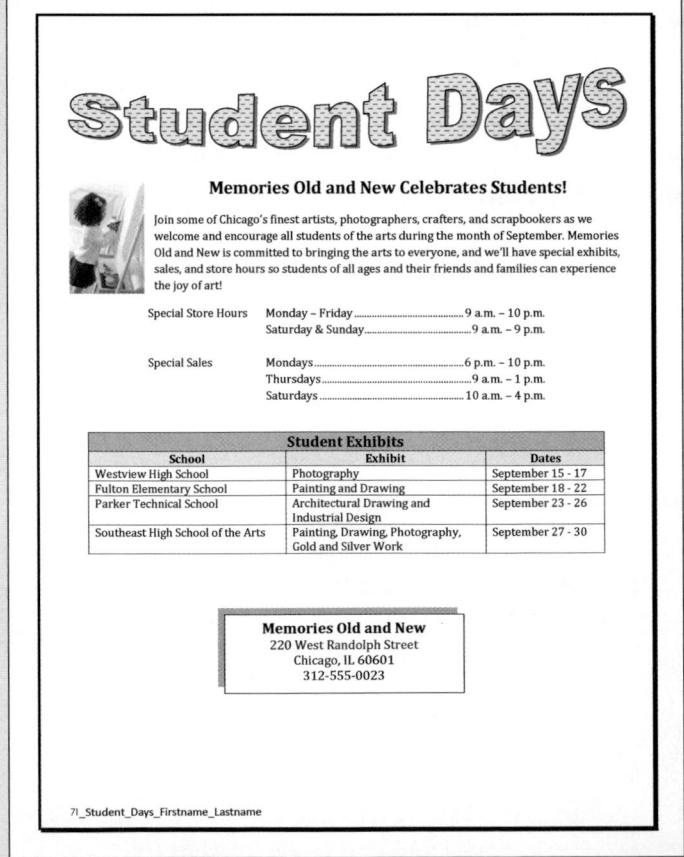

(Project 7I–Student Days continues on the next page)

Word

chapterseven

Mastering Word

(Project 7I–Student Days continued)

1. **Start** Word and be sure a new blank document is displayed. Display formatting marks and rulers. **Save** the document in your chapter folder as **7I_Student_Days_Firstname_Lastname** and add the file name to the footer. Change all four document margins to **.75 inch**. Change the **Font** to **Cambria** and be sure the **Font Size** is set to **11**.

2. **Insert** a Student Days WordArt title, using **WordArt style 23**—the fifth style in the fourth row. Change the **WordArt** size to **7 inches** wide and **1.5 inches** high.

3. Click to the right of the WordArt title, and then press Enter. Type **Memories Old and New Celebrates Students!** and press Enter. Select the text you just typed, **Center** the text, apply **Bold** emphasis, and then change the **Font Size** to **16**.

4. Position the insertion point in the blank line below the title you just typed, press Enter, and then type the following text:

   Join some of Chicago's finest artists, photographers, crafters, and scrapbookers as we welcome and encourage all students of the arts during the month of September. Memories Old and New is committed to bringing the arts to everyone, and we'll have special exhibits, sales, and store hours so students of all ages and their friends and families can experience the joy of art!

5. Press Enter. Insert a **Left tab stop** at **2.5 inches on the horizontal ruler**. Insert a **Right tab stop** at **6 inches on the horizontal ruler**. Display the **Tabs** dialog box. Add a **dot leader** to the tab stop at **6 inches**. Type the following text, pressing Tab between entries, and press Enter at the end of each line, including the last line. In the lines with no text in the first column, press Tab. Leave the third line blank:

Special Store Hours	Monday - Friday	9 a.m. - 10 p.m.
	Saturday & Sunday	9 a.m. - 9 p.m.
Special Sales	Mondays	6 p.m. - 10 p.m.
	Thursdays	9 a.m. - 1 p.m.
	Saturdays	10 a.m. - 4 p.m.

6. Starting with the text that begins *Special Store Hours*, select the text from that point to the end of the document, but do not include the blank line at the end of the document. Display the **Paragraph** dialog box, set the **Left Indentation** to **1 inch**, and set the **Spacing After** to **0**.

7. Press Ctrl + End, and then press Enter. Display the **Paragraph** dialog box and set the **Spacing After** to **0**. **Insert** a **3x6** table, and then add the following text:

Student Exhibits		
School	Exhibit	Dates
Westview High School	Photography	September 15 – 17
Fulton Elementary School	Painting and Drawing	September 18 – 22
Parker Technical School	Architectural Drawing and Industrial Design	September 23 – 26
Southeast High School of the Arts	Painting, Drawing, Photography, Gold and Silver Work	September 27 – 30

(Project 7I–Student Days continues on the next page)

Content-Based Assessments

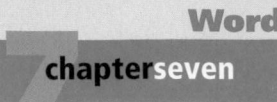
(Project 7I–Student Days continued)

8. Display the **Table Properties** dialog box and **Center** the table. Click the **Column tab**, and then set the first two columns to **2.5 inches** wide, and the third column to **1.5 inches** wide.

9. In the first row, merge the three cells, and then **Center** and **Bold** *Student Exhibits*, and change the **Font Size** to **14**. **Center** and **Bold** the text in the three cells in the second row of the table. Select the first row of the table. On the **Design tab**, display the **Shading gallery**, and add **Orange, Accent 6, Lighter 40%** shading—the fourth color in the last column. Select the second row of the table, display the **Shading gallery**, and add **Orange, Accent 6, Lighter 80%** shading— the second color in the last column. **Save** your work.

10. Place the insertion point to the left of the paragraph that begins *Join some of Chicago's*, and then from your student files, insert the picture **w07I_Student_Artist**. Change the **Height** of the picture to **1.4 inches**, and then apply **Square Text Wrapping**. Move the picture to the position shown in Figure 7.62 at the beginning of this project.

11. **Save** your changes. **Draw** a **Text Box** that is aligned with the left margin, with the top edge at **7.0 inches on the vertical ruler**. Use the **Size** buttons to change the **Height** to **1"** and the **Width** to **3"**. Select the paragraph mark in the text box, display the **Paragraph** dialog box, and then set the space **After** to **0** and the **Line Spacing** to **Single**. In the text box, type:

Memories Old and New
220 West Randolph Street
Chicago, IL 60601
312-555-0023

12. Select all of the text in the text box and **Center** the text. Change the **Font Size** to **12**. Select the top line of text in the text box, add **Bold** emphasis, and change the **Font Size** to **14**. Display the **Shadow Effects gallery**, and under **Drop Shadow**, click the first style—**Shadow Style 1**. Drag to center the text box under the table.

13. Add a **Shadow** page border, using a **2 1/4 pt** line width and the default black color.

14. Preview the document, and then print it, or submit it electronically as directed. **Save** your changes. **Close** the file, and then **Exit** Word.

End **You have completed Project 7I**

Content-Based Assessments

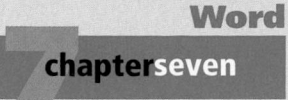

Project 7J — Business Running Case

In this project, you will apply the skills you practiced from all the Objectives in Projects 7A and 7B.

Close Word and any other open windows. Display the Start menu, click Computer, and then navigate to the student files that accompany this textbook. In the folder **03_business_running_case**, locate and open the folder for this chapter. Open and print the instructions for this project, which are provided to you in Adobe PDF format. Follow the instructions and use the skills you have gained thus far to assist Jennifer Nelson in meeting the challenges of owning and running her business.

End **You have completed Project 7J** ⸺⸺⸺⸺⸺⸺⸺

Project 7K — *GO!* Fix It

In this project, you will apply the skills you practiced from the Objectives in Projects 7A and 7B.

For Project 7K, you will need the following file:

w07K_fixit_Digital_Dog_Flyer

**You will save your document as
7K_Digital_Dog_Flyer_Firstname_Lastname**

In this project, you will edit a flyer for a workshop on digital pet photography that is being prepared for Memories Old and New. From the student files that accompany this textbook, open the folder **05_go_fix_it**. Locate and open the file **w07K_fixit_Digital_Dog_Flyer**, and then save the file in your chapter folder as **7K_Digital_Dog_Firstname_Lastname**

This document contains errors that you must find and correct. Read and examine the document, and then edit to correct the errors that you find. Types of errors could include:

- Spelling, grammar, punctuation, and usage errors such as text case, repeated text, subject-verb agreement, and meaning.

- Content errors such as missing or incorrect text, pictures, or other objects.

- Font formatting and positioning errors such as font used, style, size, color, underline style, effects, font character spacing, text effects, special characters, and styles.

- Paragraph formatting and positioning errors such as indents and spacing, tabs, line and page breaks, wordwrap, sentence spacing, missing text or unnecessary text or blank lines, or errors in footnotes or endnotes or references.

- Image or object formatting and positioning errors relating to color, lines, size, scale, layout, positioning, or picture control.

- Page setup errors such as margins, orientation, layout, or alignment.

To complete the project you should:

- Be aware that there are no errors in sentence or paragraph spacing.

- Reformat the picture style of the dog image by using *Metal Frame*.

- Modify the words *Pet Photos?* in the title by applying WordArt style 9 with 36 pt font size.

- Format the Horizontal Scroll shape by applying Shadow Style 4.

(Project 7K–*GO!* Fix It continues on the next page)

Content-Based Assessments

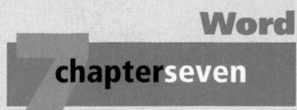
(Project 7K–*GO!* Fix It continued)

- Modify the table by merging cells, aligning text in the first row and in the second column, and by applying Table Style *Light Shading – Accent 1*.
- Center the table horizontally on the page.

Save the changes you have made, add the file name to the footer, and then submit as directed.

 You have completed Project 7K ——————————

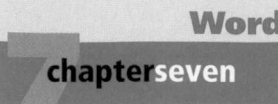

Rubric

The following outcomes-based assessments are *open-ended assessments*. That is, there is no specific correct result; your result will depend on your approach to the information provided. Make *Professional Quality* your goal. Use the following scoring rubric to guide you in *how* to approach the problem, and then to evaluate *how well* your approach solves the problem.

The *criteria*—Software Mastery, Content, Format and Layout, and Process—represent the knowledge and skills you have gained that you can apply to solving the problem. The *levels of performance*—Professional Quality, Approaching Professional Quality, or Needs Quality Improvements—help you and your instructor evaluate your result.

	Your completed project is of Professional Quality if you:	Your completed project is Approaching Professional Quality if you:	Your completed project Needs Quality Improvements if you:
1-Software Mastery	Choose and apply the most appropriate skills, tools, and features and identify efficient methods to solve the problem.	Choose and apply some appropriate skills, tools, and features, but not in the most efficient manner.	Choose inappropriate skills, tools, or features, or are inefficient in solving the problem.
2-Content	Construct a solution that is clear and well organized, contains content that is accurate, appropriate to the audience and purpose, and is complete. Provide a solution that contains no errors of spelling, grammar, or style.	Construct a solution in which some components are unclear, poorly organized, inconsistent, or incomplete. Misjudge the needs of the audience. Have some errors in spelling, grammar, or style, but the errors do not detract from comprehension.	Construct a solution that is unclear, incomplete, or poorly organized, containing some inaccurate or inappropriate content; and contains many errors of spelling, grammar, or style. Do not solve the problem.
3-Format and Layout	Format and arrange all elements to communicate information and ideas, clarify function, illustrate relationships, and indicate relative importance.	Apply appropriate format and layout features to some elements, but not others. Overuse features, causing minor distraction.	Apply format and layout that does not communicate information or ideas clearly. Do not use format and layout features to clarify function, illustrate relationships, or indicate relative importance. Use available features excessively, causing distraction.
4-Process	Use an organized approach that integrates planning, development, self-assessment, revision, and reflection.	Demonstrate an organized approach in some areas, but not others; or, use an insufficient process of organization throughout.	Do not use an organized approach to solve the problem.

Outcomes-Based Assessments

Problem Solving

Project 7L — Books

In this project, you will apply the skills you practiced from the Objectives in Projects 7A and 7B.

For Project 7L, you will need the following file:

New blank Word document

You will save your document as
7L_Books_Firstname_Lastname

Memories Old and New carries an extensive line of books and periodicals for artists, photographers, students, teachers, and hobbyists. They have recently begun stocking a full line of scrapbooking books. In this project, you will create a flyer that includes a table of popular scrapbooking books for sale in the store.

To complete this assignment:

- Include a WordArt title, either with the name of the store, or the topic that is covered in the flyer.

- Write an opening paragraph introducing the topic.

- Create a table that consists of books on scrapbooking. The table should use at least three columns, including the author's name, the title of the book, and the book price. You should include at least six books in the table—use an online book dealer to search for appropriate titles.

- Format the table with a title that spans all of the columns and include a heading for each column. The title and column headings should be formatted distinctively.

- Include a text box with instructions for placing orders by phone.

- Include a shape with the name, address, and phone number of the store.

Add the file name to the footer. Check the flyer for spelling or grammar errors. Save the document as **7L_Books_Firstname_Lastname** and submit it as directed.

End **You have completed Project 7L** ───────────────

Outcomes-Based Assessments

Problem Solving

Project 7M—Restoration Class

In this project, you will construct a solution by applying any combination of the skills you practiced from the Objectives in Projects 7A and 7B.

For Project 7M, you will need the following files:

New blank Word document
w07M_McArthur

You will save your document as
7M_Restoration_Class_Firstname_Lastname

Memories Old and New offers extensive photo restoration and photo recovery services. They also offer Beginner, Intermediate, and Advanced level classes on basic restoration techniques, using popular photograph manipulation software. Each level consists of two sessions that are four hours in length. Each session costs $50, and all six sessions can be taken for $250.

Create a flyer that can be handed out to customers in the store, and that contains information about the photo restoration classes. The flyer should include a decorative title, an introductory paragraph about Memories Old and New and photo restoration, and information about the classes. Format the information using a table, or using tab stops and dot leaders. You will need to include at least one text box with the name and address of the company, and one photo. If you have one or two old family photos that you would like to include, use those. Otherwise, use **w07M_McArthur**, which is included with your student files. Add a Picture Style or a Picture Effect to make the picture more visually interesting. The address information for Memories Old and New can be found in Activity 7.14.

Add the file name to the footer. Check the flyer for spelling or grammar errors. Save the document as **7M_Restoration_Class_Firstname_Lastname** and submit it as directed.

End **You have completed Project 7M**

Outcomes-Based Assessments

Problem Solving

Project 7N — Frames

In this project, you will construct a solution by applying any combination of the skills you practiced from the Objectives in Projects 7A and 7B.

For Project 7N, you will need the following files:

New blank Word document
w07N_Frame1
w07N_Frame2

**You will save your document as
7N_Frames_Firstname_Lastname**

Many people bring pictures to Memories Old and New for repair and restoration. Few people realize that the company employs experts in frame repair. In this project, you will create a flyer about picture frame repairs and refinishing offered by Memories Old and New.

Some of the frame repairs and enhancements offered, including minimum prices, are:

- Refinishing a wood frame, including stripping varnish or removing paint, which is priced by frame size and starts at $49.95.
- Adding a faux finish and distressing the wood, which is priced by project and starts at $29.95.
- Repairing plaster, which is priced by frame size and starts at $49.95.
- Repairing minor chips and scratches, which is priced by the project and starts at $29.95.
- Gilding and gold leaf, which is priced by project; prices vary.

To complete this assignment, create a flyer that includes the following:

- A WordArt title that describes the topic.
- An opening paragraph introducing the topic.
- A table using the information presented above. Format the table with a title that spans all of the columns. Each column should have a column heading. The title should be formatted distinctively.
- A text box or banner with instructions on getting an in-home estimate.
- At least one graphic with an introductory paragraph that wraps around the graphic or graphics. Two frame pictures are included with the student files.

(Project 7N–Frames continues on the next page)

Outcomes-Based Assessments

Problem Solving

(Project 7N–Frames continued)

Add the file name to the footer. Check the flyer for spelling or grammar errors. Save the document as **7N_Frames_Firstname_Lastname** and submit it as directed.

 You have completed Project 7N ——————————

Outcomes-Based Assessments

Problem Solving

Project 7O — Flower Show

In this project, you will construct a solution by applying any combination of the skills you practiced from the Objectives in Projects 7A and 7B.

For Project 7O, you will need the following files:

New blank Word document
w07O_Flower1
w07O_Flower2
w07O_Flower3
w07O_Flower4
w07O_Flower5
w07O_Flower6

**You will save your document as
7O_Flower_Show_Firstname_Lastname**

Memories Old and New is heavily involved in community activities. Every year, the neighborhood's small botanical garden—The Northwest Chicago Botanical Garden—sponsors a flower show, and solicits local businesses to participate and to help defray the expenses of the event. In return, participating companies receive good publicity. This year, Memories Old and New has agreed to create the event flyers.

In this project you will create a flyer advertising the event. This year's event runs from May 20 to May 25. Admission is free, and the hours are from 10 a.m. until 7 p.m. on May 20–22; 10 a.m. until 5 p.m. on May 23; and Noon to 5 p.m. on May 24–25. On the flyer, the abbreviated name of the garden—NWC Botanical Garden—should display as a decorative title. One or two paragraphs are necessary to describe the details of the event, which include a flower show and flower sale, and activities for children. A table or tabbed list is necessary to convey information about dates and times. Include at least two pictures in the flyer. You can use any flower pictures you'd like, including the six that are included with your student files. Resize the pictures as necessary, and apply special effects to the pictures that enhance the overall design of the flyer. Add a banner indicating that Memories Old and New provided the flyers and that provides information about the company. Add an appropriate page border.

Save the flyer as **7O_Flower_Show_Firstname_Lastname** and then create a footer that contains file name. Submit the document as directed.

End **You have completed Project 7O** ——————

Outcomes-Based Assessments

Problem Solving

Project 7P — Art Supplies

In this project, you will construct a solution by applying any combination of the skills you practiced from the Objectives in Projects 7A and 7B.

For Project 7P, you will need the following file:

New blank Word document

You will save your document as
7P_Art_Supplies_Firstname_Lastname

Memories Old and New started business under a different name as an artist's supply store. The business has expanded greatly, covering many more areas of the art world, but artist's supplies are still an important part of the company's business. In this project, you will create a handout of commonly used art supplies that Art Instructor Ming Han provides to her drawing students.

Create a decorative title for the handout. Include an introductory paragraph that welcomes students to the drawing class and that informs them of the types of artwork that they will learn to draw, including landscapes, still lifes, animals, and cartoons. Use the Internet to research art supplies and prices, and then use your research to create a table below the introductory paragraph that lists eight to ten popular art supplies and their prices. Examples of these supplies include paint brushes, charcoal, chalk, canvas, and drawing pads. Search the Microsoft Clip Art library for one or more graphics to add to the handout. Include a text box or shape that includes the company name and address and add a page border.

Save the price list as **7P_Art_Supplies_Firstname_Lastname** and then add the file name to the footer. Submit the document as directed.

 End **You have completed Project 7P** ——————————

Outcomes-Based Assessments

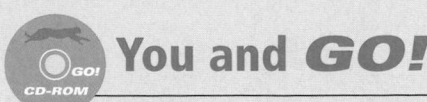 You and *GO!*

Project 7Q—You and *GO!*

In this project, you will construct a solution by applying any combination of the skills you practiced from the Objectives in Projects 7A and 7B.

Close Word and any other open windows. Display the Start menu, click Computer, and then navigate to the student files that accompany this textbook. In the folder **04_you_and_go**, locate and open the folder for this chapter. Open and print the instructions for this project, which are provided to you in Adobe PDF format. Follow the instructions to create a resume using a table.

 End You have completed Project 7Q ——————————

GO! with Help

Project 7R—*GO!* with Help

In this chapter, you inserted a table, and changed existing text into a table. A third way to create a table is to draw the outline and grid lines by hand. This enables you to create a table of any shape for any purpose.

1 **Start** Word. On the Ribbon, click the **Microsoft Office Word Help** button. In the **Search** box, type **draw table** and then click the **Search** button.

2 In the displayed **Search Results** task pane, click **Draw a table**. Maximize the displayed window, and at the top of the window, click the **Show All** link. Scroll through and read how to draw a table.

3 If you want, print a copy of the information by clicking the **Print** button at the top of **Word Help** window.

4 **Close** the **Help** window, and then **Exit** Word.

 End You have completed Project 7R ——————————

Outcomes-Based Assessments

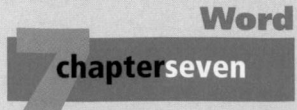

Group Business Running Case

Project 7S — Group Business Running Case

In this project, you will apply the skills you practiced from the Objectives in Projects 7A and 7B.

Your instructor may assign this group case project to your class. If your instructor assigns this project, he or she will provide you with information and instructions to work as part of a group. The group will apply the skills gained thus far to help the Bell Orchid Hotel Group achieve its business goals.

End **You have completed Project 7S**

8 chaptereight

Special Document Formats, Columns, and Mail Merge

OBJECTIVES

At the end of this chapter you will be able to:

1. Collect and Paste Text and Graphics
2. Create and Format Columns
3. Use Special Character and Paragraph Formatting
4. Create Mailing Labels Using Mail Merge

OUTCOMES

Mastering these objectives will enable you to:

PROJECT 8A
Create a Multicolumn Newsletter and Print Mailing Labels

5. Insert Hyperlinks
6. Insert a SmartArt Graphic
7. Preview and Save a Document as a Web Page

PROJECT 8B
Create and Preview a Web Page

Georgia Gardens

Gardening and lawn care in the southern United States are year-round activities. More and more people are approaching what used to be considered a chore as a rewarding and exciting hobby. Southern Home Media produces the television show *Georgia Gardens* to present information on the proven methods, newest techniques, and hottest tools for growing healthy food and creating beautiful yards and gardens. The show's hosts also travel to interesting and lovely private and public gardens throughout the United States to provide viewers a glimpse into the many possibilities that gardening provides.

Using Special Document Formats, Columns, and Mail Merge

Creating a newsletter is usually a job reserved for desktop publishing programs, such as Microsoft Publisher. Word, however, has a number of tools that enable you to create a simple and attractive newsletter that effectively communicates your message.

Newsletters consist of a number of elements, but nearly all have a title, story headlines, articles, and graphics. The text of each article is typically split into two or three columns, which is easier to read than text formatted in a single, wide column. Newsletters are often printed, but newsletters can also be designed to display as Web pages. A useful tool to couple with newsletters is mail merge, which enables you to print mailing labels.

Project 8A Garden Newsletter

In Activities 8.01 through 8.11, you will edit a newsletter for the *Georgia Gardens* subscribers. You will collect text and graphics from other documents, and then paste the collected information into a new document. You will change the text from one column to two columns, and then format the columns. You will use special text formatting features to change the font color and set off one of the paragraphs with a border and shading. Finally, you will create mailing labels for the newsletter. Your completed documents will look similar to Figure 8.1.

For Project 8A, you will need the following files:

New blank Word document

w08A_Tomatoes

w08A_Ornamental_Grasses

w08A_Pictures

w08A_Addresses

You will save your documents as
8A_Garden_Newsletter_Firstname_Lastname
8A_Mailing_Labels_Firstname_Lastname
8A_Addresses_Firstname_Lastname

Taylor Dunnahoo
189 Ventura Street
Rome, GA 30161

Daniel Echols
2000 St. Luke Place
Rome, GA 30165

Isabelle Riniker
8720 Natchez Trail
Rome, GA 30149

Byeong Chang
2221 S. Flowers Road
Atlanta, GA 30358

Ruth Thompson
4220 Thornewood Dr.
#320
Atlanta, GA 30317

Leland Wang
600 County Line NE
Atlanta, GA 30331

Julian Omdahl
34 Gloucester Pl.
Gainesville, GA 30504

Andrew Lau
975 Treetop Place
#G
Seneca, SC 29672

Anthony Blankenship
2820 Clairewood Terrace
Chattanooga, TN 37450

Phillip Scroggs
1518 Orchard Place West
Hunstville, AL 35806

Harriet Hasty
1875 Bullpen Dr.
Columbus, GA 31993

Georgia Gardens Newsletter

ORNAMENTAL GRASSES

As seen on *Georgia Gardens*, ornamental grasses can add new drama, texture, and color to your garden. Best of all, they tend to be very hardy and low-maintenance plants.

In the South, most ornamental grasses grow quickly in the spring and summer, bloom late in the summer and fall, and are dormant throughout the winter. They are very versatile—they can be annuals or perennials, and they can be ground covers or can reach up to 20 feet tall. Some have flowers and are brightly colored, and all have interesting textures and sway gracefully in the wind.

Ornamental grasses can be used as accent plants, but they can also be used to solve problems in your landscape. Try planting them to create a hedge, a border, or a groundcover.

Some dramatic ornamental grasses that do well in the South: Pampas Grass, which can reach up to 20 feet in height and has large silvery white flower plumes on long stems; Red Baron Japanese Blood Grass, which is about 12 to 18 inches tall and has bright red foliage in summer and fall; and Variegated Purple Moor Grass, which has purplish leaves with cream stripes.

To see more examples of how ornamental grasses can enhance your landscape, watch *Georgia Gardens.*

TOMATO TIPS

Few things taste more delicious than a freshly picked tomato from the garden in summer. With a little extra knowledge, you can help ensure a healthy tomato harvest this year.

After the last frost in your area, the soil should be warm enough to plant tomatoes. Choose a spot where the plants will receive at least six hours of sunlight each day. Due to the clay soil found in most of the South, it is recommended that you augment the soil with some peat moss or humus. You have the right mix if it crumbles when you squeeze a handful.

Be sure to dig a deep hole for the tomato plant. It should sit deeper in the ground than it does in the pot. This helps the roots grow stronger and produces a stronger plant. Add a little fertilizer to the soil before planting. Tomato plants can get very large and need extra support, so it is best to use stakes or a cage to hold them up so they won't fall over.

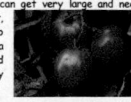

Water the plants well when you plant them, and then check them regularly to see if they need more water (wilted leaves are a sign that they need water). When you water, focus on the soil around the plant rather than watering the plant itself. Consider adding fertilizer after another six to eight weeks.

By following these tips, you should be able to enjoy a fruitful tomato season.

8A_Garden_Newsletter_Firstname_Lastname

Figure 8.1
Project 8A—Garden Newsletter

Objective 1
Collect and Paste Text and Graphics

You have already used the Office Clipboard, which is a temporary storage area maintained by your Windows operating system. When you perform the Copy command or the Cut command, the text that you select is moved to the Office Clipboard. From this Office Clipboard storage area, you can paste text into another location of your document, into another document, or into another Office program.

You can copy and then paste a single selection of text without displaying the Clipboard task pane. However, displaying the Clipboard task pane is essential if you want to *collect and paste* information—collect a group of graphics or selected text blocks and then paste them into a document at any time. The Office Clipboard holds up to 24 items, and the Clipboard task pane displays a preview of each item.

Activity 8.01 Using Collect and Paste to Gather Images and Text

Newsletters typically contain articles written by different people and contain graphics from various sources. Use the Office Clipboard to collect all of the components of the newsletter in one place.

Note — Comparing Your Screen With the Figures in This Textbook

Your screen will match the figures shown in this textbook if you set your screen resolution to 1024 x 768. At other resolutions, your screen will closely resemble, but not match, the figures shown. To view your screen's resolution, on the Windows desktop, right-click in a blank area, click Personalize and then click Display Settings.

---

1 **Start** Word and display a new blank document. Display formatting marks and rulers, and be sure your screen shows both the left and right document edges. Display the **Save As** dialog box, navigate to your storage location, create a new folder named **Word Chapter 8** and then save the document as **8A_Garden_Newsletter_Firstname_Lastname** Open the document footer and add the file name to the footer. Set the top, left, and right margins to **1 inch**, and the bottom margin to **0.5 inch**.

2 On the **Home tab**, in the **Clipboard group**, click the **Dialog Box Launcher** to display the **Clipboard** task pane. If any items display in the Clipboard, at the top of the task pane, click the **Clear All** button. At the bottom of the task pane, click the **Options** button, and then compare your screen with Figure 8.2.

The options displayed in the list enable you to display the Clipboard task pane whenever you cut or copy an object, and also enable you to collect items without displaying the Clipboard task pane.

Figure 8.2

Clipboard group
Dialog Box Launcher

Clear All button

Clipboard empty indicated

Clipboard task pane

Office Clipboard options

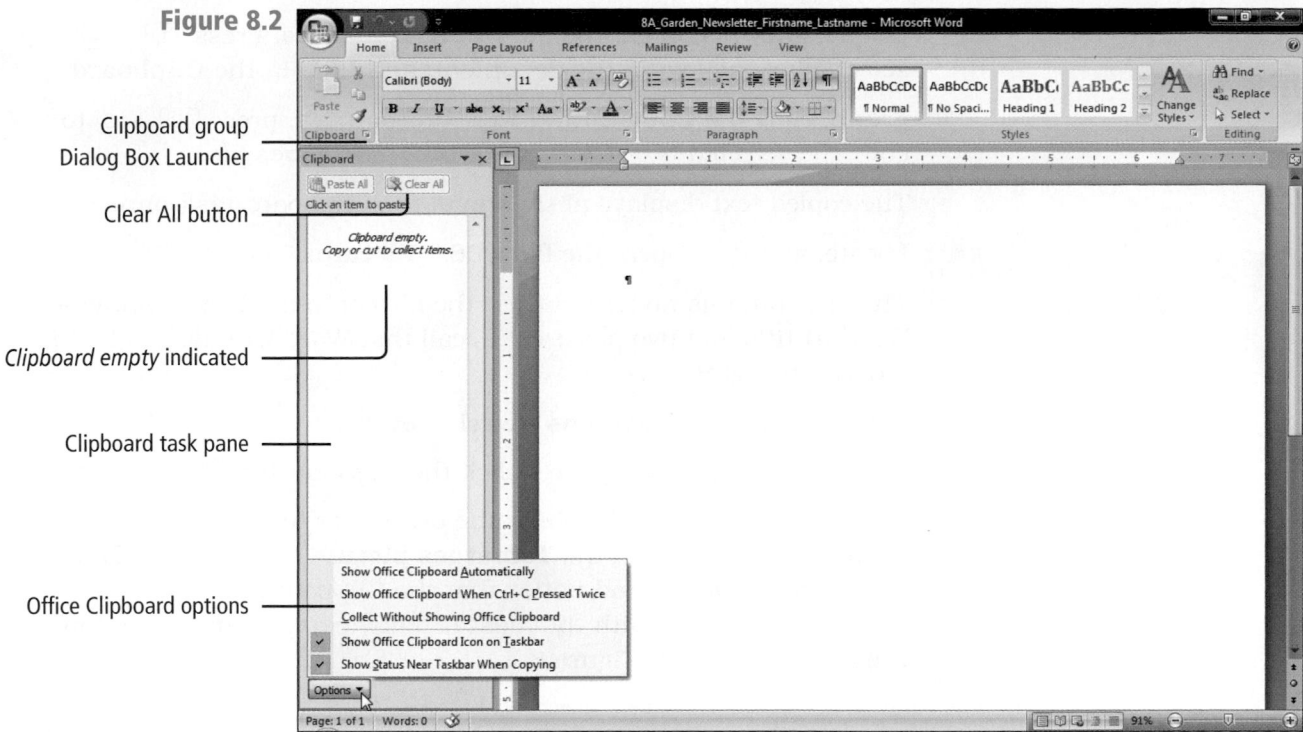

3 Click anywhere in the document to close the **Options** list. Locate and open the file **w08A_Ornamental_Grasses**. Press Ctrl + A to select all of the text in the document, and then in the **Clipboard group**, click the **Copy** button . Press Ctrl + W to close the **w08A_Ornamental_Grasses** file. Alternatively, from the Office menu, click Close. Notice that the first few lines of text display in the Clipboard task pane, as shown in Figure 8.3.

Your saved blank document displays.

Figure 8.3

Text stored in the
Office Clipboard

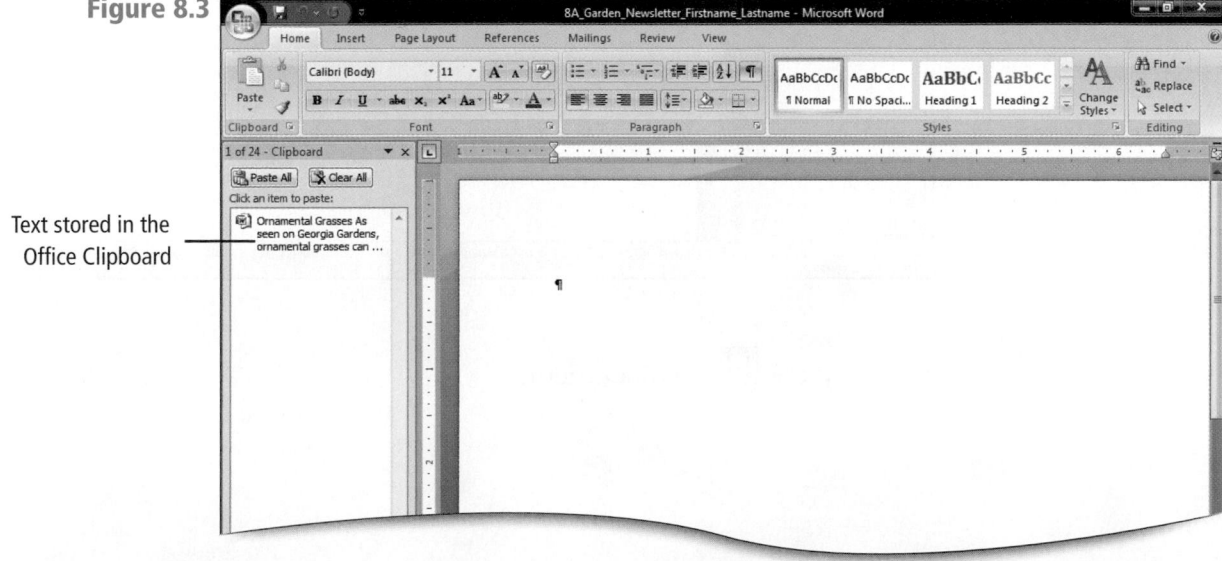

4 Locate, and then open, the file **w08A_Tomatoes**. Press ⌃Ctrl⌄ + ⌃A⌄ to select all of the text in the document, and then in the **Clipboard group**, click the **Copy** button 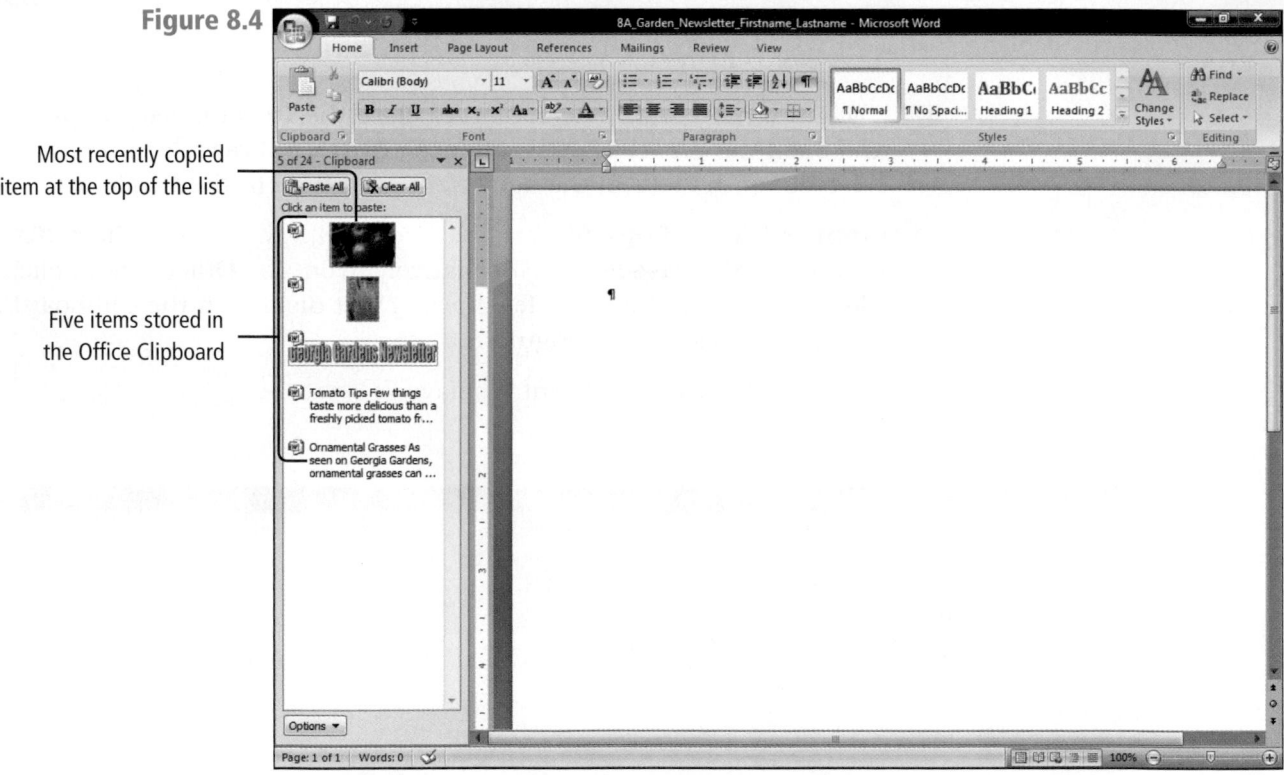. Alternatively, press ⌃Ctrl⌄ + ⌃C⌄ to copy the selected text. **Close** the **w08A_Tomatoes** file.

The copied text displays at the top of the Clipboard task pane.

5 Locate, and then open, the file **w08A_Pictures**.

This file contains no text; rather, the file contains three graphics—a WordArt title and two pictures. Recall that WordArt changes text into a decorative graphic.

6 Select the **Georgia Gardens Newsletter** WordArt title, and then in the **Clipboard group**, click the **Copy** button to copy it to the Office Clipboard. Use the same procedure to **Copy** the **Grass picture** on the left and the **Tomatoes picture** on the right. **Close** the **w08A_Pictures** file, and notice that the Clipboard task pane contains five items, with the most recently copied item at the top of the list, as shown in Figure 8.4.

Figure 8.4

Most recently copied item at the top of the list

Five items stored in the Office Clipboard

7 **Save** the document.

More Knowledge

Being Careful of Copyright Issues

You can collect and paste text and graphics from the Internet. However, nearly everything you find on the Internet is protected by *copyright* law, which protects authors of original works, including text, art, photographs, and music. If you want to use text or graphics that you find online, you will need to get permission. One of the exceptions to this law is the use of small amounts of information for educational purposes, which falls under Fair Use guidelines.

Copyright laws in the United States are open to different interpretations, and copyright laws can be very different in other countries. As a general rule, if you want to use someone else's material, always get permission first.

Activity 8.02 Pasting Information from the Clipboard Task Pane

After you have collected text and graphics from other documents or sources, you can paste them into your document.

1 With your **8A_Garden_Newsletter** file displayed, in the **Clipboard** task pane, locate and click the **Georgia Gardens Newsletter** WordArt title. Compare your screen with Figure 8.5.

The WordArt title is pasted into the document at the insertion point location, and also remains available in the Office Clipboard.

Figure 8.5

WordArt title is pasted at the insertion point location

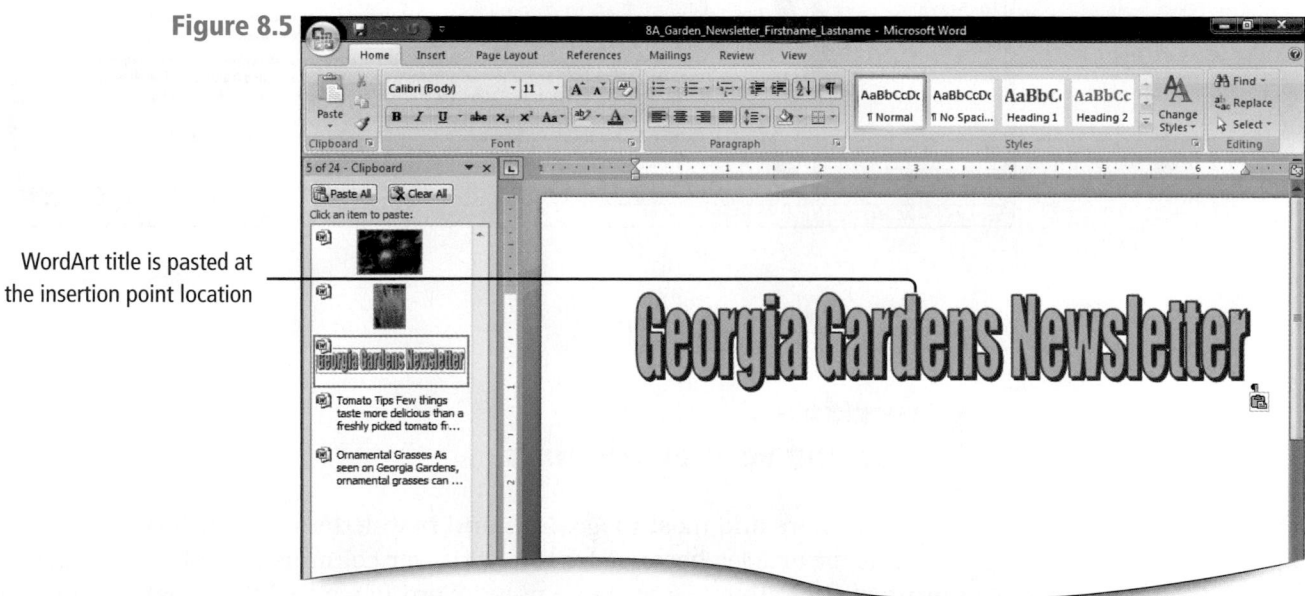

2 Press Enter. In the **Clipboard** task pane, click the text entry beginning *Ornamental Grasses* to paste the entire block of text at the insertion point.

3 In the **Clipboard** task pane, click the text entry beginning *Tomato Tips* to paste the entire block of text at the insertion point. Press ←Bksp to remove the blank line at the bottom of the inserted text.

4 Select all of the text in the document except the WordArt title. Be sure to include the paragraph mark at the end of the document.

5 Right-click the selected text, and then click **Paragraph**. In the displayed **Paragraph** dialog box, under **Spacing**, in the **After** box, click the **down spin arrow** to change the spacing to **6 pt**.

6 Under **Spacing**, click the **Line spacing arrow**, and then click **Single**. Click **OK** to close the **Paragraph** dialog box. Press Ctrl + Home to move to the top of the document, and then compare your screen with Figure 8.6.

Figure 8.6

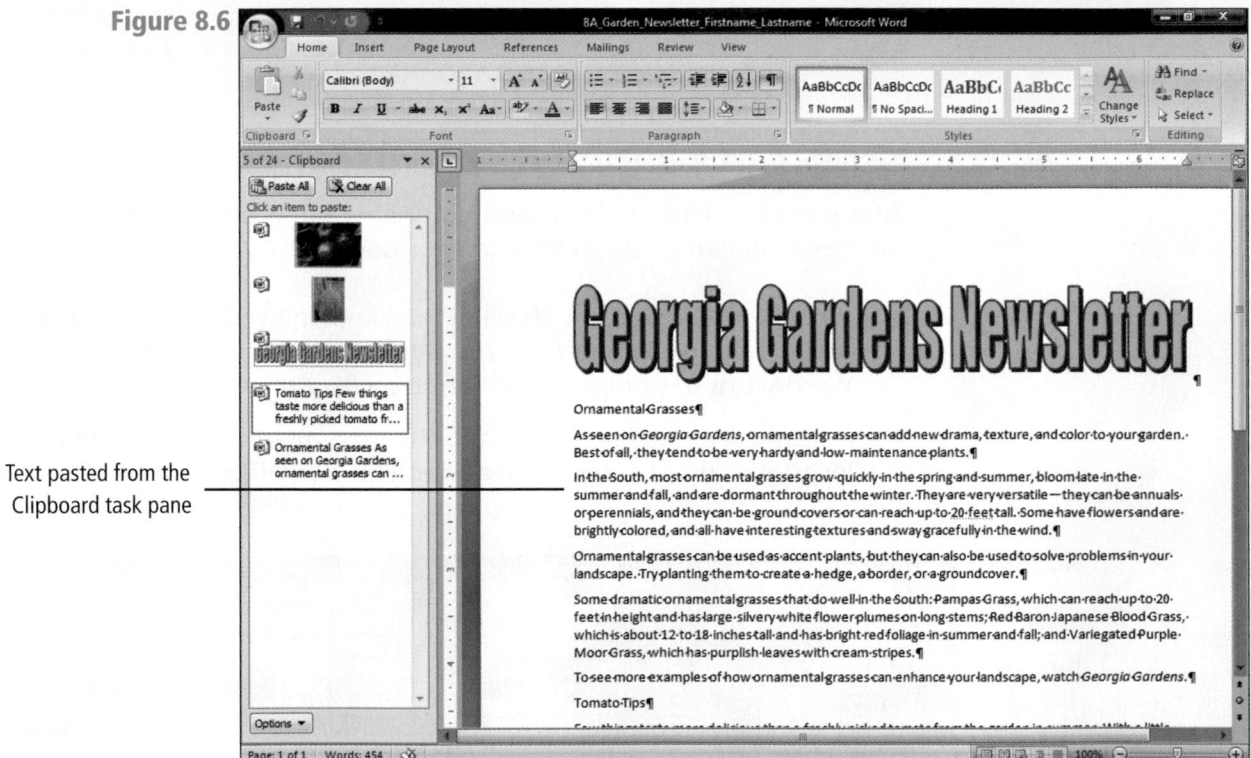

Text pasted from the Clipboard task pane

7 **Save** the document.

Objective 2
Create and Format Columns

All newspapers and most magazines and newsletters use multiple columns for articles because text in narrower columns is easier to read than text that stretches across a page. Word has a tool that enables you to change a single column of text into two or more columns, and then format the columns. If a column does not end where you want, you can end the column at a location of your choice by inserting a *manual column break*.

Activity 8.03 Changing One Column of Text to Two Columns

Newsletters are usually two or three columns wide. When using 8.5 × 11-inch paper in portrait orientation, avoid creating four or more columns because they are so narrow that word spacing looks awkward, often resulting in one long word by itself on a line.

1 Select all of the text in the document except the WordArt title. Be sure to include the paragraph mark at the end of the document.

2 Click the **Page Layout tab**, and then in the **Page Setup group**, click the **Columns** button. From the displayed **Columns gallery**, click **Two**, scroll to the top of the document, and then compare your screen with Figure 8.7.

The text is divided into two columns, and a section break is inserted below the WordArt title, dividing the one-column section of the document from the two-column section of the document. Do not be concerned if your columns do not break at the same line as shown in the figure.

Figure 8.7

Two-column format

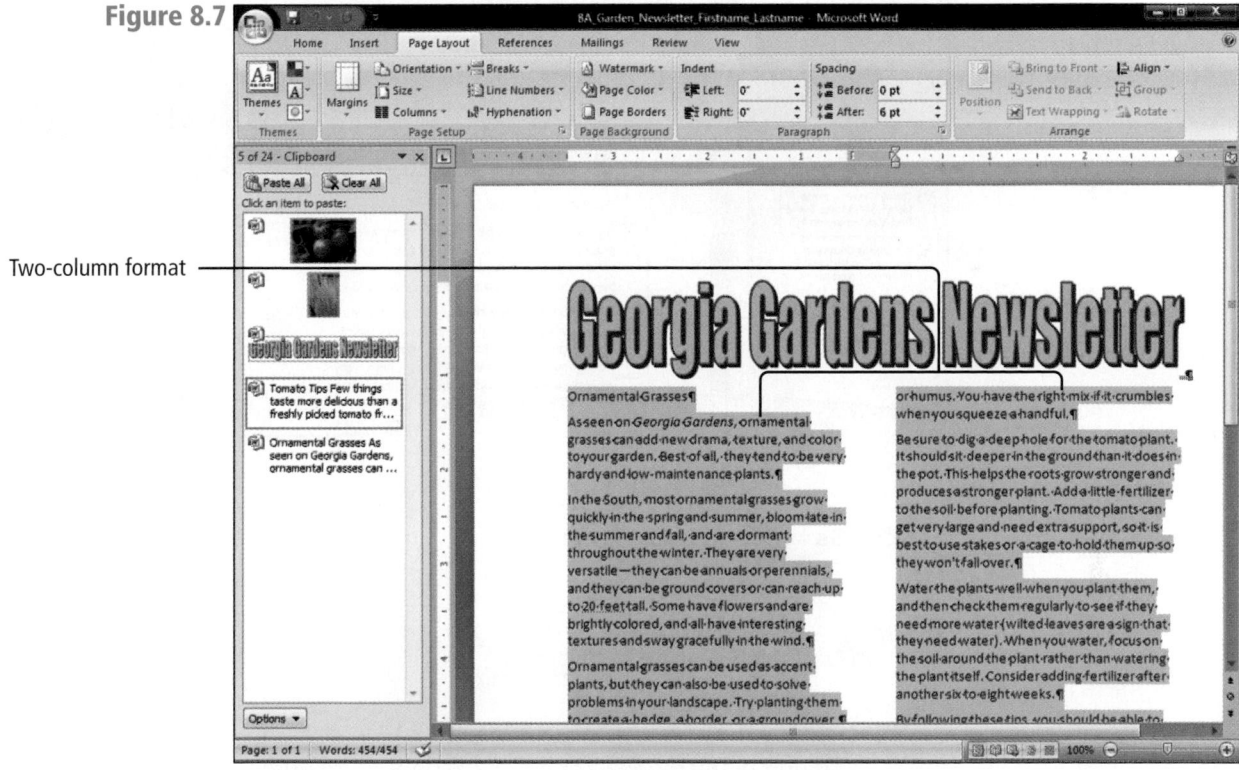

3 **Save** the document.

Activity 8.04 Formatting Multiple Columns

The uneven right edge of a single page-width column is readable. When you create narrow columns, justified text is sometimes preferable. The font you choose should also match the style of newsletter you are creating.

1 With the text still selected, click the **Home tab**. In the **Font group**, click the **Font button arrow** Cambria, scroll down the font list, and then click **Comic Sans MS**. Alternatively, you can press *c* to move to the first font beginning with that letter, and then scroll down to the desired font.

2 In the **Font group**, click the **Font Size button arrow** 12 ▾ , and then click **10**.

3 In the **Paragraph group**, click the **Justify** button ▤ . Click anywhere in the document to deselect the text, and then compare your screen with Figure 8.8.

The document displays in 10 pt. Comic Sans MS font, an informal and easy-to-read font; the text is justified.

Figure 8.8

Text justified

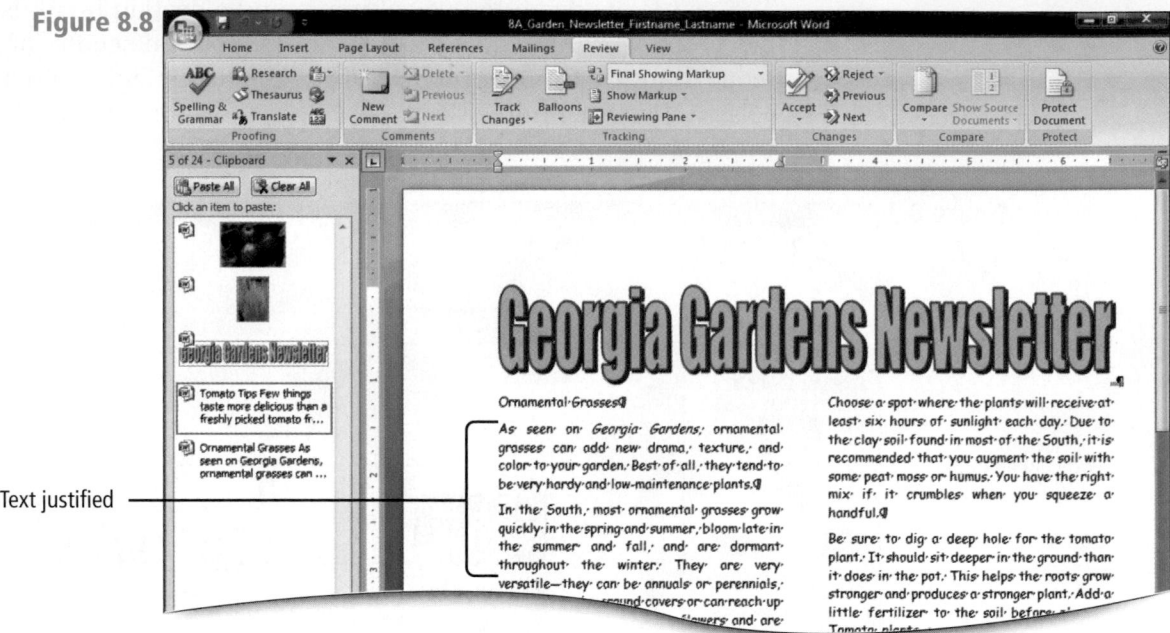

4 **Save** 🖫 the document.

More Knowledge

Justifying Column Text

Although many magazines and newspapers still justify text in columns, there is a great deal of disagreement about whether to justify the columns, or to use left alignment and leave the right edge uneven. Justified text tends to look more formal and cleaner, but it also results in uneven spacing between words, which some feel makes justified text harder to read.

Activity 8.05 Inserting a Column Break

Insert manual column breaks to adjust columns that end or begin awkwardly, or to make space for graphics or text boxes.

1 From the **Office** menu 🪟 , point to **Print**, and then click **Print Preview**. Notice that the columns end unevenly.

2 In the **Preview group**, click the **Close Print Preview** button. Scroll down, and then near the bottom of the first column, position the insertion point to the left of *Tomato Tips*.

3 Click the **Page Layout tab**, and then in the **Page Setup group**, click the **Breaks** button to display the **Page and Section Breaks gallery**, as shown in Figure 8.9.

Breaks gallery

Figure 8.9

Column break

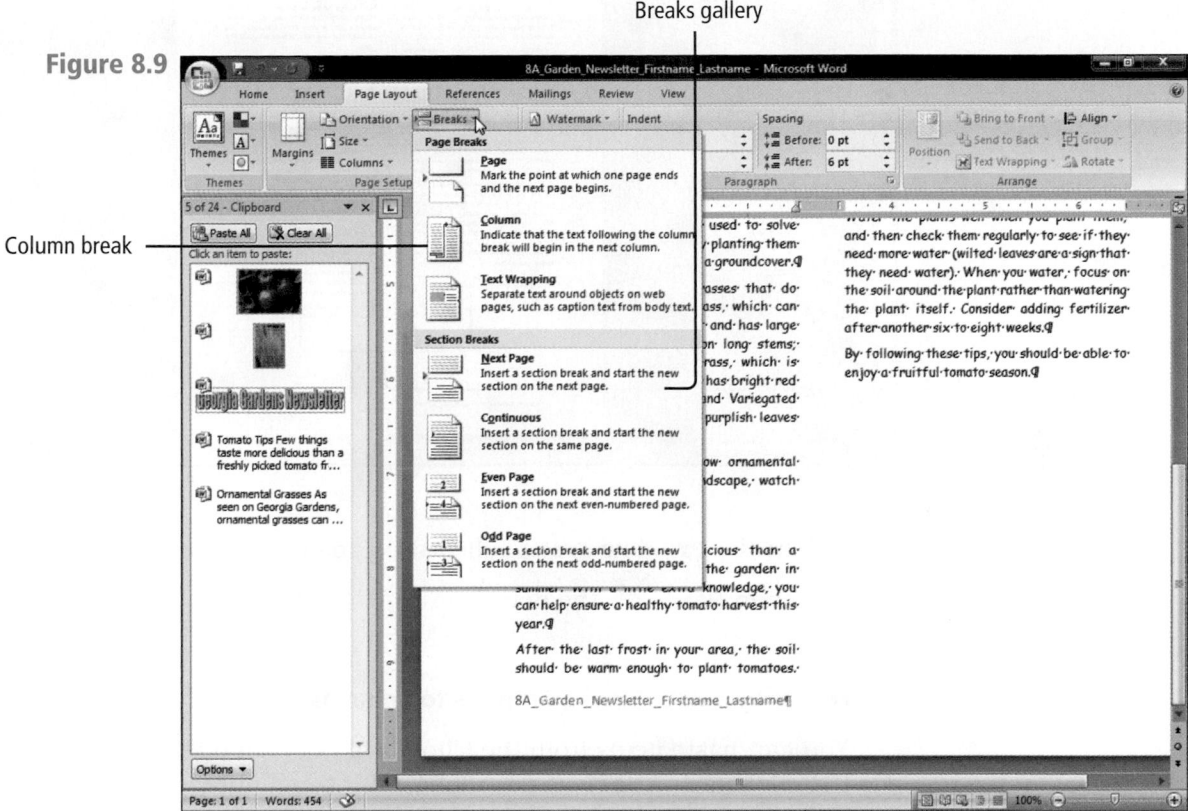

4 From the displayed **Breaks gallery**, under **Page Breaks**, click **Column**.

The column breaks at the insertion point, and the text to the right of the insertion point moves to the top of the next column.

5 From the **Office** menu , point to **Print**, and then click **Print Preview**. Compare your screen with Figure 8.10.

The columns are more even, although they still do not align at exactly the same line. The bottom alignment will be adjusted when graphics are added to the newsletter.

Figure 8.10

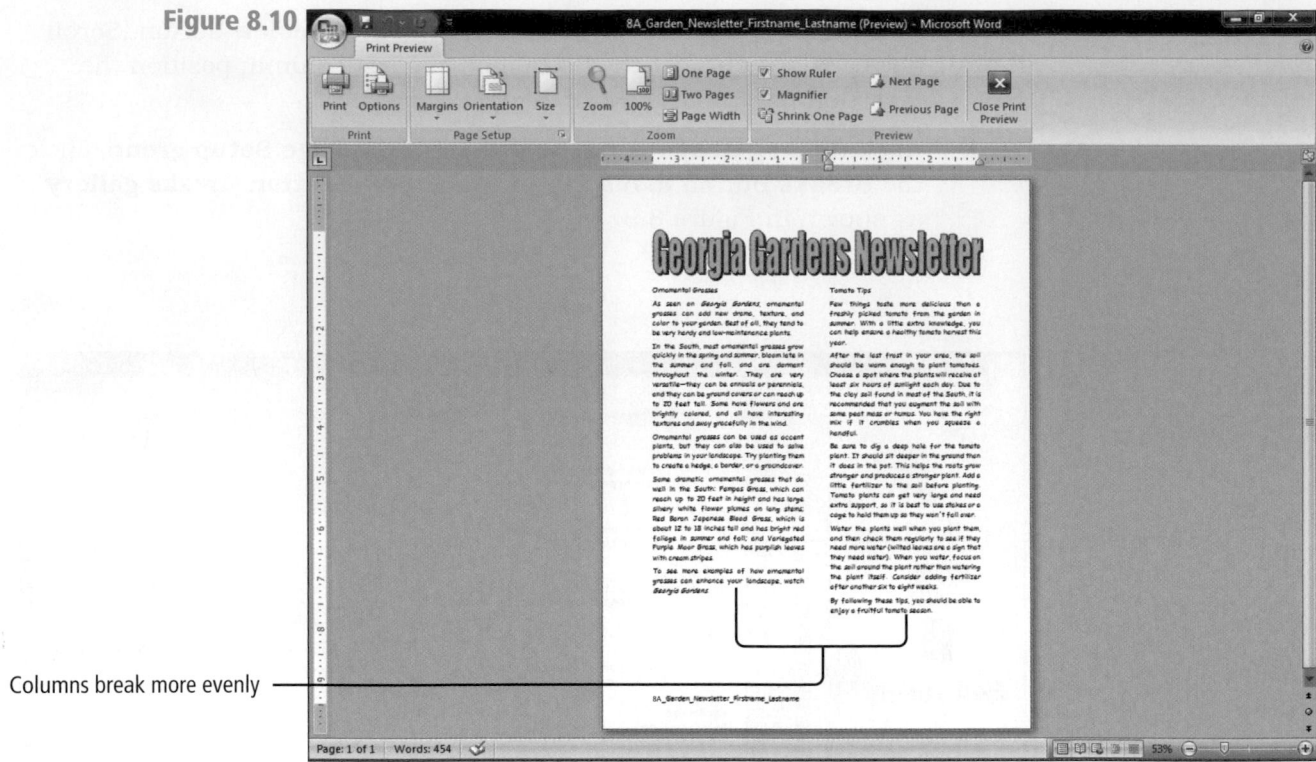

Columns break more evenly

6 In the **Preview group**, click the **Close Print Preview** button, and then **Save** the document.

Activity 8.06 Adding Graphics to Columns

You can paste items from the Clipboard task pane at any time. Items on the clipboard remain on the clipboard throughout your Word session unless you delete them. Recall that the limit for items on the Office Clipboard is 24—if you add a 25th item, the earliest item added is removed.

1 In the first column, click anywhere to position the insertion point. In the **Clipboard** task pane, click the **grass** picture to paste it at the insertion point location.

2 Right-click the **grass** picture, point to **Text Wrapping**, and then click **Square** to wrap the text around the picture.

3 Right-click the **grass** picture, and then from the shortcut menu, click **Size**. In the displayed **Size** dialog box, under **Scale**, select the **Lock aspect ratio** check box. Under **Size and rotate** click the **Height down spin arrow** as necessary to set the picture height to **2**". Alternatively, select the value in the Height box and type *2*.

Recall that the *aspect ratio* is the ratio of the height to the width of an object. Locking the aspect ratio ensures that the proportions of the object will remain unchanged when either the height or width is changed.

4 At the bottom of the **Size** dialog box, click the **Close** button. Drag the picture to the left margin of the first column, with the top edge of the picture even with the top of the paragraph beginning *In the South*.

5 In the second column, click anywhere to position the insertion point. In the **Clipboard** task pane, click the **tomatoes** picture to paste it at the insertion point location.

6 Use the procedure you just practiced to set the **Text Wrapping** to **Square**. Proportionally change the **Height** to **1.2**". Drag the picture to the right margin of the second column, with the top edge at approximately **5.5 inches on the vertical ruler**, as shown in Figure 8.11. Recall that you can more precisely adjust the position of the picture by holding down Ctrl and then pressing the arrow keys.

Figure 8.11

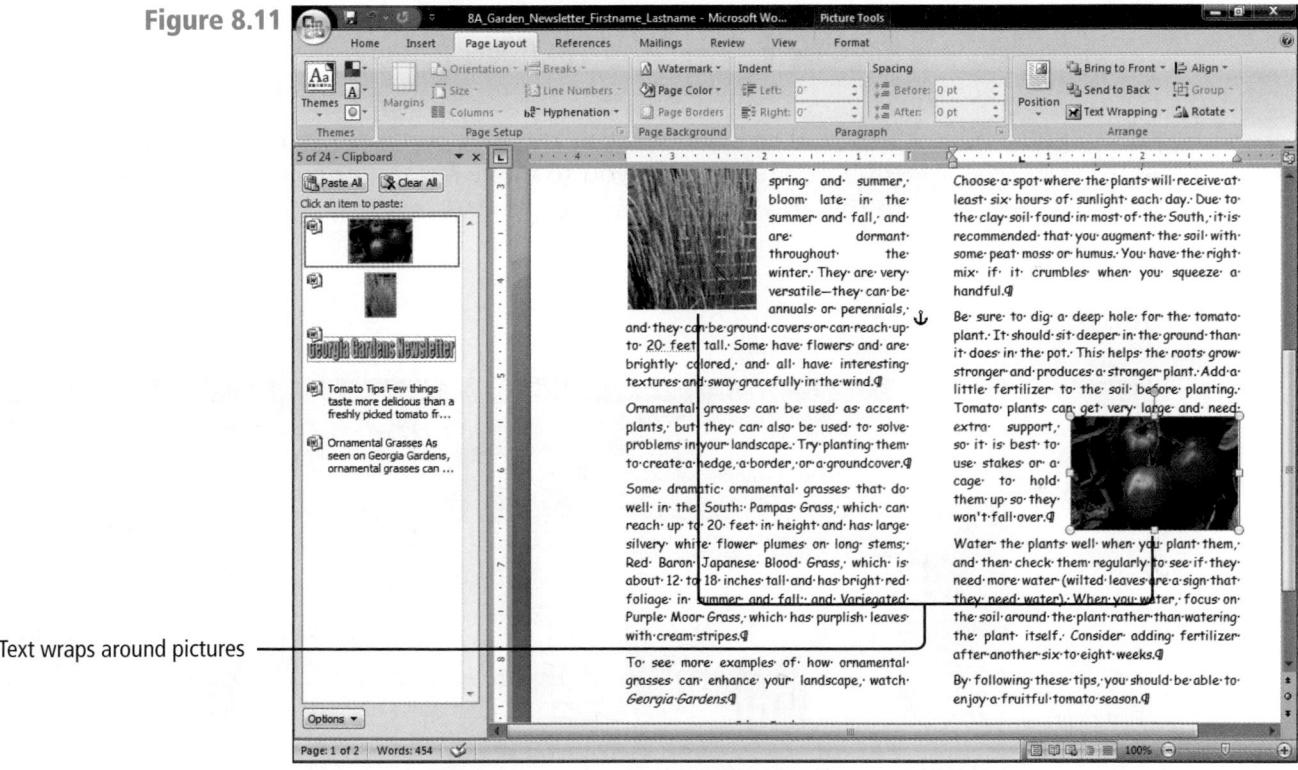

Text wraps around pictures

7 Near the top of the **Clipboard** task pane, click the **Clear All** button to remove all items from the Office Clipboard. **Close** ☒ the Clipboard task pane.

8 **Save** 🖫 the document.

Objective 3
Use Special Character and Paragraph Formatting

Special text and paragraph formatting is useful to emphasize text, and it makes your newsletter look more professional. There are various ways to call attention to specific text. One way is to place a border around a paragraph.

Another is to shade a paragraph, although use caution not to make the shade too dark, because shading can make the text difficult to read.

Activity 8.07 Using Small Caps and Changing the Font Color

For headlines and titles, **small caps** is an attractive font effect. Lowercase letters are changed to uppercase letters but remain the height of lowercase letters. Titles are frequently formatted using this style.

1 Press Ctrl + Home to move to the top of the document. At the top of the first column, select the text *Ornamental Grasses*. Be sure to include the paragraph mark.

2 Right-click the selected text, and then from the shortcut menu, click **Font**. In the displayed **Font** dialog box, click the **Font color arrow**, and then under **Theme Colors**, click **Orange, Accent 6, Darker 50%**—the bottom color in the tenth column. Under **Font style**, click **Bold**. Under **Size**, click **18**. Under **Effects**, select the **Small caps** check box. Compare your screen with Figure 8.12.

The Font dialog box gives you more options than are available on the Ribbon, and enables you to make several changes at the same time. In the Preview box, the text displays with the selected formatting options applied.

Small caps
check box   Font size

Figure 8.12

Font style

Font color

Selected text

Preview box

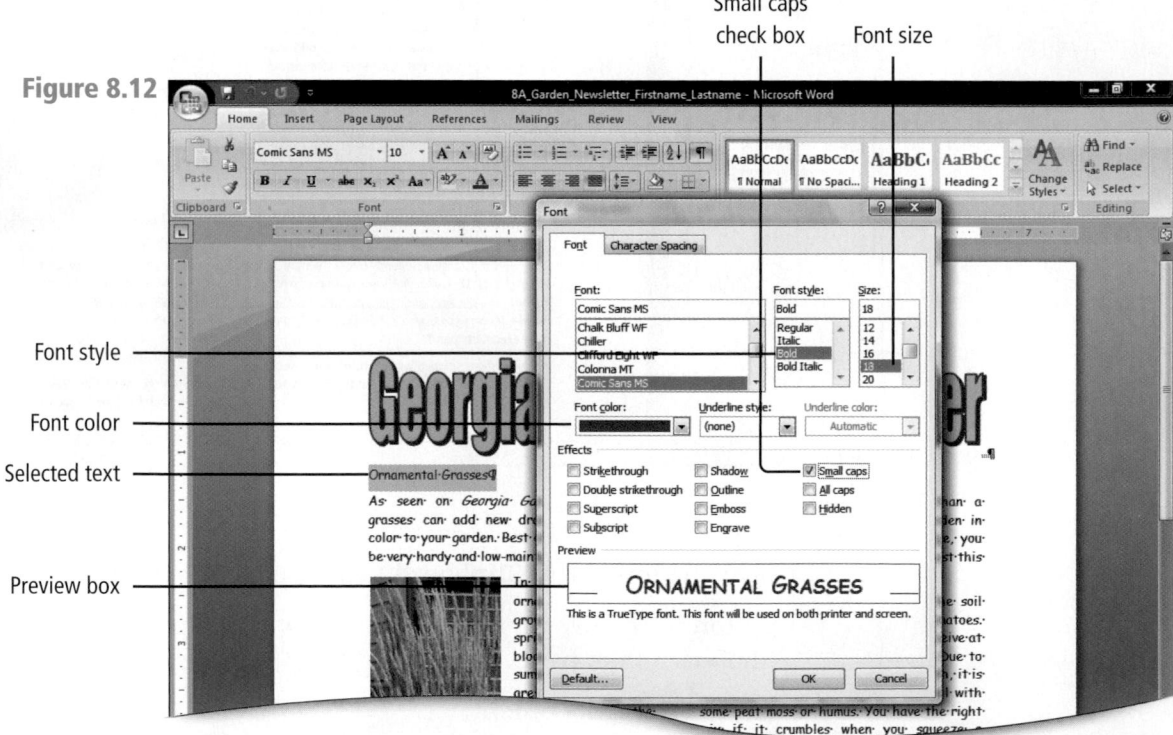

3 At the bottom of the **Font** dialog box, click **OK**.

4 At the top of the second column, select the text *Tomato Tips*. Using the technique you just practiced, apply the same formatting that you added to the title of the first column. Alternatively, use the Format Painter. Click anywhere in the document to deselect the text, and then compare your screen with Figure 8.13.

Figure 8.13

Word | chapter 8

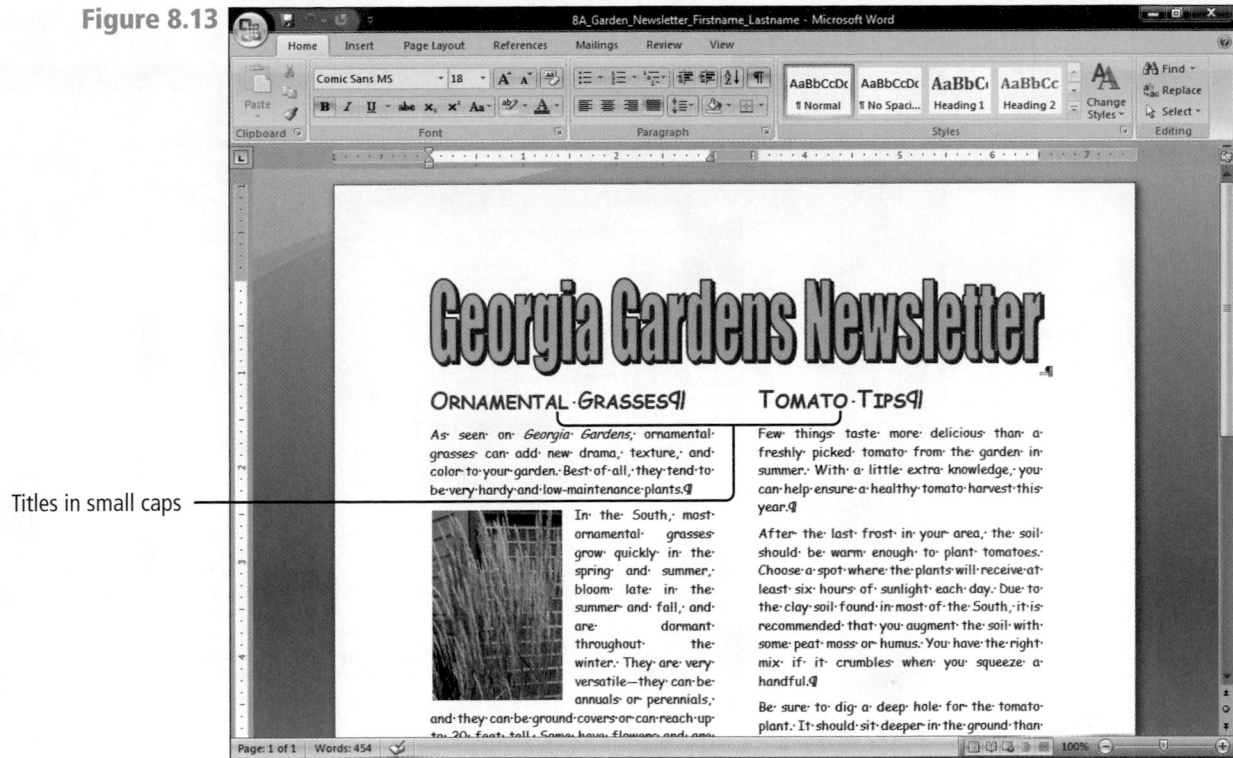

Titles in small caps

5 **Save** 📧 the document.

Activity 8.08 Adding a Border and Shading to a Paragraph

Paragraph borders provide strong visual cues to the reader. Shading can be used with or without borders. When used with a border, light shading can be very effective in drawing the reader's eye to the text.

1 At the bottom of the first column, in the paragraph that begins *To see more examples*, triple-click in the paragraph to select it. On the **Home tab**, in the **Paragraph group**, click the **Border button arrow** ⊞▾, and then click **Borders and Shading**. In the displayed **Borders and Shading** dialog box, be sure the **Borders tab** is selected. Under **Setting**, click **Box**. Click the **Width arrow**, and then click **1 1/2 pt**. Click the **Color arrow**, and then click **Orange, Accent 6, Darker 50%**—the bottom color in the tenth column. Compare your screen with Figure 8.14.

In the lower right portion of the Borders and Shading dialog box, the *Apply to* box displays *Paragraph*. The *Apply to* box directs where the border will be applied—in this instance, the border will be applied to the selected paragraph.

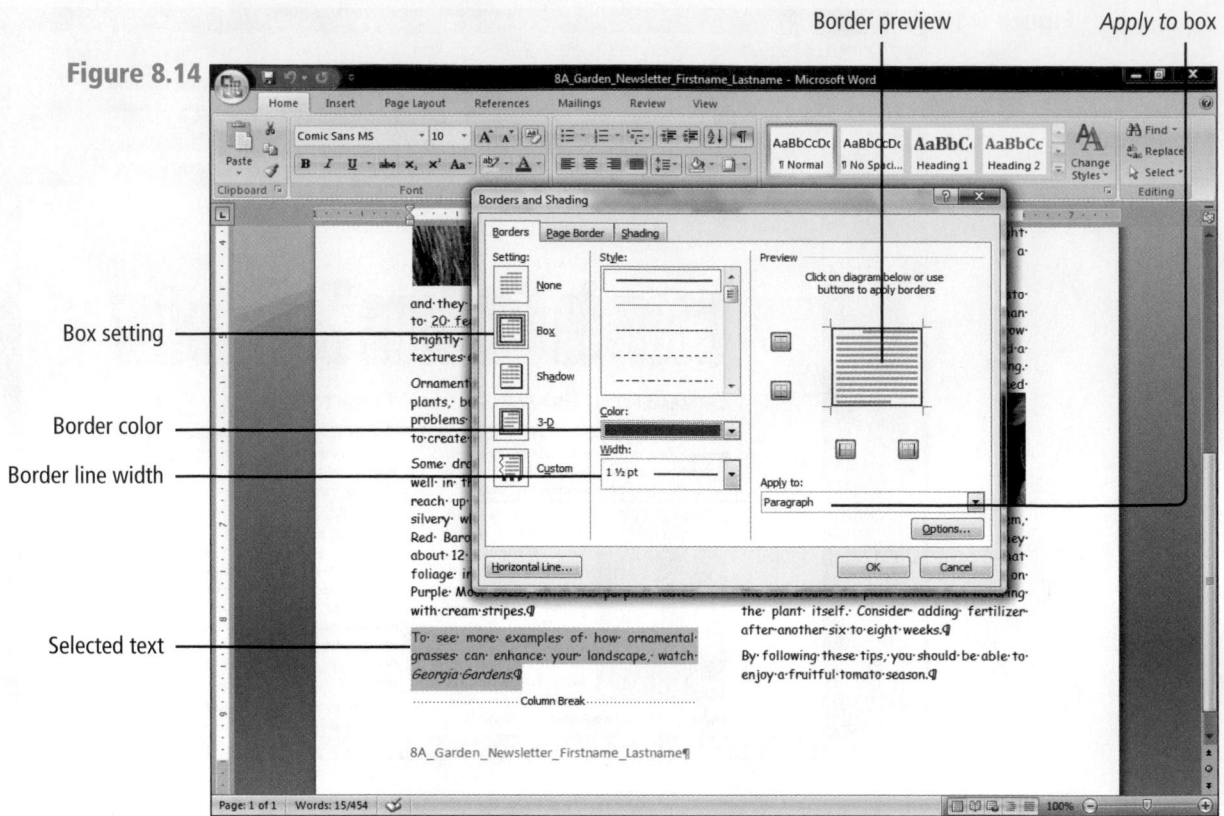

Border preview | *Apply to* box

Figure 8.14

Box setting

Border color

Border line width

Selected text

Note — Adding Simple Borders to Text

Simple borders and border edges can be added using the Border button in the Paragraph group. This button offers very little control, however, because line thickness and color depend on the previous thickness and color chosen from the Borders and Shading dialog box.

2 At the top of the **Borders and Shading** dialog box, click the **Shading tab**.

3 Click the **Fill arrow**, and then click **Orange, Accent 6, Lighter 80%**—the second color in the tenth column. At the bottom of the **Borders and Shading** dialog box, click **OK**. Click anywhere in the document to deselect the text, and then compare your screen with Figure 8.15.

Figure 8.15

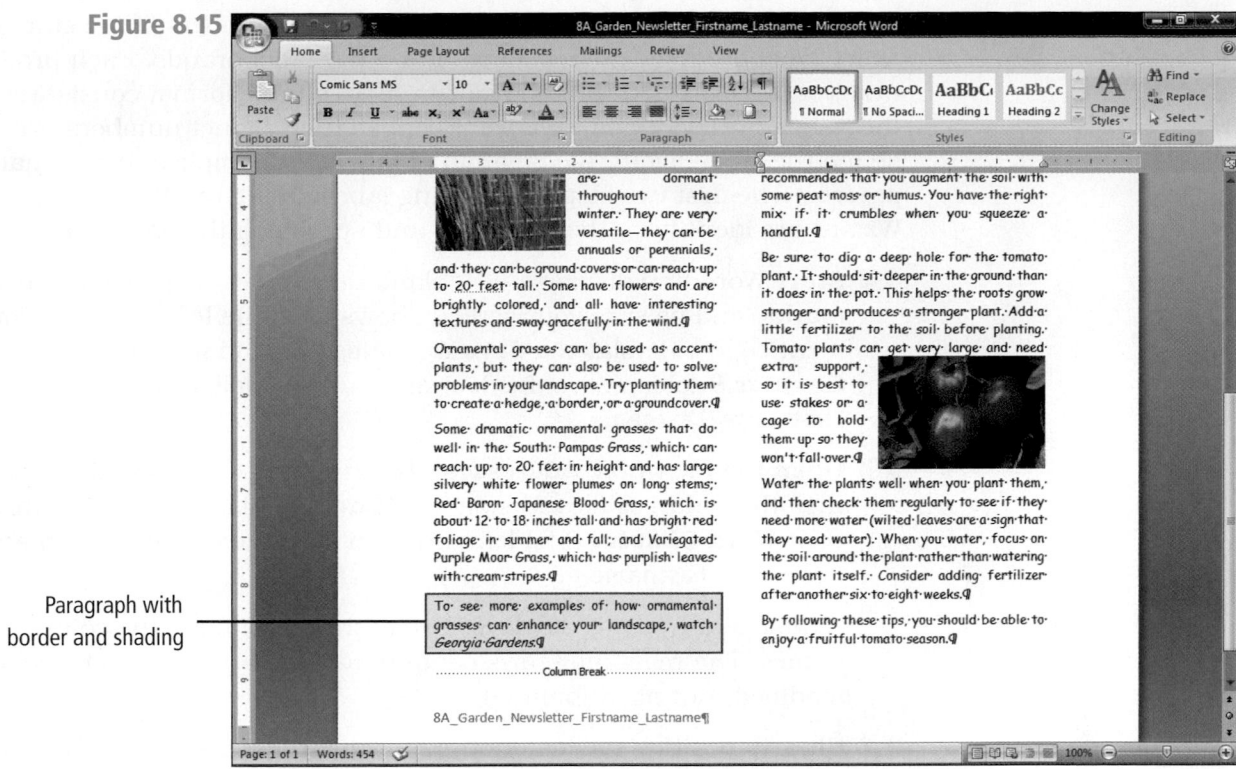

Paragraph with border and shading

4 **Save** 📄 the document, submit your file as directed, and then **Exit** Word.

Objective 4
Create Mailing Labels Using Mail Merge

Word's *mail merge* feature joins a *main document* and a *data source* to create customized letters or labels. The main document contains the text or formatting that remains constant. In the case of labels, the main document contains the formatting for a specific label size. The data source contains information including the names and addresses of the individuals for whom the labels are being created. Names and addresses in a data source might come from a Word table, an Excel spreadsheet, or an Access database.

The easiest way to perform a mail merge is to use the Mail Merge Wizard. Recall that a wizard asks you questions and, based on your answers, walks you step-by-step through a process. Labels are used to address newsletters, envelopes, postcards, disk labels, name badges, file folder labels, and so on. Sheets of precut labels can be purchased from office supply stores.

Activity 8.09 Opening the Mail Merge Wizard Template

Mail merge information can be stored in various formats and programs, including Microsoft Word tables. Such tables can be edited in the same manner as other Word tables.

The label feature in Word contains the product numbers of the standard Avery label products as well as several other label brands. Each product number is associated with a layout in Word's table format consisting of the height and width of the label. Because the product numbers pre-define the label layout, the creation of labels is a simple and automated process. The first two steps in creating labels using the Mail Merge Wizard are identifying the label type and specifying the data source.

1 **Start** Word and display a new blank document. Display formatting marks, and be sure your screen shows both the left and right document edges. Display the **Save As** dialog box and in your **Word Chapter 8** folder, save the document as **8A_Mailing_Labels_Firstname_Lastname**

2 **Open** the file **w08A_Addresses**—be sure to use w08**A** and not one of the other address files. Display the **Save As** dialog box, navigate to your **Word Chapter 8** folder, and then save the file as **8A_Addresses_Firstname_Lastname**

A table of addresses displays. The first row contains the column names. The remaining rows contain addresses. This data file will be modified, but not submitted.

3 Click to position the insertion point in the last cell in the table, and then press Tab to create a new row. Enter the following information, and then compare your table with Figure 8.16.

First Name	Duncan
Last Name	McArthur
Address 1	3336 S. Flowers Rd.
Address 2	#234
City	Macon
State	GA
ZIP Code	31217

Figure 8.16

Column names ⎯⎯⎯⎯

New row ⎯⎯⎯⎯

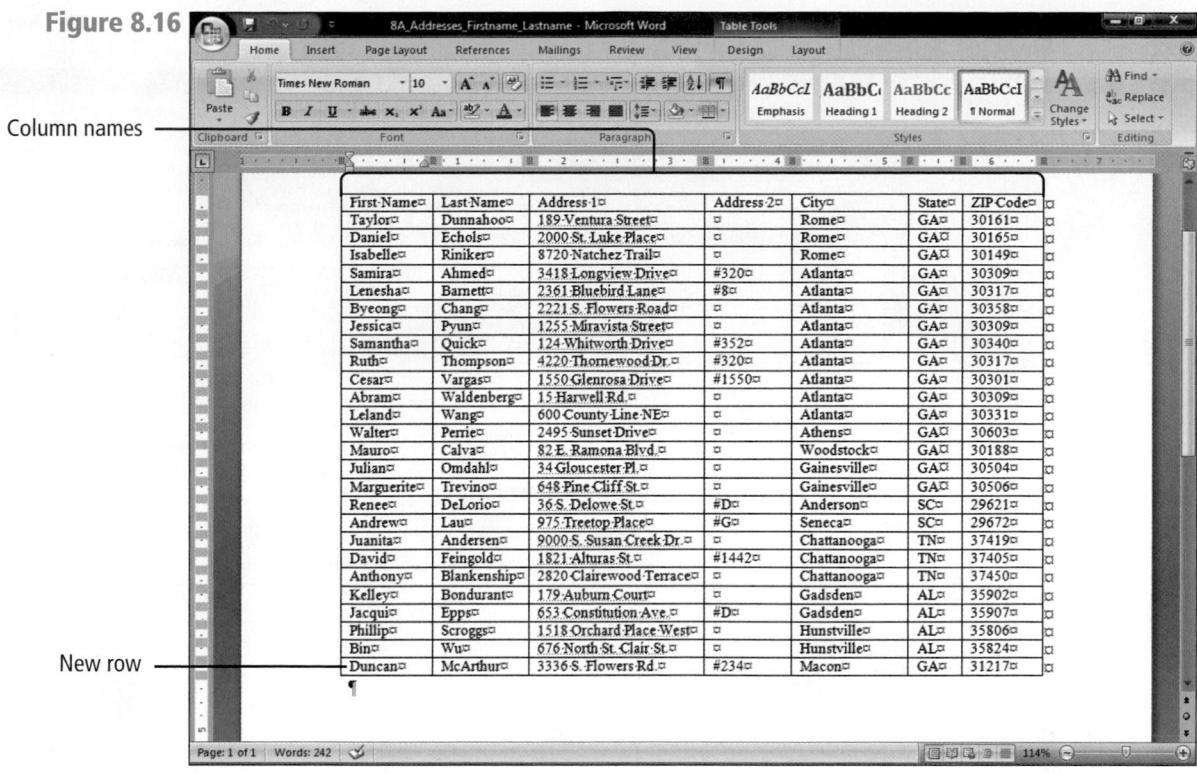

4 **Save** 🖫 , and then **Close** ❎ the table of addresses; be sure your **8A_Mailing_Labels** document displays.

5 Click the **Mailings tab**. In the **Start Mail Merge group**, click the **Start Mail Merge** button, and then click **Step by Step Mail Merge Wizard** to display the **Mail Merge** task pane. Under **Select document type**, click the **Labels** option button.

6 At the bottom of the task pane, click **Next: Starting document** to display **Step 2 of 6** of the Mail Merge Wizard. Under **Select starting document**, be sure **Change document layout** is selected, and then under **Change document layout**, click **Label options**.

7 In the **Label Options** dialog box, under **Printer information**, click the **Tray arrow**, and then click **Default tray (Automatically Select)**—your wording may vary—to print the labels on regular paper, rather than feeding label pages manually. Under **Label information**, click the **Label vendors arrow**, and then click **Avery US Letter**. Under **Product number**, scroll about halfway down the list, and then click **5160**. Compare your screen with Figure 8.17.

The Avery 5160 address label is a commonly used label. The precut sheets contain three columns of 10 labels each—for a total of 30 labels per sheet.

Mail Merge task pane

Figure 8.17

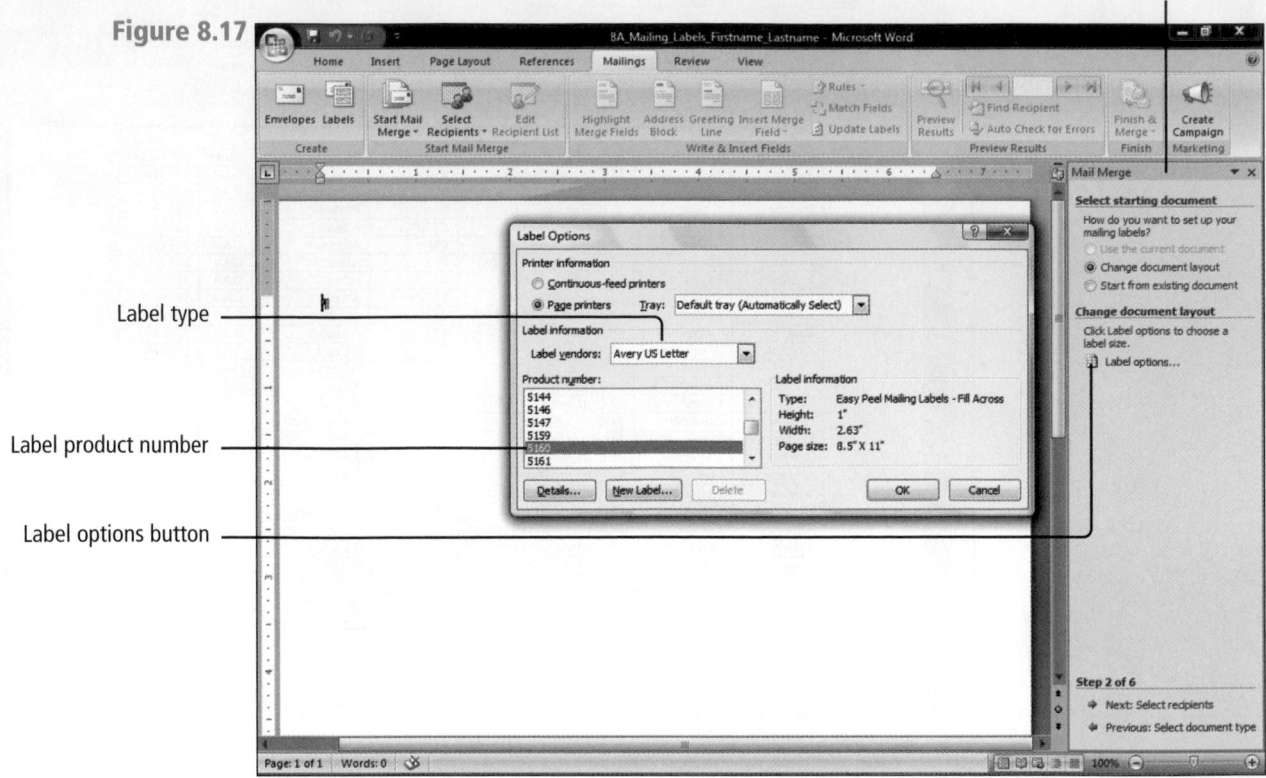

Label type

Label product number

Label options button

8 At the bottom of the **Label Options** dialog box, click **OK**. If a message box displays, click OK to set up the labels. At the bottom of the task pane, click **Next: Select recipients**.

The label page is set up with three columns and ten rows. The label borders may or may not display on your screen, depending on your setup. In Step 3 of the Mail Merge Wizard, you must identify the recipients—the data source. For your recipient data source, you can choose to use an existing list—for example, a list of names and addresses that you have in an Access database, an Excel worksheet, a Word table, or your Outlook contacts list. If you do not have an existing data source, you can type a new list at this point in the wizard.

9 Under **Select recipients**, be sure the **Use an existing list** option button is selected. Under **Use an existing list**, click **Browse**. Navigate to your **Word Chapter 8** folder, select your **8A_Addresses_Firstname_Lastname** file, and then click **Open** to display the Mail Merge Recipients dialog box, as shown in Figure 8.18.

The labels in the first row of the Word table display as the column headings in the Mail Merge Recipients dialog box. In a database or Word address table, each row of information that contains data for one person is called a *record*. The column headings—for example, *Last_Name* and *First_Name*—are referred to as *fields*. An underscore replaces the spaces between words in the field names.

Figure 8.18

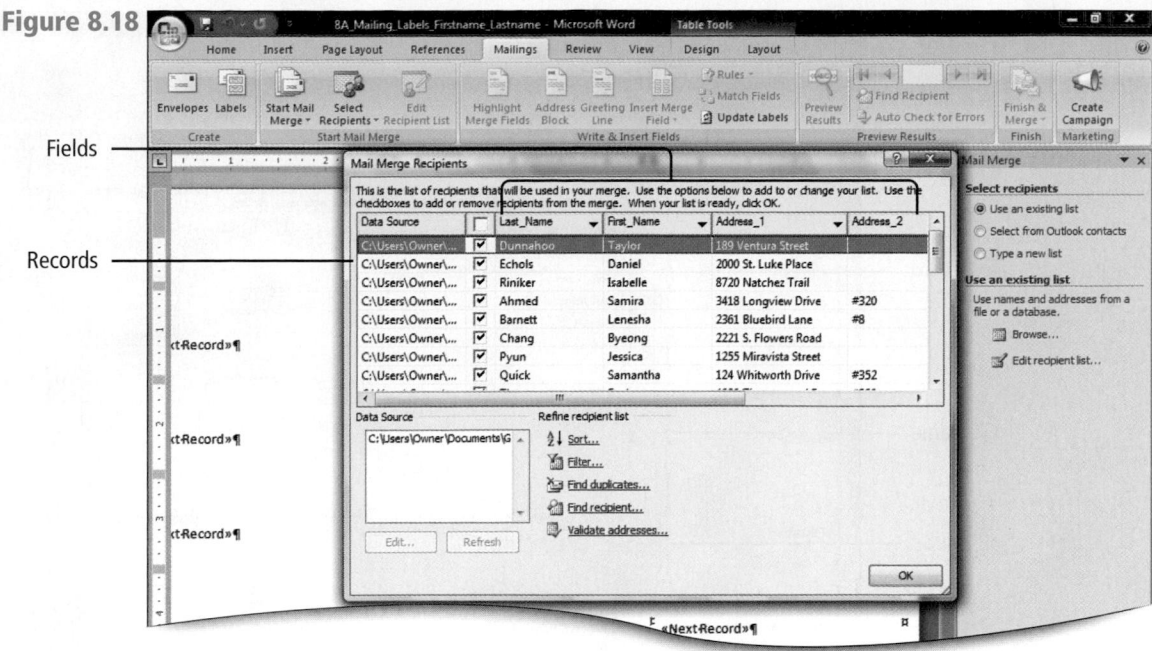

Fields

Records

Activity 8.10 Completing the Mail Merge Wizard

You can add or edit names and addresses while completing the Mail Merge Wizard. You can also match your column names with preset names used in Mail Merge; for example, if the column heading for city names was *Place*, you could match that column with the *City* field to create the correct address blocks.

1 Near the bottom of the **Mail Merge Recipients** dialog box, under **Data Source**, click the file name. At the bottom of the **Mail Merge Recipients** dialog box, click **Edit**.

The Data Form dialog box displays. You can edit or delete the selected record, or use the same dialog box to add a new recipient.

2 On the right side of the displayed **Data Form** dialog box, click **Add New**. In the displayed blank record, type the following, pressing Tab to move from field to field, and then compare your **Data Form** dialog box with Figure 8.19:

First_Name	**Harriet**
Last_Name	**Hasty**
Address_1	**1875 Bullpen Dr.**
Address_2	
City	**Columbus**
State	**GA**
ZIP_Code	**31993**

Word | chapter 8

Figure 8.19

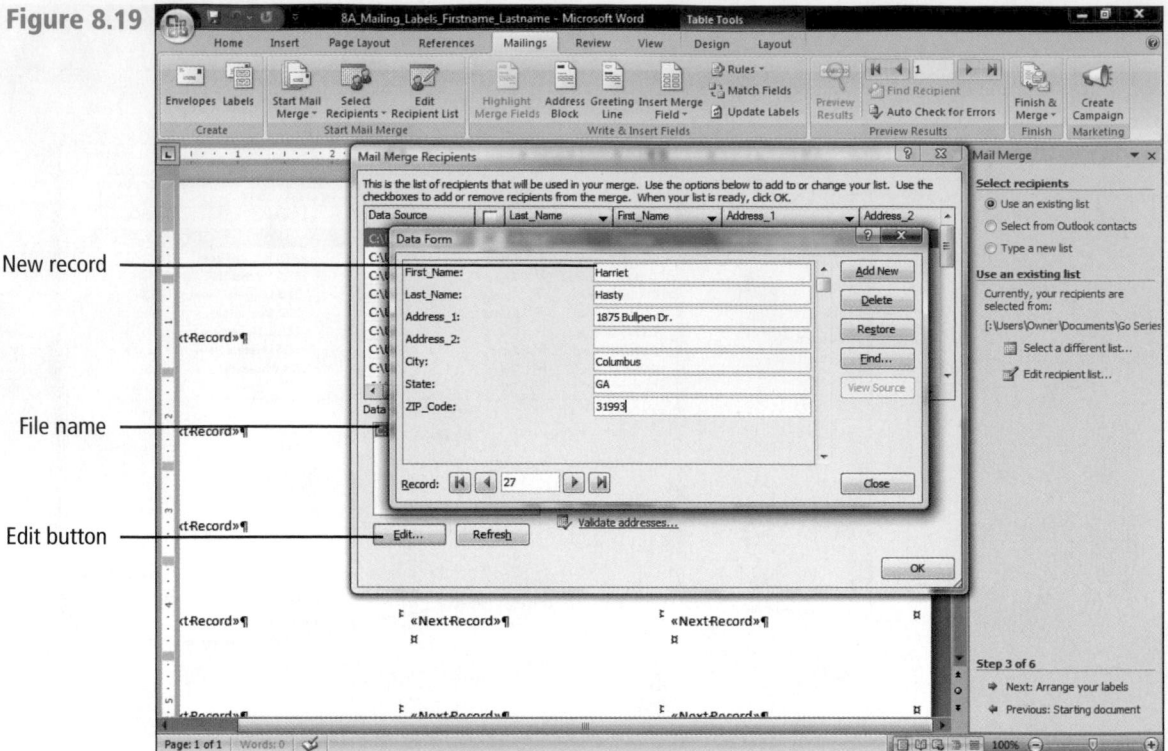

New record

File name

Edit button

---

3 At the bottom of the **Data Form** dialog box, click **Close**. Scroll to the end of the recipient list to confirm that the record you just added is in the list. At the bottom of the **Mail Merge Recipients** dialog box, click **OK**. At the bottom of the **Mail Merge** task pane, click **Next: Arrange your labels**.

At Step 4 of the Mail Merge Wizard, Word provides various ways to arrange and add features to your labels.

4 Under **Arrange your labels**, click **Address block**. In the **Insert Address Block** dialog box, under **Specify address elements**, examine the various formats for names. If necessary, under **Insert recipient's name in this format**, select the **Joshua Randall Jr.** format. Compare your dialog box with Figure 8.20.

Address block preview

Figure 8.20

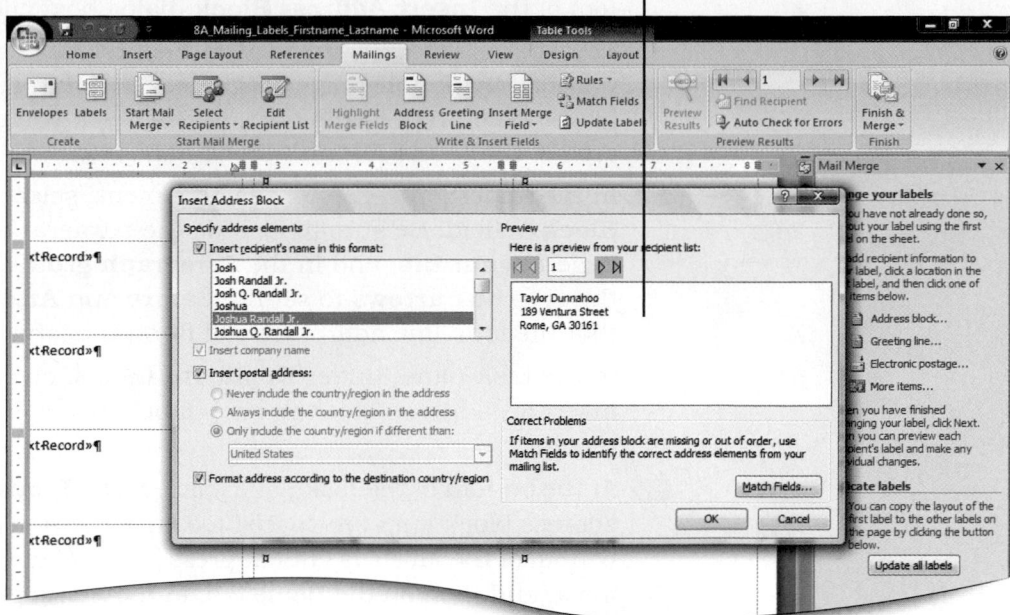

5 Near the lower right corner of the **Insert Address Block** dialog box, click **Match Fields**. Scroll down and examine the dialog box, and then compare your screen with Figure 8.21.

If your field names are descriptive, the Mail Merge program will identify them correctly, as is the case with the information in the *Required for Address Block* section. If you need to match a field, display the list to choose the correct field from your database or table.

Figure 8.21

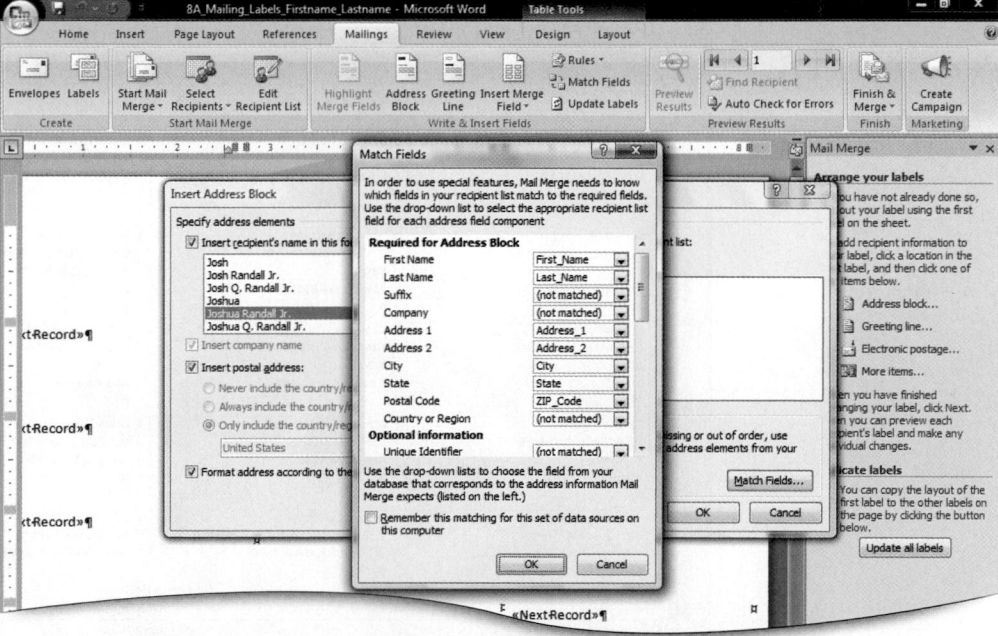

6 At the bottom of the **Match Fields** dialog box, click **OK**. At the bottom of the **Insert Address Block** dialog box, click **OK**.

The Address block is inserted in the first label space and is surrounded by double angle brackets. The *Address Block* field name displays, which represents the address block you saw in the Preview area of the Insert Address Block dialog box.

7 In the upper left corner of the document, select the <<**Address Block**>> field. Be sure to include the paragraph mark. Click the **Page Layout tab**, and in the **Paragraph group**, under **Spacing**, use the **spin box arrows** to set the **Before** and **After** boxes to **0** to ensure that the four-line addresses will fit on the labels.

8 In the task pane, under **Replicate labels**, click **Update all labels** to insert an address block in each label space for each subsequent record.

9 At the bottom of the task pane, click **Next: Preview your labels**. If the address block lines are spaced too far apart and some of the text at the bottom of the labels is cut off, press Ctrl + A to select the entire document, and then on the Home tab, in the Styles group, click the No Spacing style. If necessary, scroll to the left to view the left edge of the page, and then compare your labels with Figure 8.22.

Some Word defaults add extra spacing after paragraphs. Changing the line spacing ensures that the address blocks will fit properly on the labels. In some cases, where there is an apartment or unit number, there are addresses on two lines. The wizard creates the lines automatically when the Address Block is inserted.

Figure 8.22

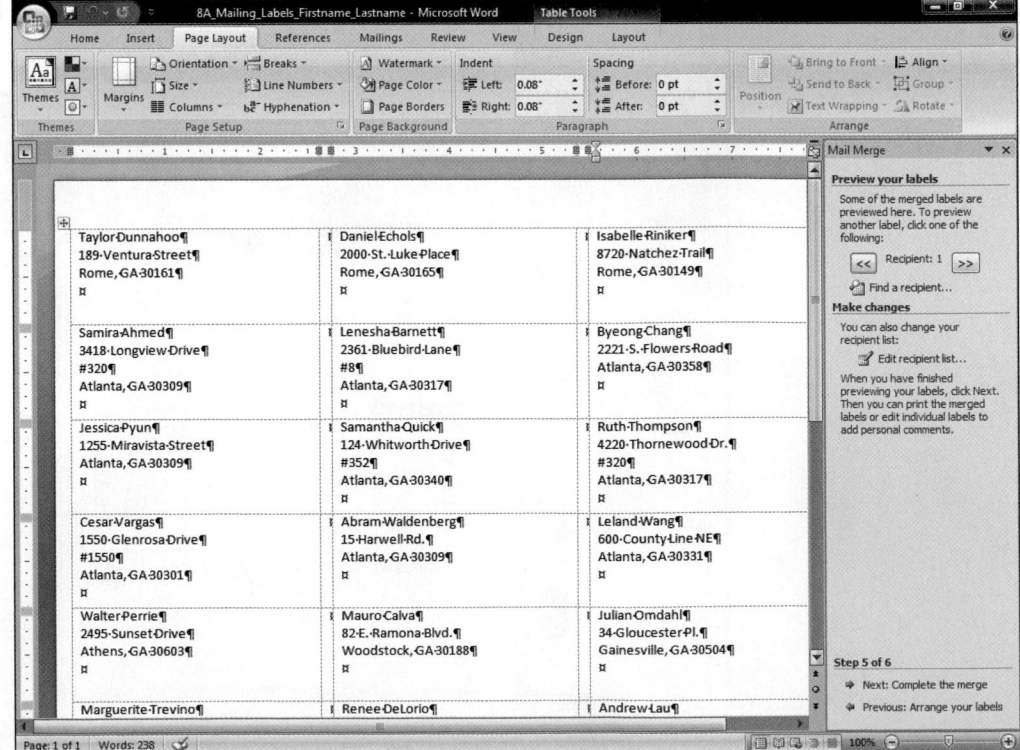

10 At the bottom of the task pane, click **Next: Complete the merge.**

Step 6 of the Mail Merge task pane displays. At this point you can print or edit your labels, although this is done more easily in the document window.

11 **Save** 💾 your labels, and then **Close** ❌ the Mail Merge task pane.

Activity 8.11 Previewing and Printing the Mail Merge Document

Before you print, preview your labels to be sure the information fits in the space reserved for each label.

1 Display the document footer and add the file name to the footer, and then close the footer area. From the **Office** menu 🗔, point to the **Print arrow**, and then click **Print Preview**. Position the 🔍 pointer over the labels and click one time. Compare your screen with Figure 8.23.

Adding footer text to a label sheet replaces the last row of labels on a page with the footer text, and moves the last row of labels to the top of the next page. In this case, a blank second page is created.

Figure 8.23

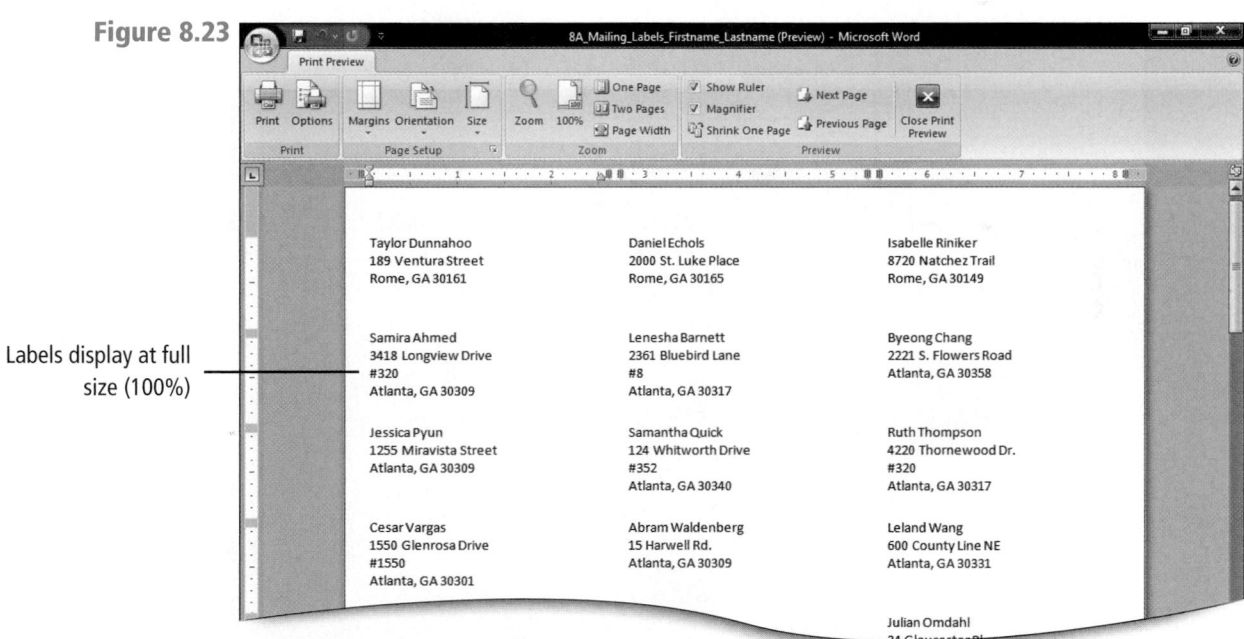

Labels display at full size (100%)

2 To submit electronically, follow your instructor's directions. Otherwise, on the **Print Preview tab**, in the **Print group**, click the **Print** button. In the **Print** dialog box, under **Page range**, click the **Current page** option button, and then click **OK**.

The labels will print on whatever paper is in the printer. In this case, unless you have preformatted labels available, you will print your labels on a sheet of paper. Printing the labels on plain paper first enables you to proofread the labels before you print them on more expensive label sheets.

3 On the **Print Preview tab**, in the **Preview group**, click the **Close Print Preview** button.

4 **Close** the document, click **Yes** to save the data source, click **Yes** to save the labels, and then **Exit** Word.

End You have completed Project 8A ——————————

Project 8B Television Hosts

In Activities 8.12 through 8.18 you will edit a document that introduces the hosts of the *Georgia Gardens* television show. You will add links to text and graphics, and you will add a SmartArt graphic. Finally, you will save the document as both a Word document and as a Web page. Your completed documents will look similar to Figure 8.24.

For Project 8B, you will need the following file:

w08B_Television_Hosts

You will save your documents as
8B_Television_Hosts_Firstname_Lastname
8B_Television_Hosts_Firstname_Lastname.mht

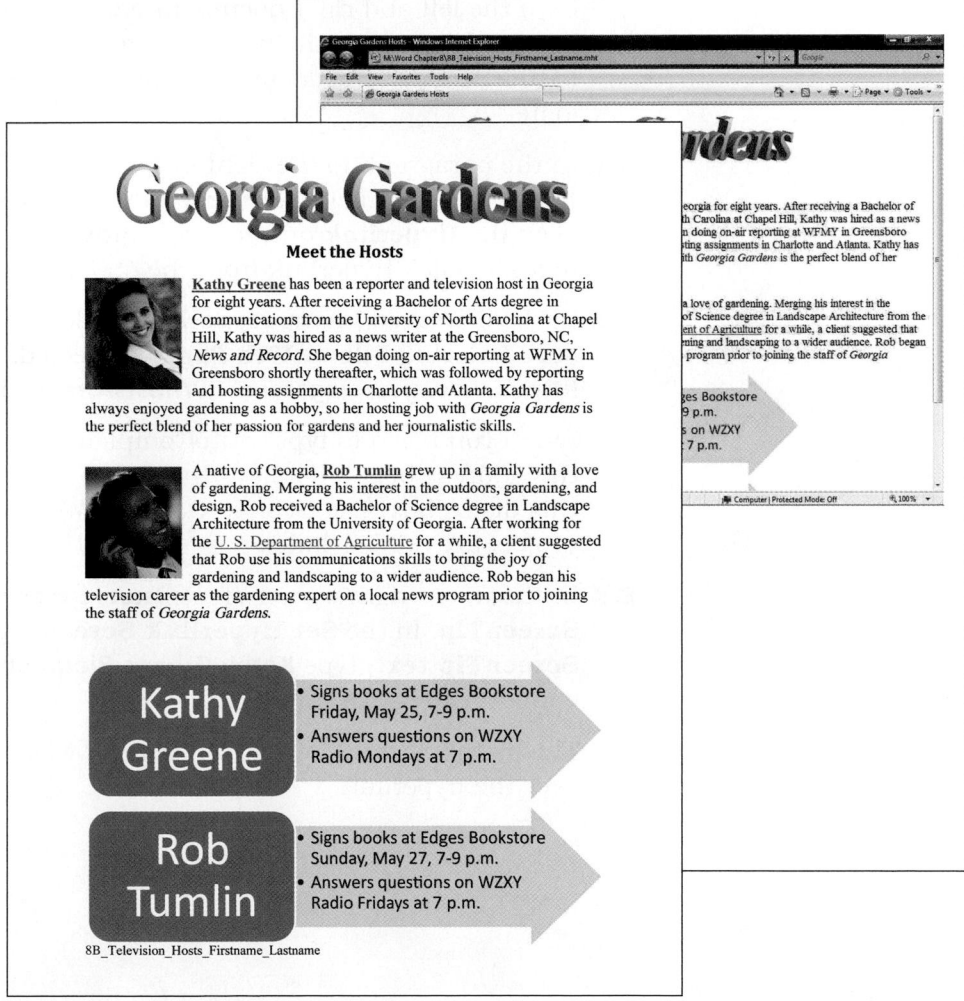

Figure 8.24
Project 8B—Television Hosts

Objective 5
Insert Hyperlinks

Organizations publish information about themselves on the Web. Microsoft Word has tools that enable the creation of Web pages directly from word processing documents. Hyperlinks can be added to move to related sites quickly. *Hyperlinks* are text or graphics that you click to move to a file, another page in a Web site, or a page in a different Web site.

Activity 8.12 Inserting Text Hyperlinks

The type of hyperlink used most frequently is one that is attached to text. Text hyperlinks usually display underlined and in blue.

1 **Start** Word. Locate and open the document **w08B_Television_ Hosts**. Display formatting marks, and be sure your screen shows both the left and right document edges. Display the **Save As** dialog box, and then save the document as **8B_Television_Hosts_Firstname_ Lastname** Open the document footer and add the file name to the footer.

2 In the paragraph to the right of the upper picture, select the text *Kathy Greene*. Click the **Insert tab**, and then in the **Links group**, click the **Hyperlink** button. Alternatively, right-click on the selected text and click Hyperlink from the shortcut menu.

3 In the displayed **Insert Hyperlink** dialog box, under **Link to**, be sure **Existing File or Web Page** is selected. In the **Address** box, type **http://www.georgiagardens.tv/hosts/greene.htm**

When you begin to type, AutoComplete may display an address in the Address box. It displays the Web address typed most recently in this dialog box. The Georgia Gardens Web addresses used in this project are not live links.

4 In the upper right corner of the **Insert Hyperlink** dialog box, click **ScreenTip**. In the **Set Hyperlink ScreenTip** dialog box, under **ScreenTip text**, type **Kathy Greene Biography** and then compare your screen with Figure 8.25.

This is the ScreenTip that will display when the pointer is moved over the hyperlink.

Figure 8.25

Web address

ScreenTip

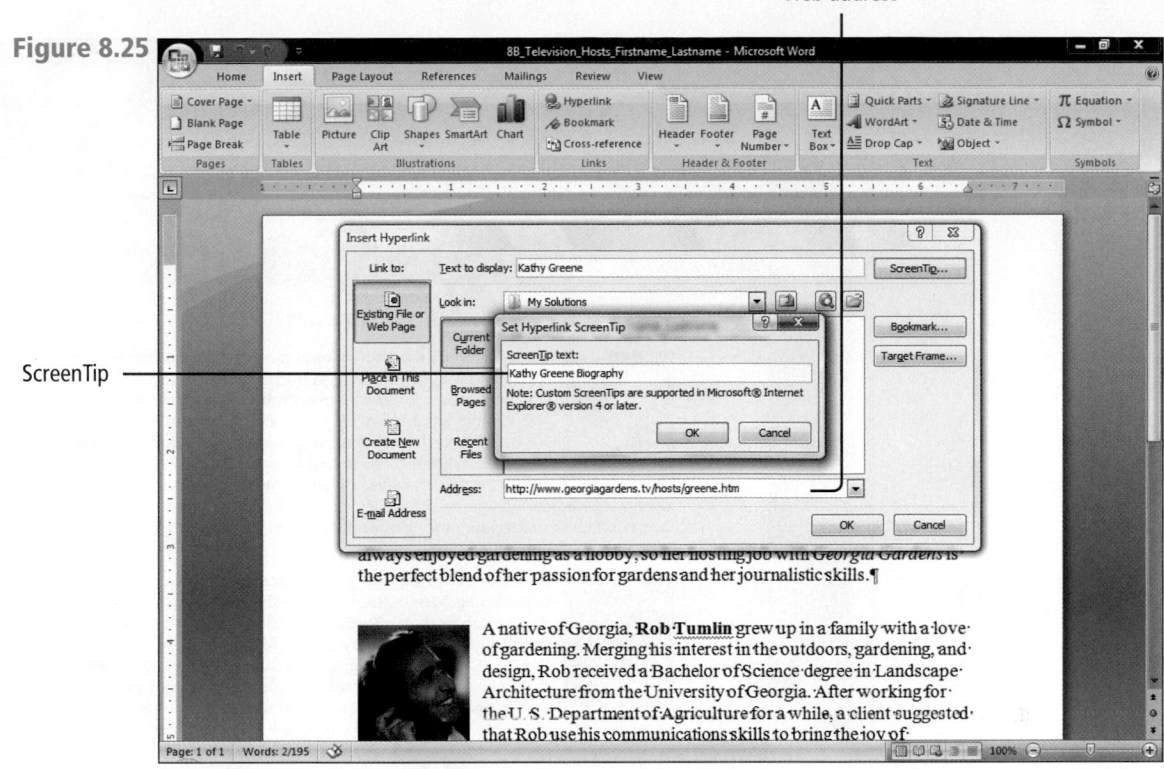

5 In the **Set Hyperlink ScreenTip** dialog box, click **OK**. At the bottom of the **Insert Hyperlink** dialog box, click **OK**.

The hyperlink is recorded, and the selected text changes to blue and is underlined.

6 In the next paragraph, in the first line, select the text *Rob Tumlin*. Using the technique you just practiced, create a hyperlink to the address **http://www.georgiagardens.tv/hosts/tumlin.htm** and then as the **ScreenTip**, type **Rob Tumlin Biography**

7 In the same paragraph, select the text *U. S. Department of Agriculture*. Using the technique you just practiced, create a hyperlink to the address **http://www.usda.gov** and then as the **ScreenTip**, type **Department of Agriculture**

8 **Save** your document, and then compare your screen with Figure 8.26.

Figure 8.26

Inserted hyperlinks

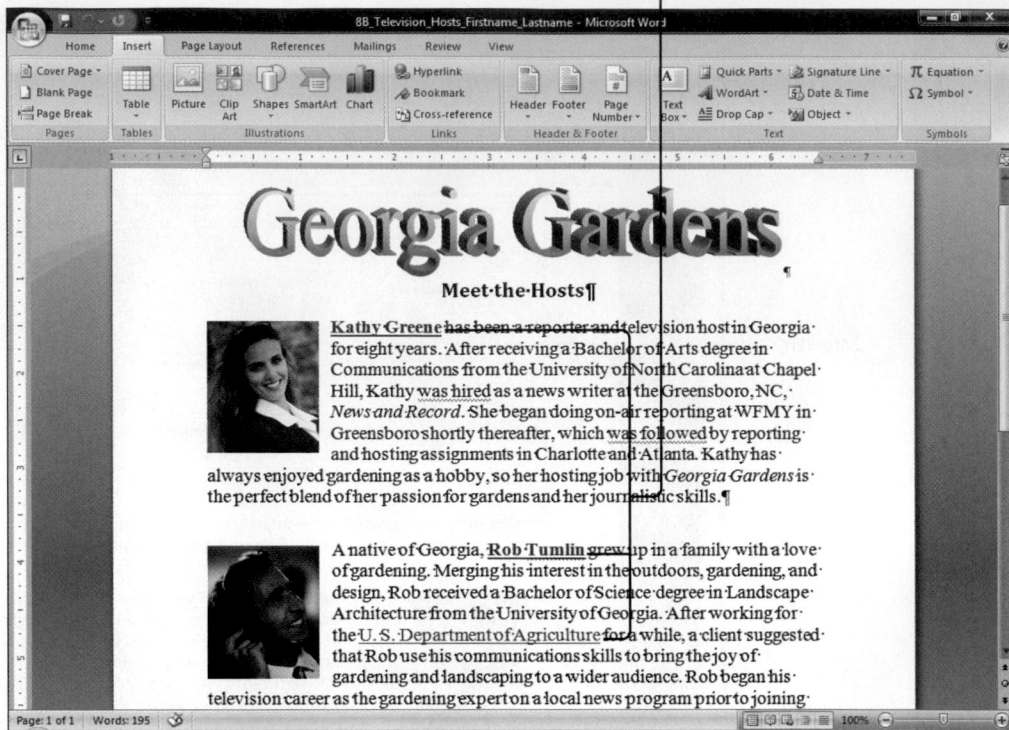

Activity 8.13 Adding a Hyperlink to a Graphic

When you point to a graphic on a Web page, if the pointer changes to the Link Select pointer ![pointer], this indicates that a hyperlink has been added to the graphic. When you point to a hyperlink in a Word document, a ScreenTip displays with instructions for accessing the link.

1 Near the top of the document, right-click the upper picture—the picture of *Kathy Greene*—and then click **Hyperlink**.

2 In the displayed **Insert Hyperlink** dialog box, under **Link to**, be sure **Existing File or Web Page** is selected. In the **Address** box, type **http://www.georgiagardens.tv/hosts/greene.htm**

This is the same address you typed for the text in the paragraph to the right of the picture. In this document, there will be two hyperlinks to the same address for each host.

3 In the upper right corner of the **Insert Hyperlink** dialog box, click **ScreenTip**. In the **Set Hyperlink ScreenTip** dialog box, under **ScreenTip text**, type **Kathy Greene Biography** and then close both dialog boxes.

4 Click to deselect the picture. Point to the *Kathy Greene* picture and notice the ScreenTip and the Web address in the status bar, as shown in Figure 8.27. Use the same procedure to check the *Kathy Greene* text hyperlink.

Hyperlink ScreenTip

Figure 8.27

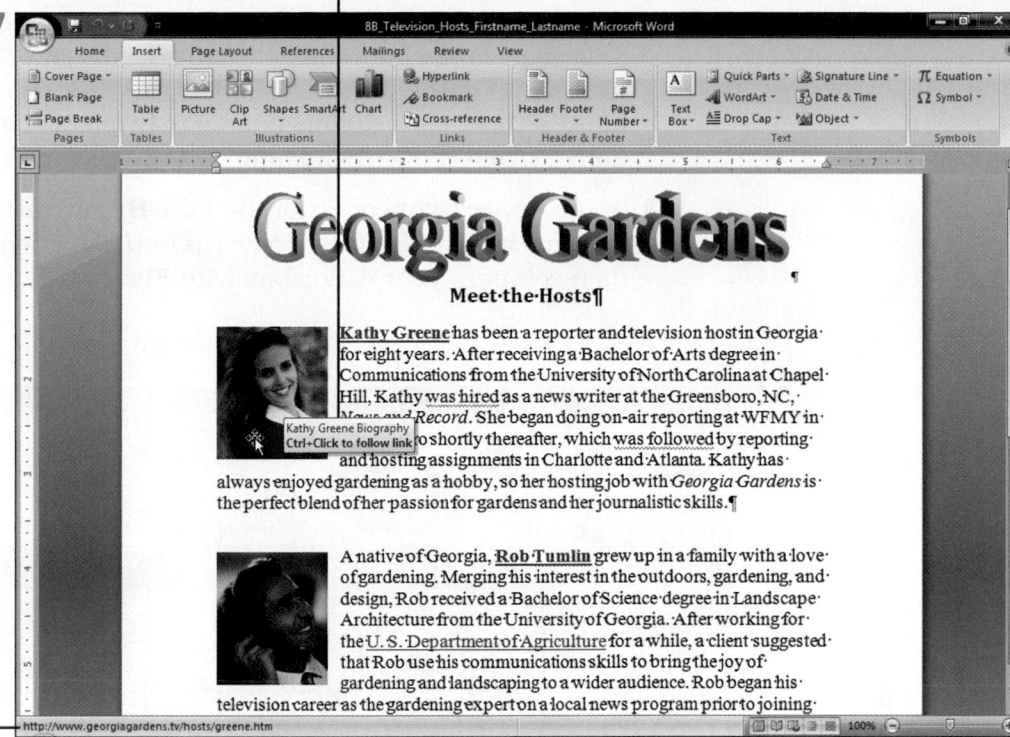

Web address in status bar ——— http://www.georgiagardens.tv/hosts/greene.htm

5 Right-click the lower picture—the picture of *Rob Tumlin*—and click **Hyperlink**. Using the technique you just practiced, create a hyperlink to the address **http://www.georgiagardens.tv/hosts/tumlin.htm** and then type **Rob Tumlin Biography** as the ScreenTip.

6 **Save** 💾 the document.

More Knowledge

Adding an E-Mail Hyperlink

You can also add a hyperlink to an e-mail address in a document. Select the text that you want to link to, and then display the Insert Hyperlink dialog box. Under Link to, click E-mail Address. Type the e-mail address, or select it from the Recently used e-mail addresses list. If desired, type a Subject line. You can also click the ScreenTip button to add a ScreenTip to the hyperlink.

Activity 8.14 Testing and Modifying Hyperlinks

Make changes to hyperlinks in the Edit Hyperlink dialog box, which is similar to the Insert Hyperlink dialog box.

1 Be sure you have an Internet connection. Point to the **U. S. Department of Agriculture** hyperlink and read the ScreenTip. Follow the ScreenTip directions to test the hyperlink.

Your computer may be configured to click to activate a hyperlink, or you may be required to hold down Ctrl, and then click the hyperlink.

2 Close ![X] your browser window and return to your Word document. Point to the **U. S. Department of Agriculture** hyperlink, and then right-click. From the shortcut menu, click **Edit Hyperlink**. At the bottom of the displayed **Edit Hyperlink** dialog box, in the **Address** box, change the address to **http://www.usna.usda.gov/ Gardens/collections/friend.html** Be sure to capitalize *Gardens*.

3 In the upper right corner of the **Edit Hyperlink** dialog box, click **ScreenTip**. Change the ScreenTip to **USDA Friendship Garden** and then compare your dialog box with Figure 8.28.

ScreenTip changed

Figure 8.28

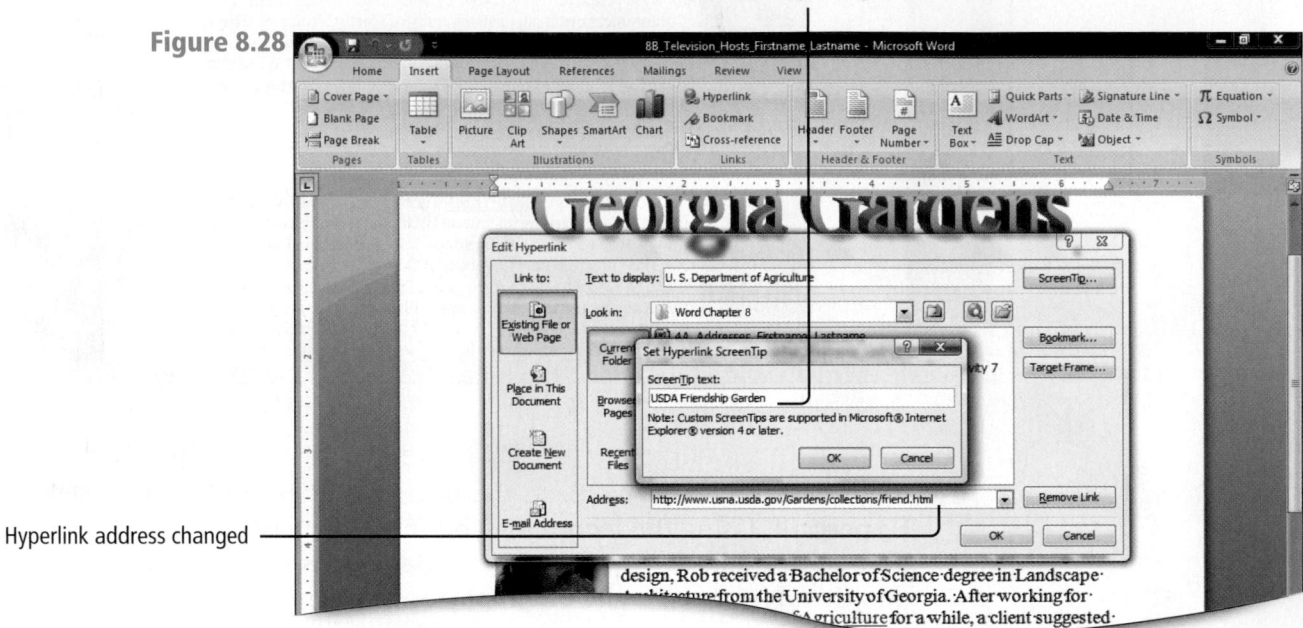

Hyperlink address changed

Note — If the Text Displays Automatically

When you begin typing the text in the text boxes of the Edit Hyperlink dialog box, the complete text may display after typing only a few letters. This indicates that another student used the computer to complete this project and that the AutoComplete feature is turned on.

4 Click **OK** to close both dialog boxes. Point to the **U. S. Department of Agriculture** hyperlink and read the new ScreenTip. Follow the ScreenTip directions to test the new hyperlink address. Close ![X] your browser window and return to your Word document.

5 **Save** ![save] the document.

Objective 6
Insert a SmartArt Graphic

SmartArt graphics are designer-quality visual representations of information that you can create by choosing from among many different layouts. Insert a SmartArt graphic to more effectively communicate your messages or ideas, and to add visual appeal to a document or a Web page.

Activity 8.15 Inserting a SmartArt Graphic

1 Press [Ctrl] + [End] to move to the end of the document, and then press [Enter].

2 Click the **Insert tab**, and then in the **Illustrations group**, point to the **SmartArt** button to display its ScreenTip. Read the ScreenTip, and then click the button.

3 In the displayed **Choose a SmartArt Graphic** dialog box, use the scroll bar to examine the types of SmartArt graphics available to you. When you are finished, scroll to the top of the list, and then click the first style in the fifth row—**Vertical Arrow List**. At the right of the dialog box, notice the preview and description of the graphic, as shown in Figure 8.29.

Preview and description

Figure 8.29

Vertical Arrow List SmartArt graphic

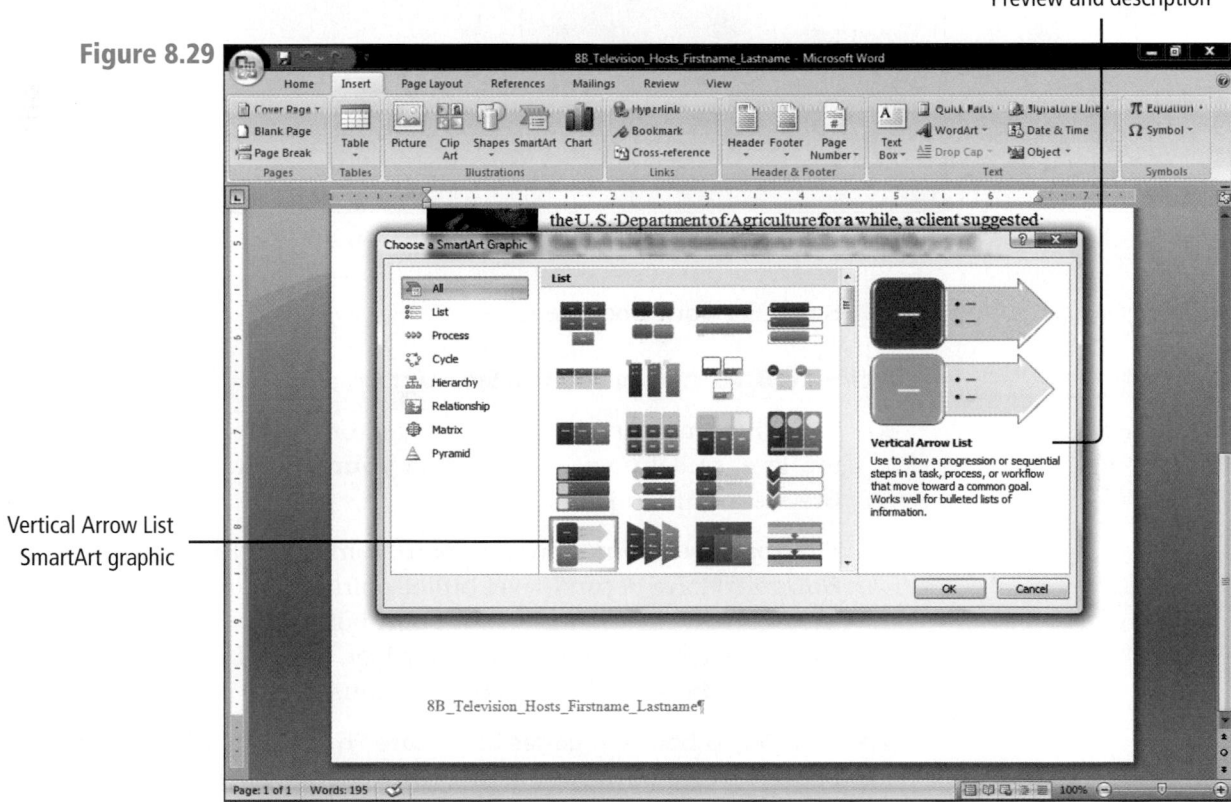

4 At the bottom of the displayed **Choose a SmartArt Graphic** dialog box, click **OK**. If the *Type your text here* box does not display, on the Design tab, in the Create Graphic group, click the Text Pane button. Compare your screen with Figure 8.30.

The SmartArt graphic is placed at the insertion point location. The graphic consists of two parts—the graphic itself, and a *Type your text here* box, into which you can type the SmartArt graphic text in outline format. On the Ribbon, two SmartArt Tools—the Design tab and the Format tab—display.

Figure 8.30

SmartArt Tools

Vertical Arrow List
SmartArt graphic

Text Pane button

Type your text here box

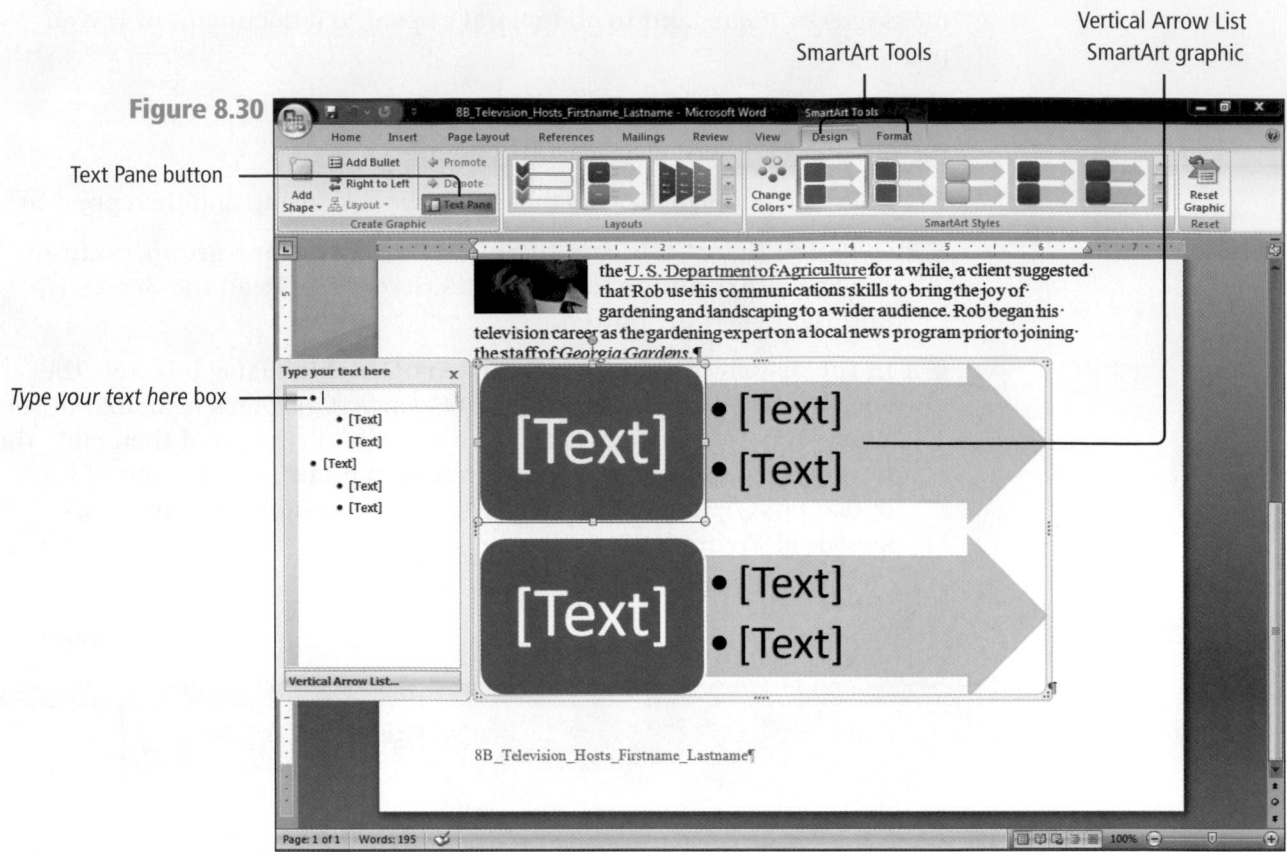

5 Save 💾 your document.

Activity 8.16 Adding Text to a SmartArt Graphic

1 With the SmartArt graphic displayed on your screen, click in the first top-level bullet point. In the **Type your text here** box, type **Kathy Greene** and then press ⬇.

The **top-level points** are the main points in a SmartArt graphic. **Subpoints** are second-level bullet points. The name displays in the left SmartArt box, and the insertion point moves to the first second-level bullet. If you press the Enter key, a new bullet point will be added at the same level as the previous bullet point.

2 Type **Signs books at Edges Bookstore Friday, May 25, 7-9 p.m.** and then press ⬇. Compare your screen with Figure 8.31.

Figure 8.31

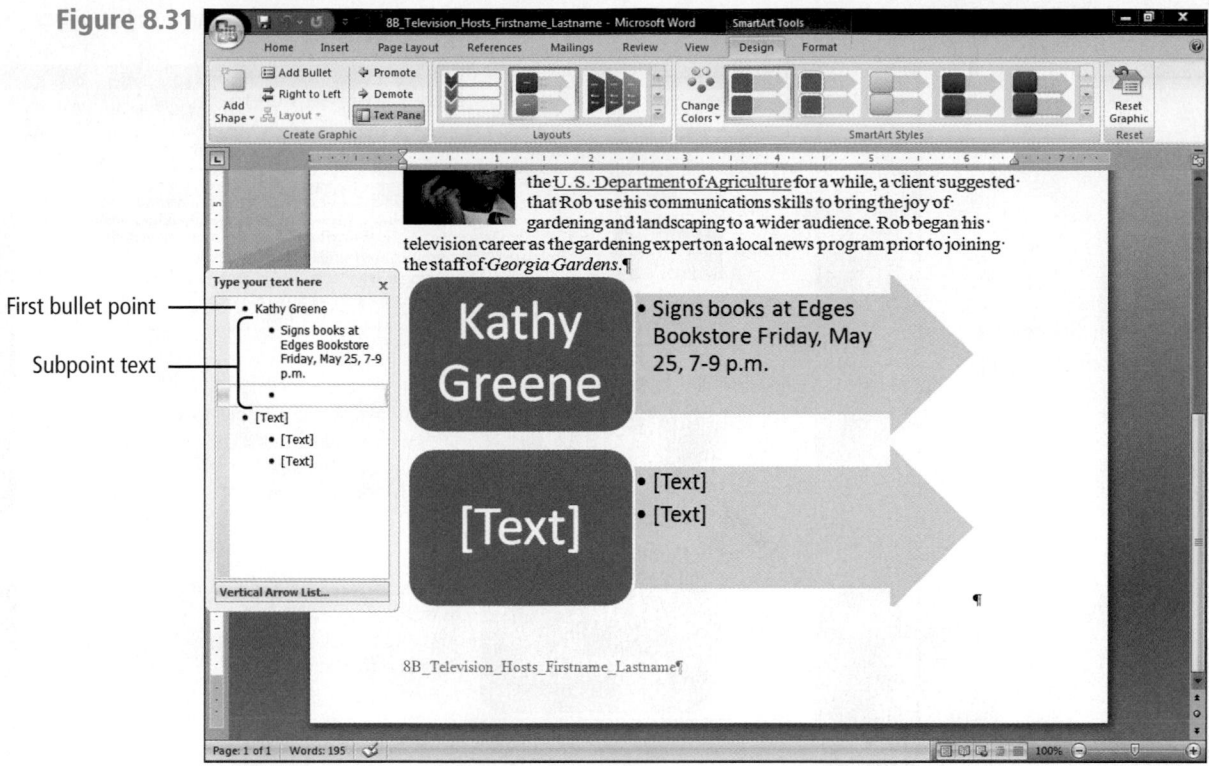

First bullet point

Subpoint text

3 Type **Answers questions on WZXY Radio Mondays at 7 p.m.** and then press ↓.

4 Type **Rob Tumlin** and then press ↓. Type **Signs books at Edges Bookstore Sunday, May 27, 7-9 p.m.** and then press ↓. Type **Answers questions on WZXY Radio Fridays at 7 p.m.** and then on the **Design tab**, in the **Create Graphic group**, click the **Text Pane** button to close the *Type your text here* box.

5 Move the pointer to the middle of the right border of the SmartArt graphic to display the ⟷ pointer, and then drag the right edge of the graphic to **6.5 inches on the horizontal ruler**. On the right side of the **Format tab**, click the **Arrange** button, click the **Position** button, and then under **With Text Wrapping**, click the **Position in Bottom Center with Square Text Wrapping** button—the middle button in the bottom row. Compare your screen with Figure 8.32.

Arrange button

Figure 8.32

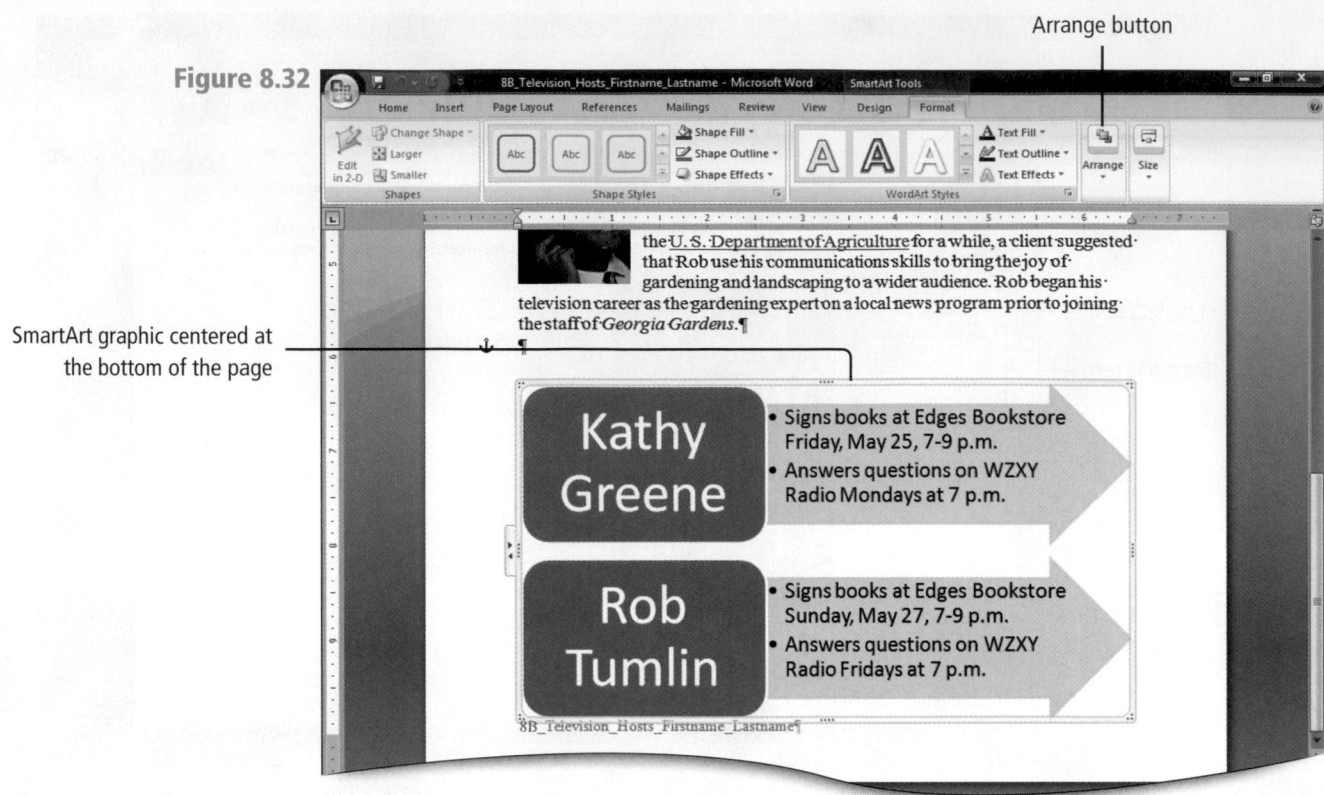

SmartArt graphic centered at the bottom of the page

6 Deselect the SmartArt graphic, and then **Save** your document.

More Knowledge

Adding More Items to a SmartArt List

After you have filled the SmartArt graphic with information, you can add new top-level points and subpoints. In the *Type your text here* box, position the insertion point where you want a new point. On the Design tab, in the Create Graphic group, click Add Bullet. To move to a first-level heading down to a subhead level, click the Demote button. To move a subpoint to a top-level heading, click the Promote button.

Objective 7
Preview and Save a Document as a Web Page

After you have created a document to be used as a Web page, you can see what the page will look like when displayed in a Web browser such as Internet Explorer. A **Web browser** is software that enables you to use the Web and navigate from page to page and site to site. You can adjust the image and preview it until you get it exactly right. After you are satisfied with the way your document looks when displayed in a Web browser, you can save the document as a Web page.

Activity 8.17 Previewing a Document as a Web Page

1 Click the **View tab**, and then in the **Document Views group**, click the **Web Layout** button. **Maximize** the screen if necessary, and then scroll to the top of the page. Compare your screen with Figure 8.33.

The document displays as a Web page, although Word does not open your Web browser. Your screen may look different from the figures shown, depending on your screen size, screen resolution, and the Web browser you use.

Document previewed as Web page—
your screen may vary

Figure 8.33

Click Web Layout button

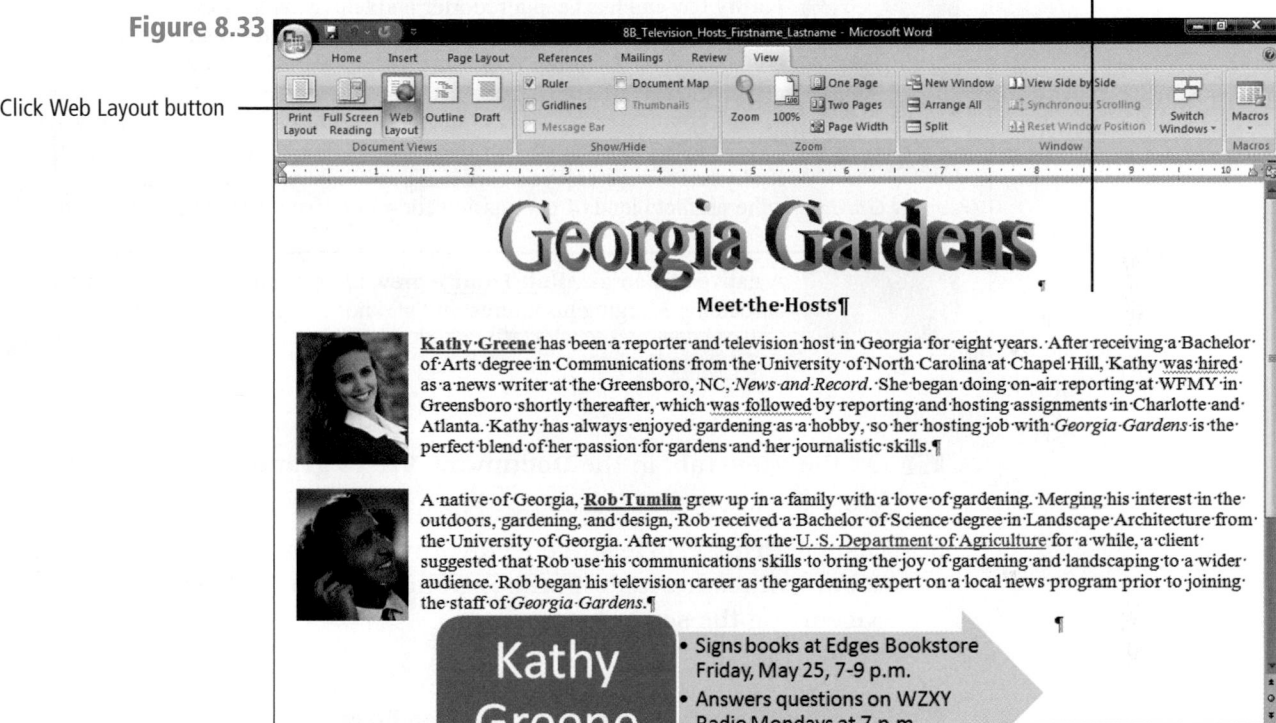

2 On the right side of the status bar, use the Zoom slider to zoom in and out to see what the Web page will look like on screens with lower or higher resolutions, or with the browser window not maximized. Notice that the font and picture sizes increase and decrease as you zoom in and out, but the word wrapping continues, and centered text remains centered. Figure 8.34 displays the look of the screen if you use a lower resolution monitor.

Figure 8.34

Zoom In button

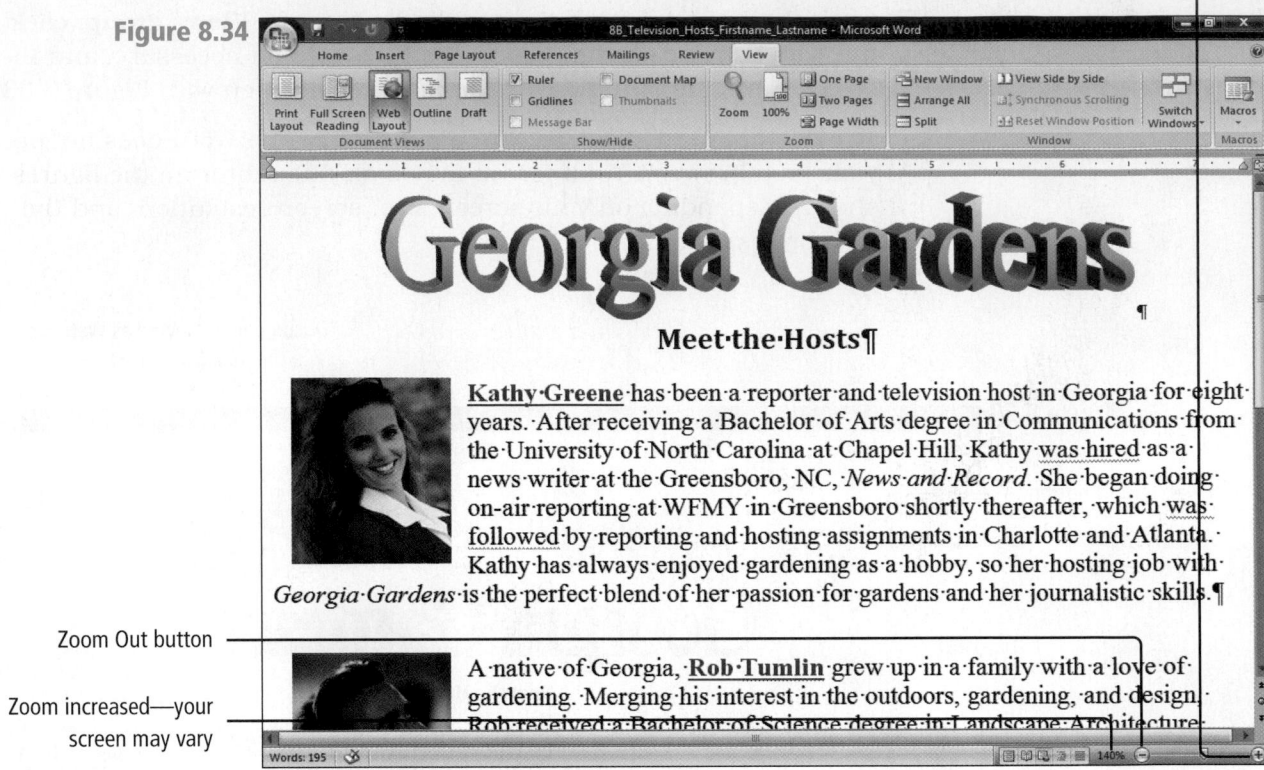

Zoom Out button

Zoom increased—your
screen may vary

3 On the **View tab**, in the **Document Views group**, click the **Print Layout** button.

4 Display **Print Preview** to check your document. Submit the Word document as directed—in the next activity, you will create a Web page using the same document.

Activity 8.18 Saving a Document as a Web Page

After you are satisfied with your document, you can save it as a Web page.

1 From the **Office** menu , click **Save As**. In the displayed **Save As** dialog box, navigate to your **Word Chapter 8** folder. Near the bottom of the **Save As** dialog box, click the **Save as type arrow**. Scroll down and click **Single File Web Page**.

The first line of the document—*Georgia Gardens*—may display as the default Page title for the Web page depending on your program settings. The default title is the first line of text in the document. If your system is set to display file extensions, *.mht* displays in place of *.docx*.

2 Near the bottom of the **Save As** dialog box, click **Change Title**. In the displayed **Set Page Title** dialog box, type **Georgia Gardens Hosts** and then click **OK**. Compare your screen with Figure 8.35.

The text that you type in the Set Page Title dialog box will become the Web page title; that is, the title that displays in the browser title bar and displays in the Web browser's history list.

Change Title button

Figure 8.35

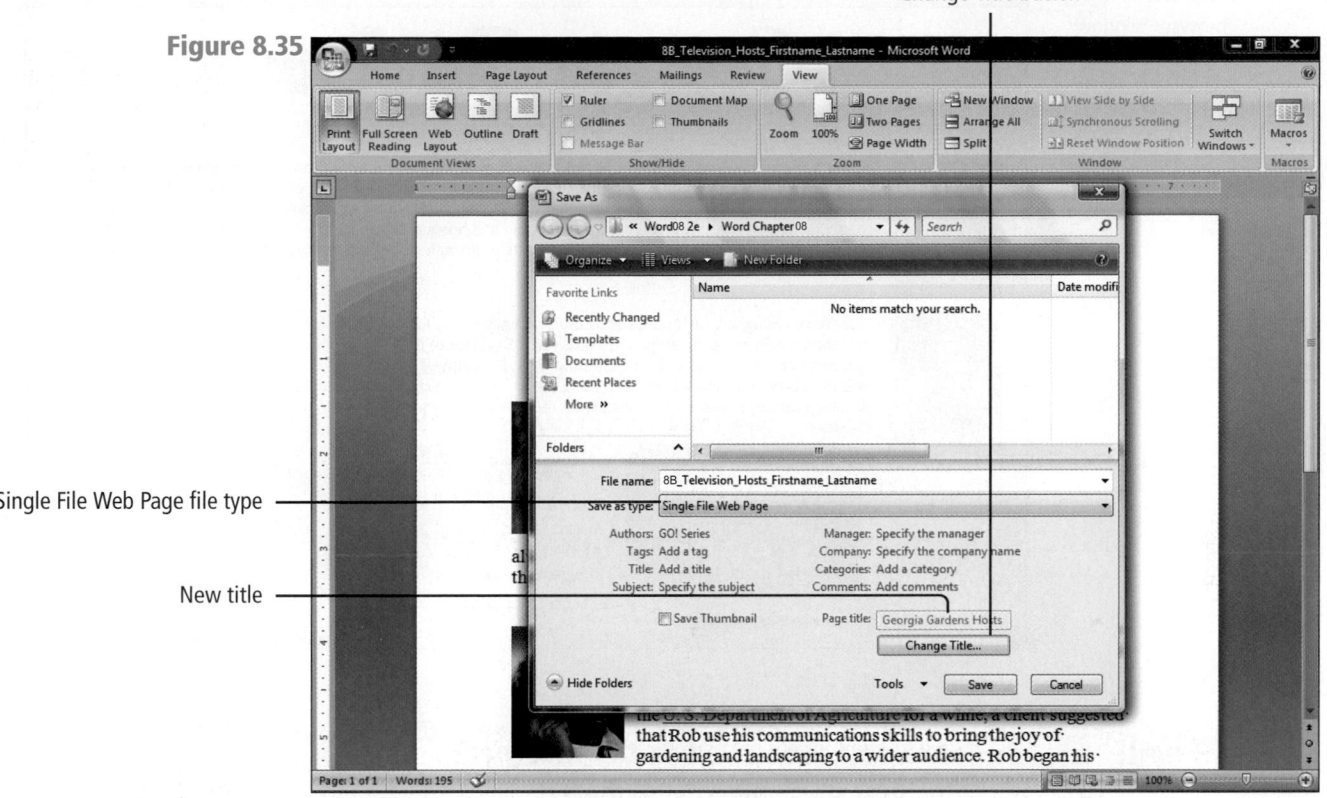

Single File Web Page file type

New title

3 At the bottom of the **Save As** dialog box, click **Save** to save the document as a Web page.

4 **Close** the document, and then **Exit** Word. Navigate to your **Word Chapter 8** folder. Locate and double-click the **8B_Television_Hosts_Firstname_Lastname.mht** file. If necessary, maximize the browser screen. Notice that the title you changed displays in the browser title bar, as shown in Figure 8.36.

The Web page you created will have a different file extension and file type icon to distinguish it from the Word document by the same name.

Word | chapter 8

Figure 8.36

Document open in
browser window

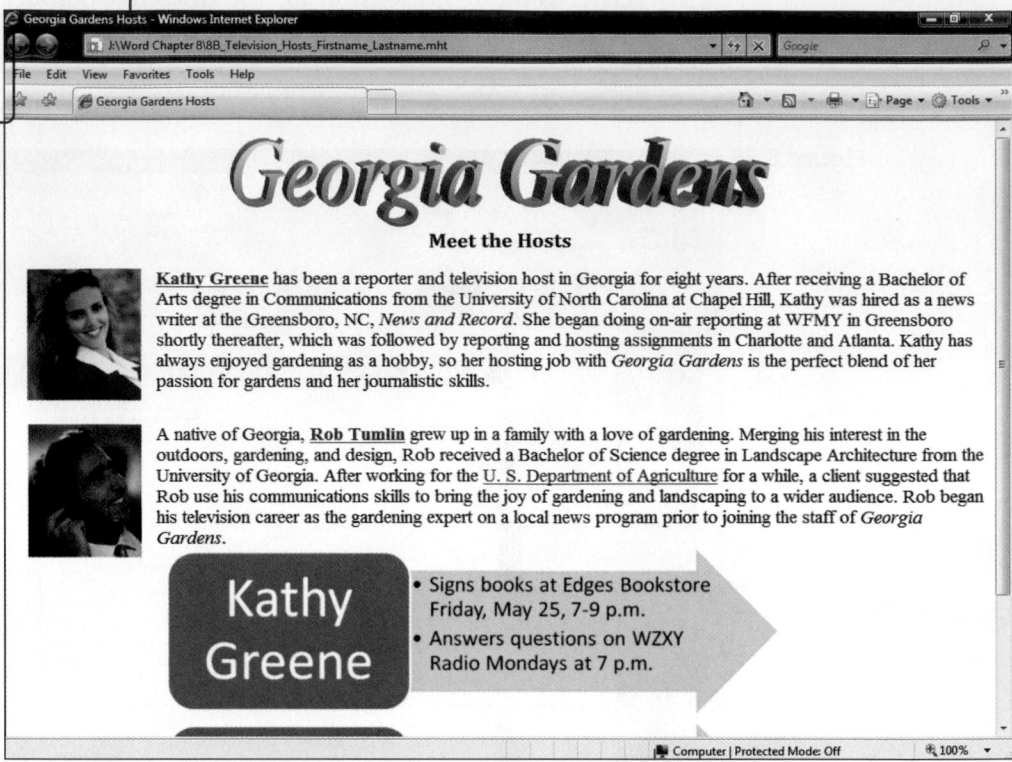

 Submit your Web page as directed, and then **Close** ▣ the Web browser.

End **You have completed Project 8B** ——————————

There's More You Can Do!

Close Word and any other open windows. Display the Start menu, click Computer, and then navigate to the student files that accompany this textbook. In the folder **02_theres_more_you_can_do**, locate and open the folder for this chapter. Open and print the instructions for this project, which are provided to you in Adobe PDF format.

Try IT! 1—Adding Comments and Tracking Changes

In this Try It! exercise, you will use Word's reviewing features to track changes made to the document and to add nonprinting comments.

Content-Based Assessments

Summary

Microsoft Word includes features you can use to create newsletters and Web pages, similar to those created by desktop publishing or Web design programs. For example, you can add borders and shading to paragraphs, and use special character formats to create distinctive headings. You can format text into multiple-column documents and add hyperlinks to a Word document and save it as a Web page. Word also assists you in creating mailing labels using the Mail Merge Wizard. Word enables you to use the collect-and-paste process to gather information from various sources and store them in the Office Clipboard. You can also create professional-looking graphics using SmartArt.

Key Terms

The ⬤ symbol represents Key Terms found on the Student CD in the 02_theres_more_you_can_do folder for this chapter.

300 **Word** | Chapter 8: Special Document Formats, Columns, and Mail Merge

Content-Based Assessments

Matching

Match each term in the second column with its correct definition in the first column. Write the letter of the term on the blank line in front of the correct definition.

_____ **1.** Laws that protect the rights of authors of original works, including text, art, photographs, and music.

_____ **2.** The Microsoft Office feature that enables you to place up to 24 objects on the Office Clipboard, and then paste them as needed, and in any order.

_____ **3.** A Microsoft Office feature with which you can turn text into decorative graphics.

_____ **4.** An artificial end to a column to balance columns or to provide space for the insertion of other objects.

_____ **5.** A font effect, usually used in titles, that changes lowercase text into capital (uppercase) letters using a reduced font size.

_____ **6.** A category of information stored in columns in a data table.

_____ **7.** All of the fields containing information about one topic (a person or organization) and stored in a row in a data table.

_____ **8.** A Word feature that joins a main document and a data source to create customized letters or labels.

_____ **9.** The document that contains the text or formatting that remains constant in a mail merge.

_____ **10.** A list of variable information, such as names and addresses, that is merged with a main document to create customized form letters or labels.

_____ **11.** Text that you click to go to another location in a document, another document, or a Web site; the text is a different color (usually blue) than the surrounding text, and is commonly underlined.

_____ **12.** A designer-quality graphic used to create visual representations of information.

_____ **13.** The main points in a SmartArt graphic.

_____ **14.** Software that enables you to use the Web and navigate from page to page and site to site.

_____ **15.** A document that has been saved with an *.mht* extension so it can be viewed with a Web browser.

A Collect and paste

B Copyright

C Data source

D Field

E Hyperlink

F Mail merge

G Main document

H Manual column break

I Record

J Small caps

K SmartArt

L Top-level point

M Web browser

N Web page

O WordArt

Content-Based Assessments

Fill in the Blank

Write the correct word in the space provided.

1. You can store up to _____ items in the Office Clipboard.

2. To remove the items in the Clipboard task pane, click the _____ _____ button.

3. WordArt changes text into a decorative _____.

4. Microsoft Publisher is a(n) _____ _____ program.

5. Use a(n) _____ _____ to change uneven columns into more equal lengths.

6. To change one column of text into two columns, use the _____ button on the Page Layout tab.

7. When you change from a one-column format to a two-column format, Word inserts a(n) _____ _____.

8. Magazines and newspapers use narrower columns of text because they are easier to _____ than text that stretches across a page.

9. All of the information about a single person or business in a mail merge address file is known as a(n) _____.

10. The column headings in a mail merge data source are known as _____.

11. In a SmartArt graphic, the main text points are the _____ points.

12. In a SmartArt graphic, the secondary points are the _____.

13. Internet Explorer is an example of _____ software.

14. To enable a user to click on text or a graphic to move to another file or a Web site, add a(n) _____ to the text or graphic.

15. When you save a Word document as a Web page, the text that you type in the Set Page Title dialog box displays in the browser _____ bar.

Content-Based Assessments

Project 8C — Trellis

In this project, you will apply the skills you practiced from the Objectives in Project 8A.

Objectives: 1. *Collect and Paste Text and Graphics;* **2.** *Create and Format Columns;* **3.** *Use Special Character and Paragraph Formatting;* **4.** *Create Mailing Labels Using Mail Merge.*

In the following Skills Review, you will use collect and paste to create a newsletter about building a trellis. You will also create mailing labels for the newsletter. Your completed documents will look similar to the ones shown in Figure 8.37.

For Project 8C, you will need the following files:

New blank Word document
w08C_Trellis_Graphics
w08C_Basic_Trellis
w08C_Rough_Trellis
w08C_Addresses

You will save your documents as
8C_Trellis_Firstname_Lastname
8C_Labels_Firstname_Lastname
8C_Addresses_Firstname_Lastname

Figure 8.37

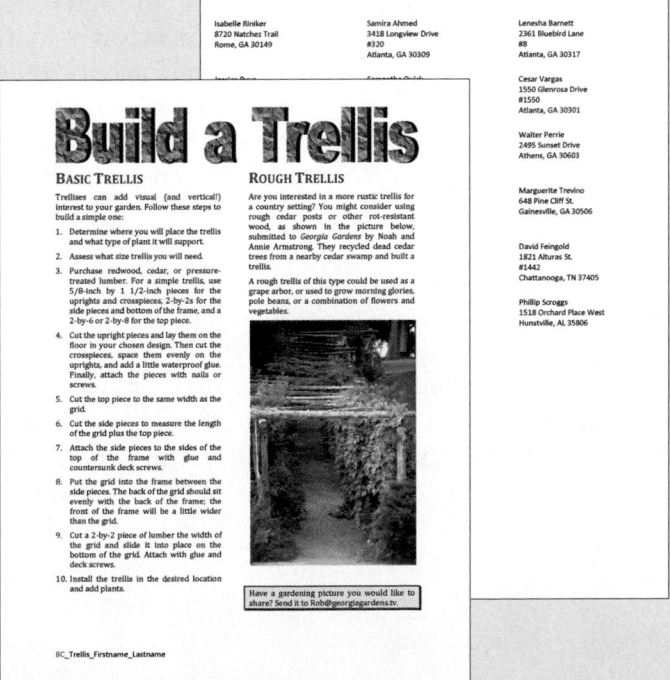

(Project 8C–Trellis continues on the next page)

Content-Based Assessments

(Project 8C–Trellis continued)

1. **Start** Word and display a new blank document. Display formatting marks and rulers. Set the left and right margins to **1**", and the top and bottom margins to **0.5**". Display the **Save As** dialog box, navigate to your **Word Chapter 8** folder, and then save the document as **8C_Trellis_Firstname_Lastname** Open the document footer and add the file name to the footer.

2. On the **Home tab**, in the **Clipboard group**, click the **Dialog Box Launcher** to display the **Clipboard** task pane. If any items display in the clipboard, at the top of the task pane, click the **Clear All** button.

3. Locate, and then open the file **w08C_Basic_Trellis**. Select all of the text in the document, and then in the **Clipboard group**, click the **Copy** button. Locate, and then open the file **w08C_Rough_Trellis**. Select, and then **Copy** all of the text in the document. Locate, and then open the file **w08C_Trellis_Graphics**. **Copy** the WordArt title and the picture. Leave the **8C_Trellis** document open, but **Close** the other three files.

4. In the **Clipboard** task pane, click the **Build a Trellis** WordArt title, and then press Enter. In the **Clipboard** task pane, click the text entry beginning *Basic Trellis* to paste the entire block of text at the insertion point. In the **Clipboard** task pane, click the text entry beginning *Rough Trellis* to paste the entire block of text at the insertion point. At the bottom of the text, click the **Paste Options** button, and then click **Paste List Without Merging**— this removes the numbered list from the last three paragraphs. Press ←Bksp to

remove the blank line at the bottom of the inserted text.

5. Select all of the text in the document except the WordArt title. Be sure to include the paragraph mark at the end of the document. Right-click the selected text, and then click **Paragraph**. In the displayed **Paragraph** dialog box, under **Spacing**, in the **After** box, click the **up spin arrow** to change the spacing to **6 pt**. Under **Spacing**, click the **Line spacing arrow**, and then click **Single**. Under **Spacing**, be sure the *Don't add space between paragraph of the same style* check box is cleared—you may have to click it two times to clear the check mark. Click **OK**, and then **Save** the document.

6. With the text still selected, click the **Page Layout tab**, and then in the **Page Setup group**, click the **Columns** button. From the displayed **Columns gallery**, click **Two**.

7. With the text still selected, click the **Home tab**. In the **Font group**, click the **Font button arrow**, and then click **Cambria**. In the **Font group**, click the **Font Size button arrow**, and then click **11**. In the **Paragraph group**, click the **Justify** button. Click anywhere in the document to deselect the text.

8. Click to the left of the *Rough Trellis* title, and then click the **Page Layout tab**. In the **Page Setup group**, click the **Breaks** button, and then under **Page Breaks**, click **Column**.

9. Press Ctrl + End to move to the end of the second column, and then press Enter. In the **Clipboard** task pane, click the **Trellis** picture. Right-click the picture, and then click **Size**. In the displayed **Size**

(Project 8C–Trellis continues on the next page)

Content-Based Assessments

(Project 8C–Trellis continued)

dialog box under **Scale**, click the **Lock aspect ratio** check box. Under **Size and rotate**, click the **Shape Width up spin arrow**, as necessary to set the picture width to **3"**. Be sure the picture sizes proportionally, and then **Close** the **Size** dialog box.

10. Near the top of the **Clipboard** task pane, click the **Clear All** button to remove all items from the Office Clipboard. **Close** the Clipboard task pane, and then **Save** the document.

11. At the top of the first column, select the text **Basic Trellis**. Be sure to include the paragraph mark. Right-click the selected text, and then click **Font**. In the displayed **Font** dialog box, click the **Font color arrow**, and then under **Theme Colors**, click **Orange, Accent 6, Darker 50%**—the bottom color in the tenth column. Under **Font style**, click **Bold**. Under **Size**, click **20**. Under **Effects**, select the **Small caps** check box, and then click **OK**. At the top of the second column, select **Rough Trellis**. Apply the same formatting you added to the title of the first column.

12. Press Ctrl + End to move to the end of the second column, and then press Enter two times. Type **Have a gardening picture you would like to share? Send it to Rob@ georgiagardens.tv.** and then select the new paragraph. On the **Home tab**, in the **Paragraph group**, click the **Border button arrow**, and then click **Borders and Shading**. In the displayed **Borders and Shading** dialog box, be sure the **Borders tab** is selected. Under **Setting**, click **Shadow**. Click the **Width arrow** and then click **1 1/2 pt**. Click the **Color arrow**, and then click **Orange, Accent 6, Darker 50%**—the bottom color in the tenth column.

13. At the top of the **Borders and Shading** dialog box, click the **Shading tab**. Click the **Fill arrow**, and then click **Orange, Accent 6, Lighter 80%**—the second color in the tenth column. At the bottom of the **Borders and Shading** dialog box, click **OK**. **Save**, and then **Close** the document.

14. Submit your file as directed. Next, you will create mailing labels for a small group of subscribers.

15. Display a new blank document. Display the **Save As** dialog box and, in your **Word Chapter 8** folder, save the document as **8C_Labels_Firstname_Lastname** Be sure all margins are set to **1"**. Locate and **Open** the file **w08C_Addresses**. Display the **Save As** dialog box, navigate to the **Word Chapter 8** folder, and then save the file as **8C_Addresses_Firstname_ Lastname**

16. Click to position the insertion point in the last cell in the table, and then press Tab to create a new row. Enter the following information:

First Name	Robert
Last Name	Hasty
Address 1	1884 Alcona Rd.
Address 2	
City	Columbus
State	GA
ZIP Code	31993

17. **Save**, and then **Close** the table of addresses; be sure your **8C_Labels** document displays. Click the **Mailings tab**. In the **Start Mail Merge group**, click the **Start Mail Merge** button, and then click **Step by Step Mail Merge Wizard** to display the **Mail Merge** task pane. Under

(Project 8C–Trellis continues on the next page)

(Project 8C–Trellis continued)

Select document type, click the **Labels** option button.

18. At the bottom of the task pane, click **Next: Starting document**. Under **Select starting document**, be sure **Change document layout** is selected, and then under **Change document layout**, click **Label options**. In the **Label Options** dialog box, under **Printer information**, click the **Tray arrow**, and then click **Default tray (Automatically Select)**—your text may vary. Under **Label information**, click the **Label vendors arrow**, and then click **Avery US Letter**. Under **Product number**, scroll as necessary and click **5160**.

19. At the bottom of the **Label Options** dialog box, click **OK**, and then at the bottom of the task pane, click **Next: Select recipients**.

20. Under **Select recipients**, be sure the **Use an existing list** option button is selected. Under **Use an existing list**, click **Browse**. Navigate to your **Word Chapter 8** folder, select your **8C_Addresses_Firstname_Lastname** file, and then click **Open**. Click **OK**.

21. At the bottom of the **Mail Merge** task pane, click **Next: Arrange your labels**. Under **Arrange your labels**, click **Address block**. In the **Insert Address Block** dialog box, under **Insert recipient's name in**

this format, if necessary, select the Joshua Randall Jr. format. Examine the **Preview** area to see how the label will look, and then click **OK**.

22. In the upper left corner of the document, select the **<<Address Block>>** field. Be sure to include the paragraph mark. Click the **Page Layout tab**, and in the **Paragraph group**, use the **spin box arrows** to set the **Before** and **After** boxes to **0** to ensure that the four-line addresses will fit on the labels.

23. In the task pane, under **Replicate labels**, click **Update all labels**. At the bottom of the task pane, click **Next: Preview your labels**. At the bottom of the task pane, click **Next: Complete the merge**. Display the document footer, and then add the file name to the footer. **Save** your labels.

24. To submit electronically, follow your instructor's directions. Otherwise, on the **Print Preview tab**, in the **Print group**, click the **Print** button. In the **Print** dialog box, under **Page range**, click the **Current page** option button, and then click **OK**. On the **Print Preview tab**, in the **Preview group**, click the **Close Print Preview** button.

25. **Close** the document, click **Yes** to save the labels, and then **Exit** Word.

 You have completed Project 8C ———————————————

Content-Based Assessments

Project 8D—Lawn Care

In this project, you will apply the skills you practiced from the Objectives in Project 8B.

Objectives: 5. *Insert Hyperlinks;* **6.** *Insert a SmartArt Graphic;* **7.** *Preview and Save a Document as a Web Page.*

In the following Skills Review, you will add hyperlinks to text and a picture in a lawn care document created by the *Georgia Gardens* staff, and then add a SmartArt graphic. You will also save the document as a Web page, to be posted on the show's Web site. Your completed documents will look similar to Figure 8.38.

For Project 8D, you will need the following file:

w08D_Lawn_Care

You will save your documents as
8D_Lawn_Care_Firstname_Lastname
8D_Lawn_Care_Firstname_Lastname.mht

Figure 8.38

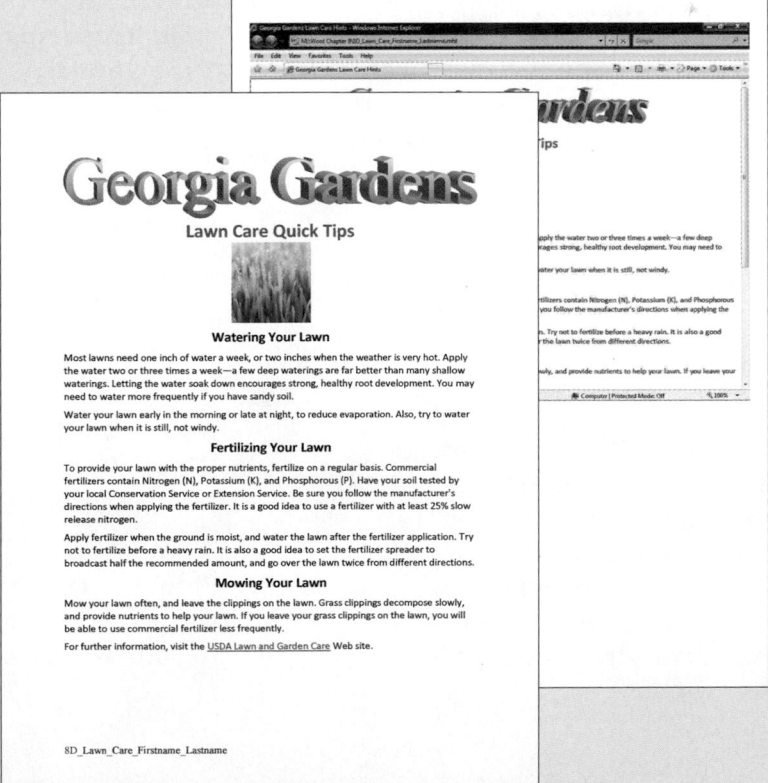

(Project 8D–Lawn Care continues on the next page)

Content-Based Assessments

(Project 8D–Lawn Care continued)

1. **Start** Word. Locate and open the document **w08D_Lawn_Care**. Display formatting marks. **Save** the document in your **Word Chapter 8** folder as **8D_Lawn_Care_ Firstname_Lastname** Open the document footer, and then add the file name to the footer.

2. In the last paragraph in the document, select the text *USDA Lawn and Garden Care*. Click the **Insert tab**, and then in the **Links group**, click the **Hyperlink** button.

3. In the displayed **Insert Hyperlink** dialog box, under **Link to**, be sure **Existing File or Web Page** is selected. In the **Address** box, type **http://www.nrcs.usda.gov/feature/ highlights/homegarden/lawn.html**

4. In the upper right corner of the **Insert Hyperlink** dialog box, click **ScreenTip**. In the **Set Hyperlink ScreenTip** dialog box, under **ScreenTip text**, type **Lawn Care Tips**

5. In the **Set Hyperlink ScreenTip** dialog box, click **OK**. At the bottom of the **Insert Hyperlink** dialog box, click **OK**. **Save** your document.

6. Near the top of the document, right-click the **grass** picture, and then click **Hyperlink**. Using the procedure you just practiced, add the same address and ScreenTip, and then return to the document.

7. Be sure you have an Internet connection. Point to the *USDA Lawn and Garden Care* text hyperlink and read the ScreenTip. Follow the directions to test the hyperlink. Close your browser window to return to your document, and then test the hyperlink associated with the picture. Close your browser window.

8. Display **Print Preview** to check your document. **Close** the **Print Preview** window.

9. Submit the Word document as directed.

10. Press Ctrl + End to move to the end of the document, and then press Enter. Click the **Insert tab**. In the **Illustrations group**, click the **SmartArt** button.

11. On the left side of the displayed **Choose a SmartArt Graphic** dialog box, click **Cycle**. In the middle of the dialog box, click the first SmartArt graphic—**Basic Cycle**. At the bottom of the displayed **Choose a SmartArt Graphic** dialog box, click **OK**, and then **Save** your document. The graphic will display on the second page of the document. If the *Type your text here* box does not display, on the Design tab, in the Create Graphic group, click the Text Pane button.

12. With the SmartArt graphic displayed on your screen, in the first bullet point in the **Type your text here** box, type **Water Regularly** and then press ↓.

13. Type **Fertilize As Needed** and then press ↓. Type **Mow Often** and then press ↓. Type **Leave Clippings** and then press ↓.

14. With the insertion point in the fifth (blank) bullet point, press ←Bksp to remove the fifth item.

15. **Close** the *Type your text here* box. Click the **View tab**, and then in the **Document Views group**, click the **Web Layout** button. **Maximize** the screen if necessary. Scroll to the view the page.

16. From the **Office** menu, click **Save As**. In the displayed **Save As** dialog box, navigate to your **Word Chapter 8** folder. Near the

(Project 8D–Lawn Care continues on the next page)

Content-Based Assessments

(Project 8D–Lawn Care continued)

bottom of the **Save As** dialog box, click the **Save as type arrow**. Scroll down, and then click **Single File Web Page**.

17. Near the bottom of the **Save As** dialog box, click **Change Title**. In the displayed **Set Page Title** dialog box, type **Georgia Gardens Lawn Care Hints** and then click **OK**. At the bottom of the **Save As** dialog box, click **Save** to save the document as a Web page.

18. **Close** the document, and then **Exit** Word. Display the **My Computer** window, and then navigate to your **Word Chapter 8** folder. Locate and double-click the **8D_Lawn_Care_Firstname_Lastname.mht** file. If necessary, maximize the browser screen. Notice that the title you changed displays in the browser title bar.

19. Submit your Web page as directed, and then **Close** the Web browser.

End **You have completed Project 8D** ——————————————————————————

Content-Based Assessments

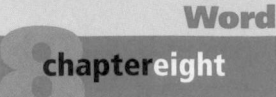
Mastering Word

Project 8E — Soil Types

In this project, you will apply the skills you practiced from the Objectives in Project 8A.

Objectives: 1. *Collect and Paste Text and Graphics;* **2.** *Create and Format Columns;* **3.** *Use Special Character and Paragraph Formatting;* **4.** *Create Mailing Labels Using Mail Merge.*

In the following Mastering Word project, you will create a newsletter for *Georgia Gardens* about dealing with different soil types. Your completed documents will look similar to Figure 8.39.

For Project 8E, you will need the following files:

New blank Word document
w08E_Soil_Types
w08E_Addresses
w08E_Soil_Graphics

**You will save your documents as
8E_Soil_Types_Firstname_Lastname
8E_Mailing_Labels_Firstname_Lastname
8E_Addresses_Firstname_Lastname**

Figure 8.39

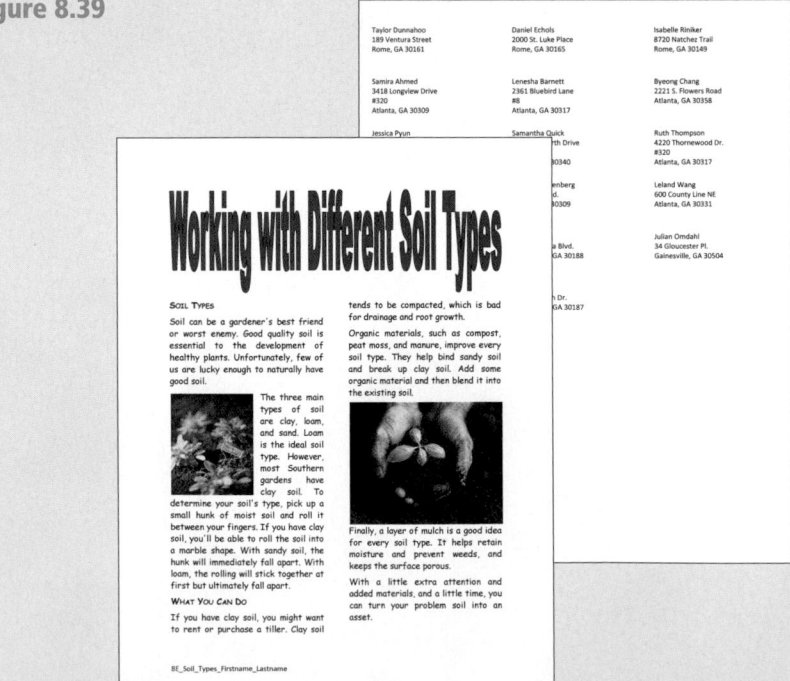

(Project 8E–Soil Types continues on the next page)

Content-Based Assessments

(Project 8E–Soil Types continued)

1. **Start** Word and be sure a new blank document is displayed. Display formatting marks, and be sure your screen displays both the left and right document edges. If necessary, set all document margins to **1**". **Save** the file as **8E_Soil_Types_Firstname_Lastname** and then add the file name to the footer.

2. Display the **Clipboard** task pane, and if necessary, **Clear All** contents. Locate and open the file **w08E_Soil_Types**. Select all of the text in the document, and then **Copy** the text to the Office Clipboard. Locate and open the file **w08E_Soil_Graphics**. Select and **Copy** the **WordArt title**, the **herb garden** picture, and the **hands** picture. Leave the **8E_Soil_Types_Firstname_Lastname** document open, but **Close** the other files.

3. In the **Clipboard** task pane, click the **WordArt title**, and then press Enter. Use the **Office Clipboard** to insert the text beginning *Soil Types*, and then remove the blank line at the bottom of the inserted text. Select all of the text except the WordArt title. On the **Page Layout tab**, change the number of **Columns** to **Two**. On the **Home tab**, change the **Font Size** to **12**, and then **Justify** the text. Single-space the text. **Save** the document.

4. Click anywhere in the first column to deselect the text. Insert the **herb garden** picture. Select the picture, display the **Format tab**, and then change the **Text Wrapping** to **Square**. Display the **Size** dialog box, and then change the **Height** to **2**", making sure that the resize is proportional. Align the top edge of the picture with the left margin of the first column and the top of the paragraph beginning *The three main types*.

5. Near the end of the document, position the insertion point at the beginning of the paragraph that begins *Finally, a layer*. Insert the **hands** picture. Display the **Format tab**, and if necessary, change the **Width** to **3**". Leave the picture as an inline object. **Clear All** the items from the Office Clipboard, and then **Close** the Clipboard task pane.

6. At the top of the first column, select the title *Soil Types*, and then display the **Font** dialog box. Add **Bold** emphasis, and then change the text to **Small Caps**. Repeat this procedure with the second title—*What You Can Do*. **Save** and **Close** the document, and then submit it as directed. Next, you will create mailing labels for a group of Georgia subscribers.

7. Display a new blank document. Display the **Save As** dialog box, and, in your **Word Chapter 8** folder, **Save** the document as **8E_Mailing_Labels_Firstname_Lastname**. Locate and **Open** the file **w08E_Addresses**. Display the **Save As** dialog box, navigate to your **Word Chapter 8** folder, and then save the file as **8E_Addresses_Firstname_Lastname**. Add the file name to the footer.

8. Add the following row to the bottom of the table:

First Name	Henry
Last Name	Clark
Address 1	61 N. Bullpen Dr.
Address 2	
City	Woodstock
State	GA
ZIP Code	30187

9. **Save** and **Close** the table of addresses. With the **8E_Mailing_Labels** document displayed, on the **Mailings tab**, start the

(Project 8E–Soil Types continues on the next page)

Content-Based Assessments

(Project 8E–Soil Types continued)

Mail Merge Wizard. Select **Labels**, click **Next**, and then click **Label options**. Select the **Default tray (Auto Select)**—your text may vary—for the printer. Select the **Avery 5160** mailing label format.

10. Select your **8E_Addresses_Firstname_ Lastname** file as the data source for the recipients. To arrange your labels, select the **Address block** option. In the upper left corner of your document, select **<<AddressBlock>>** and change the **Before**

and **After** paragraph spacing to **0**. In the Mail Merge task pane, click **Update all labels**. Preview your labels, adjust line spacing as necessary, and complete the merge. **Save** your labels.

11. To submit electronically, follow your instructor's directions. Otherwise, **Print** the first page of labels.

12. **Close** the document, click **Yes** to save the labels, and then **Exit** Word.

 End **You have completed Project 8E** ——————————————

Content-Based Assessments

Mastering Word

Project 8F—Shade Garden

In this project, you will apply the skills you practiced from the Objectives in Project 8B.

Objectives: 5. *Insert Hyperlinks;* **6.** *Insert a SmartArt Graphic;* **7.** *Preview and Save a Document as a Web Page.*

In the following Mastering Word project, you will edit a flyer about the design and use of shade gardens. Your completed documents will look similar to Figure 8.40.

For Project 8F, you will need the following file:

w08F_Shade_Garden

You will save your documents as
8F_Shade_Garden_Firstname_Lastname
8F_Shade_Garden_Firstname_Lastname.mht

Figure 8.40

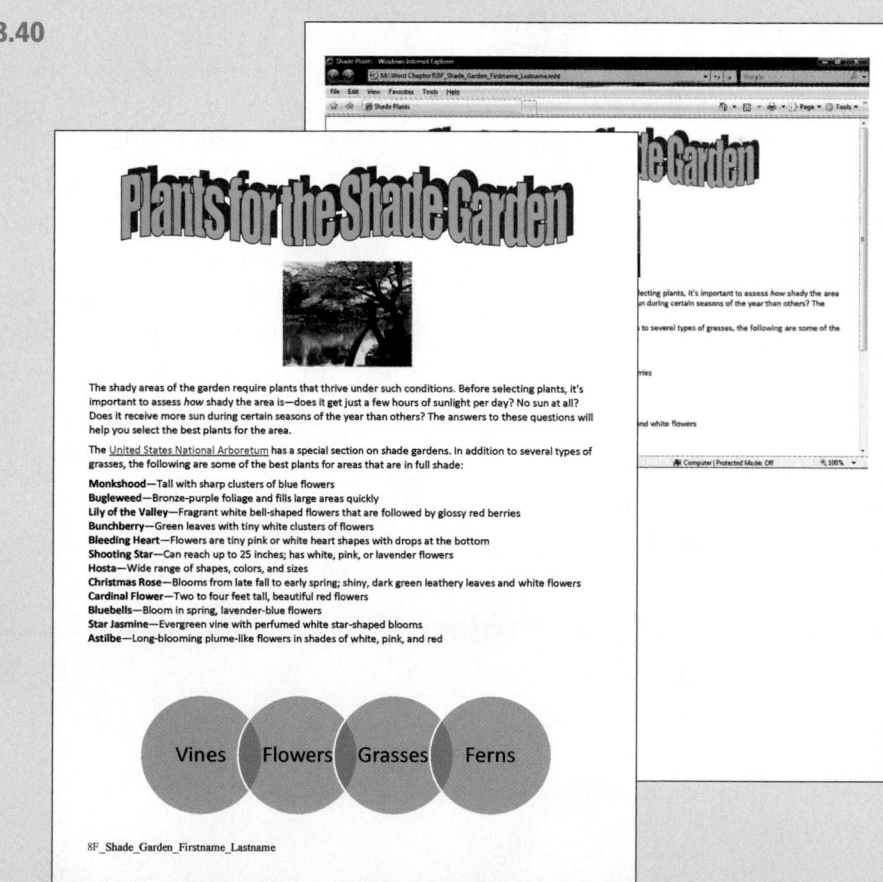

(Project 8F–Shade Garden continues on the next page)

(Project 8F–Shade Garden continued)

1. Locate and open the document **w08F_Shade_Garden**. Display formatting marks, and be sure your screen displays both the left and right document edges. **Save** the file as **8F_Shade_Garden_ Firstname_Lastname** and then add the file name to the footer. Set all document margins to **0.5**".

2. In the second paragraph in the document, select the text *United States National Arboretum*. Insert a hyperlink to the address **http://www.usna.usda.gov/ Gardens/faqs/fernsfaq2.html** Add a **Ferns in Shady Areas** ScreenTip to the hyperlink.

3. Near the top of the document, select the picture, and then insert the same hyperlink: **http://www.usna.usda.gov/ Gardens/faqs/fernsfaq2.html** Add a **Japanese Shade Garden** ScreenTip to the hyperlink. **Save** your document.

4. Be sure you have an Internet connection. Point to the *United States National Arboretum* text hyperlink and read the ScreenTip. Follow the directions to test the hyperlink. Return to your document and test the hyperlink associated with the picture.

5. Press ⌃Ctrl + End to move to the end of the document, and then press Enter. From the **Insert tab**, insert a **Linear Venn** SmartArt graphic—located near the bottom of the **Relationship** graphics.

6. If necessary, open the Text Pane. In the Text Pane, type **Vines** and then press ↓. Type **Flowers** and then press ↓. Type **Grasses** and press ↓. Type **Ferns** and then **Close** the *Type your text here box*.

7. Move the pointer to the middle of the bottom SmartArt border to display the ⬍ pointer. Drag up approximately 1 inch so that the SmartArt graphic moves to the first page of the document. On the **Format tab**, use the **Arrange** button and the **Position** options to center the SmartArt graphic at the bottom of the page, and then click anywhere in the document to deselect it. **Save** your document, and then submit it as directed.

8. Display the document in **Web Layout** view, and then return to **Print Layout** view. **Save** your document as a **Single File Web Page**, and then change the **Page Title** to **Shade Plants**

9. **Close** the document, and then **Exit** Word. Locate and double-click the **8F_Shade_ Garden_Firstname_Lastname.mht** file. If necessary, maximize the browser screen. Notice that the title you changed displays in the browser title bar.

10. Submit your Web page as directed, and then **Close** the Web browser.

End You have completed Project 8F

Content-Based Assessments

Word

chaptereight

Mastering Word

Project 8G — Itinerary

In this project, you will apply the skills you practiced from the Objectives in Projects 8A and 8B.

Objectives: 1. *Collect and Paste Text and Graphics;* **3.** *Use Special Character and Paragraph Formatting;* **5.** *Insert Hyperlinks;* **7.** *Preview and Save a Document as a Web Page.*

In the following Mastering Word project, you will collect information, and then create an itinerary for Rob Tumlin. You will save it as a document, and also as a Web page for the program's internal, private Web site. Your completed documents will look similar to Figure 8.41.

For Project 8G, you will need the following files:

New blank Word document
w08G_Itinerary
w08G_Itinerary_Graphics

You will save your documents as
8G_Itinerary_Firstname_Lastname
8G_Itinerary_Firstname_Lastname.mht

Figure 8.41

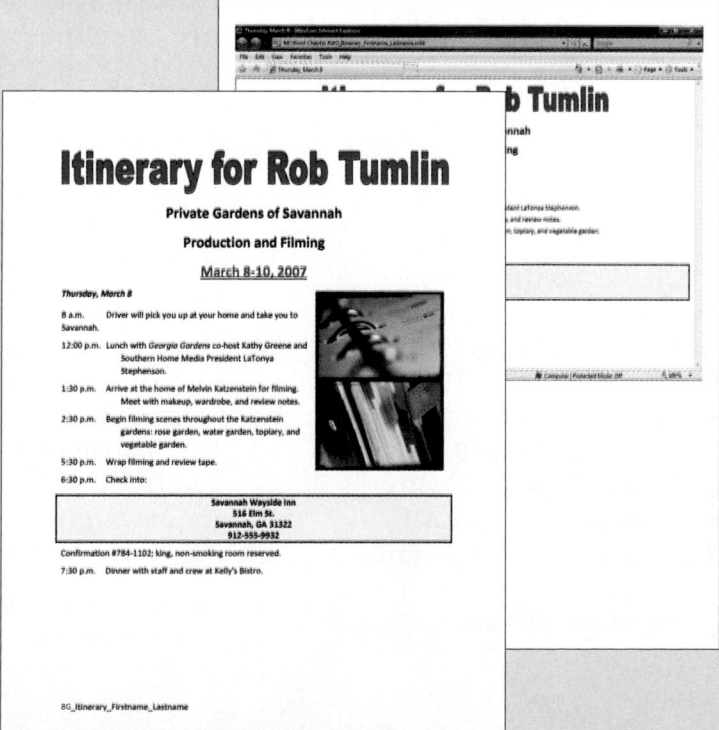

(Project 8G–Itinerary continues on the next page)

(Project 8G–Itinerary continued)

1. **Start** Word and be sure a new blank document is displayed. Display formatting marks, and be sure your screen displays both the left and right document edges and the document margins are all set to 1". **Save** the file as **8G_Itinerary_Firstname_Lastname** and then add the file name to the footer.

2. Display the **Clipboard** task pane, and if necessary, **Clear All** contents. Locate and open the file **w08G_Itinerary**. Select all of the text in the document, and then **Copy** the text to the Office Clipboard.

3. Locate, and then open the file **w08G_Itinerary_Graphics**. Select and **Copy** the **WordArt title**, and then **Copy** the **appointment book** picture. Leave the **8G_Itinerary_Firstname_Lastname** document open, but **Close** the other files.

4. In the **Clipboard** task pane, click the **WordArt title**, and then press Enter. Use the **Clipboard** task pane to insert the text beginning *Private Gardens*, and then remove the blank line at the bottom of the inserted text. **Save** the document.

5. Insert the **appointment book** picture. Right-click the picture, and then display the **Size** dialog box. Select the **Lock aspect ratio** check box so that the picture is resized proportionally, and then change the **Height** to **3**". Change the **Text Wrapping** to **Square**. Align the top edge of the picture with the top edge of the paragraph *Thursday, March 8*, and align the right edge of the picture with the right document margin. **Clear All** entries in the **Clipboard** task pane, and then **Close** the task pane. Compare the size and placement of the picture with Figure 8.41.

6. Near the bottom of the document, select the Inn address, beginning with the line *Savannah Wayside Inn* and ending with the telephone number. Display the **Borders and Shading** dialog box. Be sure the **Borders tab** is selected. Add a **Box** border to the selected text, with a **Width** of **1 1/2 pt**. If necessary, change the box Color to Black. On the **Shading tab**, fill the box using **White, Background 1, Darker 5%**—the second color in the first column.

7. With the text still selected, **Center** the text and add **Bold** emphasis. Display the **Paragraph** dialog box, and then change the **Special Indentation** to **(none)**. Change the spacing **After** to **0**, and then change the **Line spacing** to **Single**.

8. Near the top of the document, select the text *March 8–10, 2007*. Insert a hyperlink to the address **http://www.georgiagardens. tv/hosts/tumlin/schedule.htm** Add a **Rob's Full Schedule** ScreenTip to the hyperlink. Move the pointer over the new hyperlink to examine the ScreenTip, but do not click the link. **Save** your document, and then submit it as directed.

9. Select, and then delete the graphic. **Save** your document as a **Single File Web Page**, and then change the page **Title** to **Thursday, March 8**

10. **Close** the document, and then **Exit** Word. Locate and double-click the **8G_Itinerary_Firstname_Lastname.mht** file. If necessary, maximize the browser screen. Notice that the shape and position of the paragraph with the box border are different—your screen may vary.

11. Submit your Web page as directed, and then **Close** the Web browser.

 You have completed Project 8G ────────────

Mastering Word

Project 8H — Episode Guide

In this project, you will apply the skills you practiced from the Objectives in Project 8B.

Objectives: 6. *Insert a SmartArt Graphic;* **7.** *Preview and Save a Document as a Web Page.*

In the following Mastering Word project, you will create a *Georgia Gardens* episode guide document that will also be used as a Web page. The focus of the document will be a SmartArt graphic. Your completed documents will look similar to Figure 8.42.

For Project 8H, you will need the following file:

New blank Word document

You will save your documents as
8H_Episode_Guide_Firstname_Lastname
8H_Episode_Guide_Firstname_Lastname.mht

Figure 8.42

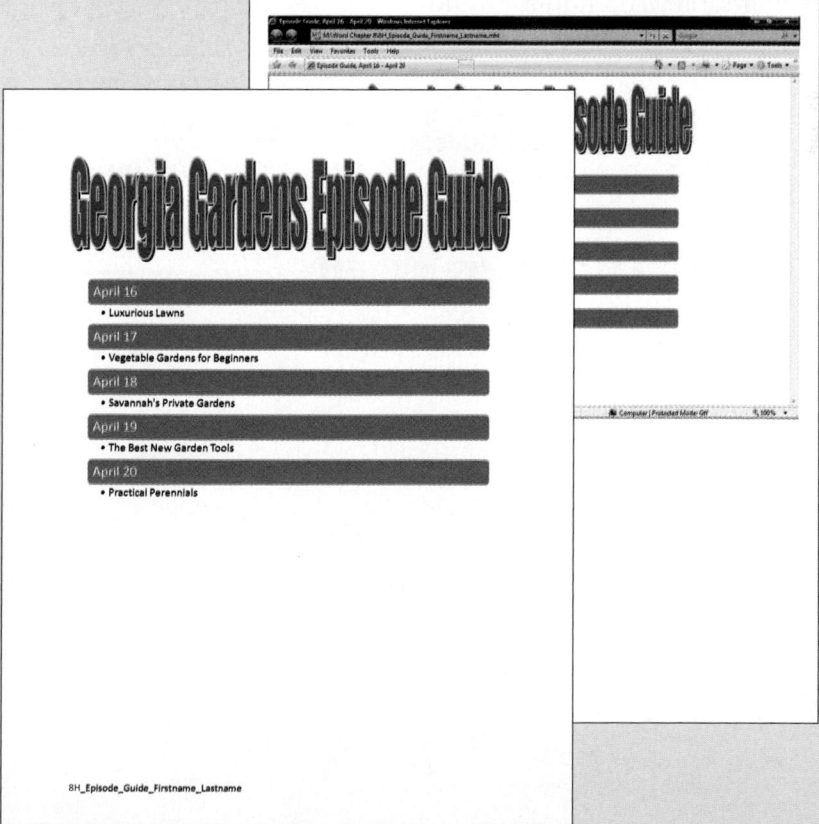

(Project 8H–Episode Guide continues on the next page)

(Project 8H–Episode Guide continued)

1. **Start** Word and be sure a new blank document is displayed. Display formatting marks, and be sure your screen displays both the left and right document edges. **Save** the document as **8H_Episode_Guide_Firstname_Lastname** Open the document footer, and then add the file name.

2. Add a **Georgia Gardens Episode Guide** WordArt title using **WordArt style 11**. Change the **Height** of the WordArt title to **1.5"** and the **Width** to **6.5"**. **Center** the WordArt title.

3. Insert a blank line below the WordArt title, and then insert a **Vertical Bullet List** SmartArt graphic—the third style in the first row of the **List** category.

4. Use the **Type your text here** box to enter the five dates and program titles shown in the following table. The dates should appear in the blue boxes, with the titles below the date in the white areas, as shown in Figure 8.42. After you have entered the first two dates and titles, on the **Design tab**, in the **Create Graphic**

group, click the **Add Bullet** button. Recall that you can change the bullet levels using the **Promote** and **Demote** buttons.

April 16	Luxurious Lawns
April 17	Vegetable Gardens for Beginners
April 18	Savannah's Private Gardens
April 19	The Best New Garden Tools
April 20	Practical Perennials

5. Close the **Type your text here** box. **Save** your document, and then submit it as directed.

6. **Save** your document as a **Single File Web Page**, and then change the **Page Title** to **Episode Guide, April 16 - April 20**

7. **Close** the document, and then **Exit** Word. Locate and double-click the **8H_Episode_Guide_Firstname_Lastname.mht** file. If necessary, maximize the browser screen.

8. Submit your Web page as directed, and then **Close** the Web browser.

End **You have completed Project 8H**

Content-Based Assessments

Mastering Word

Project 8I — Extension Service

In this project, you will apply the skills you practiced from all of the Objectives in Projects 8A and 8B.

Objectives: 1. *Collect and Paste Text and Graphics;* **2.** *Create and Format Columns;* **3.** *Use Special Character and Paragraph Formatting;* **4.** *Create Mailing Labels Using Mail Merge;* **5.** *Insert Hyperlinks;* **6.** *Insert a SmartArt Graphic;* **7.** *Preview and Save a Document as a Web Page.*

In the following Mastering Word project, you will create a newsletter and Web page about the Georgia Gardens Extension Service. You will also complete a set of name tags for people who have confirmed that they will attend an Extension Service open house. Your completed documents will look similar to Figure 8.43.

For Project 8I, you will need the following files:

New blank Word document

w08I_Extension_Service

w08I_Extension_Service_Graphics

w08I_Addresses

You will save your documents as
8I_Extension_Service_Firstname_Lastname
8I_Extension_Service_Firstname_Lastname.mht
8I_Name_Tags_Firstname_Lastname
8I_Addresses_Firstname_Lastname

Figure 8.43

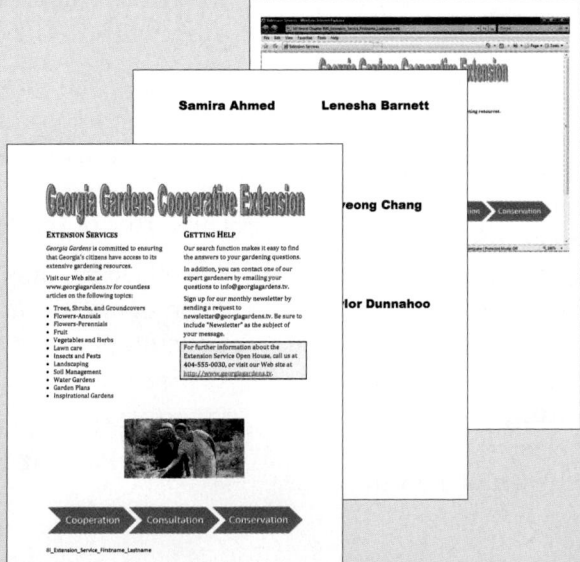

(Project 8I–Extension Service continues on the next page)

Content-Based Assessments

(Project 8I–Extension Service continued)

1. **Start** Word and be sure a new blank document is displayed. Display formatting marks, and be sure your screen displays both the left and right document edges. **Save** the file as **8I_Extension_Service_Firstname_Lastname** and then add the file name to the footer.

2. Display the **Clipboard** task pane, and if necessary, **Clear All** contents. Locate and open the file **w08I_Extension_ Service**. Select all of the text in the document, and then **Copy** the text to the Office Clipboard. Locate and open the file **w08I_Extension_Service_Graphics**. Select and **Copy** the WordArt title, and then **Copy** the **gardening** picture. Leave the **8I_Extension_Service_Firstname_Lastname** document open, but **Close** the other files.

3. In the **Clipboard** task pane, click the **WordArt title**, and then press Enter. Use the **Clipboard** task pane to insert the text beginning *Extension Services*, and then remove the blank line at the bottom of the inserted text. Select all of the text except the WordArt title. On the **Page Layout tab**, change the number of **Columns** to **Two**. Change the **Font Size** to **12**, **Center** the WordArt title, and then **Save** the document.

4. Position the insertion point to the left of *Getting Help*. On the **Page Layout tab**, insert a **Column** break. Press Ctrl + End to move to the end of the document. Press Enter, and then type **For further information about the Extension Service Open House, call us at 404-555-0030, or visit our Web site at www.georgiagardens.tv.** and then select the new paragraph. On the **Home tab**, display the **Borders and Shading** dialog box. Add a **Box** border to the selected text, with a **Width** of **1 1/2 pt**. On the **Shading tab**,

fill the box using **White, Background 1, Darker 5%**—the second color in the first column.

5. Click anywhere in the document to deselect the text. In the paragraph with the border, select the text *www.georgiagardens.tv*. Insert a hyperlink to the address http://www.georgiagardens.tv Add a **Georgia Gardens Home Page** ScreenTip to the hyperlink.

6. Click anywhere outside the bordered text, and then from the **Clipboard** task pane, insert the **gardening** picture. Display the **Format tab**, confirm that the **Width** is **3**″, and then change the **Text Wrapping** to **Square**. Align the top edge of the picture at **6 inches on the vertical ruler**, and center it horizontally on the page, as shown in Figure 8.43. **Clear All** items from the **Office Clipboard**, and then **Close** the **Clipboard** task pane. **Save** the document.

7. At the top of the first column, select the title *Extension Services*, and then display the **Font** dialog box. Change the **Font Size** to **16**, add **Bold** emphasis, and then change the text to **Small Caps**. Repeat this procedure with the second title—*Getting Help*.

8. Position the insertion point at the bottom of the first column. From the **Insert tab**, insert a **Basic Chevron Process** SmartArt graphic—located at the beginning of the third row of the **Process** graphics.

9. If necessary, display the **Text Pane**. Type **Cooperation** and then press ↓. Type **Consultation** and then press ↓. Type **Conservation**

10. With the SmartArt graphic still selected, display the **Format tab**. Change the **Position**

(Project 8I–Extension Service continues on the next page)

Content-Based Assessments

Mastering Word

(Project 8I–Extension Service continued)

to **Position in Bottom Center with Square Text Wrapping**—the middle button in the bottom row of the **Position gallery**. Close the **Text Pane**, and then change the **Width** to **6.5**″ and the **Height** to **0.7**″. **Save** your document, and submit it as directed.

11. **Save** your document as a **Single File Web Page**, and then change the **Page Title** to **Extension Services** If you see a message about Small Caps changing to All Caps, click Continue.

12. **Close** the document, and then **Exit** Word. Locate and double-click the **8I_Extension_ Service_Firstname_Lastname.mht** file. If necessary, maximize the browser screen. Notice that the graphics and columns are rearranged when displayed as a Web page.

13. **Close** the browser, and then submit the Web file as directed. Next, you will create name tags for the Extension Service open house.

14. **Start** Word and display a new blank document. Display the **Save As** dialog box, and, in your **Word Chapter 8** folder, **Save** the document as **8I_Name_Tags_ Firstname_ Lastname** Locate and **Open** the file **w08I_Addresses**. Display the **Save As** dialog box, navigate to your **Word**

Chapter **8** folder, and then save the file as **8I_Addresses_Firstname_Lastname** Add the file name to the footer.

15. **Save** and **Close** the table of addresses. With the **8I_Name_Tags** document displayed, on the **Mailings tab**, start the **Step by Step Mail Merge Wizard**. Select **Labels**, click **Next**, and then click **Label options**. Select the **Default tray (Automatically Select)**—your text may differ—for the printer. Select the **Avery 5095** name badge label format.

16. Select your **8I_Addresses_Firstname_ Lastname** file as the data source for the recipients. Select the **Address block** option. In the **Insert Address Block** dialog box, clear the **Insert postal address** check box. Then, **Update all labels**. Preview your labels, and then complete the merge. Press Ctrl + A to sclect all of the name tags. Change the **Font** to **Arial Black**, the **Font Size** to **22**, and then **Center** the names. Add the file name to the footer. **Save** your labels.

17. To submit electronically, follow your instructor's directions. Otherwise, **Print** the first page of name tags. **Close** the document, click **Yes** to save the labels, and then **Exit** Word.

End You have completed Project 8I

Content-Based Assessments

Business Running Case

Project 8J — Business Running Case

In this project, you will apply the skills you practiced in Projects 8A and 8B.

Close Word and any other open windows. Display the Start menu, click Computer, and then navigate to the student files that accompany this textbook. In the folder **03_business_running_case**, locate and open the folder for this chapter. Open and print the instructions for this project, which are provided to you in Adobe PDF format. Follow the instructions and use the skills you have gained thus far to assist Jennifer Nelson in meeting the challenges of owning and running her business.

End **You have completed Project 8J** ————————————

Content-Based Assessments

Mastering Word

Project 8K — *GO!* Fix It

In this project, you will construct a solution by applying any combination of the skills you practiced from the Objectives in Projects 8A and 8B.

For Project 8K, you will need the following files:

w08_fixit_Retail_Suppliers
w08_fixit_Addresses

You will save your documents as
8K_Retail_Suppliers_Firstname_Lastname
8K_Addresses_Firstname_Lastname
8K_Labels_Firstname_Lastname

From the student files that accompany this textbook, open the folder **05_go_fix_it**. Locate and open the files **w08_fixit_Retail_Suppliers** and **w08_fixit_Addresses**. Save the files in your chapter folder as **8K_Retail_ Suppliers_Firstname_Lastname** and **8K_Addresses_Firstname_Lastname**.

This project contains errors that you must find and correct. Read and examine the document, and then edit to correct the errors that you find. Types of errors could include:

- Spelling, grammar, punctuation, and usage errors such as text case, repeated text, subject-verb agreement, and meaning.
- Content errors such as missing or incorrect data, text, pictures, hyperlinks, or other objects.
- Font formatting and positioning errors such as font used, style, size, color, underline style, effects, font character spacing, text effects, special characters, and styles.
- Paragraph formatting and positioning errors such as indents and spacing, tabs, line and page breaks, word wrap, sentence spacing, missing text or unnecessary text or blank lines, or errors in footnotes or endnotes or references.
- Image or object formatting and positioning errors relating to color, lines, size, scale, layout, and positioning.
- Page setup errors such as margins, orientation, layout, or alignment.

To complete the project, you should:

- Make the following changes to the *Retail Suppliers* document:
  - Check spelling in the non-list portion of the document.
  - Reformat the WordArt title by using the font Times New Roman.
  - Change the SmartArt graphic to an Isosceles Triangle.
  - Activate the hyperlink.
  - For the category headings at the beginning of each list, apply the same effects to the third category heading that are applied to the first and second.

(Project 8K–*GO!* Fix It continues on the next page)

Mastering Word

(Project 8K–*GO!* Fix It continued)

- Be sure the size of all graphics is set to 35%.
- Format the layout of all the lists as two columns.
- In your 8K_Addresses file, delete any duplicate records and delete any records that are *not* in a ZIP code that begins with *30*.
- Create mailing labels as follows:
    - Open a new blank Word document and save it in your chapter folder as **8K_Labels_Firstname_Lastname**
    - Use the Mail Merge Wizard and follow the specifications and procedures described in Project 8A.
    - Use your corrected **8K_Addresses_Firstname_Lastname** file for the data source.

Save the changes you have made, add the file names to the footers, and then submit as directed.

End **You have completed Project 8K** _____

Outcomes-Based Assessments

Rubric

The following outcomes-based assessments are *open-ended assessments*. That is, there is no specific correct result; your result will depend on your approach to the information provided. Make *professional quality* your goal. Use the following scoring rubric to guide you in *how* to approach the problem and then to evaluate *how well* your approach solves the problem.

The *criteria*—Software Mastery, Content, Format and Layout, and Process—represent the knowledge and skills you have gained that you can apply to solving the problem. The *levels of performance*—Professional Quality, Approaching Professional Quality, or Needs Quality Improvements—help you and your instructor evaluate your result.

	Your completed project is of Professional Quality if you:	Your completed project is Approaching Professional Quality if you:	Your completed project Needs Quality Improvements if you:
1-Software Mastery	Choose and apply the most appropriate skills, tools, and features and identify efficient methods to solve the problem.	Choose and apply some appropriate skills, tools, and features, but not in the most efficient manner.	Choose inappropriate skills, tools, or features, or are inefficient in solving the problem.
2-Content	Construct a solution that is clear and well organized, contains content that is accurate, appropriate to the audience and purpose, and is complete. Provide a solution that contains no errors of spelling, grammar, or style.	Construct a solution in which some components are unclear, poorly organized, inconsistent, or incomplete. Misjudge the needs of the audience. Have some errors in spelling, grammar, or style, but the errors do not detract from comprehension.	Construct a solution that is unclear, incomplete, or poorly organized, containing some inaccurate or inappropriate content; and contains many errors of spelling, grammar, or style. Do not solve the problem.
3-Format and Layout	Format and arrange all elements to communicate information and ideas, clarify function, illustrate relationships, and indicate relative importance.	Apply appropriate format and layout features to some elements, but not others. Overuse features, causing minor distraction.	Apply format and layout that does not communicate information or ideas clearly. Do not use format and layout features to clarify function, illustrate relationships, or indicate relative importance. Use available features excessively, causing distraction.
4-Process	Use an organized approach that integrates planning, development, self-assessment, revision, and reflection.	Demonstrate an organized approach in some areas, but not others; or, use an insufficient process of organization throughout.	Do not use an organized approach to solve the problem.

Outcomes-Based Assessments

Problem Solving

Project 8L — Extension Classes

In this project, you will construct a solution by applying any combination of the skills you practiced from the Objectives in Projects 8A and 8B.

For Project 8L, you will need the following files:

New blank Word document
w08L_Extension_Classes

You will save your document as
8L_Extension_Classes_Firstname_Lastname

Georgia Gardens Extension Service offers classes on gardening and garden-related topics. The March and April schedule includes a wide variety of topics, ranging from *Pruning Basics* to *Attracting Butterflies to Your Garden*. All classes are single-day sessions, and are three hours long unless otherwise noted.

In this project, you will create a two-page newsletter announcing the upcoming classes and topics. Information about the classes can be found in a table in the file **w08L_Extension_Classes**. Open the Clipboard task pane and collect the information, or copy and paste the table information directly into your newsletter. Include a decorative title, information about where the classes are offered, and a link to the Georgia Gardens Extension Service Web site at **www.georgiagardens. tv/extension/classes.htm**. Locate a related picture or clip art image—a garden or a classroom—and add it to the newsletter. Put the class information in a two-column format. (Hint: For each class, you might want to have a title that includes the date and time, followed by the title of the class, and finally, the class description.) Format the class titles from the descriptions in a distinctive manner.

Add the file name to the footer. Check the newsletter for spelling and grammar errors. Save the newsletter as **8L_Extension_Classes_Firstname_ Lastname** and submit it as directed.

End **You have completed Project 8L**

Outcomes-Based Assessments

Problem Solving

Project 8M — Business Cards

In this project, you will construct a solution by applying any combination of the skills you practiced from the Objectives in Projects 8A and 8B.

For Project 8M, you will need the following files:

New blank Word document
w08M_Rob_Tumlin_Address

You will save your document as
8M_Business_Cards_Firstname_Lastname

In this project, you will create business cards for Rob Tumlin, co-host of the *Georgia Gardens* television show. Business cards are a type of label that you can create using the Mail Merge Wizard, in much the same way you created mailing labels in Project 8A. The major difference is the data source—instead of a list of different people, the data source is a Word or Access table, in this project, an Access table—that contains one name and address, repeated over and over.

Start the Step by Step Mail Merge Wizard. Using the method you practiced in Project 8A, create a set of labels that uses the default printer tray, and the 5911 Avery US Letter business card label type. As a data source, use the **w08M_Rob_Tumlin_Address** Access file. Use the Address Block format, and be sure to insert the company name. With the address block in place, press [Enter] to add a new line to the business card. In the same area where you select the Address block, select More items and add the E-mail Address field. Update all labels.

Check the business cards for spelling or grammar errors. Save the document as **8M_Business_Cards_Firstname_Lastname** and add the file name to the footer. Submit it as directed. If you are to submit a printed copy, print only records 1 through 8.

End **You have completed Project 8M**————————————

Outcomes-Based Assessments

Problem Solving

Project 8N — Gardening Web Sites

In this project, you will construct a solution by applying any combination of the skills you practiced from the Objectives in Projects 8A and 8B.

> **For Project 8N, you will need the following file:**
>
> New blank Word document

You will save your documents as
8N_Gardening_Web_Sites_Firstname_Lastname
8N_Gardening_Web_Sites_Firstname_Lastname.mht

In this project, you will create a flyer and a Web page that contains a list of gardening Web sites. To complete this project:

- Add an appropriate decorative title to the document.
- Add one or more appropriate pictures or clip art graphics.
- Include lists of gardening-related Web sites, with a link to each site, and a ScreenTip with a short description of the site.
- Include at least one SmartArt graphic. The links could all be contained in the SmartArt graphic, or the graphic could relate to a particular topic contained in one of the links.

To find the gardening sources, use a Web browser and search using terms such as *flower garden, vegetable garden, shade garden,* or some other appropriate phrase. Choose several of the sites that are of interest to you.

Save the document as **8N_Gardening_Web_Sites_Firstname_Lastname** and add the file name to the footer. Submit it as directed. Then, save the document as a Single File Web Page and test your hyperlinks. Submit the Web page as directed.

End **You have completed Project 8N** ——————

Outcomes-Based Assessments

Word

chaptereight

Problem Solving

Project 8O — Junior Master Gardeners

In this project, you will construct a solution by applying any combination of the skills you practiced from the Objectives in Projects 8A and 8B.

For Project 8O, you will need the following files:

New blank Word document
w08O_Master_Gardener

You will save your document as
8O_Junior_Master_Gardeners_Firstname_Lastname

In this project, you will write a newsletter about the Junior Master Gardeners program sponsored by *Georgia Gardens*. The newsletter should contain a short article explaining what the Master Gardener program is, and then another article describing the Junior Master Gardener program. You can find information about both programs in the file w08O_Master_Gardener.

To complete this project:

- Add an appropriate decorative title to the document.
- Add one or more appropriate pictures or clip art graphics, and wrap the column text around the graphics.
- Format the articles in two-column format.
- Keep the newsletter length to one page.
- Add and format titles for both newsletter articles.

Save the document as **8O_Junior_Master_Gardeners_Firstname_Lastname** and submit it as directed. Add the file name to the footer. Check the newsletter for spelling and grammar errors, and then submit the newsletter as directed.

 End **You have completed Project 8O** ————————————

Outcomes-Based Assessments

Word

chaptereight

Problem Solving

Project 8P — Butterflies

In this project, you will construct a solution by applying any combination of the skills you practiced from the Objectives in Projects 8A and 8B.

For Project 8P, you will need the following files:

New blank Word document
w08P_Butterfly1
w08P_Butterfly2
w08P_Butterfly3
w08P_Butterfly4
w08P_Butterflies

You will save your documents as
8P_Butterflies_Firstname_Lastname
8P_Butterflies_Firstname_Lastname.mht

Georgia Gardens provides classes on a variety of gardening topics. One of the classes describes how to attract and keep butterflies in your garden. In this project, you will create a one- or two-page newsletter about attracting butterflies that can be handed out at class or at the Georgia Gardens Open House. You can find information about butterflies in the file **w08P_Butterflies** and you can find more information on the Web.

To complete this project:

- Add an appropriate decorative title to the document.
- Format the articles in two-column format.
- Add several pictures to the document, and wrap the column text around the graphics. Four pictures are included with your student files—**w08P_Butterfly1** through **w08P_Butterfly4**.
- Divide the newsletter into at least two articles.
- Include a SmartArt graphic, which might include the major things you need to do to attract and keep butterflies in your garden.
- Add at least one Web link to an appropriate site.

Check for spelling and grammar errors. Save the document as **8P_Butterflies_Firstname_Lastname** and add the file name to the footer. Submit it as directed.

Save the document as a Web page. Test your Web link(s), and then submit the Web page as directed.

 End You have completed Project 8P ————————————

Outcomes-Based Assessments

 **Word**
chapter**eight**

 You and *GO!*

Project 8Q—You and *GO!*

In this project, you will construct a solution by applying any combination of the skills you practiced from the Objectives in Projects 8A and 8B.

Close Word and any other open windows. Display the Start menu, click Computer, and then navigate to the student files that accompany this textbook. In the folder **04_you_and_go**, locate and open the folder for this chapter. Open and print the instructions for this project, which are provided to you in Adobe PDF format. Follow the instructions to create a family newsletter and save it as a Web page.

 End **You have completed Project 8Q** —————————

GO! with Help

Project 8R — *GO!* with Help

The Word Help system is extensive and can help you as you work. In this chapter, you created a graphic using SmartArt. There are many ways you can format a SmartArt graphics to make it better fit your needs.

1 **Start** Word. At the far right end of the Ribbon, click the **Microsoft Office Word Help** button. In the **Word Help** window, click the **Search button arrow**, and then under **Content from this computer,** click **Word Help**.

2 In the **Type words to search for** box, type **SmartArt** and then press [Enter].

3 From the list of search results, click **Change the color of a shape, shape border, or entire SmartArt graphic**. Then, scroll down and read the section on how to **Change the color of an entire SmartArt graphic**.

4 In the **See Also** section at the bottom of the **Help** window, click the link that will take you to information on how to **Apply or change a Quick Style for shapes**.

5 When you are through, **Close** the Help window, and then **Exit** Word.

 End **You have completed Project 8R** —————————

Outcomes-Based Assessments

Project 8S — Group Business Running Case

In this project, you will apply the skills you practiced from the Objectives in Projects 8A and 8B.

Your instructor may assign this group case project to your class. If your instructor assigns this project, he or she will provide you with information and instructions to work as part of a group. The group will apply the skills gained thus far to help the Bell Orchid Hotel Group achieve its business goals.

 You have completed Project 8S —————————————

Excel 2007

9 chapternine

Creating a Worksheet and Charting Data

OBJECTIVES

At the end of this chapter you will be able to:

1. Create, Save, and Navigate an Excel Workbook
2. Enter and Edit Data in a Worksheet
3. Construct and Copy Formulas, Use the Sum Function, and Edit Cells
4. Format Data, Cells, and Worksheets
5. Close and Reopen a Workbook
6. Chart Data
7. Use Page Layout View, Prepare a Worksheet for Printing, and Close Excel

8. Design a Worksheet
9. Construct Formulas for Mathematical Operations
10. Format Percentages and Move Formulas
11. Create a Pie Chart and a Chart Sheet
12. Use the Excel Help System

OUTCOMES

Mastering these objectives will enable you to:

PROJECT 9A
Create a Worksheet and Chart Data

PROJECT 9B
Perform Calculations and Make Comparisons by Using a Pie Chart

Rio Rancho Auto Gallery

Rio Rancho Auto Gallery is a one-stop shop for car enthusiasts. The auto sales group sells a wide variety of manufacturer-certified pre-owned cars, cars that have passed rigorous inspection as determined by the manufacturers and that meet strict mileage and condition standards. The retail department sells automotive accessories such as custom wheels and performance parts, gadgets, gifts, books, magazines, and clothing, including branded items from major manufacturers. To complete the package, the company also offers auto financing and repairs and service.

Creating a Worksheet and Charting Data

With Microsoft Office Excel 2007, you can create and analyze data organized into columns and rows. After you have entered data in a worksheet, you can perform calculations, analyze the data to make logical decisions, and create a visual representation of the data in the form of a chart. In addition to its worksheet capability, Excel can manage your data, sort your data, and search for specific pieces of information.

In this chapter, you will create and modify Excel workbooks. You will practice the basics of worksheet design, create a footer, enter and edit data in a worksheet, and save, preview, and print your work. You will construct formulas to perform calculations, automatically complete text, use Excel's spelling tool, create a chart, and access Excel's Help feature.

Project 9A **Auto Sales**

In Project 9.01 through 9.17, you will construct an Excel worksheet for Sandy Cizek, the Auto Sales Manager for Rio Rancho Auto Gallery. The worksheet will display the first quarter sales of vehicle types for the current year, and will include a chart to visually represent the worksheet. Your completed worksheet will look similar to Figure 9.1.

For Project 9A, you will need the following file:

New Excel workbook

You will save your workbook as
9A_Auto_Sales_Firstname_Lastname

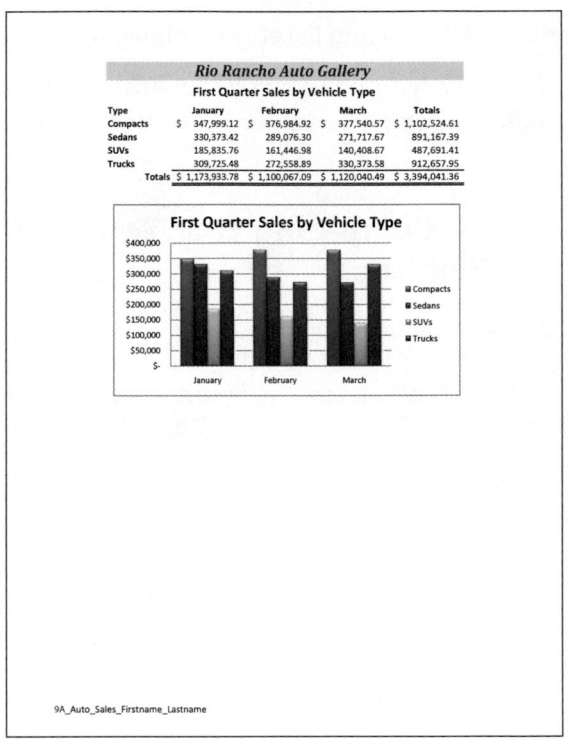

Figure 9.1
Project 9A—Auto Sales

Objective 1
Create, Save, and Navigate an Excel Workbook

When you start the Excel program, a new blank **workbook** displays. A workbook contains one or more pages called **worksheets**. A worksheet—also called a **spreadsheet**—is the primary document that you use in Excel to store and work with data.

A worksheet is formatted as a pattern of uniformly spaced horizontal and vertical lines. This grid pattern of the worksheet forms vertical columns and horizontal rows. The intersection of a column and a row forms a small rectangular box referred to as a **cell**. A worksheet is always stored in a workbook.

Activity 9.01 Starting Excel and Naming and Saving a Workbook

In this activity, you will start Excel and use the first worksheet in the workbook to prepare a report of quarterly auto sales for the current year.

Note — Comparing Your Screen With the Figures in This Textbook

Your screen will match the figures shown in this textbook if you set your screen resolution to 1024 x 768. At other resolutions, your screen will closely resemble, but not match, the figures shown. To view your screen's resolution, on the Windows desktop, right-click in a blank area, click Personalize, and then click Display Settings.

1 On the Windows taskbar, click the **Start** button ⊕, determine where the Excel program is located, point to **Microsoft Office Excel 2007**, and then click to open the program. Take a moment to compare your screen with Figure 9.2 and study the parts of the Microsoft Excel window described in the table in Figure 9.3.

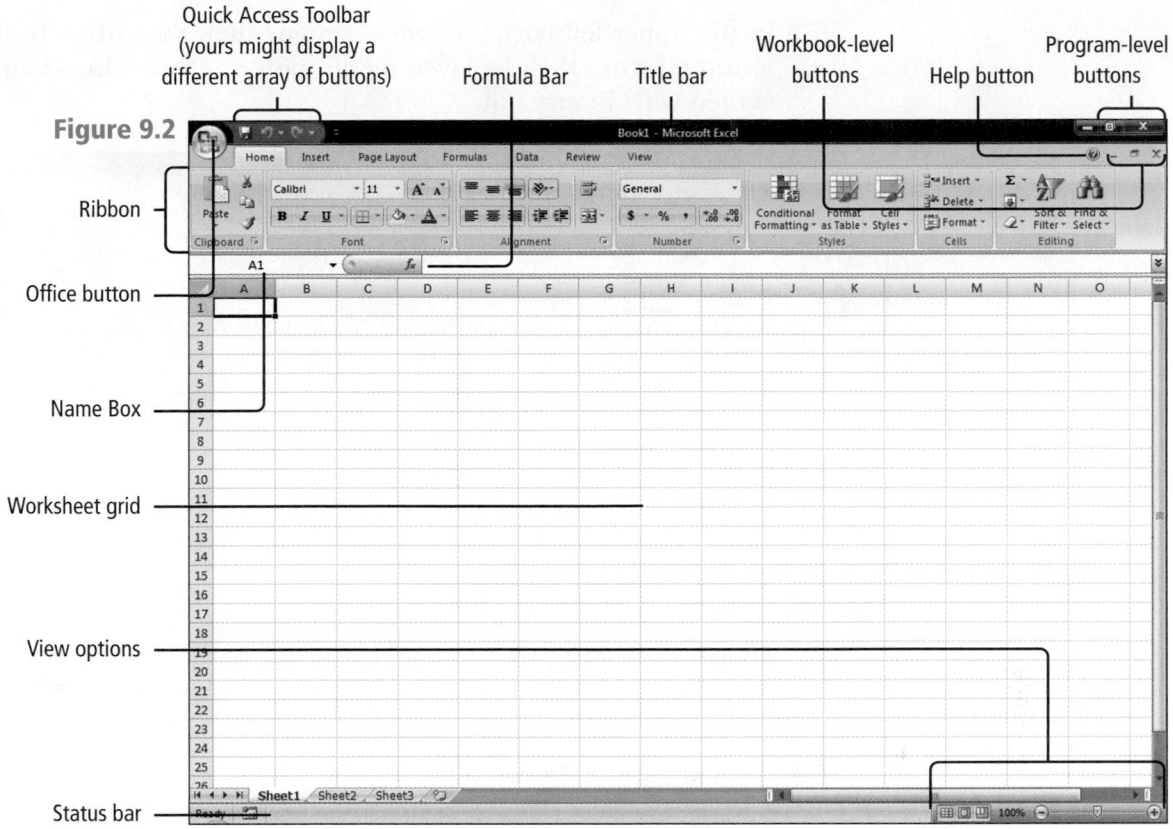

Figure 9.2

Labels around figure: Quick Access Toolbar (yours might display a different array of buttons); Formula Bar; Title bar; Workbook-level buttons; Help button; Program-level buttons; Ribbon; Office button; Name Box; Worksheet grid; View options; Status bar

Parts of the Excel Window

Screen Part	Description
Formula Bar	Displays the value or formula contained in the active cell; also permits entry or editing of values or formulas.
Help button	Displays the Help window.
Name Box	Displays the name of the selected cell, table, chart, or object.
Office button	Displays a list of commands related to things you can do *with* a workbook, such as opening, saving, printing, or sharing.
Program-level buttons	Minimizes, restores, or closes the Excel program.
Quick Access Toolbar	Displays buttons to perform frequently used commands with a single click. Frequently used commands in Excel include Save, Undo, and Redo. For commands that *you* use frequently, you can add additional buttons to the Quick Access Toolbar.
Ribbon	Groups the commands for performing related workbook tasks.
Status bar	Displays, on the left side, the current cell mode, page number, and worksheet information. On the right side, displays buttons to control how the window looks; when numerical data is selected, common calculations such as Sum and Average display.
Title bar	Indicates the name of the current workbook and the program name.
View options	Contain buttons for viewing the workbook in Normal view, Page Layout view, or Page Break Preview, and also displays controls for Zoom Out and Zoom In to increase or decrease the number of rows and columns displayed.
Workbook-level buttons	Minimizes or restores the displayed workbook.
Worksheet grid	Displays the columns and rows that intersect to form the worksheet's cells.

Figure 9.3

2 In the upper left corner of your screen, click the **Office** button 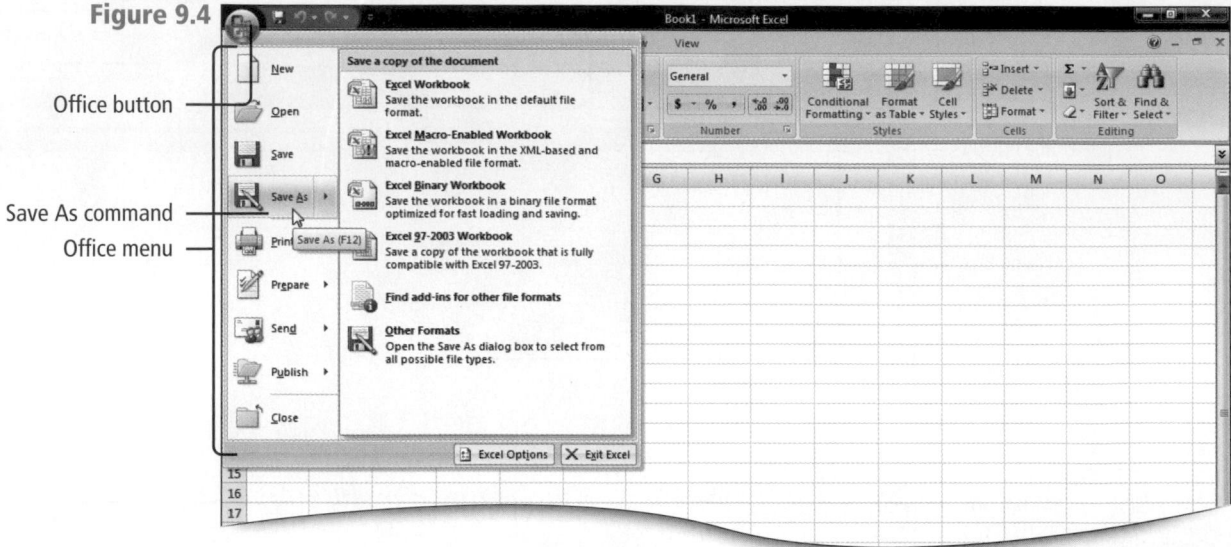, and then from the displayed menu, point to **Save As**. Compare your screen with Figure 9.4.

Figure 9.4

Office button

Save As command

Office menu

3 Click the **Save As** command. In the displayed **Save As** dialog box, if necessary, click Browse Folders to display the Navigation pane. In the **Navigation pane**, click **Computer** to view a list of the drives available to you, and then navigate to the drive on which you will be storing your folders and workbooks for this textbook—for example, a USB flash drive such as the one shown in Figure 9.5. If you are saving your files on your hard disk drive, in the Navigation pane, click Documents or the location of your choice.

Your disk or drive selected (your list of drives, drive letters, and drive names will vary)

Navigation pane expanded

Figure 9.5

Save As dialog box

Address bar displays path to your selected drive

New Folder button

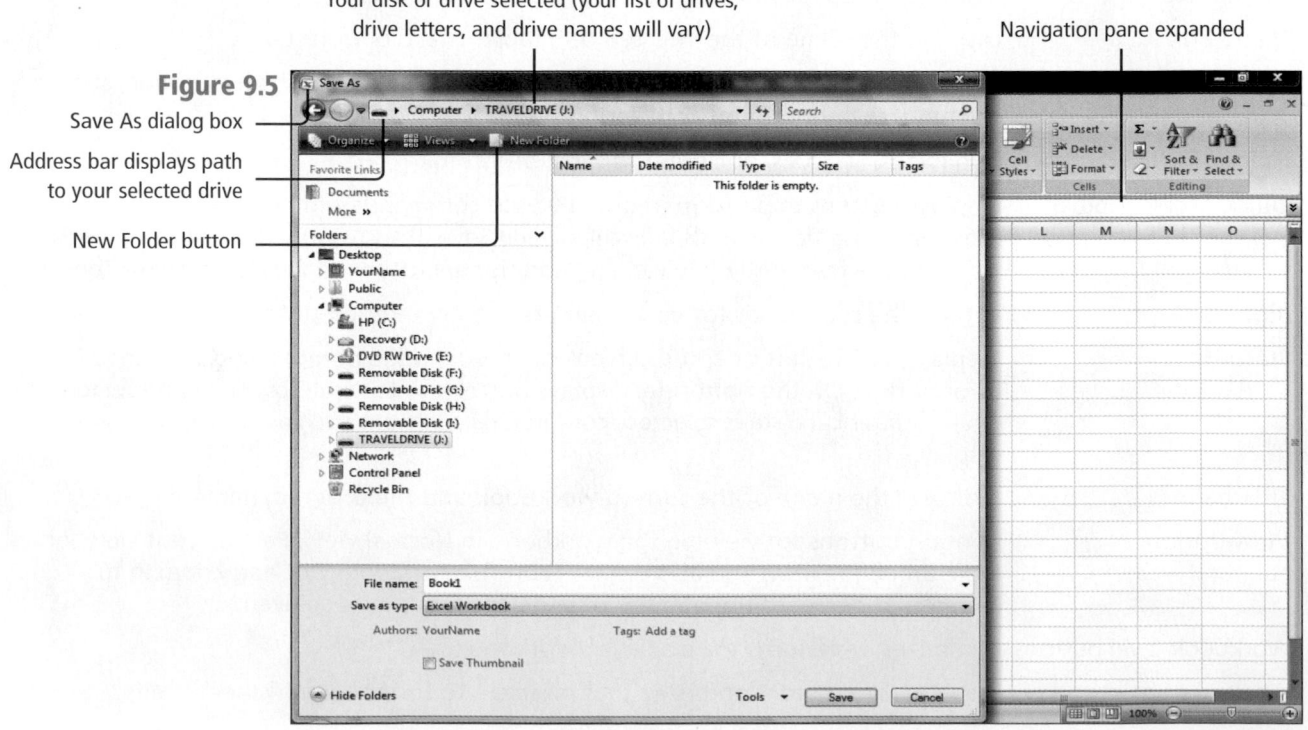

4 On the **Save As** dialog box toolbar, click the **New Folder** button.

With the text *New Folder* selected, type **Excel Chapter 9** and then press Enter.

Windows creates the *Excel Chapter 9* folder and makes it the active folder in the Save As dialog box. At the bottom of the Save As dialog box, in the File name box, *Book1* displays as the default file name.

5 In the **File name** box, using your own first and last name, delete *Book1* and type **9A_Auto_Sales_Firstname_Lastname** being sure to include the underscore (⇧ Shift + -) instead of spaces between words. Compare your screen with Figure 9.6.

Windows recognizes file names that use spaces between words, but some electronic file transfer programs do not. In this text, you will use underscores instead of spaces between words for your file names.

Your folder name

Figure 9.6

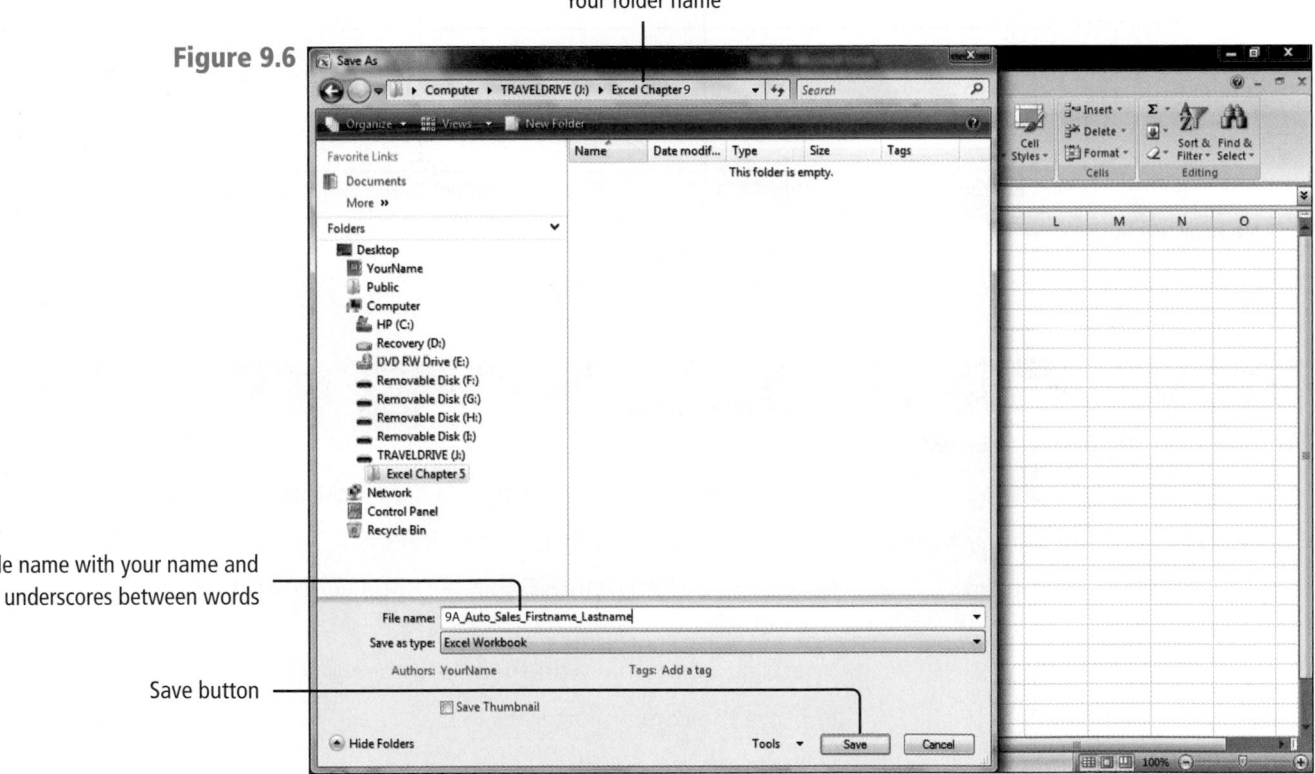

File name with your name and underscores between words

Save button

6 In the lower right corner of the **Save As** dialog box, click **Save** or press Enter.

The file is saved in the new folder with the new name. The workbook redisplays, and the new name displays in the title bar.

Activity 9.02 Navigating a Worksheet and a Workbook

1 Take a moment to study Figure 9.7 and the table in Figure 9.8 to become familiar with the Excel workbook window.

Figure 9.7

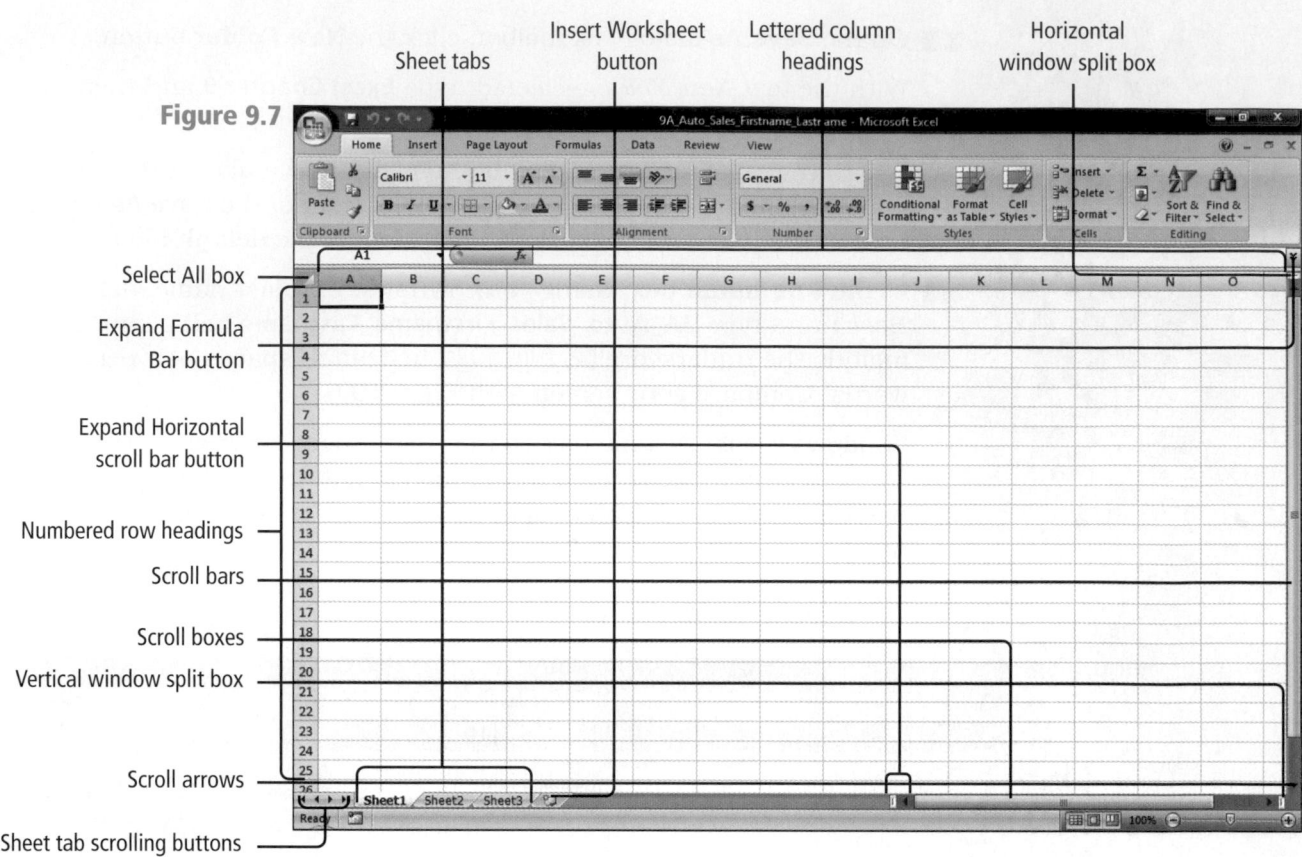

Sheet tabs

Insert Worksheet button

Lettered column headings

Horizontal window split box

Select All box

Expand Formula Bar button

Expand Horizontal scroll bar button

Numbered row headings

Scroll bars

Scroll boxes

Vertical window split box

Scroll arrows

Sheet tab scrolling buttons

Excel Workbook Window Elements

Workbook window element	Description
Expand Formula Bar button	Increases the height of the Formula Bar to display lengthy cell content.
Expand horizontal scroll bar button	Increases the width of the horizontal scroll bar.
Horizontal window split box	Splits the worksheet into two horizontal views of the same worksheet.
Insert Worksheet button	Inserts an additional worksheet into the workbook.
Lettered column headings	Indicate the column letter.
Numbered row headings	Indicate the row number.
Scroll arrows	Scroll one column or row at a time.
Scroll bars	Scroll the Excel window up and down or left and right.
Scroll boxes	Move the position of the window up and down or left and right.
Select All box	Selects all the cells in a worksheet.
Sheet tab scrolling buttons	Display sheet tabs that are not in view; used when there are more sheet tabs than will display in the space provided.
Sheet tabs	Identify the worksheets in a workbook.
Vertical window split box	Splits the worksheet into two vertical views of the same worksheet.

Figure 9.8

2 In the horizontal scroll bar, point to, and then click the **right scroll arrow**.

The workbook window shifts so that column A moves out of view. The number of times you click one of the arrows on the horizontal scroll bar determines the number of columns by which the window shifts—either to the left or to the right.

3 In the horizontal scroll bar, click the **right scroll arrow**, and then hold down the left mouse button until the columns begin to scroll rapidly to the right; release when you begin to see pairs of letters as the column headings.

The workbook window moves rapidly. This technique also works for the left scroll arrow and for the two vertical scroll arrows.

4 In the horizontal scroll bar, click the **left scroll arrow** to shift one column. Then, in the horizontal scroll bar, point to the **horizontal scroll box**. Hold down the left mouse button, *drag* the box to the left to display **column A**, and then notice that *ScreenTips* with the column letters display as you drag. Release the mouse button.

To drag is to move something from one location on the screen to another; the action of dragging includes releasing the mouse button at the desired time or location. ScreenTips display useful information when you perform various mouse actions such as pointing to screen elements or dragging.

Use the scroll boxes in this manner to move various parts of the worksheet into view. Scroll boxes change in size to indicate how the visible portion of the worksheet compares to the total amount of the worksheet in use.

5 Use the techniques you just practiced to scroll the worksheet to position **column Z** near the center of your screen.

Column headings to the right of column Z use two letters starting with AA, AB, AC, and so on. After that, columns begin with three letters beginning with AAA. This pattern is used to provide a total of 16,384 columns. The last column available is column XFD.

6 Near the lower left of the screen, point to, and then click the **Sheet2 tab**.

The second worksheet in the workbook displays and becomes the active worksheet. Column A displays at the left.

7 Click the **Sheet1 tab**.

The first worksheet in the workbook becomes the active worksheet. A workbook consists of one or more worksheets. By default, new workbooks contain three worksheets. When you save a workbook, the worksheets are contained within it and do not have separate file names.

8 In the vertical scroll bar, point to, and then click the **down scroll arrow** one time.

Row 1 moves out of view. The number of times you click the arrows on the vertical scroll bar determines the number of rows shifted either up or down. You can drag the vertical scroll box to scroll downward in a manner similar to the technique used in the horizontal scroll bar.

9 In the vertical scroll bar, point to, and then click the **up scroll arrow**.

Row 1 comes back into view. The maximum number of rows on a single Excel worksheet is 1,048,576.

10 Use the skills you just practiced to scroll horizontally to display **column A**.

Activity 9.03 Selecting Parts of a Worksheet

In the following activity, you will *select* both individual cells and groups of cells in the worksheet. Selecting refers to highlighting, by clicking or dragging with your mouse, one or more cells so that the selected cells can be edited, formatted, copied, or moved. Selected cells are indicated by a dark border, and Excel treats the selected *range*—two or more cells on a worksheet that are adjacent or nonadjacent—as a single unit; thus, you can make the same change, or combination of changes, to more than one cell at a time.

In Excel, text or numbers in a cell are referred to as *data*. Before you enter data into a worksheet, you must select the location in the worksheet where you want the data to display. After the data is in the worksheet, you can select one or more cells of data to which you can apply Excel's formatting, features, and functions.

1 In **Sheet1**, move the mouse pointer over—*point* to—the cell at the intersection of **column A** and **row 3**, and then click. Compare your screen with Figure 9.9.

A black border surrounds the cell, indicating that it is the *active cell*. The active cell in a worksheet is the cell ready to receive data or be affected by the next Excel command. A cell is identified by the intersecting column letter and row number, which forms the *cell reference*. A cell reference is also referred to as a *cell address*. The cell reference displays in the *Name Box*. Although either lowercase or uppercase letters can be used to indicate columns, uppercase letters are commonly used.

Figure 9.9

Cell A3 is selected

Cell address displays in the Name Box

Active cell

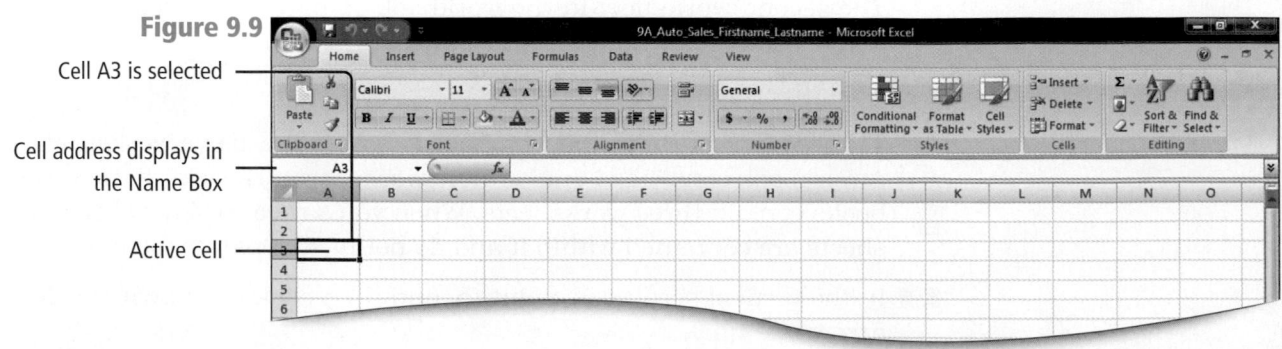

2 On the keyboard, press ⬇ three times, and then look at the cell address in the **Name Box**.

Cell A6 becomes the active cell. Pressing one of the four direction arrow keys relocates the active cell. The cell address of the active cell always displays in the Name Box.

3 Point to cell **B2**, hold down the left mouse button, drag downward to select cells **B2**, **B3**, **B4**, and **B5**, and then continue to drag across to cell **C5** and release the left mouse button. Alternatively, drag diagonally from cell B2 to C5. If you are not satisfied with your result, click anywhere and begin again. Compare your screen with Figure 9.10.

The eight cells, B2 through B5 and C2 through C5 are selected. This range of cells is referred to as *B2:C5*. When you see a colon (:) between two cell references, the range includes all the cells between the two cell references. The cell references used to indicate the range are the upper left cell and the lower right cell—in this instance, B2 and C5. When you select a range of cells, the cells are bordered by a thick black line, and the cells change color except for the first cell in the range, which displays in the Name Box.

Selected range B2:C5

Black border surrounds selected range

Figure 9.10

Name Box always indicates address of the first cell in range

First cell selected but not highlighted

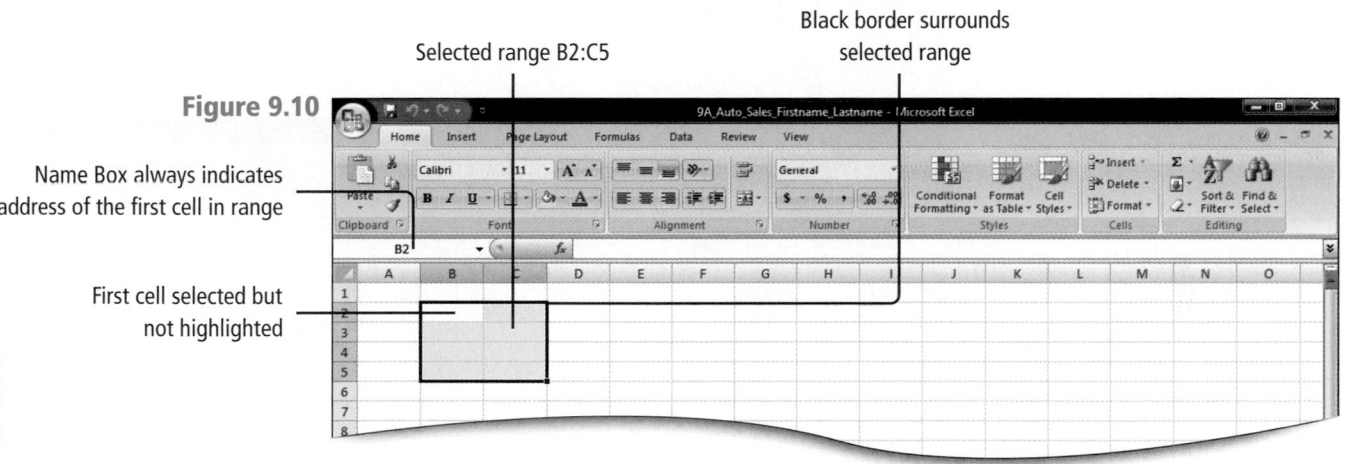

4 At the left edge of the worksheet, point to the number **3** to display the ➡ pointer, and then click the **row 3** heading.

Row 3 is selected. A *row* is a horizontal group of cells in a worksheet. Beginning with number 1, a unique number identifies each row— this is the *row heading*, located at the left side of the worksheet. All the cells in the row are selected, including those that are out of view.

5 In the upper left corner of **Sheet1**, point to the letter **A** to display the ⬇ pointer, and then click one time.

Column A is selected. A *column* is a vertical group of cells in a work- sheet. Beginning with the first letter of the alphabet, A, a unique let- ter identifies each column—this is called the *column heading*. All the cells in the column are selected, including those that are out of view.

6 Click in the **Name Box** and notice that the cell reference *A1* moves to the left edge and is highlighted in blue. In any Windows program, text highlighted in blue in this manner will be replaced by your typing. Type **d4:f6** and then compare your screen with Figure 9.11.

Figure 9.11

Range typed in Name Box—
OK to type lowercase or
uppercase letters

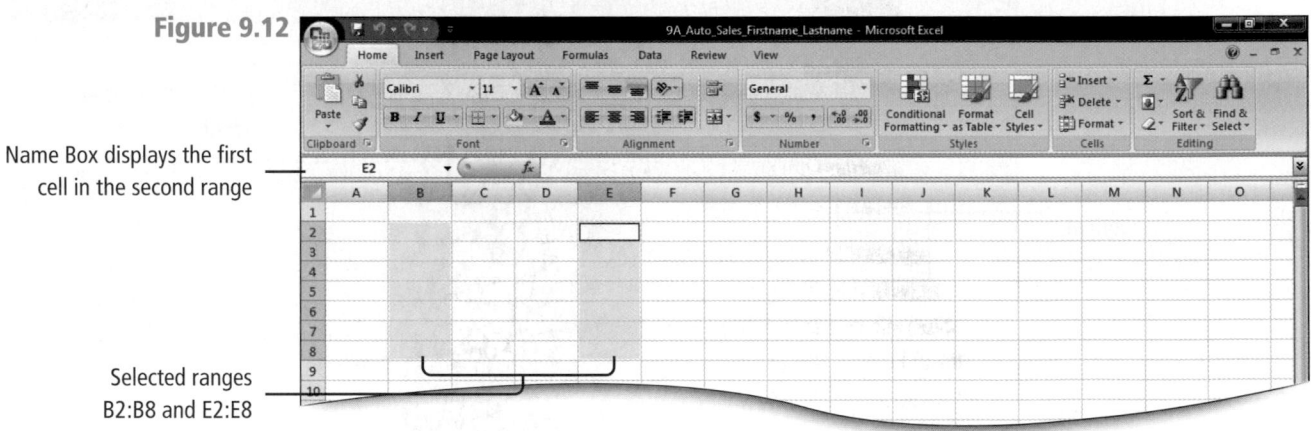

7 Press Enter to select the range. Then, click in the **Name Box**, type **b2:b8,e2:e8** press Enter, and then compare your screen with Figure 9.12.

Two *nonadjacent*—not next to each other—ranges are selected. Ranges of cells that are not *adjacent*—next to each other—can be selected by typing the ranges into the Name Box separated by a comma.

Figure 9.12

Name Box displays the first
cell in the second range

Selected ranges
B2:B8 and E2:E8

8 Select the range **C3:C5** and notice that the previously selected cells are deselected. Then, with the range selected, hold down Ctrl, and select the range **E3:E5**.

Use either technique to select cells that are nonadjacent (not next to one another). A range of cells can be adjacent or nonadjacent. Recall that a range of cells that is nonadjacent can be indicated by separating the ranges with a comma. In this instance, the selected ranges can be referred to as *c3:c5,e3:e5*.

9 At the upper left corner of your worksheet, locate, and then click the **Select All** box—the small box above **row heading 1** and to the left of **column heading A** to select all of the cells in the worksheet. Then, point to any cell on your worksheet and click to cancel the selection.

Objective 2
Enter and Edit Data in a Worksheet

Anything typed into a cell is referred to as **cell content**. Cell content can be one of two things—either a **constant value**—referred to simply as a **value**—or a **formula**. A value can be numbers, text, dates, or times of day that you type into a cell. A formula is an equation that performs mathematical calculations on values in your worksheet.

After you enter values into a cell, they can be **edited**—changed—or cleared from the cell. Words—text—typed in a worksheet usually provide information about numbers in other worksheet cells. For example, a title such as *Quarterly Auto Sales* gives the reader an indication that the data in the worksheet relates to information about sales of autos during a 3-month period.

Activity 9.04 Entering Text, Using AutoComplete, Filling a Series with Auto Fill, and Using Spelling Checker and Undo to Correct Typing Errors

To enter text into a cell, select the cell and type. In this activity, you will enter a title for the worksheet and titles for the rows and columns that will identify the types of vehicles purchased and the monthly sales amount for each vehicle type.

1 Click the **Sheet1 tab**, if necessary, so that Sheet 1 is the active sheet. Click cell **A1**, type **Rio Rancho Auto Gallery** and then press Enter.

After you type data into a cell, you must confirm the entry to store it in the cell. One way to do this is to press the Enter key, which typically moves the selection to the cell *below* to facilitate entry in a column of cells. You can also use other keyboard movements, such as Tab, or one of the arrow keys on your keyboard to make another cell active and confirm the entry.

2 Look at the text you typed in cell **A1**, and notice that the text does not fit into cell A1; the text spills over and displays in cells **B1** and **C1** to the right.

If text is too long for a cell and the cells to the right are empty, the text will display. If the cells to the right contain other data, only the text that will fit in the cell will display. Cell A2 is the active cell, as indicated by the black border surrounding it.

3 In cell **A2**, type **Monthly Sales by Vehicle Type** and then press Enter. In cell **A3**, type **Type** and then press Enter. Compare your screen with Figure 9.13.

Text too long for cell spills into adjacent
cells if the adjacent cells are empty

Figure 9.13

Cell A4 active cell

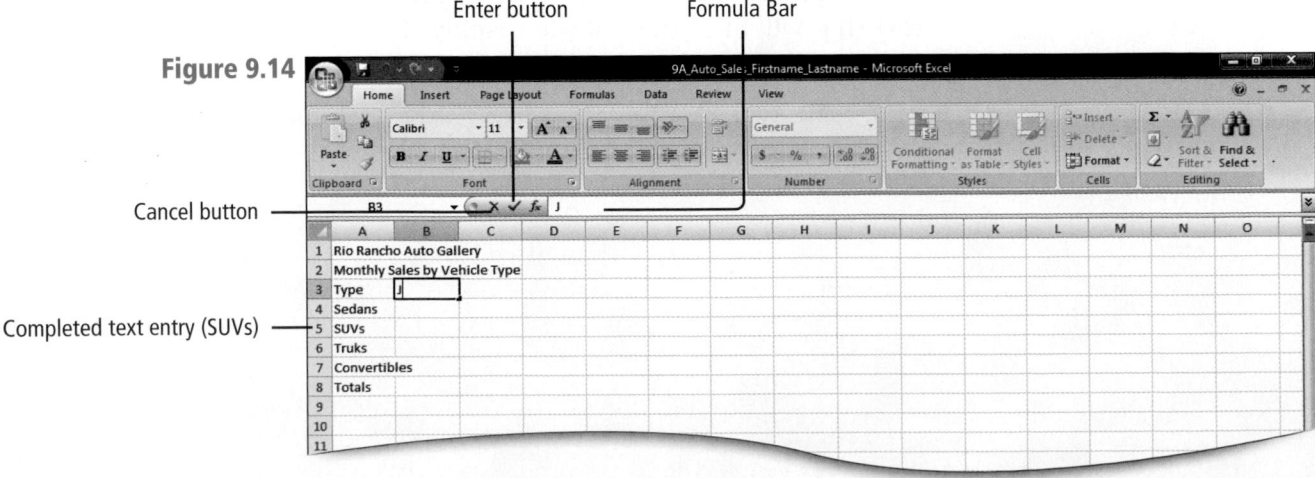

4 In cell **A4**, type **Sedans** and then press Enter.

The text is left aligned in the cell and the selection moves to cell A5. *Left alignment* —characters align at the left edge of the cell—is the default for text entries. Formatting information of this type is stored with the cell.

5 In cell **A5**, type **S** and notice the text from the previous cell displays.

Excel assists you in typing. If the first characters you type in a cell match an existing entry in the column, Excel fills in the remaining characters for you. This feature, called *AutoComplete*, speeds your typing. AutoComplete assists only with alphabetic values; it does not assist with numeric values.

6 Continue typing the remainder of the row title, **UVs** and press Enter.

As soon as the entry you are typing differs from the previous value, the AutoComplete suggestion is removed.

7 Without correcting the spelling error, in cell **A6**, type **Truks** and then press Enter. Then, in cell **A7**, type **Convertibles** and press Enter. In cell **A8**, type **Totals** and then press Enter.

8 Click cell **B3** to make it the active cell. Type **J** and notice that when you begin to type in a cell, on the **Formula Bar**, the **Cancel** and **Enter** buttons become active, as shown in Figure 9.14.

Enter button   Formula Bar

Figure 9.14

Cancel button

Completed text entry (SUVs)

9 Continue to type **anuary** and then on the **Formula Bar**, click the **Enter** button ☑ to keep cell **B3** the active cell.

Clicking the Enter button on the Formula Bar confirms the entry and maintains the current cell as the active cell. This is convenient if you want to take further action on the cell. If you mistakenly press Enter, reselect the cell.

10 With **B3** as the active cell, notice the small black square in the lower right corner of the selected cell.

You can drag the *fill handle*—the small black square in the lower right corner of a selected cell—to adjacent cells to fill the cells with values based on the first cell or cells in the series.

11 Point to the fill handle until the ⊞ pointer displays, hold down the left mouse button, drag to the right to cell **F3**, and as you drag notice the ScreenTips *February*, *March*, *April* and *May*. Release the left mouse button, point to the **Auto Fill Options** button that displays, and then compare your screen with Figure 9.15.

Excel's *Auto Fill* feature can generate a *series* of values into adjacent cells, based on the value of other cells. A series is a group of things that come one after another in succession. For example, *January*, *February*, *March*, and so on, is a series. Likewise, *1st Qtr*, *2nd Qtr*, *3rd Qtr*, and *4th Qtr* form a series.

Auto Fill Options button

Figure 9.15

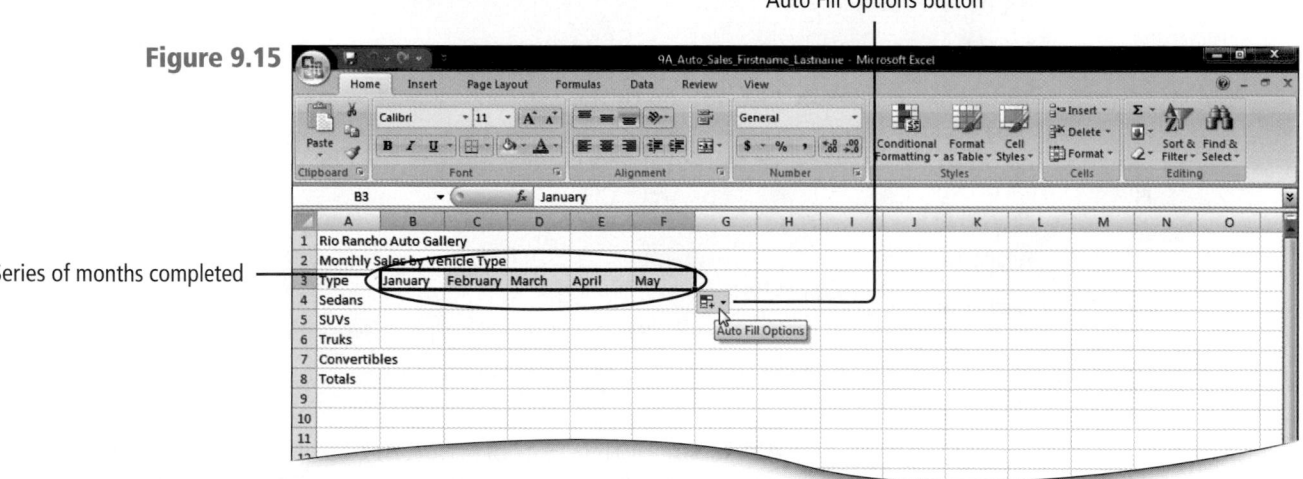

Series of months completed

12 To the right of and below the filled data, point to, and then click the **Auto Fill Options** button.

The Auto Fill Options button displays just below a filled selection after you fill data in a worksheet. When you click the button, a list displays with options to fill the data. The list of options varies depending on the content you are filling, the program you are filling from, and the format of the data you are filling.

Fill Series is selected, indicating the action that was taken. Note that you can also fill only *Formatting*. Because the options are related to the current task, the button is referred to as being *context sensitive*.

13 Click in any cell to cancel the display of the Auto Fill Options list.

The list no longer displays; the button will display until some other screen action takes place.

14 Hold down Ctrl, and then press Home to make cell **A1** the active cell—this is a *keyboard shortcut*, which is an individual keystroke or a combination of keys pressed simultaneously that can either access an Excel command or move to another location on your screen.

15 Take a moment to study the table in Figure 9.16 to become familiar with additional keyboard shortcuts with which you can navigate the Excel worksheet.

Keyboard Shortcuts to Navigate the Excel Screen

To Move the Location of the Active Cell:	Press:
Up, down, right, or left one cell	↑, ↓, →, ←
Down one cell	Enter
Up one cell	⇧ Shift + Enter
Up one full screen	Page Up
Down one full screen	PageDown
Left one full screen	Alt + Page Up
Right one full screen	Alt + PageDown
To column A of the current row	Home
To the last cell in the last column of the active area (the rectangle formed by all the rows and columns in a worksheet that contain entries)	Ctrl + End
To cell A1	Ctrl + Home
Right one cell	Tab
Left one cell	⇧ Shift + Tab

Figure 9.16

16 With cell **A1** as the active cell, on the Ribbon, click the **Review tab**, and then in the **Proofing** group, click the **Spelling** button. Alternatively, press F7, which is the keyboard shortcut for the Spelling command. Compare your screen with Figure 9.17.

Figure 9.17

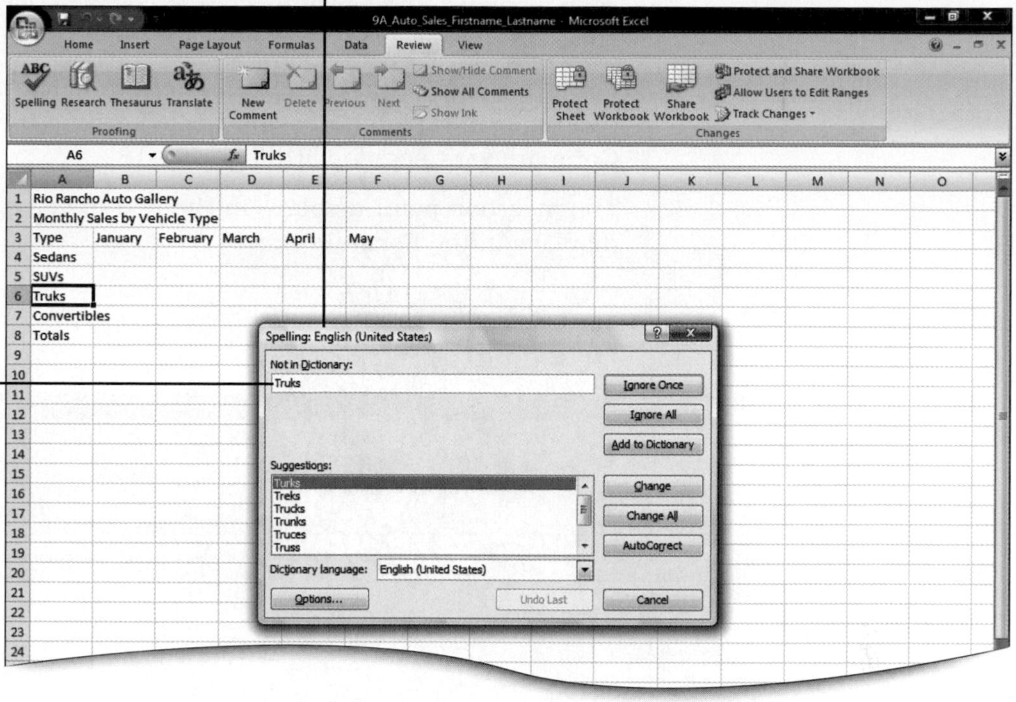

Spelling dialog box

Word indicated as *Not in Dictionary*

Does a message display asking if you want to continue checking at the beginning of the sheet?

If a message displays asking if you want to continue checking at the beginning of the sheet, click Yes. The Spelling command begins its checking process with the currently selected cell and moves to the right and down. Thus, if your active cell was a cell after A6, this message may display.

17 In the displayed **Spelling** dialog box, under **Not in Dictionary**, notice the word *Truks*.

The spelling tool does not have this word in its dictionary. Under *Suggestions*, Excel provides a list of suggested spellings.

18 Under **Suggestions**, click **Trucks**, and then click the **Change** button.

Truks, which was a typing error, is changed to *Trucks*. A message box displays *The spelling check is complete for the entire sheet.* Because the spelling check begins its checking process starting with the currently selected cell, it is a good habit to return to cell A1 before starting the Spelling command.

Note — Words Not in the Dictionary Are Not Necessarily Misspelled

Many proper nouns or less commonly used words are not in the dictionary used by Excel. If Excel indicates a correct word as *Not in Dictionary*, you can choose to ignore this word or add it to the dictionary. You may want to add proper names that you expect to use often, such as your own last name, to the dictionary if you are permitted to do so.

19 Correct any other errors that you may have made. When the message displays, *The spelling check is complete for the entire sheet,* click **OK**.

20 Point to cell **A5**, and then **double-click**—click the left mouse button two times in rapid succession while keeping the mouse still. Compare your screen with Figure 9.18.

The insertion point displays in the text in cell A5, and the text also displays in the Formula Bar.

Cell content displays
in the Formula Bar

Figure 9.18

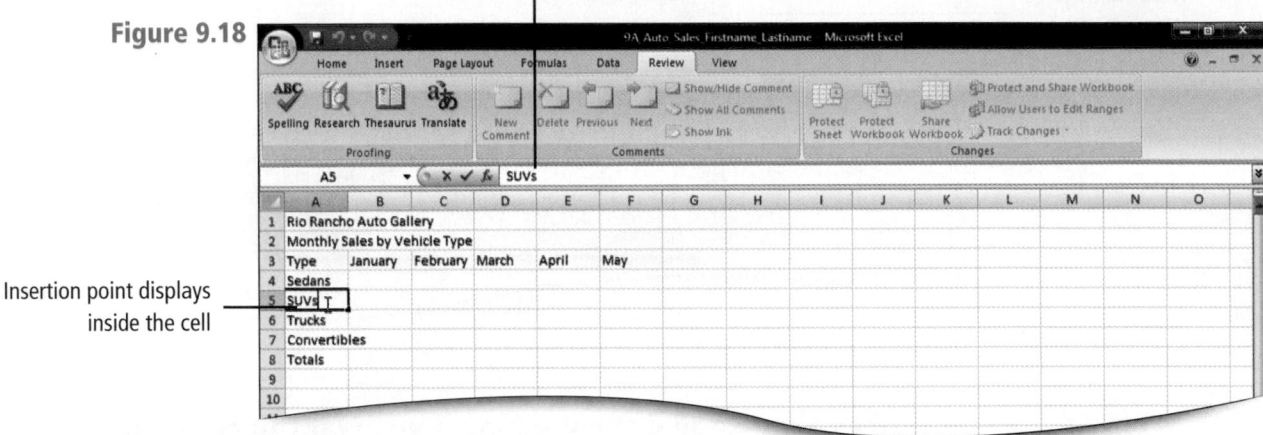

Insertion point displays
inside the cell

21 Move the mouse pointer away from the cell so that you have a clear view, and then using the arrow, Del or ←Bksp keys as necessary, edit the text and change it to **Vans** Confirm the change by pressing Enter.

22 On the **Quick Access Toolbar**, click the **Undo** button. Alternatively, you can press Ctrl + Z on the keyboard to reverse (undo) the last action.

SUVs is restored and *Vans* is deleted—your action was undone.

More Knowledge

AutoCorrect Also Assists in Your Typing

AutoCorrect assists in your typing by automatically correcting and formatting some text as you type. Excel compares your typing to a list of commonly mistyped words and when it finds a match, it substitutes the correct word. For example, if you type *monday*, Excel will automatically correct to *Monday*. To view the AutoCorrect options, display the Office menu. At the lower right, click Excel Options; on the left, click Proofing, and then click the AutoCorrect Options button.

Activity 9.05 Aligning Text and Adjusting the Size of Columns and Rows

Data typed into a cell can be aligned at the left, at the right, or centered. You can make columns wider or narrower and make rows taller or shorter. In this activity, you will adjust the size of columns and rows and right-align and center data in a cell.

1 In the **column heading area**, point to the vertical line between **column A** and **column B** to display the ⊕ pointer, press and hold down the left mouse button, and then compare your screen with Figure 9.19.

A ScreenTip displays information about the width of the column.

Figure 9.19

ScreenTip

Pointer

Dotted line indicates column divider is selected

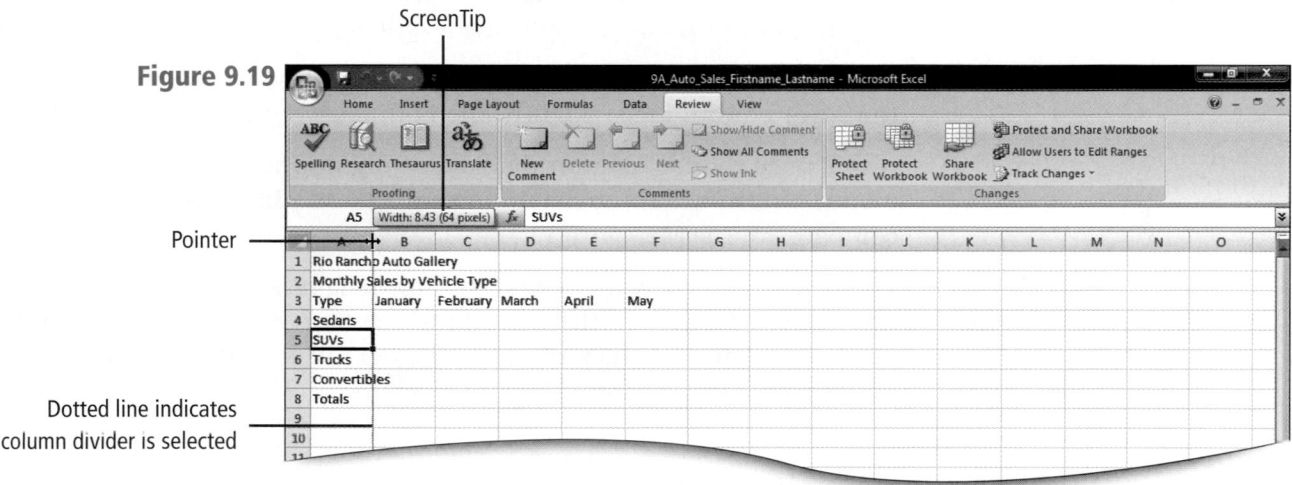

2 Drag to the right and release the mouse button when the number of pixels indicated in the ScreenTip reaches **90 pixels**, which is wide enough to display the longest row title in cells A4 through A7—the worksheet title in A1 will span more than one column and still does not fit in column A. If you are not satisfied with your result, click the Undo button and begin again.

The default width of a column is 64 **pixels**. A pixel, short for **picture element**, is a point of light measured in dots per square inch on a screen. Sixty-four pixels equals 8.43 characters, which is the average number of digits that will fit in a cell using the default **font**—a set of characters with the same design, size, and shape. The default font in Excel is Calibri, and the default **font size**—the size of characters in a font measured in **points**—is 11. There are 72 points in an inch, with 10 or 11 points being a typical font size in Excel. Point is usually abbreviated as **pt**.

3 Click cell **A8**. On the Ribbon click the **Home tab**, and then in the **Alignment group**, click the **Align Text Right** button ☰.

The row title is aligned at the right side of the cell to distinguish it from the other row titles in the column. Text can be aligned at the center, left, or right of a cell. By default, text aligns at the left, but is easily changed as you have done here.

4 Select the range **B3:F3**, and then with your pointer positioned any-where over the selected range, ***right-click***—click the right mouse button—to display a ***shortcut menu*** and a ***Mini toolbar***—both of which display commands most commonly used in the context of selected text of this type. On the Mini toolbar, click the **Center** button ![Center icon] and notice that the shortcut menu no longer displays. Then, move the mouse slightly below the displayed Mini toolbar and notice that the Mini toolbar fades so that you can see the result of your formatting. Move the pointer back into the Mini toolbar, and then notice that it displays and once again becomes a functioning toolbar.

The column titles *January – May* align in the center of each cell. A shortcut menu offers the most commonly used commands relevant to the selected area and thus is context sensitive. You can also dis-play a shortcut menu by pressing ⎇Shift + F10.

5 Click in any cell to cancel the selection and close the Mini toolbar. In the **row heading area**, point to the boundary between **row 1** and **row 2** until the ![resize pointer] pointer displays. Drag downward, release the mouse button when the height of **row 1** is **28 pixels**, and then compare your screen with Figure 9.20.

The height of the row is increased. Row height is measured in points or in pixels. Points are the units in which font size is measured and pixels are units of screen display. The default height of a row is 15.00 points or 20 pixels.

Text centered within the cells

Figure 9.20

Column A changed to 90 pixels wide

Row 1 changed to 28 pixels high

Text in cell A8 right aligned

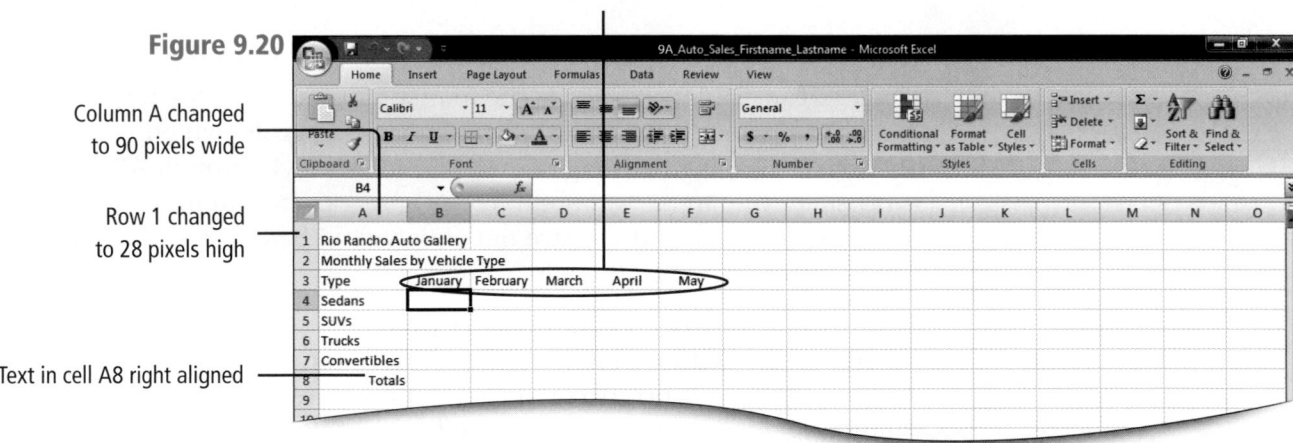

6 On the **Quick Access Toolbar**, click the **Save** button ![Save icon] to save the changes you have made to your workbook; alternatively, press Ctrl + S.

Activity 9.06 Entering Numbers

When typing numbers in an Excel worksheet, you can use either the number keys across the top of your keyboard or the number keys and Enter key on the numeric keypad. Try to develop some proficiency in touch control of the numeric keypad. In this activity, you will enter the sales amounts for Rio Rancho Auto Gallery.

1 Click cell **B4**, type **330373.42** and then on the **Formula Bar**, click the **Enter** button ☑ to maintain cell **B4** as the active cell. Compare your screen with Figure 9.21.

By default, numbers align at the right edge of the cell. The default *number format*—a specific way in which Excel displays numbers—is the *general format*. The general format has no specific characteristics —whatever you type in the cell will display, with the exception that trailing zeros to the right of a decimal point will not display. For example, if you type *125.50* the cell will display *125.5* instead.

Numbers that are too long to fit in the cell do *not* spill over into the unoccupied cell to the right in the same manner as text. Rather, the number is rounded. However, the entire number still exists and displays in the Formula Bar. Data displayed in a cell is referred to as the *displayed value*. Data displayed in the Formula Bar is referred to as the *underlying value*. The number of digits or characters that display in a cell—the displayed value—depends on the width of the column.

Cell content, in full, displays in Formula Bar

Figure 9.21

Display of number does not extend into occupied cells, number is rounded

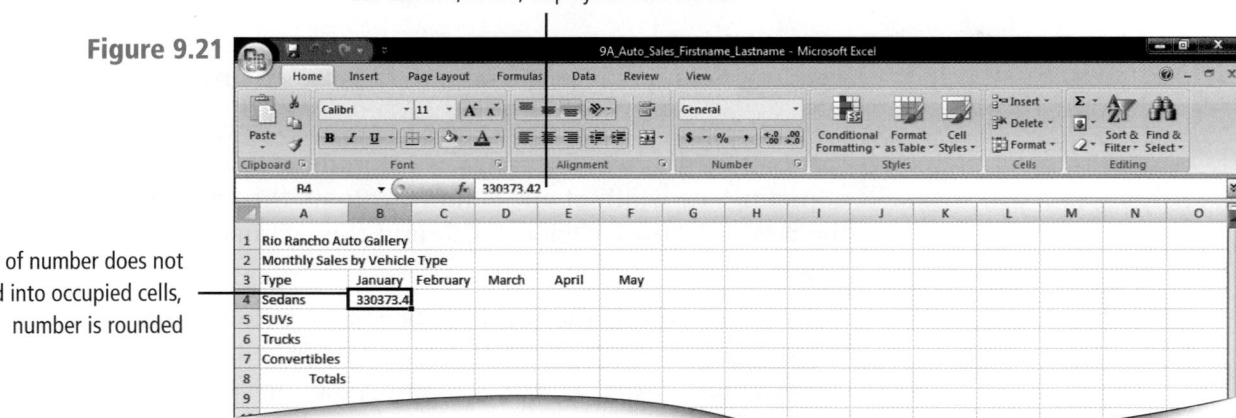

2 Enter the remaining sales figures for *Sedans* and *SUVs* in the months of January through May, as shown in the following table. Press ⬚Tab⬚ to simultaneously confirm your entry and move across the row, and then press ⬚Enter⬚ at the end of a row to move to the next row. Notice that as you type, if the column is too narrow to display all of the decimal places in a number, the display of the number will be rounded to fit the available space. When finished, compare your screen with Figure 9.22.

Rounding is a procedure in which you determine which digit at the right of the number will be the last digit displayed and then increase it by one if the next digit to its right is 5, 6, 7, 8, or 9.

Recall that trailing zeros to the right of a decimal point will not display. So for example, if you type 289076.30, the cell will display 289076.3 and if you type 297467.00, the cell will display 297467.

Calculations performed on numbers in Excel will always be based on the underlying value, not the displayed value.

	January	February	March	April	May
Sedans	330373.42	289076.30	271717.67	326243.00	297467.00
SUVs	185835.76	163446.98	140408.67	247780.87	189756.00

Figure 9.22

Values entered for Sedans and SUVs

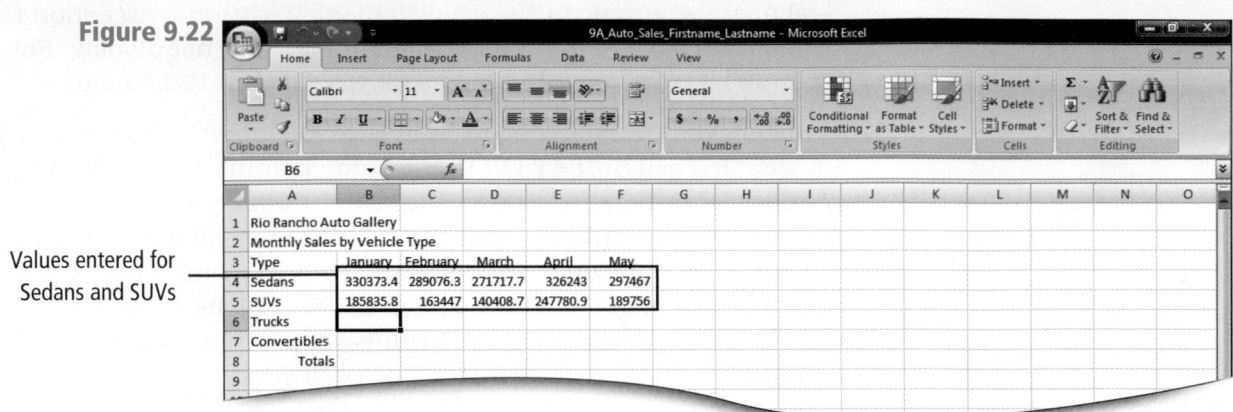

3 Click in the **Name Box**, type **b:f** and then press Enter. In the **column heading area**, point to the boundary between any two of the selected column headings to display the ✛ pointer, drag to **50** pixels, and then notice that when a range of columns is selected in this manner, adjusting the width of one column adjusts the width of all. Release the mouse button, click cell **C5**, and then compare your screen with Figure 9.23.

In this example, as the columns become narrower and the decimal places cannot fit into the cell, the numbers are rounded further to fit the available space. The underlying value, however, is unchanged.

Cell content, in full, displays in Formula Bar; displays underlying value

Figure 9.23

Display of numbers does not extend into occupied cells; rounded to 163447

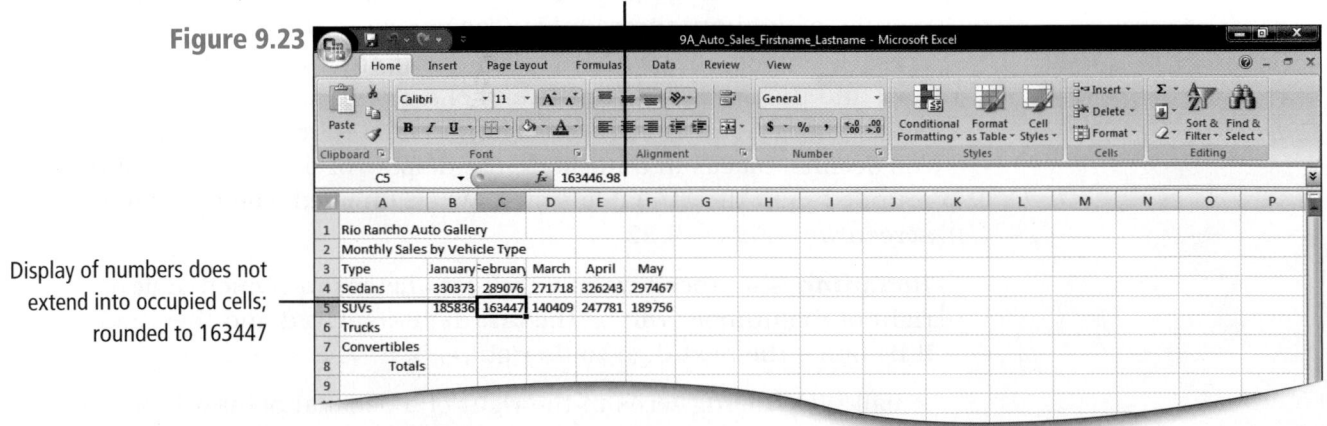

4 On the **Quick Access Toolbar**, click the **Undo** button ↶ to restore the column widths to 64 pixels. Click in any cell to deselect the columns. In the **column heading area**, point to the right boundary of **column D**, and then drag the right column border to the left to set the width of **column D** to **30 pixels**. Then, click cell **D5** and compare your screen with Figure 9.24.

If a cell width is too narrow to display all of the number, Excel displays a series of pound signs instead; displaying only a portion of a whole number would be misleading. The underlying values remain unchanged and are displayed in the Formula Bar for the selected cell. The underlying value also displays in the ScreenTip if you point to a cell containing ###.

Pound signs indicate cell is too
narrow to display the number

Figure 9.24

Underlying value displays
in the Formula Bar

Point to a cell containing
to display underlying
value in a ScreenTip

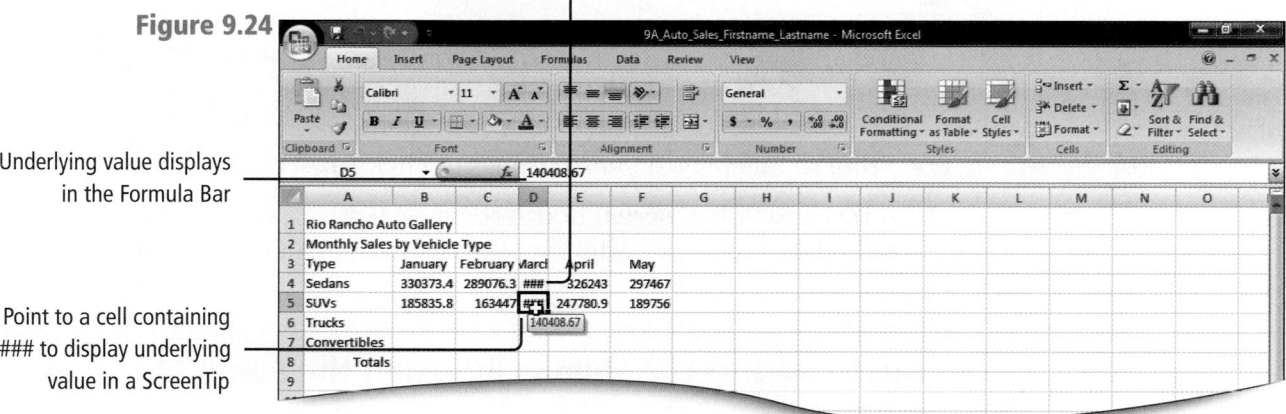

5 On the **Quick Access Toolbar**, click the **Undo** button ↶ to restore **column D** to a width of 64 pixels. Select **columns B:F**. In the **column heading area**, point to the boundary between any two of the selected column headings to display the ⟷ pointer, and then drag to **85** pixels.

Recall that in the default general number format, trailing zeros to the right of a decimal point do not display regardless of the column width.

6 Click any cell to cancel the selection, and then **Save** 💾 your workbook.

Activity 9.07 Inserting and Deleting Rows and Columns, and Using the Insert Options Button

In this activity, you will insert a new row to record sales for the vehicle type *Compacts* and delete the *Convertibles* vehicle type.

1 Point to the **row 4** heading, and then right-click to simultaneously select the row and display the shortcut menu and the Mini toolbar. Compare your screen with Figure 9.25.

You can right-click row numbers or column headings to simultaneously select and display a context-sensitive shortcut menu and the Mini toolbar.

Figure 9.25

Entire row selected

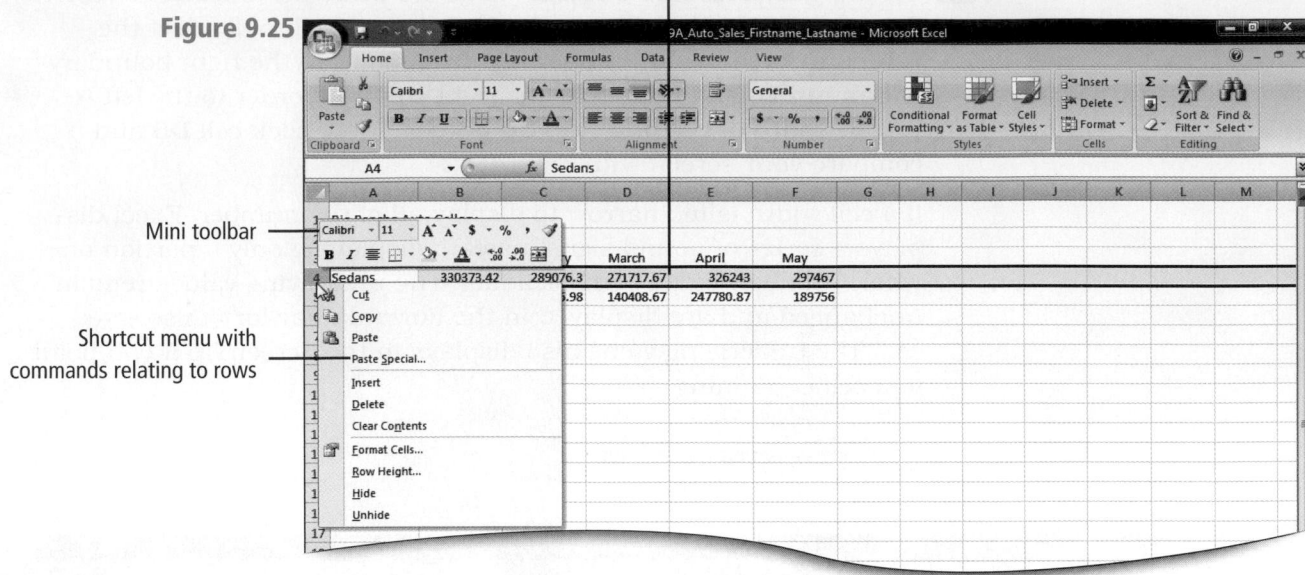

Mini toolbar

Shortcut menu with
commands relating to rows

2 From the displayed shortcut menu, click **Insert**.

A new row 4 is inserted above the selected row, and the existing rows
shift down one row. Additionally, the Insert Options button displays.

Note — Insert Columns By Using the Same Shortcut Menu Technique

Use a similar technique to insert a new column in a worksheet. That is, from
the column heading area, right-click to simultaneously select the column
and display the context-sensitive shortcut menu. Click Insert to insert a new
column and shift the remaining columns to the right. Alternatively, select
the column, and then on the Ribbon, in the Cells group, click the Insert button or the Insert button arrow for additional options.

3 Point to the **Insert Options** button to display its ScreenTip and
its arrow, and then click the button to display a list of options.

From this menu, you can format the new row like the row above or
the row below, or you can leave it unformatted. The default is *Format
Same As Above*.

4 Click **Format Same As Below**.

The new row is formatted, using the format from the row of data
below instead of the row of column titles above, which are centered.
The Insert Options button remains visible until you perform another
screen action.

5 Click cell **A4**, type **Compacts** and then press Tab. Enter the values for *Compacts* for each month, as shown in the following table. Use Tab to confirm each entry and move the active cell across the row.

Type	January	February	March	April	May
Compacts	326485.76	376984.92	367540.57	330373.58	345765.64

6 From the **row heading area**, select **row 8**. On the Ribbon, in the **Cells group**, click the **Delete button arrow**, and then from the displayed menu, click **Delete Sheet Rows**. Alternatively, click the Delete button on the Ribbon; or, right-click the row 8 heading to simultaneously select the row and display a shortcut menu, and then from the displayed shortcut menu, click Delete.

7 Enter the remaining sales figures for *Trucks* as follows, and then compare your screen with Figure 9.26.

Type	January	February	March	April	May
Trucks	309725.48	272558.89	330373.58	289076.55	319583.61

Figure 9.26

Values entered for Compacts and Trucks

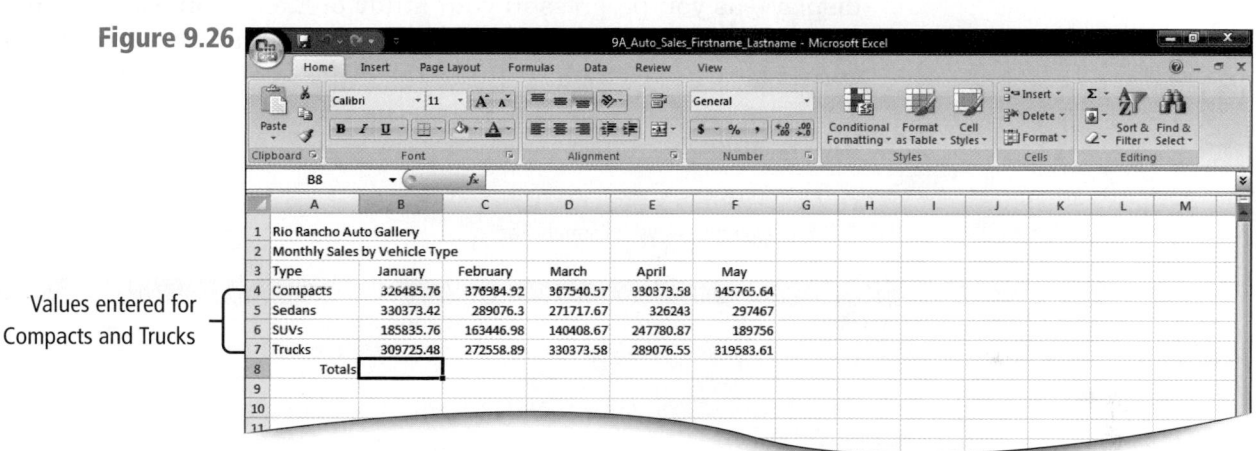

8 **Save** your workbook.

Objective 3
Construct and Copy Formulas, Use the Sum Function, and Edit Cells

Excel performs calculations on numbers; that is why you use Excel. If you make changes to the numbers, Excel automatically *re*-calculates. This is one of the most powerful and valuable features of Excel. You can arrange data in a format of columns and rows in other programs—in a word processing program, for example—and even perform simple calculations. Excel, however, performs complex calculations on numbers.

Recall that a cell contains either a constant value or a formula. Recall also that a formula is an equation that performs mathematical calculations on values in other cells, and then places the result in the cell containing the formula. You can create your own formulas, or you can use one of Excel's prewritten formulas called a ***function***. A function is a prewritten formula that takes one or more values, performs an operation, and then returns a value or values.

Activity 9.08 Constructing a Formula, Using the Sum Function, and Editing Numbers in Cells

In this activity, you will sum the sales of vehicles by month and by type and use various methods to edit numbers within a cell.

1 Click cell **B8** to make it the active cell and type **=**

The equal sign (=) displays in the cell with the insertion point blinking, ready to accept more data. All formulas begin with the = sign, which is the signal that directs Excel to begin a calculation. The Formula Bar displays the = sign, and the Formula Bar Cancel and Enter buttons display.

2 At the insertion point, type **b4** and then compare your screen with Figure 9.27.

A list of Excel functions that begin with the letter *B* may briefly display—as you progress in your study of Excel, you will use functions of this type. Cell B4 is surrounded by a blue border with small corner boxes. This indicates that the cell is part of an active formula. The color used in the box matches the color of the cell reference in the formula.

Your typing displays in Formula Bar

Figure 9.27

Cell outlined in the same color as the cell reference in the formula

Formula started in the active cell

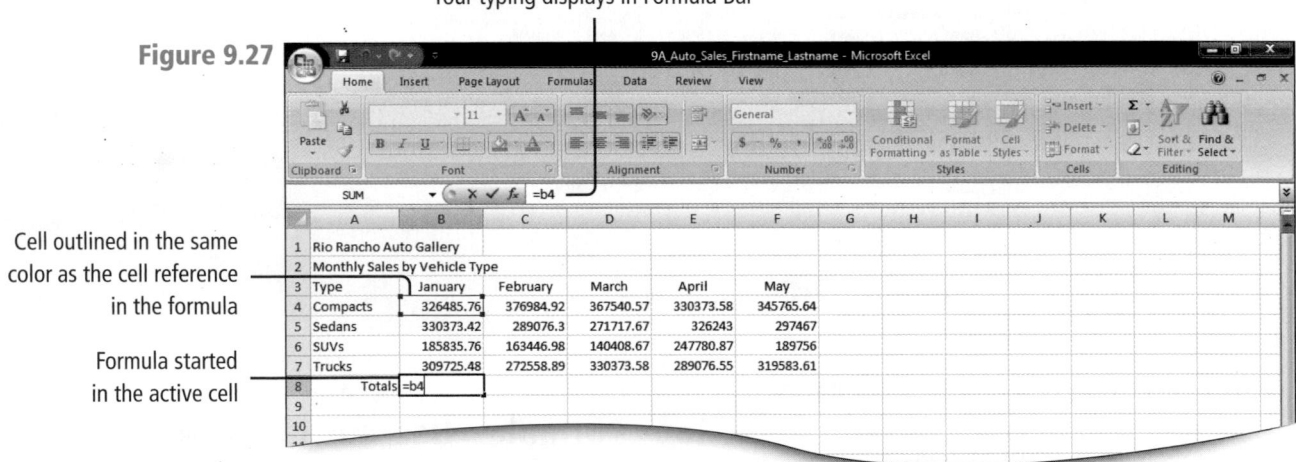

3 At the insertion point, type **+** and then type **b5** Alternatively, use the ⊕ key on your numeric keypad, which does not require the ⇧ Shift key.

A border of another color surrounds cell B5, and the color matches the color of the cell reference in the active formula. Recall that when typing cell references, it is not necessary to use uppercase letters.

4 At the insertion point, type **+b6+b7** and then press Enter.

The result of the formula calculation—*1152420.42*—displays in the cell.

5 Click cell **B8** again to make it the active cell, and then look at the **Formula Bar**. Compare your screen with Figure 9.28.

You created a formula that adds the values in cells B4 through B7, and the result of adding the values in those cells displays in cell B8. Although cell B8 displays the *result* of the formula, the formula itself is displayed in the Formula Bar. This is referred to as the **underlying formula**. Always view the Formula Bar to be sure of the exact content of a cell—*a displayed number may actually be a formula.*

Underlying formula displays in the Formula Bar

Figure 9.28

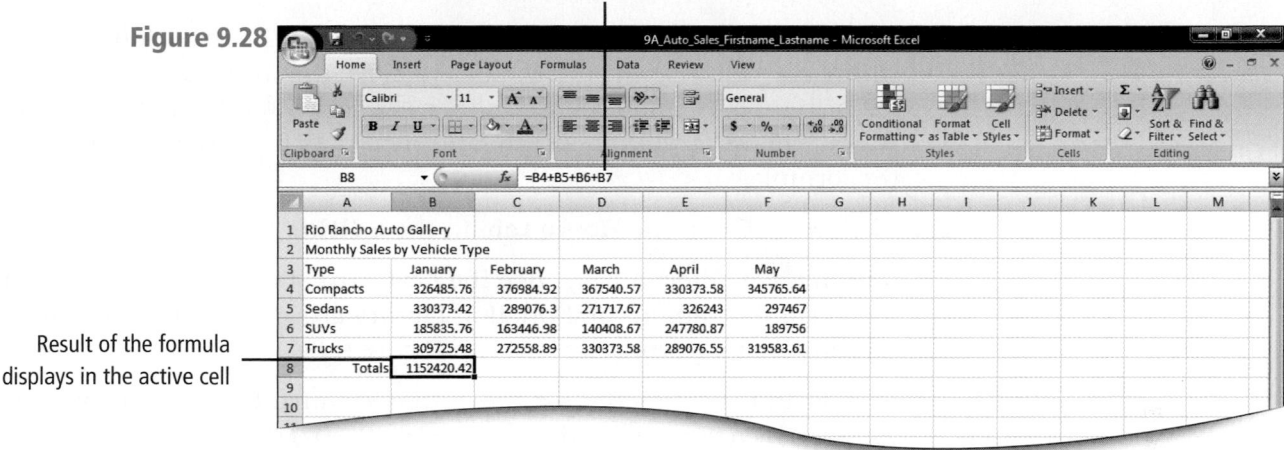

Result of the formula displays in the active cell

6 To change the value in cell B4, click cell **B4,** type **347999.12** and then watch cell **B8** as you press Enter.

Excel recalculates the formula and displays *1173933.78*. Recall that Excel formulas *recalculate* if you change values in a cell that is referenced in the formula. It is not necessary to delete the old value in a cell; selecting the cell and typing a new value replaces the old value with your new typing.

7 In cell **C8**, type **=** to signal the beginning of a formula. Then, point to cell **C4**, click once, and compare your screen with Figure 9.29.

The reference to the cell, C4, is added to the active formula. A moving border surrounds the referenced cell, and the border color and the color of the cell reference in the formula are color coded to match.

The cell referred to outlined with a moving border

Figure 9.29

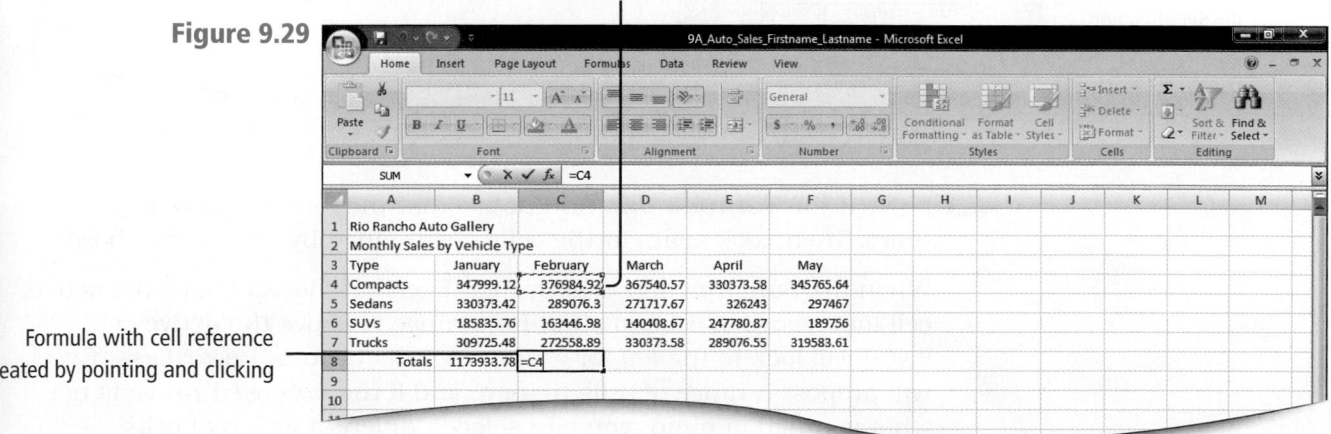

Formula with cell reference created by pointing and clicking

8 At the insertion point, type **+** and then click cell **C5**. Repeat this process to complete the formula to add cells **C4** through **C7**, and then press Enter.

The result of the formula calculation—*1102067.09*—displays in the cell. This method of constructing a formula is the **point and click method**. Constructing a formula by using the point and click method is convenient when the referenced cells are not adjacent to one another.

9 Point to cell **C6**, and then double-click to place the insertion point within the cell. Use the arrow keys to move the insertion point to the left or right of *3*, and then use either Delete or ←Bksp to change *3* to **1** Watch cell **C8** as you press Enter, and then notice the recalculation of the formula.

10 Click cell **D8**. On the **Home tab**, in the **Editing group**, click the **Sum** button Σ ▾. Alternatively, use the keyboard shortcut Alt + = or, on the Formulas tab, in the Function Library group, click the AutoSum button. Compare your screen with Figure 9.30.

Sum is an Excel function—a prewritten formula. Cells D4:D7 are surrounded by a moving border, and =*SUM(D4:D7)* displays in cell D8. The = sign signals the beginning of a formula, *SUM* indicates the type of calculation that will take place (addition), and *(D4:D7)* indicates the range of cells on which the sum operation will be performed. A ScreenTip provides additional information about the action.

Figure 9.30

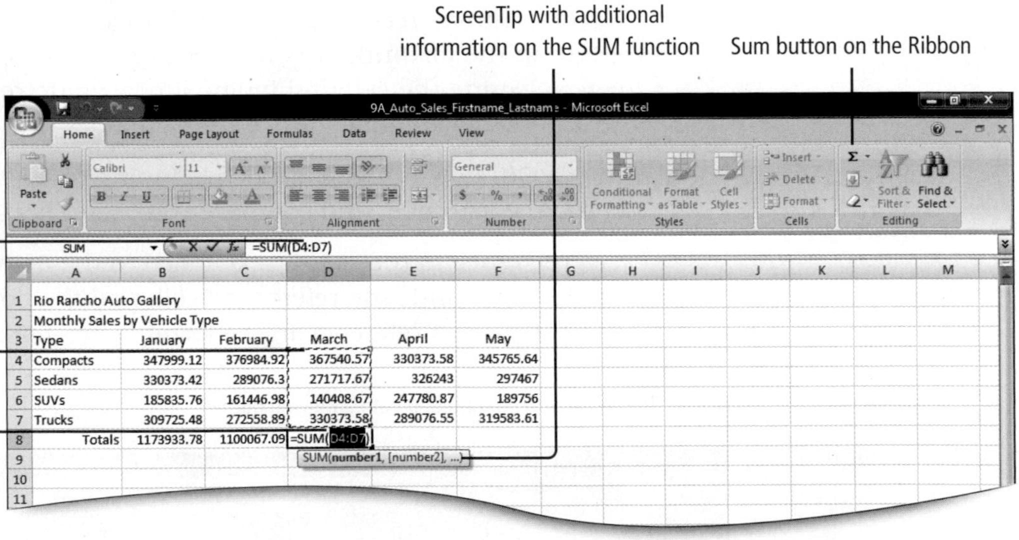

ScreenTip with additional information on the SUM function   Sum button on the Ribbon

Underlying formula displays in Formula Bar

Moving border surrounds the range selected by Sum

Formula generated by the Sum function

11 Look at the **Formula Bar**, and notice that the formula also displays there. Then, look again at the cells surrounded by the moving border.

When the Sum function is activated, Excel first looks *above* the active cell for a range of cells to sum. If no range is above the active cell, Excel will look to the *left* for a range of cells to sum. Regardless, Excel will propose a range of cells to sum, and if the proposed range is not what you had in mind, you can select a different group of cells.

12 Press [Enter] to view the sum of March sales—*1110040.49*—displayed in cell **D8**.

Because the Sum function is frequently used, it has its own button in the Editing group on the Ribbon. A larger version of the button also displays on the Formulas tab in the Function Library group. As you progress in your study of Excel, you will use additional Excel functions. This button is also referred to as ***AutoSum***.

13 Click cell **D4**, and then click in the **Formula Bar** to position the insertion point there. Change the number *6* to **7** so that the value is *377540.57*, and then press [Enter] to recalculate the formula.

The total for March is recalculated to *1120040.49*. You can edit cells in the Formula Bar or inside the cell itself.

14 Select the range **E4:F8**, look at the status bar at the lower right of your screen, and then compare your screen with Figure 9.31.

By selecting a range of cells and including the empty cells at the bottom of each column, you can apply the Sum function to sum several columns at once; the formula for adding each column will be placed in the empty cells at the bottom of each column.

Additionally, when you select a range of cells containing numbers, Excel displays the result of applying the Average, Count, or Sum functions in the status bar. You can see that if you averaged the numbers of the selected cells, the result would be 293255.7813; if you counted the cells in the selection that contain values (text or numbers), the result would be 8, and if you added the numbers in the selected cells, the total would be 2343596.25.

Selected range

Figure 9.31

Empty cells included in selected range

Status bar displays the result of the Average, Count, or Sum function

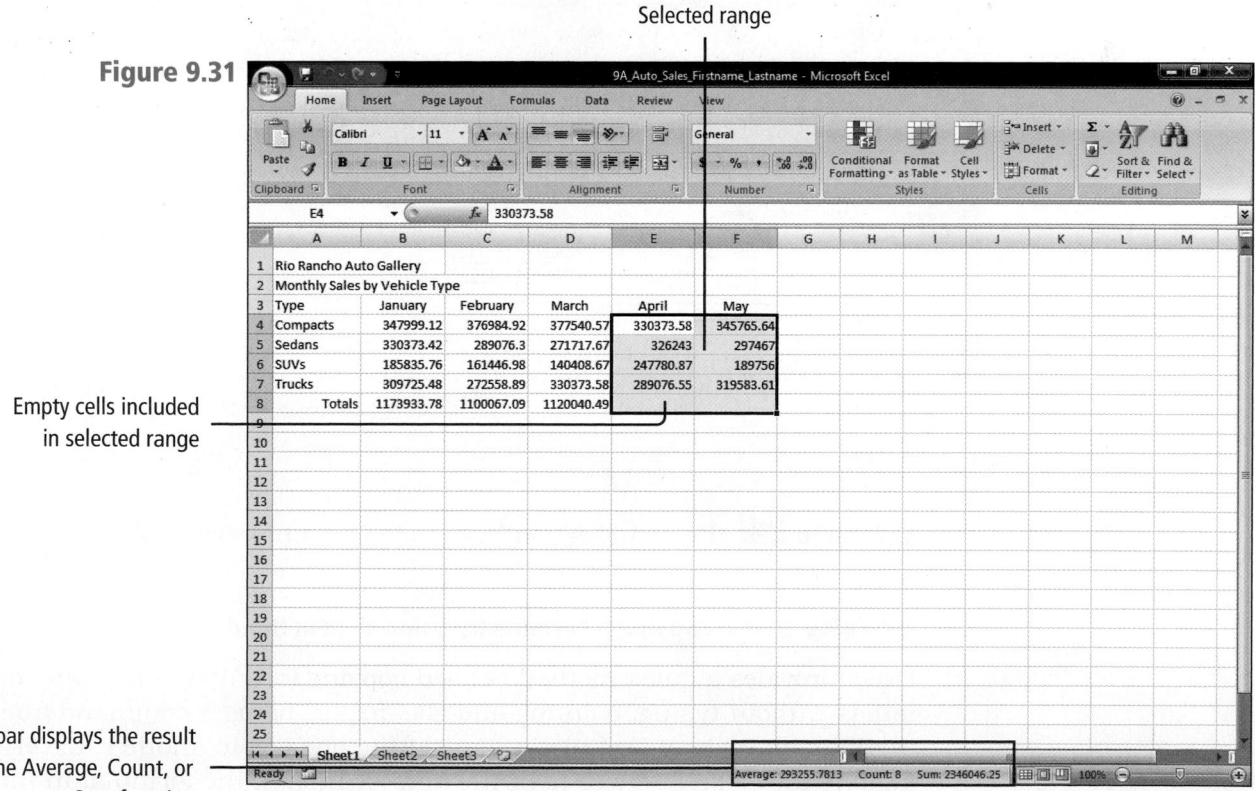

More Knowledge

Multiple Status Bar Calculations

When numerical data is selected, three calculations display in the status bar by default—Average, Count, and Sum. You can display a total of six of these calculations on the status bar by adding the Numerical Count (the number of cells within the selection that contain numbers), Minimum, and Maximum functions to the status bar. To add additional calculations, right-click the status bar and select the calculations you want to display.

15 In the **Editing group**, click the **Sum** button $\boxed{\Sigma ~\cdot}$ or press $\boxed{\text{Alt}}$ + $\boxed{=}$.

Excel places the Sum formula in cells E8 and F8 and a result displays in cells E8 and F8 indicating the sums *1193474* and *1152572.25*. Recall that in the General number format, trailing zeros do not display.

16 Click cell **E8**, and then notice the formula in the **Formula Bar**. Click cell **F8** to view the formula in the **Formula Bar**. Compare your screen with Figure 9.32.

The cells display the result of the calculated function, which is a formula that Excel has prewritten and named.

Formula indicated in Formula Bar

Figure 9.32

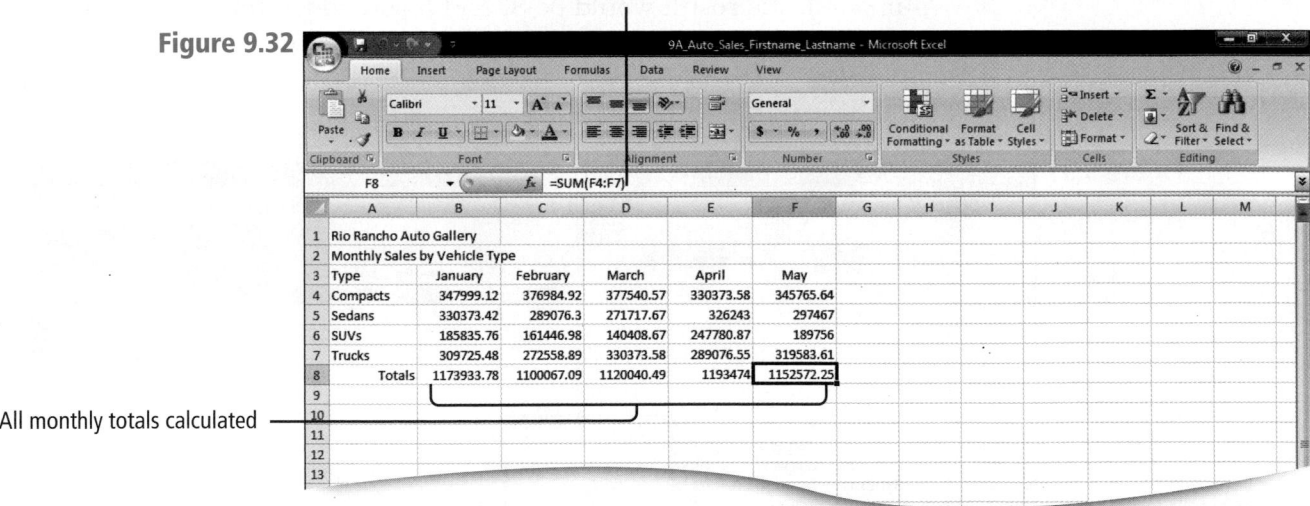

All monthly totals calculated

17 **Save** 💾 the changes you have made to your workbook.

Activity 9.09 Copying a Formula by Using the Fill Handle

Excel provides a quick method—called copying formulas—to create formulas without typing, pointing and clicking, or using a command from the Ribbon. When a formula is copied from one cell to another, Excel adjusts the cell references to fit the new location of the formula. In this activity, you will delete the columns that do not relate to the first quarter, and then copy formulas.

1 From the **column heading area**, select **columns E:F**. On the **Home tab**, in the **Cells group**, click the **Delete button arrow**, and then from the displayed list, click **Delete Sheet Columns**. Alternatively, click the Delete button; or, right-click over the selected columns to display the shortcut menu and click Delete.

Only the monthly sales for the first quarter of the year—January through March—display.

2 Click cell **E4**, hold down Alt, and then press =. Compare your screen with Figure 9.33.

Use this keyboard shortcut as the fastest way to apply the Sum function. Recall that when the Sum function is applied, Excel first looks above the selected cell for a proposed range of cells to sum, and if no data is detected, Excel then looks to the left and proposes a range of cells to sum.

Sum function applied with proposed range of cells to sum

Figure 9.33

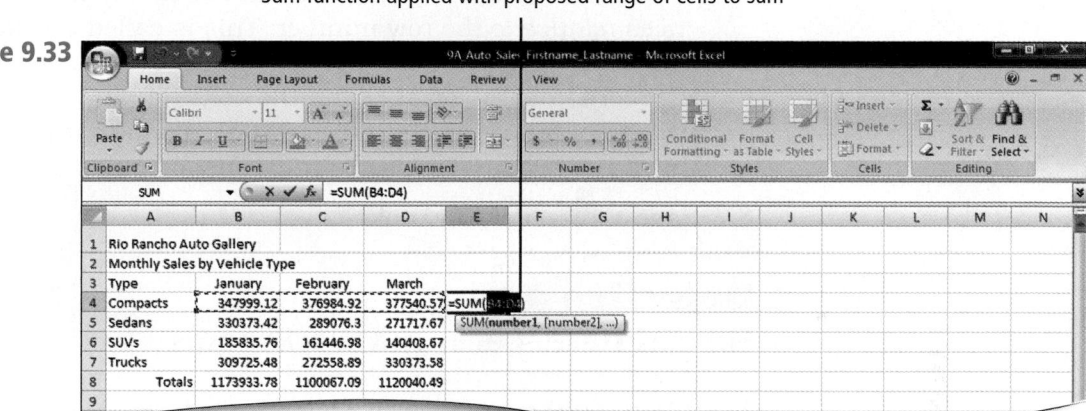

3 On the **Formula Bar**, click the **Enter** button ☑ so that cell **E4** remains the active cell.

The total dollar amount of *Compacts* sold in the quarter is *1102525*. You can see that in cells E5:E8, you need a formula similar to the one in E4, but one that refers to the cells in row 5, row 6, and so forth.

4 With cell **E4** selected, point to the fill handle in the lower right corner of the cell until the ✚ pointer displays. Then, drag downward through cell **E8**. Compare your screen with Figure 9.34.

Figure 9.34

Rows 4 – 8 summed   Auto Fill Options button

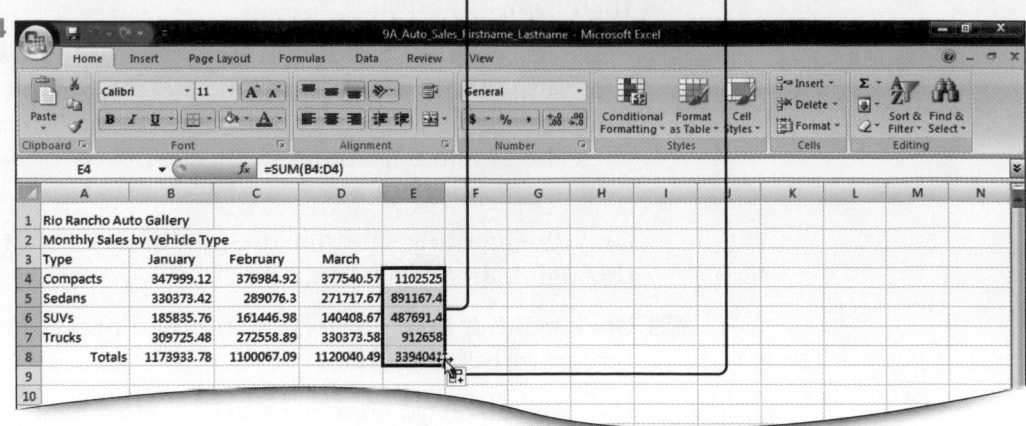

5 Click cell **E5**, look at the **Formula Bar**, and notice the formula =*SUM(B5:D5)*. Click cell **E6**, look at the **Formula Bar**, and then notice the formula =*SUM(B6:D6)*.

In each row, Excel copied the formula but adjusted the cell references *relative to* the row number. This is called a **relative cell reference**—a cell reference based on the relative position of the cell that contains the formula and the cells referred to. The calculation is the same, but it is performed on the cells in that particular row. Use this quick method to insert numerous formulas into spreadsheets.

6 **Save** your workbook.

Objective 4
Format Data, Cells, and Worksheets

Excel has many options for displaying numbers—think of percentages, fractions, or money. Recall that Excel refers to the various ways to write numbers as number formats. Some common number formats are those used for reporting financial information like monthly sales.

Formatting is the process of specifying the appearance of cells and the overall layout of a worksheet. Formatting is accomplished through various commands on the Ribbon, many of which are also available by using shortcut menus or keyboard shortcuts.

Activity 9.10 Formatting Financial Numbers, Using Column AutoFit, and Using Format Painter

The General format is the default format for a number that you type in a cell. Unless you apply a different number format to a cell, Excel will use the General format. The General format displays a number exactly as you type it—with three exceptions, as noted in the table in Figure 9.36.

1 Click cell **B4** so that a cell with numerical data is selected. On the **Home tab**, in the **Number group**, point to the **Dialog Box Launcher** button in the lower right corner, as shown in Figure 9.35.

A ScreenTip displays what the result of clicking the icon will be. A **Dialog Box Launcher** displays in some groups on the Ribbon and opens a related dialog box providing additional options and commands related to that group.

Dialog Box Launcher button

Figure 9.35

Number group on the Home tab

ScreenTip indicates what will display

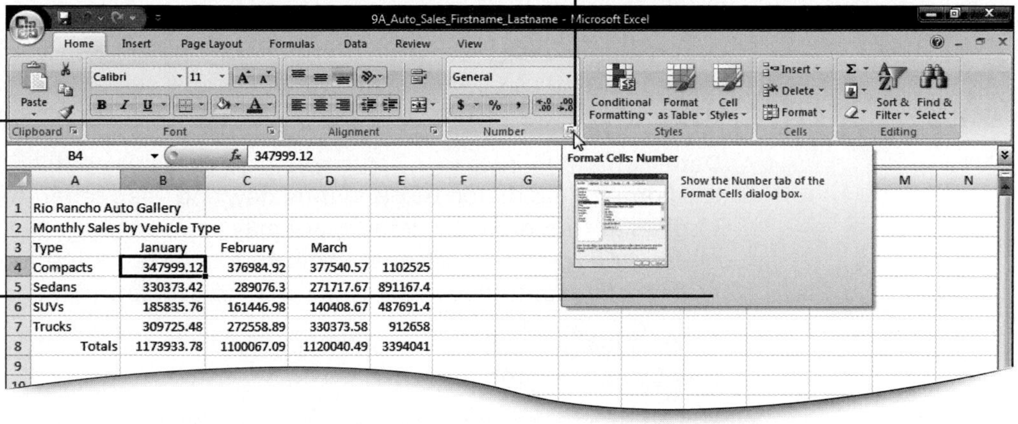

2. Click the **Dialog Box Launcher** button, and then in the displayed **Format Cells** dialog box, on the **Number tab** under **Category**, click each category. As you do so, look at the **Sample** box to view the effect that each number format will have on the selected cell, and then take a moment to study the information about each Number format in the table in Figure 9.36.

Excel Number Formats

Number Format	Description
General	The General format is the default format for a number that you type in a cell. The General format displays a number exactly as you type it—with three exceptions: 1. Extremely long numbers may be abbreviated to a shorthand version of numbers called scientific notation; Excel will still use the underlying value in any calculations. 2. Trailing zeros will not display in the General format. 3. A decimal fraction entered without a number to the left of the decimal point will display with a zero.
Number	Number format is used for the general display of non-currency numbers. The default format has two decimal places, and you may choose to check the option for using a comma as a thousand separator. Negative numbers can display in red, be preceded by a minus sign, be enclosed in parentheses, or display both in red and in parentheses.
Currency	Currency format is used for general monetary values—the U.S. dollar sign is the default symbol.

(Continued)

(Continued)

Number Format	Description
Accounting	Accounting formats line up the currency symbols and decimal points in a column. It is similar to Currency format with two differences—the dollar sign (or other currency symbol) always displays at the left edge of the cell, rather than flush against the first number. Thus, both dollar signs and numbers are vertically aligned in the same column. Also, Accounting format adds a blank space equal to the width of a closing parenthesis on the right side of positive values to ensure that decimal points align if a column has both positive and negative numbers.
Date	Date format provides many common ways to display dates. The default format in the Format Cells dialog box is month, day, and year, separated by a slash. The year displays as four digits by default, but may be changed in the Control Panel to a two-digit display. Formats that begin with an asterisk are subject to change by regional date and time settings specified in the Control Panel.
Time	Time format provides many common ways to display time; formats are subject to change in the manner described above for dates.
Percentage	Percentage format multiplies the cell value by 100 and displays the result with a percent sign. The default is two decimal places.
Fraction	Fraction format displays fractional amounts as actual fractions rather than as decimal values.
Scientific	Scientific format displays numbers in scientific (exponential) notation. This is useful for extremely large numbers.
Text	Text format treats a number as if it were text. The number is left-aligned like text.
Special	Special formats used primarily with database functions such as postal codes, telephone numbers, and taxpayer ID numbers.
Custom	Custom format is used to create your own number format.

Figure 9.36

3 In the **Format Cells** dialog box, click **Cancel**. Hold down Ctrl, select the nonadjacent ranges **B4:E4** and **B8:E8**, and then on the Ribbon, in the **Number group**, click the **Accounting Number Format** button [$ ▾]. Compare your screen with Figure 9.37.

Columns B through D are not wide enough to accommodate the newly formatted numbers and thus display # signs. The *Accounting Number Format* button formats the number with the default Accounting format that uses the U.S. dollar sign. That is, it applies a thousand comma separator where appropriate, inserts a fixed U.S. dollar sign aligned at the left edge of the cell, applies two decimal places, and leaves a small amount of space at the right edge of the cell to accommodate a parenthesis for negative numbers.

Accounting Number Format applied to selected cells

Figure 9.37

Accounting Number Format
button in Number group

Cells too narrow
for newly formatted
numbers display # signs

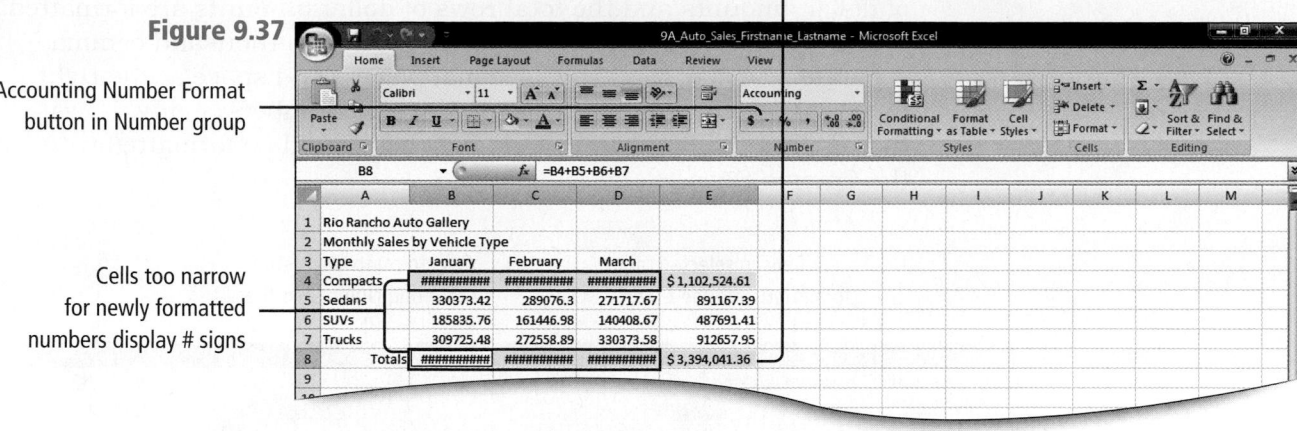

Note — Showing Fewer Decimal Places

Many financial documents do not display values with cents because either it
is unnecessary to be completely precise or it not feasible to determine the
exact number. To decrease the number of decimal places and round to the
nearest whole dollar amount, select the cells, and then on the Home tab of
the Ribbon, in the Number group, click the Decrease Decimal button two
times to show a less precise value by showing fewer decimal places.

4 Select **column B**. On the Ribbon, in the **Cells group**, click the
Format button, and then from the displayed menu, click **AutoFit
Column Width**.

The width of the column is adjusted to accommodate the longest
entry, which is the formatted total in cell B8.

5 Select **columns C:E**. In the **column heading area**, point to the right
boundary of any of the selected columns to display the ⊞ pointer,
and then double-click.

This is an alternative method to apply the AutoFit Column Width
command. Each column width adjusts to accommodate the longest
entry in its column.

6 Select the range **B5:B7**, and then in the **Number group**, click the
Comma Style button ⬚ .

The **Comma Style** inserts thousand comma separators where
appropriate and applies two decimal places. Comma Style also leaves
space at the right to accommodate a parenthesis for negative
numbers.

7 Click cell **B5**. On the Ribbon, in the **Clipboard group**, click the
Format Painter button ⬚. With the ⬚ pointer, select the range
C5:E7, and then compare your screen with Figure 9.38.

Use **Format Painter** to copy the *formatting* of one cell to other cells.
You can see that there are numerous methods to apply formatting
to cells.

When preparing worksheets with financial information, the first row of dollar amounts and the total rows of dollar amounts are formatted in the Accounting Number Format; that is, with thousand comma separators, dollar signs, two decimal places, and space at the right to accommodate a parenthesis for negative numbers, if any. Rows that are not the first row or the total row should be formatted with the Comma Style.

Cells in selected range formatted with the Comma Style

Cells formatted with the Accounting Number Format

Figure 9.38

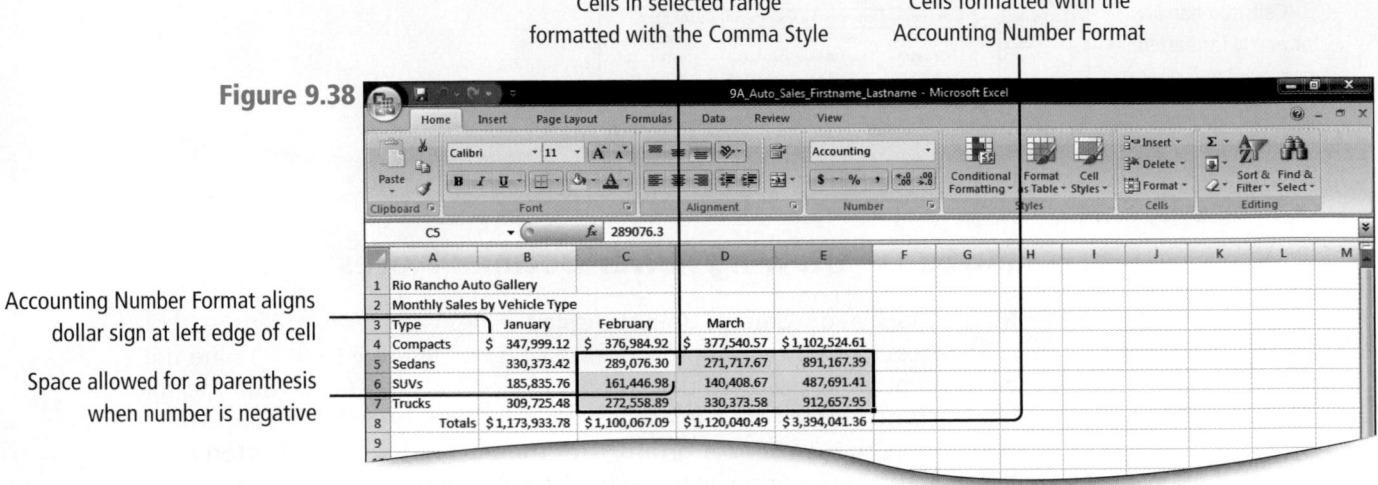

Accounting Number Format aligns dollar sign at left edge of cell

Space allowed for a parenthesis when number is negative

Note — Double-click Format Painter to Copy Formatting to Multiple Selections

Double-clicking the Format Painter button causes it to remain active until you click the button again to turn it off. Use this technique to copy cell formatting to two or more cells that are not adjacent.

8 Select the range **B8:E8**. In the **Font group**, click the **Borders button arrow** to display a *gallery* of commonly used border styles. Compare your screen with Figure 9.39.

A gallery displays a list of potential results. The Borders button displays the most recently used border style; clicking the button, rather than the arrow, applies the most recently used style as indicated by the button.

Borders arrow

Figure 9.39

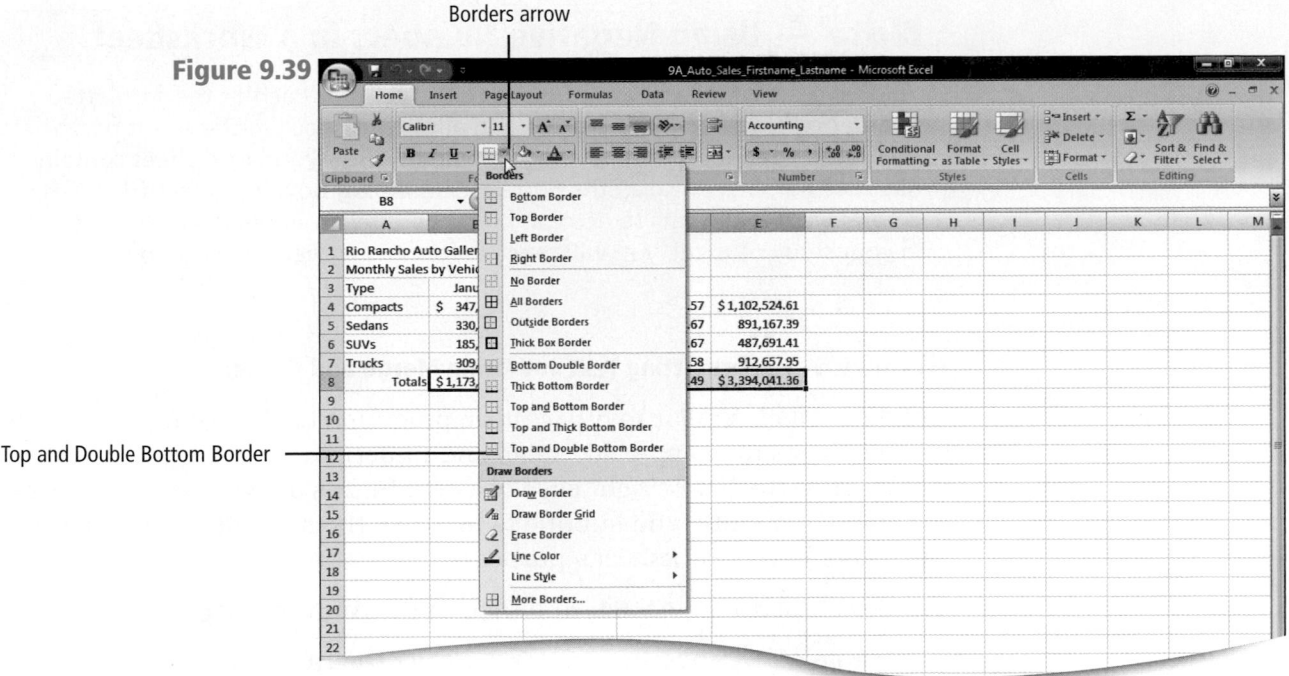

Top and Double Bottom Border

9 From the displayed list, click **Top and Double Bottom Border**. Click any empty cell to deselect the range, and then compare your screen with Figure 9.40.

This is a common way to apply borders to financial information. The single border indicates that calculations were performed on the numbers above, and the double border indicates that the information is complete.

Figure 9.40

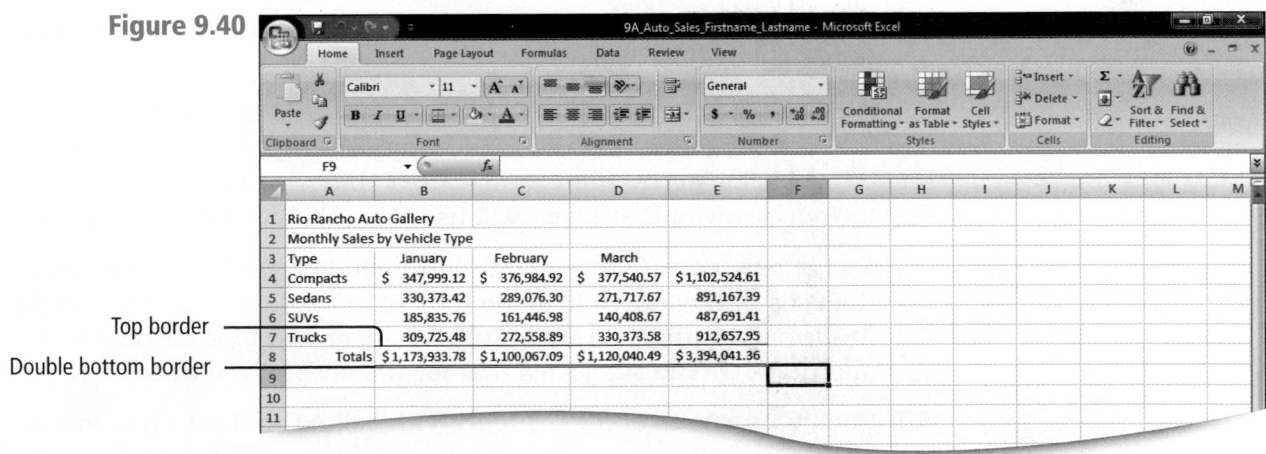

Top border
Double bottom border

10 Save 💾 your workbook.

Note — Using Negative Numbers in a Worksheet

You can see a small amount of space to the right of each of the formatted number cells. The formats you applied allow this space in the event parentheses are needed to indicate negative numbers. If your worksheet contains negative numbers, display the Format Cells dialog box and select from among various formats to accommodate negative numbers. As you progress in your study of Excel, you will practice formatting negative numbers.

Activity 9.11 Formatting Text and Using Merge and Center

Use techniques similar to other Office programs to change fonts; you can add emphasis by using bold, italic, and underline, and align text in the center, or at the left or right edge of a cell. In this activity, you will format the worksheet's title and subtitle to increase their visibility and inform the reader of the worksheet's purpose.

1 Select the range **A1:E1**, and then in the **Alignment group**, click the **Merge and Center** button. Select the range **A2:E2**, right-click over the selection to display the shortcut menu and Mini toolbar, and then on the Mini toolbar, click the **Merge and Center** button.

The Merge and Center command joins the selected cells into one larger cell and centers the contents in the new cell; cells B1:E1 can no longer be selected individually because they are merged into cell A1. Access the Merge and Center command by using either method; this command works only on a single row at a time.

2 Click cell **A1**, which contains the merged and centered text *Rio Rancho Auto Gallery*. On the **Home tab**, in the **Font group**, click the **Font button arrow** [Calibri].

3 At the top of the list, under **Theme Fonts**, point to **Cambria**, and notice *(Headings)* to the right.

A ***theme*** is a predefined set of colors, fonts, lines, and fill effects that look good together and that can be applied to your entire workbook or to specific items—for example, to a chart or table. As you progress in your study of Excel, you will use more theme features.

Cambria is a ***serif*** font—a font that includes small line extensions on the ends of the letters to guide the eye in reading from left to right. In the default theme, *Cambria* is the suggested font for headings, and *Calibri* is the suggested font for the body of the worksheet.

4 Click **Cambria** to apply the font. With cell **A1** still selected, in the **Font group**, click the **Font Size button arrow** [11], and then point to **14**, and then **16**, and then **18**, and notice how the text expands as you point to each size—this is ***Live Preview***. Click **18**.

Live Preview is a technology that shows the results of applying an editing or formatting change as you move the pointer over the items presented in the gallery or list.

5 With cell **A1** selected, in the **Font group**, click the **Bold** button **B**.

The Bold *font style* is applied to your text. Font styles are used to emphasize text by using bold, italic, and underline.

6 With cell **A1** still selected, in the lower right corner of the **Font group**, click the **Dialog Box Launcher** button to display the **Font tab** of the **Format Cells** dialog box. Notice that *Cambria* is selected and that a preview of the font is also displayed under **Preview**.

7 Under **Font style**, click **Bold Italic**, and then notice that the Preview changes to reflect your selection. Click the **Color arrow**. Under **Theme Colors**, point to the fourth box to display the ScreenTip *Dark Blue, Text 2*, and then in that column of colors, click the next to last color—**Dark Blue, Text 2, Darker 25%**—as shown in Figure 9.41.

From the Format Cells dialog box, you can apply multiple formats at one time in this manner.

Figure 9.41

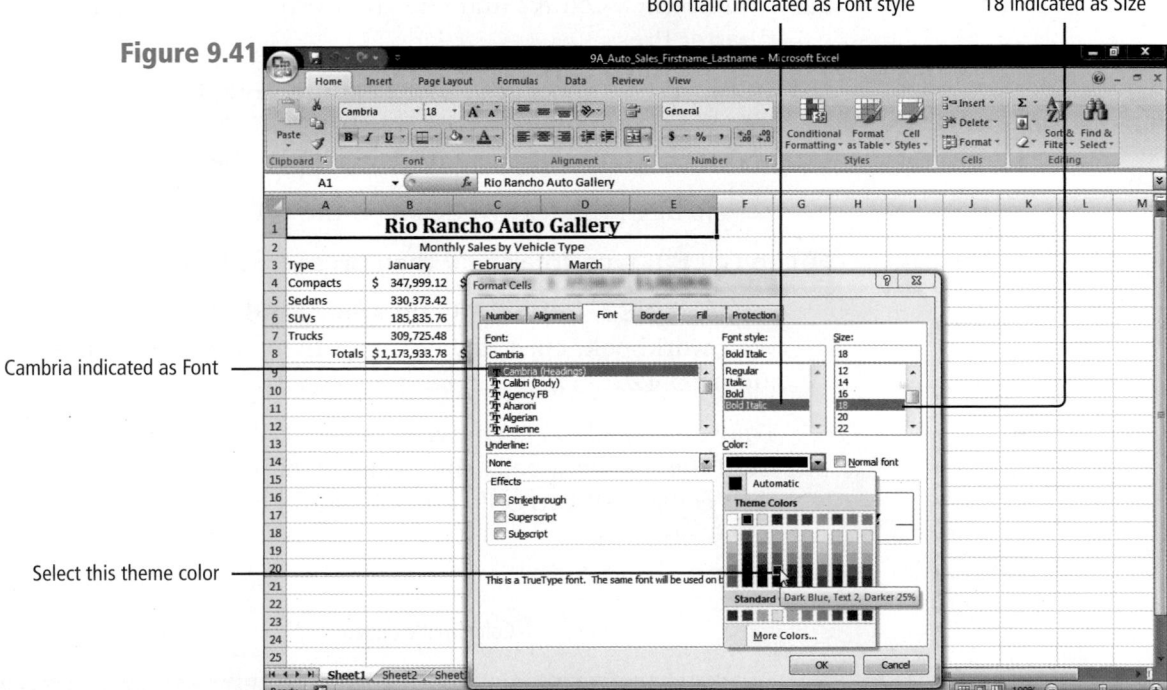

Bold Italic indicated as Font style

18 indicated as Size

Cambria indicated as Font

Select this theme color

8 Click **OK**. With cell **A1** still selected, in the **Font group** click the **Underline** button **U**.

From the Ribbon, you can apply some common formats such as this one. The **Underline** button places a single underline under the *contents* of a cell. The Bold, Italic, and Underline buttons on the Ribbon are **toggle buttons**, which means that you can click the button one time to turn the formatting on and click it again to turn it off.

9 With cell **A1** selected, in the **Font group** click the **Underline** button **U** again to turn off Underline.

The Underline font style is removed from the text, but the Bold and Italic font styles remain.

10 With cell **A1** selected, in the **Font group**, click the **Fill Color button arrow** 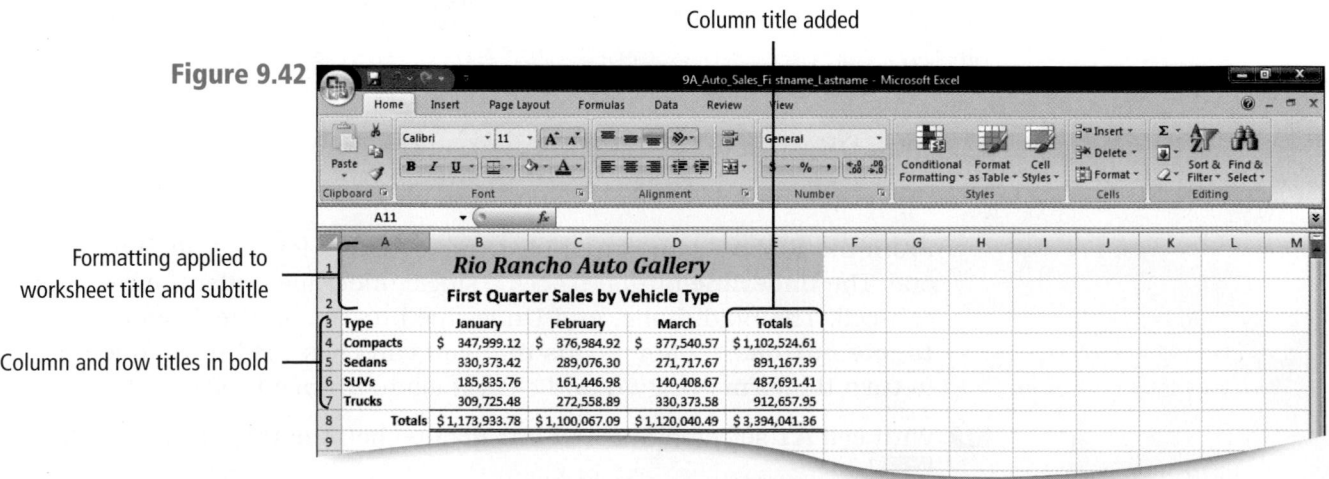. On the displayed color palette, under **Theme Colors**, in the fourth column, click the second color—**Dark Blue, Text 2, Lighter 80%**.

The background of the cell—its *fill color*—changes. If your printer does not print in color, the colors will print as shades of gray, so select light colors to provide better contrast. Colors are especially distinctive if your workbook will be viewed on a screen.

11 Point to cell **A2**, right-click, on the displayed Mini toolbar, click the **Increase Font Size** button two times, and as you click, notice that the new Font Size number displays on both the Ribbon and the Mini toolbar. Then, on the Mini toolbar, click the **Bold** button. Move the mouse pointer slightly away so that the Mini toolbar fades out, view your formatting, and then click any cell to cancel the selection and close the Mini toolbar.

12 Double-click cell **A2** and edit the word *Monthly* to change it to **First Quarter** Press Enter.

13 Select **row 2**, and in the **row heading area**, drag the lower border of **row 2** down to increase the row height to **35 pixels**. Select cell **A2**, and then in the **Alignment group**, click the **Middle Align** button to align the text vertically in the cell.

14 In cell **E3**, type **Totals** and then press Enter. Select the nonadjacent ranges **A3:E3** and **A4:A8** and apply **Bold** emphasis. **Save** your workbook, click any cell, and then compare your screen with Figure 9.42.

The text in cell E3 is centered because the centered format continues from the adjacent cell. The same formatting will be applied to adjacent cells until two cells are left blank, and then the formatting is not continued.

Column title added

Figure 9.42

Formatting applied to worksheet title and subtitle

Column and row titles in bold

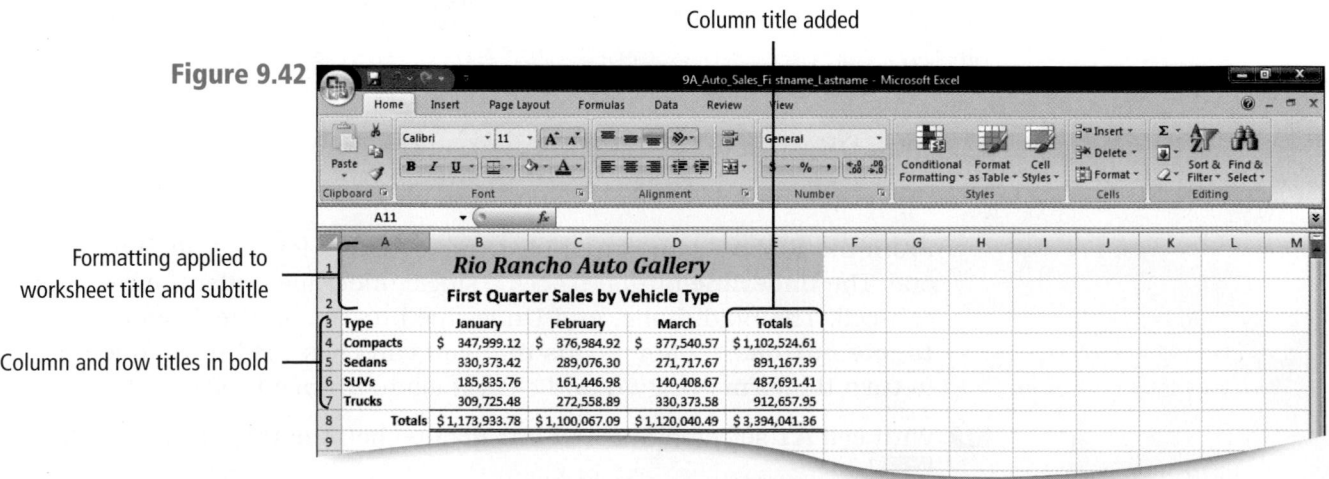

Objective 5
Close and Reopen a Workbook

You can save and close a workbook and then reopen it later to continue working. For example, at this point in this Project, you may want to close the workbook and continue working later.

Activity 9.12 Closing and Reopening an Existing Workbook

1 To close the workbook, from the **Office** menu 🗔, click **Close**—if there are changes to be saved, Excel will prompt you to save before closing. In the upper right corner of your screen, click the **Close** button **X** to exit Excel. Alternatively, from the Office menu, click Exit Excel. Or, to simultaneously close your workbook and close the Excel program, from the Office menu in the lower right corner, click Exit Excel.

2 To reopen the workbook, **start** Excel, and then display the **Office** menu 🗔. From the list of **Recent Documents**, click your workbook name if it displays. Alternatively, click the Open button and navigate to your storage location, select your workbook, and then click Open.

Objective 6
Chart Data

A **chart** is a graphic representation of data in a worksheet. For the reader, data presented as a chart is usually easier to understand than a table of numbers.

Activity 9.13 Charting Data

In this activity, you will create a column chart showing the monthly sales of vehicles by type during the first quarter. The chart will allow Sandy Cizek, the Auto Sales Manager, to see a pattern of overall monthly sales and a pattern of monthly sales by vehicle type.

1 Select the range **A3:E8**. On the Ribbon, click the **Insert tab**, and then in the **Charts group**, click **Column** to display a gallery of Column **chart types**.

Various chart types are used to chart data in a way that is meaningful to the reader—common examples are column charts, pie charts, and line charts. A **column chart** is useful for illustrating comparisons among related numbers.

2 From the displayed gallery of column chart types, under **2-D Column**, point to the first chart to display the ScreenTip *Clustered Column*, and then click to select it. Compare your screen with Figure 9.43.

A column chart displays in the worksheet, and the charted data is bordered by colored lines. Because the chart object is selected—surrounded by a border and displaying sizing handles—*contextual tools* named *Chart Tools* display and add *contextual tabs* next to the standard tabs on the Ribbon.

Contextual tools enable you to perform specific commands related to the selected object, and display one or more contextual tabs that contain related groups of commands that you will need when working with the type of object that is selected. Contextual tools display only when needed for a selected object; when you deselect the object, the contextual tools no longer display.

Cells outlined in blue represented in chart columns

Cells outlined in green represent the legend

Chart Tools indicates that tools for selected object added to the Ribbon

Chart Tools contextual tabs added to standard Ribbon tabs

Figure 9.43

Cells outlined in purple represent category labels

Clustered column chart displays in the worksheet

Border and sizing handles indicate chart is selected

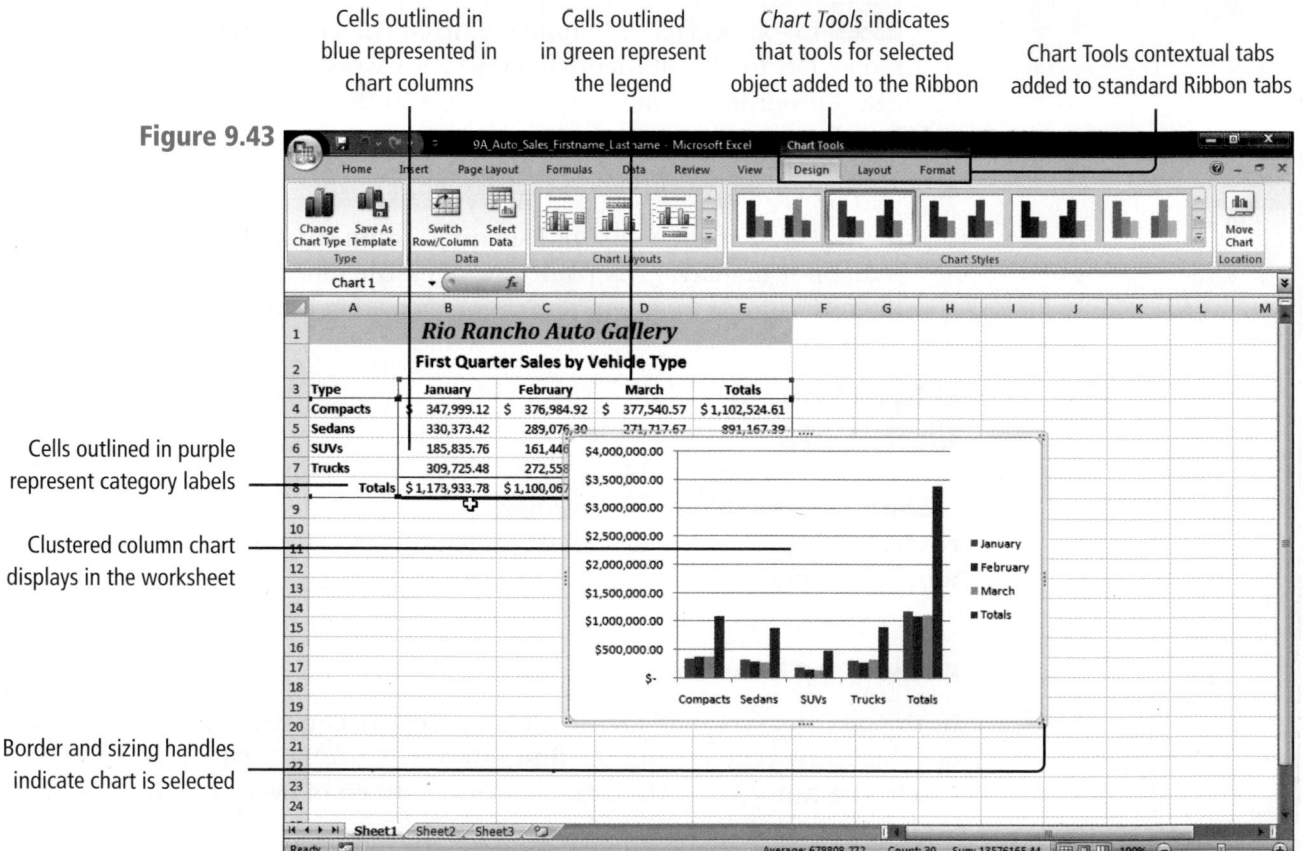

3 Point to the top border of the chart to display the pointer, hold down the left mouse button, and then drag the upper left corner of the chart just inside the upper left corner of cell **A10**, approximately as shown in Figure 9.44.

Based on the data in your worksheet, Excel constructs a column chart and adds *category labels*—the labels that display along the bottom of the chart to identify the category of data. This area is referred to as the *category axis* or the *x-axis*. Excel uses the row titles as the category names.

On the left, Excel includes a numerical scale upon which the charted data is based; this is referred to as the *value axis* or the *y-axis*. On the right, a *legend*, which identifies the patterns or colors that are assigned to the categories in the chart, displays.

Figure 9.44

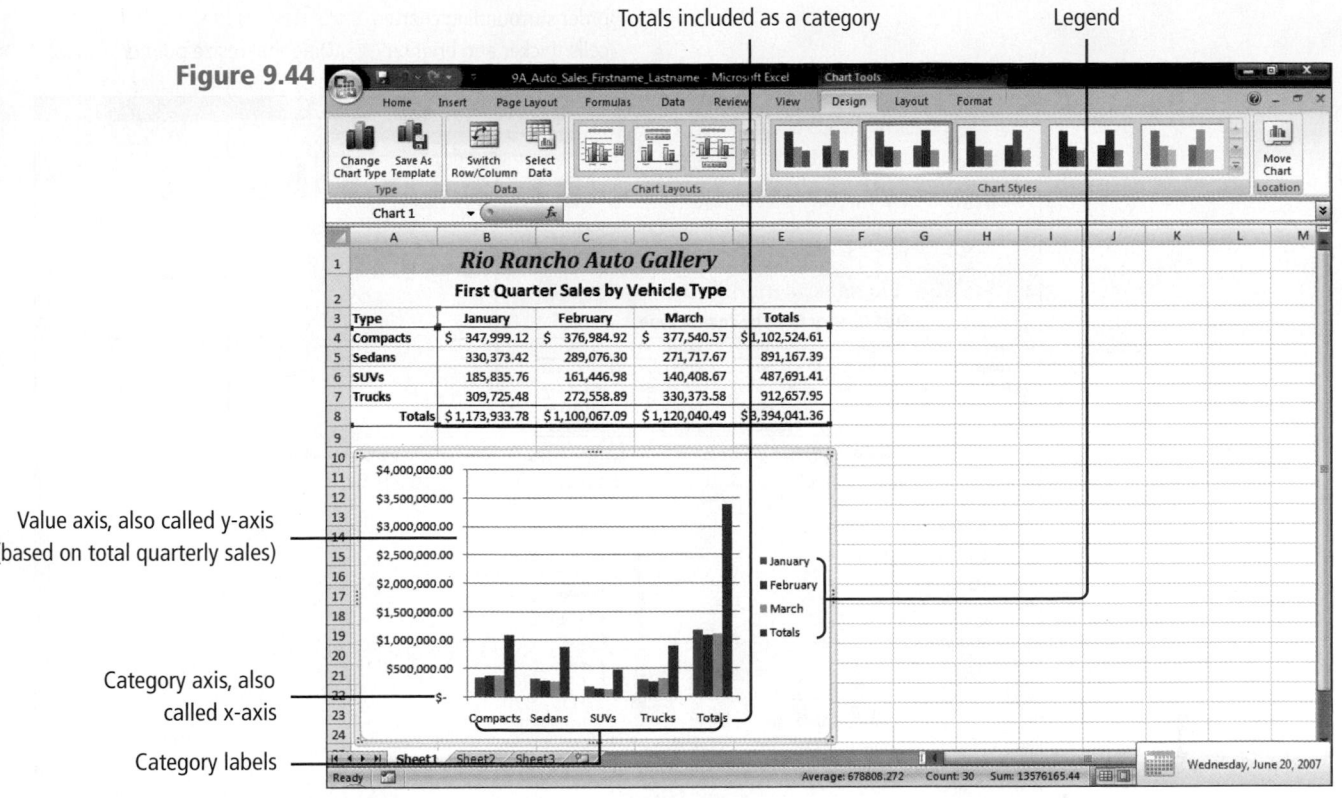

Totals included as a category

Legend

Value axis, also called y-axis (based on total quarterly sales)

Category axis, also called x-axis

Category labels

4 On the Ribbon, locate the three contextual tabs that are active under **Chart Tools—Design**, **Layout**, and **Format**.

When a chart is selected, Chart Tools become available and these three tabs—Design, Layout, and Format—provide commands for working with the chart. When the chart is not selected, the Chart Tools do not display.

5 Point to the lower right corner of cell **E8** to display the ⬉ pointer, and then notice that the blue border surrounding the group of charted cells becomes thicker and brighter in color. Compare your screen with Figure 9.45.

You can adjust the chart by selecting a different group of cells to chart. On this chart, Sandy Cizek, the Auto Sales Manager for Rio Rancho Auto Gallery, wants to see only the sales by month and not the total sales for the quarter.

When charting data, typically, you should not include totals—include only the comparable data.

Figure 9.45

Border surrounding charted cells thicker and brighter   Diagonal resize pointer

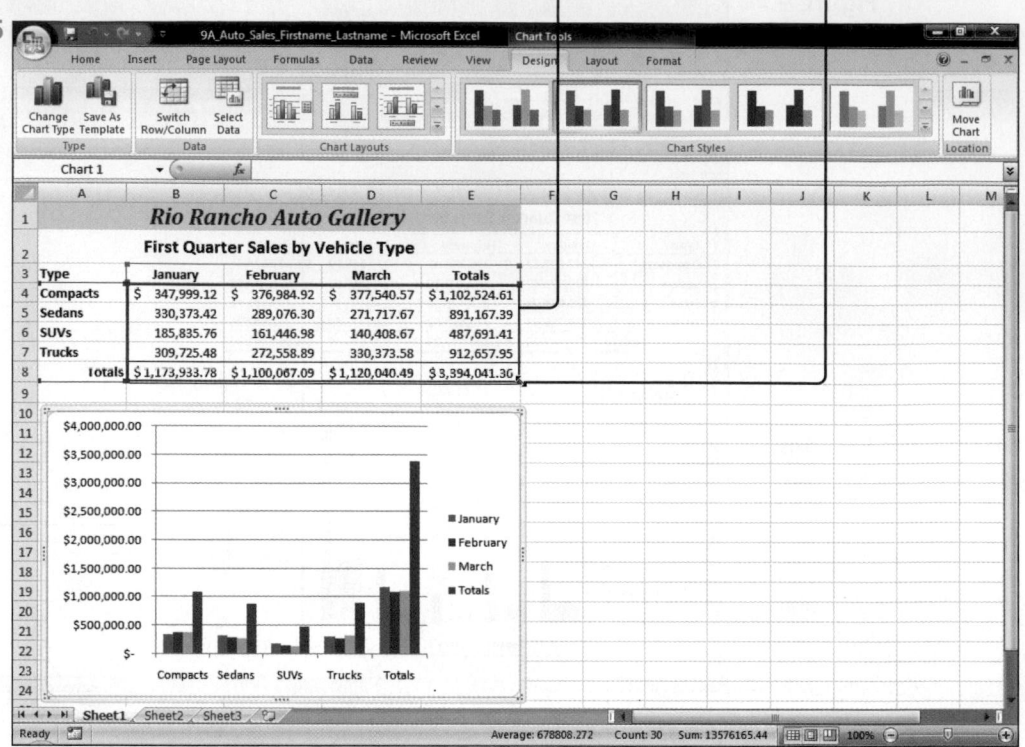

6 Drag the ⬉ pointer up and to the left until only the monthly dollar amounts in the range **B4:D7** are surrounded by the blue border. Release the left mouse button and notice the changes in your chart. Compare your screen with Figure 9.46.

Each of the twelve cells bordered in blue is referred to as a ***data point***—a value that originates in a worksheet cell. Each data point is represented in the chart by a ***data marker***—a column, bar, area, dot, pie slice, or other symbol in a chart that represents a single data point. Related data points form a ***data series***; for example, there is a data series for *January*, for *February*, and for *March*. Each data series has a unique color or pattern represented in the chart legend.

Figure 9.46

Only sales figures for January, February, and March display

Totals no longer included in the charted data

Color for each data series defined in legend

Each value in the selected range is a data point

Data markers (columns) represent each data point

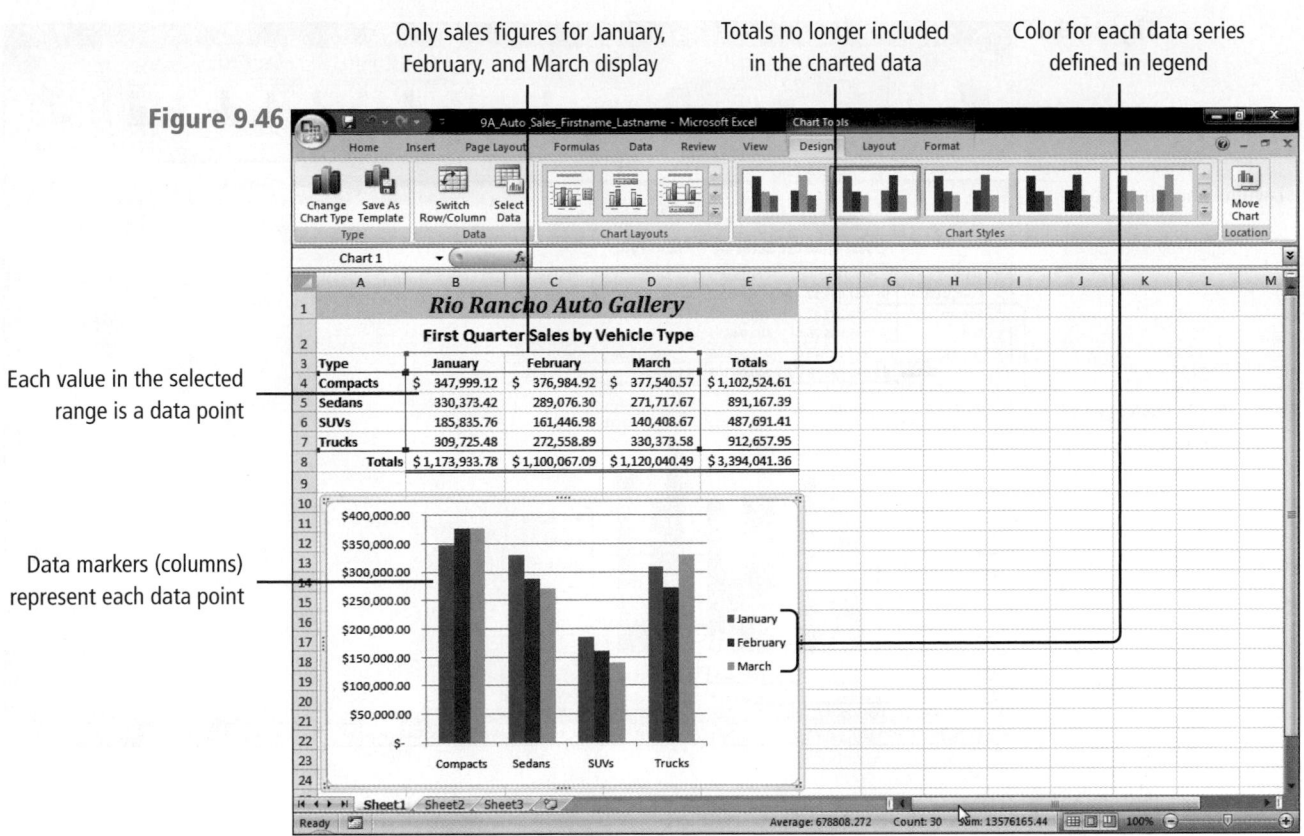

7 On the **Design tab** of the Ribbon, in the **Data group**, click the **Switch Row/Column** button, and then compare your chart with Figure 9.47.

In this manner, you can easily change the categories of data from the row titles, which is the default, to the column titles. Whether you use row or column titles as your category names depends on how you want to view your charted data. In this instance, the Sales Manager wants to see monthly sales and the breakdown of vehicle type within each month.

Figure 9.47

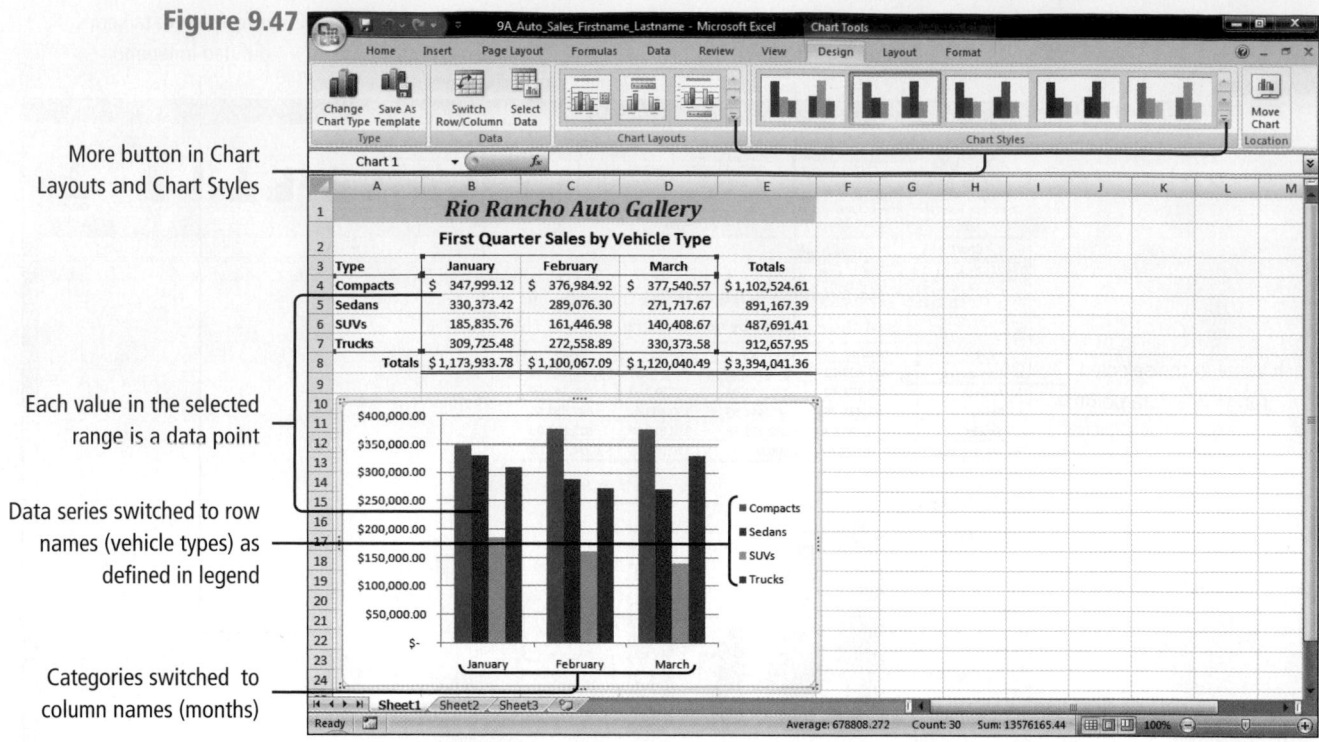

More button in Chart
Layouts and Chart Styles

Each value in the selected
range is a data point

Data series switched to row
names (vehicle types) as
defined in legend

Categories switched to
column names (months)

8 On the **Design tab** of the Ribbon, in the **Chart Layouts group**, locate, and then click the **More** button ⬇, and then compare your screen with Figure 9.48.

From the *Chart Layouts gallery*, you can select a predesigned *chart layout*—the combination of chart elements you want to display, which can include a title, legend, labels for the columns, and the table of charted cells.

Chart Layouts gallery

Figure 9.48

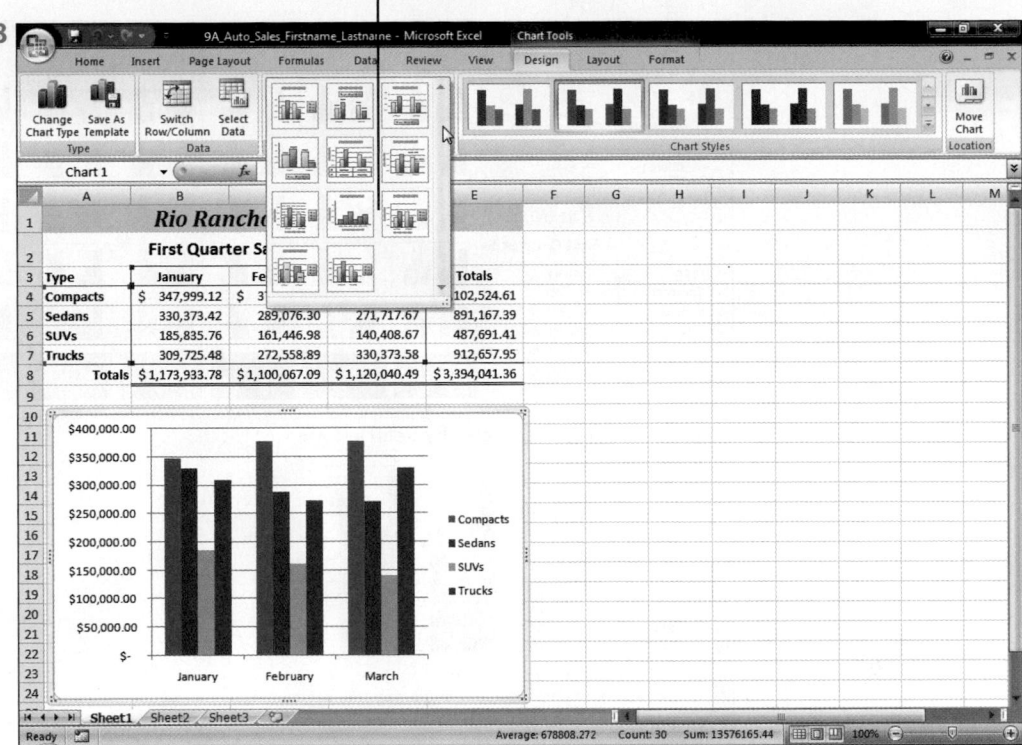

9 Click several different layouts to see the effect on your chart, and then using the ScreenTips as your guide, locate and click **Layout 1**.

10 In the chart, point to the text *Chart Title*, right-click, and then from the shortcut menu, click **Edit Text**. Alternatively, select the title and double-click. Delete the text, and then type **First Quarter Sales by Vehicle Type**

11 Click in a white area *inside* the chart to deselect the chart title, but leaving the chart itself selected. On the **Design tab**, in the **Chart Styles group**, point to, and then click the **More** button [⬇], and then compare your screen with Figure 9.49.

The **Chart Styles gallery** displays. Here you can select from among a large array of pre-defined **chart styles**—the overall visual look of the chart in terms of its graphic effects, colors, and backgrounds. For example, you can have flat or beveled columns, colors that are solid or transparent, and backgrounds that are dark or light.

Figure 9.49

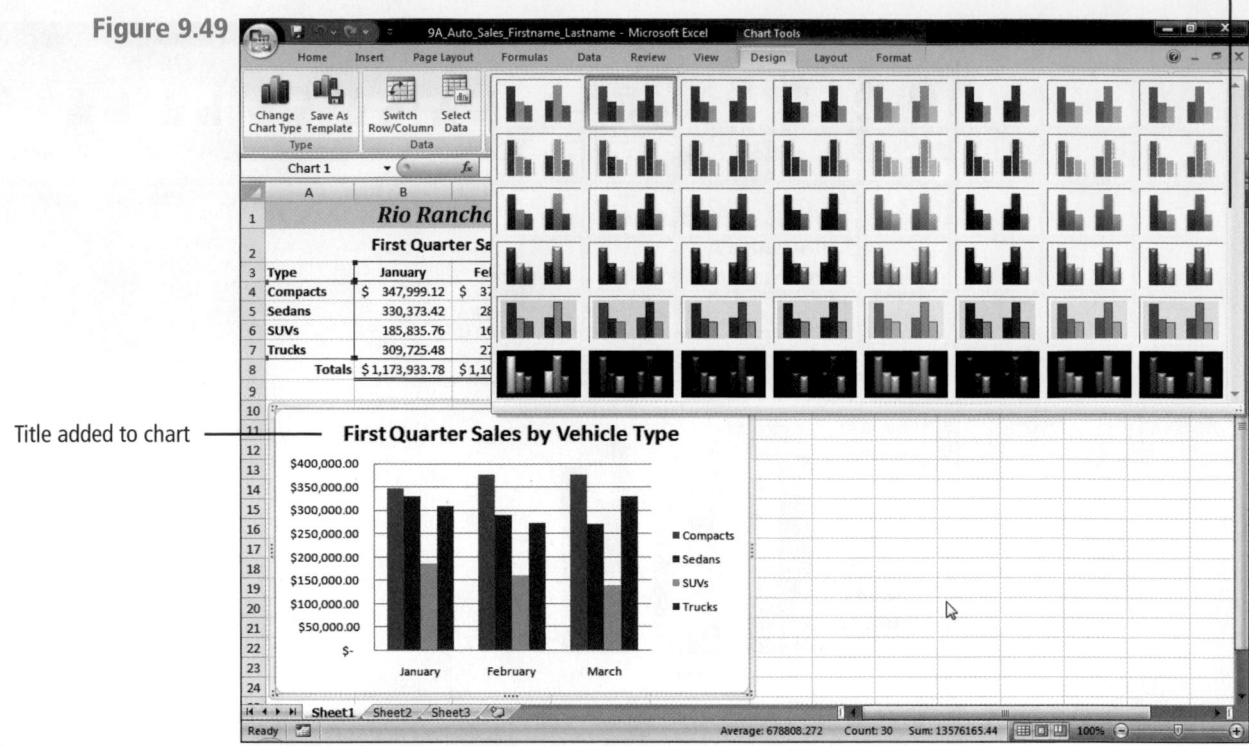

Title added to chart

12 Click several different styles to see the effect on your chart, and then using the ScreenTips as your guide, locate and click **Style 26**.

This style uses a white background, formats the columns by using theme colors, and applies a slightly beveled effect to the columns.

With this clear visual representation of the data, Mr. Cizek can see that sales of compact cars have risen in each month of the quarter. He can also see that sales of sedans and SUVs have declined steadily in each month of the quarter. Finally, Mr. Cizek can see that truck sales declined slightly, and then rose again in March, possibly due to spring demand from local ranchers and farmers.

13 In your chart, notice that the values on the **value axis** include two decimal places. Then, on the Ribbon, click the **Layout tab**. In the **Axes group**, click the **Axes** button, point to **Primary Vertical Axis**, and then compare your screen with Figure 9.50.

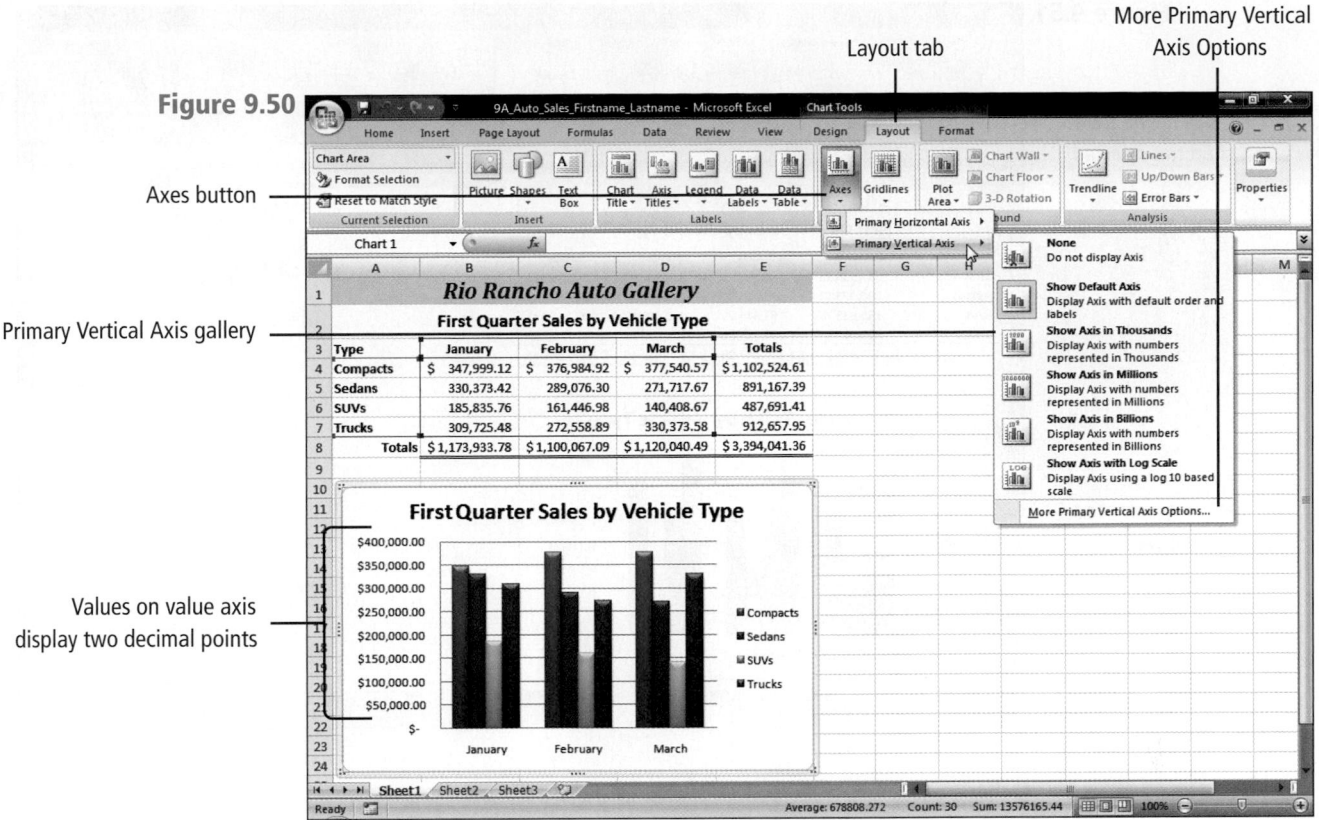

Figure 9.50

Layout tab

More Primary Vertical Axis Options

Axes button

Primary Vertical Axis gallery

Values on value axis display two decimal points

14 At the bottom of the gallery, click **More Primary Vertical Axis Options** to display the **Format Axis** dialog box. In the displayed dialog box, in the column at the left, click **Number**, and then in the **Decimal places** box, delete the existing number, type **0** and then click **Close**.

The decimal places are removed from the value axis, resulting in a less cluttered look, and the value axis area of the chart is selected.

15 Click any cell to deselect the chart, and notice that the *Chart Tools* no longer display in the Ribbon. Compare your screen with Figure 9.51.

Contextual tabs related to contextual tools in Office 2007 programs display when an object is selected, and then are removed from view when the object is deselected.

Figure 9.51

Chart Tools removed from
view when chart not selected

Decimal points removed
from value axis

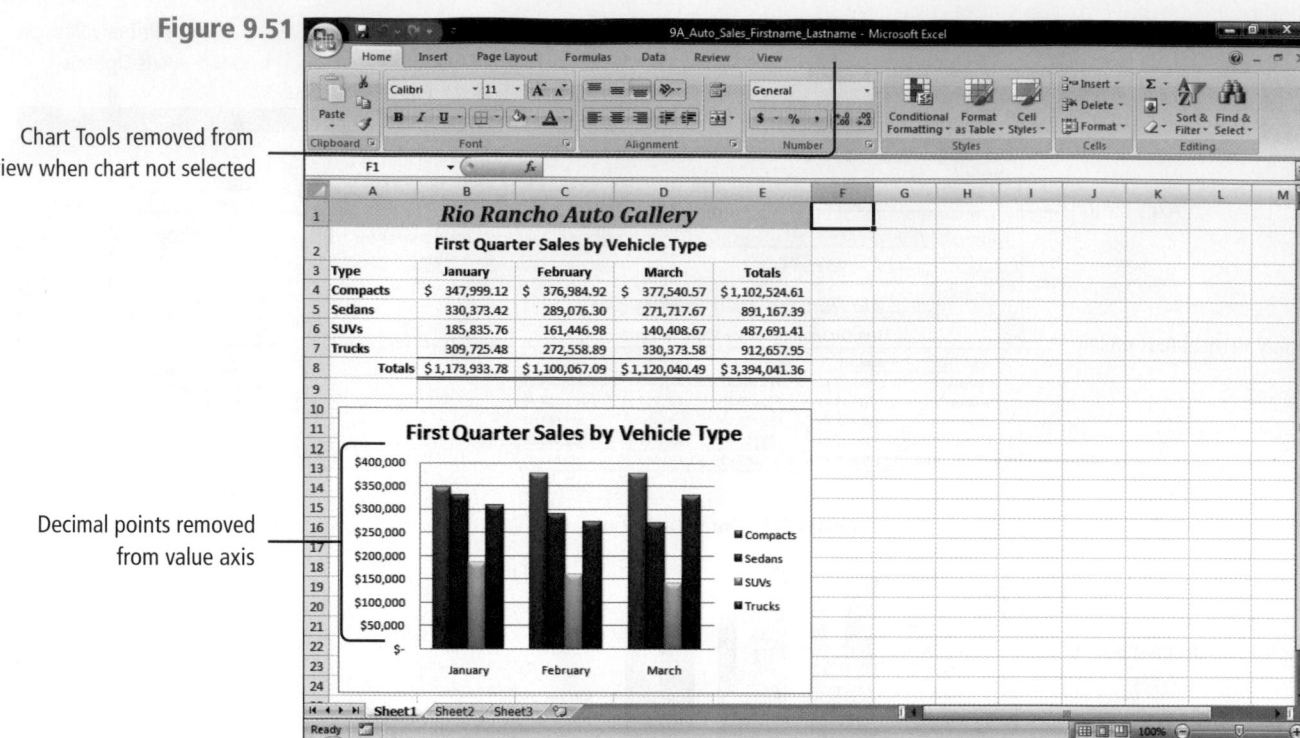

16 Save 💾 your workbook.

More Knowledge

A Chart Can Occupy a Separate Sheet in the Workbook

When a chart displays as an object within the worksheet, it is referred to as an *embedded chart*. On the Design tab of the Ribbon, the last button—Move Chart—creates a new workbook sheet and places the chart on a separate workbook sheet. An embedded chart is useful when you want to view or print a chart on the same page as its source data.

Objective 7
Use Page Layout View, Prepare a Worksheet for Printing, and Close Excel

Before you print a worksheet, use *Page Layout view* and the commands on the Page Layout tab to prepare your data for printing. In Page Layout view, you can use the rulers to measure the width and height of data, set margins for printing, hide or display the numbered row headings and the lettered column headings, and change the *page orientation*—the position of data on the paper.

In *portrait orientation*, the paper is taller than it is wide. In *landscape orientation*, the paper is wider than it is tall. In Page Layout view, you can also add *headers* or *footers* which are text, page numbers, graphics, and formatting that print at the top (header) or bottom (footer) of every page of a worksheet. Finally, you can see how the data and chart are centered on the page and if everything fits onto one page.

Activity 9.14 Changing Views, Creating a Footer and Using Print Preview

For each of your projects in this textbook, you will create a footer containing your name and the project name. This will make it easy for you to identify your printed documents in a shared printer environment such as a lab or classroom, or if you or your instructor view your completed work electronically.

1 On the Ribbon, click the **Insert tab**, and then in the **Text group**, click **Header & Footer** to switch to **Page Layout view** and open the **Header area**. Compare your screen with Figure 9.52.

In this view you can see the edges of the paper of multiple pages, the margins, and the rulers. You can also insert a header or footer by typing in the areas indicated and using the Header & Footer Tools. Recall that contextual tools and tabs of this type become available when an object requiring the related commands is selected—in this instance the Header area object.

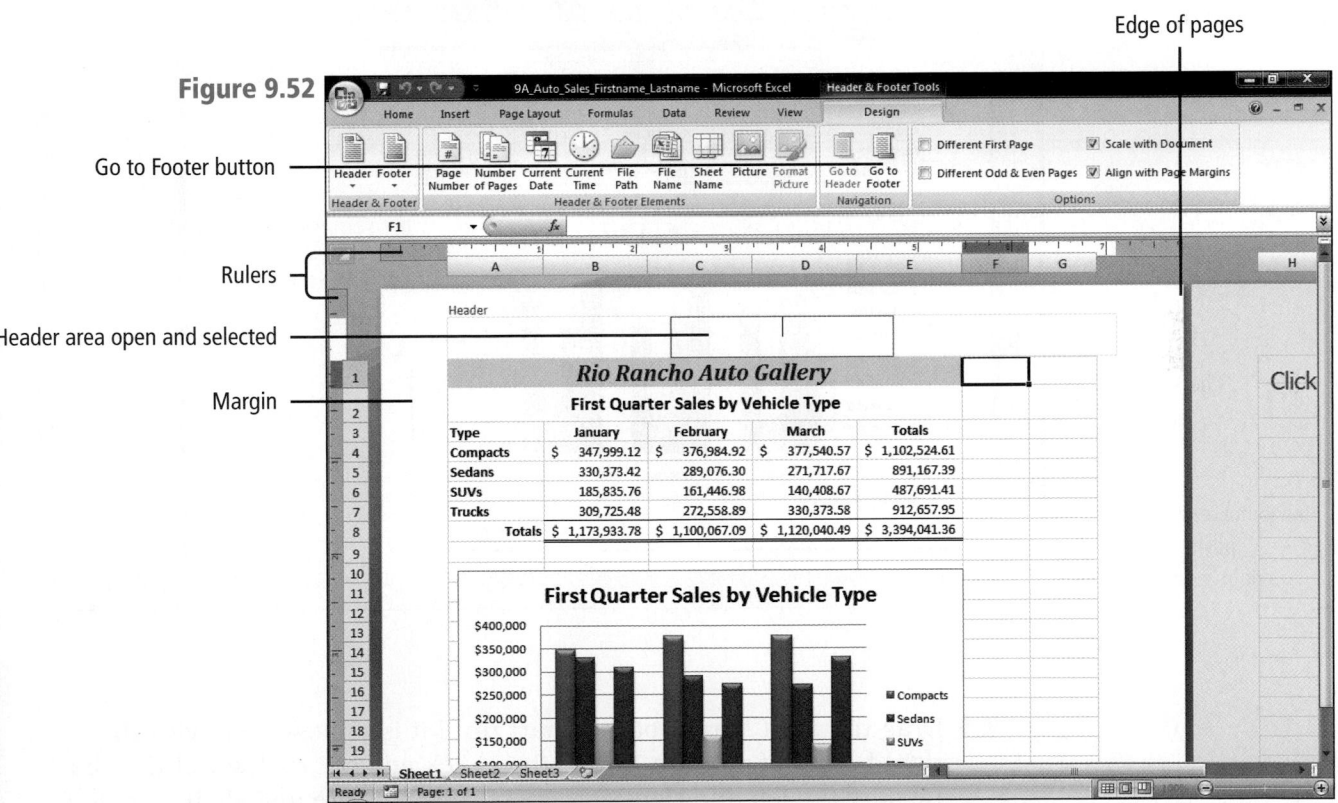

Figure 9.52

2 In the **Navigation group**, click the **Go to Footer** button to move to the bottom of the page and open the **Footer area**, and then click just above the word *Footer* to place the insertion point in the left section of the **Footer area**.

The Header and Footer areas have three distinct sections—left, center, and right.

3 On the Ribbon, in the **Header & Footer Elements group**, click the **File Name** button to add the name of your file to the footer—&*[File]* displays in the left section of the **Footer area**. Then, click in a cell just above the footer to exit the **Footer area** and view your file name.

The Header & Footer Tools are removed from view. In Page Layout View, you can also type a header or footer directly into the areas indicated, but use this technique to automatically insert the file name.

4 Scroll up to view your chart, click the upper right corner of the chart to select it, and then check to see if the chart is centered under the data in the cells. If necessary, point to the **right resize handle** to display the ⟷ pointer, as shown in Figure 9.53.

Figure 9.53

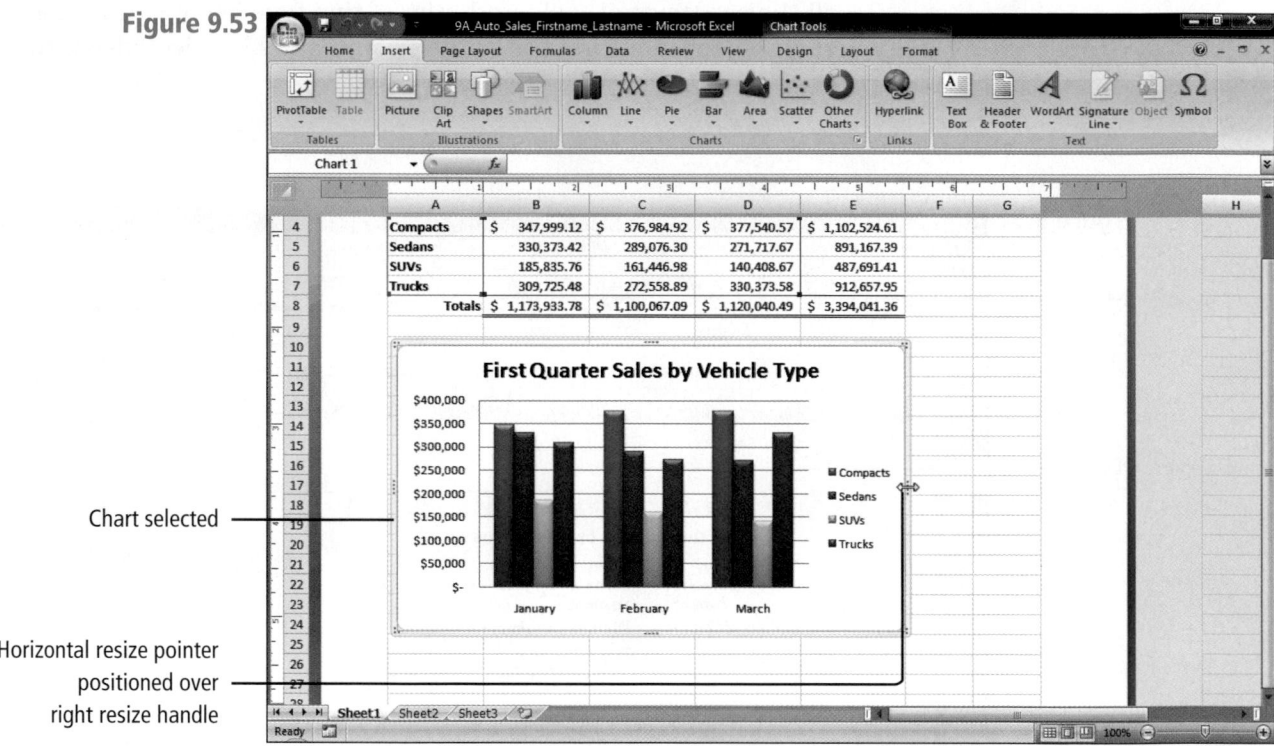

Chart selected

Horizontal resize pointer
positioned over
right resize handle

5 Drag the right border of the chart until it is almost even with the right border of **column E**, and then click any cell to deselect the chart. Be sure the left and right borders of the chart are just slightly inside the left border of **column A** and the right border of **column E**—adjust as necessary.

6 Click any cell to deselect the chart. Click the **Page Layout tab**, in the **Page Setup group**, click the **Margins** button, and then at the bottom of the **Margins gallery**, click **Custom Margins**. In the displayed **Page Setup** dialog box, under **Center on page**, select the **Horizontally** check box.

This action will center the data and chart horizontally on the page, as shown in the Preview area. Alternatively, you can display the Page Setup dialog box by clicking the Dialog Box Launcher in the Page Setup group, and then clicking the desired tab within the dialog box.

7 In the lower right corner of the **Page Setup** dialog box, click **OK**. In the upper left corner of your screen, click the **Office** button , from the displayed menu, point to the **Print button**, and then click **Print Preview**. Alternatively, press Ctrl + F2 to view the Print Preview. Compare your screen with Figure 9.54.

The Ribbon displays the Print Preview program tab, which replaces the standard set of tabs when you switch to Print Preview.

Figure 9.54

Print Preview tab

Close Print Preview button

Document displayed
in Print Preview

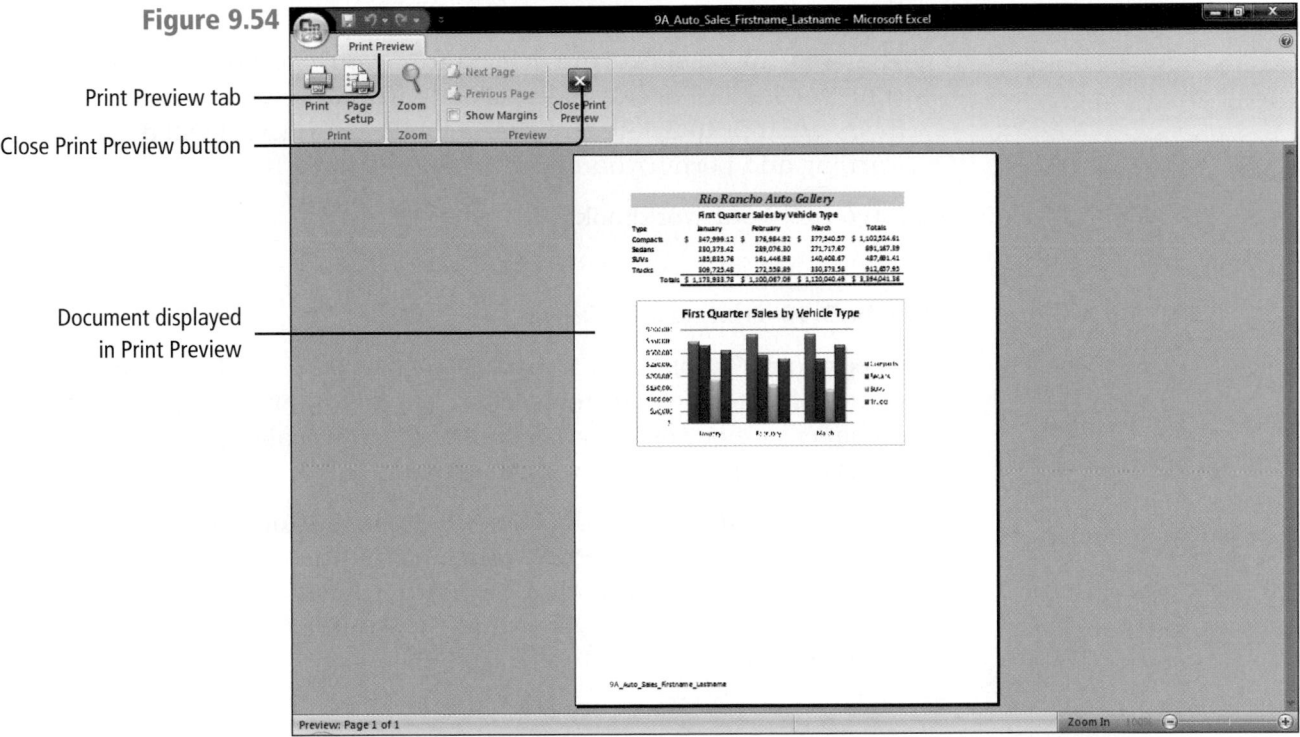

8 Note any adjustments that need to be made, and then on the Ribbon, click the **Close Print Preview** button. On the right side of the status bar, click the **Normal** button to return to the Normal view, and then press Ctrl + Home to return to cell **A1**.

The **Normal view** maximizes the number of cells visible on your screen and keeps the column letters and row numbers closer. The vertical dotted line between columns indicates that as currently arranged, only the columns to the left of the dotted line will print on the first page. The exact position of the vertical line will depend on your default printer setting—yours may fall elsewhere.

9 **Save** your workbook.

Activity 9.15 Deleting Unused Sheets in a Workbook

By default, each new Excel workbook contains three blank worksheets. Although it is not necessary to delete unused sheets, doing so saves storage space and removes any doubt that additional information is in the workbook.

1 At the bottom of your worksheet, click the **Sheet2 tab** to display Sheet 2 and make it the active worksheet.

2 Hold down Ctrl, and then click the **Sheet3 tab**. With both sheets selected (tab background is white, not blue, on the selected sheets), display the **Home tab**. In the **Cells group**, click the **Delete button arrow**, and then click **Delete Sheet**. Alternatively, point to either of the selected sheet tabs, right-click, and then click Delete to delete the sheets.

The two unused sheets are deleted from your workbook. Do not be concerned about accidentally deleting worksheets that contain data. If you attempt to delete a worksheet with data, Excel will display a warning and permit you to cancel the deletion.

3 **Save** your workbook.

Activity 9.16 Printing a Worksheet

1 Check your *Chapter Assignment Sheet* or *Course Syllabus*, or consult your instructor, to determine if you are to submit your assignments on paper or electronically. To submit electronically, follow the instructions provided by your instructor.

2 From the **Office** menu, click the **Print** button. In the displayed **Print** dialog box, under **Print range**, verify that the **All** option button is selected. Under **Print what**, verify that **Active sheet(s)** is selected, and then under **Copies**, verify that the **Number of copies** is **1**. Compare your screen with Figure 9.55.

Figure 9.55

Print dialog box

Your default printer

Print all pages

Print currently
active worksheet

One copy

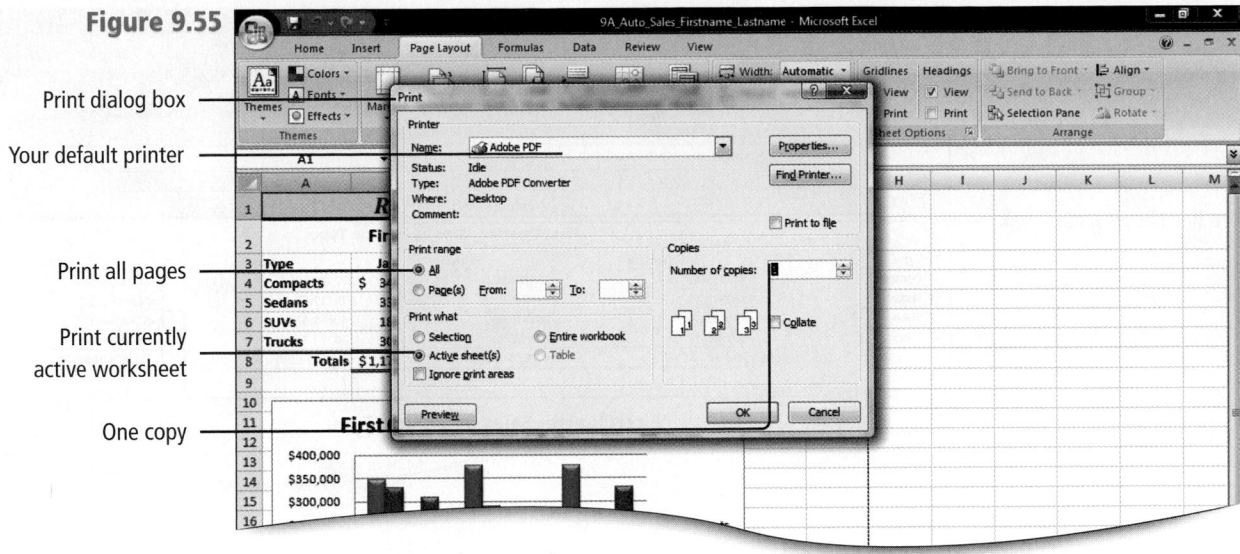

3 Click **OK** to print your worksheet, and then **Save** ![save icon] your
workbook.

Alert!

Is your printed result centered horizontally?

If your worksheet does not appear to be centered horizontally on the page,
reduce the width of the chart by a small amount so that its borders fall
slightly inside the left and right columns with which they are aligned.

Activity 9.17 Displaying, Printing, and Hiding Formulas

When you have a formula in a cell, the cell displays the results of the formula. Recall that this value is called the ***displayed value***. You can view
and print the underlying formulas in the cells. When you do so, a formula often takes more horizontal space to display than the result of the
calculation. Thus, the landscape orientation is usually a better choice
than portrait orientation to fit the formulas on one page. In this activity,
you will print the formulas in Sheet1 in landscape orientation and then
close the workbook without saving the changes.

1 Because you will make some temporary changes to your workbook,

on the **Quick Access Toolbar**, click the **Save** button ![save icon] to be sure
that you have saved your work up to this point.

2 Hold down Ctrl, and then press ` (usually located below Esc), and
then compare your screen with Figure 9.56. Alternatively, on the
Formulas tab, in the Formula Auditing group, click the Show
Formulas button.

Figure 9.56

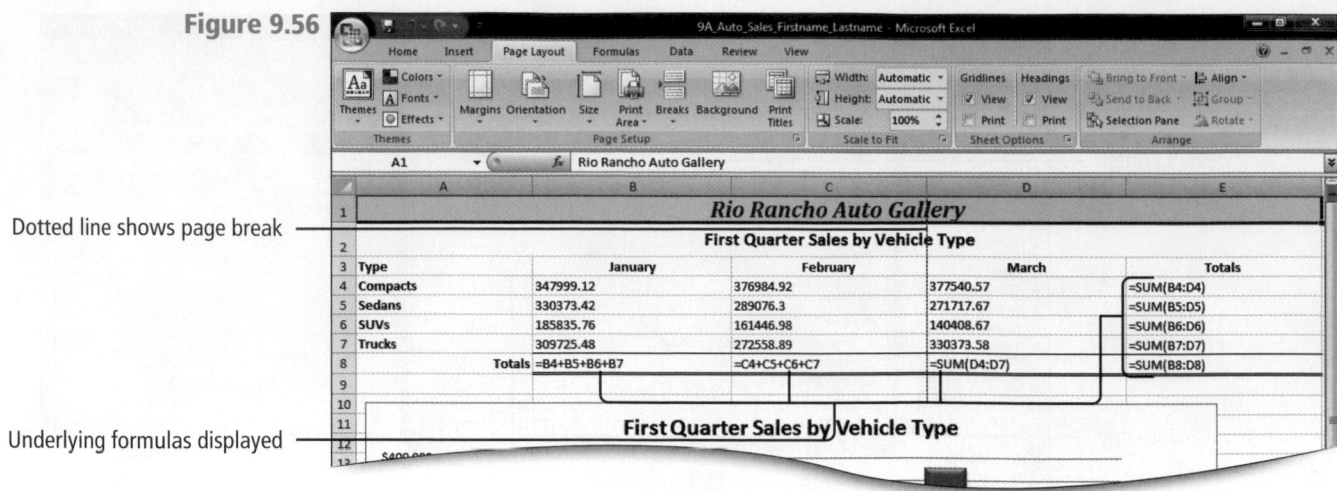

Dotted line shows page break

Underlying formulas displayed

3. From the **column heading area**, select columns **A:E**. Point to the column heading boundary between any two of the selected columns and double-click to AutoFit the selected columns.

4. Display the **Page Layout tab**. In the **Page Setup group**, click the **Orientation** button, and then click **Landscape**. In the **Scale to Fit group**, click the **Dialog Box Launcher** button ⊞ to display the **Page tab** of the **Page Setup** dialog box.

5. Under **Scaling**, click the **Fit to** option button, and then in the lower right corner, click the **Print Preview** button—this is another point from which you can display the Print Preview.

Scaling adjusts the size of the printed worksheet to fit on the page, and is convenient for printing formulas. Although it is not always the case, formulas frequently take up more space than the actual data.

6. Click **Close Print Preview**. Check your *Chapter Assignment Sheet* or *Course Syllabus*, or consult your instructor, to determine if you are to submit your printed formulas on paper or electronically. To submit electronically, follow the instructions provided by your instructor.

7. From the **Office** menu 🔘, click the **Print** button. In the displayed **Print** dialog box, under **Print range**, verify that the **All** option button is selected. Under **Print what**, verify that **Active sheet(s)** is selected, and then under **Copies**, verify that the **Number of copies** is **1**.

8. Click **OK** to print your worksheet. From the **Office** menu 🔘, click **Close**, and when prompted, click **No** so that you do *not* save the changes you made—displaying formulas, changing column widths and orientation, and scaling—to print your formulas.

9. In the upper right corner of your screen, click the **Close** button  to close Excel.

End **You have completed Project 9A**

Project 9B Safety Products

In Project 9.18 through 9.25, you will create a workbook for Arthur Potempa, the Retail Sales Manager for Rio Rancho Auto Gallery. One of the retail areas in the Auto Gallery carries an inventory of safety products. Mr. Potempa wants to calculate the retail value of the inventory of safety products and then, using a pie chart, display how each item's retail value contributes to the total retail value. Your completed worksheet and chart will look similar to Figure 9.57.

For Project 9B, you will need the following file:

New blank Excel workbook

You will save your workbook as
9B_Safety_Products_Firstname_Lastname

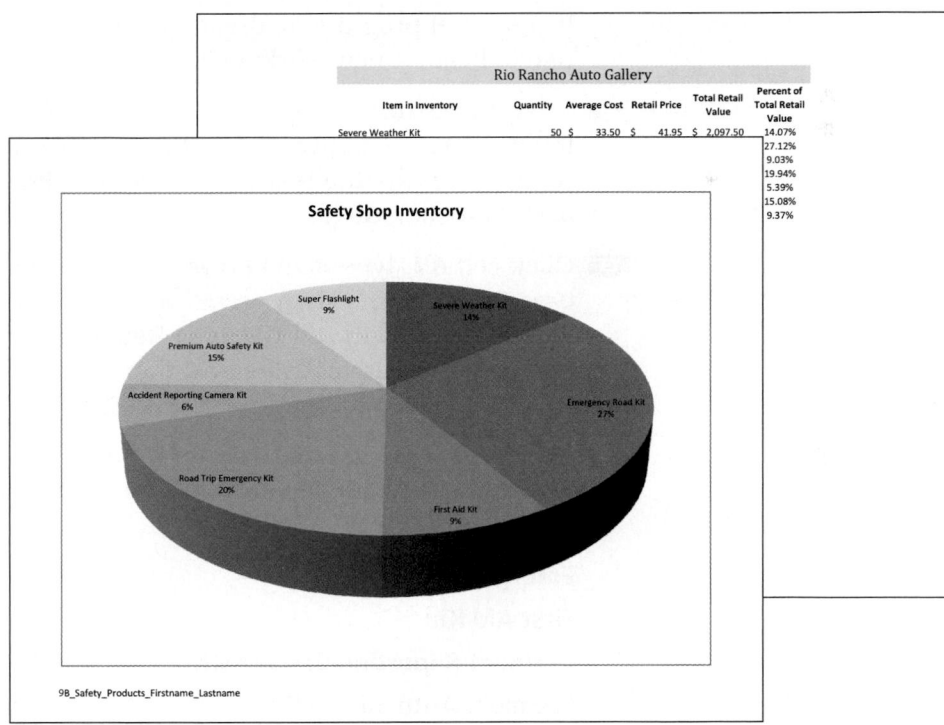

Figure 9.57
Project 9B—Safety Products

Objective 8
Design a Worksheet

Good design techniques, which make your worksheet useful to the reader, include the following: generally it is best to use rows rather than columns for the most abundant data; if you will print the worksheet, consider how it will look on paper; and, arrange the data so that it is easily charted.

Activity 9.18 Setting Column Widths and Creating Row and Column Titles

The worksheet title is typically placed in the first row and centered above the columns of data.

1 With **Excel** open, from the **Office** menu , click **New**. In the **New Workbook** dialog box, under **Blank and recent**, click **Blank Workbook**, and then in the lower right corner, click the **Create** button. Alternatively, press Ctrl + N.

If the Excel program is already open, these are techniques you can use to begin a new workbook.

2 From the **Office** menu , display the **Save As** dialog box, navigate to your **Excel Chapter 9 folder**, and then in the **File name** box, replace the existing text with **9B_Safety_Products_Firstname_Lastname** and then click **Save**.

3 Click cell **A2**, type **Item in Inventory** and then press Tab. In cell **B2**, type **Quantity** and then press Tab. In cell **C2**, type **Average Cost** and then press Tab. In cell **D2**, type **Retail Price** and then press Tab. In cell **E2**, type **Total Retail Value** and then press Tab. In cell **F2**, type **Percent of Total Retail Value** and then press Enter.

4 In cell **A3**, type **Severe Weather Kit** and then press Enter. Type the remaining row titles in cells **A4:A9**, and then compare your screen with Figure 9.58.

Emergency Road Kit

First Aid Kit

Accident Reporting Camera Kit

Premium Auto Safety Kit

Super Flashlight

Total Retail Value for All Products

Figure 9.58

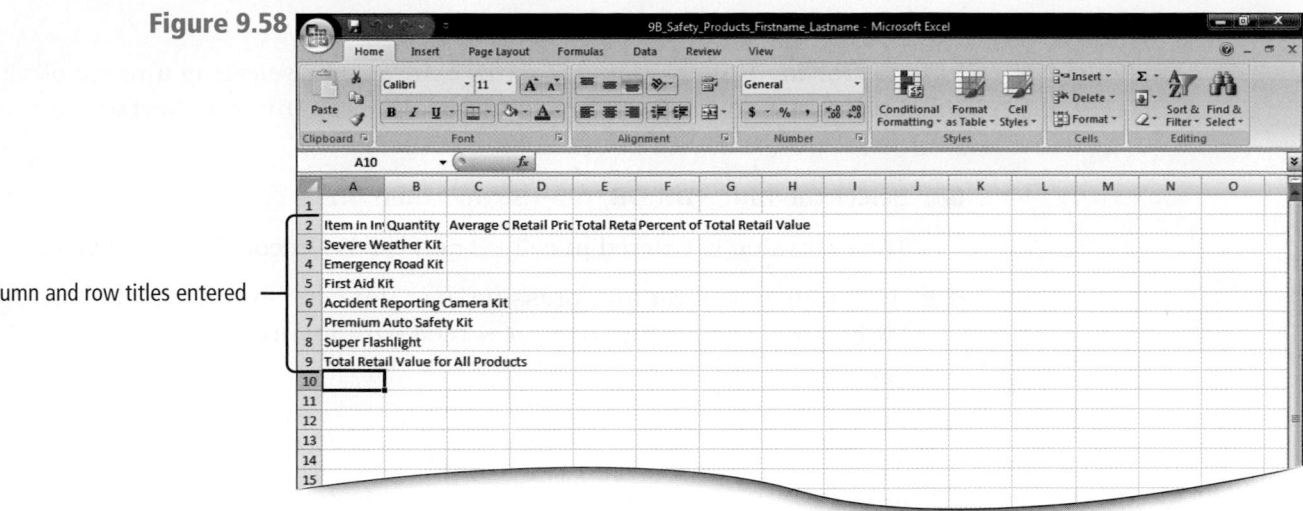

Column and row titles entered

5 Right-click cell **A9** and on the Mini toolbar, click **Bold** B .

6 Select **columns A:F**, position the ⊞ pointer over the right boundary of any of the selected column heading letters, and then double-click to apply **AutoFit Column Width**. Alternatively, click the Format button arrow, and then click AutoFit Column Width.

7 Click cell **A1** and type **Rio Rancho Auto Gallery** and then on the **Formula Bar**, click the **Enter** button ✓. Select the range **A1:F1**, and then right-click over the selection.

On the Mini toolbar, click the **Merge and Center** button ⊞ ▾, change the **Font** Calibri ▾ to **Cambria**, and then change the **Font Size** 11 ▾ to **16**.

8 With cell **A1** still selected, click the **Fill Color arrow** 🎨 ▾ . Under **Theme Colors**, in the first row, point to the seventh box to display the ScreenTip *Olive Green, Accent 3*, and then in that column of colors, click the third color—**Olive Green, Accent 3, Lighter 60%**.

Click anywhere to deselect cell **A1**, **Save** 💾 your workbook, and then compare your screen with Figure 9.59.

The worksheet title is formatted with a different font, font size, and fill color to distinguish it visually from the worksheet data.

Figure 9.59

Column widths adjusted

Worksheet title entered and formatted

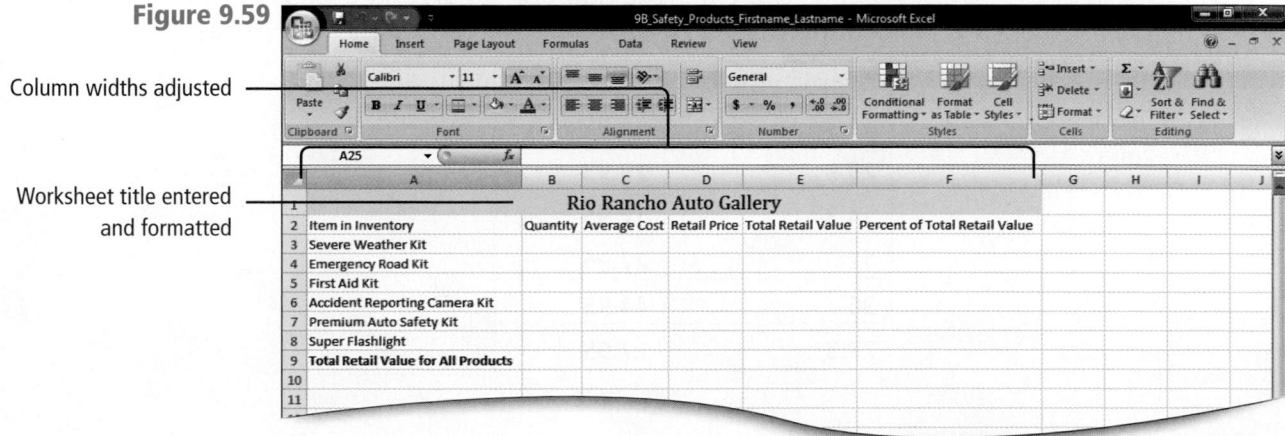

Activity 9.19 Entering Data by Range

In the following activity, you will enter data by first selecting a range of cells; this can be a time-saving technique. Use the numeric keypad on your keyboard to make this technique even faster.

1 Select the range **B3:D8**, type **50** and then press ⏎.

The first value is entered in cell B3 and cell B4 becomes the active cell.

2 Beginning in cell **B4** and pressing ⏎ after each entry, type the following, and then compare your screen with Figure 9.60:

135

75

35

50

50

After you enter the last value and press ⏎, the active cell moves to the top of the next column within the selected range. Selecting the range in this manner—before you enter data—saves time because it confines the movement of the active cell to the selected range.

Figure 9.60

Active cell moves to the next column

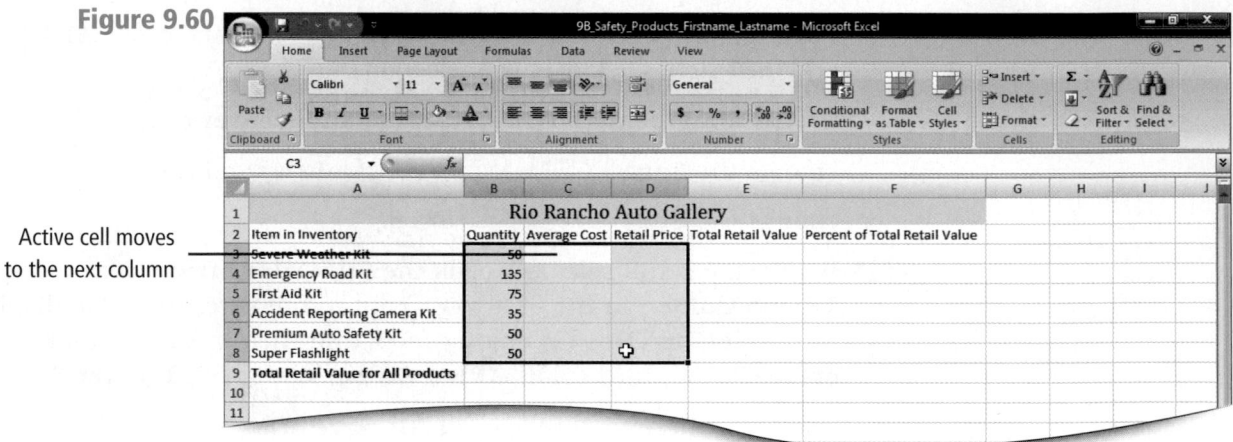

3 From the following table, beginning in cell **C3** and pressing ⏎ after each entry, enter the data for the **Average Cost** and **Retail Price** columns. Then compare your screen with Figure 9.61.

Average Cost	Retail Price
33.5	41.95
23.9	29.95
14.3	17.95
12	22.95
36	44.95
23.3	27.95

Recall that the default number format for cells is the *General* number format, in which numbers display exactly as you type them and trailing zeros do not display, even if you type them.

Figure 9.61

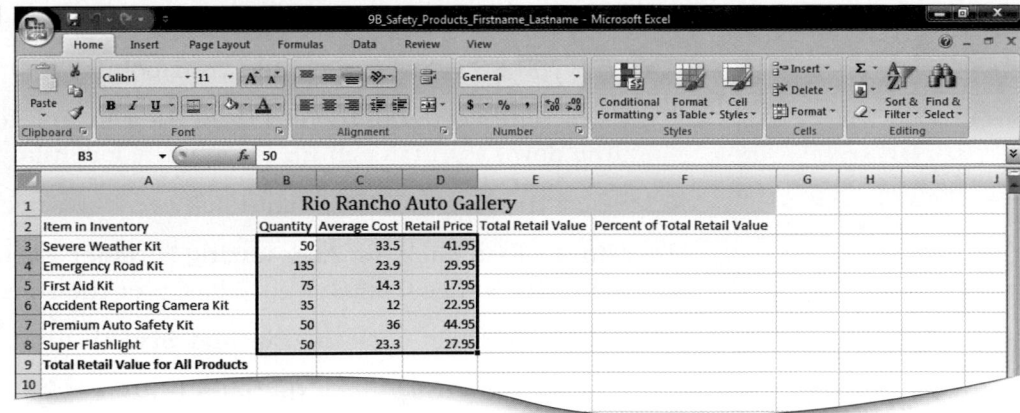

4 Save your workbook.

Objective 9
Construct Formulas for Mathematical Operations

Operators are symbols with which you can specify the type of calculation you want to perform in a formula.

Activity 9.20 Using Arithmetic Operators

1 In cell **E3**, type **=b3*d3** and press Enter.

The *Total Retail Value* of all *Severe Weather Kit* items in the shop—2097.5—equals the *Quantity* (50) times the *Retail Price* (selling price) of 41.95. In Excel, the asterisk (*) represents multiplication.

2 Take a moment to study the symbols you will use to perform basic mathematical operations in Excel, as shown in the table in Figure 9.62—these are referred to as *arithmetic operators*.

Symbols Used in Excel for Arithmetic Operators

Operator Symbol	Operation
+	Addition
-	Subtraction (also negation)
*	Multiplication
/	Division
%	Percent
^	Exponentiation

Figure 9.62

3 Click cell **E3**.

You can see that in cells E4:E8, you need a formula similar to the one in E3, but one that refers to the cells in row 4, row 5, and so forth. Recall that you can copy formulas and the cell references will change *relative to* the row number.

4 With cell **E3** selected, position your pointer over the fill handle in the lower right corner of the cell until the ➕ pointer displays. Then, drag down through cell **E8** to copy the formula.

5 Select the range **C3:E3**, right-click over the selection, and then on the Mini toolbar, click the **Accounting Number Format** button $ ▾ . Select the range **C4:E8**, right-click over the selection, and then on the Mini toolbar, click the **Comma Style** button ❟ . Click cell **E9**, in the **Editing group**, click the **Sum** button Σ ▾ , and then press Enter. **Save** 💾 your workbook, and then compare your screen with Figure 9.63.

Your result is *$11,935.25*. The Accounting Number Format is automatically applied to cell E9. The format of the cell containing the formula is the same as the format of the cells used in the formula. If the formula references a range of cells and those cells contain a mix of formats, the format from the cell in the upper left corner of the range is applied.

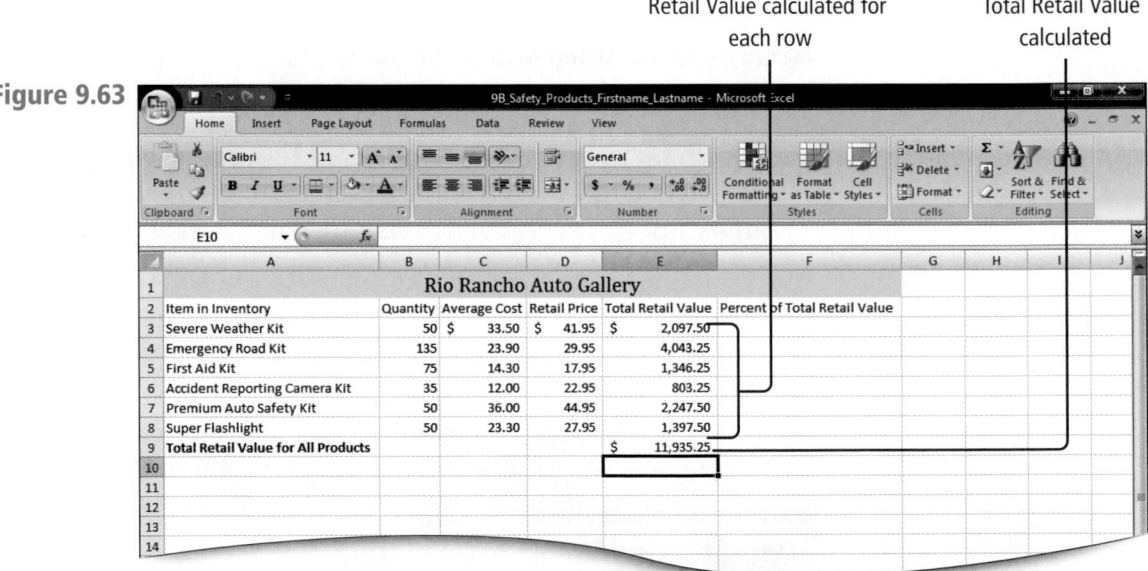

Retail Value calculated for each row   Total Retail Value calculated

Figure 9.63

Activity 9.21 Copying Formulas Containing Absolute Cell References

You have seen that a relative cell reference refers to cells by their position in relation to the cell that contains the formula. ***Absolute cell references***, on the other hand, refer to cells by their *fixed* position in the worksheet, for example, the total in cell E9.

A relative cell reference automatically adjusts when a formula is copied. An absolute cell reference does *not* adjust; rather, it remains the same when the formula is copied—and there are times when you will want to do this.

1 Click cell **F3**, type = and then click cell **E3**. Type / and then click cell **E9**.

The formula created, *=E3/E9*, indicates that the value in cell E3 will be divided by the value in cell E9. Why? Because Mr. Potempa wants to know the percentage by which each product's Total Retail Value makes up the Total Retail Value for All Products. Arithmetically, the percentage is computed by dividing the *Total Retail Value* for each product by the *Total Retail Value for All Products*. The result will be a percentage expressed as a decimal.

Workshop

Calculate a Percentage if You Know the Total and the Amount

Using the equation *amount/total = percentage*, you can calculate the percentage by which a part makes up a total—with the percentage formatted as a decimal.

For example, if on a quiz you score 42 points correctly out of 50, your percentage of correct answers is 42/50 = 0.84 or 84%.

2 Press [Enter]. Click cell **F3** and notice that the formula displays in the **Formula Bar**. Then, point to cell **F3** and double-click.

The formula, with the two referenced cells displayed in color and bordered with the same color, displays in the cell. This is the ***range finder***, and is useful for verifying formulas or quickly positioning the insertion point within the cell to perform editing directly in the cell.

3 Press [Enter] to redisplay the result of the calculation in the cell, and notice that approximately 17% of the total retail value of the inventory is made up of Severe Weather Kits. Then, click cell **F3** again, and drag the fill handle down through cell **F8**. Compare your screen with Figure 9.64.

Each cell displays an error message—*#DIV/0!* and a green triangle in the upper left corner of each cell indicates an error has been found. Like a grammar checker, Excel uses rules to check for formula errors and flags them in this manner. Additionally, the Auto Fill Options button displays, from which you can select formatting options for the copied cells.

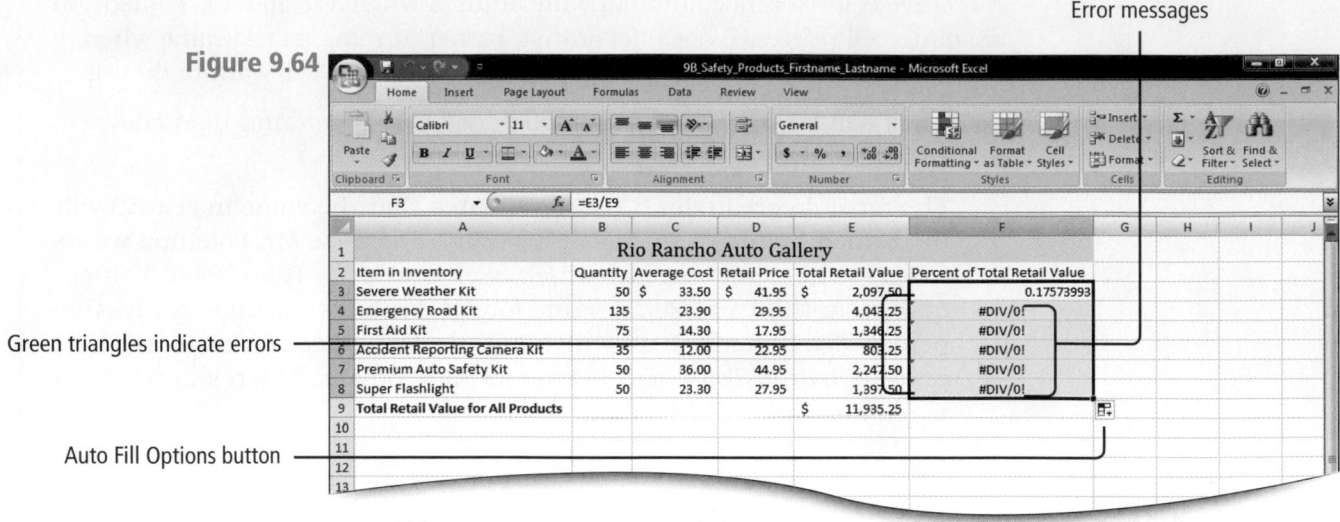

Figure 9.64

Error messages

Green triangles indicate errors

Auto Fill Options button

4 Click cell **F4**, and to the left of the cell, point to the displayed **Error Checking** button ◈ to display its ScreenTip—*The formula or function used is dividing by zero or empty cells.*

In this manner, Excel suggests the cause of an error.

5 Look at the **Formula Bar** to examine the formula.

The formula is *=E4/E10*. The cell reference to *E4* is correct, but the cell reference following the division operator (/) is *E10*, and E10 is an *empty* cell.

6 Click cell **F5**, point to the **Error Checking** button ◈, and in the **Formula Bar** examine the formula.

Because the cell references are relative, Excel attempts to build the formulas by increasing the row number for each equation. In this particular calculation, however, the divisor must always be the value in cell E9—the *Total Retail Value for All Products*.

7 Point to cell **F3**, and then double-click to have the range finder display the cell's formula and place the insertion point within the cell.

8 Within the cell, be sure the insertion point is blinking to the right of *E9*, and then press F4. Alternatively edit the formula so that it indicates **=E3/$E$9** Compare your screen with Figure 9.65.

To make a cell reference absolute, dollar signs are inserted into the cell reference. The use of the dollar sign to denote an absolute reference is not related in any way to whether or not the values you are working with are currency values. It is simply the symbol used by Excel to denote an absolute cell reference.

Edited formula with dollar signs denoting
an absolute cell reference

Figure 9.65

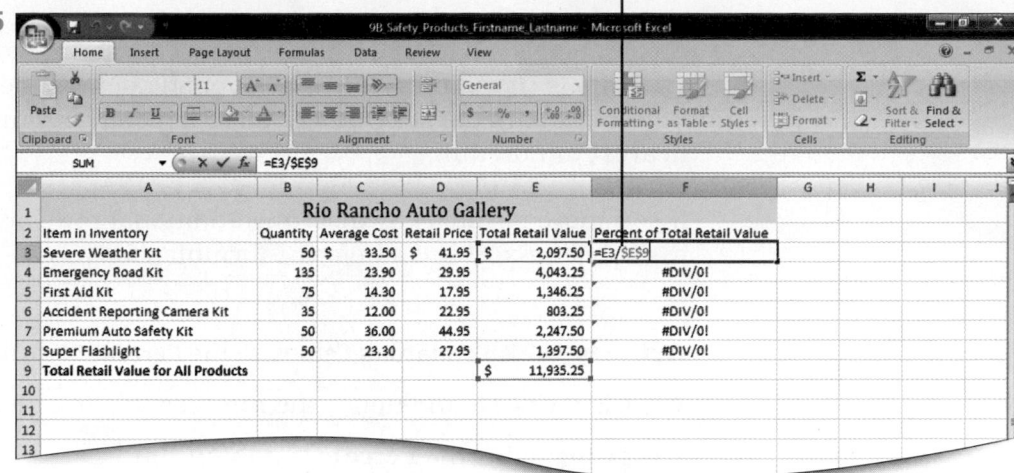

On the **Formula Bar**, click the **Enter** button ✓ so that **F3** is still
the active cell. Then, drag the fill handle to copy the formula down
through cell **F8**. Compare your screen with Figure 9.66, and then
click cell **F4**, examine the formula in the **Formula Bar**, and then
examine the formulas for cells **F5**, **F6**, **F7**, and **F8**.

You can see that for each formula, the cell reference for the *Total
Retail Value* of each product changed relative to its row; however, the
value used as the divisor—*Total Retail Value for All Products* in cell
E9—remained absolute. Thus, using either relative or absolute cell
references, it is easy to duplicate formulas without typing them.

Absolute cell reference   Percentages calculated for each product

Figure 9.66

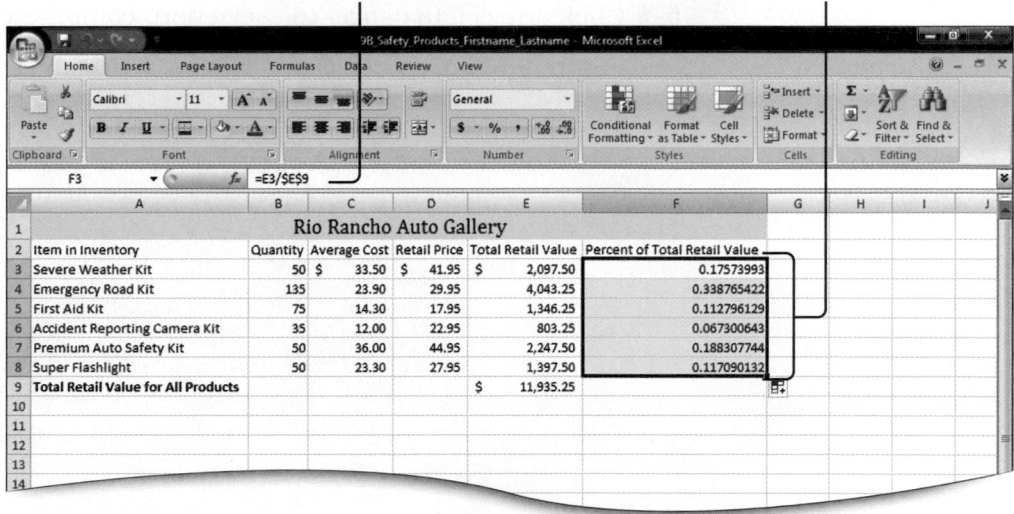

10 **Save** 💾 your workbook.

Objective 10
Format Percentages and Move Formulas

A percentage is part of a whole expressed in hundredths. For example, 75 cents is the same as 75 percent of one dollar. The Percent Style button formats the selected cell as a percentage rounded to the nearest hundredth.

If you move formulas by inserting additional rows or columns in your worksheet, Excel will adjust the formulas for you.

Activity 9.22 Formatting Cells with the Percent Style Button

1 Click cell **F3** and notice the number *0.17573993*. In the **Number group**, click the **Percent Style** button %.

Your result is 18%, which is *0.17573993* rounded up to the nearest hundredth and expressed as a percentage. Percent Style displays the value of a cell as a percentage.

2 Select the range **F3:F8**, right-click over the selection, and then on the Mini toolbar click the **Percent Style** button %, click the **Increase Decimal** button two times, and then click the **Center** button. Alternatively, click the commands in the appropriate groups on the Ribbon.

Percent Style may not offer a percentage precise enough to analyze important financial information—adding additional decimal places to a percentage makes data more precise. For example, with additional decimal places, Mr. Potempa can see a slight difference in the percentage of First Aid Kits and Super Flashlights.

3 Click any cell to cancel the selection, compare your screen with Figure 9.67, and then **Save** your workbook.

Figure 9.67

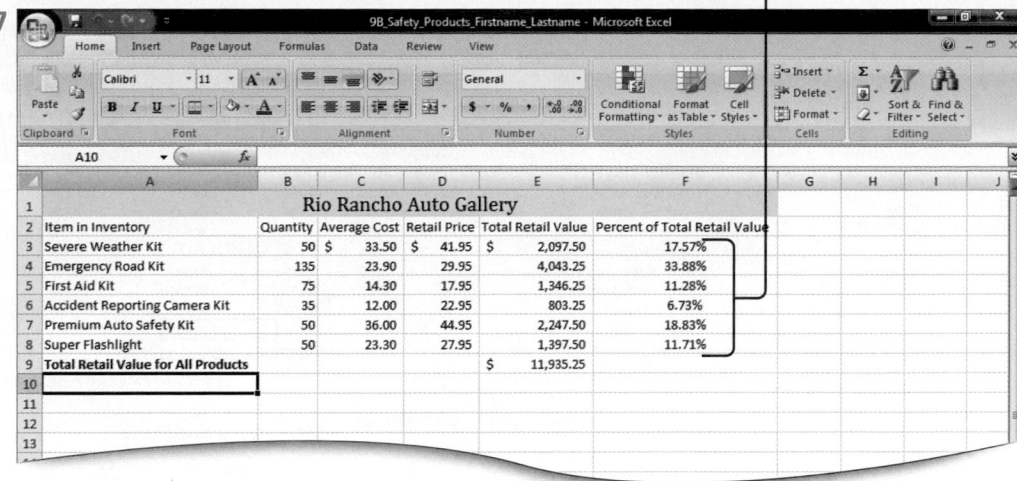

Percentages formatted

Activity 9.23 Inserting Rows in a Worksheet Containing Formulas and Wrapping Text in a Cell

You can edit formulas in the same manner as you edit text. In this activity, you will add a row for Road Trip Emergency Kits, which is another item carried by the Safety Shop, and wrap text.

1 Double-click cell **E9** and confirm that the range finder shows the formula to be the sum of cells *E3:E8*. Press Enter. Click cell **E6**. On the **Home tab**, in the **Cells group**, click the **Insert button arrow**, and then from the displayed list, click **Insert Sheet Rows**.

Another Way — To Insert Rows

Click the row heading and then in the Cells group, click the Insert button; or, right-click the cell, click Insert, and then click Entire row.

2 Click cell **E10**. On the **Formula Bar**, notice that the range was edited and changed to sum the newly expanded range **E3:E9**.

3 In the range **A6:D6**, type the following:

Road Trip Emergency Kit   35   67.96   84.95

4 Select the range **E5:F5** to select the two formulas above the new row, and then drag the fill handle to fill both formulas down to cells **E6** and **F6**.

5 Click cell **E10**. Move the pointer to the bottom edge of the cell until the ⬚ pointer displays, and then drag downward until cell **E11** is outlined, as shown in Figure 9.68.

Figure 9.68

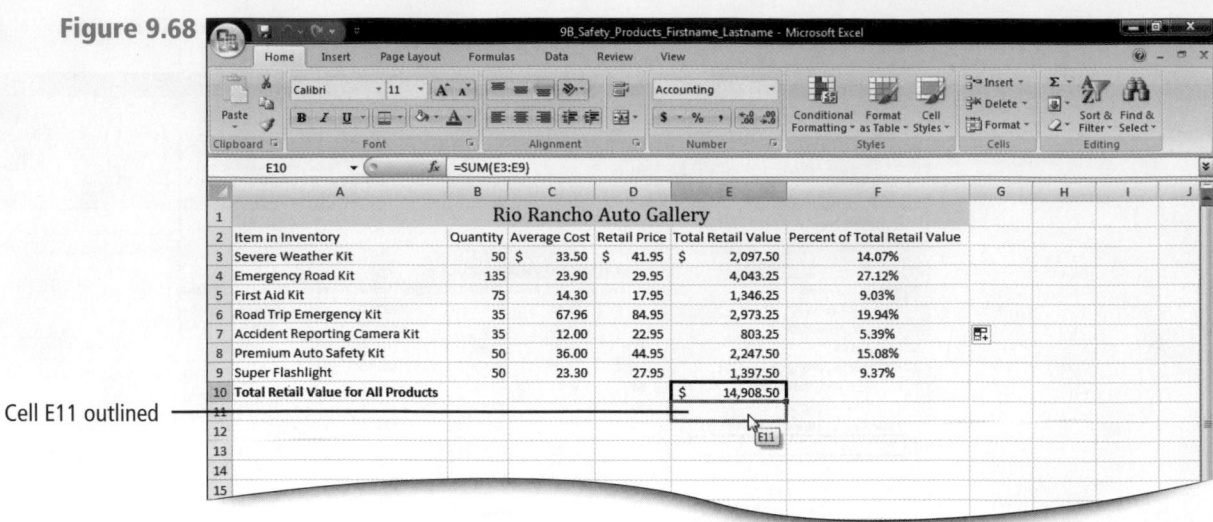

Cell E11 outlined

6 Release the mouse button, double-click cell **E11** to display the range finder, and then in cell **E11** and on the **Formula Bar**, notice that the range, **E3:E9**, did not change when you moved the formula.

If you move a formula to another cell, the cell references do not change.

7 Press ⌈Esc⌉ to cancel the range finder, and then on the **Quick Access Toolbar**, click **Undo** to return the formula to cell **E10**. **Save** your workbook.

8 In the **row heading area**, point to the lower boundary of **row 2** to display the ⧢ pointer, and then drag downward until the row is **60 pixels** high. Select **columns B:F**, and then from the **column heading area**, drag the right border of one of the selected columns to **80 pixels**.

9 Select the range **C2:F2**, and then in the **Alignment group**, click the **Wrap Text** button.

Use the Wrap Text command to display text on multiple lines within a single cell when the column is not wide enough to display all of the cell's content.

10 Select the range **A2:F2**. In the **Font group**, click the **Bold** button **B**; in the **Alignment group**, click the **Center** button and the **Middle Align** button. Click cell **E10**. In the **Font** group, click the **Borders button arrow**, and then from the displayed list, click **Top and Double Bottom Border**. Click any cell to cancel the selection from cell E10. **Save** your workbook, and then compare your screen with Figure 9.69.

Figure 9.69

Column widths adjusted

Text wrapped and centered
Row height increased

Border added

Percents formatted

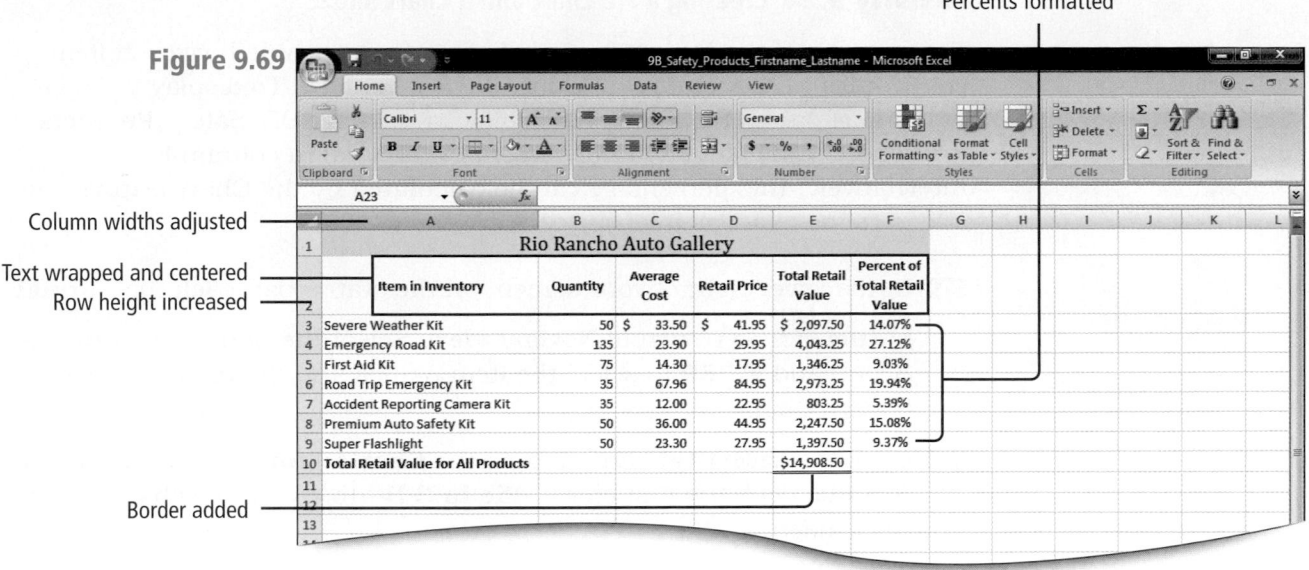

11 On the Ribbon, click the **Insert tab**, and then in the **Text group**, click **Header & Footer** to switch to **Page Layout view** and open the **Header area**. On the **Design tab**, in the **Navigation group**, click the **Go to Footer** button. Click just above the word *Footer* to place your insertion point in the left section of the **Footer area**, and then in the **Header & Footer Elements group**, click the **File Name** button. Click any cell above the footer to exit the **Footer area** and view your file name.

12 Press Ctrl + Home to move to cell **A1** and display the upper portion of your worksheet. Click the **Page Layout tab**. In the **Page Setup group**, click the **Orientation** button, and then click **Landscape**. Click the **Margins** button, and then at the bottom of the **Margins gallery**, click **Custom Margins**. In the displayed **Page Setup** dialog box, under **Center on page**, select the **Horizontally** check box. Click **OK**, and then **Save** the changes to your workbook.

Objective 11
Create a Pie Chart and a Chart Sheet

Pie charts show the relationship of each part to a whole. To create a pie chart, you must select two ranges. One range contains the labels for each slice of the pie chart, and the other range contains the values that add up to a total. The two ranges must have the same number of cells and the range with the values should *not* include the cell with the total. You can use a legend to identify the slices of the pie by using colors, but it is usually more effective to place the labels within or close to each pie slice.

Activity 9.24 Creating a Pie Chart and a Chart Sheet

The purpose of the inventory worksheet is to determine how each item contributes to the total retail value of the inventory. To display the relationship of parts to a whole, use a pie chart. In the 9B_Safety_Products worksheet, you calculated the percent of the total in column F. Alternatively, this percentage can be calculated by the Chart feature and added to the chart as a label.

1 In the lower right of your screen, on the status bar, click the **Normal** button ⊞ to return to **Normal view**. Select the nonadjacent ranges **A3:A9** and **E3:E9** to select the item names and the total retail value of each item.

2 Click the **Insert tab**, and then in the **Charts group**, click **Pie**. Under **3-D Pie**, click the first chart—**Pie in 3-D**—to create the chart on your worksheet.

3 On the **Design tab**, in the **Location group**, click the **Move Chart** button. In the displayed **Move Chart** dialog box, click the **New sheet** option button. Replace the highlighted text *Chart1* by typing **Inventory Chart** and then click **OK**.

A ***chart sheet*** is created in your workbook, which is a workbook sheet that contains only a chart and is useful when you want to view a chart separately from the worksheet data. The sheet tab indicates *Inventory Chart*.

4 On the **Design tab**, in the **Chart Layouts group**, click the first layout—**Layout 1**. Right-click over the text *Chart Title*, click **Edit Text**, delete the existing text, and then type **Safety Shop Inventory**

In this layout, the legend is removed and the category labels and the percentages—calculated by the chart feature—display on the pie slices. Recall that *chart layout* refers to the combination of chart elements—title, legend, labels—that you want to display. If you plan to print a chart sheet on a printer that does not print in color, it is better to label each pie slice individually rather than use a legend.

5 In the **Chart Styles group**, click the **More** button ⏷ , and then click **Style 5**. Click anywhere in the white area of the chart to deselect the Chart Title, and then compare your screen with Figure 9.70.

To print on paper, the paler colors will display well. To present this chart in a PowerPoint presentation, you would likely pick one of the more vibrant styles with multiple colors.

Figure 9.70

Excel | chapter 9

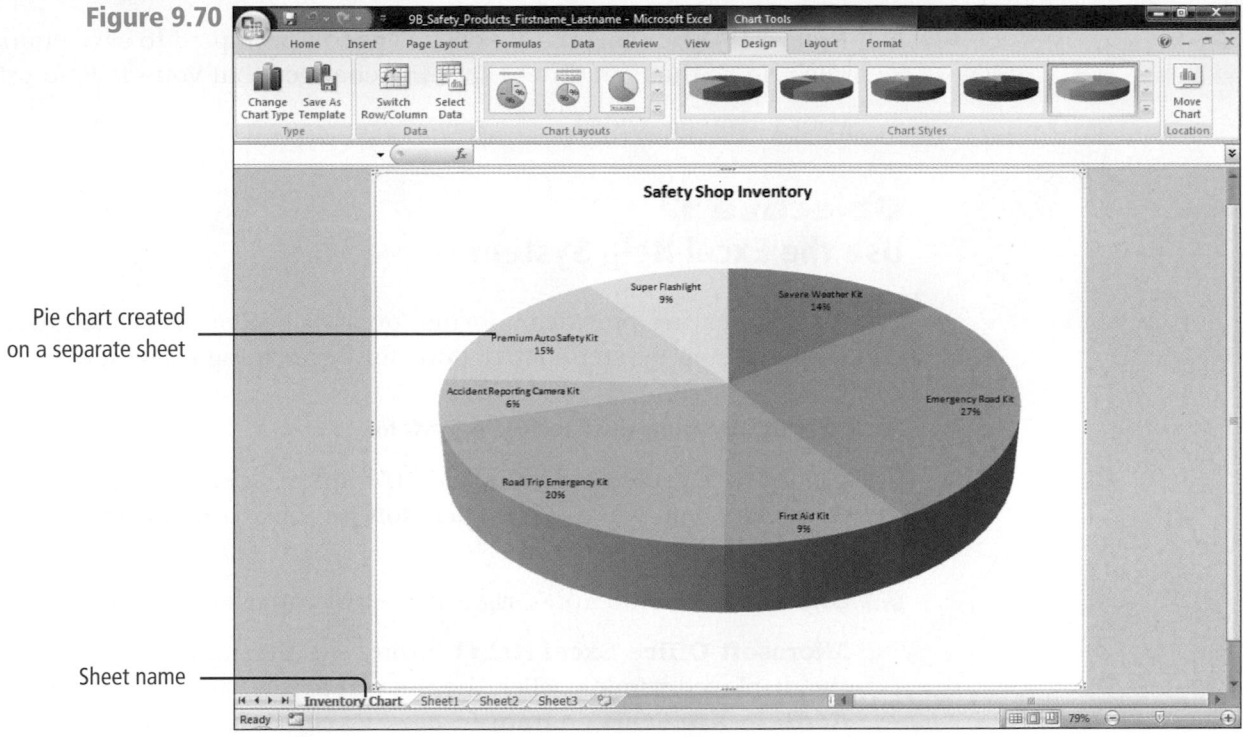

Pie chart created
on a separate sheet

Sheet name

6 Click the **Insert tab**. In the **Text group**, click **Header & Footer**, and
then in the **Page Setup** dialog box, click the **Custom Footer** button.
With the insertion point positioned in the **Left section**, click the

Insert File Name button , and then click **OK** two times.

Use the Page Setup dialog box in this manner to insert a footer on a
chart sheet, which has no Page Layout view in which you can see the
Header and Footer areas.

7 To delete the unused worksheets, click the **Sheet2 tab**, hold down
Ctrl, and then click the **Sheet3 tab**. Right-click over one of the
selected sheet tabs, and then from the shortcut menu, click **Delete**.
Be sure **Sheet1** is the active sheet, and then press Ctrl + Home to cancel the selections and make cell **A1** the active cell.

8 **Save** your workbook. Check your *Chapter Assignment Sheet* or
Course Syllabus, or consult your instructor, to determine if you are
to submit your assignments on paper or electronically. To submit
electronically, follow the instructions provided by your instructor.

9 To print, from the **Office** menu , click **Print**. In the displayed
Print dialog box, under **Print what**, click the **Entire workbook**
option button. In the lower left corner of the dialog box, click
Preview, and notice in the status bar, *Preview: Page 1 of 2* displays.

10 Review the preview of your chart sheet, and then in the **Preview
group**, click the **Next Page** button to preview the worksheet containing your data. In the **Print group**, click **Print** to print the two pages.

11 **Save** your workbook. If you are instructed to print your formulas on Sheet1, follow the instructions in Activity 9.17 to do so, and
then redisplay the worksheet by pressing Ctrl + `.

12 From the **Office** menu, click **Close**. If prompted to save changes, click **No** so that you do not save the changes that you made to print your formulas. **Close** ☒ Excel.

Objective 12
Use the Excel Help System

Excel's Help feature provides information about all of Excel's features and displays step-by-step instructions for performing many tasks.

Activity 9.25 Using the Excel Help System

Workbooks that you create in Excel 2007 can be opened in Excel 2003. In this activity, you will use the Microsoft Help feature to learn more about this feature.

1 **Start** Excel. In the upper right corner of your screen, click the **Microsoft Office Excel Help** button ⊙. Alternatively, press F1. In the displayed window, click the **Search arrow**, and then under **Content from this computer**, click **Excel Help**. In the white box on the left, type **open an Excel 2007 workbook in Excel 2003**.

2 Click **Search** or press Enter. On the list of results, click **Open an Office Excel 2007 workbook in an earlier version of Excel**.

3 If you want to do so, click the **Print** button to print a copy of this information for your reference. Your name will not print.

4 On the title bar of the Excel Help window, click the **Close** button ☒. On the right side of the Microsoft Excel title bar, click the **Close** button ☒ to close Excel.

End **You have completed Project 9B** ————————————

There's More You Can Do!

Close Excel and any other open windows. Display the Start menu, click Computer, and then navigate to the student files that accompany this textbook. In the folder **02_theres_more_you_can_do**, locate and open the folder for this chapter. Open and print the instructions for this project, which are provided to you in Adobe PDF format.

Try IT! 1—Change a Chart Type

In this Try It! exercise, you will change the chart type of an existing chart from a column chart to a bar chart.

Summary

In this chapter, you used Microsoft Office Excel 2007 to create and analyze data organized into columns and rows and to chart and perform calculations on the data. By organizing your data with Excel, you will be able to make logical decisions and create visual representations of your data in the form of charts.

Key Terms

The 🔘 symbol represents Key Terms found on the Student CD in the 02_theres_more_you_can_do folder for this chapter.

Content-Based Assessments

Key Terms

Content-Based Assessments

Matching

Match each term in the second column with its correct definition in the first column by writing the letter of the term on the blank line in front of the correct definition.

_____ **1.** An Excel file that contains one or more worksheets.

_____ **2.** The primary document that you use in Excel to store and work with data, and which is formatted as a pattern of uniformly spaced horizontal and vertical lines.

_____ **3.** The intersection of a row and column in an Excel worksheet.

_____ **4.** An element in the Excel window that displays the value or formula contained in the active cell, and in which you can enter or edit values or formulas.

_____ **5.** The box to the left of the Formula Bar that identifies the selected cell, table, chart, or object.

_____ **6.** The user interface in Office 2007 that groups the commands for performing related tasks on tabs across the upper portion of the program window.

_____ **7.** Buttons on the right side of the status bar for viewing in Normal, Page Layout View, or Page Break Preview; also displays controls for zoom out and zoom in.

_____ **8.** The letters at the top of an Excel worksheet that designate the columns.

_____ **9.** Two or more selected cells on a worksheet that are adjacent or nonadjacent, and treated by Excel as a single unit for the purpose of editing.

_____ **10.** The cell, surrounded by a black border, ready to receive data or be affected by the next Excel command.

_____ **11.** The identification of a specific cell by its intersecting column letter and row number.

_____ **12.** Anything typed into a cell.

_____ **13.** Numbers, text, dates, or times of day that you type into a cell.

_____ **14.** An equation that performs mathematical calculations on values in a worksheet.

_____ **15.** The small black square in the lower right corner of a selected cell.

A Active cell

B Cell

C Cell content

D Cell reference

E Column headings

F Constant value

G Fill handle

H Formula

I Formula Bar

J Name Box

K Range

L Ribbon

M View options

N Workbook

O Worksheet

Content-Based Assessments

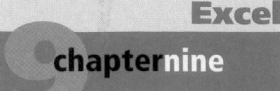

Fill in the Blank

Write the correct answer in the space provided.

1. A set of characters with the same design, size, and shape is called a _____.

2. A specific way in which Excel displays numbers in a cell is referred to as the _____ _____.

3. The default format that Excel applies to numbers, which has no specific characteristics except that trailing zeros to the right of a decimal point will not display, is the _____ format.

4. The data that displays in the Formula Bar is referred to as the _____ _____.

5. A formula prewritten by Excel is a _____.

6. In a formula, the address of a cell based on the relative position of the cell that contains the formula and the cell referred to is a _____ cell reference.

7. The Excel number format that applies a thousand comma separator where appropriate, inserts a fixed U.S. dollar sign aligned at the left edge of the cell, applies two decimal places, and leaves a small amount of space at the right edge of the cell to accommodate a parenthesis for negative numbers is the _____ _____ format.

8. The Excel number format that inserts thousand comma separators where appropriate, applies two decimal places, and leaves space at the right to accommodate a parenthesis for negative numbers is the _____ _____.

9. The area along the bottom of a chart that identifies the categories of data, and which is also referred to as the x-axis, is the _____ axis.

10. A numerical scale on the left side of a chart that shows the range of numbers for the data points, and also referred to as the y-axis, is the _____ axis.

11. In a chart, an explanation of the patterns or colors that are assigned to a data series that represents a category is called the _____.

(Fill in the Blank continues on the next page)

Fill in the Blank

12. Related data points represented by data markers in a chart, each of which has a unique color or pattern represented in the chart legend, are referred to as a _____ _____.

13. The combination of chart elements that can be displayed in a chart such as a title, legend, labels for the columns, and the table of charted cells is referred to as the _____ _____.

14. Symbols that specify addition, subtraction, multiplication, division, percentage, and exponentiation in an Excel formula are called _____ _____.

15. A cell reference that refers to cells by their fixed position in a work-sheet and which remain the same when the formula is copied is referred to as an _____ cell reference.

Content-Based Assessments

Skills Review

Project 9C — Service

In this project, you will apply the skills you practiced from the Objectives in Project 9A.

Objectives: 1. *Create, Save, and Navigate an Excel Workbook;* **2.** *Enter and Edit Data in a Worksheet;* **3.** *Construct and Copy Formulas, Use the Sum Function, and Edit Cells;* **4.** *Format Data, Cells, and Worksheets;* **5.** *Close and Reopen a Workbook;* **6.** *Chart Data;* **7.** *Use Page Layout View, Prepare a Worksheet for Printing, and Close Excel.*

In the following Skills Review, you will create a worksheet for Ellie Rose, Service Manager at the Rio Rancho Auto Gallery, to track weekly service revenue. Your completed worksheet will look similar to the one shown in Figure 9.71.

For Project 9C, you will need the following file:

New blank Excel workbook

You will save your workbook as
9C_Service_Firstname_Lastname

Figure 9.71

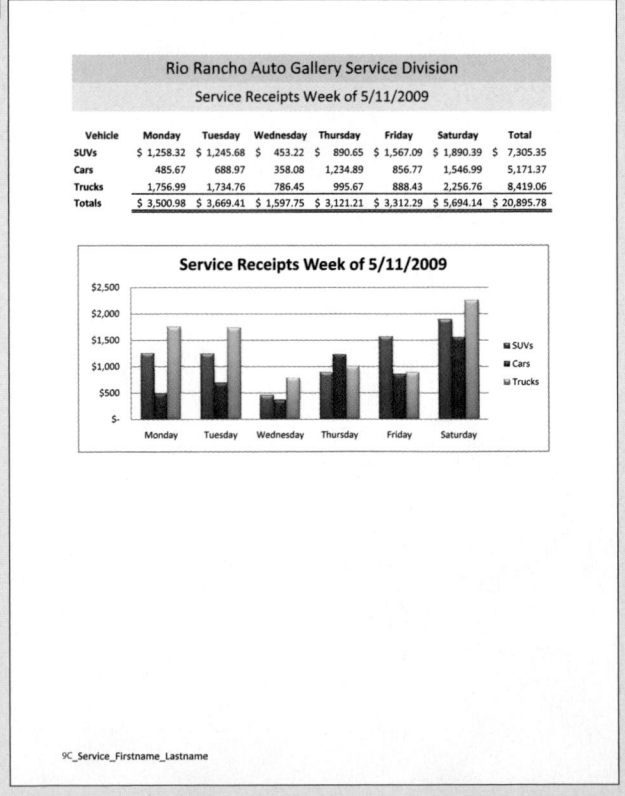

(Project 9C–Service continues on the next page)

Content-Based Assessments

(Project 9C–Service continued)

1. **Start** Excel. In cell **A1**, type **Rio Rancho Auto Gallery Service Division** and then press Enter. In cell **A2**, type **Service Receipts Week of 5/11/2009** and then press Enter. Display the **Save As** dialog box, navigate to your **Excel Chapter 9** folder, and then using your own first and last name, **Save** the workbook as 9C_Service_Firstname_Lastname

2. In cell **A3**, type **Vehicle** and then press Enter. Type **SUVs** and then press Enter. Type **Cars** and then press Enter. Type **Trucks** and then press Enter. In cell **A7**, type **Totals** and then press Enter.

3. In cell **B3**, type **Monday** and then press Enter. Click in cell **B3** again to make it the active cell. In the lower right corner of cell **B3**, point to the fill handle to display the ⊞ pointer, drag the fill handle to the right to cell **G3** so that the last ScreenTip that displays is *Saturday*, and then release the mouse button to fill the days of the week. In cell **H3**, type **Total** and then press Enter.

4. Press Ctrl + Home to move to cell **A1**, and then on the Ribbon, click the **Review tab**. In the **Proofing group**, click **Spelling**, and then correct any spelling errors that you may have made while typing. Beginning in cell **B4**, type the following data:

Vehicle	Monday	Tuesday	Wednesday	Thursday	Friday	Saturday
SUVs	1258.32	1245.68	453.22	890.65	1567.09	1890.39
Cars	485.67	688.97	358.08	1234.89	856.77	1546.99
Trucks	1756.99	1734.76	786.45	995.67	888.43	2256.76

5. From the **column heading area**, select **columns A:G**, and then point to the right boundary of any of the selected column letters to display the ↔ pointer. Drag to the right until the ScreenTip indicates **75 pixels**, and then release the mouse button to resize the selected columns.

6. Point to the **row 3** heading, and then right-click to simultaneously select the row and display the shortcut menu and the Mini toolbar. From the displayed shortcut menu, click **Insert** to insert a blank row—this will add some space between the worksheet titles and the column titles.

7. Click cell **H5**. On the **Home tab**, in the **Editing group**, click the **Sum** button, and then press Enter to enter the function—a prewritten formula. Your result is *7305.35*. Click cell **H5**, and then drag the fill handle down to cell **H7** to copy the formula. Recall that the cell references will adjust relative to their row.

8. Select the range **B5:H8**, which includes the columns to be totaled and the cells in which each total will display. Hold down Alt, and then press = to enter the Sum function in cells **B8:H8**. **Save** your workbook.

9. Select the range **A1:H1**, and then on the **Home tab**, in the **Alignment group**, click the **Merge and Center** button. Select the range **A2:H2**, right-click over the selection to display the short-cut menu and Mini toolbar, and then on the Mini toolbar, click the **Merge and Center** button. Both worksheet titles are centered over the worksheet.

(Project 9C–Service continues on the next page)

Content-Based Assessments

(Project 9C–Service continued)

10. Right-click cell **A1** to display the shortcut menu and the Mini toolbar. On the Mini toolbar, click the **Font Size arrow**, and then click **18**. Then, click the **Fill Color button arrow**, and under **Theme Colors**, in the next to last column, click the third color—**Aqua, Accent 5, Lighter 60%**.

11. Right-click cell **A2**. On the Mini toolbar, change the **Font Size** to **16**. Click the **Fill Color button arrow**, and then under **Theme Colors**, in the next to last column, click the second color—**Aqua, Accent 5, Lighter 80%**.

12. Select **rows 1** and **2**. Position the ⊕ pointer over the lower border of either of the selected rows, and then drag downward to increase the row height of both rows to **40 pixels**. Then, in the **Alignment group**, click the **Middle Align** button to center the titles vertically in the cells. Select **rows 4:8**, and then increase the row height of all of the selected rows to **24 pixels**.

13. Select the range **A4:H4**. Then, hold down Ctrl, and select the nonadjacent range **A5:A8**, so that both the column and row titles are selected. On the **Home tab**, in the **Font group**, click the **Bold** button. Select the range **A4:H4**, and then in the **Alignment group**, click the **Center** button.

14. Select the range **B5:H5**. Then, hold down Ctrl and select the nonadjacent range **B8:H8**. In the **Number group**, click the **Accounting Number Format** button to apply the format to the selected ranges. Select the range **B6:H7**, and then in the **Number group**, click the **Comma Style** button. Select the range **B8:H8**. In the **Font group**, click the **Borders button arrow**, and then click **Top and Double Bottom Border**. **Save** your workbook.

15. To chart the week's receipts by day and vehicle type, select the range **A4:G7**. On the Ribbon, click the **Insert tab**, and then in the **Charts group**, click **Column**. Under **2-D Column**, click the first chart type—**Clustered Column**. Point to the top border of the chart to display the ⊡ pointer, and then drag to position the chart so that its upper left corner is positioned inside the upper left corner of cell **A11**.

16. On the **Design tab**, in the **Chart Layouts group**, click **Layout 1**. Click in the **Chart Title**, delete the existing text, and then type **Service Receipts Week of 5/11/2009** Click in a white area slightly *inside* the chart's border to deselect the chart title, but leave the chart itself selected. On the **Design tab**, in the **Chart Styles group**, click the **More** button to display the gallery of chart styles. Click **Style 26**.

17. Click the **Layout tab**, and then, in the **Axes group**, click the **Axes** button. Point to **Primary Vertical Axis**, and then click **More Primary Vertical Axis Options**. In the **Format Axis** dialog box, in the column at the left, click **Number**. In the **Decimal places** box, change the number to **0** and then click **Close**.

18. Click any cell to deselect the chart. Click the **Insert tab**, and then in the **Text group**, click the **Header & Footer** button to switch to **Page Layout view** and open the **Header area**. In the **Navigation group**, click the **Go to Footer** button, click just above the word *Footer*, and then in the **Header & Footer Elements group**, click the **File Name** button. Click in a cell just above the footer to exit the footer area and view your file name.

(Project 9C–Service continues on the next page)

Content-Based Assessments

(Project 9C–Service continued)

19. Scroll up to view your chart. Click the chart to select it, and notice that the chart is not centered under the data in the cells. Position the pointer over the **right resize handle**, which will display the $\leftrightarrow$ pointer, and then drag to the right so that the right border of the chart is just inside the right border of **column H**. Release the mouse button to resize the chart.

20. Click any cell to deselect the chart. Click the **Page Layout tab**. In the **Page Setup group**, click the **Margins** button, and then at the bottom of the **Margins gallery**, click **Custom Margins**. In the displayed **Page Setup** dialog box, under **Center on page**, select the **Horizontally** check box. Click **OK** to close the dialog box, and then **Save** the changes to your workbook.

21. On the status bar, click the **Normal** button to return to **Normal view**, and then press Ctrl + Home to move to the top of your worksheet. At the lower edge of the window, click to select the **Sheet2 tab**, hold down Ctrl and click the **Sheet3 tab** to select the two unused sheets. On the **Home tab**, in the **Cells group**, click the **Delete button arrow**, and then from the displayed list, click **Delete Sheet**.

22. **Save** the changes you have made to your workbook. Check your *Chapter Assignment Sheet* or *Course Syllabus* or consult your instructor to determine if you are to submit your assignments on paper or electronically. To submit electronically, follow the instructions provided by your instructor.

23. From the **Office** menu, point to the **Print button**, and then click **Print Preview** to check the placement of your worksheet. In the **Print group**, click the **Print** button. In the displayed **Print** dialog box, under **Print range**, verify that the **All** option button is selected. Under **Print what**, verify that **Active sheet(s)** is selected, and then under **Copies**, verify that the **Number of copies** is **1**. Click **OK** to print your worksheet. If you are directed to submit printed formulas, refer to Activity 9.17 to do so.

24. If you printed your formulas, be sure to redisplay the worksheet by pressing Ctrl + `. From the **Office** menu, click **Close**. If the dialog box displays asking if you want to save changes, click **No** so that you do *not* save the changes you made for printing formulas. **Exit** Excel.

End **You have completed Project 9C**

Content-Based Assessments

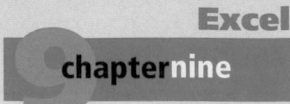
Skills Review

Project 9D — Tires

In this project, you will apply the skills you practiced from the Objectives in Project 9B.

Objectives: 8. *Design a Worksheet;* **9.** *Construct Formulas for Mathematical Operations;* **10.** *Format Percentages and Move Formulas;* **11.** *Create a Pie Chart and a Chart Sheet.*

In the following Skills Review, you will create a worksheet for Arthur Potempa, Retail Sales Manager of the Rio Rancho Auto Gallery, to track the sales of two different types of tires at the four subsidiary stores that sell only tires. Your completed worksheet will look similar to the one shown in Figure 9.72.

For Project 9D, you will need the following file:

New blank Excel workbook

You will save your workbook as 9D_Tires_Firstname_Lastname

Figure 9.72

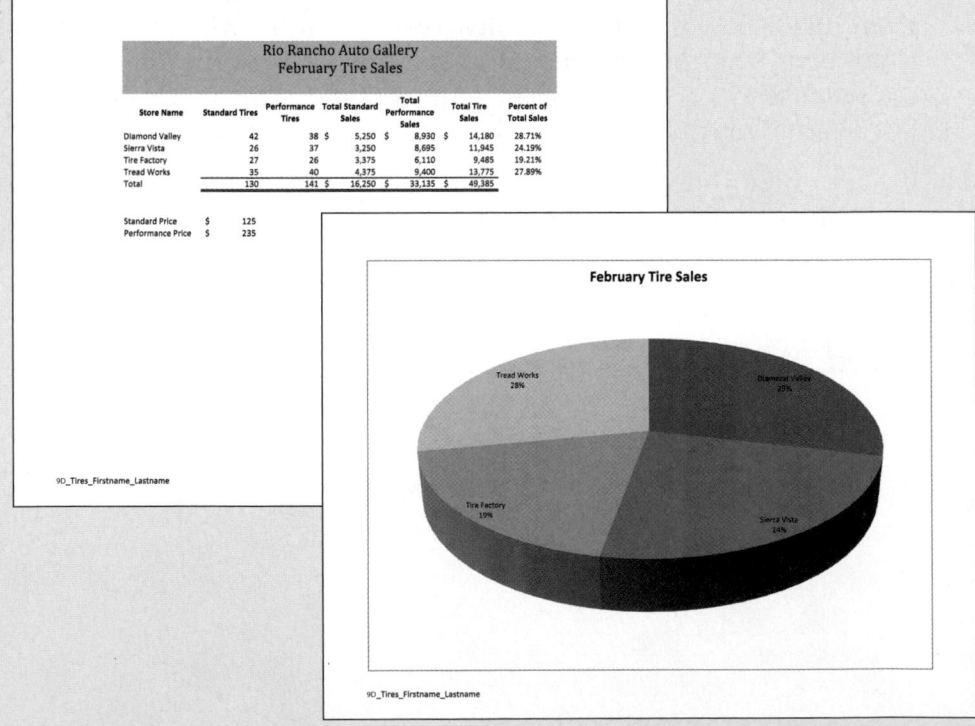

(Project 9D–Tires continues on the next page)

Content-Based Assessments

(Project 9D–Tires continued)

1. **Start** Excel so that a new blank workbook displays. In cell **A1**, type **Rio Rancho Auto Gallery** and then press Enter. In cell **A2**, type **February Tire Sales** and then press Enter. Select the range **A1:A2**. In the **Font group**, click the **Font arrow**, and then click **Cambria**. Click the **Font Size arrow**, and then click **18**. Display the **Save As** dialog box, navigate to your **Excel Chapter 9** folder, and then using your own first and last name, **Save** the workbook as 9D_Tires_ Firstname_Lastname

2. In cell **A3**, type **Store Name** and then press Tab. In cell **B3**, type **Standard Tires** and then press Tab. In cell **C3**, type **Performance Tires** and then press Tab. In cell **D3**, type **Total Standard Sales** and then press Tab. In cell **E3**, type **Total Performance Sales** and then press Tab. In **F3**, type **Total Tire Sales** and then press Tab. In cell **G3**, type **Percent of Total Sales** and then press Enter.

3. In the **column heading area**, point to the right boundary of **column A** to display the ⟷ pointer, and then drag to the right to widen the column to **120 pixels**. Select the range **A3:G3**, and then in the **Font group**, click the **Bold** button. In the **Alignment group**, click the **Wrap Text** button, click the **Center** button, and then click the **Middle Align** button. Select **columns B:G**. In the **column heading area**, point to the right boundary of any of the selected columns to display the ⟷ pointer, and then drag to the right to increase the column width to **90 pixels**.

4. Select the range **A4:C6**, and then type the following data, pressing Enter to move from cell to cell within the selected range.

Store Name	Standard Tires	Performance Tires
Diamond Valley	42	38
Sierra Vista	26	37
Tread Works	35	40

5. In the range **A10:B11** type the following:

Standard Price	125
Performance Price	235

6. Click cell **D4** and type = to begin a formula. Click cell **B4**, type * and then click cell **B10** to construct a formula that will multiply the number of Standard Tires sold at the Diamond Valley store by the Standard Price, which is 125. Then, press F4 to make the reference to cell **B10** absolute so that your formula indicates =B4*$B$10

   Because you will copy the formula down for the other two stores, the first cell reference should change relative to each row, but the price, located in cell B10, should remain the same for each formula.

7. Press Enter; your result is *5250*. Select cell **D4** again, and then drag the fill handle downward through cell **D6**. Check each formula to be sure that the first cell reference changed relative to the row and that the second cell reference remained absolute—in each formula referring to the price in cell **B10**.

8. In cell **E4**, construct a similar formula to calculate the total sales of Performance Tires at Diamond Valley, using the Performance Price in cell **B11**. Then, copy the formula down through cell **E6** to compute the sales of Performance Tires for the other locations.

9. In cell **F4**, type = and then use the point and click method to construct a formula to add the Total Standard Sales and the Total

(Project 9D–Tires continues on the next page)

(Project 9D–Tires continued)

Performance Sales at the Diamond Valley store; your formula should indicate =*D4+E4*, and then click the **Enter** button on the **Formula Bar**. Your result is *14180*. With cell **F4** still selected, use the fill handle to copy the formula down to compute the Total Tire Sales for the Sierra Vista store and the Tread Works store.

10. In cell **A7**, type **Total** and then press Enter. Select the range **B4:F7**. On the **Home tab**, in the **Editing group**, click the **Sum** button to calculate totals for each column. Click any cell to deselect. Select the range **D4:F4**, and then hold down Ctrl and select the nonadjacent ranges **D7:F7** and **B10:B11**. On the **Home tab**, in the **Number group**, click **Accounting Number Format**, and then click the **Decrease Decimal** button two times to format the numbers with zero decimal places.

11. Select the range **D5:F6**, in the **Number group**, click **Comma Style**, and then click the **Decrease Decimal** button two times to format the numbers with comma separators and zero decimal places. Select the range **B7:F7**. In the **Font group**, click the **Borders button arrow**, and then from the displayed list, click **Top and Double Bottom Border**.

12. Point to the **row 6** heading and right-click to select the row and display the shortcut menu. Click **Insert** to insert a blank row, and as you type the following data in **A6:C6**, notice that the Total in cell **B8** and cell **C8** recalculates:

Tire Factory   27   26

13. Select the range **D5:F5**, and then drag the fill handle down to fill the three formulas to the range **D6:F6**, which will calculate the sales for the Tire Factory store and recalculate the column totals.

14. Click in cell **G4**, type = click cell **F4**, type / click cell **F8**, and then press F4 . Your formula =*F4/$F$8* will calculate the percentage by which Diamond Valley's sales contributes to the Rio Rancho Auto Gallery's total tire sales. Press Enter; your result is *0.28713172* or approximately 29 percent. Click cell **G4**, and then use the fill handle to copy the formula down through cell **G7**. In each formula, the first cell reference will change relative to its row, and the second cell reference will remain absolute—referring to the total in cell **F8**.

15. If necessary, select the range **G4:G7**. Right-click over the selection, on the Mini toolbar, click the **Percent Style** button, click the **Center** button, and then click the **Increase Decimal** button two times. Recall that for precise information, you can increase the decimal places in a percentage.

16. Select the range **A1:G1**, and then on the **Home tab**, in the **Alignment group**, click **Merge and Center**. Repeat this formatting for cells **A2:G2**. Select the range **A1:A2**, click the **Fill Color arrow**, and then under **Theme Colors**, in the last column, click **Orange**, **Accent 6**, **Lighter 40%**. Right-click the **row 3** heading and insert a blank row to create space between the worksheet titles and the column titles—recall that the formulas will be moved and adjusted accordingly. On the **Insert tab**, in the **Text group**, click the **Header & Footer** button. In the **Navigation group**, click the **Go to Footer** button. Click just above the word *Footer* in the left section of the **Footer area**, and then in the **Header & Footer Elements group**, click the **File Name** button. Click any cell just above the **Footer area** to deselect the footer and view your file name, and then press Ctrl + Home to move to the top of your worksheet.

(Project 9D–Tires continues on the next page)

Content-Based Assessments

(Project 9D–Tires continued)

17. Click the **Page Layout tab**. In the **Page Setup group**, click the **Orientation** button, and then click **Landscape**. Click the **Margins** button, and then at the bottom of the **Margins gallery**, click **Custom Margins**. In the displayed **Page Setup** dialog box, under **Center on page**, select the **Horizontally** check box. Click **OK**.

18. **Save** the changes you have made. On the right edge of the status bar, click the **Normal** button to return to **Normal view**. Select the range **A4:A8**, hold down (Ctrl), and then select the range **F4:F8**. Click the **Insert tab**. In the **Charts group**, click **Pie**, and then under **3-D Pie**, click the first chart—**Pie in 3-D**. On the **Design tab**, in the **Location group**, click the **Move Chart** button. In the **Move Chart** dialog box, click the **New sheet** option button and replace the highlighted text *Chart1* by typing **Tire Sales Chart** Click **OK** to move the pie chart to a separate chart sheet in the workbook.

19. On the **Design tab**, in the **Chart Layouts group**, click **Layout 1**. Click the text *Total Tire Sales*, and then edit to indicate **February Tire Sales** Click inside the white area of the chart to deselect the title. In the **Chart Styles group**, click the **More** button, and then click **Style 8**.

20. To create a footer on your chart sheet, click the **Insert tab**. In the **Text group**, click the **Header & Footer** button, and then in the displayed **Page Setup dialog box**, click the **Custom Footer** button. With the insertion point positioned in the

Left section, click the seventh button— **Insert File Name**, and then click **OK** two times.

21. Click the **Sheet1 tab** and press (Ctrl) + (Home) to cancel the selections. Click the **Sheet2** tab, hold down (Ctrl) and click the **Sheet3 tab**, right-click over the selected sheet tabs, and then click **Delete**.

22. **Save** your workbook. Check your *Chapter Assignment Sheet* or *Course Syllabus* or consult your instructor to determine if you are to submit your assignments on paper or electronically. To submit electronically, follow the instructions provided by your instructor.

23. To print, from the **Office** menu, click the **Print** button. In the displayed **Print** dialog box, under **Print what**, click the **Entire workbook** option button. In the lower left corner of the dialog box, click **Preview**, and notice in the status bar, *Preview: Page 1 of 2* displays. Check the preview, in the **Preview group**, click the **Next Page** button, and then in the **Print group**, click **Print** to print the two pages. If you are directed to submit printed formulas, refer to Activity 9.17 to do so.

24. If you printed your formulas, be sure to redisplay the worksheet by pressing (Ctrl) + (´). From the **Office** menu, click **Close**. If the dialog box displays asking if you want to save changes, click **No** so that you do *not* save the changes you made for printing formulas. **Exit** Excel.

End **You have completed Project 9D**

Content-Based Assessments

Mastering Excel

Project 9E — Analysis

In this project, you will apply the skills you practiced from the Objectives in Project 9A.

Objectives: 1 *Create, Save, and Navigate an Excel Workbook;* **2.** *Enter and Edit Data in a Worksheet;* **3.** *Construct and Copy Formulas, Use the Sum Function, and Edit Cells;* **4.** *Format Data, Cells, and Worksheets;* **5.** *Close and Reopen a Workbook;* **6.** *Chart Data;* **7.** *Use Page Layout View, Prepare a Worksheet for Printing, and Close Excel.*

In the following Mastering Excel project, you will create a year-end sales analysis worksheet for Tony Konecki, President of Rio Rancho Auto Gallery, which will compare revenue from the organization's products and services. Your completed worksheet will look similar to Figure 9.73.

For Project 9E, you will need the following file:

New blank Excel workbook

You will save your workbook as
9E_Analysis_Firstname_Lastname

Figure 9.73

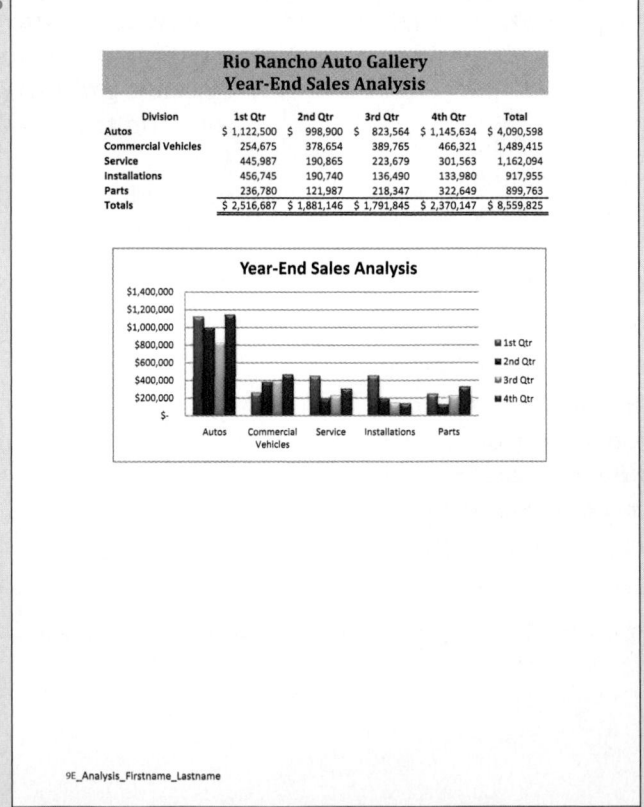

(Project 9E–Analysis continues on the next page)

Content-Based Assessments

(Project 9E–Analysis continued)

1. **Start** Excel and display a new blank workbook. In cell **A1**, type **Rio Rancho Auto Gallery** and in cell **A2**, type **Year-End Sales Analysis** In cell **A3**, type **Division** In cell **B3**, type **1st Qtr** select the cell, and then use the fill handle to create a series in the range **B3:E3** so that *2nd Qtr* through *4th Qtr* displays in the cells. In cell **F3**, type **Total** and then in your **Excel Chapter 9** folder, **Save** the workbook as **9E_Analysis_Firstname_Lastname**

2. Select the range **A4:E8**, and then enter the following data, pressing Enter to move from cell to cell within the selected range.

Division	1st Qtr	2nd Qtr	3rd Qtr	4th Qtr
Autos	1122500	998900	823564	1145634
Commercial Vehicles	254675	378654	389765	466321
Service	445987	190865	223679	301563
Installations	456745	190740	136490	133980
Parts	236780	121987	218347	322649

3. Adjust the width of **column A** so that the row title *Commercial Vehicles* displays fully— approximately **140 pixels**. Use the **Sum** function to calculate the total for the Autos Division, and then copy the formula down for the remaining divisions. Then use the **Sum** function to total the columns—recall that you can select the range **B4:F9** and click the Sum button one time. In cell **A9**, type **Totals**

4. Insert a row above **row 3** to create space between the worksheet titles and the column titles— your formulas will move and adjust accordingly. Use the **Merge and Center** command to center the worksheet titles in cells **A1** and **A2** over the column titles. Select and format the two worksheet titles as follows: change the **Font** to **Cambria**, the **Font Size** to **18**, apply **Bold**, and then apply a **Fill Color**, using the **Theme Color Purple, Accent 4, Lighter 60%**.

5. Select the range **B6:F9**, apply **Comma Style**, and then **Decrease Decimal** to zero decimals. Select the nonadjacent ranges **B5:F5** and **B10:F10**, apply **Accounting Number Format**, and **Decrease Decimal** to zero decimals. Apply the appropriate **Top and Double Bottom Border** to the totals. **Center** the column titles in **Row 4**, apply **Bold** to the column titles and row titles, and then **AutoFit** columns **B:F**. Compare your formatting to Figure 9.73 if necessary.

6. Select the range **A4:E9**, and then **Insert** a **2-D Clustered Column chart**. Position the chart approximately two rows below the worksheet data slightly inside the left edge of **column A**. Be sure that the chart is selected so that the **Chart Tools** display. On the **Design tab**, in the **Chart Layouts group**, click **Layout 1**, and then in the **Chart Styles group**, click **Style 26**. Change the **Chart Title** to **Year-End Sales Analysis**

7. **Save** your workbook. Click any cell to deselect the chart. On the **Insert tab**, in the **Text group**, click the **Header & Footer** button to switch to **Page Layout view** and open the **Header area**. In the **Navigation group**, click the **Go to Footer** button, click just above the word *Footer*, and then in the **Header & Footer Elements group**, click the **File Name** button. Click in a cell just above the footer to deselect the **Footer area** and view your file name.

(Project 9E–Analysis continues on the next page)

Content-Based Assessments

(Project 9E–Analysis continued)

8. Scroll up to view your chart. Select the chart, and then drag the right sizing handle of the chart as necessary to widen the chart so that the right border of the chart is slightly inside the right border of **column F**. Deselect the chart. On the **Page Layout tab**, in the **Page Setup group**, click the **Margins** button, and then at the bottom of the **Margins gallery**, click **Custom Margins**. Under **Center on page**, select the **Horizontally** check box, click **OK**, and then **Save** the changes to your workbook. Return to **Normal view** and scroll up as necessary to view the top of your worksheet. Select and delete **Sheet2** and **Sheet3**.

9. **Save** the changes to your workbook. Check your *Chapter Assignment Sheet* or *Course Syllabus* or consult your instructor to determine if you are to submit your assignments on paper or electronically. To submit electronically, follow the instructions provided by your instructor.

10. From the **Office** menu, preview, and then print your worksheet. If you are directed to submit printed formulas, refer to Activity 9.17 to do so. If you printed your formulas, be sure to redisplay the worksheet by pressing Ctrl + ` . From the **Office** menu click **Close**. If the dialog box displays asking if you want to save changes, click **No** so that you do *not* save the changes you made for printing formulas. **Exit** Excel.

End **You have completed Project 9E** ——————————————————

Content-Based Assessments

Mastering Excel

Project 9F—4th Quarter Sales

In this project, you will apply the skills you practiced from the Objectives in Project 9B.

Objectives: 8. *Design a Worksheet;* **9.** *Construct Formulas for Mathematical Operations;* **10.** *Format Percentages and Move Formulas;* **11.** *Create a Pie Chart and a Chart Sheet.*

In the following Mastering Excel project, you will create a worksheet and chart sheet for Sandy Cizek, the Auto Sales Manager for Rio Rancho Auto Gallery, to analyze fourth quarter vehicle sales. Your completed worksheet and chart will look similar to Figure 9.74.

For Project 9F, you will need the following file:
New blank Excel workbook

You will save your workbook as 9F_4th_Quarter_Sales_Firstname_Lastname

Figure 9.74

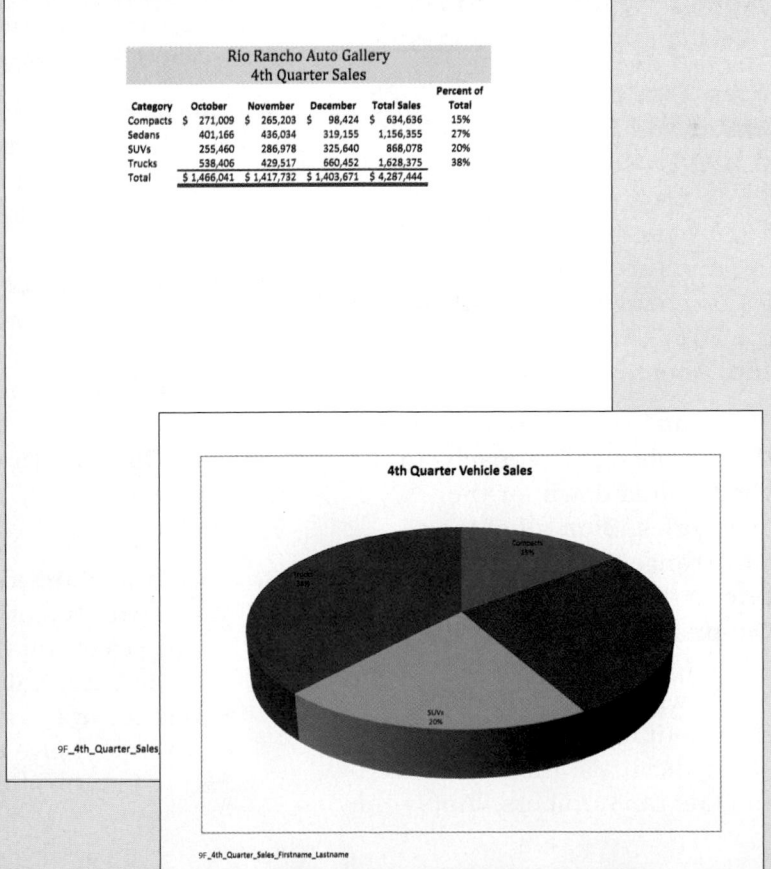

(Project 9F–4th Quarter Sales continues on the next page)

Content-Based Assessments

(Project 9F–4th Quarter Sales continued)

1. **Start** Excel and display a new blank workbook. In cell **A1**, type **Rio Rancho Auto Gallery** and in cell **A2**, type **4th Quarter Sales** In cell **A3**, type **Category** In cell **B3**, type **October** Select cell **B3**, and then use the fill handle to create a series in the range **C3:D3** so that *November* and *December* display in the cells. In cell **E3**, type **Total Sales** and in cell **F3**, type **Percent of Total** In your **Excel Chapter 9** folder, **Save** the workbook as 9F_4th_Quarter_Sales_Firstname_Lastname

2. In the range **A4:D6**, type the following data; if you want to do so, select the range first and use Enter to confine the movement of the active cell within the range.

Category	October	November	December
Compacts	271009	265203	98424
Sedans	401166	436034	319155
Trucks	538406	429517	660452

3. Apply the **Wrap Text** command to cell **F3**, and then **Center** and **Bold** all the column titles in **row 3**. Adjust the width of **columns B:F** to **80 pixels**. **Merge and Center** the two worksheet titles over columns **A:F**, and then select and format the two titles by changing the **Font** to **Cambria**, the **Font Size** to **16**, and the **Fill Color** to **Blue, Accent 1, Lighter 80%**.

4. In cell **A7**, type **Total** In cell **E4**, **Sum** the three month's of sales for Compacts, and then copy the formula down for the remaining categories. **Sum** all of the columns in the range **B4:E7**. Apply the **Comma Style** to the range **B5:E6** and **Decrease Decimals** to zero decimals. (Hint: Recall that pound signs indicate that a cell is not wide enough to display the number without distortion; however after decreasing decimals, the cell width will accommodate the numbers.) Apply the

Accounting Number Format to the ranges **B4:E4,B7:E7**, and then **Decrease Decimals** to zero decimals. Apply the appropriate border to the totals.

5. Insert a row above *Trucks* and enter the following data—recall that Excel will move and adjust formulas when rows are inserted. After you enter the data, use the fill handle to copy the formula from **E5** to **E6**.

   SUVs   255460   286978   325640

6. In cell **F4**, type = and then construct a formula to calculate the percentage by which fourth quarter sales of Compacts makes up the Total Sales. (Hint: Divide the Total Sales of Compacts by the Total for all categories.) Use F4 to apply absolute cell referencing where necessary. To your result, apply **Percent Style** formatting with zero decimals, and then fill the formula down to cell **F7**. **Center** the percentages.

7. On the **Insert tab**, in the **Text group**, click **Header & Footer** to switch to **Page Layout View**. In the **Navigation group**, click the **Go to Footer** button, click just above the word *Footer*, and then in the **Header & Footer Elements group**, click the **File Name** button. Click a cell just above the footer to deselect the **Footer area** and view your file name. On the **Page Layout tab**, display the **Margins gallery**, click **Custom Margins**, and then under **Center on page**, select the **Horizontally** check box.

8. Switch to **Normal view** and press Ctrl + Home to move to the top of your worksheet. Select the vehicle categories in **A4:A7** and the Total Sales amounts in **E4:E7**. **Insert** a **Pie** chart, using the **Pie in 3-D** chart type. Move the chart to a new sheet and name the sheet **4th Quarter Chart**

(Project 9F–4th Quarter Sales continues on the next page)

Content-Based Assessments

(Project 9F–4th Quarter Sales continued)

Apply **Chart Layout 1**, **Chart Style 2**, and change the **Chart Title** to 4th Quarter Vehicle Sales Deselect the chart title. To create a footer on the chart sheet, on the **Insert tab**, click the **Header & Footer** button, and then create a **Custom Footer** with the file name in the **Left section**.

9. Click the **Sheet1 tab** and press Ctrl + Home to cancel the selections. Select and delete **Sheet2** and **Sheet3**.

10. **Save** your workbook. Check your *Chapter Assignment Sheet* or *Course Syllabus* or consult your instructor to determine if you are to submit your assignments on paper or electronically. To submit electronically, follow the instructions provided by your instructor.

11. To print, from the **Office** menu, click the **Print** button. In the displayed **Print** dialog box, under **Print what**, click the **Entire workbook** option button. In the lower left corner of the dialog box, click **Preview**, and notice in the status bar, *Preview: Page 1 of 2* displays. Check the preview, in the **Preview group**, click the **Next Page** button, and then in the **Print group**, click **Print** to print the two pages. If you are directed to submit printed formulas, refer to Activity 9.17 to do so.

12. If you printed your formulas, be sure to redisplay the worksheet by pressing Ctrl + `. From the **Office** menu, click **Close**. If the dialog box displays asking if you want to save changes, click **No** so that you do *not* save the changes you made for printing formulas. **Exit** Excel.

End You have completed Project 9F

Mastering Excel

Project 9G — Compensation

In this project, you will apply the skills you practiced from the Objectives in Projects 9A and 9B.

Objectives: 1. *Create, Save, and Navigate an Excel Workbook;* **2.** *Enter and Edit Data in a Worksheet;* **3.** *Construct and Copy Formulas, Use the Sum Function, and Edit Cells;* **4.** *Format Data, Cells, and Worksheets;* **7.** *Use Page Layout View, Prepare a Worksheet for Printing, and Close Excel;* **9.** *Construct Formulas for Mathematical Operations;* **10.** *Format Percentages and Move Formulas.* **11.** *Create a Pie Chart and a Chart Sheet.*

In the following Mastering Excel project, you will create a worksheet for Clint Williams, Truck Sales Manager of Rio Rancho Auto Gallery. Members of the sales staff are paid a 5 percent commission on their total sales and also receive a small expense allowance to purchase pro-motional items like mugs, license plate holders, and key chains to give to customers. Your completed worksheet will look similar to Figure 9.75.

For Project 9G, you will need the following file:

New blank Excel workbook

You will save your workbook as
9G_Compensation_Firstname_Lastname

Figure 9.75

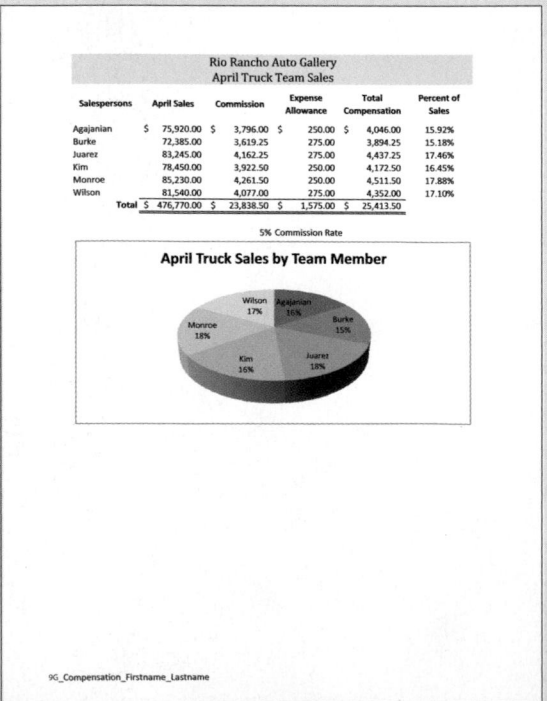

(Project 9G–Compensation continues on the next page)

Content-Based Assessments

Excel
chapter nine   Mastering Excel

(Project 9G–Compensation continued)

1. **Start** Excel and display a new blank workbook. In cell **A1**, type **Rio Rancho Auto Gallery** and in cell **A2**, type **April Truck Team Sales** In cell **A3**, type **Salespersons** and then press Tab. In cell **B3**, type **April Sales** In cell **C3**, type **Commission** In cell **D3**, type **Expense Allowance** In cell **E3**, type **Total Compensation** In cell **F3**, type **Percent of Sales** In your **Excel Chapter 9** folder, **Save** the workbook as 9G_Compensation_Firstname_Lastname

2. Beginning in cell **A4**, enter the following data:

Salespersons	April Sales	Commission	Expense Allowance
Agajanian	75920		250
Burke	72385		275
Juarez	83245		275
Kim	78450		250
Monroe	85230		250
Wilson	81540		275

3. Apply the **Wrap Text** command to the range **D3:F3**. Widen all the columns to approximately **95 pixels**, and then select the column titles and apply **Bold**, **Center**, and **Middle Align**. **Merge and Center** cells **A1** and **A2** over the column titles. Select the two worksheet titles and change the **Font** to **Cambria**, the **Font Size** to **14**, and apply a **Fill Color** of **Olive Green, Accent 3, Lighter 60%**.

4. In cell **C12**, type **5%** and in cell **D12**, type **Commission Rate** In cell **C4**, construct a formula to calculate the Commission for Agajanian—April Sales times the 5% rate in cell **C12**, using absolute cell references where necessary so that you can copy the formula down. Your result is *3796*. Copy the formula down for the remaining salespersons. In cell **E4**, construct a formula to calculate Agajanian's Total Compensation

by adding the Commission plus the Expense Allowance. Your result is *4046*. Copy the formula down for the remaining salespersons.

5. In cell **A10**, type **Total** Then, **Align Text Right** and apply **Bold**. Calculate totals for each of the four columns. Using financial formatting for the appropriate numbers, first apply **Comma Style**, next apply **Accounting Number Format**, and then apply a **Top and Double Bottom Border** to the total row.

6. In cell **F4**, construct a formula to calculate Agajanian's Percent of Sales by dividing Agajanian's April Sales in **B4** by Total April Sales in **B10**, using absolute cell references as necessary so that you copy the formula. Your result is *0.159238207*. Apply **Percent Style**, increase the decimal places to two, and then **Center** the percentage. Fill the formula down for the remaining salespersons.

7. Select the range of data containing the name of each salesperson and each salesperson's April Sales. **Insert** a **Pie** chart, using the **Pie in 3-D** chart type. Position the upper left corner of the chart just inside the upper left corner of cell **A13**. Apply **Chart Layout 1**, **Chart Style 5**, and as the **Chart Title** type **April Truck Sales by Team Member**

8. **Save** your workbook. Click any cell to deselect the chart. On the **Insert tab**, in the **Text group**, click **Header & Footer** to switch to **Page Layout view** and open the **Header area**. In the **Navigation group**, click the **Go to Footer** button, click just above the word *Footer*, and then in the **Header & Footer Elements group**, click the **File Name** button. Click in a cell just

(Project 9G–Compensation continues on the next page)

Content-Based Assessments

(Project 9G–Compensation continued)

above the footer to deselect the **Footer area** and view your file name.

9. Scroll up to view your chart. Select the chart, and then using the ↔ pointer, drag the right sizing handle of the chart as necessary to widen the chart so that the right border of the chart is just inside the right border of **column F**. Deselect the chart. On the **Page Layout tab**, in the **Page Setup group**, click the **Margins** button, and then at the bottom of the **Margins gallery**, click **Custom Margins**. Under **Center on page**, select the **Horizontally** check box, click **OK**, and then **Save** your workbook. Return to **Normal view** and scroll up as necessary to view the top of

your worksheet. Select and delete **Sheet2** and **Sheet3**.

10. **Save** the changes to your workbook. To submit electronically, follow the instructions provided by your instructor. To print on paper, from the **Office** menu, preview and then print your worksheet. If you are directed to submit printed formulas, refer to Activity 9.17 to do so. If you printed your formulas, be sure to redisplay the worksheet by pressing Ctrl + `. **Close** your workbook. If the dialog box displays asking if you want to save changes, click **No** so that you do *not* save the changes you made for printing formulas. **Exit** Excel.

End **You have completed Project 9G** ──────────────

Mastering Excel

Project 9H — Warranties

In this project, you will apply the skills you practiced from the Objectives in Projects 9A and 9B.

Objectives: 1. *Create, Save, and Navigate an Excel Workbook;* **2.** *Enter and Edit Data in a Worksheet;* **3.** *Construct and Copy Formulas, Use the Sum Function, and Edit Cells;* **4.** *Format Data, Cells, and Worksheets;* **7.** *Use Page Layout View, Prepare a Worksheet for Printing, and Close Excel;* **8.** *Design a Worksheet;* **9.** *Construct Formulas for Mathematical Operations;* **11.** *Create a Pie Chart and a Chart Sheet.*

In the following Mastering Excel project, you will create a workbook for Sandy Cizek, the Auto Sales Manager, which summarizes both the sales of vehicle warranties and the commissions paid on the warranties that were sold. Your completed worksheets will look similar to Figure 9.76.

For Project 9H, you will need the following file:

New blank Excel workbook

**You will save your workbook as
9H_Warranties_Firstname_Lastname**

Figure 9.76

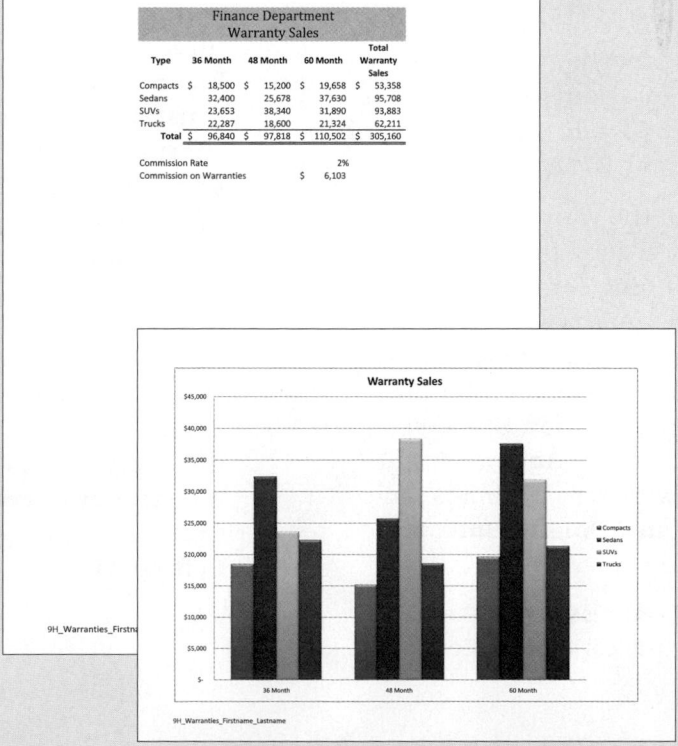

(Project 9H–Warranties continues on the next page)

Content-Based Assessments

(Project 9H–Warranties continued)

1. **Start** Excel and display a new blank workbook. In cell **A1**, type **Finance Department** and in cell **A2**, type **Warranty Sales** In cell **A3**, type **Type** and press Tab. In cell **B3**, type **36 Month** In cell **C3**, type **48 Month** In cell **D3**, type **60 Month** In cell **E3**, type **Total Warranty Sales** In your **Excel Chapter 9** folder, **Save** the workbook as **9H_Warranties_Firstname_Lastname**

2. In the range **A4:D7** type the following data; if you want to do so, select the range first and use Enter to confine the movement of the active cell within the range.

Type	36 Month	48 Month	60 Month
Compacts	18500	15200	19658
Sedans	32400	25678	37630
SUVs	23653	38340	31890
Trucks	22287	18600	21324

3. Apply the **Wrap Text** command to cell **E3**. Format all the column titles in **row 3** with **Center**, **Middle Align**, and **Bold**. Adjust the width of **columns B:E** to **80 pixels**. **Merge and Center** the two worksheet titles over columns **A:E**, and then select and format the two titles by changing the **Font** to **Cambria**, the **Font Size** to **16**, and the **Fill Color** to **Red, Accent 2, Lighter 60%**.

4. In cell **E4**, **Sum** all the warranties sold for Compacts, and then copy the formula down for the remaining vehicle types. **Sum** the columns. In cell **A8**, type **Total** and apply **Bold** and **Align Text Right**. Using financial formatting for the appropriate numbers, first apply **Comma Style** with zero decimals, next apply **Accounting Number Format** with zero decimals, and then apply a **Top and Double Bottom Border** to the total row.

5. In cell **A10**, type **Commission Rate** and in cell **D10**, type **2%** In cell **A11**, type

Commission on Warranties In cell **D11**, construct a formula that multiplies the Total Warranty Sales in cell **E8** by the Commission Rate in **D10**, and then apply **Accounting Number Format** with zero decimals.

6. On the **Insert tab**, in the **Text group**, click **Header & Footer** to switch to **Page Layout view**. In the **Navigation group**, click the **Go to Footer** button, click just above the word *Footer*, and then in the **Header & Footer Elements group**, click the **File Name** button. Click a cell just above the footer to deselect the **Footer area** and view your file name. On the **Page Layout tab**, display the **Margins gallery**, click **Custom Margins**, and then under **Center on page**, select the **Horizontally** check box.

7. Switch to **Normal view** and scroll to the top of your worksheet. Select the range of data that represents the types of vehicles and the warranty sales for each of the three types, including the column titles. **Insert** a **Column** chart, using the **2-D Clustered Column** chart type. Move the chart to a new sheet and name the sheet **Warranty Sales Chart** On the **Design tab**, in the **Data group**, click the **Switch Row/Column** button to display the warranty periods as the categories. Apply **Chart Layout 1**, **Chart Style 26**, and change the **Chart Title** to **Warranty Sales** Deselect the chart by clicking in an area outside of the chart. To create a footer on the chart sheet, on the **Insert tab**, click the **Header & Footer** button, create a **Custom Footer** with the file name in the **Left section**.

(Project 9H–Warranties continues on the next page)

Content-Based Assessments

(Project 9H–Warranties continued)

8. Click the **Sheet1 tab** and press Ctrl + Home to cancel the selections. Select and delete **Sheet2** and **Sheet3**.

9. **Save** your workbook. To submit electronically, follow the instructions provided by your instructor. To print, from the **Office** menu, click the **Print** button. In the displayed **Print** dialog box, under **Print what**, click the **Entire workbook** option button. In the lower left corner of the dialog box, click **Preview**, and notice in the status bar, *Preview: Page 1 of 2* displays. Check the preview, in the **Preview group**, click the **Next Page** button, and then in the **Print group**, click **Print** to print the two pages. If you are directed to submit printed formulas, refer to Activity 9.17 to do so.

10. If you printed your formulas, be sure to redisplay the worksheet by pressing Ctrl + `. From the **Office** menu, click **Close**. If the dialog box displays asking if you want to save changes, click **No** so that you do *not* save the changes you made for printing formulas. **Exit** Excel.

 You have completed Project 9H ——————————————————————

Mastering Excel

Project 9I—Team Comparison

In this project, you will apply the skills you practiced from all the Objectives in Projects 9A and 9B.

In the following Mastering Excel project, you will create a workbook for Sandy Cizek, Auto Sales Manager, which summarizes the monthly team sales for one of the three auto sales teams at Rio Rancho Auto Gallery. Your completed worksheet will look similar to Figure 9.77.

For Project 9I, you will need the following file:

New blank Excel workbook

**You will save your workbook as
9I_Team_Comparison_Firstname_Lastname**

Figure 9.77

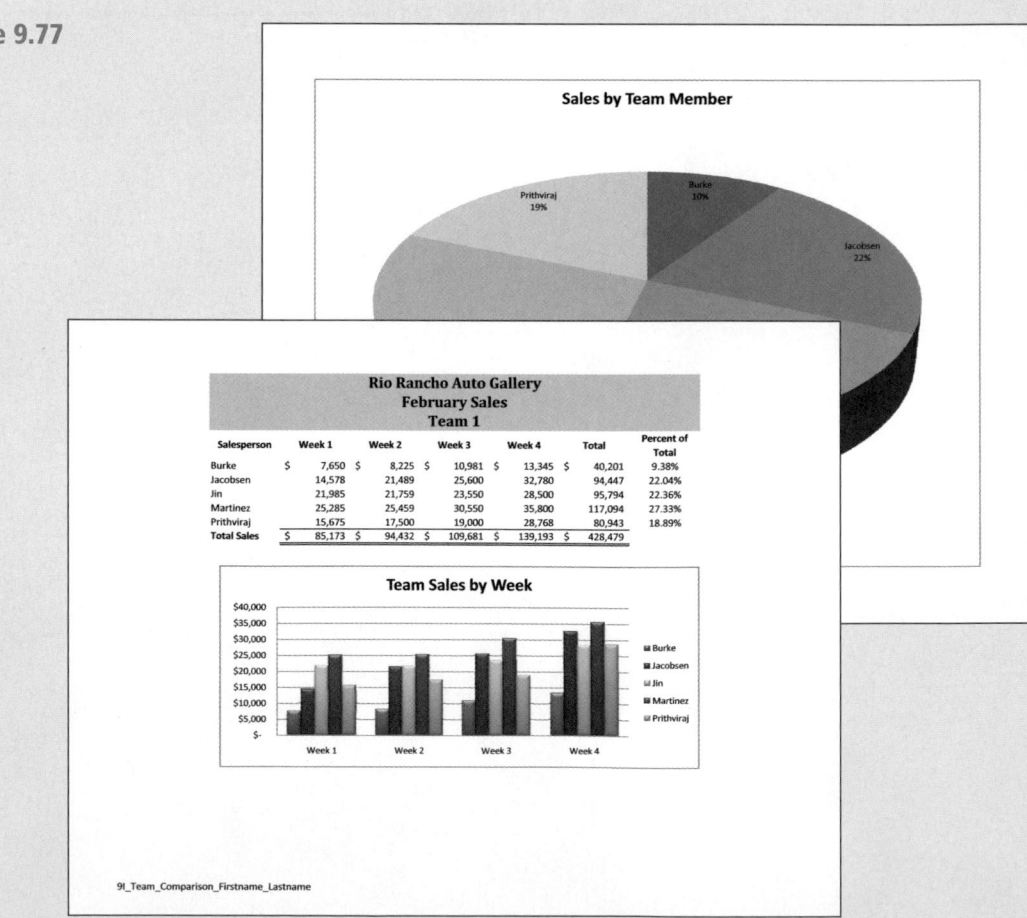

(Project 9I–Team Comparison continues on the next page)

Content-Based Assessments

(Project 9I–Team Comparison continued)

1. **Start** Excel and display a new blank workbook. In cell **A1**, type **Rio Rancho Auto Gallery** In cell **A2**, type **February Sales** In cell **A3**, type **Team 1** In cell **A4**, type **Salesperson** and then press Tab. In cell **B4**, type **Week 1** Select cell **B4**, and then use the fill handle to create a series in the range **B4:E4** so that *Week 2* and *Week 3* and *Week 4* display in the cells. In cell **F4**, type **Total** and then in cell **G4**, type **Percent of Total** In your **Excel Chapter 9** folder, **Save** the workbook as 9I_Team_Comparison_Firstname_Lastname

2. In the range **A5:E8**, type the following data; if you want to do so, select the range first and use Enter to confine the movement of the active cell within the range.

Sales-person	Week 1	Week 2	Week 3	Week 4
Burke	7650	8225	10981	13345
Jacobsen	14578	21489	25600	32780
Jin	21985	21759	23550	28500
Prithviraj	15675	17500	19000	28768

3. Apply the **Wrap Text** command to cell **G4**. To all the column titles in **row 4**, apply the **Bold**, **Center**, and **Middle Align** commands. Adjust the width of **columns A:G** to **90 pixels**. **Merge and Center** the three worksheet titles over columns **A:G**, and then format the three titles by changing the **Font** to **Cambria**, the **Font Size** to **16**, the **Fill Color** to **Aqua, Accent 5, Lighter 40%** and applying **Bold**.

4. In cell **A9**, type **Total Sales** and format the cell with **Bold**. **Sum** the rows for each salesperson, and then **Sum** the columns for each week and for the Total. Insert a row above *Prithviraj* and enter the following data—recall that Excel will move and adjust formulas when rows are inserted.

After you enter the data, use the fill handle to copy the formula from **F7** to **F8**.

Martinez 25285 25459 30550 35800

5. Using financial formatting for the appropriate numbers, first apply **Comma Style** with zero decimals, next apply **Accounting Number Format** with zero decimals, and then apply a **Top and Double Bottom Border** to the total row.

6. In cell **G5**, construct a formula to calculate the percentage by which Burke's total sales makes up the Total in cell **F10**. Use F4 to apply absolute cell referencing where necessary. Apply **Percent Style** formatting with two decimals, and then fill the formula down to cell **G9**. **Center** the percentages.

7. Select the range of data that represents the names and each week's sales of each salesperson including the column titles. **Insert** a **2-D Clustered Column** chart, and then click the **Switch Row/Column** button so that the chart displays the weeks on the category axis and the salespersons as the data points. Position the upper left corner of the chart in the upper left corner of cell **A12**.

8. Click any cell to deselect the chart. On the **Insert tab**, click the **Header & Footer** button to switch to **Page Layout view**. Click the **Go to Footer** button, click just above the word *Footer*, and then click the **File Name** button. Click a cell just above the footer to deselect the **Footer area** and view your file name. On the **Page Layout tab**, change the **Orientation** to **Landscape**. Display the **Margins gallery**, click **Custom Margins**, and then under **Center on page**, select the **Horizontally** check box.

(Project 9I–Team Comparison continues on the next page)

(Project 9I–Team Comparison continued)

9. Scroll up, and then use the pointer to resize the chart so that its right edge is even with the right side of the data. Format the chart, using **Chart Layout 1**, **Chart Style 26** and then change the **Chart Title** to Team Sales by Week

10. **Save** your workbook, click any cell to deselect the chart, switch to **Normal view**, and then press Ctrl + Home to move to the top of your worksheet. Select the range of data that represents each salesperson's name and his or her Total for the month. **Insert** a **Pie** chart, using the **Pie in 3-D** chart type. Move the chart to a new sheet, and then name the sheet **Team Chart** Apply **Chart Layout 1**, **Chart Style 7**, and then change the **Chart Title** to Sales by Team Member Deselect the chart by clicking outside of the chart. To create a footer on the chart sheet, on the **Insert tab**, click the **Header & Footer** button, and then create a **Custom Footer** with the file name in the **Left section**.

11. Click the **Sheet1 tab**, and press Ctrl + Home to cancel the selections. Select and delete

Sheet2 and **Sheet3**. **Save** your workbook. Check your *Chapter Assignment Sheet* or *Course Syllabus* or consult your instructor to determine if you are to submit your assignments on paper or electronically. To submit electronically, follow the instructions provided by your instructor.

12. To print, from the **Office** menu, click the **Print** button. In the displayed **Print** dialog box, under **Print what**, click the **Entire workbook** option button. In the lower left corner of the dialog box, click **Preview**, and notice in the status bar, *Preview: Page 1 of 2* displays. Check the preview, in the **Preview group**, click the **Next Page** button, and then in the **Print group**, click **Print** to print the two pages. If you are directed to submit printed formulas, refer to Activity 9.17 to do so.

13. If you printed your formulas, be sure to redisplay the worksheet by pressing Ctrl + '. From the **Office** menu, click **Close**. If the dialog box displays asking if you want to save changes, click **No** so that you do *not* save the changes you made for printing formulas. **Exit** Excel.

End **You have completed Project 9I**

Content-Based Assessments

  **Business Running Case**

Project 9J — Business Running Case

In this project, you will apply the skills you practiced in Projects 9A and 9B.

Close Excel and any other open windows. Display the Start menu, click Computer, and then navigate to the student files that accompany this textbook. In the folder **03_business_running_case**, locate and open the folder for this chapter. Open and print the instructions for this project, which are provided to you in Adobe PDF format. Follow the instructions and use the skills you have gained thus far to assist Jennifer Nelson in meeting the challenges of owning and running her business.

 You have completed Project 9J ————————————

Content-Based Assessments

Project 9K — *GO!* Fix It

In this project, you will construct a solution by applying any combination of the skills you practiced from the Objectives in Projects 9A and 9B.

For Project 9K, you will need the following file:

e09_fixit_Accessories

**You will save your workbook as
9K_Accessories_Firstname_Lastname**

From the student files that accompany this textbook, open the folder **05_go_fix_it**. Locate and open the file **w09_fixit_Accessories**, and then save the file in your chapter folder as **9K_Accessories_Firstname_Lastname**

In this project, you will edit the first draft of an Excel workbook that contains information about sales of automotive electronic accessories. The workbook was prepared for Arthur Potempa, Retail Accessories Manager of Rio Rancho Auto Gallery.

This workbook contains **ten errors** that you must find and correct. Read and examine the document, and then edit to correct the errors that you find. Types of errors could include:

- Spelling, grammar, and punctuation errors in cells, charts, worksheet tabs, or file names.
- Errors in data entry and workbook layout. Formatting errors in text, numbers, alignment, indents and spacing, tabs, wrapping, merge and center, text direction and orientation, fonts, borders, patterns, protection, AutoFormat, conditional formatting, data sort, filter, and validation.
- Formula and function errors such as incorrect and missing formulas, error indicators and values, relative vs. absolute cell referencing, What-If Analysis, Paste Special, function arguments, and Goal Seek.
- Errors in object design, layout, and formatting, for example chart type, location, data source, elements, size, scale, positioning, pictures, and hyperlinks.
- Row and column formatting errors such as height, width, and AutoFit.
- Worksheet, tab design, and formatting errors such as missing or blank worksheets, worksheet tab colors, and locations.
- Page setup errors such as page orientation and scaling, margins and centering, headers and footers, sheet gridlines, and row and column headings.

(Project 9K–*Go!* Fix It continues on the next page)

Content-Based Assessments

(Project 9K–*GO!* Fix It continued)

To complete the project you should know that in this workbook:

- There are no errors in data entry, font size, color and shading, row and column format, chart location, or page setup.
- Formula errors in a *range* of cells count as a *single* error.
- Cell A2 should be centered horizontally and vertically.
- Chart design should be Style 3.
- Chart title should be changed to February Sales Chart.

Save the changes you have made, add the filename to the worksheet footers, and then submit as directed.

 You have completed Project 9K ———————————————

Outcomes-Based Assessments

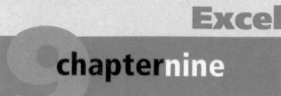

Rubric

The following outcomes-based assessments are *open-ended assessments*. That is, there is no specific correct result; your result will depend on your approach to the information provided. Make *Professional Quality* your goal. Use the following scoring rubric to guide you in *how* to approach the problem and then to evaluate *how well* your approach solves the problem.

The *criteria*—Software Mastery, Content, Format and Layout, and Process—represent the knowledge and skills you have gained that you can apply to solving the problem. The *levels of performance*—Professional Quality, Approaching Professional Quality, or Needs Quality Improvements—help you and your instructor evaluate your result.

	Your completed project is of Professional Quality if you:	Your completed project is Approaching Professional Quality if you:	Your completed project Needs Quality Improvements if you:
1-Software Mastery	Choose and apply the most appropriate skills, tools, and features and identify efficient methods to solve the problem.	Choose and apply some appropriate skills, tools, and features, but not in the most efficient manner.	Choose inappropriate skills, tools, or features, or are inefficient in solving the problem.
2-Content	Construct a solution that is clear and well organized, contains content that is accurate, appropriate to the audience and purpose, and is complete. Provide a solution that contains no errors of spelling, grammar, or style.	Construct a solution in which some components are unclear, poorly organized, inconsistent, or incomplete. Misjudge the needs of the audience. Have some errors in spelling, grammar, or style, but the errors do not detract from comprehension.	Construct a solution that is unclear, incomplete, or poorly organized, containing some inaccurate or inappropriate content; and contains many errors of spelling, grammar, or style. Do not solve the problem.
3-Format and Layout	Format and arrange all elements to communicate information and ideas, clarify function, illustrate relationships, and indicate relative importance.	Apply appropriate format and layout features to some elements, but not others. Overuse features, causing minor distraction.	Apply format and layout that does not communicate information or ideas clearly. Do not use format and layout features to clarify function, illustrate relationships, or indicate relative importance. Use available features excessively, causing distraction.
4-Process	Use an organized approach that integrates planning, development, self-assessment, revision, and reflection.	Demonstrate an organized approach in some areas, but not others; or, use an insufficient process of organization throughout.	Do not use an organized approach to solve the problem.

Outcomes-Based Assessments

Excel

chapternine

Problem Solving

Project 9L—Rims

In this project, you will construct a solution by applying any combination of the skills you practiced from the Objectives in Projects 9A and 9B.

For Project 9L, you will need the following file:

New blank Excel workbook

**You will save your workbook as
9L_Rims_Firstname_Lastname**

Rio Rancho Auto Gallery stocks one brand of tire rims and in January sold 10 16-inch rims priced at $150 each, 20 18-inch rims priced at $225 each, 32 20-inch rims priced at $375 each, and 16 22-inch rims priced at $500 each. The installation fee for all rims is $50 each.

Create a spreadsheet detailing this information and include a column that calculates the Installed Price for each rim size (Price + Installation Fee) and the Total Sales for each rim size (Installed Price times Number Sold). Total the columns to calculate the total number of rims sold and the Total Sales of all rims. Add an additional column in which you create a formula that calculates the Percent of Sales that each Rim Size is of the Total Sales of all rim sales. Create a 3-D pie chart that compares the Total Sales generated by each rim size. Position the pie chart below the data on the worksheet.

Create a title that identifies the worksheet and apply appropriate formats to the data and the pie chart. Use borders, fill colors, and font styles and sizes to format a professional worksheet. Add a footer that includes the file name and center the worksheet on the page. Save the workbook as **9L_Rims_Firstname_Lastname** and submit it as directed.

 End **You have completed Project 9L** ⎯⎯⎯⎯⎯⎯⎯⎯⎯⎯

Outcomes-Based Assessments

Excel
chapternine

Problem Solving

Project 9M—Finance

In this project, you will construct a solution by applying any combination of the skills you practiced from the Objectives in Projects 9A and 9B.

For Project 9M, you will need the following file:

New blank Excel workbook

You will save your workbook as
9M_Finance_Firstname_Lastname

In this project, you will create a worksheet for Tony Konecki, President of Rio Rancho Auto Gallery, which specifies, by quarter, the amount of credit extended to customers on vehicle purchases during the past fiscal year. The data is organized according to customer credit scores—overall, more credit was given to customers with higher credit scores. Create a worksheet with appropriate titles, and then enter the following data for Quarters 1 through 4.

Credit Score	Quarter 1	Quarter 2	Quarter 3	Quarter 4
750 or Above	350190	322489	368700	385644
700- 749	425654	496451	485200	501780
650- 699	328976	298560	316789	335679
600- 649	489561	462312	475232	490520
550- 599	182597	215600	202450	228600
Under 550	162487	175800	186532	188423

Calculate totals for each quarter and for each credit score, and then create a column chart that compares the amounts for each quarter by credit score. A chart layout that places the legend at the bottom of the chart will allow more space for the columns. Use formatting and editing techniques that you learned in this chapter so that the worksheet and chart are professional and accurate. Add the file name to the footer and save the workbook as **9M_Finance_Firstname_Lastname** Submit the project as directed.

End **You have completed Project 9M**

Outcomes-Based Assessments

Problem Solving

Project 9N—Service

In this project, you will construct a solution by applying any combination of the skills you practiced from the Objectives in Projects 9A and 9B.

> ### For Project 9N, you will need the following file:
>
> New blank Excel workbook

You will save your workbook as
9N_Service_Firstname_Lastname

In this project, you will create a worksheet for the service department to analyze the labor costs associated with different types of repairs during the current month. Create an appropriate worksheet title and then enter the following data and column headings.

Service	Hours to Complete Service	Cost for Service at Standard Rate	Number Completed During June	Total Labor Cost
Valve replacement	8		13	
Head gasket	12		12	
Transmission	15		10	
Engine replacement	15		11	
Total Labor Cost				

Two rows below the Total Labor Cost row, in column A, type the **Standard Labor Rate** and in column B, type **35.75** In the Cost for Service at Standard Rate column, construct a formula to calculate the cost to complete each type of service at the standard rate. In the Total Labor Cost column, construct a formula to calculate the total labor cost for each of the services completed during the month.

Add a column to the worksheet with the column heading **Percent of Total Labor Cost** and calculate the percent that each service is of the Total Labor Cost. Create a pie chart on a separate chart sheet that compares the Total Labor Costs by Service. Add the file name to the footer in both sheets and check for spelling errors. Save the workbook as **9N_Service_Firstname_Lastname** and submit it as directed.

End You have completed Project 9N ——————————

Outcomes-Based Assessments

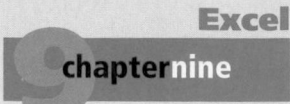

Problem Solving

Project 9O — Incentives

In this project, you will construct a solution by applying any combination of the skills you practiced from the Objectives in Projects 9A and 9B.

For Project 9O, you will need the following file:

New blank Excel workbook

You will save your workbook as
9O_Incentives_Firstname_Lastname

In this project, you will create a worksheet for Ray Justham, the Finance Manager for Rio Rancho Auto Gallery, to track the cost of incentives offered to clients who purchase vehicles. Create an appropriate title for the worksheet and then enter the data below.

Vehicle Type	Dealer Rebates	Service Certificates	Complimentary Gas
New Cars	10500	8320	4380
New Trucks	12300	6350	3325
New SUVs	18650	13480	5825
Used Vehicles	11800	5650	1250

Sum the incentives by vehicle type and by incentive type. Then create a column chart comparing the data, switching rows and columns as necessary so that the vehicle types are the data series and placing the incentive type on the category axis. A chart layout that places the legend at the bottom of the chart will allow more space for the columns. Add the file name to the footer and check the workbook for spelling errors. Save the workbook as **9O_Incentives_Firstname_Lastname** and submit it as directed.

 End **You have completed Project 9O** _____

Outcomes-Based Assessments

Problem Solving

Project 9P—Rental

In this project, you will construct a solution by applying any combination of the skills you practiced from the Objectives in Projects A and B.

For Project 9P, you will need the following file:

New blank Excel workbook

You will save your workbook as 9P_Rental_Firstname_Lastname

Rio Rancho Auto Gallery rents motorcycles, vans, SUVs, convertibles, pickup trucks, and motor scooters for short-term use by vacationers, tourists, and others who want to experience a different kind of drive. Create a workbook that Jane Gelson, Rental and Lease Manager for Rio Rancho Auto Gallery, can use to track the fees collected on the different types of vehicles rented by Rio Rancho customers in the month of August. Create an appropriate title for the worksheet and then enter the data below.

	Daily Rental Fee	Number of Days Rented	Rental Fees Collected
Motorcycle	35	22	
Van	45	30	
SUV	45	25	
Convertible	40	30	
Pickup truck	42	15	
Motor scooter	30	12	

Calculate the Rental Fees Collected by vehicle type and then total the Rental Fees Collected column. Create a 3-D pie chart to compare Rental Fees Collected by each vehicle. Add the file name to the footer and check the workbook for spelling errors. Save the workbook as **9P_Rental_Firstname_Lastname** and submit it as directed.

End **You have completed Project 9P** ———————

Outcomes-Based Assessments

  **You and *GO!***

Project 9Q — You and *GO!*

In this project, you will construct a solution by applying any combination of the skills you practiced from the Objectives in Projects 9A and 9B.

Close Excel and any other open windows. Display the Start menu, click Computer, and then navigate to the student files that accompany this textbook. In the folder **04_you_and_go**, locate and open the folder for this chapter. Open and print the instructions for this project, which are provided to you in Adobe PDF format. Follow the instructions to create a budget for yourself over a three month period.

 You have completed Project 9Q ————————

GO! with Help

Project 9R — *GO!* with Help

The Excel Help system is extensive and can help you as you work. In this chapter, you used the Quick Access Toolbar on several occasions. You can customize the Quick Access Toolbar by adding buttons that you use regularly, making them quickly available to you from any tab on the Ribbon. In this exercise, you will use Help to find out how to add buttons.

1 **Start** Excel. At the far right end of the Ribbon, click the **Microsoft Office Excel Help** button ⓘ. In the **Excel Help** dialog box, click the **Search button arrow**, and then, under **Content from this computer**, click **Excel Help**.

2 In the **Search** box, type **Quick Access Toolbar** and then press Enter. From the list of search results, click **Customize the Quick Access Toolbar**. Click each of the links to find out how to add buttons from the Ribbon and from the **Excel Options** dialog box.

3 When you are through, **Close** the Help window, and then **Exit** Excel.

 You have completed Project 9R ————————

Outcomes-Based Assessments

Group Business Running Case

Project 9S — Group Business Running Case

In this project, you will apply the skills you practiced from the Objectives in Projects 9A and 9B.

Your instructor may assign this group case project to your class. If your instructor assigns this project, he or she will provide you with information and instructions to work as part of a group. The group will apply the skills gained thus far to help the Bell Orchid Hotel Group achieve its business goals.

End **You have completed Project 9S** ————————

10 chapterten

Managing Workbooks and Analyzing Data

OBJECTIVES

At the end of this chapter you will be able to:

1. Create and Save a Workbook from an Existing Workbook
2. Navigate a Workbook and Rename Worksheets
3. Enter Dates, Clear Contents, and Clear Formats
4. Move, Copy, and Paste Cell Contents
5. Edit and Format Multiple Worksheets at the Same Time
6. Create a Summary Sheet
7. Format and Print Multiple Worksheets in a Workbook

8. Design a Worksheet for What-If Analysis
9. Perform What-If Analysis
10. Compare Data with a Line Chart

OUTCOMES

Mastering these objectives will enable you to:

PROJECT 10A
Create a Summary Sheet from Multiple Worksheets

PROJECT 10B
Make Projections Using What-If Analysis

The City of Golden Grove

Golden Grove is a California city located between Los Angeles and San Diego, about 20 miles from the Pacific shore. Ten years ago the population was just over 200,000; today it has grown to over 300,000. Community leaders focus on quality and economic development in decisions about housing, open space, education, and infrastructure, making the city a model for other communities its size. The city provides many recreational and cultural opportunities with a large park system and a thriving arts community.

Managing Workbooks and Analyzing Data

Organizations typically create workbooks that contain multiple worksheets. In such a workbook, the first worksheet usually summarizes the detailed information in the other worksheets. To make it easier to work with multiple worksheets, there are techniques to enter data into multiple worksheets simultaneously by grouping the worksheets. You can also copy, and then paste information from one worksheet to another. Additional techniques for managing workbooks with multiple worksheets include naming and color coding the sheet tabs so that you can quickly locate the detailed information you are looking for.

In Excel, you can explore options by recalculating formulas that depend on other formulas. For example, you can change the interest rate in a table of loan payments to determine the amount of monthly payments based on differing interest rates.

In this chapter, you will work with workbooks that contain multiple worksheets and analyze data by making projections of future growth.

Project 10A Ticket Sales

In Activities 10.01 through 10.10, you will edit an existing Excel workbook for Judith Amaya, the Director of Arts and Parks for Golden Grove. The annual Summer Fair and Arts Festival will be held during the last week in August. During the first week in August, the city is preselling tickets at three locations in the city. The four worksheets of your completed workbook will look similar to Figure 10.1.

For Project 10A, you will need the following file:

e10A_Ticket_Sales

You will save your workbook as
10A_Ticket_Sales_Firstname_Lastname

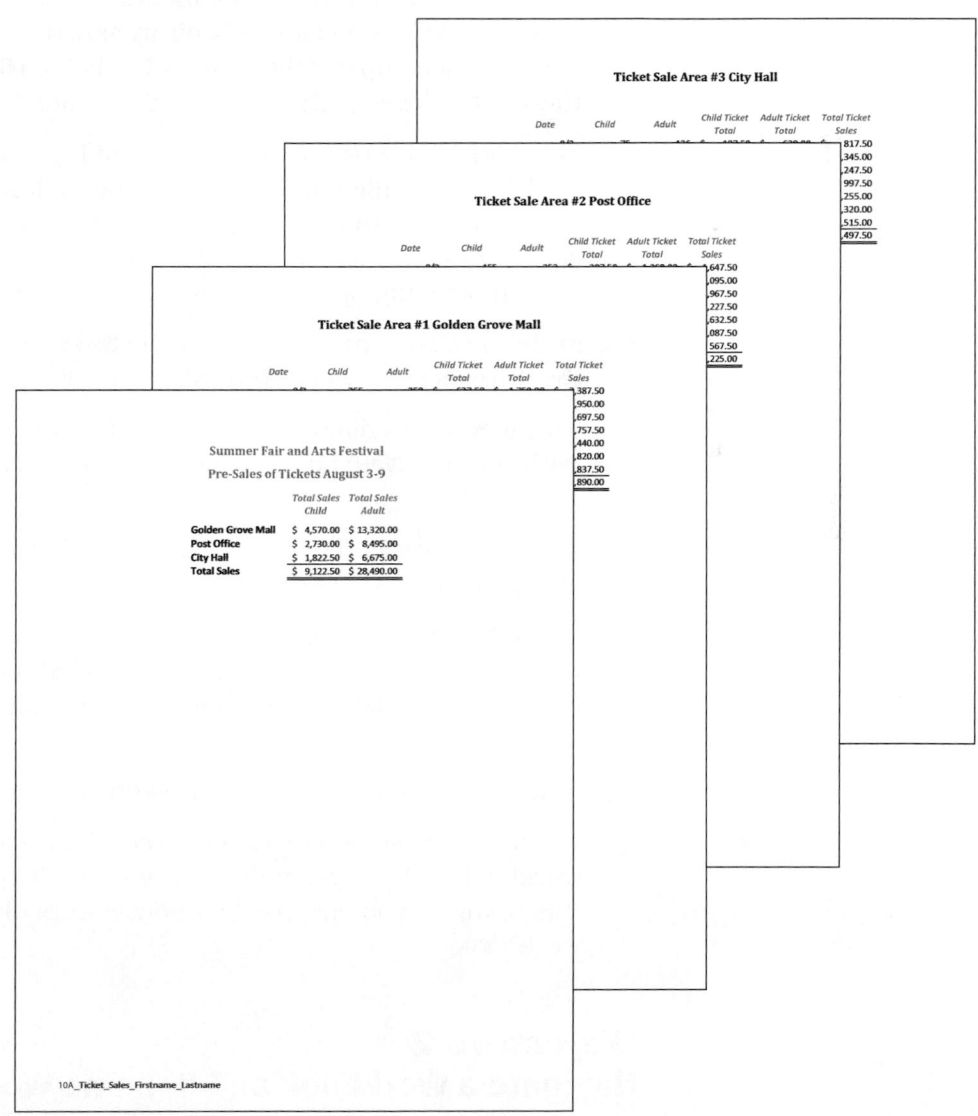

Figure 10.1
Project 10A—Ticket Sales

Objective 1
Create and Save a Workbook from an Existing Workbook

Within a workbook, individual worksheets may contain data for separate topics, locations, or periods of time related to the workbook's data. In such a workbook, it is common practice to have one worksheet that summarizes information from the other worksheets.

Activity 10.01 Creating and Saving a Workbook from an Existing Workbook

Judith has created a workbook with worksheets into which she can record the number of tickets sold at the three locations during the first week in August. In this activity, you will open the workbook and save it in your chapter folder with a different name.

1 **Start** Excel. From the **Office** menu 📇, click **Open**. In the displayed **Open** dialog box, click the **Look in arrow**, navigate to the student files that accompany this textbook, click **e10A_Ticket_Sales**, and then in the lower right corner of the dialog box, click **Open**.

The workbook e10A_Ticket_Sales displays. Alternatively, you can double-click a file name to open it. Some information has already been entered into the worksheets. For example, on the first worksheet, the dates for the one-week period have been entered, along with information about the dates and ticket prices.

2 From the **Office** menu 📇, click the **Save As** command. Navigate to the drive location where you will store your projects for this chapter.

On the **Save As** dialog box toolbar, click the **New Folder** button 📁. With the text *New Folder* selected, type **Excel Chapter 10** and then press [Enter].

Windows creates the *Excel Chapter 10* folder and makes it the active folder in the Save As dialog box.

3 In the **File name** box, edit as necessary to indicate, using your own first and last name, **10A_Ticket_Sales_Firstname_Lastname** Be sure to include the underscore ([⇧ Shift] + [-]) instead of spaces between words.

4 In the lower right corner of the **Save As** dialog box, click **Save**.

Excel saves the file in your chapter folder with the new name. The workbook redisplays, and the new name displays in the title bar. In this manner, you can create a new workbook from an existing workbook.

Objective 2
Navigate a Workbook and Rename Worksheets

The default setting for the number of worksheets in a workbook is three. You can add additional worksheets or delete unused worksheets. Using multiple worksheets in a workbook is frequently a logical approach to arranging data.

Activity 10.02 Navigating Among Worksheets, Renaming Worksheets, and Changing the Tab Color of a Worksheet

When you have more than one worksheet in a workbook, you can **navigate** (move) among worksheets by clicking the **sheet tabs**. Sheet tabs identify each worksheet in a workbook and are located along the lower left edge of the workbook window. When you have more worksheets in the workbook than can be displayed in the sheet tab area, use the four sheet tab scrolling buttons to move sheet tabs into and out of view.

Excel names the first worksheet in a workbook *Sheet1* and each additional worksheet in order—*Sheet2*, *Sheet3*, and so on. Most Excel users rename the worksheets with names that are more meaningful. In this activity, you will navigate among three worksheets. You will also rename each worksheet and change the tab color of the sheet tabs.

1 Along the bottom of the Excel window, point to and then click the **Sheet2 tab**. Compare your screen with Figure 10.2.

The second worksheet in the workbook displays and becomes the active worksheet. *Sheet2* displays in bold.

Sheet tabs with *Sheet2* active sheet

Figure 10.2

Sheet tab scrolling buttons

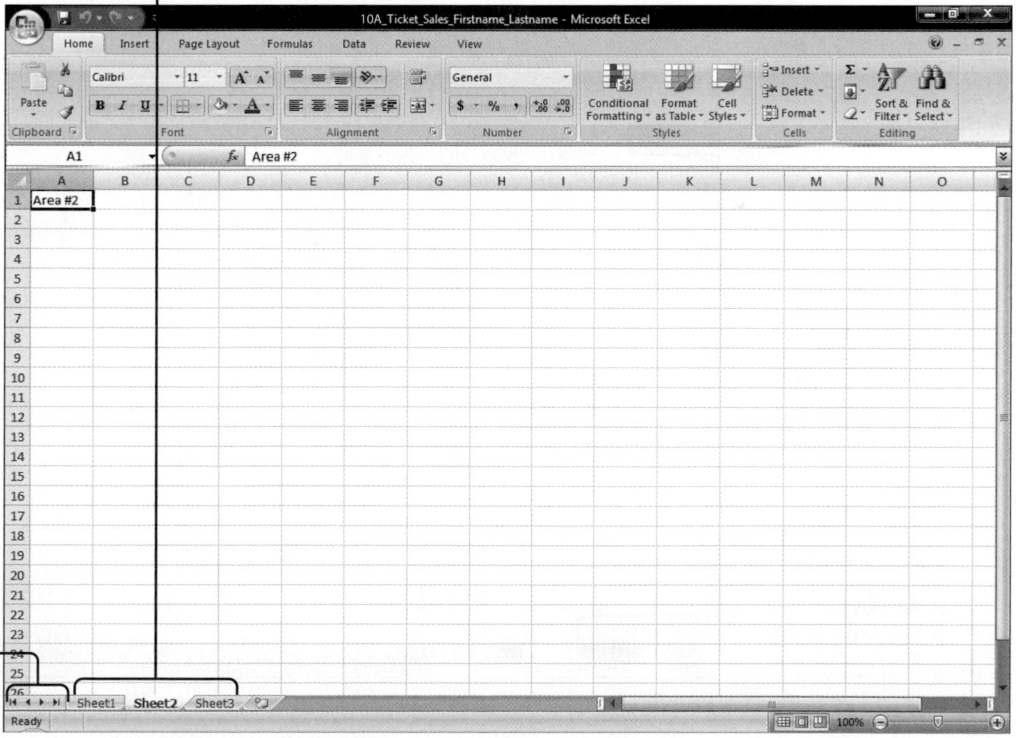

2 In cell **A1**, notice the text *Area #2*—this worksheet will contain data for Summer Fair tickets purchased at the Area #2 location. Click the **Sheet1 tab**.

The first worksheet in the workbook becomes the active worksheet, and cell A1, which is formatted with an orange background, displays *Area #1*.

3 Point to the **Sheet3 tab**, and then right-click. From the displayed shortcut menu, click **Rename**. With *Sheet3* selected, type **City Hall** and then press [Enter].

4 Point to the **Sheet1 tab**, and then double-click to select its name. Type **Golden Grove Mall** and then press [Enter]. Using either of the two methods you just practiced, rename **Sheet2** as **Post Office**

5 Right-click the **Golden Grove Mall sheet tab**, and then from the displayed shortcut menu, point to **Tab Color** to display the colors associated with the workbook's theme. Under **Theme Colors**, locate and click **Purple, Accent 4, Lighter 40%**.

When the sheet is active, the tab color displays as an underline.

6 Click the **Post Office** sheet to make it the active sheet. On the Ribbon's **Home tab**, in the **Cells group**, click the **Format** button, and then from the displayed list, point to **Tab Color**. Under **Theme Colors**, click **Aqua, Accent 5, Lighter 40%**. Using either of the two techniques you have just practiced, change the **Tab Color** of the **City Hall** worksheet to **Orange, Accent 6, Lighter 40%**. Compare your screen with Figure 10.3.

Figure 10.3

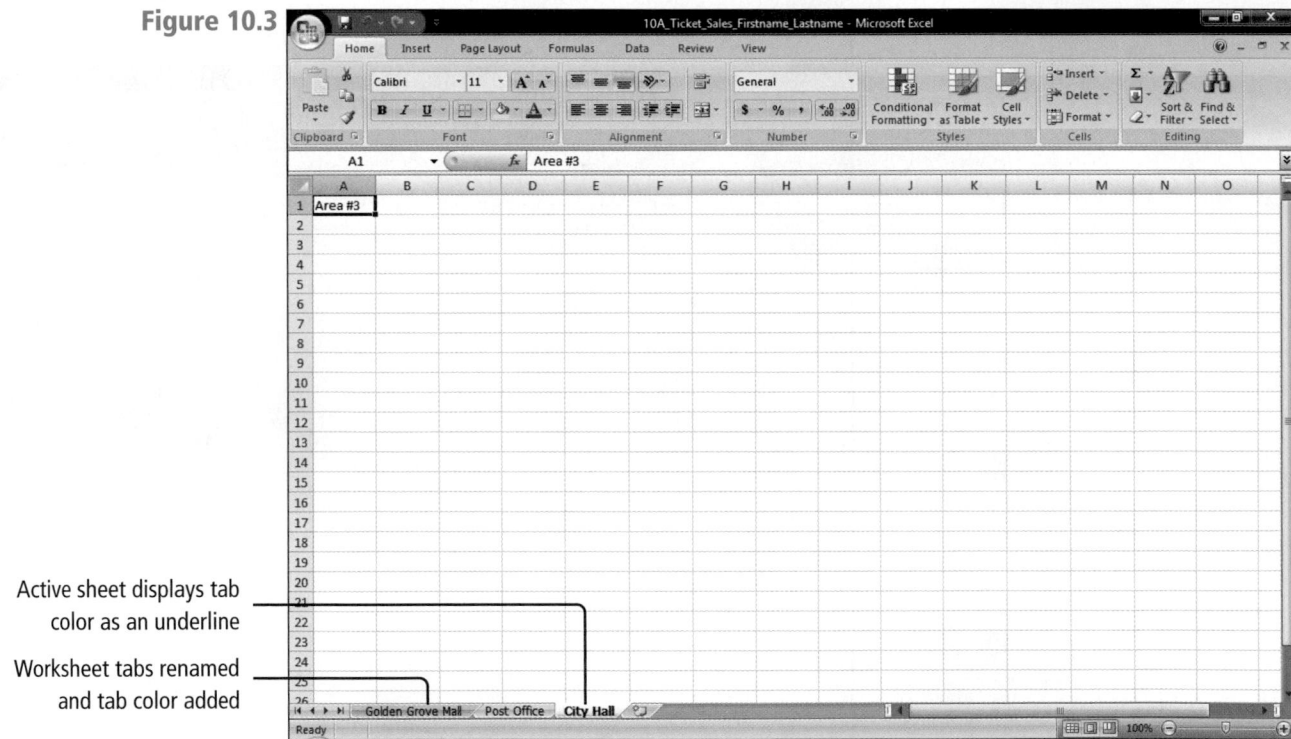

Active sheet displays tab color as an underline

Worksheet tabs renamed and tab color added

7 **Save** the changes you have made to your workbook.

Objective 3
Enter Dates, Clear Contents, and Clear Formats

Dates represent a type of value that you can enter in a cell. When you enter a date, Excel assigns a serial value—a number—to the date. This makes it possible to treat dates like other numbers. For example, if two cells contain dates, you can find the number of days between the two dates by subtracting the older date from the more recent date.

Activity 10.03 Entering and Formatting Dates

In this activity, you will examine the various ways that Excel can format a date that you type into a cell.

Date values entered in any of the following formats will be recognized by Excel as a date:

Format	Example
m/d/yy	7/4/09
d-mmm	4-Jul
d-mmm-yy	4-Jul-09
mmm-yy	Jul-09

On your keyboard, ⬚ (the hyphen key) and ⬚ (the forward slash key) function identically in any of these formats and can be used interchangeably. You can abbreviate the month name to three characters or spell it out. You can enter the year as two digits, four digits, or even leave it off. When left off, the current year is assumed but does not display in the cell.

A two-digit year value of 30 through 99 is interpreted by the Windows operating system as the four-digit years of 1930 through 1999. All other two-digit year values are assumed to be in the 21st century. If you always type year values as four digits, even though only two digits may display in the cell, you can be sure that Excel interprets the year value as you intended. See the table in Figure 10.4 for examples.

How Excel Interprets Dates

Date Typed As:	Completed by Excel As:
7/4/09	7/4/2009
7-4-98	7/4/1998
7/4	4-Jul (current year assumed)
7-4	4-Jul (current year assumed)
July 4	4-Jul (current year assumed)
Jul 4	4-Jul (current year assumed)
Jul/4	4-Jul (current year assumed)
Jul-4	4-Jul (current year assumed)
July 4, 1998	4-Jul-98
July 2009	Jul-09 (first day of month assumed)
July 1998	Jul-98 (first day of month assumed)

Figure 10.4

1 Click the **Golden Grove Mall sheet tab** to make it the active sheet. Click cell **A5** and notice that the cell indicates *8/3* (August 3). In the **Formula Bar**, notice that the full date of August 3, 2009 displays in the format *8/3/2009*.

2 With cell **A5** selected, on the Ribbon, in the **Number group**, click the **Number Format arrow**. From the bottom of the displayed menu, click **More Number Formats** to display the **Number tab** of the **Format Cells** dialog box. Compare your screen with Figure 10.5.

Under Category, *Date* is selected, and under Type, *3/14* is selected. All of the dates in Column A were formatted using this format type; that is, only the month and day display in the cell.

3/14 indicated as Type

Figure 10.5

Format Cells dialog box

Number tab active

8/3 displays in Sample box

Date category selected

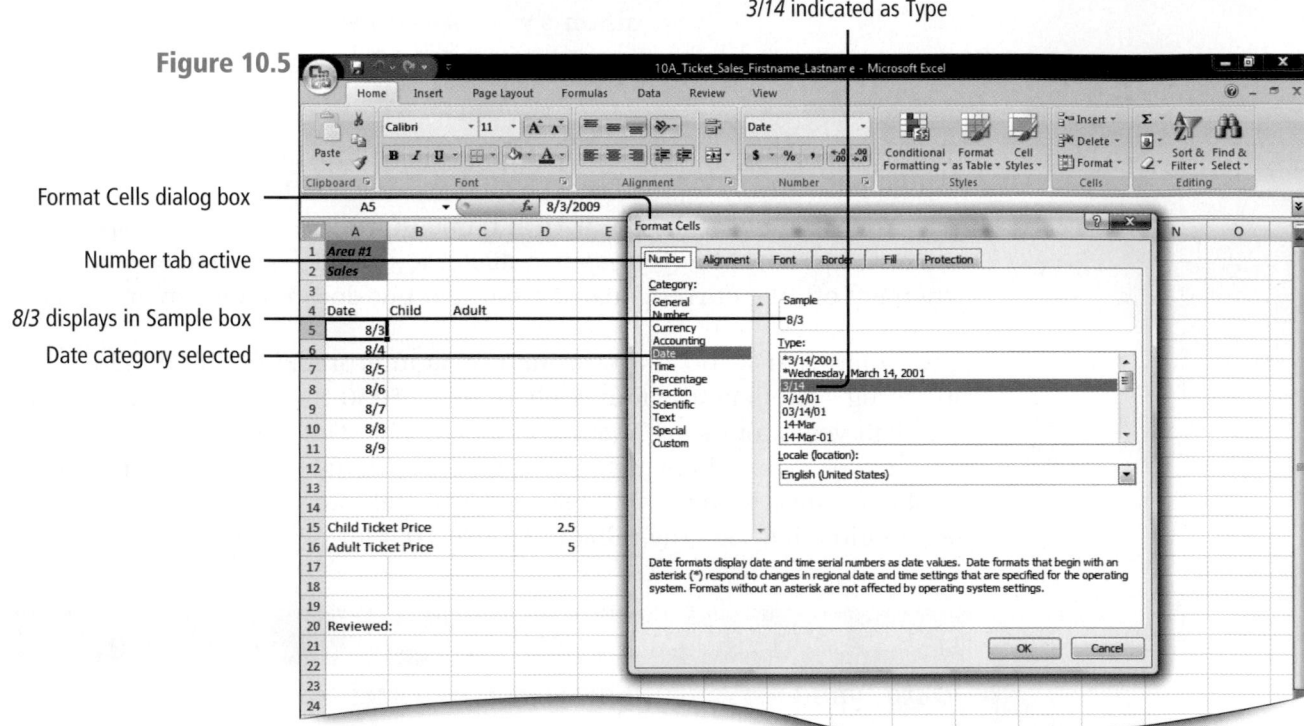

3 In the displayed dialog box, under **Type**, click several other date types and watch the **Sample** area to see how applying the selected date format would format your cell. When you are finished, click the **3/14** type, and then at the bottom of the dialog box, click **OK**.

4 Click cell **A21**, type **8/10/2009** and then press Enter.

Cell A21 has no special date formatting applied, and thus displays in the default date format *8/10/2009*.

Alert | **The date does not display as 8/10/2009?**
Settings in your Windows operating system determine the default format for dates. If your result is different, it is likely that the formatting of the default date was adjusted on the computer at which you are working.

5 Click cell **A21** again. Hold down Ctrl and press ; (the semicolon key) on your keyboard. Press Enter to confirm the entry.

Excel enters the current date, obtained from your computer's internal calendar, into the selected cell using the default date format. Ctrl + ; is a convenient keyboard shortcut for entering the current date.

6 Click cell **A21** again, type **8/10/09** and then press Enter.

Because the year *09* is less than 30, Excel assumes a 21st century date and changes *09* to *2009* to complete the four-digit year. Typing *98* would result in *1998*. For two-digit years that you type that are between 30 and 99, Excel assumes a 20th century date.

7 Click cell **A5**, and then on the **Home tab**, in the **Clipboard group**, click the **Format Painter** button. Click cell **A21**, and notice that the date format from cell **A5** is copied to cell **A21**. **Save** your workbook.

Activity 10.04 Clearing Cell Contents and Formats

A cell has contents—a value or a formula—and a cell may also have one or more formats applied, for example bold and italic font style, fill color, font color, and so on. You can choose to clear the contents of a cell, the formatting of a cell, or both. You can clear—delete—the contents of a selected cell in two ways: Press Delete or use the Clear Contents command available both from the Editing group on the Ribbon and from a shortcut menu.

Clearing the contents of a cell deletes the value or formula typed there, but it does *not* clear formatting applied to a cell. In this activity, you will clear the contents of a cell and then clear the formatting of a cell that contains a date to see its underlying content.

1 On the **Golden Grove Mall** worksheet, click cell **A1**. On the Ribbon, in the **Editing group**, click the **Clear** button. From the displayed list, click **Clear Contents**. Click cell **A2**, and then press Delete.

You can use either of these two methods to delete the *contents* of a cell. Deleting the contents does not, however, delete the formatting of the cell; you can see that the orange fill color format applied to the two cells still displays.

2 In cell **A1**, type **Area #1** and then on the **Formula Bar**, click the **Enter** button so that cell **A1** remains the active cell. In the **Editing group**, click the **Clear** button, and then from the displayed menu, click **Clear Formats**.

Clearing the Formats deletes formatting from the cell—the orange fill color and the bold and italic font styles—but does not delete the cell's contents.

3 Use the same technique to clear the orange fill color from cell **A2**.

4 Click cell **A5**, click the **Clear** button ⟨2·⟩, and then click **Clear Formats**. In the **Number group**, notice that *General* displays as the number format of the cell.

The box at the top of the Number group indicates the current Number format of the selected cell. Clearing the date formatting from the cell displays the date's serial number. The date, August 3, 2009, is stored as a serial number that indicates the number of days since January 1, 1900. This date is the 40,028th day since the reference date of January 1, 1900.

5 On the **Quick Access Toolbar**, click the **Undo** button ⟨↶⟩ to restore the date format. **Save** 🖫 your workbook, and then compare your screen with Figure 10.6.

Date indicated as the Number format

Figure 10.6

Date in Formula Bar ————

Orange fill color and bold italic
font style cleared from cell A1 ————

Contents of cell A2 deleted ————

A5 reformatted as a date ————

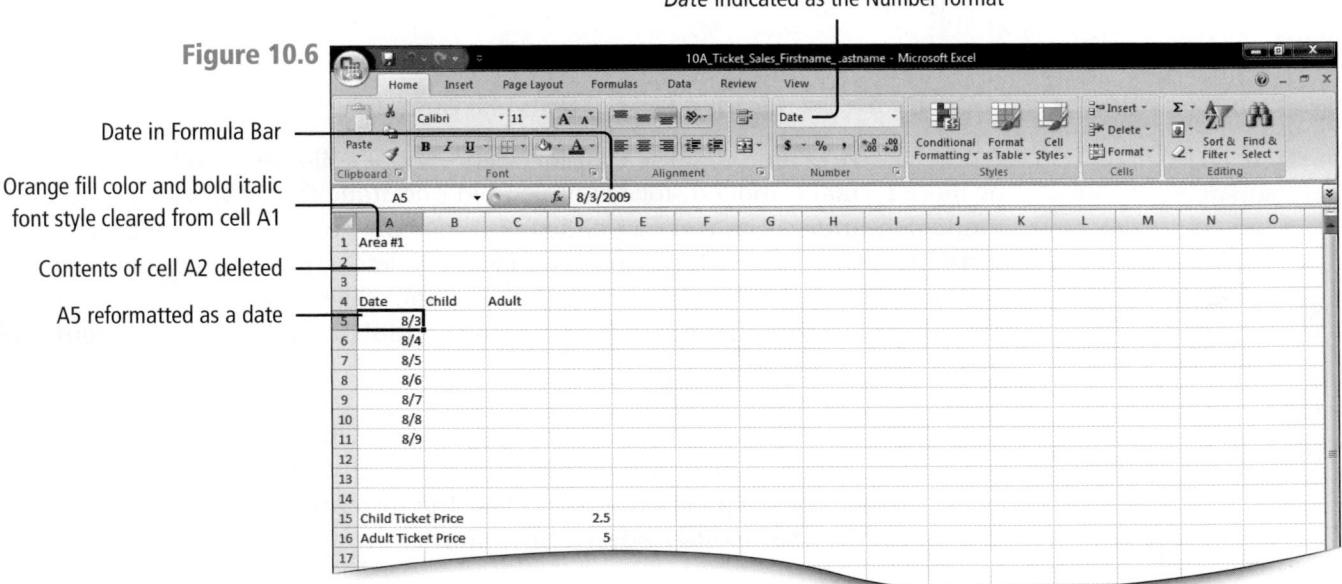

Objective 4
Move, Copy, and Paste Cell Contents

Data from individual cells and groups of cells can be copied to other cells in the same worksheet, to other sheets in the same workbook, or to sheets in another workbook. Likewise, data can be moved from one place to another. The action of placing cell contents that have been copied or moved to the Office Clipboard to another location is called *paste*.

Activity 10.05 Copying, Pasting, and Moving Cell Contents

The *Office Clipboard* is a temporary storage area maintained by your Windows operating system. When you select one or more cells, and then perform the Copy command or the Cut command, the selected data is placed on the Office Clipboard. From the Office Clipboard storage area, the data is available for pasting into other cells, other worksheets, other workbooks, and even into other Office programs.

1 On the **Golden Grove Mall** sheet, select the range **A20:A21**. Point to the upper edge of the black border surrounding the selected cells until the [pointer] pointer displays. Drag upward until the ScreenTip displays *A18:A19*, as shown in Figure 10.7, and then release the mouse button to complete the move.

Using this technique, cell contents can be moved from one location to another; this is referred to as ***drag and drop***.

Figure 10.7

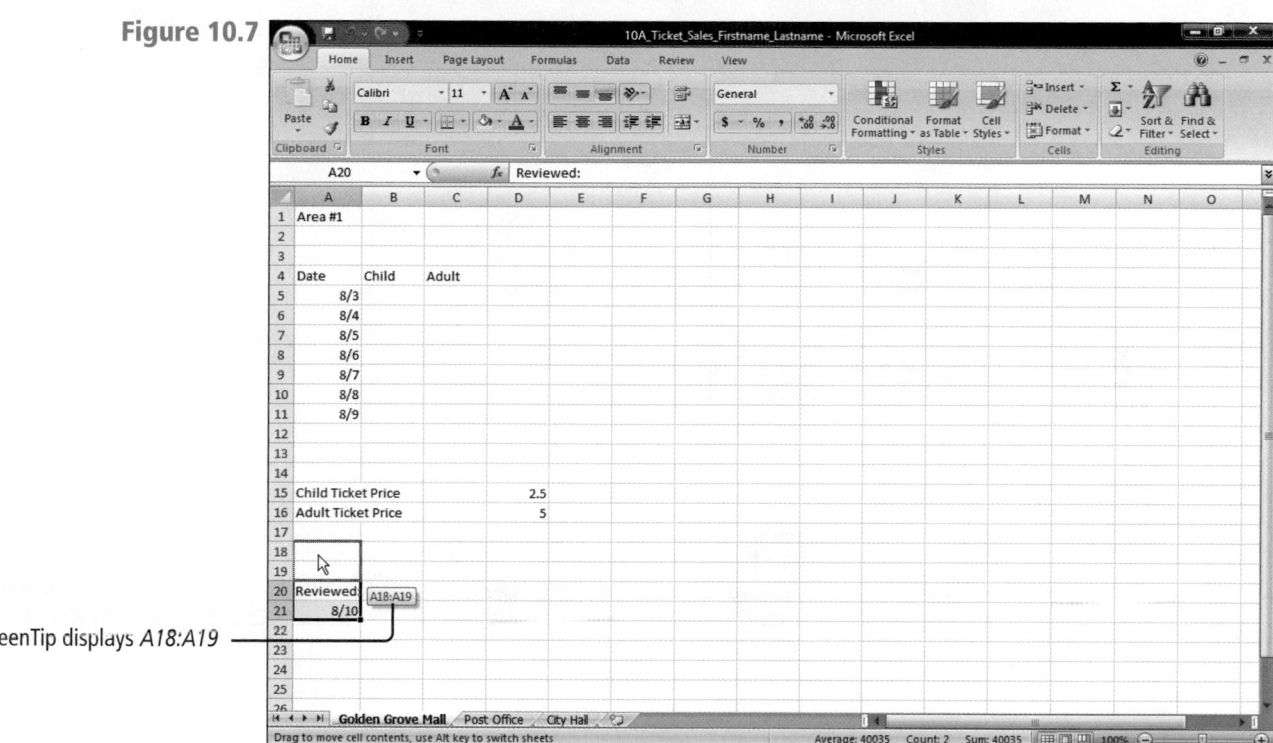

ScreenTip displays *A18:A19*

2 Select the range **A4:D16**.

A range of cells identical to this one is required for the *Post Office* worksheet and the *City Hall* worksheet.

3 On the **Home tab**, in the **Clipboard group**, click the **Copy** button [icon] to place a copy of the selected cells on the Office Clipboard. Alternatively, press Ctrl + C; or, right-click over the selected range, and then click Copy from the shortcut menu.

A moving border surrounds the selected range, and a message on the left side of the status bar indicates *Select destination and press ENTER or choose Paste*. These two results confirm that your selected range has been placed on the Office Clipboard.

4 At the bottom of the workbook window, click the **Post Office sheet tab** to make it the active worksheet. Click cell **A4**, and then on the **Home tab**, in the **Clipboard group**, click the **Paste** button. Alternatively, use the keyboard shortcut for Paste, which is Ctrl + V. Compare your screen with Figure 10.8.

The selected cells from the first worksheet are copied from the Office Clipboard to the second worksheet. When pasting a range of cells, you need only select the cell in the upper left corner of the *paste area*—the target destination for data that has been cut or copied using the Office Clipboard.

Figure 10.8

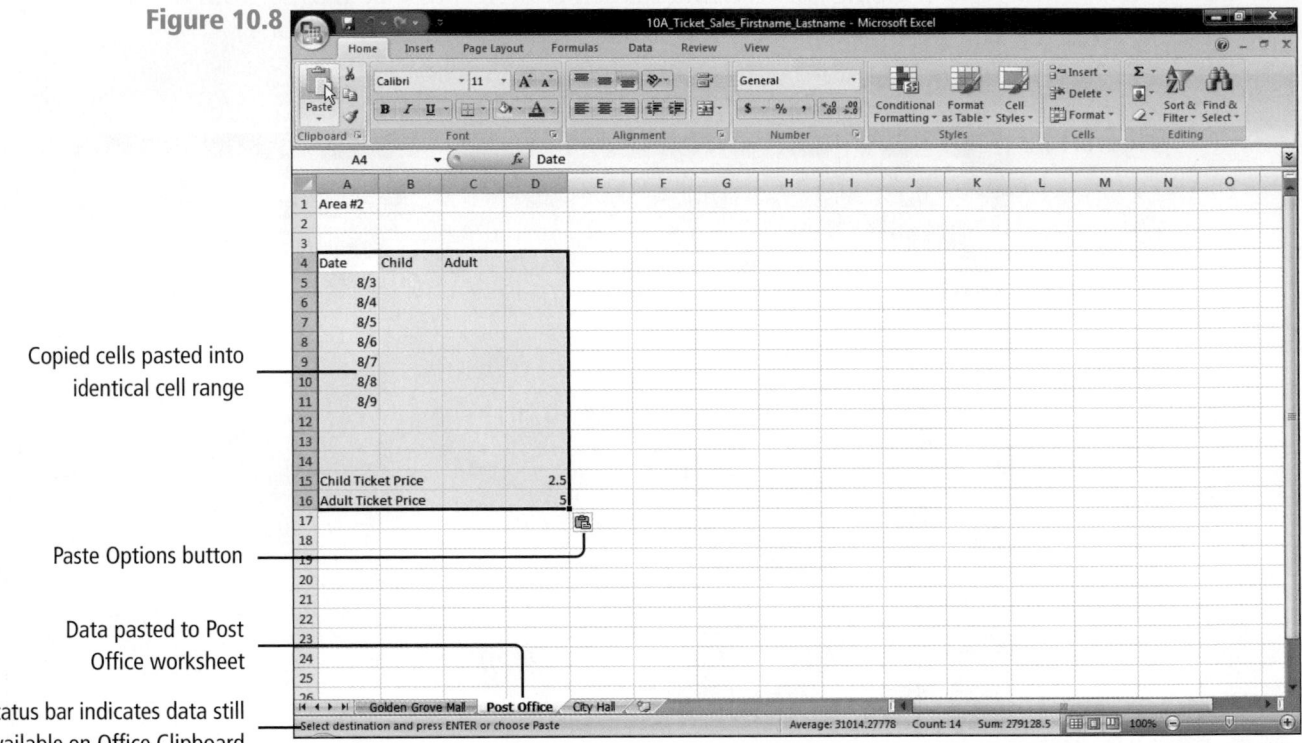

Copied cells pasted into identical cell range

Paste Options button

Data pasted to Post Office worksheet

Status bar indicates data still available on Office Clipboard

Note — Pressing Enter to Complete a Paste Action

Pressing Enter pastes the text and removes it from the Office Clipboard. Thus, if you want to paste the same text more than one time, click the Paste button so that the copied text remains available on the Office Clipboard.

5 In the lower right corner of the paste area, click the **Paste Options** button.

The *Paste Options button*, which displays just below your pasted selection after you perform the paste operation, displays a list of options that lets you determine how the information is pasted into your worksheet. The list varies depending on the type of content you are pasting and the program you are pasting from.

6 Click any cell to close the list and deselect the paste area. In the status bar, notice that the message still displays, indicating that your selected range remains on the Office Clipboard. Click the **City Hall sheet tab** to make it the active sheet, and then click cell **A4**. In the **Clipboard group**, click the **Paste** button.

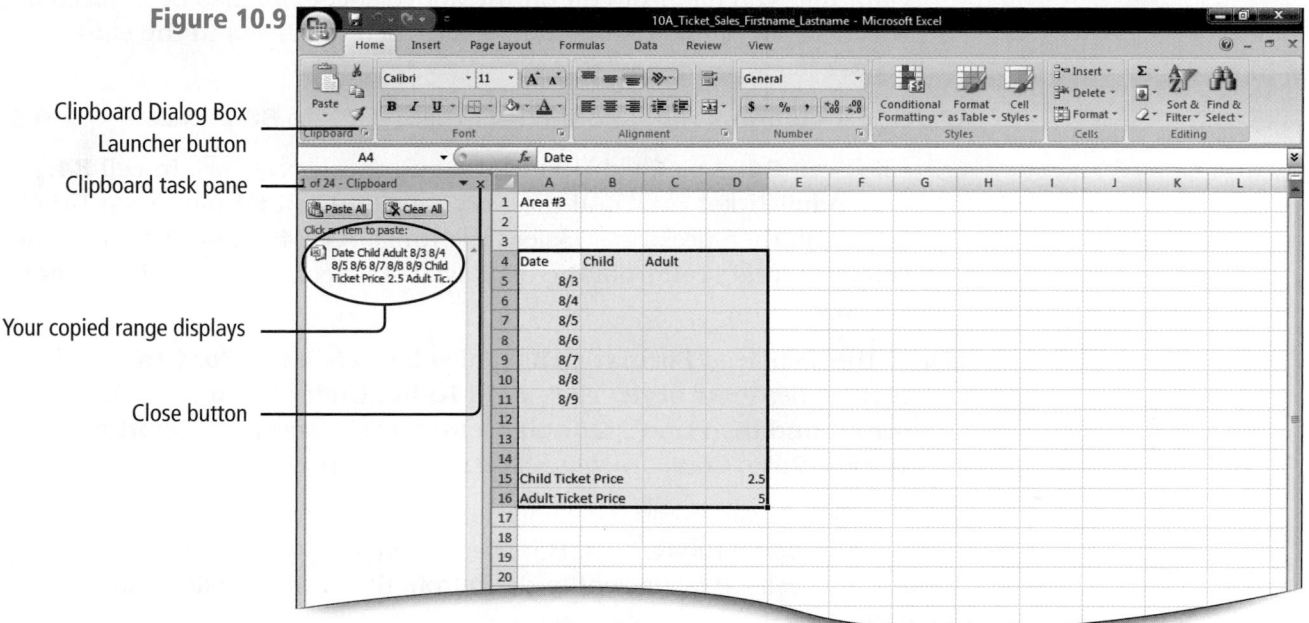

7 On the **Home tab**, in the **Clipboard group**, click the **Clipboard Dialog Box Launcher** button ⬚, and then compare your screen with Figure 10.9.

The Clipboard task pane displays, and you can view your selection on the Clipboard. Here you can clear your selection from the Clipboard, although it is not necessary to do so.

Figure 10.9

Clipboard Dialog Box Launcher button

Clipboard task pane

Your copied range displays

Close button

8 In the upper right corner of the **Office Clipboard task pane**, click the **Close** button ⊠. Display the **Golden Grove Mall** sheet. Press Esc to cancel the moving border.

The status bar no longer displays the message.

9 **Save** 💾 your changes.

Objective 5
Edit and Format Multiple Worksheets at the Same Time

You can enter or edit data on several worksheets at the same time by selecting and grouping multiple worksheets. Data that you enter or edit on the active sheet is reflected in all selected sheets. If you apply color to the sheet tabs, the name of the sheet tab will be underlined in the color you selected. If the sheet tab displays with a background color, the sheet has not been selected.

Activity 10.06 Wrapping Text in a Cell in Several Worksheets at the Same Time

If you want text to appear on multiple lines within a single cell, you can format the cell so that the text wraps automatically, or you can enter a manual line break. In this activity, you will group the worksheets for the three ticket sales locations, and then format additional column titles with wrapped text on all the worksheets at the same time.

1 With the **Golden Grove Mall** worksheet as the active sheet, press Ctrl + Home to make cell **A1** the active cell. Point to the sheet tab, right-click, and then from the displayed menu, click **Select All Sheets**. At the top of your screen, look at the title bar and notice that *[Group]* displays.

All the worksheets are selected, as indicated by *[Group]* in the title bar and the sheet tab names underlined in the selected tab color. Data that you enter or edit on the active sheet will also be entered or edited in the same manner on all the selected sheets in the same cells.

2 Select **columns A:F**, and then set their width to **83 pixels**.

3 Click cell **D4**, type **Child Ticket Total** and then press Tab. In cell **E4**, type **Adult Ticket Total** and then press Tab. In cell **F4** type **Total Ticket Sales** and then press Enter. Select the range **A4:F4**, right-click over the selection, and then from the displayed shortcut menu, click **Format Cells**.

4 In the displayed **Format Cells** dialog box, click the **Font tab**, and then under **Font style**, click **Bold Italic**. Under **Color**, click the arrow, and then under **Theme Colors**, click **Orange, Accent 6, Darker 25%**. Compare your screen with Figure 10.10.

Recall that commonly used Font formats are also available from the Font group on the Ribbon. However, when applying multiple formats to selected cells, it is efficient to do so from the Format Cells dialog box.

[Group] in title bar

Figure 10.10

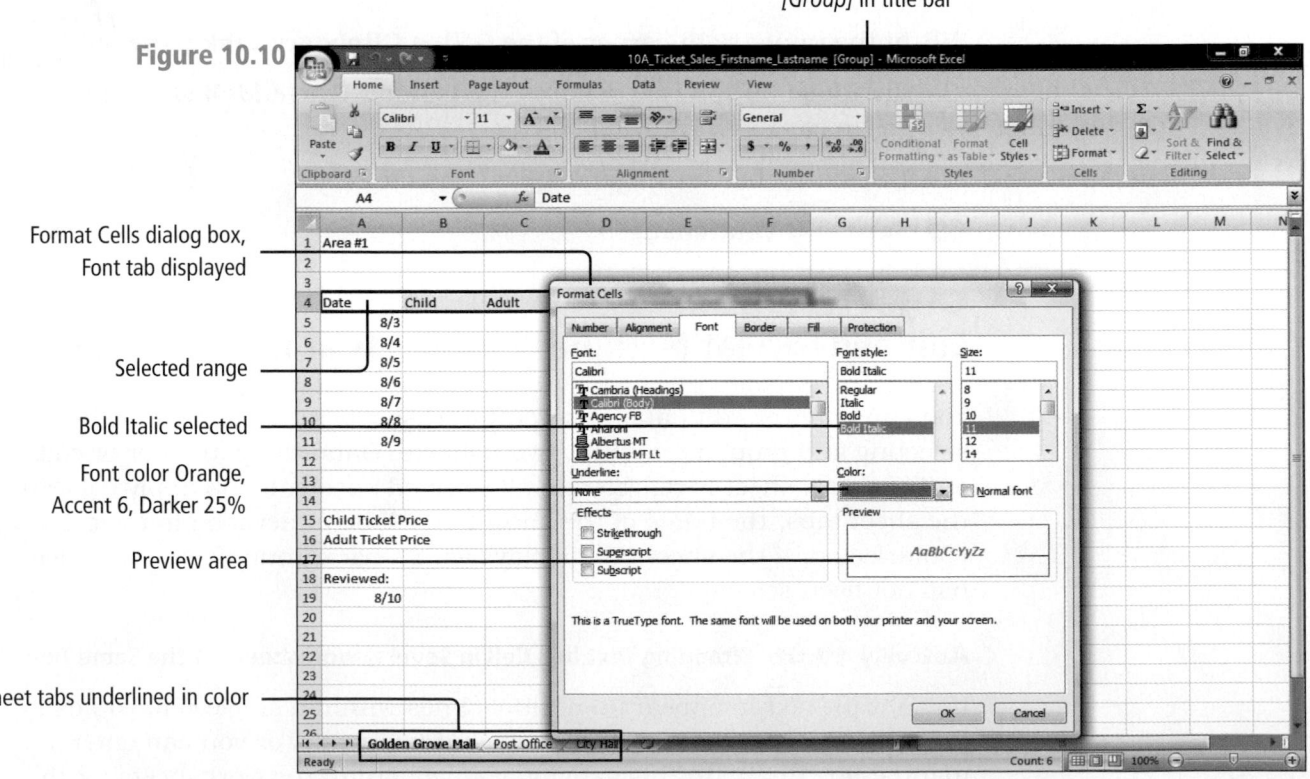

Format Cells dialog box, Font tab displayed

Selected range

Bold Italic selected

Font color Orange, Accent 6, Darker 25%

Preview area

Sheet tabs underlined in color

5 In the **Format Cells** dialog box, click the **Alignment tab**.

Here you can change the alignment of text in the selected range.

6 Under **Text alignment**, click the **Horizontal arrow**, and then from the displayed list, click **Center**. Click the **Vertical arrow**, and then from the displayed list, click **Center**. Under **Text control**, click to select—place a check mark in—the **Wrap text** check box.

Data in the cell will wrap to fit the column width; a change in column width will automatically adjust the wrapping of the text.

Another Way — **To Wrap Text in a Cell**

To wrap text in a cell or range of cells, select the specific cells, and then in the Alignment group, click the Wrap Text button.

To start a new line of text at a specific point in a cell, regardless of column width, double-click the cell, click the location where you want to break the line in the cell, and then press [Alt] + [Enter] to insert a line break.

---

7 At the bottom of the dialog box, click **OK**, and then compare your screen with Figure 10.11.

All the formats that you selected in the Format Cells dialog box are applied to the selected range of cells. Those formats that have buttons on the Ribbon are shown as being selected.

Wrap Text button selected

Figure 10.11

Center and Middle Align buttons selected

Bold and Italic buttons selected

Dialog Box Launcher button

All formats selected in Format Cells dialog box applied to range

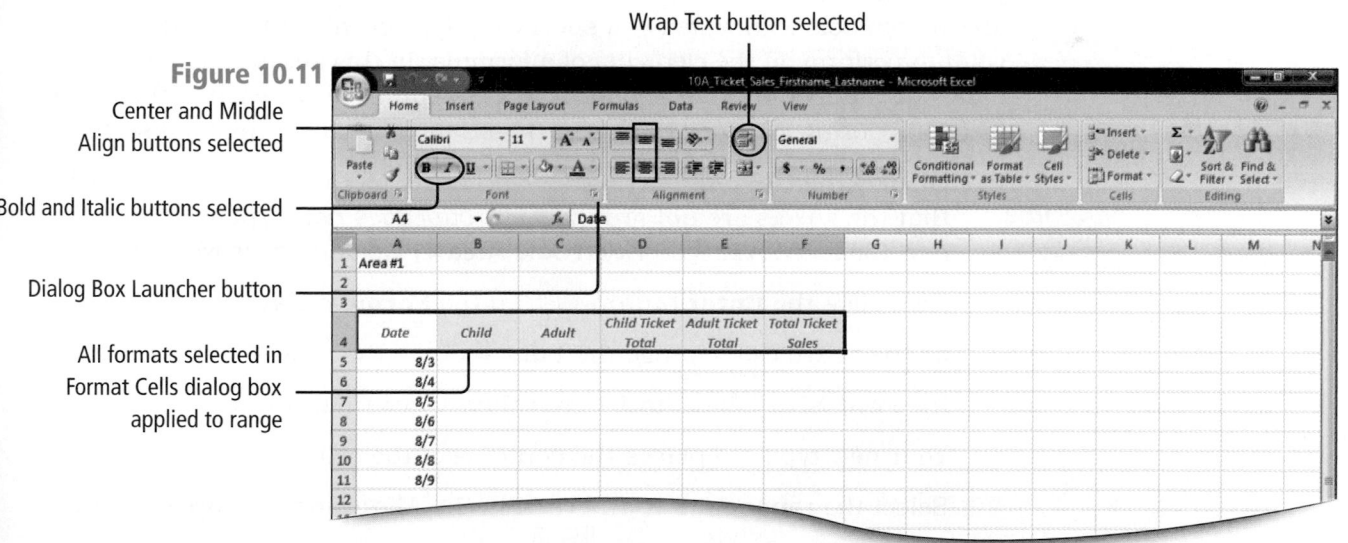

8 In the **Font group**, click the **Dialog Box Launcher** button.

The Font tab of the Format Cells dialog box displays. The most commonly used settings from this tab are displayed as buttons on the Ribbon.

9 Click **Cancel** to close the dialog box. On the Ribbon, in the **Alignment group**, click the **Dialog Box Launcher** button ⌧.

The Alignment tab of the Format Cells dialog box displays. The most commonly used settings from the Alignment tab are displayed as buttons in the Alignment group on the Ribbon. In this manner, Excel makes frequently used commands quickly available to you on the Ribbon. To perform multiple commands, use either the Ribbon buttons or the Format Cells dialog box. To use commands that are not commonly used and thus not displayed on the Ribbon, use the Format Cells dialog box.

10 Click **Cancel** to close the dialog box. Display the **Post Office** worksheet.

As soon as you select a single sheet, the grouping of the sheets is canceled and *[Group]* no longer displays in the title bar. Because the sheets were grouped, the same new text and formatting was applied to all of the selected sheets. In this manner, you can make the same changes to all the sheets in a workbook at one time.

11 Display the **City Hall** worksheet, and then verify that the changes have also been made to this worksheet. **Save** 💾 your workbook.

Activity 10.07 Entering Data and Constructing Formulas on Multiple Worksheets

Recall that formulas are equations that perform calculations on values in your worksheet, and that a formula starts with an equal sign (=). Operators are the symbols with which you specify the type of calculation that you want to perform on the elements of a formula. In this activity, you will enter the number of Child and Adult tickets purchased at each of the three locations during the week of August 3, and then calculate the total sales.

1 Display the **Golden Grove Mall** worksheet as the active sheet. Verify that the sheets are not grouped—*[Group]* does *not* display in the title bar. Click cell **A1**, type **Ticket Sale Area #1 Golden Grove Mall** and then click the **Enter** button ✓ on the **Formula Bar**. With cell **A1** as the active cell, change the **Font** Calibri ▾ to **Cambria**, the **Font Size** 11 ▾ to **14**, and then apply **Bold** **B**.

Your new typing replaces the contents of the cell.

2 Select the range **A1:F1**, and then in the **Alignment group**, click the **Merge and Center** button ⊞ ▾.

3 Select the range **B5:C11**, type **255** and then press Enter Type **350** and then press Enter.

Although it is not required that you do so, recall that selecting a range in this manner lets you enter columns of data by pressing Enter after each entry, and keeps the entries within the defined range of cells. After you type in the last selected cell in column B, which is B11, pressing Enter will make cell C5 the active cell.

4 Type the remaining number of tickets sold as shown in the following table, pressing [Enter] after each entry, and then compare your screen with Figure 10.12.

	Child	Adult
8/3	255	**350**
8/4	350	**415**
8/5	**295**	**392**
8/6	**115**	**294**
8/7	**214**	**381**
8/8	**304**	**412**
8/9	**295**	**420**

Number of tickets sold at this location entered

Figure 10.12

Worksheet title formatted

Typing and pressing Enter keeps data within selected range

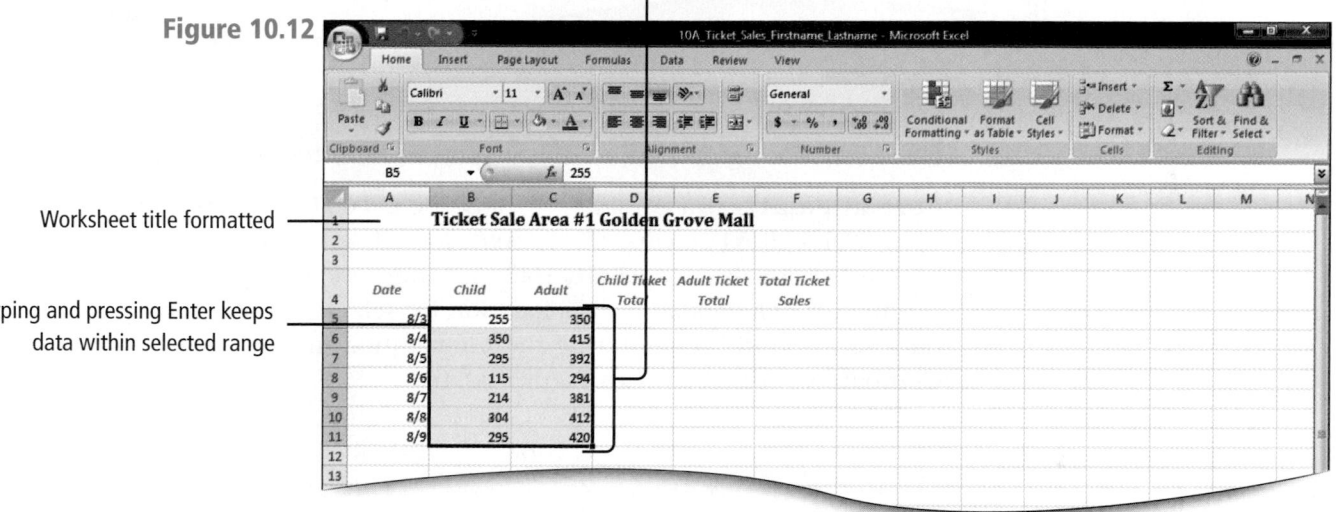

5 Click cell **A1**, and then in the **Clipboard group**, click the **Format Painter** button. Click the **Post Office sheet tab**, and then click cell **A1** in the active sheet to apply the formatting. In cell **A1**, replace *Area #2* by typing **Ticket Sale Area #2 Post Office** and then pressing [Enter].

6 Select the range **B5:C11**, enter the number of tickets purchased at this location as shown in the following table, and then compare your screen with Figure 10.13.

	Child	Adult
8/3	155	252
8/4	210	314
8/5	195	296
8/6	95	198
8/7	87	283
8/8	195	320
8/9	55	36

Number of tickets sold
at this location entered

Figure 10.13

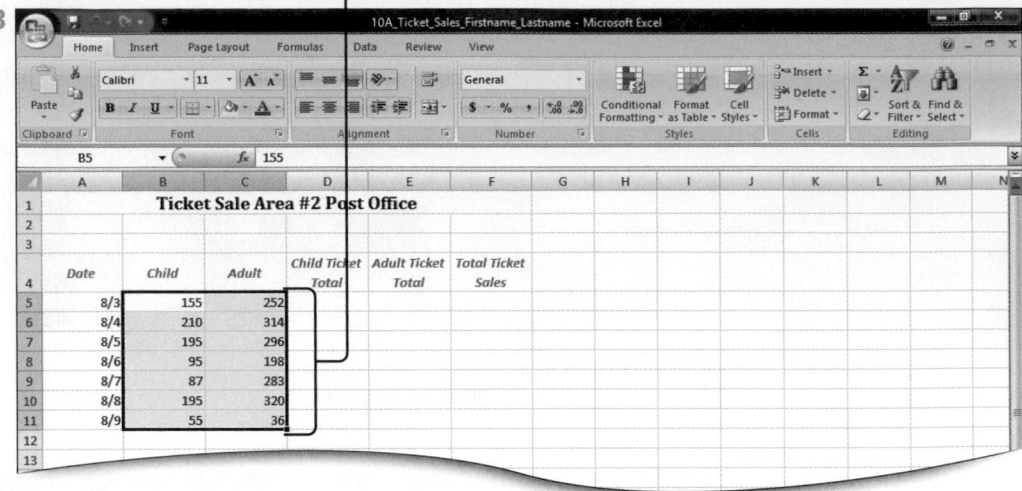

7 Click cell **A1**, right-click, on the displayed Mini toolbar, click the

Format Painter button [icon], display the **City Hall** worksheet, and
then click cell **A1** to copy the format. In cell **A1**, replace *Area #3* by
typing **Ticket Sale Area #3 City Hall** and then pressing Enter. Enter the
number of tickets sold at this location by selecting the appropriate
data range, and then entering the information in the following table.
Compare your screen with Figure 10.14.

	Child	Adult
8/3	75	126
8/4	110	214
8/5	105	197
8/6	85	157
8/7	92	205
8/8	104	212
8/9	158	224

Figure 10.14

Number of tickets sold
at this location entered

8 **Save** 🖫 your changes. Right-click the **Golden Grove Mall sheet tab**, and then from the displayed shortcut menu, click **Select All Sheets**.

The first worksheet becomes the active sheet, and the worksheets are grouped. *[Group]* displays in the title bar, and the sheet tabs are underlined in the tab color to indicate they are selected as part of the group. Recall that when grouped, any editing or data entry that you perform on the active worksheet is *also* performed on the other selected worksheets.

9 Click cell **D5** and type **=** to begin a formula. Click cell **B5**, type ***** click cell **D15**, and then compare your screen with Figure 10.15.

Recall that the symbols + and − and * and / are used in formulas to perform addition, subtraction, multiplication, and division. This formula will calculate the total amount from the sale of Child tickets on August 3 at the Golden Grove Mall location.

Recall that in the General number format, trailing zeroes do not display.

Figure 10.15

Formula to multiply 255 Child tickets times price of 2.50

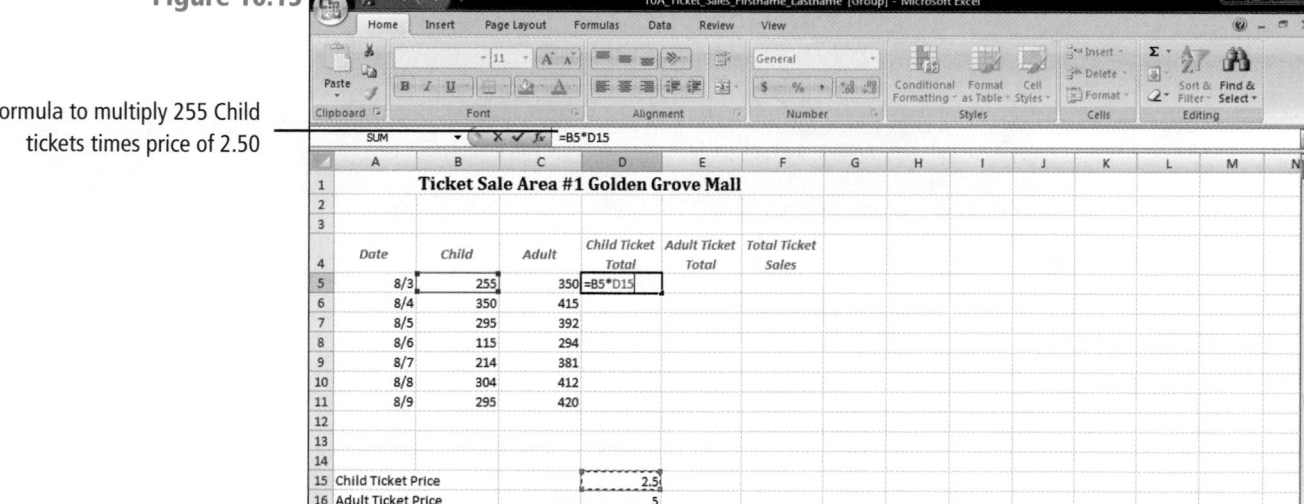

10 Press F4 to make the reference to **Child Ticket Price** in cell **D15** absolute.

Recall that when you copy formulas down to other cells in a column, the cell references change relative to the row number, and for the reference to each date in column A, that is the desired result. For the cell reference to the ticket price in cell D15, the cell reference should remain the same for each date.

11 On the **Formula Bar**, click the **Enter** button ✓ to display the formula result of *637.5* and then use the fill handle to copy the formula down for the remaining dates. Compare your screen with Figure 10.16.

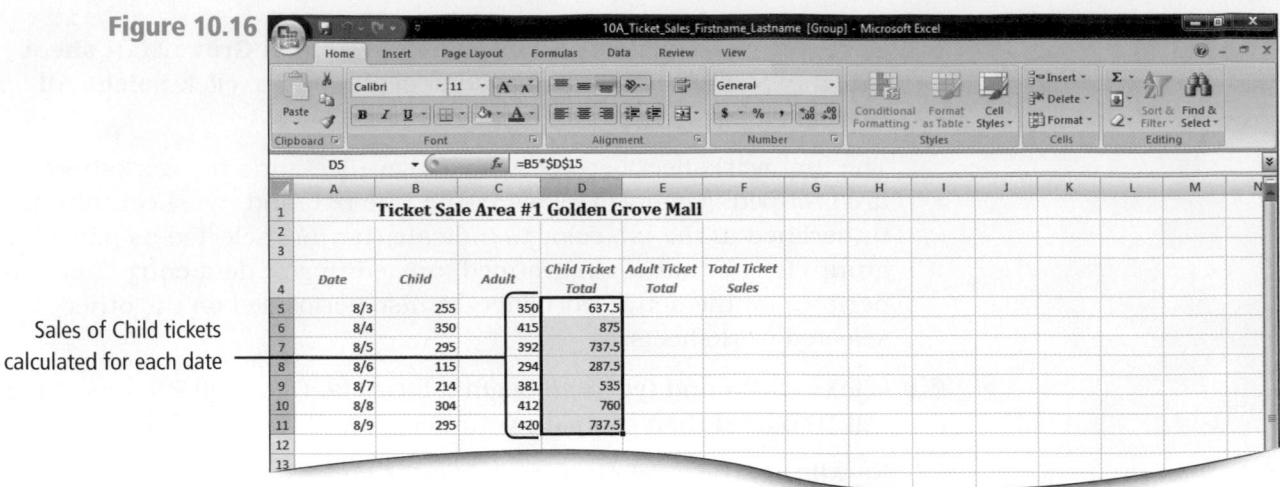

Figure 10.16

Sales of Child tickets calculated for each date

---

12 In cell **E5**, construct a similar formula to multiply the number of **Adult** tickets sold on August 3 times the **Adult Ticket Price** in cell **D16**. Make the reference to cell **D16** absolute so that each day's sales are multiplied by the **Adult Ticket Price** in cell **D16**. Copy the formula down for the remaining dates, and then compare your screen with Figure 10.17.

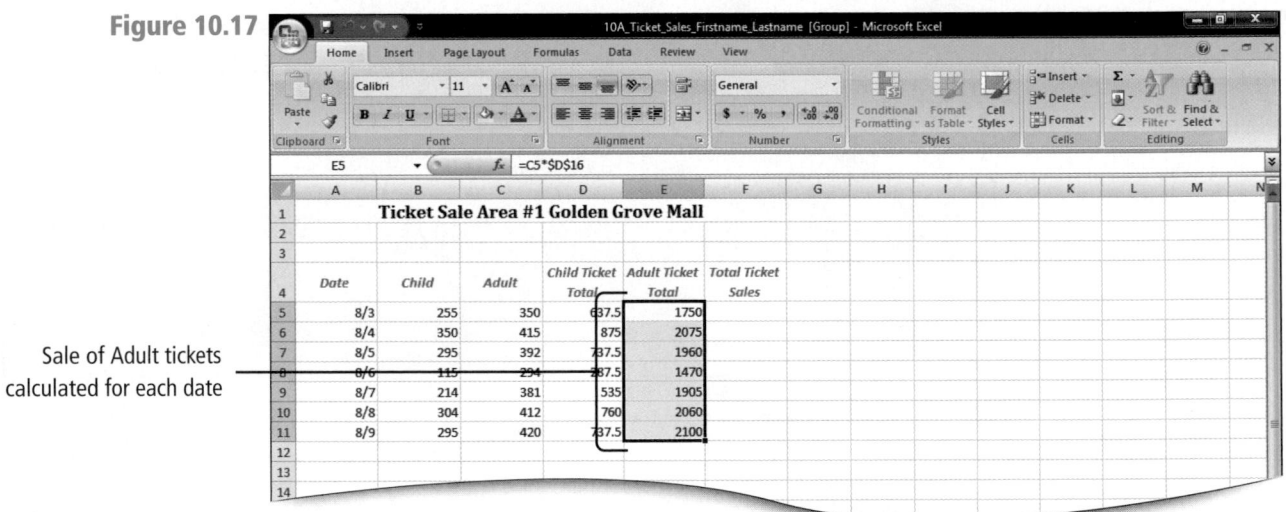

Figure 10.17

Sale of Adult tickets calculated for each date

---

13 Click cell **F5**, and then in the **Editing group**, click the **Sum** button Σ ▾. Notice that Excel selects all the numeric values—but not the date values—in the row. To Sum only the values in **D5** and **E5**—the **Child Total** and the **Adult Total**—with your mouse, select the range **D5:E5**, and then compare your screen with Figure 10.18.

Recall that the Sum function first looks above the selected cell for a range of numbers to sum. If no values display above the selected cell, Excel looks to the left for a range of numbers to sum. You can change the range to which you want to apply the Sum function by simply selecting the desired range.

Figure 10.18

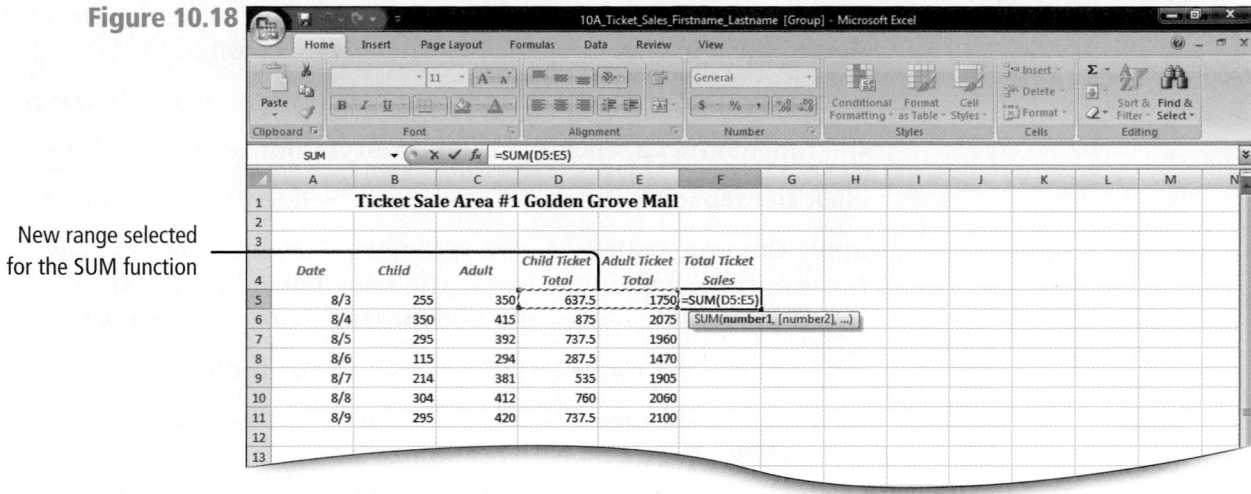

New range selected
for the SUM function

14 On the **Formula Bar**, click the **Enter** button ☑, and then copy the formula down for the remaining dates. Compare your screen with Figure 10.19.

Recall that because your worksheets are grouped, the calculations on the first worksheet are also being performed on the other two worksheets.

Daily totals for Child
and Adult tickets sold

Figure 10.19

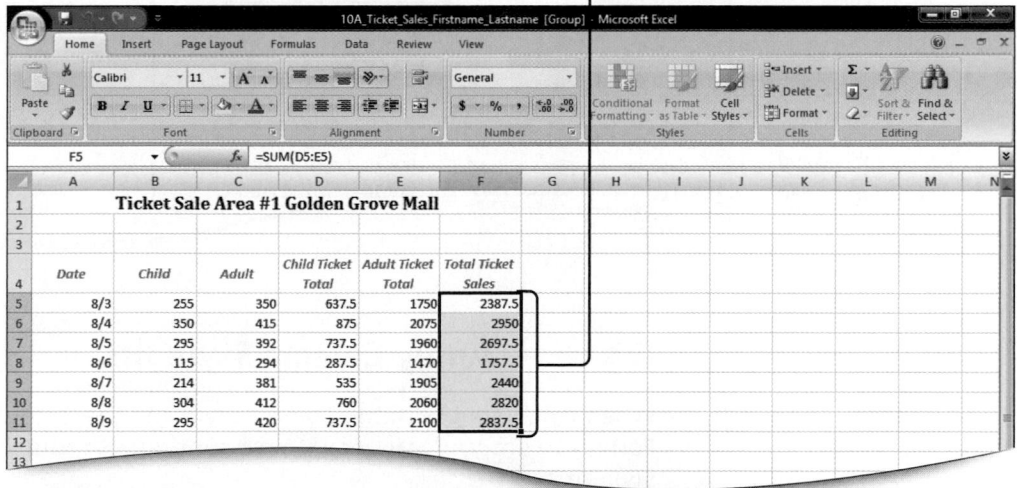

15 Click cell **F12**, and then in the **Editing group**, click the **Sum** button Σ ▾. Be sure the range **F5:F11** is selected, and then press Enter.

Excel looks above the selected cell and proposes a range to sum. Your result is *17890*.

16 In cell **A12** type **Totals** and then on the **Formula Bar**, click the **Enter** button ☑ to confirm the entry and keep **A12** as the active cell. Then apply the **Align Text Right** ≣ format and **Bold** **B** to the cell.

17 Select the range **B5:E12**, and then in the **Editing group**, click the **Sum** button to apply the Sum function to the range.

Recall that selecting a range in this manner will place the Sum function in the empty cells at the bottom of each column.

18 Apply appropriate number and financial formatting as follows: Select the range **B5:C12**, click the **Comma Style** button [,], and then click **Decrease Decimal** [.00→.0] two times. Select the range **D6:F11** and apply **Comma Style** [,]—leave the two decimal places displayed in these currency amounts. Select the nonadjacent ranges **D5:F5** and **D12:F12**, and then click the **Accounting Number Format** button [$ ▾]. Select the range **B12:F12**, in the **Font group** click the **Borders button arrow** [▢ ▾], and then click **Top and Double Bottom Border** to apply the common format for financial numbers. Click any blank cell to deselect, and then compare your screen with Figure 10.20.

Accounting Number Format applied

Figure 10.20

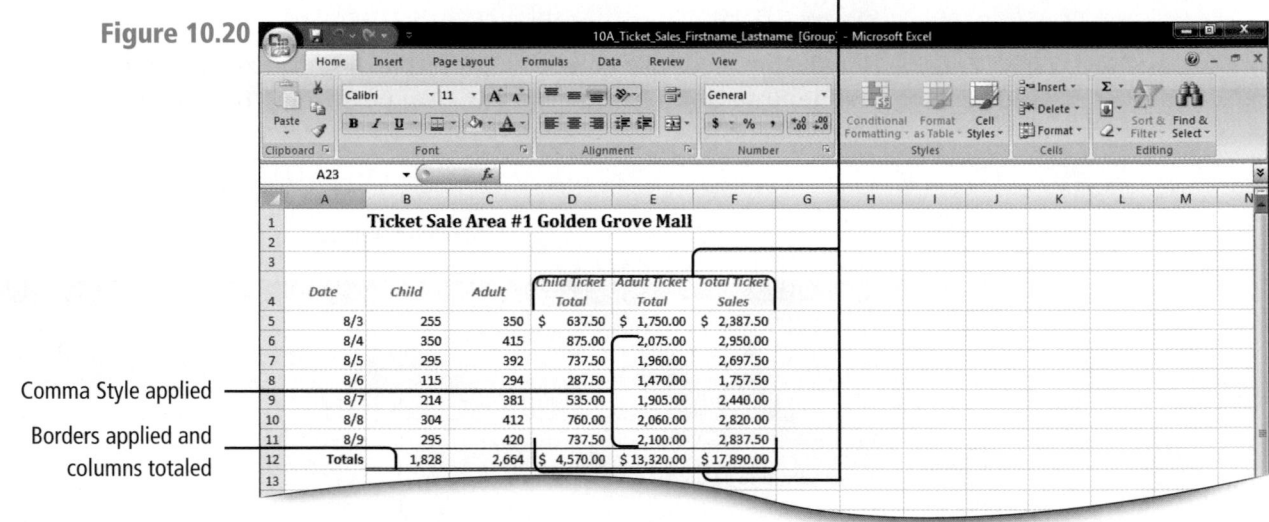

Note — Apply Comma Style first

When combining both the Comma Style and the Accounting Number Format to different ranges within a contiguous group of cells, apply Comma Style first.

19 Select the range **D15:D16**, right-click over the selection, and then on the Mini toolbar, click the **Accounting Number Format** [$ ▾] button.

20 Display the **Post Office** worksheet to examine the totals, and then compare your screen with Figure 10.21.

Recall that because your worksheets were grouped while making the calculations, all the calculations and formatting on the first worksheet were also being performed on the other two worksheets.

As soon as you select an individual sheet, as you have done here, the grouping is canceled. *[Group]* no longer displays in the title bar.

Figure 10.21

Totals calculated for Area #2

[Group] no longer displays
(sheets are ungrouped)

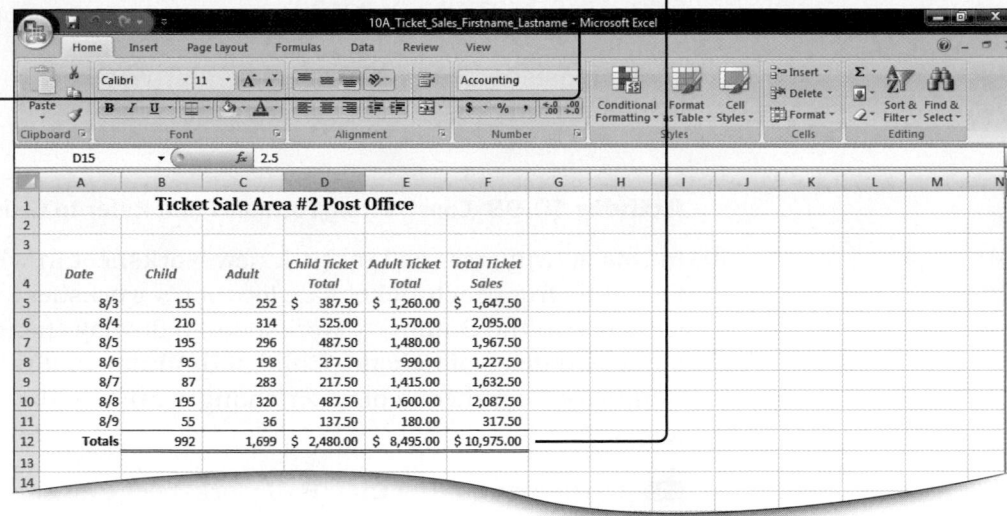

21 Display the **City Hall** worksheet to examine the totals, and then compare your screen with Figure 10.22.

You can see that by grouping sheets and copying formulas, it is easy to make multiple calculations in Excel without typing formulas multiple times.

Totals calculated for Area #3

Figure 10.22

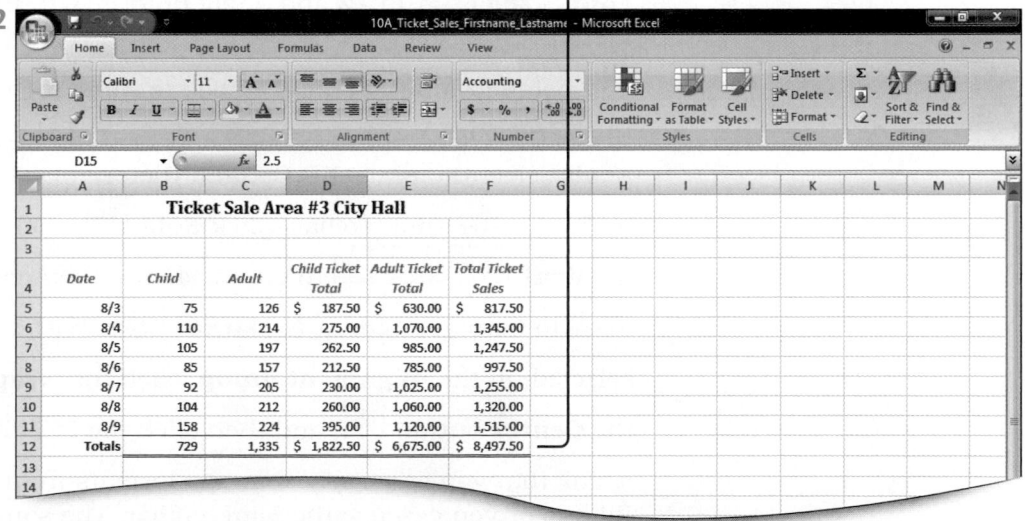

22 **Save** 💾 the changes you have made to your workbook.

Objective 6
Create a Summary Sheet

You can create a summary sheet as a place where totals from other worksheets are displayed and summarized.

Activity 10.08 Constructing Formulas that Refer to Cells in Another Worksheet

In this activity, you will insert a new worksheet in which you will place the totals from each ticket sale location's worksheet. You will construct formulas in the Summary worksheet to display the total revenue for each of the two types of tickets—Child and Adult—that will update the Summary worksheet whenever changes are made to the other worksheet totals.

1 To the right of the **City Hall** worksheet tab, click the **Insert Worksheet** button 🗐.

A new worksheet displays with the name *Sheet1* or *Sheet2* or some other number, depending on whether the other worksheets have been renamed and how many times a new worksheet has been inserted.

2 Rename the new worksheet **Summary** and then change the **Tab Color** to **Olive Green, Accent 3, Lighter 40%**. In cell **A4**, type **Golden Grove Mall** In cell **A5**, type **Post Office** and then in cell **A6**, type **City Hall** Select the range **A4:A6**, right-click, and then on the Mini toolbar, change the **Font Size** 11 ▾ to **12** and apply **Bold** **B**. In the **column heading area**, point to the right border of **column A** to display the ╫ pointer, and then double-click to AutoFit the column.

3 In cell **B3**, type **Total Sales Child** and then in cell **C3**, type **Total Sales Adult** Select the range **B3:C3**, and then right-click over the selection to display the Mini toolbar. Click **Bold** **B**, click **Italic** **I**, change the **Font** Calibri ▾ to **Cambria**, and then change the **Font Color** **A** ▾ to **Orange, Accent 6, Darker 25%**. With the two cells still selected, in the **Alignment group**, click the **Wrap Text** button 🗐, the **Center** button ≡, and then click the **Middle Align** ≡ button.

Recall that you can apply common formats from the buttons on the Ribbon or you can use the Mini toolbar. The same formats can also be applied from the Format Cells dialog box. Additionally, the Format Cells dialog box contains some formatting commands that are not commonly used enough to warrant a button on the Ribbon or Mini toolbar.

4 Click cell **B4**. Type **=** and then click the **Golden Grove Mall sheet tab**. On the **Golden Grove Mall** worksheet, click cell **D12**, and then press Enter to redisplay the **Summary** worksheet.

5 Click cell **B4** to select it again. Look at the **Formula Bar** and notice that instead of a value, the cell contains a formula that is equal to the value in another cell in another worksheet. Compare your screen with Figure 10.23.

The value in this cell is equal to the value in cell D12 of the *Golden Grove Mall* worksheet. The Accounting Number Format applied to the referenced cell is carried over. By using a formula of this type, changes in cell D12 on the *Golden Grove Mall* worksheet will be automatically updated in this *Summary* worksheet.

Cell value equal to cell D12 in
the Golden Grove Mall worksheet

Figure 10.23

Column titles formatted

Accounting Number
Format retained

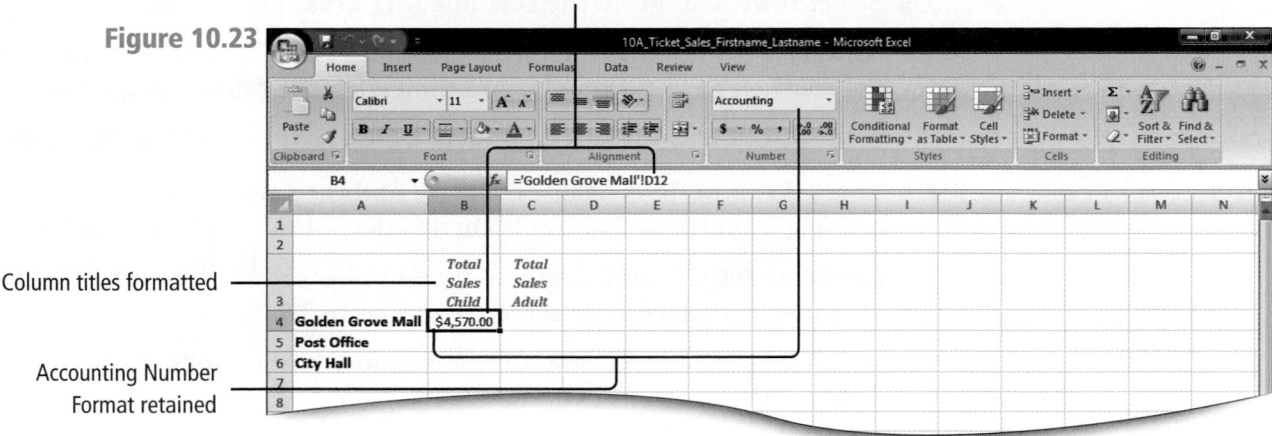

6 Click cell **C4**. Type **=** and then click the **Golden Grove Mall sheet tab**. Click cell **E12**, and then press Enter. Then, use the technique you just practiced to copy the week's total for **Child** and **Adult** ticket sales for the **Post Office worksheet** and the **City Hall worksheet**. Compare your screen with Figure 10.24.

The formulas in cells B4:C6 display the totals from the other three worksheets. Changes made to any of the other three worksheets—sometimes referred to as a ***detail worksheet*** because the details of the information are contained there—that affect their totals will display on this Summary worksheet. In this manner, the summary worksheet accurately displays the current totals from the other worksheets.

Total Child and Adult sales from each location

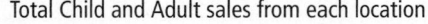

Figure 10.24

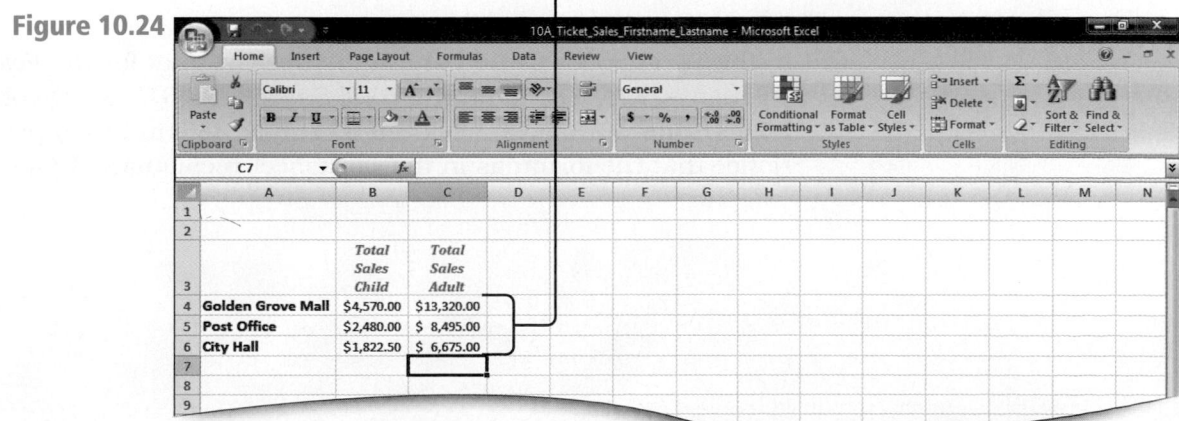

7 In cell **A1** type **Summer Fair and Arts Festival** and then **Merge and Center** the text over the range **A1:C1**. In cell **A2** type **Pre-Sales of Tickets August 3-9** and then **Merge and Center** the text over the range **A2:C2**. Select the two worksheet titles and change the Font Calibri to **Cambria**, change the **Font Color** to **Orange, Accent 6, Darker 25%**, change the **Font Size** 11 to **14**, and apply **Bold B**.

8 Select **rows 1:2**. From the **row heading area**, point to the lower boundary of either selected row to display the ⊕ pointer, increase the row height to **35 pixels**, and then click the **Middle Align** button. Select **columns B:C**, and then set the column width to **80 pixels**.

9 In cell **A7**, type **Total Sales** press Enter, and then notice that the formatting from the cell above is carried down to the new cell. Select the range **B4:C7**, and then use the **Sum** button Σ ▾ to total the two columns. Compare your screen with Figure 10.25.

Recall that cell formatting carries over to adjacent cells unless two cells are left blank.

Worksheet titles formatted

Figure 10.25

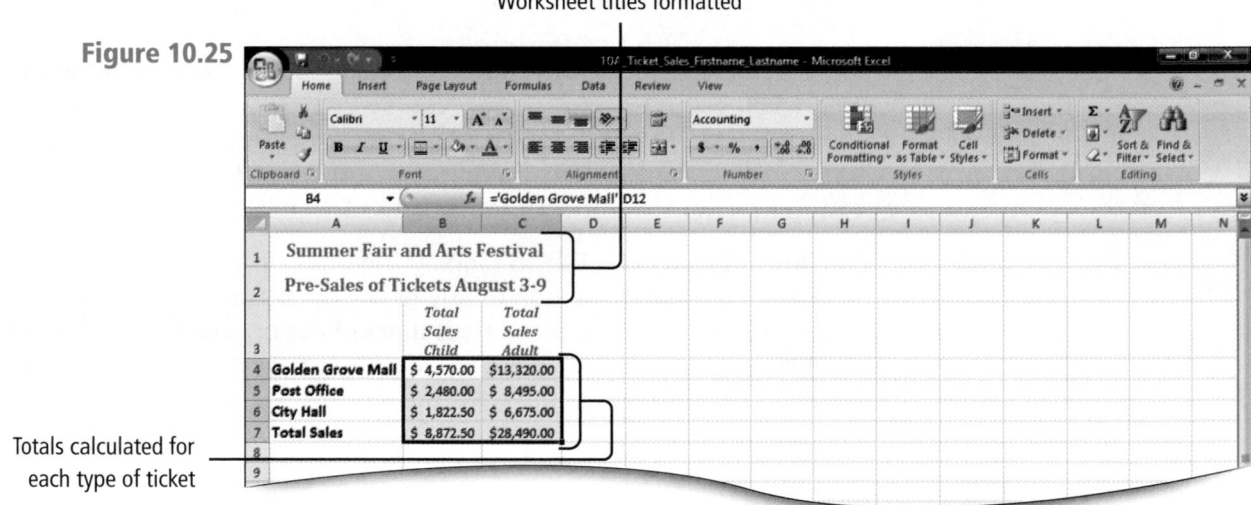

Totals calculated for each type of ticket

10 In the **Total Sales Child column**, notice the total for the *Post Office* location is *$2,480.00* and the *Total Sales* is *$8,872.50*. Display the **Post Office** worksheet, click cell **B11**, type **155** and then press Enter. Notice that the formulas in the worksheet recalculate. Display the

Summary worksheet, and notice that in the **Total Sales Child column**, both the total for the *Post Office* location and the *Total Sales* also recalculated. Compare your screen with Figure 10.26.

In this manner, a Summary sheet recalculates any changes made in the other worksheets.

Figure 10.26

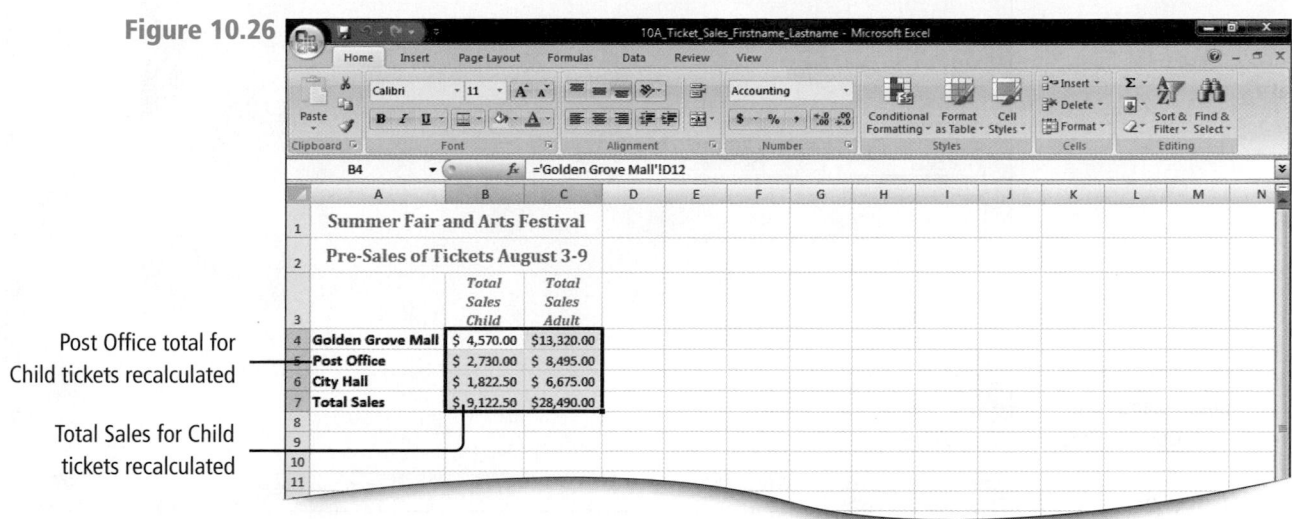

Post Office total for
Child tickets recalculated

Total Sales for Child
tickets recalculated

[11] Select the range **B7:C7**, and then apply a **Top and Double Bottom** border.

[12] **Save** your workbook.

Objective 7
Format and Print Multiple Worksheets in a Workbook

Each worksheet within a workbook can have different formatting, for example different headers or footers. If all the worksheets in the workbook will have the same header or footer, you can select all the worksheets and apply formatting common to all of the worksheets; for example, you can set the same footer in all of the worksheets.

Activity 10.09 Moving and Formatting Worksheets in a Workbook

In this activity, you will move the Summary sheet to become the first worksheet in the workbook. Then you will format and prepare your workbook for printing. The four worksheets containing data can be formatted simultaneously.

[1] Point to the **Summary sheet tab**, hold down the left mouse button to display a small black triangle—a caret—and then notice that a small paper icon attaches to the mouse pointer. Drag to the left until the caret and mouse pointer are to the left of the **Golden Grove Mall sheet tab**, as shown in Figure 10.27, and then release the left mouse button.

Use this technique to rearrange the order of worksheets within a workbook.

Figure 10.27

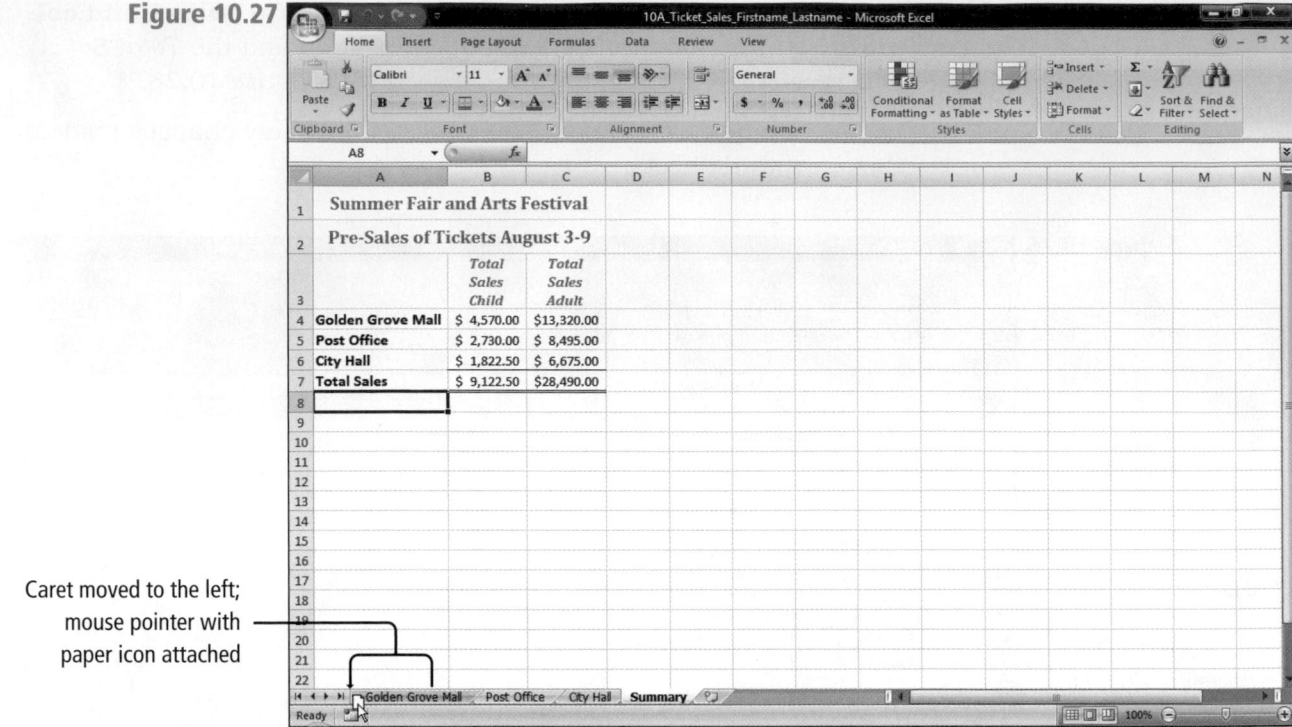

Caret moved to the left;
mouse pointer with
paper icon attached

2 Be sure the **Summary** worksheet is the active sheet. Then point to its sheet tab, right-click, and then click **Select All Sheets** to display *[Group]* in the title bar. On the Ribbon, click the **Insert tab**, and then in the **Text group**, click the **Header & Footer** button. In the **Navigation group**, click the **Go to Footer** button, click in the **left section** above the word *Footer*, and then in the **Header & Footer Elements group**, click the **File Name** button.

3 Click in a cell above the footer to deselect the **Footer area** and view your file name. On the Ribbon, click the **Page Layout tab**. In the **Page Setup group**, click the **Margins** button, and then at the bottom of the **Margins gallery**, click **Custom Margins**. In the displayed **Page Setup** dialog box, under **Center on page**, select the **Horizontally** check box. Click **OK**, and then on the status bar, click the **Normal** button ⊞ to return to Normal view.

After displaying worksheets in Page Layout View, dotted lines display to indicate the page breaks when you return to Normal view.

4 Press (Ctrl) + (Home) to move to the top of the worksheet. Verify that *[Group]* still displays in the title bar.

Recall that by selecting all sheets, you can apply the same formatting to all the worksheets at the same time.

5 **Save** 🖫 your changes. From the **Office** menu 🗔, point to the **Print** button, and then from the displayed menu, click **Print Preview**. Alternatively, press (Ctrl) + (F2) to display the Print Preview. Compare your screen with Figure 10.28.

With all the sheets grouped, you can view all of the sheets in Print Preview. If you do not see *Page 1 of 4* in the status bar, close the Preview, select all the sheets again, and then redisplay Print Preview.

Figure 10.28

Excel | chapter 10

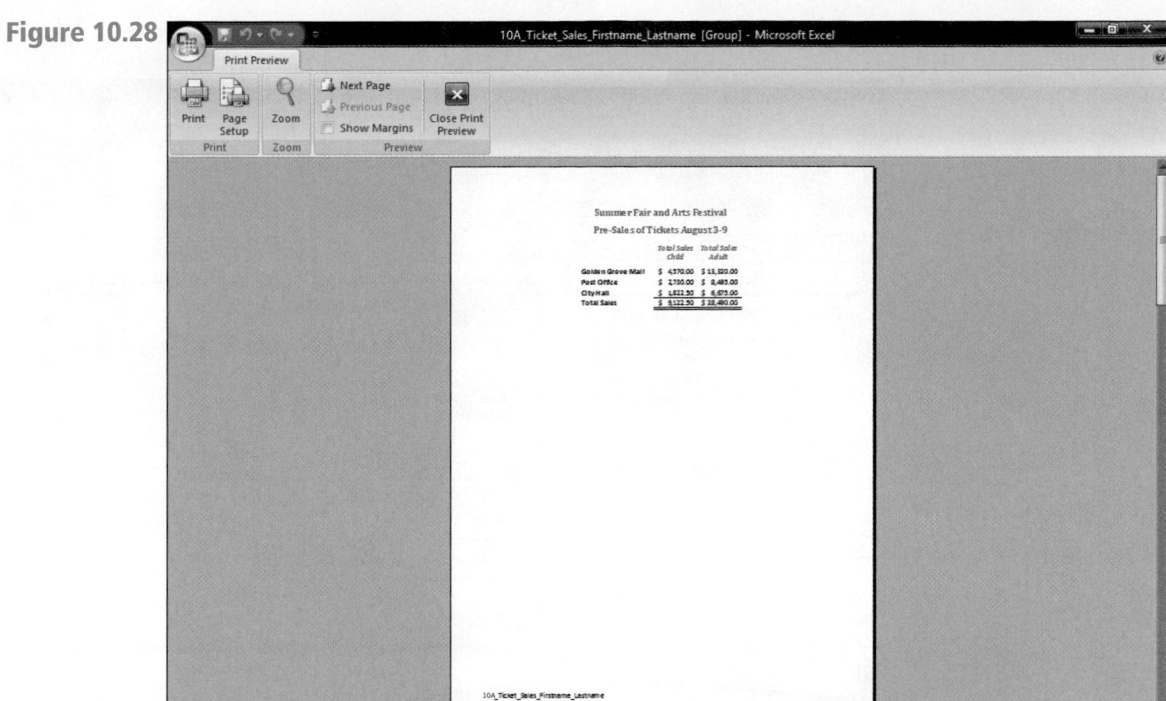

6 On the Ribbon, in the **Preview group**, click the **Next Page** button as necessary and take a moment to view each page of your workbook. After viewing all the worksheets, click the **Close Print Preview** button.

Activity 10.10 Printing All the Worksheets in a Workbook

1 **Save** your workbook before printing. Check your *Chapter Assignment Sheet* or *Course Syllabus*, or consult your instructor, to determine if you are to submit your assignments on paper or electronically. To submit electronically, follow the instructions provided by your instructor.

2 Verify that the worksheets in your workbook are still grouped—

[Group] displays in the title bar. From the **Office** menu , click the **Print** button. In the displayed **Print** dialog box, under **Print range**, verify that the **All** option button is selected. Under **Print what**, verify that **Active sheet(s)** is selected. Alternatively, if your worksheets are not grouped, you can click Entire workbook in this dialog box to print all the worksheets in the workbook. Under **Copies**, verify that the **Number of copies** is **1**. Compare your screen with Figure 10.29.

[Group] displays in the title bar

Figure 10.29

Default printer (yours will vary) ⎯

One copy ⎯

Active sheets(s) selected ⎯

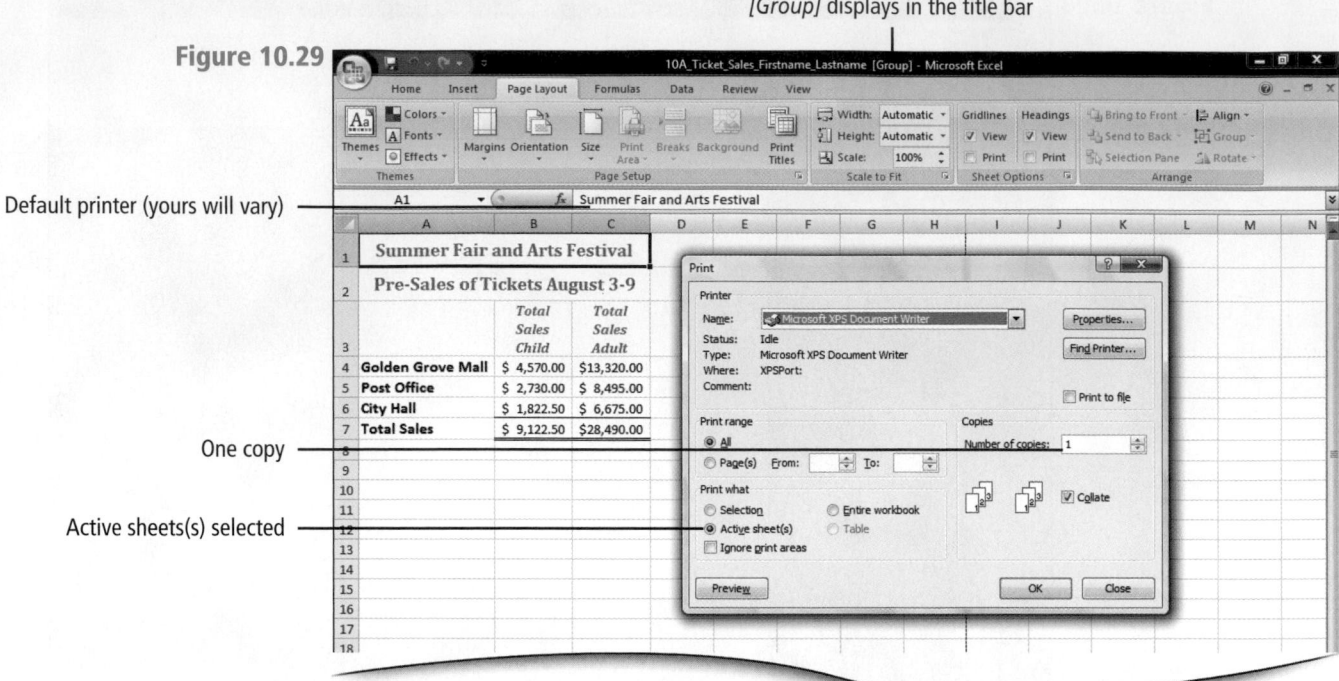

3 Click **OK** to print your worksheets. Determine if you are to print formulas for any or all of the worksheets in this workbook. To print formulas, refer to Activity 5.17 in Project 5A.

4 If you printed your formulas, be sure to redisplay the worksheet by pressing Ctrl + `. From the **Office** menu, click **Close**. If you are prompted to save changes, click **No** so that you do not save the changes to the Print layout that you used for printing formulas. **Close** Excel.

End **You have completed Project 10A**

Project 10B Growth Projection

In Activities 10.11 through 10.15, you will assist Mervyn Aghazarian, the City Planner for Golden Grove, in creating a workbook to estimate future population growth based on three different growth rates. Your resulting worksheet and chart will look similar to Figure 10.30.

For Project 10B, you will need the following file:

New blank Excel workbook

You will save your workbook as
10B_Growth_Projection_Firstname_Lastname

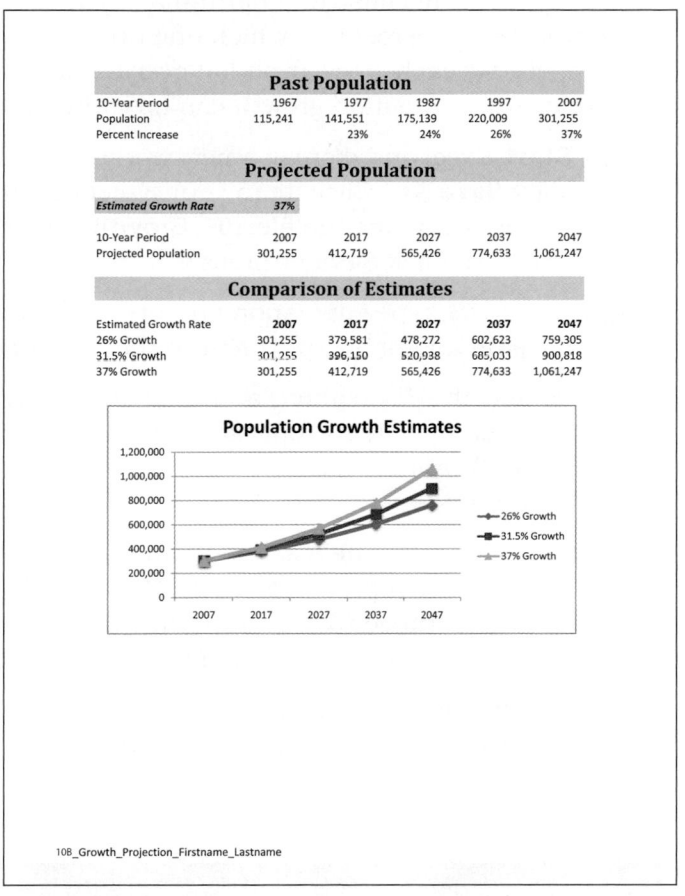

Figure 10.30
Project 10B—Growth Projection

Objective 8
Design a Worksheet for What-If Analysis

Excel recalculates; if you change the value in a cell referenced in a formula, the result of the formula is automatically recalculated. Thus, you can change cell values to see *what* would happen *if* you tried different values. This process of changing the values in cells to see how those changes affect the outcome of formulas in your worksheet is called **what-if analysis**.

Activity 10.11 Using Parentheses in a Formula

Mr. Aghazarian has the city's population figures for the past five 10-year periods. In each 10-year period, the population has increased. In this activity, you will construct a formula to calculate the **percentage rate of increase**—the percent by which one number increases over another number—for each 10-year period over the past years. From this information, future population growth can be estimated.

1 **Start** Excel and display a new workbook. From the **Office** menu , click **Save As**. Navigate to your Excel Chapter 10 folder, in the **File name** box, name the file **10B_Growth_Projection_Firstname_Lastname** and then click **Save** or press Enter.

2 In cell **A3**, type **Population** and press Enter. In cell **A4**, type **Percent Increase** and press Enter. Point to the right boundary of **column A** to display the pointer, and then double-click to AutoFit the column to accommodate its longest entry. Alternatively, on the Home tab, in the Cells group, click the Format button, and then click AutoFit Column Width.

3 In cell **A2**, type **10-Year Period** and then press Tab. In cell **B2**, type **1967** and then press Tab. In cell **C2**, type **1977** and then press Tab. Select the range **B2:C2**, drag the fill handle to the right through cell **F2**, and then compare your screen with Figure 10.31.

By establishing a pattern of 10-year intervals with the first two cells, you can use the fill handle to continue the series. The Auto Fill fea-

Figure 10.31

Pattern used to fill 10-year periods to create column titles

Row titles entered

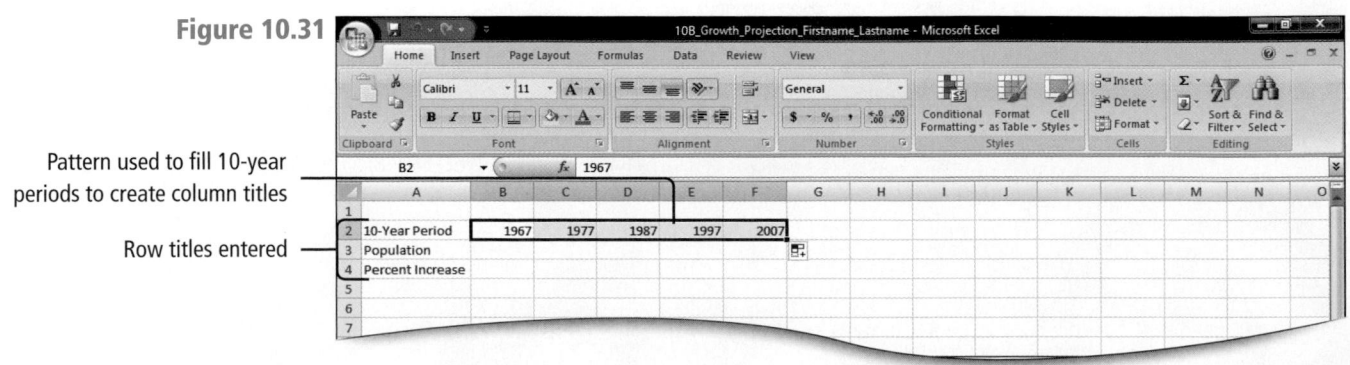

ture will do this for any pattern that you establish with two or more cells.

4 Click cell **A1**. Type **Past Population** and press Enter. Select the range **A1:F1**, and then right-click to display the Mini toolbar. Click the **Merge and Center** button ⊞▾, apply **Bold** **B**, change the Font Calibri ▾ to **Cambria**, and then change the **Font Size** 11 ▾ to **18**.

5 Beginning in cell **B3**, and then pressing Tab to move across the row, enter the following values for the population in the years listed:

1967	1977	1987	1997	2007
115241	**141551**	**175139**	**220009**	**301255**

6 Select the range **B3:F3**, right-click, on the Mini toolbar, click **Comma Style** ▾ , and then **Decrease Decimal** ▾ two times.

7 Click cell **C4**. Being sure to include the parentheses, type **=(c3-b3)/b3** and then press Enter. Click cell **C4**. In the **Number group**, click the **Percent Style** button % , and then examine the formula in the **Formula Bar**.

The mathematical formula to calculate the percentage rate of population increase from 1967 to 1977 is *rate = amount of increase/base*.

The first step is to determine the *amount of increase*. This is accomplished by subtracting the ***base***—the starting point represented by the 1967 population—from the 1977 population. Thus, the *amount of increase* = 141,551 – 115,241 or 26,310. Between 1967 and 1977, the population increased by 26,310 people. In the formula, this calculation is represented by *c3-b3*.

The second step is to calculate the *rate*—what the amount of increase (26,310) represents as a percentage of the base (1967's population of 115,241). Determine this by dividing the amount of increase (26,310) by the base (115,241). Thus, 26,310 divided by 115,241 is equal to 0.22830416 or, when rounded to a percent—23%.

8 In the **Formula Bar**, locate the parentheses enclosing *C3-B3*.

Excel follows a set of mathematical rules called the ***order of operations***, which has four basic parts:

- Expressions within parentheses are processed first.

- Exponentiation, if present, is performed before multiplication and division.

- Multiplication and division are performed before addition and subtraction.

- Consecutive operators with the same level of precedence are calculated from left to right.

9 Click cell **D4**, type = and then by typing, or using a combination of typing and clicking cells to reference them, construct a formula similar to the one in cell **C4** to calculate the rate of increase in population from 1977 to 1987. Compare your screen with Figure 10.32.

Recall that the first step is to determine the *amount of increase—* 1987 population minus 1977 population—and then to write the calculation so that Excel performs this operation first; that is, place it in parentheses.

The second step is to divide the result of the calculation in parentheses by the *base—*the population for 1977.

Figure 10.32

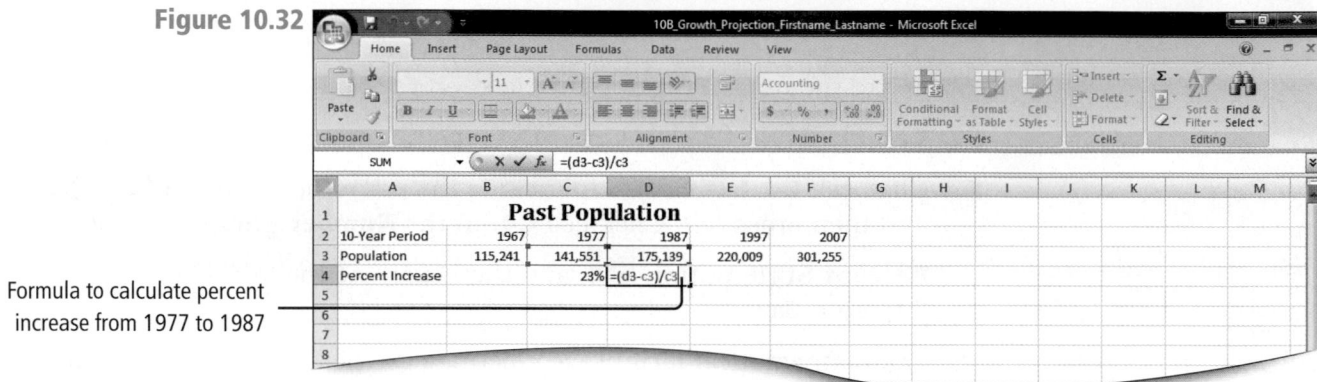

Formula to calculate percent increase from 1977 to 1987

10 Press Enter, and then format cell **D4** with the **Percent Style** %.

Your result is *24%*.

11 With cell **D4** selected, drag the fill handle to the right through cell **F4**. Click any empty cell to cancel the selection, **Save** your workbook, and then compare your screen with Figure 10.33.

Because this formula uses relative cell references—that is, for each year, the formula is the same but the values used are relative to the formula's location—you can copy the formula in this manner. For example, the result for 1987 uses 1977 as the base, the result for 1997 uses 1987 as the base, and the result for 2007 uses 1997 as the base.

The formula results show the percent of increase for each 10-year period between 1967 and 2007. You can see that in each 10-year period, the population has grown as much as 37%—between 1997 and 2007—and as little as 23%—between 1967 and 1977.

Percent increase calculated for the past 10-year periods

Figure 10.33

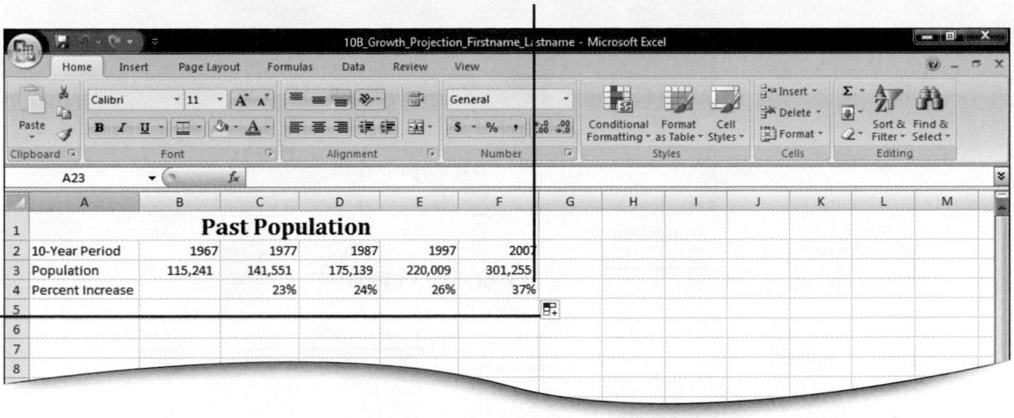

Auto Fill Options
button displays

Workshop

Use of Parentheses in a Formula

When writing a formula in Excel, use parentheses to communicate the order in which the operations should occur. For example, to average three test scores of 100, 50, and 90 that you scored on three different tests in a class, you would add the test scores and then divide by the number of test scores in the list. If you write this formula as =100+50+90/3, the result would be 180, because Excel would first divide 90 by 3 and then add 100+50+30. Excel would do so because the order of operations states that multiplication and division are calculated *before* addition and subtraction.

The correct way to write this formula is =(100+50+90)/3. Excel will add the three values, and then divide the result by 3, or 240/3 resulting in a correct average of 80. Parentheses play an important role in assuring that you get the correct result in your formulas.

Activity 10.12 Formatting as You Type

You can format numbers as you type them. When you type numbers in a format that Excel recognizes, Excel automatically applies that format to the cell. Recall that once applied, cell formats remain with the cell, even if the cell contents are deleted. In this activity, you will format cells by typing the numbers with percent signs and use the Format Painter to copy text (non-numeric) formats.

1 In cell **A6**, type **Projected Population** and then press Enter. Click cell **A1**. On the **Home tab**, in the **Clipboard group**, click the **Format Painter** button , and then click cell **A6**.

The format of cell A1 is *painted* or applied to cell A6, including the merging and centering of the text across cells A6:F6.

2 In cell **A8**, type **Estimated Growth Rate** and then press Enter. AutoFit **column A** to accommodate the new longer entry.

3 In cell **A10**, type **10-Year Period** and then in cell **A11**, type **Projected Population** In cell **B10**, type **2007** and then press Tab. In cell **C10**, type **2017** and then press Enter. Select the range **B10:C10**, and then drag the fill handle through cell **F10** to extend the pattern of years to *2047*. Compare your screen with Figure 10.34.

Figure 10.34

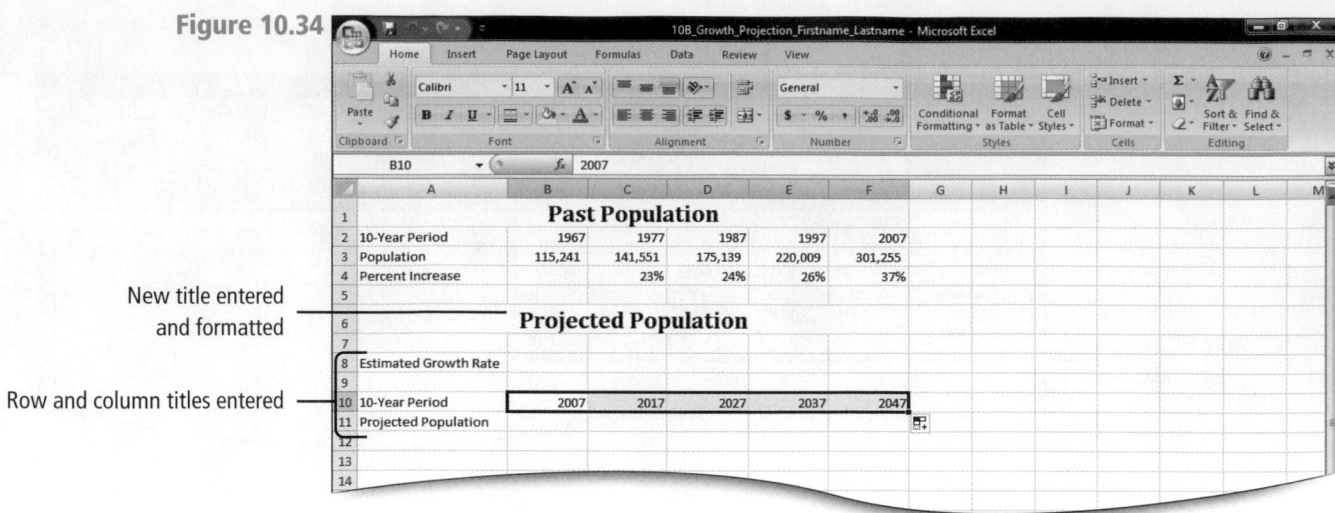

New title entered and formatted

Row and column titles entered

(Spreadsheet contents:)

	A	B	C	D	E	F
1		**Past Population**				
2	10-Year Period	1967	1977	1987	1997	2007
3	Population	115,241	141,551	175,139	220,009	301,255
4	Percent Increase		23%	24%	26%	37%
5						
6		**Projected Population**				
7						
8	Estimated Growth Rate					
9						
10	10-Year Period	2007	2017	2027	2037	2047
11	Projected Population					
12						
13						
14						

4 Click cell **B11**, and then in the **Number group**, notice that the format indicates *General*. Including the comma, type **301,255** On the **Formula Bar**, click the **Enter** button ✓ to keep the cell active, and then in the **Number group**, notice that the format changed to *Number*. Then, press Delete, and in the **Number group**, notice that the *Number* format is still indicated.

Recall that deleting the contents of a cell does not delete the cell's formatting.

5 *Without* typing a comma, in cell **B11** type **301255** and then press Enter.

The comma is inserted even though you did not type it. When you type a number and include a formatting symbol such as a comma, dollar sign, or percent sign, Excel applies the format to the cell. Thus, if you delete the contents of the cell and type in the cell again, the format you established remains applied to the cell. This is referred to as *format as you type*.

6 Examine the format of the value in cell **B11**, and then compare it to the format in cell **B3** where you used the Comma Style button to format the cell. Notice that the number in cell **B11** is flush with the right edge of the cell, but the number in cell **B3** leaves a small space on the right edge.

When you type commas as you enter numbers, Excel applies the *Number* format, which does *not* leave a space at the right of the number for a closing parenthesis in the event of a negative number. This is different from the format that is applied when you use the *Comma Style* button on the Ribbon or Mini toolbar, as you did for the numbers entered in row 3. Recall that the Comma Style format applied from either the Ribbon or the Mini toolbar leaves space on the right for a closing parenthesis in the event of a negative number.

7 In cell **B8**, type **26%** and then on the **Formula Bar**, click **Enter** ✓. Then, press Delete and *without* typing a percent sign, type **26** and then press Enter.

The percent sign is inserted even though you did not type it—this is another example of the *format as you type* feature.

8 Select the range **A8:B8**, and then apply **Bold** [B] and *Italic* [I].

9 **Save** [💾] your workbook.

More Knowledge

Percentage Calculations

When you type a percentage into a cell—for example *26%*—the percentage format, without decimal points, displays in both the cell and the Formula Bar. Excel will, however, use the decimal value of *0.26* for actual calculations.

Activity 10.13 Calculating a Value After an Increase

A growing population results in increased use of streets, schools, and other city services. Thus, city planners in Golden Grove must estimate how much the population will increase in the future. The calculations you made in the previous activity show that the population has increased at varying rates during each 10-year period, ranging from a low of 23% to a high of 37% per 10-year period.

Population data from the state and surrounding areas suggests that future growth will trend closer to that of the recent past. To plan for the future, Mr. Aghazarian wants to prepare three forecasts of the city's population based on the percentage increases in 1997, in 2007, and for a percentage increase halfway between the two, that is, for 26%, 31.5%, and 37%. In this activity, you will calculate the population that would result from a 26% increase.

1 Click cell **C11**. Type **=b11*(100%+b8)** and then on the **Formula Bar**, click the **Enter** [✓] button. Compare your screen with Figure 10.35.

This formula calculates what the population will be in the year 2017 assuming an increase of 26% over 2007's population. The mathematical formula to calculate a value after an increase is ***value after increase = base x percent for new value***.

The first step is to establish the *percent for new value*. The ***percent for new value = base percent + percent of increase***. The *base percent* of 100% represents the base population and the *percent of increase* in this instance is 26%. Thus, the population will equal 100% of the base year plus 26% of the base year. This can be expressed as 126% or 1.26. In this formula, you will use 100% + the rate in cell B8, which is 26%, to equal 126%.

The second step is to enter a reference to the cell that contains the *base*—the population in 2007. The base value resides in cell B11—301,255.

The third step is to calculate the *value after increase*. Because in each future 10-year period the increase will be based on 26%—an absolute value located in cell B8—this cell reference can be formatted as absolute with the use of dollar signs.

Figure 10.35

Absolute reference to cell B8 ——

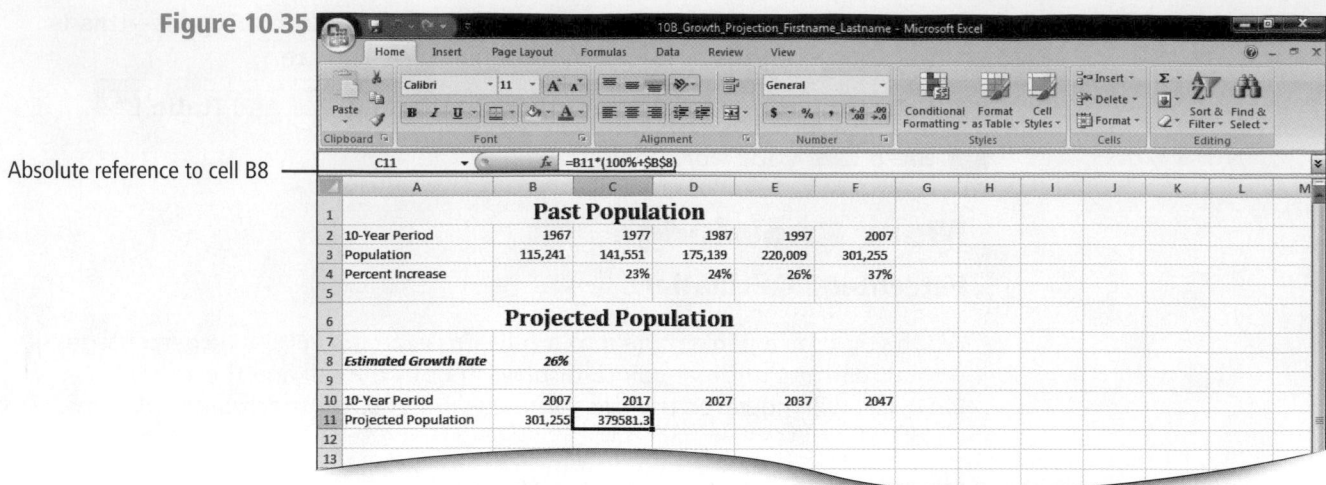

---

2 With cell **C11** as the active cell, drag the fill handle to copy the formula to the range **D11:F11**. Click cell **B11**, click the **Format Painter** button, and then select the range **C11:F11**. Click an empty cell to cancel the selection, and then compare your screen with Figure 10.36.

This formula uses a relative cell address—B11—for the *base*; the population in the previous 10-year period is used in each of the formulas in cells D11:F11 as the *base* value. Because the reference to the *percent of increase* in cell B8 is an absolute reference, each *value after increase* is calculated with the value from cell B8.

The population projected for 2017—*379,581*—is an increase of 26% over the population in 2007. The projected population in 2027—*478,272*—is an increase of 26% over the population in 2017 and so on.

Figure 10.36

Each value represents a 26% increase over the previous base year ——

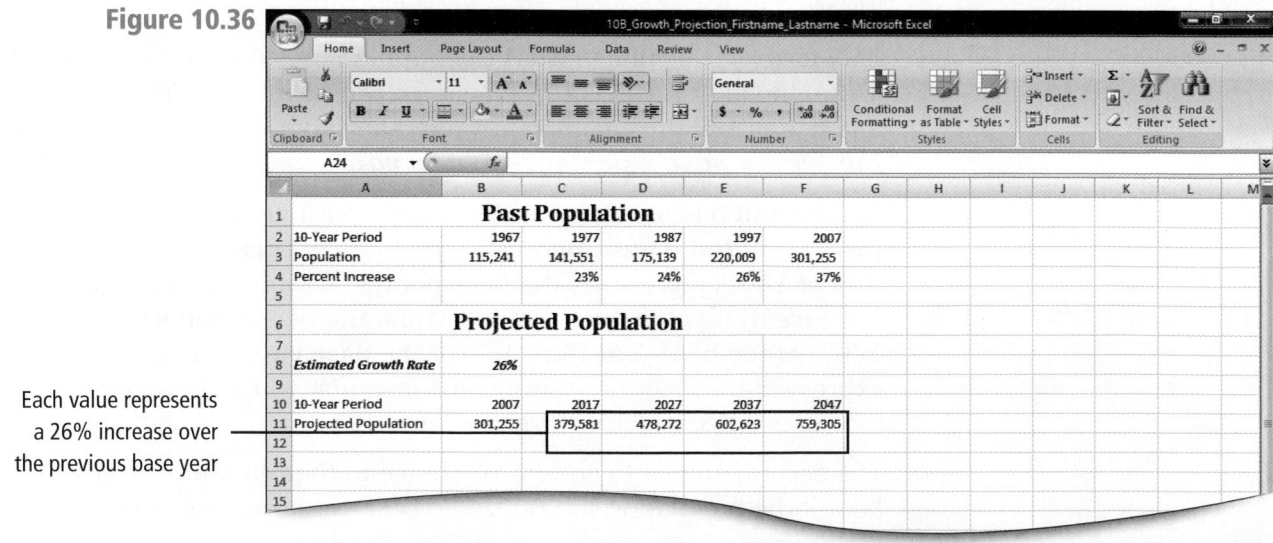

3 **Save** your workbook.

Workshop

Calculating Percent Increase or Decrease

The basic formula for calculating an increase or decrease can be done in two parts. First determine the percent by which the base value will be increased or decreased, and then add or subtract the results to the base. The formula can be simplified by using (1+amount of increase) or (1–amount of decrease), where 1 represents the whole, rather than 100%. Thus, the formula used in Step 1 of Activity 10.13 could also be written =b11*(1+b8), or =(b11*b8)+b11.

Objective 9
Perform What-If Analysis

If a formula depends on the value in a cell, you can see what effect it will have if you change the value in that cell. Then, you can copy the value computed by the formula and paste it into another part of the worksheet where it can be compared and charted. This can be done for multiple formulas.

Activity 10.14 Performing What-If Analysis and Using Paste Special

Mr. Aghazarian can see that a growth rate of 26% in each 10-year period will result in a population of almost 760,000 people by 2047. The city planners will likely ask him what the population might be if population grows at the highest rate (37%) or at a rate that is halfway between the 1997 and 2007 rates (31.5%). Because the formulas are constructed to use the growth rate displayed in cell B8, Mr. Aghazarian can answer these questions quickly by entering different percentages into that cell. To keep the results of each set of calculations so they can be compared, you will paste the results of each what-if analysis into another area of the worksheet.

1 In cell **A13**, type **Comparison of Estimates** and then press Enter. Click cell **A6**, click **Format Painter** 🖌, and then click cell **A13**. Select the range **A8:B8**, right-click to display the Mini toolbar, click the **Fill Color button arrow** 🎨▾, and then under **Theme Colors**, apply **Olive Green, Accent 3, Lighter 40%**. Click cell **A1**, hold down Ctrl, and then click cells **A6** and **A13**. In the **Font group**, click the **Fill Color** button 🎨▾ to apply the same fill color to these titles.

Recall that the Fill Color button retains its most recent color.

2 In the range **A15:A18** type the following row titles:

Estimated Growth Rate
26% Growth
31.5% Growth
37% Growth

3 Select the range **B10:F10**. On the **Home tab**, in the **Clipboard group**, click the **Copy** 📋 button, click cell **B15**, and then in the **Clipboard group**, click the **Paste** button.

Recall that when pasting a group of copied cells to a target range, you need only select the first cell of the range.

4 Select the range **B11:F11**, click **Copy** 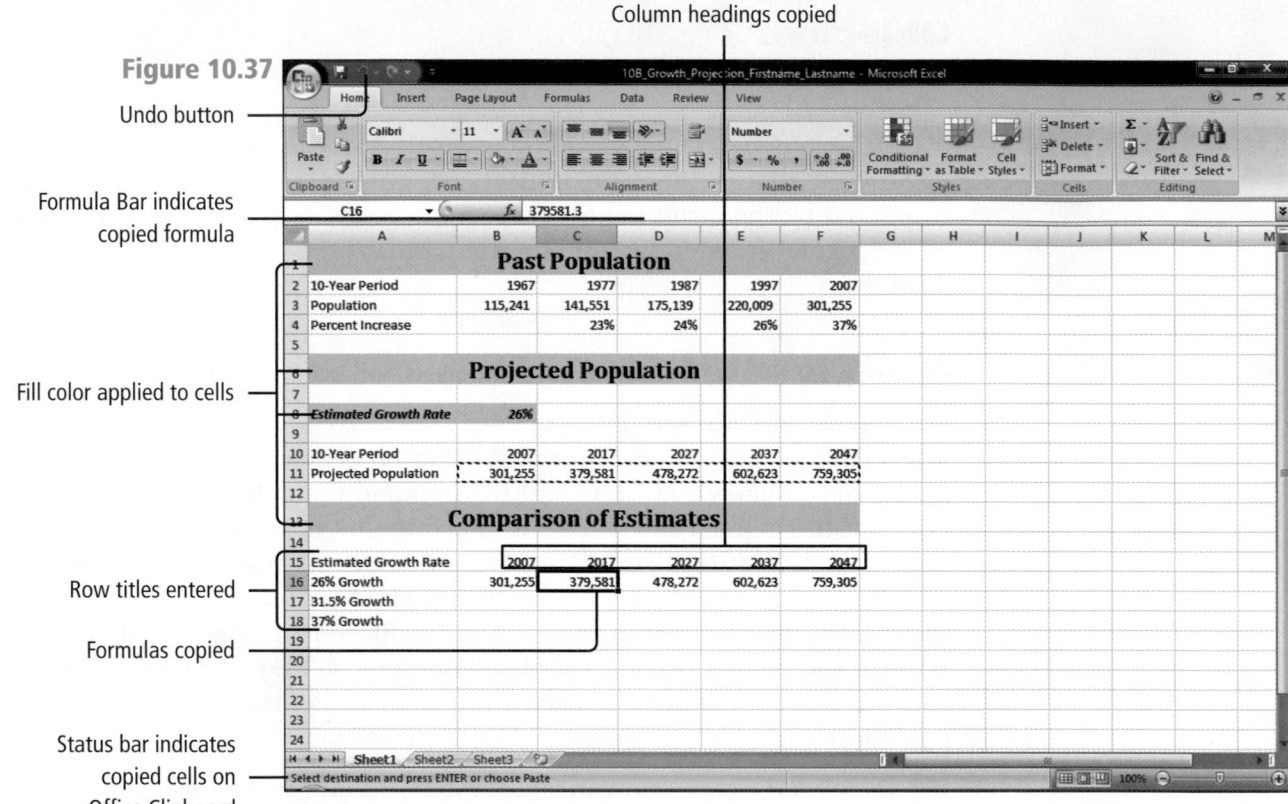, click cell **B16**, and then click the **Paste** button. Click cell **C16**, and notice on the **Formula Bar** that the *formula* was pasted into the cell. Compare your screen with Figure 10.37.

This is *not* the desired result. The actual *calculated values*—not the formulas—are needed in the range B16:F16.

Column headings copied

Figure 10.37

Undo button —

Formula Bar indicates copied formula —

Fill color applied to cells —

Row titles entered —

Formulas copied —

Status bar indicates copied cells on Office Clipboard

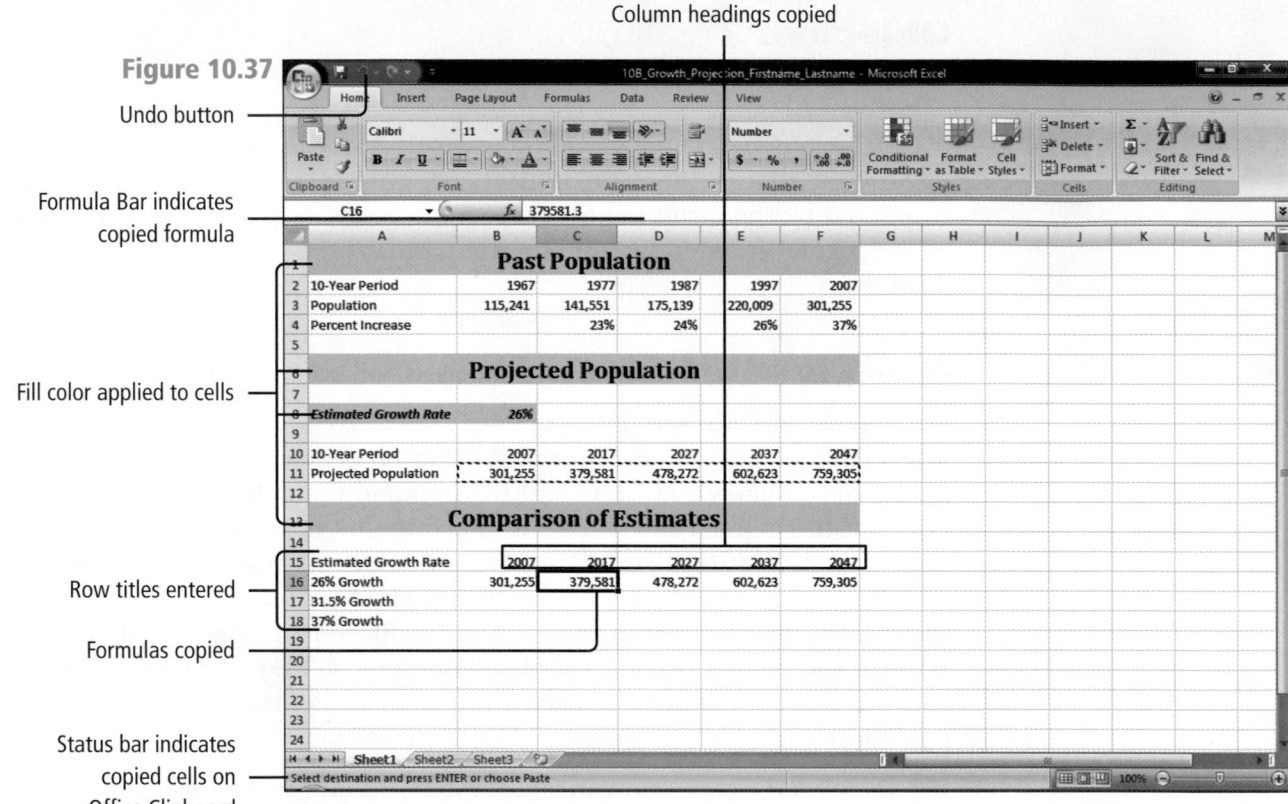

5 On the **Quick Access Toolbar**, click the **Undo** button. With the range **B11:F11** still copied to the Clipboard—as indicated by the message in the status bar and the moving border—in the **Clipboard group**, click the **Paste button arrow**. From the displayed menu, click **Paste Special**. In the displayed **Paste Special** dialog box, under **Paste**, click the **Values and number formats** option button.

The *Paste Special* dialog box offers various options for the manner in which you can paste the contents of the Office Clipboard. The *Values and number formats* command pastes the *calculated values* that result from the calculation of formulas into other cells—along with the formatting applied to the copied cells.

6 In the displayed **Paste Special** dialog box, click **OK**. Click cell **C16**. Notice on the **Formula Bar** that the cell contains a value, not a formula. Press [Esc] to cancel the moving border and then compare your screen with Figure 10.38.

The calculated estimates based on a 26% growth rate are pasted along with their formatting.

Figure 10.38

Formula Bar indicates the value ———

Calculated value pasted ———

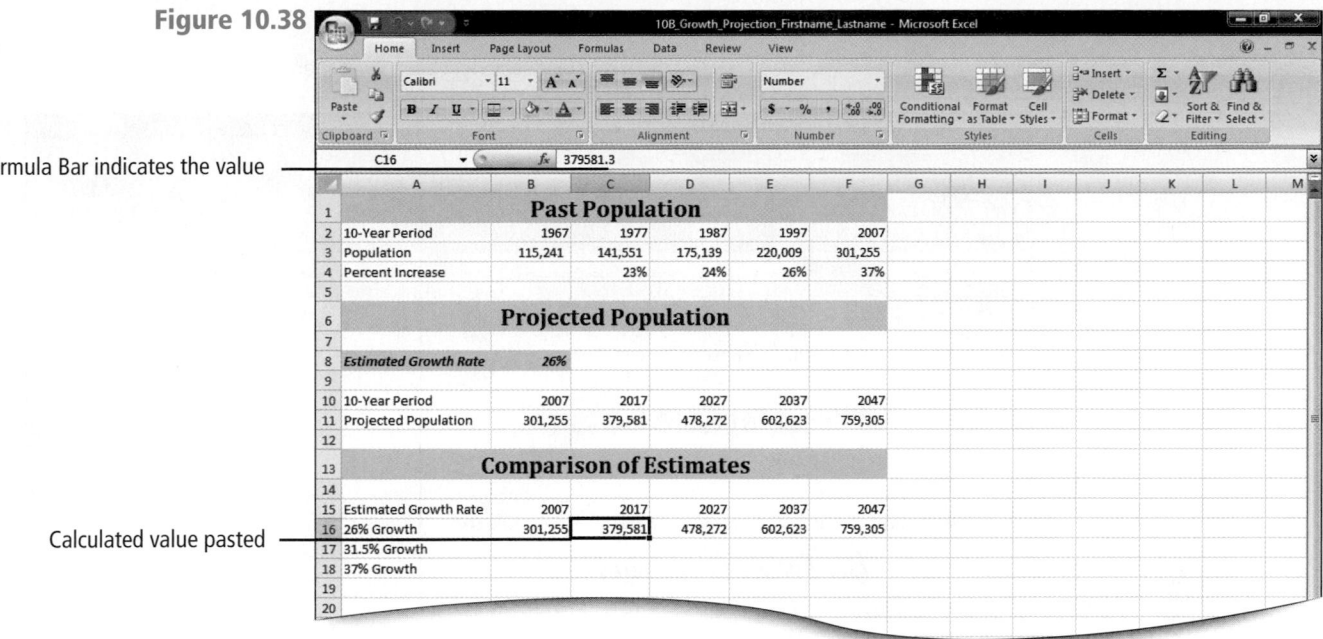

7 Click cell **B8**. Type **31.5** and then watch the values in **C11:F11** recalculate as, on the **Formula Bar**, you click the **Enter** button ☑.

The value *31.5%* is halfway between 26% and 37%—the growth rates from the two most recent 10-year periods. Although the cell may display 32%, you can see that the underlying value is 31.5%.

8 Select the range **B11:F11**, and then press ⌃Ctrl + ⃝C, which is the keyboard shortcut for the Copy command. Click cell **B17**. In the **Clipboard group**, click the **Paste button arrow**, and then click **Paste Special**. In the **Paste Special** dialog box, click the **Values and number formats** option button, and then click **OK**.

9 In cell **B8**, type **37** and then press ⏎Enter. Notice that the projected values in **C11:F11** are recalculated.

10 Using the skills you just practiced, copy the range **B11:F11**, and then paste the **values and number formats** of the copied range to the range **B18:F18**.

11 Press ⎋Esc to cancel the moving border, and then click an empty cell to cancel the selection. In **rows 15:18**, notice that the data and titles are arranged in simple rows and columns in adjacent cells for convenient charting. Compare your screen with Figure 10.39.

With this information, Mr. Aghazarian can answer several what-if questions about the future population of the city and provide a range of population estimates based on the rates of growth over the past 10-year periods.

Values copied for each what-if analysis

Figure 10.39

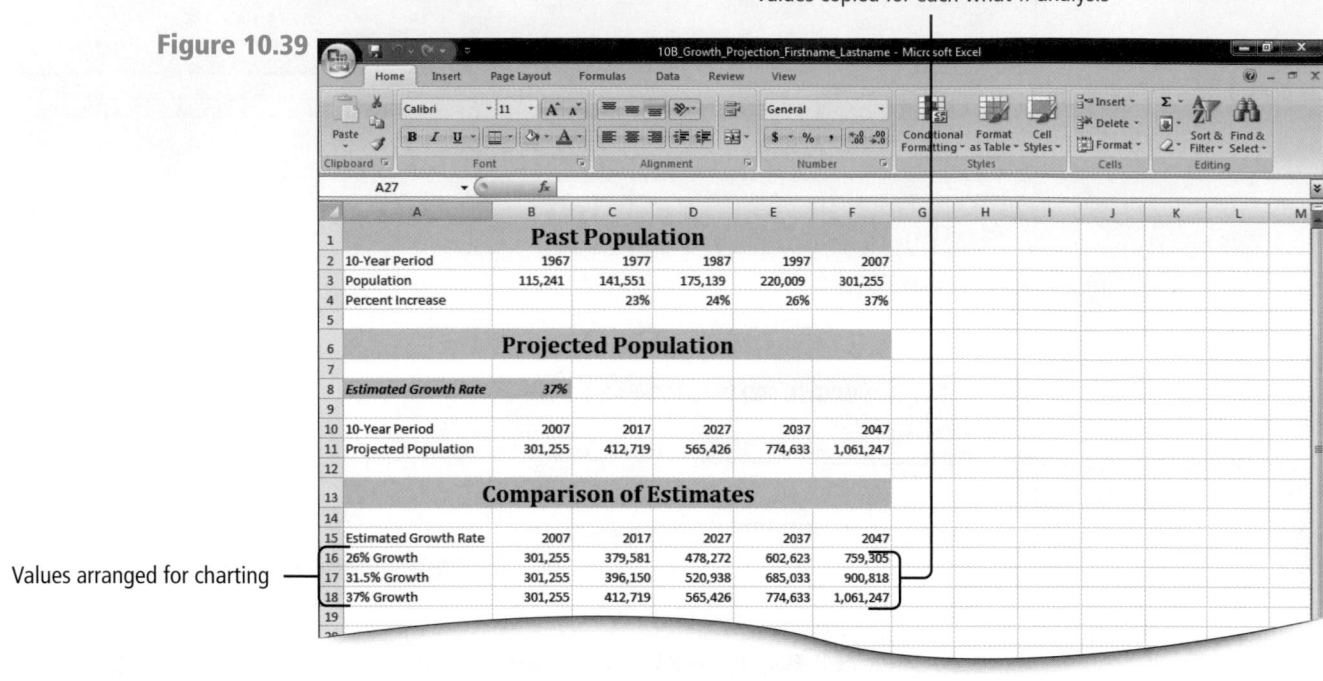

Values arranged for charting

12 **Save** 💾 your workbook.

Another Way ── **To Display the Paste Special Dialog Box**

Right-click over the target area, and then from the shortcut menu, click Paste Special. In many instances, using this method shortens the distance your mouse must travel in order to select an option from this dialog box.

Objective 10
Compare Data with a Line Chart

A **_line chart_** displays trends over time. Time is displayed along the bottom axis and the data point values are connected with a line. If you want to compare more than one set of values, each group is connected by a different line. The curves and directions of the lines make trends obvious to the reader.

Activity 10.15 Creating a Line Chart

In this activity, you will chart the values that represent the three different possible rates of population growth for Golden Grove. The 10-year periods will form the categories of time along the bottom of the chart and each set of values corresponding to a different growth rate will be represented by a line.

1 Select the range **B15:F15** and apply **Bold** **B**.

2 Select the range **A16:F18**. On the **Insert tab**, in the **Charts group**, click the **Line** button. From the displayed gallery of line charts, in the second row, point to the first chart type to display the ScreenTip *Line with Markers* as shown in Figure 10.40.

Figure 10.40

Line with Markers chart type —

Data selected for charting —

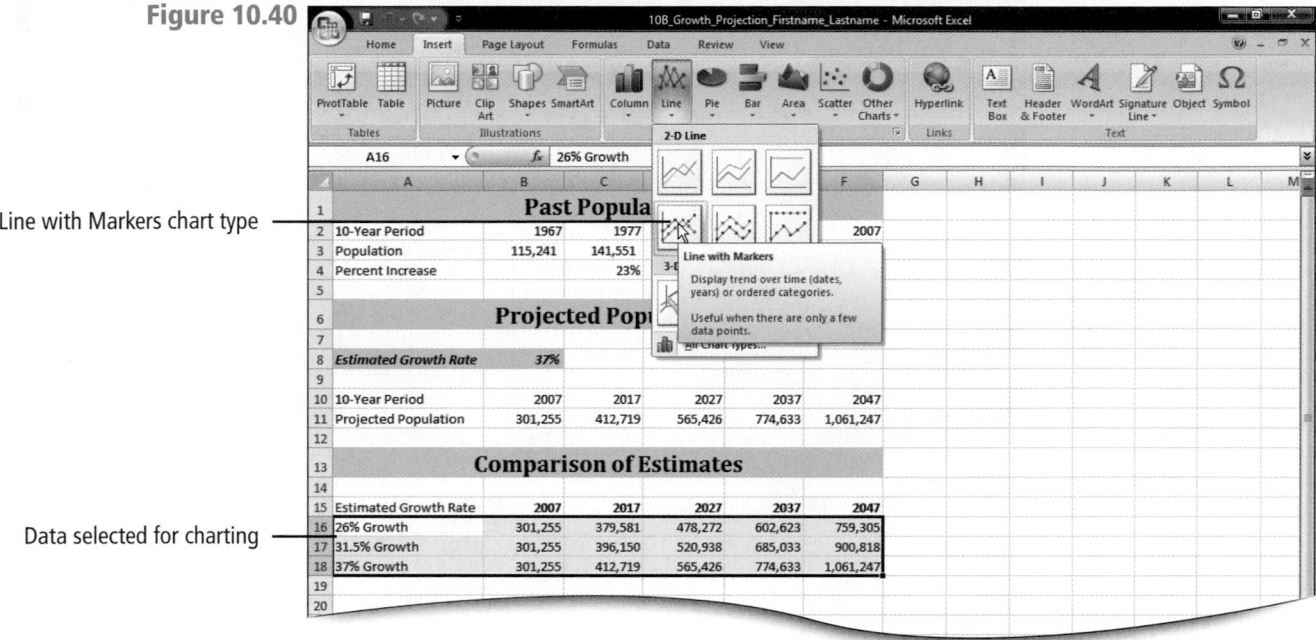

3 Click the **Line with Markers** chart type to create the chart as an embedded chart in the worksheet. Use the ⬚ pointer to move the upper left corner of the chart just inside the upper left corner of cell **A20**. Then, scroll down so that you can view both the data and the chart on your screen. Compare your screen with Figure 10.41.

The chart still requires appropriate time labels along the category axis.

Line representing each growth rate

Figure 10.41

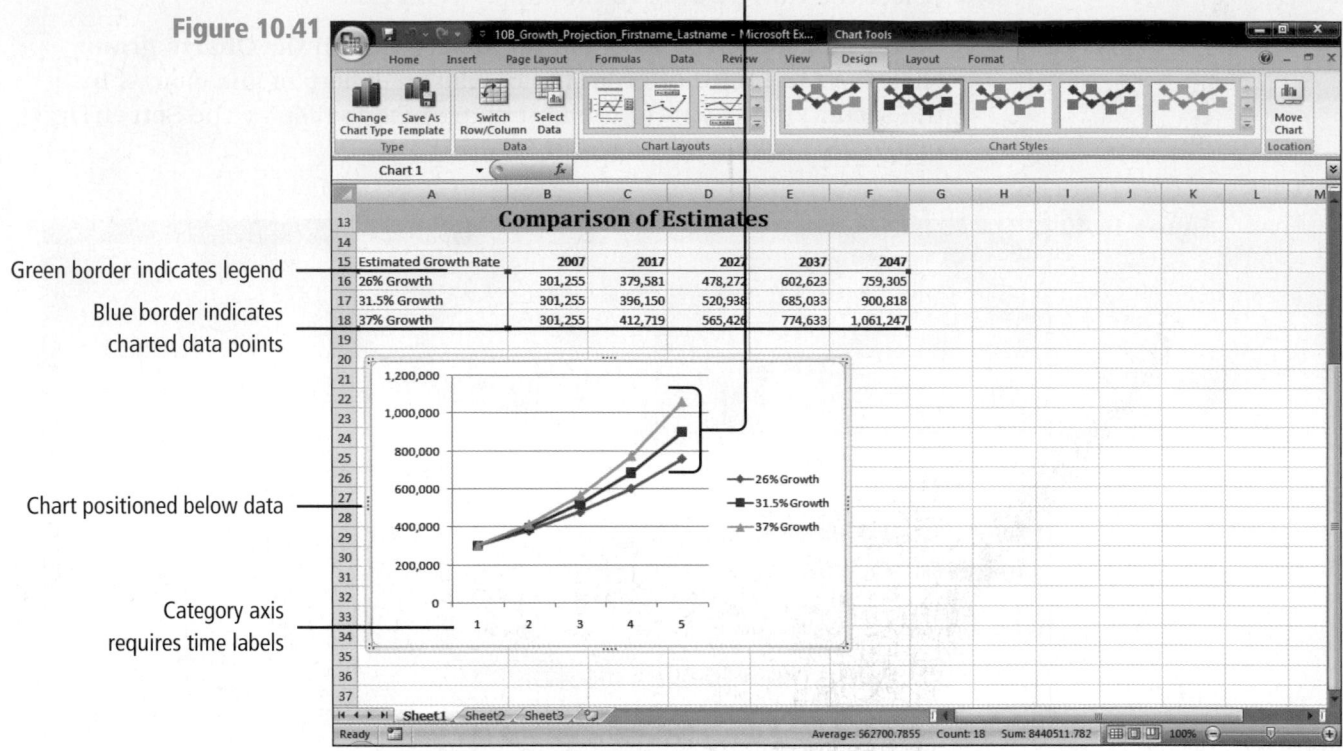

Green border indicates legend

Blue border indicates
charted data points

Chart positioned below data

Category axis
requires time labels

---

4 Be sure the chart is still selected. In the lower left corner of the
chart, point to where the vertical and horizontal axis lines intersect
near the *0* until the ScreenTip *Horizontal (Category) Axis* displays.
Then, right-click, and from the displayed shortcut menu, click
Select Data.

5 On the right side of the displayed **Select Data Source** dialog box,
under **Horizontal (Category) Axis Labels**, locate the **Edit** button, as
shown in Figure 10.42.

Figure 10.42

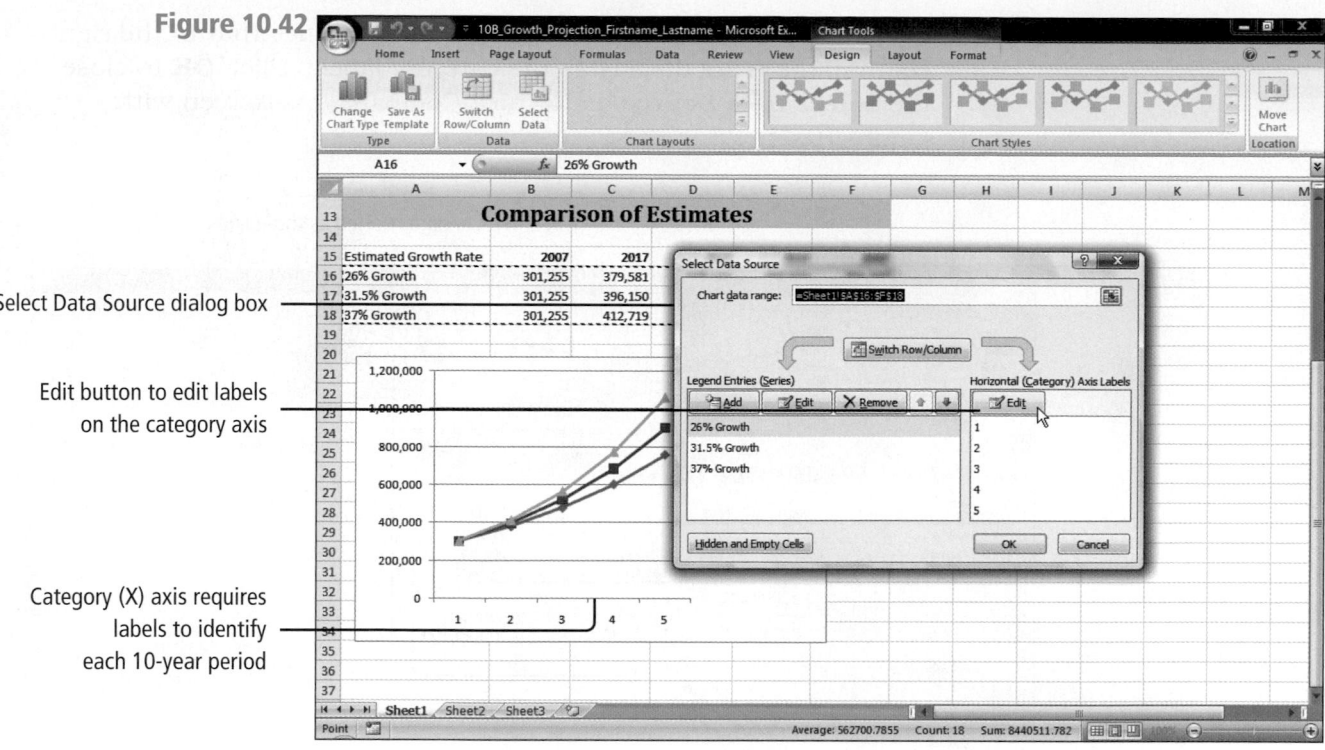

Select Data Source dialog box

Edit button to edit labels on the category axis

Category (X) axis requires labels to identify each 10-year period

6 In the right column, click the **Edit** button. Drag the title bar of the **Axis Labels** dialog box to the right of the chart as necessary so that it is not blocking your view of the data, and then select the range **B15:F15**. Compare your screen with Figure 10.43.

Figure 10.43

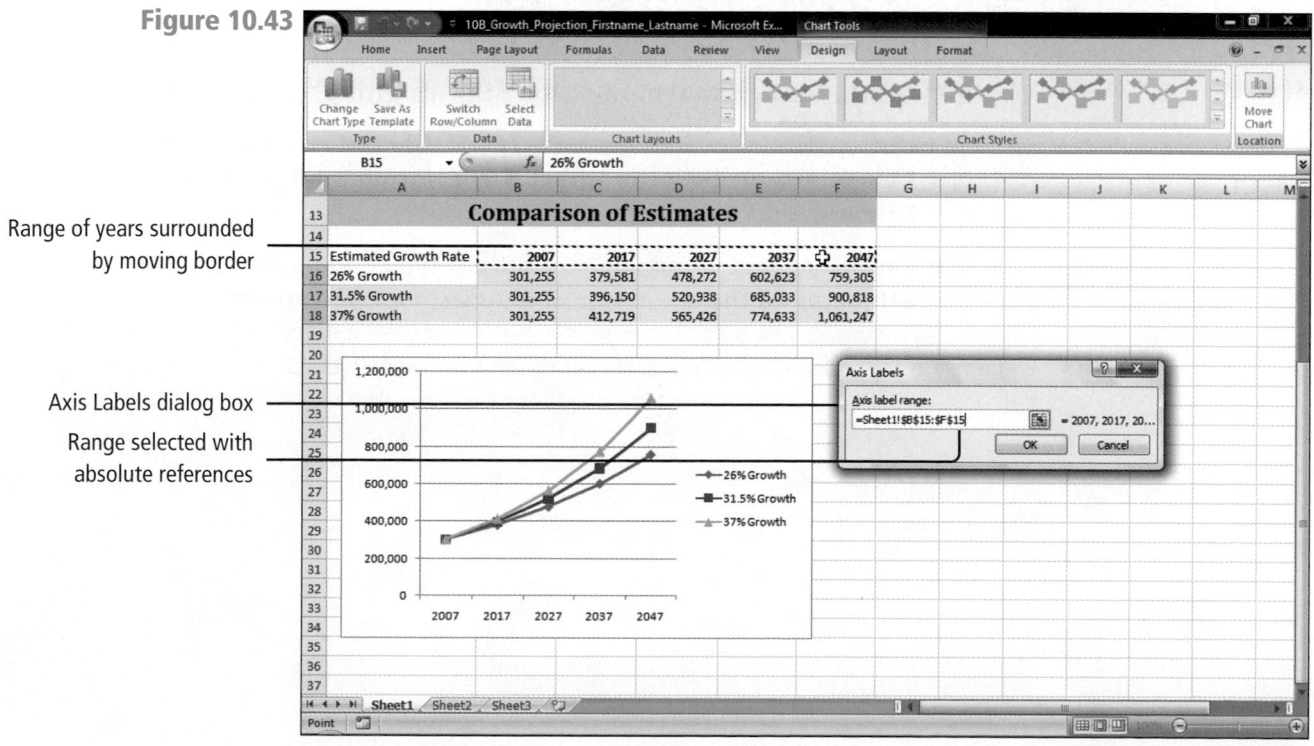

Range of years surrounded by moving border

Axis Labels dialog box

Range selected with absolute references

7 In the **Axis Labels** dialog box, click **OK**, and notice that in the right column, the years display as the category labels. Click **OK** to close the **Select Data Source** dialog box. Compare your screen with Figure 10.44.

Three rows of data charted as three lines

Figure 10.44

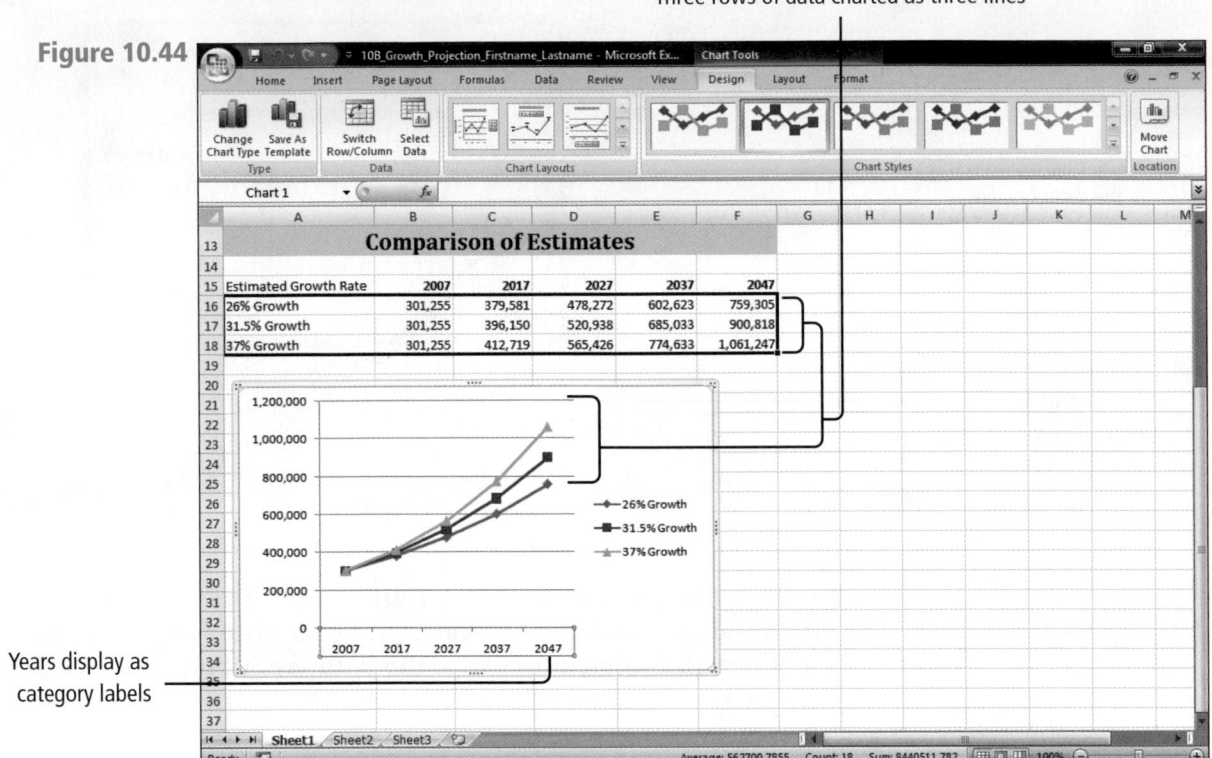

Years display as category labels

8 On the **Design tab**, in the **Chart Styles group**, click the **More** button ⯆, and then click **Style 10**. Click the **Layout tab**. In the **Labels group**, click the **Chart Title** button, and then click **Above Chart**.

9 Delete the text *Chart Title*, and then type **Population Growth Estimates** as the chart title. Compare your screen with Figure 10.45.

Based on the chart, city planners can see that the population will probably double between now and 2037 and could more than triple between now and 2047.

Figure 10.45

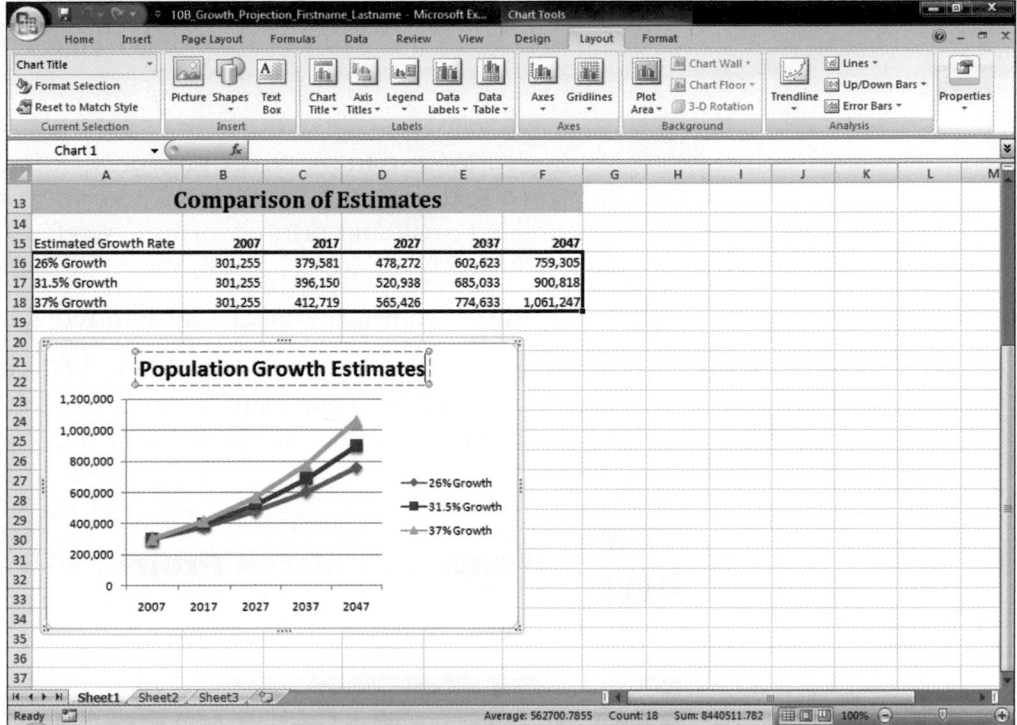

10 Click any cell to deselect the chart. Click the **Insert tab**, and then in the **Text group**, click **Header & Footer** to switch to **Page Layout View** and open the **Header area**. In the **Navigation group**, click the **Go to Footer** button, click just above the word *Footer*, and then in the **Header & Footer Elements group**, click the **File Name** button. Click in a cell just above the footer to exit the **Footer area** and view your file name.

11 Scroll up and to the left as necessary to view your chart. Click the chart to select it, and notice that the chart is not centered under the data in the cells. Position the pointer over the **right resize handle** to display the ↔ pointer, and then drag to the right so that the right border of the chart is just inside the right border of **column F**. Release the mouse button to resize the chart.

12 Click any cell to deselect the chart. Click the **Page Layout tab**. In the **Page Setup group**, click the **Margins** button, and then at the bottom of the **Margins gallery**, click **Custom Margins**. In the displayed **Page Setup** dialog box, under **Center on page**, select the **Horizontally** check box. Click **OK** to close the dialog box, and then **Save** 🖫 the changes to your workbook.

13 On the status bar, click the **Normal** button 🁢 to return to Normal view, and then press Ctrl + Home to move to the top of your worksheet. At the lower edge of the window, click to select the **Sheet2 tab**, hold down Ctrl, and then click the **Sheet3 tab** to select the two unused sheets. Right-click over the selected sheet tabs, and then on the displayed shortcut menu, click **Delete**.

14 **Save** the changes you have made to your workbook. Check your *Chapter Assignment Sheet* or *Course Syllabus* or consult your instructor to determine if you are to submit your assignments on paper or electronically. To submit electronically, follow the instructions provided by your instructor.

15 Press [Ctrl] + [F2] to display the **Print Preview** to check the placement of your worksheet. In the **Print group**, click the **Print** button. In the displayed **Print** dialog box, click **OK** to print your worksheet. If you are directed to submit printed formulas, refer to Activity 5.17 to do so.

16 If you printed your formulas, be sure to redisplay the worksheet by pressing [Ctrl] + [`]. From the **Office** menu 🏢 , click **Close**. If the dialog box displays asking if you want to save changes, click **No** so that you do *not* save the changes you made for printing formulas. **Exit** Excel.

End **You have completed Project 10B** ————————————

There's More You Can Do!

Close Excel and any other open windows. Display the Start menu, click Computer, and then navigate to the student files that accompany this textbook. In the folder **02_theres_more_you_can_do**, locate and open the folder for this chapter. Open and print the instructions for this project, which are provided to you in Adobe PDF format.

Try IT! 1—Change the Office Theme in an Excel Workbook

In this Try It! exercise, you will change an Office theme in an Excel workbook.

Content-Based Assessments

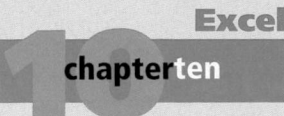

Summary

In this chapter, you created and saved a workbook from an existing workbook, renamed worksheets, and color-coded worksheet tabs. You examined and practiced the various ways that Excel formats numbers in a worksheet. You moved, copied, and pasted cell contents using the Office Clipboard. Workbooks frequently contain multiple worksheets, and when they do, a Summary sheet is often included to summarize the data on the individual worksheets. You practiced grouping worksheets to enter and format data simultaneously on multiple worksheets, and then created a summary worksheet to summarize the data.

What-if analysis is used to determine what would happen to one value if another value changes. In this chapter, you used a what-if analysis process to project future trends, and then created a line chart to visually represent those trends.

Key Terms

The ⏺ symbol represents Key Terms found on the Student CD in the 02_theres_more_you_can_do folder for this chapter.

Content-Based Assessments

Excel
chapterten   **Matching**

Match each term in the second column with its correct definition in the first column. Write the letter of the term on the blank line to the left of the correct definition.

_____ **1.** To move within a document or workbook.

_____ **2.** The labels along the lower border of the worksheet window that identify each worksheet.

_____ **3.** The action of placing cell contents that have been copied or moved to the Office Clipboard to another location.

_____ **4.** A temporary storage area maintained by your Windows operating system.

_____ **5.** A method of moving or copying the content of selected cells in which you point to the selection and then drag it to a new location.

_____ **6.** The target destination for data that has been cut or copied using the Office Clipboard.

_____ **7.** A button that displays in the lower right corner of a pasted selection and that displays a list of options that lets you determine how the information is pasted into your worksheet.

_____ **8.** Within a workbook of multiple worksheets, a worksheet that contains the details of information summarized on a summary worksheet.

_____ **9.** The process of changing the values in cells to see how those changes affect the outcome of formulas in your worksheet.

_____ **10.** The percent by which one number increases over another.

_____ **11.** The mathematical formula to calculate a rate of increase.

_____ **12.** The starting point when you divide the amount of increase by it to calculate the rate of increase.

_____ **13.** The mathematical rules for performing multiple calculations within a formula.

_____ **14.** The Excel feature by which a cell takes on the formatting of the number typed into the cell.

_____ **15.** The formula for calculating the value after an increase by multiplying the original value—the base—by the percent for new value.

A Base

B Detail worksheet

C Drag and drop

D Format as you type

E Navigate

F Office Clipboard

G Order of operations

H Paste

I Paste area

J Paste Options

K Percent rate of increase

L Rate = amount of increase/base

M Sheet tabs

N Value after increase = base X percent for new value

O What-if analysis

Content-Based Assessments

Fill in the Blank

Write the correct answers in the space provided.

1. When a worksheet is active, its tab color displays as an _____.

2. When you enter a date, Excel assigns a _____ value to the date, which makes it possible to treat dates like other numbers for the purpose of calculating the number of days between two dates.

3. A two-digit year value of 30 through 99 is interpreted by the Windows operating system as the four-digit years 1930 through _____.

4. The keyboard shortcut Ctrl + ; enters the _____ _____, which is obtained from your computer's internal calendar.

5. Clearing the contents of a cell does not clear the _____ of a cell—for example fill color applied to the cell.

6. You can view selections stored on the Office Clipboard by displaying its _____ _____ from the Dialog Box Launcher in the Clipboard group.

7. According to the order of operations for formulas, the first expressions calculated are those within _____.

8. According to the order of operations, _____ and division are performed before addition and subtraction.

9. According to the order of operations, consecutive operators with the same level of _____ are calculated from left to right.

10. The symbol used to indicate the multiplication operation is the _____ symbol.

11. In the formula *percent for new value = base percent + percent of increase*, the base percent is usually _____ %.

12. When pasting a group of copied cells to a target range, you need only select the _____ cell of the target range.

13. The chart type that displays trends over time and that connects data point values with a line is called a _____ chart.

14. In the formula *=(B3-C4)*D3* the mathematical operation that is performed first is _____.

15. When copying the formula *=(B3-B4)*$A$2* to the right, the formula in column C would be _____.

Skills Review

Project 10C — Permit Sales

In this project, you will apply the skills you practiced from the Objectives in Project 10A.

Objectives: 1. *Create and Save a Workbook from an Existing Workbook;* **2.** *Navigate a Workbook and Rename Worksheets;* **3.** *Enter Dates, Clear Contents, and Clear Formats;* **4.** *Move, Copy, and Paste Cell Contents;* **5.** *Edit and Format Multiple Worksheets at the Same Time;* **6.** *Create a Summary Sheet;* **7.** *Format and Print Multiple Worksheets in a Workbook.*

In the following Skills Review, you will edit a workbook for the Golden Grove Parks and Recreation Director to summarize the sales of weekly and daily campground permits for the three city campgrounds in the month of June. The four worksheets of your completed workbook will look similar to those shown in Figure 10.46.

For Project 10C, you will need the following file:

e10C_Permit_Sales

You will save your workbook as
10C_Permit_Sales_Firstname_Lastname

Figure 10.46

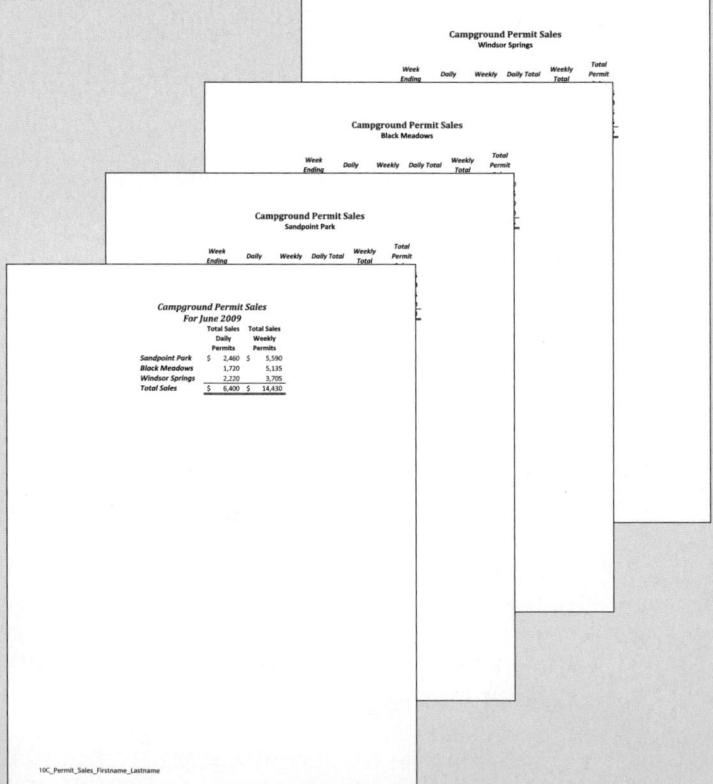

(Project 10C–Permit Sales continues on the next page)

Content-Based Assessments

(Project 10C–Permit Sales continued)

1. **Start** Excel. From the **Office** menu, click **Open**, and then navigate to the student files that accompany this textbook. Locate, select, and then open the file **e10C_Permit_Sales**. **Save** the file in your Excel Chapter 10 folder as **10C_Permit_Sales_Firstname_Lastname** Take a moment to examine the data in each of the three worksheets.

2. Point to the **Sheet1 tab**, and then double-click to select its name. Type **Sandpoint Park** and then press Enter to rename the sheet. Right-click the **Sandpoint Park sheet tab**, and then from the displayed shortcut menu, point to **Tab Color** to display the colors associated with the workbook's theme. Under **Theme Colors**, click **Purple, Accent 4, Lighter 40%**.

3. Point to the **Sheet2 tab**, right-click to display the shortcut menu, and then click **Rename**. Type **Black Meadows** and then press Enter to rename the sheet. On the **Home tab**, in the **Cells group**, click the **Format** button, and then from the displayed list, point to **Tab Color**. Under **Theme Colors**, click **Aqua, Accent 5, Lighter 40%**.

4. Using either of the two techniques you just practiced, change the name of the **Sheet3 tab** to **Windsor Springs** and then change the **Tab Color** to **Orange, Accent 6, Lighter 40%**.

5. Display the **Sandpoint Park** worksheet, and then select the range **A13:D14**. On the **Home tab**, in the **Clipboard group**, click the **Copy** button to place a copy of the selected cells on the Office Clipboard.

6. Click the **Black Meadows sheet tab** to make it the active worksheet. Click cell **A13**, and then on the **Home tab**, in the **Clipboard group**, click the **Paste** button. Click the **Windsor Springs sheet tab** to make it the active worksheet, and then click cell **A13**. In the **Clipboard group**, click the **Paste** button. Click the **Sandpoint Park sheet tab** to make it the active worksheet, and then press Esc to cancel the moving border.

7. Right-click the **Sandpoint Park sheet tab**, and then from the displayed shortcut menu, click **Select All Sheets** to group the sheets—[Group] displays in the title bar. Select the range **A5:A8**. On the **Home tab**, in the **Number group**, click the **Number Format arrow**, at the bottom click **More Number Formats**, under **Category**, click **Date**, and then under **Type**, click **3/14** and click **OK**. The date format for the selected range of cells is changed for all three worksheets.

8. With the worksheets still grouped, click cell **D4**, type **Daily Total** and then press Tab. In cell **E4**, type **Weekly Total** and then press Tab. In cell **F4**, type **Total Permit Sales** and then press Enter. Select the range **A4:F4**, right-click over the selection, and then from the displayed shortcut menu, click **Format Cells**. Click the **Font tab**, and then under **Font style**, click **Bold Italic**. Click the **Alignment tab**. Under **Text alignment**, click the **Horizontal arrow**, and then from the displayed list, click **Center**. Click the **Vertical arrow**, and then from the displayed list, click **Center**. Under **Text control**, select the **Wrap text** check box. Click **OK**.

9. With the worksheets still grouped, select the range **A1:F1**, and then in the **Alignment group**, click the **Merge and Center** button. Change the **Font** to **Cambria**, the **Font Size** to **14**, and then apply **Bold**. Select the range **A2:F2**, right-click over the selection, and then on the Mini toolbar, click the **Merge and Center** button, change the **Font Size** to **12**, and then apply **Bold**.

(Project 10C–Permit Sales continues on the next page)

(Project 10C–Permit Sales continued)

10. With the worksheets still grouped, click cell **D5** and construct a formula to calculate the total sales of *Daily* permits for the week ending June 6 as follows: type = to begin a formula, click cell **B5**, type * click cell **D13**, and then press F4 to make the reference to cell **D13** absolute. On the **Formula Bar**, click the **Enter** button. Your result is *340*. Use the fill handle to copy the formula down for the remaining dates.

11. In cell **E5**, construct a similar formula to multiply the number of *Weekly* permits sold during the week of June 6 in cell **C5** times the *Weekly Permit Price* in cell **D14**. Make the reference to cell **D14** absolute so that each week's sales are multiplied by the *Weekly Permit Price* in cell **D14**. Your result is *585*. Copy the formula down for the remaining dates.

12. Click cell **A9**, and then apply **Align Text Right** and **Bold**. Select the range **B5:E9**, and then in the **Editing group**, click the **Sum** button to sum each column.

13. With the worksheets still grouped, select the range **D5:F9**, and then in the **Editing group**, click the **Sum** button to sum the rows for *Total Permit Sales* for each week.

14. With the worksheets still grouped, select the nonadjacent ranges **B5:C9** and **D6:F8**, and then apply the **Comma Style** with **zero decimal places**. Select the nonadjacent ranges **D5:F5** and **D9:F9**, and then apply **Accounting Number Format** with **zero decimal places**. Select the range **B9:F9**, in the **Font group**, click the **Borders button arrow**, and then click **Top and Double Bottom Border**. Select **columns B:F**, and then set the width to **70 pixels**.

15. Click the **Black Meadows sheet tab**, and then verify that the formulas and format-

ting that you applied in Steps 7–14 were applied to the worksheet—recall that selecting an individual worksheet ungroups the sheets. Click the **Windsor Springs sheet tab,** and then verify that the formulas and formatting that you applied in Steps 7–14 were applied.

16. **Save** your workbook. To the right of the **Windsor Springs** worksheet tab, click the **Insert Worksheet** button. Rename the new worksheet **Summary** and then change the **Tab Color** to **Olive Green, Accent 3, Lighter 40%**. In cell **A4** type **Sandpoint Park** In cell **A5** type **Black Meadows** In cell **A6** type **Windsor Springs** In cell **A7** type **Total Sales** Select the range **A4:A7**, change the **Font Size** to **12**, and then apply **Bold** and **Italic**. **AutoFit column A**.

17. In cell **B3**, type **Total Sales Daily Permits** and then in cell **C3**, type **Total Sales Weekly Permits** Select the two cells, and then in the **Alignment group**, click the **Wrap Text** button and the **Center** button. In the **Font group**, click **Bold**.

18. Click cell **B4**. Type = and then click the **Sandpoint Park sheet tab**. On the **Sandpoint Park** worksheet, click cell **D9**, and then press Enter to create a formula that references the *Daily Total Sales* for *Sandpoint Park*.

19. Click cell **C4**. Type = and then click the **Sandpoint Park sheet tab**. Click cell **E9** and then press Enter to create a formula that references the *Weekly Total Sales* for *Sandpoint Park*. Then, use the same technique to copy the totals for *Daily* and *Weekly* permit sales for the **Black Meadows worksheet** and the **Windsor Springs worksheet**.

20. In cell **A1**, type **Campground Permit Sales** and then **Merge and Center** the text over

(Project 10C–Permit Sales continues on the next page)

(Project 10C–Permit Sales continued)

the range **A1:C1**. Change the **Font** to **Cambria**, the **Font Size** to **14**, and apply **Bold** and **Italic**. In cell **A2**, type **For June 2009** and then use the **Format Painter** to apply the format from cell **A1**.

21. Select the range **B4:C7**, click the **Sum** button to total the two columns. Format the range **B5:C6** with **Comma Style** and **zero decimal places**. Format the nonadjacent ranges **B4:C4** and **B7:C7** with the **Accounting Number Format** and **zero decimal places**. Apply a **Top and Double Bottom** border to the range **B7:C7**.

22. Point to the **Summary sheet tab**, hold down the left mouse button to display a small black caret symbol, and then drag to the left until the caret is positioned to the left of the **Sandpoint Park sheet tab**; release the left mouse button to make the Summary sheet the first sheet in the workbook.

23. Be sure the **Summary** worksheet is the active sheet. Then point to its sheet tab, right-click, and click **Select All Sheets** to display *[Group]* in the title bar. Click the **Insert tab**, and then in the **Text group**, click the **Header & Footer** button. In the **Navigation group**, click the **Go to Footer** button, click in the **left section** above the word *Footer*, and then in the **Header & Footer Elements group**, click the **File Name** button.

24. Click in a cell above the footer to deselect the **Footer area** and view your file name. Click the **Page Layout tab**. In the **Page Setup group**, click the **Margins** button, and then at the bottom of the **Margins**

gallery, click **Custom Margins**. In the displayed **Page Setup** dialog box, under **Center on page**, select the **Horizontally** check box. Click **OK**, and then on the status bar, click the **Normal** button. Press Ctrl + Home to move to the top of the worksheet. Verify that *[Group]* still displays in the title bar.

25. **Save** your workbook. Check your *Chapter Assignment Sheet* or *Course Syllabus*, or consult your instructor, to determine if you are to submit your assignments on paper or electronically. To submit electronically, follow the instructions provided by your instructor.

26. From the **Office** menu, point to the **Print arrow**, and then from the displayed menu, click **Print Preview**. At the top of the screen, click the **Next Page** button as necessary to view and check each page of your workbook.

27. Click the **Print** button. Under **Print range**, verify that the **All** option button is selected. Under **Print what**, click **Active sheet(s)** (assuming your worksheets are still grouped) and then under **Copies**, verify that the **Number of copies** is **1**. Click **OK** to print your workbook. Determine if you are to print formulas for any or all of the worksheets in this workbook. To print formulas, refer to Activity 5.17 in Project 5A.

28. If you printed your formulas, be sure to redisplay the worksheet by pressing Ctrl + `. From the **Office** menu, click **Close**. If you are prompted to save changes, click **No**. **Exit** Excel.

End **You have completed Project 10C**

Content-Based Assessments

Excel

chapter**ten**

Skills Review

Project 10D — Property Tax

In this project, you will apply the skills you practiced from the Objectives in Project 10B.

Objectives: 8. *Design a Worksheet for What-If Analysis;* **9.** *Perform What-If Analysis;* **10.** *Compare Data with a Line Chart.*

In the following Skills Review, you will create a worksheet for the Controller of Golden Grove to forecast property tax revenue for the next 10 years. Your completed worksheet will look similar to the one shown in Figure 10.47.

For Project 10D, you will need the following file:

New blank Excel workbook

You will save your workbook as
10D_Property_Tax_Firstname_Lastname

Figure 10.47

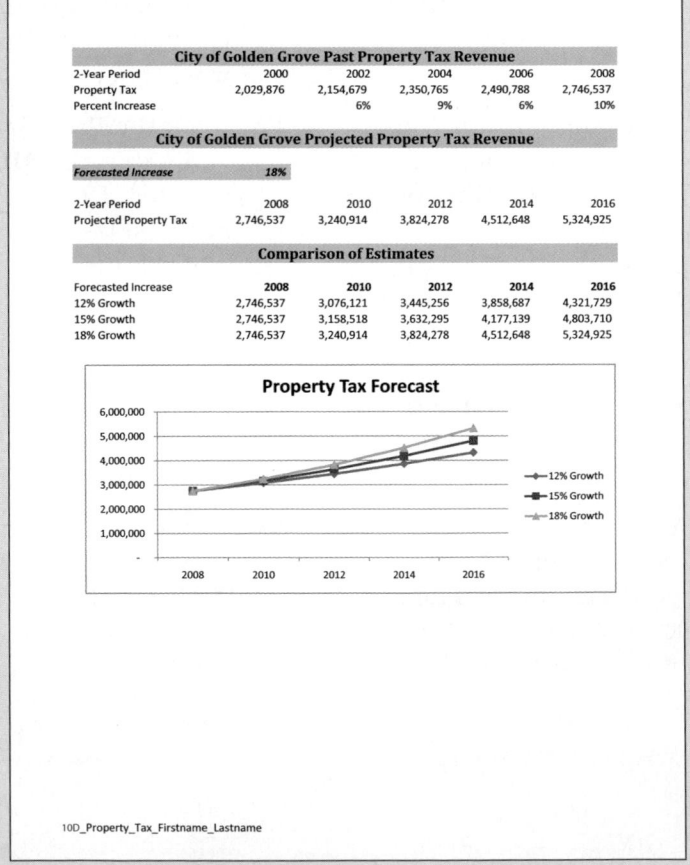

(Project 10D–Property Tax continues on the next page)

Content-Based Assessments

(Project 10D–Property Tax continued)

1. **Start** Excel and display a new workbook. In cell **A1**, type **City of Golden Grove Past Property Tax Revenue** and then press Enter. Adjust the width of **column A** to **155 pixels**. Select the range **A1:F1**, right-click over the selection, and then on the Mini toolbar, apply **Bold**, change the **Font** to **Cambria**, change the **Font Size** to **14**, and then click the **Merge and Center** button. From the **Office** menu, click **Save As**, navigate to your Excel Chapter 10 folder, in the **File name** box, name the file **10D_Property_Tax_Firstname_Lastname** and then click **Save**.

2. In cell **A2**, type **2-Year Period** In cell **B2**, type **2000** and then press Tab. In cell **C2**, type **2002** and then press Tab. Select the range **B2:C2**, and then drag the fill handle to the right through cell **F2** to enter years through *2008*.

3. In cell **A3**, type **Property Tax** and then press Enter. In cell **A4**, type **Percent Increase** and then press Enter. Beginning in cell **B3** and pressing Tab to move across the row, enter the following values for property tax revenue in the years listed:

2000	2002	2004	2006	2008
2029876	2154679	2350765	2490788	2746537

4. Select the range **B3:F3**, and then right-click over the selection. On the Mini toolbar, apply the **Comma Style**, and then click **Decrease Decimal** two times to apply **zero decimal places**.

5. Click cell **C4**. Type **=(c3-b3)/b3** and then press Enter to calculate the *Percent Increase* from the year 2000 to the year 2002. Point to cell **C4** and right-click, and then on the Mini toolbar, click the **Percent Style** button. Your result is *6%*.

6. Click cell **D4**, type **=** and then by either typing, or using a combination of typing and clicking cells to reference them, construct a formula similar to the one in cell **C4** to calculate the rate of increase in property tax from 2002 to 2004. Press Enter, and then format cell **D4** with the **Percent Style**. With cell **D4** selected, drag the fill handle to the right through cell **F4** to calculate the property tax *Percent Increase* for each 2-year period.

7. In cell **A6**, type **City of Golden Grove Projected Property Tax Revenue** and then press Enter. Click cell **A1**. On the **Home tab**, in the **Clipboard group**, click the **Format Painter** button, and then click cell **A6**.

8. In cell **A8**, type **Forecasted Increase** and then press Enter. In cell **A10**, type **2-Year Period** and then in cell **A11**, type **Projected Property Tax** In cell **B10**, type **2008** and then press Tab. In cell **C10**, type **2010** and then press Enter. Select the range **B10:C10**, and then drag the fill handle through cell **F10** to extend the pattern of years to **2016**.

9. **Save** the changes you have made to your workbook thus far. In cell **B8**, type **12%** and then press Enter. Select the range **A8:B8**, right-click, and then on the Mini toolbar, click **Bold** and **Italic**.

10. In cell **B11**, type **=** click cell **F3**, and then press Enter to create a formula that references the 2008 Property Tax collected by the city.

11. Click cell **C11**. Type **=b11*(100%+b8)** and then on the **Formula Bar**, click the **Enter** button to create a formula that calculates the city's projected property tax revenue based on a forecasted increase of 12%. With cell **C11** as the active cell, drag the fill handle to copy the formula to **D11:F11**. Click cell **B11**, click the **Format Painter** button, and then select the range **C11:F11** to copy the formatting.

(Project 10D–Property Tax continues on the next page)

Content-Based Assessments

(Project 10D–Property Tax continued)

12. In cell **A13**, type **Comparison of Estimates** and then press Enter. Click **A6**, click the **Format Painter** button, and then click cell **A13**. Select the range **A8:B8**, right-click to display the Mini toolbar, click the **Fill Color button arrow**, and then under **Theme Colors**, click **Aqua, Accent 5, Lighter 40%**. Click cell **A1**, and then hold down Ctrl and click **A6** and **A13**. In the **Font group**, click the **Fill Color** button to apply the same fill color to these titles.

13. In cells **A15:A18**, type the following row titles:

    Forecasted Increase

    12% Growth

    15% Growth

    18% Growth

14. Select the range **B10:F10**. On the **Home tab**, in the **Clipboard group**, click the **Copy** button, click cell **B15**, and then in the **Clipboard group**, click the **Paste** button.

15. Select the range **B11:F11**, and then click **Copy**. Click cell **B16**, and then in the **Clipboard group**, click the **Paste button arrow**. From the displayed menu, click **Paste Special**. In the displayed **Paste Special** dialog box, under **Paste**, click the **Values and number formats** option button. Click **OK** to paste the values in the cells rather than the formulas.

16. Press Esc to cancel the moving border. Click cell **B8**. Type **15** and then press Enter to recalculate the values in cells **C11:F11** for a 15% increase.

17. Select the range **B11:F11**, and then press Ctrl + C to copy the selection. Click cell **B17**. In the **Clipboard group**, click the **Paste button arrow**, and then click **Paste**

Special. In the **Paste Special** dialog box, click the **Values and number formats** option button, and then click **OK**.

18. In cell **B8**, change the **Forecasted Increase** to **18** and press Enter. Using the skills you just practiced, copy the values and number formats in the range **B11:F11** to the range **B18:F18**. Press Esc to cancel the moving border.

19. **Save** your changes thus far. Select the range **B15:F15** and apply **Bold**.

20. Select the range **A16:F18**. On the **Insert tab**, in the **Charts group**, click the **Line** button. Click the **Line with Markers** chart type to create the chart as an embedded chart in the worksheet. Drag to position the upper left corner of the chart slightly inside the upper left corner of cell **A20**.

21. Along the lower portion of the chart, point to any of the category axis numbers such as *1* or *2* to display the ScreenTip *Horizontal (Category) Axis* displays. Then, right-click, and from the displayed short-cut menu, click **Select Data**. On the right side of the displayed **Select Data Source** dialog box, under **Horizontal (Category) Axis Labels**, click the **Edit** button. Drag the title bar of the **Axis Labels** dialog box to the right of the chart as necessary so that it is not blocking your view of the data, and then select the range **B15:F15**. Click **OK** two times so that the years display on the horizontal axis.

22. On the **Design tab**, in the **Chart Styles group**, click the **More** button, and then click **Style 2**. Click the **Layout tab**. In the **Labels group**, click the **Chart Title** button, and then click **Above Chart**. Delete the text *Chart Title*, and then type **Property Tax Forecast**

(Project 10D–Property Tax continues on the next page)

Content-Based Assessments

(Project 10D–Property Tax continued)

23. Click any cell to deselect the chart. Click the **Insert tab**, and then in the **Text group**, click **Header & Footer**. In the **Navigation group**, click the **Go to Footer** button, click just above the word *Footer*, and then in the **Header & Footer Elements group**, click the **File Name** button. Click in a cell just above the footer to exit the **Footer area** and view your file name.

24. Scroll up to view your chart, click an edge of the chart to select it, position the pointer over the right resize handle to display the  pointer, and then drag to the right so that the right border of the chart is just inside the right border of **column F**.

25. Click any cell to deselect the chart. Click the **Page Layout tab**. In the **Page Setup group**, click the **Margins** button, and then at the bottom of the **Margins gallery**, click **Custom Margins**. In the displayed **Page Setup** dialog box, under **Center on page**, select the **Horizontally** check box. Click **OK** to close the dialog box.

26. On the status bar, click the **Normal** button to return to Normal view, and then press Ctrl + Home to move to the top of your worksheet. At the lower edge of the window,

click to select the **Sheet2 tab**, hold down Ctrl, and then click the **Sheet3 tab** to select the two unused sheets. Right-click, and then click **Delete** to delete the unused sheets.

27. **Save** the changes you have made to your workbook. Check your *Chapter Assignment Sheet* or *Course Syllabus* or consult your instructor to determine if you are to submit your assignments on paper or electronically. To submit electronically, follow the instructions provided by your instructor.

28. From the **Office** menu, point to the **Print button arrow**, and then click **Print Preview** to check the placement of your worksheet. In the **Print group**, click the **Print** button. In the displayed **Print** dialog box, click **OK** to print your worksheet. If you are directed to submit printed formulas, refer to Activity 5.17 to do so.

29. If you printed your formulas, be sure to redisplay the worksheet by pressing Ctrl + `. From the **Office** menu, click **Close**. If the dialog box displays asking if you want to save changes, click **No** so that you do *not* save the changes you made for printing formulas. **Exit** Excel.

End **You have completed Project 10D**

Content-Based Assessments

Mastering Excel

Project 10E — Summer Camp

In this project, you will apply the skills you practiced from the Objectives in Project 10A.

Objectives: 1. *Create and Save a Workbook from an Existing Workbook;* **2.** *Navigate a Workbook and Rename Worksheets;* **3.** *Enter Dates, Clear Contents, and Clear Formats;* **4.** *Move, Copy, and Paste Cell Contents;* **5.** *Edit and Format Multiple Worksheets at the Same Time;* **6.** *Create a Summary Sheet;* **7.** *Format and Print Multiple Worksheets in a Workbook.*

The city of Golden Grove offers summer camp for children at three different parks. Children are enrolled on a daily or a weekly basis. In the following Mastering Excel assessment, you will edit a workbook that summarizes the enrollments and fees at the three summer camp locations. Your completed worksheets will look similar to Figure 10.48.

For Project 10E, you will need the following file:

e10E_Summer_Camp

**You will save your workbook as
10E_Summer_Camp_Firstname_Lastname**

Figure 10.48

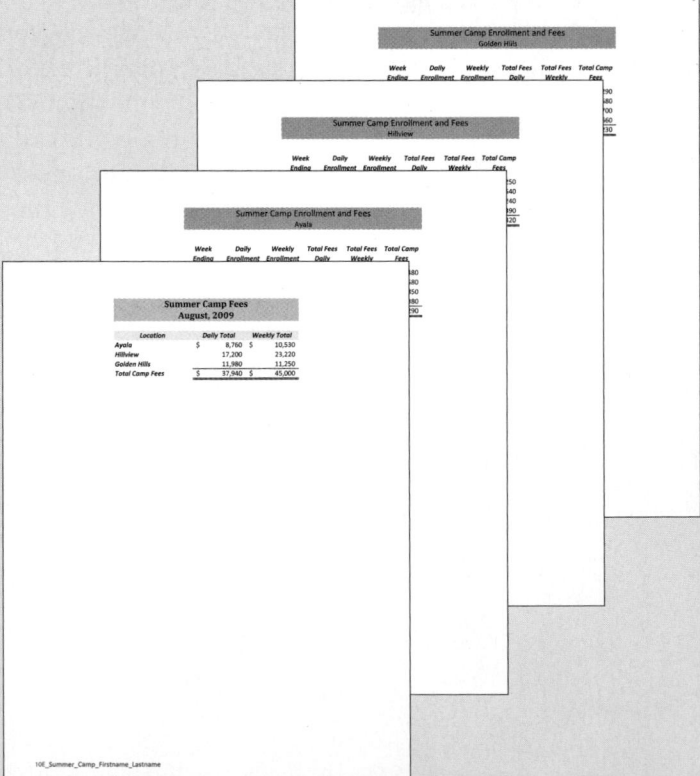

(Project 10E–Summer Camp continues on the next page)

Content-Based Assessments

(Project 10E–Summer Camp continued)

1. **Start** Excel and from your student files, open **e10E_Summer_Camp**. **Save** the workbook in your Excel Chapter 10 folder as **10E_Summer_Camp_Firstname_Lastname** Take a moment to examine the data in the three worksheets.

2. Rename the **Sheet1 tab** as **Ayala** and then change its **Tab Color** to **Blue, Accent 1, Lighter 40%**. Rename **Sheet2** as **Hillview** and then change its **Tab Color** to **Red, Accent 2, Lighter 40%**. Rename **Sheet3** as **Golden Hills** and then change its **Tab Color** to **Olive Green, Accent 3, Lighter 40%**.

3. Right-click the **Ayala sheet tab**, and then click **Select All Sheets** so that the three sheets are grouped. In cell **D4**, type **Total Fees Daily** in cell **E4**, type **Total Fees Weekly** and in cell **F4**, type **Total Camp Fees** Select the range **A4:F4**, and then apply the following formats: **Wrap Text**, **Center**, **Middle Align**, **Bold**, and **Italic**. Widen columns **A:F** to **75 pixels**.

4. With the worksheets still grouped, select the dates in the range **A5:A8**, display the **Format Cells** dialog box, and then on the **Number tab**, apply the third **Date** format—**3/14**. Right-click a sheet tab and click **Ungroup Sheets**. In the **Ayala sheet**, select, and then **Copy** the range **A12:D13**. Paste the selected range in the same location in both the **Hillview sheet** and the **Golden Hills sheet**. Make the **Ayala** sheet active, and then press [Esc] to cancel the moving border.

5. Right-click the **Ayala sheet tab**, and then click **Select All Sheets** to group the three sheets. In cell **D5**, construct a formula to multiply the *Daily Enrollment* for the week ending *8/7* in cell **B5** times the *Daily Summer Camp Fee* in cell **D12**. Be sure to

make the reference to cell **D12** absolute. Copy the formula down for the remaining weeks. In cell **E5**, construct a similar formula to multiply the *Weekly Enrollment* during the week of *8/7* in cell **C5** times the *Weekly Summer Camp Fee* in cell **D13**. Make the reference to cell **D13** absolute. **Copy** the formula down for the remaining dates.

6. With the worksheets still grouped, **Sum** the columns. Then, in each row, **Sum** the Daily and Weekly fees. Apply appropriate financial formatting to the range **D5:F9**, applying **Comma Style** first, using **zero decimal places**, and then applying a **Top and Double Bottom Border** to all appropriate cells. With the worksheets still grouped, **Merge and Center** the titles in **row 1** and **row 2** across columns **A:F**. To the two worksheet titles, apply a **Fill Color** using **Purple, Accent 4, Lighter 40%**.

7. **Save** the changes you have made to your workbook thus far. **Ungroup** the worksheets, and then view the **Hillview** and **Golden Hills** worksheets to verify that the formulas and formatting that you applied in the previous steps were applied to both worksheets. Insert a new worksheet, name the worksheet **Summary** and then change its **Tab Color** to **Orange, Accent 6, Lighter 40%**. In cell **A4**, type **Location** In cell **A5**, type **Ayala** In cell **A6**, type **Hillview** In cell **A7**, type **Golden Hills** In cell **A8**, type **Total Camp Fees** Select the range **A5:A8**, and then apply **Bold** and **Italic**. Adjust the width of **column A** to **150 pixels**.

8. In cell **B4**, type **Daily Total** and then in cell **C4**, type **Weekly Total** Adjust the width of **columns B:C** to **100 pixels**. Select the range **A4:C4**, and then apply **Center**, **Bold**, **Italic**, and a **Fill Color** of **Orange**,

(Project 10E–Summer Camp continues on the next page)

Content-Based Assessments

Mastering Excel

(Project 10E–Summer Camp continued)

Accent 6, Lighter 80%. Beginning in cell **B5** and using the techniques you have practiced to create a summary sheet, create a formula to reference the *Total Fees Daily* in **row 9** from the **Ayala** worksheet. In cell **C5**, create a similar formula to reference the *Total Fees Weekly* in **row 9** of the **Ayala** worksheet. In the range **B6:C7**, create similar formulas to reference the appropriate cells in the **Hillview** and **Golden Hills** worksheets.

9. Calculate the *Total Camp Fees* for both *Daily* and *Weekly* enrollments, and then apply appropriate financial formatting to the numbers and the totals; first apply **Comma Style** and decrease to **zero decimal places**. In cell **A1**, type **Summer Camp Fees** and then **Merge and Center** the text over the range **A1:C1**. Change the **Font** to **Cambria**, the **Font Size** to **14**, and then apply **Bold**. In cell **A2**, type **August, 2009** and then use **Format Painter** to copy the format from cell **A1** to cell **A2**. Select both cells, and then apply a **Fill Color** of **Orange, Accent 6, Lighter 40%**.

10. Move the **Summary sheet** so that it is the first worksheet in the workbook. Group the worksheets again, insert a footer on the left side with the **File Name**, and then center the worksheets **Horizontally**. Return to **Normal** view and display the top of the worksheet.

11. **Save** your workbook, and then view the worksheets in **Print Preview**. Check your *Chapter Assignment Sheet* or *Course Syllabus*, or consult your instructor, to determine if you are to submit your assignments on paper or electronically. To submit electronically, follow the instructions provided by your instructor.

12. **Print** the entire workbook, either by grouping the sheets or by clicking **Entire workbook** in the **Print** dialog box. Determine if you are to print formulas for any or all of the worksheets in this workbook. To print formulas, refer to Activity 5.17 in Project 5A.

13. If you printed your formulas, be sure to redisplay the worksheet by pressing Ctrl + `. From the **Office** menu, click **Close**. If you are prompted to save changes, click **No**. **Exit** Excel.

 End You have completed Project 10E

Excel

chapterten

Mastering Excel

Project 10F — Gardens

In this project, you will apply the skills you practiced from the Objectives in Project 10B.

Objectives: 8. *Design a Worksheet for What-If Analysis;* **9.** *Perform What-If Analysis;* **10.** *Compare Data with a Line Chart.*

The city of Golden Grove is home to the Golden Botanical Gardens—a tourist attraction that draws visitors from around the world. The Board of Directors for the Gardens is considering an expansion plan for this popular attraction and wants to examine past attendance data and an estimate of future attendance. In the following Mastering Excel Assessment, you will create a worksheet with a line chart that projects future attendance based on varying estimates. Your completed worksheet will look similar to Figure 10.49.

For Project 10F, you will need the following file:

New blank Excel workbook

You will save your workbook as 10F_Gardens_Firstname_Lastname

Figure 10.49

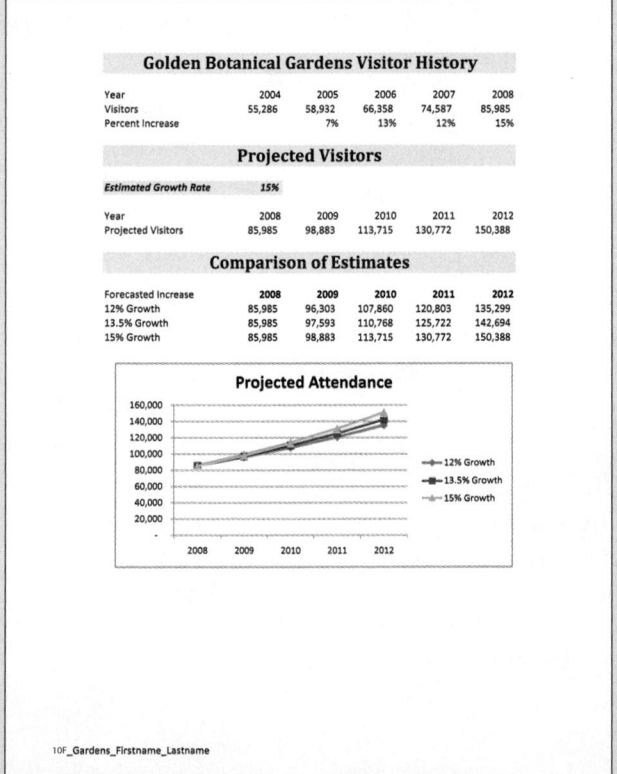

(Project 10F– Gardens continues on the next page)

(Project 10F–Gardens continued)

1. **Start** Excel and display a new workbook. Adjust the width of **column A** to **155 pixels**. In cell **A1**, type **Golden Botanical Gardens Visitor History** and then **Merge and Center** the title over **A1:F1**. Apply **Bold**, change the **Font** to **Cambria**, change the **Font Size** to **18**, and then apply a **Fill Color** of **Orange, Accent 6, Lighter 80%**. **Save** the file in your Excel Chapter 10 folder as **10F_Gardens_Firstname_Lastname**

2. In cell **A3**, type **Year** In cell **B3**, type **2004** and in cell **C3** type **2005** Select the range **B3:C3**, and then fill the years through *2008* in cell **F3**. In cell **A4**, type **Visitors** and then in cell **A5**, type **Percent Increase**

3. Enter the following attendance data in the range **B4:F4**, and then apply **Comma Style** with **zero decimal places** to the data.

2004	2005	2006	2007	2008
55286	58932	66358	74587	85985

4. In cell **C5**, construct a formula to calculate the *Percent Increase* in attendance from 2004 to 2005. Recall that you must first calculate the difference between 2005 and 2004 attendance figures by placing the expression in parentheses, and then divide the result by the base year attendance of 2004. Your result is *0.065948*. Apply **Percent Style** for a result of *7%*, and then fill the formula through cell **F5** to calculate the *Percent Increase* for the remaining years.

5. In cell **A7**, type **Projected Visitors** and then use **Format Painter** to copy the format from cell **A1** to cell **A7**. In cell **A9**, type **Estimated Growth Rate** In cell **A11**, type **Year** and then in cell **A12**, type **Projected Visitors** In cell **B11**, type **2008** and in cell **C11** type **2009** and then extend the pattern of years to *2012*. In cell **B12**, type **=f4** to

create a reference to the attendance in year 2008.

6. **Save** the changes you have made to your workbook thus far. In cell **B9**, type **12%** Select the range **A9:B9**, and then apply **Bold**, **Italic**, and a **Fill Color** of **Orange, Accent 6, Lighter 80%**. The first projection will be based on an estimated growth in attendance of 12%.

7. In cell **C12**, construct a formula to calculate the 2009 estimated attendance based on an increase of 12% over the 2008 attendance—a value after an increase—as follows: multiply the base value in cell **B12** times 100% plus the value in cell **B9**. Place the second expression in parentheses so that addition is performed first, and make the reference to the value in **B9** absolute so you can copy the formula. Your result is *96303.2*. Copy the formula for the remaining years, and then use the **Format Painter** to apply the format of cell **B12** to the range **C12:F12**.

8. In cell **A14** type **Comparison of Estimates** and then use **Format Painter** to copy the formatting from **A7** to cell **A14**. **Copy** the dates in the range **B11:F11**, and then paste them in the range **B16:F16**. Apply **Bold** to the pasted range.

9. Board members want to look at estimates in visitor growth between 12% and 15% (the rates for the past two years) and the rate halfway between those two rates, which is 13.5%. In the range **A16:A19**, type the following row titles.

   Forecasted Increase
   12% Growth
   13.5% Growth
   15% Growth

(Project 10F–Gardens continues on the next page)

(Project 10F–Gardens continued)

10. **Copy** the first set of projections in the range **B12:F12**, point to cell **B17** and right-click, from the shortcut menu click **Paste Special**, and then from the **Paste Special** dialog box, paste the **Values and number formats**—rather than the formulas—to the range **B17:F17**.

11. In cell **B9**, change the projected rate to **13.5** to recalculate the values in the range **C12:F12**. Copy the values and number formats in the range **B12:F12** to the range **B18:F18**. In cell **B9**, change the rate to **15** Copy the values and formats in the range **B12:F12** to the range **B19:F19**. Press (Esc) to cancel the moving border.

12. Using the data in the range **A17:F19**, insert a line chart using the **Line with Markers** chart type, and then position the upper left corner of the chart inside the upper left corner of cell **A21**. Right-click one of the numbers along the **Horizontal (Category) Axis**, and then click **Select Data**. From the **Select Data Source** dialog box, **Edit** the **Horizontal (Category) Axis Labels** by selecting the years in the range **B16:F16** as the category labels.

13. Apply **Chart Style 2**, and then click the **Layout tab**. In the **Labels group**, click the **Chart Title** button, and then click **Above Chart**. As the chart title, type **Projected**

Attendance Click any cell to deselect the chart, and then **Insert** a footer in the left section with the **File Name**. Scroll up to view the chart, and then widen the chart to display attractively below the data. Deselect the chart, and then center the worksheet **Horizontally** on the page. Switch to **Normal** view, **Delete** the extra worksheets in the workbook, and then press (Ctrl) + (Home) to display the top of the worksheet.

14. **Save** the changes you have made to your workbook. Check your *Chapter Assignment Sheet* or *Course Syllabus* or consult your instructor to determine if you are to submit your assignments on paper or electronically. To submit electronically, follow the instructions provided by your instructor.

15. Display your worksheet in **Print Preview**, and then **Print**. If you are directed to submit printed formulas, refer to Activity 5.17 to do so. If you printed your formulas, be sure to redisplay the worksheet by pressing (Ctrl) + (`). From the **Office** menu, click **Close**. If the dialog box displays asking if you want to save changes, click **No** so that you do *not* save the changes you made for printing formulas. **Exit** Excel.

End You have completed Project 10F ——————————

Excel
chapterten

Mastering Excel

Project 10G — Operations Costs

In this project, you will apply the skills you practiced from the Objectives in Projects 10A and 10B.

Objectives: 1. *Create and Save a Workbook from an Existing Workbook;* **2.** *Navigate a Workbook and Rename Worksheets;* **3.** *Enter Dates, Clear Contents, and Clear Formats;* **4.** *Move, Copy, and Paste Cell Contents;* **5.** *Edit and Format Multiple Worksheets at the Same Time;* **6.** *Create a Summary Sheet;* **7.** *Format and Print Multiple Worksheets in a Workbook.* **10.** *Compare Data with a Line Chart.*

In the following Mastering Excel assessment, you will edit a workbook that summarizes and charts the operations costs of Golden Grove's Public Works Department. The department's three divisions are Engineering, Contract Administration, and Street Services. Your completed worksheet will look similar to Figure 10.50.

For Project 10G, you will need the following file:

e10G_Operations_Costs

You will save your workbook as
10G_Operations_Costs_Firstname_Lastname

Figure 10.50

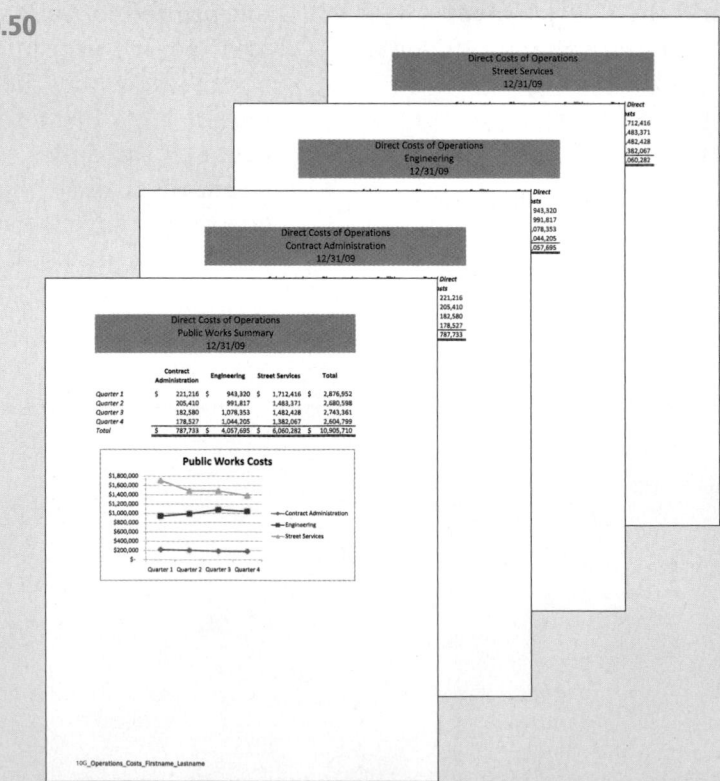

(Project 10G–Operations Costs continues on the next page)

(Project 10G–Operations Costs continued)

1. Start Excel and from your student files, open **e10G_Operations_Costs**. **Save** the workbook in your Excel Chapter 10 folder as **10G_Operations_Costs_Firstname_ Lastname**

2. Rename the **Sheet1 tab** as **Contract Administration** and then change its **Tab Color** to **Purple, Accent 4, Lighter 40%**. Rename **Sheet2** as **Engineering** and then change its **Tab Color** to **Aqua, Accent 5, Lighter 40%**. Rename **Sheet3** as **Street Services** and then change its **Tab Color** to **Orange, Accent 6, Lighter 40%**.

3. Point to the **Contract Administration** sheet tab, right-click, and then select all of the sheets so that they are grouped. **Merge and Center** the titles in **A1** and **A2** over **columns A:E**. In cell **A3**, type **12/31/2009** and then apply the **03/14/01** date format to the cell. **Merge and Center** cell **A3** over **columns A:E**, and then change the **Font Size** to **16**. Select the range **A1:A3**, and then apply a **Fill Color** of **Red, Accent 2, Lighter 40%**.

4. With the worksheets still grouped, in **row 5**, apply **Wrap Text** formatting to the column titles, and then apply **Bold** and **Italic**. **Center** the column titles.

5. With the worksheets still grouped, sum the columns and then sum the rows. Beginning with **Comma Style**, apply appropriate financial formatting using **zero decimal places**, and then change the width of **column A** to **110 pixels**. Select cell **A10** and **Clear Formats** so that the text is aligned at the left and not bold.

6. Ungroup the worksheets and verify that the formulas and formatting applied in Steps 3 through 5 were applied to the **Engineering** and **Street Services** sheets. Insert a new worksheet and **Rename** it

Summary Change the **Tab Color** to **Olive Green, Accent 3, Lighter 40%**.

7. Display the **Contract Administration** worksheet. Select and **Copy** the range **A1:A3**, and then **Paste** the selection to the **Summary** worksheet in cell **A1**. In the **Summary** worksheet, click cell **A2**, and then type **Public Works Summary**

8. Display the **Contract Administration** worksheet. **Copy** the range **A6:A9**, **Paste** the selection to the **Summary** worksheet in cell **A6**, and then in the **Summary** worksheet, adjust the width of **column A** to **110 pixels** and the width of **columns B:E** to **100 pixels**. In cell **A10**, type **Total**— italic emphasis will carry forward from the cell above.

9. In cell **B5**, type **Contract Administration** In cell **C5**, type **Engineering** In cell **D5**, type **Street Services** In cell **E5**, type **Total Center** and apply **Wrap Text** formatting to the column titles in **row 5**, apply **Bold**, and then apply **Middle Align**.

10. Save the changes you have made to your workbook thus far. In the **Summary** worksheet in cell **B6**, create a formula that references the **Contract Administration** worksheet *Quarter 1 Total Direct Costs* in cell **E6**. Fill the formula down through **B9** to create formulas that reference the remaining quarter's *Total Direct Costs*. Create similar formulas for the **Engineering** and **Street Services** quarterly *Total Direct Costs*. Sum the columns and then sum the rows. Beginning with **Comma Style**, apply appropriate financial formatting using **zero decimal places**.

11. Select the range **A5:D9**, and then insert a line chart using the **Line with Markers** chart type. Position the upper left corner

(Project 10G–Operations Costs continues on the next page)

Excel

chapterten

Mastering Excel

(Project 10G–Operations Costs continued)

of the chart inside the upper left corner of cell **A12**. Apply **Chart Style 10**, and then add a **Chart Title—Public Works Costs** in the **Above Chart** position. From the status bar, click the **Page Layout View** button, widen the chart to display attractively below the data, and then click any cell to deselect the chart. **Move** the **Summary** worksheet so that it is the first sheet in the workbook.

12. Group the worksheets, insert a footer with the **File Name** on the left, and then center the worksheets **Horizontally**. Return to **Normal** view and display the upper portion of the worksheet.

13. **Save** your workbook, and then examine your grouped worksheets in **Print Preview**. Print or submit electronically as directed. If the worksheets are grouped, all the worksheets will print. If the worksheets are not grouped, click Entire workbook to print all the sheets. Determine if you are to print formulas for any or all of the worksheets in this workbook. To print formulas, refer to Activity 5.17 in Project 5A.

14. If you printed your formulas, be sure to redisplay the worksheet by pressing Ctrl + `. From the **Office** menu, click **Close**. If you are prompted to save changes, click **No**. **Exit** Excel.

 You have completed Project 10G

Excel

Mastering Excel

Project 10H — Venue Revenue

In this project, you will apply the skills you practiced from the Objectives in Projects 10A and 10B.

Objectives: 3. *Enter Dates, Clear Contents, and Clear Formats;* **8.** *Design a Worksheet for What-If Analysis;* **9.** *Perform What-If Analysis;* **10.** *Compare Data with a Line Chart.*

In the following Mastering Excel assessment, you will complete a workbook for the Director of Conventions, Culture, and Leisure, which shows revenue estimates for city-owned venues for conventions, cultural events, and leisure activities and their associated parking structures. Your resulting worksheet and chart will look similar to Figure 10.51.

For Project 10H, you will need the following file:

New blank Excel workbook

You will save your workbook as
10H_Venue_Revenue_Firstname_Lastname

Figure 10.51

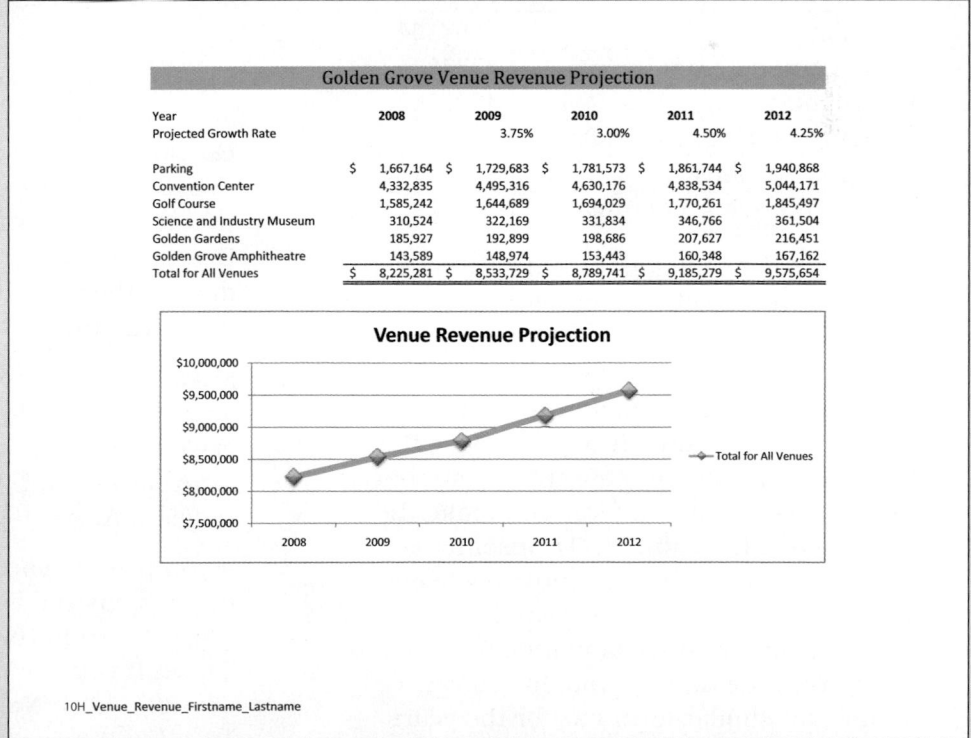

(Project 10H–Venue Revenue continues on the next page)

(Project 10H–Venue Revenue continued)

1. **Start** Excel and display a new blank work-book. **Save** the workbook in your Excel Chapter 10 folder as **10H_Venue_Revenue_Firstname_Lastname**

2. In cell **A1**, type **Golden Grove Venue Revenue Projection** and then **Merge and Center** the title across cells **A1:F1**. Change the **Font** to **Cambria**, the **Font Size** to **16**, and then apply the **Olive Green, Accent 3 Fill Color**. In cell **A3**, type **Year** In the range **B3:F3**, create a pattern of years from 2008 through 2012. Format the years with **Bold** and **Center**.

3. In cell **A4**, type **Projected Growth Rate** In the range **C4:F4**, type the following percentages: **3.75% 3.0% 4.5% 4.25%**

4. Widen **column A** to **200 pixels** and widen columns **B:F** to **100 pixels**. In the range **A6:B11**, enter the following data:

Parking	1667164
Convention Center	4332835
Golf Course	1585242
Science and Industry Museum	310524
Golden Gardens	185927
Golden Grove Amphitheatre	143589

5. In cell **C6**, construct a formula that calculates the year *2009* revenue for *Parking* assuming an increase of 3.75% (the rate in cell C4) over the previous year. That is, multiply the base value in cell **B6** times 100% plus the value in cell **C4**. Place the second expression in parentheses so that addition is performed first, and make the reference to the value in **C4** absolute so that you can copy this formula down column C. In cell **D6**, for the year *2010*, construct a similar formula using the previous year's revenue and the rate in cell **D4**. Construct similar formulas for the years

2011 and *2012* using the previous year's revenue and the projected growth rate for the year indicated. **Copy** the formulas in **row 6** down through **row 11**.

6. In cell **A12**, type **Total for All Venues** and then in **row 12**, sum the values in **columns B:F**. Beginning with **Comma Style**, apply appropriate financial formatting with **zero decimal places**.

7. **Save** the changes you have made to your workbook thus far. Using the data in the range **A12:F12**, insert a line chart using the **Line with Markers** chart type, and then apply **Chart Style 29**. Edit the data source so that the **Horizontal (Category) Axis** uses the years in the range **B3:F3** as the labels. Change the chart title to **Venue Revenue Projection** Position the upper left corner of the chart inside the upper left corner of cell **A14**.

8. Click any cell to deselect the chart. Change the **Orientation** to **Landscape**, and then center the worksheet on the page **Horizontally**. Insert a footer with the **File Name** on the left side. Widen the chart so that it displays attractively under the data. Deselect the chart, return to **Normal** view, display the top of the worksheet, and then delete the unused sheets in the workbook.

9. **Save** your workbook, and then examine your worksheet in **Print Preview**. Print or submit electronically as directed. To print formulas, refer to Activity 5.17 in Project 5A.

10. If you printed your formulas, be sure to redisplay the worksheet by pressing [Ctrl] + [`]. From the **Office** menu, click **Close**. If you are prompted to save changes, click **No. Exit** Excel.

 End **You have completed Project 10H**

Content-Based Assessments

Project 10I — Analysis

In this project, you will apply the skills you practiced from all the Objectives in Projects 10A and 10B.

Objectives: 1. *Create and Save a Workbook from an Existing Workbook;* **2.** *Navigate a Workbook and Rename Worksheets;* **3.** *Enter Dates, Clear Contents, and Clear Formats;* **4.** *Move, Copy, and Paste Cell Contents;* **5.** *Edit and Format Multiple Worksheets at the Same Time;* **6.** *Create a Summary Sheet;* **7.** *Format and Print Multiple Worksheets in a Workbook;* **8.** *Design a Worksheet for What-If Analysis;* **9.** *Perform What-If Analysis;* **10.** *Compare Data with a Line Chart.*

In the following Mastering Excel assessment, you will complete a workbook for the Director of Parks and Recreation, which shows departmental expenses for the three departments reporting to the director. Your resulting worksheet and chart will look similar to Figure 10.52.

For Project 10I, you will need the following file:

e10I_Analysis

You will save your workbook as
10I_Analysis_Firstname_Lastname

Figure 10.52

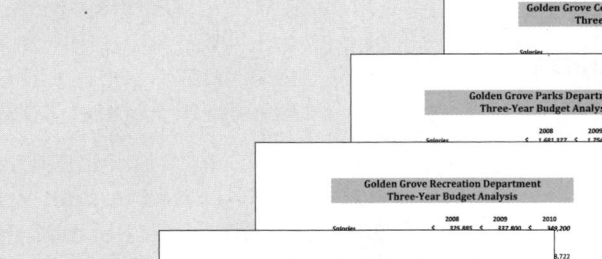

(Project 10I– Analysis continues on the next page)

(Project 10I–Analysis continued)

1. **Start** Excel, and then from your student files, open the file **e10I_Analysis**. **Rename Sheet1** as **Recreation** and then change the **Tab Color** to **Blue, Accent 1, Lighter 40%**. **Rename Sheet2** as **Parks** and then change the **Tab Color** to **Red, Accent 2, Lighter 40%**. **Rename Sheet3** as **Community Outreach** and then change the **Tab Color** to **Olive Green, Accent 3, Lighter 40%**. **Save** the workbook in your Excel Chapter 10 folder as **10I_Analysis_ Firstname_Lastname**

2. Display the **Recreation** worksheet, and then group the three worksheets. Select the range **A1:A2**, change the **Font** to **Cambria**, the **Font Size** to **16**, apply **Bold**, and then apply a **Fill Color** of **Aqua, Accent 5, Lighter 40%**. **Merge and Center** the two worksheet titles across the ranges **A1:D1** and **A2:D2**. Select the years in the range **B4:D4** and apply **Bold**, and **Center** alignment. Select the **Salaries** data in the range **B5:D5**, apply **Accounting Number Format** with **zero decimal places**, and then select the range **A5:D5** and apply **Bold** and **Italic**. Use **Format Painter** to copy the formatting from cell **A5** to cell **A7** and to cell **A14**.

3. Verify that the worksheets are still grouped, and then in **row 14**, sum each year's data for *Expenses*. Apply **Bold** and **Italic** to the totals. Beginning with **Comma Style** and using **zero decimal places**, apply appropriate financial formatting to the *Expenses* data, *without* a Top and Double Bottom Border. Instead, to the range **B14:D14**, apply only a **Top Border**.

4. Ungroup the worksheets and verify that the formatting and editing changes that you made in Steps 2 and 3 were applied to all three worksheets. On the **Recreation** worksheet, **Copy** the text in cell **A16**, and

then **Paste** it to the same location in the **Parks** worksheet and **Community Outreach** worksheet.

5. Display the **Recreation** worksheet and press Esc to cancel the moving border. Group the three worksheets. In cell **B16**, construct a formula that adds the *2008 Salaries* in cell **B5** and the *2008 Total Expenses* in cell **B14**. Fill the formula across the remaining two years, and then with the range **B16:D16** still selected, apply a **Bottom Double Border**. Select the range **A16:D16**, and then apply **Bold** and **Italic**.

6. With the worksheets still grouped, in cell **A18** type **Total Departmental Increase** In cell **C18**, construct a formula that calculates the percent increase of the *Total Departmental Increase* for *2009* from *2008*. Your result is *0.003307521*, an increase of less than 1%. Apply **Percent Style** formatting with **two decimal places** for a result of *0.33%*. Copy the formula to the right for the year 2010; in this year, the percentage increase was more significant—*8.27%*. To the range **A18:D18**, apply **Bold**, **Italic**, and a **Fill Color** using **Aqua, Accent 5, Lighter 40%**.

7. With the worksheets still grouped, in cell **A20** type **Projected Budget Years 2010 – 2012** and then use **Format Painter** to copy the format from cell **A1** to cell **A20**. In cell **A22**, type **Forecasted Increase** In cell **A24**, type **Year** and in cell **A25**, type **Forecasted Total Budget** Apply **AutoFit** to **column A**. In the range **B24:D24**, enter a pattern of years from 2010 through 2012, and then **Center** and **Bold** the years. In cell **B22**, type **8.5%** which will display as *8.50%*. To the range **A22:B22**, apply **Bold** and **Italic**.

8. With the worksheets still grouped, in cell **B25** construct a formula that references cell **D16**—the *Total Department* expenses for *2010*. In cell **C25**, construct a formula

(Project 10I–Analysis continues on the next page)

(Project 10I–Analysis continued)

that calculates the *Forecasted Total Budget* for *2011* based on the 8.5% increase in cell **B22**. Be sure to make the reference to cell **B22** absolute. (The result displays as being too wide for the cell.) Copy the formula to cell **D25**, and then use **Format Painter** to copy the formatting from cell **B25** to the range **C25:D25**.

9. **Save** the changes you have made thus far. Insert a new worksheet, rename the worksheet **Summary** and then change the **Tab Color** to **Orange, Accent 6, Lighter 40%**. In cell **A1**, type **Golden Grove Parks and Recreation** In cell **A2**, type **Forecast Summary** In cell **A3**, type **Years 2010 to 2012** In the range **B5:D5**, enter the years **2010** and **2011** and **2012 Bold** and **Center** the years. In the range **A6:A9**, enter the row titles **Recreation** and **Parks** and **Community Outreach** and **Total** Widen columns **B:D** to **95 pixels**.

10. **Merge and Center** each of the three worksheet titles across columns **A:D**, and then change the **Font** to **Cambria**, the **Font Size** to **16**, and apply a **Fill Color** of **Aqua, Accent 5, Lighter 40%**.

11. In cell **B6**, enter a formula that references the **Forecasted Total Budget** for **2010** from cell **B25** in the **Recreation** worksheet. Fill the formula across through cell **D6**, and then construct similar formulas for the **Forecasted Total Budget** amounts from the **Parks** worksheet and the **Community Outreach** worksheet. Calculate totals for each year in **row 9**. Beginning with **Comma Style**, apply appropriate financial formatting to the data with **zero decimal places**.

12. **Save** your changes. Using the data in the range **A6:D8**, insert a line chart using the **Line with Markers** chart type. Position the upper left corner of the chart inside the upper left corner of cell **A11**, apply **Chart Style 2**, and then edit the data source so that the **Horizontal (Category) Axis** displays the years in the range **B5:D5**. Insert a chart title in the **Above Chart** position with the text **Three-Year Budget Forecast**

13. Click any cell to deselect the chart. Move the **Summary** worksheet to become the first worksheet in the workbook, and then group the worksheets. Center the worksheets in the workbook **Horizontally** on the page. Insert a footer on the left side with the **File Name**. Ungroup the worksheets. Adjust the width of the chart so that it is slightly inside the right boundary of **column D** to display attractively below the data. Return to **Normal** view, deselect the chart, and display the top of the worksheet.

14. **Save** your workbook, and then examine your worksheets in **Print Preview**. Print or submit electronically as directed. If the worksheets are grouped, all the worksheets will print. If the worksheets are not grouped, click **Entire workbook** to print all the sheets. Determine if you are to print formulas for any or all of the worksheets in this workbook. To print formulas, refer to Activity 5.17 in Project 5A.

15. If you printed your formulas, be sure to redisplay the worksheet by pressing Ctrl + [`]. From the **Office** menu, click **Close**. If you are prompted to save changes, click **No**. **Exit** Excel.

End You have completed Project 10I

Content-Based Assessments

 Excel

chapterten

 Business Running Case

Project 10J—Business Running Case

In this project, you will apply the skills you practiced in Projects 10A and 10B.

From My Computer, navigate to the student files that accompany this textbook. In the folder **03_business_running_case**, locate and open the folder for this chapter. Open and print the instructions for this project, which are provided to you in Adobe PDF format. Follow the instructions and use the skills you have gained thus far to assist Jennifer Nelson in meeting the challenges of owning and running her business.

 End **You have completed Project 10J** ———————

Content-Based Assessments

Mastering Excel

Project 10K — *GO!* Fix It

In this project, you will construct a solution by applying any combination of the skills you practiced from the Objectives in Projects 10A and 10B.

The Golden Grove City Council has maintained the same pool pass fee structure for the past six years. It has asked staff to provide information on attendance and receipts, to see if an increase in fees is warranted. Your task is to review and correct a draft workbook containing this information and to make revenue projections.

For Project 10K, you will need the following file:

e10k_fixit_Pool_Passes

You will save your workbook as
10K_Pool_Passes_Firstname_Lastname

From the student files that accompany this textbook, open the folder **05_go-fix_it**. Locate and open the file **e10K_fixit_Pool_Passes**, and then save the file in your chapter folder as **10K_Pool_Passes_Firstname_Lastname**

This workbook contains **five errors** that you must find and correct. Read and examine the document, and then edit to correct the errors that you find. Types of errors could include:

- Spelling, grammar, and punctuation errors in cells, charts, worksheet tabs, or file names.
- Errors in data entry and workbook layout. Formatting errors in text, numbers, alignment, indents and spacing, tabs, wrapping, merge and center, text direction and orientation, fonts, borders, patterns, protection, AutoFormat, conditional formatting, data sort, filter, and validation.
- Formula and function errors such as incorrect and missing formulas, error indicators and values, relative vs. absolute cell referencing, What-If Analysis, Paste Special, function arguments, and Goal Seek.
- Errors in object design, layout, and formatting, for example chart type, location, data source, elements, size, scale, positioning, pictures, and hyperlinks.
- Row and column formatting errors such as height, width, and AutoFit.
- Worksheet, tab design, and formatting errors such as missing or blank worksheets, worksheet tab colors, and locations.
- Page setup errors such as page orientation and scaling, margins and centering, headers and footers, sheet gridlines, and row and column headings.

(Project 10K–*GO!* Fix It continues on the next page)

Content-Based Assessments

Mastering Excel

(Project 10K–*GO!* Fix It continued)

To complete the project you should know:

- In your finished workbook, the grand total in Cell E36 on the Summary worksheet should be $6,193,765.
- It is efficient to work from the last worksheet to the first when looking for errors.
- Formula errors and omissions in a range of cells count as a single error.
- A chart title should be inserted above the chart, entitled *Revenue from Pool Passes 2003–2008* and formatted as Verdana, 18 pt bold.
- All the workbook pages should be centered horizontally.

Save the changes you have made, add the file name to the footers, and then submit as directed.

 You have completed Project 10K ——————————

Outcomes-Based Assessments

Rubric

The following outcomes-based assessments are *open-ended assessments*. That is, there is no specific correct result; your result will depend on your approach to the information provided. Make *Professional Quality* your goal. Use the following scoring rubric to guide you in *how* to approach the problem and then to evaluate *how well* your approach solves the problem.

The *criteria*—Software Mastery, Content, Format and Layout, and Process—represent the knowledge and skills you have gained that you can apply to solving the problem. The *levels of performance*—Professional Quality, Approaching Professional Quality, or Needs Quality Improvements—help you and your instructor evaluate your result.

	Your completed project is of Professional Quality if you:	Your completed project is Approaching Professional Quality if you:	Your completed project Needs Quality Improvements if you:
1-Software Mastery	Choose and apply the most appropriate skills, tools, and features and identify efficient methods to solve the problem.	Choose and apply some appropriate skills, tools, and features, but not in the most efficient manner.	Choose inappropriate skills, tools, or features, or are inefficient in solving the problem.
2-Content	Construct a solution that is clear and well organized, contains content that is accurate, appropriate to the audience and purpose, and is complete. Provide a solution that contains no errors of spelling, grammar, or style.	Construct a solution in which some components are unclear, poorly organized, inconsistent, or incomplete. Misjudge the needs of the audience. Have some errors in spelling, grammar, or style, but the errors do not detract from comprehension.	Construct a solution that is unclear, incomplete, or poorly organized, containing some inaccurate or inappropriate content; and contains many errors of spelling, grammar, or style. Do not solve the problem.
3-Format and Layout	Format and arrange all elements to communicate information and ideas, clarify function, illustrate relationships, and indicate relative importance.	Apply appropriate format and layout features to some elements, but not others. Overuse features, causing minor distraction.	Apply format and layout that does not communicate information or ideas clearly. Do not use format and layout features to clarify function, illustrate relationships, or indicate relative importance. Use available features excessively, causing distraction.
4-Process	Use an organized approach that integrates planning, development, self-assessment, revision, and reflection.	Demonstrate an organized approach in some areas, but not others; or, use an insufficient process of organization throughout.	Do not use an organized approach to solve the problem.

Outcomes-Based Assessments

Problem Solving

Project 10L — Fire Stations

In this project, you will construct a solution by applying any combination of the skills you practiced in the Objectives covered in Projects 10A and 10B.

> ### For Project 10L, you will need the following file:
>
> New blank Excel workbook

You will save your workbook as
10L_Fire_Stations_Firstname_Lastname

The City of Golden Grove has approved a bond measure for the construction of three new fire stations. Using the information provided, create a workbook that the City Controller can present to the City Council that details construction costs covered by the bond measure. Design your workbook so that the data for each fire station is on a separate worksheet. First, group the sheets to apply formatting and type the row and column titles that will be the same across all sheets; this will help you avoid unnecessary typing and formatting. Then, ungroup the sheets, include the fire station location at the top of each worksheet, and type the costs into each sheet. To type the costs, it may be helpful to select the range first so that the movement of the insertion point is confined to the range.

Grand Avenue Fire Station	Land Costs	Design Costs	Construction Costs
Phase 1	13840320	343900	2209384
Phase 2	1102984	230098	3384950
Phase 3	1920384	119739	6937409

South Edison Fire Station	Land Costs	Design Costs	Construction Costs
Phase 1	1866428	459320	1938400
Phase 2	293040	664739	6790474
Phase 3	288730	193804	8498502

Hill Street Fire Station	Land Costs	Design Costs	Construction Costs
Phase 1	394058	484927	1849023
Phase 2	1293846	559680	7593084
Phase 3	129800	583920	5890503

For all of the worksheets, calculate totals for each Phase (rows) and for each type of cost (columns). Insert a worksheet that summarizes, for each fire station, the total costs by type of cost (Land, Design, and Construction). Sum the columns. On each worksheet, use borders, fill colors, and font styles and sizes to create a professional worksheet. Add a footer to each worksheet that includes the file name and center the worksheets on the page. Save the workbook as **10L_Fire_Stations_Firstname_Lastname** and submit it as directed.

End You have completed Project 10L

Problem Solving

Project 10M—Water Usage

In this project, you will construct a solution by applying any combination of the skills you practiced in the Objectives covered in Projects 10A and 10B.

For Project 10M, you will need the following file:

New blank Excel workbook

You will save your workbook as
10M_Water_Usage_Firstname_Lastname

Golden Grove is a growing community and the City Council has requested an analysis of future water needs. In this project, you will create a worksheet for the Department of Water and Power that contains data regarding past residential water usage and that forecasts water usage in the future. Create a worksheet with the following data:

Year	2002	2004	2006	2008	2010
Water Use in Acre Feet	62500	68903	73905	76044	80342

Calculate the percent increase in water usage from 2002 to 2004, and then for 2006, 2008, and 2010. Using Project 10B as a guide, add a section to the worksheet to calculate the projected water usage for the years 2010 to 2018 in two-year increments. The 2010 amount is 80,342. Add a comparison of estimates section to the worksheet with three forecasted increases: 4%, 6%, and 9%. Include a worksheet title and use formatting and editing techniques that you practiced in this chapter so that the worksheet looks attractive and professional. Add the file name to the footer. Save the workbook as **10M_Water_Usage_Firstname_Lastname** and submit it as directed.

End **You have completed Project 10M**————————

Outcomes-Based Assessments

Problem Solving

Project 10N — Schools

In this project, you will construct a solution by applying any combination of the skills you practiced in the Objectives in Projects 10A and 10B.

For Project 10N, you will need the following file:

New blank Excel workbook

You will save your workbook as
10N_Schools_Firstname_Lastname

As the city of Golden Grove grows, the school district must plan for additional students that will enroll in the elementary, middle, and high schools. In this project, you will create a workbook that contains enrollment projections for the next four years. First, create three worksheets containing the following information:

Elementary Schools	2008	2009	2010	2011	2012
Projected Increase		2%	3.5%	7%	5%
Wyndham	1350				
Warm Creek	956				
Los Serranos	1175				
Hidden Canyon	1465				
Butterfield	854				

Middle Schools	2008	2009	2010	2011	2012
Projected Increase		4.5%	5.75%	3%	3.5%
Townsend	1194				
Canyon Hills	1575				
Golden Springs	1392				

High Schools	2008	2009	2010	2011	2012
Projected Increase		6%	7.5%	4%	2.75%
Poppy Hills	2276				
Diamond Ranch	3150				

On each sheet, create formulas in the 2009 column that increase the 2008 enrollment by the Projected Increase percent. Create similar formulas for each year, increasing the previous year's enrollment by the Projected Increase percent. Calculate totals by year. Insert a line chart on each sheet with the years on the category horizontal axis. Create a summary sheet that includes the total enrollment by year for each *type* of school—Elementary Schools, Middle Schools, and High Schools—and then calculate totals for each year. Use formatting and editing techniques that you practiced in this chapter so that the workbook looks attractive and professional. Add the file name to the footer. Save the workbook as **10N_Schools_Firstname_Lastname** and submit it as directed.

 End **You have completed Project 10N**

Outcomes-Based Assessments

Problem Solving

Project 10O — Park Acreage

In this project, you will construct a solution by applying any combination of the skills you practiced in the Objectives covered in Projects 10A and 10B.

For Project 10O, you will need the following file:

New blank Excel workbook

You will save your workbook as
10O_Park_Acreage_Firstname_Lastname

The city of Golden Grove wants to maintain a high ratio of parkland to residents and has established a goal of maintaining a minimum of 50 parkland acres per 1,000 residents. The following table contains the park acreage and the population, in thousands, since 1970. Enter the data in a worksheet, and then calculate the *Acres per 1,000 residents* by dividing the *Park acreage* by the *Population in thousands*. Create a line chart that displays the Acres per 1,000 residents for each year in the table. Use formatting and editing techniques that you practiced in this chapter so that the worksheet looks attractive and professional. On your worksheet, apply yellow fill color to any year in which the goal of a minimum of 50 parkland acres per 1,000 residents was not achieved. Add the file name to the footer. Save the workbook as **10O_Park_Acreage_Firstname_Lastname** and submit it as directed.

	1970	1980	1990	2000	2010
Population in thousands	116.3	145.4	180.2	225.3	304.5
Park acreage	5,800	7,250	10,050	11,250	12,240
Acres per 1,000 residents					

 You have completed Project 10O _____

Outcomes-Based Assessments

Problem Solving

Project 10P — Transportation

In this project, you will construct a solution by applying any combination of the skills you practiced in the Objectives covered in Projects 10A and 10B.

For Project 10P, you will need the following file:

New blank Excel workbook

**You will save your workbook as
10P_Transportation_Firstname_Lastname**

The Public Transportation Director for the city of Golden Grove would like to compare the sources of funding for public transportation in the current year (2009) and the forecasted amounts for 2010, 2011, and 2012. The 2009 sources of funding are:

	2009
Passenger fares	1,524,630
City appropriation	2,358,796
State appropriation	1,857,942
Federal grants	1,564,894
Other funding sources	978,623

The projected increase for 2010 is 5% for passenger fares and 2% for all other categories. The projected increase from the 2010 forecast for 2011 is 3.5% for passenger fares and 1.5% for all other categories. The projected increase from the 2011 forecast for 2012 is 6% for passenger fares and 3% for all other categories. Create a worksheet with formulas that calculate the forecasted funding amounts and that totals each year and each funding source. Then, insert a line chart that illustrates the total funding for each year. Use formatting and editing techniques that you practiced in this chapter so that the worksheet and chart look attractive and professional. Add the file name to the footer and save the workbook as **10P_Transportation_Firstname_Lastname** and submit it as directed.

End **You have completed Project 10P** —————————

Outcomes-Based Assessments

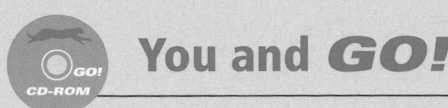

Project 10Q — You and *GO!*

In this project, you will construct a solution by applying any combination of the skills you practiced in the Objectives covered in Projects 10A and 10B.

From My Computer, navigate to the student files that accompany this textbook. In the folder **04_you_and_go**, locate and open the folder for this chapter. Open and print the instructions for this project, which are provided to you in Adobe PDF format. Follow the instructions to create a budget for yourself over a three-month period.

End You have completed Project 10Q ————————————

GO! with Help

Project 10R — *GO!* with Help

In this chapter, you inserted line charts with markers that identified the data points for each data series. You can add data labels to a line chart so that the value of each data point displays adjacent to the data marker. In this exercise, you will use Help to find out how to add data labels to a chart.

1 **Start** Excel. At the far right end of the Ribbon, click the **Microsoft Office Excel Help** button . Click the **Search arrow**, and then under **Content from this computer**, click **Excel Help**.

2 In the **Search** box, type **insert data labels** and then press Enter. Click **Edit titles or data labels in a chart** and then click **Add or remove data labels in a chart**.

3 Read the information under **Add data labels to a chart**, print the information if you want to do so, close the Help window, and then **Exit** Excel.

End You have completed Project 10R ————————————

Outcomes-Based Assessments

Group Business Running Case

Project 10S — Group Business Running Case

In this project, you will apply the skills you practiced from the Objectives in Projects 10A and 10B.

Your instructor may assign this group case project to your class. If your instructor assigns this project, he or she will provide you with information and instructions to work as part of a group. The group will apply the skills gained thus far to help the Bell Orchid Hotel Group achieve its business goals.

 End **You have Completed Project 10S** ———————————

11 chaptereleven

Using Functions and Tables

OBJECTIVES

At the end of this chapter you will be able to:

1. Use SUM, AVERAGE, MEDIAN, MIN, and MAX Functions
2. Use COUNTIF and IF Functions, and Apply Conditional Formatting
3. Use a Date Function
4. Freeze Panes and Create an Excel Table
5. Format and Print a Large Worksheet

6. Use Financial Functions
7. Use Goal Seek
8. Create a Data Table

OUTCOMES

Mastering these objectives will enable you to:

PROJECT 11A
Track Inventory by Using Math, Logical, and Statistical Functions and by Creating an Excel Table

PROJECT 11B
Make Financial Decisions by Using Financial Functions and What-If Analysis

Adamantine Jewelry, Inc.

Adamantine Jewelry is based in Milan, Italy, one of the world's leading centers for fashion and design. The company's designers take inspiration from nature, cultural artifacts, and antiquities to produce affordable, fashionable jewelry that is sold through major retailers around the world. With a 40-year history, the company is well respected among its retail customers and has recently expanded to online and television retailers. In addition to women's bracelets, necklaces, rings, and earrings, the company also produces sport and fashion watches for men and women.

Using Functions and Tables

In this chapter, you will design worksheets that use the library of formulas and procedures provided with Excel to perform specific functions. You will also use more What-If Analysis tools. Using these tools will make your worksheets valuable tools for analyzing data and making financial decisions.

Project 11A **Milan Inventory**

In Activities 11.01 through 11.13, you will edit a worksheet for Rose Elleni, Vice President of Production, detailing the current inventory of two product types at the Milan production facility. Your completed worksheet will look similar to Figure 11.1.

For Project 11A, you will need the following file:

e011A_Milan_Inventory

You will save your workbook as
11A_Milan_Inventory_Firstname_Lastname

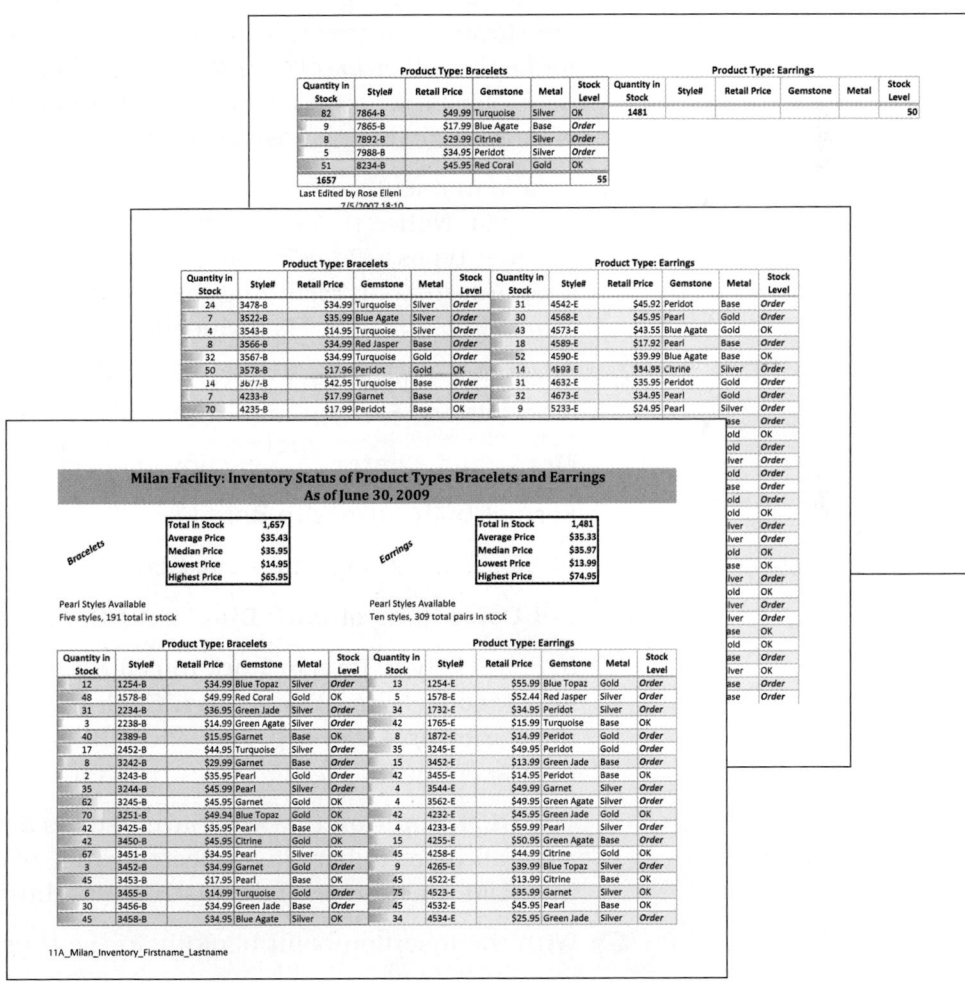

Figure 11.1
Project 11A—Milan Inventory

Objective 1
Use SUM, AVERAGE, MEDIAN, MIN, and MAX Functions

A *function* is a predefined formula—a formula that Excel has already built for you—that performs calculations by using specific values in a particular order or structure.

Activity 11.01 Using the SUM, AVERAGE, and MEDIAN Functions

Rose has a worksheet with information about the inventory of two product types—Bracelets and Earrings—currently in stock at the Milan facility. In this activity, you will use the SUM and AVERAGE functions to gather information about the product inventory.

1 **Start** Excel. From the student files that accompany this text, locate and open **e11A_Milan_Inventory**. From the **Office** menu 🗔, display the **Save As** dialog box, and then navigate to the location where you are storing your projects for this chapter. Click the **New Folder** button, name the folder **Excel Chapter 11** and then press ⏎ to make your new folder the active folder. In the **File name** box, type **11A_Milan_Inventory_Firstname_Lastname** and then click **Save** or press ⏎.

2 Take a moment to scroll down the worksheet to become familiar with the data. Notice that the worksheet contains data related to two product types—*Bracelets* and *Earrings*—and then for each product type, information regarding the *Quantity in Stock*, *Style#*, *Retail Price*, *Gemstone*, and *Metal* is included.

3 In cell **A1**, type **Milan Facility: Inventory Status of Product Types Bracelets and Earrings** and in cell **A2** type **As of June 30, 2009**

Merge and Center 🔲 each worksheet title across the columns **A:L**. Format both titles with **Bold** **B**, change the **Font** Calibri to **Cambria**, change the **Font Size** 11 to **16**, and then apply a **Fill Color** 🖌 of **Dark Blue, Text 2, Lighter 60%**.

4 In cell **A4**, type **Total in Stock** In cell **A5**, type **Average Price** In cell **A6**, type **Median Price** Click cell **B4**. Click the **Formulas tab**, and then in the **Function Library group**, click the **AutoSum** button. Compare your screen with Figure 11.2.

The **SUM function** that you have used is a predefined formula that adds all the numbers in a selected range of cells. You can also insert the SUM function from the Math & Trig button.

5 With the insertion point blinking in the function, select the range

Figure 11.2

AutoSum button   Formulas tab selected   Worksheet titles formatted

Function Library group

SUM function started in cell

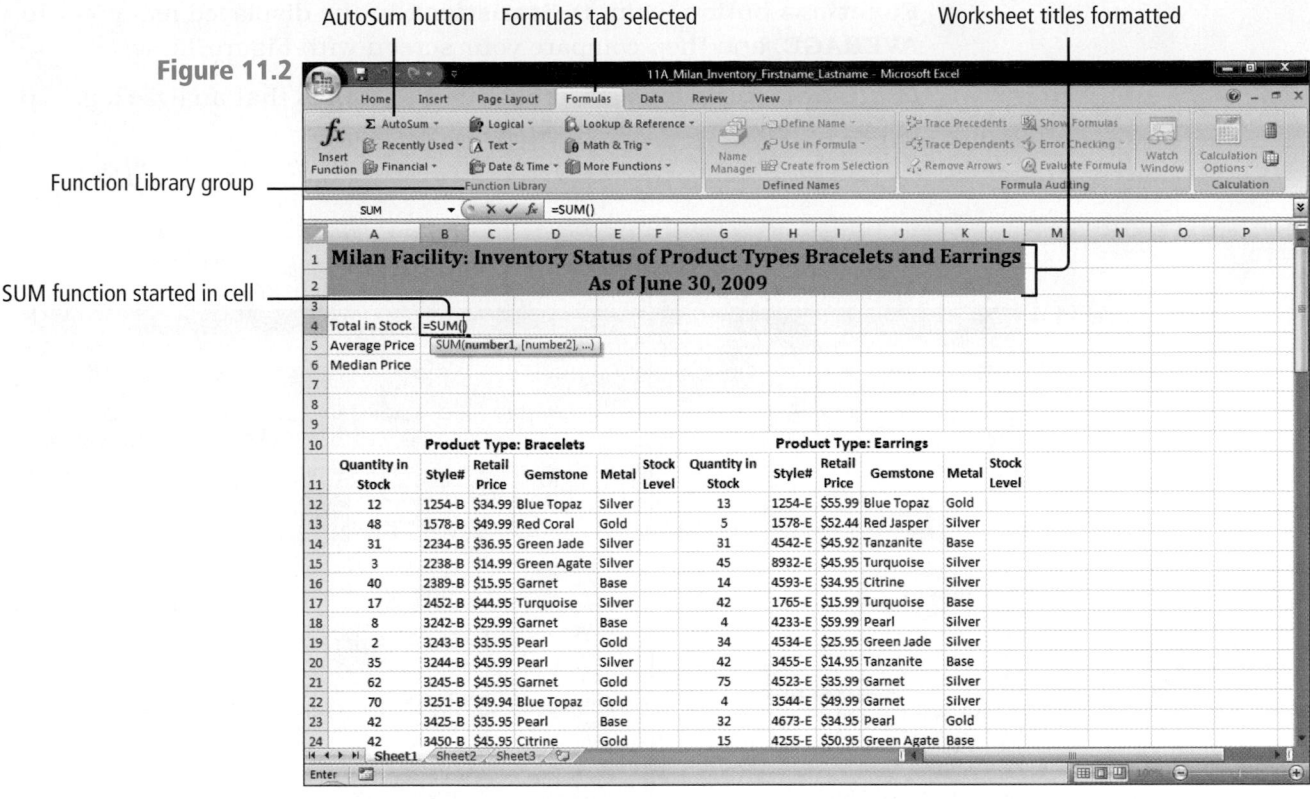

A12:A66, dragging downward as necessary, and then press ⟨Enter⟩. Scroll up to view the top of your worksheet, and notice your result in cell **B4**, *1657*. Click cell **B4**, look at the **Formula Bar**, and compare your screen with Figure 11.3.

The values in parentheses are the *arguments*—the values that an Excel function uses to perform calculations or operations. In this instance, the argument consists of the values in the range A12:A66.

6 Click cell **B5**. In the **Function Library group**, click the **More**

Argument in parentheses

Figure 11.3

SUM function in Formula Bar

Number of Bracelets in stock

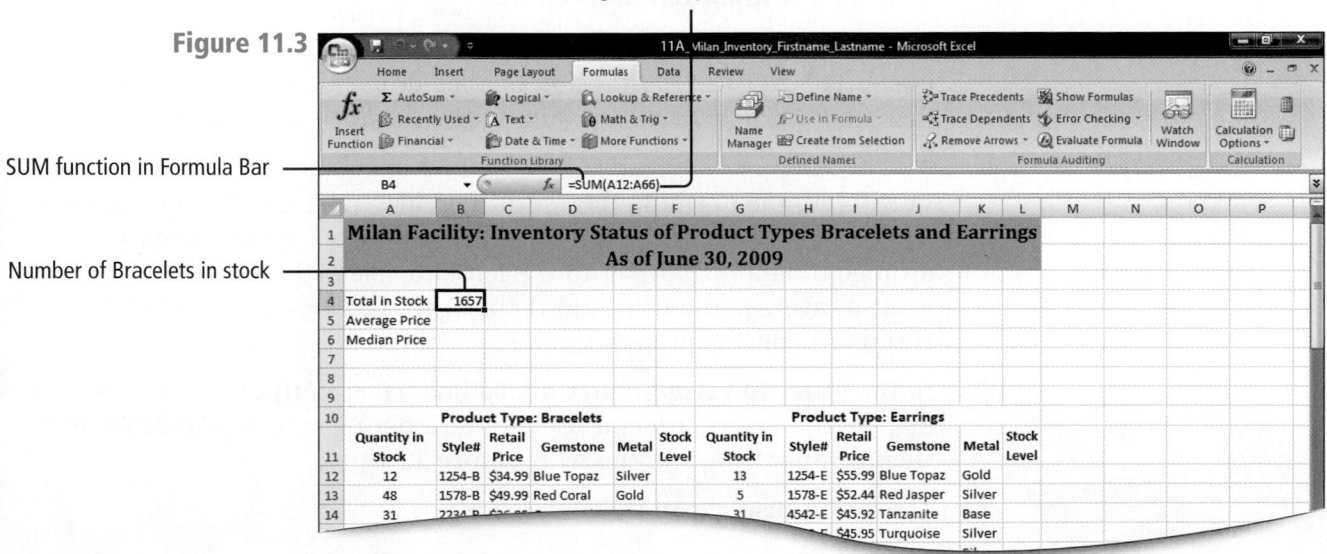

Functions button, point to **Statistical**, in the displayed list, point to **AVERAGE**, and then compare your screen with Figure 11.4.

Statistical functions are pre-written formulas that analyze a group of measurements.

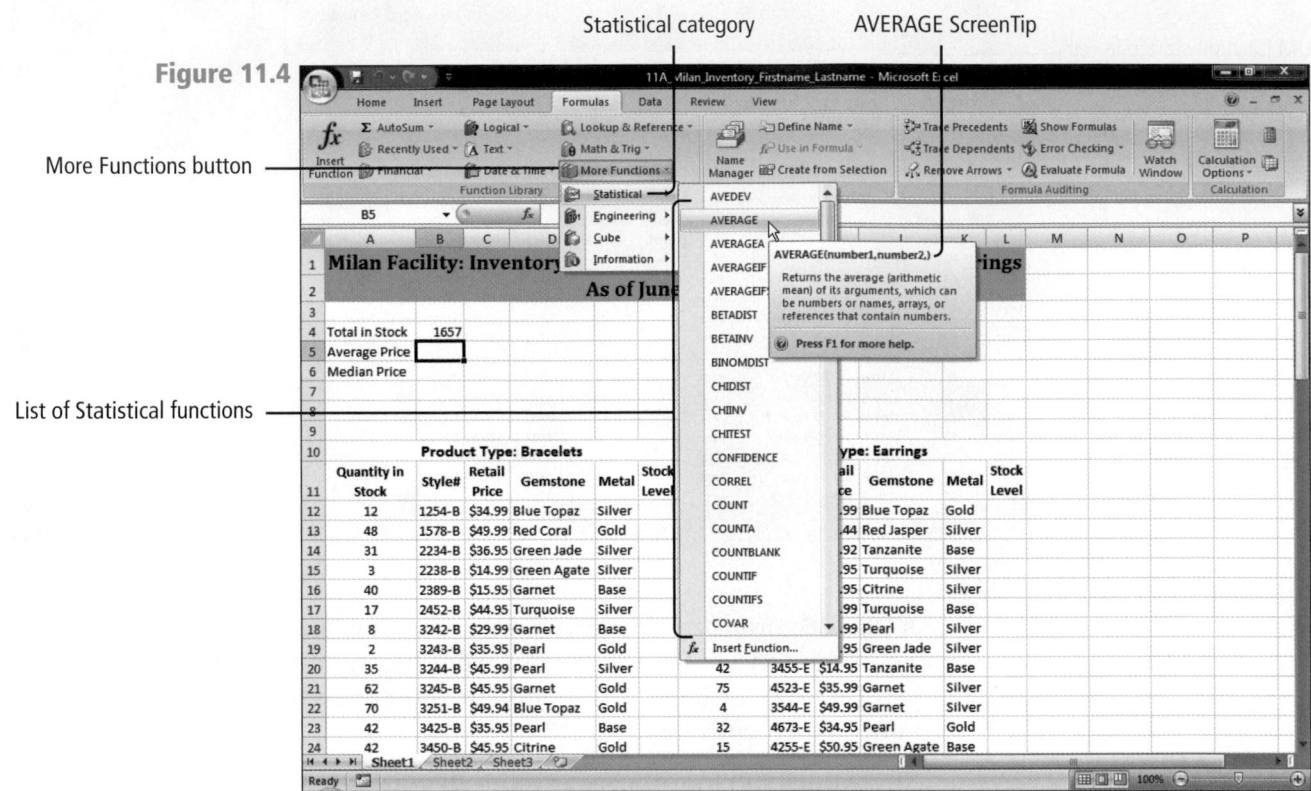

Figure 11.4

Statistical category

AVERAGE ScreenTip

More Functions button

List of Statistical functions

7 Click **AVERAGE**, and then if necessary, drag the title bar of the **Function Arguments** dialog box down and to the right so you can view the **Formula Bar** and cell **B5**.

The Function Arguments dialog box for the AVERAGE function displays. The *AVERAGE function* is a formula that adds a group of values, and then divides the result by the number of values in the group.

In the cell, the Formula Bar, and the dialog box, Excel proposes to average the value in cell B4. Recall that Excel functions will propose a range if data is above or to the left of a selected cell. Because you want to average the values in the range C12:C66—and *not* cell B4— you must edit the proposed range.

8 In the **Function Arguments** dialog box, click in the **Number1** box to display the insertion point. Delete the existing text, type **c12:c66** and then compare your screen with Figure 11.5.

The result displays in the dialog box.

Formula Bar displays
function and argument

Range of cells
to average

Figure 11.5

Function Arguments dialog
box for AVERAGE function

Result displays

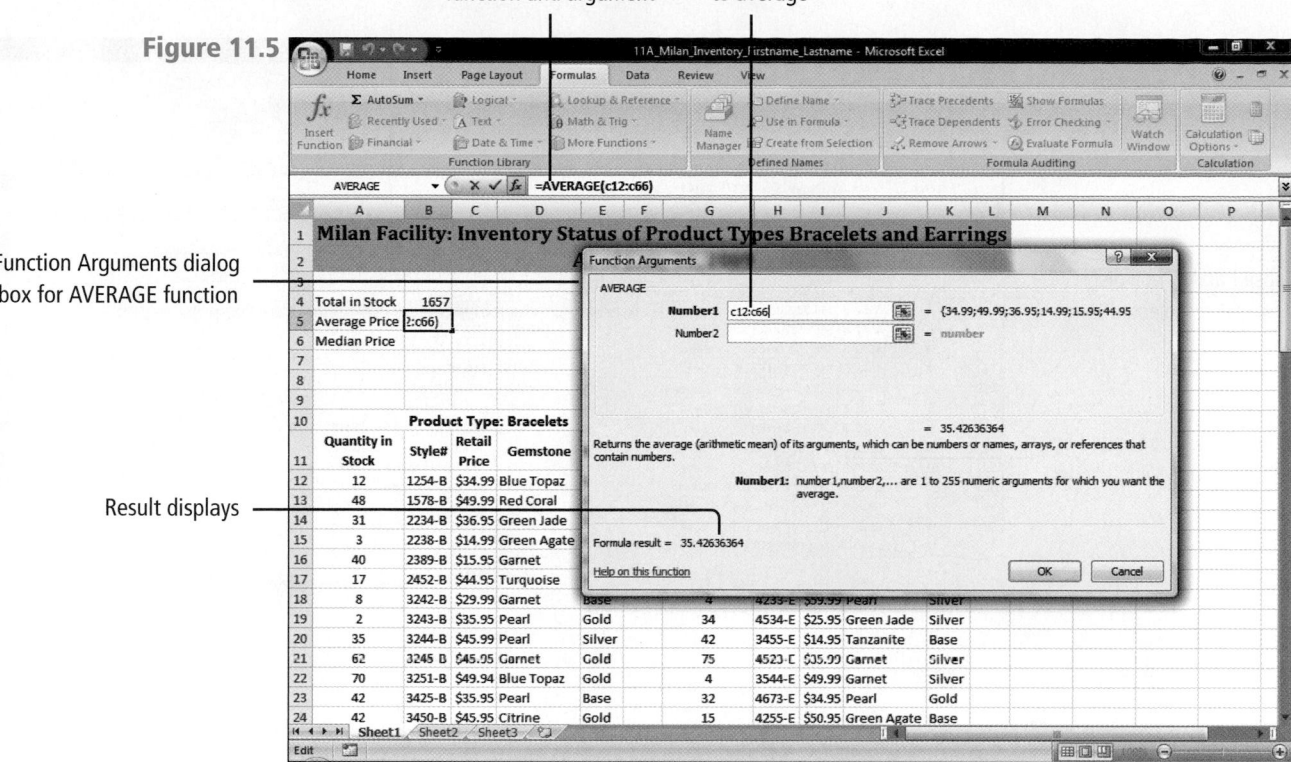

9 In the **Function Arguments** dialog box, click **OK**.

The result indicates that the average Retail Price of all Bracelets is
$35.43.

10 Click cell **B6**. In the **Function Library group**, click the **More
Functions** button, display the list of **Statistical** functions, scroll
down as necessary, and then click **MEDIAN**.

The **MEDIAN function** is a statistical function commonly used to
describe a group of data—you have likely seen it used to describe the
price of houses in a particular geographical area. The MEDIAN function finds the *middle value* that has as many values *above* it in the
group as are *below* it. It differs from AVERAGE in that the result is
not affected as much by a single value that is greatly different from
the others.

11 In the displayed **Function Arguments** dialog box, to the right of the
Number1 box, click the **Collapse Dialog** button —the square
with the red arrow.

The dialog box collapses to a small size containing only space for the
first argument. With the dialog box collapsed, you can see more of
your worksheet data.

12 Select the range **C12:C66**, and then compare your screen with
Figure 11.6.

Figure 11.6

Formula Bar displays function and argument

Dialog box collapsed to a small size

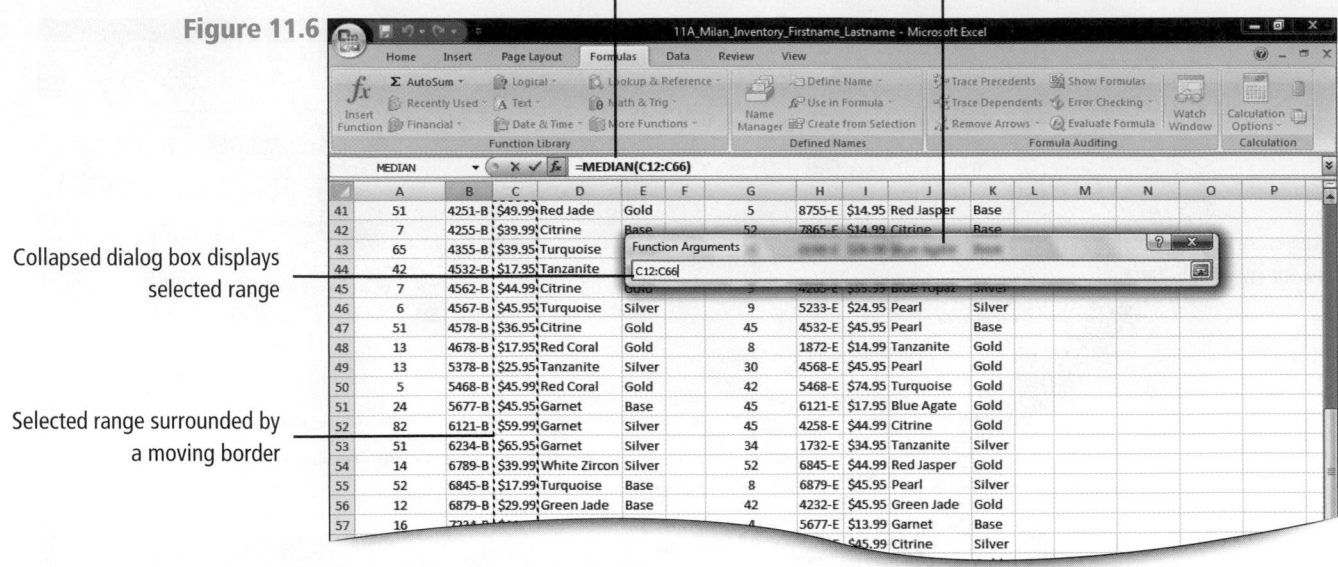

Collapsed dialog box displays selected range

Selected range surrounded by a moving border

13 Press [Enter].

The dialog box expands to its original size and the selected range displays as the argument in the Number1 box. When entering arguments into a Function Arguments dialog box, you can either select the range of cells in this manner, or type the range into the argument box.

14 In the lower right corner of the **Function Arguments** dialog box, click **OK**. **Save** 💾 your workbook.

Your result is *$35.95*—in the range of prices, $35.95 is the middle value. Half of all Bracelet products are priced *above* $35.95 and half are priced *below* $35.95.

15 Select the range **A4:A6**, right-click over the selection, and then from the displayed shortcut menu, click **Copy**. Point to cell **G4**, right-click, and then click **Paste**. Press [Esc] to cancel the moving border.

16 Scroll to the bottom of your worksheet and notice that the **Earrings** product type ends in **row 61**. Then, in cell **H4**, use the technique you just practiced to **SUM** the total number of **Earrings** in stock. In cell **H5**, use the **AVERAGE** function to display the average **Retail Price** of the **Earrings** product type. In cell **H6**, use the **MEDIAN** function to display the median value of the **Retail Price** for **Earrings**.

17 Select cells **B4** and **H4**, apply **Comma Style** with **zero decimal places**, click any cell to deselect, and then compare your screen with Figure 11.7.

Figure 11.7

Comma style applied

Functions used to calculate
Earrings product information

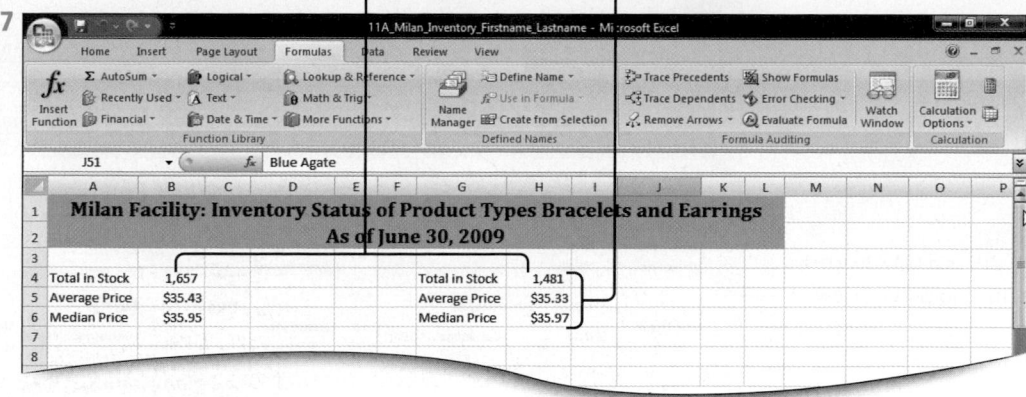

18 **Save** 💾 your workbook.

Activity 11.02 Using the MIN and MAX Functions

The **MIN function** determines the smallest value in a selected range of values. The **MAX function** determines the largest value in a selected range of values.

1 In cell **A7**, type **Lowest Price** and then in cell **A8**, type **Highest Price**

2 Click cell **B7**. On the **Formulas tab**, in the **Function Library group**, click the **More Functions** button, display the list of **Statistical** functions, scroll as necessary, and then click **MIN**. At the right end of the **Number1** box, click the **Collapse Dialog** button 📉, select the range **C12:C66**, and then press Enter. Click **OK**.

The lowest retail price in the Bracelets product group is *$14.95*.

3 In cell **B8**, using a similar technique, insert the **MAX** function to determine the highest **Retail Price** in the **Bracelets** product type.

The highest Retail Price in the Bracelets product type is *$65.95*.

4 Copy the range **A7:A8** and paste it in cell **G7**. Then in cells **H7** and **H8**, use the **MIN** and **MAX** functions to calculate the lowest and highest **Retail Price** for products in the **Earrings** product type. Compare your screen with Figure 11.8.

Figure 11.8

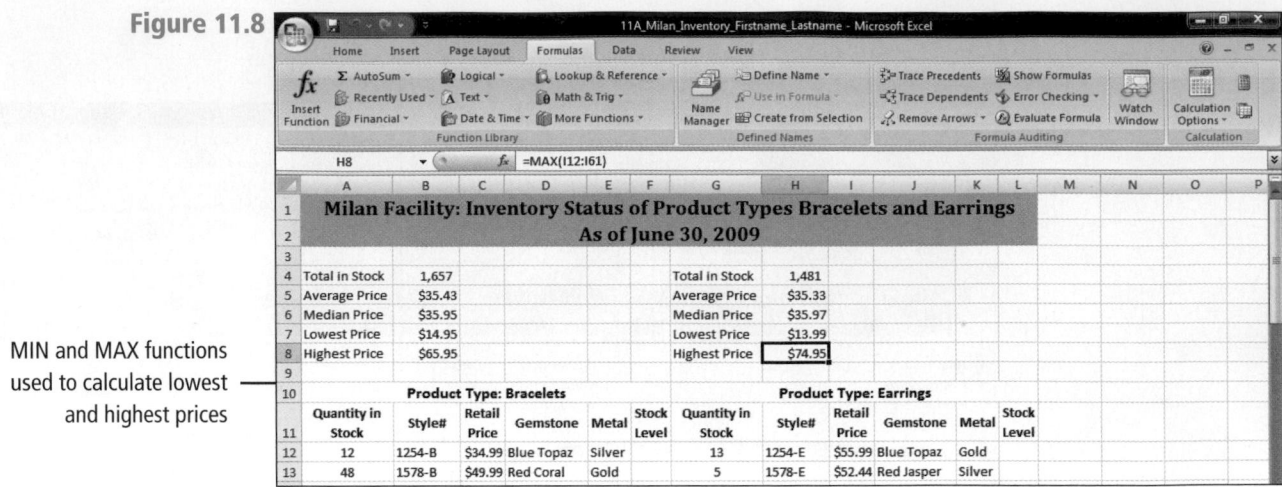

MIN and MAX functions used to calculate lowest and highest prices

5 **Save** 💾 the changes you have made to your workbook.

To Insert a Function

There are several ways to begin a function in Excel. Because the functions are grouped into categories such as *Financial*, *Logical* and so on, it is efficient to locate and insert functions from the Function Library. You can also click the Insert Function button 🔣 on the Formula Bar; or, type = in the cell, type the first letter of the function, and then select the function from the list that displays. This feature is called *Formula AutoComplete*. You can also copy a similar function from another cell and edit the arguments within the cell or on the Formula Bar. Finally, you can access the Insert Function dialog box by selecting Insert Function from any of the displayed menus in the Function Library group or by pressing ⇧Shift + F3 .

Activity 11.03 Moving Data, Adding Borders, and Rotating Text

Recall that you can select and move a range of cells containing formulas or functions (prewritten formulas). Use borders to emphasize a range of cells—bordered data draws the reader's eye to a specific portion of a worksheet. Similarly, use rotated text to draw attention to data on your worksheet.

1 Select the range **A4:B8**. Point to the right edge of the selected range to display the 🔣 pointer, and then compare your screen with Figure 11.9.

Figure 11.9

Move pointer

Selected range

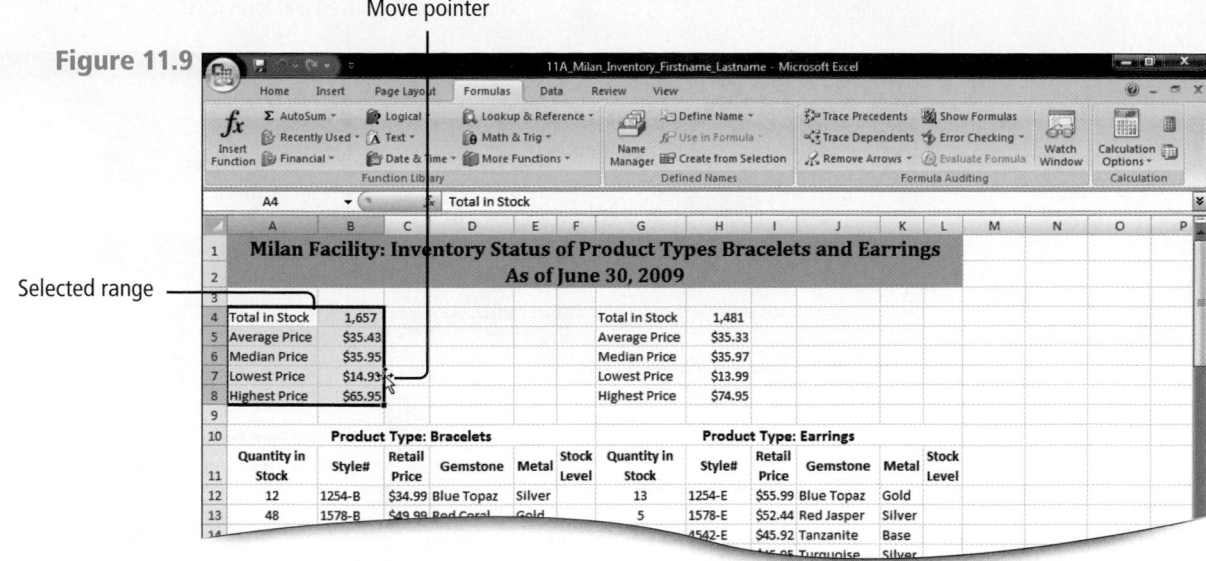

2 Drag the selected range to the right until the ScreenTip displays *C4:D8*, and then release the mouse button. Select **columns C:D**, and then apply **AutoFit** to adjust the column widths. Then, use the same technique to move the range **G4:H8** to the range **I4:J8**. Select **columns I:J**, and then apply **AutoFit**.

3 Select the nonadjacent ranges **C4:D8** and **I4:J8**, right-click to display the Mini toolbar, and then apply **Bold** [B] and a **Thick Box Border** [⊞ ▾].

4 In cell **A6**, type **Bracelets** Select the range **A5:A7**, right-click over the selection, and then from the shortcut menu, click **Format Cells**. In the displayed **Format Cells** dialog box, click the **Alignment tab**. Under **Text control**, select the **Merge cells** check box.

5 In the upper right portion of the dialog box, under **Orientation**, point to the **red diamond**, and then drag the diamond upward until the **Degrees** box indicates **30**. Alternatively, type the number of degrees directly into the Degrees box. Compare your screen with Figure 11.10.

Figure 11.10

Range of cells moved and formatted

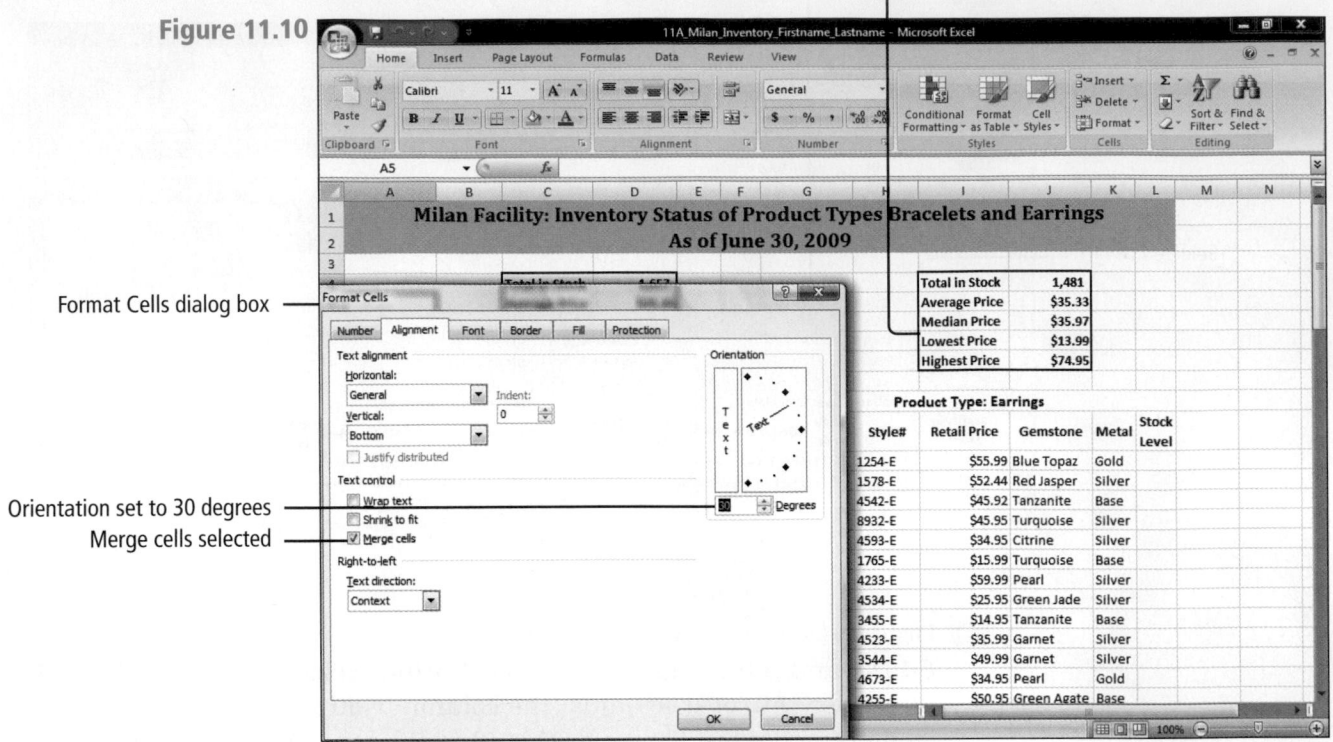

Format Cells dialog box

Orientation set to 30 degrees

Merge cells selected

6. In the lower right corner of the **Format Cells** dialog box, click **OK**. With the merged cell still selected, display the Mini toolbar, change the **Font Size** 11 to **12**, and then apply **Bold** B and **Italic** I. On the **Home tab**, in the **Alignment group**, apply **Center** alignment and **Middle Align**.

7. In cell **G5** type **Earrings** Point to the merged cell **A5** and right-click. On the Mini toolbar, click the **Format Painter** button, and then click cell **G5** to copy the formatting. Compare your screen with Figure 11.11.

Text rotated and formatted

Figure 11.11

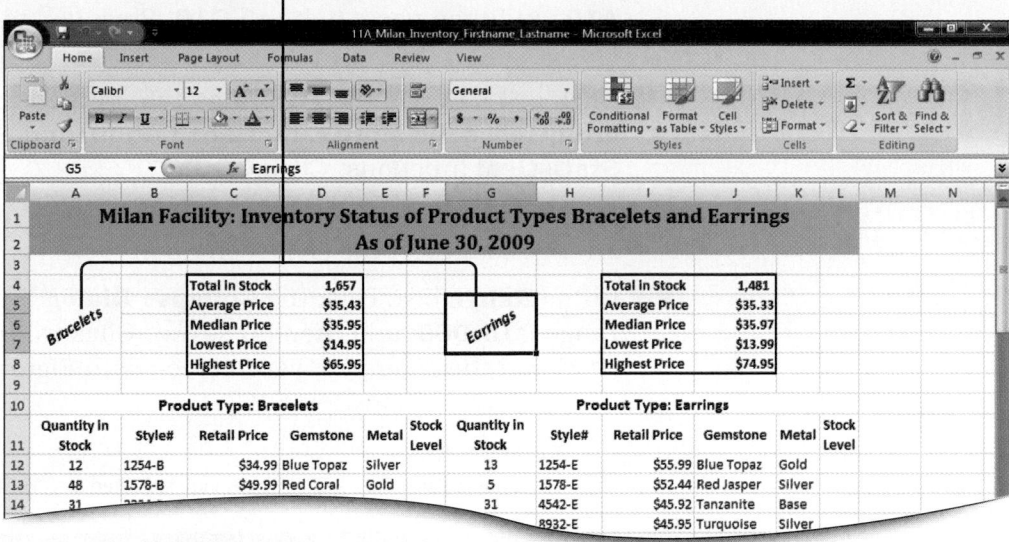

8 **Save** 💾 your workbook.

Objective 2
Use COUNTIF and IF Functions, and Apply Conditional Formatting

Recall that statistical functions analyze a group of measurements. Another group of Excel functions, referred to as *logical functions*, test for specific conditions. Logical functions typically use conditional tests to determine whether specified conditions—called *criteria*—are true or false.

Activity 11.04 Using the COUNTIF Function

The *COUNTIF function* counts the number of cells within a range that meet the given condition—the criteria that you provide. The COUNTIF function has two arguments—the range of cells to check and the criteria.

Rose has learned that Adamantine's pearl bracelets and earrings will be featured on an upcoming segment of a TV shopping channel in Italy. In this activity, you will use the COUNTIF function to determine the number of pearl styles currently available in inventory.

1 From the **row heading area**, point to **row 10**, and then right-click. From the shortcut menu, click **Insert**. Press [F4] two times to repeat the last action and thus insert three blank rows. Click cell **D4**, look at the **Formula Bar**, and then notice that the arguments of the **SUM** function adjusted and refer to **rows 15:69**.

The referenced range updates to A15:A69 after you insert the three new rows. In this manner, Excel adjusts the cell references in a formula relative to their new locations.

2 In cell **A10**, type **Pearl Styles Available:** and then press ⏎. Copy cell **A10**, and then paste it to cell **G10**. Press Esc to cancel the moving border.

3 Click cell **A11**. On the **Formulas tab**, in the **Function Library group**, click the **More Functions** button, and then display the list of **Statistical** functions. Click **COUNTIF**.

Recall that the COUNTIF function counts the number of cells within a range that meet the given condition.

4 In the **Range** box, click the **Collapse Dialog** button ▦, select the range **D15:D69**, and then press ⏎. Click in the **Criteria** box, type **Pearl** and then compare your screen with Figure 11.12.

Function displays
in Formula Bar

Range indicated as *D15:D69*

Figure 11.12

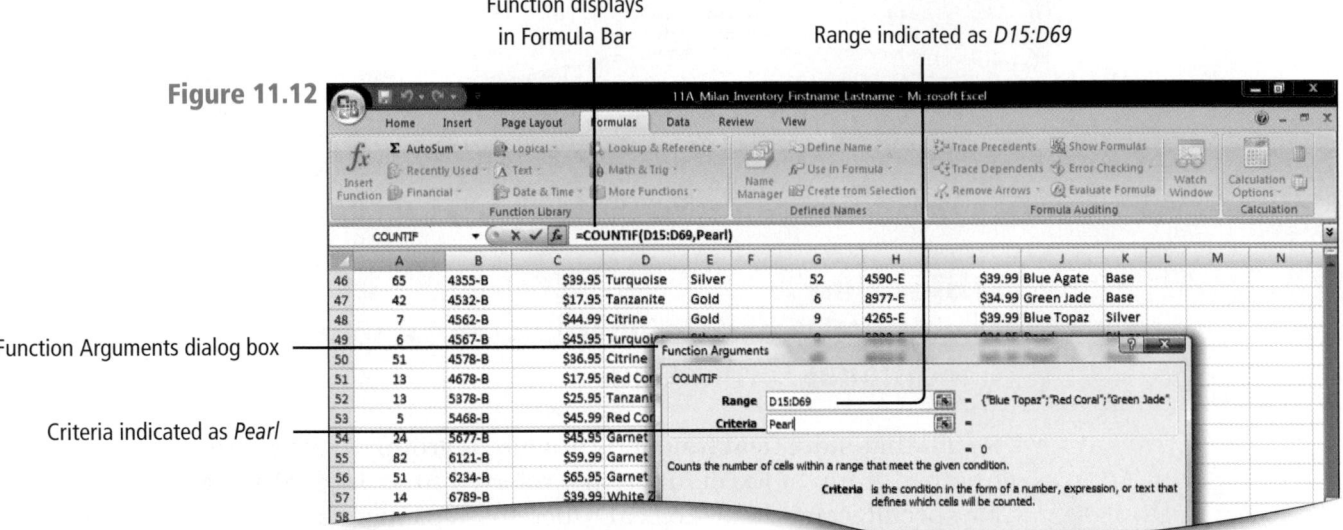

Function Arguments dialog box

Criteria indicated as *Pearl*

5 In the lower right corner of the **Function Arguments** dialog box, click **OK**.

Five different styles of Pearl bracelets are available to feature on the TV show.

6 Using the technique you just practiced, in cell **G11**, count the number of **Pearl** styles available in the **Earrings** product type.

Ten different styles of Pearl earrings are available to feature on the TV show.

7 Select cells **A11** and **G11**, and then on the **Home tab**, in the **Alignment group**, click the **Align Text Left** button ▤.

8 **Save** 💾 your workbook.

Activity 11.05 Using the IF Function and Applying Conditional Formatting

A **logical test** is any value or expression that can be evaluated as being true or false. The **IF function** uses a logical test to check whether a condition is met, and then returns one value if true, and another value if false. For example, *C8=100* is an expression that can be evaluated as true or false. If the value in cell C8 is equal to 100, the expression is true. If the value in cell C8 is not 100, the expression is false.

In this activity, you will use the IF function to determine the inventory stock levels and determine if more products should be ordered.

1 Click cell **F15**. On the **Formulas tab**, in the **Function Library group**, click the **Logical** button, and then in the displayed list, click **IF**. If necessary, drag the title bar of the displayed **Function Arguments** dialog box up so that you can view **row 15** on your screen.

2 With the insertion point in the **Logical_test** box, click cell **A15**, and then type **<40**

This logical test will look at the value in cell A15, the value of which is *12*, and then determine if the number is less than 40. The expression *<40* includes the < **comparison operator**, which means *less than*. Comparison operators compare values.

3 Take a moment to examine the table in Figure 11.13 for a list of comparison operator symbols and their definitions.

Comparison Operators

Comparison Operator Symbol	Definition
=	Equal to
>	Greater than
<	Less than
>=	Greater than or equal to
<=	Less than or equal to
<>	Not equal to

Figure 11.13

4 Press ⎡Tab⎤ to move the insertion point to the **Value_if_true** box, and then type **Order**

If the result of the logical test is true—the Quantity in Stock is less than 40—the cell will display the text *Order* indicating that additional product must be ordered.

5 Press ⎡Tab⎤ to move the insertion point to the **Value_if_false** box, type **OK** and then compare your dialog box with Figure 11.14.

If the result of the logical test is false—the Quantity in Stock is *not* less than 40—then Excel will display *OK* in the cell.

Figure 11.14

Value if true (less than 40) will indicate *Order*

Logical test will determine if value in A15 is less than 40

Value if false (40 or more) will indicate *OK*

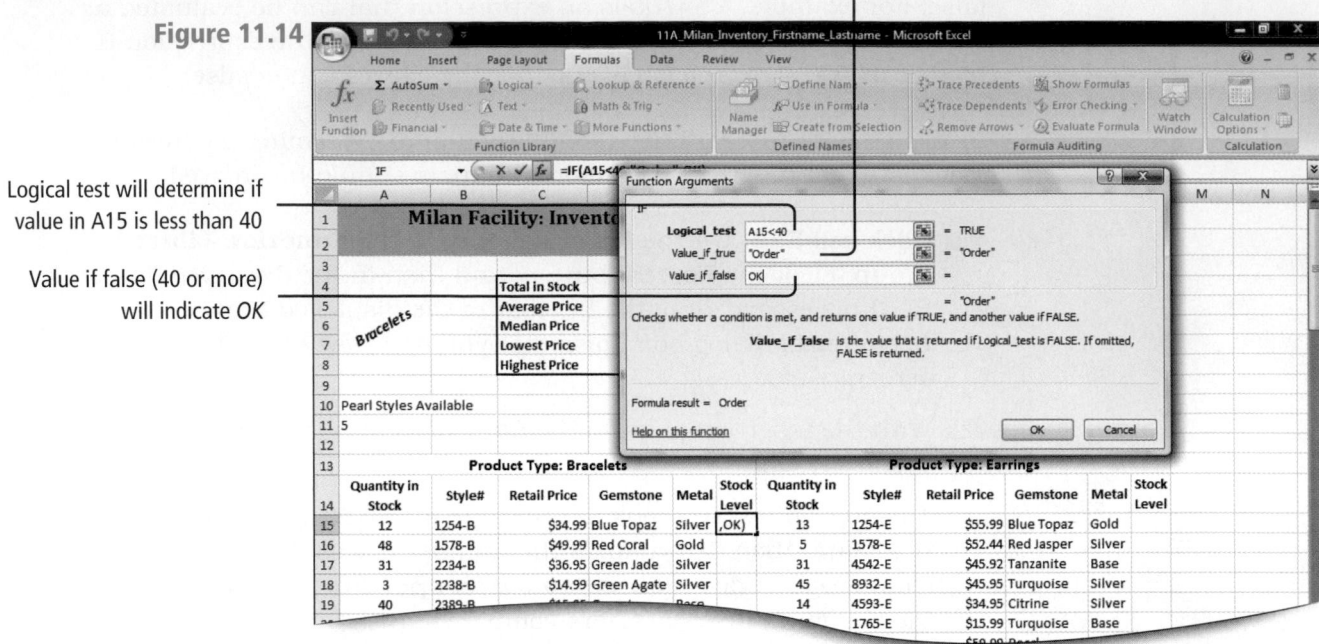

6 Click **OK** to display the result *Order* in cell **F15**. Then, using the fill handle, copy the function down through cell **F69**. Look at cell **A19**, and then look at cell **F19** and notice that the **Stock Level** is indicated as *OK*.

The comparison operator indicated <40 (less than 40) and thus a value of *exactly* 40 is indicated as OK.

7 Click cell **L15**, and then using the technique you just practiced and a quantity *less than* 40, conduct a logical test on the quantities of **Earrings** in stock. Then, scroll to the upper portion of your worksheet, click cell **L15**, look at the **Formula Bar**, and then compare your screen with Figure 11.15.

Note

You can also copy the function in cell F15 to cell L15 and the cell references will adjust accordingly.

Figure 11.15

Formula Bar displays formula

Stock Level status
indicated for Earrings

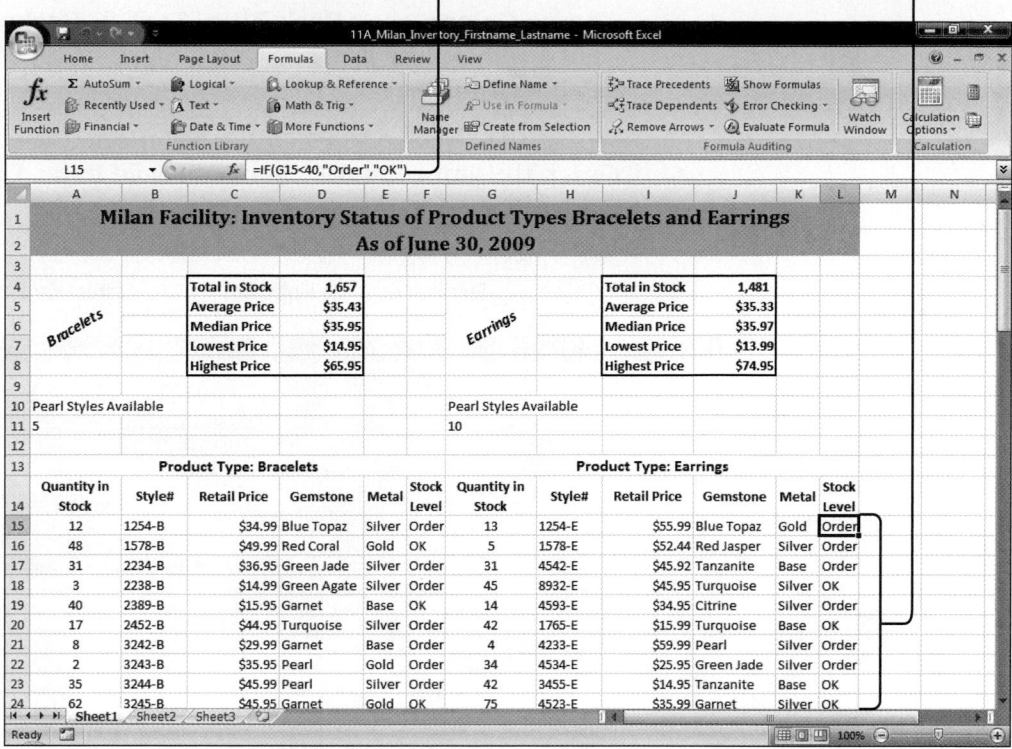

B Save 💾 your workbook.

Activity 11.06 Applying Conditional Formatting Using Custom Formats and Data Bars

A **conditional format** changes the appearance of a cell range based on a condition—a criteria. If the condition is true, the cell range is formatted based on that condition; if the condition is false, the cell range is *not* formatted based on the condition. In this activity, you will use conditional formatting as another way to draw attention to the Stock Level of products.

1 Select the range **F15:F69**. On the **Home tab**, in the **Styles group**, click the **Conditional Formatting** button. In the displayed list, point to **Highlight Cells Rules**, and then click **Text that Contains**. In the **Text That Contains** dialog box, with the insertion point blinking in the first box, type **Order** In the second box, click the arrow, and then in the displayed list, click **Custom Format**.

The Format Cells dialog box displays. Here you can select any combination of formats to apply to the cell if the condition is true. The custom format that you specify will be applied to any cell in the selected range if it contains the specific text *Order*.

2 In the displayed **Format Cells** dialog box, on the **Font tab**, under **Font style**, click **Bold Italic**. Click the **Color arrow**, and then under **Theme Colors**, click **Dark Blue, Text 2, Darker 25%**. In the lower right corner of the **Format Cells** dialog box, click **OK**. Compare your screen with Figure 11.16.

Within the selected range, if the cell meets the condition of containing *Order*, the font color will change to Bold Italic, Dark Blue, Text 2 Darker 25%.

Text That Contains dialog box   *Custom Format* indicated

Figure 11.16

Only cells with the text *Order* will be formatted

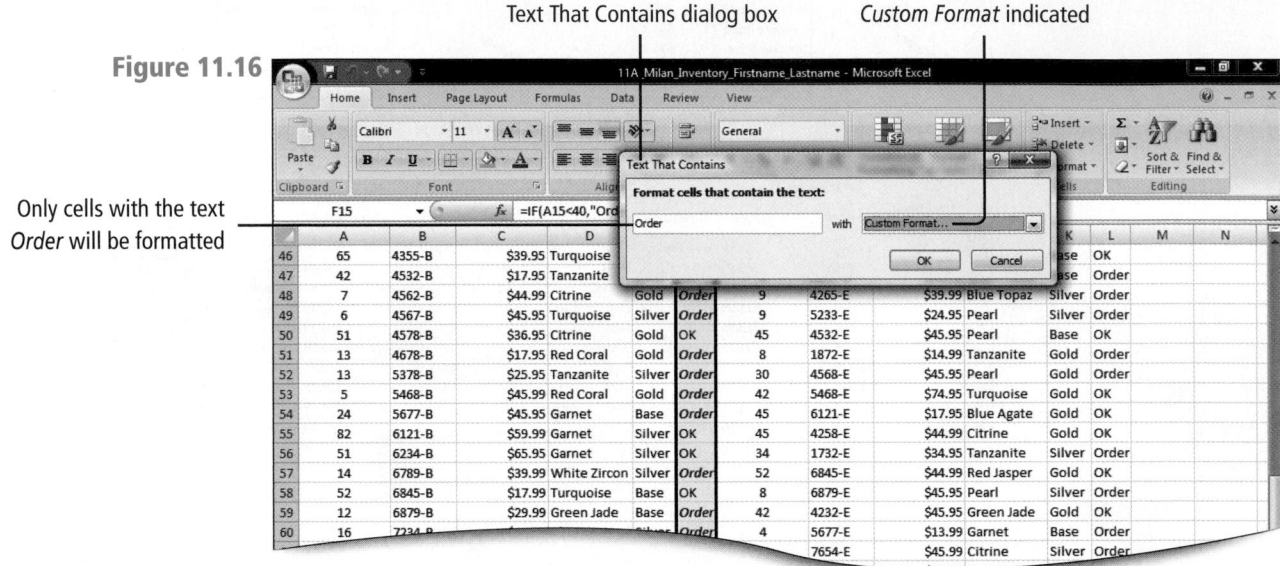

3 In the **Text That Contains** dialog box, click **OK** to apply the conditional formatting.

4 Select the range **A15:A69**. In the **Styles group**, click the **Conditional Formatting** button. In the displayed list, point to **Data Bars**, and then in the displayed gallery, click **Orange Data Bar**.

A **data bar** provides a visual cue to the reader about the value of a cell relative to other cells. The length of the data bar represents the value in the cell. A longer bar represents a higher value and a shorter bar represents a lower value. Data bars are useful to quickly identify higher and lower numbers within a large group of data, such as very high or very low levels of inventory.

5 Using the techniques you just practiced, apply the same conditional formatting to the *Stock Level* column for the **Earrings** product type, and then apply the same data bars to indicate the *Quantity of Stock* in inventory. Press [Ctrl] + [Home] to make cell **A1** the active cell, and then compare your screen with Figure 11.17.

Conditional font formatting applied to *Order*

Figure 11.17

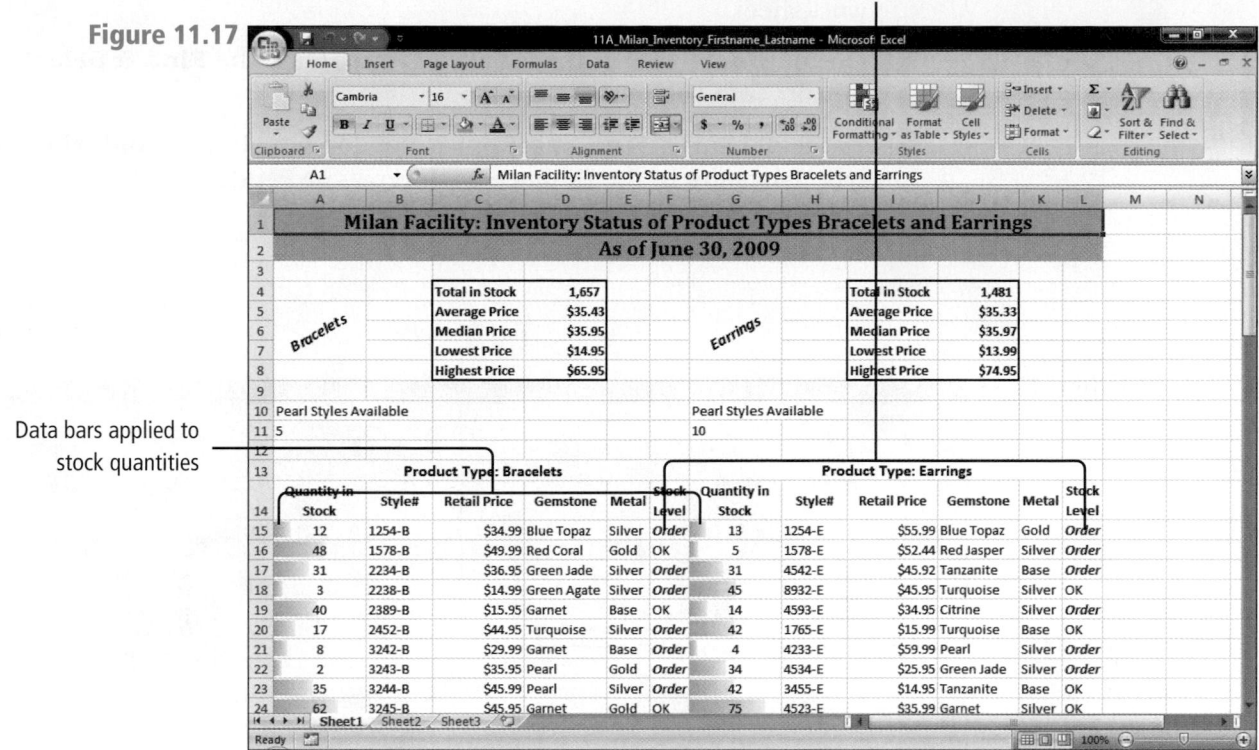

Data bars applied to stock quantities

---

6 **Save** 💾 your workbook.

More Knowledge

Use Format Painter to Copy Conditional Formatting

You can also use Format Painter to apply the same conditional formatting from one range of cells to another.

Activity 11.07 Using Find and Replace

The ***Find and Replace*** feature searches the cells in a worksheet—or in a selected range—for matches, and then replaces each match with a replacement value of your choice.

Rose was just informed that because a quality grade of Tanzanite was not readily available for manufacturing, the pieces listed as having a gemstone of Tanzanite were actually set with Peridot. In this activity, you will replace all occurrences of *Tanzanite* with *Peridot*.

1 To the left of the **Formula Bar**, click in the **Name Box**, type **d15:d69,j15:j64** and then press Enter. Alternatively, select the nonadjacent ranges of Gemstones with your mouse pointer.

The range of cells that contains the gemstone names for both product types is selected. Restrict the find and replace operation to a specific range if there is a possibility that the name occurs elsewhere in the worksheet.

2 On the **Home tab**, in the **Editing group**, click the **Find & Select** button, and then click **Replace**.

3 In the displayed **Find and Replace** dialog box, in the **Find what** box, type **Tanzanite** In the **Replace with** box type **Peridot** and then compare your screen with Figure 11.18.

Find *Tanzanite*

Find & Select button in the Editing group

Figure 11.18

Replace with *Peridot*

Replace All button

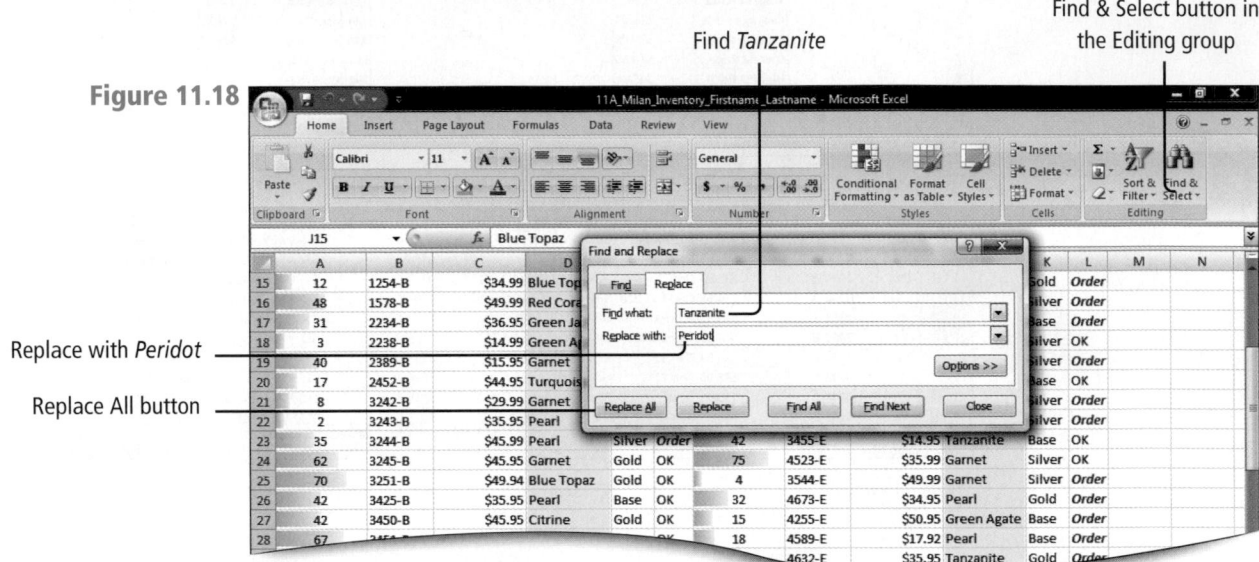

4 Click the **Replace All** button. In the displayed message box, notice that *12 replacements* were made, and then click **OK**. In the lower right corner of the **Find and Replace** dialog box, click the **Close** button. Click any cell to deselect the ranges.

5 **Save** 💾 your workbook.

Objective 3
Use a Date Function

Excel can obtain the date and time from the computer's calendar and clock and display this information on your worksheet.

Activity 11.08 Using the NOW Function

The **NOW function** retrieves the date and time from your computer's calendar and clock and inserts the information into the selected cell. The result is formatted as a date and time, rather than in the sequential number that Excel uses for dates. This feature is useful to date stamp a worksheet to record when it was last edited.

1 Scroll down to view **row 71**. Click cell **A71**, type **Last Edited by Rose Elleni** and then press Enter.

2 With cell **A72** as the active cell, on the **Formulas tab**, in the **Function Library group**, click the **Date & Time** button. In the displayed list of functions, click **NOW**. Compare your screen with Figure 11.19.

No specific arguments for this function

Figure 11.19

Function Arguments
dialog box for
NOW function

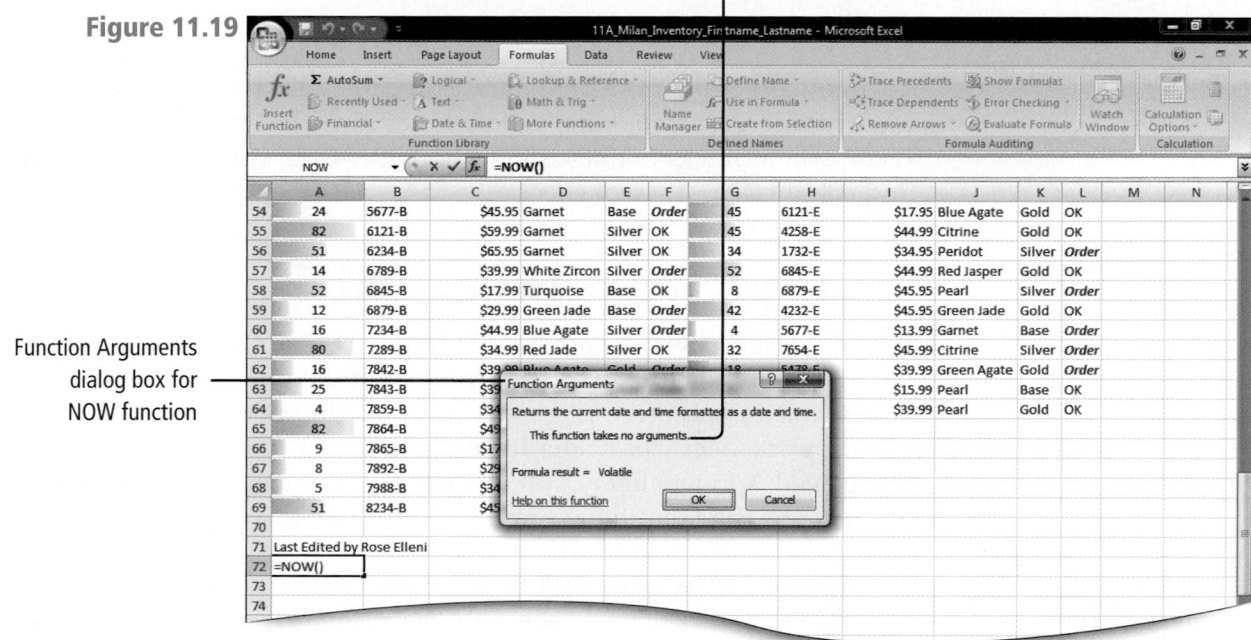

3 Take a moment to read the description in the displayed **Function Arguments** dialog box, and notice that this result is *Volatile*.

The Function Arguments dialog box displays a message indicating that this function does not require an argument. It also states that this function is **volatile**, meaning the date and time will not remain as entered, but rather the date and time will be updated each time you open this workbook.

4 In the **Function Arguments** dialog box, click **OK** to close the dialog box to display the current date and time in cell **A72**.

5 **Save** your workbook.

Note — NOW Function Recalculates When the Workbook Opens

The NOW function places a sequential number in the cell that corresponds to the date and time at the moment. The NOW function updates this number each time the workbook is opened. If you open a workbook with the NOW function in it and then close the workbook, you will see a message that asks if you want to save the changes. The change to which this message refers is the new date that has been inserted by the NOW function. With the workbook open, you can force the NOW function to update by pressing F9, for example, to update the time.

Objective 4
Freeze Panes and Create an Excel Table

By freezing or splitting panes, you can view two areas of a worksheet and lock rows and columns in one area. When you freeze panes, you select the specific rows or columns that you want to remain visible when scrolling in your worksheet.

To analyze a group of related data, you can convert a range of cells to an *Excel table*. An Excel table is a series of rows and columns that contains related data that is managed independently from the data in other rows and columns in the worksheet.

Activity 11.09 Freezing and Unfreezing Panes

In a large worksheet, if you scroll down more than 25 rows or scroll beyond column O (the exact row number and column letter varies, depending on your screen resolution), you will no longer see the top rows of your worksheet where identifying information about the data is usually placed. You will likely find it easier to work with your data if you can always view the identifying row or column titles.

The *Freeze Panes* command enables you to select one or more rows or columns and freeze (lock) them into place. The locked rows and columns become separate panes. A *pane* is a portion of a worksheet window bounded by and separated from other portions by vertical or horizontal bars.

1 Press Ctrl + Home to make cell **A1** the active cell. Scroll down until **row 40** displays at the top of your screen, and notice that all of the identifying information in the column titles is out of view.

2 Press Ctrl + Home again, and then select **row 15**. Click the **View tab**, and then in the **Window group**, click the **Freeze Panes** button. In the displayed list, click **Freeze Panes**. Click any cell to deselect the row, and then notice that a line displays along the upper border of **row 15**.

By selecting row 15, the rows above—rows 1–14—are frozen (locked) in place and will not move as you scroll down the worksheet.

3 Watch the row numbers below **row 14**, and then begin to scroll down to bring **row 40** into view again. Compare your screen with Figure 11.20.

Rows 1:14 remain frozen in place and the remaining rows of data continue to scroll. Use this feature when you have long or wide worksheets.

Figure 11.20

Freeze Panes button in Window group

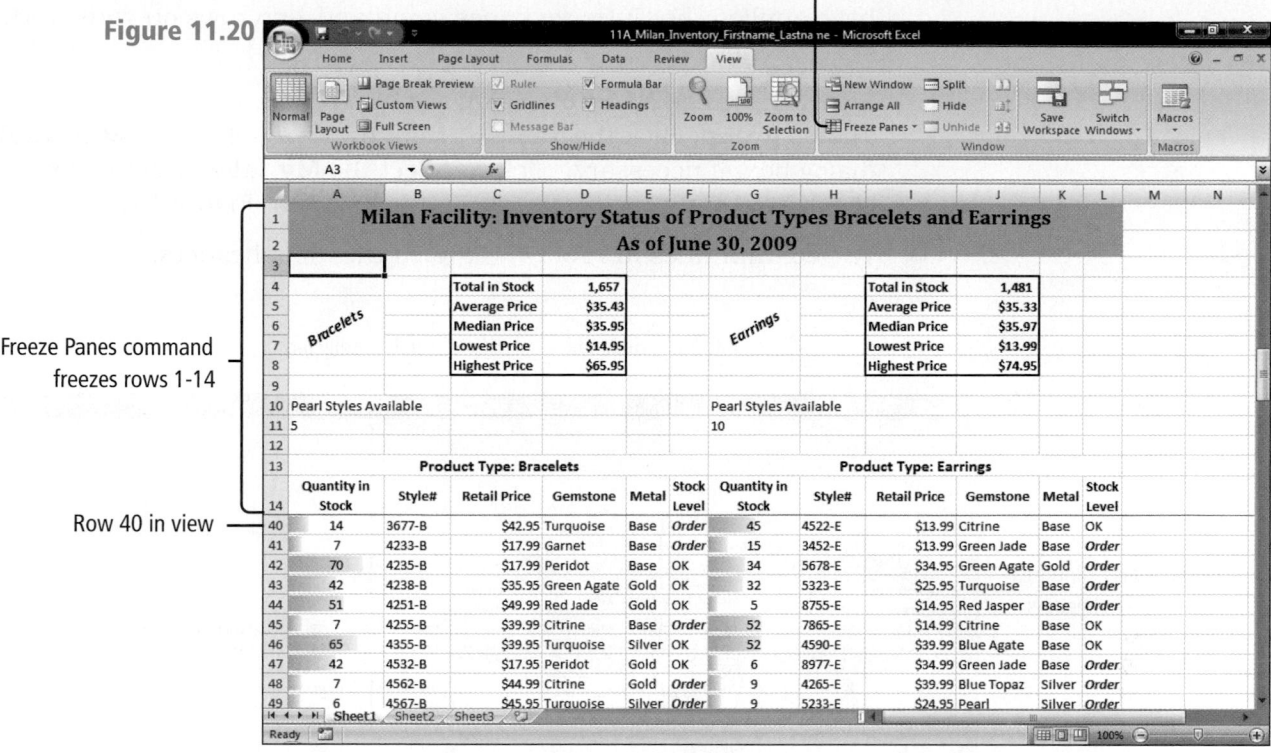

Freeze Panes command freezes rows 1-14

Row 40 in view

4 In the **Window group**, click the **Freeze Panes** button, and then click **Unfreeze Panes** to unlock all rows and columns.

5 **Save** your workbook.

More Knowledge

Freeze Columns or Freeze both Rows and Columns

You can freeze columns that you want to remain in view on the left. Select the column to the right of the column(s) that you want to remain in view while scrolling to the left, and then click the Freeze Panes command. You can also use the command to freeze both rows and columns; click a *cell* to freeze the rows *above* the cell and the columns to the *left* of the cell.

Activity 11.10 Sorting and Filtering In an Excel Table

Recall that an Excel table is a series of rows and columns with related data that can be managed independently from the data in other rows and columns. For example, in your 11A_Milan_Inventory workbook, you have data for two product types—*Bracelets* and *Earrings*.

To manage several groups of data, you can insert more than one table in the same worksheet. In Activities 11.10 and 11.11, you will create an Excel table for each of the two product types, and then work with each set of data independently of the other.

1 Press `Ctrl` + `Home` to make cell **A1** the active cell. Be sure that you have applied the Unfreeze Panes command—no rows on your worksheet are locked.

2 Select the range **A14:F69**. Click the **Insert tab**, and then in the **Tables group**, click the **Table** button. In the displayed **Create Table** dialog box, if necessary, click to select the **My table has headers** check box, and then compare your screen with Figure 11.21.

The column titles in row 14 will form the table headers.

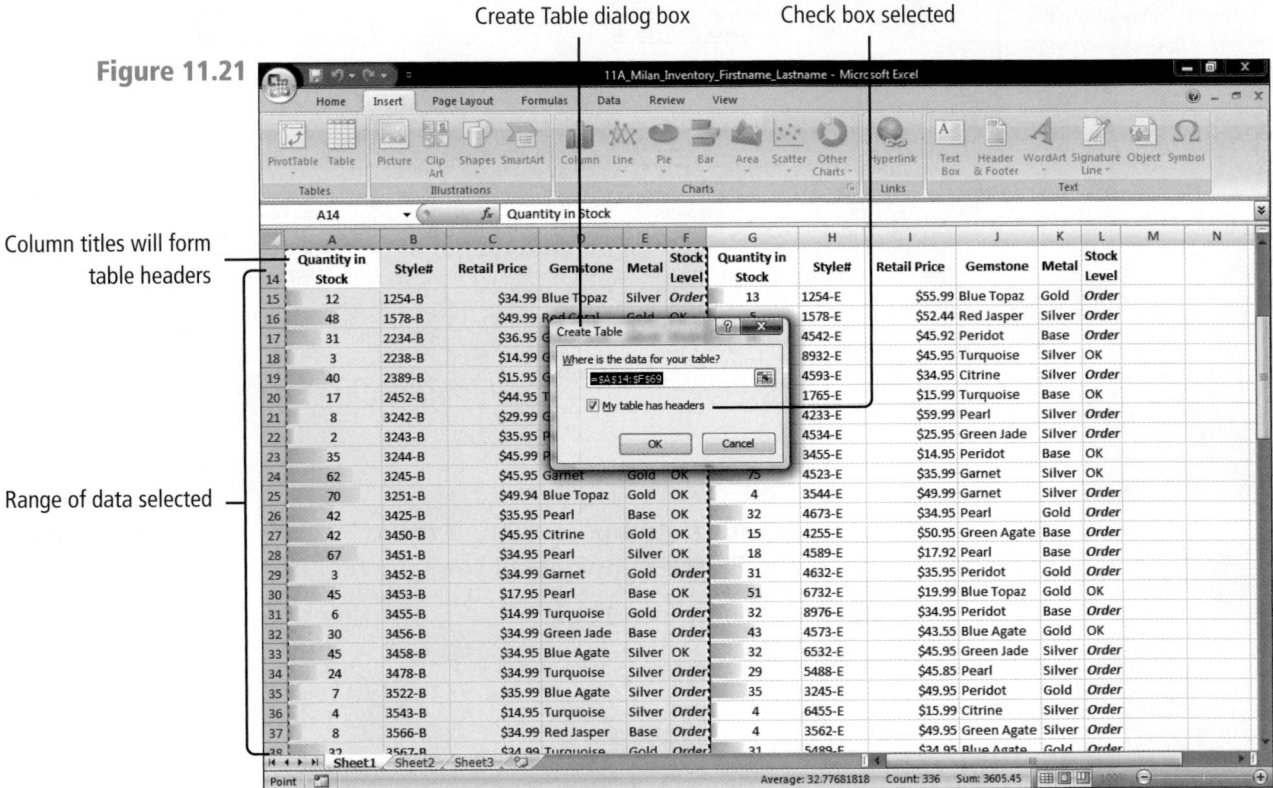

Figure 11.21

Create Table dialog box

Check box selected

Column titles will form table headers

Range of data selected

3 In the **Create Table** dialog box, click **OK**. With the range still selected, on the Ribbon notice that the **Table Tools** are active. On the **Design tab**, in the **Table Styles group**, click the **More** button, and then under **Light**, locate and click **Table Style Light 16**. Press `Ctrl` + `Home` to make cell **A1** the active cell and to cancel the selection, and then compare your screen with Figure 11.22.

Sorting and filtering arrows display in the table's header row. You can sort tables in ascending or descending order or by color. You can filter tables to show only the data that meets the criteria that you specify, or you can filter by color.

Figure 11.22

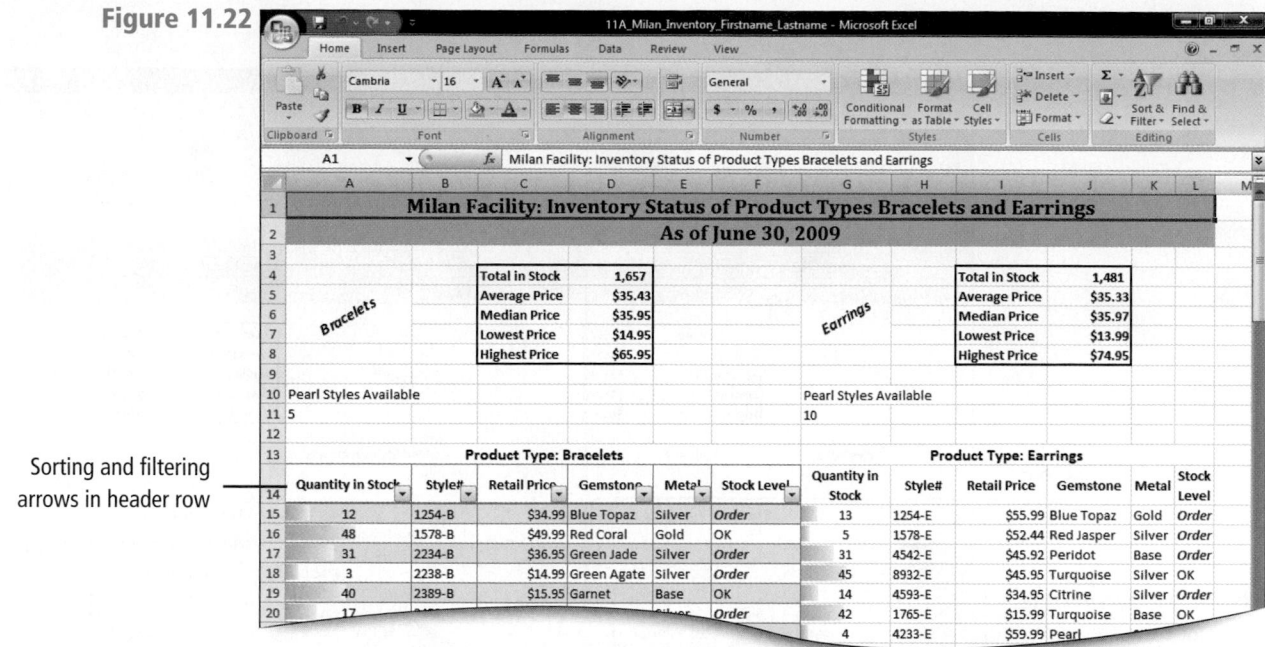

Sorting and filtering arrows in header row

4 In the header row of the table, click the **Retail Price arrow**, and then from the displayed menu, click **Sort Smallest to Largest**. Next to the arrow, notice the small **up arrow** indicating the sort.

The rows in the table, which includes only columns A:F, are sorted from the lowest retail price to highest retail price. Cells in the same rows in columns G:L are not affected by the sort because the table feature isolates the table cells and treats them independently of other cells outside of the table.

5 In the header row of the table, click the **Gemstone arrow**. From the displayed menu, click **Sort A to Z**. Next to the arrow, notice the small **up arrow** indicating an ascending (A to Z) sort.

The rows in the table are sorted alphabetically by Gemstone.

6 Click the **Gemstone arrow** again, and then sort from **Z to A**.

The rows in the table are sorted in reverse alphabetic order by Gemstone name, and the small arrow points downward, indicating a descending (Z to A) sort.

7 Click the **Gemstone arrow** again. On the displayed menu, click the **(Select All)** check box to clear all the check boxes. Click to select only the **Pearl** check box, and then click **OK**. Compare your screen with Figure 11.23.

Only the rows containing *Pearl* in the Gemstone column display, and the remaining rows are hidden from view. A small funnel in the Gemstone arrow indicates that a filter is applied to the data in the table. Additionally, the row numbers display in blue to indicate that some rows are hidden from view. A filter hides the entire row in the worksheet.

Only bracelets that have *Pearl* as the gemstone display

Figure 11.23

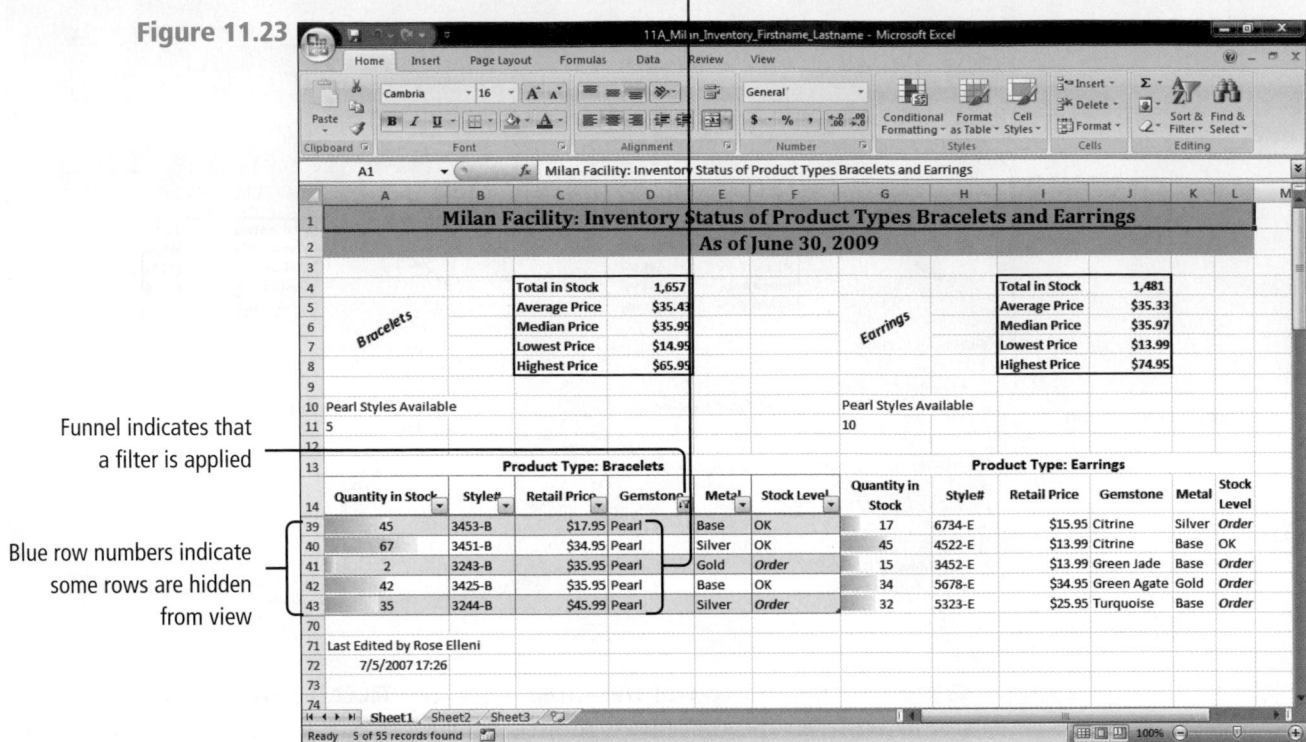

Funnel indicates that a filter is applied

Blue row numbers indicate some rows are hidden from view

8 Click any cell in the table so that the table is selected. On the Ribbon, click the **Design tab**, and then in the **Table Style Options group**, click to select the **Total Row** check box.

Total displays in cell A70, and in cell F70, the number *5* indicates that five rows are currently displayed.

9 Click cell **A70**, click the arrow that displays to the right of cell A70, and then in the displayed list, click **Sum**.

Excel sums only the visible rows in Column A, and indicates that *191* bracelets containing the Gemstone *Pearl* are in stock. In this manner, you can use an Excel table to quickly find information about a group of data.

10 Click cell **A11**, type **Five styles, 191 total in stock** and then press Enter.

11 In the table header row, click the **Gemstone arrow**, and then in the displayed menu, click **Clear Filter From "Gemstone"**.

All the rows in the table redisplay. The Z to A sort on Gemstone remains in effect.

12 Click the **Metal arrow**, click the **(Select All)** check box to clear all the check boxes, and then click to select the **Gold** check box. Click **OK**. Click the **Gemstone arrow**, click the **(Select All)** check box to clear all the check boxes, and then click the **Red Coral** check box. Click **OK**, and then compare your screen with Figure 11.24.

By applying multiple filters, Rose can quickly determine that among the Bracelets product type, four styles have a Red Coral gemstone in a Gold setting and there are 117 total in stock.

Four bracelet styles have *Red Coral* as *Gemstone* and *Gold* as *Metal*

Figure 11.24

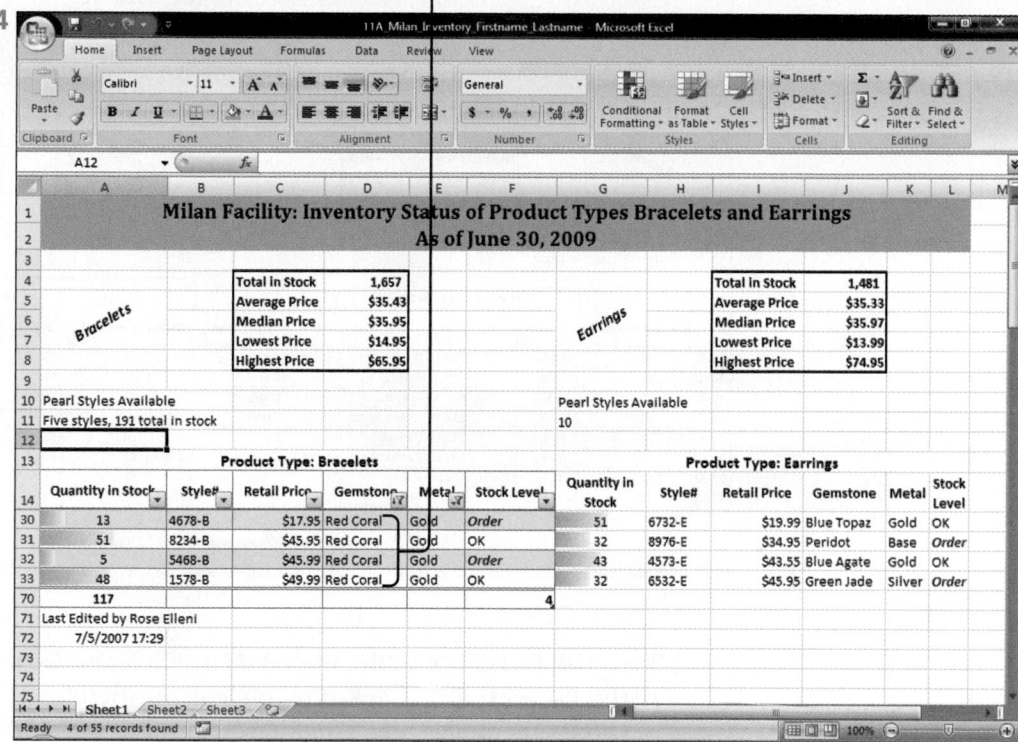

13 Click the **Gemstone arrow**, and then click **Clear Filter from "Gemstone"**. Use the same technique to remove the filter from the **Metal** column.

14 In the table header row, click the **Style# arrow**, and then click **Sort A to Z**, which will apply an ascending sort to the *Style#* column.

15 **Save** the changes to your workbook.

Activity 11.11 Inserting a Second Table in a Worksheet

In this activity, you will format the product information for *Earrings* as a table.

1 Select the range **G14:L64**. On the **Insert tab**, in the **Tables group**, click the **Table** button. Be sure the **My table has headers** check box is selected, and then click **OK**. In the **Table Styles group**, click the

More button , and then under **Light**, click **Table Style Light 18**. Press Ctrl + Home, and then compare your screen with Figure 11.25.

Figure 11.25

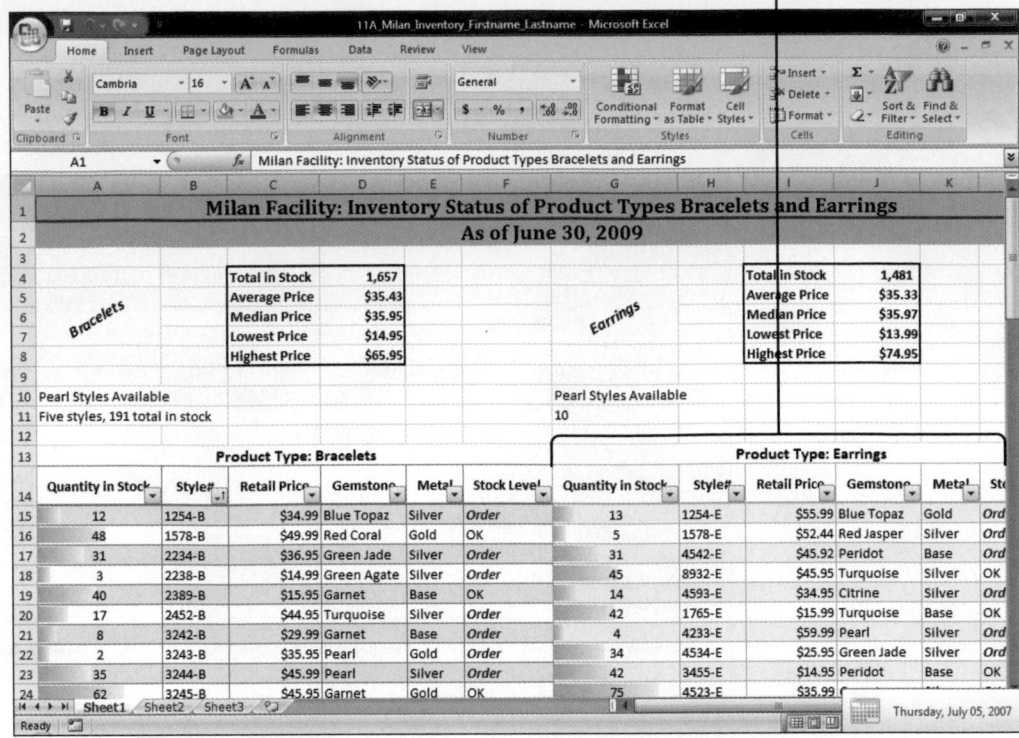

2 In the **Earrings** table, in cell **J14**, click the **Gemstone arrow**, click the **(Select All)** check box to clear all the check boxes, and then click the **Pearl** check box. Click **OK**. Scroll down and to the right as necessary so that you can view the table on your screen.

In the worksheet, rows within the Earrings table that do not contain *Pearl* as the gemstone are hidden.

3 Click any cell in the **Earrings** table to select the table, click the **Design tab**, and then in the **Table Style Options group**, click to select the **Total Row** check box.

Total displays in cell G65, and in cell L65, the number *10* indicates that ten rows are currently displayed.

4 Click cell **G65**, click the arrow that displays to the right of cell G65, and then in the displayed list, click **Sum**. Compare your screen with Figure 11.26.

Excel sums only the visible rows in Column G, and indicates that *309* earrings containing the Gemstone *Pearl* are in stock. Recall that in this manner, you can use an Excel table to quickly find information about a group of data.

Figure 11.26

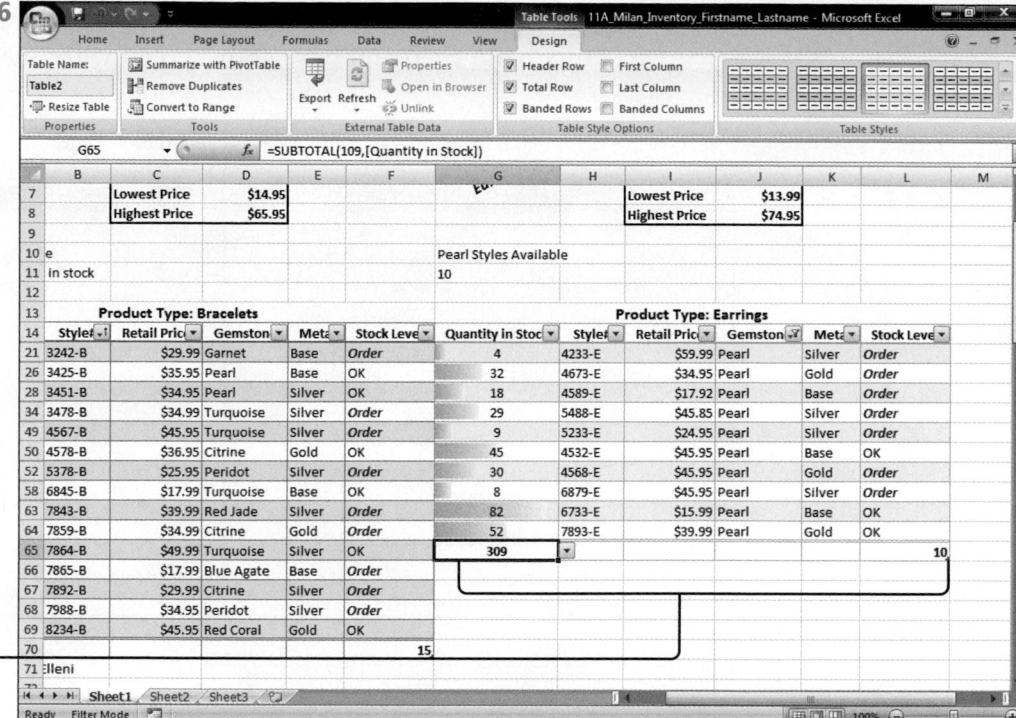

309 total Pearl earrings in stock; 10 Pearl styles

5 Click cell **G11**, type **Ten styles, 309 total pairs in stock** and then press Enter.

6 In the table header row, click the **Gemstone arrow**, and then in the displayed menu, click **Clear Filter From "Gemstone"** to redisplay all the rows in the table.

7 In the table header row of the **Earrings** table, click the **Style# arrow**, and then click **Sort A to Z**, which will apply an ascending sort to the **Style#** column.

8 **Save** 💾 the changes to your workbook.

Activity 11.12 Converting a Table to a Range of Data

When you are finished answering questions about the data in a table by sorting, filtering, and totaling, you no longer need the table. You can remove a table by converting it back to a normal range.

1 Click anywhere in the **Bracelets** table to activate the table and display the **Table Tools** on the Ribbon.

2 On the **Design tab**, in the **Tools group**, click the **Convert to Range** button. In the displayed message box, click **Yes**.

The list arrows are removed from the column titles; the color and shading formats applied from the table style remain.

3 Use the technique you just practiced to convert the **Earrings** table to a range, and then compare your screen with Figure 11.27.

Both tables converted to a range

Figure 11.27

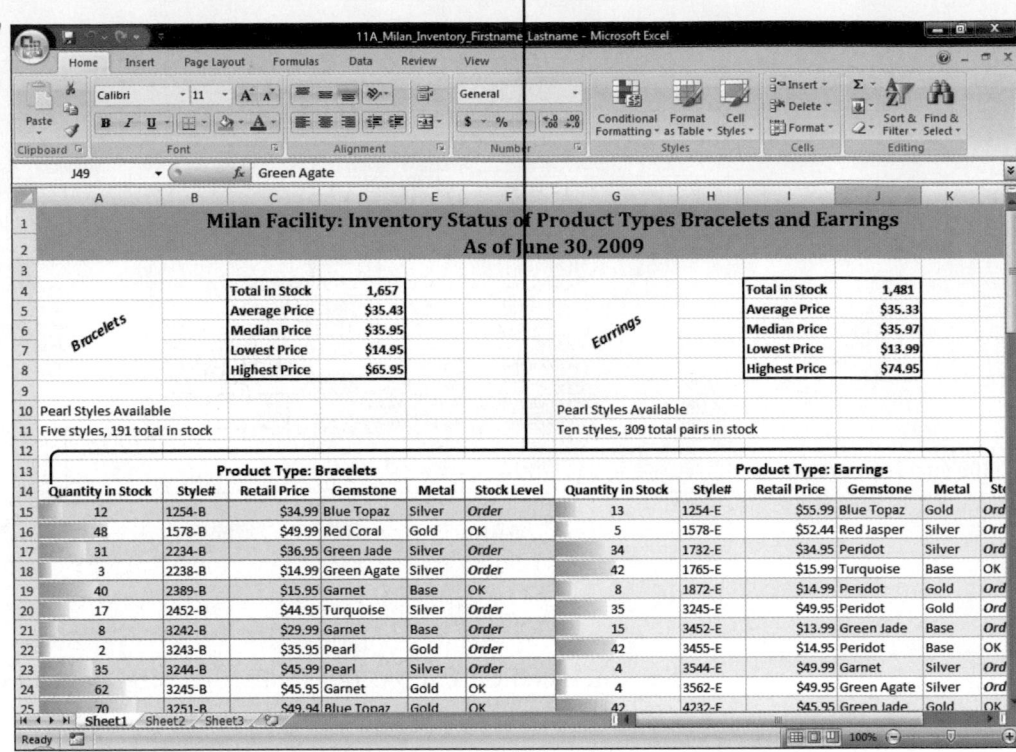

4 Save your workbook.

More Knowledge

To Remove Shading Formats From a Table

If you do not want to retain the shading and other formats applied from a table style, apply the *None* table style before converting back to a range.

Objective 5
Format and Print a Large Worksheet

A large worksheet will be too wide, too long—or both—to print on a single page. To make reading multiple printed pages easier, Excel features let you print row and column headings on each page of a worksheet.

Activity 11.13 Printing Large Worksheets

In this activity, you will adjust the column widths, change the Page Layout so that column titles display on every page, and print the worksheet.

1 Hold down Ctrl, select the nonadjacent **columns C** and **I**, and then set their width to **90 pixels**. Select **column A**, hold down Ctrl and select columns **D**, **G**, and **J**, and then set their width to **80 pixels**. Select **column B**, hold down Ctrl and select **column H**, and then set their width to **70 pixels**.

2 Select **columns E**, **F**, **K**, and **L** and set their width to **55 pixels**. Select the range **A72:B72**, right-click, click **Format Cells**, and then on the **Alignment tab** of the **Format Cells** dialog box, under **Text control**, select the **Merge cells** check box. Click **OK**.

The merged cell is widened so that it can display the result of the NOW function that it contains.

3 Select the column titles in **Row 14**, and then on the **Home tab,** in the **Alignment group**, click the **Wrap Text** button ![wrap text icon]. Look at the column titles in Row 14 and either verify that the the full column titles display in each cell, or if necessary, click the **Wrap Text** button again so that the full titles display.

4 Press Ctrl + Home to display the top of your worksheet.

5 On the **Insert tab**, in the **Text group**, click **Header & Footer** to switch to **Page Layout view**. In the **Navigation group**, click the **Go to Footer** button, click just above the word *Footer*, and then in the **Header & Footer Elements group**, click the **File Name** button. Click a cell just above the footer to deselect the **Footer area** and view your file name.

6 Click the **Page Layout tab**. In the **Page Setup group**, click the **Orientation** button, and then click **Landscape**. In the same group, click the **Print Titles** button. Under **Print titles**, click in the **Rows to repeat at top** box, and then at the right, click the **Collapse Dialog** button ![collapse dialog icon]. From the **row heading area**, select **rows 13:14**, and then compare your screen with Figure 11.28.

Collapsed dialog box displays
the row numbers as an absolute reference

Figure 11.28

Rows 13 and 14 selected;
surrounded by moving border

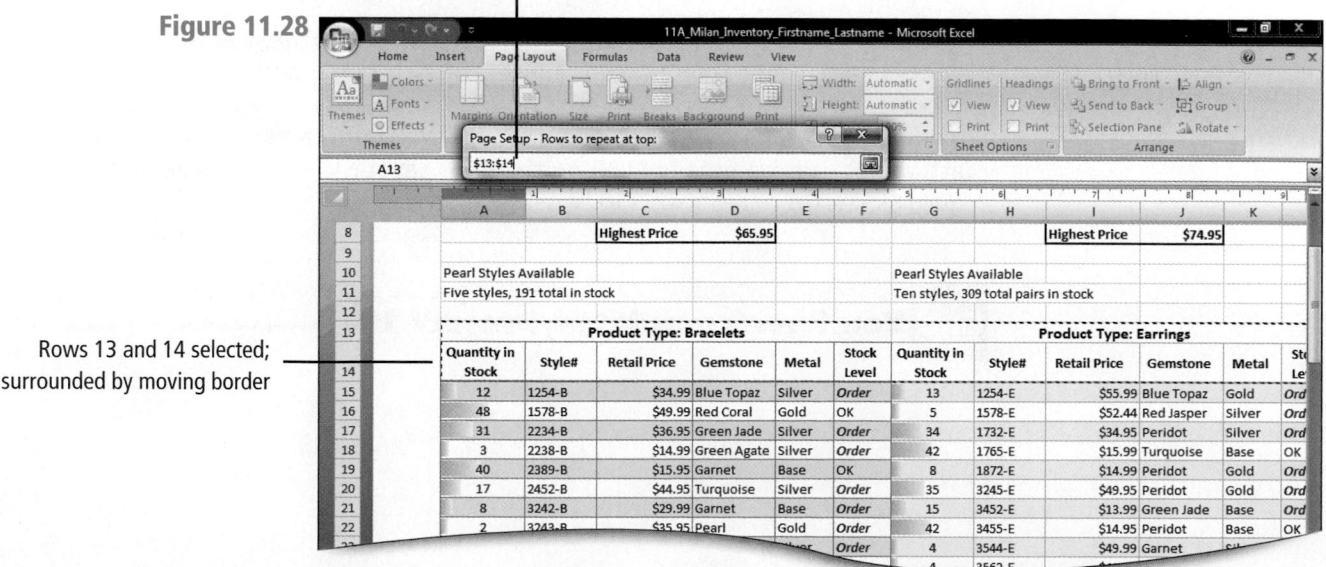

7 Press Enter, and then in the displayed **Page Setup** dialog box, click the **Margins tab**. Under **Center on page**, select the **Horizontally** check box, and then click **OK**. Delete the unused sheets **Sheet2** and **Sheet3**. On the right edge of the status bar, click the **Normal** button ▦, and then press Ctrl + Home to display the top of your worksheet.

8 From the **Office** menu 🔘, point to **Print**, and then click **Print Preview**. On your screen, it is possible that the *Earrings Stock Level* column does not display. In the **Preview Group**, click **Next Page** several times to determine if the *Stock Level column* displays on separate pages. Close the **Print Preview**.

9 If necessary, on the **Page Layout tab**, in the **Scale to Fit group**, click the **Width button arrow**, and then click **1 page**.

Excel will make the necessary adjustments to fit the worksheet columns to one page.

10 **Save** 💾 your workbook. To submit electronically, follow the instructions provided by your instructor. To print, from the **Office** menu 🔘, point to the **Print** button, and then click **Print Preview**. In the **Preview group**, click the **Next Page** and **Previous Page** buttons as necessary to view and check each page. Be sure the two header rows and the footer display on each page, and then click the **Print** button. In the displayed **Print** dialog box, under **Print range**, be sure that **All** is selected, and then click **OK**. If you are directed to submit printed formulas, refer to Activity 5.17 to do so.

11 If you printed your formulas, be sure to redisplay the worksheet by pressing Ctrl + `. From the **Office** menu, click **Close**. If the dialog box displays asking if you want to save changes, click **No** so that you do *not* save the changes you made for printing formulas. **Close** Excel.

More Knowledge

Adjust Scaling for Data That is Slightly Larger Than the Printed Page

If your data is just a little too large to fit on a printed page, you can scale the worksheet to make it fit. Scaling reduces the horizontal and vertical size of the printed data to a percentage of its original size or by the number of pages that you specify. To adjust the printed output to a percentage of its actual size, for example to 80%, on the Page Layout tab, in the Scale to Fit group, click the Scale arrows to select a percentage.

End You have completed Project 11A ——————

Project 11B Loan Payment

In Activities 11.14 through 11.19, you will create a worksheet for Wattana Dithasaro, International Sales Director, that details the loan information to purchase furniture and fixtures for a new Adamantine Jewelry store in Mexico City. Wattana plans to borrow money to pay for the new store furniture and fixtures, and then pay off the loan in monthly payments. She must decide how to arrange the loan to buy the furniture and fixtures she needs and still keep the monthly payment within her budget for new store openings. You will create a worksheet containing payments for combinations of time periods and interest rates so Wattana can identify what range of rates and time periods will meet her requirements. The worksheets of your workbook will look similar to Figure 11.29.

For Project 11B, you will need the following file:

New blank Excel workbook

You will save your workbook as
11B_New_Store_Loan_Firstname_Lastname

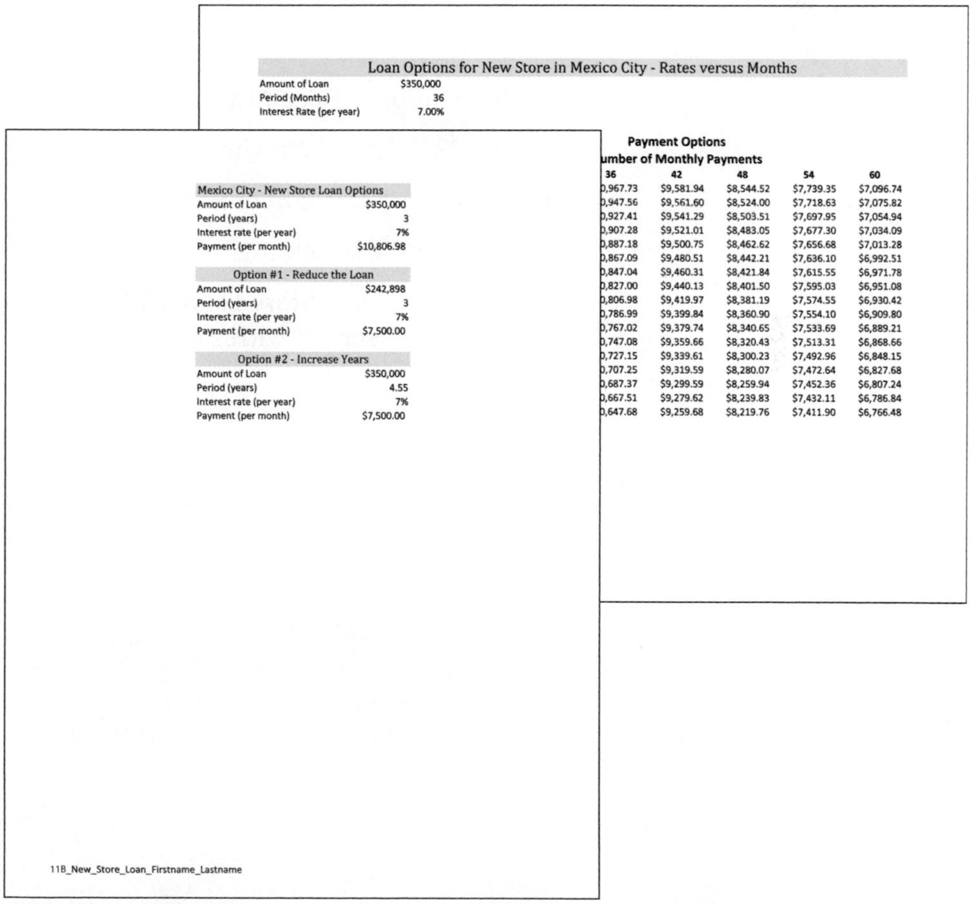

Figure 11.29
Project 11B—Loan Payment

Objective 6
Use Financial Functions

Financial functions perform common business calculations such as calculating a loan payment on a vehicle or calculating how much to save each month to buy something. Financial functions commonly involve a period of time such as months or years.

Activity 11.14 Designing a Loan Worksheet

1 **Start** Excel and display a new blank workbook. From the **Office** menu 🗔, display the **Save As** dialog box, navigate to your **Excel Chapter 11** folder, and then in the **File name** box, name the file **11B_New_Store_Loan_Firstname_Lastname**

2 Widen **column A** to **180 pixels** and **column B** to **100 pixels**. In the range **A2:B5**, enter the following row titles and data. Recall that you can format the numbers as you type by typing them with their symbols as shown:

Amount of Loan	$350,000
Period (years)	3
Interest rate (per year)	7%
Payment (per month)	

3 In cell **A1**, type **Mexico City - New Store Loan Options Merge and Center** 🔲 ▾ the title in the range **A1:B1**, add a **Fill Color** of **Olive Green, Accent 3, Lighter 60%**, change the **Font** [Calibri ▾] to **Cambria**, and then change the **Font Size** [11 ▾] to **12**. Rename the worksheet tab **New Store Loan** and then **Save** 🖫 your workbook. Compare your screen with Figure 11.30.

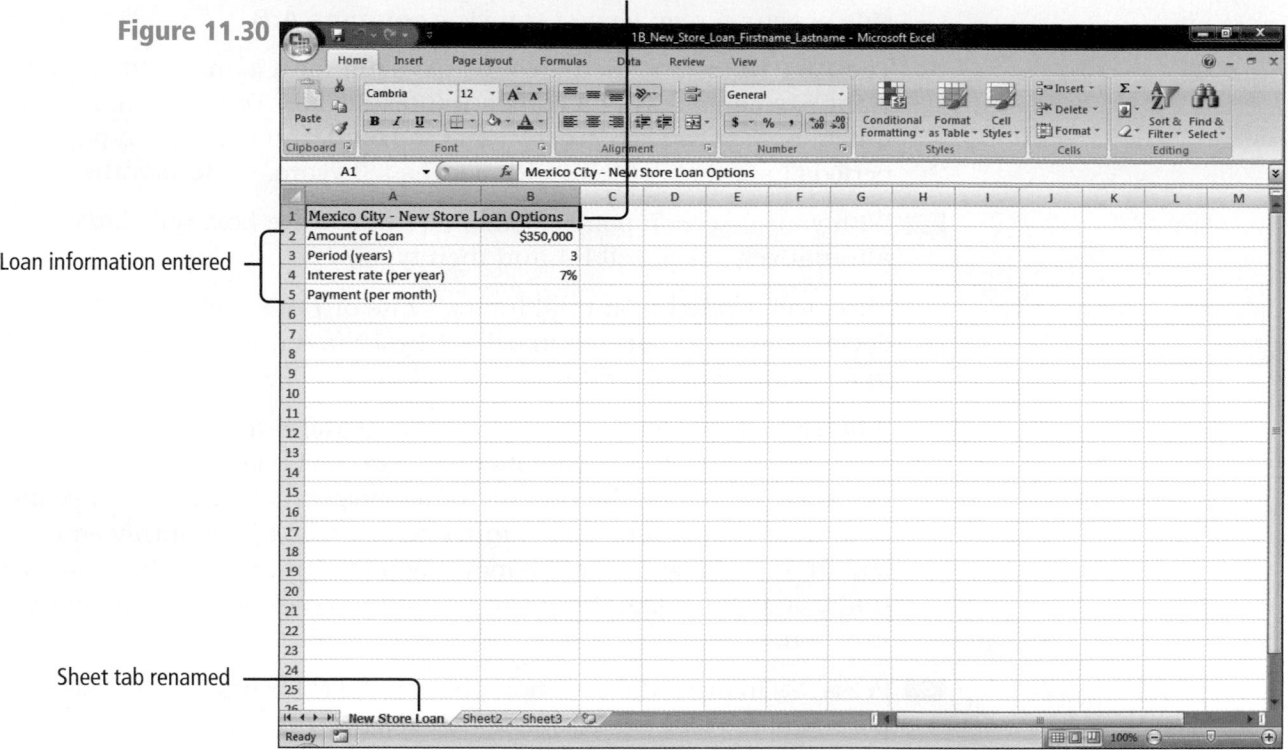

Worksheet title centered with fill color

Figure 11.30

Loan information entered

Sheet tab renamed

Activity 11.15 Inserting the PMT Financial Function

When you borrow money from a bank or a similar lending institution, the amount charged to you for your use of the borrowed money is called *interest*. Loans are typically made for a period of years, and the interest that must be paid is a percentage of the loan amount that is still owed. In Excel, this percentage is called the *rate*. The initial amount of the loan is called the *Present value (Pv)*, which is the total amount that a series of future payments is worth now, and is also known as the *principal*. When you borrow money, the loan amount is the *present value* to the lender. The number of time periods—number of payments—is abbreviated *nper*. The value at the end of the time periods is the *Future value (Fv)*—the cash balance you want to attain after the last payment is made. The future value is usually zero for loans.

In this activity, you will calculate the monthly payments that Adamantine Jewelry will have to make to finance the purchase of the furniture and fixtures for the new store in Mexico City, the total cost of which is $350,000. You will calculate the monthly payments, including interest, for a three-year loan at an annual interest rate of 7.0%. To stay within Wattana's budget, the monthly payment must be approximately $7,500.

1 Click cell **B5**. On the **Formulas tab**, in the **Function Library group**, click the **Financial** button. In the displayed list, scroll down as necessary, and then click **PMT**.

The Function Arguments dialog box displays. Recall that arguments are the values that an Excel function uses to perform calculations or operations.

2 If necessary, drag the **Function Arguments** dialog box to the right side of your screen so you can view **columns A:B**.

The *PMT function* calculates the payment for a loan based on constant payments and at a constant interest rate. To complete the PMT function, first you must determine the total number of loan payment periods (months), which is 12 months × 3 years, or 36 months.

3 With your insertion point positioned in the **Rate** box, type **b4/12** Alternatively, click cell B4 and then type */12*.

Excel will divide the annual interest rate of 7%, which is 0.070 in decimal notation, located in cell B4 by 12 (months), which will result in a *monthly* interest rate.

When borrowing money, the interest rate and number of periods are quoted in years. The payments on a loan, however, are usually made monthly. Therefore, the number of periods, which is stated in years, and the *annual* interest rate, must be changed to a monthly equivalent in order to calculate the monthly payment amount. You can see that calculations like these can be made as part of the argument in a function.

4 Press Tab to move the insertion point to the **Nper** box. In the lower portion of the dialog box, notice that *Nper is the total number of payments for the loan* (number of periods). Type **b3*12** to have Excel convert the number of years in the loan (3) to the total number of months.

Recall that the PMT function calculates a *monthly* payment. Thus, all values in the function must be expressed in months.

5 Press Tab to move to the **Pv** box, and then type **b2**

Pv represents the present value—the amount of the loan before any payments are made—in this instance $350,000.

6 In cell **B5** and on the **Formula Bar**, notice that the arguments that comprise the PMT function are separated by commas. Notice also, in the **Function Arguments** dialog box, that the value of each argument displays to the right of the argument box. Compare your screen with Figure 11.31.

Figure 11.31

Cell references entered for PMT function   Argument values

Formula displayed in
Formula Bar; arguments
separated by commas

Optional arguments

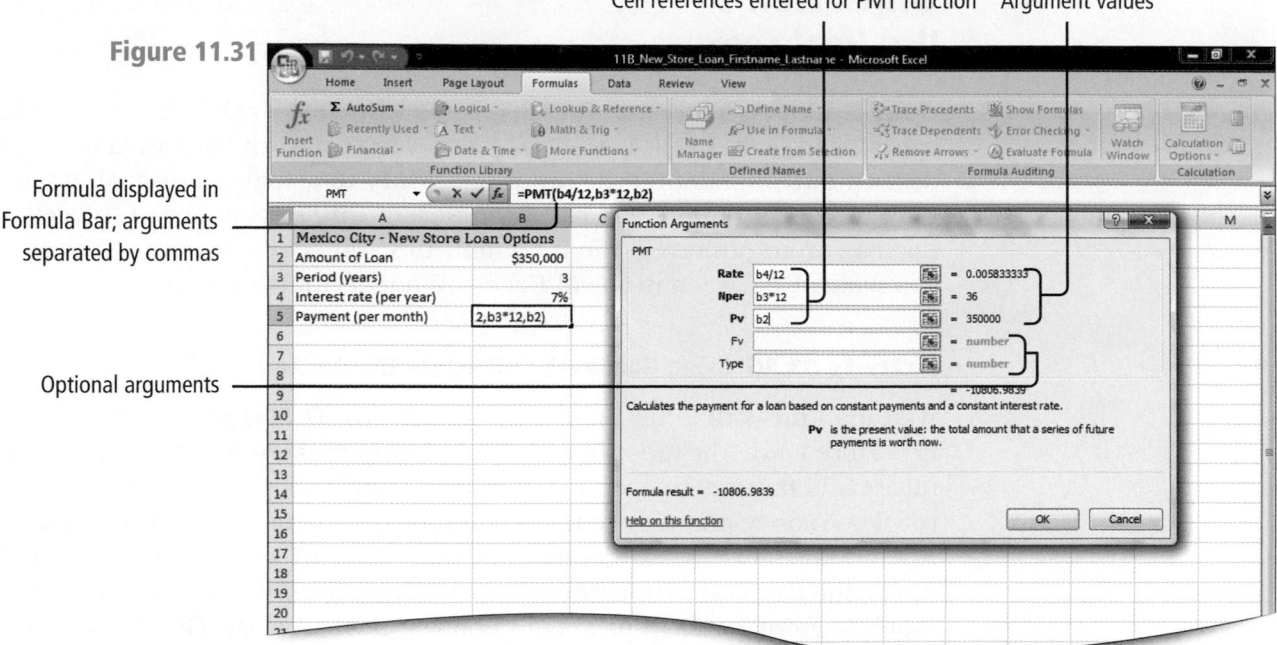

Note — Optional Arguments

The PMT function has two arguments not indicated by bold; these are optional. The Future value (Fv) argument assumes that the unpaid portion of the loan should be zero at the end of the last period. The *Type argument* assumes that the payment will be made at the end of each period. These default values are typical of most loans and may be left blank.

7 In the displayed dialog box, click **OK**.

The monthly payment amount, ($10,806.98), displays in cell B5. The amount displays in red and in parentheses to show that it is a negative number, a number that will be *paid out*. This monthly payment of $10,806.98 is over the budget of $7,500 per month that Wattana has in mind.

8 Click in the **Formula Bar**, and then use the arrow keys on the keyboard as necessary to position the insertion point between the equal sign and *PMT*. Type – (minus sign) to insert a minus sign into the formula, and then press [Enter]. **Save** your workbook.

By placing a minus sign in the formula, the monthly payment amount, $10,806.98, displays in cell B5 as a *positive* number, which is more familiar and less distracting to work with.

Objective 7
Use Goal Seek

Goal Seek is a method to find a specific value for a cell by adjusting the value of one other cell. With Goal Seek, you can work backward from the desired outcome to find the input necessary to achieve your goal. If you have a result in mind, you can try different numbers in one of the cells used as an argument in the function until you get close to the answer you want. Goal Seek is one of Excel's What-If Analysis tools.

Activity 11.16 Using Goal Seek to Produce the Desired Result

Wattana knows that her budget cannot exceed $7,500 per month for the new store loan. The amount of $350,000 is necessary to purchase the furniture and fixtures to open the new store. Now she has two options—borrow less money and reduce the amount or quality of the furniture and fixtures in the store, or extend the time to repay the loan. To find out how much she can borrow for three years to stay within the budget, or how much to increase the repayment period, you will use the Goal Seek tool.

1 Click cell **B5**. On the **Data tab**, in the **Data Tools group**, click the **What-If Analysis** button, and then in the displayed list, click **Goal Seek**. In the displayed **Goal Seek** dialog box, in the **Set cell** box, confirm that *B5* displays.

The cell address in this box is the cell that displays the desired result.

2 Press ⇥Tab. In the **To value** box, type the payment goal of **7500.00** and press ⇥Tab. In the **By changing cell** box, type **b2** which is the amount of the loan, and then compare your dialog box with Figure 11.32. Alternatively, you can click cell B2.

In the By changing cell box, if you click cell B2, Excel will make the cell reference absolute.

Figure 11.32

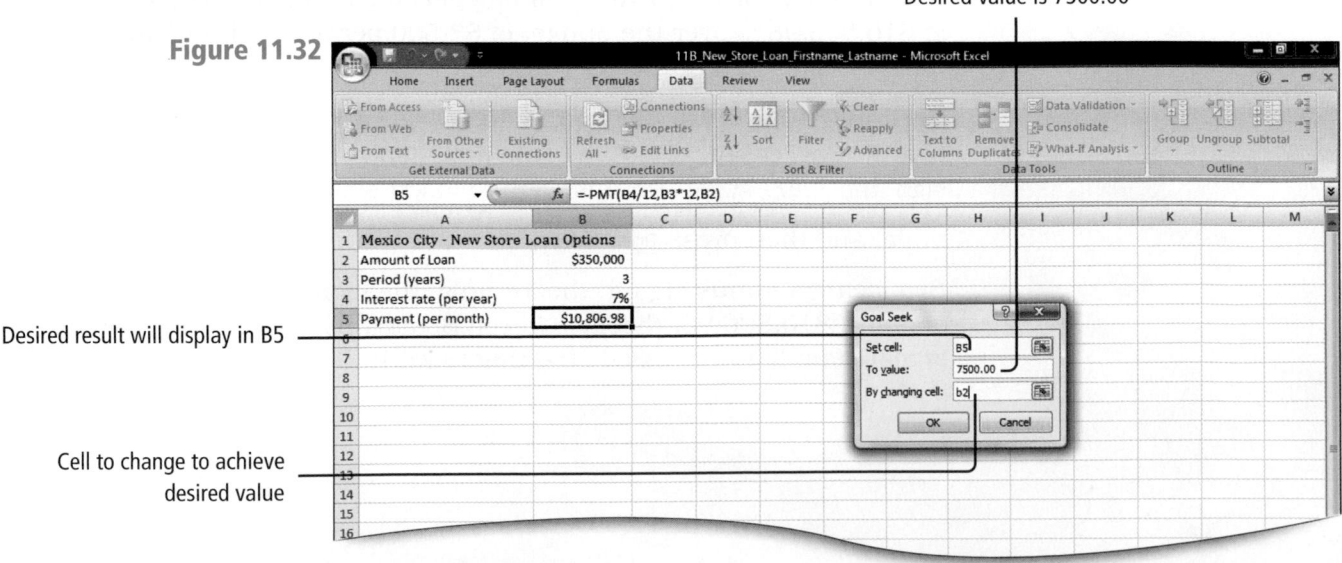

Desired value is 7500.00

Desired result will display in B5

Cell to change to achieve desired value

3 In the displayed **Goal Seek** dialog box, click **OK**. In the displayed **Goal Seek Status** dialog box, click **OK**.

Excel's calculations indicate that to achieve a monthly payment of $7,500.00 using a 3-year loan, Wattana can borrow only *$242,898*—not $350,000.

4 Click cell **A7**. Type **Option #1 - Reduce the Loan** and press Enter. Right-click cell **A7**. On the Mini toolbar, apply a **Fill Color**  of **Olive Green, Accent 3, Lighter 60%**, change the **Font** Calibri to **Cambria** and the **Font Size** 11 to **12**. **Merge and Center** the title across the range **A7:B7**.

5 Select the range **A2:B5**, right-click, and then click **Copy**. Click cell **A8**, right-click, and then from the shortcut menu, click **Paste Special**. In the **Paste Special** dialog box, under **Paste**, click the **Values and number formats** option button, and then click **OK**.

Press Esc to cancel the moving border. **Save** your workbook, click anywhere to deselect, and then compare your worksheet with Figure 11.33.

Recall that with the Paste Special command, you can copy the *value* in a cell, rather than the formula, and the cell formats are retained—cell B5 contains the PMT function formula, and here you need only the value that *results* from that formula.

Values and formats pasted

Figure 11.33

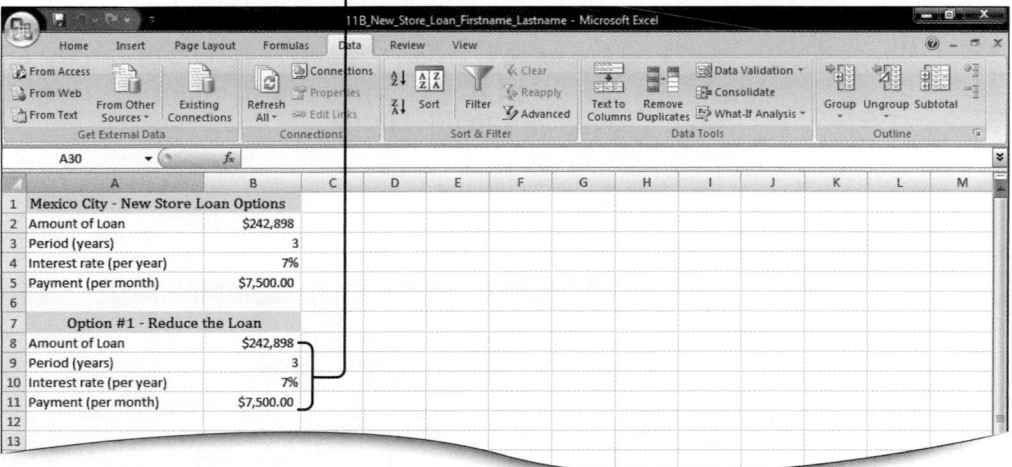

Savings Accounts—Using the Future Value Function

Another commonly used financial function, similar to the PMT function, is the Future Value function. The function has three required arguments: Rate, Nper, and Pmt. The Rate argument is the interest rate paid to you by the financial institution; the Nper is the number of periods; and Pmt is the amount you deposit into the account each period. The function also has two optional arguments—Pv and Type. The Pv argument is the amount you start with in the account. Excel assumes this is zero if you do not provide a starting amount. The Type argument assumes that the payment is made at the beginning of the time period.

For example, in the FV Function Arguments dialog box, enter a rate of 6%/12 (6% annually divided by 12 months), enter 60 (5 years or 60 months) as the number of periods, enter 100 ($100) as the monthly deposit you will make, and enter a present value of 1500 ($1,500 opening deposit in the account). Excel will calculate that at the end of 5 years, you will have $9,000.28 in your savings account.

Activity 11.17 Using Goal Seek to Find an Increased Period

For Wattana's purchase of furniture and fixtures for the new store in Mexico City, an alternative to borrowing less money—which would mean buying fewer items or items of lesser quality—would be to increase the number of years of payments.

1 In cell **B2**, type **350000** and then press Enter to restore the original loan amount. Click cell **B5**. On the **Data tab**, in the **Data Tools group**, click the **What-If Analysis** button, and then click **Goal Seek**.

2 In the **Set cell** box, confirm that **B5** displays. Press Tab. In the **To value** box, type **7500.00** Press Tab. In the **By changing cell** box, type **b3** which is the number of years for the loan. Compare your dialog box with Figure 11.34.

Value of $350,000 restored

Cell with the number of payment periods indicated as the *change* cell

Figure 11.34

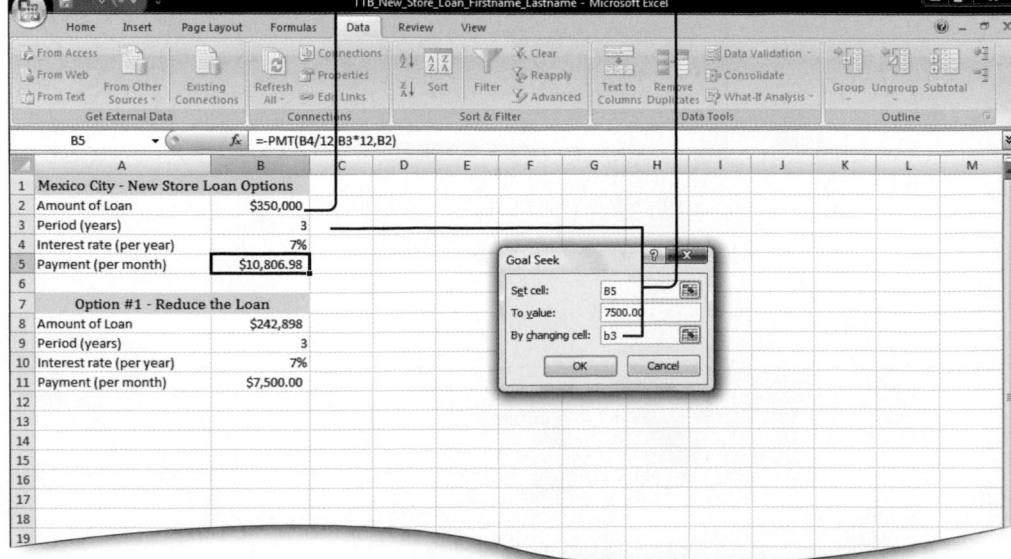

3 Click **OK** two times to close the two dialog boxes.

Excel's calculations indicate that by making payments for 4.5 years—4.552648969—a monthly payment of $7,500.00 is achieved.

4 Click **A13**. Type **Option #2 - Increase Years** and then press Enter. Right-click click cell **A7**, on the Mini toolbar, click the **Format Painter** button , and then click cell **A13** to copy the formats.

5 Select the range **A2:B5,** and then right-click. From the displayed shortcut menu, click **Copy** , and then click cell **A14**. Right-click, click **Paste Special**, and then paste the **Values and number formats**. Press Esc to cancel the moving border.

6 Click cell **B15**, right-click to display the Mini toolbar, and then click the **Decrease Decimal** button until the number of decimal places is two. Click cell **B3**. Type **3** and then press Enter to restore the original value. Compare your worksheet with Figure 11.35.

Figure 11.35

Option 1: Reduce the amount of the loan

Option 2: Increase the number of years to pay off the loan

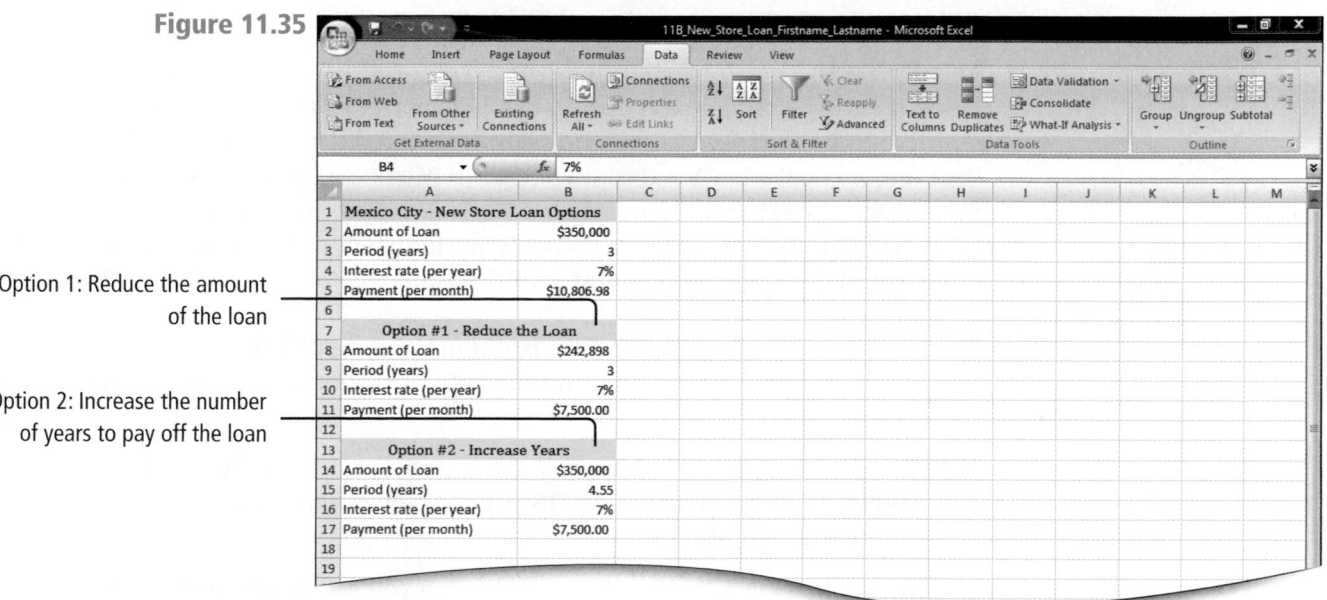

7 Click the **Insert tab**, and then in the **Text group**, click the **Header & Footer** button to switch to **Page Layout View** and open the **Header area**. In the **Navigation group**, click the **Go to Footer** button, click just above the word *Footer*, and then in the **Header & Footer Elements group**, click the **File Name** button. Click in a cell just above the footer to exit the **Footer area** and view your file name.

8 Click the **Page Layout tab**. In the **Page Setup group**, click the **Margins** button, and then at the bottom of the **Margins gallery**, click **Custom Margins**. In the displayed **Page Setup** dialog box, under **Center on page**, select the **Horizontally** check box. Click **OK**, and then on the status bar, click the **Normal** button . Press Ctrl + Home to move to the top of the worksheet.

9 **Save** your workbook.

Objective 8
Create a Data Table

A *data table* is a range of cells that shows how changing certain values in your formulas affects the results of those formulas. Data tables make it easy to calculate multiple versions in one operation, and then to view and compare the results of all the different variations.

For example, banks may offer loans at different rates for different periods of time, which require different payments. Using a data table, you can calculate the possible values for each argument.

A *one-variable data table* changes the value in only one cell. For example, use a one-variable data table if you want to see how different interest rates affect a monthly payment. A *two-variable data table* changes the values in two cells—for example, you can see how both different interest rates *and* different payment periods will affect a monthly payment.

Activity 11.18 Designing a Two-Variable Data Table

Recall that the PMT function has three required arguments: Present value (Pv), Rate, and Number of periods (Nper). Because Wattana would still like to borrow $350,000 and purchase the fixtures and furniture that she has selected for the new store in Mexico City, in this data table the present value will not change. The two values that will change are the Rate and Number of periods. Possible periods will range from 24 months (2 years) to 60 months (5 years) and the Rate will vary from 8% to 6%.

1 Double-click the **Sheet2 tab**, rename it **Payment Table** and then press Enter. Right-click the **Sheet3 tab**, and then from the shortcut menu, click **Delete**.

2 With the **Payment Table** worksheet active, widen **column A** to **165 pixels**. Widen **column B** to **80 pixels**. Select **columns C:I**, and then widen them to **85 pixels**.

3 In the range **A2:B4**, enter the following row titles and data. Recall that you format numbers as you type by typing them with their symbols as shown:

Amount of Loan	$350,000
Period (months)	36
Interest rate (per year)	7.00%

4 Click cell **C8**. Type **24** and then press Tab. Type **30** and then press Tab. Select the range **C8:D8**. Point to the fill handle, and then drag to the right through cell **I8** to fill in a pattern of months from 24 to 60 in increments of six months.

5 In cell **B9**, type **8.000%** and then press Enter. Type **7.875%** and then press Enter.

The display of both values is rounded to two decimal places.

6 Select the range **B9:B10**. Point to the fill handle, and then drag down through cell **B25** to fill in a pattern of interest rates in increments of .125 from 8.00% down to 6.00%. With the range **B9:B25** still selected, right-click anywhere over the range, and then on the Mini toolbar, click the **Increase Decimal** button one time. Compare your screen with Figure 11.36.

Row 8 represents the number of monthly payments, and column B represents a range of possible annual interest rates. These two arguments will be used to calculate varying payment arrangements for a loan of $350,000.

Varying arguments for months

Figure 11.36

Varying arguments for rates

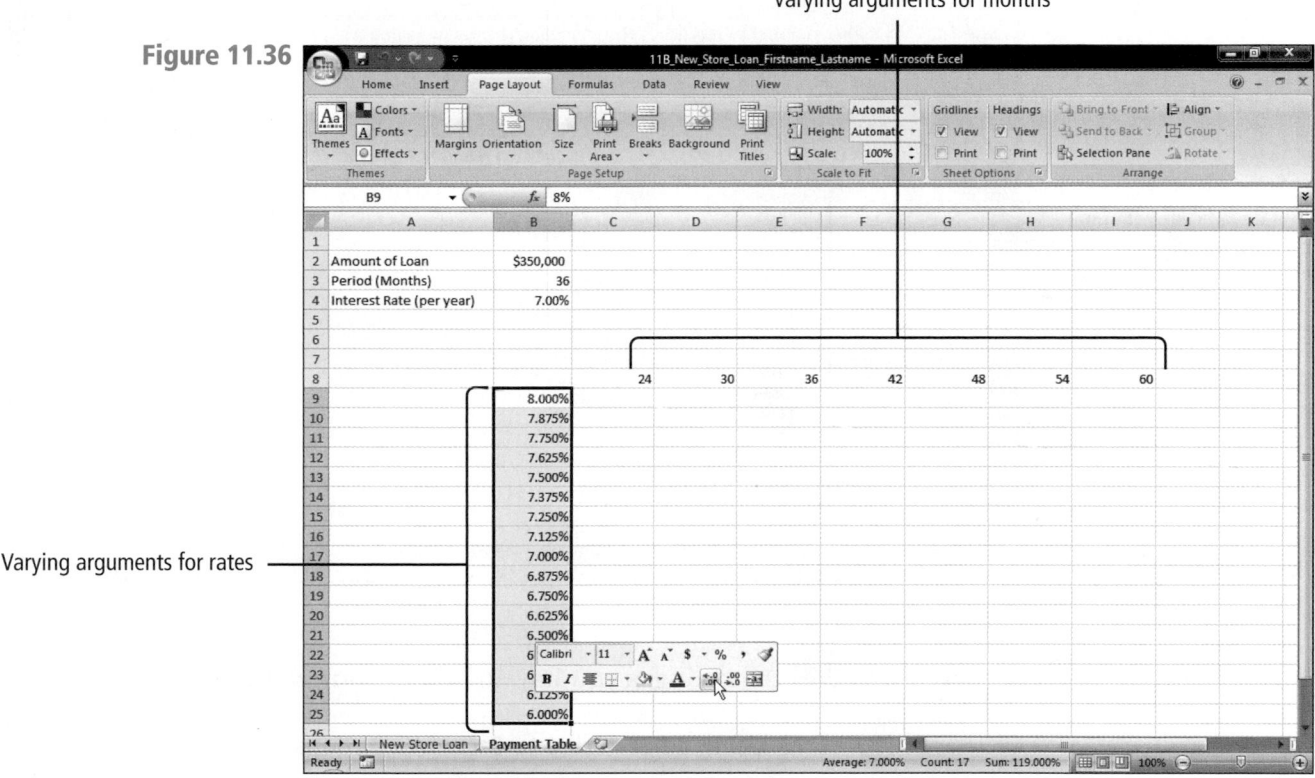

7 Click cell **A1**. Type **Loan Options for New Store in Mexico City - Rates versus Months** and then press Enter. **Merge and Center** this title across the range **A1:I1**. Change the **Font** Calibri to **Cambria**, the **Font Size** 11 to **16**, and then apply a **Fill Color** of **Olive Green, Accent 3, Lighter 60%**.

8 Click cell **C6**. Type **Payment Options** and then press Enter. **Merge and Center** this title across the range **C6:I6**. Change the **Font Size** 11 to **14**, and then apply **Bold**.

9 Click cell **C7**. Type **Number of Monthly Payments** and then use the **Format Painter** to apply the format of cell **C6** to cell **C7**.

10 Click cell **A9**, type **Rates** and then press [Enter]. Select the range **A9:A25**. On the **Home tab**, in the **Alignment group**, click the **Merge and Center** button ⬚▾, click the **Align Text Right** button ▤, and then click the **Middle Align** button ▤. Change the **Font Size** ⌊11 ▾⌋ to **14**, and then apply **Bold** ⬚. Compare your screen with Figure 11.37.

Figure 11.37

Merged cells with right alignment and vertical centering

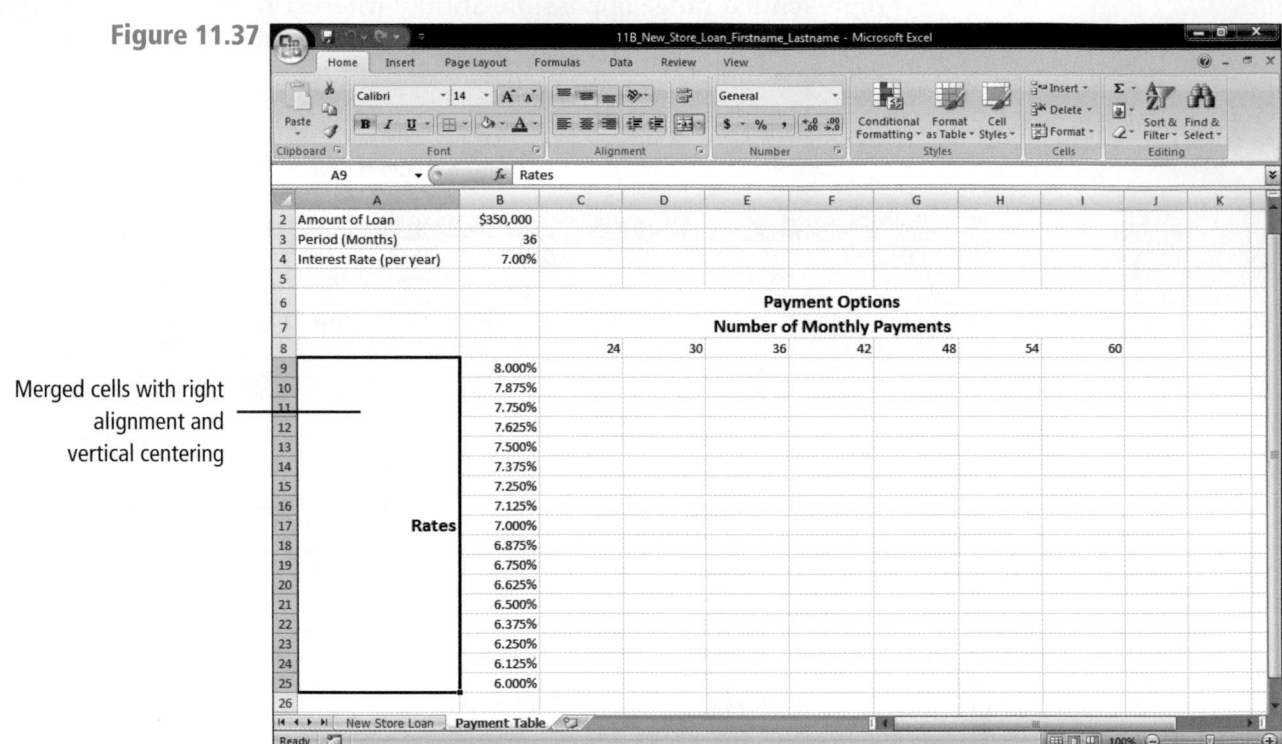

11 **Save** 🖫 the changes you have made to your workbook.

Activity 11.19 Using a Data Table to Calculate Options

Recall that a data table is a range of cells that shows how changing certain values in your formulas affects the results of those formulas. In this activity, you will create a table of payments for every combination of payment periods, which are represented by the column titles under *Number of Monthly Payments*, and interest rates, which are represented by the row titles to the right of *Rates*. From the resulting table, Wattana can find a combination of payment periods and interest rates that will enable her to go forward with her plan to borrow $350,000 to purchase the necessary furniture and fixtures for the new store in Mexico City.

1 Click cell **B8**, type **=** and notice that in the upper left corner of your screen, in the **Name Box**, *PMT* displays indicating the most recently used function. Click in the **Name Box** to open the **Function Arguments** dialog box for the **PMT** function. Alternatively, use one of the other methods you have practiced to insert the PMT function.

The PMT function is entered in the upper left corner of your range of data, so that when the data table is completed, the months in row 8 and the rates in column B will be substituted into each cell's formula to fill the table with the range of months and interest rate options that are displayed.

2 In the **Rate** box, type **b4/12** to divide the interest rate per year by 12 and convert it to a monthly interest rate.

3 Press [Tab] to move the insertion point to the **Nper** box. Type **b3** and then press [Tab].

The periods in cell B3 are already stated in months and need not be changed.

4 In the **Pv** box, type **-b2** and then click **OK**.

The payment—$10,806.98—is calculated for the values in cells B2, B3, and B4. This is the same payment that you calculated on the first worksheet. Now it displays as a positive number because you entered the loan amount in cell B2 as a negative number.

5 Select the range **B8:I25**. On the **Data tab**, in the **Data Tools group**, click the **What-If Analysis** button, and then in the displayed list, click **Data Table**. In the **Data Table** dialog box, in the **Row input cell** box, type **b3** and then press [Tab]. In the **Column input cell** box, type **b4** and then compare your screen with Figure 11.38.

The row of months will be substituted for the value in cell B3, and the column of interest rates will be substituted for the value in cell B4.

Column values substituted for interest rates

Figure 11.38

Row values substituted for months

Selected area indicates data table range

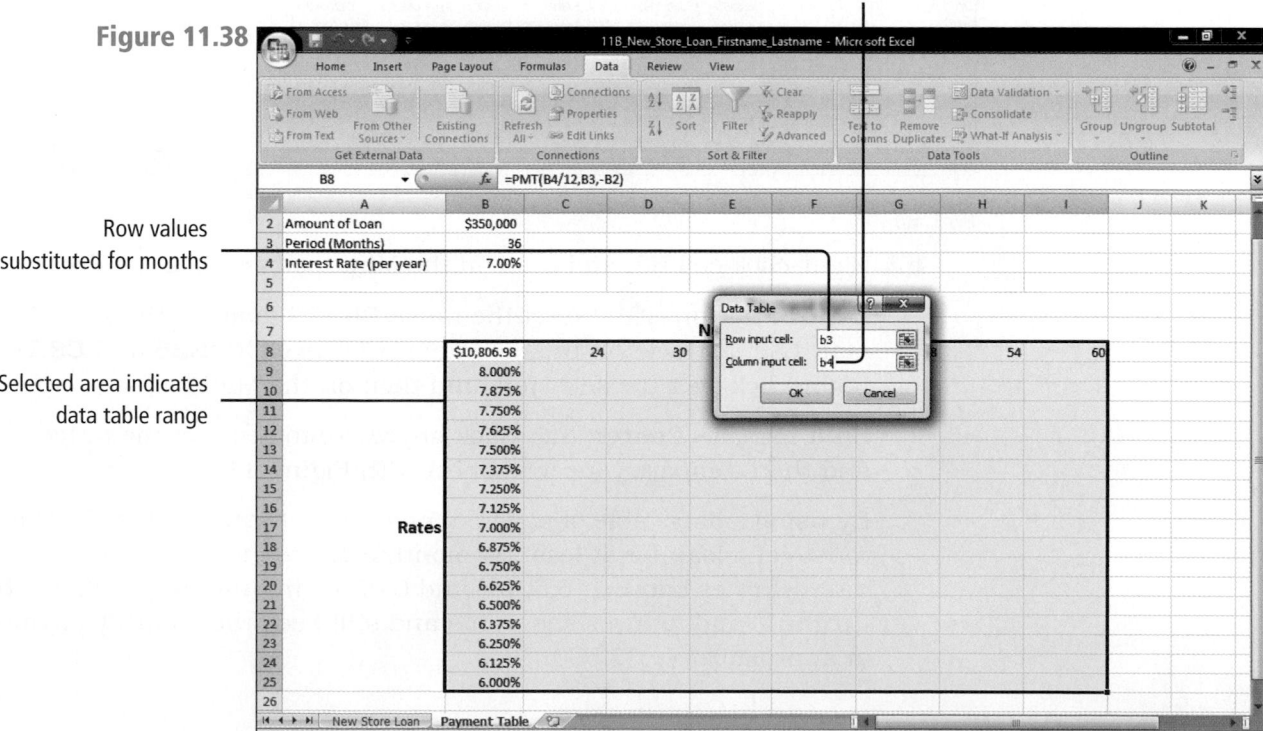

6 In the **Data Table** dialog box, click **OK**. Click cell **H21**, and then examine the formula in the **Formula Bar**. Compare your screen with Figure 11.39.

The table is filled with payment options that use the month and interest rate corresponding to the position in the table. Thus, if Wattana chooses a combination of 54 months at an interest rate of 6.5%, the monthly payment will be $7,492.96.

The data table is one of a group of Excel's What-If Analysis tools.

Period of 54 months, at 6.500% interest, results in $7,492.96 payment

Figure 11.39

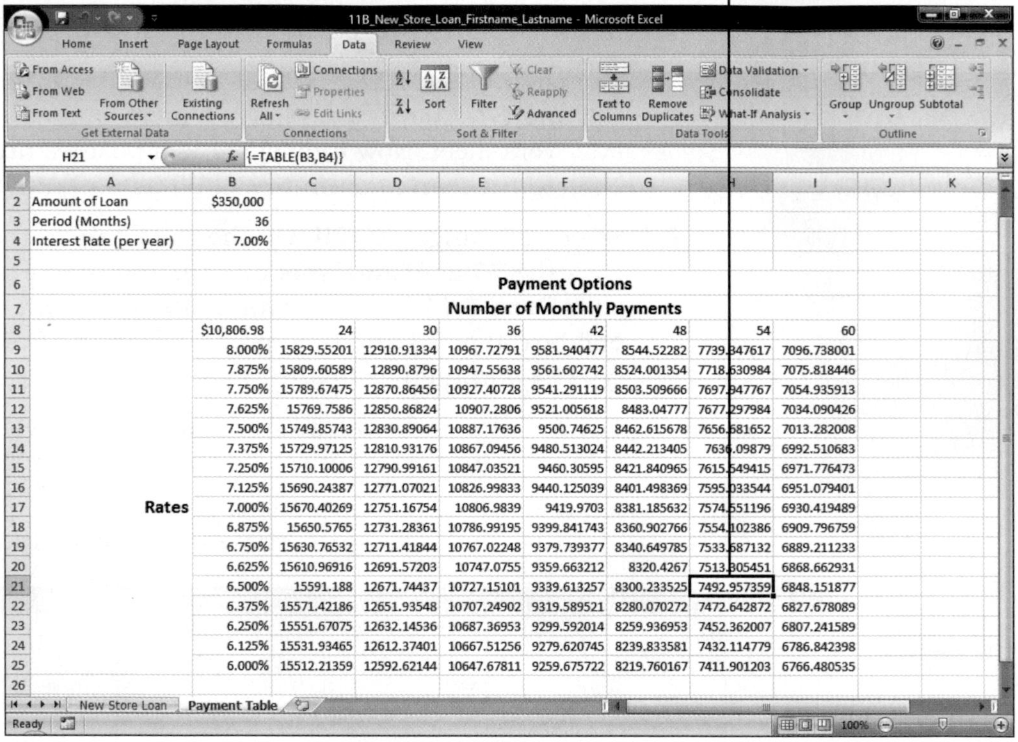

7 Right-click cell **B8**, and then on the Mini toolbar, click the **Format Painter** button. Select the range **C9:I25** to apply the same format. Use Ctrl to select the non-adjacent ranges **B9:B25** and **C8:I8**. Right-click over the selection, and then on the Mini toolbar, apply **Bold** B and **Center**. Click anywhere to deselect the range, and then compare your worksheet with Figure 11.40.

By using a data table of payment options, you can see that Wattana must get a loan for at least 54 months (4.5 years) for any of the interest rates between 6.500% and 6.000% in order to purchase the furniture and fixtures she wants and still keep the monthly payment at approximately $7,500.

For a 54-month period, loan options in this range will be within the budget

Figure 11.40

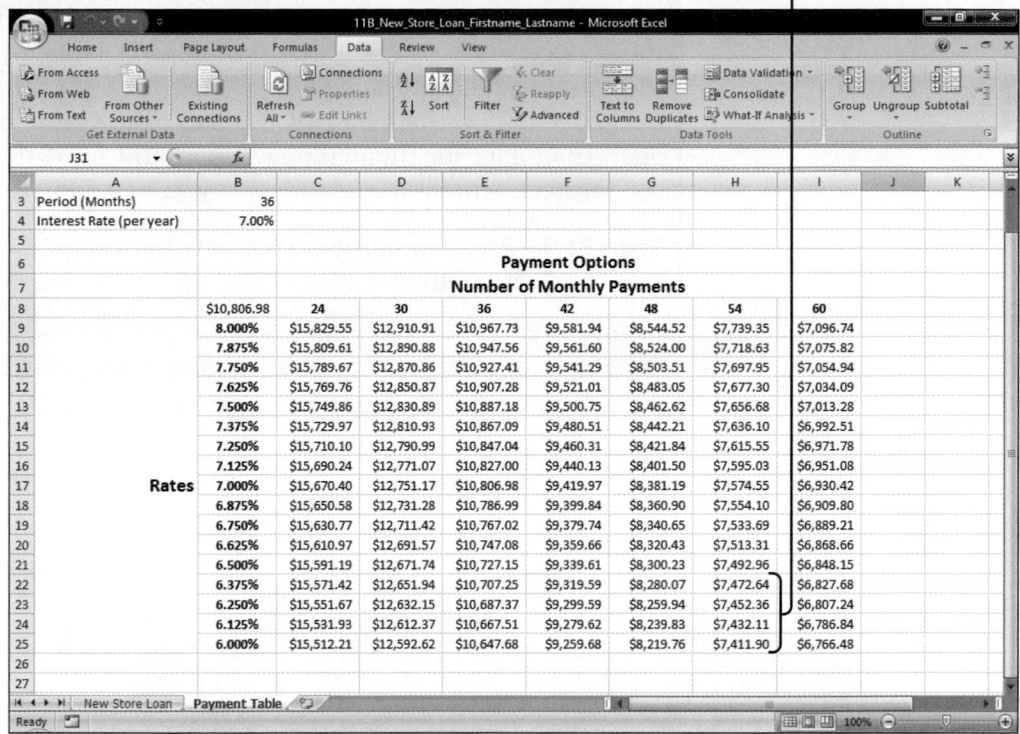

	A	B	C	D	E	F	G	H	I	J	K
3	Period (Months)	36									
4	Interest Rate (per year)	7.00%									
5											
6						Payment Options					
7						Number of Monthly Payments					
8		$10,806.98	24	30	36	42	48	54	60		
9		8.000%	$15,829.55	$12,910.91	$10,967.73	$9,581.94	$8,544.52	$7,739.35	$7,096.74		
10		7.875%	$15,809.61	$12,890.88	$10,947.56	$9,561.60	$8,524.00	$7,718.63	$7,075.82		
11		7.750%	$15,789.67	$12,870.86	$10,927.41	$9,541.29	$8,503.51	$7,697.95	$7,054.94		
12		7.625%	$15,769.76	$12,850.87	$10,907.28	$9,521.01	$8,483.05	$7,677.30	$7,034.09		
13		7.500%	$15,749.86	$12,830.89	$10,887.18	$9,500.75	$8,462.62	$7,656.68	$7,013.28		
14		7.375%	$15,729.97	$12,810.93	$10,867.09	$9,480.51	$8,442.21	$7,636.10	$6,992.51		
15		7.250%	$15,710.10	$12,790.99	$10,847.04	$9,460.31	$8,421.84	$7,615.55	$6,971.78		
16		7.125%	$15,690.24	$12,771.07	$10,827.00	$9,440.13	$8,401.50	$7,595.03	$6,951.08		
17	Rates	7.000%	$15,670.40	$12,751.17	$10,806.98	$9,419.97	$8,381.19	$7,574.55	$6,930.42		
18		6.875%	$15,650.58	$12,731.28	$10,786.99	$9,399.84	$8,360.90	$7,554.10	$6,909.80		
19		6.750%	$15,630.77	$12,711.42	$10,767.02	$9,379.74	$8,340.65	$7,533.69	$6,889.21		
20		6.625%	$15,610.97	$12,691.57	$10,747.08	$9,359.66	$8,320.43	$7,513.31	$6,868.66		
21		6.500%	$15,591.19	$12,671.74	$10,727.15	$9,339.61	$8,300.23	$7,492.96	$6,848.15		
22		6.375%	$15,571.42	$12,651.94	$10,707.25	$9,319.59	$8,280.07	$7,472.64	$6,827.68		
23		6.250%	$15,551.67	$12,632.15	$10,687.37	$9,299.59	$8,259.94	$7,452.36	$6,807.24		
24		6.125%	$15,531.93	$12,612.37	$10,667.51	$9,279.62	$8,239.83	$7,432.11	$6,786.84		
25		6.000%	$15,512.21	$12,592.62	$10,647.68	$9,259.68	$8,219.76	$7,411.90	$6,766.48		
26											
27											

New Store Loan   Payment Table

8 Click the **Insert tab**, and then in the **Text group**, click the **Header & Footer** button to switch to **Page Layout View** and open the **Header area**. In the **Navigation group**, click the **Go to Footer** button, click just above the word *Footer*, then in the **Header & Footer Elements group**, click the **File Name** button. Click in a cell just above the footer to exit the **Footer area** and view your file name.

9 Click the **Page Layout tab**. In the **Page Setup group**, click the **Orientation** button, and then click **Landscape**. Click the **Margins** button, and then at the bottom of the **Margins gallery**, click **Custom Margins**. In the displayed **Page Setup** dialog box, under **Center on page**, select the **Horizontally** check box. Click **OK**, and then on the status bar, click the **Normal** button. Press Ctrl + Home to move to the top of the worksheet.

10 **Save** 💾 your workbook. Press Ctrl + F2 to display the worksheet in **Print Preview**. To print, in the **Print group**, click the **Print** button, under **Print what**, click the **Entire workbook** option button, and then click **OK**. To submit electronically, follow your instructor's directions. Determine if you are to print formulas for any or all of the worksheets in this workbook. To print formulas, refer to Activity 5.17 in Project 5A.

11 If you printed your formulas, be sure to redisplay the worksheet by pressing Ctrl + `. From the **Office** menu, click **Close**. If you are prompted to save changes, click **No**. **Close** Excel.

End **You have completed Project 11B**

There's More You Can Do!

Close Excel and any other open windows. Display the Start menu, click Computer, and then navigate to to the student files that accompany this textbook. In the folder **02_theres_more_you_can_do**, locate and open the folder for this chapter. Open and print the instructions for this project, which are provided to you in Adobe PDF format.

Try IT! 1—Apply Conditional Formats by Using Color Scales, Icon Sets, and Top/Bottom Rules

In this Try It! exercise, you will use Color Scales, Icon Sets, and Top/Bottom rules to help you visualize data distribution and variation.

Content-Based Assessments

Summary

Predefined formulas, referred to as functions, are available in Excel in various categories including Statistical, Logical, Date & Time, and Financial. Such functions enable you to make complex calculations without having to build the formulas yourself. Conditional formatting enables you to highlight interesting cells based on criteria, emphasize unusual values, and visualize data using Data Bars. The DATE function adds the current date to a workbook. Financial functions, along with the Goal Seek tool and data tables, are useful when making choices among various financing options.

Key Terms

The 🔘 symbol represents Key Terms found on the Student CD in the 02_theres_more_you_can_do folder for this chapter.

Content-Based Assessments

Matching

Match each term in the second column with its correct definition in the first column by writing the letter of the term on the blank line in front of the correct definition.

_____ **1.** A predefined formula—a formula that Excel has already built for you—that performs calculations by using specific values in a particular order.

_____ **2.** The values that an Excel function uses to perform calculations or operations.

_____ **3.** A statistical function that adds a group of values, and then divides the result by the number of values in the group.

_____ **4.** A statistical function that determines the smallest value in a group of values.

_____ **5.** An Excel feature which, after typing an = (equal sign) and the beginning letter or letters of a function name, displays a list of function names that match the typed letter(s), and from which you can insert the function by pointing to its name, and then pressing the Tab key or double-clicking.

_____ **6.** Conditions that you specify in a logical function.

_____ **7.** Any value or expression that can be evaluated as being *true* or *false*.

_____ **8.** The symbols < (less than), > (greater than), and = (equal) that evaluate each field value to determine if it is the same, greater than, less than, or in between a range of values as specified by the criteria.

_____ **9.** A cell format consisting of a shaded bar that provides a visual cue to the reader about the value of a cell relative to other cells; the length of the bar represents the value in the cell—a longer bar represents a higher value and a shorter bar represents a lower value.

_____ **10.** A function within the *Date & Time* category that retrieves the date and time from your computer's calendar and clock and inserts the information into the selected cell.

_____ **11.** A series of rows and columns in a worksheet that contains related data, and that is managed independently from the data in other rows and columns in the worksheet.

_____ **12.** A portion of a worksheet window bounded by and separated from other portions by vertical and horizontal bars.

_____ **13.** The amount charged for the use of borrowed money.

_____ **14.** The total amount that a series of future payments is worth now; also known as the principal.

_____ **15.** An Excel function that calculates the payment for a loan based on constant payments and at a constant rate of interest.

A Arguments

B AVERAGE

C Comparison operators

D Criteria

E Data Bar

F Excel table

G Formula AutoComplete

H Function

I Interest

J Logical test

K MIN

L NOW

M Pane

N PMT

O Present value

Content-Based Assessments

Excel
chapter eleven | **Fill in the Blank**

Write the correct answer in the space provided.

1. The Excel function that adds all the numbers in a selected range of cells is the _____ function.

2. Prewritten formulas that analyze a group of measurements are _____ functions.

3. A statistical function commonly used to describe a group of data, and which finds the middle value in a group of values that has as many values above it in the group as are below it is the _____ function.

4. The MAX function determines the _____ value in a selected range of values.

5. Prewritten formulas that test for specific conditions, and which typically use conditional tests to determine whether specified conditions, referred to as criteria, are true or false, are _____ functions.

6. To count the number of cells within a range that meets the given condition, use the _____ function.

7. The IF function uses a logical test to check whether a condition is met, and then returns one value if true, and another value if _____.

8. A format that changes the appearance of a cell range—for example by adding cell shading or font color—based on a condition is a _____ format.

9. The command that searches the cells in a worksheet—or in a selected range—for matches, and then replaces each match with a replacement value of your choice is called _____ _____ _____.

10. The term used to describe an Excel function that is subject to change each time the workbook is reopened; for example, when the NOW function updates itself to the current date and time each time the workbook is opened, is _____.

11. The command that enables you to select one or more rows or columns and freeze (lock) them into place as separate panes is _____ _____.

12. The group of functions in Excel that performs common business calculations, such as calculating a loan payment on a vehicle, and that

Fill in the Blank | **Excel**   579

Content-Based Assessments

Fill in the Blank

commonly involves a period of time such as months or years, are called _____ functions.

13. The value at the end of the time periods in an Excel function is known as the _____ _____.

14. One of Excel's What-If Analysis tools, which provides a method to find a specific value for a cell by adjusting the value of one other cell, is _____ _____.

15. A range of cells that shows how changing certain values in your formulas affects the results of those formulas, and that makes it easy to calculate multiple versions in one operation, is a _____ _____.

Skills Review

Project 11C—Pendants

In this project, you will apply the skills you practiced from the Objectives in Project 11A.

Objectives: 1. *Use SUM, AVERAGE, MEDIAN, MIN, and MAX Functions;*
2. *Use COUNTIF and IF Functions, and Apply Conditional Formatting;*
3. *Use a Date Function;* **4.** *Freeze Panes and Create an Excel Table;*
5. *Format and Print a Large Worksheet.*

Adamantine Jewelry creates castings, which it sells to other jewelry makers. In the following Skills Review, you will edit a worksheet for Rose Elleni, Vice President of Production, detailing the current inventory of pendant castings at the Milan production facility. Your completed worksheet will look similar to the one shown in Figure 11.41.

For Project 11C, you will need the following file:

e11C_Pendants

**You will save your workbook as
11C_Pendants_Firstname_Lastname**

Figure 11.41

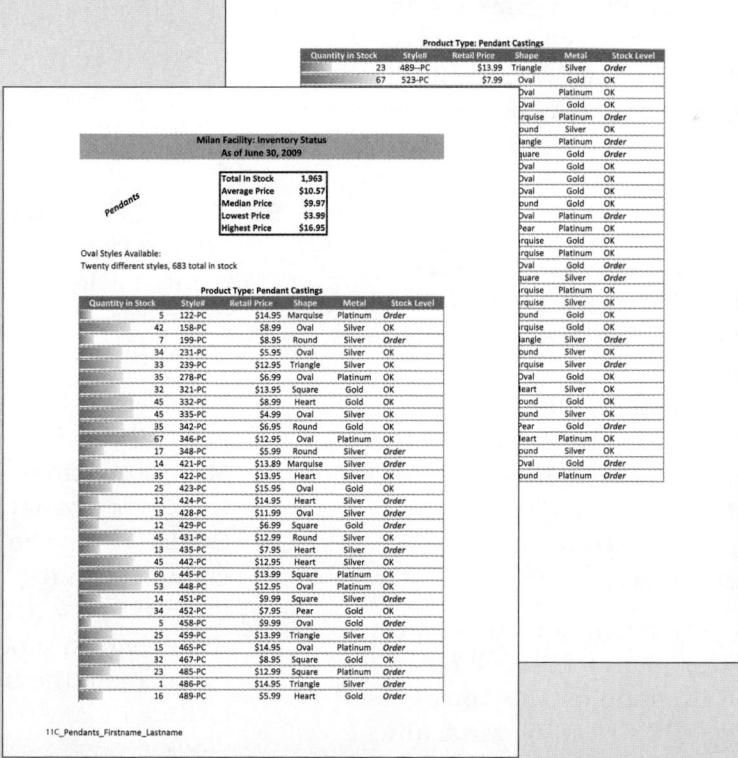

(Project 11C–Pendants continues on the next page)

Content-Based Assessments

(Project 11C–Pendants continued)

1. **Start** Excel. From the student files that accompany this text, locate and open **e11C_Pendants**. From the **Office** menu, display the **Save As** dialog box, click the **Save in arrow**, and then navigate to your **Excel Chapter 11** folder. In the **File name** box, type **11C_Pendants_Firstname_Lastname** and then click **Save** or press Enter.

2. Click cell **B4**. Click the **Formulas tab**, and then in the **Function Library group**, click the **AutoSum** button. Select the range **A12:A77**, dragging downward as necessary, and then press Enter. Right-click cell **B4**, and then apply **Comma Style** with zero decimal places.

3. Click cell **B5**. In the **Function Library group**, click the **More Functions** button, and then point to **Statistical**. Click **AVERAGE**, and then if necessary, drag the title bar of the **Function Arguments** dialog box down and to the right so you can view the **Formula Bar** and cell **B5**. In the **Function Arguments** dialog box, in the **Number1** box, delete the existing text, and then type **c12:c77** Click **OK** to calculate the average product price.

4. Click cell **B6**. In the **Function Library group**, click the **More Functions** button, display the list of **Statistical** functions, scroll down as necessary, and then click **MEDIAN**. In the displayed **Function Arguments** dialog box, to the right of the **Number1** box, click the **Collapse Dialog** button. Select the range **C12:C77**, and then press Enter. Click **OK** to calculate the median product price.

5. Using either of the techniques that you practiced in Steps 3 and 4, in cell **B7**, insert the **MIN** function for the range **C12:C77**. In cell **B8** insert the **MAX** function for the range **C12:C77**.

6. Select the range **A4:B8**. Point to the right edge of the selected range to display the ⬚ pointer. Drag the selected range to the right until the ScreenTip displays *C4:D8*, and then release the mouse button. Select **columns C:D**, and then apply **AutoFit** to adjust the column widths. Select the range **C4:D8**, and then apply **Bold** and a **Thick Box Border**.

7. In cell **A6**, type **Pendants** Select the range **A5:A7**, right-click over the selection, and then from the shortcut menu, click **Format Cells**. In the displayed **Format Cells** dialog box, click the **Alignment tab**. Under **Text control**, select the **Merge cells** check box. In the upper right portion of the dialog box, under **Orientation**, point to the **red diamond**, and then drag the diamond upward until the **Degrees** box indicates *30*. Click **OK**.

8. With the cell still selected, click the **Home tab**, change the **Font Size** to **12**, and then apply **Bold** and **Italic**. In the **Alignment group**, apply **Center** alignment and **Middle Align**.

9. From the **row heading area**, point to **row 10** and right-click. From the shortcut menu, click **Insert**. Press F4 two times to insert two more rows. In cell **A10** type **Oval Styles Available:** and press Enter.

10. With cell **A11** active, on the **Formulas tab**, in the **Function Library group**, click the **More Functions** button, and then display the list of **Statistical** functions. Click **COUNTIF**. In the **Range** box, click the **Collapse Dialog** button, select the range **D15:D80**, and then press Enter. Click in the **Criteria** box, type **Oval** and then click **OK** to calculate the number of Oval pendant castings that Adamantine Jewelry has in stock.

(Project 11C–Pendants continues on the next page)

(Project 11C–Pendants continued)

11. Click cell **F15**. On the **Formulas tab**, in the **Function Library group**, click the **Logical** button, and then in the displayed list, click **IF**. With the insertion point in the **Logical_test** box, click cell **A15**, and then type **<25** Press [Tab] to move the insertion point to the **Value_if_true** box, and then type **Order** Press [Tab] to move the insertion point to the **Value_if_false** box, and then type **OK** Click **OK** to display the result *Order* in cell **F15**. Then, using the fill handle, copy the function down through cell **F80** to indicate the order status for each Style#.

12. Be sure the range **F15:F80** is selected. On the **Home tab**, in the **Styles group**, click the **Conditional Formatting** button. In the displayed list, point to **Highlight Cells Rules**, and then click **Text that Contains**. In the **Text That Contains** dialog box, with the insertion point blinking in the first box, type **Order** In the second box, click the arrow, and then in the displayed list, click **Custom Format**. On the **Font tab**, under **Font style**, click **Bold Italic**. Click the **Color arrow**, and then under **Theme Colors**, click **Dark Blue, Text 2, Darker 25%**. Click **OK**, and then click **OK** again to apply the formatting to the items that need to be ordered.

13. Select the range **A15:A80**. In the **Styles group**, click the **Conditional Formatting** button. In the displayed list, point to **Data Bars**, and then in the displayed gallery, click **Blue Data Bar** to visually indicate the quantity in stock for each item.

14. To the left of the **Formula Bar**, in the **Name Box**, type **e15:e80** and then press [Enter]. On the **Home tab**, in the **Editing group**, click the **Find & Select** button. From the displayed menu, click **Replace** to display the **Find and Replace** dialog box. In the **Find what** box, type **Base** In the

Replace with box, type **Platinum** Click the **Replace All** button, and then click **OK** to replace 16 occurrences of *Base* with *Platinum*. Click **OK** to close the displayed message box. **Close** the **Find and Replace** dialog box.

15. Scroll down to view **row 81**. Click cell **A81**, type **Last Edited by Rose Elleni** and then press [Enter]. With cell **A82** as the active cell, on the **Formulas tab**, in the **Function Library group**, click the **Date & Time** button. In the displayed list of functions, click **NOW**. In the **Function Arguments** dialog box, click **OK** to close the dialog box. Adjust the width of **column A** to **127 pixels** to display the current date and time. Apply **Align Text Left** to cell **A82**.

16. **Save** your changes up to this point. Press [Ctrl] + [Home] to make cell **A1** the active cell. Select the range **A14:F80**. Click the **Insert tab**, and then in the **Tables group**, click the **Table** button. In the displayed **Create Table** dialog box, if necessary, click to select the **My table has headers** check box. Click **OK** to create the table.

17. On the **Design tab**, in the **Table Styles group**, click the **More** button, and then under **Light**, locate and click **Table Style Light 9**.

18. In the header row of the table, click the **Retail Price arrow**, and then from the displayed menu, click **Sort Smallest to Largest** to rearrange the data so that the products display in ascending order with the lowest price item first and the highest price item last.

19. In the header row of the table, click the **Shape arrow**. From the displayed menu, click **Sort A to Z**. Click the **Shape arrow** again. On the displayed menu, click the **(Select All)** check box to clear all the

(Project 11C–Pendants continues on the next page)

Content-Based Assessments

(Project 11C–Pendants continued)

check boxes. Then, click to select only the **Oval** check box, and then click **OK** to display only the **Oval** products.

20. Click any cell in the table so that the table is selected. On the Ribbon, click the **Design tab**, and then in the **Table Style Options group**, click to select the **Total Row** check box. Click cell **A81**, click the arrow that displays, and then in the displayed list, click **Sum** to display *683*—the total number of oval shaped pendant castings in stock. Click cell **A11**, type **Twenty different styles, 683 total in stock** and then press Enter.

21. Click any cell in the table. On the Ribbon, click the **Design tab**, and then in the **Table Style Options group**, click the **Total Row** check box to clear it and remove the Total row from the bottom of the table. In the displayed message box, click **Yes**. In the table header row, click the **Shape arrow**, and then in the displayed menu, click **Clear Filter From "Shape"** to redisplay all of the products.

22. In the table header row, click the **Style# arrow**, and then click **Sort A to Z**, which will apply an ascending sort to the **Style#** column. In the **Tools group**, click the **Convert to Range** button. In the displayed message box, click **Yes**.

23. Press Ctrl + Home to display the top of your worksheet. On the **Insert tab**, in the **Text group**, click **Header & Footer** to switch to **Page Layout view**. In the **Navigation group**, click the **Go to Footer** button, click just above the word *Footer*, and then in the **Header & Footer Elements group**, click the **File Name** button. Click a cell

just above the footer to deselect the **Footer area** and view your file name.

24. Press Ctrl + Home to display the top of your worksheet. On the **Page Layout tab**, in the **Page Setup group**, click the **Print Titles** button. Under **Print titles**, click in the **Rows to repeat at top** box, and then at the right, click the **Collapse Dialog** button. From the **row heading area**, select **rows 13:14**. Press Enter, and then in the displayed **Page Setup** dialog box, click the **Margins tab**. Under **Center on page**, click the **Horizontally** check box, and then click **OK**. Delete the unused sheets **Sheet2** and **Sheet3**. On the right edge of the status bar, click the **Normal** button.

25. **Save** your workbook. To submit electronically, follow the instructions provided by your instructor. To print, from the **Office** menu, point to the **Print** button, and then click **Print Preview**. In the **Preview group**, click the **Next Page** and **Previous Page** buttons as necessary to view and check each page. Be sure the two header rows and the footer display on each page, and then click the **Print** button. In the displayed **Print** dialog box, under **Print range**, be sure that **All** is selected, and then click **OK**. If you are directed to submit printed formulas, refer to Activity 5.17 to do so.

26. If you printed your formulas, be sure to redisplay the worksheet by pressing Ctrl + `. From the **Office** menu, click **Close**. If the dialog box displays asking if you want to save changes, click **No** so that you do *not* save the changes you made for printing formulas. **Close** Excel.

End **You have completed Project 11C** ——————————

Content-Based Assessments

Project 11D—Auto Loan

In this project, you will apply the skills you practiced from the Objectives in Project 11B.

Objectives: 6. *Use Financial Functions;* **7.** *Use Goal Seek;* **8.** *Create a Data Table.*

In the following Skills Review, you will create a worksheet for Jennifer Bernard, U.S. Sales Director, that details loan information for purchasing eight automobiles for Adamantine Jewelry sales representatives. The monthly payment for the eight automobiles cannot exceed $3,000. The two worksheets in your workbook will look similar to Figure 11.42.

> ### For Project 11D, you will need the following file:
>
> New blank Excel workbook

You will save your workbook as
11D_Auto_Loan_Firstname_Lastname

Figure 11.42

Loan Options for Automobile Purchase - Rates versus Months

Amount of Loan	$125,000
Period (months)	36
Interest rate (per year)	5.50%

Payment Options
Number of Monthly Payments

36	42	48	54	60
3,859.64	$3,364.28	$2,993.28	$2,705.20	$2,475.15
3,831.13	$3,335.58	$2,964.37	$2,676.06	$2,445.77
3,802.74	$3,307.03	$2,935.63	$2,647.11	$2,416.60
3,774.49	$3,278.63	$2,907.06	$2,618.35	$2,387.65
3,746.36	$3,250.38	$2,878.66	$2,589.79	$2,358.90
3,718.37	$3,222.28	$2,850.44	$2,561.42	$2,330.38
3,690.50	$3,194.33	$2,822.38	$2,533.24	$2,302.07
3,662.76	$3,166.54	$2,794.50	$2,505.26	$2,273.97

Adamantine Jewelry - Auto Purchase

Amount of Loan	$125,000
Period (years)	3
Interest rate (per year)	5.50%
Payment (per month)	$3,774.49

Option #1 - Reduce the Loan

Amount of Loan	$99,351
Period (years)	3
Interest rate (per year)	5.50%
Payment (per month)	$3,000.00

Option #2 - Increase Years

Amount of Loan	$125,000
Period (years)	3.86
Interest rate (per year)	5.50%
Payment (per month)	$3,000.00

11D_Auto_Loan_Firstname_Lastname

(Project 11D–Auto Loan continues on the next page)

Content-Based Assessments

(Project 11D–Auto Loan continued)

1. **Start** Excel and display a new blank workbook. From the **Office** menu, display the **Save As** dialog box, navigate to your **Excel Chapter 11** folder, and then in the **File name** box, type **11D_Auto_Loan_Firstname_Lastname** Click **Save** or press Enter.

2. Widen **column A** to **180 pixels** and **column B** to **100 pixels**. In cell **A1**, type **Adamantine Jewelry – Auto Purchase Merge and Center** the worksheet title in the range **A1:B1**, change the **Font** to **Cambria**, the **Font Size** to **12**, and then add a **Fill Color** of **Orange, Accent 6, Lighter 40%**. Rename the worksheet tab as **Auto Loan** In the range **A2:B5**, enter the following row titles and data.

Amount of Loan	$125,000
Period (years)	3
Interest rate (per year)	5.5%
Payment (per month)	

3. Click cell **B5**. On the **Formulas tab**, in the **Function Library group**, click the **Financial** button, and then click **PMT**. Drag the **Function Arguments** dialog box to the right side of your screen so you can view **columns A:B**.

4. In the **Rate** box, type **b4/12** to convert the annual interest rate to a monthly interest rate. Press Tab, and then in the **Nper** box, type **b3*12** to have Excel convert the number of years in the loan (3) to the total number of months. Press Tab, and then in the **Pv** box, type **b2** to enter the present value of the loan. Click **OK** to create the function. In the **Formula Bar**, between the equal sign and *PMT*, type – (minus sign) to insert a minus sign into the formula, and then press Enter to display the loan payment as a positive number.

5. The result of *$3,774.49* is higher than the monthly payment of $3,000 that Jennifer wants. One option is to reduce the amount of money that she is going to borrow; she can determine the maximum amount that she can borrow and still keep the payment at $3,000 by using Goal Seek. Click cell **B5**. On the **Data tab**, in the **Data Tools group**, click the **What-If Analysis** button, and then in the displayed list, click **Goal Seek**. In the displayed **Goal Seek** dialog box, in the **Set cell** box, confirm that *B5* displays.

6. Press Tab. In the **To value** box, type the payment goal of **3000** and then press Tab. In the **By changing cell** box, type **b2** which is the amount of the loan. Click **OK** two times. For three years at 5.5%, Jennifer can borrow only $99,351 if she maintains a monthly payment of $3,000.

7. Click cell **A7**. Type **Option #1 - Reduce the Loan** and then press Enter. Right-click cell **A1**, on the Mini toolbar, click the **Format Painter** button, and then click cell **A7** to copy the formats.

8. Select the range **A2:B5**, right-click, and then click **Copy**. Click cell **A8**, right-click, and then from the shortcut menu, click **Paste Special**. In the **Paste Special** dialog box, under **Paste**, click the **Values and number formats** option button, and then click **OK**. Press Esc to cancel the moving border.

9. In cell **B2**, type **125000** and then press Enter to restore the original loan amount. Another option that Jennifer can explore with Goal Seek is to increase the number of years over which she finances the automobiles. Click cell **B5**. On the **Data tab**, in the **Data Tools group**, click the **What-If Analysis** button, and then click **Goal Seek**.

(Project 11D–Auto Loan continues on the next page)

Content-Based Assessments

(Project 11D–Auto Loan continued)

10. In the **Set cell** box, confirm that **B5** displays. Press Tab. In the **To value** box, type **3000** Press Tab. In the **By changing cell** box, type **b3** which is the number of years for the loan. Click **OK** two times. Extending the loan over 3.86 years will maintain a monthly payment of $3,000 at the current interest rate.

11. Click **A13**. Type **Option #2 - Increase Years** and then press Enter. Use the **Format Painter** to copy the formats from cell **A7** to cell **A13**. Select the range **A2:B5**, right-click, click **Copy**, and then click cell **A14**. Right-click, click **Paste Special**, and then paste the **Values and number formats**. Press Esc to cancel the moving border.

12. Click cell **B15**, right-click to display the Mini toolbar, and then click the **Decrease Decimal** button until the number of decimal places is two. Click cell **B3**. Type **3** and then press Enter to restore the original value.

13. Click the **Insert tab**, and then in the **Text group**, click **Header & Footer** to switch to **Page Layout View** and open the **Header area**. In the **Navigation group**, click the **Go to Footer** button, click just above the word *Footer*, then in the **Header & Footer Elements group**, click the **File Name** button. Click in a cell just above the footer to exit the **Footer area** and view your file name.

14. Click the **Page Layout tab**. In the **Page Setup group**, click the **Margins** button, and then at the bottom of the **Margins gallery**, click **Custom Margins**. In the displayed **Page Setup** dialog box, under **Center on page**, select the **Horizontally** check box. Click **OK**, and then on the status bar, click the **Normal** button. Press Ctrl + Home to move to the top of the worksheet.

15. **Save** the changes you have made thus far. To determine how variable interest rates and a varying number of payments affect the payment amount, Jennifer will set up a two-variable data table. Double-click the **Sheet2 tab**, rename it **Payment Table** and then press Enter. In cell **A1** type **Loan Options for Automobile Purchase - Rates versus Months** and then press Enter. **Merge and Center** this title across the range **A1:I1**. Change the **Font** to **Cambria**, the **Font Size** to **16**, and apply a **Fill Color** of **Orange, Accent 6, Lighter 40%**.

16. Widen **column A** to **165 pixels**. Widen **column B** to **80 pixels**. Select **columns C:I** and widen them to **85 pixels**. In the range **A2:B4**, enter the following row titles and data.

Amount of Loan	$125,000
Period (months)	36
Interest rate (per year)	5.5%

17. Click cell **C8**. Type **24** and then press Tab. Type **30** and then press Tab. Select the range **C8:D8**. Drag the fill handle to the right through cell **I8** to fill a pattern of months from 24 to 60 in increments of six months.

18. In cell **B9**, type **7.0%** and press Enter. Type **6.5%** and press Enter. Select the range **B9:B10**, and then drag the fill handle down through cell **B16** to fill a pattern of interest rates in increments of .5% from 7.00% down to 3.50%.

19. Click cell **C6**. Type **Payment Options** and then press Enter. **Merge and Center** this title across the range **C6:I6**. Change the **Font Size** to **14** and apply **Bold**. Click cell **C7**. Type **Number of Monthly Payments** and then use the **Format Painter** to apply the format of cell **C6** to cell **C7**.

(Project 11D–Auto Loan continues on the next page)

(Project 11D–Auto Loan continued)

20. Click cell **A9**, type **Rates** and then press ⟨Enter⟩. Select the range **A9:A16**. On the **Home tab**, in the **Alignment group**, click the **Merge and Center** button, click the **Align Text Right** button, and then click the **Middle Align** button. Change the **Font Size** to **14** and apply **Bold**.

21. Click cell **B8**. On the **Formulas tab**, in the **Function Library group**, click the **Financial** button, and then click **PMT**. In the **Rate** box, type **b4/12** to divide the interest rate per year by 12 to convert it to a monthly interest rate. Press ⟨Tab⟩, and then in the **Nper** box, type **b3** Press ⟨Tab⟩. In the **Pv** box, type **-b2** and then click **OK**.

22. Select the range **B8:I16**. On the **Data tab**, in the **Data Tools group**, click the **What-If Analysis** button, and then in the displayed list, click **Data Table**. In the **Data Table** dialog box, in the **Row input cell** box, type **b3** and then press ⟨Tab⟩. In the **Column input cell** box, type **b4** In the **Data Table** dialog box, click **OK** to create the data table.

23. Click cell **B8**, and then right-click to display the Mini toolbar. Click the **Format Painter** button. Select the range **C9:I16** to apply the same format. Select the ranges **B9:B16** and **C8:I8** and apply **Bold** and **Center**. Notice that in cell **G9**, the payment is *$2,993.28*, which is close to Jennifer's goal of a monthly payment of $3,000. At any of the interest rates, she will have to extend the loan over at least 48 months to stay within her goal of $3,000 per month.

24. Click the **Insert tab**, and then in the **Text group**, click **Header & Footer** to switch to **Page Layout View** and open the **Header area**. In the **Navigation group**, click the **Go to Footer** button, click just above the word *Footer*, then in the **Header & Footer Elements group**, click the **File Name** button. Click in a cell just above the footer to exit the **Footer area** and view your file name.

25. Click the **Page Layout tab**. In the **Page Setup group**, change the **Orientation** to **Landscape**. Click the **Margins** button, and then at the bottom of the **Margins gallery**, click **Custom Margins**. In the displayed **Page Setup** dialog box, under **Center on page**, select the **Horizontally** check box. Click **OK**, and then on the status bar, click the **Normal** button. Press ⟨Ctrl⟩ + ⟨Home⟩ to move to the top of the worksheet. Delete **Sheet3** from the workbook.

26. **Save** your workbook. Press ⟨Ctrl⟩ + ⟨F2⟩ to display the worksheet in **Print Preview**. To print, in the **Print group**, click the **Print** button, under **Print what**, click the **Entire workbook** option button, and then click **OK**. To submit electronically, follow your instructor's directions. Determine if you are to print formulas for any or all of the worksheets in this workbook. To print formulas, refer to Activity 5.17 in Project 5A.

27. If you printed your formulas, be sure to redisplay the worksheet by pressing ⟨Ctrl⟩ + ⟨`⟩. From the **Office** menu, click **Close**. If you are prompted to save changes, click **No**. **Close** Excel.

 You have completed Project 11D

Content-Based Assessments

chapter eleven   Excel

Mastering Excel

Project 11E—Castings

In this project, you will apply the skills you practiced from the Objectives in Project 11A.

Objectives: 1. *Use SUM, AVERAGE, MEDIAN, MIN, and MAX Functions;* **2.** *Use COUNTIF and IF Functions, and Apply Conditional Formatting;* **3.** *Use a Date Function;* **4.** *Freeze Panes and Create an Excel Table;* **5.** *Format and Print a Large Worksheet.*

Adamantine Jewelry manufactures castings, which it sells to other jewelry makers. In the following Skills Review, you will edit a worksheet for Rose Elleni, Vice President of Production, detailing the current inventory of ring and earring castings at the Milan production facility. Your completed worksheet will look similar to the one shown in Figure 11.43.

For Project 11E, you will need the following file:

e11E_Castings

You will save your workbook as 11E_Castings_Firstname_Lastname

Figure 11.43

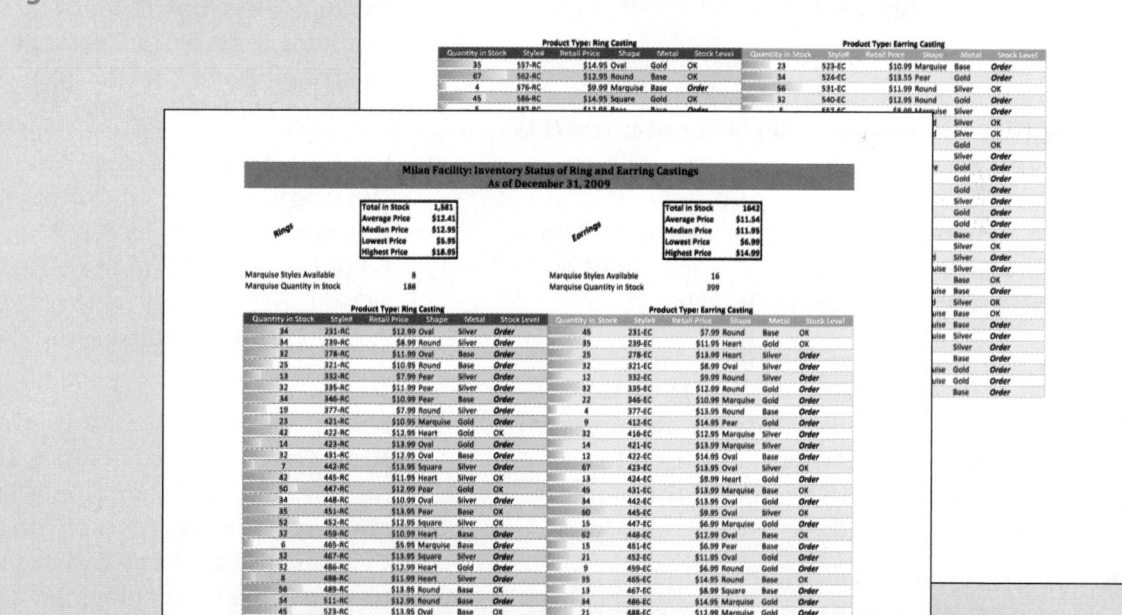

(Project 11E–Castings continues on the next page)

(Project 11E–Castings continued)

1. **Start** Excel. From the student files that accompany this text, locate and open **e11E_Castings**. In your **Excel Chapter 11** folder, save the file as **11E_Castings_Firstname_Lastname**

2. In cell **B4**, enter a function that sums the range **A12:A70**, and then apply **Comma Style** with zero decimal places. In cell **B5**, enter a function to calculate the average ring casting price in the range **C12:C70**. In cells **B6**, **B7**, and **B8**, use statistical functions to calculate the median ring casting price, the lowest ring casting price, and the highest ring casting price.

3. In the range **H4:H8** and by using the **Earring Casting** data, insert functions to make calculations similar to those you created in Step 2. The *Total in Stock* data is located in **column G** and the *Price* data is located in **column I**.

4. Move the range **A4:B8** to the range **C4:D8**, and then apply **Bold** and a **Thick Box Border** to the range. **AutoFit columns C:D**. In cell **A6**, type **Rings** Select the range **A5:A7**, merge the cells, and then change the **Orientation** to **30 Degrees**. Change the **Font Size** to **12**, and then apply **Bold** and **Italic**. **Center** and **Middle Align** the text.

5. Move the range **G4:H8** to the range **I4:J8**, and then apply **Bold** and a **Thick Box Border** to the range. **AutoFit columns I:J**. In cell **G5**, type **Earrings** and then use **Format Painter** to format in the same manner as cell **A5**.

6. Insert 3 rows above **row 10**. In cell **A10**, type **Marquise Styles Available** and then in cell **A11**, type **Marquise Quantity in Stock** Copy the two cells that you just typed, and then paste to the range **G10:G11**. In cell **C10**, enter a **COUNTIF** function that

counts **Marquise** items in the range **D15:D73**, and then create a similar formula in cell **I10** to count the **Marquise** items in the range **J15:J73**.

7. In cell **F15**, insert an **IF** function, and then test whether the value in cell **A15** is less than **35**. If true, display **Order** and if false, display **OK** Copy the function down through cell **F73**. Insert a similar **IF** function in **L15** to test whether the value in cell **G15** is less than **35**. If true, display **Order** and if false, display **OK** Copy the function down through cell **L73**.

8. To the range **F15:F73**, apply **Conditional Formatting** consisting of **Bold Italic** to any text that displays *Order*. Then, use the same **Conditional Formatting** rules to format the range **L15:L73**. Use **Conditional Formatting** to apply an **Orange Data Bar** to all of the quantities in stock for both **Ring Castings** and **Earring Castings**. **Save** the changes you have made to your workbook.

9. For both **Ring Castings** and **Earring Castings**, replace all occurrences of **Triangle** with **Pear** In cell **A74**, type **Last Edited by Rose Elleni** In cell **A75**, insert the **NOW** function. Adjust the width of **column A** to **127 pixels** so that the date and time display fully.

10. Select the range of data that comprises the **Ring Casting** data, insert a **Table** with a header row, and then apply **Table Style Medium 5**. **Sort** the table on the **Retail Price** from **Smallest to Largest**. Then filter the table by displaying only the **Marquise** shapes.

11. Click any cell in the table so that the table is selected, and then modify the **Table Style Options** to include a **Total Row**. In cell

(Project 11E–Castings continues on the next page)

Content-Based Assessments

(Project 11E–Castings continued)

A74, calculate the **Sum** for the *Quantity in Stock* column. In cell **C11**, type the value that displays in cell **A74**. Clear the **Total Row** from the table, and then clear the filter from the **Shape** column. **Sort** the table from **A to Z** on the **Style#** column, and then convert the table to a range.

12. Select the range of data that comprises the **Earring Casting** data, insert a **Table** with a header row, and then apply **Table Style Medium 4**. **Sort** the table on the **Retail Price** from **Smallest to Largest**. Then filter the table by displaying only the **Marquise** shapes.

13. Modify the **Table Style Options** to include the **Total Row**, and then in cell **G74**, calculate the **Sum** for the *Quantity in Stock* column. In cell **I11**, type the value that displays in cell **G74**. Clear the **Total Row** from the table, and then clear the filter from the **Shape** column. **Sort** the table from **A to Z** on the **Style#** column, and then convert the table to a range.

14. Insert a **Footer** with the **File Name** in the left section. On the **Page Layout tab**, change the **Orientation** to **Landscape**. Change the **Print Titles** option by repeating rows **13:14** at the top of each page, and then **Center** the worksheet **Horizontally**. On the **Page Layout tab**, in the **Scale to Fit group**, click the **down Scale arrow** several times to display **80%**. Delete the unused worksheets, and then return to **Normal** view.

15. **Save** 🖫 your workbook. **Print** the worksheet, or submit electronically. If you are directed to submit printed formulas, refer to Activity 5.17 to do so.

16. If you printed your formulas, be sure to redisplay the worksheet by pressing [Ctrl] + [`]. From the **Office** menu, click **Close**. If the dialog box displays asking if you want to save changes, click **No** so that you do *not* save the changes you made for printing formulas. **Close** Excel.

End **You have completed Project 11E**

Content-Based Assessments

Mastering Excel

Project 11F — Studio

In this project, you will apply the skills you practiced from the Objectives in Project 11B.

Objectives: 6. *Use Financial Functions;* **7.** *Use Goal Seek;* **8.** *Create a Data Table.*

In the following Mastering Excel project, you will create a worksheet for Marco Canaperi, President of Adamantine Jewelry, that analyzes loan options for a house in Maine that the company is considering purchasing and converting to a design studio. Marco wants to establish a design facility in the United States, but would like to keep the monthly loan payment below $6,000. The worksheets of your workbook will look similar to Figure 11.44.

For Project 11F, you will need the following file:

New blank Excel workbook

You will save your workbook as
11F_Studio_Loan_Firstname_Lastname

Figure 11.44

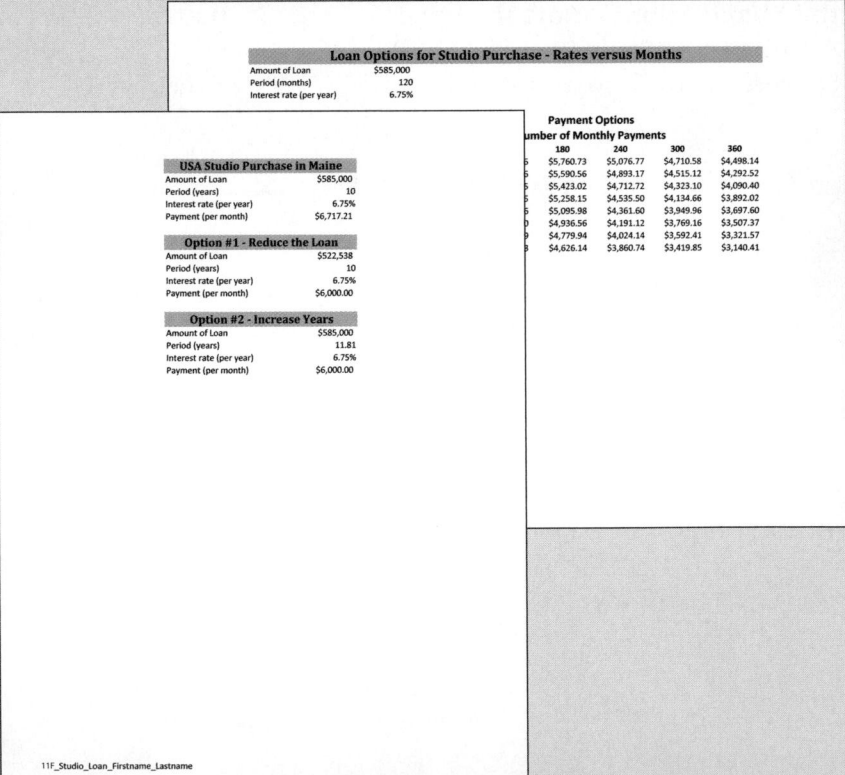

(Project 11F–Studio continued)

1. **Start** Excel and display a new blank workbook. **Save** the workbook in your **Excel Chapter 11** folder as **11F_Studio_Loan_ Firstname_Lastname** Widen **column A** to **185 pixels** and **column B** to **100 pixels**. In cell **A1**, type **USA Studio Purchase in Maine Merge and Center** the title in the range **A1:B1**, change the **Font** to **Cambria**, change the **Font Size** to **14**, apply **Bold**, and then add a **Fill Color** of **Blue, Accent 1, Lighter 40%**. Rename the worksheet tab as **Studio Purchase** In the range **A2:B5**, enter the following row titles and data.

Amount of Loan	$585,000
Period (years)	10
Interest rate (per year)	6.75%
Payment (per month)	

2. In cell **B5**, insert the **PMT** function using the data from the range **A2:B5**. Be sure that you divide the interest rate by 12 and multiply the years by 12, and that the payment displays as a positive number. The result is *$6,717.21*. Recall that Marco would prefer to keep the monthly payment below $6,000. Use **Goal Seek** to reduce the loan amount so that the payment does not exceed $6,000.

3. In **A7**, type **Option #1 - Reduce the Loan** Copy the format from cell **A1** to cell **A7**. Copy the range **A2:B5**, and then paste the **Values and number formats** to cell **A8**.

4. In cell **B2**, type **585000** to restore the original loan amount. Then use **Goal Seek** to increase the number of years in which to finance the studio so that the payment does not exceed $6,000. In **A13**, type **Option #2 - Increase Years** Format the cell the same as cell **A7**. Copy the range **A2:B5**, and then paste the **Values and number formats** to cell **A14**. Display the

value in **B15** with two decimal places, and then in cell **B3**, type **10** to restore the original value. Insert a footer with the **File Name** in the left section, and then **Center** the worksheet **Horizontally** on the page.

5. **Save** your workbook and return to **Normal** view. To determine how changes in interest rates and number of payments affect the payment amount, Marco will set up a two-variable data table. Rename the **Sheet2 tab** to **Studio Payment Table**

6. In the new worksheet, widen **column A** to **165 pixels**. Widen **column B** to **80 pixels**. In cell **A1**, type **Loan Options for Studio Purchase - Rates versus Months Merge and Center** this title across the range **A1:H1**. Change the **Font** to **Cambria**, the **Font Size** to **16**, apply **Bold**, and then apply a **Fill Color** of **Blue, Accent 1, Lighter 40%**.

7. Widen **columns C:H** to **85 pixels**. In the range **A2:B4**, enter the following row titles and data.

Amount of Loan	$585,000
Period (months)	120
Interest rate (per year)	6.75%

8. The lender with whom Adamantine Jewelry is financing the studio purchase has loan programs based on 5-, 10-, 15-, 20-, 25-, and 30-year terms. In cell **C8**, type **60**—the number of months in a 5-year loan. In **D8**, type **120**—the number of months in a 10-year loan. Then, fill the series across for the remaining four terms. **Center** and **Bold** the series information.

9. Beginning in cell **B9**, enter varying interest rates in increments of .5% beginning with **8.5%** and ending with **5%**. Format all the interest rates with two decimal places, and then **Center** and **Bold** the rates. In cell **C6**, type **Payment Options** and then **Merge**

(Project 11F–Studio continues on the next page)

Content-Based Assessments

(Project 11F–Studio continued)

and **Center** the title across the range **C6:H6**. Change the **Font Size** to **14**, and then apply **Bold**. In cell **C7**, type **Number of Monthly Payments** and then copy the format of cell **C6** to cell **C7**.

10. In cell **B8**, enter a **PMT** function using the information in cells **B2:B4**. Be sure that you convert the interest rate to a monthly rate and that the result displays as a positive number. Create a **Data Table** in the range **B8:H16** using the information in cells **B2:B4** in which the **Row input cell** is the **Period** and the **Column input cell** is the **Interest rate**. Copy the format from **B8** to the results in the data table. Insert a

footer with the **File Name** in the left section. Change the **Orientation** to **Landscape**, and then **Center** the worksheet **Horizontally** on the page. Delete **Sheet3** from the workbook, and then return to **Normal** view.

11. **Save** your workbook. **Print** the **Entire workbook**, or, submit electronically. If you are directed to submit printed formulas, refer to Activity 5.17 to do so.

12. If you printed your formulas, be sure to redisplay the worksheet by pressing Ctrl + `. From the **Office** menu, click **Close**. If you are prompted to save changes, click **No**. **Close** Excel.

 You have completed Project 11F

Mastering Excel

Project 11G — Sales

In this project, you will apply the skills you practiced from the Objectives in Project 11A and 7B.

Objectives: 1. *Use SUM, AVERAGE, MEDIAN, MIN, and MAX Functions;* **2.** *Use COUNTIF and IF Functions, and Apply Conditional Formatting;* **3.** *Use a Date Function;* **4.** *Freeze Panes and Create an Excel Table;* **5.** *Format and Print a Large Worksheet;* **7.** *Use Goal Seek.*

In the following Mastering Excel assessment, you will edit a worksheet for Jennifer Bernard, U.S. Sales Director for Adamantine Jewelry, that calculates the October sales commission and bonuses for the U.S. sales representatives. The sales representatives earn 15% commission and those whose sales exceed $20,000 per month earn a bonus of $750. The worksheet will also provide sales statistics for the month of October and will detail November sales goals. The worksheets of your workbook will look similar to Figure 11.45.

For Project 11G, you will need the following file:

e11G_Sales

You will save your workbook as 11G_Sales_Firstname_Lastname

Figure 11.45

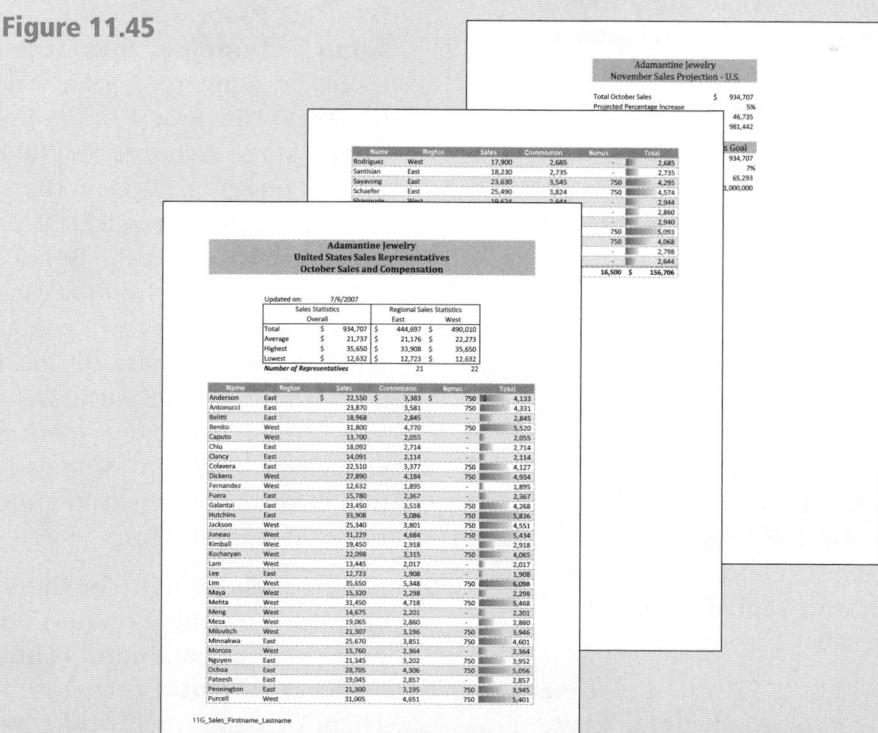

(Project 11G–Sales continues on the next page)

(Project 11G–Sales continued)

1. **Start** Excel, locate and open the file **e11G_Sales**, and then save the file in your **Excel Chapter 11** folder as **11G_Sales_ Firstname_Lastname** Rename **Sheet1** as Sales Data In cell **C6**, enter the **NOW** function, and then on the **Home tab**, in the **Number group**, click the **Number Format arrow** and apply the **Short Date** format to the date. In cell **C9**, enter a function that sums the total sales in the range **C16:C58**. In cells **C10**, **C11**, and **C12**, use statistical functions to calculate the average sales, the highest sales, and the lowest sales.

2. In cell **D16**, construct a formula to calculate the commission on sales earned by **Anderson** by using a commission formula of *Sales times 15%*. Format the result with **Comma Style** and **zero decimal places**. Copy the formula down for each sales representative. In cell **E16**, enter an **IF** function and test whether the sales value in cell **C16** is greater than **20000**. If true, display **750** and if false, display **0** Format the result as **Comma Style**, with **zero decimal places**, and then fill the formula down for each sales representative. Those representatives who receive no bonus will display – in the cell.

3. In cell **F16**, construct a formula to calculate the total compensation by adding the **Commission** and **Bonus** amounts for **Anderson**. The format of Comma Style and zero decimal places will be applied based on the reference to cell D16. Fill the formula down for each sales representative. With the range **F16:F58** still selected, apply **Light Blue Data Bar Conditional Formatting** to the **Total** column. In cell **D13**, enter a **COUNTIF** function to count the number of sales representatives in the **East** region. Enter a similar function in cell **E13** for the **West** region.

4. Select the range **A15:F58** and then **Insert** a **Table** with headers. Apply **Table Style**

(Project 11G–Sales continues on the next page)

Medium 7. In the **Name** column, **Sort** the table **A to Z**. Change the **Table Style Options** to display the **Total Row**.

5. If necessary, scroll up so that you can view **rows 1:18** on your screen. Then, select **row 16**, click the **View tab**, in the **Window group**, click the **Freeze Panes** button, and then click **Freeze Panes**. Scroll to bring the **Total row** at the bottom of the table closer to **row 15**—it is OK to leave three or four rows visible for visual reference. Recall that you can freeze panes in this manner to keep row titles visible while scrolling down through a large amount of data.

6. Filter the table to display only the sales representatives in the **East** region—the table will be filtered even though not all rows are in view. Click cell **C59**, and then by using the functions available from the **Total row arrow** in the **Sales** column, **Sum** the **Sales** for the **East** region. Right-click over the result, **Copy** the result, right-click over cell **D9**, click **Paste Special**, and then **Paste** its **value and number format** to cell **D9**. Using the same technique, and by using the **Total row arrow** in the **Sales** column, calculate the **Average** for the **East** region, and then copy and paste the **value and number format** to cell **D10**. By using the **Total row arrow** in the **Sales** column, calculate the highest and lowest sales amount for the **East** region, and paste the **values and number formats** to cells **D11** and **D12**. You can see that by freezing panes and using the shortcut menus, you can easily copy and paste values from one section of your worksheet to another without unnecessary scrolling.

7. Filter the **Sales** data for the **West** region, scroll to view the data and notice that the Freeze Panes command is still in effect. Position the **Total row** close to **row 15**. Then, by using the **Total row arrow** in the

(Project 11G–Sales continued)

Sales column in the manner you did in the previous step, make similar calculations and then copy and paste the **values and number formats** into the range **E9:E12**.

8. Clear the filter to redisplay all of the data in the table, and then in the **Total** row, **Sum** the **Sales**, **Commission**, **Bonus**, and **Total** columns. Select the four totals, right-click, and then apply **Accounting Number Format** with **zero decimal places**. Click the **View tab**, in the **Window group**, click the **Freeze Panes** button, and then click **Unfreeze Panes**. Click inside the table, and then on the **Design tab**, convert the table to a range. To the ranges **C9:E12** and **C16:F16**, apply **Accounting Number Format** with **zero decimal places**.

9. Insert a **Footer** with the **File Name** in the left section, and then **Center** the worksheet **Horizontally**. Click the **Print Titles** button and repeat **row 15** at the top of each page. Return to **Normal** view and display the top of your worksheet.

10. **Save** your work up to this point. **Rename Sheet2** as **November Sales Goal** In cell **A1**, type **Adamantine Jewelry** and then adjust the column width of **column A** to **220 pixels**. **Merge and Center** the title across **A1:B1**. Change the **Font** to **Cambria**, change the **Font Size** to **14**, and then add a **Fill Color** of **Orange, Accent 6, Lighter 40%**. In cell **A2**, type **November Sales Projection – U.S.** Copy the format from cell **A1** to cell **A2**. In the range **A4:B7**, enter the following data.

Total October Sales	
Projected Percentage Increase	5%
Projected November Increase	
Sales Projection November 2010	

11. Click cell **B4**, type = to begin a formula, click the **Sales Data worksheet** to make it the active sheet, click cell **C9**, and then press Enter to return to the **November Sales Goal** worksheet and reference the **Total October Sales** in cell **B4**. Format the result with **Accounting Number Format** with **zero decimal places**.

12. In cell **B6**, construct a formula to multiply the **Total October Sales** times the **Projected Percentage Increase**, and then format the result the same as cell **B4**. In cell **B7**, construct a formula to add the **Total October Sales** and the **Projected November Increase**.

13. Jennifer's sales goal for the U.S. sales representatives is $1,000,000. Use **Goal Seek** to determine the **Projected Percentage Increase** if the **Sales Projection November 2010** value is **1,000,000**. In cell **A9**, type **Increase Needed to Reach Sales Goal** and then format the cell the same as cell **A1**. **Copy** the range **A4:B7**, and then paste the **Values and number formats** to cell **A10**. In cell **B5**, reset the original value to **5%** and press Enter.

14. Insert a **Footer** in the left section with the **File Name**, and then **Center** the worksheet **Horizontally** on the page. Return to **Normal** view and display the top of the worksheet. Delete **Sheet3** from the workbook.

15. **Save** your workbook. **Print** the **Entire workbook** or submit electronically as directed. If you are directed to submit printed formulas, refer to Activity 5.17 to do so. If you printed your formulas, be sure to redisplay the worksheet by pressing Ctrl + `. From the **Office** menu, click **Close**. If you are prompted to save changes, click **No**. **Close** Excel.

End **You have completed Project 11G**

chaptereleven

Excel

Mastering Excel

Project 11H — Retirement

In this project, you will apply the skills you practiced from the Objectives in Projects 11A and 11B.

Objectives: 3. *Use a Date Function;* **6.** *Use Financial Functions;* **8.** *Create a Data Table.*

In the following Mastering Excel project, you will create a data table for Rosetta Caputo, the Chief Financial Officer for Adamantine Jewelry, that she will use to consider investment alternatives for the employee benefits retirement fund. Your workbook will look similar to Figure 11.46.

For Project 11H, you will need the following file:

New blank Excel workbook

You will save your workbook as
11H_Retirement_Firstname_Lastname

Figure 11.46

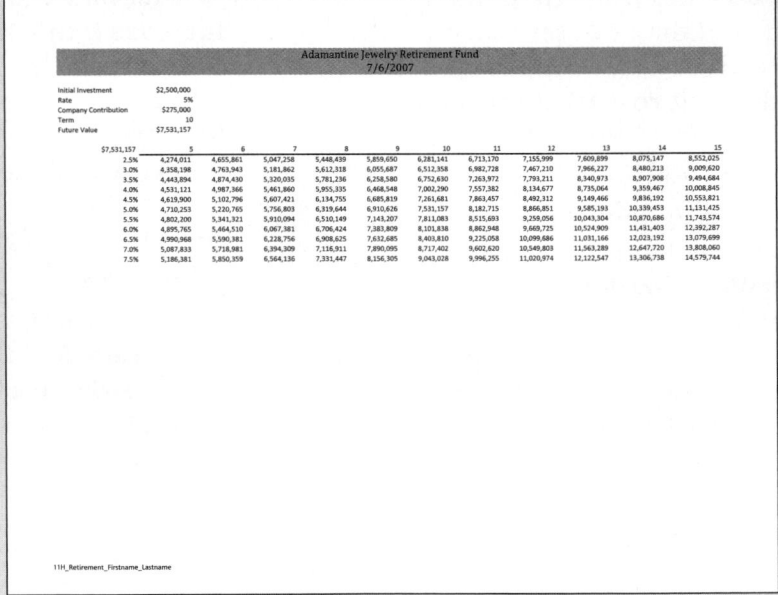

(Project 11H–Retirement continues on the next page)

Content-Based Assessments

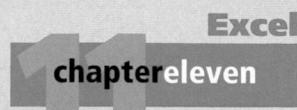
(Project 11H–Retirement continued)

1. **Start** Excel and display a new blank workbook. In your **Excel Chapter 11** folder, **Save** the file as **11H_Retirement_Firstname_Lastname** In cell **A1**, type **Adamantine Jewelry Retirement Fund** and then **Merge and Center** the text across **A1:L1**. Change the **Font** to **Cambria**, change the **Font Size** to **16**, and then apply a **Fill Color** of **Red, Accent 2, Lighter 40%**.

2. Copy the formatting from cell **A1** to cell **A2**. Then, in cell **A2**, enter the **NOW** function. On the **Home tab**, in the **Number group**, click the **Number Format arrow**, and then apply the **Short Date** format. In the range **A4:B8**, enter the following row titles and data and then **AutoFit column A**.

Initial Investment	$2,500,000
Rate	5%
Company Contribution	$275,000
Term	10
Future Value	

3. Click cell **B8**. Click the **Formulas tab**, and then insert the **Financial** function **FV** to calculate the future value of the retirement fund based on the data that you entered in Step 2. Complete the arguments as follows: the **Rate** is the value in cell **B5**, and **Nper** is the value in cell **B7**. **Pmt** is the amount of the **Company contribution** in cell **B6**, and **Pv** is the **Initial Investment** in cell **B4**. Click **OK**, and then edit the formula in the **Formula Bar** so that the result displays as a positive number. Format the **Future Value** with **zero decimal places**. Based on the calculations, at the end of ten years, the fund will have a value of *$7,531,157*.

4. In the range **B10:L10**, in 1-year increments, use **AutoFill** to enter a series of

years from **5** to **15**, indicating the term of the retirement fund. Apply a **Thick Bottom Border** to the range. Beginning in cell **A11**, enter the possible interest rates for the fund beginning with **2.5%** and increasing in increments of .5% up to 7.5%. Format the interest rates with **one decimal place**.

5. In cell **A10** type **=b8** to enter a formula that references cell **B8**. Select the range **A10:L21**, and then create a **Data Table** with a **Row input cell** that references cell **B7** and a **Column input cell** that references **B5**. Format the results in the data table with **Comma Style, zero decimal places**. You can see by the resulting data table, that the higher the interest rate that can be obtained for the investment, the higher the value of the fund will be in future years.

6. Insert a footer in the left section with the **File Name**, exit the **Footer area**, display the **Page Layout tab**, and then **Center** the worksheet **Horizontally** on the page. Change the **Orientation** to **Landscape**. In the **Scale to Fit group**, set the **Width** to **1 page** and the **Height** to **1 page** (or scale to 70%). Return to **Normal** view, display the top of the worksheet, and then delete the extra worksheets from the workbook.

7. **Save** your workbook. **Print** the worksheet, or submit electronically as directed. If you are directed to submit printed formulas, refer to Activity 5.17 to do so.

8. If you printed your formulas, be sure to redisplay the worksheet by pressing [Ctrl] + [`]. From the **Office** menu, click **Close**. If you are prompted to save changes, click **No**. **Close** Excel.

 You have completed Project 11H

Content-Based Assessments

Mastering Excel

Project 11I — Opals

In this project, you will apply the skills you practiced from all of the Objectives in Projects 11A and 11B.

Objectives: 1. *Use SUM, AVERAGE, MEDIAN, MIN, and MAX Functions;* **2.** *Use COUNTIF and IF Functions, and Apply Conditional Formatting;* **3.** *Use a Date Function;* **4.** *Freeze Panes and Create an Excel Table;* **5.** *Format and Print a Large Worksheet;* **6.** *Use Financial Functions;* **7.** *Use Goal Seek;* **8.** *Create a Data Table.*

In the following Mastering Excel assessment, you will edit a worksheet for Adamantine Jewelry's Chief Financial Officer, Rosetta Caputo. Adamantine Jewelry is considering the purchase of Opal Industries—a large distributor of elegant and expensive opal jewelry. The purchase includes the entire current inventory held by Opal Industries. Rosetta wants to compute the value of the Opal Industries inventory and determine which items are still in production and which items are in a warehouse. She must also explore alternatives for financing the purchase. Your completed workbook will look similar to Figure 11.47.

For Project 11I, you will need the following file:

e11I_Opals

You will save your workbook as 11I_Opals_Firstname_Lastname

Figure 11.47

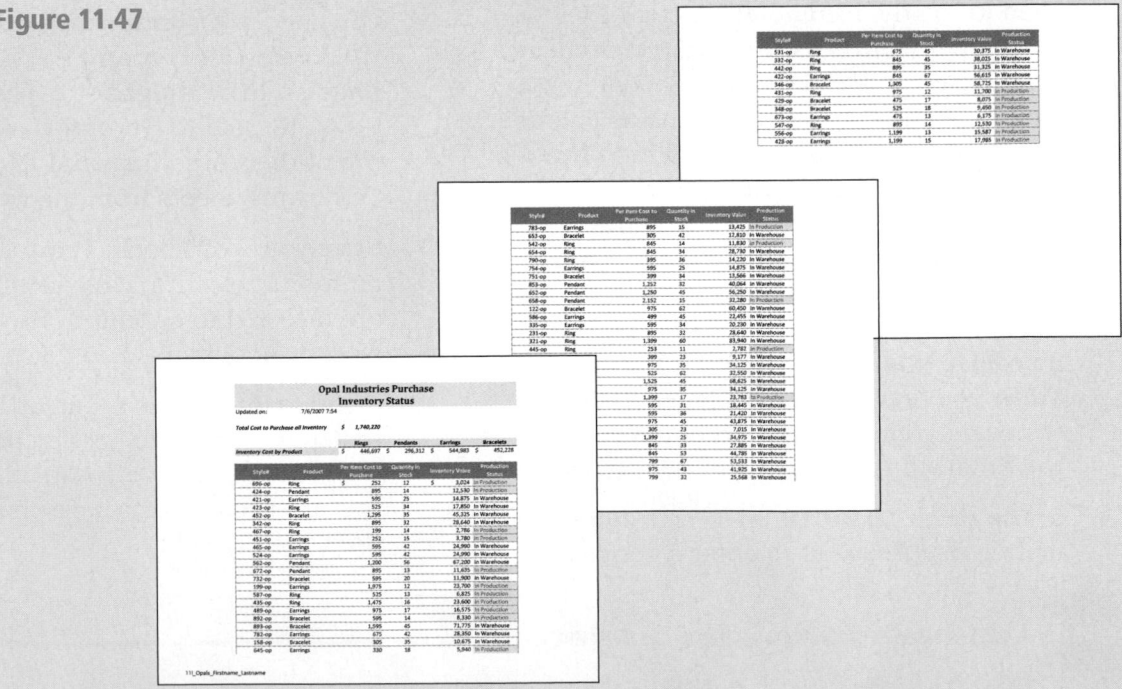

(Project 11I–Opals continues on the next page)

(Project 11I–Opals continued)

1. **Start** Excel. From the student files that accompany this text, locate and open the file **e11I_Opals**, and then save it in your **Excel Chapter 11** folder as 11I_Opals_Firstname_Lastname

2. In cell **B3**, insert the **NOW** function. In cell **E11**, construct a formula to calculate the **Inventory Value** of the first Style# by multiplying the **Per Item Cost to Purchase** times the **Quantity in Stock**, and then copy the formula down through **row 76**. Format the selected range with **Comma Style** and **zero decimal places**.

3. Opal Industries moves stock from the production facility to the warehouse after 20 items are produced. In cell **F11**, enter an **IF** function to test whether the **Quantity in Stock** value in cell **D11** is **greater than or equal to 20**. If true, display In **Warehouse** and if false, display In **Production** Copy the formula down through **row 76**. With the range still selected, use the **Text that Contains** conditional formatting to apply **Green Fill with Dark Green Text** to cells that contain In Production

4. Select the range **A10:F76**, and then **Insert** a **Table** with headers. Apply **Table Style Light 9**. Change the **Table Style Options** to display the **Total Row**. Press Ctrl + Home to deselect the table and view **row 1** on your screen. Select **row 11**, click the **View tab**, in the **Window group**, click the **Freeze Panes** button, and then click **Freeze Panes**.

5. Filter the table to display only the **Ring** products, and then scroll so that the **Total row** is closer to the column titles in **row 14**. In the **Total row**, calculate the **Sum** for the **Inventory Value** of Rings, right-click over the result, click **Copy**, right-

click over cell **C8**, right-click, click **Paste Special**, and then click **Values and number formats**. Even though some rows are out of view, the calculation is made on the appropriate rows. Recall that by freezing panes and using shortcut menus in this manner, you minimize the amount of scrolling necessary to perform actions.

6. Repeat Step 5 for the **Pendant**, **Earrings**, and **Bracelet** products in the appropriate cells. Then clear any filters to display all of the data in the table. Click any table cell, click the **Design tab**, remove the **Total Row** from the table, and then convert the table to a range. In cell **C5**, enter a function to calculate the cost to purchase the total inventory, which is the sum of the range **C8:F8**. Your result is 1,740,220. On the **View tab**, in the **Window group**, click the **Freeze Panes** button, and then click **Unfreeze Panes**. Hold down Ctrl and select cell **C11**, cell **E11**, cell **C5**, and the range **C8:F8**. To the selected cells, apply **Accounting Number Format** with **zero decimal places**. Set **columns C:F** to **100 pixels**.

7. Insert a footer with the **File Name** in the left section, and then **Center** the sheet **Horizontally**. Set the **Print Titles** option to repeat **row 10** at the top of each page. Change the **Orientation** to **Landscape**, return to **Normal** view, and then display the top of your worksheet. **Save** your workbook.

8. **Copy** cell **C5**, display the **Goal** sheet, and then use **Paste Special** to paste the **Values and number formats** to cell **B2** in the **Goal** sheet. In cell **B5**, insert the **PMT** function using the data from the range **B2:B4**. Be sure that you convert the interest rate and period to reflect monthly payments by dividing the interest rate by 12

(Project 11I–Opals continues on the next page)

Excel
chaptereleven **Mastering Excel**

(Project 11I–Opals continued)

and multiplying the years by 12. Display the result as a positive number. Apply the **Accounting Number Format** with **zero decimal places** to cell **B5**—your result is *$52,548.*

9. Rosetta prefers that the monthly payment not exceed $40,000. Use **Goal Seek** to determine the amount of money that Adamantine Jewelry can finance to keep the payment at $40,000. The interest rate and period will not change. The result is *$1,324.683.07.*

10. **Copy** the range **B2:B5**, and then paste the **Values and number formats** to cell **B8**. In cell **B2** type **1740220** to restore the original amount.

11. Insert a footer in the left section with the **File Name**, and then **Center** the sheet **Horizontally** on the page. Display the sheet in **Normal** view, and then **Save** your workbook.

12. **Copy** cell **B8**, display the **Financing** sheet, and then in cell **B3**, paste the value and number format; this will reference the amount that Rosetta has decided to finance as the **Amount of Loan**. In cell **B7**, enter a **PMT** function using the data in the range **B3:B5**. The period is already expressed in months, but the rate is not. Be sure that the result displays as a positive number. To determine how changes in interest rates and number of payments affect the payment amount, Rosetta will set up a two-variable data table. Rosetta is exploring loan programs from 12 to 60 months in duration and at rates of 2.5% to 6.5%.

13. Select the range **B7:G16**, and then create a **Data Table** using the information in cells **B3:B5** in which the **Row input cell** is the **Period** and the **Column input cell** is the **Interest rate**. Format the data with **Comma Style** and **zero decimal** places. Format cell **B7** with **Accounting Number Format** and **zero decimal places**.

14. Select the data table results—the range **C8:G16**. Recall that Rosetta prefers a monthly payment that does not exceed $40,000. Apply **Conditional Formatting** using the **Highlight Cells Rules Less Than** option. In the **Format cells that are LESS THAN** box, type **40000** and use **Light Red Fill with Dark Red Text**. Click any cell to deselect. Rosetta can clearly see which financing rates and terms are acceptable.

15. Insert a footer in the left section with the **File Name**, and then **Center** the sheet **Horizontally** on the page. Display the sheet in **Normal** view and press Ctrl + Home to display the top of the worksheet.

16. **Save** your workbook. **Print** the **Entire workbook**, or submit electronically as directed. If you are directed to submit printed formulas, refer to Activity 5.17 to do so.

17. If you printed your formulas, be sure to redisplay the sheet by pressing Ctrl + ꞌ. From the **Office** menu, click **Close**. If you are prompted to save changes, click **No**. **Close** Excel.

 End **You have completed Project 11I** ⎯⎯⎯⎯⎯⎯⎯⎯⎯⎯⎯⎯⎯

Content-Based Assessments

Project 11J—Business Running Case

In this project, you will apply the skills you practiced in Projects 11A and 11B.

From My Computer, navigate to the student files that accompany this textbook. In the folder **03_business_running_case**, locate and open the folder for this chapter. Open and print the instructions for this project, which are provided to you in Adobe PDF format. Follow the instructions and use the skills you have gained thus far to assist Jennifer Nelson in meeting the challenges of owning and running her business.

End **You have completed Project 11J** ⎯⎯⎯⎯⎯⎯

Content-Based Assessments

Mastering Excel

Project 11K — *GO!* Fix It

In this project, you will construct a solution by applying any combination of the skills you practiced from the Objectives in Projects 11A and 11B.

For Project 11K, you will need the following file:

e11K_fixit_Ruby_Inventory

**You will save your document as
11K_Ruby_Inventory_Firstname_Lastname**

From the student files that accompany this textbook, open the folder **05_go_fix_it**. Locate and open the file **e11K_fixit_Ruby_Inventory**, and then save the file in your chapter folder as **11K_Ruby_Inventory_Firstname_Lastname**

Adamantine Jewelry maintains a large stock of rubies for use in its retail business. In this project, you will edit and complete an Inventory and Reorder List and Loan Information tables.

This document contains **five errors** that you must find and correct. Read and examine the workbook, and then edit to correct the errors that you find. Types of errors could include:

- Spelling, grammar, and punctuation errors in cells, charts, worksheet tabs, or file names.
- Errors in data entry and workbook layout. Formatting errors in text, numbers, alignment, indents and spacing, tabs, wrapping, merge and center, text direction and orientation, fonts, borders, patterns, protection, AutoFormat, conditional formatting, data sort, filter, and validation.
- Formula and function errors such as incorrect and missing formulas, error indicators and values, relative vs. absolute cell referencing, What-If Analysis, Paste Special, function arguments, and Goal Seek.
- Errors in object design, layout, and formatting.
- Row and column formatting errors such as height, width, and AutoFit.
- Worksheet, tab design, and formatting errors such as missing or blank worksheets, worksheet tab colors, and locations.
- Page setup errors such as page orientation and scaling, margins and centering, headers and footers, sheet gridlines, and row and column headings.

(Project 11K–*GO!* Fix It continues on the next page)

Mastering Excel

(Project 11K–*GO!* Fix It continued)

To complete this project you should know:

- There are no spelling, grammar, punctuation, usage, font, font size, or border errors in the body of the worksheets.
- All the errors in the Inventory & Reorder List are in the top portion of the worksheet.

Save the changes you have made, add the file name to the footers, and then submit as directed.

End You have completed Project 11K————————

Outcomes-Based Assessments

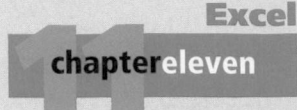

Excel

chaptereleven

Rubric

The following outcomes-based assessments are *open-ended assessments*. That is, there is no specific correct result; your result will depend on your approach to the information provided. Make *Professional Quality* your goal. Use the following scoring rubric to guide you in *how* to approach the problem, and then to evaluate *how well* your approach solves the problem.

The *criteria*—Software Mastery, Content, Format and Layout, and Process—represent the knowledge and skills you have gained that you can apply to solving the problem. The *levels of performance*—Professional Quality, Approaching Professional Quality, or Needs Quality Improvements—help you and your instructor evaluate your result.

	Your completed project is of Professional Quality if you:	Your completed project is Approaching Professional Quality if you:	Your completed project Needs Quality Improvements if you:
1-Software Mastery	Choose and apply the most appropriate skills, tools, and features and identify efficient methods to solve the problem.	Choose and apply some appropriate skills, tools, and features, but not in the most efficient manner.	Choose inappropriate skills, tools, or features, or are inefficient in solving the problem.
2-Content	Construct a solution that is clear and well organized, contains content that is accurate, appropriate to the audience and purpose, and is complete. Provide a solution that contains no errors of spelling, grammar, or style.	Construct a solution in which some components are unclear, poorly organized, inconsistent, or incomplete. Misjudge the needs of the audience. Have some errors in spelling, grammar, or style, but the errors do not detract from comprehension.	Construct a solution that is unclear, incomplete, or poorly organized, containing some inaccurate or inappropriate content; and contains many errors of spelling, grammar, or style. Do not solve the problem.
3-Format and Layout	Format and arrange all elements to communicate information and ideas, clarify function, illustrate relationships, and indicate relative importance.	Apply appropriate format and layout features to some elements, but not others. Overuse features, causing minor distraction.	Apply format and layout that does not communicate information or ideas clearly. Do not use format and layout features to clarify function, illustrate relationships, or indicate relative importance. Use available features excessively, causing distraction.
4-Process	Use an organized approach that integrates planning, development, self-assessment, revision, and reflection.	Demonstrate an organized approach in some areas, but not others; or, use an insufficient process of organization throughout.	Do not use an organized approach to solve the problem.

Outcomes-Based Assessments

chaptereleven

Problem Solving

Project 11L — Capital Equipment

In this project, you will construct a solution by applying any combination of the skills you practiced from the Objectives in Projects 11A and 11B.

For Project 11L, you will need the following file:

New blank Excel workbook

You will save your workbook as
11L_Capital_Equipment_Firstname_Lastname

Adamantine Jewelry plans to renovate the Milan production facility. The renovation consists primarily of the purchase and installation of new capital equipment used in the production of earrings and pendants. The renovation and equipment will cost $1,500,000. Rosetta Caputo, Chief Financial Officer, is exploring financing options for the purchase of the equipment. Create a workbook with two worksheets that Rosetta can use to analyze loan payment information. In the first worksheet, enter a title in cell A1. In A2:A5 enter the following row titles: Amount of Loan, Period (years), Interest Rate (per year), and Payment (per month). In B2:B4 enter the loan amount, $1,500,000; the Period, 10 years; and the Interest rate, 6.5%. Adjust the column widths as necessary. In B5 use the preceding data to construct a PMT function to calculate the monthly loan payment, converting the interest rate and the period to reflect monthly payments.

Marco Canaperi, the company president, has asked Rosetta to keep the loan payments below $15,000. Use Goal Seek to explore two options for reducing the loan payment, either by reducing the loan or by increasing the number of years. Arrange the worksheet so that the two loan options display similar to Project 11B in the chapter.

In the second worksheet, using your work in Project 11B as a guide, create a data table to calculate payments over 10, 15, 20, and 25 years with varying interest rates from 3.5% to 8.5% in .5% increments. In A2:B4 enter the row titles and the loan information. In C6:C7 enter titles that describe the data table. In C8:F8 enter the yearly increments. In B9:B19 enter the interest rates in .5% increments. In B8 construct the PMT function, and then create the data table. On each worksheet, apply appropriate number formatting, use borders, fill colors, and font styles and sizes to create a professional worksheet. Add a footer to each worksheet that includes the file name, center the worksheets on the page, and delete unused sheets. Save the workbook as **11L_Capital_Equipment_Firstname_Lastname** and submit it as directed.

End You have completed Project 11L —————————

Outcomes-Based Assessments

Problem Solving

Project 11M — Commission

In this project, you will construct a solution by applying any combination of the skills you practiced from the Objectives in Projects 11A and 11B.

For Project 11M, you will need the following file:

e11M_Commission

You will save your workbook as
11M_Commission_Firstname_Lastname

The U.S. Sales Director for Adamantine Jewelry, Jennifer Bernard, wants a report on the December sales and compensation for the U.S. sales representatives. From your student files, open e11M_Commissions. Calculate the Commission (Commission Rate times Sales) for each sales representative, using absolute cell references as necessary. Sales representatives whose sales exceed $20,000 receive a bonus of $750. In the Bonus column, use an IF function to calculate bonuses—the value_if_true is 750 and the value_if_false is 0. Then calculate the total Compensation (Commission + Bonus) for each sales representative. Use Conditional Formatting to apply Data Bars to the Total Compensation column. In the range B8:C12, enter functions to calculate the total sales and commission, the average sales and commission, the median sales and commission, and the highest and lowest sales and commission.

Insert a table using the range of data A16:F59. Sort the table from A to Z on the Name column. Add a Total Row to the table, freeze panes if you want to do so, and then filter the table for each region. Calculate the total Sales and Commissions for each region and enter the amounts in cells F8:G11 being sure to paste the value and number format. Then, total the Sales and Commissions in F12:G12. Convert the table to a range and unfreeze panes if necessary. Use the NOW function to enter the current date in cell B5 and apply the Short Date format. Add the file name to the footer, delete unused sheets, set up for printing appropriately, including printing the table header row on each page. Save the workbook as **11M_Commission_Firstname_Lastname** and submit it as directed.

 You have completed Project 11M

Outcomes-Based Assessments

Excel
chapter eleven

Problem Solving

Project 11N—Truck Purchase

In this project, you will construct a solution by applying any combination of the skills you practiced from the Objectives in Projects 11A and 11B.

For Project 11N, you will need the following file:

New blank Excel workbook

You will save your workbook as
11N_Truck_Purchase_Firstname_Lastname

Rosetta Caputo, Chief Financial Officer for Adamantine Jewelry, is exploring financing options for the purchase of five new delivery trucks for the Milan production facility. The cost of the five trucks is $150,000.

Rosetta wants to look at various loan arrangements by creating a data table. In A1 enter an appropriate title for the worksheet. In A2:A4 enter the following row titles: Amount of Loan, Period (months), Interest Rate (per year). In B2:B4 enter the financing data: $150,000; 36; 4.5%. In C6 fill the payment periods in six-month increments beginning with 24 and concluding with 60. In the column beginning in cell B7, create a list of varying interest rates from 4.5% to 8% in .5% increments. In B6 construct a PMT function using the data in cells B2:B4, then create the data table. Use formatting and editing techniques that you practiced in this chapter so that the workbook looks professional and is easy to read. Add the file name to the footer, delete unused sheets, and then arrange for attractive printing. Save the workbook as **11N_Truck_Purchase_Firstname_Lastname** and submit it as directed.

End **You have completed Project 11N** ─────────

Outcomes-Based Assessments

Problem Solving

Project 11O — Watches

In this project, you will construct a solution by applying any combination of the skills you practiced from the Objectives in Projects 11A and 11B.

> **For Project 11O, you will need the following file:**
>
> e11O_Watches

You will save your workbook as
11O_Watches_Firstname_Lastname

Rose Elleni, Vice President of Production, has requested a worksheet detailing the current inventory of watches at the Milan production facility. She wants the worksheet to include quantities, styles, prices, product descriptions, and stock levels. Open **e11O_Watches** and complete the worksheet as follows: In the Stock Level column, enter an IF function that tests the Quantity in Stock. Items with less than 35 in stock must be ordered. If the items do not need to be ordered, the Stock Level is OK. Use Conditional Formatting to apply bold and italic to the items in the Stock Level column designated as Order. In B5 use a function to sum the Quantity in Stock column. In B6:B9 use functions to calculate the Average, Median, Lowest, and Highest values in the Retail Price column.

Insert a table using the range A12:F65. Sort the table from Smallest to Largest on Style# and then use filters to display and calculate the Quantity in Stock for each type of Band and enter the values and number formats in F6:F8. In F9, construct a formula to calculate the total Quantity in Stock. Convert the table to a range. Add the file name to the footer, delete unused pages, print the table headers and use the Print Titles option so that row 12 prints at the top of every page. Save the workbook as **11O_Watches_Firstname_Lastname** and submit it as directed.

 End **You have completed Project 11O** ———

Outcomes-Based Assessments

Problem Solving

Project 11P — Sales Directors

In this project, you will construct a solution by applying any combination of the skills you practiced from the Objectives in Projects 11A and 11B.

For Project 11P, you will need the following file:

e11P_Sales_Directors

You will save your workbook as
11P_Sales_Directors_Firstname_Lastname

The U.S. Regional Directors for Adamantine Jewelry are responsible for maximizing profits at several retail locations. Jennifer Bernard, the U.S. Sales Director, has requested an annual profit analysis. Open the file **e11P_Sales_Directors**, which contains summary information about the sales, expenses, and profits in the Eastern Region. Apply Data Bars to the Profit column. Insert a table and then sort the table from A to Z on the City column. Sort again from Smallest to Largest on the Sales Director column. Filter the table by each region and then calculate the total profit by region and enter the results in the range C5:C8. Convert the table to a range and if necessary wrap the text in row 10. Use formatting and editing techniques that you learned in this chapter so that the worksheet is attractive and easy to read. Add the file name to the footer and save the workbook as **11P_Sales_Directors_Firstname_Lastname** and submit it as directed.

End **You have completed Project 11P** ————————————

Outcomes-Based Assessments

 **Excel**
chapter**eleven**

 You and *GO!*

Project 11Q—You and *GO!*

In this project, you will construct a solution by applying any combination of the Objectives found in Projects 11A and 11B.

From My Computer, navigate to the student files that accompany this textbook. In the folder **04_you_and_go**, locate and open the folder for this chapter. Open and print the instructions for this project, which are provided to you in Adobe PDF format. Follow the instructions to create a data table to compare vehicle loan terms.

 End **You have completed Project 11Q** ————————————

GO! with Help

Project 11R—*GO!* with Help

In this chapter, you practiced using statistical, logical, and financial functions. Sometimes a single function is not sufficient to complete a calculation. For example, when you create an IF function, you must specify the value_if_true and the value_if_false. Either of these values may require that you sum a range of cells. You can nest (combine) the functions by making the sum function a part of the IF function argument. In this exercise, you will use Help to find out how to nest functions.

1 **Start** Excel. At the far right end of the Ribbon, click the **Microsoft Office Excel Help** button 🔘.

2 Click the **Search arrow**, and then under **Content from this computer**, click **Excel Help**. In the search box, type **IF Function** and then press ⏎. Click the link for **Nest a function within a function**.

3 Read the information that displays. When you are finished, close the Help window, and then **Close** Excel.

 End **You have completed Project 11R** ————————————

Outcomes-Based Assessments

Group Business Running Case

Project 11S — Group Business Running Case

In this project, you will apply all the Objectives found in Projects 11A and 11B.

Your instructor may assign this group case project to your class. If your instructor assigns this project, he or she will provide you with information and instructions to work as part of a group. The group will apply the skills gained thus far to help the Bell Orchid Hotel Group achieve its business goals.

 You have completed Project 11S ——————————

chapter twelve

Getting Started with Access Databases and Tables

OBJECTIVES

At the end of this chapter you will be able to:

1. Start Access and Create a New Blank Database
2. Add Records to a Table
3. Rename Table Fields in Datasheet View
4. Modify the Design of a Table
5. Add a Second Table to a Database
6. Print a Table
7. Create and Use a Query
8. Create and Use a Form
9. Create and Print a Report
10. Close and Save a Database

11. Create a Database Using a Template
12. Organize Database Objects in the Navigation Pane
13. Create a New Table in a Database Created With a Template
14. View a Report and Print a Table in a Database Created With a Template
15. Use the Access Help System

OUTCOMES

Mastering these objectives will enable you to:

PROJECT 12A
Create a New Blank Database

PROJECT 12B
Create a Database from a Template

Texas Lakes Medical Center

Texas Lakes Medical Center is an urban hospital serving the city of Austin and surrounding Travis County, an area with a population of over 1 million people. Texas Lakes is renowned for its cardiac care unit, which is rated among the top 10 in Texas. The hospital also offers state-of-the-art maternity and diagnostic services, a children's center, a Level II trauma center, and a number of specialized outpatient services. Physicians, nurses, scientists, and researchers from around the world come together at Texas Lakes to provide the highest quality patient care.

Getting Started with Access Databases and Tables

Do you have a collection of belongings that you like, such as a coin or stamp collection, a box of favorite recipes, or a stack of music CDs? Do you have an address book with the names, addresses, and phone numbers of your friends, business associates, and family members? If you collect something, chances are you have made an attempt to keep track of and organize the items in your collection. If you have an address book, you have probably wished it was better organized. A program like Microsoft Office Access can help you organize and keep track of information.

Microsoft Office Access 2007 is a program to organize a collection of related information about a particular topic, such as an inventory list, a list of people in an organization, or the students who are enrolled in classes in a college. Whether you use Access for personal or business purposes, it is a powerful program that helps you organize, search, sort, retrieve, and present information about a particular subject in an organized manner.

Project 12A Doctor and Patient Contact Information

In Activities 12.01 through 12.14, you will assist June Liu, Chief Administrative Officer at Texas Lakes Medical Center, in creating a new database for tracking the contact information for doctors and patients. June has a list of doctors and their contact information and a list of patients and their contact information. Using June's lists, you will create an Access database to track this information and use it to prepare a report. Your results will look similar to Figure 12.1.

For Project 12A, you will need the following file:

New blank Access database

You will save your database as
12A_Contact_Information_Firstname_Lastname

Figure 12.1
Project 12A—Contact Information

Objective 1
Start Access and Create a New Blank Database

A **database** collects and organizes **data**—facts about people, events, things, or ideas—related to a particular topic or purpose. Data that has been organized in a useful manner is referred to as **information**.

Many databases start as a simple list on paper, in a Word document, or in an Excel spreadsheet. As the list grows bigger and the data becomes more difficult to keep track of, it is a good idea to transfer the data to a database management system (**DBMS**) such as Access.

Examples of data that could be in a database include the titles and artists of all the CDs in a collection or the names and addresses of all the doctors and patients at a medical facility. A database includes not only the data, but also the tools for organizing the data in a way that is useful to you.

The first step in creating a new database from data that you already have is to plan your database on paper. Determine what information you want to track, and then ask yourself, *What questions should this database be able to answer for me?*

For example, in the Contact Information database for the Texas Lakes Medical Center, the questions to be answered may include:

- How many doctors and patients are there at the Texas Lakes Medical Center?

- Which and how many patients live in Austin?

- Is any doctor or patient listed twice?

- Which and how many patients have a balance owed?

Activity 12.01 Starting Access, Creating and Naming a Folder, and Creating a Database from a New Blank Database

There are two methods to create a new Access database: create a new database using a **template**—a preformatted database designed for a specific purpose—or create a new **blank database**. A blank database has no data and has no database tools; you create the data and the tools as you need them. In this activity, you will create a new blank database.

Regardless of which method you use, you must name and save the database before you can create any **objects** in the database. Objects are the basic parts of a database; you will create objects to store your data and work with your data. Think of an Access database as a container for the database objects that you will create.

1 On the left side of the Windows taskbar, click the **Start** button , determine where the **Access** program is located, point to **Microsoft Office Access 2007**, and then click one time to open the program. Take a moment to compare your screen with Figure 12.2 and study the parts of the Microsoft Access window described in the table in Figure 12.3.

From this Access starting point, you can open an existing database, start a new blank database, or begin a new database from one of the available database templates.

Figure 12.2

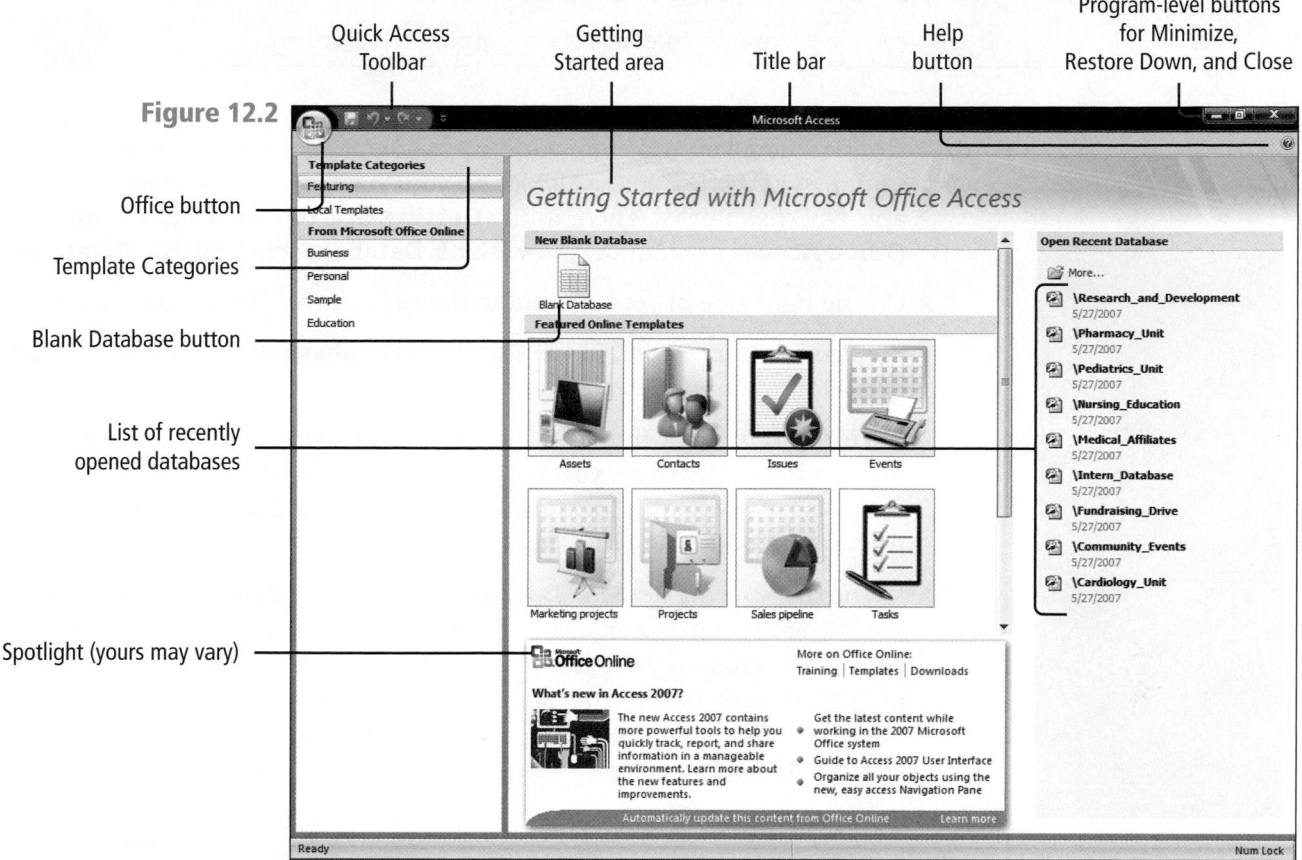

| Quick Access Toolbar | Getting Started area | Title bar | Help button | Program-level buttons for Minimize, Restore Down, and Close |

- Office button
- Template Categories
- Blank Database button
- List of recently opened databases
- Spotlight (yours may vary)

The Access Getting Started Screen

Window Part	Description
Blank Database button	Starts a new blank database.
Getting Started area	Contains the starting point to begin a New Blank Database or view new information from Microsoft Office Online.
Help button	Displays the Access Help window.
Open Recent Database	Displays a list of the most recently opened databases on the computer at which you are working.
Office button	Displays a menu of commands related to things you can do *with* a database, such as opening, saving, printing, or managing.
Program-level buttons for Minimize, Restore Down, and Close	Minimizes, restores, or closes the Access program.
Quick Access Toolbar	Displays buttons to perform frequently used commands with a single click. Frequently used commands in Access include Save, Undo, and Redo. You can add commands that you use frequently to the Quick Access Toolbar.
Spotlight	Displays the latest online content, such as new templates, articles about Access, and tips from Microsoft's Web site.

(Continued)

Window Part	Description
Template Categories	Displays a list of available database templates.
Title bar	Displays the program name and the program-level buttons.

Figure 12.3

2 Decide where you will store your Access databases for this textbook—for example, in the *Documents* folder on your hard disk drive or on a removable USB flash drive. Then, in the **Getting Started with Microsoft Office Access** area, under **New Blank Database**, click **Blank Database**.

3 On the right side of your screen, to the right of the **File Name** box, click the **Browse** button 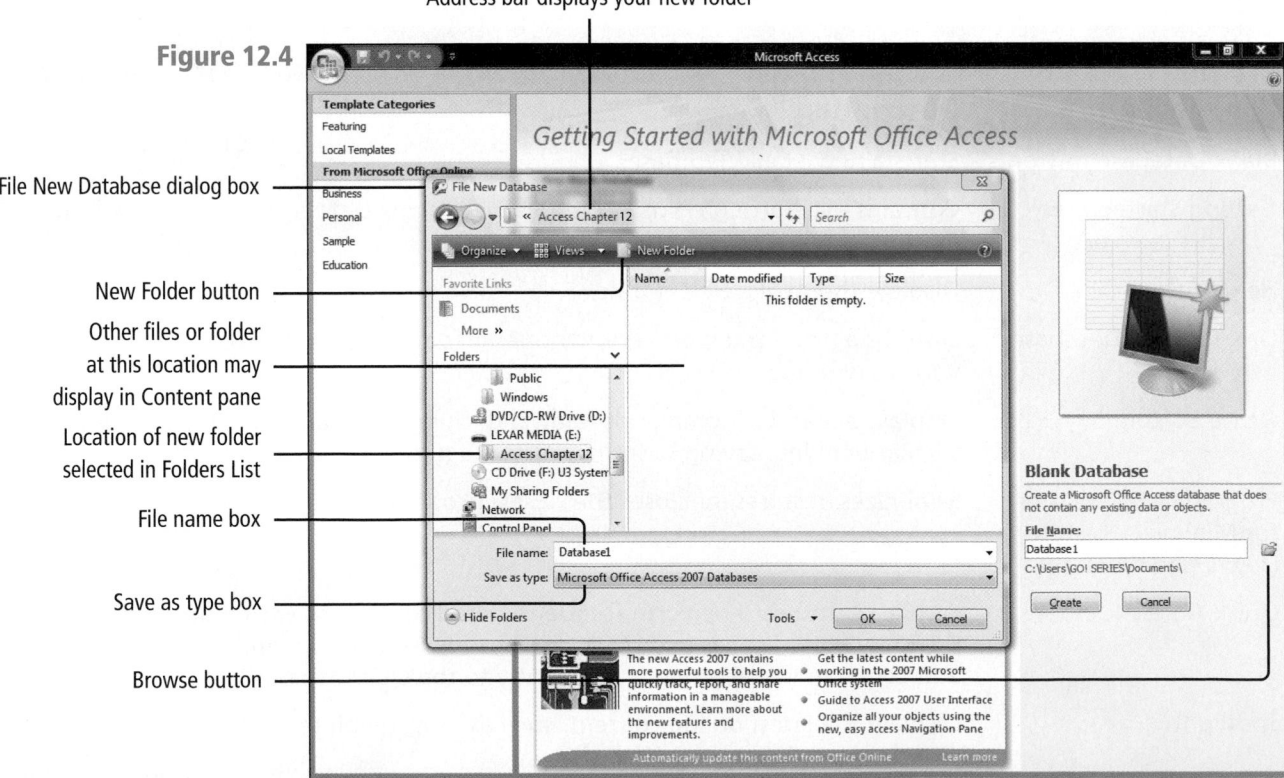. In the **File New Database** dialog box, notice the default location in the **Address bar**.

A *dialog box* is a window containing commands or that asks you to make a decision. Here, you indicate where you will save your new database. The default location for saving a new database file is your *Documents* folder on your hard disk drive.

4 In the displayed **File New Database** dialog box, navigate to the location where you are storing your projects for this chapter, for example, *Documents* on your hard disk drive or *LEXAR MEDIA (E:)* to store on a USB flash drive—the exact name and drive letter will vary. Then, on the toolbar, click the **New Folder** button. Type **Access Chapter 12** and press [Enter]. Compare your screen with Figure 12.4.

Address bar displays your new folder

Figure 12.4

File New Database dialog box —

New Folder button —

Other files or folder at this location may display in Content pane

Location of new folder selected in Folders List —

File name box —

Save as type box —

Browse button —

5 In the lower portion of the dialog box, in the **File name** box, select the existing text, and then type **12A_Contact_Information_Firstname_Lastname** Press ⏎, and then compare your screen with Figure 12.5.

Text that you select is replaced by new text that you type. The Microsoft Windows operating system recognizes file names with spaces. However, some Internet file transfer programs do not. To facilitate sending your files over the Internet, in this textbook you will save files using an underscore rather than a space. On most keyboards, the underscore key is the shift of the hyphen key, which is to the right of the zero key.

Figure 12.5

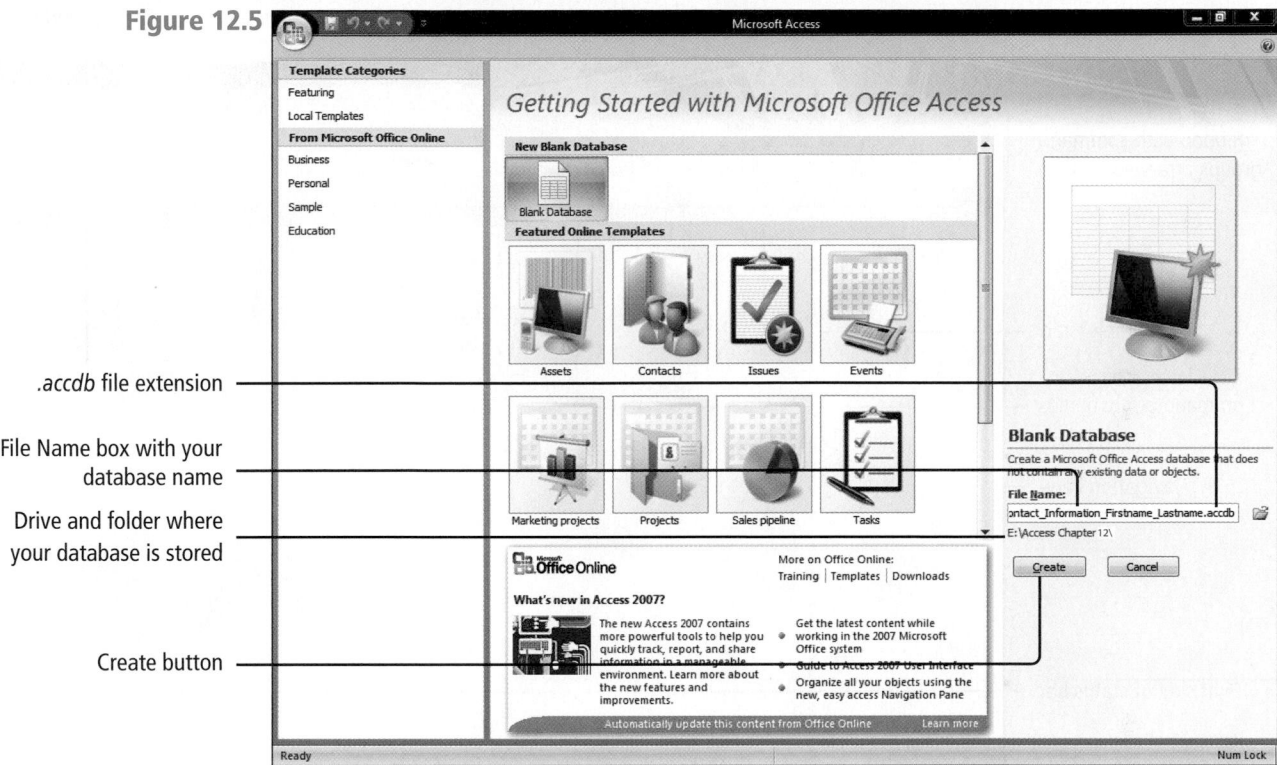

.*accdb* file extension

File Name box with your database name

Drive and folder where your database is stored

Create button

6 In the lower right corner, click the **Create** button, compare your screen with Figure 12.6, and then take a moment to study the screen elements described in the table in Figure 12.7.

Access creates the new database and opens a ***table*** named *Table1*. A table is the Access object that stores your data organized in an arrangement of columns and rows. Recall that *object* is the term used to refer to the parts of an Access database that you will use to store and work with your data.

Table objects are the foundation of your Access database because tables store the actual data.

Note — Comparing Your Screen With the Figures in This Textbook

Your screen will match the figures shown in this textbook if you set your screen resolution to 1024 × 768. At other resolutions, your screen will closely resemble, but not match, the figures shown. To view your screen's resolution, on the Windows desktop, right-click in a blank area, click Personalize and then click Display Settings.

Figure 12.6

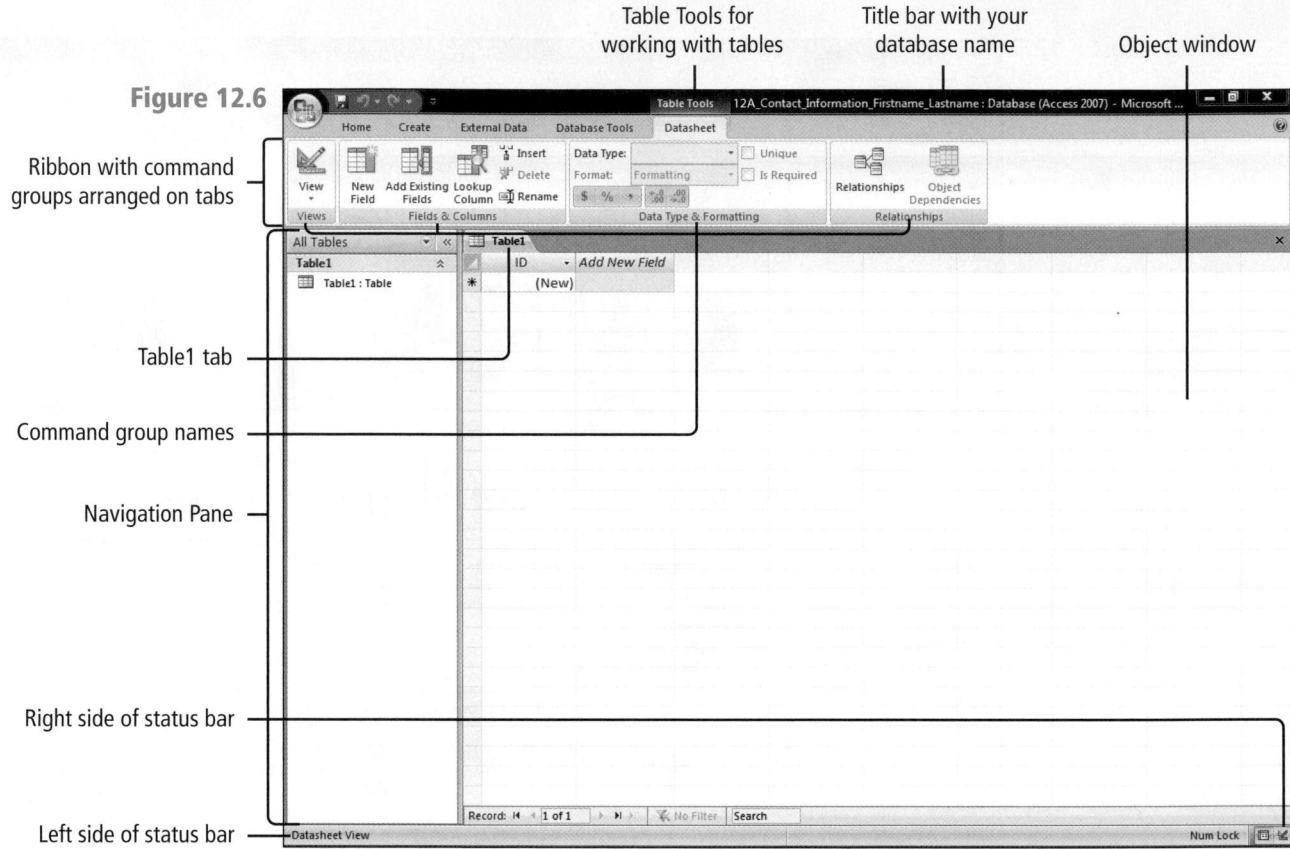

Table Tools for working with tables

Title bar with your database name

Object window

Ribbon with command groups arranged on tabs

Table1 tab

Command group names

Navigation Pane

Right side of status bar

Left side of status bar

Parts of the Access Window

Window Part	Description
Command group names	Contains groups of related command buttons associated with the selected command tab.
Left side of status bar	Indicates the active view and the status of actions occurring within the database.
Navigation Pane	Displays the database objects; from here you open the database objects to display in the object window at the right.
Object window	Displays the open table object.
Ribbon with command groups arranged on tabs	Groups the commands for performing related database tasks on tabs.
Right side of status bar	Provides buttons to switch between Datasheet View and Design View.
Table Tools for working with tables	Provides tools for working with a table object; Table Tools are available only when a table is displayed.
Table1 tab	Enables you to select the table object.
Title bar with your database name	Displays the name of your database.

Figure 12.7

7 Leave your database open for the next activity.

Objective 2
Add Records to a Table

After you have saved and named the database, the next step is to plan and create the tables in which to record your data. Recall that tables are the foundation of your database because the actual data is stored there.

Limit the data in each table to one subject. For example, think of all the data at your college; there is likely one table for student information, another table for course information, another table for classroom information, and so on.

Within each table, create columns that are broken down into the smallest usable part. For example, instead of a complete address, break the address down into a part for the street address, a part for the city, a part for the state, and a part for the postal code. With small usable parts, you can, for example, find all of the people who live in a particular city or state or postal code.

To answer all the questions you want your database to answer, in this project you will create a database with two tables. One table will list the names and contact information for patients at Texas Lakes Medical Center and the other table will list the names and contact information for doctors at Texas Lakes Medical Center.

Activity 12.02 Adding Records to a Table

In a table object, each column contains a category of data called a *field*. Fields are categories that describe each piece of data stored in the table. You can add the field names, which display at the top of each column of the table, before or while you are entering your data. Each row in a table contains a **record**—all of the categories of data pertaining to one person, place, thing, event, or idea. Your *table design* refers to the number of fields, the names of fields, and the type of content within a field, for example numbers or text.

There are two ways to view a table—in **Datasheet view** or in **Design view**. Datasheet view displays the table data organized in a format of columns and rows similar to an Excel spreadsheet. Design view displays the underlying structure of the table object.

When you buy a new address book, it is not very useful until you fill it with names, addresses, and phone numbers. Likewise, a new database is not useful until you **populate**, or fill, a table with data. You can populate a table with records by typing data directly into the table.

In this activity, you will populate a table in Datasheet view that will list contact information for patients at Texas Lakes Medical Center.

1 Look at your screen and notice that the Datasheet view for a table displays. Then, take a moment to study the elements of the table object window as shown in Figure 12.8.

When you create a new blank database, only one object—a new blank table—is created. You will create the remaining database objects as you need them.

Because you have not yet named this table, the Table tab indicates the default name *Table1*. Access creates the first field and names it *ID*. In the ID field, Access will assign a unique sequential number—each number incremented by one—to each record as you type it into the table.

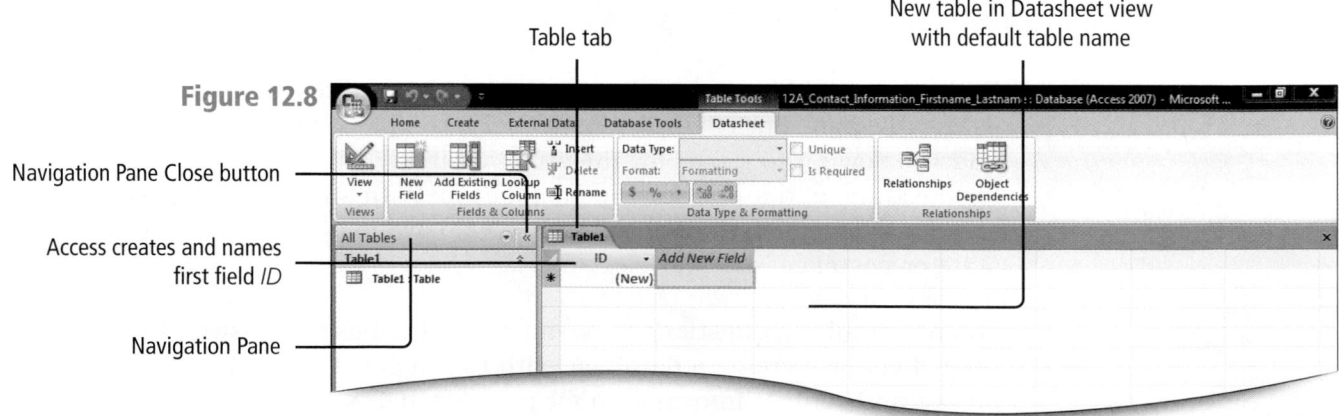

Figure 12.8

Table tab

New table in Datasheet view with default table name

Navigation Pane Close button

Access creates and names first field *ID*

Navigation Pane

2 In the **Navigation Pane**, click the **Open/Close** button [«] to collapse the **Navigation Pane** into a narrow bar at the left side of your screen.

Collapsing the Navigation Pane in this manner gives you more screen space in which to work with your database.

3 In the second column, click in the **cell**—the box formed by the intersection of a row and a column—under *Add New Field*, type **Elena** and then press [Tab] or [Enter]. Click in the **ID** field. On the **Datasheet tab**, in the **Data Type & Formatting group**, click the **Data Type arrow**, and then click **Text**. Type **1248-P** and then to the right of *Elena*, click in the **Add New Field** cell. Type **L** and then press [Tab]. Compare your screen with Figure 12.9.

As soon as information is entered, Access assigns the name *Field1* to the field and enters an AutoNumber of 1 in the ID field. The ID field is automatically created by Access. By default, Access creates this field for all new tables and sets the data type for the field to **AutoNumber**, which sequentially numbers each entry. Changing the ID field data type from *AutoNumber* to *Text* enables you enter a custom patient number. As you enter data, Access assigns Field names as *Field1*, *Field2*, and so on; you can rename the fields when it is convenient for you to do so.

The pencil icon in the **record selector box**—the small box at the left of a record in Datasheet view which, when clicked, selects the entire record—indicates that a new record is being entered.

Field named *Field1*

Figure 12.9

Pencil icon indicates a new record is being entered

Record selector boxes

First patient ID is *1248-P*

First name of first patient entered

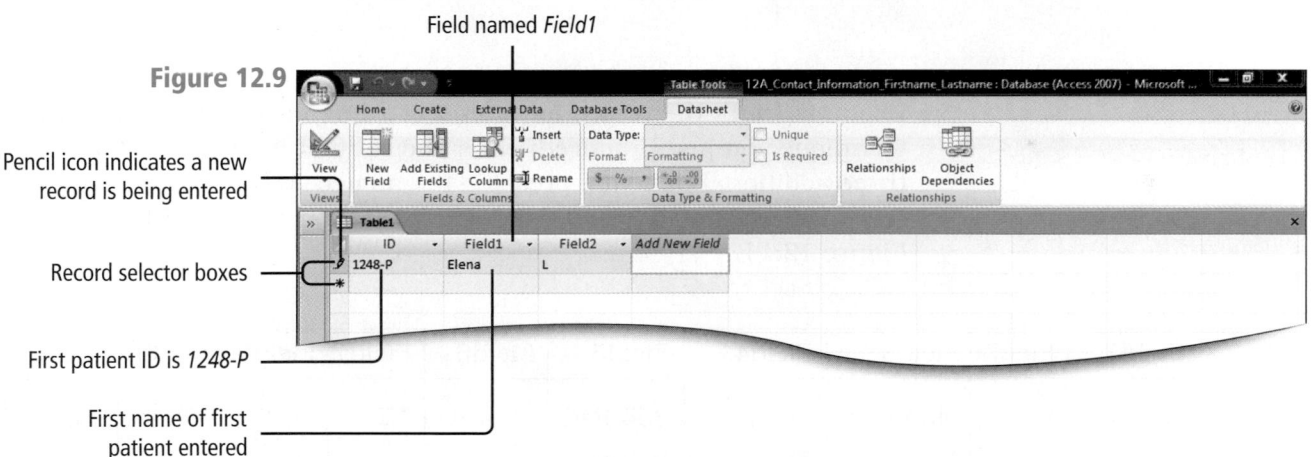

4 With the insertion point positioned in the fourth column, in the cell under *Add New Field*, type **Montoya** and then press [Tab] or [Enter].

5 Type **(512) 555-0723** and then press [Enter]. Type **854 Red Willow Drive** and then press [Enter] to form *Field5*.

Do not be concerned if the data does not completely display in the column. As you progress in your study of Access, you will adjust the column widths so that you can view the data.

6 Type **Austin** and then press [Enter] to form *Field6*. Type **TX** and then press [Enter] to form *Field7*.

7 Type **78754** and then press [Enter] to form *Field8*. Type **Wilcox** and then press [Enter] to form *Field9*. Type **150** and then press [Enter] two times. Compare your screen with Figure 12.10.

To move across the row, you can press [Tab] or [Enter]. Pressing [Enter] two times moves the insertion point to the next row to begin a new record. As soon as you move to the next row, the record is saved— you do not have to take any specific action to save the record.

First record entered

Figure 12.10

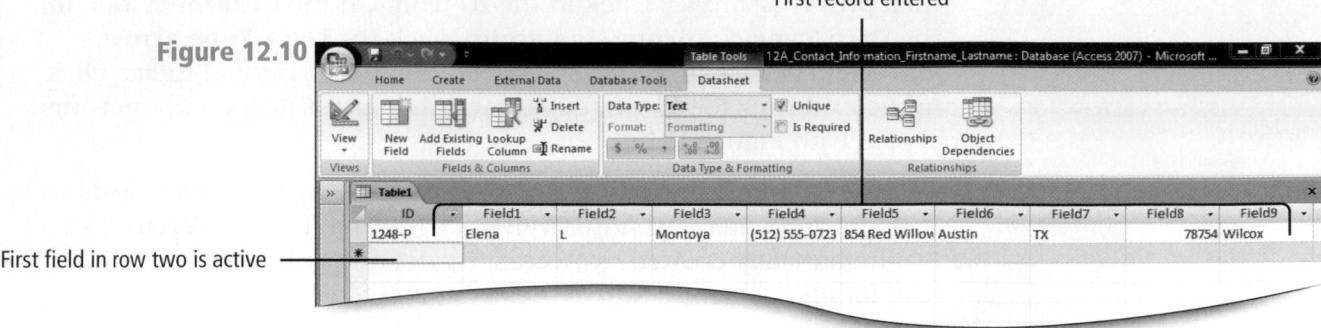

First field in row two is active

Note — Correct Typing Errors by Using Techniques Similar to Documents and Worksheets

If you make a mistake while entering data, you can correct the error by using [←Bksp] to remove characters to the left, [Delete] to remove characters to the right, or select the text you want to replace and type the correct information. You can also press [Esc] to exit out of a new record.

8 Beginning with the record for *Margaret E Fitzpatrick*, and using the technique you just practiced, enter the contact information for three additional patients, pressing [Enter] as necessary after entering the information in *Field10*. Then compare your screen with Figure 12.11.

ID	Field1	Field2	Field3	Field4	Field5	Field6	Field7	Field8	Field9	Field10
1248-P	Elena	L	Montoya	(512) 555-0723	854 Red Willow Drive	Austin	TX	78754	Wilcox	150
1252-P	Margaret	E	Fitzpatrick	(512) 555-0199	601 Meadow Drive	Abbott	TX	76621	Lee	486
1253-P	Jerry	R	Chung	(512) 555-0144	7094 Leland Avenue	Abilene	TX	79608	Wilcox	144
1257-P	Emily	A	Rhoades	(512) 555-0135	67 Bolivar Drive	Amarillo	TX	79101	Woods	298

Field 10 out of view (your screen may
vary in how many columns are shown)

Figure 12.11

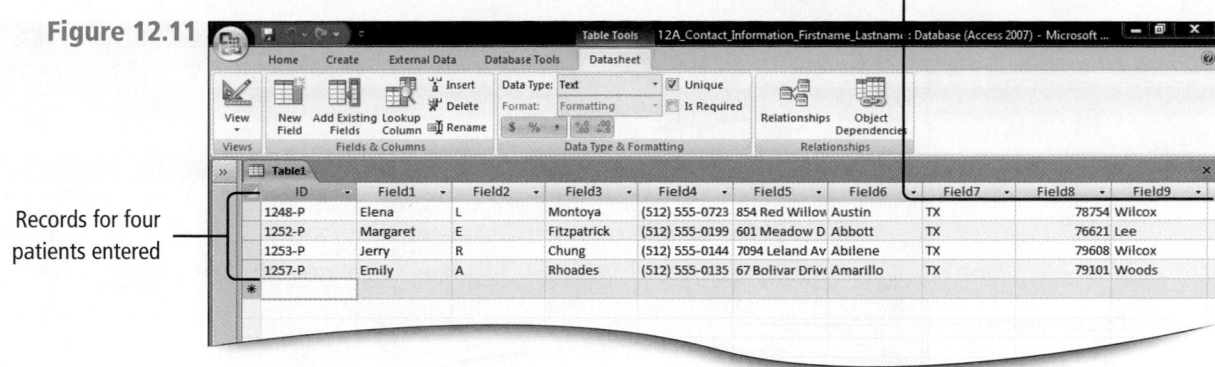

Records for four
patients entered

More Knowledge
Format for Typing Telephone Numbers in Access

Access does not require any specific format for entering telephone numbers
in a database. The examples in this project use the format used in Microsoft
Outlook. Using such a format facilitates easy transfer of Outlook information
to and from Access.

Objective 3
Rename Table Fields in Datasheet View

Recall that each column in a table contains a category of data called a
field, and that field names display at the top of each column of the table.
Recall also that each row contains a *record*—all of the data pertaining to
one person, place, thing, event, or idea—and that each record is broken
up into small parts—the *fields*.

Activity 12.03 Renaming the Fields In a Table in Datasheet View

In this activity, you will rename fields in your table to give the fields more
meaningful names.

1 At the top of the second column, point to the text *Field1* to display

the 🔽 pointer and click. Compare your screen with Figure 12.12.

Figure 12.12

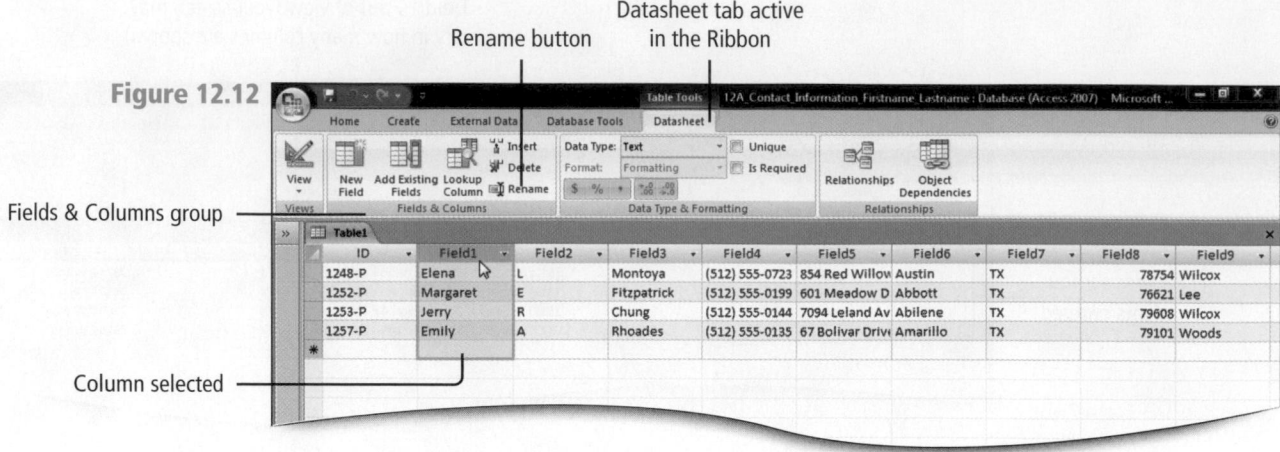

Rename button

Datasheet tab active
in the Ribbon

Fields & Columns group

Column selected

2 On the Ribbon, notice that **Table Tools** display above the **Datasheet tab**. In the **Fields & Columns group**, click the **Rename** button, and notice that the text *Field1* is selected.

3 Type **First Name** as the field name, and then press Enter. Point to the text *Field2*, click to select the column, and then in the **Fields & Columns group**, click the **Rename** button. Type **Middle Initial** and then press Enter.

4 Point to the text *Field3* and *double-click* to select the text. With the text selected, type **Last Name** and then press Enter. Point to the text *Field4* and right-click. From the displayed shortcut menu, click **Rename Column**, and then type **Phone Number** and press Enter.

5 Using any of the techniques you just practiced, rename the remaining fields as follows, and then compare your screen with Figure 12.13.

Field5	**Address**
Field6	**City**
Field7	**State/Province**
Field8	**ZIP/Postal Code**
Field9	**Doctor**
Field10	**Amount Owed**

Fields renamed

Figure 12.13

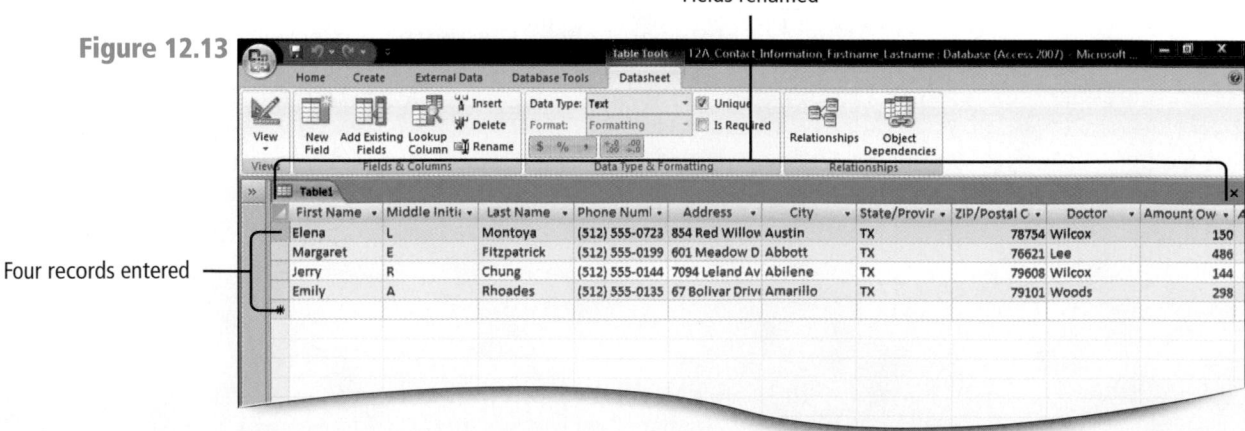

Four records entered

Activity 12.04 Changing the Data Type of a Field in Datasheet View

Data type is the characteristic that defines the kind of data that can be entered into a field, such as numbers, text, or dates. A field in a table can have only one data type. Based on the data you type into a field, Access assigns a data type, but you can change the data type if another type more accurately describes your data. In this activity, you will change the data type of fields.

1 In any of the four records that you have entered, click in the **ID field**. On the Ribbon, on the **Datasheet tab**, in the **Data Type & Formatting group**, notice that in the **Data Type** box, *Text* displays. Compare your screen with Figure 12.14.

Recall that the ID field has been changed from *AutoNumber*, which sequentially numbers each entry to *Text* so that a custom ID number for patients can be assigned.

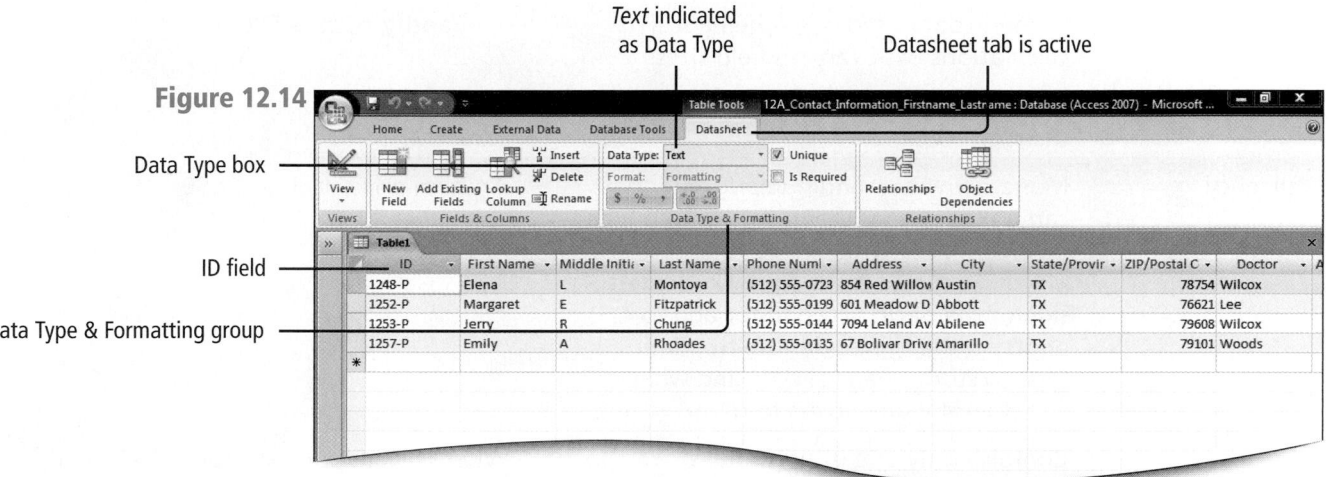

Text indicated as Data Type

Datasheet tab is active

Figure 12.14

Data Type box

ID field

Data Type & Formatting group

2 In any record, click in the **Last Name** field, and then on the **Datasheet tab**, notice that the **Data Type** indicates *Text.* Click the **Data Type arrow** to display a list of data types as shown in Figure 12.15 and take a moment to study the table in Figure 12.16 that describes the different data types.

Data Type arrow

Figure 12.15

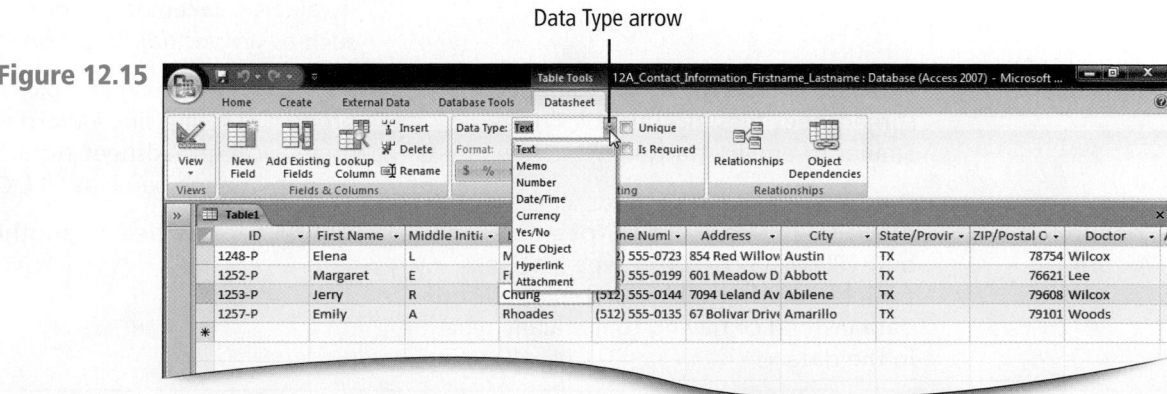

Data Types

Data Types	Description	Example
AutoNumber	Available in Design view. A unique sequential or random number assigned by Access as each record is entered and that cannot be updated.	An inventory item number, such as 1, 2, 3 or a randomly assigned employee number, such as 3852788.
Text	Text or combinations of text and numbers; also numbers that are not used in calculations. Limited to 255 characters or length set on field, whichever is less. Access does not reserve space for unused portions of the text field. This is the default data type.	An inventory item such as a computer, or a phone number or postal code that is not used in calculations, and which may contain characters other than numbers.
Memo	Lengthy text or combinations of text and numbers up to 65,535 characters or limitations of database size.	Description of a product or information pertaining to a patient.
Number	Numeric data used in mathematical calculations with varying field sizes.	A quantity, such as 500.
Date/Time	Date and time values for the years 100 through 9999.	An order date, such as 11/10/2009 3:30 P.M.
Currency	Monetary values and numeric data that can be used in mathematical calculations involving data with one to four decimal places. Accurate to 15 digits on the left side of the decimal separator and to 4 digits on the right side. Use this data type to store financial data and when you do not want Access to round values.	An item price, such as $8.50.
Yes/No	Contains only one of two values—Yes/No, True/False, or On/Off. Access assigns -1 for all Yes values and 0 for all No values.	Whether an item was ordered—Yes or No.
OLE Object	An object created by programs other than Access that is linked to or embeddedin the table. *OLE* is an abbreviation for *object linking and embedding*, a technology for transferring and sharing information among programs.	A graphics file, such as a picture of a product, a sound file, a Word document, or an Excel spreadsheet stored as a bitmap image.
Hyperlink	Web or email addresses.	An email address, such as dwalker@txlakemed.org or a Web page, such as *www.txlakemed.org*.
Attachment	Any supported type of file—images, spreadsheet files, documents, charts. Similar to email attachments.	A graphics file, such as a picture of a product, a sound file, a Word document, or an Excel spreadsheet stored as a bitmap image—same as OLE Object.
Lookup Wizard	Available in Design view. Not a data type, but will display on Data Type list. Links to fields in other tables to display a list of data instead of having to manually type in the data.	Link to another field in another table.

Figure 12.16

3 Click the **Data Type arrow** again to close the list without changing the data type. In any record, click in the **Address** field, and notice that the **Data Type** box indicates *Text*.

As described in the table in Figure 12.16, Access assigns a data type of *Text* to combinations of letters and numbers.

4 Scroll to the right as necessary, in any record click in the **Amount Owed** field, and then in the **Data Type** box, notice that Access assigned the data type of *Number*. Click the **Data Type arrow** to the right of *Number*, and then from the displayed list, click **Currency**.

Based on your typing, Access determined this data type to be *Number*. However, Amount Owed refers to a monetary value, so the data type must be defined as *Currency*. When you click the Currency data type, Access automatically adds a U.S. dollar sign ($) and two decimal places to all the fields in the column. Compare your screen with Figure 12.17.

Data Type box indicates *Currency*

Amount Owed field data type changed to *Currency*

Figure 12.17

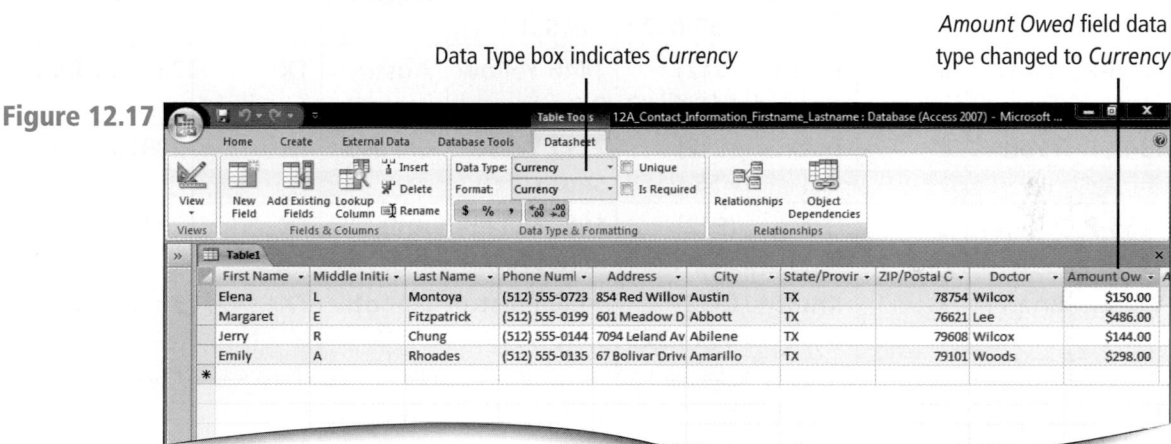

5 Scroll to the left as necessary, and in any record, click in the **ID** field.

In a database, each record should, in some way, be different from all the other records. What is important is that the number is unique; no other record in the table will be assigned this number.

You are probably familiar with unique numbers. For example, at your college, no two students have the same Student ID number, although they could have the same name, such as *David Michaels*.

When records in a database have *no* unique number, for example the CDs in your personal collection probably have no unique number, the AutoNumber data type is a useful way to automatically create a unique number so that you have a way to ensure that every record is unique.

6 Change the name of the **ID** field to **Patient ID**. In the new record row, which is indicated by an asterisk (*) in the record selector box on the left, click in the **Patient ID** field, and then type the records shown in the following list. When you are finished, compare your screen with Figure 12.18.

Recall that you need not be concerned if the data does not completely display in the column. Also, as soon as you move to the next row, the record is saved—you do not have to take any specific action to save the record. Correct typing mistakes using ordinary methods you have practiced in this and other programs.

Patient ID	First Name	Middle Initial	Last Name	Phone Number	Address	City	State/ Province	ZIP/ Postal Code	Doctor Name	Amount Owed
1260-P	Maria	S	Flores	(512) 555-0177	1 Casa Del Sol	Austin	TX	78715	Ruiz	37.50
1265-P	Joan	M	Curtis	(512) 555-0192	1446 Yellow Rose Lane	Austin	TX	78715	Ruiz	255
1342-P	Yvonne	L	Dubois	(512) 555-0155	2117 West Smith Trail	El Paso	TX	79973	Woods	147.56
1385-P	Joseph	C	Ortega	(512) 555-0245	1923 Village Park West	Amarillo	TX	79101	Wilcox	200
1423-P	Brian	K	Khuu	(512) 555-0323	1130 Preston Way SE	Abbott	TX	76621	Lee	568.12

Figure 12.18

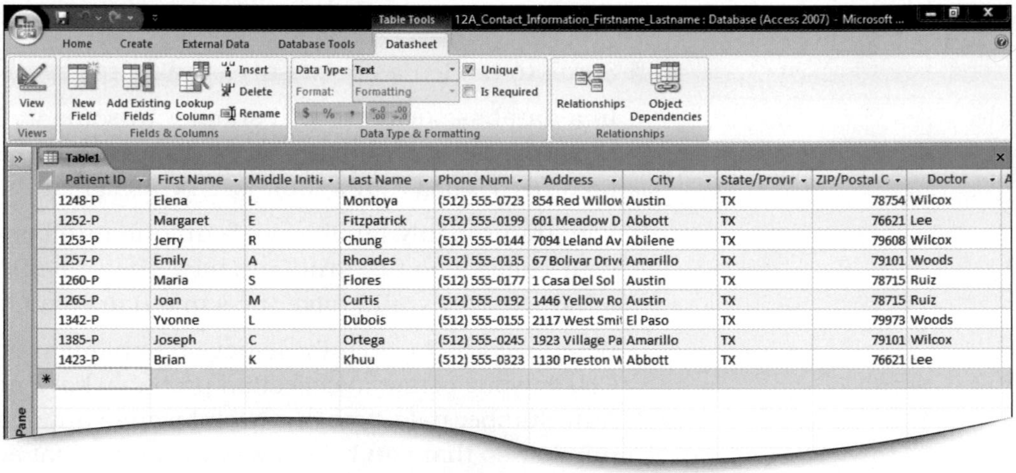

7 On the **Quick Access Toolbar**, click the **Save** button ⊞.

The Save As dialog box displays. Recall that an individual record is saved as soon as you move to another row in the table. However, because you have changed the table *design* by changing field names and data types, Access will prompt you to save the design changes made to the table.

Here you can also give the table a more meaningful name if you want to do so. In the Table Name box, a suggested name of *Table1* displays and is selected—yours may differ depending on the number of tables you have attempted to create in this database.

You will likely want to give your table a name that describes the information it contains. You can use up to 64 characters (letters or numbers), including spaces, to name a table.

8 In the **Save As** dialog box, in the **Table Name** box and using your first and last name, type **12A Patients Firstname Lastname** and then click **OK**. Compare your screen with Figure 12.19.

The table tab displays the new table name.

When you save objects within a database, it is not necessary to use underscores. Your name is included as part of the object name so that you and your instructor will be able to identify your printouts and electronic files.

Table name

Figure 12.19

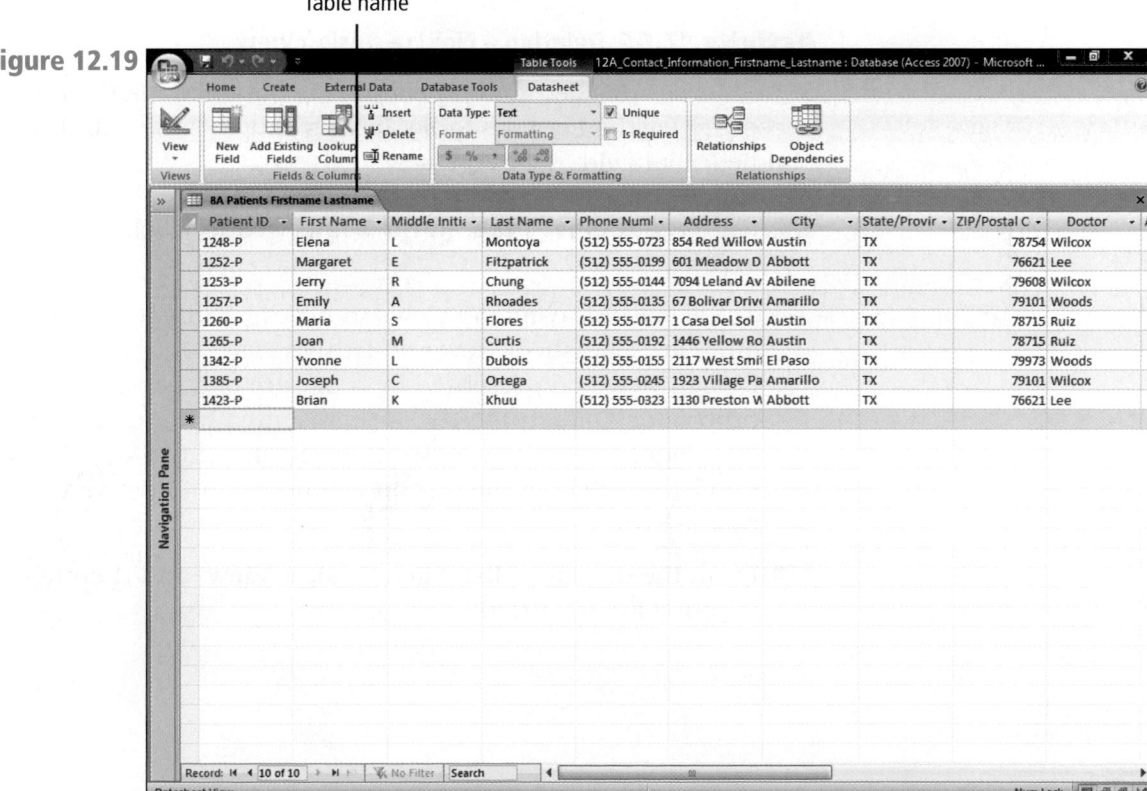

Objective 4
Modify the Design of a Table

When you create and populate a new table in Datasheet view, the data that you type for the first record determines the number and content of the fields in the table. Recall that the number and names of the fields and the data type of each field is referred to as the *table design*. After you have created a table, you may find that you need to make changes to the design of the table by adding or deleting fields, or changing the order of the fields within a table. You can modify a table in Datasheet view, but you may prefer to modify the table in Design view where you have additional options.

Activity 12.05 Deleting a Field in Design View

June Liu has decided that a field for the patient's middle initial is not necessary for the Patients table. In this activity, you will delete the Middle Initial field in Design view.

1 On the **Datasheet tab**, in the **Views group**, click the **View button arrow**.

There are four common views in Access, but two that you will use often are Datasheet view and Design view. On the displayed list, Design view is represented by a picture of a pencil, a ruler, and a protractor. Datasheet view is represented by a small table of rows and columns. When you see these icons on the View button, you will know that clicking the button will take you to the view represented by the icon.

2 From the displayed list, click **Design View**, and then take a moment to study Figure 12.20.

Design view displays the underlying structure of your table. Each field name is listed, along with its data type. A column to add a Description—information about the data in the field—is provided. At the bottom of the Design view window, you can make numerous other decisions about how each individual field will look and behave. For example, you can set a specific field size.

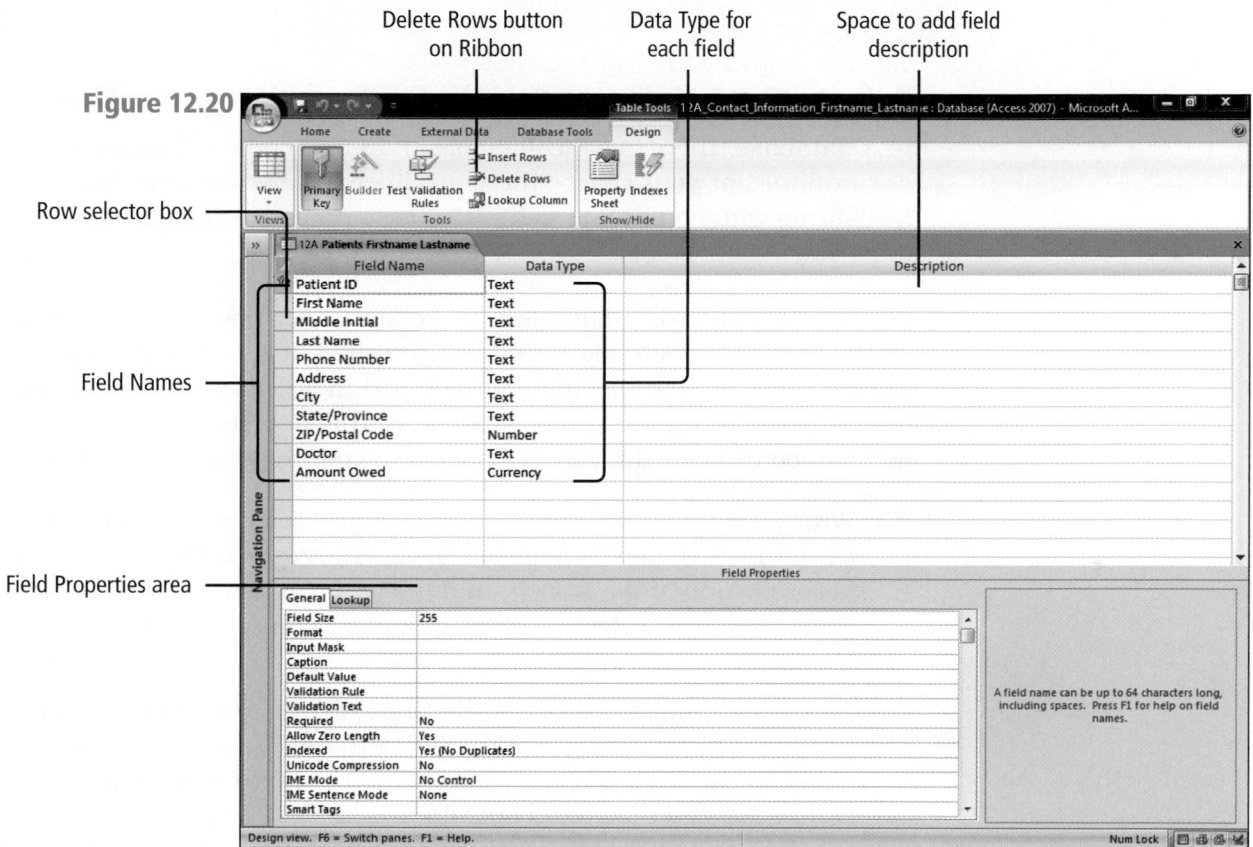

Delete Rows button on Ribbon · Data Type for each field · Space to add field description

Figure 12.20

Row selector box

Field Names

Field Properties area

3 In the **Field Name** column, to the left of **Middle Initial**, point to the row selector box to display the ➡ pointer, and then click to select—outline in orange—the entire row. On the **Design tab**, in the **Tools group**, click the **Delete Rows** button, read the message in the displayed dialog box, and then click **Yes**.

If the field is deleted, both the field and its data will be deleted; you cannot undo this action. If you change your mind after deleting the field, you will have to add the field back into the table and then reenter the data for that field in each record.

More Knowledge

Choosing the Proper View to Make Changes

You can make design changes in Datasheet view or Design view. Design view provides more flexibility in the types of design changes you can make, and you will become familiar with these as you progress in your study of Access.

Activity 12.06 Modifying a Field Size and Description in Design View

In a database, there is typically more than one person entering data. For example, at your college there are likely numerous Registration Assistants who enter and modify student and course information every day.

When you design your database, there are things you can do to help yourself and others to always enter accurate data. Two ways to ensure accuracy are to restrict what can be typed in a field and to communicate information within the database itself. In this activity, you will modify fields to control the data entry process to ensure greater accuracy.

1 With your table still displayed in **Design view**, in the **Field Name** column, click anywhere in the **State/Province** field name. In the lower portion of the screen, under **Field Properties**, click in the **Field Size** box, select the text *255*, and then type **2** Compare your screen with Figure 12.21.

This action limits the size of the State/Province field to no more than two characters—the size of the two-letter state abbreviations provided by the United States Postal Service. **Field properties** are characteristics of a field that control how the field will display and how the data can be entered in the field. Using this portion of the Design view screen, you can define properties for each field.

The default field size for a text field is 255. By limiting the field size property to 2, you ensure that only two characters can be entered for each state. A primary goal of any database is to ensure the accuracy of the data that is entered. Setting the proper data type for the field and limiting the field size are two ways to help to reduce errors.

Figure 12.21

Field Properties Field Size changed to 2

State/Province field selected —

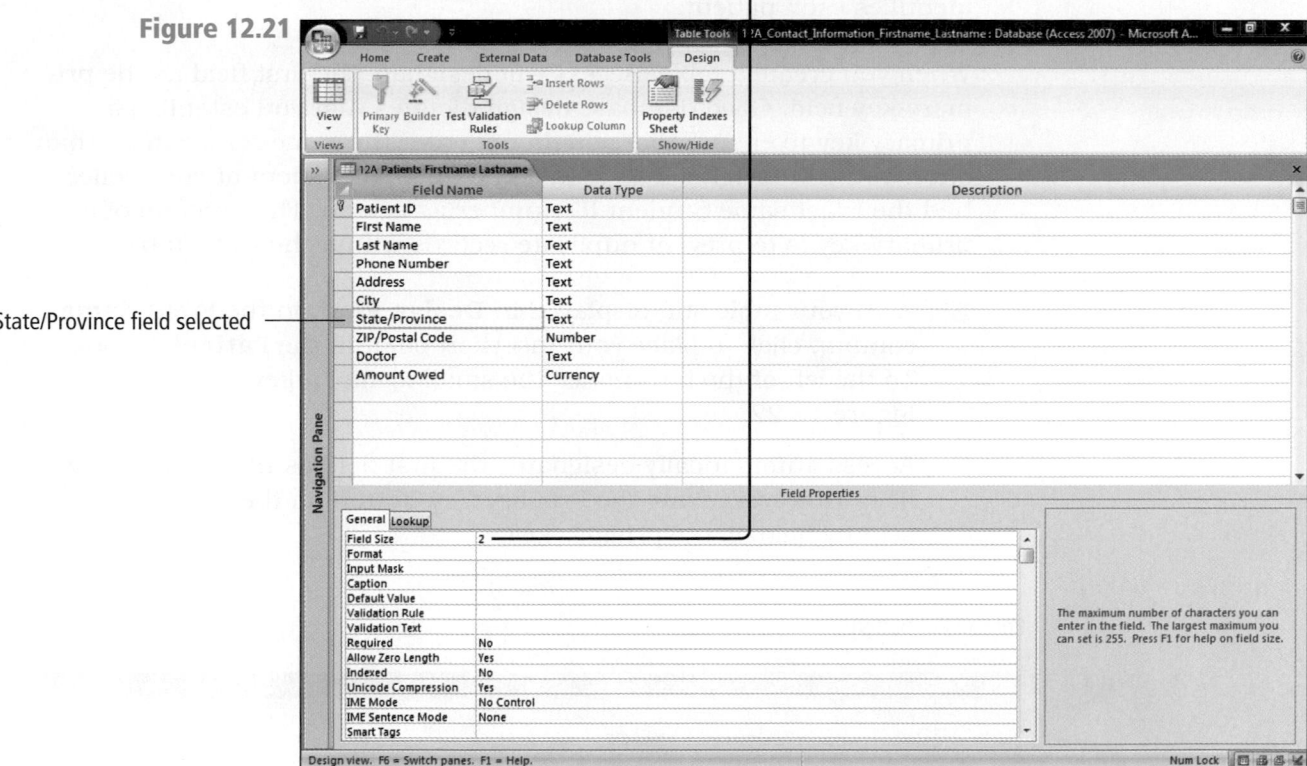

2 In the **State/Province** field name row, click in the **Description** column, and then type **Two-character state abbreviation**

Descriptions for fields in a table are not required. Include a description if the field name does not provide an obvious explanation of the field. Information typed in the description area displays in the status bar of the Datasheet view when the field is active. In this manner, the description communicates additional information to individuals who are entering data.

3 For the **Amount Owed** field name, click in the **Description** column, and then type **Outstanding balance**

4 On the **Quick Access Toolbar**, click the **Save** button [icon], and then click **Yes** when the message box displays. Leave your table in Design view for the next activity.

The changes you have made to the fields and their properties will help to ensure accurate data entry and provide communication to users of the database. The warning indicates that if more than two characters are currently present in the State/Province field, the data could be lost because the field was not previously restricted to two characters.

Activity 12.07 Setting a Primary Key and Saving a Table

A **primary key** is the field that uniquely identifies a record in a table. For example, in a college registration system, your Student ID number uniquely identifies you—no other student at the college has your exact student number. In your 12A Patients table, the Patient ID uniquely identifies each patient.

When you create a table, Access will designate the first field as the primary key field. Good database design dictates that you establish a primary key to ensure that you do not enter the same record more than once. You can imagine the confusion if another student at your college had the exact same Student ID number as you do. The function of a primary key is to prevent duplicate records within the same table.

1 With your table still displayed in **Design view**, in the **Field Name** column, click to place your insertion point in the **Patient ID** box. To the left of the box, notice the small icon of a key, as shown in Figure 12.22.

Access automatically designates the first field as the primary key field. However, using the Primary Key button on the Ribbon, you can set any field as the primary key.

Primary Key button

Figure 12.22

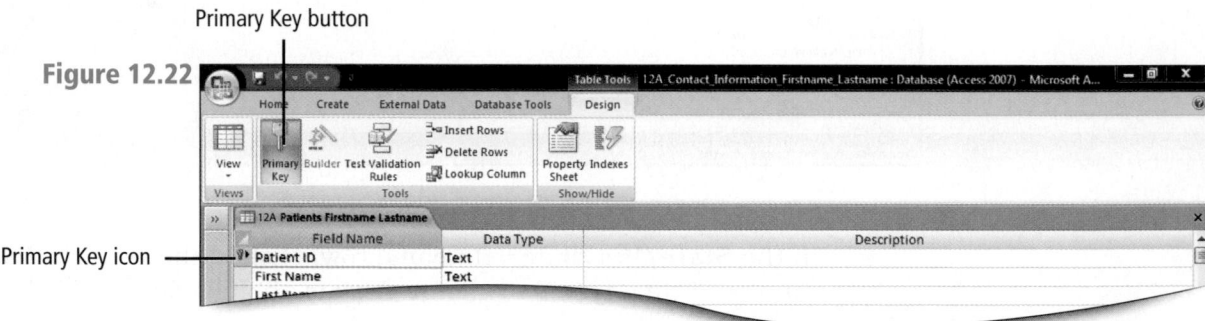

Primary Key icon

2 On the **Design tab**, in the **Views group**, notice that the **View** button contains a picture of a Datasheet, indicating that clicking the button will return you to Datasheet view. Click the **View** button; if prompted, click **Yes** to save the changes you have made to the design of your table.

Objective 5
Add a Second Table to a Database

Access includes a *table template*—a pre-built table format for common topics such as contacts, issues, and tasks. You can use the table template as it is or customize it to suit your needs. Using a table template is a fast way to add an additional table to your database.

Activity 12.08 Adding a Second Table to a Database

In this activity, you will add a second table in your database. The table will contain contact information for the doctors at the medical center. You will create the table using a table template specifically designed for contact information.

1 With your **12A Patients** table displayed in Datasheet view, on the Ribbon, click the **Create tab**. In the **Tables group**, click **Table Templates**, and then from the displayed list, click **Contacts**. Compare your screen with Figure 12.23.

A new table with pre-defined fields displays in the object window. Your 12A Patients table is still open—its tab is visible—but is behind the new table. The Contacts Table Template most closely matches the business need to track doctor information.

New Table1 added
with pre-defined fields

Table Templates button

Figure 12.23

12A Patients table still open

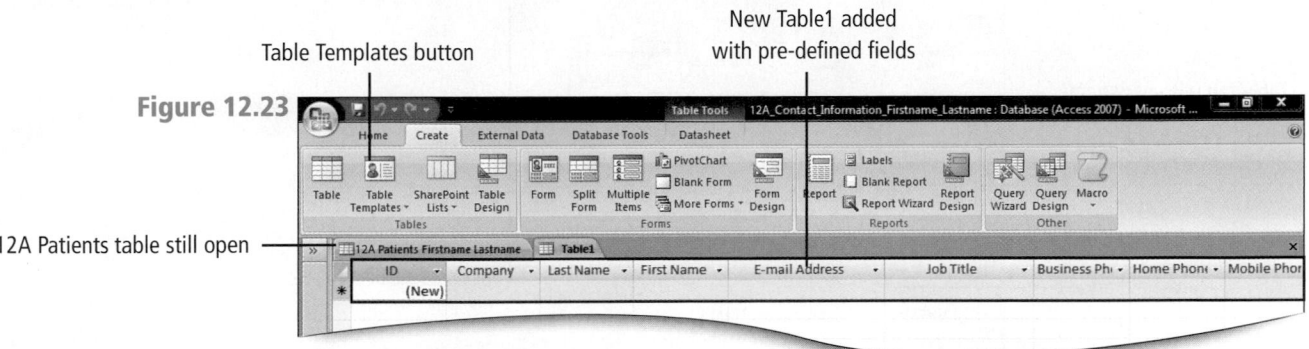

2 On the Ribbon, click the **Datasheet tab** to display the groups of Datasheet commands. In the second column, point to the **Company** field name, click to select the field, and then on the **Datasheet tab**, in the **Fields & Columns group**, click the **Delete** button. Alternatively, right-click on the selected field name, and from the displayed shortcut menu, click Delete Column.

You can delete fields in Design view, in the manner you did in a previous activity, or you can delete fields directly in Datasheet view as you have done here.

3 Point to the **E-mail Address** field, and then with your ⬇ pointer displayed, drag to the right to select both the **E-mail Address** field and the **Job Title** field. Right-click over the selected field names, and then from the displayed shortcut menu, click **Delete Column**.

4 Using the techniques you have just practiced, delete the following fields: **Business Phone**, **Home Phone**, **Fax Number**, **Country/Region**, **Web Page**, and **Notes**.

The field that displays a paperclip is the *Attachments* field. Recall that an attachment field can contain a graphics file such as a picture, a sound file, a Word document, or an Excel spreadsheet. In the future, June may attach a picture and a biography of each doctor to this field, so do not delete it.

5 On the **Datasheet tab**, in the **Views group**, click the **View** button to switch to **Design view**. In the **Save As** dialog box, in the **Table Name** box, type **12A Doctors Firstname Lastname** and then click **OK**.

This action will save the changes you have made to the design of the table—deleting fields—and provide a more meaningful table name. Your table displays in Design view, where you can see the names of each field and the data types assigned to the fields.

6 In the **Field Name** column, click anywhere in the **Attachments** box, and then on the **Design tab**, in the **Tools group**, click **Insert Rows**. In the newly inserted field name box, type **Specialty** In the **Description** box, type **Medical field specialty** and then compare your screen with Figure 12.24.

Description for new field

Figure 12.24

Table tab with new name

New field added

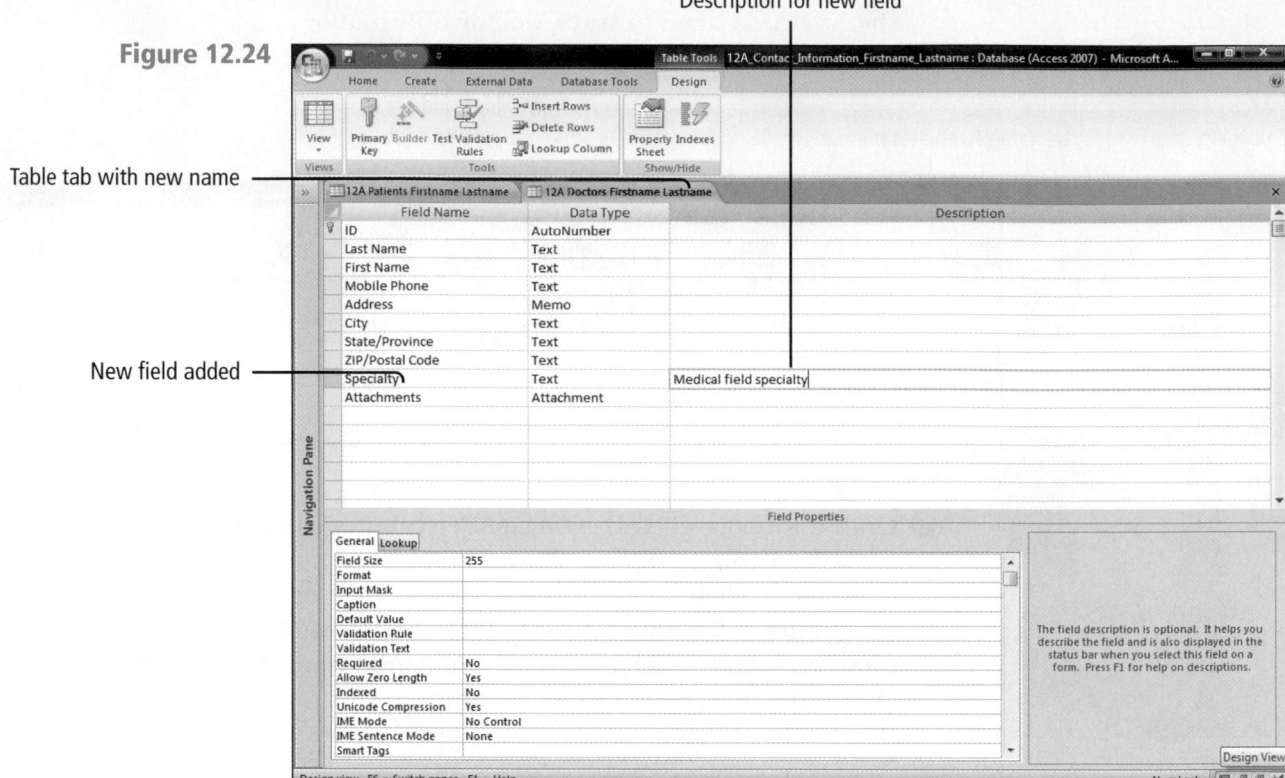

7 In the **Field Name** column, click in the **ID** box, and then replace the text with **Doctor ID** Press ⎇Tab to move to the **Data Type** column, click the arrow, and then from the displayed list, click **Text**. Press ⎇Tab to move to the **Description** column, and then type **Physician ID Number**

Because the medical center assigns a unique ID number to each doctor, you will use that number as the Primary Key instead of the AutoNumber generated by Access. Recall that AutoNumber is useful only when no other unique number for a record is available.

8 Click in the **State/Province** box, and then in the lower portion of the screen, under **Field Properties**, change the **Field Size** to **2** Compare your screen with Figure 12.25.

Figure 12.25

Description for Doctor ID

Doctor ID Data Type set to *Text*

Doctor ID field name

Descriptions added for two fields

State/Province Field Size changed to 2

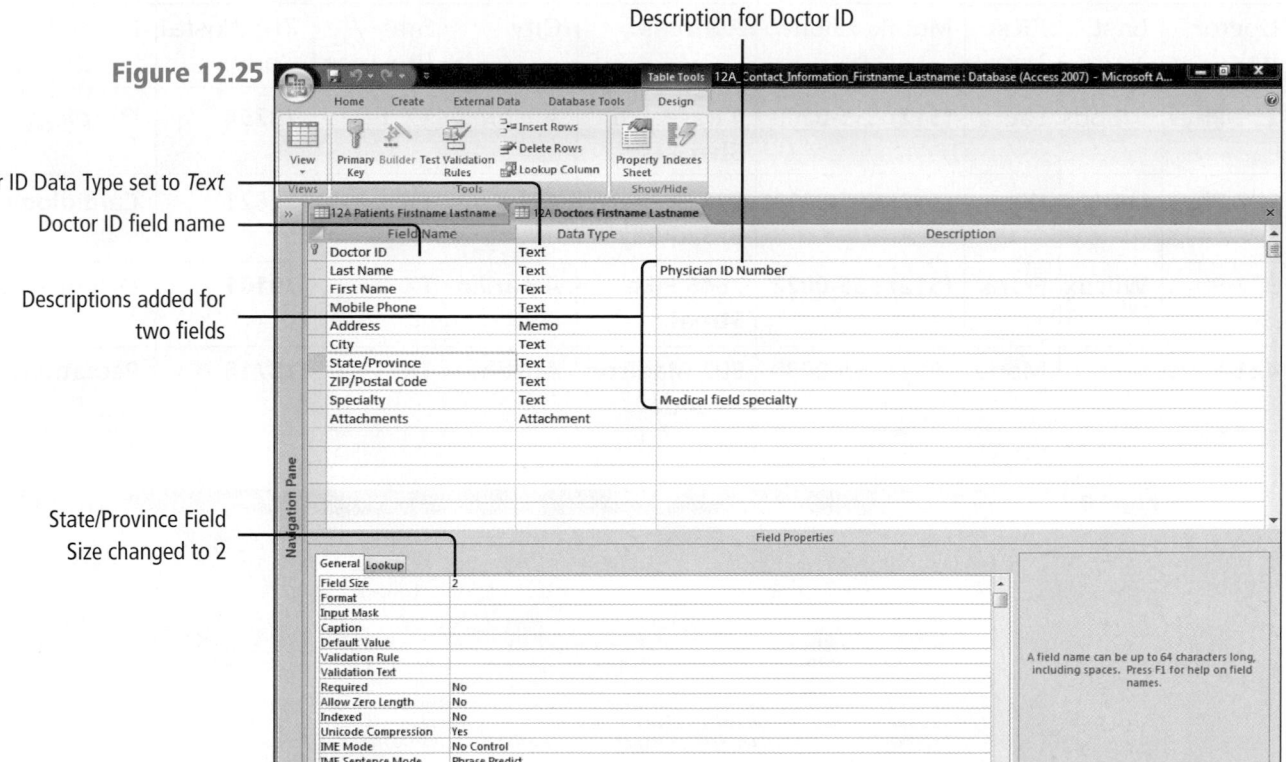

9 On the **Design tab**, in the **Views group**, click the **View** button to switch to Datasheet view—the picture of a datasheet reminds you that clicking the button will switch you to Datasheet view. Click **Yes** to save the changes you have made to the design of your table.

Activity 12.09 Adding Records to a Second Table

In this activity, you will add the records for the doctors' contact information.

1 With your **12A Doctors** table displayed in Datasheet view, beginning in the first row under **Doctor ID**, use the techniques you have practiced to enter the following four records, and then compare your screen with Figure 12.26.

As you type in the Doctor ID field, *Physician ID Number* displays in the status bar. As you type in the Specialty field, *Medical field specialty* displays in the status bar.

Doctor ID	Last Name	First Name	Mobile Phone	Address	City	State/Province	ZIP/Postal Code	Specialty
239-Phys	Woods	Laura	(512) 555-0100	4 Research Blvd	Austin	TX	78754	Oncology
287-Phys	Lee	Kim	(512) 555-0111	809 Broadway	Abbott	TX	76621	Cardiology
327-Phys	Wilcox	Frank	(512) 555-0022	7646 Pike Street	Amarillo	TX	79101	Orthopedics
421-Phys	Ruiz	Maria	(512) 555-0030	902 Madison Avenue	Austin	TX	78715	Pediatrics

Figure 12.26

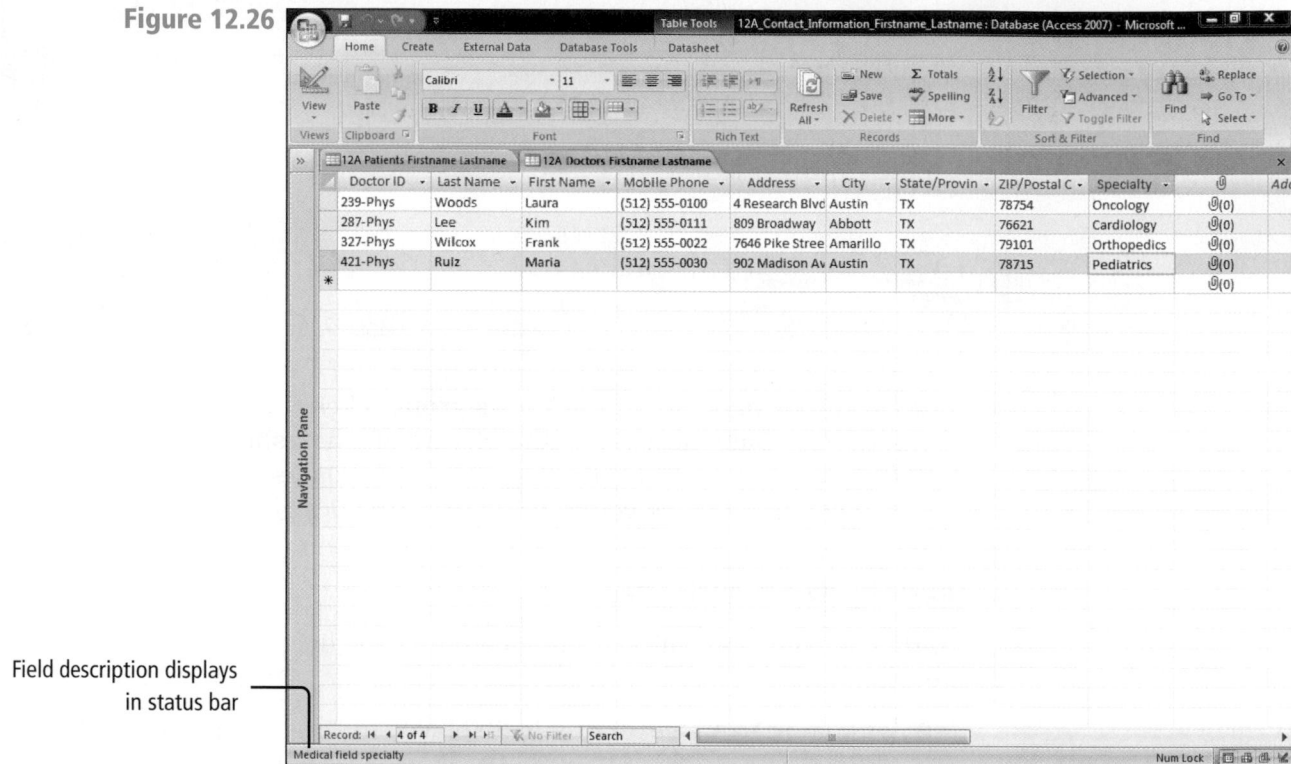

Field description displays in status bar

Objective 6
Print a Table

A printed table is not as professional looking as a formal report, but there are times when you may want to print your table in this manner as a quick reference or to proofread the data you have entered.

Activity 12.10 Adjusting Column Widths and Printing a Table

1 In the object window, click the tab for your **12A Patients** table.

By clicking the tabs along the top of the object window, you can display open objects so that you can work with them.

In the table, you can see that all of the columns are the same width regardless of the amount of data that is entered in the field or the field size that was set. If you print the table as currently displayed, some of the fields in some records may not fully display. Thus, it is recommended that you adjust the column widths.

2 Change the field name of the **State/Province** field to **State** and change the name of the **ZIP/Postal Code** field to **ZIP**

3 In the row of field names, point to the right boundary of the **Address** field to display the ⟨+|+⟩ pointer, and then compare your screen with Figure 12.27.

Pointer positioned on right boundary of Address field

Figure 12.27

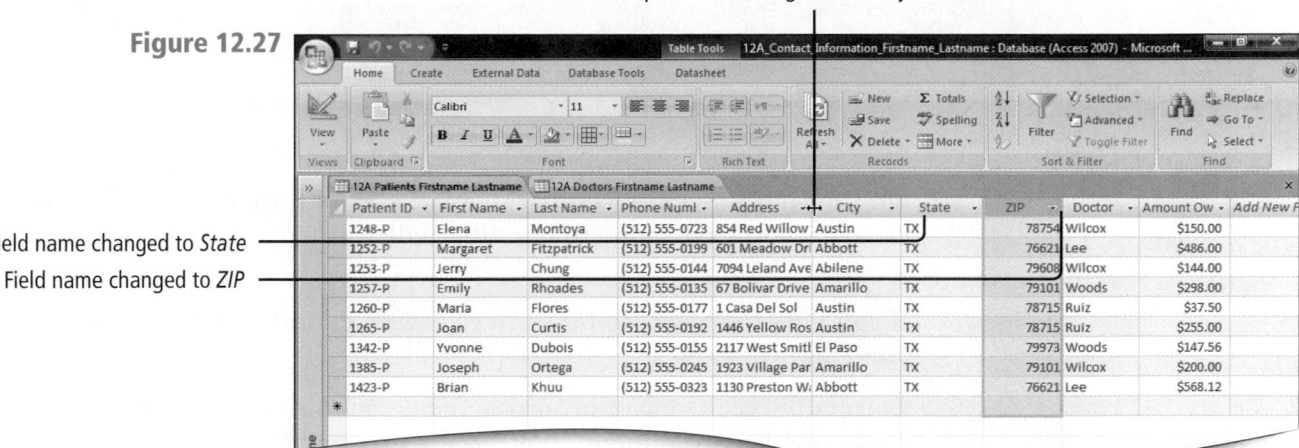

Field name changed to *State*
Field name changed to *ZIP*

4 With your ⟨+|+⟩ pointer positioned as shown in Figure 12.27, double-click the right boundary of the **Address** field.

The column width of the Address field widens to fully display the field name and the longest entry in the column. In this manner, the width of a column can be increased or decreased to fit its contents.

5 In the field headings row, point to the right border of the **City** field, and then with the ⟨+|+⟩ pointer, hold down the left mouse button and drag to the left to visually narrow the column width to accommodate only the widest entry in that column.

Adjusting the width of columns does not change the data contained in the table's records. It changes only your view of the data.

Another Way — **To Adjust Column Widths**

You can select multiple columns, and then in the heading area, double-click the right boundary of any selected column to adjust all widths, in a manner similar to an Excel spreadsheet. Or, you can select one or more columns, right-click over the selection, from the displayed menu click Column Width, and then in the Column Width dialog box, click Best Fit.

6 Using any of the techniques you have practiced or described above, adjust all the column widths, and then compare your screen with Figure 12.28.

All column widths adjusted to fit longest entry in the column

Figure 12.28

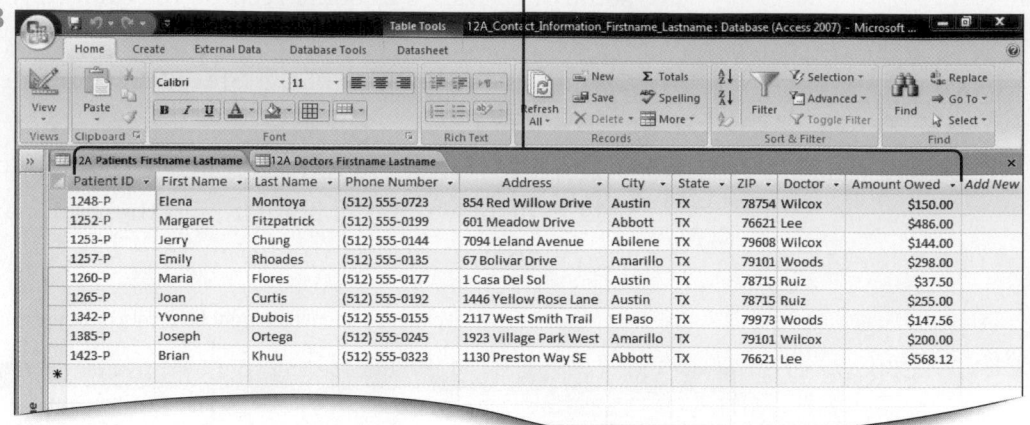

7 On the **Quick Access Toolbar**, click the **Save** button to save the changes you have made to the table's design—changing the column widths.

If you forget to save the table, Access will remind you to save when you close the table.

8 In the upper left corner of your screen, click the **Office** button. From the displayed menu, point to **Print**, click **Print Preview**, and then compare your screen with Figure 12.29.

Figure 12.29

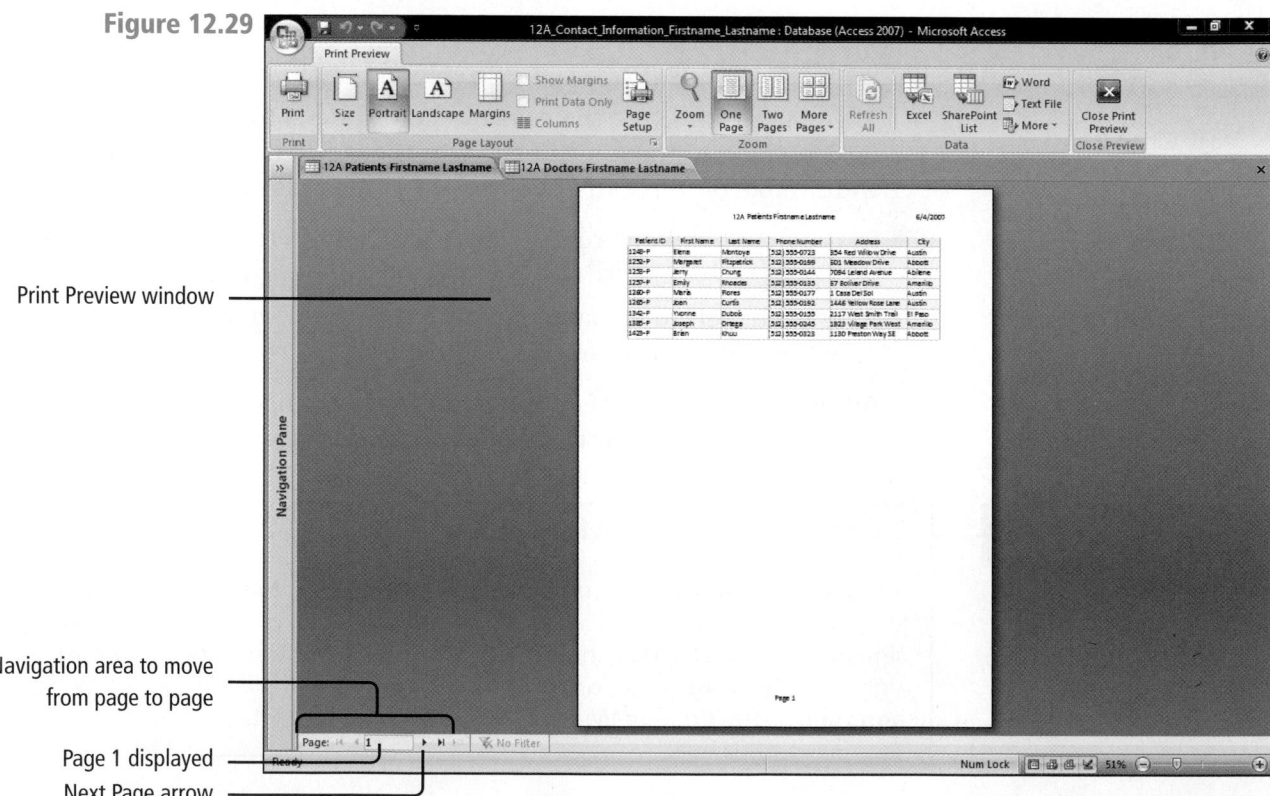

Print Preview window

Navigation area to move from page to page

Page 1 displayed

Next Page arrow

9 In the navigation area in the lower left of your screen, click the **Next Page arrow**, point to the displayed data at the top of the page to display the 🔍 pointer, click one time to zoom in, and then compare your screen with Figure 12.30.

The second page of the table displays the last four field columns.

Figure 12.30

Last four fields display on a second page

Previous Page arrow

Page 2

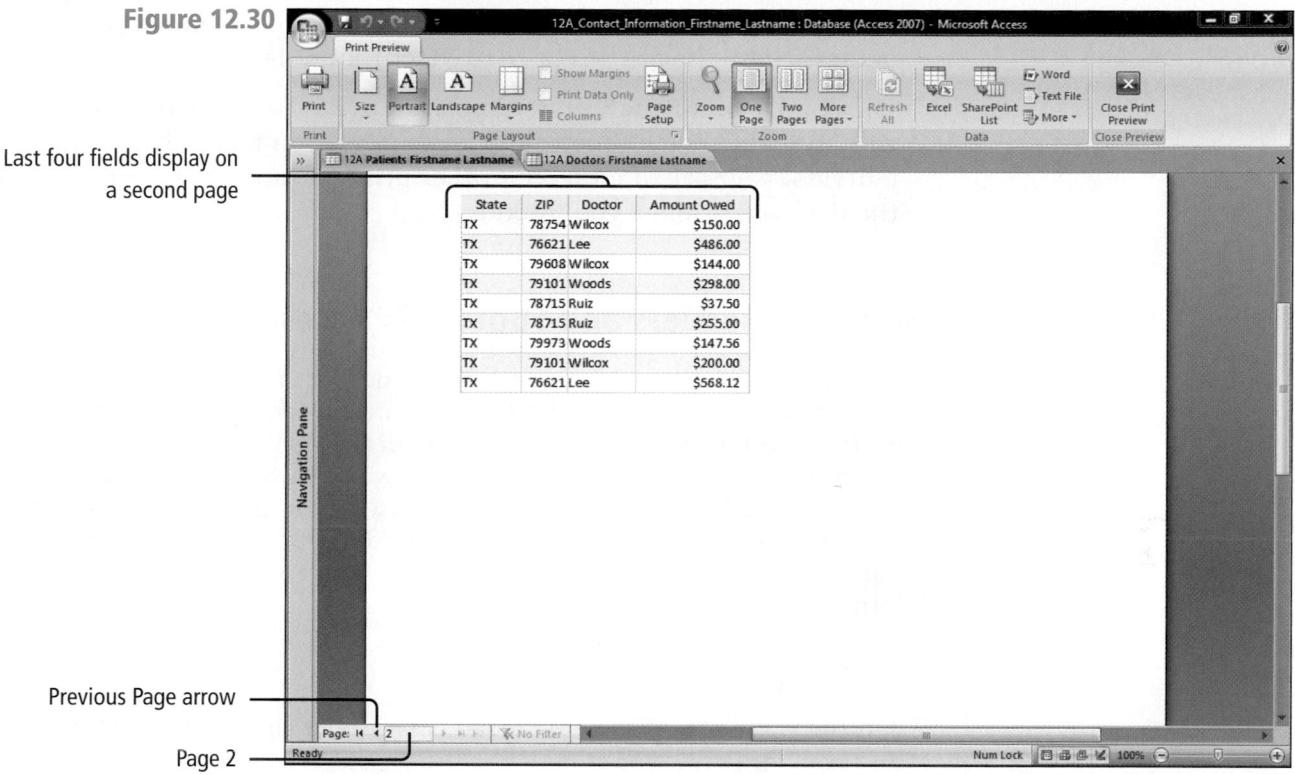

10 On the Ribbon, in the **Zoom group**, click the **Zoom** button to zoom back to Fit to Window view. In the **Page Layout group**, click the **Margins** button. In the displayed **Margins gallery**, point to **Wide**, and then compare your screen with Figure 12.31.

Wide gallery choice

Figure 12.31

Margins button

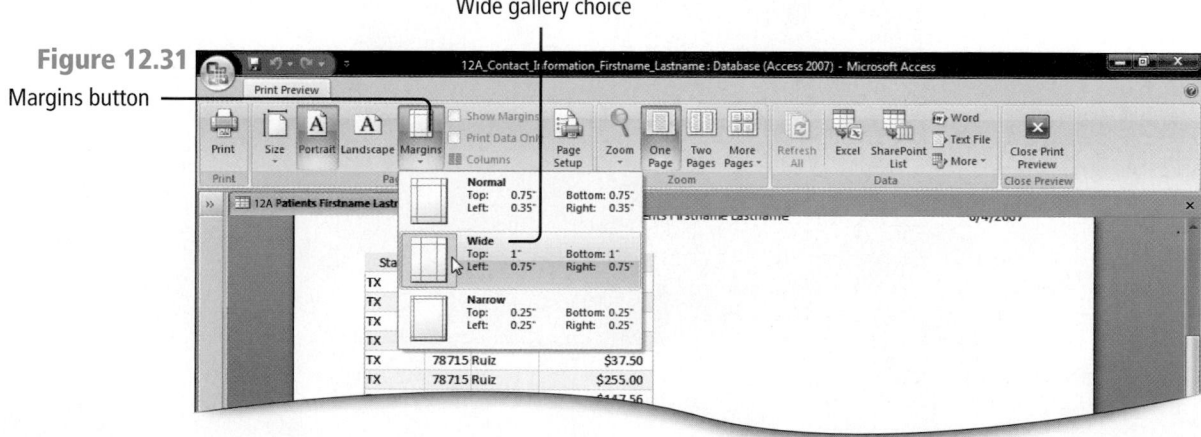

11 Click **Wide**. Then, in the **Page Layout group**, click the **Landscape** button.

The orientation of the printout changes, and the navigation arrows are inactive because all of the fields and all of the records display on one page. Additionally, the table name and current date display at the top of the page, and the page number displays at the bottom.

By default, Access prints in *portrait orientation*—the printed page is taller than it is wide. An alternate orientation is *landscape orientation*—the printed page is wider than it is tall.

The change in orientation from portrait to landscape is not saved with the table. Each time you want to print, you must check the margins, page orientation, and other print parameters to ensure that the data will print as you intend.

Note — Headers and Footers in Access Objects

The headers and footers in Access tables and queries are controlled by default settings; you cannot add additional information or edit the information. The object name displays in the center of the header area with the date on the right—that is why adding your own name to the object name is helpful to identify your paper or electronic results. The page number displays in the center of the footer area. The headers and footers in Access reports and forms, however, are more flexible; you can add to and edit the information.

12 On the right side of the status bar, just to the right of the **View** buttons, drag the **Zoom** slider to the right—or click the **Zoom In** button—until you have zoomed to approximately **120%**, as shown in Figure 12.32.

To *zoom* means to increase or to decrease the viewing area of the screen. You can zoom in to look closely at a particular section of a document, and then zoom out to see a whole page on the screen. You can also zoom to view multiple pages on the screen.

Figure 12.32

Zoom In button

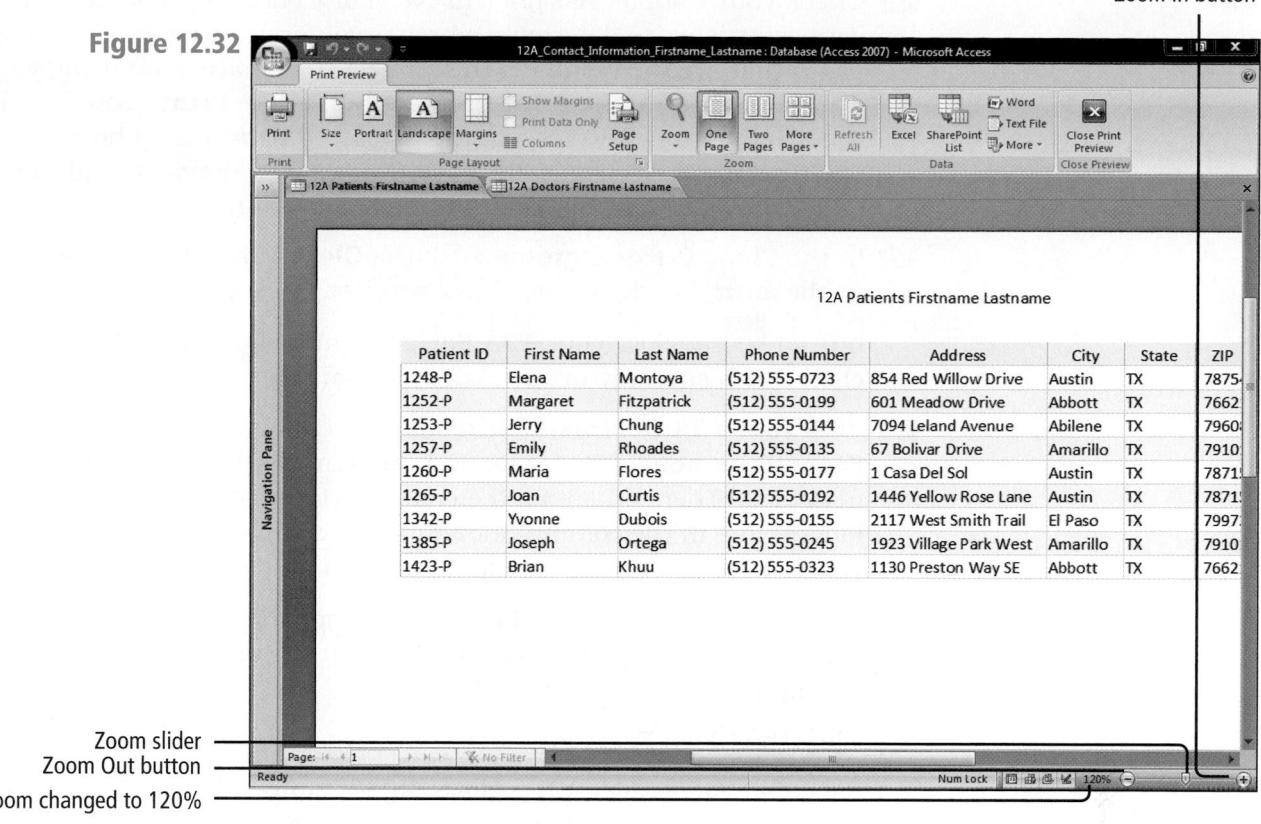

Zoom slider
Zoom Out button
Zoom changed to 120%

13 Drag the **Zoom** slider to the left—or click the **Zoom Out** button—until you have zoomed to approximately **50%**, as shown in Figure 12.33.

Figure 12.33

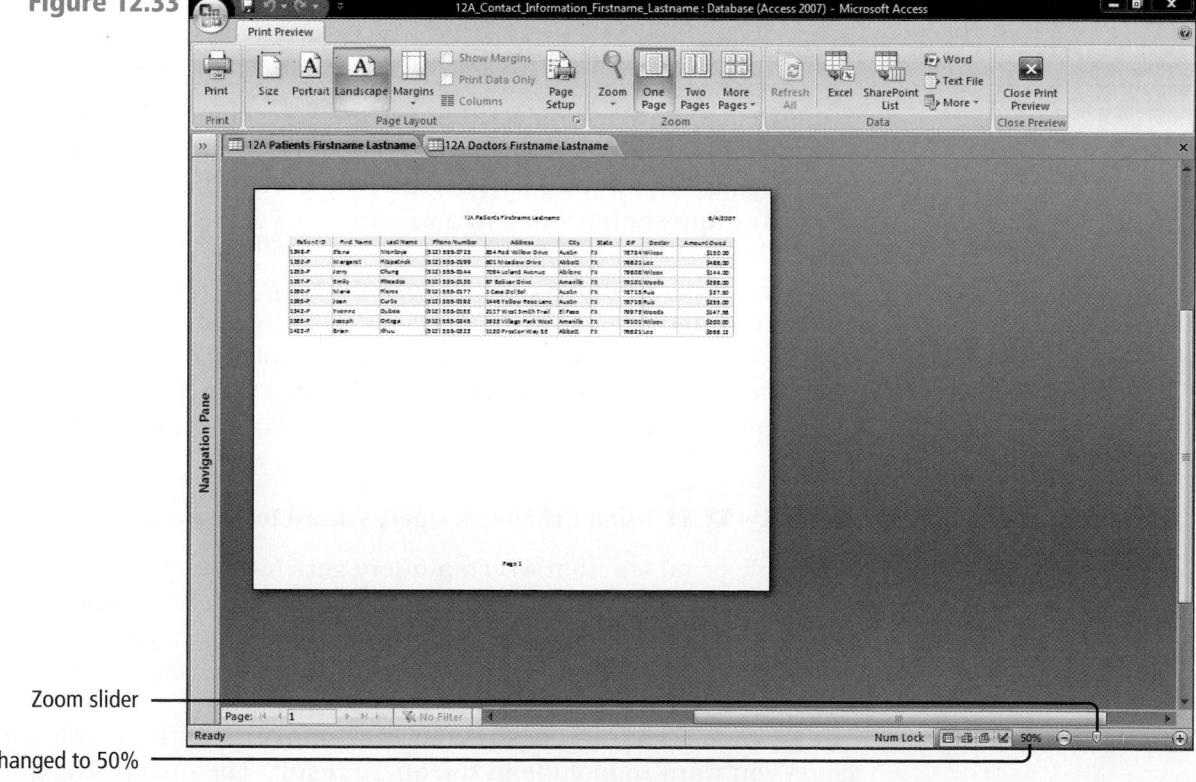

Zoom slider

Zoom changed to 50%

14 Check your *Chapter Assignment Sheet* or *Course Syllabus*, or consult your instructor, to determine whether you are to submit the printed pages that are the results of this project. If you are submitting your work on paper, on the **Print Preview tab**, in the **Print group**, click the **Print** button, and then in the displayed **Print** dialog box, click **OK**. To submit electronically, click **Close Print Preview**, and then follow the directions provided by your instructor.

15 In the **Close Preview group**, click the **Close Print Preview** button. At the far right edge of the object window, click the **Close Object** button ☒ to close your **12A Patients** table. If prompted to do so, click Yes to save any unsaved design changes.

16 With your **12A Doctors** table displayed, change the name of the **State/Province** field to **State** and the name of the **ZIP/Postal Code** field to **ZIP** Then, adjust all the column widths to accommodate the longest line in the column, including the **Attachments** column, which displays a paperclip icon.

17 Display the table in **Print Preview**. Change the **Margins** to **Wide** and the orientation to **Landscape**. Print if you are directed to do so, or submit your work electronically.

18 Click the **Close Print Preview** button, and then at the far right of the object window, click the **Close Object** button ☒. Click **Yes** to save the changes you made to the layout—changing the column widths.

All of your database objects—the 12A Patients table and the 12A Doctors table—are closed, and the object window is empty.

Objective 7
Create and Use a Query

A *query* is a database object that retrieves specific data from one or more tables and then, in a single datasheet, displays only the data you specified. Because the word *query* means *to ask a question*, you can think of a query as a question formed in a manner that Access can interpret.

One type of query in Access is a *select query*. A select query, also called a *simple select query*, retrieves (selects) data from one or more tables and makes it available for use in the format of a datasheet. A select query is used to create subsets of data that you can use to answer specific questions; for example, *Which patients live in Austin, TX?*

Activity 12.11 Using the Simple Query Wizard to Create a Query

The table or tables from which a query gets its data are referred to as the query's *data source*. In the following activity, you will create a simple select query using a *wizard*. A wizard is a feature in Microsoft Office programs that walks you step by step through a process.

The process involves choosing the data source, and then indicating the fields you want to include in the query result. The query—the question that you want to ask—is *What is the name, complete mailing address, and Patient ID of every patient in the database?*

1 On the Ribbon, click the **Create tab**, and then in the **Other group**, click the **Query Wizard** button. In the **New Query** dialog box, click **Simple Query Wizard**, and then click **OK**. Compare your screen with Figure 12.34.

Figure 12.34

Simple Query Wizard dialog box

Tables/Queries arrow

Add Field button

No database objects display in object window; all are closed

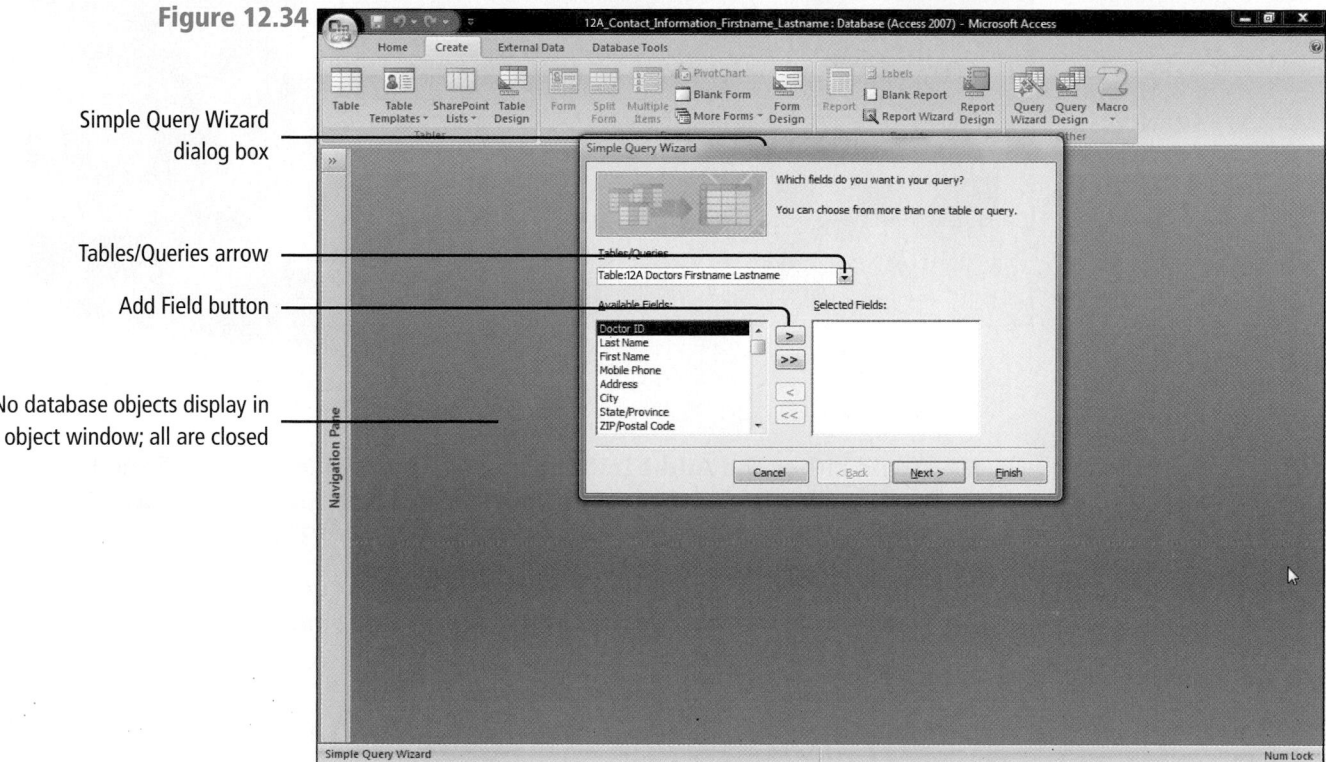

2 Click the **Tables/Queries arrow**, and then click your **Table: 12A Patients**.

To create a query, first choose the data source—the tables or queries from which you will select the data you want. To find the name and complete mailing address of every patient, you will need the 12A Patients table.

3 Under **Available Fields**, click **Patient ID**, and then click the **Add Field** button **>** to move the field to the **Selected Fields** list on the right. Using the same technique, add the **Last Name** field to the list. Alternatively, double-click the field name to move it to the Selected Fields list. Compare your screen with Figure 12.35.

Recall that the second step is to choose the fields that you want to include in your resulting query.

Two fields added to Selected Fields list

Figure 12.35

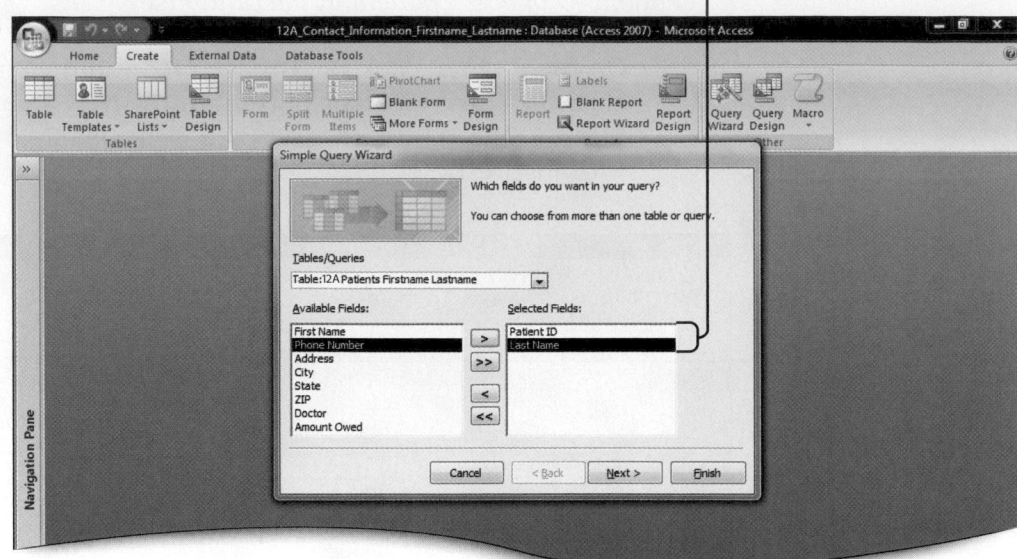

4 Using either the **Add Field** button [>] or double-click, add the following fields to the **Selected Fields** list: **First Name**, **Address**, **City**,
State, **ZIP**. Compare your screen with Figure 12.36.

Choosing these seven fields will give you the query result that you
want—it will answer the question, *What is the name, address, and
Patient ID of every patient in the database?*

Seven fields added to the List

Figure 12.36

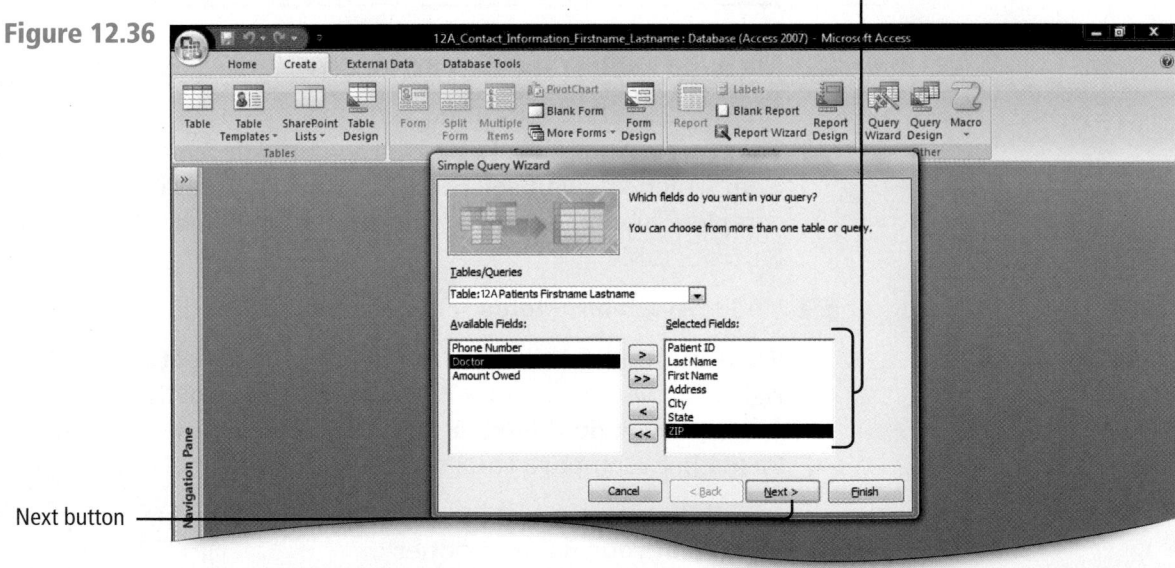

Next button

5 In the lower right corner, click the **Next** button. Be sure that the
option for **Detail (shows every field of every record)** is selected,
and then in the lower right corner, click the **Next** button. Click in
the **What title do you want for your query?** box, and then edit as

necessary so that the query name, using your own first and last name, is **12A ALL Patients Firstname Lastname Query** Compare your screen with Figure 12.37.

Name of query

Figure 12.37

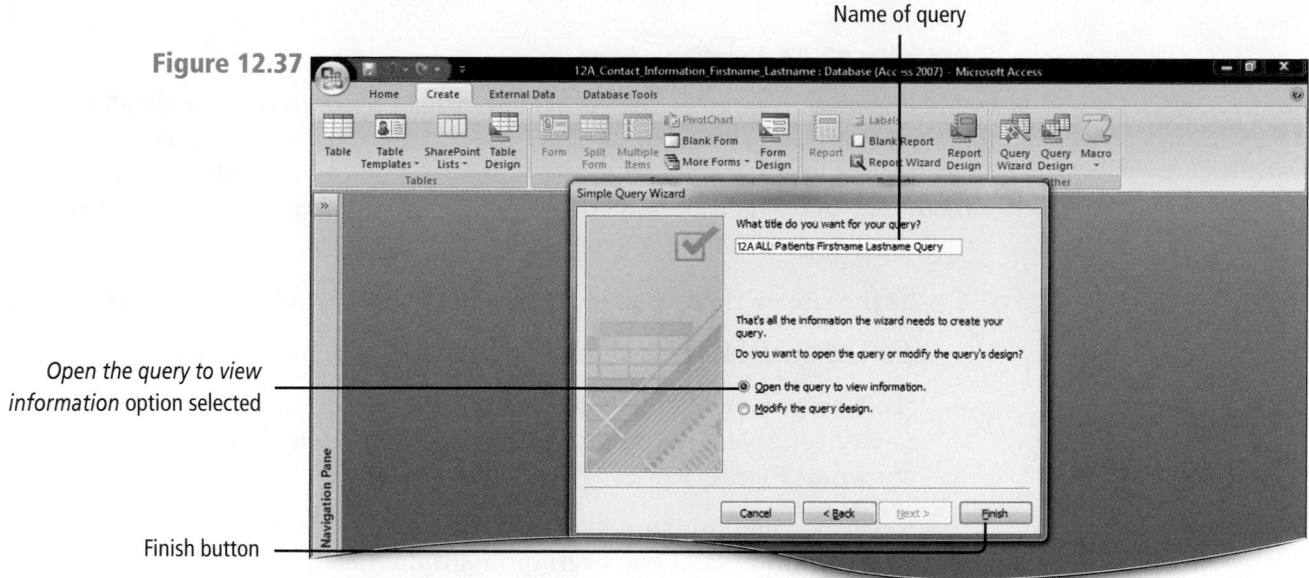

Open the query to view information option selected

Finish button

6 Click **Finish**.

Access **runs** the query—performs the actions indicated in your query design by searching the table of records included in the query, finding the records that match the criteria, and then displaying the records in a datasheet—so that you can see the results. In this manner, a select query *selects*—pulls out and displays—*only* the information from the table that you requested.

In the object window, Access displays every patient record in Datasheet view, but displays only the seven fields that you included in the Selected Fields list in the query wizard.

7 Display the query in **Print Preview**, and then print or submit electronically as directed. Click the **Close Print Preview** button; leave the query object open.

Objective 8
Create and Use a Form

A **form** is an Access object with which you can enter data, edit data, or display data from a table or a query. Think of a form as a window through which you and others can view and work with the data. In a form, the fields are laid out in a visually attractive format on the screen, which makes working with the database more pleasant and more efficient.

One type of Access form displays only one record in the database at a time. Such a form is useful not only to the individual who performs the data entry—typing in the actual records—but also to anyone who has the job of viewing information in a database.

For example, when you visit the Records office at your college to obtain a transcript, someone displays your record on a screen. For the viewer, it is much easier to look at one record at a time, using a form, than to look at all the student records in the database table.

Activity 12.12 Creating a Form

The Form command on the Ribbon creates a form that displays all the fields from the underlying data source (table) on the form, and does so one record at a time. You can use this new form immediately, or you can modify it. Records that you edit or create by using a form automatically update the underlying table or tables.

1 In the upper right corner of the object window, click the **Close Object** button ⊠ to close your query. Then, at the top of the **Navigation Pane**, click the **Open** button ⟩⟩. Point to your **12A Patients** table, and then right-click to display a shortcut menu as shown in Figure 12.38.

In the Navigation Pane, a table displays a datasheet icon and a query displays an icon of two overlapping datasheets.

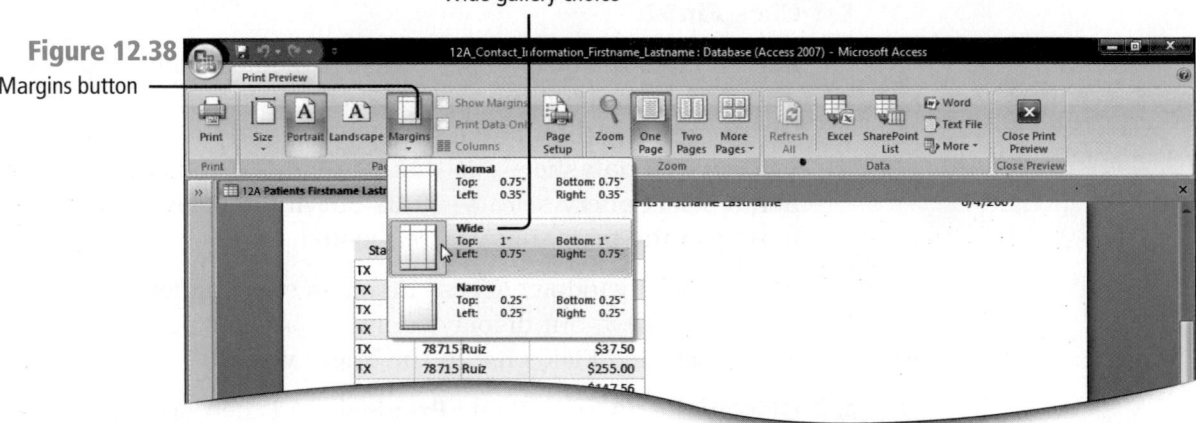

Figure 12.38

Margins button

Wide gallery choice

2 From the displayed menu, click **Open** to display the table in the object window, and then in the upper right corner of the **Navigation Pane**, click the **Close** button ⟨⟨ to maximize your screen space.

3 Notice that there are 10 fields in your table. On the Ribbon, click the **Create tab**, and then in the **Forms group**, click the **Form** button. Compare your screen with Figure 12.39.

Access creates a form based on the currently selected object—your 12A Patients table. Access creates the form in a simple top-to-bottom format, with all the fields in the table lined up in a single column.

The form displays in Layout view, which means you can make modifications to the form on this screen. The data for the first record in the table—for *Elena Montoya*—displays in each field.

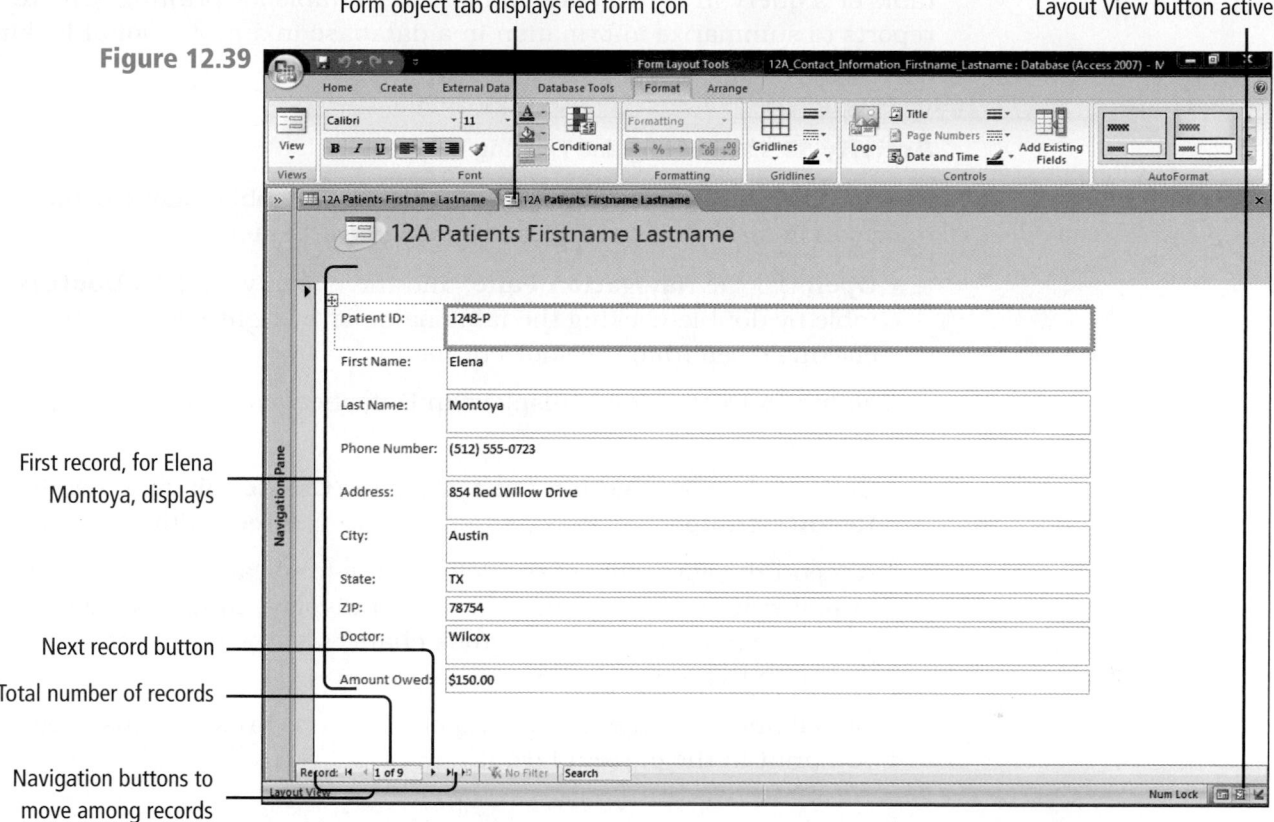

Figure 12.39

Form object tab displays red form icon

Layout View button active

First record, for Elena Montoya, displays

Next record button

Total number of records

Navigation buttons to move among records

4 In the lower right corner of the screen, at the right edge of the status bar, notice that the **Layout View** button ⬚ is active, indicating the form is displayed in Layout view.

5 At the right edge of the status bar, click the **Form View** button ⬚. Alternatively, on the Home tab, in the Views group, click the View button, which displays an icon of a form indicating the Form view.

In this view, you can view the records, but you cannot change the layout of the form.

6 In the navigation area, click the **Next record** button ▶ three times.

The fourth record—for *Emily Rhoades*—displays. The navigation buttons are useful to scroll among the records to select any single record you need to display.

7 On the **Quick Access Toolbar**, click the **Save** button ⬚. In the displayed **Save As** dialog box, accept the default name for the form—

12A Patients Firstname Lastname—by clicking **OK**. **Close** ⬚ the form object.

Your 12A Patients Firstname Lastname table remains open in the object window.

Objective 9
Create and Print a Report

A *report* is a database object that displays the fields and records from a table or a query in an easy-to-read format suitable for printing. Create reports to summarize information in a database in a professional-looking manner.

Activity 12.13 Creating and Printing a Report

In this activity, you will create a report that lists mobile phone contact information for doctors at Texas Lakes Medical Center.

1 **Open** ⏵⏵ the **Navigation Pane**, and then open your **12A Doctors** table by double-clicking the table name or by right-clicking and clicking Open from the shortcut menu.

Your 12A Doctors table displays in Datasheet view in the object window.

2 **Close** ⏴⏴ the **Navigation Pane**. Click the **Create tab**, and then in the **Reports group**, click **Report**. Compare your screen with Figure 12.40.

A report displays each of the fields in the table laid out in a report format suitable for printing. The report displays in Layout view, which means you can make quick changes to the design of the report on this screen.

Dotted lines indicate how the report would be broken across pages if you print in the current layout.

Report Layout Tools available

Figure 12.40

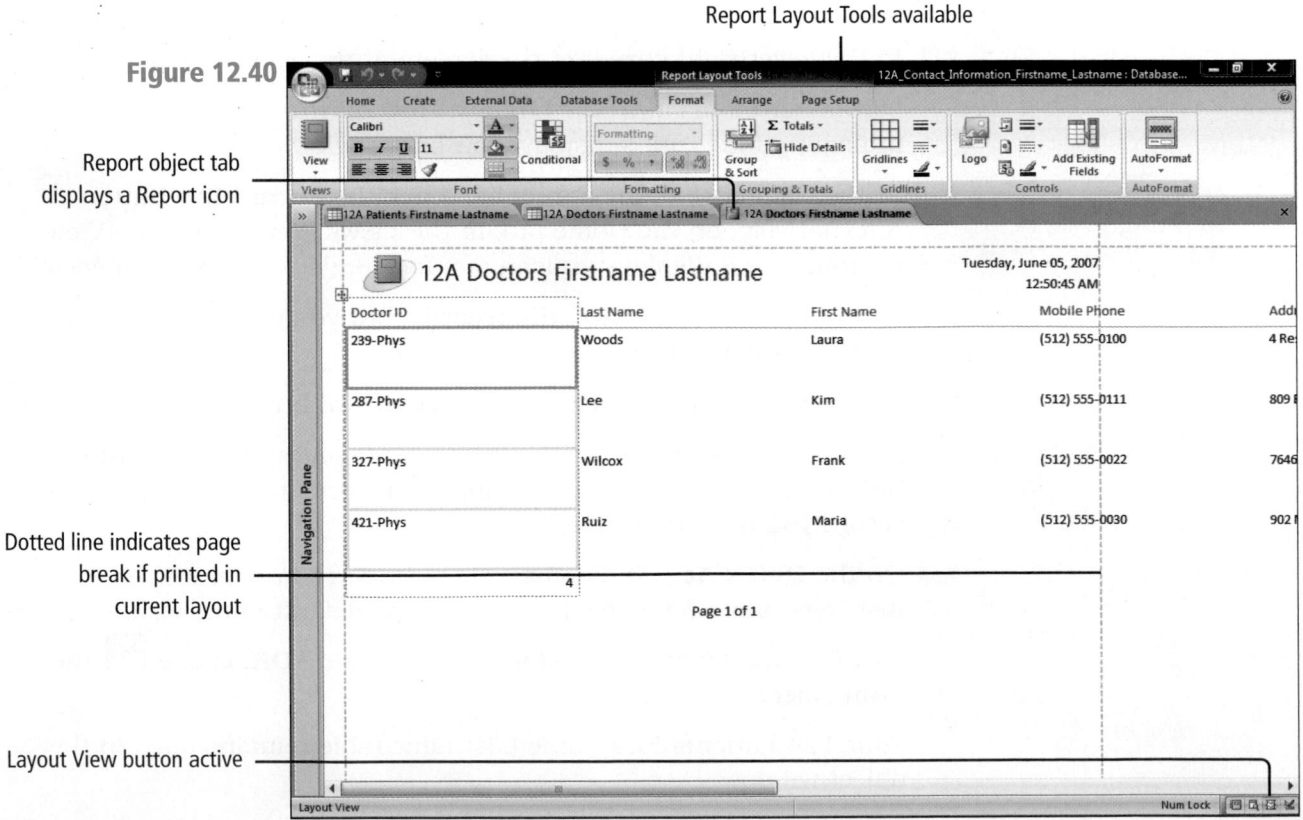

Report object tab displays a Report icon

Dotted line indicates page break if printed in current layout

Layout View button active

3 Scroll to the right as necessary, point to the **Address** field, right-click, and then from the displayed shortcut menu, click **Delete**.

The Address field and data are deleted and the report readjusts to accommodate the deletion.

4 Use the same technique to delete the following fields on the report layout: **City**, **State**, **ZIP**, **Specialty**, and **Attachments**.

This report will provide June with a quick list of each doctor and his or her ID and mobile phone number.

5 Click the **Page Setup tab**, and then in the **Page Layout group**, click the **Landscape** button. Scroll to the left, and then compare your screen with Figure 12.41.

Figure 12.41

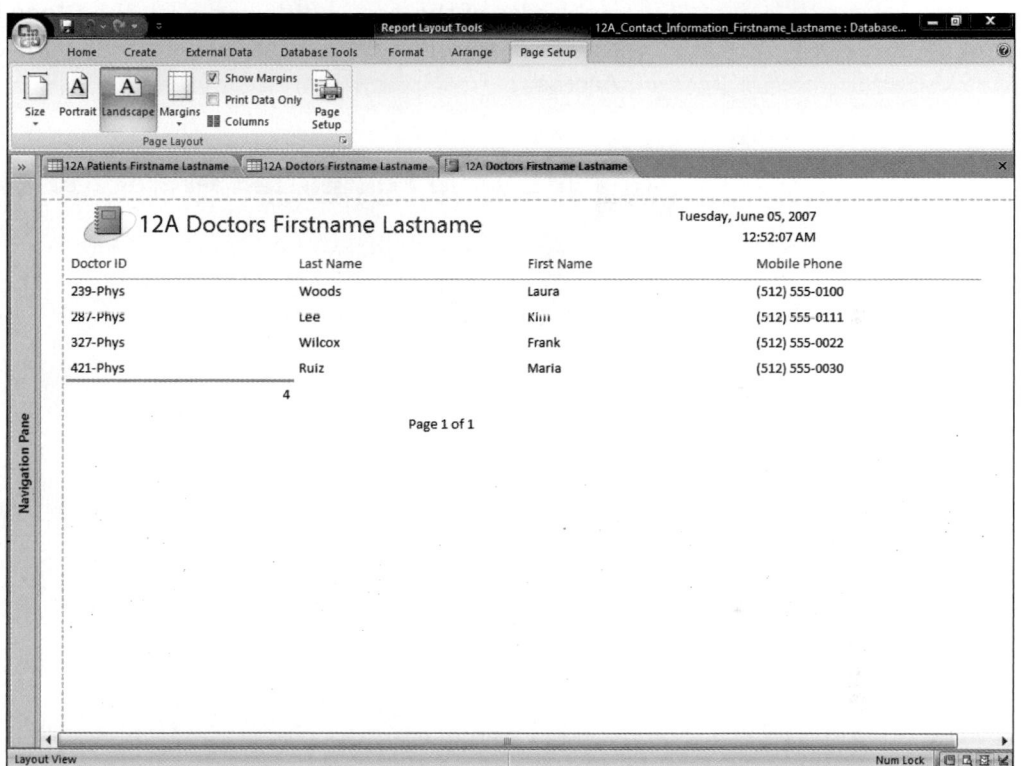

6 If you are submitting your results from this project on paper, from the **Office** menu , point to **Print**, click **Print Preview**, and then in the **Print group**, click **Print**. To submit electronically, follow the directions provided by your instructor.

7 Click the **Close Print Preview** button. Click the **Close Object** button to close the report. In the **Microsoft Office Access** dialog box, click **Yes** to save the report. In the **Save As** dialog box, click **OK** to accept the report name.

8 **Close** all the open objects so that there are no objects displayed in the object window.

Objective 10
Close and Save a Database

When you close an Access table, any changes made to the records are saved automatically. If you have changed the design of the table, or have changed the layout of the Datasheet view, such as adjusting the column widths, you will be prompted to save your changes. At the end of your Access session, close your database, and then close Access.

Activity 12.14 Closing and Saving a Database

1 Be sure all objects are closed.

2 From the **Office** menu, click **Close Database**, and then at the right edge of the Access title bar, click the **Close** button ☒ to close the Access program. Alternatively, from the Office menu, click Exit Access.

End **You have completed Project 12A**

Project 12B **Health Seminars**

In Activities 12.15 through 12.21, you will assist June Liu, Chief Administrative Officer, in creating a database to store information about community health seminars presented by Texas Lakes Medical Center. You will use a database template that tracks event information. You will add seminar information to the database and print a page displaying the results. Your printout will look similar to Figure 12.42.

For Project 12B, you will need the following file:

New Access database using the Events template

You will save your database as
12B_Health_Seminars_Firstname_Lastname

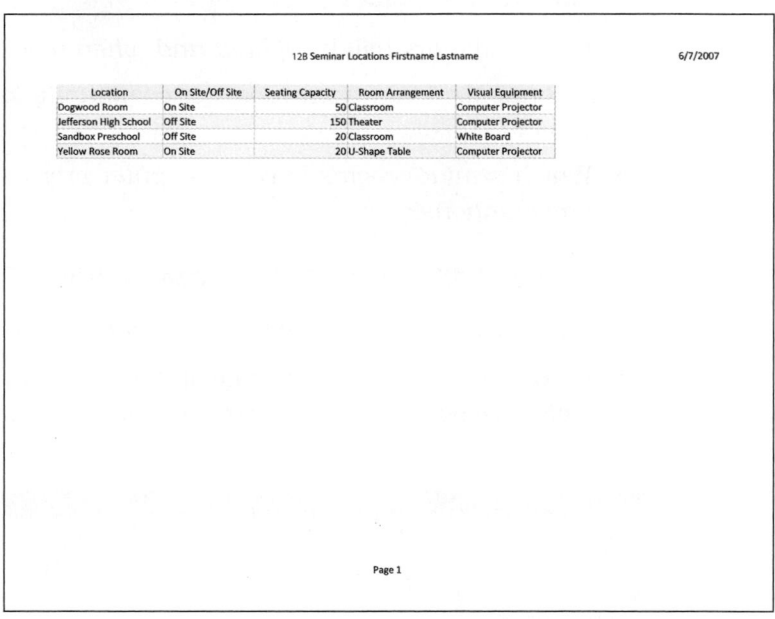

	12B Seminar Locations Firstname Lastname				6/7/2007
Location	On Site/Off Site	Seating Capacity	Room Arrangement	Visual Equipment	
Dogwood Room	On Site	50	Classroom	Computer Projector	
Jefferson High School	Off Site	150	Theater	Computer Projector	
Sandbox Preschool	Off Site	20	Classroom	White Board	
Yellow Rose Room	On Site	20	U-Shape Table	Computer Projector	

Page 1

Figure 12.42
Project 12B—Health Seminars

Objective 11
Create a Database Using a Template

A database template contains pre-built tables, queries, forms, and reports to perform a specific task, such as tracking a large number of events. For example, your college probably holds a large number of events, such as athletic contests, plays, lectures, concerts, and club meetings. Using a pre-defined template, your college Activities Director could quickly establish a database to manage such events.

The advantage of using a template to start a new database is that you do not have to create the objects—all you need to do is enter your data and modify the pre-built objects to suit your needs.

The purpose of the database in this project is to track the health seminars offered by Texas Lakes Medical Center. The questions to be answered may include:

- *What seminars will be offered and when will they be offered?*
- *In what Medical Center rooms or community locations will the seminars be held?*
- *Which seminar rooms have a computer projector for PowerPoint presentations?*

Activity 12.15 Creating a New Database Using a Template

In this activity, you will create a new database using the Events template.

1 **Start** Access. On the left side of the screen, under **Template Categories**, click **Local Templates**. Compare your screen with Figure 12.43.

Figure 12.43

Local Templates

Available Local Templates

Events template

2 Under **Local Templates**, click **Events**. In the right portion of your screen, to the right of the **File Name** box, click the **Browse** button 📂, and then navigate to your **Access Chapter 12** folder that you created in Project 12A.

3 At the bottom of the **File New Database** dialog box, delete any text in the **File name** box, and then, using your own information, type **12B_Health_Seminars_Firstname_Lastname** and press Enter.

4 On the right side of your screen, click the **Create** button.

Your 12B Health Seminars database is created, and the name displays in the title bar.

5 Directly below the Ribbon, on the **Message Bar**, check to see if a **Security Warning** displays.

Note

If no Security Warning displays, skip the next step and move to Activity 12.16.

6 On the **Message Bar**, click the **Options** button. In the displayed **Microsoft Office Security Options** dialog box, click the **Enable this content** option button, and then click **OK** or press Enter. Compare your screen with Figure 12.44.

Databases provided by Microsoft are safe to use on your computer.

Figure 12.44

Database name displays in the title bar

Multiple items form pre-named as *Event List*

Form icon indicates a form object

Total line displays by default

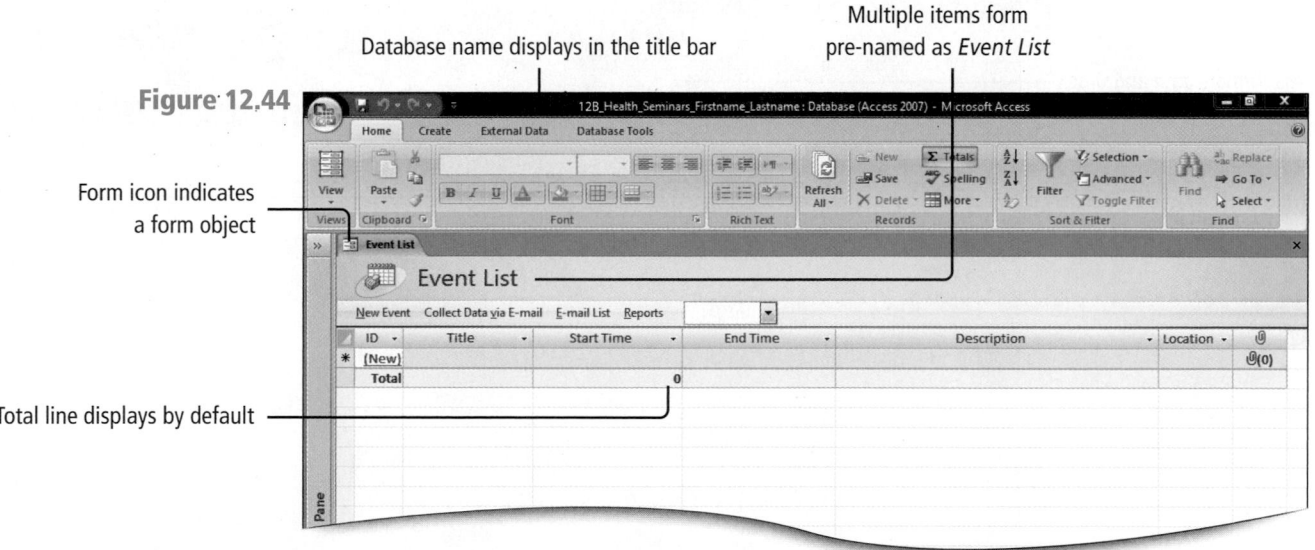

Activity 12.16 Building a Table by Entering Records in a Multiple Items Form

The purpose of a form is to simplify the entry of data into a table—either for you or for others who enter data. In Project 12A, you created a simple form, in which you can display or enter records in a table one record at a time.

The Events template creates a **multiple items form**, a form in which you can display or enter *multiple* records in a table, but still with an easier and more simplified screen than typing directly into the table itself.

1 Click in the first empty **Title** field. Type **Repetitive Stress Injuries** and then press Tab. In the **Start Time** field, type **3/9/09 7p** and then press Tab.

Access formats the date and time. As you enter dates and times, a small calendar displays to the right of the field, which you can click to select a date instead of typing.

2 In the **End Time** field, type **3/9/09 9p** and then press Tab. In the **Description** field, type **Workplace Health** and then press Tab. In the **Location** field, type **Yellow Rose Room** and then press Tab three times to move to the new record row. Compare your screen with Figure 12.45.

Because the seminars have no unique number, the AutoNumber feature of Access is useful to assign a unique number to each seminar.

Figure 12.45

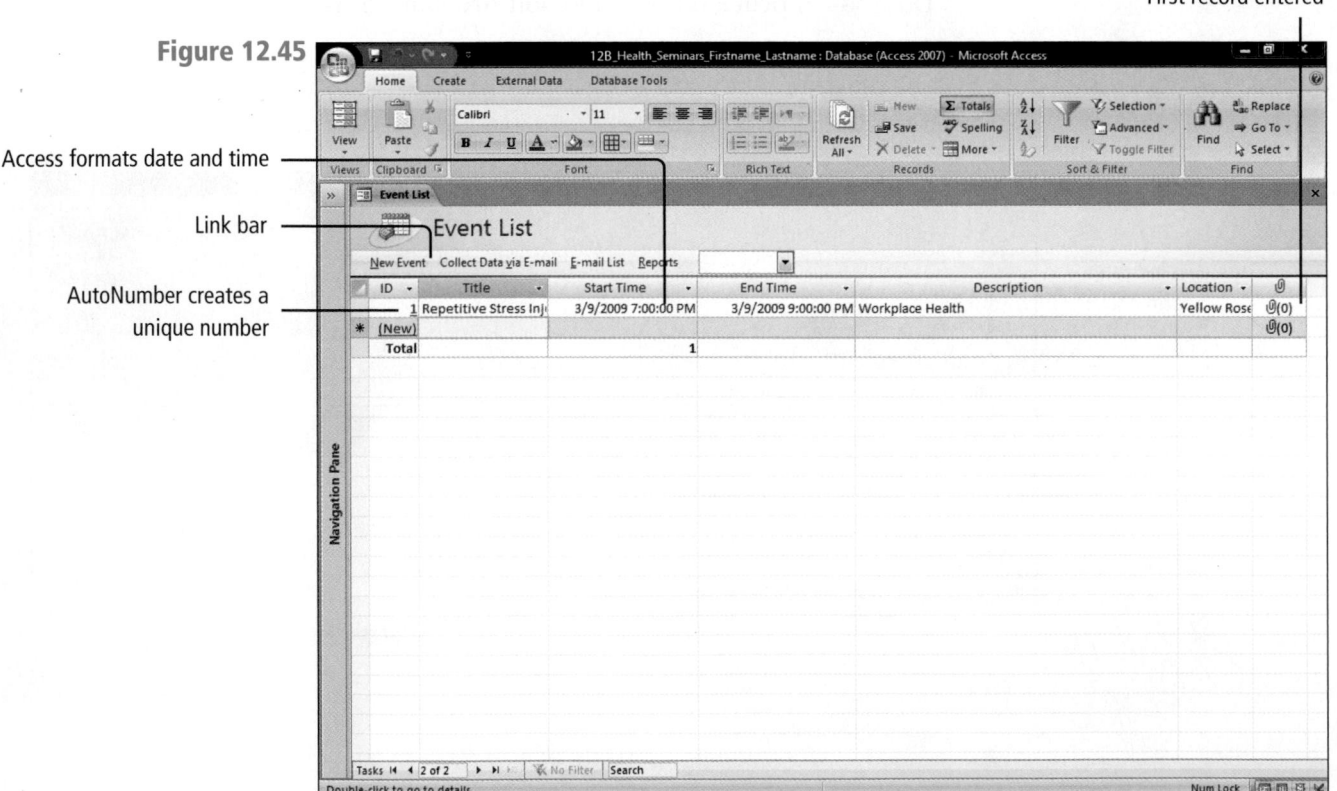

Access formats date and time

Link bar

AutoNumber creates a unique number

First record entered

3 In the **Link bar**, just above the field names, click **New Event**.

A single-record form displays, similar to the simple form you created in Project 12A.

4 Using [Tab] to move from field to field, enter the following record— press [Tab] three times to move from the **End Time** field to the **Description** field. Compare your screen with Figure 12.46.

Title	Location	Start Time	End Time	Description
First Aid for Teens	**Jefferson High School**	**3/10/09 4p**	**3/10/09 6p**	**Teen Health**

Single-record form   Close button

Figure 12.46

Save and New button

New Event button on Link bar

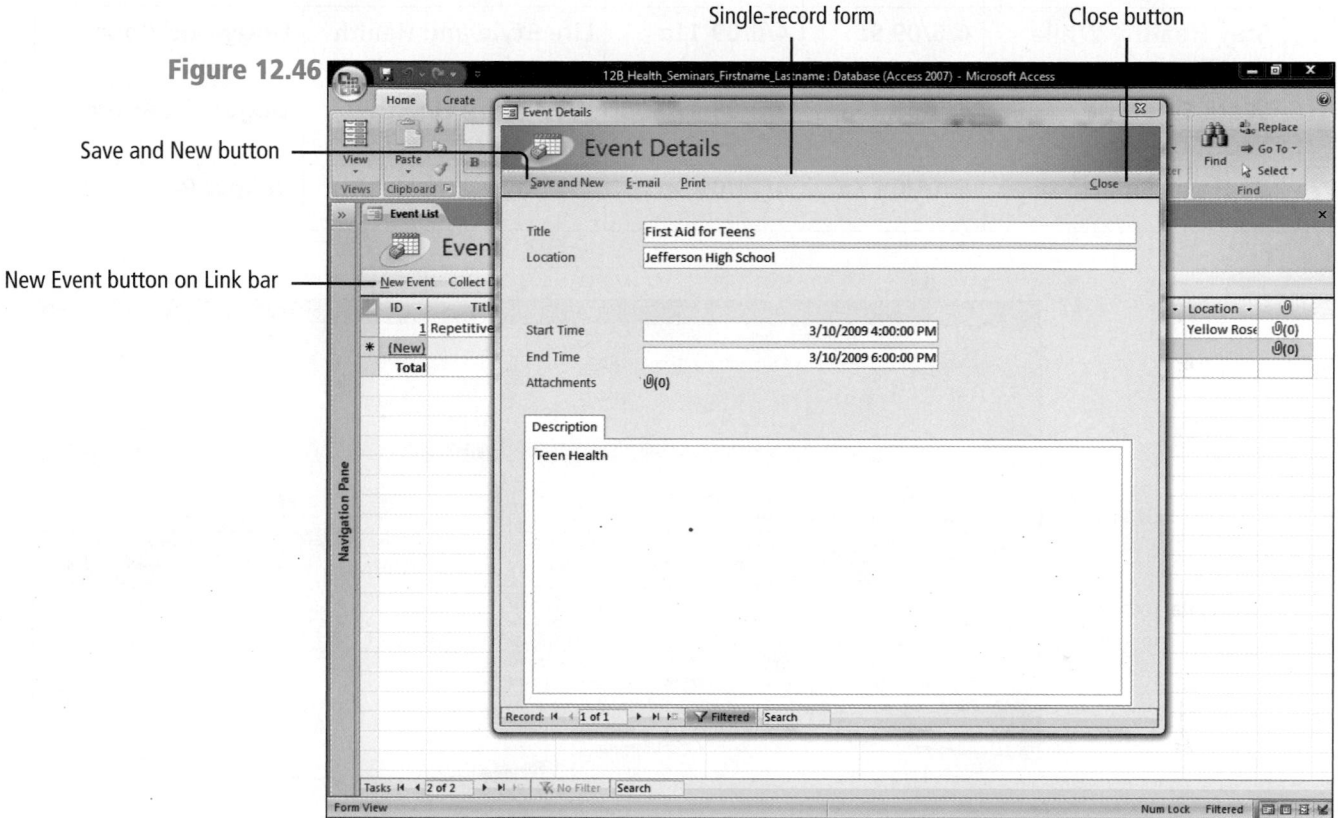

5 In the upper right corner of the single-record form, click **Close**, and notice that the new record displays in your Multiple Items form. Using either the rows on the Multiple Items form or the New Event single-record form, enter the following records, and then compare your screen with Figure 12.47.

Does a Single Record Form Open?

When entering records in the multiple items form, pressing [Enter] three times at the end of a row to begin a new record may display the single-record New Event form. If you prefer to use the multiple items form, close the single-record form and continue entering records, using the [Tab] key to move from field to field.

ID	Title	Start Time	End Time	Description	Location
3	**Safety on the Job**	**3/18/09 2p**	**3/18/09 4p**	**Workplace Health**	**Yellow Rose Room**
4	**Nutrition for Toddlers**	**3/19/09 1p**	**3/19/09 3p**	**Child Health and Development**	**Sandbox Preschool**
5	**Stay Healthy While You Travel**	**4/6/09 9a**	**4/6/09 11a**	**Life Style and Health**	**Dogwood Room**
6	**Work Smart at Your Computer**	**4/8/09 11a**	**4/8/09 12:30p**	**Workplace Health**	**Dogwood Room**
7	**Be Heart Smart**	**4/14/09 7p**	**4/14/09 9p**	**Life Style and Health**	**Yellow Rose Room**

Figure 12.47

Seven total records entered in form

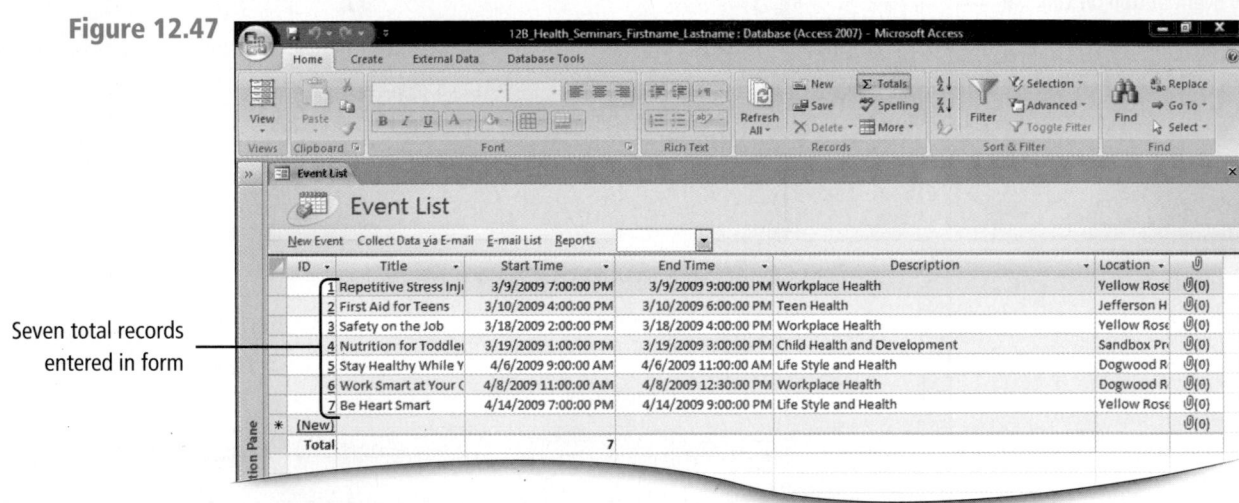

Objective 12
Organize Database Objects in the Navigation Pane

Use the Navigation Pane to organize your database objects, to open them for use, and to perform common tasks like renaming an object. So far, your databases have had only a few objects, but databases can have a large number of tables and other objects. Thus, the Navigation Pane will become your tool for organizing your database objects.

Activity 12.17 Organizing Database Objects in the Navigation Pane

The Navigation Pane groups and displays your database objects, and can do so in predefined arrangements. In this activity, you will group your database objects using the *Tables and Views category*, an arrangement that groups objects by the table to which they are related. Because all of your data must be stored in one or more tables, this is a useful arrangement.

1 **Open** 》 the **Navigation Pane**. At the top of the **Navigation Pane**, click the **Navigation arrow** ⊙, and then from the displayed list, under **Navigate To Category**, click **Tables and Related Views**.

Click the **Navigation arrow** ⊙ to display the list again, and then under **Filter By Group**, point to **All Tables**. Compare your screen with Figure 12.48.

Figure 12.48

All Tables displays

Tables and Related Views selected

All Tables selected

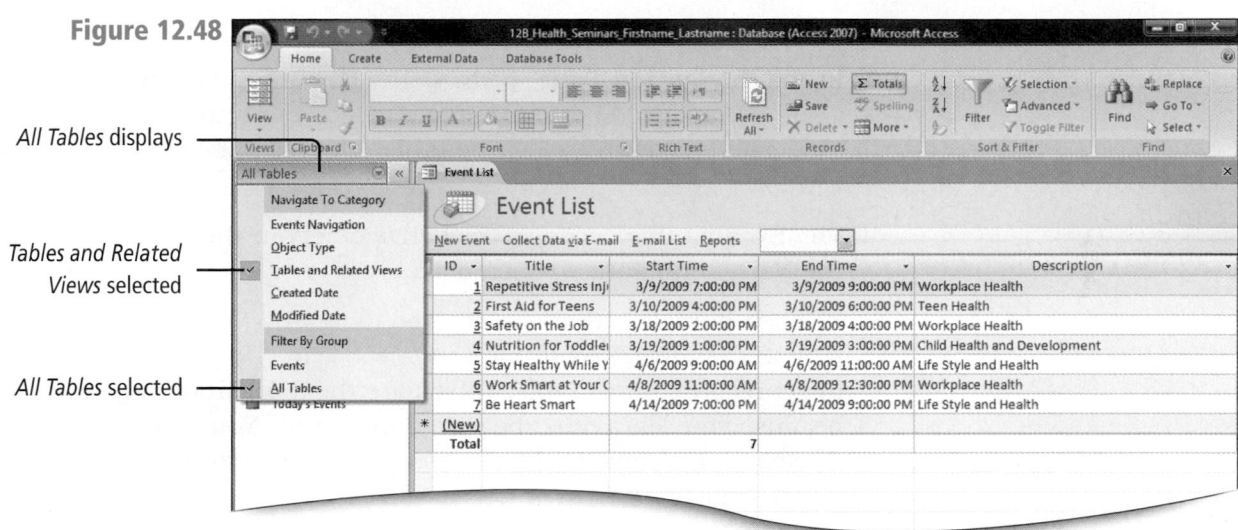

2 Click **All Tables** to close the list, and then confirm that *Events* displays in the blue bar at the top of the **Navigation Pane**. Compare your screen with Figure 12.49.

The icons to the left of the objects listed in the Navigation Pane indicate that the Events template created a number of objects for you—among them, one table titled *Events*, five reports, two forms, and one query. The Event List Multiple Items form, which is currently displayed in the object window, is included in the list.

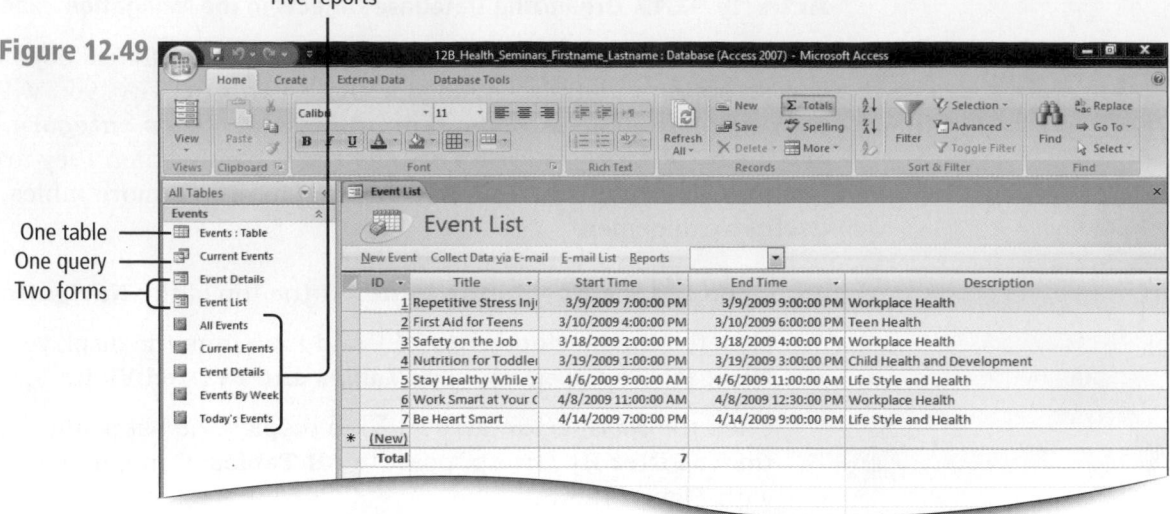

Five reports

Figure 12.49

One table
One query
Two forms

---

3 In the **Navigation Pane**, point to the **Events** *table*, and then right-click to display a shortcut menu. On the shortcut menu, click **Open**. Alternatively, double-click the table name to open it in the object window.

The Events table becomes the active object in the object window. Use the Navigation Pane to open objects for use.

The seven records that you entered using the Multiple Items *form* display in the *table*. Recall that the purpose of a form is to make it easy to get records into a table. Tables are the foundation of your database because your data must be stored in a table. You can enter records directly into a table in the manner you did in Project 12A, or you can use a single item form or a multiple items form to enter records.

4 In the object window, click the **Event List form tab** to bring it into view and make it the active object.

Recall that a form presents a more user-friendly screen with which to enter records into a table.

5 In the **Navigation Pane**, right-click the report named **Current Events**, and then click **Open**. Alternatively, double-click the report name to open it. Compare your screen with Figure 12.50.

An advantage of using a template to begin a database is that many objects, such as attractively formatted reports, are already designed for you.

Current Events report preformatted
and designed by the template

Figure 12.50

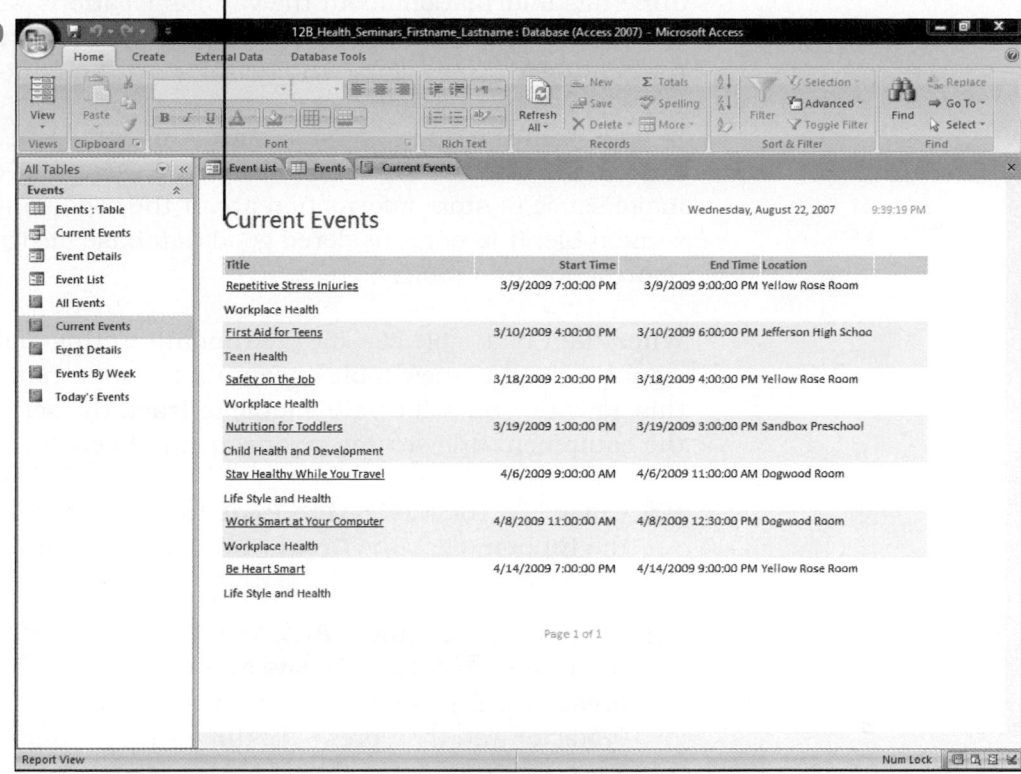

6 In the object window, **Close** [×] the **Current Events** report.

7 From the **Navigation Pane**, open the **Events By Week** report.

In this predesigned report, the events are displayed by week. These are among the reports that are predesigned and come with the template. After you enter your records, these preformatted reports are instantly available to you.

8 In the object window, **Close** [×] the **Events By Week** report. Then **Close** [×] the remaining two open objects. Leave the **Navigation Pane** fully displayed.

There are no open objects in your object window.

Objective 13
Create a New Table in a Database Created With a Template

The Events template created only one table—the *Events* table. Although the database was started from a template and contains many necessary objects, you can add additional objects as you need them.

Create a new table in a database when you begin to see repeated information. Repeated information is a good indication that an additional table is needed. For example, in the Events database, both the Yellow Rose Room and the Dogwood Room are listed more than one time.

Activity 12.18 Creating a New Table and Changing Its Design

June has information about the various locations where seminars are held. For example, for the Yellow Rose Room, she has information about the seating arrangements, number of seats, and audio-visual equipment.

In your database, three seminars are currently scheduled in the Yellow Rose Room and two are scheduled in the Dogwood Room. It would not make sense to store information about the rooms multiple times in the same table. It is *not* considered good database design to have duplicate information in a table.

When data in a table becomes redundant in this manner, it is usually a signal to create a new table to contain the information about the topic. In this activity, you will create a table to track the seminar locations and the equipment and seating arrangements in each location.

1 **Close** ⟪ the **Navigation Pane** to maximize your screen space. On the Ribbon, click the **Create tab**, and then in the **Tables group**, click the **Table** button.

2 Click in the cell under **Add New Field**, type **Yellow Rose Room** and then press [Tab]. Type **On Site** and then press [Tab]. Type **20** and then press [Tab]. Type **U-Shape Table** and then press [Tab]. Type **Computer Projector** and then press [Tab] three times. Compare your screen with Figure 12.51.

Access assigns an AutoNumber in the ID field.

Figure 12.51

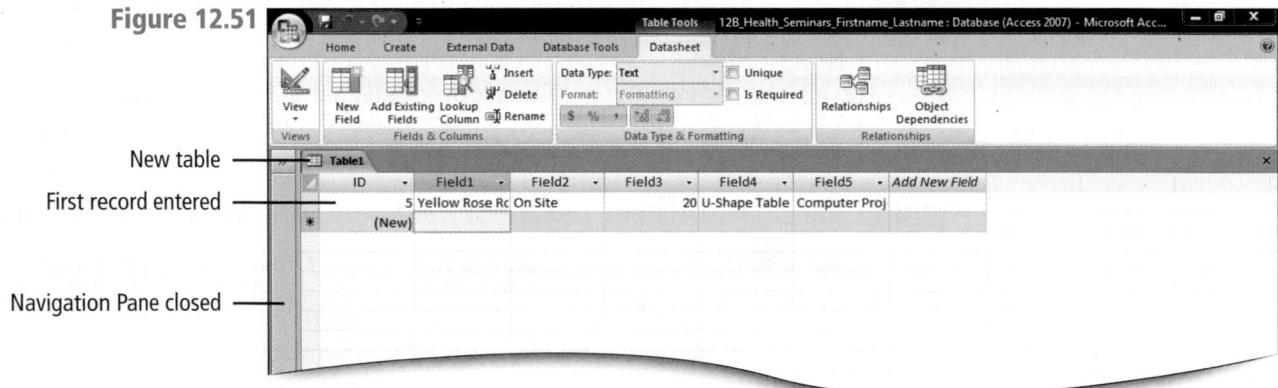

New table

First record entered

Navigation Pane closed

3 Point to the text *Field1*, right-click, and then from the displayed shortcut menu, click **Rename Column**. Type **Location** Point to the text *Field2*, double-click, and then type **On Site/Off Site** Point to and click *Field3*, click the **Datasheet tab**, and then in the **Fields & Columns group**, click **Rename**. Type **Seating Capacity** Using any of the techniques you have practiced, change *Field4* to **Room Arrangement** and *Field5* to **Visual Equipment**

4 In the **Views group**, click the **View** button to switch to **Design view**. **Save** the table as **12B Seminar Locations Firstname Lastname** and then click **OK**.

5 In **Design view**, in the **Field Name** column, click in the **Location** box. Then, on the **Design tab**, in the **Tools group**, click the **Primary Key** button.

The key icon moves to the left of the Location field. Recall that the Primary Key is the field that contains a unique identifier for the record. In the Seminar Locations table, the Location name is unique; no other record will have the same Location name.

6 Point to the **row selector box** for the **ID** field to display the ➡ pointer, and then click to select the entire row. On the **Design tab**, in the **Tools group**, click the **Delete Rows** button, and then click **Yes** in the message box.

Because the Location name will serve as the primary key field, the ID field is not necessary.

7 On the **Design tab**, in the **Views group**, click the **View** button, which by its icon indicates that you will return to the Datasheet view of the table. Click **Yes** to save the changes you have made to the table design.

8 Enter the remaining records in the table:

Location	On Site/ Off Site	Seating Capacity	Room Arrangement	Visual Equipment
Jefferson High School	**Off Site**	**150**	**Theater**	**Computer Projector**
Dogwood Room	**On Site**	**50**	**Classroom**	**Computer Projector**
Sandbox Preschool	**Off Site**	**20**	**Classroom**	**White Board**

9 Point to the field name *Location* to display the ⬇ pointer, hold down the left mouse button, and then drag across to select all of the columns, as shown in Figure 12.52.

All the columns selected

Figure 12.52

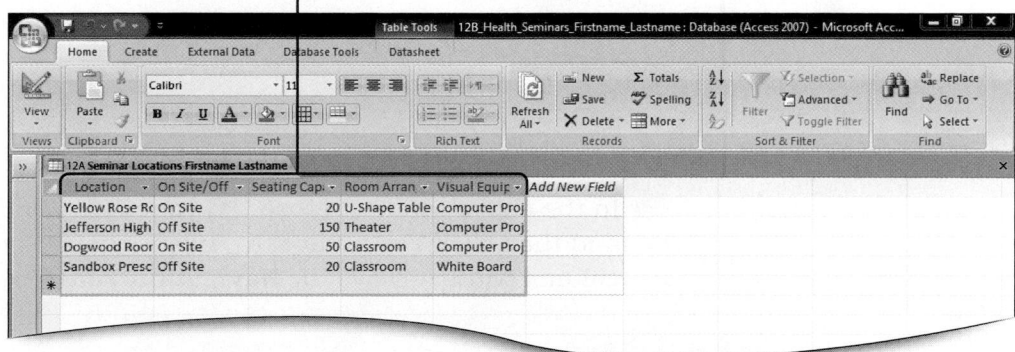

10 Point to any of the selected field names in the top row, right-click, and then from the displayed shortcut menu, click **Column Width**. In the displayed **Column Width** dialog box, click **Best Fit**. Alternatively, with the columns selected, in the field heading row, point to the right boundary of any of the selected rows to display the ⟨+⟩ pointer, and then double-click to apply Best Fit to all of the selected columns.

All of the columns widths are adjusted to accommodate the longest entry in the column.

11 Click in any record to cancel the selection of the columns. **Open** ⟨≫⟩ the **Navigation Pane**, locate the name of your new table, and then compare your screen with Figure 12.53.

Recall that as it is currently arranged, the Navigation Pane organizes the objects by table name. The Events table is listed first, followed by its associated objects, and then the Seminar Locations table is listed. Currently, there are no other objects associated with the Seminar Locations table.

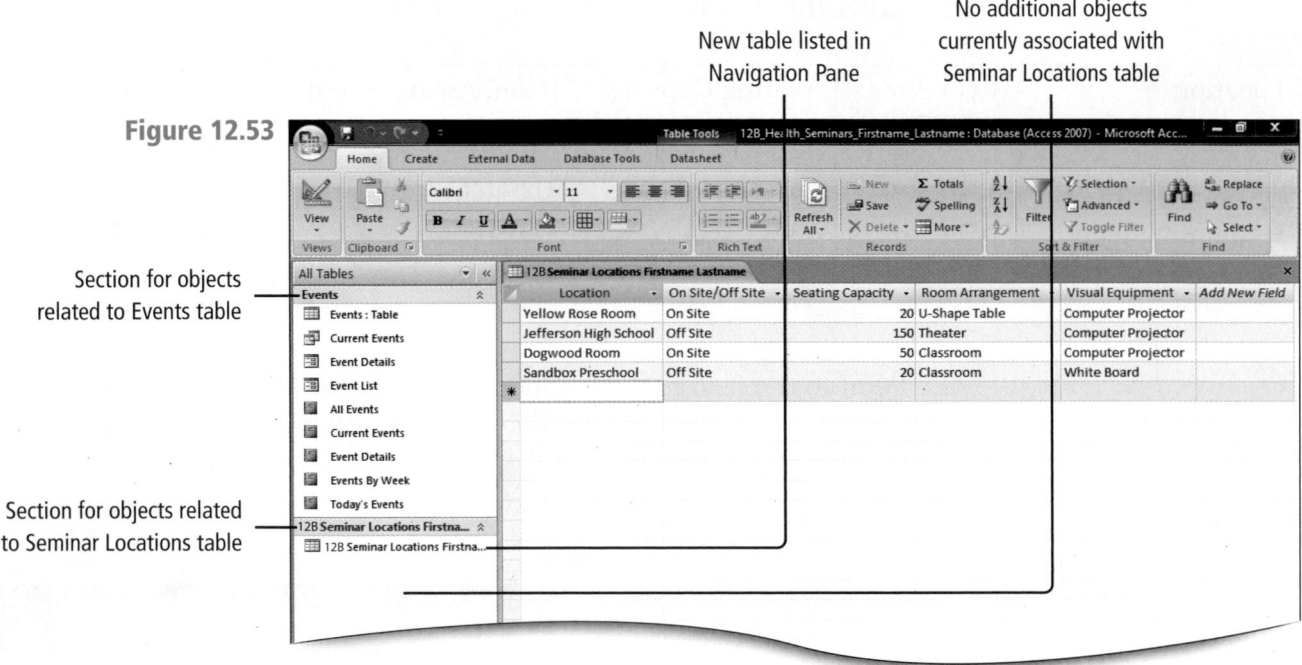

Figure 12.53

Section for objects related to Events table

Section for objects related to Seminar Locations table

New table listed in Navigation Pane

No additional objects currently associated with Seminar Locations table

12 In the object window, **Close** ⟨×⟩ your **12B Seminar Locations** table, and then click **Yes** to save the layout changes you made to the column widths. Leave the **Navigation Pane** open.

Objective 14
View a Report and Print a Table in a Database Created With a Template

Recall that an advantage to starting a new database with a template is that many report objects are already created for you.

Activity 12.19 Viewing a Report

1 From the **Navigation Pane**, open the **All Events** report. Compare your screen with Figure 12.54.

The All Events report displays in an attractively arranged pre-built report.

All Events report

Figure 12.54

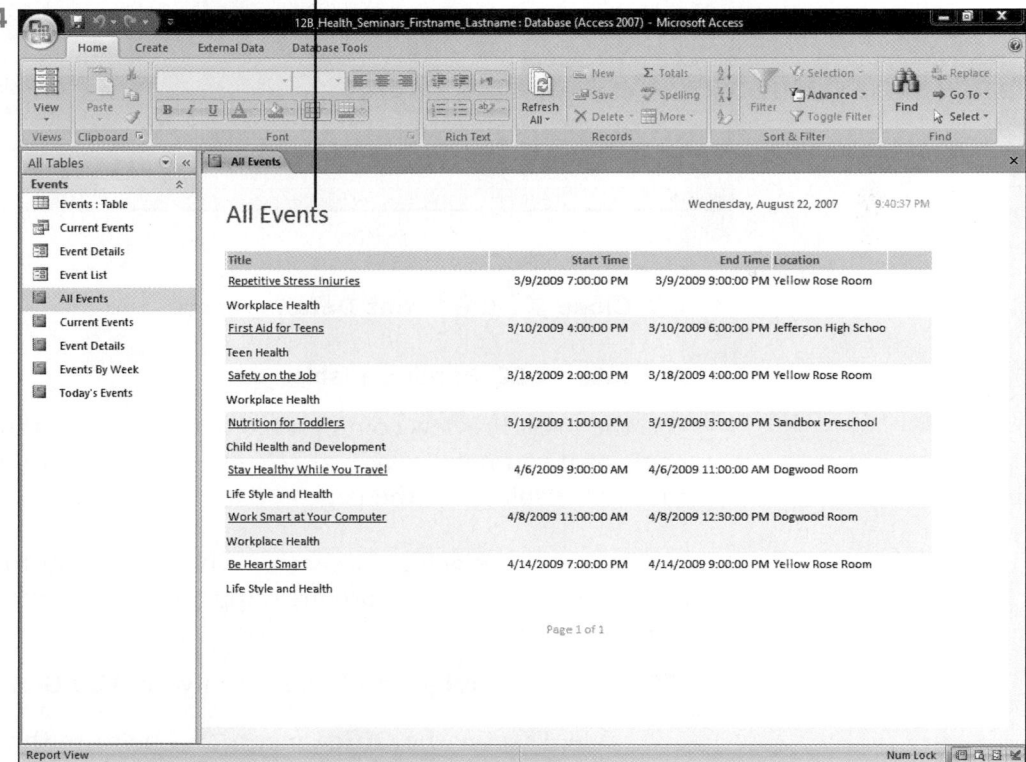

2 **Close** the **All Events** report.

3 Open the **Event Details** report and compare your screen with Figure 12.55.

The Event Details report displays in a pre-built report. Each report displays the records in the table in different useful formats.

Event Details report

Figure 12.55

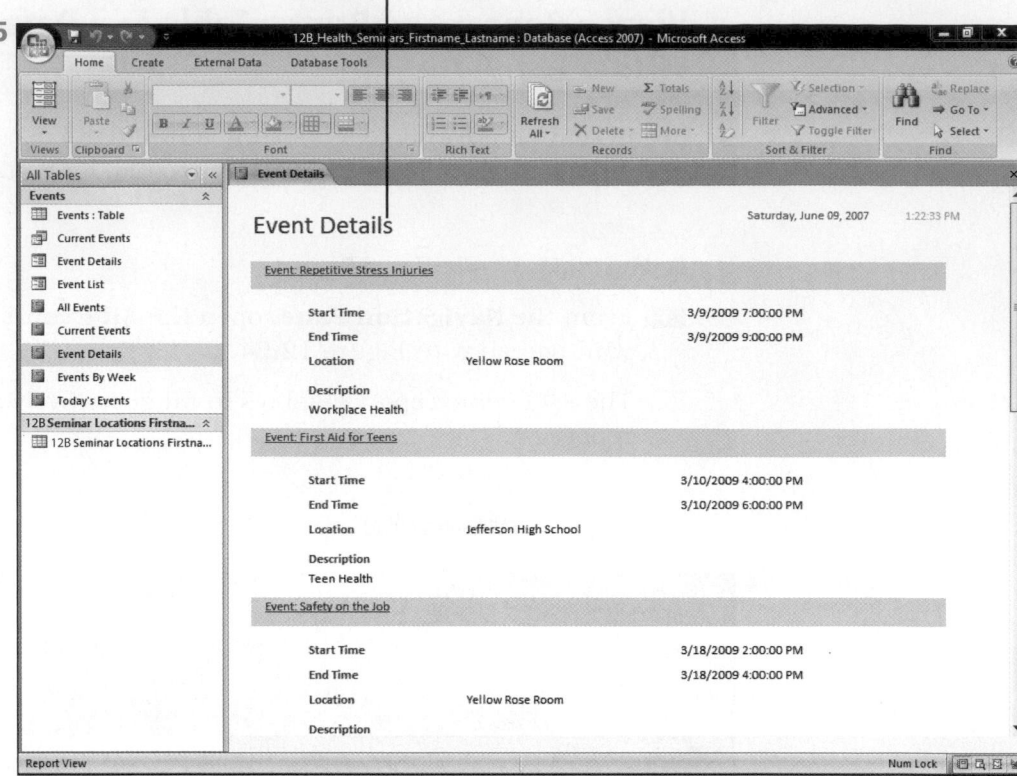

4 Close ☒ the **Event Details** report.

Activity 12.20 Printing a Table

Use the Print Preview command to determine if a table will print on one page, or if you need to adjust column widths, margins, or the direction the data displays on the page.

Recall that there will be occasions when you want to print your table for a quick reference or for proofreading. For more formal-looking information, print a report.

1 From the **Navigation Pane**, open your **12B Seminar Locations** table. Display the **Office** menu 🔘 , point to the **Print** button, and then click **Print Preview**.

The table displays in the Print Preview window so you can see how it will look when it is printed. The name of the table displays at the top of the page. The navigation area at the bottom of the window displays *1* in the Pages box, and the right-pointing arrow—the Next arrow—is active. Recall that when you are in the Print Preview window, the navigation arrows are used to navigate from one page to the next, rather than from one record to the next.

2 In the navigation area, click the **Next Page** arrow.

The second page of the table displays the last field column. Whenever possible, try to print all of the fields horizontally on one page. Of course, if you have many records you may need more than one page to print all of the records.

3 On the **Print Preview tab**, in the **Page Layout group**, click **Margins**, and then click **Wide**. Then, click the **Landscape** button and compare your screen with Figure 12.56.

Table in landscape orientation

Figure 12.56

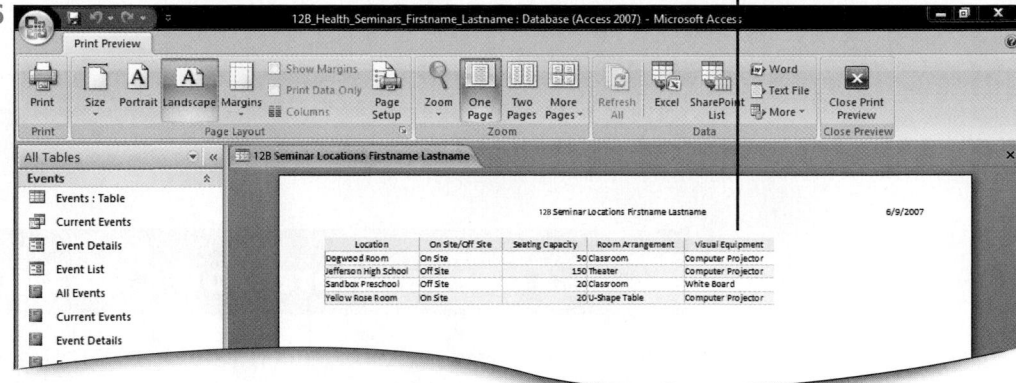

4 Check your *Chapter Assignment Sheet* or *Course Syllabus*, or consult your instructor, to determine whether you are to submit the printed pages that are the results of this project. To submit your work on paper, on the **Print Preview tab**, in the **Print group**, click the **Print** button. To submit electronically, close the Print Preview window and follow the directions provided by your instructor.

5 On the **Print Preview tab**, click **Close Print Preview**. **Close** your **12B Seminar Locations** table.

6 Close any open objects, and then **Close** the **Navigation Pane**.

From the **Office** menu , click **Close Database**. From the **Getting Started** screen, display the **Office** menu , and then click **Exit Access**.

Objective 15
Use the Access Help System

Access has a Help feature to assist you when performing a task in Access or to get more information about a particular topic in Access. You can activate the Help feature by clicking the Help button or by pressing F1.

Activity 12.21 Using the Access Help System

1 **Start** Access. In the upper right corner of the Access window, click the **Microsoft Office Access Help** button . In the **Access Help** window, click the **Search arrow**, and then under **Content from this computer**, click **Access Help**.

2 Click in the **Search** box, type **database design** and then press Enter. In the list that displays, click **Database design basics**.

This information is an informative overview of how to design a database from the beginning—from the stage where you are just writing your ideas on paper. If desired, print this information by clicking the Print button.

3 In the upper right corner of the **Access Help** window, click the **Close** button ▣.

End You have completed Project 12B ———————————

There's More You Can Do!

Close Access and any other open windows. Display the Start menu, click Computer, and then navigate to the student files that accompany this textbook. In the folder **02_theres_more_you_can_do**, locate and open the folder for this chapter. Open and print the instructions for this project, which are provided to you in Adobe PDF format.

Try IT 1—Convert a Database to a Different Format

In this Try It! exercise, you will convert an Access 2007 database to a database that others can view and edit in Access 2002 or Access 2003.

Content-Based Assessments

Access

chapter twelve

Summary

Microsoft Office Access is a database management system that uses various objects—tables, forms, queries, reports—to organize a database. Data is stored in tables in which you establish fields, set the data type and field size, and create a primary key. Data from a database can be reported and printed.

Key Terms

The ⊛ symbol represents Key Terms found on the Student CD in the 02_theres_more_you_can_do folder for this chapter.

Content-Based Assessments

Access

chapter twelve

Matching

Match each term in the second column with its correct definition in the first column. Write the letter of the term on the blank line in front of the correct definition.

_____ **1.** An organized collection of facts about people, events, things, or ideas related to a particular topic or purpose.

_____ **2.** Facts about people, events, things, or ideas.

_____ **3.** Data that is organized in a useful manner.

_____ **4.** The basic parts of a database, which include tables, forms, queries, reports, and macros.

_____ **5.** The Access object that stores your data organized in an arrangement of columns and rows.

_____ **6.** The area of the Access window that displays and organizes the names of the objects in a database, and from where you open objects for use.

_____ **7.** The portion of the Access window that displays open objects.

_____ **8.** A category that describes each piece of data stored in a table.

_____ **9.** All of the categories of data pertaining to one person, place, thing, event, or idea.

_____ **10.** The number of fields, and the type of content within each field, in an Access table.

_____ **11.** The Access view that displays an object organized in a format of columns and rows similar to an Excel spreadsheet.

_____ **12.** The Access view that displays the underlying structure of an object.

_____ **13.** The action of filling a database table with records.

_____ **14.** The characteristic that defines the kind of data that can be entered into a field, such as numbers, text, or dates.

_____ **15.** An Access feature that sequentially numbers entered records creating a unique number for each field and which is useful for data that has no distinct field that is unique.

A AutoNumber

B Data

C Data type

D Database

E Datasheet view

F Design view

G Field

H Information

I Navigation Pane

J Object window

K Objects

L Populate

M Record

N Table

O Table design

Content-Based Assessments

Fill in the Blank

Write the correct word in the space provided.

1. DBMS is an acronym for _____ _____ _____ .

2. A preformatted database designed for a specific purpose is a database _____ .

3. A database that has no data and has no database tools, in which you create the data and the tools as you need them, is referred to as a(n) _____ database.

4. Characteristics of a field that control how the field will display and how data can be entered in a field are known as the _____ _____ .

5. The field that uniquely identifies a record in a table is the _____ _____ .

6. A pre-built table format for common topics such as contacts, issues, and tasks is a(n) _____ _____ .

7. A database object that retrieves specific data from one or more tables, and then displays the specified data in Datasheet view is a(n) _____ .

8. A type of query that retrieves data from one or more tables and makes it available for use in the format of a datasheet is a(n) _____ query.

9. The table or tables from which a query gets its data is the _____ _____

10. A feature in Microsoft Office programs that walks you step by step through a process is a(n) _____ .

11. To search a table of records included in a query, find the records that match the criteria, and then display the records, _____ the query.

12. An Access object with which you can enter new records into a table, edit existing records in a table, or display existing records from a table is a(n) _____ .

13. The Access object that displays data in a formatted manner for printing and publication is a(n) _____ .

14. The Access form object in which multiple records can be entered into or displayed from a table is a(n) _____ _____ form.

15. An arrangement of objects in the Navigation Pane in which the objects are grouped by the table to which they are related is the _____ _____ _____ category.

Content-Based Assessments

Project 12C—Departments

In this project, you will apply the skills you practiced from the Objectives in Project 12A.

Objectives: 1. *Start Access and Create a New Blank Database;* **2.** *Add Records to a Table;* **3.** *Rename Table Fields in Datasheet View;* **4.** *Modify the Design of a Table;* **5.** *Add a Second Table to a Database;* **6.** *Print a Table;* **7.** *Create and Use a Query;* **8.** *Create and Use a Form;* **9.** *Create and Print a Report;* **10.** *Close and Save a Database.*

In the following Skills Review, you will assist Kendall Walker, the CEO of Texas Lakes Medical Center, in creating a database to store information about the Departments and Department Directors at Texas Lakes Medical Center. Your printed results will look similar to those in Figure 12.57.

For Project 12C, you will need the following file:

New blank Access database

You will save your database as
12C_Departments_Firstname_Lastname

Figure 12.57

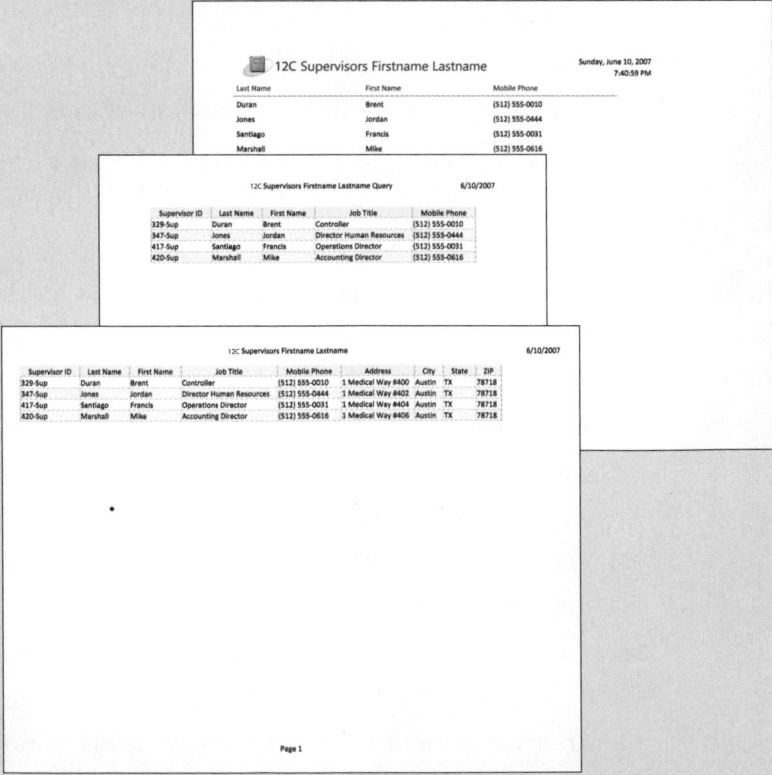

(Project 12C–Departments continues on the next page)

Content-Based Assessments

(Project 12C–Departments continued)

1. **Start** Access and create a new **Blank Database**. In the lower right portion of the screen, click the **Browse** button, navigate to your **Access Chapter 12** folder, and then in the **File New Database** dialog box, name the database **12C_Departments_Firstname_Lastname** Press Enter. In the lower right corner, click the **Create** button.

2. In the **Navigation Pane**, click the **Close** button to collapse the **Navigation Pane** and maximize your screen space. Click in the first **Add New Field** box, type **Accounting** and then click in the **ID** field. To assign custom Department IDs, on the **Datasheet tab**, in the **Data Type & Formatting group**, click the **Data Type arrow**, and then click **Text**. Type **1212-D** and then click in the next **Add New Field** box to the right of *Accounting*, and complete the entry of this record and the next record as follows.

ID	Field1	Field2	Field3	Field4	Field5	Field6	Field7	Field8	Field9	Field10
1212-D	Accounting	Jennifer	R	Lee	(512) 555-0987	1 Medical Way #216	Austin	TX	78718	Duran
1233-D	Employee Benefits	Mike	M	Hernandez	(512) 555-0344	1 Medical Way #214	Austin	TX	78718	Duran

3. Point to the text *ID*, and then click to select the column. On the **Datasheet tab**, in the **Fields & Columns group**, click the **Rename** button, type **Dept ID** and press Enter. Point to the text *Field1*, right-click, and from the displayed menu, click **Rename Column**. Type **Department** and press Enter. Point to the text *Field2* and double-click. With the text selected, type **Director First Name** and press Enter. Using any of these techniques, rename *Field3* as **Director Middle Initial** Rename *Field4* as **Director Last Name** Rename *Field5* as **Mobile Phone** Rename *Field6* as **Address** Rename *Field7* as **City** Rename *Field8* as **State** Rename *Field9* as **ZIP** Rename *Field10* as **Supervisor**

4. Enter the following additional records:

Dept ID	Department	Director First Name	Director Middle Initial	Director Last Name	Mobile Phone	Address	City	State	ZIP	Supervisor
1259-D	Emergency Room	Paul	S	Roberts	(512) 555-0234	1 Medical Way #212	Austin	TX	78718	Marshall
1265-D	Nursing Services	Andrea	T	McMillan	(512) 555-0233	1 Medical Way #302	Austin	TX	78718	Jones

(Project 12C–Departments continues on the next page)

(Project 12C–Departments continued)

1313-D	Finance	Beth	N	Crosby	(512) 555-0266	1 Medical Way #301	Austin	TX	78718	Duran
1355-D	Physician Services	Laura	O	Klein	(512) 555-0277	1 Medical Way #146	Austin	TX	78718	Jones
1459-D	Facilities	Mario	B	Bartello	(512) 555-0211	1 Medical Way #236	Austin	TX	78718	Santiago

5. On the **Datasheet tab**, in the **Views group**, click the **View button arrow**. From the displayed list, click **Design View**. To save the changes you made to the field names and data types, and to give the table a more meaningful name, save the table, using your own first and last name, as **12C Departments Firstname Lastname** and then click **OK**.

6. In the **Field Name** column, click the row selector box to the left of the **Director Middle Initial** field name to select the entire row. Then, on the **Design tab**, in the **Tools group**, click the **Delete Rows** button, read the message in the displayed dialog box, and then click **Yes**. For this table, Kendall decides that having the Director's middle initial is not necessary.

7. With your table still displayed in Design view, in the **Field Name** column, click in the **Dept ID** box. To the left of the box, notice the small icon of a key representing the primary key. Recall that the primary key is the field that uniquely identifies each individual record—no two records in the database will have the same Dept ID.

8. In the **Field Name** column, click in the **State** field, and then in the **Field Properties** area, set the **Field Size** to **2** In the **Description** column, click in the **Address** row, and then type **Include the Room number** Recall that descriptions entered here will display in the status bar when entering records using a form. This will communicate additional information to the person entering data about how to enter data in the field.

9. Click the **View** button to return to Datasheet view, and then click **Yes** two times to save the changes you have made to the design of your table—deleting a field, adding a description, and changing a field property.

10. With your **12C Departments** table displayed in Datasheet view, notice that in the **Supervisor** field, several names are repeated. Thus, it would not make sense to include information about these individuals multiple times in the same table. Recall that when you see repeated information, it is likely that an additional table should be added to your database. On the Ribbon, click the **Create tab**. In the **Tables group**, click **Table Templates**, and then from the displayed list, click **Contacts**.

11. Click the **Datasheet tab** to display the groups of Datasheet commands. In the second column, point to the text *Company*, click to select the field, and then on the **Datasheet tab**, in the **Fields & Columns group**, click **Delete**.

(Project 12C–Departments continues on the next page)

Content-Based Assessments

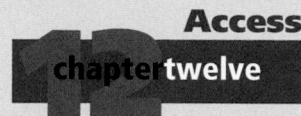
(Project 12C–Departments continued)

12. Delete the **E-mail Address** field. With your mouse, drag to the right to select the **Business Phone** field and **Home Phone** field. Right-click over the field names, and then from the displayed shortcut menu, click **Delete Column**. Delete the **Fax Number** field. Then, delete the fields **Country/Region**, **Web Page**, **Notes**, and **Attachments** (the field with the paper clip icon).

13. On the **Datasheet tab**, in the **Views group**, click the **View** button to switch to **Design view**. To save the changes you made to the field arrangement and to give the table a more meaningful name, save the table, using your own first and last name, as **12C Supervisors Firstname Lastname** and then click **OK**.

14. In the **Field Name** column, click the **ID** box, delete the text, and then type **Supervisor ID** Click in the **Data Type** box, click the **Data Type arrow**, and then from the displayed list, click **Text**. Click in the **Description** column, and type **Supervisor's ID number** The medical center assigns a unique ID number to each Supervisor, which you will use as the primary key instead of the AutoNumber.

15. In the **Field Name** column, click in the **State/Province** field, and then in the **Field Properties** area, set the **Field Size** to **2** Click the **View** button to switch to Datasheet view, and then click **Yes** to save the changes you have made to the design of your table—changing a field name, adding a description, and changing a field property.

16. With your **12C Supervisors** table displayed in Datasheet view, in the new record row which is indicated by an asterisk (*) in the record selector box on the left, click in the **Supervisor ID** field, and then add the following records:

Supervisor ID	Last Name	First Name	Job Title	Mobile Phone	Address	City	State/ Province	ZIP/Postal Code
329-Sup	Duran	Brent	Controller	(512) 555-0010	1 Medical Way #400	Austin	TX	78718
347-Sup	Jones	Jordan	Director Human Resources	(512) 555-0444	1 Medical Way #402	Austin	TX	78718
417-Sup	Santiago	Francis	Operations Director	(512) 555-0031	1 Medical Way #404	Austin	TX	78718
420-Sup	Marshall	Mike	Accounting Director	(512) 555-0616	1 Medical Way #406	Austin	TX	78718

17. Change the field name **State/Province** to **State** and **ZIP/Postal Code** to **ZIP** Select all of the columns, and then apply **Best Fit** either by double-clicking the right border of any selected column or by displaying the shortcut menu, clicking Column Width, and then clicking Best Fit. On the **Quick Access Toolbar**, click the **Save** button to save the changes you have made to the layout of the table.

(Project 12C–Departments continues on the next page)

Content-Based Assessments

(Project 12C–Departments continued)

18. From the **Office** menu, point to the **Print** button, and then click **Print Preview**. In the **Page Layout group**, click the **Margins** button, and then click **Normal**. Click the **Landscape** button. If you are submitting paper results, click the **Print** button, and in the displayed **Print** dialog box, click **OK**. To submit electronically, follow the directions provided by your instructor. Click **Close Print Preview**.

19. **Close** your **12C Supervisors** table and **Close** your **12C Departments** table. Click the **Create tab**, and then in the **Other group**, click **Query Wizard**. In the **New Query** dialog box, click **Simple Query Wizard**, and then click **OK**. Click the **Tables/Queries arrow**, and then click your **Table: 12C Supervisors**. Under **Available Fields**, click **Supervisor ID**, and then click the **Add Field** button to move the field to the **Selected Fields** list on the right. Add the **Last Name**, **First Name**, **Job Title**, and **Mobile Phone** fields to the **Selected Fields** list. Recall that you can also double-click a field name to move it.

This query will answer the question *What is the Supervisor ID, name, job title, and mobile phone number of every Supervisor in the database?* Click the **Next** button. Be sure that the option **Open the query to view information** is selected. Click **Finish**. Display the query in Print Preview, use the default margins and orientation, and then print or submit electronically. **Close** the Print Preview.

20. **Close** your query. **Open** the **Navigation Pane**, click to select your **12C Supervisors** table. You need not open the table, just select it. **Close** the **Navigation Pane**. On the Ribbon, click the **Create tab**, and then in the **Forms group**, click **Form**. The form displays in Layout view, in which you can make changes to the layout of the form. Because no changes are necessary, on the **Home tab**, in the **Views group**, click the **View button arrow**, and then from the displayed list, click **Form View**. From the **Office** menu, click **Save** to save your newly designed form, and then click **OK** to accept the default name. **Close** the form object. Recall that you typically create forms to make data entry easier for the individuals who enter new records into your database.

21. **Open** the **Navigation Pane**, locate your **12C Supervisors** table—recall that a table displays a small icon of a datasheet, a query displays a small icon of two datasheets, and a form displays a red form icon. Open the table either by double-clicking the table name or right-clicking and clicking Open from the shortcut menu. **Close** the **Navigation Pane**. On the **Create tab**, in the **Reports group**, click **Report**.

22. Point to the **Supervisor ID** column heading, right-click, and then click **Delete**. Delete the **Job Title**, **Address**, **City**, **State**, and **ZIP** fields from the report layout. From the **Office** menu, display **Print Preview**. In the **Page Layout group**, click the **Margins** button, and then click **Wide**. Click the **Landscape** button. If you are submitting paper results, click the **Print** button. To submit electronically, follow the instructions provided by your instructor. Click the **Close Print Preview** button.

23. **Close** your **12C Supervisors** report, and then click **Yes** to save the design changes. In the **Save As** dialog box, click **OK** to save the report with the default name. If necessary, close any remaining objects and **Close** the **Navigation Pane**. From the **Office** menu, click **Exit Access**.

End **You have completed Project 12C** ――――――――――――――――――――

Content-Based Assessments

Project 12D — Benefits Fair

In this project, you will apply the skills you practiced from the Objectives in Project 12B.

Objectives: 11. *Create a Database Using a Template;* **12.** *Organize Database Objects in the Navigation Pane;* **13.** *Create a New Table in a Database Created With a Template;* **14.** *View a Report and Print a Table in a Database Created With a Template.*

In the following Skills Review, you will assist Sharon Fitzgerald, the Human Resources Director at Texas Lakes Medical Center, in creating a database to store information about the Employee Benefits Fair at Texas Lakes Medical Center. Your printed result will look similar to Figure 12.58.

For Project 12D, you will need the following file:

New Access database using the Events Template

**You will save your database as
12D_Benefits_Fair_Firstname_Lastname**

Figure 12.58

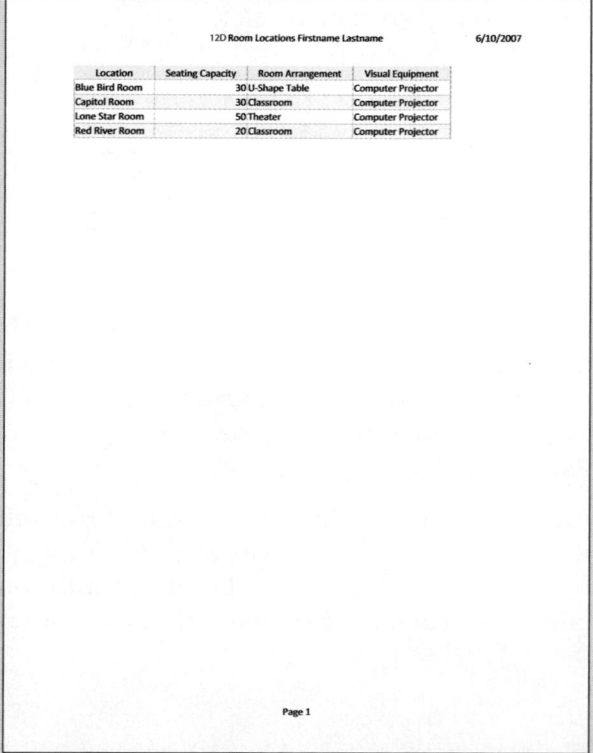

(Project 12D–Benefits Fair continues on the next page)

Content-Based Assessments

(Project 12D–Benefits Fair continued)

1. **Start** Access. Under **Template Categories**, click **Local Templates**, and then click **Events**. In the lower right portion of the screen, click the **Browse** button 📁, navigate to your **Access Chapter 12** folder, and then save the database as **12D_Benefits_Fair_Firstname_Lastname** Press ⏎. In the lower right corner, click the **Create** button. If necessary, to the right of the **Security Warning**, click **Options**, click **Enable this content**, and then click **OK**.

2. Recall that a template opens with a pre-built Multiple Items form into which you can enter records to build a table. In the **Event List** Multiple Items form, enter the following records, pressing ⇥ to move across the row:

ID	Title	Start Time	End Time	Description	Location
1	Medical Plan	5/1/09 8a	5/1/09 5p	Health Benefits	Lone Star Room
2	Eye Care Plan	5/1/09 9a	5/1/09 3p	Health Benefits	Red River Room
3	Prescription Plan	5/1/09 8a	5/1/09 8p	Health Benefits	Lone Star Room
4	Pension Plan	5/1/09 10a	5/1/09 7:30p	Retirement Benefits	Capitol Room
5	Life Insurance Plan	5/1/09 1p	5/1/09 5p	Life Insurance Benefits	Blue Bird Room
6	Deferred Compensation Plan	5/1/09 10a	5/1/09 3p	Compensation Benefits	Red River Room

3. In the **Link bar**, just above the Field names, click **New Event**, and then enter the following record using the single record form. Recall that you can also use this form to enter records into a table:

Title	Location	Start Time	End Time	Description
Dental Plan	Blue Bird Room	5/1/09 8a	5/1/09 5p	Health Benefits

4. **Close** the single record form. **Close** the **Event List** form. **Open** the **Navigation Pane**. At the top of the **Navigation Pane**, click the **Navigation arrow**. Under **Navigate To Category**, click **Tables and Related Views**. Click the **Navigation arrow** again, and then in the **Filter By Group** section, notice that **All Tables** is selected. Recall that this arrangement organizes the database objects by the table to which they are related.

5. From the **Navigation Pane**, right-click the **Events** table, and then click **Open**—or double-click the table name to open it. This is the table that was built from the records you entered into the form. Rather than enter information about the Locations multiple times in this table, you will create another table for the Location information. **Close** the **Events** table, and then **Close** the **Navigation Pane**.

(Project 12D–Benefits Fair continues on the next page)

(Project 12D–Benefits Fair continued)

6. On the Ribbon, click the **Create tab**, and then in the **Tables group**, click the **Table** button. Enter the following records, pressing Tab or Enter to move across the row. Recall that Access will assign unique numbers; your assigned numbers may vary.

ID	Field1	Field2	Field3	Field4
4	Blue Bird Room	30	U-Shape Table	Computer Projector
5	Red River Room	20	Classroom	Computer Projector
6	Capitol Room	30	Classroom	Computer Projector

7. Point to the text *Field1* and click to select the column. On the **Datasheet tab**, in the **Fields & Columns group**, click **Rename**, and then type **Location** Point to the text *Field2*, right-click, and then from the displayed menu, click **Rename Column**. Type **Seating Capacity** Point to the text *Field3* and double-click. With the text selected, type **Room Arrangement** Using any of these techniques, rename *Field4* as **Visual Equipment**

8. Enter one additional record as follows:

ID	Location	Seating Capacity	Room Arrangement	Visual Equipment
7	Lone Star Room	50	Theater	Computer Projector

9. On the **Home tab**, in the **Views group**, click the **View button arrow**, and then click **Design View**. **Save** the table as **12D Room Locations Firstname Lastname** and then click **OK**.

10. In the **Field Name** column, click in the **Location** box, and then on the **Design tab**, click the **Primary Key** button. Point to the row selector box for the **ID** field, and then click to select the entire row. On the **Design tab**, click the **Delete Rows** button, and then click **Yes**. The Location name will serve as the primary key for this table. In the **Views group**, click the **View** button, and then click **Yes** to save the changes you made to the table design.

11. On the field name row, drag across to select all of the columns. Right-click over any column heading, click **Column Width**, and then in the displayed **Column Width** dialog box, click **Best Fit**.

12. **Close** the **12D Room Locations** table, and then click **Yes** to save the layout changes you made to the column widths. From the **Navigation Pane**, open the **All Events** report. Open the **Event Details** report. The pre-built reports are arranged in various useful formats. **Close** both reports.

13. From the **Navigation Pane**, open your **12D Room Locations** table. From the **Office** menu, point to **Print**, and then click **Print Preview**. Check your *Chapter Assignment Sheet* or *Course Syllabus*, or consult your instructor, to determine whether you are to submit the printed page.

(Project 12D–Benefits Fair continues on the next page)

Content-Based Assessments

(Project 12D–Benefits Fair continued)

If you are submitting your work on paper, on the **Print Preview tab**, in the **Print group**, click the **Print** button. To submit electronically, follow the directions provided by your instructor.

14. Close Print Preview, and then **Close** your **12D Room Locations** table. **Close** the **Navigation Pane**. Be sure all database objects are closed. From the **Office** menu, click **Exit Access**.

 You have completed Project 12D ————————————————————————

Content-Based Assessments

Project 12E—Orthopedic Supplies

In this project, you will apply the skills you practiced from the Objectives in Project 12A.

Objectives: 1. *Start Access and Create a New Blank Database;* **2.** *Add Records to a Table;* **3.** *Rename Table Fields in Datasheet View;* **4.** *Modify the Design of a Table;* **5.** *Add a Second Table to a Database;* **6.** *Print a Table;* **7.** *Create and Use a Query;* **8.** *Create and Use a Form;* **9.** *Create and Print a Report;* **10.** *Close and Save a Database.*

In the following Mastering Access assessment, you will assist Kelley Martin, the Orthopedics Director of Texas Lakes Medical Center, in creating a database to store information about medical suppliers and supplies. Your printed results will look similar to those shown in Figure 12.59.

For Project 12E, you will need the following file:

New blank Access database

You will save your database as
12E_Orthopedic_Supplies_Firstname_Lastname

Figure 12.59

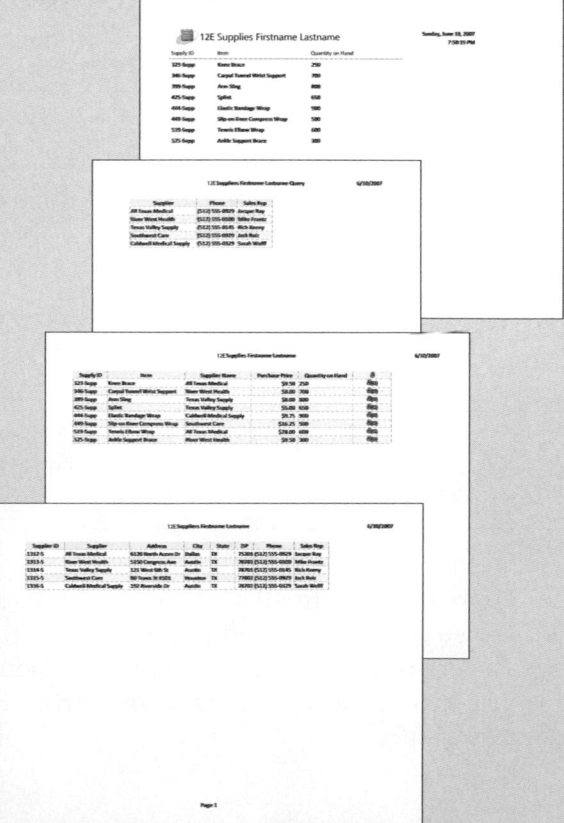

(Project 12E–Orthopedic Supplies continues on the next page)

(Project 12E–Orthopedic Supplies continued)

1. **Start** Access, create a new **Blank Database**, use the **open folder icon** to navigate to your **Access Chapter 12** folder, and then name the new database **12E_Orthopedic_Supplies_ Firstname_Lastname Close** the **Navigation Pane**, and then beginning in the first new field, add the following records:

ID	Field1	Field2	Field3	Field4	Field5	Field6	Field7	Field8	Field9
9	1312-S	All Texas Medical	6120 North Acorn Dr	Dallas	TX	75201	(512) 555-0929	Jacque Ray	14-O
10	1313-S	River West Health	5150 Congress Ave	Austin	TX	78701	(512) 555-0100	Mike Frantz	16-R

2. Rename *Field1* as **Supplier ID** Rename *Field2* as **Supplier** Rename *Field3* as **Address** Rename *Field4* as **City** Rename *Field5* as **State** Rename *Field6* as **ZIP** Rename *Field7* as **Phone** Rename *Field8* as **Sales Rep** Rename *Field9* as **Sales Code**

3. Click **View** to open the table in **Design view**. Name the table **12E Suppliers Firstname Lastname** Set the **Supplier ID** field as the **Primary Key**, and then delete the **ID** field. Set the **Field Size** for the **State** field to **2** Return to **Datasheet view**, **Save** the changes, and then, beginning with *Supplier ID 1314-S*, enter the following records:

Supplier ID	Supplier	Address	City	State	ZIP	Phone	Sales Rep	Sales Code
1312-S	All Texas Medical	6120 North Acorn Dr	Dallas	TX	75201	(512) 555-0929	Jacque Ray	14-O
1313-S	River West Health	5150 Congress Ave	Austin	TX	78701	(512) 555-0100	Mike Frantz	16-R
1314-S	Texas Valley Supply	121 West 6th St	Austin	TX	78701	(512) 555-0145	Rich Keeny	12-R
1315-S	Southwest Care	80 Travis St #101	Houston	TX	77002	(512) 555-0929	Jack Ruiz	14-O
1316-S	Caldwell Medical Supply	192 Riverside Dr	Austin	TX	78701	(512) 555-0329	Sarah Wolff	16-O

4. **Delete** the **Sales Code** field. Apply **Best Fit** to all of the columns to accommodate their data and column headings. If you are submitting printed pages, display the **Print Preview**, change the margins to **Wide**, change the orientation to **Landscape**, and then **Print** the table. For electronic submissions, follow your instructor's directions. **Close Print Preview**, and then **Save** the changes you have made to your table.

(Project 12E–Orthopedic Supplies continues on the next page)

(Project 12E–Orthopedic Supplies continued)

5. Close your **12E Suppliers** table. Create a second table using the **Table Templates Assets** template to record the information about the orthopedic supplies that have been purchased by the medical center. Delete the following fields from the template: **Category**, **Condition**, **Acquired Date**, **Current Value**, **Location**, **Manufacturer**, **Model**, **Comments**, and **Retired Date**.

6. Rename the **Description** field as **Supplier Name** and then rename the **ID** field as **Supply ID** On the **Datasheet tab**, set the **Data Type** for the **Supply ID** field to **Text**. On the **Home tab**, switch to **Design view**, save the table as **12E Supplies Firstname Lastname** and then in the **Field Name** column, insert a new row above **Attachments**. Name the new field **Quantity on Hand** Click the **Supply ID** field, and then change its **Field Size** to **8** Return to **Datasheet** view, save your changes, and then add the following records:

Supply ID	Item	Supplier Name	Purchase Price	Quantity on Hand
323-Supp	Knee Brace	All Texas Medical	9.50	250
346-Supp	Carpal Tunnel Wrist Support	River West Health	8	700
399-Supp	Arm Sling	Texas Valley Supply	8	800
425-Supp	Splint	Texas Valley Supply	5	650
444-Supp	Elastic Bandage Wrap	Caldwell Medical Supply	9.75	900
449-Supp	Slip-on Knee Compress Wrap	Southwest Care	16.25	500
519-Supp	Tennis Elbow Wrap	All Texas Medical	28	600
525-Supp	Ankle Support Brace	River West Health	9.50	300

7. Select all of the columns, and then apply **Best Fit**. Display the table in **Print Preview**, and then select **Wide** margins and **Landscape** orientation. If you are submitting printed pages, print the table. To submit electronically, follow the directions provided by your instructor.

8. **Close Print Preview**, **Close** the **12E Supplies** table, and then **Save** the changes. On the **Create tab**, use the **Query Wizard** to create a **Simple Query** based on the **12E Suppliers** table. The query will answer the question *What is the name of every supplier, their phone number, and their Sale Rep's name?* Add the **Supplier** field, **Phone** field, and **Sales Rep** field. Title the query as **12E Suppliers Firstname Lastname Query** Print and then close the query.

9. From the **Navigation Pane**, select your **12E Supplies** table—you do not need to open the table, just be sure that it is selected. **Create** a **Form** based on the table, click the **View button**

(Project 12E–Orthopedic Supplies continues on the next page)

Content-Based Assessments

Access

chapter twelve

Mastering Access

(Project 12E–Orthopedic Supplies continued)

arrow and then click **Form View**. When needed, the form can be used to enter or view records one record at a time.

10. **Close** the form, and then save it with the default name. **Create** a **Report** based on your **12E Supplies** table. Delete the **Supplier Name** field, the **Purchase Price** field, and the **Attachments** field from the report. In **Print Preview**, set the **Margins** to **Wide** and the orientation to **Landscape**. If you are submitting printed pages, print the table. To submit electronically, follow the directions provided by your instructor.

11. **Close Print Preview**, **Close** and **Save** the report with the default name. **Close** any open objects, **Close** the **Navigation Pane**, and then from the **Office** menu, click **Exit Access**.

 End **You have completed Project 12E**

Mastering Access

Project 12F — Fundraisers

In this project, you will apply the skills you practiced from the Objectives in Project 12B.

Objectives: 11. *Create a Database Using a Template;* **12.** *Organize Database Objects in the Navigation Pane;* **13.** *Create a New Table in a Database Created With a Template;* **14.** *View a Report and Print a Table in a Database Created With a Template.*

In the following Mastering Access project, you will assist Kirk Shaw, the Development Director for Texas Lakes Medical Center, in creating a database to store information about the various fundraising events held throughout the year. Your printed results will look similar to those shown in Figure 12.60.

For Project 12F, you will need the following file:

New Access database using the Events Template

You will save your database as
12F_Fundraisers_Firstname_Lastname

Figure 12.60

12F Locations Firstname Lastname   Sunday, June 10, 2007
7:53:46 PM

Location	Special Amenities	Notes
Wildflower Hotel	Large indoor atrium	Can set up long or round tables
Community Park	Bleachers and ball fields	Ample sporting facilities
Medical Center Park	Band shell, large stage, large grassy area	Park-like setting

3

12F Locations Firstname Lastname   6/10/2007

Location	Parking Capacity	Special Amenities	Notes
Community Park	850	Bleachers and ball fields	Ample sporting facilities
Medical Center Park	650	Band shell, large stage, large grassy area	Park-like setting
Wildflower Hotel	1000	Large indoor atrium	Can set up long or round tables

Page 1

(Project 12F–Fundraisers continues on the next page)

Content-Based Assessments

(Project 12F—Fundraisers continued)

1. **Start** Access, and then from **Local Templates**, create a new database using the **Events** database template. In the lower right portion of the screen, click the **Browse** button , navigate to your **Access Chapter 12** folder, and then name the new database **12F_Fundraisers_ Firstname_Lastname** In the lower right corner, click the **Create** button. If necessary, to the right of the **Security Warning**, click **Options**, click **Enable this content**, and then click **OK**.

2. To build the **Event List** table, enter the following records using either the displayed Multiple Items form or the single record form, which is available by clicking **New Event** in the **Link bar**:

ID	Title	Start Time	End Time	Description	Location
1	Heart Ball	2/14/09 6p	2/14/09 11p	Gala Ball	Wildflower Hotel
2	Auto Raffle	3/30/09 4p	3/30/09 6p	Raffle	Medical Center Park
3	Spring Book Sale	4/5/09 8a	4/5/09 8p	New and Used Book Sale	Wildflower Hotel
4	Softball Contest	6/10/09 11a	6/10/09 6p	Softball games	Community Park
5	Taste of Texas	8/28/09 11a	8/28/09 11p	Food and music festival	Community Park
6	Holiday Kids Fair	12/15/09 1p	12/15/09 7p	Children's Rides and Games	Medical Center Park

3. **Close** the **Event List** form. **Open** the **Navigation Pane**, and then using the **Navigation arrow**, arrange the **Navigation Pane** by **Tables and Related Views.** From the **Navigation Pane**, open the **Events** table that you created by entering records in the form. Select all of the columns in the table, apply **Best Fit**, and then **Close** the table and save the changes to the layout. **Close** the **Navigation Pane**, and then **Create** a second **Table**. Enter the following records. Recall that Access will assign unique ID numbers; yours may vary.

ID	Field1	Field2	Field3	Field4
4	Wildflower Hotel	1000	Large indoor atrium	Can set up long or round tables
5	Community Park	850	Bleachers and ball fields	Ample sporting facilities
6	Medical Center Park	650	Band shell, large stage, large grassy area	Park-like setting

4. Rename *Field1* as **Location** Rename *Field2* as **Parking Capacity** Rename *Field3* as **Special Amenities** Rename *Field4* as **Notes** Display the table in **Design view**, and then name it **12F Locations Firstname Lastname** Set the **Location** field as the **Primary Key**—no two locations will have the same name. Delete the **ID** field row.

5. Return to Datasheet view, **Save** the design changes, select all the table columns, and then apply **Best Fit**. Display the table in **Print Preview**; select **Wide** margins and **Landscape**

(Project 12F—Fundraisers continues on the next page)

(Project 12F—Fundraisers continued)

orientation. If you are submitting printed pages, print the table. To submit electronically, follow the directions provided by your instructor. **Close** the table and save the changes to the layout.

6. Be sure your **12F Locations** table is still active, **Create** a **Report** based on the table. In the report, delete the **Parking Capacity** field, and then display the report in **Print Preview**. Select **Landscape** orientation, **Wide** margins, and then **Print** the report. To submit electronically, follow the directions provided by your instructor.

7. **Close Print Preview**, **Close** the report, save the changes to the design, and then accept the default report name. Close and save any open objects, and then **Exit Access**.

 End **You have completed Project 12F**—————————————————

Content-Based Assessments

Mastering Access

Project 12G — Gift Shop

In this project, you will apply skills you practiced from the Objectives in Projects 12A and 12B.

Objectives: 1. *Start Access and Create a New Blank Database;* **2.** *Add Records to a Table;* **3.** *Rename Table Fields in Datasheet View;* **4.** *Modify the Design of a Table;* **5.** *Add a Second Table to a Database;* **6.** *Print a Table;* **7.** *Create and Use a Query;* **8.** *Create and Use a Form;* **9.** *Create and Print a Report;* **10.** *Close and Save a Database;* **12.** *Organize Database Objects in the Navigation Pane.*

In the following Mastering Access project, you will assist Scott Williams, the Gift Shop Manager of Texas Lakes Medical Center, in creating a database to store information about gift items in the shop's inventory. Your printed results will look similar to those shown in Figure 12.61.

For Project 12G, you will need the following file:

New Access database

**You will save your database as
12G_Gift_Shop_Firstname_Lastname**

Figure 12.61

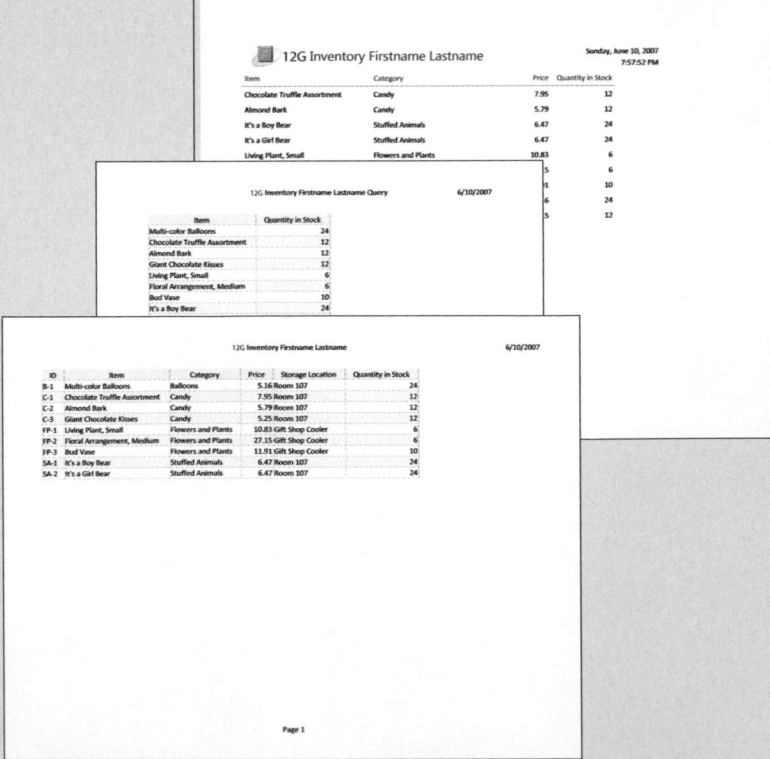

(Project 12G—Gift Shop continues on the next page)

Content-Based Assessments

(Project 12G—Gift Shop continued)

1. **Start** Access, create a new **Blank Database**, and then store it in your **Access Chapter 12** folder as **12G_Gift_Shop_Firstname_Lastname**

2. **Close** the **Navigation Pane**. Change the **ID** field **Data Type** to **Text**. Enter the following records:

ID	Field1	Field2	Field3	Field4	Field5
C-1	Chocolate Truffle Assortment	Candy	7.95	Room 107	12
C-2	Almond Bark	Candy	5.79	Room 107	12
SA-1	It's a Boy Bear	Stuffed Animals	6.47	Room 107	24
SA-2	It's a Girl Bear	Stuffed Animals	6.47	Room 107	24
FP-1	Living Plant, Small	Flowers and Plants	10.83	Gift Shop Cooler	6
FP-2	Floral Arrangement, Medium	Flowers and Plants	27.15	Gift Shop Cooler	6
FP-3	Bud Vase	Flowers and Plants	11.91	Gift Shop Cooler	10
B-1	Multi-color Balloons	Balloons	5.16	Room 107	24
C-3	Giant Chocolate Kisses	Candy	5.25	Room 107	12

3. Rename *Field1* as **Item** Rename *Field2* as **Category** Rename *Field3* as **Price** Rename *Field4* as **Storage Location** Rename *Field5* as **Quantity in Stock** Select all the table columns, and then apply **Best Fit**. **Save** the table, and name it **12G Inventory Firstname Lastname** Display the table in **Print Preview**, set the margins to **Wide** and the orientation to **Landscape**. If you are submitting printed pages, click Print; or submit electronically as directed by your instructor. **Close Print Preview**; close the table and save any changes.

4. **Create** a second **Table** to record the information about the storage of inventory categories. Add the following records to the new table. Recall that Access will assign unique ID numbers; yours may vary.

ID	Field1	Field2	Field3
3	Candy	Room 107	North Zone 1
4	Stuffed Animals	Room 107	South Zone 2
5	Flowers and Plants	Gift Shop Coolers	Cooler 1
6	Balloons	Room 107	East Zone 3

(Project 12G–Gift Shop continues on the next page)

(Project 12G–Gift Shop continued)

5. Rename *Field1* as **Category** Rename *Field2* as **Storage Location** Rename *Field3* as **Location Detail** Switch to **Design** view, name the table **12G Categories Firstname Lastname** Set the **Category** field as the **Primary Key**—each category of inventory items is unique. Delete the **ID** field. Switch back to **Datasheet** view and save the changes. Select all the columns, and then apply **Best Fit**. **Close** your **12G Categories** table, and then save the changes to the layout.

6. **Create**, using the **Query Wizard**, a **Simple Query** based on your **12G Inventory** table. Include only the **Item** and **Quantity in Stock** fields in the query result. The query will answer the question *How many of each item do we currently have in stock?* Accept the default name, and then **Print** and **Close** the query.

7. **Create** a **Report** based on your **12G Inventory** table. Delete the **ID** field and the **Storage Location** field. Display the report in **Print Preview**, set the margins to **Wide** and the orientation to **Landscape**. If you are submitting printed pages, print the table. To submit electronically, follow the directions provided by your instructor. **Close** the report, save the design changes, and then accept the default name. Close any open objects and close the **Navigation Pane**. From the **Office** menu, **Exit Access**.

 End **You have completed Project 12G**

Content-Based Assessments

Mastering Access

Project 12H — Recruiting Events

In this project, you will apply skills you practiced from the Objectives in Projects 12A and 12B.

Objectives: 2. *Add Records to a Table;* **6.** *Print a Table;* **7.** *Create and Use a Query;* **10.** *Close and Save a Database;* **11.** *Create a Database Using a Template;* **12.** *Organize Database Objects in the Navigation Pane;* **13.** *Create a New Table in a Database Created With a Template;* **14.** *View a Report and Print a Table in a Database Created With a Template.*

In the following Mastering Access project, you will assist Serge Juco, Vice President of Human Resources, in creating a database to track recruiting events that are scheduled to attract new employees to careers at the medical center. Your printed results will look similar to those shown in Figure 12.62.

For Project 12H, you will need the following file:

New Access database using the Events Template

You will save your database as
12H_Recruiting_Events_Firstname_Lastname

Figure 12.62

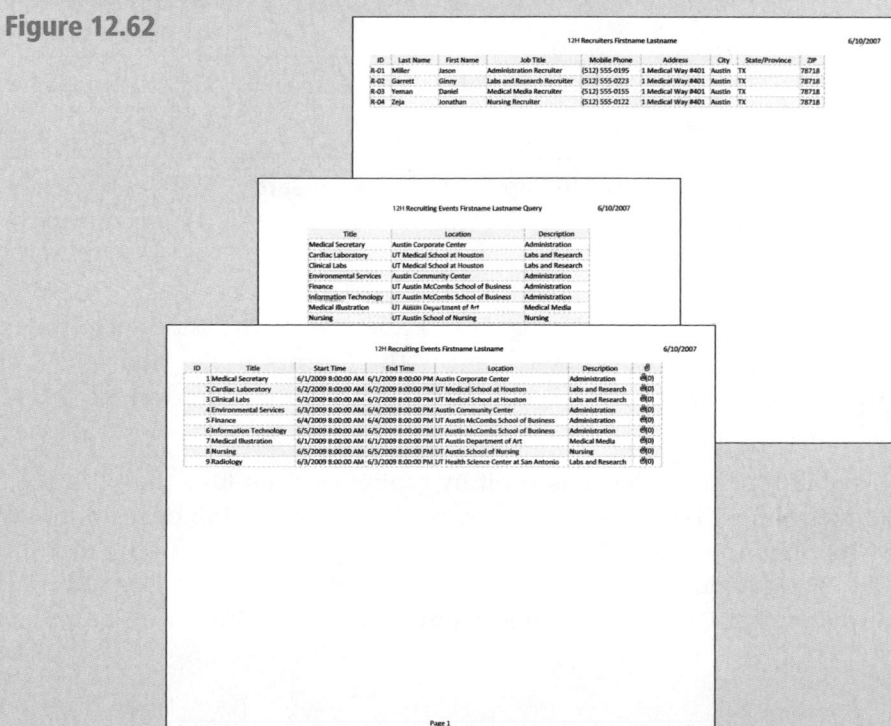

(Project 12H–Recruiting Events continues on the next page)

Content-Based Assessments

(Project 12H–Recruiting Events continued)

1. **Start** Access and then from **Local Templates**, create a new database based on the **Events** template. In your **Access Chapter 12** folder, name the new database **12H_Recruiting_Events_ Firstname_Lastname** In the lower right corner, click the **Create** button. If necessary, to the right of the **Security Warning**, click **Options**, click **Enable this content**, and then click **OK**.

2. In the **Multiple Items** form, enter the following records to build the Event List table; if you prefer, use the **New Event** single record form available on the **Link bar**:

ID	Title	Start Time	End Time	Description	Location
1	Medical Secretary	6/1/09 8a	6/1/09 8p	Administration	Austin Corporate Center
2	Cardiac Laboratory	6/2/09 8a	6/2/09 8p	Labs and Research	UT Medical School at Houston
3	Clinical Labs	6/2/09 8a	6/2/09 8p	Labs and Research	UT Medical School at Houston
4	Environmental Services	6/3/09 8a	6/4/09 8p	Administration	Austin Community Center
5	Finance	6/4/09 8a	6/4/09 8p	Administration	UT Austin McCombs School of Business
6	Information Technology	6/5/09 8a	6/5/09 8p	Administration	UT Austin McCombs School of Business
7	Medical Illustration	6/1/09 8a	6/1/09 8p	Medical Media	UT Austin Department of Art
8	Nursing	6/5/09 8a	6/5/09 8p	Nursing	UT Austin School of Nursing
9	Radiology	6/3/09 8a	6/3/09 8p	Labs and Research	UT Health Science Center at San Antonio

3. **Close** the form, and then display the **Navigation Pane**. Using the **Navigation arrow**, organize the objects by **Tables and Related Views**. Point to the **Events** table, right-click, click **Rename**, and then type **12H Recruiting Events Firstname Lastname** and press Enter to rename the table.

4. **Open** the table; recall that the table was built by typing records into the Multiple Items form. Leave the Attachments field because Serge may decide to attach job description brochures for each event. The AutoNumber ID will serve as the primary key—the unique identifier for each record. **Close** the **Navigation Pane**. Select all the columns and apply **Best Fit**. Display the table in **Print Preview**, set the margins to **Normal** and the orientation to **Landscape**. Print if

(Project 12H–Recruiting Events continues on the next page)

Content-Based Assessments

(Project 12H–Recruiting Events continued)

you are submitting paper results; or, follow your instructor's directions for electronic submission. **Close Print Preview**, and then **Close** the table, saving the changes to the layout.

5. **Create** a new table using the **Contacts Table Template**. Delete the **Company** field. Delete the **E-mail Address** field. Delete the **Business Phone** and **Home Phone** fields. Delete the **Fax Number** field. Delete the **Country/Region**, **Web Page**, **Notes**, and **Attachments** fields. Click in the first **ID** field, from the **Datasheet tab**, change the **Data Type** of the **ID** field to **Text**, and then enter the following records:

ID	Last Name	First Name	Job Title	Mobile Phone	Address	City	State/ Province	ZIP/ Postal Code
R-01	Miller	Jason	Administration Recruiter	(512) 555-0195	1 Medical Way #401	Austin	TX	78718
R-02	Garrett	Ginny	Labs and Research Recruiter	(512) 555-0223	1 Medical Way #401	Austin	TX	78718
R-03	Yeman	Daniel	Medical Media Recruiter	(512) 555-0155	1 Medical Way #401	Austin	TX	78718
R-04	Zeja	Jonathan	Nursing Recruiter	(512) 555-0122	1 Medical Way #401	Austin	TX	78718

6. **Close** the table, save the changes, and then name the table **12H Recruiters Firstname Lastname Create**, using the **Query Wizard**, a **Simple Query** based on your **12H Recruiting Events** table. Add the appropriate fields to the query to answer the question *What is the title, location, and description of all the recruiting events?* Accept the default name for the query. **Print** and then **Close** the query.

7. From the **Navigation Pane**, open your **12H Recruiters** table. Change the name of the **ZIP/Postal Code** field to **ZIP** Select all the columns in the table and apply **Best Fit**. Display the table in **Print Preview**, set the margins to **Normal** and the orientation to **Landscape** and then either print or submit electronically.

8. **Close Print Preview**, and then **Close** the table, saving the layout changes. From the **Navigation Pane**, open the **All Events** report. Then, open the **Events By Week** report. Recall that one advantage of starting a database from a database template is that many objects, such as attractively arranged reports, are provided.

9. **Close** the reports and any other open objects. **Close** the **Navigation Pane**. From the **Office** menu, **Exit Access**.

End **You have completed Project 12H**

Content-Based Assessments

Mastering Access

Project 12I — Facility Expansion

In this project, you will apply all the skills you practiced from the Objectives in Projects 12A and 12B.

Objectives: 1. *Start Access and Create a New Blank Database;* **2.** *Add Records to a Table;* **3.** *Rename Table Fields in Datasheet View;* **4.** *Modify the Design of a Table;* **5.** *Add a Second Table to a Database;* **6.** *Print a Table;* **7.** *Create and Use a Query;* **8.** *Create and Use a Form;* **9.** *Create and Print a Report;* **10.** *Close and Save a Database;* **11.** *Create a Database Using a Template;* **12.** *Organize Database Objects in the Navigation Pane;* **13.** *Create a New Table in a Database Created With a Template;* **14.** *View a Report and Print a Table in a Database Created With a Template.*

In the following Mastering Access project, you will assist Jerry Lopez, the Budget Director, in creating a database to store information about the facility expansion at Texas Lakes Medical Center and in creating a separate database to store information about public events related to the expansion. Your printed results will look similar to the ones shown in Figure 12.63.

For Project 12I, you will need the following files:

New Access database
New Events database

You will save your databases as
12I_Facility_Expansion_Firstname_Lastname
12I_Public_Events_Firstname_Lastname

Figure 12.63

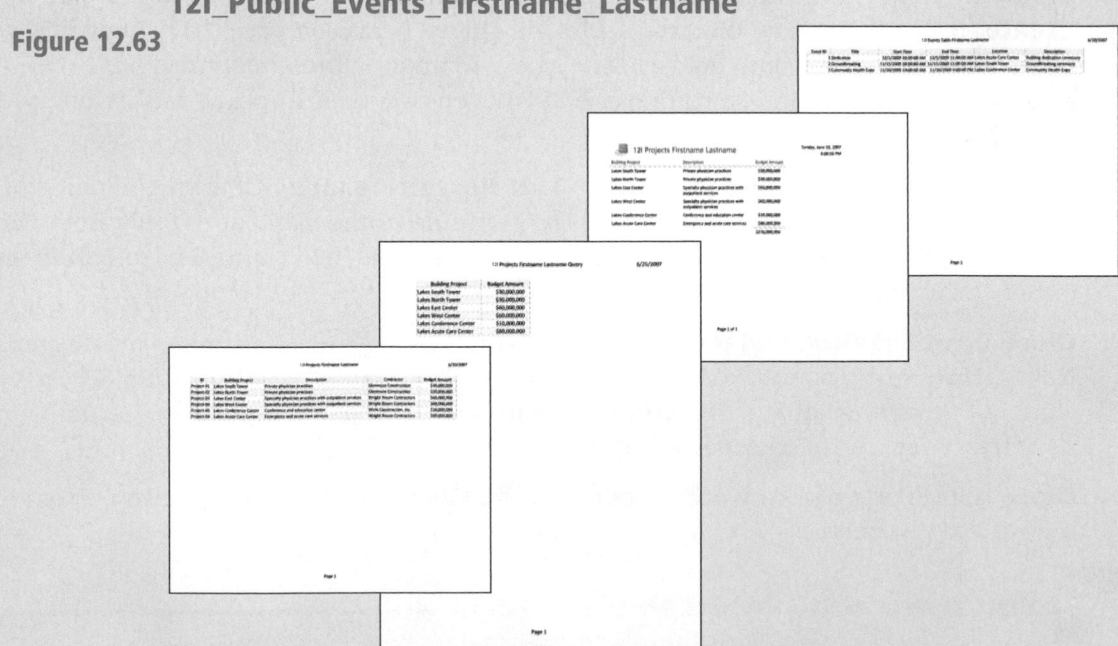

(Project 12I—Facility Expansion continues on the next page)

(Project 12I—Facility Expansion continued)

1. **Start** Access, create a new **Blank Database**, and store it in your **Access Chapter 12** folder as **12I_Facility_Expansion_Firstname_Lastname**

2. **Close** the **Navigation Pane**. Change the **ID** field **Data Type** to **Text**. Enter the following records:

ID	Field1	Field2	Field3	Field4
Project-01	**Lakes South Tower**	**Private physician practices**	**Glenmore Construction**	**30,000,000**
Project-02	**Lakes North Tower**	**Private physician practices**	**Glenmore Construction**	**30,000,000**
Project-03	**Lakes East Center**	**Specialty physician practices with outpatient services**	**Wright Rosen Contractors**	**60,000,000**
Project-04	**Lakes West Center**	**Specialty physician practices with outpatient services**	**Wright Rosen Contractors**	**60,000,000**
Project-05	**Lakes Conference Center**	**Conference and education center**	**Wells Construction, Inc.**	**10,000,000**
Project-06	**Lakes Acute Care Center**	**Emergency and acute care services**	**Wright Rosen Contractors**	**80,000,000**

3. Rename *Field1* as **Building Project** Rename *Field2* as **Description** Rename *Field3* as **Contractor** Rename *Field4* as **Budget Amount** Change the **Data Type** of the **Budget Amount** field to **Currency**. Apply **Best Fit** to all the columns in the table. **Save** the table as **12I Projects Firstname Lastname** In **Print Preview**, set the margins to **Wide** and the orientation to **Landscape**. If you are submitting printed pages, click **Print**; or submit electronically as directed by your instructor. **Close Print Preview** and then close your **12I Projects** table.

4. **Create** a second **Table** to record the information about the contractors for the facility expansion. Add the following records to the new table. Recall that Access will assign unique ID numbers; your numbers may vary.

ID	Field1	Field2	Field3
3	**Glenmore Construction**	**Bob Ballard**	**(512) 555-0900**
4	**Wright Rosen Contractors**	**Lisa Li**	**(512) 555-0707**
5	**Wells Construction, Inc.**	**Frank Levin**	**(512) 555-0444**

5. Rename *Field1* as **Contractor** Rename *Field2* as **Project Manager** Rename *Field3* as **Phone Number** Switch to **Design** view, name the table **12I Contractors Firstname Lastname** Set the **Contractor** field as the **Primary Key**—each contractor name is unique. Delete the **ID** field. Switch back to **Datasheet** view and save the changes. Apply **Best Fit** to all the columns. **Close** your **12I Contractors** table and save the changes to the layout—the column widths.

(Project 12I—Facility Expansion continues on the next page)

Content-Based Assessments

(Project 12I—Facility Expansion continued)

6. **Create**, using the **Query Wizard**, a **Simple Query** based on your **12I Projects** table. Include only the appropriate fields to answer the question *For each Building Project, what is the Budget Amount?* Accept the default name, display the query in **Print Preview**, and then print or submit electronically. **Close Print Preview**, and then **Close** the query.

7. In the **Navigation Pane**, select your **12I Projects** table. **Create** a **Form**, close the **Navigation Pane**, view and then **Close** the form. Save and accept the default name.

8. **Open** your **12I Projects** table from the **Navigation Pane**. With the table open, **Create** a **Report**. Delete the **ID** field and the **Contractor** field. Display the report in **Print Preview**, set the margins to **Wide** and the orientation to **Landscape**. If you are submitting printed pages, print the report. To submit electronically, follow the directions provided by your instructor. **Close Print Preview**, close the report, save the changes, and accept the default name. **Close** any open objects and close the **Navigation Pane**. From the **Office** menu, click **Close Database**.

9. From the **Local Templates**, create a new database using the **Events template**. Create the database in your chapter folder and name it **12I_Public_Events_Firstname_Lastname** If necessary, enable the content.

10. To build the **Events** table, enter the following records using either the displayed Multiple Items Event List form or the single record form, which is available by clicking **New Event** in the **Link bar**:

Title	Start Time	End Time	Description	Location
Dedication	12/1/09 10a	12/1/09 11a	Building dedication ceremony	Lakes Acute Care Center
Groundbreaking	11/15/09 10a	11/15/09 11a	Groundbreaking ceremony	Lakes South Tower
Community Health Expo	11/30/09 10a	11/30/09 9p	Community Health Expo	Lakes Conference Center

11. **Close** the **Event List** form. **Open** the **Navigation Pane**, and then using the **navigation arrow**, arrange the **Navigation Pane** by **Tables and Related Views**. From the **Navigation Pane**, point to the **Events** table and right-click. From the shortcut menu, click **Rename**, type **12I Events Table Firstname Lastname** and then press Enter. Then open the table. Recall that the table was created by entering records in the form. Change the field name **ID** to **Event ID** Delete the **Attachments** field. Select all the columns in the table, apply **Best Fit**, and then display the table in **Print Preview**. Set the margins to **Normal** and the orientation to **Landscape**. Print or submit electronically, **Close Print Preview**, and then **Close** the table and **Save** the changes to the layout.

12. If necessary, close the Navigation Pane and close any open objects. **Close** the database and **Exit Access**.

 End **You have completed Project 12I**

Content-Based Assessments

 Business Running Case

Project 12J—Business Running Case

In this project, you will apply the skills you practiced in Projects 12A and 12B.

Close Access and any other open windows. Display the Start menu, click Computer, and then navigate to to the student files that accompany this textbook. In the folder **03_business_running_case**, locate and open the folder for this chapter. Open and print the instructions for this project, which are provided to you in Adobe PDF format. Follow the instructions and use the skills you have gained thus far to assist Jennifer Nelson in meeting the challenges of owning and running her business.

 End **You have completed Project 12J** —————

Content-Based Assessments

Mastering Access

Project 12K — GO! Fix It

In this project, you will apply the skills you practiced from the Objectives in Projects 12A and 12B.

For Project 12K, you will need the following file:

a012K_fixit_Cardiac_Patients

You will save your database as 12K_Cardiac_Patients_Firstname_Lastname

In this project, you will edit a draft of an Access database that will be used by the Cardiac Unit nursing staff at the Texas Lakes Medical Center. From the student files that accompany this textbook, open the folder **05_go_fix_it**. Locate and make a copy of the database **a012K_fixit_Cardiac_Patients** in your chapter folder. Name the copy **12K_Cardiac_ Patients_Firstname_Lastname**

This database contains errors that you must find and correct. Examine the database, and then correct the errors that you find. Types of errors could include:

- Spelling, grammar, punctuation, and usage errors such as text case.
- Missing or incorrect data in tables, queries, forms, and reports such as filenames, field names, types, descriptions, properties, records, and criteria.
- Table design errors such as primary key.
- Query design errors such as field, table, show, sort, and criteria.
- Page setup errors such as margins, orientation, layout, or alignment.

Things you should know to complete this project:

- The primary key in the table should be Patient ID.
- Field names in the table should be properly spelled.
- Martin Harris is 68 years old.
- Both Age and Monitor Level should have a Data Type of Text.
- The following record is missing: Elizabeth Norton, Patient Id: 2008-0911-056, Room #: 3006A, Age: 82, Monitor Level: 3, Attending Physician: Obester M, Secondary Physician: Ovitz J, and 2nd Physician Specialty: Gerontology

Add your first name and last name to the name of the table. Print the table in Landscape orientation or submit your database as directed.

End You have completed Project 12K

Outcomes-Based Assessments

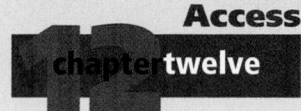

Rubric

The following outcomes-based assessments are *open-ended assessments*. That is, there is no specific correct result; your result will depend on your approach to the information provided. Make *Professional Quality* your goal. Use the following scoring rubric to guide you in *how* to approach the problem and then to evaluate *how well* your approach solves the problem.

The *criteria*—Software Mastery, Content, Format and Layout, and Process—represent the knowledge and skills you have gained that you can apply to solving the problem. The *levels of performance*—Professional Quality, Approaching Professional Quality, or Needs Quality Improvements—help you and your instructor evaluate your result.

	Your completed project is of Professional Quality if you:	Your completed project is Approaching Professional Quality if you:	Your completed project Needs Quality Improvements if you:
1-Software Mastery	Choose and apply the most appropriate skills, tools, and features and identify efficient methods to solve the problem.	Choose and apply some appropriate skills, tools, and features, but not in the most efficient manner.	Choose inappropriate skills, tools, or features, or are inefficient in solving the problem.
2-Content	Construct a solution that is clear and well organized, contains content that is accurate, appropriate to the audience and purpose, and is complete. Provide a solution that contains no errors of spelling, grammar, or style.	Construct a solution in which some components are unclear, poorly organized, inconsistent, or incomplete. Misjudge the needs of the audience. Have some errors in spelling, grammar, or style, but the errors do not detract from comprehension.	Construct a solution that is unclear, incomplete, or poorly organized, containing some inaccurate or inappropriate content; and contains many errors of spelling, grammar, or style. Do not solve the problem.
3-Format and Layout	Format and arrange all elements to communicate information and ideas, clarify function, illustrate relationships, and indicate relative importance.	Apply appropriate format and layout features to some elements, but not others. Overuse features, causing minor distraction.	Apply format and layout that does not communicate information or ideas clearly. Do not use format and layout features to clarify function, illustrate relationships, or indicate relative importance. Use available features excessively, causing distraction.
4-Process	Use an organized approach that integrates planning, development, self-assessment, revision, and reflection.	Demonstrate an organized approach in some areas, but not others; or, use an insufficient process of organization throughout.	Do not use an organized approach to solve the problem.

Outcomes-Based Assessments

Access

chapter twelve

Problem Solving

Project 12L — Public Seminars

In this project, you will construct a solution by applying any combination of the skills you practiced from the Objectives in Projects 12A and 12B.

For Project 12L, you will need the following files:

New Access database
a012L_Public_Seminars (Word document)

You will save your database as
12L_Public_Seminars_Firstname_Lastname

Texas Lakes Medical Center has developed a series of public health seminars. The information about the seminars is located in your student files, in the Word document **a012L_Public_Seminars**.

Using the data in the Word document and a new database created from the Events database template, enter the data into the Multiple Items form. Each seminar will begin at 7 p.m. and end at 9 p.m. After entering the records, in the Navigation Pane, point to the name of the table that was created as a result of entering the records into the Multiple Items form, click Rename, and then name the table **12L Seminars Firstname Lastname** Open the table, apply Best Fit to the table's columns, and then display and modify the Print Preview so that that all the columns fully display on a single sheet. Print the table or submit electronically. Save the database with the name **12L_Public_Seminars_Firstname_Lastname** and then close the database.

End **You have completed Project 12L** ——————————

Outcomes-Based Assessments

Access
chaptertwelve

Problem Solving

Project 12M — Media Contacts

In this project, you will construct a solution by applying any combination of the skills you practiced from the Objectives in Projects 12A and 12B.

For Project 12M, you will need the following files:

New Access database
a012M_Media_Contacts (Word document)

You will save your database as
12M_Media_Contacts_Firstname_Lastname

The Public Relations Department at Texas Lakes Medical Center maintains a list of media contacts who receive e-mail notification when press releases regarding the Medical Center are issued. The information about the media contacts is located in your student files, in the Word document **a012M_Media_Contacts**.

Create a new blank database, and then close the default Table1. Create a new table using the Contacts table template, and then use the data in the Word document to enter the records. Delete the unneeded fields from the table. As necessary, rename fields to match those in the Word document. Change the data type of the ID field to Text, and use the IDs provided. Close the table, and save it as **12M Media Contacts Firstname Lastname** Create a report and delete the Media ID column. In Page Setup or Print Preview, use narrow margins and landscape orientation to arrange the report. Print or submit the report electronically. Close the database.

End You have completed Project 12M ————————————

Outcomes-Based Assessments

Access

Problem Solving

Project 12N—Billing Rates

In this project, you will construct a solution by applying any combination of the skills you practiced from the Objectives in Projects 12A and 12B.

For Project 12N, you will need the following files:

New Access database
a012N_Billing_Rates (Word document)

**You will save your database as
12N_Billing_Rates_Firstname_Lastname**

Physicians at Texas Lakes Medical Center have varying billing rates. The information about the physician names and billing rates is located in your student files, in the Word document **a012N_Billing_Rates**.

Create a new blank database. Create a table with the Physician IDs and billing rates. For the rates, change data type to Currency. Apply Best Fit to the columns, save and name the table **12N Rates Firstname Lastname** and then print the table, or submit electronically as directed. From the table, create a query indicating only the Physician ID and the rate, and print or submit the query electronically. Create a second table using the Contacts table template, enter the names and phone numbers of the physicians, and delete unneeded columns. Apply Best Fit to the columns, save and name the table **12N Physicians Firstname Lastname** Print the table or submit electronically. Save the database with the name **12N_Billing_Rates_Firstname_Lastname** and then close the database.

 End **You have completed Project 12N** ———————

Outcomes-Based Assessments

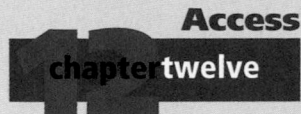

Access

chapter twelve

Problem Solving

Project 12O — Training

In this project, you will construct a solution by applying any combination of the skills you practiced from the Objectives in Projects 12A and 12B.

> **For Project 12O, you will need the following files:**
>
> New Access database
> a012O_Training (Word document)

**You will save your database as
12O_Training_Firstname_Lastname**

Texas Lakes Medical Center has developed a series of training seminars to increase the skills of staff members in making public presentations and in dealing with the media. The information about the seminars is located in your student files, in the Word document **a012O_Training**.

Using the data in the Word document and a new database created from the Events database template, enter the data into the Multiple Items form. Each seminar will begin at 8:30 a.m. and end at 11:30 a.m. After entering the records, in the Navigation Pane, point to the name of the table that was created as a result of entering the records into the Multiple Items form, click Rename, and then name the table **12O Training Firstname Lastname** Open the table, apply Best Fit to the table's columns, and then display and modify the Print Preview so that that all the columns fully display on a single sheet. Print the table or submit electronically. Close the database.

End **You have completed Project 12O** ————————

Outcomes-Based Assessments

Problem Solving

Project 12P — Nurses

In this project, you will construct a solution by applying any combination of the skills you practiced from the Objectives in Projects 12A and 12B.

For Project 12P, you will need the following files:
New Access database
a012P_Nurses (Word document)

You will save your database as 12P_Nurses_Firstname_Lastname

The Nursing Supervisor at Texas Lakes Medical Center maintains a list of nurses and the departments to which they are assigned. The information about the nurses is located in your student files, in the Word document **a012P_Nurses**.

Create a new blank database, and then close the default Table1. Create a new table using the Contacts table template, and then use the data in the Word document to enter the records. Use the Department data for the Company field, and change the field name accordingly. Delete the unneeded fields from the table. Change the ID field name to Emp#, and use the Employee numbers provided. Close the table, and save it as **12P Nurses Firstname Lastname** Based on the table, create a report and print it or submit the report electronically. Close the database.

 End **You have completed Project 12P** _____

Outcomes-Based Assessments

 **You and** *GO!*

Project 12Q — You and *GO!*

In this project, you will construct a solution by applying any combination of the skills you practiced from the Objectives in Projects 12A and 12B.

Close Access and any other open windows. Display the Start menu, click Computer, and then navigate to the student files that accompany this textbook. In the folder **04_you_and_go**, locate and open the folder for this chapter. Open and print the instructions for this project, which are provided to you in Adobe PDF format. Follow the instructions to create a personal inventory database for insurance purposes.

 End **You have completed Project 12Q** ——————————

GO! with Help

Project 12R — *GO!* with Help

1 **Start** Access and in the upper right corner, click the **Microsoft Office Access Help** button ⓘ. Click the **Search arrow**, and then under **Content from this computer**, click **Access Help**. In the **Search** box, type **Help** and then press [Enter].

2 From the displayed list, scroll down as necessary, and then locate and click **What's new in Microsoft Office Access 2007**. Maximize the displayed window. Scroll through and read all the various features of **Microsoft Office Access 2007**.

3 If you want to do so, print a copy of the information by clicking the printer button at the top of the Access Help window. **Close** the Help window, and then **Exit** Access.

 End **You have completed Project 12R** ——————————

Outcomes-Based Assessments

Access

chapter twelve

Group Business Running Case

Project 12S — Group Business Running Case

In this project, you will apply the skills you practiced from the Objectives in Projects 12A and 12B.

Your instructor may assign this group case project to your class. If your instructor assigns this project, he or she will provide you with information and instructions to work as part of a group. The group will apply the skills gained thus far to help the Bell Orchid Hotel Group achieve its business goals.

 End **You have completed Project 12S** ————————————————

chapterthirteen

Sort and Query a Database

OBJECTIVES

At the end of this chapter, you will be able to:

1. Open an Existing Database
2. Create Table Relationships
3. Sort Records in a Table
4. Create a Query in Design View
5. Create a New Query from an Existing Query
6. Sort Query Results
7. Specify Criteria in a Query

8. Create a New Table by Importing an Excel Spreadsheet
9. Specify Numeric Criteria in a Query
10. Use Compound Criteria
11. Create a Query Based on More Than One Table
12. Use Wildcards in a Query
13. Use Calculated Fields in a Query
14. Group Data and Calculate Statistics in a Query

OUTCOMES

Mastering these objectives will enable you to:

PROJECT 13A

Sort and Query a Database

PROJECT 13B

Create a Database Table from an Excel Spreadsheet and Create Complex Queries

Florida Port Community College

Florida Port Community College is located in St. Petersburg, Florida, a coastal port city located near the Florida High Tech Corridor. With 60 percent of Florida's high tech companies and a third of the state's manufacturing companies located in the St. Petersburg and Tampa Bay areas, the college partners with businesses to play a vital role in providing a skilled workforce. The curriculum covers many areas including medical technology, computer science, electronics, aviation and aerospace, and simulation and modeling. The college also serves the community through cultural, athletic, and diversity programs, and provides adult basic education.

Sort and Query a Database

To convert data into meaningful information, you must manipulate the data in a way that you can answer questions. For example, you might ask the question, *What are the names and addresses of students who are enrolled in the Business Information Technology program and who have a grade point average of 3.0 or higher?* With such information, you could send the selected students information about scholarships that might be available to them.

Questions concerning the data in database tables can be answered by sorting the data or by creating a query. Access queries enable you to isolate specific data in database tables by limiting the fields that display and by setting conditions that limit the records to those that match specified conditions. You can also use a query to create calculations. In this chapter, you will sort Access database tables. You will also create and modify queries in an Access database.

Project 13A **Instructors and Courses**

Florida Port Community College uses sorting techniques and queries to locate information about data in their databases. In Activities 13.01 through 13.13, you will assist Lydia Barwari, Dean, in locating information about the records in the Instructors and Courses database in the Business Information Technology Department. Your completed queries and report will look similar to those in Figure 13.1.

For Project 13A, you will need the following file:

a13A_Instructors_and_Courses

**You will save your database as
13A_Instructors_and_Courses_Firstname_Lastname**

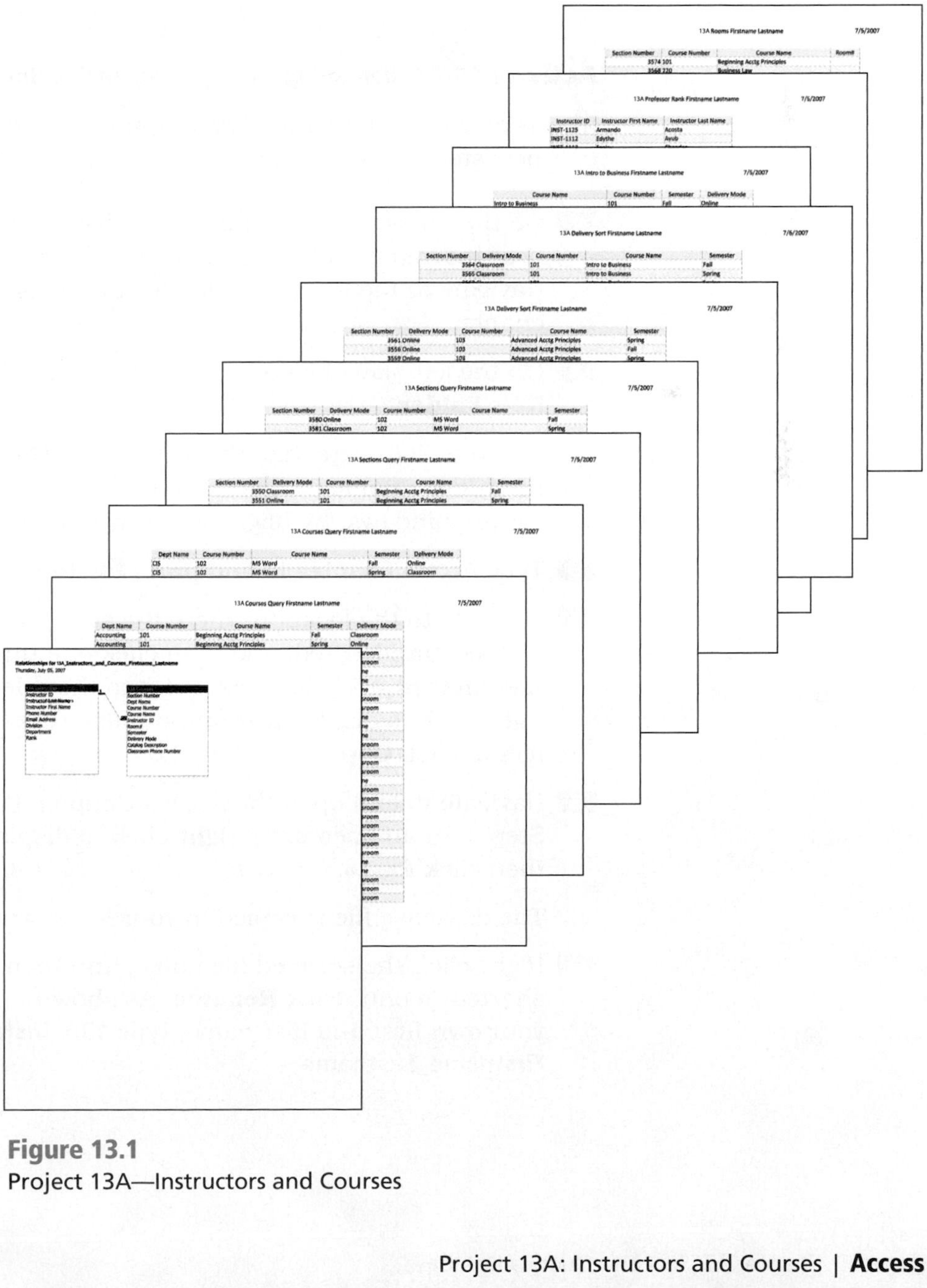

Figure 13.1
Project 13A—Instructors and Courses

Objective 1
Open an Existing Database

In other Microsoft Office 2007 applications, when you open a file, your computer loads the program and the file into random access memory (RAM). When you save and close, the file is transferred to a permanent storage location that you designate, such as a removable USB flash drive or your hard disk drive.

Because database files are typically very large, the entire database file is *not* loaded to RAM; rather, you work with the file from its permanent storage location. For this reason, Access does not have a Save As command with which you can save an entire database file with a new name. Thus, to work with the student files that accompany this textbook, you will use commands within your Windows operating system to copy the file to your chapter folder, and then rename the file before opening it.

Activity 13.01 Renaming and Opening an Existing Database

In this activity, you will use the Computer window to copy a database file to a new storage location and then rename the database.

1 On the left side of the Windows taskbar, click the **Start** button ⊛ , and near the middle of the right side of the **Start menu**, click **Computer**. Navigate to the location where you are storing your projects for this chapter.

2 On the left side of your screen, click **Organize**, and then click **New Folder**.

A new folder is created, the words *New Folder* display highlighted in the folder's name box, and the insertion point is blinking. Recall that within Windows, highlighted text will be replaced by your typing.

3 Type **Access Chapter 13** and press Enter to rename the folder.

4 Navigate to the location where the student files that accompany this textbook are located, and then click one time to select the file **a13A_Instructors_and_Courses**. Point to the selected file name, and then right-click to display a shortcut menu. On the displayed shortcut menu, click **Copy**.

5 Navigate to and open the Access Chapter 13 folder you created in Step 3. In an open area, right-click to display a shortcut menu, and then click **Paste**.

The database file is copied to your folder and is selected.

6 Right-click the selected file name, and then from the displayed shortcut menu, click **Rename**. As shown in Figure 13.2, and using your own first and last name, type **13A_Instructors_and_Courses_Firstname_Lastname**

Alert! Does your system display file extensions?

If the Windows operating system on the computer at which you are working is set to display file extensions, be sure to type the new file name in front of the extension, for example: 13A_Instructors_and_Courses_Firstname_Lastname.accdb

Access Chapter 13
indicated in the title bar

Figure 13.2

Your name here

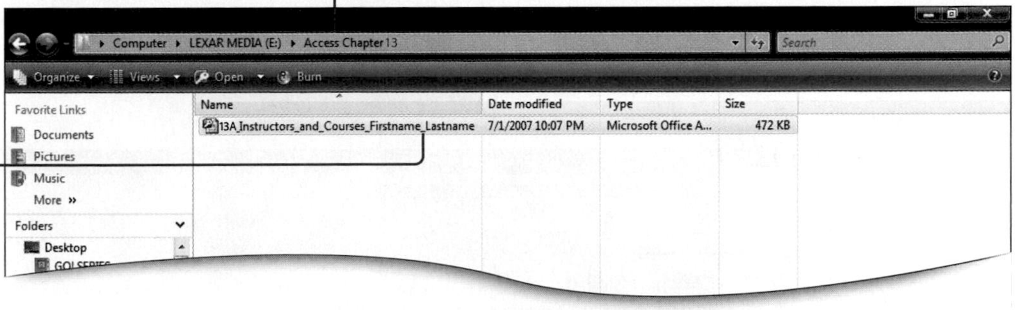

7 Press [Enter] to save the file with the new name. On the title bar, click the **Close** button [X] to close the **Computer** window.

Alert! Does a Confirm File Rename message display?

If the file you have copied has a Read-only property applied, a message box will display to alert you when you attempt to rename a file. In the message box, click Yes to rename the file. Then, right-click the file name, and from the shortcut menu, click Properties. In the displayed Properties dialog box, on the General tab under Attributes, click to clear the Read-only check mark. Click OK to accept the change, and then close the dialog box.

Activity 13.02 Opening an Existing Database and Resolving Security Alerts

The **Message Bar** is the area directly below the Ribbon that displays information such as security alerts when there is potentially unsafe, active content in an Office 2007 document that you open. Settings that determine which alerts display on your Message Bar are set in the Access **Trust Center**. The Trust Center is an area of the Access program where you can view the security and privacy settings for your Access installation.

You may or may not be able to change the settings in the Trust Center, depending upon decisions made within your organization's computing environment. To display the Trust Center, from the Office menu, in the lower right corner click Access Options, and then click Trust Center.

1 **Start** Access. From the **Office** menu [icon], click **Open**. In the displayed **Open** dialog box, navigate to your Access Chapter 13 folder.

2 Locate the database file that you saved and renamed with your name in Activity 13.01. Click your **13A_Instructors_and_Courses_Firstname_Lastname** database file one time to select it, and then, in the lower right corner, click the **Open** button. Alternatively, double-click the name of the database to open it.

The database window opens, and the database name displays in the title bar.

3 Directly below the Ribbon, on the **Message Bar**, check to see if a **Security Warning**, similar to the one shown in Figure 13.3, displays.

Database name in title bar

Figure 13.3

Security Warning message

Message Bar

Options button

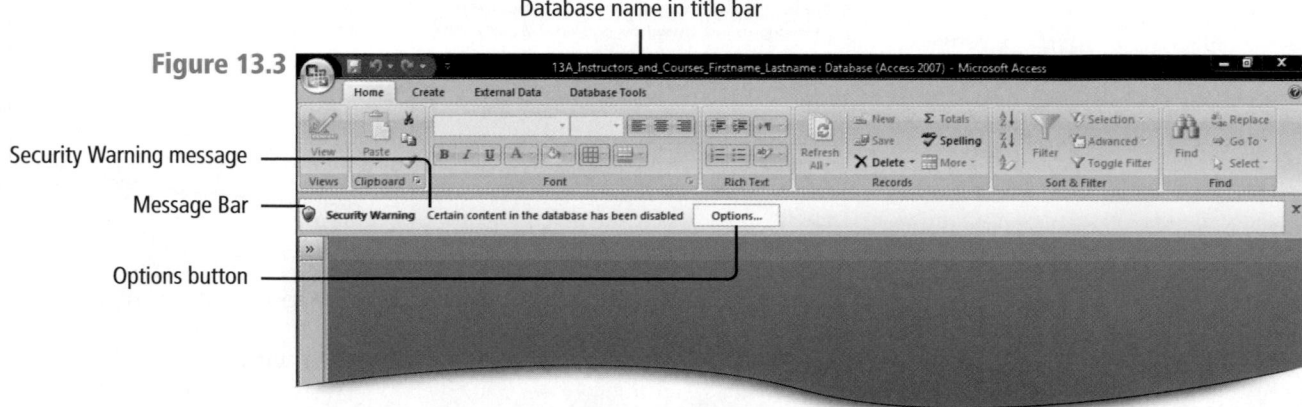

4 On the **Message Bar**, click the **Options** button. In the displayed **Microsoft Office Security Options** dialog box, click the **Enable this content** option button, and then click **OK** or press Enter.

When working with the student files that accompany this textbook, repeat these actions each time you see this security warning. Databases provided with this textbook are safe to use on your computer.

Objective 2
Create Table Relationships

Access databases are *relational databases* because the tables in the database can relate—actually *connect*—to other tables through *common fields*. Common fields are fields that contain the same data in more than one table.

After you have set up a table for each different subject in your database, you must provide a way to bring that data back together again when you need to create meaningful information. To do this, place common fields in tables that are related and then define table *relationships*. A relationship is an association that you establish between two tables based on common fields. After the relationship is established, you can create a query, a form, or a report that displays information from more than one table.

Activity 13.03 Creating Table Relationships and Enforcing Referential Integrity

In this activity, you will connect a field in one table with a field in another table to create a relationship. The common field between the two tables is Instructor ID; that is, Instructor ID is the field that appears in both tables. By connecting this information, you could identify the name, and not just the Instructor ID, of an instructor for a course section.

1 **Open** [»] the **Navigation Pane**. At the top of the **Navigation Pane**, click the **Navigation Pane menu arrow** [⊙], and then look at the displayed menu to verify that the objects are organized by **Tables and Related Views**. Click outside the menu to close it, and then compare your screen with Figure 13.4.

Two objects—the *13A Instructors* table and the *13A Courses* table—display in the Navigation Pane.

No objects open in
the object window

Figure 13.4

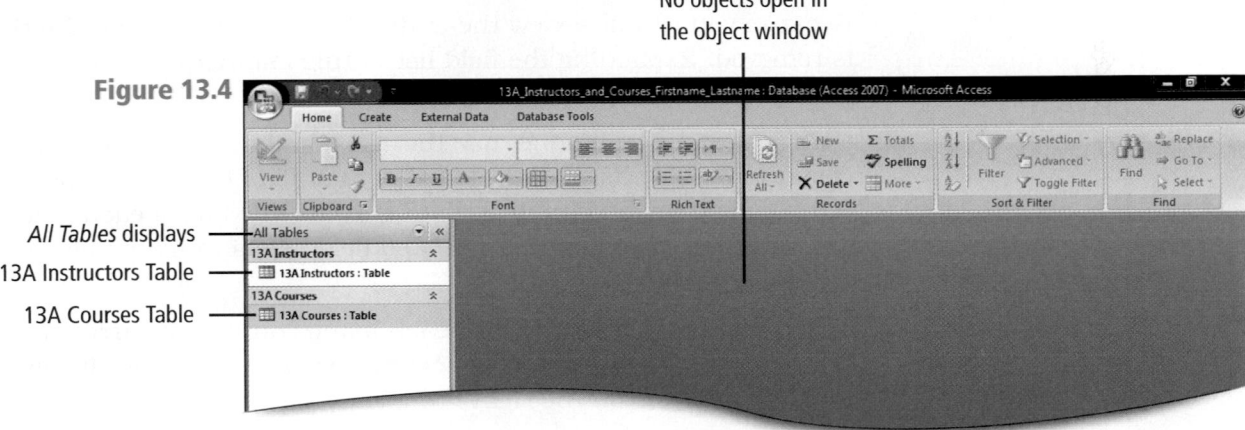

All Tables displays

13A Instructors Table

13A Courses Table

2 By right-clicking and clicking **Open**, or by double-clicking, open the **13A Instructors** table and take a moment to examine its contents. Then, open the **13A Courses** table and examine its contents.

In the 13A Instructors table, Instructor ID is the primary key field, which ensures that each individual instructor will appear in the table only one time. In the 13A Courses table, Section Number is the primary key. Each course's record includes the Instructor ID of the instructor who teaches the course.

Because *one* instructor can teach *many* different courses, *one* instructor's Instructor ID number can appear *many* times in the 13A Courses table. Thus, the relationship between each instructor and the courses is referred to as a ***one-to-many relationship***. This is the most common type of relationship in Access.

3 **Close** [✕] both tables so that the object window is empty; leave the **Navigation Pane** displayed. On the Ribbon, click the **Database Tools tab**. In the **Show/Hide group**, click the **Relationships** button to open the Relationships window and display the **Relationship Tools** on the Ribbon.

4 On the **Design tab**, in the **Relationships group**, click the **Show Table** button to display the **Show Table** dialog box. In the **Show Table** dialog box, in the list of table objects, click **13A Courses**, and then at the bottom of the dialog box, click **Add**.

5 In the **Show Table** dialog box, point to the **13A Instructors** table, double-click to add the table to the **Relationships** window, and then click **Close** to close the **Show Table** dialog box.

Use either technique to add a table to the Relationships window. A *field list*—a list of the field names in a table—for each of the two table objects displays and each table's primary key is identified. Although this database currently has only two tables, larger databases can have many tables.

6 In the **13A Courses** field list, position your mouse pointer over the lower right corner of the field list to display the 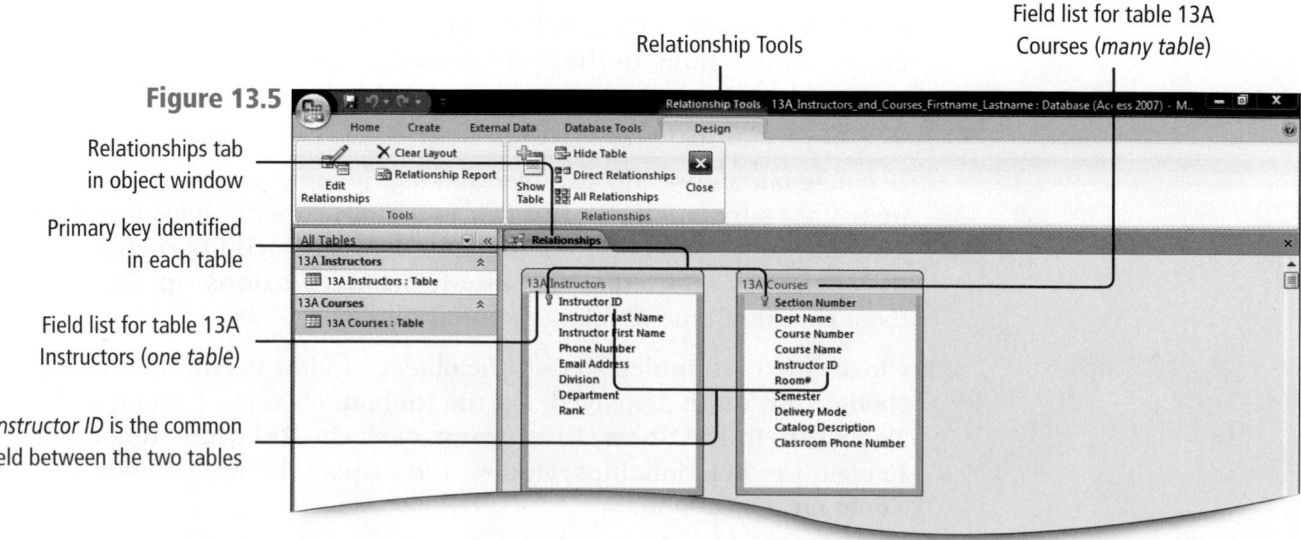 pointer, and then drag downward and to the right as necessary to display the names of each field completely.

Because you can now view the entire list, the scroll bar on the right is removed. Expanding the field list in this manner enables you to see all of the available fields.

7 Using the same technique, use the pointer to resize the **13A Instructors** field list as necessary so that all of the field names are completely visible. Then, by pointing to the title bar of each field list and dragging, position the expanded field lists approximately as shown in Figure 13.5.

Recall that *one* instructor can teach *many* courses. By arranging the tables in this manner on your screen, the *one table* is on the left and the *many table* is on the right.

Recall that the primary key in each table is the field that uniquely identifies the record in each table. For example, in the Instructors table, each instructor is uniquely identified by the Instructor ID. In the Courses table, each course section offered is uniquely identified by the Section Number.

Relationship Tools

Field list for table 13A Courses (*many table*)

Figure 13.5

Relationships tab in object window

Primary key identified in each table

Field list for table 13A Instructors (*one table*)

Instructor ID is the common field between the two tables

Note — Highlighted Field Does Not Matter

As you rearrange the two field lists in the Relationships window, the highlighted field indicates which field list and which field is active. This is of no consequence for completing the activity. It simply indicates which of the field lists you moved last.

 In the **13A Instructors** field list, point to **Instructor ID**, hold down the left mouse button, and then drag to the right to the **13A Courses** field list until your mouse pointer is on top of **Instructor ID** as shown in Figure 13.6. Then release the mouse button.

As you drag, a small graphic displays to indicate that you are dragging the Instructor ID primary key from the Instructors table to the Instructor ID field in the Courses table. The Edit Relationships dialog box displays.

A table relationship works by matching data in two fields—typically two fields with the same name in both tables.

Icon indicates you are dragging the
primary key field to another table

Figure 13.6

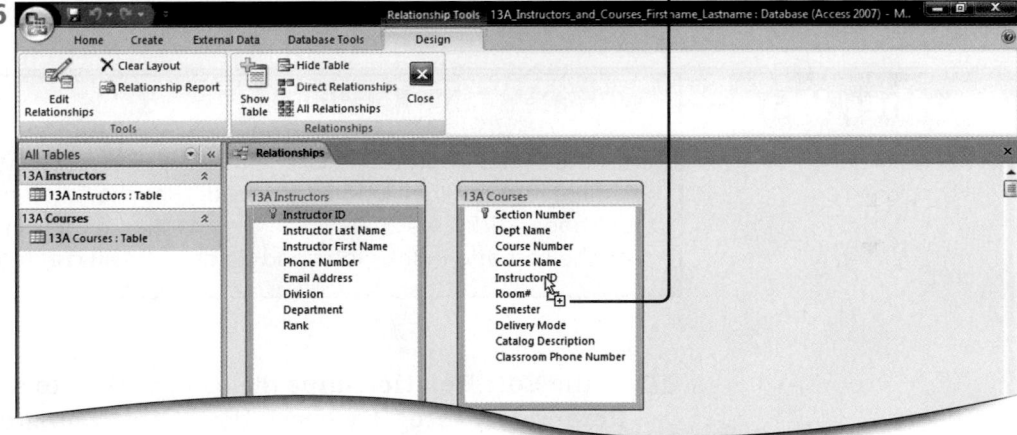

 Point to the title bar of the **Edit Relationships** dialog box, and then drag the dialog box below the two field lists as shown in Figure 13.7.

Both tables include the Instructor ID field—that is the common field between the two tables. By dragging, you created the one-to-many relationship. In the Instructors table, Instructor ID is the primary key. In the Courses table, Instructor ID is referred to as the ***foreign key*** field. The foreign key is the field that is included in the related table so the field can be joined with the primary key in another table.

The field on the *one* side of the relationship is typically the primary key. Recall that *one* instructor can teach *many* courses. Thus, *one* instructor record in the Instructors table can be related to *many* course records in the Courses table.

Figure 13.7

13A Courses table indicated on
the right as Related Table/Query

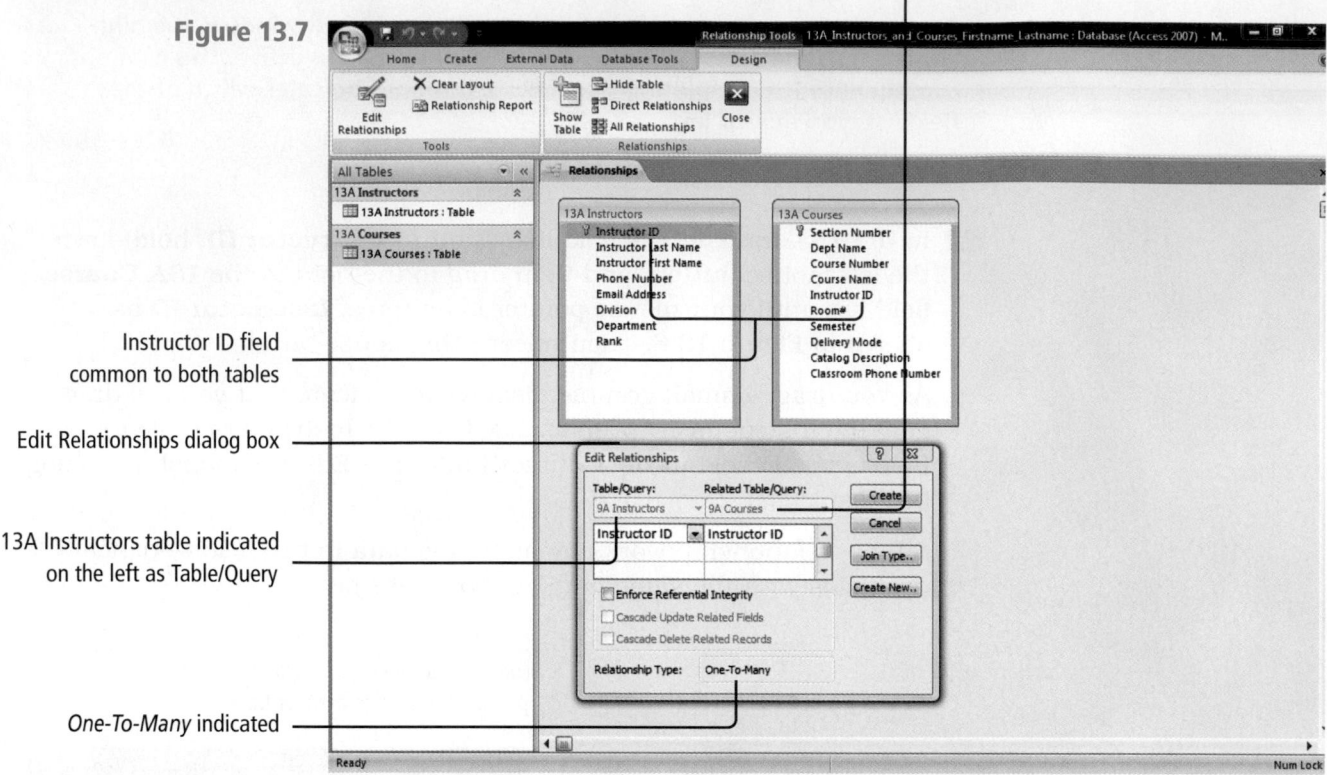

Instructor ID field
common to both tables

Edit Relationships dialog box

13A Instructors table indicated
on the left as Table/Query

One-To-Many indicated

Another Way ── **To Create a Table Relationship**

With the tables displayed in the Relationships window, rather than dragging one field into another field list, instead, click the Edit Relationships button on the Ribbon, click Create New, and then in the Create New dialog box, designate the Left and Right tables and fields that will create the relationship.

---

10 In the **Edit Relationships** dialog box, click to select the **Enforce Referential Integrity** check box—as you progress in your study of Access, you will use the Cascade options.

Referential integrity is a set of rules that Access uses to ensure that the data between related tables is valid. Enforcing referential integrity ensures that a course cannot be added to the 13A Courses table with the name of an instructor who is *not* included in the 3A Instructors table. In this manner, you ensure that you do not have courses listed in the 13A Courses table with no corresponding instructor in the 13A Instructors table. Similarly, you will not be able to delete an Instructor from the 13A Instructors table if there is a course listed for that instructor in the 13A Courses table.

11 In the upper right corner of the **Edit Relationships** dialog box, click the **Create** button, and then compare your screen with Figure 13.8.

A *join line*—the line joining two tables—displays between the two tables. On the line, *1* indicates the *one* side of the relationship, and the infinity symbol (∞) indicates the *many* side of the relationship. These symbols display when referential integrity has been enforced.

Figure 13.8

Common field in both tables

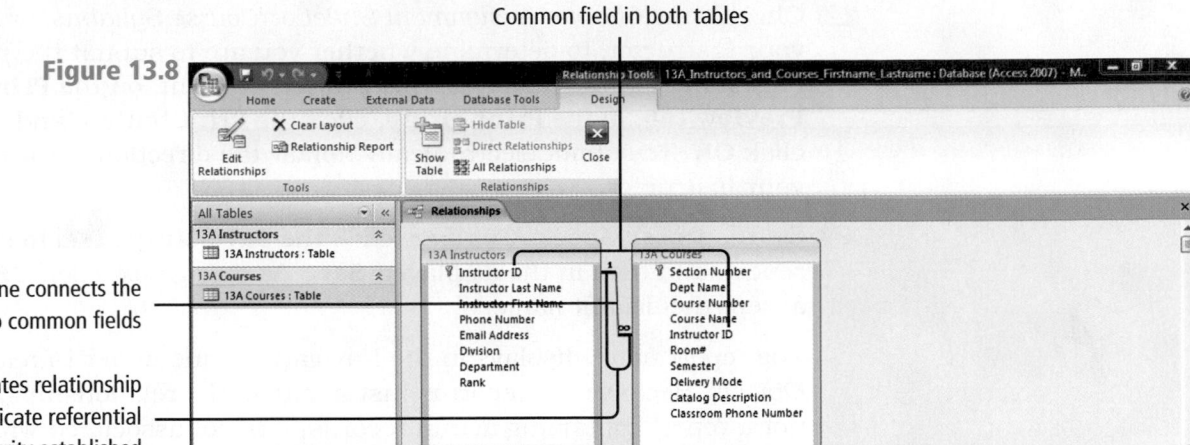

Join line connects the two common fields

Line indicates relationship and 1 and ∞ indicate referential integrity established

More Knowledge

Fields in a Relationship

To create a relationship, the two connected fields must have the same data type and the same field size, but they need not have the exact same field name.

Activity 13.04 Printing a Relationship Report

Table relationships provide a map of how your database is organized, and you can print this information as a report. In this activity, you will print your relationship report.

1 With the **Relationships** window open, on the **Design tab**, in the **Tools group**, click the **Relationship Report** button to create the report and display it in Print Preview. On the displayed **Print Preview tab**, in the **Page Layout group**, click the **Margins** button, and then click **Normal**. Compare your screen with Figure 13.9 .

Print Preview tab

Figure 13.9

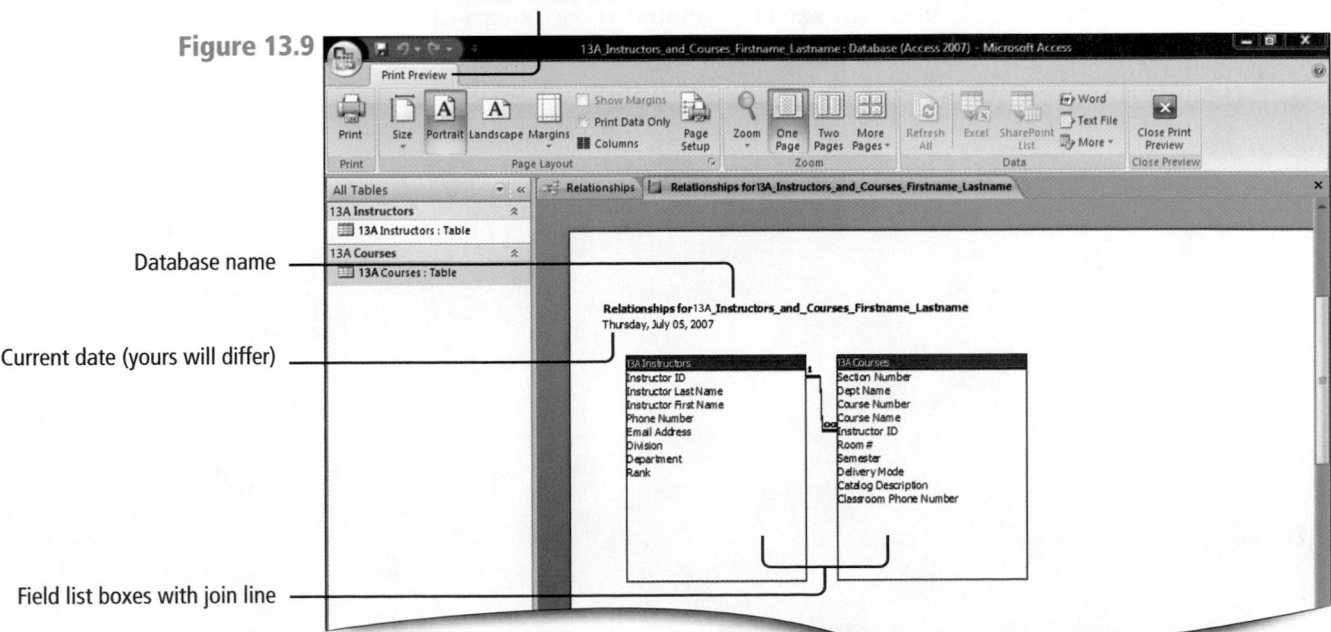

Database name

Current date (yours will differ)

Field list boxes with join line

2 Check your *Chapter Assignment Sheet* or *Course Syllabus*, or consult your instructor, to determine whether you are to submit the printed pages that are the results of this project. To print, on the **Print Preview tab**, in the **Print group**, click the **Print** button, and then click **OK**. To submit electronically, follow the directions provided by your instructor.

3 On the **Quick Access Toolbar**, click the **Save** button to save the report, and then in the displayed **Save As** dialog box, click **OK** to accept the default name.

The report name displays in the Navigation Pane under *Unrelated Objects*. Because the report is just a map of the relationships, and not a report containing actual records, it is not associated with either of the tables.

4 Click the **Close Print Preview** button. In the object window, **Close** the **Relationships** report, and then **Close** the **Relationships** window.

Note

The report may briefly display in the Design view (with dotted grid lines) as you close the report.

---

5 In the **Navigation Pane**, open your **13A Instructors** table. On the left side of the table, in the first record, point to the **plus sign**, and then click one time. If the Field List pane displays on the right, click the Close button to remove it from the screen. Compare your screen with Figure 13.10.

Plus signs to the left of a record in a table indicate that related records exist in a *related* table. In the first record for *Julie Adeeb*, you can see that related records exist in the Courses table. The relationship displays because you created a relationship between the two tables using the Instructor ID field.

Figure 13.10

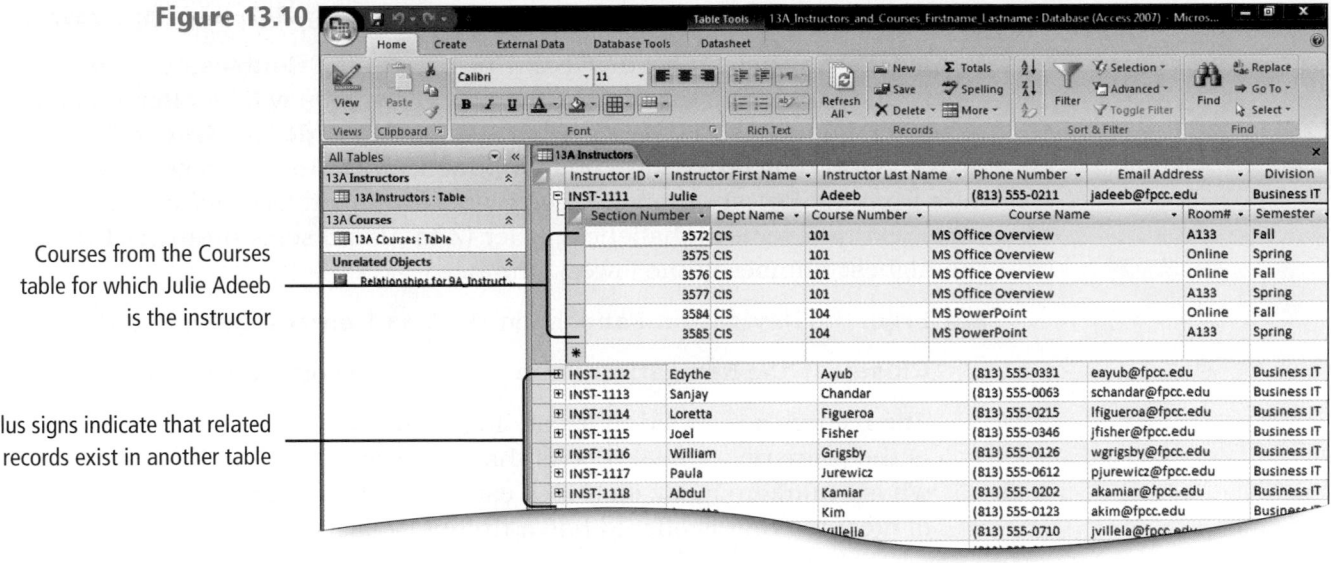

Courses from the Courses table for which Julie Adeeb is the instructor

Plus signs indicate that related records exist in another table

6 **Close** ☒ the **13A Instructors** table.

More Knowledge

Other Types of Relationships: One-to-One and Multiple One-to-Many

There are other relationships that can be created using the same process in the Relationships window. The type of relationship is determined by the placement of the primary key field. A one-to-one relationship exists between two tables when a record in one table is related to a single record in a second table. In this case, both tables use the same field as the primary key. This is most often used when data is placed in a separate table because access to the information is restricted. You can also create multiple one-to-many relationships between tables in a database simply by adding more tables to the Relationships window and creating a join line between the tables based on their common field. A primary key field from one table can be joined to the same field in more than one table.

Objective 3
Sort Records in a Table

Sorting is the process of arranging data in a specific order based on the value in each field. For example, you could sort the names in your address book alphabetically by each person's last name, or you could sort your CD collection by the date of purchase.

Initially, records in an Access table display in the order in which they are entered into the table. After a primary key is established, the records are displayed in order based on the primary key field.

Activity 13.05 Sorting Records in a Table in Ascending or Descending Order

In the following activity, you will sort records in the Courses table to determine which courses in the Business IT Division will be offered each semester. You can sort data in either *ascending order* or *descending order*. Ascending order sorts text alphabetically (A to Z) and sorts numbers from the lowest number to the highest number. Descending order sorts text in reverse alphabetical order (Z to A) and sorts numbers from the highest number to the lowest number.

1 From the **Navigation Pane**, open the **13A Courses** table, and then **Close** « the **Navigation Pane** to maximize your screen space.

The records are sorted in ascending order by Section Number, which is the primary key field. Recall that the primary key is the field whose value uniquely identifies each record in a table—each section of a course that is offered has a unique section number.

2 At the top of the **Dept Name** column, click the **Dept Name arrow**. In the displayed list, click **Sort A to Z**, and then compare your screen with Figure 13.11.

To sort records in a table, click the arrow to the right of the field name in the column on which you want to sort, and then choose the sort order you prefer. After a field is sorted in ascending or descending order, a small arrow in the field name indicates its sort order.

The records display in alphabetical order by Dept Name. Because like names are now grouped together, you can quickly scroll the length of the table and see how many courses are offered by each department.

Figure 13.11

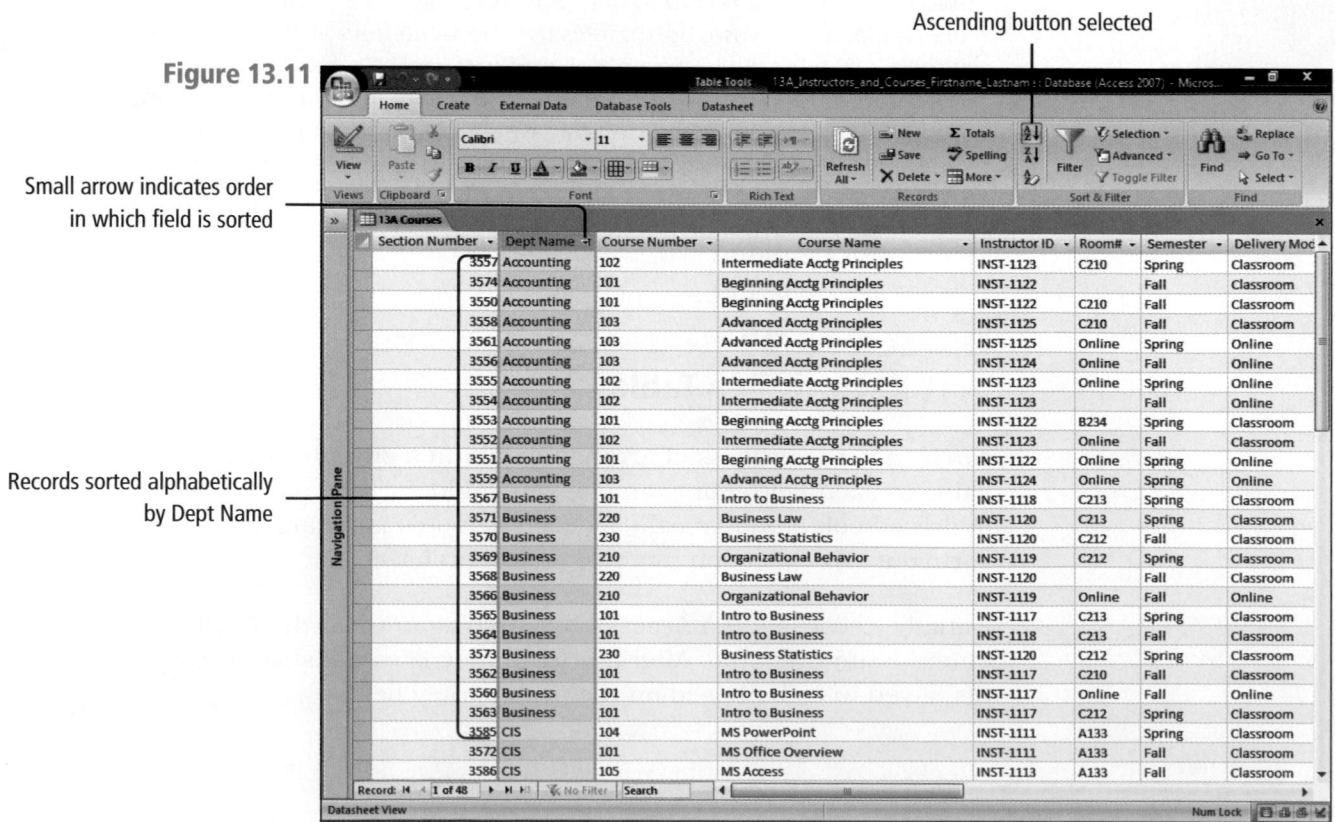

Ascending button selected

Small arrow indicates order in which field is sorted

Records sorted alphabetically by Dept Name

3 In the **Sort & Filter group**, click the **Clear All Sorts** button [icon] to clear all the sorts and return the records to the default sort order, which is by the primary key field—*Section Number*. Scroll to the right if necessary, click the **Semester arrow**, and then click **Sort Z to A**.

The records in the table are sorted by semester in reverse alphabetical order; thus *Spring* courses are listed before *Fall* courses. The small arrow in the Field name points downward indicating a descending sort, and in the Ribbon, the Descending button is selected.

Activity 13.06 Sorting Records in a Table on Multiple Fields

To sort a table on two or more fields, first identify the fields that will act as the ***outermost sort field*** and the ***innermost sort field***. The outermost sort field is the first level of sorting, and the innermost sort field is the second level of sorting. After you identify your outermost and innermost sort fields, sort the innermost field first, and then sort the outermost field.

Lydia Barwari, the Dean, would like to view the course names in alphabetical order by delivery mode, with online classes listed first. Access enables you to sort on two or more fields in a table in this manner.

1 Click the **Clear All Sorts** button [icon] to clear any sorts from the previous activity. In the **Delivery Mode** column, click any record. In the **Sort & Filter group**, click the **Descending** button [icon] .

The records are sorted in descending alphabetical order by Delivery Mode, with Online courses listed before Classroom courses.

2 Point anywhere in the **Course Name** column, and then right-click. From the displayed shortcut menu, click **Sort A to Z**. Notice the first four records in the **Course Name** column, for *Advanced Acctg Principles*, and then compare your screen with Figure 13.12.

The records are sorted first by Course Name—the *outermost* sort field—and then within a specific Course Name grouping, the sort continues in descending alphabetical order by Delivery Mode—the *innermost* sort field.

In this manner, you can perform a sort on multiple fields using both ascending and descending order.

Figure 13.12

Within each *Course Name*,
Online and *Classroom* sorted
in descending order

Small arrows indicate sort
order in each column

Course Name column
sorted in ascending order

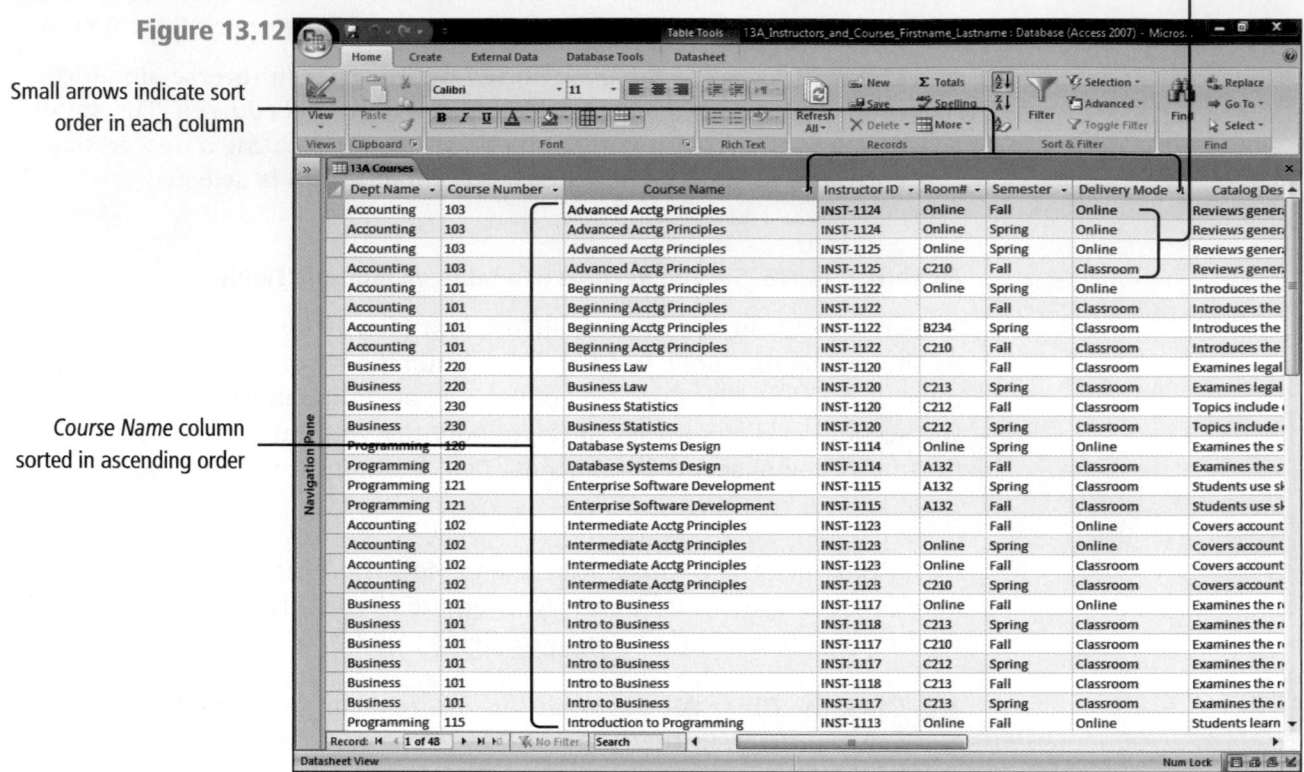

3 In the **Sort & Filter group**, click the **Clear All Sorts** button. In the object window, **Close** the table, and then click **No**; you need not save any changes made to the design.

Objective 4
Create a Query in Design View

Recall that a ***select query*** is a database object that retrieves (selects) specific data from one or more tables and then displays the specified data in datasheet view. A query answers a question such as *Which instructors are teaching CIS courses in the Fall semester?* Unless a query has already been set up to ask this question, you must create a new query.

Individuals who use databases rarely need to see all of the records in all of the tables. That is why a query is so useful; it creates a subset of records according to your specifications and then displays only those records—and does so in a useful manner.

Activity 13.07 Creating a New Select Query in Design View

Previously, you practiced creating a query using the Query Wizard. In this chapter, you will create queries in Design view, in which you can create queries that are more complex. Recall that the table or tables from which a query selects its data is referred to as the **data source**.

1 On the Ribbon, click the **Create tab**, and then in the **Other group**, click the **Query Design** button. Compare your screen with Figure 13.13.

A new query opens in Design view and the Show Table dialog box displays. The Show Table dialog box lists all of the tables in the database.

Available tables

Figure 13.13

Query1 tab

Show Table dialog box

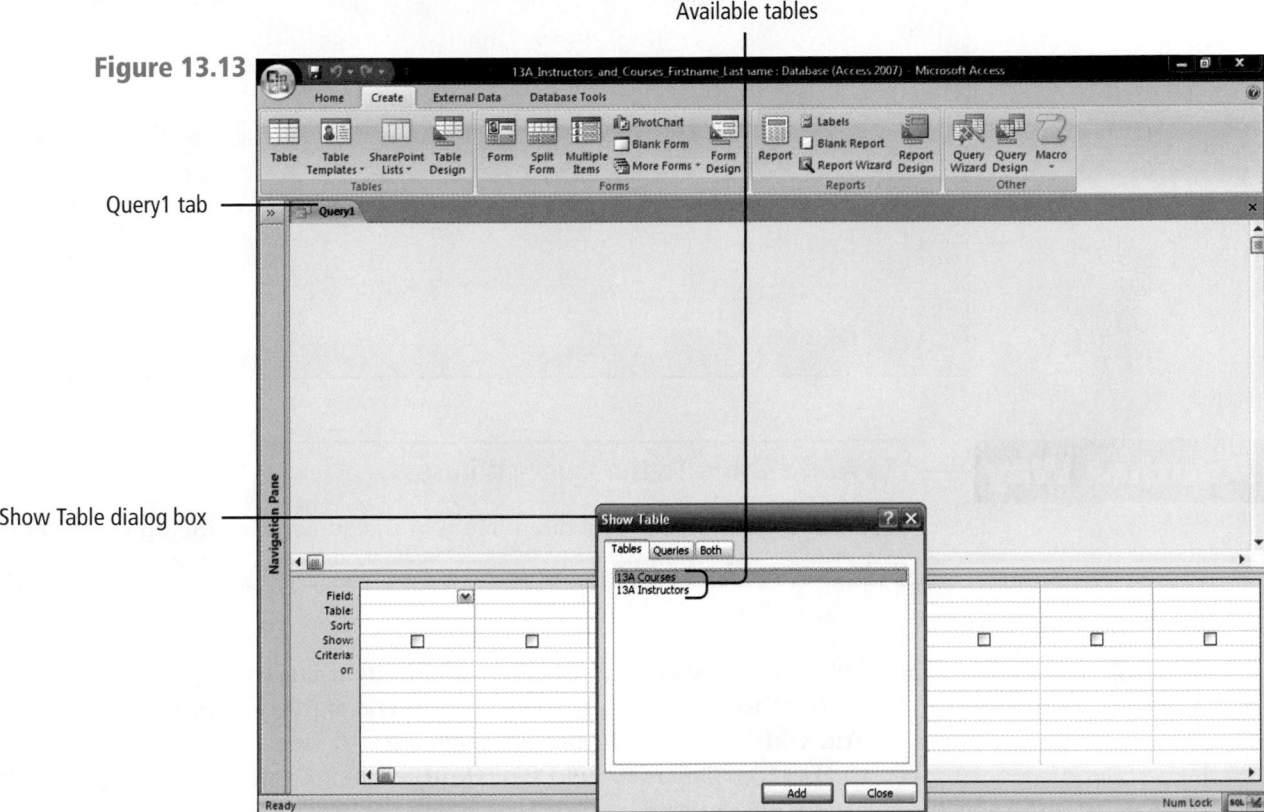

2 In the **Show Table** dialog box, click **13A Courses**, click the **Add** button, and then **Close** the **Show Table** dialog box. Compare your screen with Figure 13.14.

A field list for the 13A Courses table displays in the upper pane of the Query window. The Section Number field is indicated as the primary key field in this table. The Query window has two parts: the **table area** (upper pane) displays the field lists for tables that are used in the query, and the **design grid** (lower pane) displays the design of the query.

Figure 13.14

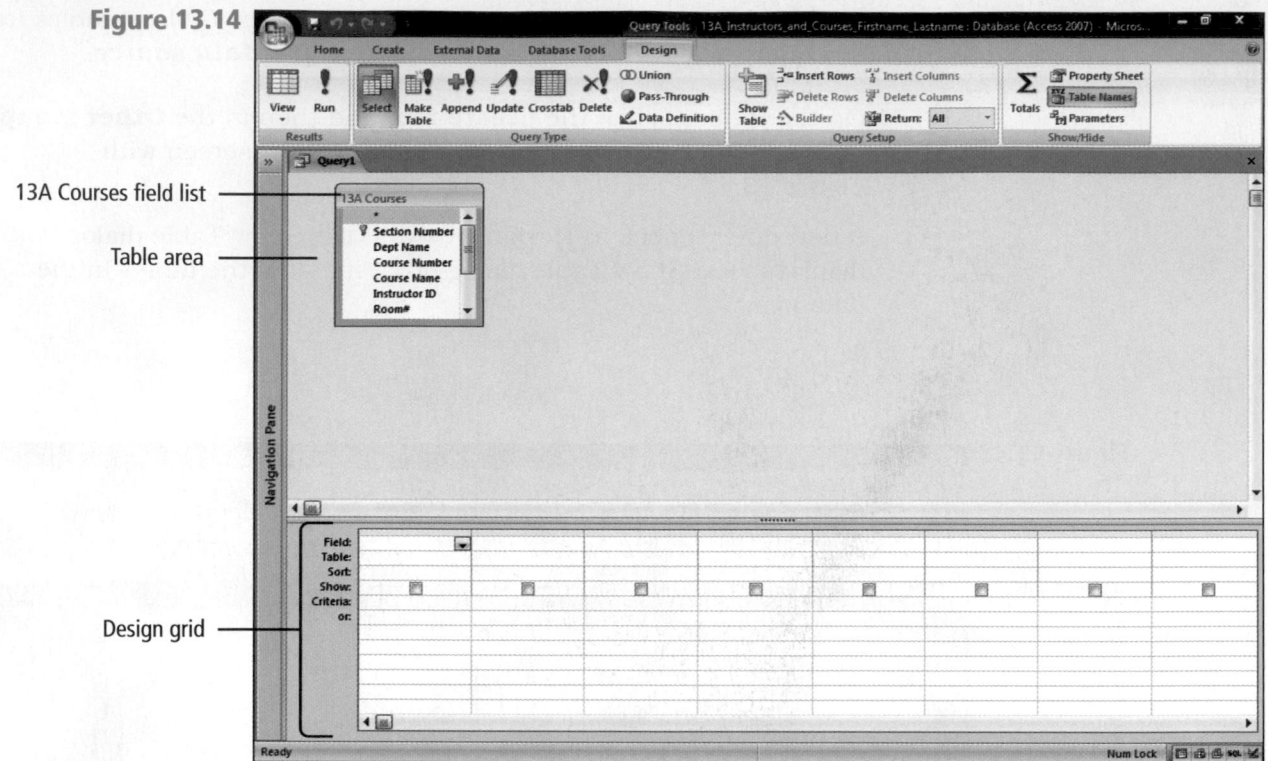

13A Courses field list

Table area

Design grid

![Another Way] **To Add a Table to the Query Window**

You can also double-click a table name in the Show Table dialog box to add it to the Query window.

3 Point to the lower right corner of the field list to display the ⬉ pointer, and then drag down and to the right to expand the height and width of the field list as necessary to view all of the field names. In the **13A Courses** field list, double-click **Dept Name**, and then look at the design grid.

The Dept Name field displays in the design grid in the Field row. By designing a query in Design view, you can limit the fields that display in the result by placing only the fields you want in the design grid.

4 In the **13A Courses** field list, point to **Course Number**, hold down the left mouse button, and then drag down into the design grid until you are pointing to the **Field** row in the next available column. Release the mouse button, and then compare your screen with Figure 13.15.

This is another way to add field names to the design grid. As you drag the field, a small rectangular shape attaches to the mouse pointer. When you release the mouse button, the field name displays in the Field row.

Figure 13.15

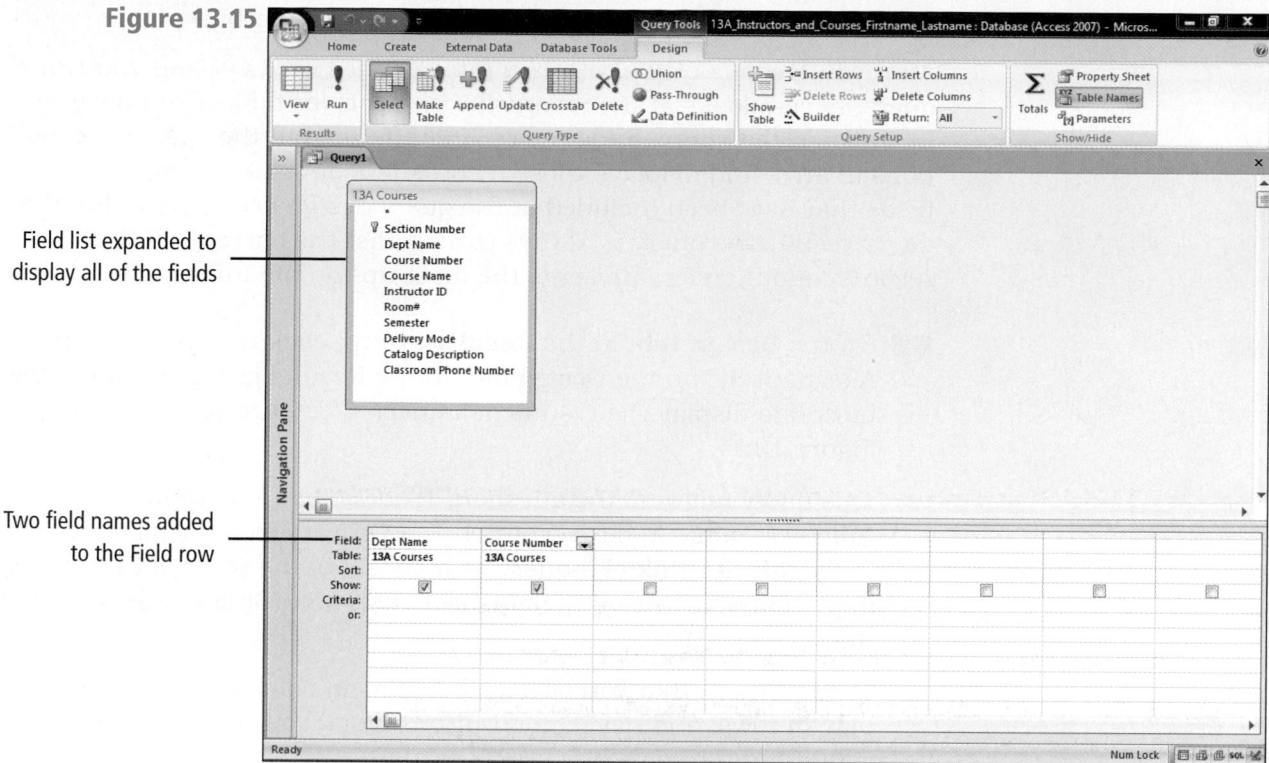

Field list expanded to
display all of the fields

Two field names added
to the Field row

5 In the **Field** row of the design grid, click in the third column, and
then click the **arrow** that displays. From the displayed list, click
Course Name to add this field to the design grid, which is another
way to add a field to the design of the query.

6 Using one of the methods you just practiced, add the **Semester** field
as the fourth column in the design grid, and then add the **Delivery
Mode** field as the fifth column in the design grid. Compare your
screen with Figure 13.16.

Figure 13.16

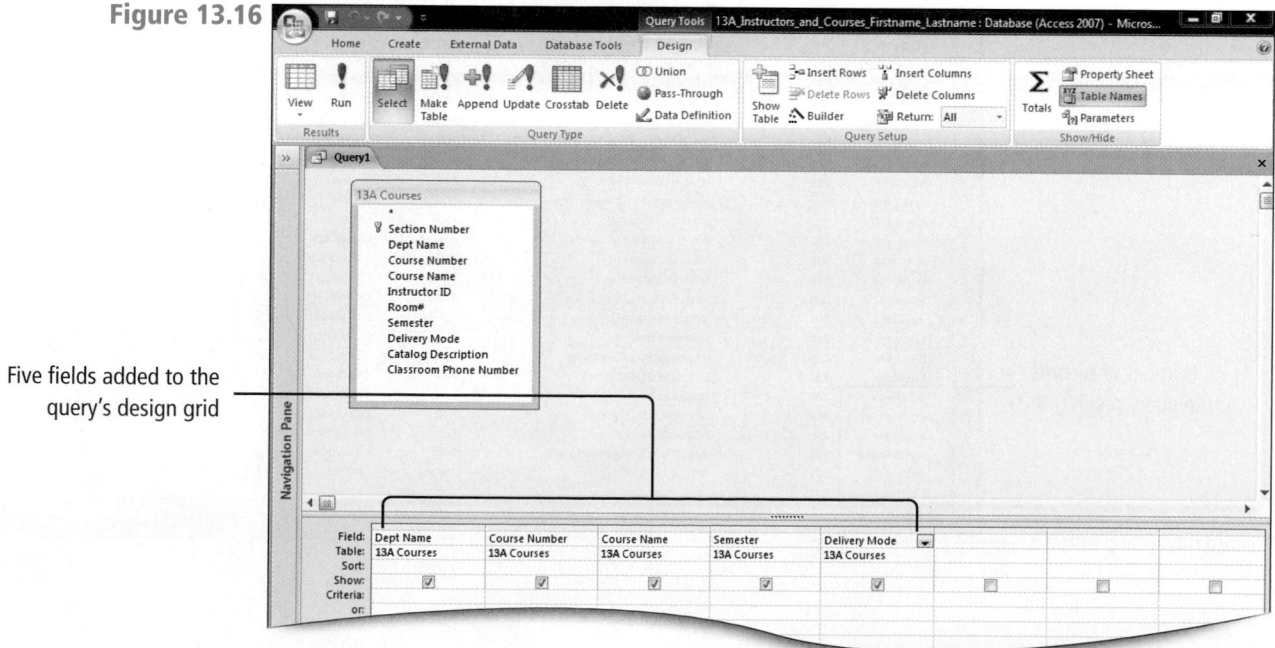

Five fields added to the
query's design grid

Activity 13.08 Running, Saving, Printing, and Closing a Query

After you create a query, you *run* it to see the results. When you run a query, Access looks at the records in the table (or tables) you have included in the query, finds the records that match the specified conditions (if any), and displays those records in a datasheet view. Only the fields that have been included in the query design are displayed in the query result. The query is always run against the current table of records, and therefore presents the most up-to-date information.

1 On the **Design tab**, in the **Results group**, click the **Run** button. Alternatively, on the Design tab, in the Results group, click the View button to display the results of a query. Compare your screen with Figure 13.17.

This query answers the question, *What is the Dept Name, Course Number, Course Name, Semester, and Delivery Mode of all the courses in the table?* Think of a query as a subset of the records in one or more tables, arranged in datasheet view, according to the conditions that you specify.

The five fields that you specified display in columns, the records display in rows, and navigation buttons display at the bottom of the window in the same manner as in a table.

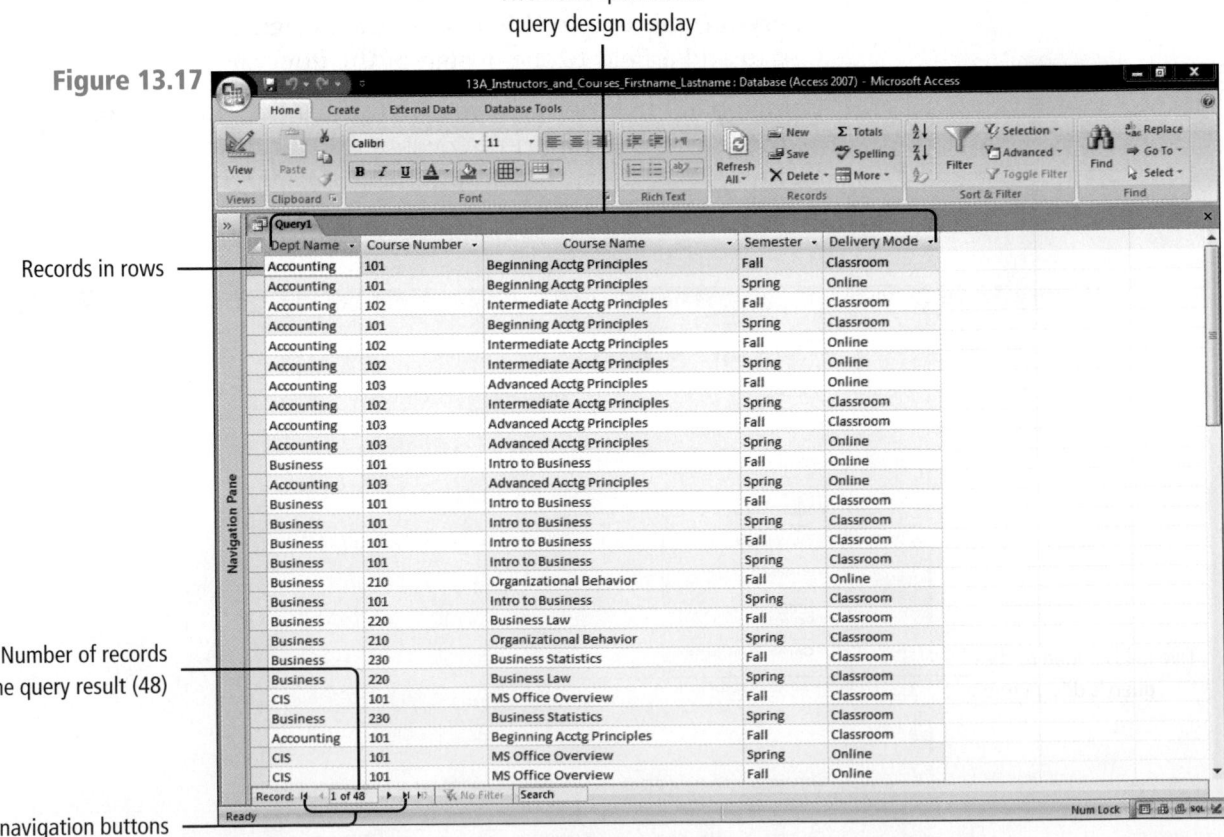

Five fields specified in query design display

Figure 13.17

Records in rows

Number of records in the query result (48)

Record navigation buttons

2 On the **Quick Access Toolbar**, click the **Save** button 🔲 to display the **Save As** dialog box. Type **13A Courses Query Firstname Lastname** and then click **OK**.

It is not necessary to save all queries, but save your queries if it is likely that you will need to ask the same question again. Doing so will save you the effort of creating the query again to answer the same question.

3 From the **Office** menu 🔘, point to the **Print** button, and then click **Print Preview**. In the **Page Layout group**, click the **Landscape** button. In the **Zoom group**, click the **Two Pages** button to see how your query will print on two pages. If you are printing your assignments on paper, click the **Print** button, and then in the displayed **Print** dialog box, click **OK**. To submit electronically, follow the directions provided by your instructor.

Two pages will print. Queries are created to answer questions and to create information from the data contained in the tables. Queries are typically created as a basis for a report. As you have just done here, however, the actual query result can be printed in a manner similar to tables and other database objects.

4 Click the **Close Print Preview** button. In the object window, **Close** ❌ the query. **Open** ⏩ the **Navigation Pane**, and then compare your screen with Figure 13.18.

The query is saved and closed. The new query name displays in the Navigation Pane under the table with which it is associated—the *Courses* table. When you save a query, only the design of the query is saved. The records still reside in the table object. Each time you open the query, Access runs it again and displays the results based on the data stored in the associated table(s). Thus, the results of a query always reflect the latest information in the associated tables.

Figure 13.18

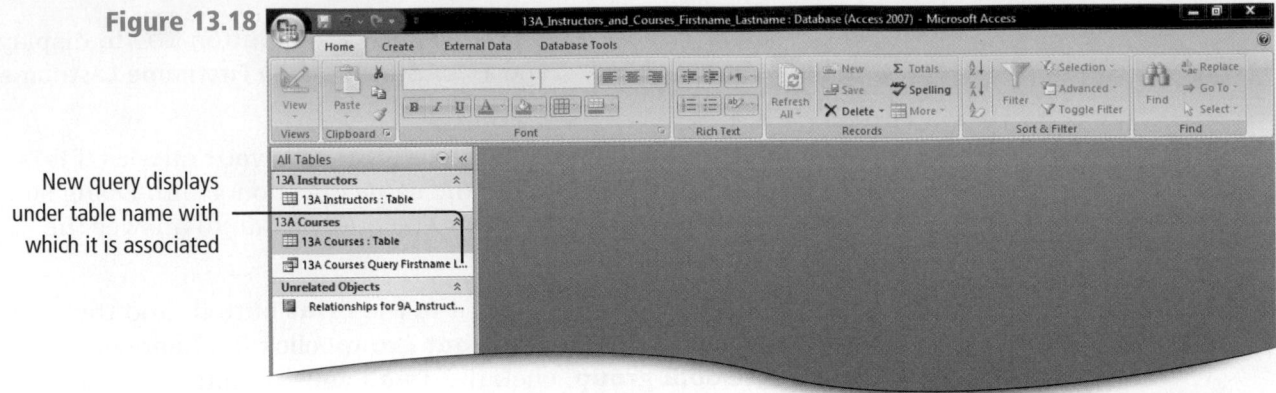

New query displays
under table name with
which it is associated

Objective 5
Create a New Query from an Existing Query

In this activity, you will begin with an existing query, save it with a new name, and then create a new query from the existing one.

Activity 13.09 Creating a New Query From an Existing Query

1 From the **Navigation Pane**, open your **13A Courses Query** by either double-clicking the name or right-clicking and clicking Open.

The query opens in the Datasheet view, which is the view used to display the records in a query result.

2 From the **Office** menu, click **Save As**, which will save the current database object—a query—as a new object. In the **Save As** dialog box, edit as necessary to name the new query **13A Sections Query Firstname Lastname** and then click **OK**. On the **Home tab**, in the **Views group**, click the **View** button to switch to Design view. Compare your screen with Figure 13.19 .

A new query, based on a copy of your 13A Courses Query, is created and displays in the object window and is added to the Navigation Pane. Your query displays in Design view.

Figure 13.19

New 13A *Sections* query in object window

New query 13A *Sections* displays in Navigation Pane

Selection bar in design grid

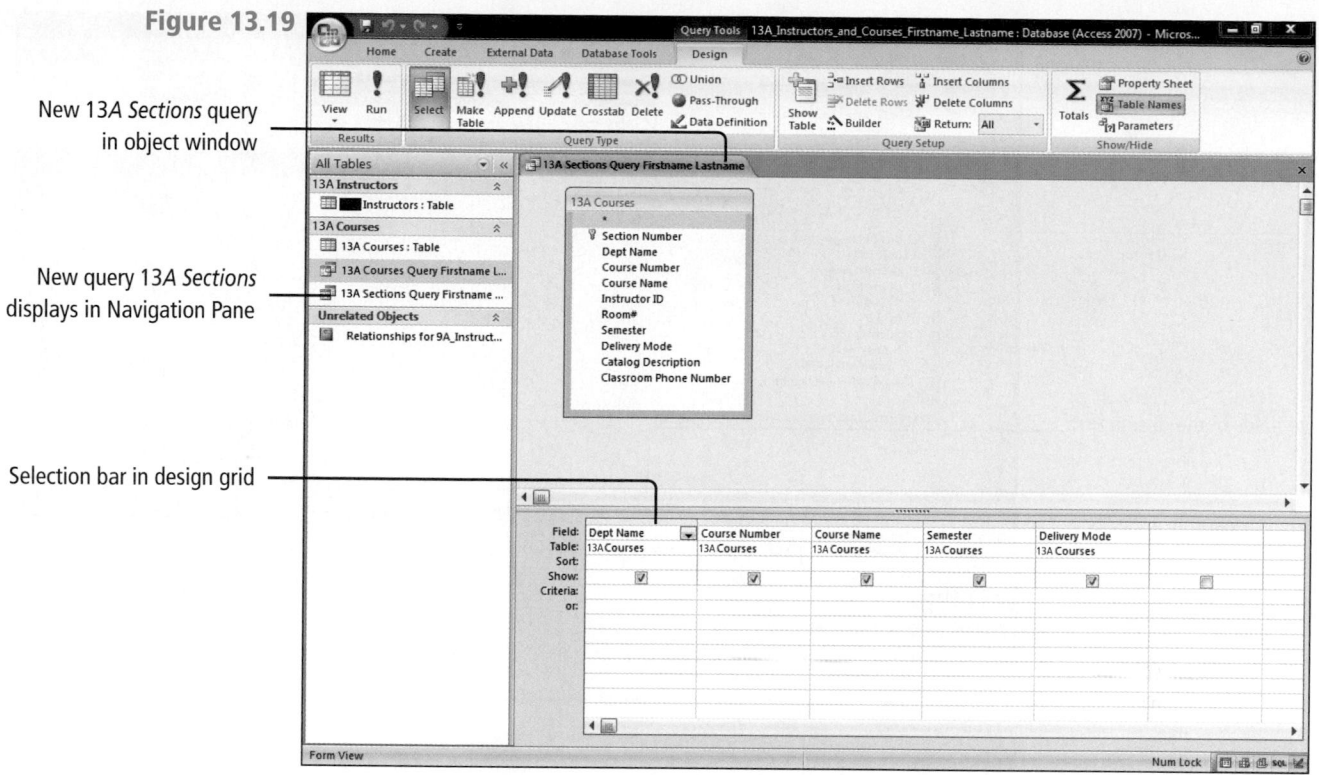

3 **Close** ≪ the **Navigation Pane**. In the design grid, point to the thin gray selection bar above the **Dept Name** field until the ↓ pointer displays. Click to select the **Dept Name** column, and then press Delete.

The Dept Name field is removed from the design grid and the Delivery Mode field moves to the fourth column in the design grid. This action deletes the field from the query design only—it has no effect on the underlying 13A Courses table.

4 Using a similar technique, from the gray selection bar, select the **Delivery Mode** column. Then, point to the **selection bar** at the top of the selected column to display the ↖ pointer, and drag to the left to position **Delivery Mode** in the first column.

To rearrange fields in the query design, first select the field you want to move, and then drag it to a new position in the design grid.

5 From the field list, add the **Section Number** field as the fifth column in the design grid. Then using the technique you just practiced, select and move the **Section Number** field to the first column in the design grid. Click outside of the grid to cancel the selection, and then compare your screen with Figure 13.20.

Figure 13.20

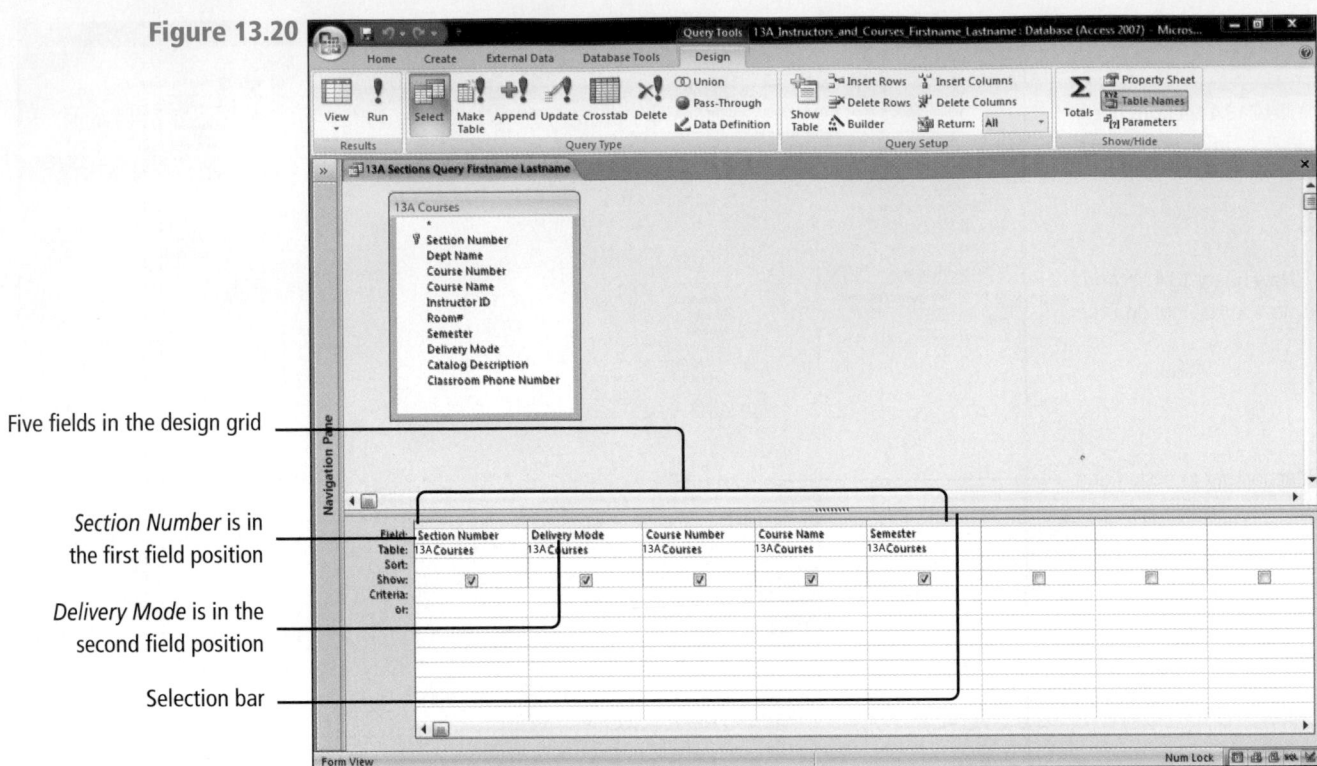

Five fields in the design grid

Section Number is in the first field position

Delivery Mode is in the second field position

Selection bar

6   On the **Query Tools Design tab**, in the **Results group**, click the **Run** button. The result of the query displays five fields in the new arrangement. Compare your screen with Figure 13.21.

This query answers the question, *What is the Section Number, Delivery Mode, Course Number, Course Name, and Semester of every course?* Recall that you can think of a query as a subset of the records in one or more tables, arranged in datasheet view, according to the conditions that you specify.

Figure 13.21

7 From the **Office** menu, point to the **Print** button, and then click **Print Preview**. On the **Print Preview tab**, in the **Page Layout group**, click **Landscape**. In the **Zoom group**, click the **Two Pages** button to view how your query will print on two pages. If you are printing on paper, in the **Print group**, click the **Print** button. In the displayed **Print** dialog box, click **OK**. To submit electronically, follow your instructor's directions.

8 Click the **Close Print Preview** button. In the object window, **Close** ☒ the query, and then click **Yes** to save the changes to the design. **Open** ⏩ the **Navigation Pane**, and then compare your screen with Figure 13.22.

The query is saved and closed. The new query name displays in the Navigation Pane under the table with which it is associated. Recall that when you save a query, only the design of the query is saved. The records still reside in the respective table objects.

Each time you open the query, Access runs it again and displays the results based on the records stored in the associated table(s).

Figure 13.22

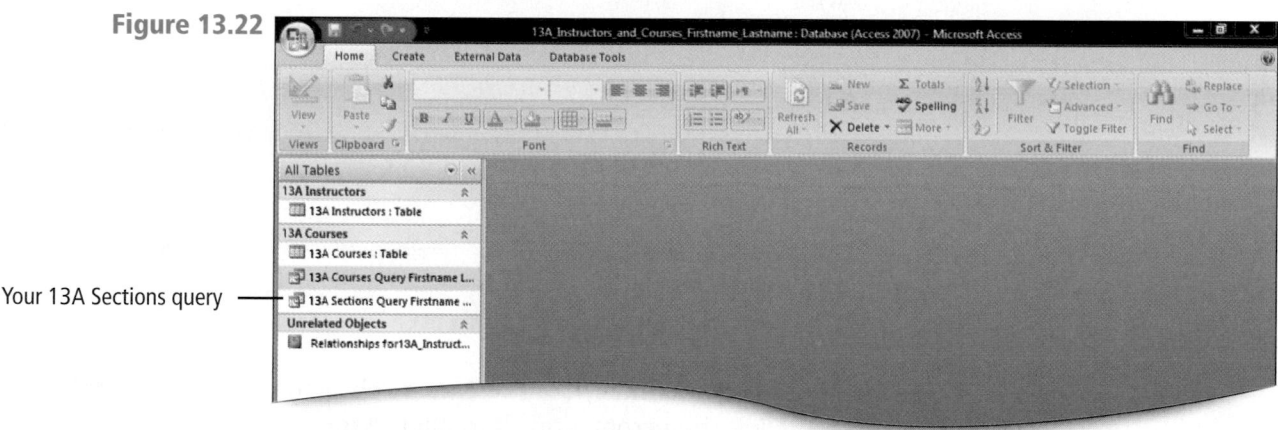

Your 13A Sections query

Objective 6
Sort Query Results

You can sort the results of a query. Because the results of a query are formatted like a table in Datasheet view, the process for sorting is similar to sorting in a table. Records can be sorted in ascending or descending order. Data in a query can be sorted from the Datasheet view or from the Design view.

Activity 13.10 Sorting Query Results

In this activity, you will open an existing query, save it with a new name, and then sort the query results in a new arrangement.

1 From the **Navigation Pane**, open your **13A Sections Query**. From the **Office** menu, click **Save As**. In the **Save As** dialog box, edit as necessary to name the query **13A Delivery Sort Firstname Lastname** and then click **OK**.

Access creates a new query, based on a copy of your 13A Sections Query.

2 **Close** « the **Navigation Pane**, and then in the **Views group**, click the **View** button to switch to Design view. In the design grid, in the **Sort** row, click in the **Delivery Mode** field to place the insertion point there and display an arrow. Click the **Sort arrow**, and then in the displayed list, click **Descending**. Compare your screen with Figure 13.23.

Figure 13.23

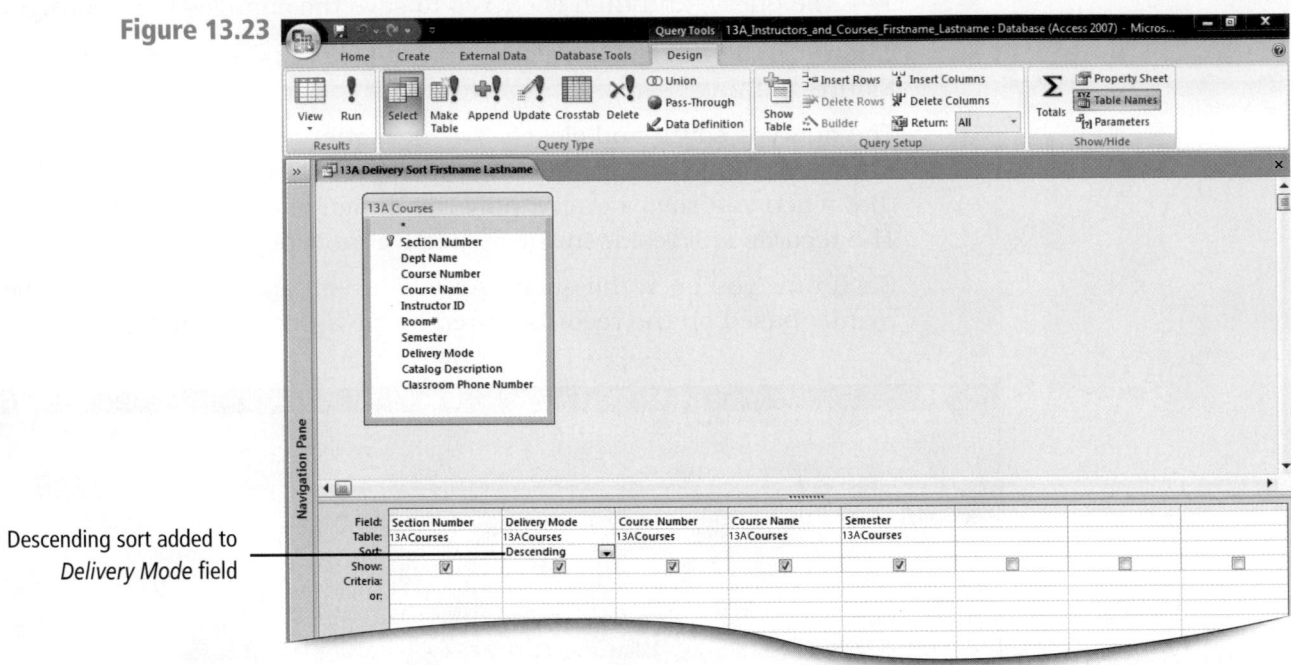

Descending sort added to
Delivery Mode field

3 In the **Sort** row, under **Course Name**, click to display the **Sort arrow**, click the arrow, and then click **Ascending**.

4 On the **Design tab**, in the **Results group**, click the **Run** button, and then compare your screen with Figure 13.24.

Fields that have a Sort designation are sorted from left to right. That is, the sorted field on the left becomes the outermost sort field, and the sorted field on the right becomes the innermost sort field. Thus, the records are sorted first in descending alphabetical order by the Delivery Mode field—the leftmost indicated sort field. Then in the Course Name field, within the Online records, the Course Names are sorted in ascending alphabetical order.

Figure 13.24

Within Course Name, records sorted in ascending order

Within Delivery Mode, records sorted in descending order

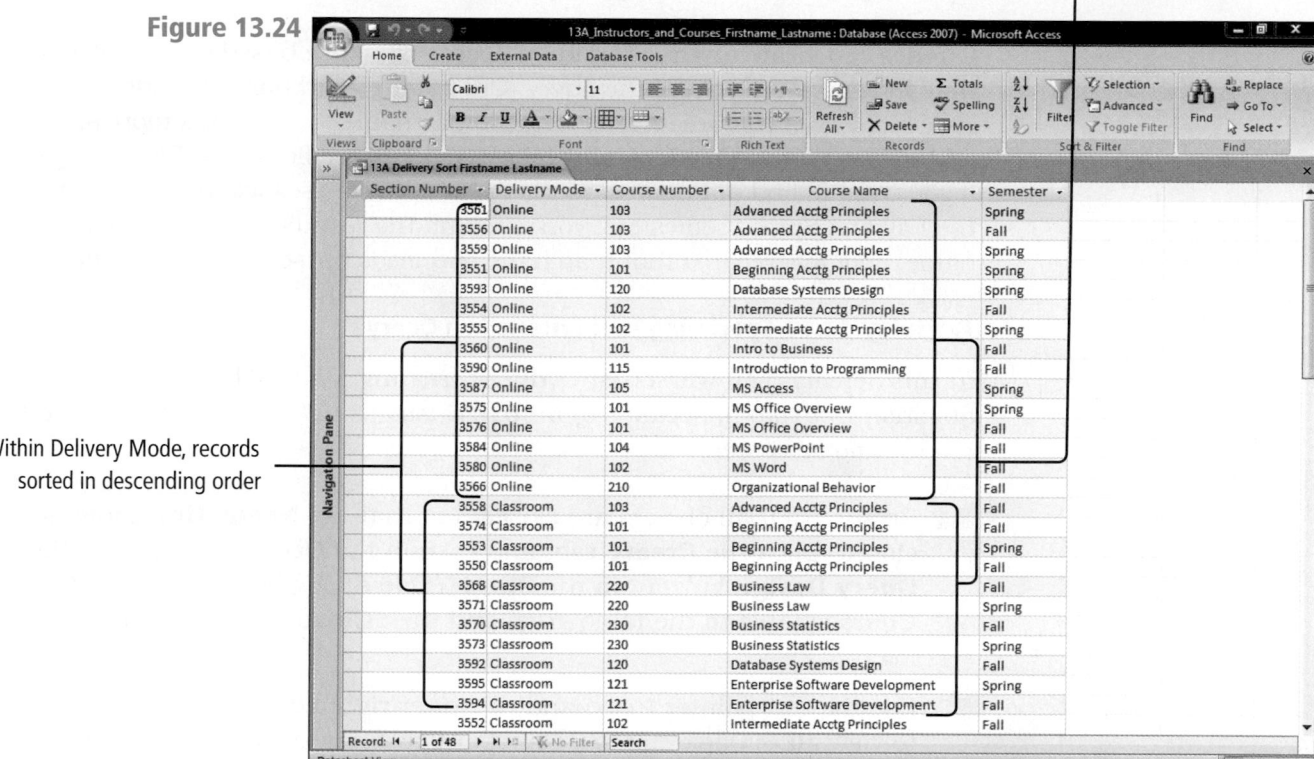

5 From the **Office** menu , point to the **Print** button, and then click **Print Preview**. On the **Print Preview tab**, in the **Page Layout group**, click **Landscape**. In the **Zoom group**, click the **Two Pages** button to view the layout of the pages. If you are printing on paper, in the **Print group**, click the **Print** button. In the displayed **Print** dialog box, click **OK**. To submit electronically, follow your instructor's directions.

6 Click the **Close Print Preview** button. **Close** ✕ the query, and then click **Yes** to save the changes to this query's design.

More Knowledge
Sorting

If you add a sort order to the *design* of a query, it remains as a permanent part of the query design. If you use the sort buttons in the Datasheet view, it will override the sort order of the query design, and can be saved as part of the query. A sort order designated directly in datasheet view will not display in the Sort row of the query design grid.

Objective 7
Specify Criteria in a Query

Queries can locate information in an Access database based on **criteria** that you specify as part of the query. Criteria are conditions that identify the specific records you are looking for. Criteria enable you to ask a more specific question, and therefore you will get a more specific result. For example, if you want to find out how many *Business Law* courses will be offered in the Fall and Spring semesters, you can limit the results to a specific course name, and only records that match the specified course name will display.

Activity 13.11 Specifying Text Criteria in a Query

In this activity, you will assist Lydia in creating a query to answer the question *How many sections of Intro to Business will be offered in the Fall and Spring semesters?*

1 Be sure that all objects are closed and that the **Navigation Pane** is closed. Click the **Create tab**, and then in the **Other group**, click the **Query Design** button. In the **Show Table** dialog box, **Add** the **13A Courses** table to the table area, and then **Close** the **Show Table** dialog box.

2 Use the ⬉ pointer to expand the lower right corner of the field list to view all the field names. Using any technique, add the following fields to the design grid in the order listed: **Course Name**, **Course Number**, **Semester**, and **Delivery Mode**.

3 In the **Criteria** row of the design grid, click in the **Course Name** field, type **Intro to Business** and then press ⏎. Compare your screen with Figure 13.25.

Access places quote marks around your criteria. Use the Criteria row to specify the criteria that will limit the results of the query to your exact specifications. Access adds quote marks to text criteria in this manner to indicate that this is a **text string**—a sequence of characters—that must be matched.

Figure 13.25

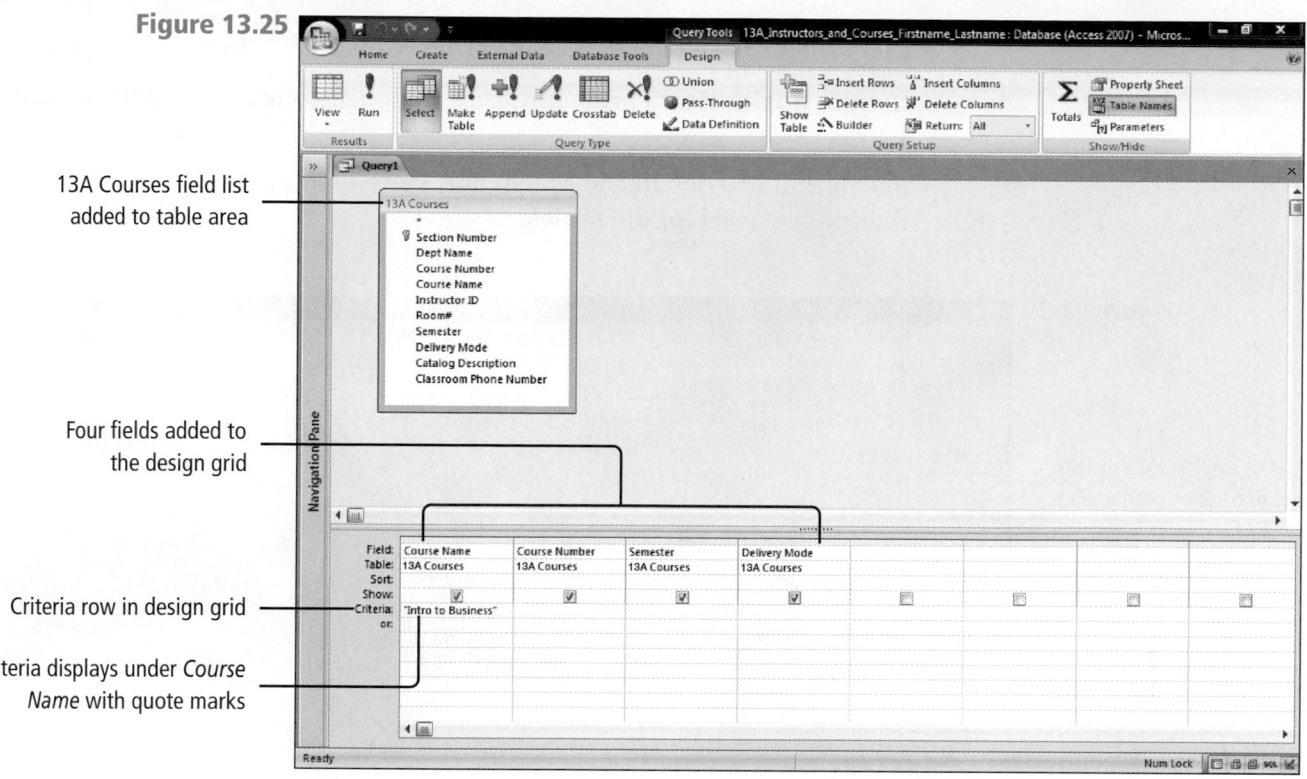

13A Courses field list added to table area

Four fields added to the design grid

Criteria row in design grid

Criteria displays under *Course Name* with quote marks

4 **Run** the query, and then compare your screen with Figure 13.26.

Six records display that meet the specified criteria—records that have *Intro to Business* in the Course Name field.

Figure 13.26

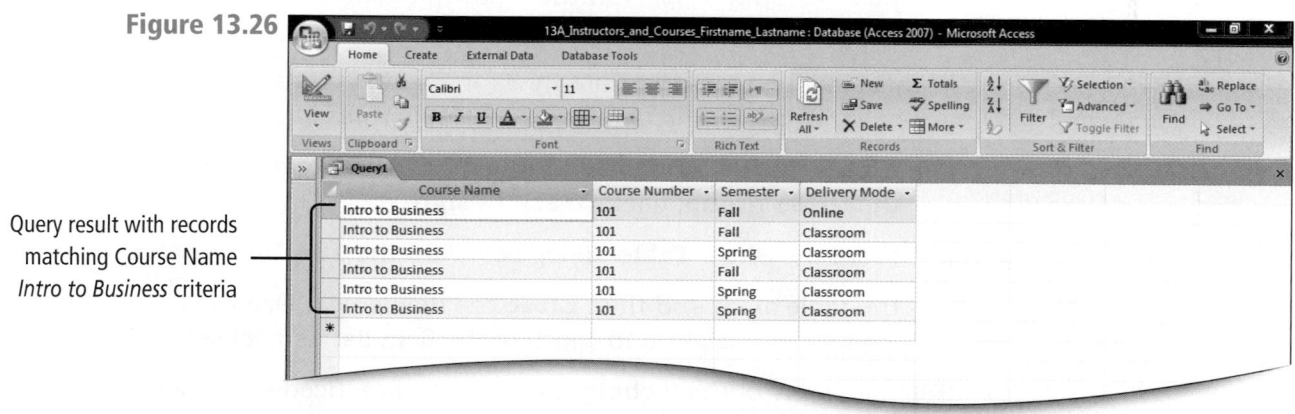

Query result with records matching Course Name *Intro to Business* criteria

5 On the **Quick Access Toolbar**, click the **Save** button [image], and then in the **Save As** dialog box, type **13A Intro to Business Firstname Lastname** and then click **OK**.

6 From the **Office** menu [image], point to the **Print** button, and then click **Print Preview**. If you are printing your assignments on paper, in the **Print group**, click the **Print** button. In the displayed **Print** dialog box, click **OK**. Or, submit electronically as directed.

7 Click the **Close Print Preview** button. **Close** ☒ the query, **Open** ⊡ the **Navigation Pane**, and then compare your screen with Figure 13.27.

Recall that queries in the Navigation Pane display a distinctive icon—that of two overlapping tables.

Figure 13.27

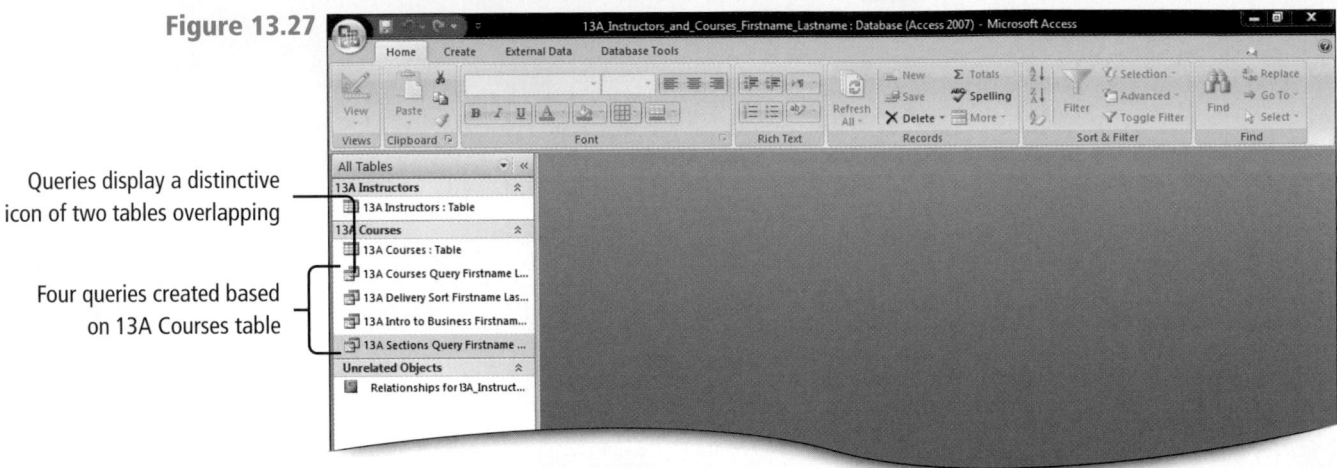

Queries display a distinctive icon of two tables overlapping

Four queries created based on 13A Courses table

Activity 13.12 Specifying Criteria Using a Field Not Displayed in the Query Result

So far, all of the fields that you included in the query design have also been included in the query result. It is not required to have every field in the query actually display in the result. In fact, there will be times when you will want to prevent some fields from displaying in the result.

In this activity, you will assist Lydia in creating a query to answer the question, *Which instructors have a rank of Professor?*

1 **Close** ⊡ the **Navigation Pane**. Click the **Create tab**, and then in the **Other group**, click **Query Design**.

2 From the **Show Table** dialog box, **Add** the **13A Instructors** table to the table area, and then **Close** the dialog box. Use the ⬎ pointer to expand the height and width of the field list as necessary.

3 Using any of the techniques you have practiced—double-clicking, dragging, or displaying the arrow, and then selecting in the list—add the following fields, in the order listed, to the design grid: **Instructor ID**, **Instructor First Name**, **Instructor Last Name**, and **Rank**.

4 In the **Sort** row, click in the **Instructor Last Name** field, click the **arrow**, and then click **Ascending**.

5 In the **Criteria** row, click in the **Rank** field, type **Professor** and then press ⏎. Compare your screen with Figure 13.28.

When you press ⏎, the insertion point moves to the next criteria box and quote marks are added around the text you entered. Recall that Access adds quote marks to text criteria to indicate that this is a text string—a sequence of characters—that must be matched.

Figure 13.28

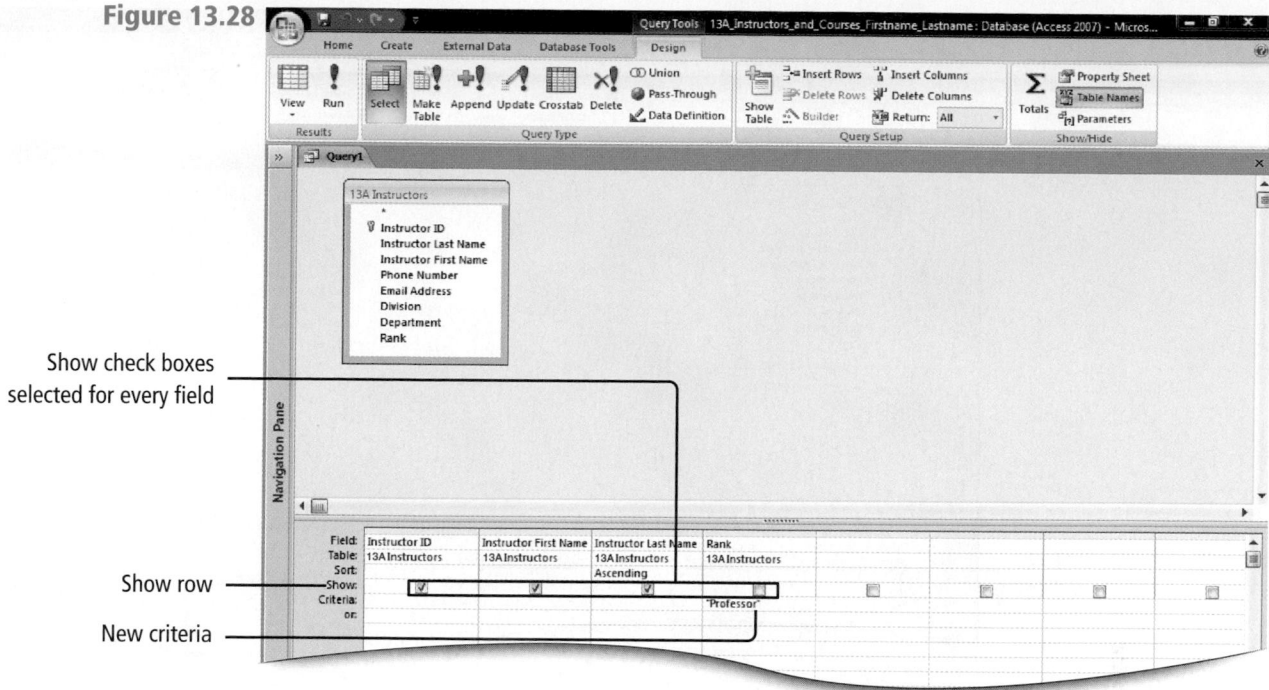

Show check boxes selected for every field

Show row

New criteria

6 In the design grid, in the **Show** row, notice that the check box is selected for every field. **Run** the query to view the result of the query.

Six records meet the criteria, and each of the six records displays *Professor* in the Rank column.

Alert! — **Do your query results differ?**

If you mistype the criteria, enter it under the wrong field, or make some other error, the result will display no records. This indicates that there are no records in the table that match the criteria as you entered it. If this occurs, return to the Design view and reexamine the query design. Verify that the criteria are typed on the Criteria row, under the correct field, and that there are no spelling errors. Then rerun the query.

7 On the **Home tab**, in the **Views group**, click the **View** button to return to Design view. In the design grid, under **Rank**, in the **Show** row, click to clear the check box, and then compare your screen with Figure 13.29.

Because it is repetitive and not particularly useful to have *Professor* display for each record in the query result, you can clear this check box so that the field does not display.

Figure 13.29

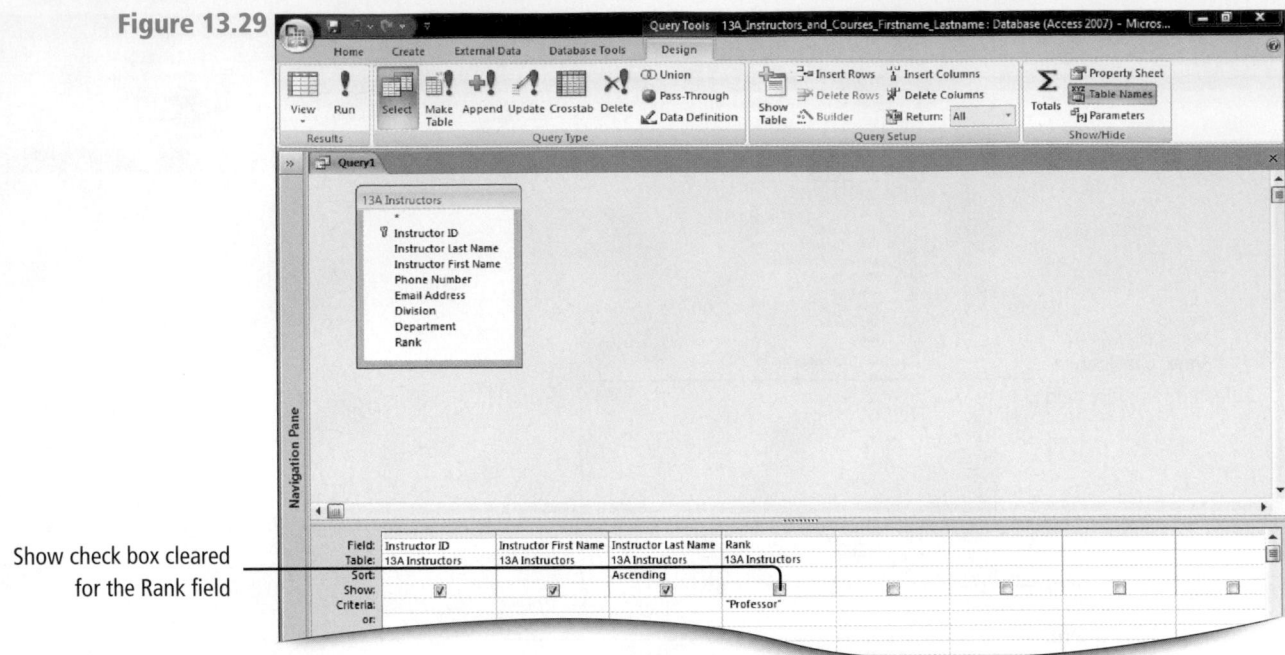

Show check box cleared for the Rank field

8 **Run** the query again, and then compare your screen with Figure 13.30.

The query results display the same six records, but the *Rank* field does not display. Although the Rank field was still included in the query criteria for the purpose of identifying specific records, it is not necessary to display the field in the result.

Clear the Show check box when necessary to avoid cluttering the query results with redundant data.

Rank field not displayed in the result

Figure 13.30

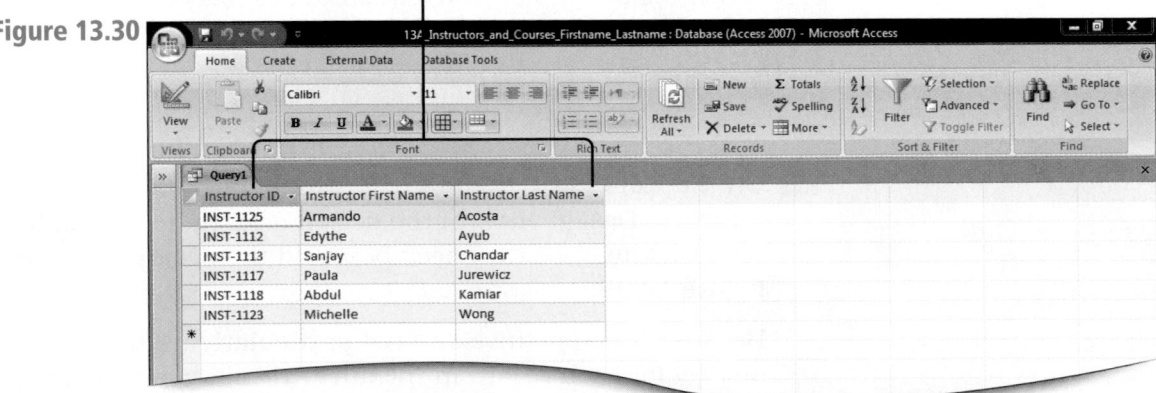

9 On the **Quick Access Toolbar**, click the **Save** button , and then in the **Save As** dialog box, type **13A Professor Rank Firstname Lastname** Click **OK**.

10 From the **Office** menu , point to the **Print** button, and then click **Print Preview**. If you are printing your assignments on paper, in the

Print group, click the **Print** button. In the displayed **Print** dialog box, click **OK**. To submit electronically, follow your instructor's directions.

11 Click the **Close Print Preview** button. **Close** ☒ the query, **Open** ⟫ the **Navigation Pane**, and then notice the query listed under the table with which it is associated—the 13A Instructors table.

Activity 13.13 Using Is Null Criteria to Find Empty Fields

Sometimes you must locate records where specific data is missing. You can locate such records by using *is null*—empty—as a criteria in a field. Additionally, you can display only the records where a value *has* been entered in a field by using *is not null* as a criteria, which will exclude records where the specified field is empty.

In this activity, you will help Lydia run a query to find out *Which course sections have not yet had a classroom assigned?*

1 **Close** ⟪ the **Navigation Pane**. Click the **Create tab**, and then in the **Other group**, click the **Query Design** button to begin a new query. **Add** the **13A Courses** table, and then **Close** the **Show Table** dialog box. Use the ⬉ pointer as necessary to expand the height and width of the field list.

2 Using any of the techniques you have practiced, add the following fields to the design grid in the order given: **Section Number**, **Course Number**, **Course Name**, and **Room#**.

3 On the **Criteria** row, click in the **Room#** field, type **Is Null** and press Enter. Alternatively, type *is null* and Access will change the criteria to display with capital letters. Compare your screen with Figure 13.31.

The criteria *Is Null* examines the field and looks for records that do *not* have any values entered in the Room# field. In this manner, you can determine which courses still need to have a classroom assigned.

Figure 13.31

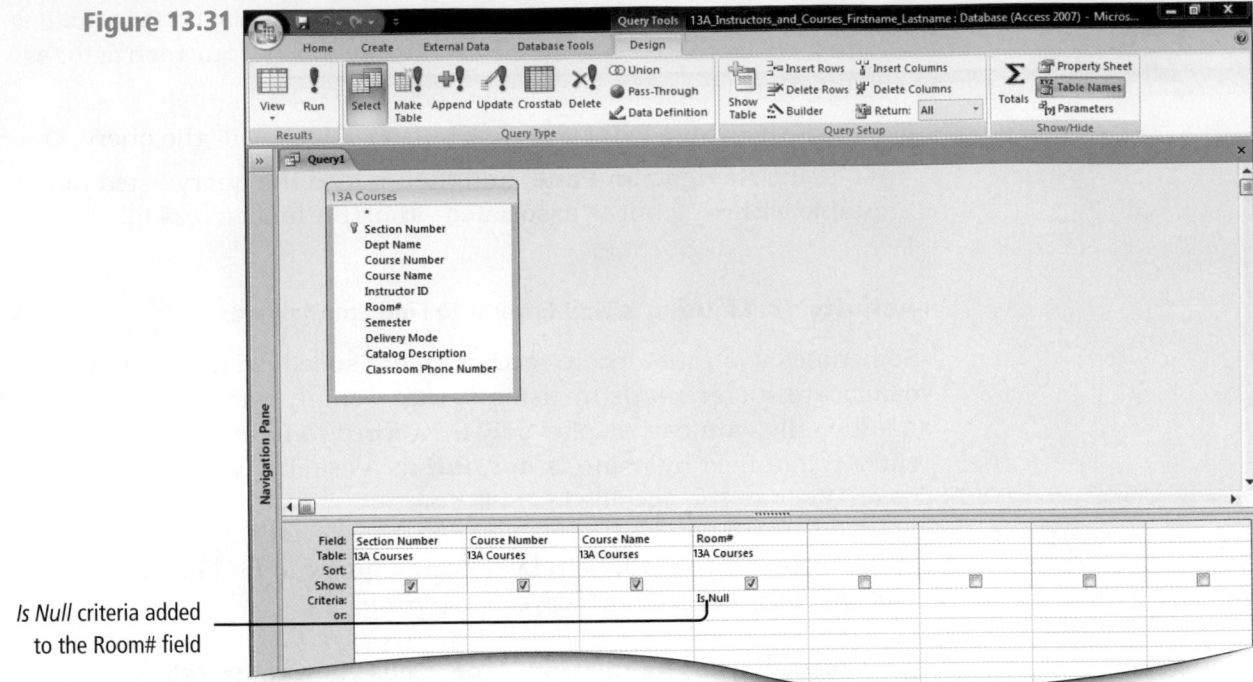

Is Null criteria added to the Room# field

---

4 On the **Sort** row, click in the **Course Name** field, click the **Sort arrow**, and then click **Ascending**. **Run** the query to see the results, and then compare your screen with Figure 13.32.

Five course sections do not have a Room# assigned—the Room# field is empty for these course sections. The course names are sorted in ascending (alphabetical) order.

Figure 13.32

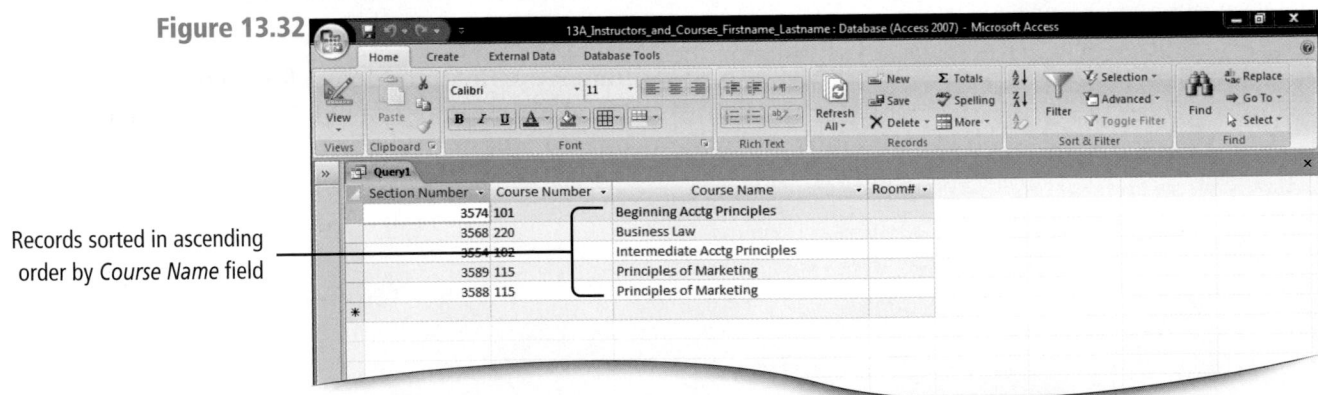

Records sorted in ascending order by *Course Name* field

---

5 **Save** your query, and then in the **Save As** dialog box, type **13A Rooms Firstname Lastname** Click **OK**.

6 From the **Office** menu, point to the **Print** button, and then click **Print Preview**. If you are printing your assignments on paper, in the **Print group**, click the **Print** button. In the displayed **Print** dialog box, click **OK**. To submit electronically, follow your instructor's directions.

7 Click the **Close Print Preview** button, and then **Close** ☒ the query.

Open ⏩ the **Navigation Pane**, and then compare your screen with Figure 13.33.

Each query that you created displays under the table with which it is associated. The objects display in alphabetical order.

Figure 13.33

Query objects display, in alphabetical order, with table on which they are based

8 **Close** ⏪ the **Navigation Pane** and be sure all objects are closed.

9 From the **Office** ⊕ menu, click **Close Database**, and then at the right edge of the Access title bar, click the **Close** button ☒ to close the Access program. Alternatively, from the Office menu, click Exit Access.

End **You have completed Project 13A** ─────────

13B

Project 13B Athletes and Scholarships

In Activities 13.14 through 13.25, you will assist Marcus Simmons, Athletic Director for Florida Port Community College, in developing and querying his Athletes and Scholarships database. In this database, Mr. Simmons tracks the scholarships awarded to student athletes. Your completed Relationships report and queries will look similar to those in Figure 13.34.

For Project 13B, you will need the following files:

a13B_Athletes_and_Scholarships

a13B_Athletes (Excel file)

You will save your database as
13B_Athletes_and_Scholarships_Firstname_Lastname

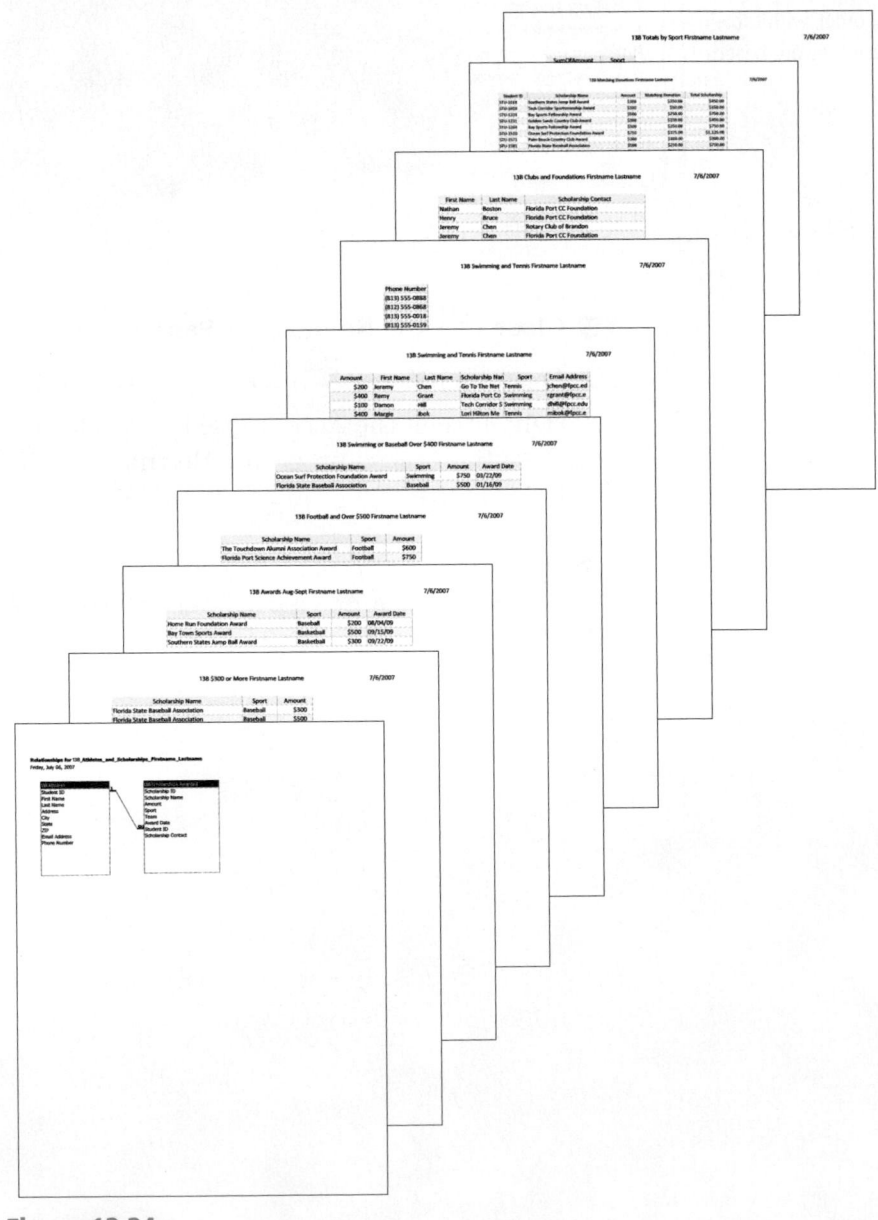

Figure 13.34
Project 13B—Athletes and Scholarships

Objective 8
Create a New Table by Importing an Excel Spreadsheet

Many users of Microsoft Office track their data in an Excel spreadsheet. The sorting and filtering capabilities of Excel are useful enough for a simple database where all the information can reside in one large table, which is the Excel spreadsheet itself.

Excel is limited as a database management program because it cannot support multiple tables nor can it *relate* the information so that you can retrieve information from multiple spreadsheets using a query. However, data in an Excel spreadsheet can easily become an Access table by importing the spreadsheet, because Excel's format of columns and rows is similar to that of an Access table.

Activity 13.14 Opening an Existing Database and Preparing to Import an Excel Spreadsheet

In this activity, you will open, rename, and save an existing database, and then examine an Excel spreadsheet that Mr. Simmons wants to bring into Access as a new table.

1 On the left side of the Windows taskbar, click the **Start** button , and near the middle of the right side of the **Start menu**, click **Computer**. Navigate to the location where the student files that accompany this textbook are stored, and then click one time to select the file **a13B_Athletes_and_Scholarships**.

2 Point to the selected file name, right-click to display a shortcut menu, and then click **Copy**. Navigate to and open the **Access Chapter 13** folder you created in Project 13A. In an open area, right-click to display a shortcut menu, and then click **Paste**.

3 Right-click the selected file name, click **Rename**, and then using your own first and last name type **13B_Athletes_and_Scholarships_Firstname_Lastname** Press Enter to save the new file name. On the title bar, **Close** ⬛X⬛ the **Computer** window.

4 **Start** Access. From the **Office** menu , click **Open**. In the displayed **Open** dialog box, navigate to your **Access Chapter 13** folder, and then open your **13B_Athletes_and_Scholarships** database file.

5 If necessary, on the **Message Bar**, click the **Options** button, and then in the **Microsoft Office Security Options** dialog box, click the **Enable this content** option button. Click **OK**.

6 **Open** ⟩⟩ the **Navigation Pane**, open the **13B Scholarships Awarded** table, **Close** ⟨⟨ the **Navigation Pane**, and then take a moment to examine the data in the table. Compare your screen with Figure 13.35.

In this table, Mr. Simmons tracks the name and amount of scholarships awarded to student athletes. In the table, the students are identified only by their Student ID numbers; the table's primary key is the Scholarship ID field.

Student ID of student receiving scholarship

Figure 13.35

Scholarship Name field

Amount field

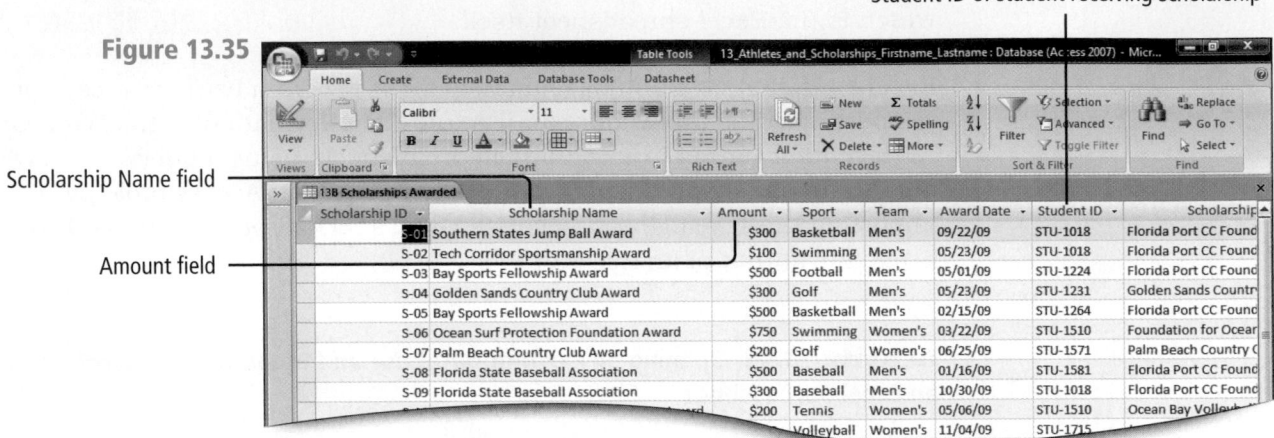

7 **Close** ☒ the table. From the Windows taskbar, click the **Start** button 🪟 , and then locate and open **Microsoft Office Excel 2007**. In Excel, from the **Office** menu 🗔 , click **Open**, navigate to the location where the student files for this textbook are stored, and then open the file **a13B_Athletes**. Compare your screen with Figure 13.36.

Mr. Simmons created an Excel spreadsheet to store the names, addresses, and other information of all the student athletes. Because *one* athlete can receive *many* scholarships, Mr. Simmons can see that using Access, rather than Excel, and having two *related* tables of information, will enable him to track and query this information more efficiently.

Figure 13.36

Excel spreadsheet containing student information

Student ID field

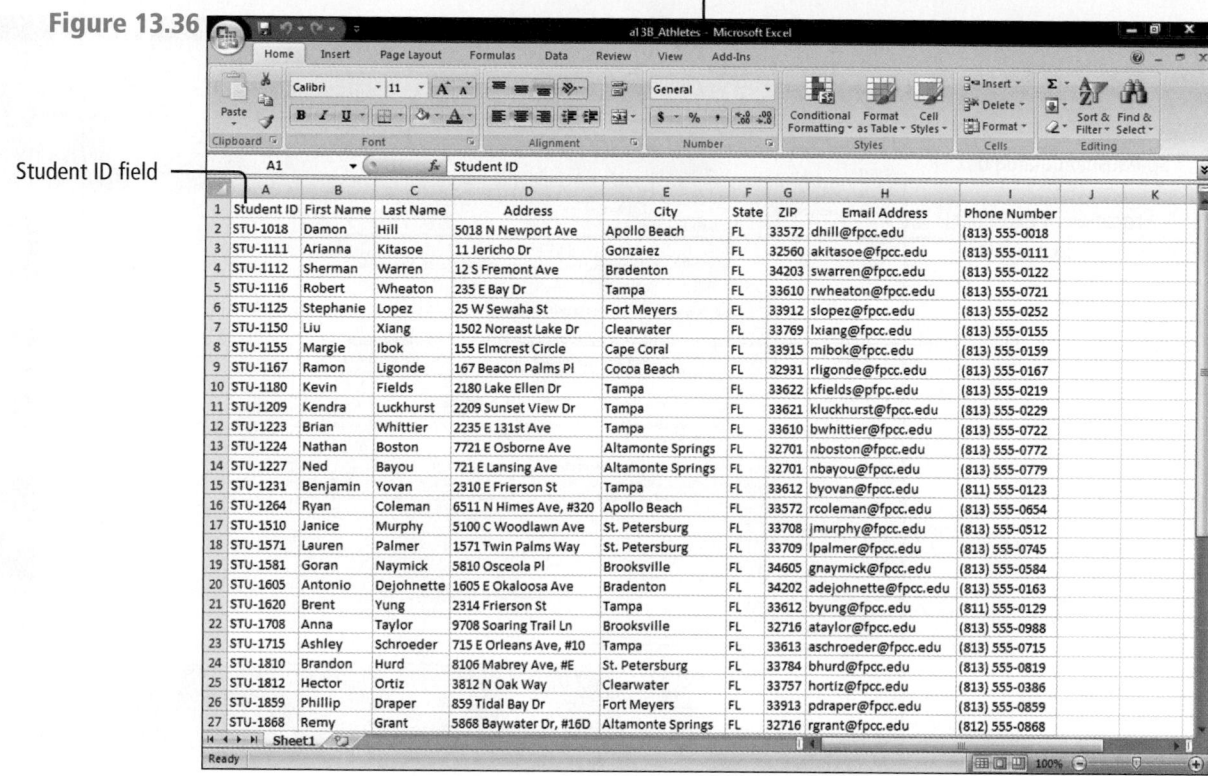

8 In the Excel spreadsheet, notice that in **row 1**, the column titles are similar to the field names in an Access table, and that each row contains the information for one student in a manner similar to a record in Access. Then, display the **Office** menu , and in the lower right corner of the menu, click **Exit Excel**.

Activity 13.15 Creating a New Table by Importing an Excel Spreadsheet

In this activity, you will create a new Access table by importing the Excel spreadsheet containing the names and addresses of the student athletes, create a one-to-many relationship between the new table and the 13A Scholarships Awarded table, enforce referential integrity, and then print a Relationship report.

1 Open ≫ the **Navigation Pane**. On the Ribbon, click the **External Data tab**, and then in the **Import group**, click **Excel**. In the displayed **Get External Data – Excel Spreadsheet** dialog box, to the right of the **File name** box, click the **Browse** button.

2 In the displayed **File Open** dialog box, navigate to the location where the student files for this textbook are stored, and then click the Excel file **a13B_Athletes**. In the lower right corner, click **Open**, and then compare your screen with Figure 13.37.

Browse button

Figure 13.37

Get External Data – Excel Spreadsheet dialog box

Location of Excel file displays here (yours may vary)

Option button selected

OK button

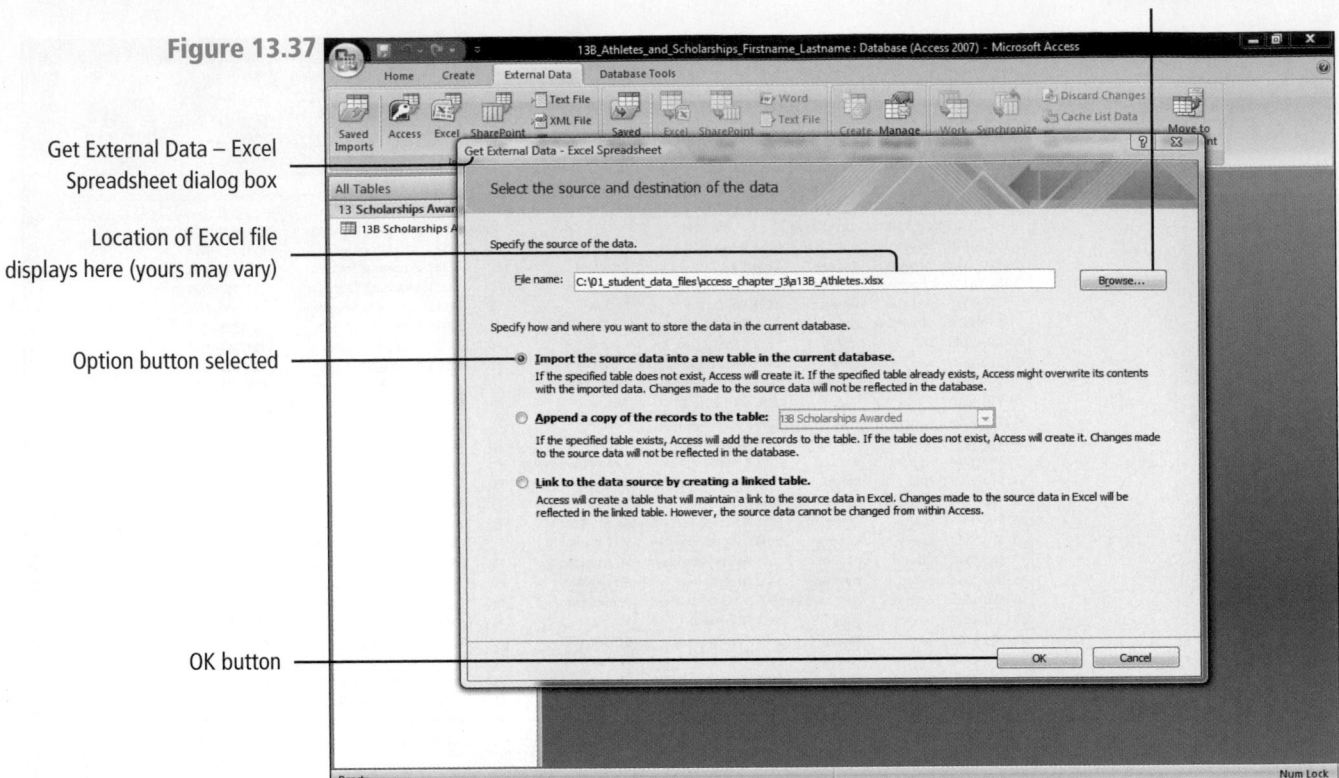

3 Be sure the **Import the source data into a new table in the current database** option button is selected, and then in the lower right corner, click **OK**.

The Import Spreadsheet Wizard opens and displays the worksheet data.

4 In the upper portion of the **Import Spreadsheet Wizard**, click to select the **First Row Contains Column Headings** check box.

The Excel data in the lower portion of the dialog box is framed so that the first row of Excel column titles can become the Access table field names, and the remaining rows can become the individual records for the new Access table.

5 In the lower right corner, click **Next**. Notice that the first column is selected, and in the upper portion of the dialog box, the **Field Name** is indicated and the **Data Type** is indicated. Click anywhere in the **First Name** column, and then compare your screen with Figure 13.38.

Here you can review and change the field properties of each field (column).

Excel column titles
become Field Names

Figure 13.38

Import Spreadsheet Wizard

Data type of selected
field identified

Spreadsheet data displays

Excel rows become records

Next button

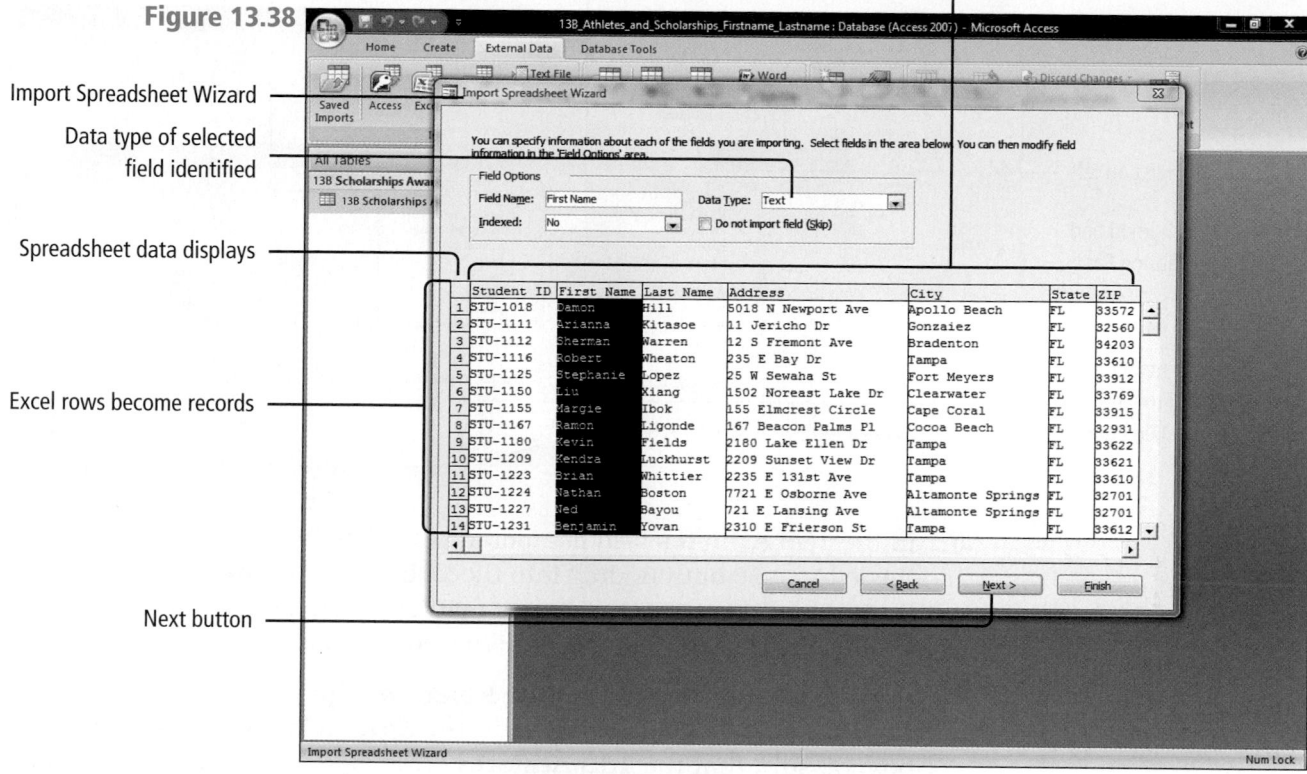

6 Under **Field Options**, make no changes for any of the fields, and then in the lower right corner, click **Next**. In the upper portion of the dialog box, click the **Choose my own primary key** option button, and then be sure that **Student ID** displays.

In the new table, Student ID will be the primary key. No two students will have the same Student ID. By default, Access selects the first field as the primary key.

7 In the lower right corner, click **Next**. In the **Import to Table** box, type **13B Athletes** and then click **Finish**. In the lower right corner of the **Get External Data – Excel Spreadsheet** dialog box, click **Close**.

That is all the information the Wizard needs to import your data. In the Navigation Pane, your new table displays.

8 On the Ribbon, click the **Database Tools tab**, and then in the **Show/Hide group**, click the **Relationships** button. On the **Design tab**, in the **Relationships group**, click the **Show Table** button. In the **Show Table** dialog box, **Add** the **13B Athletes** table, and then **Add** the **13B Scholarships Awarded** table. **Close** the **Show Table** dialog box.

9 Use the ⬉ pointer as necessary to expand the height and width of the field lists, position the field lists as necessary so that the **13B Athletes** table is on the left, and allow approximately 1 inch of space between the two field lists. Compare your screen with Figure 13.39.

Positioning the field lists in this manner is not required, but while studying Access, it makes it easier for you to view while creating the relationships.

Figure 13.39

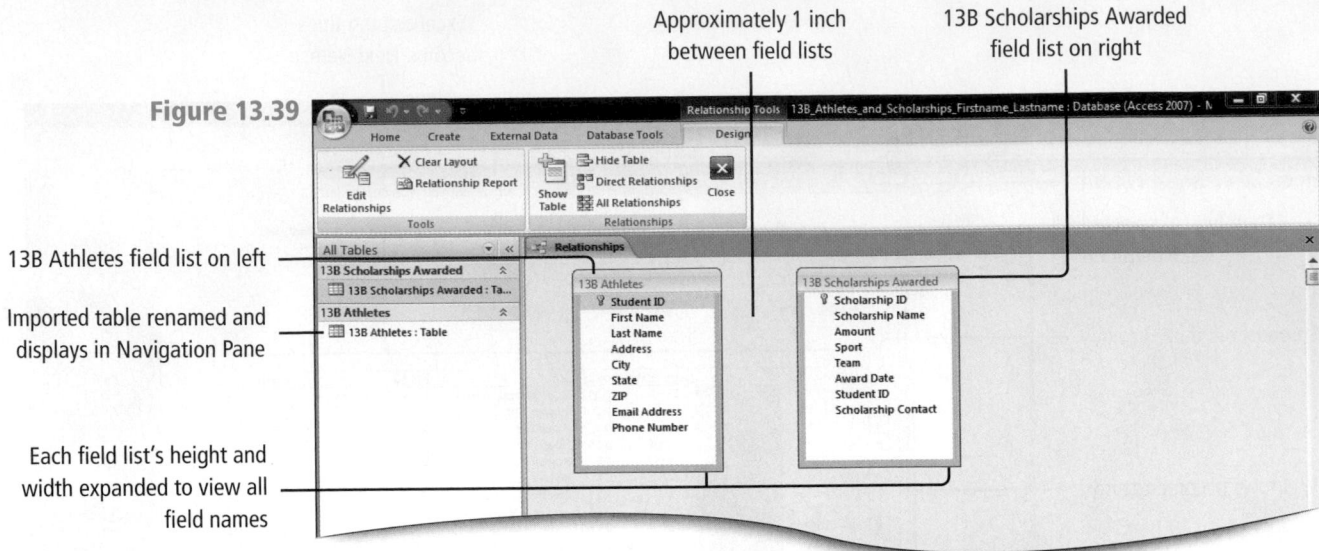

Approximately 1 inch between field lists

13B Scholarships Awarded field list on right

13B Athletes field list on left

Imported table renamed and displays in Navigation Pane

Each field list's height and width expanded to view all field names

10 In the **13B Athletes** field list, point to the **Student ID** field, hold down the left mouse button, drag into the **13B Scholarships Awarded** field list, and then position the mouse pointer on top of the **Student ID** field near the bottom of the list. Release the mouse button.

11 Point to the title bar of the **Edit Relationships** dialog box, and then drag it below the two field lists. In the **Edit Relationships** dialog box, be sure that the **13B Athletes** table is indicated on the left, that the **13B Scholarships Awarded** table is indicated on the right, and that **Student ID** is indicated as the field for both the *Table* and the *Related Table*.

The two tables are related in a one-to-many relationship—*one* athlete can be awarded *many* scholarships. The common field between the two tables is the Student ID field. In the 13B Athletes table, Student ID is the primary key. In the 13B Scholarships Awarded table, Student ID is the foreign key.

12 In the **Edit Relationships** dialog box, select the **Enforce Referential Integrity** check box, click the **Create** button, and then compare your screen with Figure 13.40.

The one-to-many relationship is established, and the *1* and ∞ indicate that referential integrity is enforced. Enforcing referential integrity ensures that a scholarship cannot be awarded to a student whose name does not appear in the 13B Athletes table. Similarly, you will not be able to delete a student athlete from the 13B Athletes table if there is a scholarship listed for that student in the 13B Scholarships Awarded table.

Join line indicates relationship established
using *Student ID* as common field

Foreign key field in
the *many* table

Figure 13.40

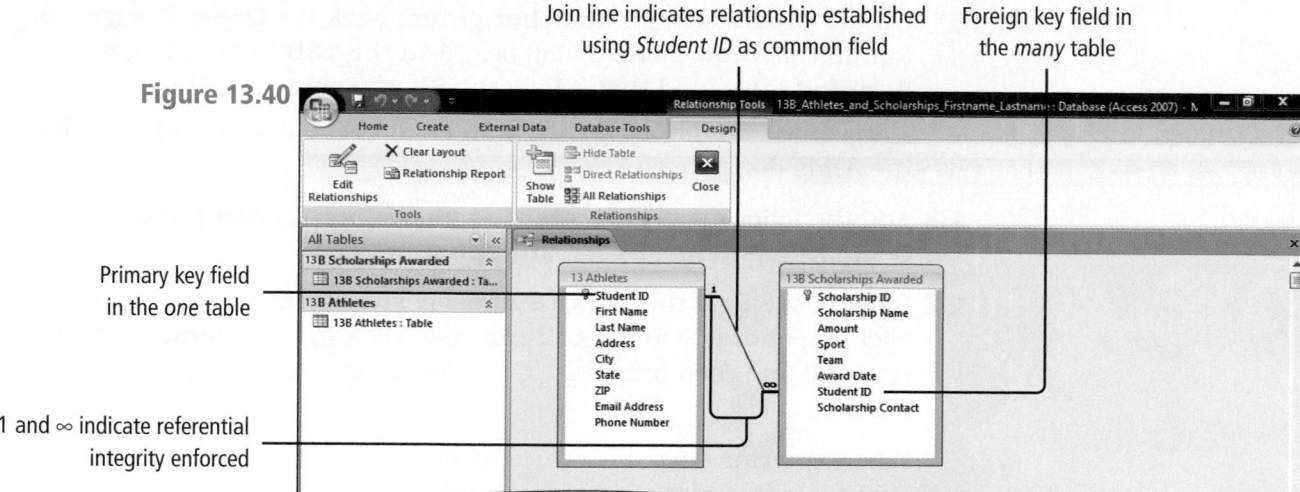

Primary key field
in the *one* table

1 and ∞ indicate referential
integrity enforced

13 On the **Design tab**, in the **Tools group**, click the **Relationship Report** button. On the displayed **Print Preview tab**, in the **Page Layout group**, click **Margins**, and then click **Normal**. Submit electronically as directed, or, if you are printing your assignments on paper, click the **Print** button, and then click **OK**. Click **Close Print Preview**. On the **Quick Access Toolbar**, click the **Save** button 🖫 to save the report. With the text in the **Save As** dialog box highlighted, type **13B Relationships Firstname Lastname** and then click **OK**.

14 Close ☒ the report and the Relationships window. From the **Navigation Pane**, open the **13B Athletes** table. On the left side of the table, in the first record, point to the **plus sign**, and then click one time.

In the first record—for *Damon Hill*—you can see that three related records exist in the 13B Scholarships Awarded table. The relationship displays because you created a relationship between the two tables using the Student ID field as the common field.

15 Close ☒ the **13B Athletes** table, and then **Close** « the **Navigation Pane**.

Objective 9
Specify Numeric Criteria in a Query

Criteria can be set for fields that contain numeric data. When you design your table, set the appropriate data type for fields that will contain numbers, currency, or dates so that mathematical calculations can be performed.

Activity 13.16 Specifying Numeric Criteria in a Query

Mr. Simmons wants to know *Which scholarships, and for which sport, are in the amount of $300?* In this activity, you will specify criteria in the query so that only the records of scholarships in the amount of $300 will display.

1 On the **Create tab**, in the **Other group**, click the **Query Design** button. In the **Show Table** dialog box, **Add** the **13B Scholarships Awarded** table, and then **Close** the **Show Table** dialog box. With the 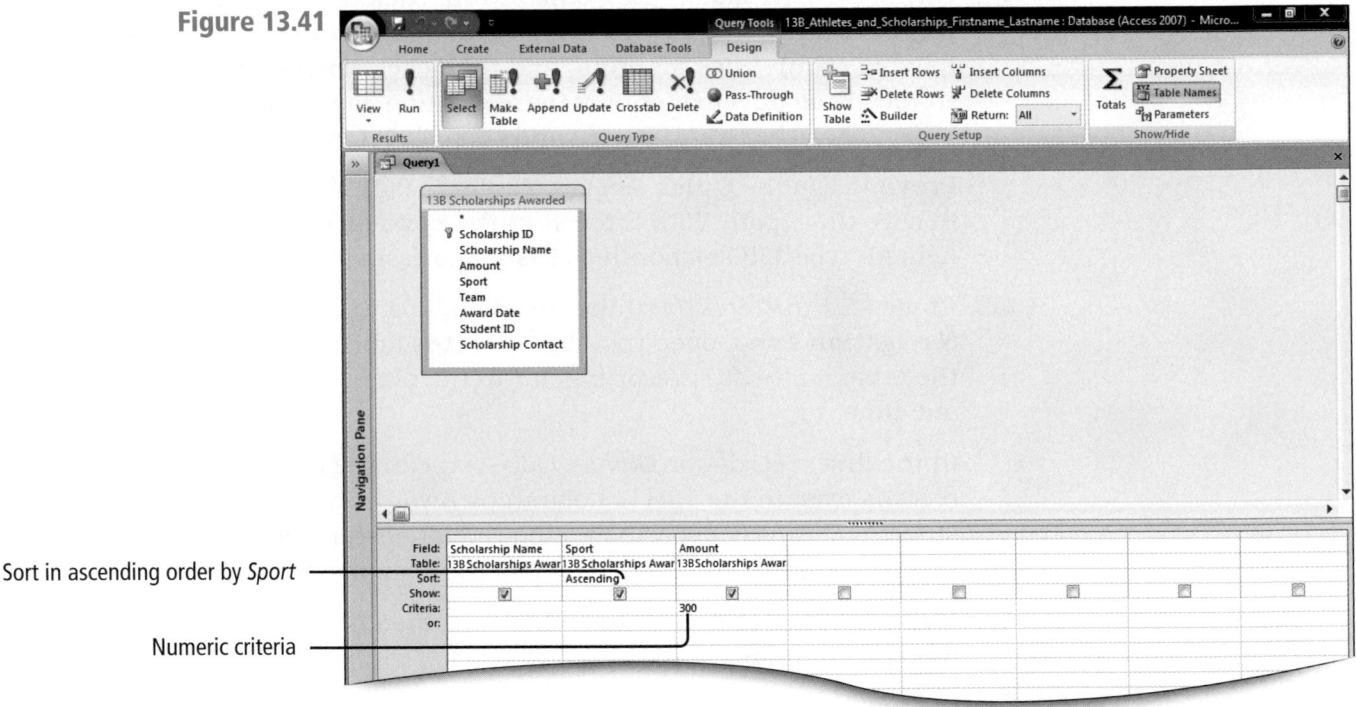 pointer, adjust the height and width of the field list so that all of the fields display.

2 Add the following fields to the design grid in the order given: **Scholarship Name**, **Sport**, and **Amount**.

3 Click in the **Sort** row under **Sport**, click the **Sort arrow**, and then click **Ascending**. On the **Criteria** row, click in the **Amount** field, type **300** and then press Enter. Compare your screen with Figure 13.41.

When entering currency values as criteria in the design grid, do not type the dollar sign, and include a decimal point only if you are looking for a specific amount that includes cents—for example 300.50.

Figure 13.41

Sort in ascending order by *Sport*

Numeric criteria

4 On the **Design tab**, in the **Results group**, click the **Run** button to view the results. Alternatively, click the View button.

Five scholarships awarded were in the exact amount of $300. At the bottom of the datasheet, *1 of 5* displays to indicate the number of records that match the criteria.

5 On the **Home tab**, in the **Views group**, click the **View** button to return to Design view. Leave the query open in Design view for the next activity.

Activity 13.17 Using Comparison Operators

Comparison operators are symbols that evaluate each field value to determine if it is the same (=), greater than (>), less than (<), or in between a range of values as specified by the criteria.

If no comparison operator is specified, equal (=) is assumed. For example, in the previous activity, you created a query to display only records where the *Amount* was 300. The comparison operator of = was assumed, and Access displayed only records that had entries equal to 300.

In this activity, you will specify criteria in the query to display records from the 13B Scholarships Awarded table that have scholarships that are *greater* than $300 and then to display scholarships that are *less* than $300.

1 Be sure your query from the last activity is displayed in Design view. On the **Criteria** row, click in the **Amount** field, delete the existing criteria, type **>300** and then press Enter. Compare your screen with Figure 13.42.

Unlike a field with a data type of *Text*, Access does not add quote marks around criteria entered in a field that has a data type of *Number* or *Currency*.

Figure 13.42

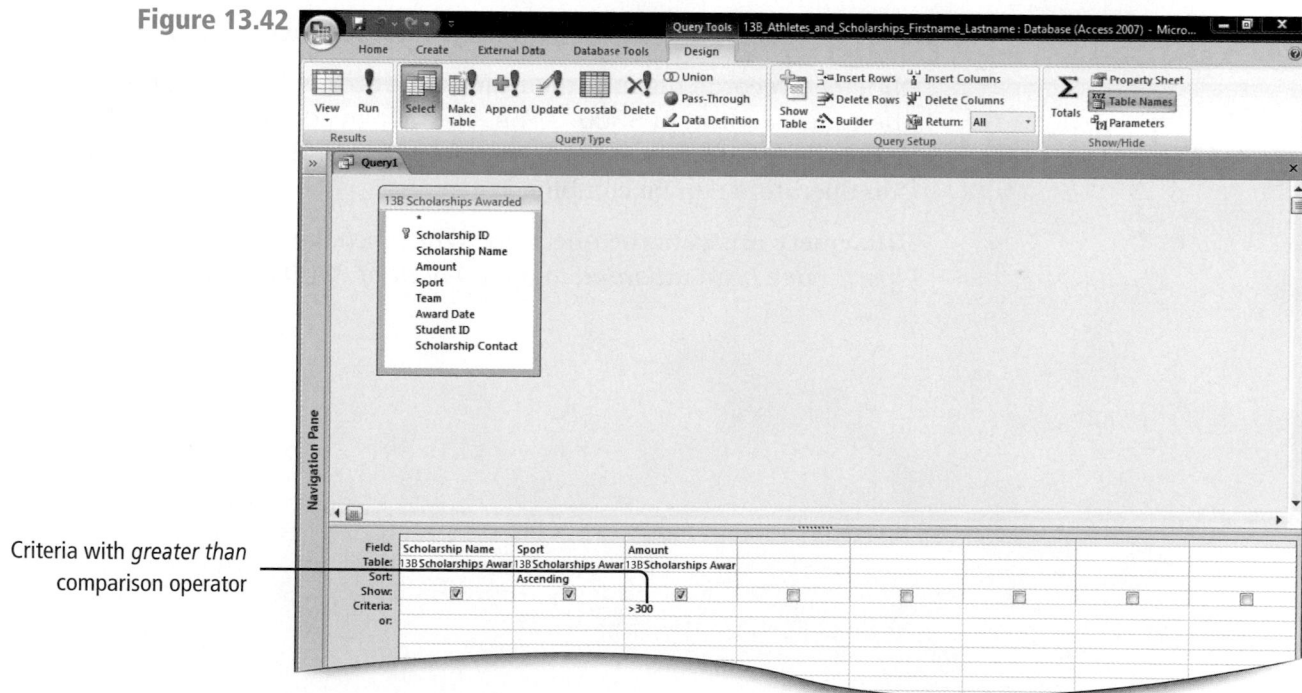

Criteria with *greater than* comparison operator

2 Click the **Design tab**, and then in the **Results group**, click the **Run** button.

Fourteen records match the criteria for an Amount that is greater than $300. The results show the records for which the Amount is *greater than* $300, but not *equal* to $300.

3 Click the **View** button to return to Design view. On the **Criteria** row, under **Amount**, delete the existing criteria, type **<300** Press ⏎, and then on the **Design tab**, in the **Results group**, click the **Run** button.

Eleven records display and each has an Amount less than $300. The results show the records for which the Amount is *less than* $300, but not *equal to* $300.

4 Switch to Design view. On the **Criteria** row, click in the **Amount** field, delete the existing criteria, type **>=300** and then press ⏎.

Note — Pressing Enter After Criteria is Added

If you press ⏎ or click in another column or row in the query design grid after you have added your criteria, you can see how Access alters the criteria so it can interpret what you have typed. Sometimes, there is no change, such as when a number is added to a number or currency field. Other times, Access may capitalize a letter or add quote marks or other symbols to clarify the criteria. Whether or not you press ⏎ after criteria is added does not affect the query results. It is used in this text to help you see how the program behaves.

---

5 **Run** the query, and then compare your screen with Figure 13.43.

Nineteen records display, including the records for scholarships in the exact amount of $300. Thus, the displayed records include scholarships *equal to* or *greater than* $300. In this manner, comparison operators can be combined.

This query answers the question, *Which scholarships, and for which sport, have been awarded in the amount of $300 or more?*

Figure 13.43

Records with a scholarship amount of $300 or more

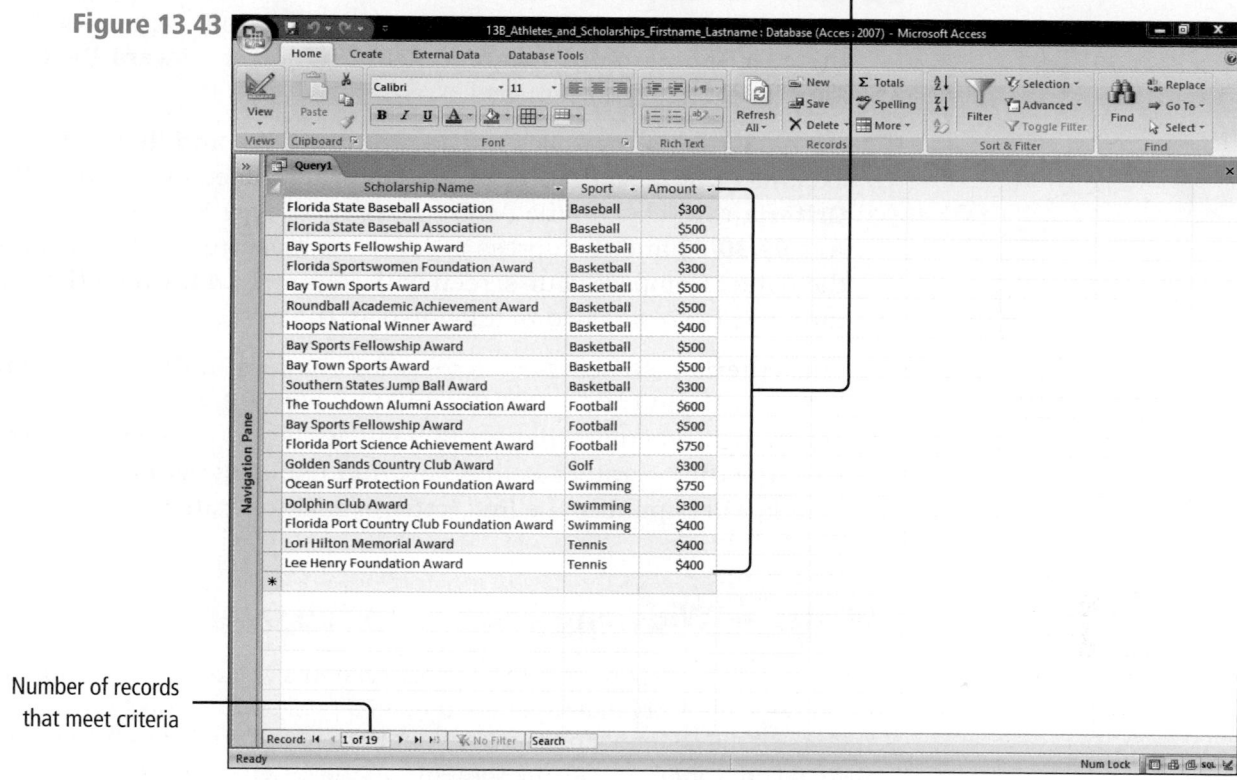

Number of records that meet criteria

6 On the **Quick Access Toolbar**, click the **Save** button 💾, and then in the **Save As** dialog box, type **13B $300 or More Firstname Lastname** Click **OK**.

7 From the **Office** menu 🔘, point to the **Print** button, and then click **Print Preview**. If you are printing your assignments on paper, in the **Print group**, click the **Print** button. In the displayed **Print** dialog box, click **OK**. To submit electronically, follow your instructor's directions.

8 Click the **Close Print Preview** button, and then **Close** ❌ the query. **Open** ⏩ the **Navigation Pane**, and notice that your new query displays under the table from which it retrieved the records.

Activity 13.18 Using the Between. . . And Comparison Operator

The ***Between . . . And operator*** is a comparison operator that looks for values within a range. It is particularly useful when you need to locate records that are within a range of dates, for example, scholarships awarded between August 1 and September 30. In this activity, you will create a new query from an existing query, and then add criteria to look for values within a range of dates. The query will answer the question *Which scholarships were awarded between August 1 and September 30?*

1 From the **Navigation Pane**, open your **13B $300 or More** query. From the **Office** menu 🔘, click **Save As**. In the **Save As** dialog box, type **13B Awards Aug-Sept Firstname Lastname** and then click **OK**.

2 Close [X] the **Navigation Pane**, and then on the **Home tab**, in the **Views group**, click the **View** button to switch to Design view. From the **13B Scholarships Awarded** field list, add the **Award Date** as the fourth field in the design grid.

3 On the **Criteria** row, click in the **Amount** field, and then delete the existing criteria so that the query is not restricted by amount. On the **Criteria** row, click in the **Award Date** field, type **Between 08/01/09 And 09/30/09** and then press [Enter]. Access places quote marks around the dates. Compare your screen with Figure 13.44, where the column has been widened to fully display the criteria.

This criteria instructs Access to look for values in the Award Date field that begin with 08/01/09 and end with 09/30/09. Both the beginning and ending dates will be included in the query results. If you type the operators *Between. . . And* using lowercase letters, Access will capitalize the first letter of each operator.

> ## Note — Widening Columns in the Query Grid
>
> For a better view of your criteria, you can widen a column in the design grid using the same techniques that are used in a table. In the selection bar at the top of the column, point to the right border and double-click to expand the column to fully display the contents on the criteria row. You can also drag the right border to the width you want.

Figure 13.44

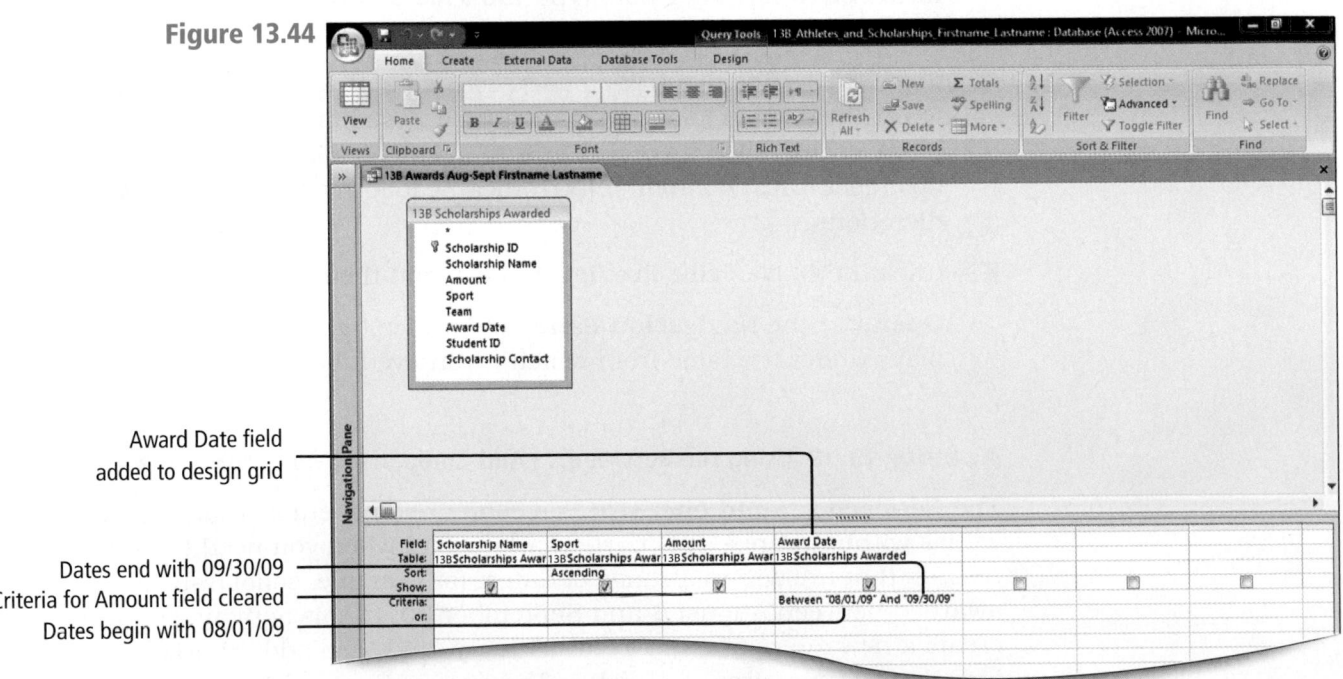

Award Date field added to design grid

Dates end with 09/30/09

Criteria for Amount field cleared

Dates begin with 08/01/09

4 **Run** the query and notice that three scholarships were awarded between the dates you specified in your criteria.

5 From the **Office** menu , point to the **Print** button, and then click **Print Preview**. If you are printing your assignments on paper, in the **Print group**, click the **Print** button. In the displayed **Print** dialog box, click **OK**. To submit electronically, follow your instructor's directions.

6 Click the **Close Print Preview** button. In the object window, **Close** the query, and then click **Yes** to save the changes to the design.

Open the **Navigation Pane**, and notice that your new query displays under the table from which it retrieved records.

Objective 10
Use Compound Criteria

You can specify more than one condition—criteria—in a query; this is called **compound criteria**. Compound criteria enable you to create queries that are quite specific. Two types of compound criteria used in queries are AND and OR, which are **logical operators**. Logical operators allow you to enter criteria for the same field or different fields.

Activity 13.19 Using AND Criteria in a Query

Compound criteria that create an AND condition will display the records in the query result that meet *both* parts of the specified criteria. In this activity, you will help Mr. Simmons answer the question *Which scholarships over $500 were awarded for Football?* The results will match the criteria >$500 *and* Football.

1 **Close** the **Navigation Pane**, and then from the **Create tab**, open a new query in Design view. **Add** the **13B Scholarships Awarded** table to the table area, **Close** the **Show Table** dialog box, and then adjust the height and width of the field list with the pointer.

2 Add the following fields to the design grid in the order given: **Scholarship Name**, **Sport**, and **Amount**.

3 On the **Criteria** row, click in the **Sport** field, type **Football** and then press (Tab). On the **Criteria** row, in the **Amount** field, type **>500** press (Enter), and then compare your screen with Figure 13.45.

The AND condition is created by placing the criteria for both fields on the same line in the Criteria row. The results will display records that contain *Football* and an amount greater than *$500*.

Figure 13.45

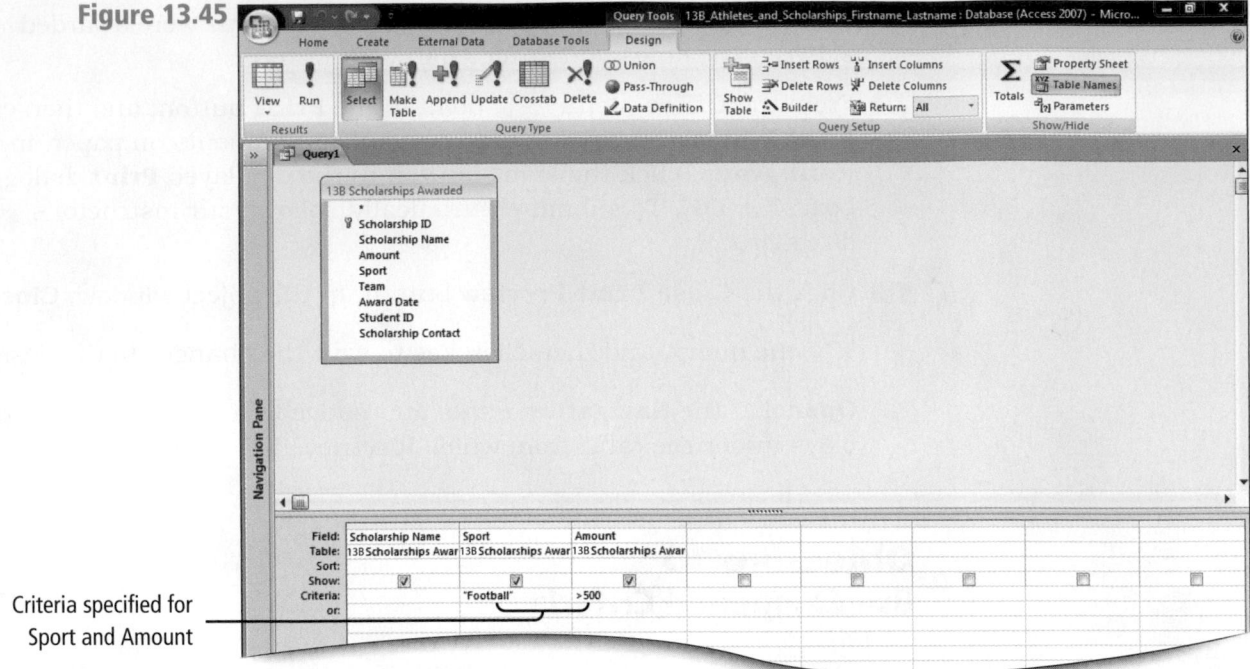

Criteria specified for
Sport and Amount

4 On the **Design tab**, in the **Results group**, click the **Run** button.

Two records display that match both conditions—Football in the Sport field and greater than $500 in the Amount field.

5 **Close** ❌ the query, click **Yes** to save changes to the query, and then in the **Save As** dialog box, type **13B Football and Over $500 Firstname Lastname** as the query name. Click **OK** or press Enter.

6 **Open** ≫ the **Navigation Pane**, click one time to select the query you just named and saved, and then from the **Office** menu 🗔, point to the **Print** button and click **Print Preview**. If you are printing your assignments on paper, in the **Print group**, click the **Print** button. In the displayed **Print** dialog box, click **OK**. To submit electronically, follow your instructor's directions.

7 Click the **Close Print Preview** button, and then **Close** ≪ the **Navigation Pane**.

You can print any selected object from the Navigation Pane in this manner—the object does not have to be displayed on your screen to print.

Activity 13.20 Using OR Criteria in a Query

Use the OR condition to specify multiple criteria for a single field, or multiple criteria on different fields when you want the records that meet either condition to display in the results. In this activity, you will help Mr. Simmons answer the question *Which scholarships over $400 were awarded in the sports of Baseball or Swimming?*

1 From the **Create tab**, open a new query in Design view. **Add** the **13B Scholarships Awarded** table, **Close** the dialog box, expand the field list, and then add the following four fields to the design grid in the order given: **Scholarship Name**, **Sport**, **Amount**, and **Award Date**.

2 On the **Criteria** row, click in the **Sport** field, and then type **Baseball**

3 In the design grid, locate the **or** row. On the **or** row, click in the **Sport** field, type **Swimming** and then press Enter. **Run** the query.

The query results display seven scholarship records whose Sport is either Baseball *or* Swimming. Use the OR condition in this manner to specify multiple criteria for a single field.

4 Return to Design view. Under **Sport**, on the **or** row, delete the text. Under **Sport**, click in the **Criteria** row, delete the existing text, and then type **Swimming Or Baseball** On the **Criteria** row, under **Amount**, type **>400** press Enter, and then compare your screen with Figure 13.46.

This is an alternative way to use the OR compound operator. Because criteria has been entered for two different fields, Access will return the records that are Baseball *or* Swimming and that have a scholarship awarded in an amount greater than $400.

In this manner, you can type multiple criteria for the same field on the Criteria row.

Figure 13.46

OR condition for two criteria in the same field

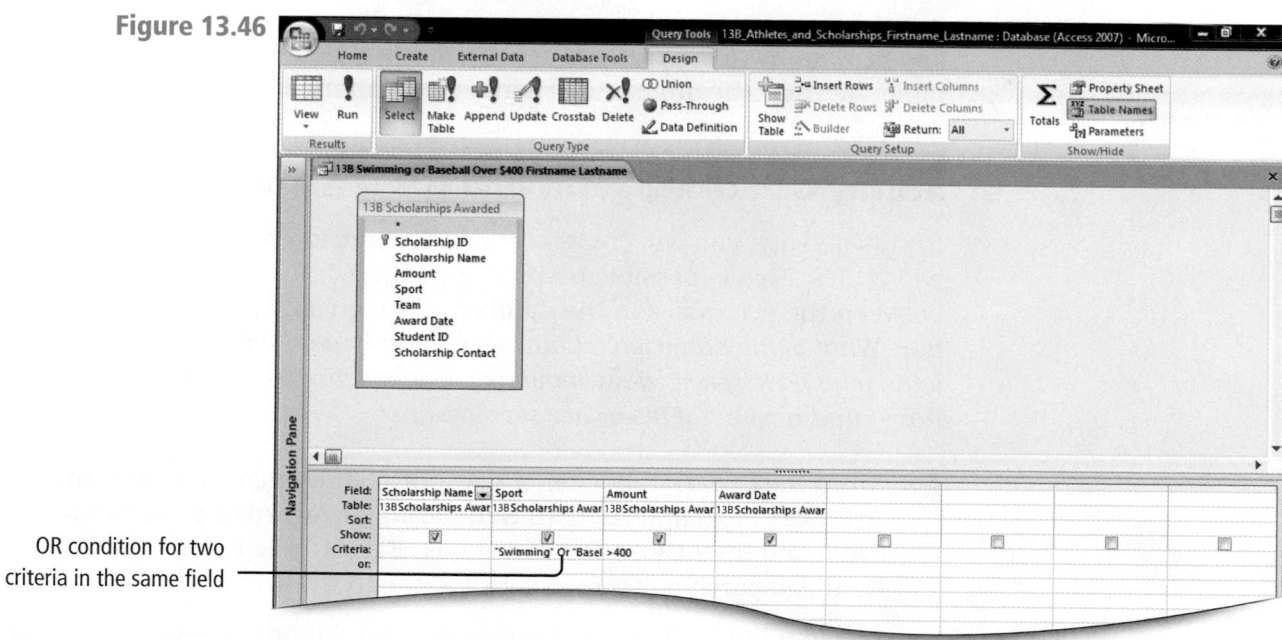

5 **Run** the query to display the two records that match the conditions.

6 **Close** ⊠ the query, click **Yes** to save changes to the query, and then in the **Save As** dialog box, type **13B Swimming or Baseball Over $400 Firstname Lastname** as the query name. Click **OK** or press Enter.

7 **Open** >> the **Navigation Pane**, click one time to select the query you just named and saved, and then from the **Office** menu 🖳, display the **Print Preview**. If you are printing your assignments on paper, in the **Print group**, click the **Print** button, and then click **OK**. To submit electronically, follow your instructor's directions.

8 Click the **Close Print Preview** button, and then **Close** « the **Navigation Pane**.

Objective 11
Create a Query Based on More Than One Table

In a relational database, you can retrieve information from more than one table. Recall that each table in a relational database contains all of the records about a single topic. Tables are joined by relating the primary key field in one table to a foreign key field in another table. This common field creates a relationship, which enables you to include data from more than one table in a query.

For example, the Athletes table contains all of the information about the student athletes—name, address, and so on. The Scholarships Awarded table includes the scholarship name, amount, award date, and so on. When an athlete receives a scholarship, only the Student ID field is included with the scholarship to identify who received the scholarship. It is not necessary to include, and would result in repeated information, if any other athlete information appeared in the Scholarships Awarded table, because the athlete information is contained in the Athletes table.

Activity 13.21 Creating a Query Based on More Than One Table

In this activity, you will create a query that retrieves information from two tables. This is possible because a relationship has been established between the two tables in the database. The query will answer the question *What is the name, email address, and phone number of student athletes who have received swimming or tennis scholarships, and what is the name and amount of his or her scholarship?*

1 From the **Create tab**, open a new query in Design view. **Add** the **13B Athletes** table and the **13B Scholarships Awarded** table to the table area, and then **Close** the dialog box. Expand the two tables, and then compare your screen with Figure 13.47.

The join line indicates the one-to-many relationship—one athlete can have many scholarships. Student ID is the common field in the two tables. Notice that Student ID is designated by a key in the Athletes table where it is the primary key field, but it is not designated by a key in the Scholarships Awarded table where it is the foreign key field.

Join line

Figure 13.47

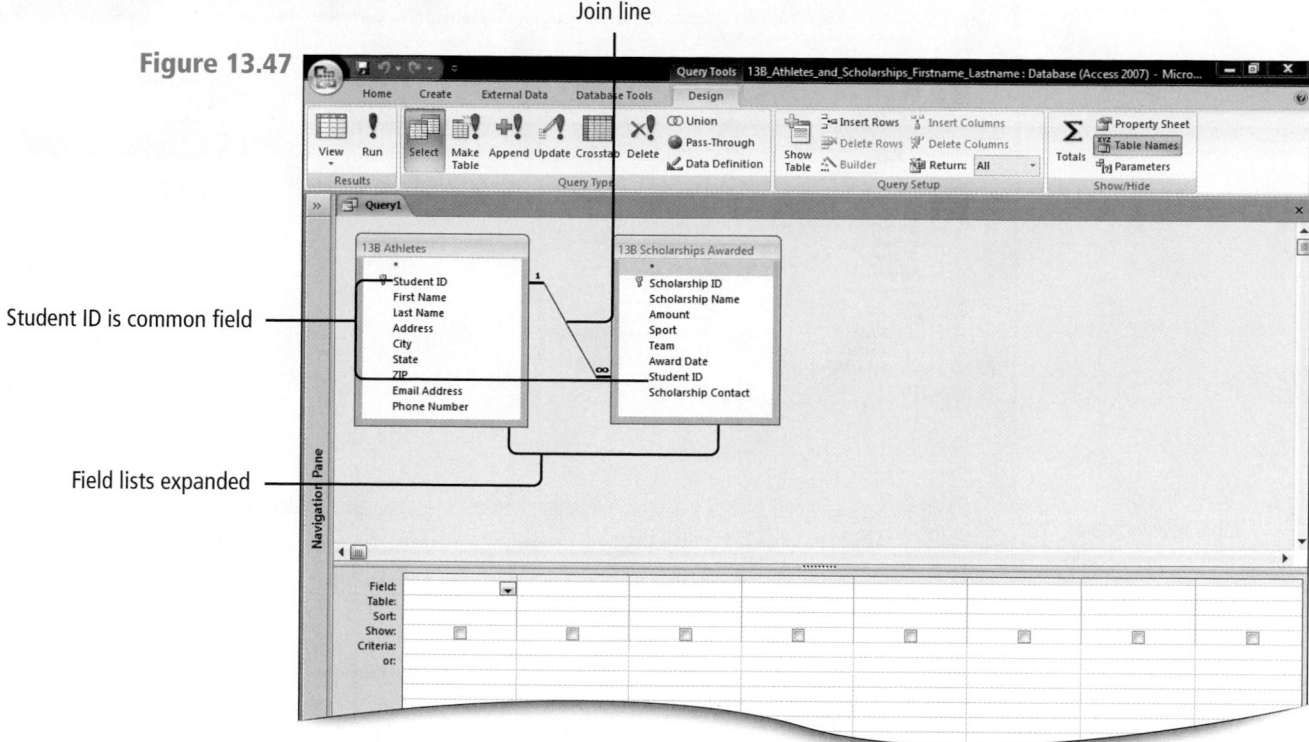

Student ID is common field

Field lists expanded

Navigation Pane

2 From the **13B Athletes** field list, add the following fields in the order given: **First Name**, **Last Name**, **Address**, **City**, **State**, and **ZIP**. On the **Sort** row, under **Last Name**, click to select **Ascending** to sort the records in alphabetical order by last name.

3 From the **13B Scholarships Awarded** field list, add **Scholarship Name**, **Sport**, and **Amount** to the design grid. On the **Criteria** row, under **Sport**, type **Swimming** On the **or** row, under **Sport**, type **Tennis** and then press Enter.

4 In the design grid, locate the second row—the **Table** row, and notice that for each field, the table from which the field was added is indicated. Compare your screen with Figure 13.48.

When using multiple tables in a query, this information is helpful, especially when some tables may include the same field names, such as address, but different data, such as a student's address or a coach's address.

Figure 13.48

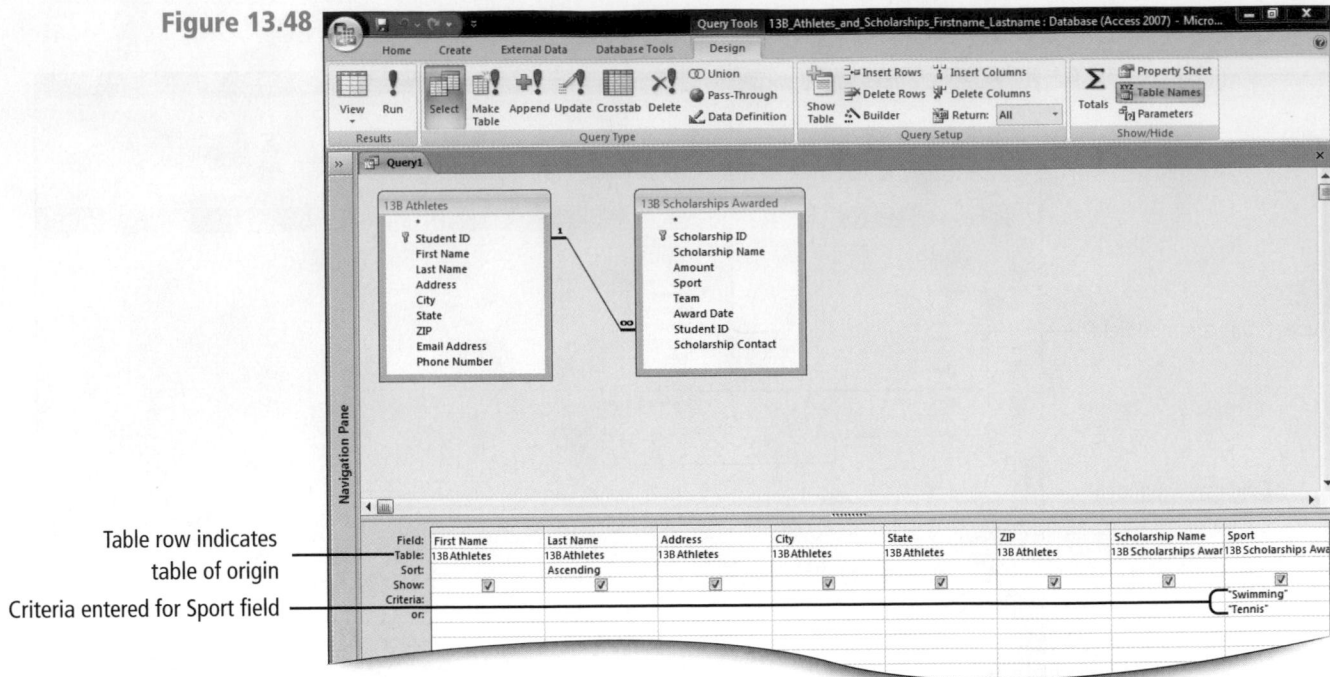

Table row indicates table of origin

Criteria entered for Sport field

5 **Run** the query.

The names and addresses of eight student athletes display. Notice that the First Name and Last Name is included in the query results even though the common field—Student ID—was *not* included in the query design. Because Student ID is included in both tables, and a one-to-many relationship was created between the tables, you can display data from both tables in one query.

Two students—*Arianna Kitasoe* and *Janice Murphy*—received scholarships in both Swimming and Tennis. Recall that *one* student athlete can have *many* scholarships.

6 Return to Design view. From the **Athletes** field list, add **Phone Number** to the design grid. Point to **Email Address**, drag it to the design grid on top of **Amount**, and then release the mouse button.

When you release the mouse button, Email Address is inserted to the left of the Amount field.

7 In the design grid, select, by dragging in the gray selection bar, the **Address**, **City**, **State**, and **ZIP** fields, and then press Delete. In the design grid, select the **Amount** field, and then drag it to the first field position in the grid. Click outside of the grid to cancel the selection, and then compare your screen with Figure 13.49.

Phone Number is added as the last field in the design grid. The Address, City, State, and ZIP fields are deleted. The Amount field is in the first position. In this manner, you can modify your query design.

Figure 13.49

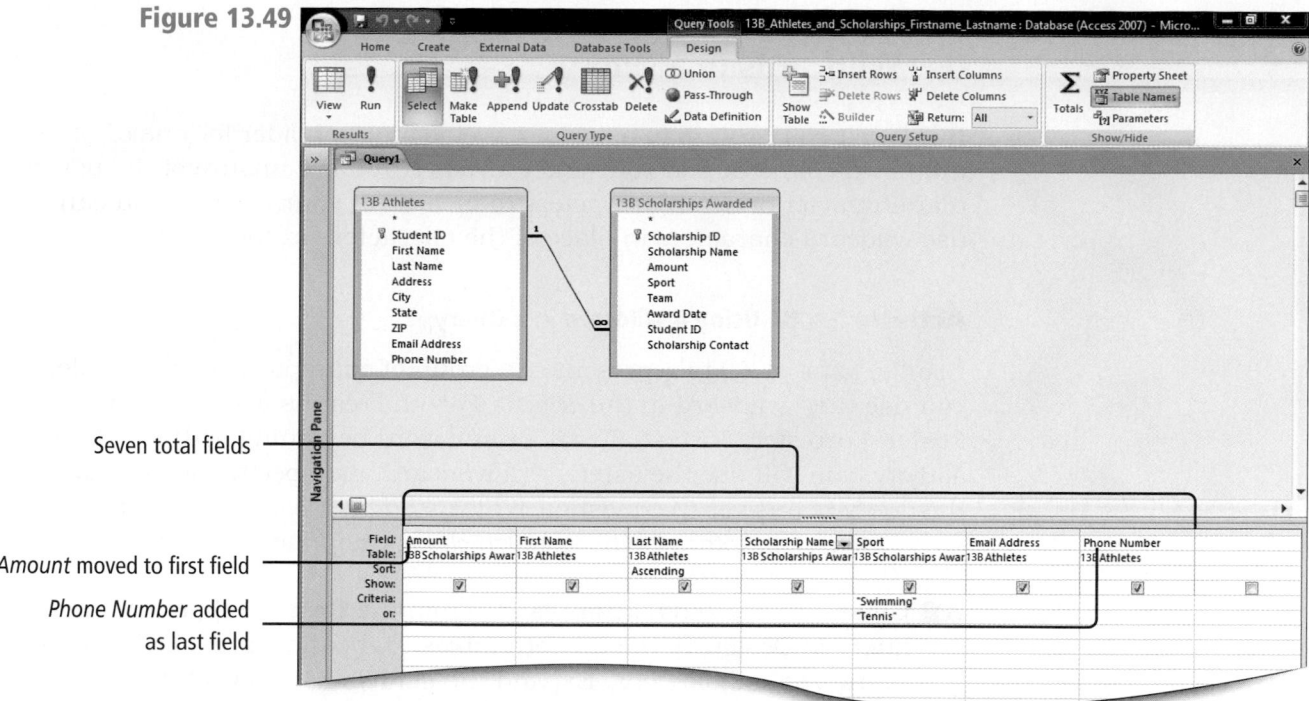

Seven total fields

Amount moved to first field

Phone Number added
as last field

8 **Run** the query again. Using techniques similar to that of a table, select all the columns in the query and apply **Best Fit** (with the columns selected, in the field heading row, point to the right boundary of any of the selected rows to display the ⊞ pointer, and then double-click to apply Best Fit to all of the selected columns).

9 On the **Quick Access Toolbar**, click the **Save** button 🖫, type **13B Swimming and Tennis Firstname Lastname** and then click **OK**. Display the query in **Print Preview**, set the **Margins** to **Normal**, and then change the orientation to **Landscape**. Print or submit electronically as directed.

10 **Close Print Preview**, close the query, open the **Navigation Pane**, and notice that your new query displays under *both* tables from which it retrieved records.

In the Tables and Related Views arrangement of the Navigation Pane, any object that references a table will display with that table.

More Knowledge

Add a Table to the Table Area

To add another table to the table area, in the Query Setup group, click Show Table; or, right-click in the table area, and from the shortcut menu, click Show Table.

Objective 12
Use Wildcards in a Query

Wildcard characters in a query serve as a placeholder for one or more unknown characters in your criteria. When you are unsure of the particular character or set of characters to include in your criteria, you can use wildcard characters in place of the characters in the criteria.

Activity 13.22 Using a Wildcard in a Query

Use the asterisk (*) to represent any group of characters. For example, if you use the * wildcard in the criteria Fo*, the results would return Foster, Forrester, Forrest, Fossil, or any word beginning with *Fo*. In this activity, you will use the asterisk (*) wildcard and specify the criteria in the query to answer the question *Which student athletes received scholarships from local Rotary Clubs, country clubs, and foundations?*

1 **Close** `«` the **Navigation Pane**. From the **Create tab**, start a new query in Design view, add both tables to the table area, and close the **Show Table** dialog box. Expand the field lists to view all the field names. Add the following fields to the design grid: **First Name** and **Last Name** from the **13B Athletes** table, and **Scholarship Contact** from the **13B Scholarships Awarded** table. On the **Sort** row, sort the query results in **Ascending** order by **Last Name**.

2 On the **Criteria** row, under **Scholarship Contact**, type **Rotary*** and then press Enter.

The wildcard character * is used as a placeholder to match any number of characters. When you press Enter, *Like* is added by Access at the beginning of the criteria. This is used to compare a sequence of characters and test whether or not the text matches a pattern.

Access will automatically insert expressions similar to this when creating queries.

3 **Run** the query to display the three student athletes who received scholarships from Rotary Clubs.

4 Return to the Design view. On the **or** row, under **Scholarship Contact**, type ***Country Club** and then press Enter.

The * can be used at the beginning or end of the criteria. The position of the wildcard determines the location of the unknown characters. Here you will search for records that end in *Country Club*.

5 **Run** the query to display a total of six records.

6 Return to Design view. In the next available row under **Scholarship Contact**, type ***Foundation*** press Enter, and then compare your screen with Figure 13.50.

In this manner, the query will return records that have the word *Foundation* anywhere—beginning, middle, or end—in the field. You can also see that you can combine many *or* criteria in a query.

Figure 13.50

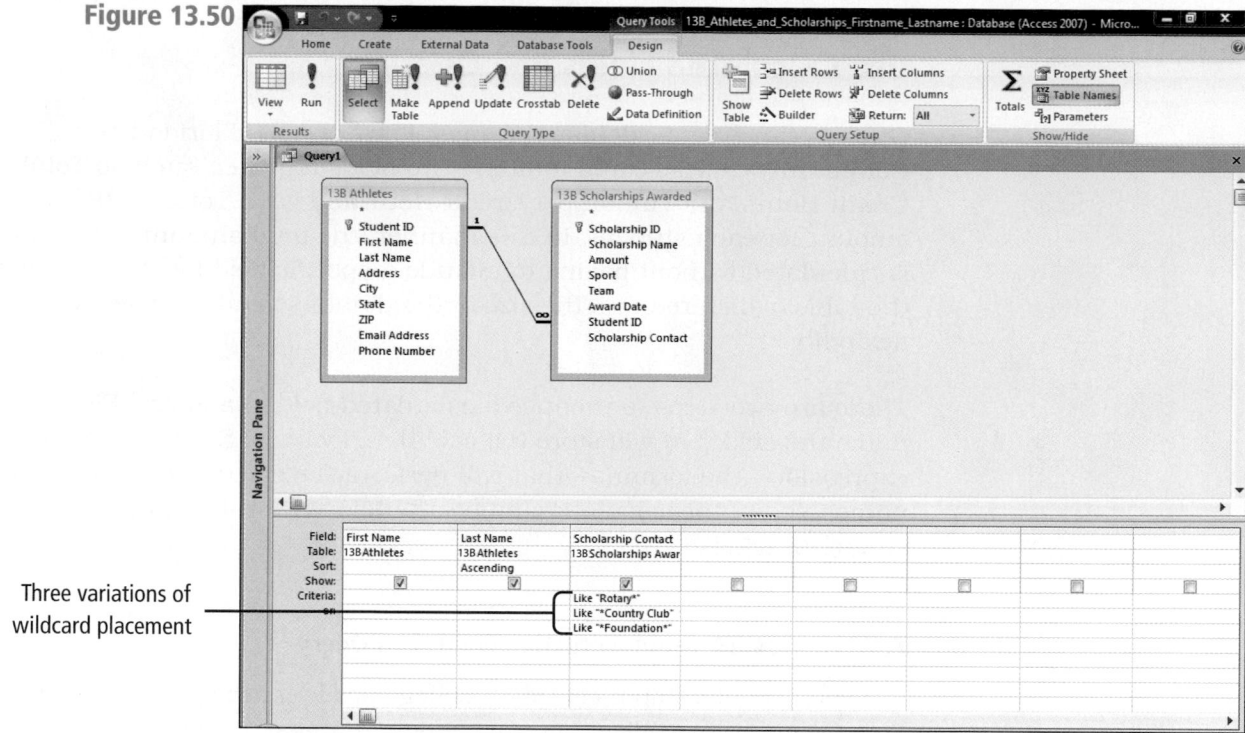

Three variations of wildcard placement

7 **Run** the query to display a total of 28 records.

Twenty-eight scholarships were awarded from either a Country Club, a Rotary Club, or a Foundation.

8 On the **Quick Access Toolbar**, click the **Save** button ⊞, and name the query **13B Clubs and Foundations Firstname Lastname** Display the **Print Preview**, and print your result if you are submitting paper assignments, or submit electronically as directed. **Close Print Preview**, **Close** the query ☒, and then **Open** ⟫ the **Navigation Pane**.

Because the query retrieved data from two tables, the query displays below each table's name.

More Knowledge

Search for a Single Unknown Character by Using the ? Wildcard

The question mark (?) is another wildcard that is used to search for unknown single characters. For each question mark included in a criteria, any character can be inserted. For example, if you used *b?d* as a criteria, the query could locate bid, bud, bed or any three-character word beginning with *b* and ending with *d*. If *b??d* is entered as the criteria, the results could include bind, bend, bard or any four-character word beginning with *b* and ending with *d*.

Objective 13
Use Calculated Fields in a Query

Queries can create calculated values. For example, Florida Port Community College could multiply two fields together, such as Total Credit Hours and Tuition per Credit Hour and get a Total Tuition Due amount for each student. In this manner, the total amount of tuition due is calculated without having to include a specific field for this amount in the table, which reduces the size of the database and provides more flexibility.

There are two steps to produce a calculated field in a query. First, name the field that will store the calculated values. Second, write the expression—the formula—that will perform the calculation. Each field name used in the calculation must be enclosed within its own pair of square brackets.

Activity 13.23 Using Calculated Fields in a Query

For each scholarship received by college student athletes, the Florida Port Community College Alumni Association has agreed to donate an amount equal to 50 percent of each scholarship. In this activity, you will create a calculated field to determine the additional amount each scholarship is worth. The query will answer the question *What will the value of each scholarship be if the Alumni Association makes a matching 50% donation?*

1 **Close** « the **Navigation Pane**. From the **Create tab**, start a new query in Design view. **Add** the **13B Scholarships Awarded** table, close the **Show Table** dialog box, and expand the field list. Add the following fields to the design grid: **Student ID**, **Scholarship Name**, and **Amount**.

2 Click in the **Sort** row under **Student ID**, click the **Sort arrow**, and then click **Ascending**. In the **Field** row, right-click in the first empty column to display a shortcut menu, and then click **Zoom**.

The Zoom dialog box that displays gives you working space so that you can see the calculation as you type it. The calculation can also be typed directly in the empty Field box in the column.

3 In the **Zoom** dialog box, type **Matching Donation: [Amount]*0.5** and then compare your screen with Figure 13.51.

The first element, *Matching Donation*, is the new field name where the calculated amounts will display. Following that is a colon (:). A colon in a calculated field separates the new field name from the expression. *Amount* is in square brackets because it is an existing field name from the 13B Scholarships Awarded table. It contains the information on which the calculation will be performed. Following the square brackets is an asterisk (*), which in math calculations signifies multiplication. Finally, the percentage (50% or 0.5) is indicated.

Figure 13.51

Calculated value

New field name

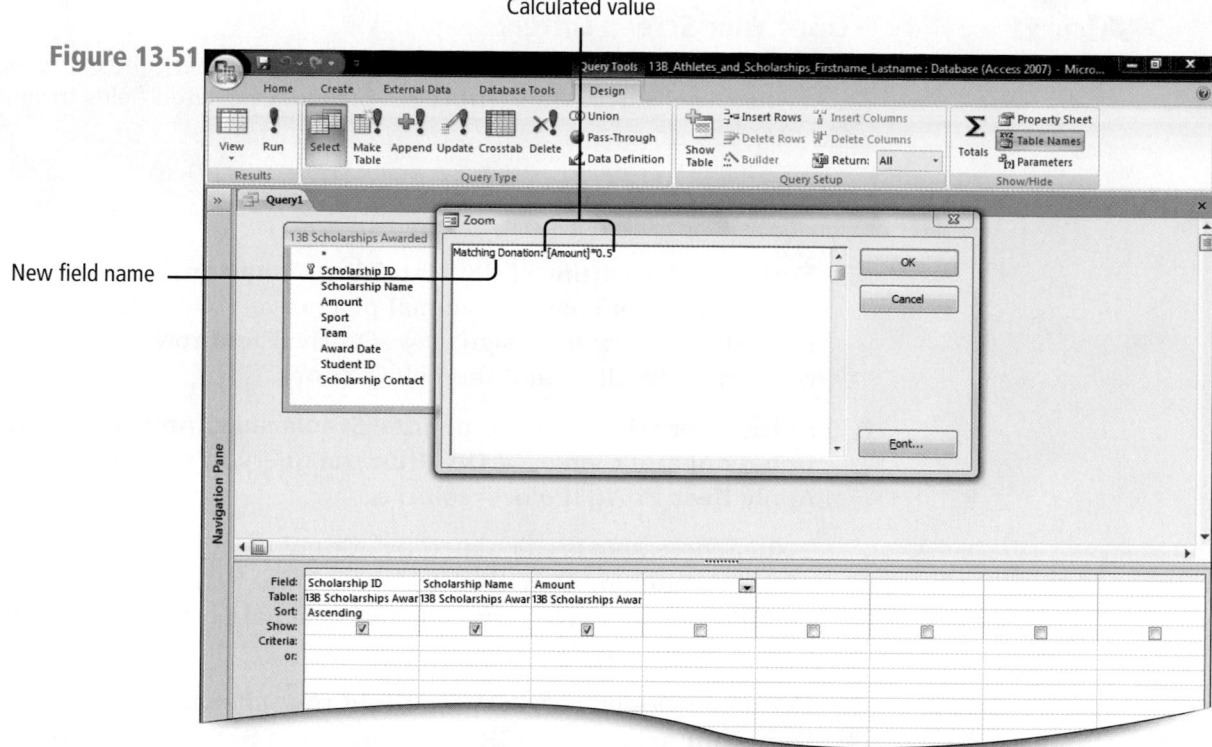

4 In the **Zoom** dialog box, click **OK**, and then **Run** the query. Select all the columns and apply **Best Fit**. Compare your screen with Figure 13.52.

The query results display the three fields from the 13B Scholarships Awarded table plus a fourth field—Matching Donation—in which a calculated amount displays. Each calculated amount equals the amount in the Amount field multiplied by 0.5.

Figure 13.52

New calculated field created (50% of Amount)

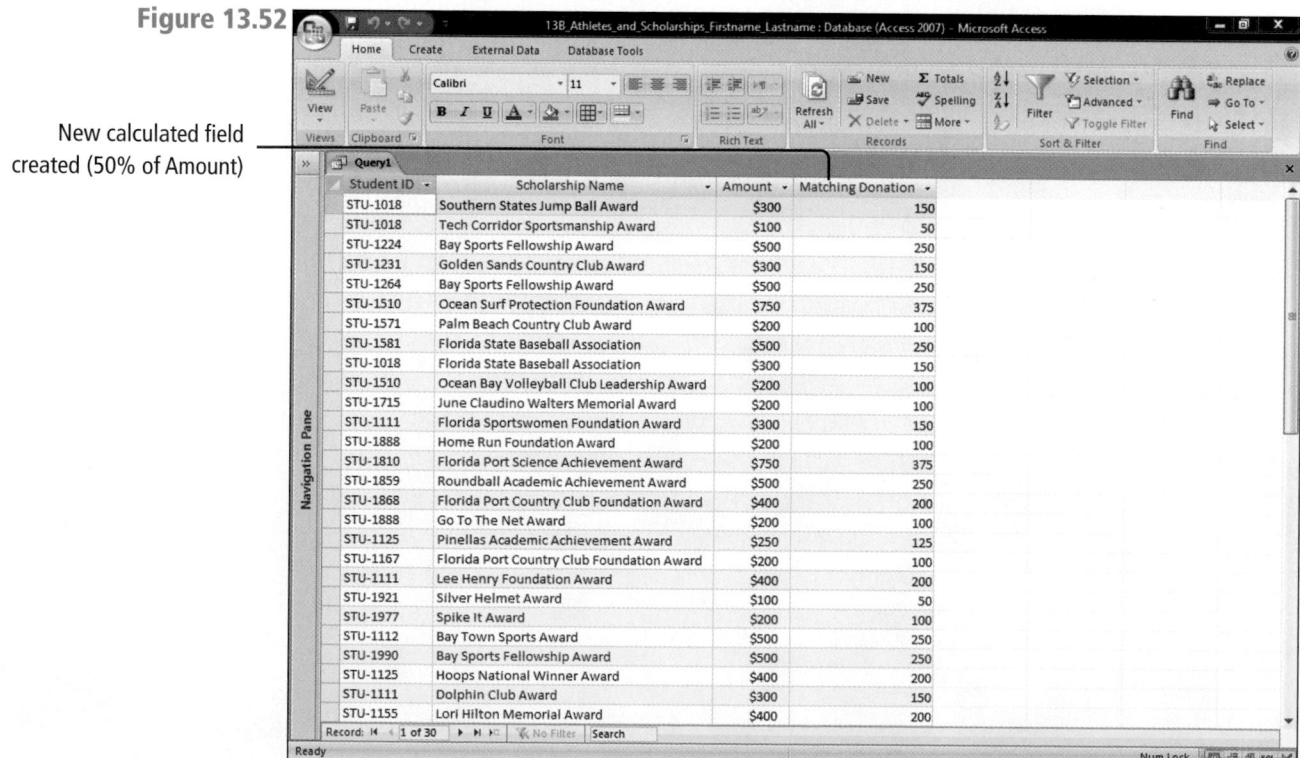

Alert! **Does Your Screen Differ?**

If your calculations in a query do not work, carefully check the expression you typed. Spelling or syntax errors will prevent calculated fields from working properly.

5 Notice the formatting of the **Matching Donation** field—there are no dollar signs, commas, or decimal places; you will adjust this formatting later. Return to Design view. On the **Field** row, in the first empty column, right-click, and then click **Zoom**.

6 In the **Zoom** dialog box, type **Total Scholarship: [Amount]+[Matching Donation]** and then click **OK**. **Run** the query to view the results. Apply **Best Fit** to the new column.

Total Scholarship is calculated by adding together the Amount field and the Matching Donation field. The Total Scholarship column includes dollar signs, commas, and decimal points, which carried over from the Amount field.

7 Return to Design view. On the **Field** row, click in the **Matching Donation** field. On the **Design tab**, in the **Show/Hide group**, click the **Property Sheet** button. Alternatively, right-click the Matching Donation field, and then click Properties.

The Property Sheet task pane displays on the right side of your screen. Here you can customize fields in a query, for example, the format of numbers in the field.

8 In the **Property Sheet** task pane, on the **General tab**, click the text *Format*, and then click the **arrow** that displays. Compare your screen with Figure 13.53.

A list of possible formats for this field displays.

Figure 13.53

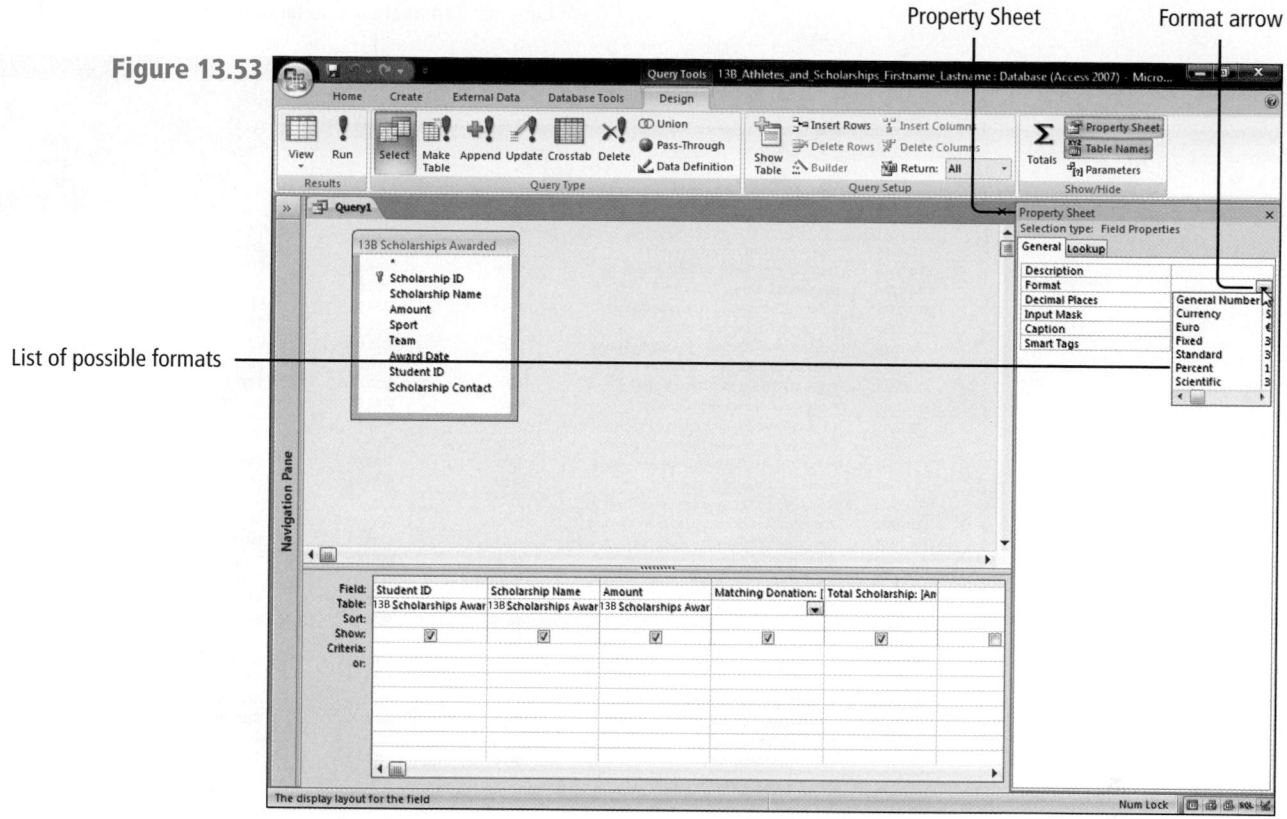

Property Sheet

Format arrow

List of possible formats

[9] In the list of formats, click **Currency**, and then **Close** ⊠ the **Property Sheet** task pane.

[10] **Run** the query to view the results. If necessary, select all the columns, and apply **Best Fit**. Click in any record to cancel the selection, and then compare your screen with Figure 13.54.

The Matching Donation column displays with currency formatting—a dollar sign, thousands comma separators, and two decimal places.

Currency format applied to all columns

Figure 13.54

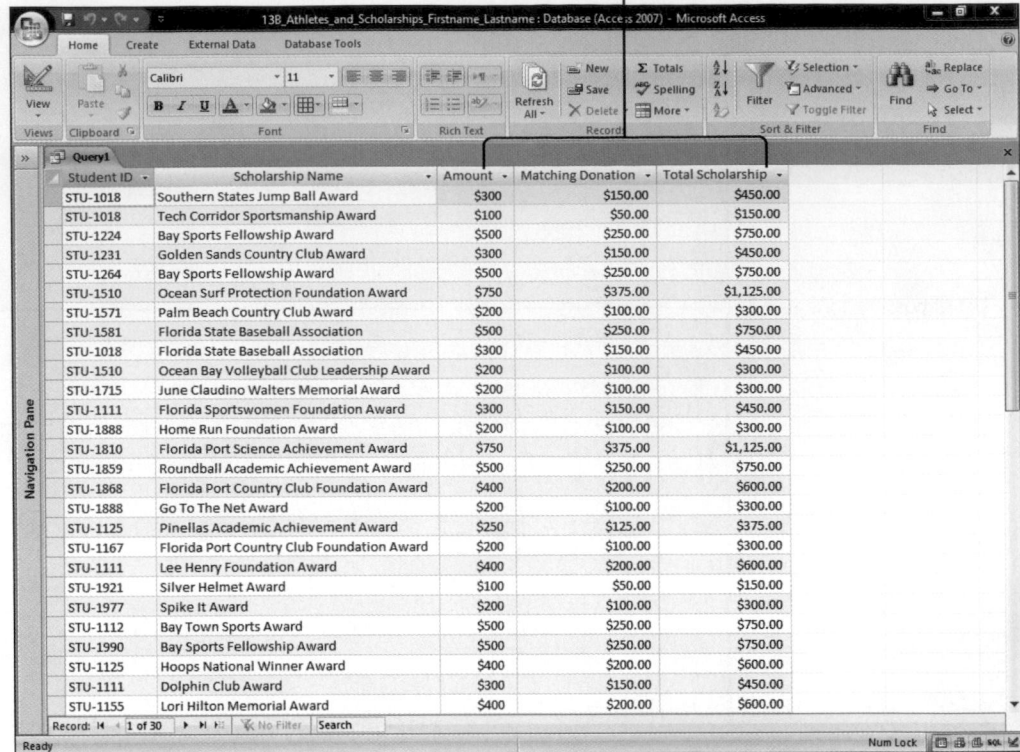

11 On the **Quick Access Toolbar**, click the **Save** button, and then name the query **13B Matching Donations Firstname Lastname** Display the **Print Preview**, change the **Orientation** to **Landscape**, and then print or submit electronically as directed. **Close Print Preview**, and then **Close** the query.

Objective 14
Group Data and Calculate Statistics in a Query

In Access queries, you can perform statistical calculations on a group of records. Calculations that are performed on a group of records are called *aggregate functions*. In the activities that follow, you will use AVG, SUM, MAX, and MIN functions. As you progress in your study of Access, you will use other functions.

Activity 13.24 Using the MIN, MAX, AVG and SUM Functions in a Query

In this activity, you will use the average, sum, maximum, and minimum functions in a query to examine the amounts of scholarships awarded. The last query will answer the question *What is the total amount of scholarships awarded?*

1 From the **Create tab**, create a new query in Design view. **Add** the **13B Scholarships Awarded** table, close the **Show Table** dialog box, and then expand the field list. Add **Amount** to the design grid.

When you want to summarize a field, include only the field you want to summarize in the query, so that the aggregate function (sum, average, minimum, maximum, and so forth) is applied to that single field.

2 On the **Design tab**, in the **Show/Hide group**, click the **Totals** button to add a **Total** row as the third row in the design grid. Notice that in the design grid, on the **Total** row, under **Amount**, *Group By* displays.

Here you select the function—such as Avg, Sum, Min, or Max—that you want to use for this field.

3 In the **Total** row, under **Amount**, click in the **Group By** box, and then click the **arrow** to display the list of functions. Access supports the aggregate functions summarized in the table shown in Figure 13.55. Take a moment to review this table, and then compare your screen with Figure 13.56.

Aggregate Functions

Function Name	What It Does
Sum	Totals the values in a field.
Avg	Averages the values in a field.
Min	Locates the smallest value in a field.
Max	Locates the largest value in a field.
Count	Counts the number of records in a field.
StDev	Calculates the Standard Deviation on the values in a field.
Var	Calculates the Variance on the values in a field.
First	Displays the First value in a field.
Last	Displays the Last value in a field.
Expression	Creates a calculated field that includes an aggregate function.
Where	Limits records displayed to those that match a condition specified on the Criteria row.

Figure 13.55

Figure 13.56

List of aggregate functions

Totals button in the Show/Hide group

Total row added to design grid

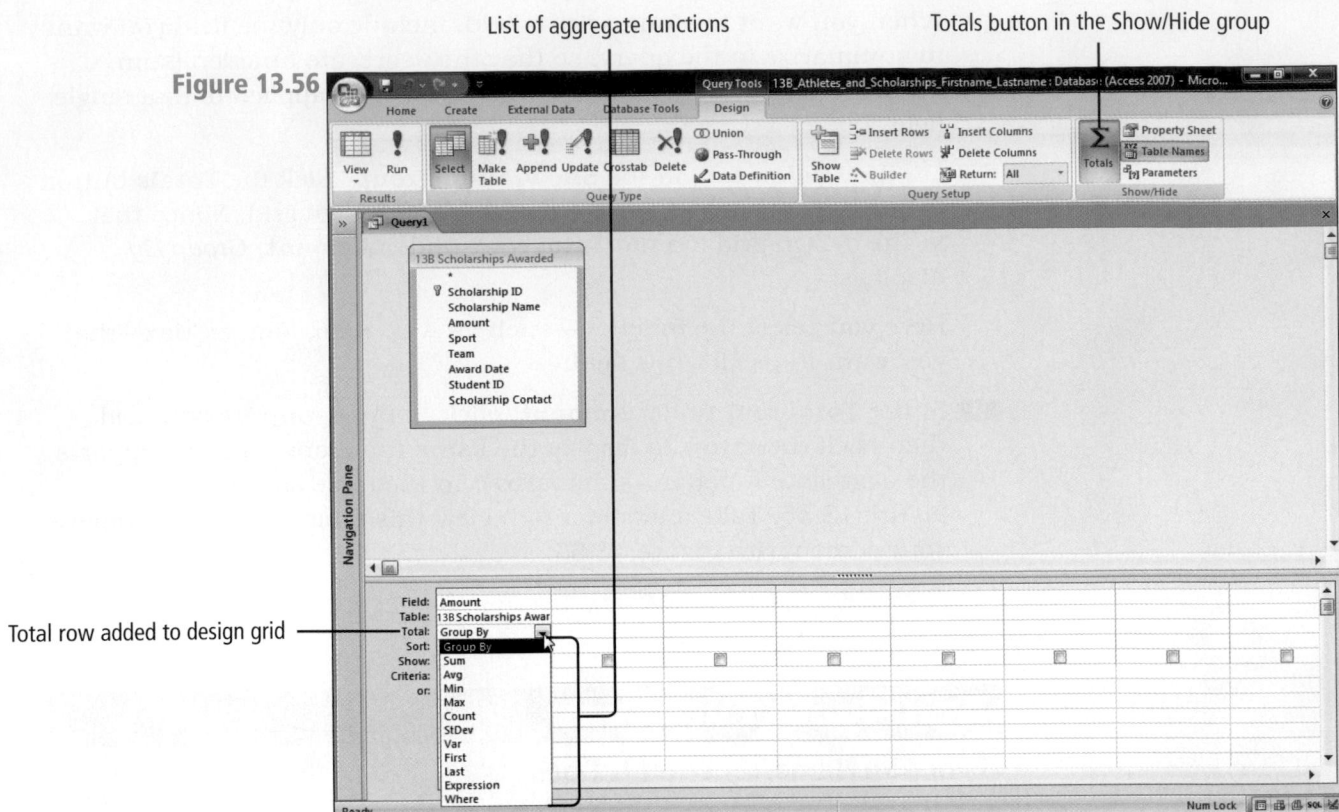

4 From the list of functions, click **Min**, and then **Run** the query. Double-click the right boundary of the column heading to widen the column.

Access calculates the minimum (smallest) scholarship award—$100.00. The field name, *MinOfAmount* displays for the calculation. This query answers the question, *What is the minimum (smallest) scholarship amount awarded?*

5 Return to Design view. Using the technique you just practiced, select the **Max** function, and then **Run** the query.

The maximum (largest) scholarship amount is $750.00.

6 Switch to Design view, select the **Avg** function, and then **Run** the query.

The average scholarship amount awarded is $358.33.

7 Return to Design view. Select the **Sum** function. **Run** the query.

Access sums the Amount field for all records and displays a result of *$10,750.00*. The field name, SumOfAmount, displays. This query answers the question, *What is the total of all the scholarships awarded?*

Activity 13.25 Grouping Data in a Query

The aggregate functions can also be used to calculate totals by groups of data. For example, if you wanted to group (summarize) the amount of scholarships awarded to each student, you would include the Student ID field, in addition to the Amount field, and then group all of the records for each student together to calculate a total awarded to each student. Similarly, you could calculate how much money was awarded to each sport.

1 Switch to Design view. Add the **Student ID** field to the design grid.

On the Total row, under Student ID, *Group By* displays by default. The design of this query will group—summarize—the records by StudentID and calculate a total Amount for each student.

2 **Run** the query to display the results, apply **Best Fit** to the columns, click any record to deselect, and then compare your screen with Figure 13.57.

The query calculates totals for each student.

Figure 13.57

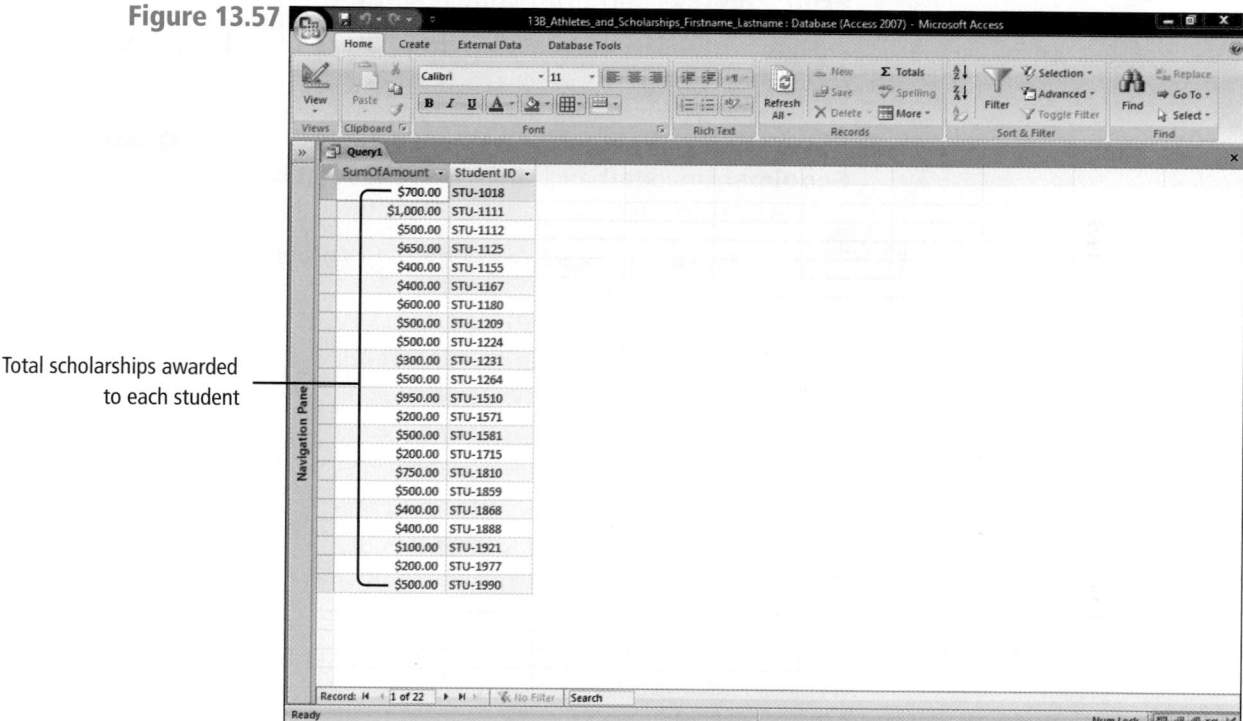

Total scholarships awarded to each student

3 Switch to Design view. In the design grid, select and delete the **Student ID** field, and then add the **Sport** field to the design grid. **Run** the query to see the results. Compare your screen with Figure 13.58.

Access summarizes the data by each sport. You can see that Basketball received the largest total Amount—$3,500.00.

Figure 13.58

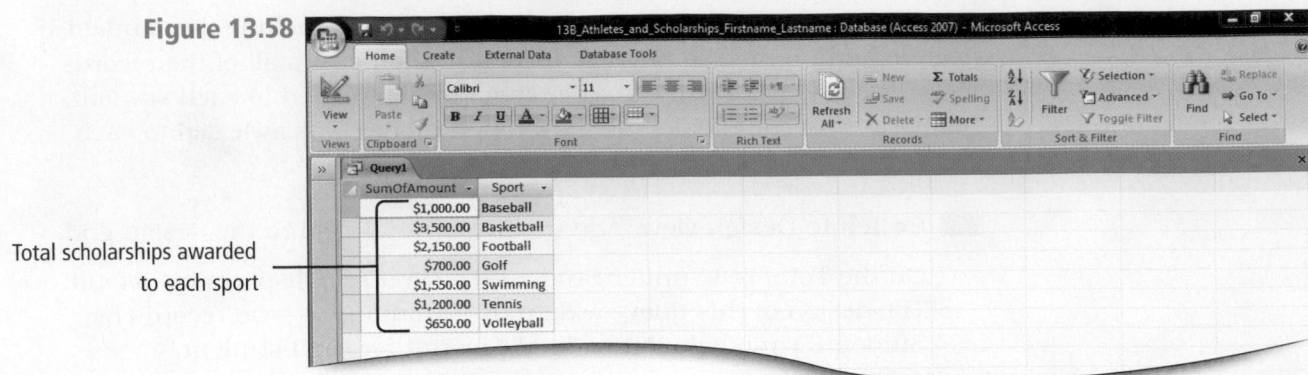

Total scholarships awarded to each sport

SumOfAmount	Sport
$1,000.00	Baseball
$3,500.00	Basketball
$2,150.00	Football
$700.00	Golf
$1,550.00	Swimming
$1,200.00	Tennis
$650.00	Volleyball

4 On the **Quick Access Toolbar**, click the **Save** button, and then name the query **13B Totals by Sport Firstname Lastname** Display the **Print Preview**, and print your result if you are submitting paper assignments. **Close Print Preview**, **Close** ✕ the query, and then **Open** » the **Navigation Pane** to view the queries you have created.

5 **Close** « the **Navigation Pane**, **Close** your **13B_Athletes_ Scholarships** database, and then **Exit Access**.

End You have completed Project 13B ——————

There's More You Can Do!

Close Access and any other open windows. Display the Start menu, click Computer, and then navigate to the student files that accompany this textbook. In the folder **02_theres_more_you_can_do**, locate and open the folder for this chapter. Open and print the instructions for this project, which are provided to you in Adobe PDF format.

Try IT! 1— Password Protect Your Database

In this Try It! exercise, you will encrypt and password protect your database to conceal data and prevent unwanted users from opening your database.

Content-Based Assessments

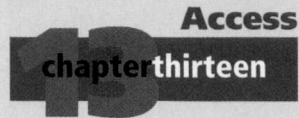

Summary

Importing an Excel spreadsheet is an efficient way to create new tables in an Access database. Sorting data in a table reorders the records based on one or more fields and is a quick way to alphabetize records or to find the highest or lowest amount in a numeric, currency, or date field. Use queries to ask complex questions about the data in a database in a manner that Access can interpret. Save queries so they can be run as needed against current records. By using queries, you can limit the fields that display, add criteria to restrict the number of records in the query result, create calculated values, and include data from more than one table.

Key Terms

Content-Based Assessments

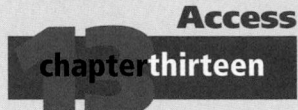

Matching

Match each term in the second column with its correct definition in the first column. Write the letter of the term on the blank line in front of the correct definition.

_____ **1.** The area directly below the Ribbon that displays information such as security alerts when there is potentially unsafe, active content in an Office 2007 document that you open.

_____ **2.** An area of the Access program where you can view the security and privacy settings for your Access installation.

_____ **3.** A type of database in which the tables in the database can relate or connect to other tables through common fields.

_____ **4.** Fields that contain the same data in more than one table.

_____ **5.** An association that is established between two tables using common fields.

_____ **6.** A relationship between two tables where one record in the first table corresponds to many records in the second table—the most common type of relationship in Access.

_____ **7.** A list of the field names in a table.

_____ **8.** The field that is included in the related table so that it can be joined to the primary key in another table for the purpose of creating a relationship.

_____ **9.** A set of rules that Access uses to ensure that the data between related tables is valid.

_____ **10.** In the Relationships window, the line joining two tables that visually indicates the related field and the type of relationship.

_____ **11.** The process of arranging data in a specific order based on the value in each field.

_____ **12.** A sorting order that arranges text in alphabetical order (A to Z) or numbers from the lowest to highest number.

_____ **13.** A database object that retrieves (selects) specific data from one or more tables and then displays the specified data in datasheet view.

_____ **14.** When sorting on multiple fields in datasheet view, the field that will be used for the first level of sorting.

_____ **15.** The table or tables from which a query selects its data.

A Ascending

B Common fields

C Data source

D Field list

E Foreign key

F Join line

G Message Bar

H One-to-many

I Outermost sort field

J Referential integrity

K Relational

L Relationship

M Select query

N Sorting

O Trust Center

Content-Based Assessments

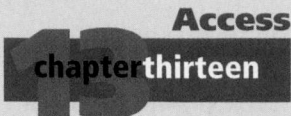
Fill in the Blank

Write the correct answer in the space provided.

1. The upper pane of the Query window, which displays the field lists for tables that are used in the query is the _____ _____.

2. The lower pane of the Query window, which displays the design of the query is the _____ _____.

3. The process in which Access searches the records in the table(s) included in a query design, finds the records that match the specified criteria, and then displays those records in a datasheet is called _____.

4. Conditions that identify the specific records you are looking for are called _____.

5. Each time you open a saved query, Access _____ the query again and displays the results based on the data stored in the associated tables; thus, the results always reflect the latest information in the tables.

6. A sequence of characters, which when used in query criteria, must be matched, is referred to as a _____ _____.

7. A criteria that searches for fields that are empty is called _____ _____.

8. A criteria that searches for fields that are *not* empty is called _____ _____.

9. Symbols that evaluate each field value to determine if it is the same (=), greater than (>), less than (<), or in between a range of values as specified by the criteria are referred to as _____ _____.

10. In a(n) _____ condition, both parts of the query must be met.

11. In a(n) _____ condition, either part of the query must be met.

12. Multiple conditions in a query or filter are called _____ _____.

13. In a query, a character that serves as a placeholder for one or more unknown characters is a _____.

14. Calculations that are performed on a group of records are called _____ _____.

15. To locate the largest value in a group of records, use the _____ function.

Content-Based Assessments

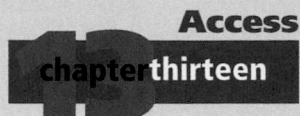

Skills Review

Project 13C — Music Department

In this project, you will apply the skills you practiced from the Objectives in Project 13A.

Objectives: 1. *Open an Existing Database;* **2.** *Create Table Relationships;* **3.** *Sort Records in a Table;* **4.** *Create a Query in Design View;* **5.** *Create a New Query from an Existing Query;* **6.** *Sort Query Results;* **7.** *Specify Criteria in a Query.*

In the following Skills Review, you will assist Pascal Sanchez, Florida Port Community College Music Director, in using his database to answer various questions about the instruments in the Music Department's inventory. Your query results will look similar to those shown in Figure 13.59.

For Project 13C, you will need the following file:

a13C_Music_Department

**You will save your database as
13C_Music_Department_Firstname_Lastname**

Figure 13.59

(Project 13C–Music Department continues on the next page)

Content-Based Assessments

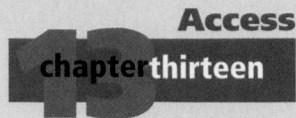
(Project 13C–Music Department continued)

1. From the student files that accompany this textbook, locate the file **a13C_Music_Department**. Copy and then paste the file to your **Access Chapter 13** folder. Rename the file 13C_Music_Department_Firstname_Lastname Start Access, open your database, and then enable the content.

2. Click the **Database Tools tab**. In the **Show/Hide group**, click the **Relationships** button. On the **Design tab**, in the **Relationships group**, click the **Show Table** button. Click the **13C Student Musicians** table, and then at the bottom of the dialog box, click **Add**. Point to the **13C Instruments Inventory** table, and then double-click to add the table to the Relationships window. **Close** the **Show Table** dialog box. In each table, use the pointer to resize the field list as necessary to display the table name and all the field names completely.

3. In your **13C Student Musicians** field list, point to **Student ID**, hold down the left mouse button, and then drag to the right to the **13C Instruments Inventory** field list until your mouse pointer is on top of **Student ID**. Release the mouse button, and then drag the **Edit Relationships** dialog box below the two field lists. The relationship between the two tables is a one-to-many relationship; *one* student can play *many* instruments. The common field is Student ID.

4. Click to select the **Enforce Referential Integrity** check box, and then click the **Create** button. With the **Relationships** window open, on the **Design tab**, in the **Tools group**, click **Relationship Report**. To print, on the **Print Preview tab**, in the **Print group**, click the **Print** button, and then click **OK**, or submit electronically as

directed. Click **Close Print Preview**. On the **Quick Access Toolbar**, click the **Save** button, and then in the displayed **Save As** dialog box, click **OK** to accept the default name. Close all open objects.

5. **Open** the **13C Instruments Inventory** table, and then **Close** the **Navigation Pane**. In the **Condition** field, click any record. In the **Sort & Filter group**, click the **Descending** button to sort the records from *Poor* to *Excellent*. Point anywhere in the **Category** field, and then right-click. From the displayed shortcut menu, click **Sort A to Z**. The records are sorted first by **Category**, the outermost sort field, and then within categories, by **Condition**, the innermost sort field. In the **Sort & Filter group**, click the **Clear All Sorts** button. **Close** the table, and then click **No**; you need not save the changes to the design after viewing a sort.

6. Click the **Create tab**, and then in the **Other group**, click the **Query Design** button. From the **Show Table** dialog box, **Add** the **13C Instruments Inventory** table, and then **Close** the **Show Table** dialog box. Use the pointer to adjust the height and width of the field list as necessary.

7. In the **13C Instruments Inventory** field list, double-click **Instrument ID** to add it to the design grid. In the **13C Instruments Inventory** field list, point to **Category**, hold down the left mouse button, and then drag down into the design grid until you are pointing to the **Field** row in the next available column. Release the mouse button. In the **Field** row of the design grid, click in the third column, and then click the **arrow** that displays. From the displayed list, click

(Project 13C–Music Department continues on the next page)

Content-Based Assessments

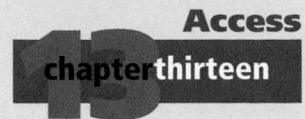
(Project 13C–Music Department continued)

Instrument to add this field to the design grid.

8. Using any technique, add the **Student ID** and **Condition** fields as the fourth and fifth fields in the design grid. On the **Query Tools Design tab**, in the **Results group**, click the **Run** button. This query answers the question, *What is the Instrument ID, Category, Instrument, Student ID, and Condition of all the instruments in the inventory?* On the **Quick Access Toolbar**, click the **Save** button to display the **Save As** dialog box. Type **13C All Instruments Query Firstname Lastname** and then click **OK**.

9. From the **Office** menu, point to the **Print** button, and then click **Print Preview**. Click the **Print** button; or, submit electronically as directed. Click the **Close Print Preview** button. Leave the query open. From the **Office** menu, click **Save As**. In the **Save As** dialog box, type **13C Condition Query Firstname Lastname** and then click **OK**. Recall that you can create a new query based on an existing query in this manner.

10. On the **Home tab**, in the **Views group**, click the **View** button to switch to Design view. In the design grid, point to the thin gray selection bar above the **Student ID** field until the ⬇ pointer displays. Click to select the **Student ID** column, and then press Delete. From the gray selection bar, select the **Instrument ID** column. Then, point to the selection bar at the top of the selected column to display the ⬉ pointer, and drag to the right to position **Instrument ID** as the fourth (last) column.

11. **Run** the query. The results of the query display four fields in the new arrangement. This query answers the question, *What is*

the Category, Instrument, Condition, and Instrument ID of every instrument in the inventory? **Close** the query, and then click **Yes**. Open the **Navigation Pane**, select the query name, display the **Print Preview**, and then print or submit electronically as directed. **Close Print Preview**.

12. **Open** your **13C All Instruments Query**, and then save it as **13C Instrument Sort Firstname Lastname** Switch to Design view. In the design grid, delete the **Student ID** field. In the **Category** field, click in the **Sort** row, click the **Sort arrow**, and then click **Descending**. Under **Condition**, click to display the **Sort arrow**, and then click **Ascending**. **Run** the query. This query answers the question *Within each category (with Category in descending alphabetical order), what instruments are in the inventory and what is the instrument's condition (with the condition listed in ascending alphabetic order)?* Print the query or submit electronically as directed. **Close** the query, and then click **Yes** to save the changes.

13. Close any open objects and **close** the **Navigation Pane**. **Create** a new query in Design view, and then **Add** the **13C Instruments Inventory** table. Add the following fields to the design grid: **Instrument ID**, **Category**, **Instrument**, and **Condition**. On the **Criteria** row of the design grid, under **Condition**, type **Fair** and then press Enter. **Run** the query. This query answers the question, *What is the Instrument ID, Category, and Instrument type of instruments that are in Fair condition?* Click the **Save** button, and then name the query **13C Fair Condition Firstname Lastname** Print or submit the query electronically, and then **Close** the query.

(Project 13C–Music Department continues on the next page)

Content-Based Assessments

(Project 13C–Music Department continued)

14. Create a new query in Design view, **Add** the **13C Instruments Inventory** table, and then add the following fields to the design grid: **Category**, **Instrument**, and **Condition**. On the **Criteria** row, under **Category**, type **Woodwinds** and then press Enter. Under **Category**, click to clear the **Show** check box, and then **Run** the query. This query answers the question, *What is the condition of the woodwind instruments in the inventory?* Recall that if all results are of the same criteria, it is not necessary to display the field name of the criteria. **Save** the query with the name **13C Woodwinds Condition Firstname Lastname** Print or submit electronically as directed, and then **Close** the query.

15. Create a new query in Design view, **Add** the **13C Student Musicians** table, and then add the following fields to the design grid in the order listed: **First Name**, **Last Name**, **Email Address**, and **Phone Number**. On the **Criteria** row, under the **Phone Number** field, type **Is Null** and then press Enter. On the **Sort** row, click in the **Last Name** field, click the **Sort arrow**, and then click **Ascending**. **Run** the query. This query answers the question, *For which student musicians are phone numbers missing?* **Save** the query as **13C Missing Phone Numbers Firstname Lastname** Print or submit electronically as directed, and then **Close** the query.

16. If necessary, close any open objects and **Close** the **Navigation Pane**. From the **Office** menu, click **Close Database**, and then at the right end of the Access title bar, click the **Close** button to close the Access program. Alternatively, from the Office menu, click **Exit Access.**

 You have completed Project 13C

Content-Based Assessments

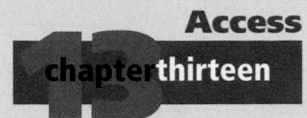
Project 13D — Concerts and Sponsors

In this project, you will apply the skills you practiced from the Objectives in Project 13B.

Objectives: 8. *Create a New Table by Importing an Excel Spreadsheet;* **9.** *Specify Numeric Criteria in a Query;* **10.** *Use Compound Criteria;* **11.** *Create a Query Based on More Than One Table;* **12.** *Use Wildcards in a Query;* **13.** *Use Calculated Fields in a Query;* **14.** *Group Data and Calculate Statistics in a Query.*

In the following Skills Review, you will assist Pascal Sanchez, College Music Director, in answering questions about concerts, sponsors, box office receipts, dates, and concert locations. Your query results will look similar to those shown in Figure 13.60.

For Project 13D, you will need the following files:

a13D_Concerts_Sponsors
a13D_Sponsors (Excel file)

You will save your database as
13D_Concerts_Sponsors_Firstname_Lastname

Figure 13.60

(Project 13D–Concerts and Sponsors continues on the next page)

Content-Based Assessments

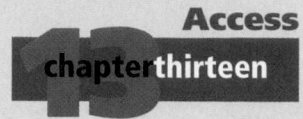
(Project 13D–Concerts and Sponsors continued)

1. From the student files that accompany this textbook, locate the file **a13D_Concerts_Sponsors**. Copy and paste the file to your **Access Chapter 13** folder. Rename the file **13D_Concerts_Sponsors_Firstname_Lastname Start** Access, open your database, and then enable the content.

2. **Open** the **Navigation Pane**. On the Ribbon, click the **External Data tab**, and then in the **Import group**, click the **Excel** button. In the displayed **Get External Data – Excel Spreadsheet** dialog box, to the right of the **File name** box, click the **Browse** button. Navigate to the location where the student files for this textbook are stored, and then click the Excel file **a13D_Sponsors**. In the lower right corner, click **Open**. Be sure the **Import the source data into a new table in the current database** option button is selected, and then in the lower right corner, click **OK**.

3. In the upper portion of the **Import Spreadsheet Wizard**, click to select the **First Row Contains Column Headings** check box. In the lower right corner, click **Next**. Under **Field Options**, make no changes for any of the fields, and then in the lower right corner, click **Next**. In the upper portion of the dialog box, click the **Choose my own primary key** option button, and then be sure that **Sponsor ID** displays. Click **Next**. In the **Import to Table** box, type **13D Sponsors** and then in the lower right corner, click **Finish**. In the displayed dialog box, in the lower right corner, click **Close**. The imported Excel spreadsheet becomes the second table in the database.

4. Click the **Database Tools tab**, and then in the **Show/Hide group**, click the

Relationships button. On the **Design tab**, in the **Relationships group**, click **Show Table**. **Add** the **13D Concerts** table, and then **Add** the **13D Sponsors** table. **Close** the **Show Table** dialog box. Expand the height and width of the field lists and position the field lists as necessary so that the **13D Sponsors** table is on the left. In the **13D Sponsors** field list, point to the **Sponsor ID** field, hold down the left mouse button, drag into the **13D Concerts** field list, position the mouse pointer on top of the **Sponsor ID** field, and then release the mouse button. Click to select the **Enforce Referential Integrity** check box, and then click the **Create** button. A one-to-many relationship is established; *one* sponsor organization can sponsor *many* concerts.

5. On the **Design tab**, in the **Tools group**, click the **Relationship Report** button. On the displayed **Print Preview tab**, click **Print**; or, submit electronically as directed. Click the **Save** button, and then click **OK** to accept the default name. **Close Print Preview**, close all open objects, and then **Close** the **Navigation Pane**.

6. On the **Create tab**, in the **Other group**, click the **Query Design** button. **Add** the **13D Concerts** table, close the **Show Table** dialog box, and then add the following fields to the design grid in the order given: **Concert Name**, **Box Office Receipts**, and **Concert Location**. Click in the **Sort** row under **Concert Location**, click the **arrow**, and then click **Ascending**. On the **Criteria** row, under **Box Office Receipts**, type **800** and then press Enter. **Run** the query. Only one concert—*Southern Hospitality Tour*— had Box Office Receipts of exactly $800.

7. On the **Home tab**, in the **Views group**, click the **View** button to return to Design view. On the **Criteria** row, under **Box**

(Project 13D–Concerts and Sponsors continues on the next page)

Content-Based Assessments

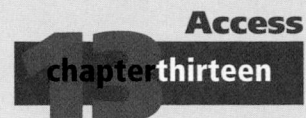
(Project 13D–Concerts and Sponsors continued)

Office Receipts, delete the existing criteria, type **>800** and then press Enter. **Run** the query again. Eight concerts had Box Office Receipts greater than $800. Return to Design view, change the **Box Office Receipts** criteria to **<800** and then run the query. Eight concerts had Box Office Receipts less than $800. Return to Design view, change **Box Office Receipts** criteria to **>=800** and then run the query. Nine records meet the criteria. This query answers the question, *Which concerts had Box Office Receipts of $800 or more, what was the amount of the Box Office Receipts, and where was each concert held?* **Save** the query as **13D $800 or More Firstname Lastname** Print or submit electronically as directed. Leave the query open. From the **Office** menu, click **Save As**, and then type **13D Concerts Jan-Apr Firstname Lastname** and click **OK**.

8. Return to Design view. From the **13D Concerts** field list, add the **Date** as the fourth field in the design grid. On the **Criteria** row, under **Box Office Receipts**, delete the existing criteria so that the query is not restricted by receipts. Under **Concert Location**, in the **Sort** row, click the arrow, and then click **(not sorted)**. Under **Date**, in the **Sort** row, click the arrow, and then click **Ascending**. Under **Date**, in the **Criteria** row, type **Between 01/01/2009 And 04/30/2009** and then press Enter. **Run** the query; five records meet the criteria. This query answers the question, *What is the name, box office receipts, location, and date, in chronological order, of concerts held between January 1, 2009 and April 30, 2009?* Print or submit electronically as directed. **Close** the query, and click **Yes** to save the changes to the design.

9. Create a new query in Design view. From the **13D Concerts** table, add the following fields to the design grid in the order given: **Concert Name**, **Concert Location**, and **Box Office Receipts**. In the **Criteria** row, under **Concert Location**, type **Port Community Theater** and then press Tab. In the **Criteria** row under **Box Office Receipts**, type **<=1000** and then press Enter. **Run** the query; two records display. This query answers the question, *Which concerts that were held at the Port Community Theater had Box Office Receipts of $1,000 or less?* Return to Design view, and then in the **Concert Location** field, clear the **Show** check box. **Run** the query. Recall that if all the records have the same criteria in one of the fields, it is not necessary to display that field in the query results. **Save** the query and name it **13D Port Community Theater $1000 or Less Firstname Lastname** Print or submit electronically, and then **Close** the query.

10. Create a new query in Design view. From the **13D Concerts** table, add the following four fields to the design grid in the order given: **Concert Name**, **Concert Location**, **Box Office Receipts**, and **Date**. On the **Criteria** row, under **Concert Location**, type **Port Community Theater** In the design grid, locate the **or** row. On the **or** row, under **Concert Location**, type **Mitchell Events Center** and then press Enter. **Run** the query. This query answers the question, *How many concerts were held at either the Port Community Theater or the Mitchell Events Center?* Twelve records meet the criteria. Return to Design view.

11. Under **Concert Location**, on the **or** row, delete the text. Under **Concert Location**, click in the **Criteria** row, delete the existing text, and then type **Port Community**

(Project 13D–Concerts and Sponsors continues on the next page)

Content-Based Assessments

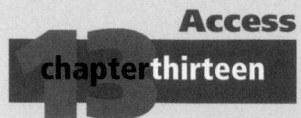

chapter**thirteen**   Skills Review

(Project 13D–Concerts and Sponsors continued)

Theater Or Mitchell Events Center On the **Criteria** row, under **Box Office Receipts**, type **>1000** and then press Enter. **Run** the query. Four records display. This query answers the question, *Which concerts held at either the Mitchell Events Center or the Port Community Theater had Box Office Receipts of more than $1,000 and on what dates were the concerts held?* **Save** the query as **13D PCT or Mitchell Over $1000 Firstname Lastname** Print or submit the query electronically as directed. **Close** the query.

12. Create a new query in Design view and add both tables. From the **13D Sponsors** field list, add the following fields: **Sponsor ID**, **Sponsor Name**, and **Phone Number**. On the **Sort** row, under **Sponsor Name**, click to select **Ascending** to sort the results in alphabetical order by Sponsor Name. From the **13D Concerts** field list, add **Concert Name**, **Concert Location**, **Box Office Receipts**, and **Date** to the design grid.

13. On the **Criteria** row, under **Concert Location**, type **Port Community Theater** On the **or** row, under **Concert Location**, type **Mitchell Events Center** and then press Enter. **Run** the query. Twelve records display. Return to the Design view. From the **Sponsors** field list, drag **Web Address** to the design grid on top of **Phone Number** and release the mouse button to insert the new field to the right of **Sponsor Name**. Select the **Sponsor ID** field and delete it.

14. In the design grid, select the **Box Office Receipts** field, and then drag it to the first field position in the grid. Delete the **Phone Number** and **Date** fields. **Run** the query. This query answers the question, *What were the box office receipts, sponsor name, sponsor Web address, concert name, and*

concert location of all concerts held at either the Port Community Theater or the Mitchell Events center, sorted alphabetically by sponsor name? Using techniques similar to that of a table, select all the columns in the query, and then apply **Best Fit**.

15. **Save** the query and name it **13D Receipts and Sponsors PCT and Mitchell Firstname Lastname** In **Print Preview**, change the orientation to **Landscape**, change the **Margins** to **Normal**, and then print the query or submit electronically as directed. **Close Print Preview** and **Close** the query. **Open** the **Navigation Pane** and notice that your new query displays under *both* tables from which it retrieved records. **Close** the **Navigation Pane**.

16. Create a new query in Design view, add both tables, and then add the following fields to the design grid: From the **13D Sponsors** table, add the **Sponsor Name** field. From the **13D Concerts** table, add the **Concert Name** field. On the **Criteria** row, under **Sponsor Name**, type **Florida*** and then press Enter. **Run** the query and widen the **Sponsor Name** column to view all of the data. Three sponsors have names that begin with *Florida*.

17. Return to Design view. On the **Criteria** row, under **Sponsor Name**, delete the text. On the **Criteria** row, under **Concert Name**, type ***Festival** and then press Enter. **Run** the query; five Concert Names end with the word *Festival*. Return to Design view. On the **Criteria** row, under **Sponsor Name**, type ***Radio*** and then press Enter. **Run** the query; two records have the word *Radio* somewhere in the Sponsor Name and the word *Festival* at the end of the Concert Name. This query answers the question, *Which radio stations are sponsor-*

(Project 13D–Concerts and Sponsors continues on the next page)

788   Access | Chapter 13: Sort and Query a Database

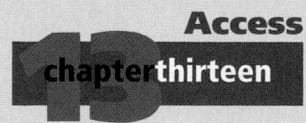

(Project 13D—Concerts and Sponsors continued)

ing Festival-type concerts? **Save** the query and name it **13D Radio Festivals Firstname Lastname** Print or submit the query electronically as directed, and then **Close** the query.

18. Create a new query in Design view, add both tables, and then add the following fields to the design grid: **Concert ID**, **Sponsor Name**, and **Box Office Receipts**. Click in the **Sort** row under **Concert ID**, click the **Sort arrow**, and then click **Ascending**. Sponsors have indicated that they will donate an additional amount to the Music Department based on 50% of the **Box Office Receipts**. On the **Field** row, right-click in the first empty column to display a shortcut menu, and then click **Zoom**. In the **Zoom** dialog box, type **Matching Donation: [Box Office Receipts]*0.5** In the **Zoom** dialog box, click **OK**, and then **Run** the query to view the new field— *Matching Donation.* Return to Design view.

19. In the **Field** row, in the first empty column, right-click, and then click **Zoom**. In the **Zoom** dialog box, type **Total Receipts: [Box Office Receipts]+[Matching Donation]** and then click **OK**. In the **Field** row, click in the **Matching Donation** field (fourth column), and then in the **Show/Hide group**, click the **Property Sheet** button. In the **Property Sheet** task pane, click in the white text box next to **Format**, click the **arrow** that displays, and then from the displayed list of formats, click **Currency**. **Close** the **Property Sheet** task pane.

20. **Run** the query to view the results. This query answers the question, *In ascending order by Concert ID, assuming each sponsor makes a matching 50% donation based on each concert's Box Office Receipts, what is the Sponsor Name, Box Office Receipts, Matching Donation, and Total Receipts for*

each concert? Select all the columns, and then apply **Best Fit**. **Save** the query and name it **13D Matching Sponsor Donation Firstname Lastname** In **Print Preview**, change the orientation to **Landscape**, and then print or submit the query electronically. **Close Print Preview** and then **Close** the query.

21. Create a new query in Design view, **Add** the **13D Concerts** table, and then add the **Box Office Receipts** field to the design grid. On the **Design tab**, in the **Show/Hide group**, click the **Totals** button to add a **Total** row as the third row in the design grid. On the **Total** row, under **Box Office Receipts**, click in the **Group By** box, and then click the **arrow** to display the list of functions. In the list of functions, click **Min**, and then **Run** the query. The lowest amount of Box Office Receipts for any concert was *$400.00.*

22. Return to Design view. Using the technique you just practiced, select the **Max** function, and then **Run** the query. The highest amount of Box Office Receipts for any concert was *$2,500.00.* Switch to **Design** view, select the **Avg** function, and then **Run** the query. The average Box Office Receipts for each concert was *$1,027.94.* Using the same technique, select the **Sum** function and **Run** the query. The total Box Office Receipts for all the concerts was *$17,475.00.*

23. Apply **Best Fit** to the **SumOfBox Office Receipts** column. Switch to Design view. Add the **Sponsor ID** field to the design grid. **Run** the query; concerts sponsored by SPONSOR-101 had the largest amount of Box Office Receipts—*$4,975.00.*

24. Switch to Design view. In the design grid, select and delete the **Sponsor ID** field from

(Project 13D—Concerts and Sponsors continues on the next page)

Content-Based Assessments

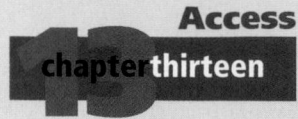
(Project 13D–Concerts and Sponsors continued)

the query design, and then add the **Concert Location** field to the design grid. **Run** the query. This query answers the question *What are the total Box Office Receipts for each concert location?* **Save** the query and name it **13D Totals by Concert Location Firstname Lastname** Print or submit the query electronically. **Close** the query. From the **Office** menu, click **Close Database**, and then at the right end of the Access title bar, click the **Close** button to close the Access program. Alternatively, from the Office menu, click **Exit Access.**

 End You have completed Project 13D _____

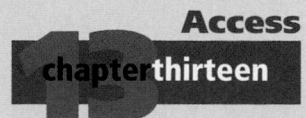

Project 13E — Lab Administrators

In this project, you will apply the skills you practiced from the Objectives in Project 13A.

Objectives: 1. *Open an Existing Database;* **2.** *Create Table Relationships;* **3.** *Sort Records in a Table;* **4.** *Create a Query in Design View;* **5.** *Create a New Query from an Existing Query;* **6.** *Sort Query Results;* **7.** *Specify Criteria in a Query.*

In the following Mastering Access project, you will assist Stephanie Cannon, Computing Services Director at the college, in querying the database to answer questions about computer lab administrators and their skill specialties. Your query results will look similar to those shown in Figure 13.61.

For Project 13E, you will need the following file:

a13E_Lab_Administrators

You will save your database as 13E_Lab_Administrators_Firstname_Lastname

Figure 13.61

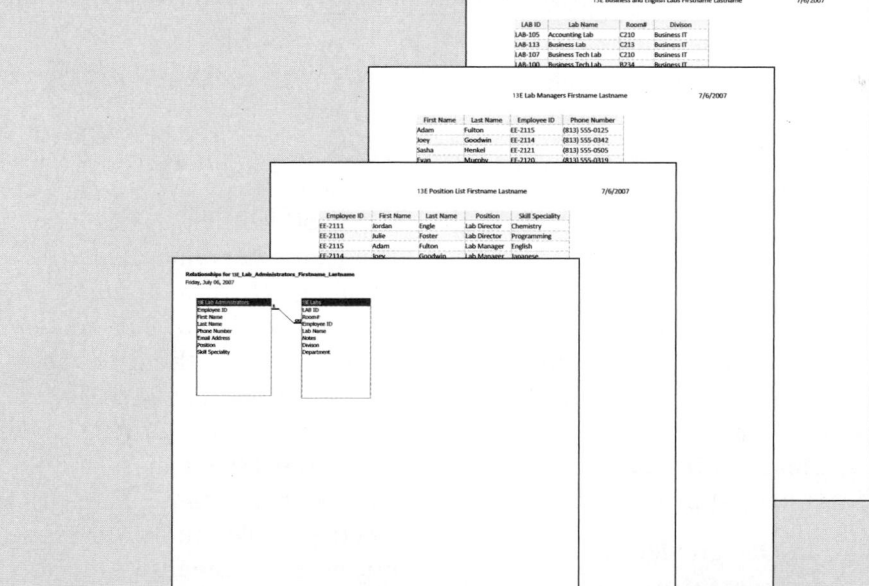

(Project 13E–Lab Administrators continues on the next page)

Content-Based Assessments

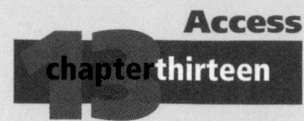

Mastering Access

(Project 13E–Lab Administrators continued)

1. From the student files that accompany this textbook, locate the file **a13E_Lab_Administrators**. Copy and paste the file to your **Access Chapter 13** folder. Rename the file **13E_Lab_Administrators_Firstname_Lastname Start** Access, open your database, and then enable the content.

2. Open the database tables and examine their fields and records to become familiar with the data; then **Close** the tables. Create a one-to-many relationship between the **13E Lab Administrators** table and the **13E Labs** table based on the **Employee ID** field and enforce referential integrity; *one* Lab Administrator can be responsible for *many* Labs. Create the **Relationship Report** and save it with the default name. Print the report, or submit electronically as directed, and then close all open objects.

3. Display the **13E_Lab_Administrators** table; **Close** the **Navigation Pane**. Notice the + signs that indicate the relationships you created. Perform a multiple-field sort on the table as follows, and remember to sort *first* by the innermost sort field: sort the table in **Ascending** order by **Last Name** (*innermost* sort field) and then sort in **Descending** order by **Position** (*outermost* sort field). The result is that your table is sorted by Position, with Lab Managers listed first, Lab Directors second, and Lab Assistants third, and within each Position, the names are alphabetized by Last Name. After examining the organization of the data, **Clear All Sorts**, **Close** the table, and do not save the changes.

4. Create a new query in Design view and add the **13E Lab Administrators** table. Add fields to the design grid so that your query will answer the question, *What is the Employee ID, First Name, and Last Name of each Lab Administrator in alphabetical order by Last Name, and what is each Lab Administrator's Position and Skill Specialty if any?* **Run** the query, save it with the name **13E Position List Firstname Lastname** Print or submit the query electronically as directed. Leave the query open.

5. From the previous query, create a new query and name it **13E Lab Managers Firstname Lastname** Switch to Design view, and then edit the design so that the query will answer the question, *What is the First Name, Last Name, Employee ID, and Phone Number of those who have the Position of Lab Manager, sorted alphabetically by Last Name?* Display the fields in the order listed in the question, display *only* the fields listed in the question, and do *not* show the **Position** field in the query result. Six employees have the position of Lab Manager. Print or submit the query electronically; **Close** the query, and then save any changes to the design.

6. Create a new query in Design view based on the **13E Labs** table to answer the uestion, *What is the LAB ID, Lab Name, and Room# of every lab in the Business IT Division and the English Division, sorted alphabetically by Lab Name?* Display the fields in the order listed in the question. Eight records meet the criteria. Save the query with the name **13E Business and English Labs Firstname Lastname** Print or submit electronically, and then **Close** the query. **Exit Access**.

End **You have completed Project 13E**

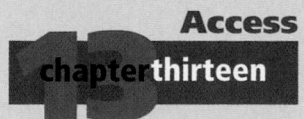

Project 13F—Bookstore Inventory

In this project, you will apply the skills you practiced from the Objectives in Project 13B.

Objectives: 8. *Create a New Table by Importing an Excel Spreadsheet;* **9.** *Specify Numeric Criteria in a Query;* **10.** *Use Compound Criteria;* **11.** *Create a Query Based on More Than One Table;* **12.** *Use Wildcards in a Query;* **13.** *Use Calculated Fields in a Query;* **14.** *Group Data and Calculate Statistics in a Query.*

In the following Mastering Access project, you will assist Nancy Pelo, College Bookstore Manager, in using her database to answer questions about the bookstore inventory. Your query results will look similar to those shown in Figure 13.62.

For Project 13F, you will need the following files:

a13F_Bookstore_Inventory

a13F_Vendors (Excel file)

You will save your database as
13F_Bookstore_Inventory_Firstname_Lastname

Figure 13.62

(Project 13F—Bookstore Inventory continues on the next page)

Content-Based Assessments

(Project 13F–Bookstore Inventory continued)

1. From the student files that accompany this textbook, locate the file **a13F_Bookstore_Inventory**. Copy and paste the file to your **Access Chapter 13** folder. Rename the file **13F_Bookstore_Inventory_Firstname_Lastname Start** Access, open your database, and then enable the content.

2. From the student files that accompany this textbook, import the Excel spreadsheet **a13F_Vendors**. Use the first row of the spreadsheet as the column headings, and choose the **Vendor ID** column as the primary key. Name the table **13F Vendors**

3. Open the database tables and examine their fields and records to become familiar with the data; then **Close** the tables. Create a one-to-many relationship between the **13F Vendors** table and the **13F Purchase Orders** table based on the **Vendor ID** field, and then enforce referential integrity; *one* Vendor can have *many* Purchase Orders. Create the **Relationship Report**, saving it with the default name. Print the report or submit electronically as directed, and then close all open objects.

4. Create a new query in Design view to answer the question, *What is the Vendor ID, Purchase Amount, Purchase Order Number, and Store Category for purchases greater than $10,000?* Display the fields in the order listed in the question. Eleven records meet the criteria. Save the query as **13F Purchases Over $10K Firstname Lastname** Print or submit electronically as directed; leave the query open.

5. Create a new query from the existing query and save it as **13F Purchases 1st Quarter Firstname Lastname** Redesign the query to answer the question, *In chronological order by Date Issued, which Purchase Order Numbers were issued between 01/01/2009 and 03/31/2009, for what amount, and to which Vendor ID?* Display the fields in the order listed in the question, display *only* the fields listed in the question, and do not restrict the purchase amount. Seventeen records meet the criteria. Print or submit electronically as directed; **Close** the query and save the design changes.

6. Create a new query in Design view to answer the question, *Which Purchase Order Numbers issued for the Textbooks department had a Purchase Amount greater than $30,000 and for what amount?* Do *not* show the **Dept** field in the result. Two records meet the criteria. Save the query as **13F Textbook Orders Over $30K Firstname Lastname** Print or submit electronically as directed; **Close** the query and save any changes.

7. Create a new query in Design view to answer the question, *Which Purchase Order Numbers were issued for either the Supplies Department or the Sundries Department and for what amount, with the amounts listed in descending order?* Display the results in the order listed in the question. Fourteen records meet the criteria. Save the query as **13F Supplies and Sundries Firstname Lastname** Print or submit electronically as directed; **Close** the query and save any changes.

8. By using both tables, create a new query to answer the question, *Which Purchase Order Numbers were issued for either the Textbooks Department or Technology Department, sorted in Ascending order by Department name, and what is the Vendor Name and amount of each purchase order?*

(Project 13F–Bookstore Inventory continues on the next page)

Content-Based Assessments

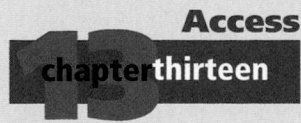
(Project 13F–Bookstore Inventory continued)

Apply **Best Fit** to the columns in the query result. Twelve records meet the criteria. Save the query as **13F Textbooks and Technology Firstname Lastname** Print or submit electronically as directed; **Close** the query and save any changes.

9. Create a new query in Design view, and then by using a wildcard in the format of *C**, answer the following question: *What is the Vendor Name, Address, City, State, and Zip of all vendors in the cities of Clearwater, Cape Coral or Cocoa Beach, and who is their Sales Rep?* Five records meet the criteria. Apply **Best Fit** to the columns in the query result, and then save the query as **13F Rep Names Firstname Lastname** Print or submit electronically as directed; **Close** the query and save any changes.

10. Create a new query in Design view, and then by using the **Sum** aggregate function, answer the question, *What are the total Purchase Order Amounts for each Department?* Apply **Best Fit** to the columns in the result, and then save the query as **13F Totals by Department**

Firstname Lastname Print or submit electronically as directed; **Close** the query and save any changes.

11. The state government announced a reduction in the tax rate applied to college bookstore purchases of 1%. Create a query to answer the question, *For each Purchase Order Number, assuming the state reduces each Purchase Amount by 1%, what will be the Amount of Reduction and the New Purchase Amount?* (Hint: First compute the amount of the reduction, naming the new field **Amount of Reduction** Then calculate the new purchase amount, naming the new field **New Purchase Amount**) As necessary, change the properties of all the new fields so that the **Format** is **Currency** and the **Decimal Places** are set to **2**. Apply **Best Fit** to the columns in the query result. **Save** the query as **13F Cost Reduction Firstname Lastname** In **Print Preview**, set the orientation to **Landscape**. Print or submit electronically as directed; **Close** the query and save any changes. **Exit Access**.

End You have completed Project 13F ————————————————————

Content-Based Assessments

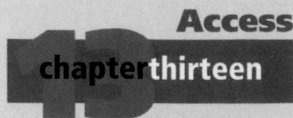
Mastering Access

Project 13G—Grants and Organizations

In this project, you will apply the skills you practiced from the Objectives in Projects 13A and 13B.

Objectives: 1. *Open an Existing Database;* **2.** *Create Table Relationships;* **4.** *Create a Query in Design View;* **5.** *Create a new Query from an Existing Query;* **6.** *Sort Query Results;* **7.** *Specify Criteria in a Query;* **8.** *Create a New Table by Importing an Excel Spreadsheet;* **9.** *Specify Numeric Criteria in a Query;* **10.** *Use Compound Criteria;* **11.** *Create a Query Based on More Than One Table;* **12.** *Use Wildcards in a Query;* **14.** *Group Data and Calculate Statistics in a Query.*

In the following Mastering Access project, you will assist Peter Donahue, Director of Grants for the college, in using his database to answer questions about public and private grants awarded to college departments. Your query results will look similar to those shown in Figure 13.63.

> ### For Project 13G, you will need the following files:
>
> a13G_Grants_Organizations
> a13G_Organizations (Excel file)

You will save your database as
13G_Grants_Organizations_Firstname_Lastname

Figure 13.63

(Project 13G–Grants and Organizations continues on the next page)

Content-Based Assessments

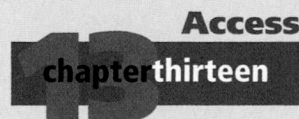

(Project 13G–Grants and Organizations continued)

1. From the student files that accompany this textbook, locate the file **a13G_Grants_Organizations**. Copy and paste the file to your **Access Chapter 13** folder. Rename the file **13G_Grants_Organizations_Firstname_Lastname Start** Access, open your database, and then enable the content.

2. From the student files that accompany this textbook, import the Excel spreadsheet **a13G_Organizations**. Use the first row of the spreadsheet as the column headings, and then choose the **Organization ID** column as the primary key. Name the table **13G Organizations**

3. Open the database tables, and then examine their fields and records to become familiar with the data; then **Close** the tables. Create a one-to-many relationship between the **13G Organizations** table and the **13G Grants Awarded** table based on the **Organization ID** field and enforce referential integrity; *one* Organization can give *many* Grants. Create the **Relationship Report**, saving it with the default name. Print the report or submit electronically as directed, and then close all open objects.

4. Create a new query in Design view to answer the question, *What is the Organization ID and Award Amount for grants greater than $10,000 and, in alphabetical order, to what Departments were the grants awarded?* Display the fields in the order listed in the question. Twelve records meet the criteria. Save the query as **13G Grants Over $10K Firstname Lastname** Print or submit electronically as directed; leave the query open.

5. Create a new query from the existing query and save it as **13G Grants 1st Quarter Firstname Lastname** Redesign the query to answer the question, *In chronological order by Award Date, which Grants were awarded between 01/01/2009 and 03/31/2009, from which Organization ID, for what amount, and to which Department?* Display the fields in the order listed in the question, display *only* the fields listed in the question, sort *only* on one field, and do *not* restrict the amount. Seven records meet the criteria. Apply **Best Fit** to the columns in the query result. In **Print Preview**, set the print to **Landscape**, and then print or submit electronically as directed; **Close Print Preview**, **Close** the query, and then save any design changes.

6. Create a new query in Design view to answer the question, *What are the names of privately funded grants awarded to either the Humanities or Social Science department, on what date were they awarded, and with the largest grants listed first, for what amount?* Display the results in the order listed in the question, and do not show the type of grant in the query result. Nine records meet the criteria. Save the query as **13G Private HMN and SS Grants Firstname Lastname** In **Print Preview**, set the print to **Landscape**, and then print or submit electronically as directed. **Close Print Preview**; **Close** the query, and then save any changes.

7. Create a new query in Design view using both tables to answer the question, *Which grants were awarded to either the Science or Health Technology department, for what amount, and, in alphabetical order, from which Organization Name?* Seven records meet the criteria. Apply **Best Fit** to the columns in the result. Save the query as **13G Science and Health Tech Firstname Lastname** In **Print Preview**, set the print to

(Project 13G–Grants and Organizations continues on the next page)

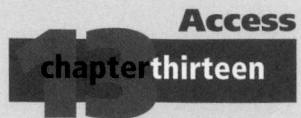
(Project 13G–Grants and Organizations continued)

Landscape, and then print or submit electronically as directed. **Close Print Preview**, **Close** the query, and then save any changes.

8. Using both tables, create a new query to answer the question, *Which grants were awarded from organizations that are Foundations, what is the name of the organization, what is the amount of the grant listed in descending order by amount, and what is the name and phone number of the organization contact?* Hint: Use a wildcard in the format of *Foundation* to find organization names containing the word *Foundation*. Fourteen records meet the criteria. Apply **Best Fit** to the columns in the result, and then save the query as **13G**

Foundation Grants Firstname Lastname Change the orientation to **Landscape**, set the **Margins** to **Normal**, and then print or submit electronically as directed; **Close** the query, and then save any changes.

9. Create a new query in Design view, and then by using the **Sum** aggregate function, answer the question, *Listed from the largest amounts to the smallest, what are the total Award Amounts for each Department?* Apply **Best Fit** to the columns in the result, and then save the query as **13G Totals by Department Firstname Lastname Print** or submit electronically as directed; **Close** the query, and then save any changes. **Exit Access**.

 End **You have completed Project 13G**

Content-Based Assessments

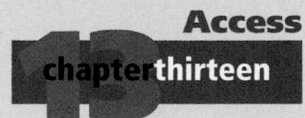
Mastering Access

Project 13H — Events and Clients

In this project, you will apply skills you practiced from the Objectives in Projects 13A and 13B.

Objectives: 1. *Open an Existing Database;* **2.** *Create Table Relationships;* **4.** *Create a Query in Design View;* **5.** *Create a New Query from an Existing Query;* **6.** *Sort Query Results;* **7.** *Specify Criteria in a Query;* **8.** *Create a New Table by Importing an Excel Spreadsheet;* **9.** *Specify Numeric Criteria in a Query;* **10.** *Use Compound Criteria;* **11.** *Create a Query Based on More Than One Table;* **12.** *Use Wildcards in a Query;* **13.** *Use Calculated Fields in a Query;* **14.** *Group Data and Calculate Statistics in a Query.*

In the following Mastering Access project, you will assist Peter Steinmetz, Facilities Manager at the college, in using his database to answer questions about facilities that the college rents to community and private organizations. Renting the facilities at times when they are not in use for college activities provides additional funding to maintain and staff the facilities. Your query results will look similar to those shown in Figure 13.64.

For Project 13H, you will need the following files:

a13H_Events_Clients

a13H_Rental_Clients (Excel file)

You will save your database as 13H_Events_Clients_Firstname_Lastname

Figure 13.64

(Project 13H–Events and Clients continues on the next page)

Content-Based Assessments

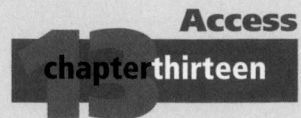
(Project 13H–Events and Clients continued)

1. From the student files that accompany this textbook, locate the file **a13H_Events_Clients**. Copy and paste the file to your **Access Chapter 13** folder. Rename the file **13H_Events_Clients_Firstname_Lastname Start** Access, open your database, and then enable the content.

2. From the student files that accompany this textbook, import the Excel spreadsheet **a13H_Rental_Clients**. Use the first row of the spreadsheet as the column headings, and then choose the **Rental Client ID** column as the primary key. Name the table **13H Rental Clients**

3. Open the database tables, and then examine their fields and records to become familiar with the data; and then **Close** the tables. Create a one-to-many relationship between the **13H Rental Clients** table and the **13H Events** table based on the **Rental Client ID** field and enforce referential integrity; *one* Rental Client can have *many* Events. Create the **Relationship Report**, print or submit electronically as directed, and then save it with the default name. Close all open objects.

4. Create a new query in Design view to answer the question, *What is the Event Name, Rental Client ID, and Rental Fee for events with fees greater than or equal to $500, in ascending order by Rental Client ID, and in which Facility was the event held?* Display the fields in the order listed in the question. Eleven records meet the criteria. Save the query as **13H Fees $500 or More Firstname Lastname** Print or submit electronically as directed; leave the query open.

5. Create a new query from the existing query, and save it as **13H Afternoon Events**

Firstname Lastname Redesign the query to answer the question, *Which Events were held in the Afternoon between 07/01/2009 and 08/31/2009, in chronological order by date, what was the Rental Fee, and what was the Event ID?* Display the fields in the order listed in the question, but do *not* display the **Time** field in the result. Do *not* restrict the result by Rental Fee. Four records meet the criteria. Print or submit electronically as directed; **Close** the query, and then save the design changes.

6. Create a new query in Design view to answer the question, *Which Events and Event Types were held in either the White Sands Music Hall or the Theater that had Rental Fees greater than $500?* Three records meet the criteria. Apply **Best Fit** to the columns, save the query as **13H White Sands and Theater Over $500 Firstname Lastname** Print or submit electronically as directed; **Close** the query and save any changes.

7. Using both tables, create a new query in Design view to answer the question *Which Events were held on one of the sports Fields, for which Renter Name, and what was the Rental Fee in order of lowest fee to highest fee?* Hint: Use a wildcard with the word *Field*. Five records meet the criteria. Apply **Best Fit** to the columns in the result. Save the query as **13H Field Usage Firstname Lastname** Print or submit electronically as directed; **Close** the query, and then save any changes.

8. Create a new query in Design view, and then by using the **Sum** aggregate function, answer the question *In descending order by total, what are the total Rental Fees for each Event Type?* As necessary, change the properties of all appropriate fields to

(Project 13H–Events and Clients continues on the next page)

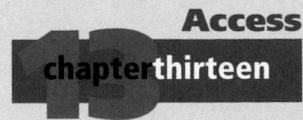

(Project 13H–Events and Clients continued)

display in **Currency** format with **0** decimal places. Apply **Best Fit** to the columns in the result, and then save the query as **13H Totals by Event Type Firstname Lastname** Print or submit electronically as directed; **Close** the query, and then save any changes.

9. The college Alumni Association will donate money to the Building Fund in an amount based on 10% of total facility rental fees. Create a query to answer the question, *In ascending order by Event ID, what will the total of each Rental Fee be if the Alumni*

Association donates an additional 10% of each fee? Hint: First compute the amount of the donation and name the new field **Amount of Donation** Then calculate the new rental fee and name the new field **New Rental Fee Amount** As necessary, change the properties of the all appropriate fields to display in **Currency** format with **0** decimal places. Apply **Best Fit** to the columns in the query result. Save the query as **13H Alumni Donation Firstname Lastname** Print or submit electronically as directed; **Close** the query, and then save any changes. **Exit Access**.

End **You have completed Project 13H**

Content-Based Assessments

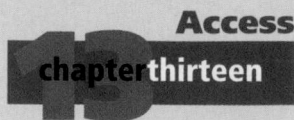
Project 13I — Students and Scholarships

In this project, you will apply the skills you practiced from all the Objectives in Projects 13A and 13B.

Objectives: 1. *Open an Existing Database;* **2.** *Create Table Relationships;* **3.** *Sort Records in a Table;* **4.** *Create a Query in Design View;* **5.** *Create a New Query From an Existing Query;* **6.** *Sort Query Results;* **7.** *Specify Criteria in a Query;* **8.** *Create a New Table by Importing an Excel Spreadsheet;* **9.** *Specify Numeric Criteria in a Query;* **10.** *Use Compound Criteria;* **11.** *Create a Query Based on More Than One Table;* **12.** *Use Wildcards in a Query;* **13.** *Use Calculated Fields in a Query;* **14.** *Group Data and Calculate Statistics in a Query.*

In the following Mastering Access project, you will assist Diane Nguyen, Director of Academic Scholarships, in using her database to answer questions about academic scholarships awarded to students. Your query results will look similar to those shown in Figure 13.65.

For Project 13I, you will need the following files:

a13I_Students_Scholarships
a13I_Students (Excel file)

You will save your database as
13I_Students_Scholarships_Firstname_Lastname

Figure 13.65

(Project 13I–Students and Scholarships continues on the next page)

Content-Based Assessments

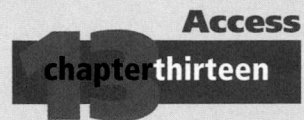

Mastering Access

(Project 13I–Students and Scholarships continued)

1. From the student files that accompany this textbook, locate the file **a13I_Students_Scholarships**. Copy and paste the file to your **Access Chapter 13** folder. Rename the file **13I_Students_Scholarships_Firstname_Lastname Start** Access, open your database, and then enable the content.

2. From the student files that accompany this textbook, import the Excel spreadsheet **a13I_Students**. Use the first row of the spreadsheet as the column headings, and then choose the **Student ID** column as the primary key. Name the table **13I Students**

3. Open the database tables and examine their fields and records to become familiar with the data; then **Close** the tables. Create a one-to-many relationship between the **13I Students** table and the **13I Scholarships** table based on the **Student ID** field and enforce referential integrity; *one* student can have *many* scholarships. Create the **Relationship Report**, print or submit electronically as directed, and then save it with the default name. Close all open objects.

4. Display the **13I Students** table; notice the + signs that indicate the relationships you created. Perform a multiple-field sort on the table to sort students in alphabetic order by Last Name within groups of cities, and sort the City names in alphabetical order. Remember to sort *first* by the innermost sort field. After examining the sorted table, **Clear All Sorts**, **Close** the table, and do not save the changes.

5. Create a new query in Design view, based on the **13I Scholarships Awarded** table, to answer the question, *In alphabetical order by Scholarship Name, what is the* *Scholarship Name, Amount, and Major for scholarships greater than or equal to $500?* Display the fields in the order listed in the question. Ten records meet the criteria. Save the query as **13I Scholarships $500 or More Firstname Lastname** Print or submit electronically as directed; leave the query open.

6. Create a new query from the existing query, and then save it as **13I Scholarships 1st Quarter Firstname Lastname** Add the **13I Students** table to the table area, and then redesign the query to answer the question, *In chronological order by Award Date, which scholarships were awarded between 01/01/2009 and 03/31/2009, for what amount, and what was the name of the student?* Be sure the fields display in the order listed in the question, display *only* the fields listed in the question, do not restrict the amount, and sort only by date. Eight records meet the criteria. In **Print Preview**, set **Wide** margins and **Landscape** orientation. Print or submit electronically as directed; **Close** the query, and then save the design changes.

7. Create a new query in Design view to answer the question, *Which scholarships were awarded for either CIS or Nursing majors for amounts of $100 or more, listed in descending order by amount?* Four records meet the criteria. Save the query as **13I Nursing and CIS $100 and Over Firstname Lastname** Print or submit electronically as directed; **Close** the query, and then save any changes.

8. Create a new query in Design view using only the 13I Students table, and then by using a wildcard, answer the question, *In alphabetical order by Last Name, what is the Student ID, First Name, Last Name, and*

(Project 13I–Students and Scholarships continues on the next page)

Content-Based Assessments

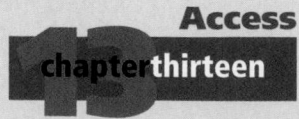
(Project 13I–Students and Scholarships continued)

City of all students in cities that begin with the letter B? Five records meet the criteria. Save the query as **13I Cities Firstname Lastname** Print or submit electronically as directed; **Close** the query, and then save any changes.

9. Create a new query in Design view based on the **13I Students** table, and that includes all the table's fields, to answer the question *For which students is the Address missing?* Three students are missing addresses. Apply **Best Fit** to the columns, and save the query as **13I Missing Addresses Firstname Lastname** Print or submit electronically as directed; **Close** the query, and then save any changes.

10. Create a new query in Design view, and then by using the **Sum** aggregate function, answer the question, *In descending order by amount, what are the total scholarship amounts for each Major?* Use the Property Sheet as necessary to display the sums with **0** decimal places and in **Currency** format. Apply **Best Fit** to the columns in the result, and then save the query as **13I**

Totals by Major Firstname Lastname Print or submit electronically as directed; **Close** the query, and then save any changes.

11. For each academic scholarship received by students, the Board of Trustees of the college will donate an amount equal to 50% of each scholarship. By using a calculated field and both tables, answer the question, *In alphabetical order by scholarship name, and including the first and last name of the scholarship recipient, what will the value of each scholarship be if the Board of Trustees makes a matching 50% donation?* Hint: First compute the amount of the donation, and then name the new field **Donation** Then calculate the new scholarship value and name the new field **New Value** As necessary, change the properties of all the fields to display in **Currency** format. Apply **Best Fit** to the columns in the query result. Save the query as **13I Trustee Donation Firstname Lastname** Print in **Landscape** or submit electronically as directed. **Close** the query, and then save any changes. **Exit Access**.

End **You have completed Project 13I**

Content-Based Assessments

 **Business Running Case**

Project 13J—Business Running Case

In this project, you will apply the skills you practiced in Projects 13A and 13B.

Close Access and any other open windows. Display the Start menu, click Computer, and then navigate to the student files that accompany this textbook. In the folder **03_business_running_case**, locate and open the folder for this chapter. Open and print the instructions for this project, which are provided to you in Adobe PDF format. Follow the instructions and use the skills you have gained thus far to assist Jennifer Nelson in meeting the challenges of owning and running her business.

 End **You have completed Project 13J** ————————————

Mastering Access

Project 13K — *GO!* Fix It

In this project, you will apply the skills you practiced from the Objectives in Projects 13A and 13B.

For Project 13K, you will need the following file:

a13K_fixit_Division_Social_Science

**You will save your document as
13K_Division_Social_Science_Firstname_Lastname**

From the student files that accompany this textbook, open the folder **05_go_fix_it**. Locate and make a copy of the database **a13K_fixit_Division_Social_Science** in your chapter folder. Name the copy **13K_Division_Social_Science_Firstname_Lastname**

This database contains **five errors** that you must find and correct. Read and examine the document, and then edit to correct the errors that you find. Types of errors could include:

- Missing or incorrect data in tables, queries, forms, and reports such as file names, field names, types, descriptions, properties, records, and criteria.
- Table design errors such as primary key.
- Query design errors such as field, table, show, sort, and criteria.
- Forms design errors such as form header and footer, page header and footer, detail, and layout.
- Reports design errors such as report header and footer, page header and footer, detail, and layout.
- Page setup errors such as margins, orientation, layout, or alignment.

To complete the project, you should know:

- There is no table relationship between the Faculty table and the Course Schedule table. Create the relationship and the report; one faculty member can teach many courses.
- Examine and correct any queries that do not accurately reflect the query name. Add your first name and last name to the query name.

Print the relationship report and the four queries or submit your database as directed.

 End **You have completed Project 13K** ——————————

Outcomes-Based Assessments

Rubric

The following outcomes-based assessments are *open-ended assessments*. That is, there is no specific correct result; your result will depend on your approach to the information provided. Make *Professional Quality* your goal. Use the following scoring rubric to guide you in *how* to approach the problem and then to evaluate *how well* your approach solves the problem.

The *criteria*—Software Mastery, Content, Format and Layout, and Process—represent the knowledge and skills you have gained that you can apply to solving the problem. The *levels of performance*—Professional Quality, Approaching Professional Quality, or Needs Quality Improvements—help you and your instructor evaluate your result.

	Your completed project is of Professional Quality if you:	Your completed project is Approaching Professional Quality if you:	Your completed project Needs Quality Improvements if you:
1-Software Mastery	Choose and apply the most appropriate skills, tools, and features and identify efficient methods to solve the problem.	Choose and apply some appropriate skills, tools, and features, but not in the most efficient manner.	Choose inappropriate skills, tools, or features, or are inefficient in solving the problem.
2-Content	Construct a solution that is clear and well organized, contains content that is accurate, appropriate to the audience and purpose, and is complete. Provide a solution that contains no errors of spelling, grammar, or style.	Construct a solution in which some components are unclear, poorly organized, inconsistent, or incomplete. Misjudge the needs of the audience. Have some errors in spelling, grammar, or style, but the errors do not detract from comprehension.	Construct a solution that is unclear, incomplete, or poorly organized, containing some inaccurate or inappropriate content; and contains many errors of spelling, grammar, or style. Do not solve the problem.
3-Format and Layout	Format and arrange all elements to communicate information and ideas, clarify function, illustrate relationships, and indicate relative importance.	Apply appropriate format and layout features to some elements, but not others. Overuse features, causing minor distraction.	Apply format and layout that does not communicate information or ideas clearly. Do not use format and layout features to clarify function, illustrate relationships, or indicate relative importance. Use available features excessively, causing distraction.
4-Process	Use an organized approach that integrates planning, development, self-assessment, revision, and reflection.	Demonstrate an organized approach in some areas, but not others; or, use an insufficient process of organization throughout.	Do not use an organized approach to solve the problem.

Outcomes-Based Assessments

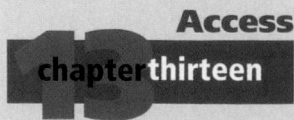

Access
Problem Solving

Project 13L — Student Refunds

In this project, you will construct a solution by applying any combination of the skills you practiced from the Objectives in Projects 13A and 13B.

For Project 13L, you will need the following files:

a13L_Student_Refunds
a13L_Student_Refunds (Word document)

You will save your database as
13L_Student_Refunds_Firstname_Lastname

Start Microsoft Word, and then from your student files, open the Word document **a13L_Student_Refunds**. Use the skills you have practiced in this chapter to assist Kathy Knudsen, the Associate Dean of Student Services, in answering questions about student refunds in your database **13L_Student_Refunds_Firstname_Lastname**. Save any queries that you create, include your name in the query title, and submit your queries as directed by your instructor. Record your answers to the questions in the Word document.

 End You have completed Project 13L ————————

Outcomes-Based Assessments

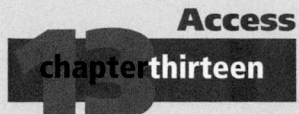
Problem Solving

Project 13M — Leave

In this project, you will construct a solution by applying any combination of the skills you practiced from the Objectives in Projects 13A and 13B.

For Project 13M, you will need the following files:

a13M_Leave
a13M_Leave (Word document)

You will save your database as
13M_Leave_Firstname_Lastname

Start Microsoft Word, and then from your student files, open the Word document **a13M_Leave**. Use the skills you have practiced in this chapter to assist Gabe Stevens, the Director of Human Resources, in answering questions about employee leave time in your database **13M_Leave_ Firstname_Lastname**. Save any queries that you create, include your name in the query title, and submit your queries as directed by your instructor. Record your answers to the questions in the Word document.

End **You have completed Project 13M** ————————

Outcomes-Based Assessments

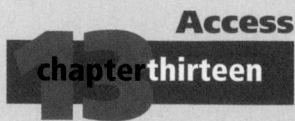

Access

Problem Solving

Project 13N — Coaches

In this project, you will construct a solution by applying any combination of the skills you practiced from the Objectives in Projects 13A and 13B.

> ### For Project 13N, you will need the following files:
>
> a13N_Coaches
> a13N_Coaches (Word document)
>
> **You will save your database as**
> **13N_Coaches_Firstname_Lastname**

Start Microsoft Word, and then from your student files, open the Word document **a13N_Coaches**. Use the skills you have practiced in this chapter to assist Marcus Simmons, the Athletic Director, in answering questions about the coaches in your database **13N_Coaches_Firstname_Lastname**. Save any queries that you create, include your name in the query title, and submit your queries as directed by your instructor. Record your answers to the questions in the Word document.

End **You have completed Project 13N** ———————————

Outcomes-Based Assessments

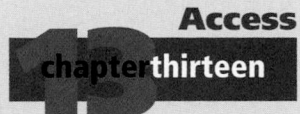

Problem Solving

Project 13O — Faculty Awards

In this project, you will construct a solution by applying any combination of the skills you practiced from the Objectives in Projects 13A and 13B.

For Project 13O, you will need the following files:

a13O_Faculty_Awards
a13O_Faculty_Awards (Word document)

You will save your database as
13O_Faculty_Awards_Firstname_Lastname

Start Microsoft Word, and then from your student files, open the Word document **a13O_Faculty_Awards**. Use the skills you have practiced in this chapter to assist Angela Ta, President of the Faculty Association, in answering questions about faculty awards in your database **13O_Faculty_Awards_Firstname_Lastname**. Save any queries that you create, include your name in the query title, and submit your queries as directed by your instructor. Record your answers to the questions in the Word document.

 End **You have completed Project 13O** _____

Outcomes-Based Assessments

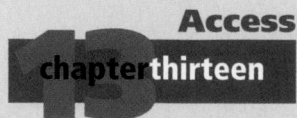

Access
chapterthirteen

Problem Solving

Project 13P — Club Donations

In this project, you will construct a solution by applying any combination of the skills you practiced from the Objectives in Projects 13A and 13B.

For Project 13P, you will need the following files:

a13P_Club_Donations
a13P_Club_Donations (Word document)

You will save your database as
13P_Club_Donations_Firstname_Lastname

Start Microsoft Word, and then from your student files, open the Word document **a13P_Club_Donations**. Use the skills you have practiced in this chapter to assist Kathy Durbin, Director of Student Activities, in answering questions about donations to student clubs in your database **13P_Club_Donations_Firstname_Lastname**. Save any queries that you create, include your name in the query title, and submit your queries as directed by your instructor. Record your answers to the questions in the Word document.

 End **You have completed Project 13P** ——————————

Outcomes-Based Assessments

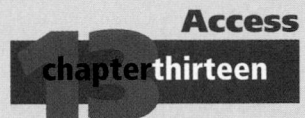
 You and *GO!*

Project 13Q—You and *GO!*

In this project, you will construct a solution by applying any combination of the Objectives found in Projects 13A and 13B.

Close Access and any other open windows. Display the Start menu, click Computer, and then navigate to the student files that accompany this textbook. In the folder **04_you_and_go**, locate and open the folder for this chapter. Open and print the instructions for this project, which are provided to you in Adobe PDF format. Follow the instructions to create queries for your personal database.

 You have completed Project 13Q ——————————

GO! with Help

Project 13R—*GO!* with Help

There are numerous wildcards that you can use in your queries. Use the Access Help system to find out more about wildcards in Access.

1 **Start** Access. Click the **Microsoft Office Access Help** button 🔘. Click the **Search arrow**, and then under **Content from this computer**, click **Access Help**. In the **Search box**, type **wildcards** and then press [Enter]. Scroll the displayed list as necessary, and then click **Using Wildcard Characters in String Comparisons**. Review the information shown in this topic.

2 If you would like to keep a copy of this information, click the **Print** button 🖫. Click the **Close** button [✖] in the top right corner of the Help window to close the Help window, and then **Exit** Access.

 You have completed Project 13R ——————————

Outcomes-Based Assessments

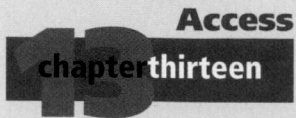

Group Business Running Case

Project 13S—Group Business Running Case

In this project, you will apply the skills you practiced from the Objectives in Projects 13A and 13B.

Your instructor may assign this group case project to your class. If your instructor assigns this project, he or she will provide you with information and instructions to work as part of a group. The group will apply the skills gained thus far to help the Bell Orchid Hotel Group achieve its business goals.

 End **You have completed Project 13S** ————————————

chapterfourteen

Forms, Filters, and Reports

OBJECTIVES

At the end of this chapter you will be able to:

1. Create a Form
2. Use a Form to Add and Delete Records
3. Create a Form by Using the Form Wizard
4. Modify a Form in Design View and in Layout View
5. Filter Records

OUTCOMES

Mastering these objectives will enable you to:

PROJECT 14A

Create Forms to Enter and Display Data in a Database

6. Create a Report by Using the Report Tool
7. Create a Report by Using the Blank Report Tool
8. Create a Report by Using the Report Wizard
9. Modify the Design of a Report
10. Print a Report and Keep Data Together

PROJECT 14B

Create Reports to Display Database Information

Baltimore Area Job Fair

The Baltimore Area Job Fair is a nonprofit organization that brings together employers and job seekers in the Baltimore and Washington, DC metropolitan areas. Each year the organization holds a number of targeted job fairs and the annual Greater Baltimore Job Fair draws over 1,000 employers in more than 70 industries and registers more than 4,000 candidates. Candidates pay a small registration fee. Employers pay to display and present at the fairs and to have access to candidate resumes. Candidate resumes and employer postings are managed by a state-of-the-art database system, allowing participants quick and accurate access to job data and candidate qualifications.

Forms, Filters, and Reports

You can both enter and view information directly in the database tables. However, for entering and viewing information, it is usually easier to use an Access form. You can design forms to display one record at a time, with fields placed in the same order to match a paper source document. When the form on the screen matches the pattern of information on the paper form, it is easier to enter the new information. In a form or table, you can also filter records to display only a portion of the total records based on matching specific values.

When viewing information, it is usually easier to view only one record at a time. For example, your college counselor can look at your college transcript in a nicely laid out form on the screen without seeing the records of other students at the same time.

In Access, reports summarize the data in a database in a professional looking manner suitable for printing. The design of a report can be modified so that the final report is laid out in a format that is useful to the person reading it. In this chapter, you will create and modify both forms and reports for Access databases.

Project 14A Candidate Interviews

Local employers and candidates who are seeking jobs get together at the two-day Greater Baltimore Job Fair. In Activities 14.01 through 14.10, you will assist Janna Sorokin, database manager for the Job Fair, in using an Access database to track the job candidates and the job interviews they have scheduled with employers during the fair event. Your completed database objects will look similar to those in Figure 14.1.

For Project 14A, you will need the following file:

a14A_Candidate_Interviews

You will save your database as
14A_Candidate_Interviews_Firstname_Lastname

14A Candidates Input Form

Candidate ID#:	22155
First Name	Firstname
Last Name	Lastname

14A Candidates

Candidate ID#:	22155
Candidate First Name:	Firstname
Candidate Last Name:	Lastname
College Major:	Business
Internships Completed:	Government
Phone Number:	(443) 555-0765
Registration Fee:	$10.00
Date Fee Collected:	10/10/2009

Figure 14.1
Project 14A—Candidate Interviews

Objective 1
Create a Form

A *form* is an Access object with which you can enter, edit, or display data from a table or a query. One typical use of a form is to control access to the data. For example, in a college registration system, you could design a form for Registration Assistants who could see and enter the courses scheduled and fees paid by an individual student. However, they could not see or enter grades or other personal information in the student's record. In this manner, think of a form as a window through which others see and reach your database.

Some Access forms display only one record at a time; other form types display multiple records at the same time. A form that displays only one record at a time is useful not only to the individual who performs the *data entry*—typing in the actual records—but also to anyone who has the job of viewing information in a database. For example, when you visit the Records office at your college to obtain a transcript, someone displays your record on a screen. For the viewer, it is much easier to look at one record at a time, using a form, than to look at all of the student records in the database.

Activity 14.01 Creating a Form

There are various ways to create a form in Access, but the fastest and easiest is to use the *Form tool*. With a single mouse click, all the fields from the underlying data source (table or query) are placed on the form. Then you can use the new form immediately, or you can modify it in Layout view or in Design view.

The Form tool incorporates all of the information, both the field names and the individual records, from an existing table or query and then instantly creates the form for you. Records that you edit or create using a form automatically update the underlying table or tables. In this activity, you will create a form, and then use it to add new interview records to the database.

1 By using the technique you practiced in Chapter 8, open **Computer**, and then navigate to the location where you will store your projects for this chapter. Create a new folder and name it **Access Chapter 14**

2 From the student files that accompany this text, locate the file **a14A_Candidate_Interviews**. Copy and then paste the file to the **Access Chapter 14** folder you created in Step 1. **Rename** the file **14A_Candidate_Interviews_Firstname_Lastname Start** Access, open your **14A_Candidate_Interviews** database, and then if necessary, enable the content.

3 **Open** the **Navigation Pane**. Click the **Database Tools tab**, and then in the **Show/Hide group**, click the **Relationships** button. Compare your screen with Figure 14.2. If your relationships do not display, in the Relationships group, click the **All Relationships** button.

At the Job Fair event, *one* candidate can have interviews with *many* organizations. Thus, a one-to-many relationship has been established between the 14A Candidates table and the 14A Interviews table using Candidate ID# as the common field—the field that displays in both tables.

Join line with symbols indicating one-to-many relationship and referential integrity

Figure 14.2

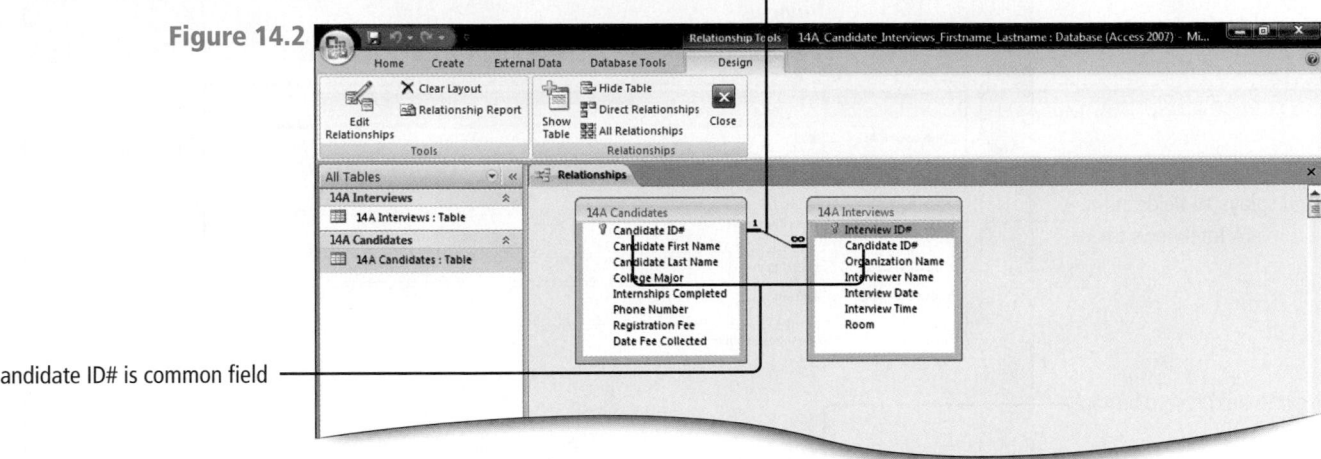

Candidate ID# is common field

4 In the **Relationships group**, click the **Close** button ☒ to close the **Relationships window**. If prompted to save your changes, click No. From the **Navigation Pane**, open the **14A Interviews** table, and notice the seven fields—*Interview ID#, Candidate ID#, Organization Name, Interviewer Name, Interview*

Date, Interview Time, and *Room.* **Close** ☒ the **14A Interviews** table.

5 Be sure the **14A Interviews table** is still selected in the **Navigation Pane**. Click the **Create tab**, and then in the **Forms group**, click

Form. Close ☒ the **Navigation Pane**, and then compare your screen with Figure 14.3.

Access creates the form based on the currently selected object—the 14A Interviews table—and displays the form in ***Layout view***. In Layout view, you can make design changes to the form while it is displaying data. For example, you can adjust the size of the text boxes to fit the data. You can use Layout view for many of the changes you might need to make to a form.

Access creates the form in a simple top-to-bottom layout, with all seven fields in the table lined up in a single column. The data for the first record in the table displays in the fields.

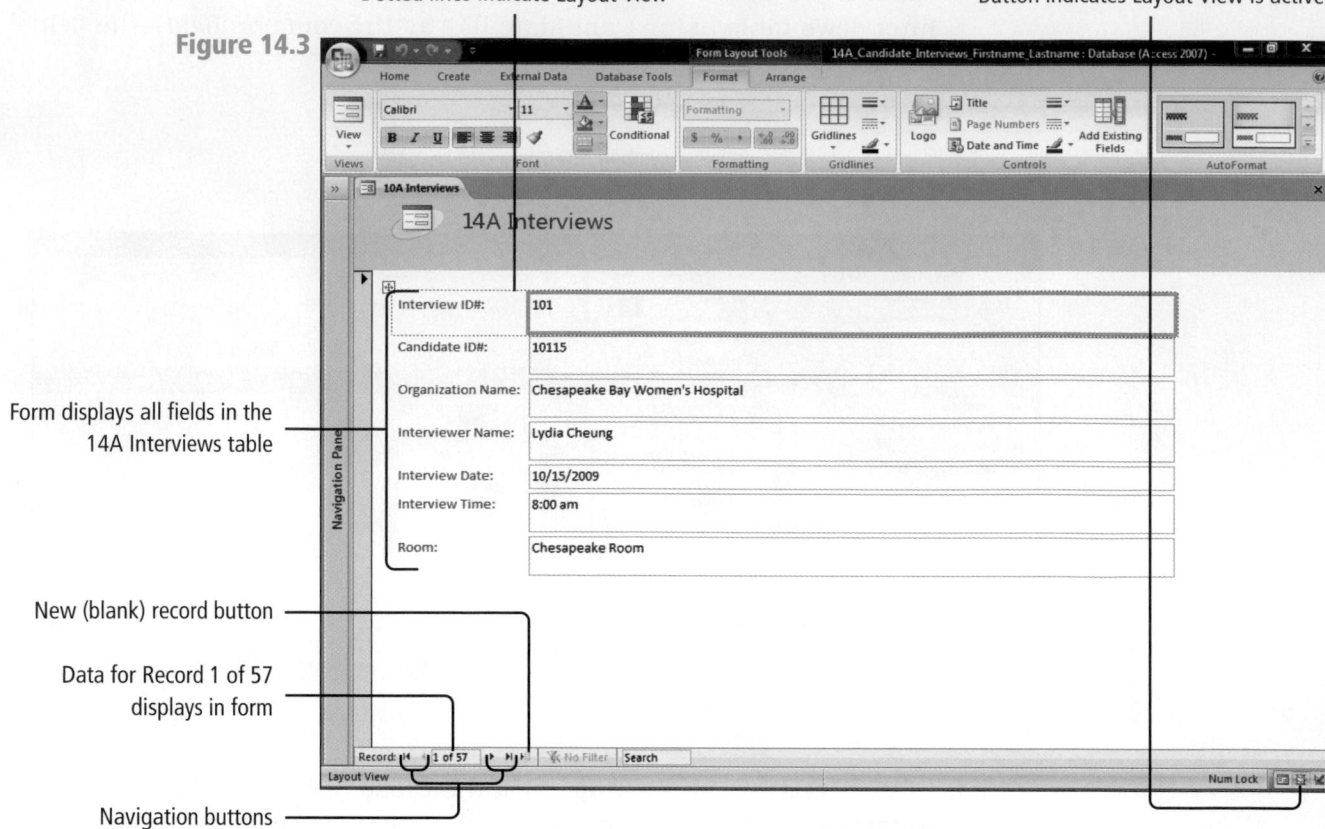

Figure 14.3

Dotted lines indicate Layout View

Button indicates Layout View is active

Form displays all fields in the 14A Interviews table

New (blank) record button

Data for Record 1 of 57 displays in form

Navigation buttons

6 In the navigation area, click the **Next record** button ▶ four times.

The fifth record—for *Interview ID# 105*—displays. Use the navigation buttons to scroll among the records to display any single record you want to view.

7 In the navigation area, click the **Last record** button ▶| to display the record for *Interview ID# 157*, and then click the **First record** button |◀ to display the record for *Interview ID# 101*.

8 From the **Office** menu , click **Save** 🖫 to save this form for future use. In the displayed **Save As** dialog box, edit as necessary to name the form **14A Interviews Form** and click **OK**. **Close** ✖ the form object.

9 **Open** » the **Navigation Pane**, and notice that your new form displays under the table with which it is associated—the **14A Interviews table**. Notice also that your new form displays the form icon, which identifies it as a form.

10 From the **Navigation Pane**, select the **14A Candidates table**, click the **Create tab**, and then in the **Forms group**, click **Form**. **Close** « the **Navigation Pane**, and then compare your screen with Figure 14.4.

If a record has related records in another table, the related records display in the form. You can scroll down and see that *Candidate ID# 10115*, for *Sally Marques*, has five interviews scheduled during the two-day Job Fair event.

Figure 14.4

14A Candidates form

Layout View button active

Candidate has related records (interviews scheduled)

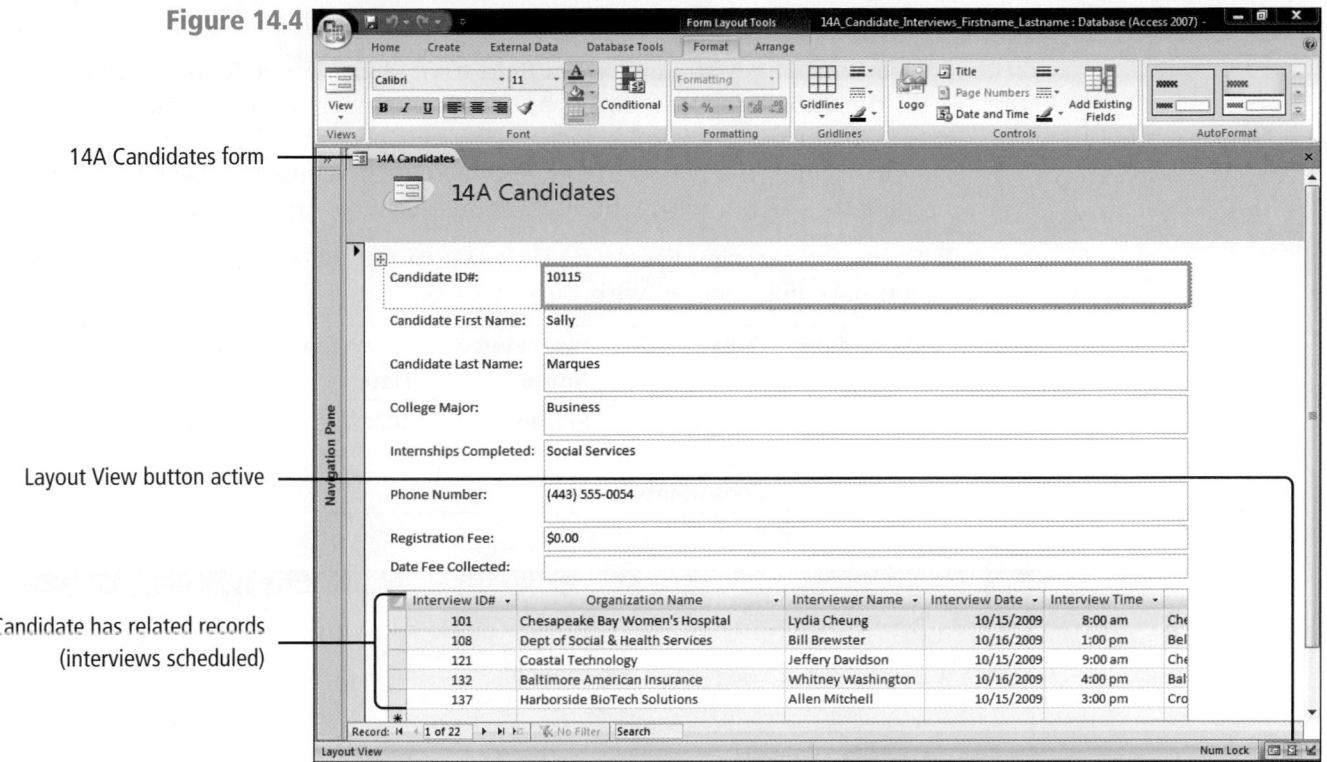

11 **Close** ☒ the **14A Candidates form**, click **Yes**, edit as necessary to name the form **14A Candidates Form** and then click **OK**.

Objective 2
Use a Form to Add and Delete Records

Adding and deleting records using a single-record form helps to prevent data entry errors, because the person performing the data entry is looking at only one record at a time. Recall that your database is useful only if the information is accurate—just like your personal address book is useful only if it contains accurate addresses and phone numbers.

Activity 14.02 Adding Records to a Table by Using a Form

Forms are based on, also referred to as **bound** to, the table where the records are stored. That is, when a record is entered in a form, the new record is added to the corresponding table. The reverse is also true—when a record is added to a table, the new record can be viewed in the corresponding form. In this activity, you will add a new record to the 14A Interviews table by using the form that you just created.

1 **Open** ☒ the **Navigation Pane**, and then open the **14A Interviews Form**. **Close** ☒ the **Navigation Pane**. In the navigation area at the bottom of the form, click the **New (blank) record** button 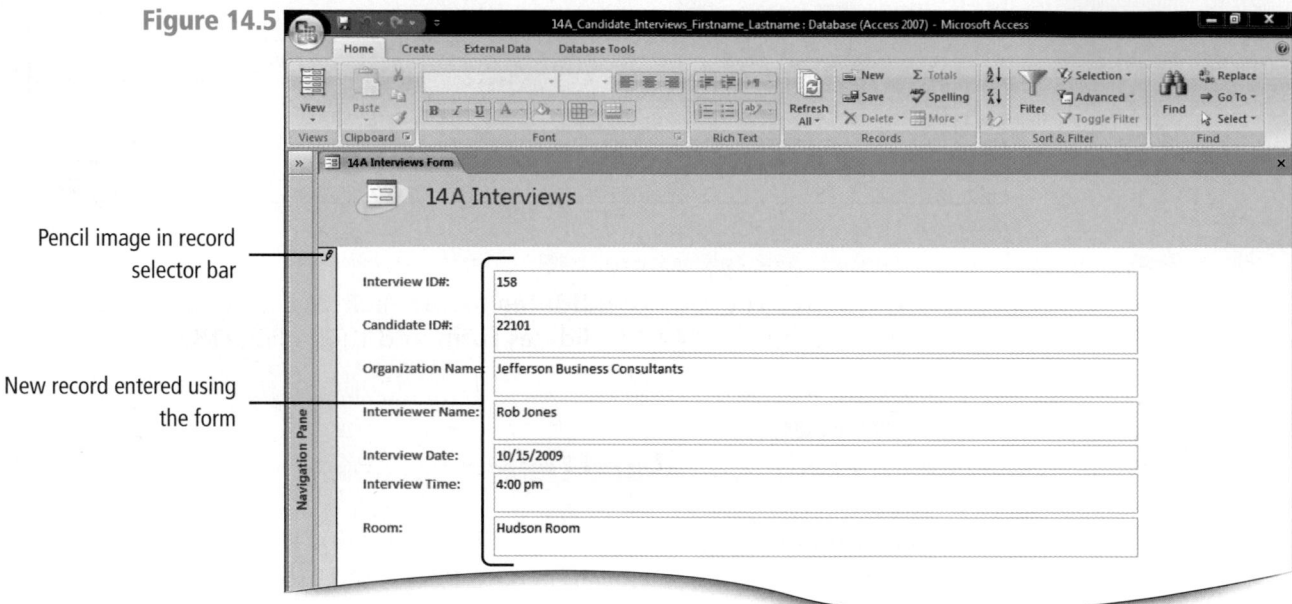.

A new blank form displays, indicated in the navigation area by *58 of 58*. Adding a new record will increase the number of records in the table to 58.

▣ In the **Interview ID#** field, type **158** and then press ⌨Tab⌨.

Use the ⌨Tab⌨ key to move from field to field in a form. This is known as the ***tab order***—the order in which the insertion point moves from one field to the next on a form when you press the ⌨Tab⌨ key. After you start typing, the pencil image displays in the ***record selector*** bar at the left—the bar with which you can select an entire record.

▣ Continue entering the data as shown in the following table, and then compare your screen with Figure 14.5.

Candidate ID#	Organization Name	Interviewer Name	Interview Date	Interview Time	Room
22101	Jefferson Business Consultants	Rob Jones	10/15/2009	4:00 pm	Hudson Room

Figure 14.5

Pencil image in record selector bar

New record entered using the form

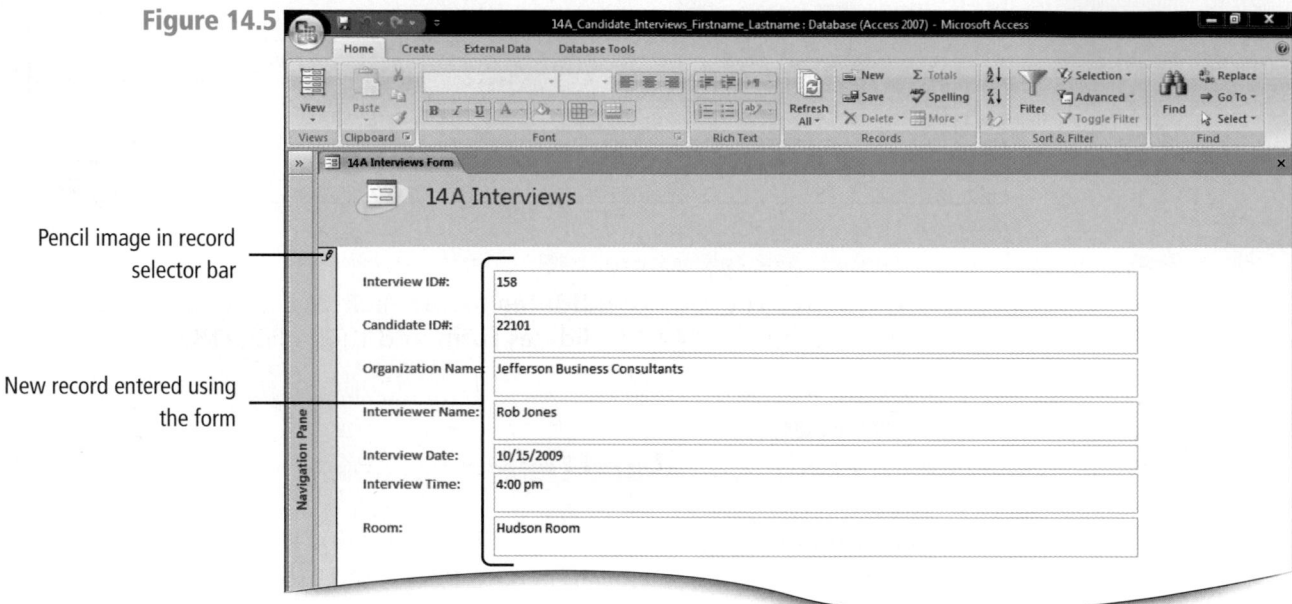

▣ **Close** ❌ the **14A Interviews Form**—the new record is stored in the table. **Open** ❯❯ the **Navigation Pane**, open the **14A Candidates Form**, and then **Close** ❮❮ the **Navigation Pane**.

▣ At the bottom of the screen, in the navigation area, click the **New (blank) record** button 🔳. In the displayed blank form, and using your own first and last name, fill in the form using the information in the following table:

Candidate ID#	Candidate First Name	Candidate Last Name	College Major	Internships Completed	Phone Number	Registration Fee	Date Fee Collected
22155	Firstname	Lastname	Business	Government	(443) 555-0765	$10.00	10/10/2009

6 Close ☒ the **14A Candidates Form**, **Open** ☒ the **Navigation Pane**, open the **14A Candidates table**, and then verify that your record as a candidate displays as the last record in the table. **Close** ☒ the table.

Activity 14.03 Deleting Records from a Table by Using a Form

You can delete records from a database table by using a form. In this activity, you will delete Interview ID# 103, because Jennifer Lee has notified Janna that she will be unable to meet with AAA Telecom at that time.

1 From the **Navigation Pane**, open the **14A Interviews Form**, click in the **Interview ID#** field, and then on the **Home tab**, in the **Find group**, click the **Find** button. Alternatively, press ⌃Ctrl + F to open the Find and Replace dialog box.

2 In the **Look In** box, notice that *Interview ID#* is indicated, and then in the **Find What** box, type **103** Click **Find Next**, and then compare your screen with Figure 14.6 and confirm that the record for **Interview ID# 103** displays.

Record for *Interview ID# 103* displays

Figure 14.6

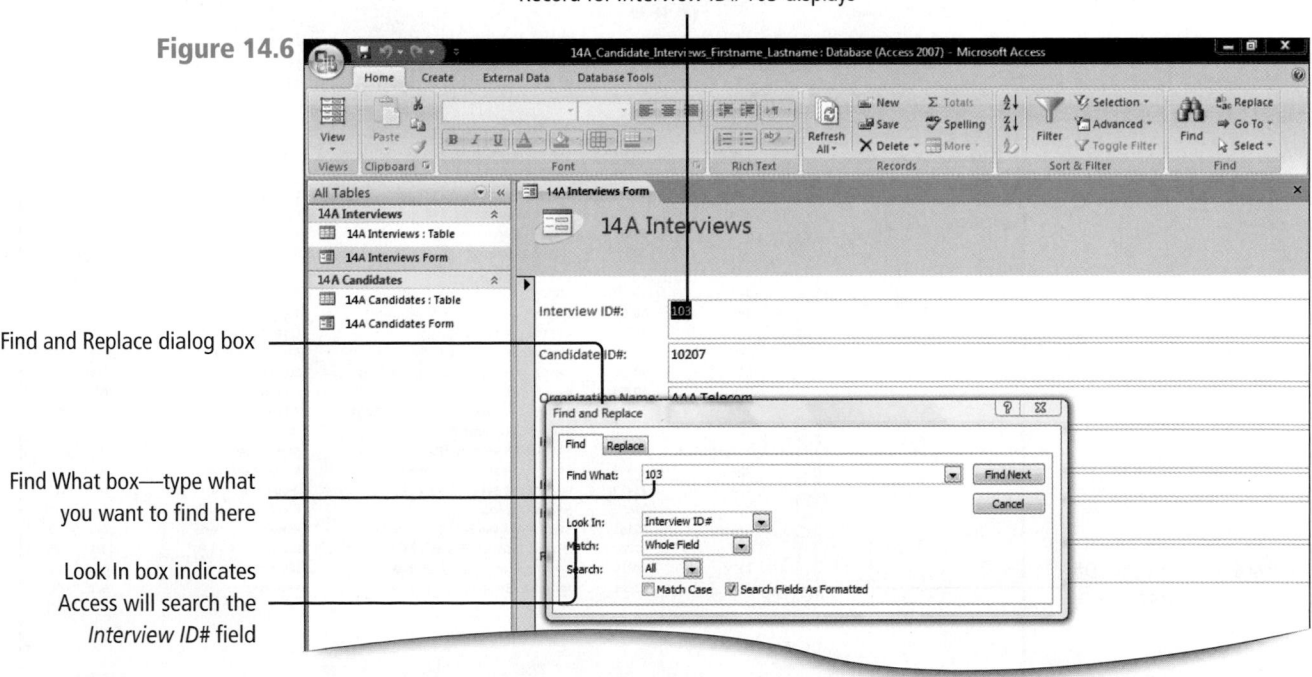

Find and Replace dialog box

Find What box—type what you want to find here

Look In box indicates Access will search the *Interview ID#* field

3 **Close** 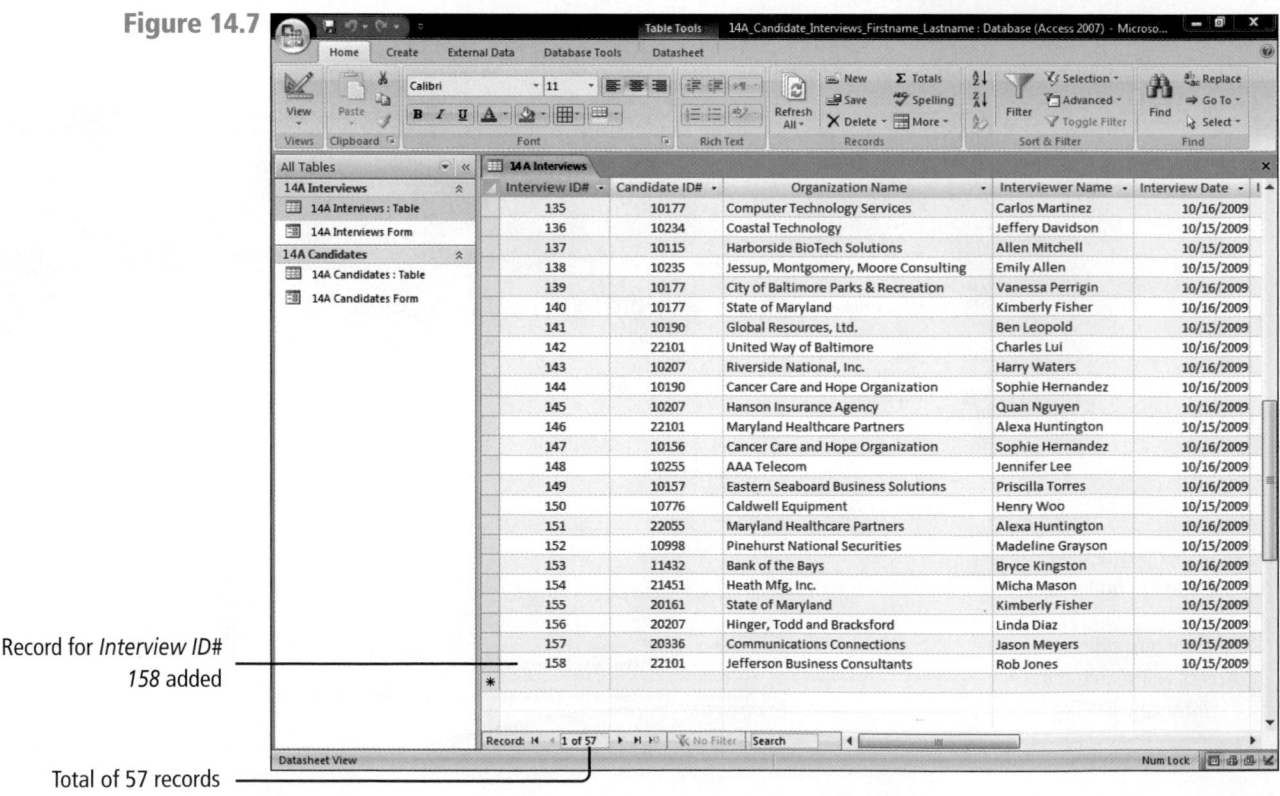 the **Find and Replace** dialog box.

4 On the **Home tab**, in the **Records group**, click the **Delete button arrow**, and then in the displayed list, click **Delete Record** to delete the record for Interview ID# 103.

The record is removed and a message displays alerting you that you are about to delete *1 record*. If you click Yes and delete the record, you cannot use the Undo button to reverse the action. If you delete a record by mistake, you must re-create the record by reentering the data.

5 Click **Yes** to delete the record, and then in the navigation area at the bottom of the screen, notice that the number of records in the table is *57*. **Close** the form object.

6 From the **Navigation Pane**, open the **14A Interviews table**.

7 Examine the table and verify that the record for *Interview ID# 103* no longer displays—by default, tables are sorted in ascending order by their primary key field, which in this table is the **Interview ID#** field. Then, scroll down and verify that the new record you added for **Interview ID# 158** is included in the table. Compare your screen with Figure 14.7.

Your actions of adding and deleting records using the 14A Interviews Form updates the records stored in the 14A Interviews table.

Figure 14.7

Record for *Interview ID# 158* added

Total of 57 records

⃞8 **Close** ☒ the table.

Activity 14.04 Printing a Form

Like other Access objects, forms can be printed. If you click the Print button, *all* of the records will print in the form layout that you selected.

⃞1 From the **Navigation Pane**, open the **14A Candidates Form**. Press Ⓒtrl + Ⓕ to display the **Find and Replace** dialog box. In the **Find What** box, type **22155** In the **Look In** box, be sure that *Candidate ID#* is indicated, and then click **Find Next** to display the record with your name. **Close** ☒ the dialog box.

⃞2 From the **Office** menu 🔘, click **Print**. In the displayed **Print** dialog box, under **Print Range**, click the **Selected Record(s)** option button. In the lower left corner of the dialog box, click the **Setup** button.

⃞3 In the displayed **Page Setup** dialog box, click the **Columns tab**, and then under **Column Size**, in the **Width** box, delete the existing text and type **7"** Compare your screen with Figure 14.8.

Column Width set to 7"

Figure 14.8

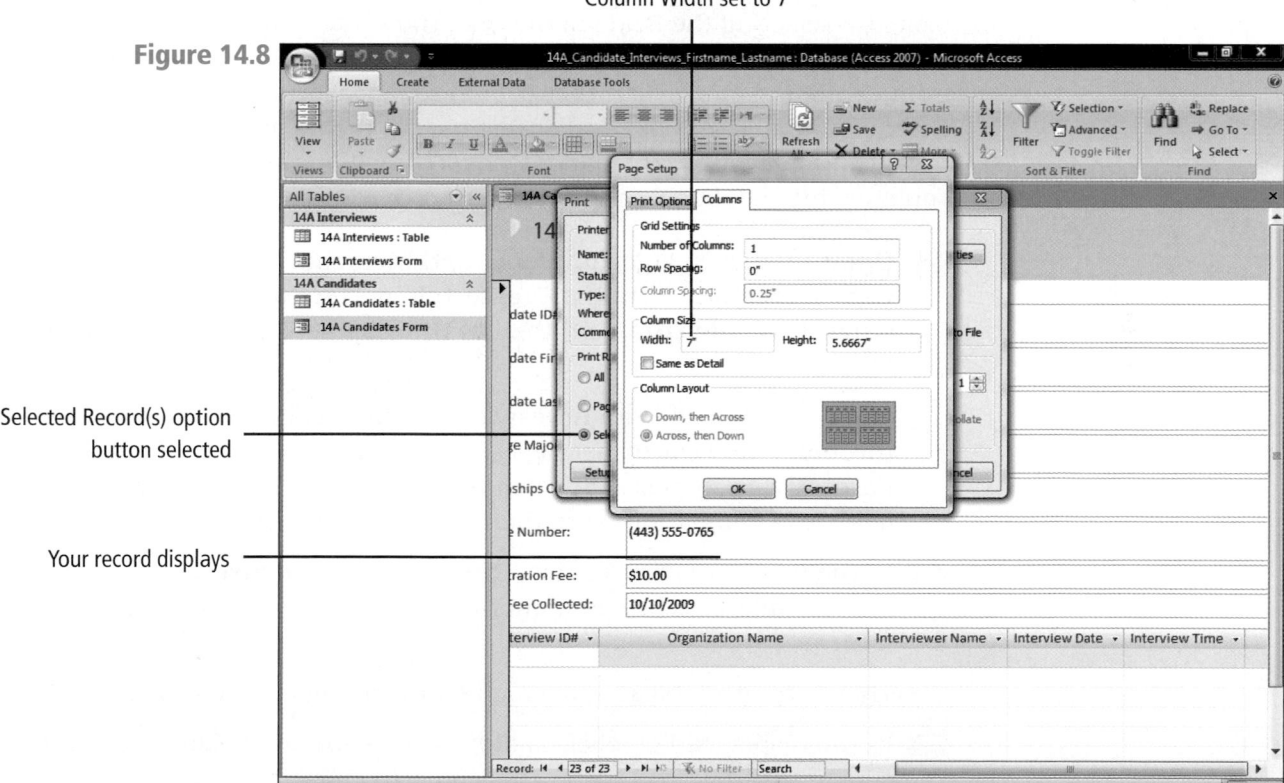

Selected Record(s) option button selected

Your record displays

4 Click **OK** two times to print only your record in the form layout, or submit electronically as directed.

5 **Close** ⊠ the **14A Candidates Form**, and then **Close** « the **Navigation Pane**.

Objective 3
Create a Form by Using the Form Wizard

The Form tool creates an instant form in a simple top-to-bottom layout with all the fields lined up in a single column. The Form Wizard, on the other hand, creates a form quickly, but does so in a manner that gives you more flexibility in the design, layout, and number of fields included.

The design of the form should be planned for the individuals who use the form—either for entering new records or viewing records. For example, when your college counselor displays your information to answer a question for you, it is easier for her or him to view the information spread out in a logical pattern across the screen rather than in one long column.

Activity 14.05 Creating a Form by Using the Form Wizard

By using the Form Wizard to create your form, you control how the form looks by selecting the fields to include, the style to apply, and the layout. When candidates register to attend the Job Fair and view job openings from exhibiting employers, they fill out a paper form. To make it easier to enter candidates into the database, you will create an Access form that matches the layout of the paper form. This will make it easier for the person entering the data into the database.

1 **Open** » the **Navigation Pane**, and then click to select the **14A Candidates** table. On the **Create tab**, in the **Forms group**, click the **More Forms button**, and then in the displayed gallery, click **Form Wizard**.

The Form Wizard is an Access feature that walks you step by step through a process by asking questions. In the first screen of the Form Wizard, you select which fields you want on your form, and the fields can come from more than one table or query.

2 In the text box below **Tables/Queries**, click the **arrow** to display a list of available tables and queries from which you can create the form.

There are two tables from which you can create a new form.

3 In the displayed list, click **Table: 14A Candidates**. Compare your screen with Figure 14.9.

The field names from the 14A Candidates table display in the Available Fields box.

Figure 14.9

One Field button   Next button

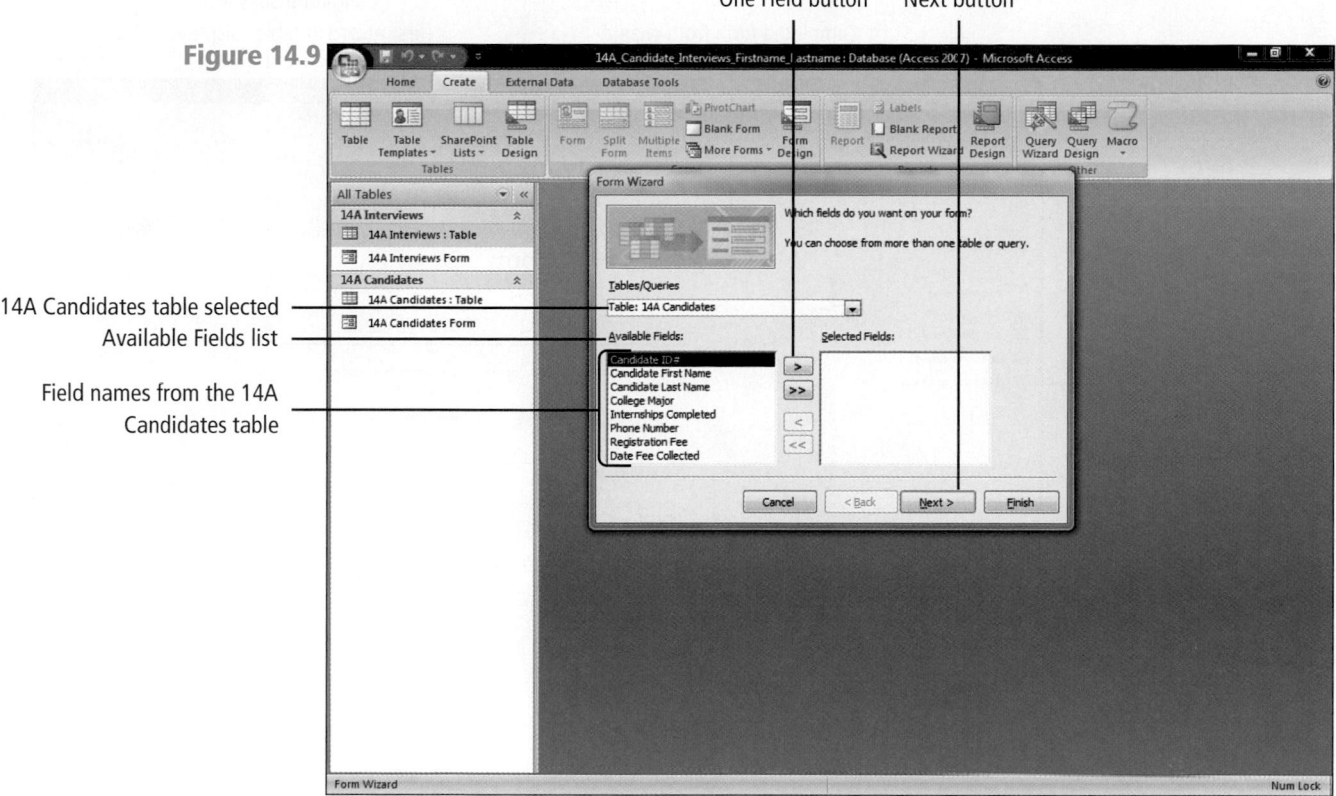

14A Candidates table selected
Available Fields list

Field names from the 14A
Candidates table

4️⃣ Using the **One Field** button ▶, move the following fields to the **Selected Fields** list: **Candidate First Name**, **Candidate Last Name**, **College Major**, **Internships Completed**, and **Phone Number**. Alternatively, double-click a field name to move it to the Selected Fields box.

5️⃣ Click **Next**. Be sure **Columnar** is selected as the layout for your form, and then click **Next**.

Here you select the style you would like for your form. The style controls the font, font size, font color, and background.

6️⃣ Click several of the styles to see how they are formatted, and then scroll as necessary and click **Trek**. Click **Next** to move to the final step; here you name your form. In the box at the top, edit as necessary to name the form **14A Candidates Input Form** and then click **Finish** to close the wizard and create the form. Compare your screen with Figure 14.10.

In the final step of the Form Wizard, when you name the form and click Finish, the form is saved and added to the Navigation Pane. Leave the new form open for the next activity.

Figure 14.10

Completed form from wizard

Candidate Sally Marques
(first record in table) displays in form

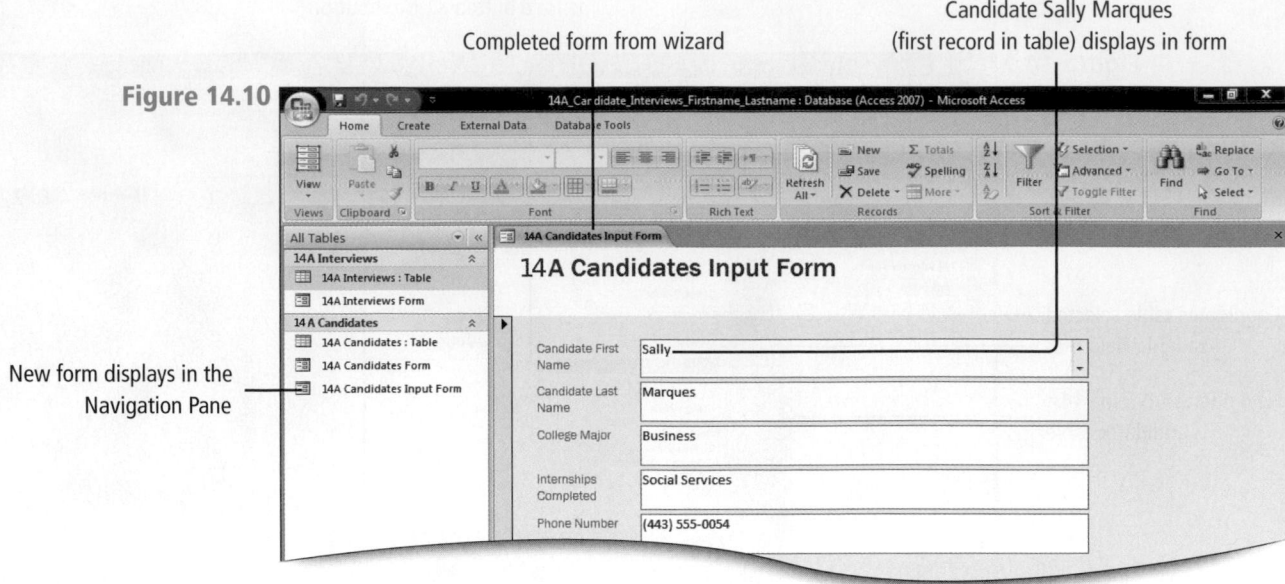

New form displays in the
Navigation Pane

Objective 4
Modify a Form in Design View and in Layout View

After you create a form, Access provides tools with which you can make additional changes. For example, you can resize the fields on the form for easier viewing or more efficient data entry.

Activity 14.06 Modifying a Form in Design View

Design view presents a detailed view of the structure of your form. Because the form is not actually running when displayed in Design view, you cannot see the underlying data. However, some tasks, such as resizing sections, must be completed in Design view.

1 **Close** ⟪ the **Navigation Pane** and be sure your **14A Candidates Input Form** displays. In the lower right corner of your screen, on the right end of the status bar, click the **Design View** button ⬛. Alternatively, in the Views group, click the View button arrow, and then click Design View. Compare your screen with Figure 14.11.

A form is divided into three sections—**Form Header**, **Detail**, and **Form Footer**—each designated by a bar called a **section bar**. **Controls** are objects on a form that display data, perform actions, and let you view and work with information; controls make the form easier to use for the person who is either using the form to enter data or to view data.

The most commonly used control is the **text box control**, which typically displays data from the underlying table, in which case it is referred to as a **bound control**—its source data comes from a table or query. Access places a **label** to the left of a text box control, which contains descriptive information that appears on the form, usually the field names. A control that does not have a source of data, for example a label that displays the title of the form, is an **unbound control**.

Figure 14.11

Text box controls

Form Header section bar ——

Detail section bar ——

Labels for text box controls ——

Form Footer section bar ——

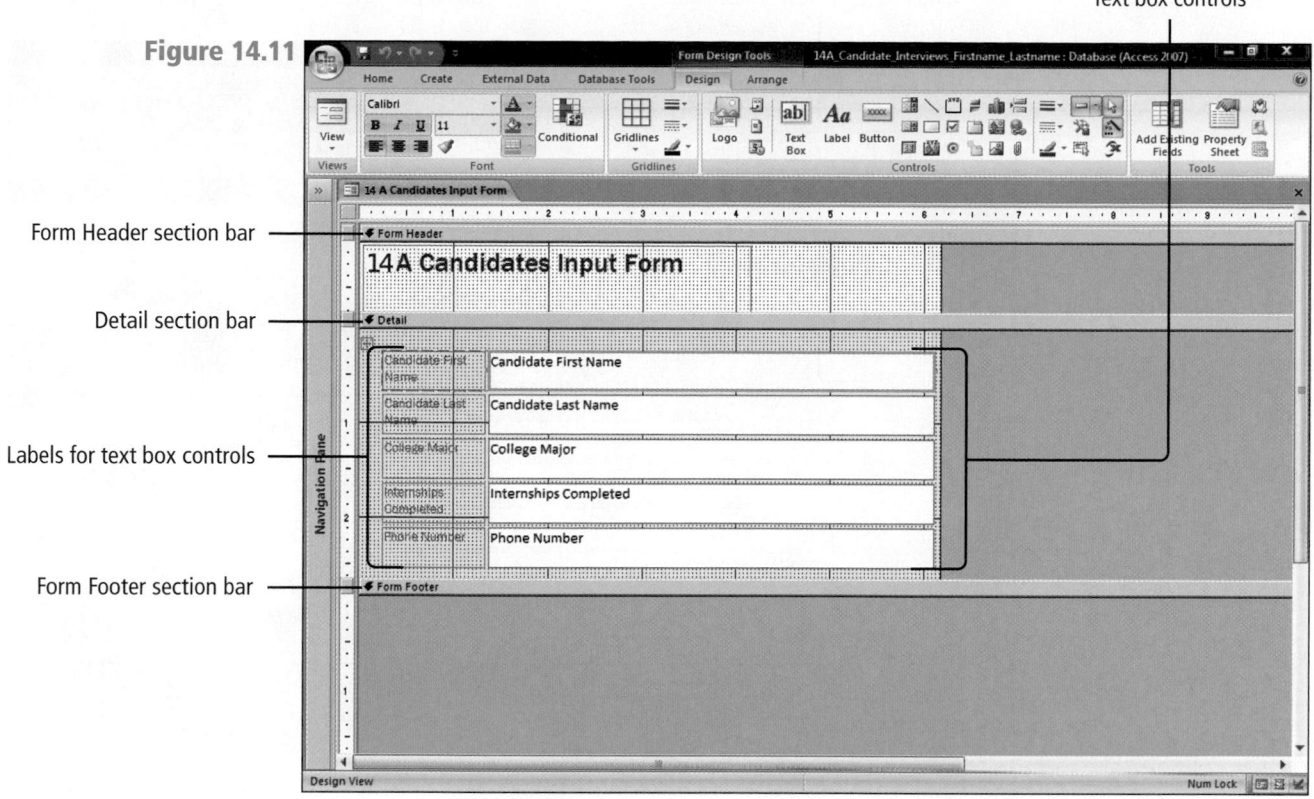

Alert! **Does the field list display?**

If the Field List pane displays on the right, in the upper right corner, click its Close button.

---

2 Point to upper edge of the **Detail section bar** to display the ⊞ pointer, and then drag downward approximately **0.5 inches**. Compare your screen with Figure 14.12.

The Form Header expands—do not be concerned if your expanded Form Header area does not match Figure 14.12 exactly; you will adjust it later. The background grid is dotted and divided into 1-inch squares by horizontal and vertical grid lines to help you place and align controls on the form precisely. You can also use the vertical and horizontal rulers to guide the placement of a control on the form.

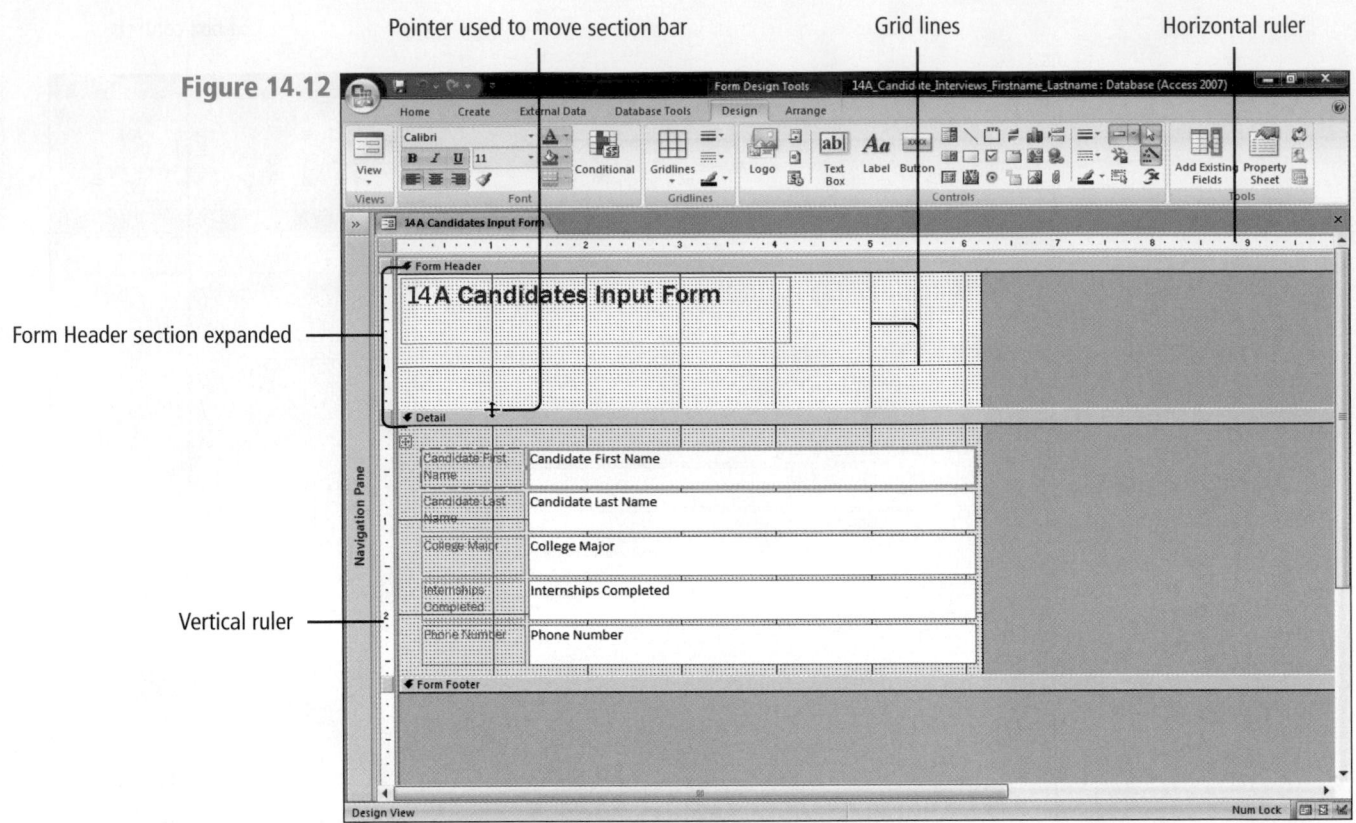

Figure 14.12

Pointer used to move section bar

Grid lines

Horizontal ruler

Form Header section expanded

Vertical ruler

Alert!

Are the rulers missing?

If the horizontal and vertical rulers do not display, on the Arrange tab, in the Show/Hide group, click Ruler.

3 In the **Form Header section**, click anywhere in the title *14A Candidates Input Form* to select it. On the **Design tab**, in the **Font group**, click the **Font Size arrow** [11 ▼], and then click **18**. Click the **Bold** button [**B**] to add bold emphasis to the text. Click the **Font Color button arrow** [**A** ▼], and then under **Access Theme Colors**, in the second row, click the ninth color—**Access Theme 9**.

The label is selected as indicated by the orange border surrounding it. The border displays small boxes called *sizing handles*, which are used to resize the control.

4 On the right side of the selected label control, point to the **middle sizing handle** to display the [↔] pointer—or point to one of the other sizing handles to display a resize pointer—and then double-click to adjust the size of the label control. Compare your screen with Figure 14.13.

The size of the label resizes to fit the text as it has been reformatted.

Figure 14.13

Form Header text—*14A Candidates Input Form*—modified

Sizing handles indicate label is selected

Label formatted and resized

0.50 inch on the vertical ruler

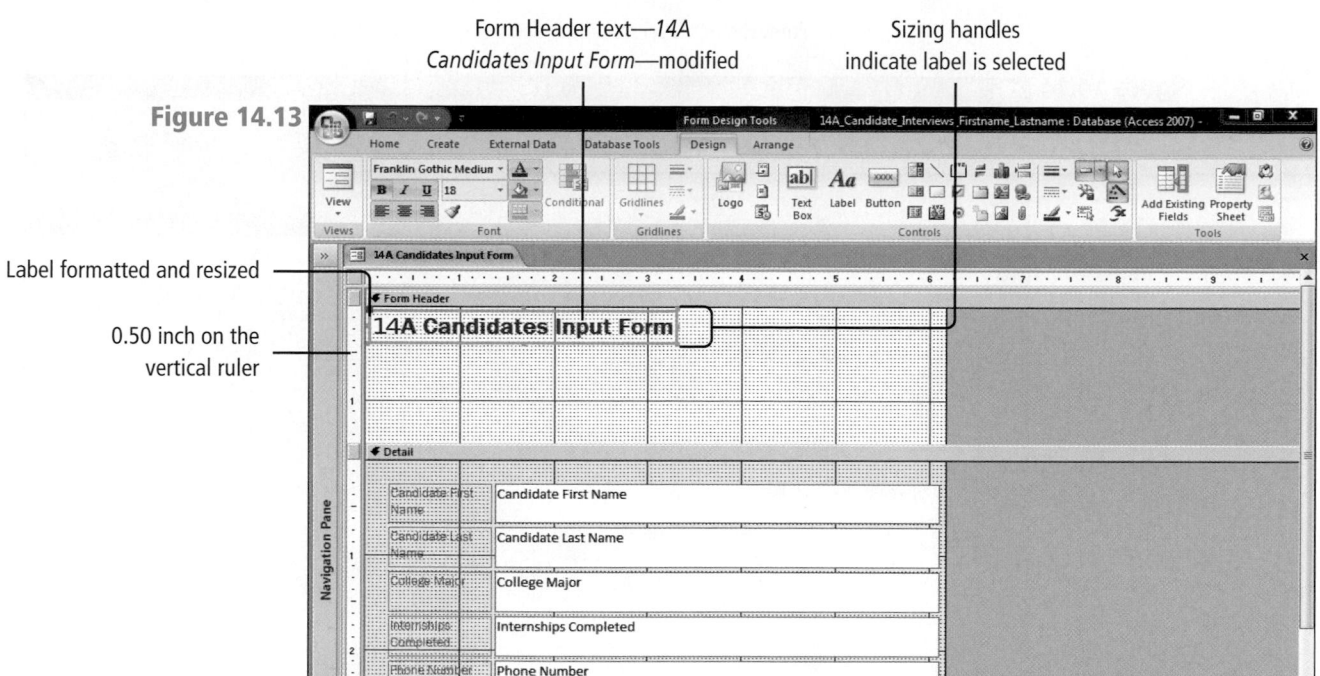

5. Point to the upper edge of the **Detail section bar** to display the ⊕ pointer, and then drag upward until the bar is at **0.50 inch on the vertical ruler**—allowing approximately two rows of dots between the lower edge of the label control border and the upper edge of the **Detail section bar**.

6. At the bottom of the form, point to the lower edge of the **Form Footer section bar** to display the ⊕ pointer, and then drag downward approximately **0.50 inch** to expand this section of the form.

7. On the **Design tab**, in the **Controls group**, click the **Label** button. Position the plus sign of the ⌶A pointer in the **Form Footer** section at approximately **0.25 inch on the horizontal ruler** and even with the top edge of the section. Drag to the right to **5 inches on the horizontal ruler**, and then downward approximately **0.25 inch**. If you are not satisfied with your result, click Undo and begin again.

8. Using your own name, type **14A Candidates Input Form Firstname Lastname** and then press Enter. Point to a sizing handle to display one of the resize pointers, and then double-click to fit the control to the text you typed. On the right end of the status bar, click the **Form View** button 🔲. Compare your screen with Figure 14.14.

Form Footer text displays on the screen at the bottom of the form, and prints only on the last page when all the forms are printed as a group.

Figure 14.14

Form Header label modified

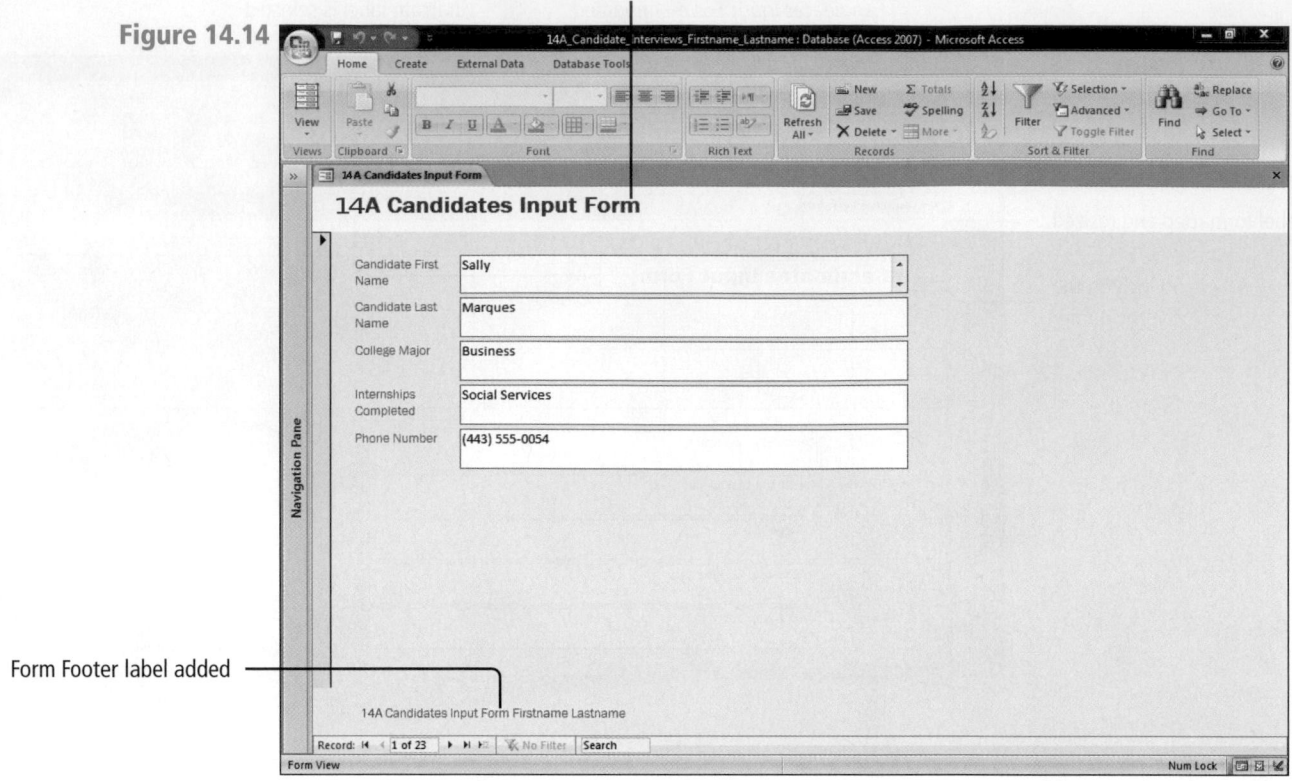

14A Candidates Input Form

Form Footer label added

14A Candidates Input Form Firstname Lastname

---

9 On the **Quick Access Toolbar**, click the **Save** button 💾 to save the changes you have made to the design of your form. Leave the **14A Candidates Input Form** open for the next activity.

Activity 14.07 Adding, Resizing, and Moving Controls in Layout View

Use the Layout view to change the form's ***control layout***—the grouped arrangement of controls on a form in Layout view. Use Layout view to make quick changes to the form's design by adding or moving controls.

1 In the lower right corner of your screen, at the right end of the status bar, click the **Layout View** button 🔳.

On the Ribbon, the Format tab is selected. A dotted line surrounds the first control—label and text box—and the white text box is surrounded by a solid orange border. In the upper left corner, the ***layout selector*** displays, with which you can select and move the entire group of controls in this view.

2 In the **Controls group**, click the **Add Existing Fields** button to display the **Field List** pane. Compare your screen with Figure 14.15.

Figure 14.15

First label and control selected

Field List pane displays

Layout selector

Layout View button in status bar selected

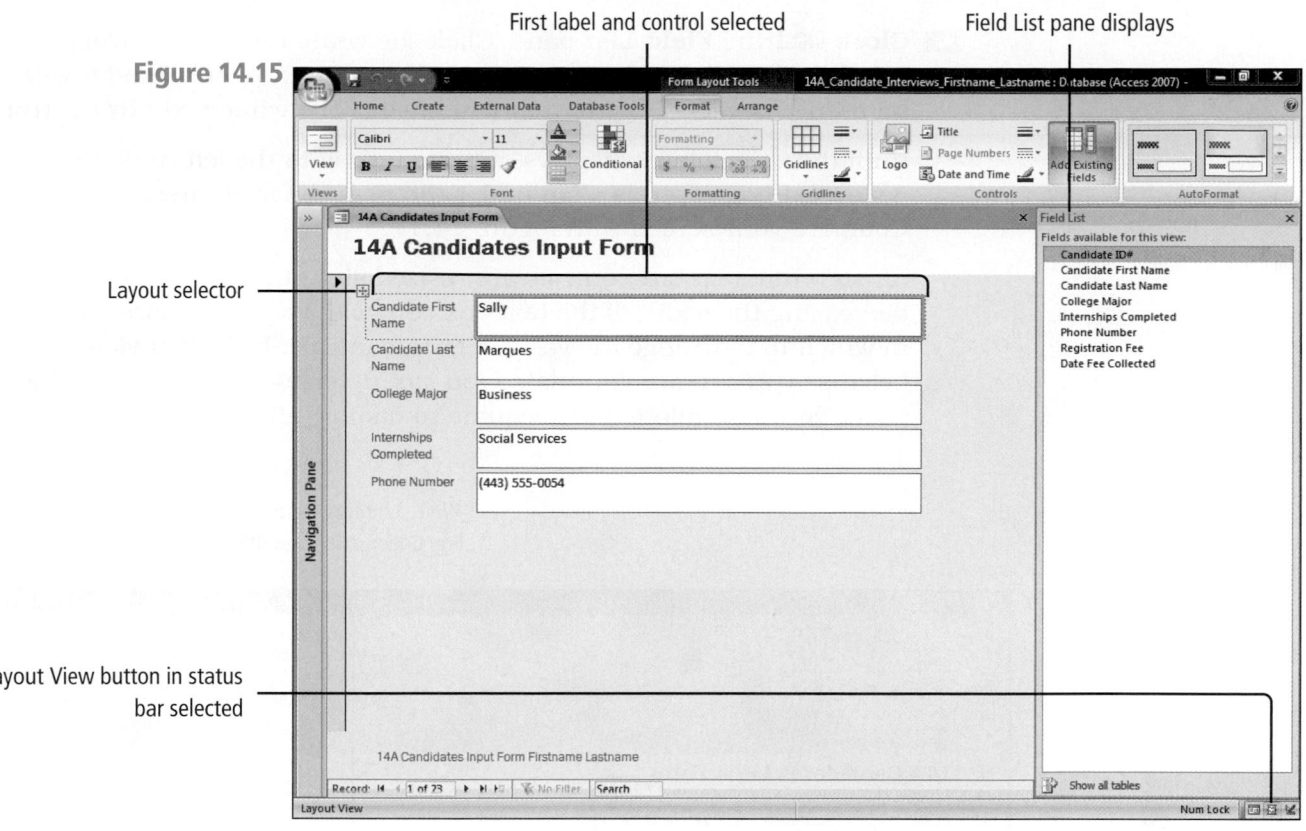

In the displayed **Field List**, point to **Candidate ID#**, hold down the left mouse button, and then drag until the pointer is in the upper portion of the *Candidate First Name* text box control and a thick orange line displays above the control. Release the mouse button, and then compare your screen with Figure 14.16. If you are not satisfied with your result, click Undo and begin again.

The Candidate ID# text box control is added to the form; recall that Access also places a label to the left of the text box. In this manner, you can add a bound text box to a form by dragging a field from the Field List pane.

Candidate ID# text box control added to the form

Figure 14.16

Access adds label to the text box control

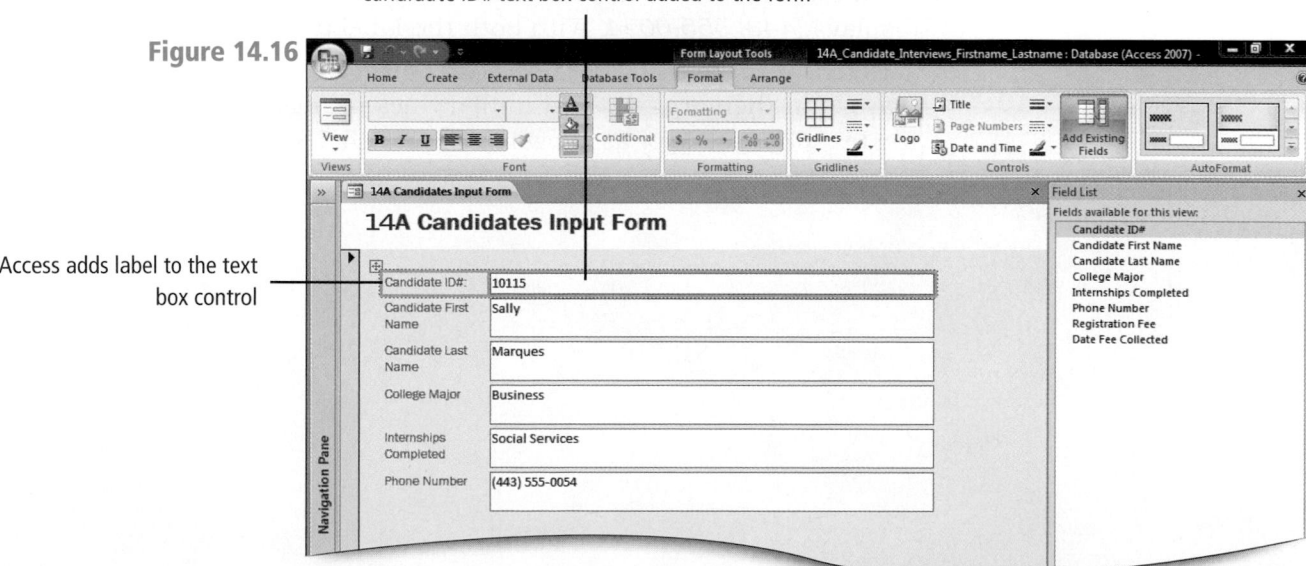

4 **Close** ❌ the **Field List** pane. Click the white text box control for **Candidate ID#**, which currently displays *10115*, to surround it with an orange border. Point to the right edge of the white text box control until the ↔ pointer displays, and then drag to the left until all the white text box controls align under the *m* in the form title above. Compare your screen with Figure 14.17.

All six white text box controls are resized simultaneously. By decreasing the width of the text box controls, you have more space in which to rearrange the various form controls. In Layout view, because you can see your data, you can determine visually that the space you have allotted is adequate to display all records.

White text box controls
align under *m* in form title

Figure 14.17

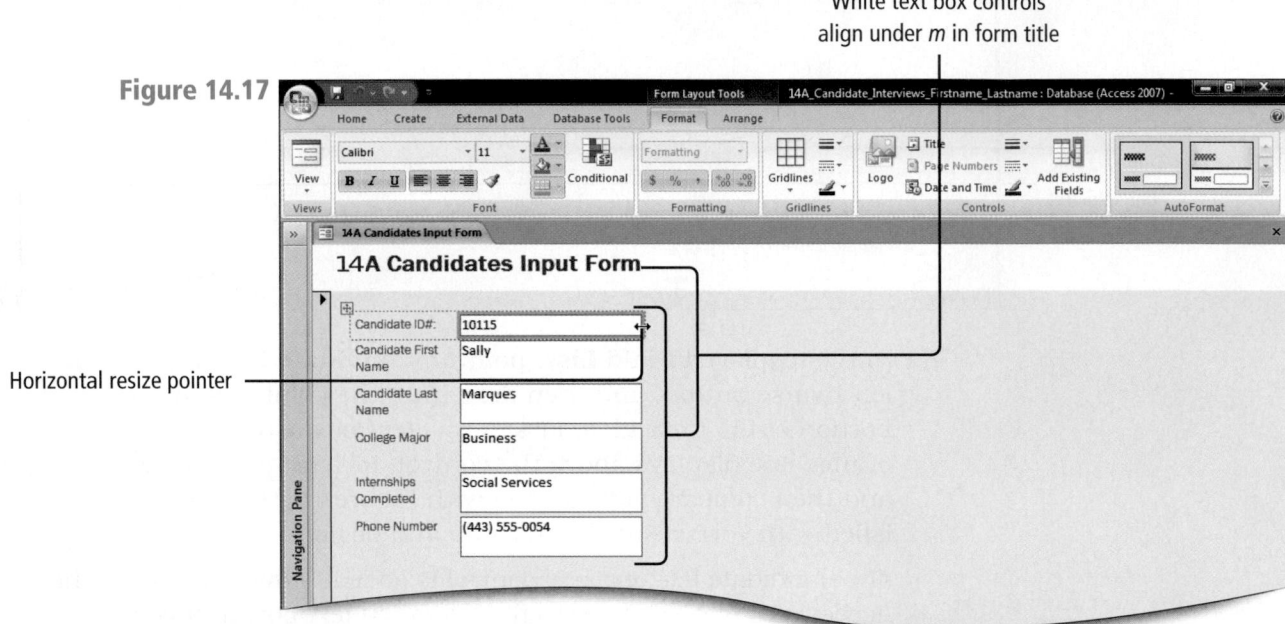

Horizontal resize pointer

5 Click the white text box control for **Phone Number**, which currently displays *(443) 555-0054*. With both the label and the text box control selected, point to the white text box control until the 🖑 pointer displays, and then drag upward until a thick orange line displays above the text *College Major* as shown in Figure 14.18.

Figure 14.18

Move pointer

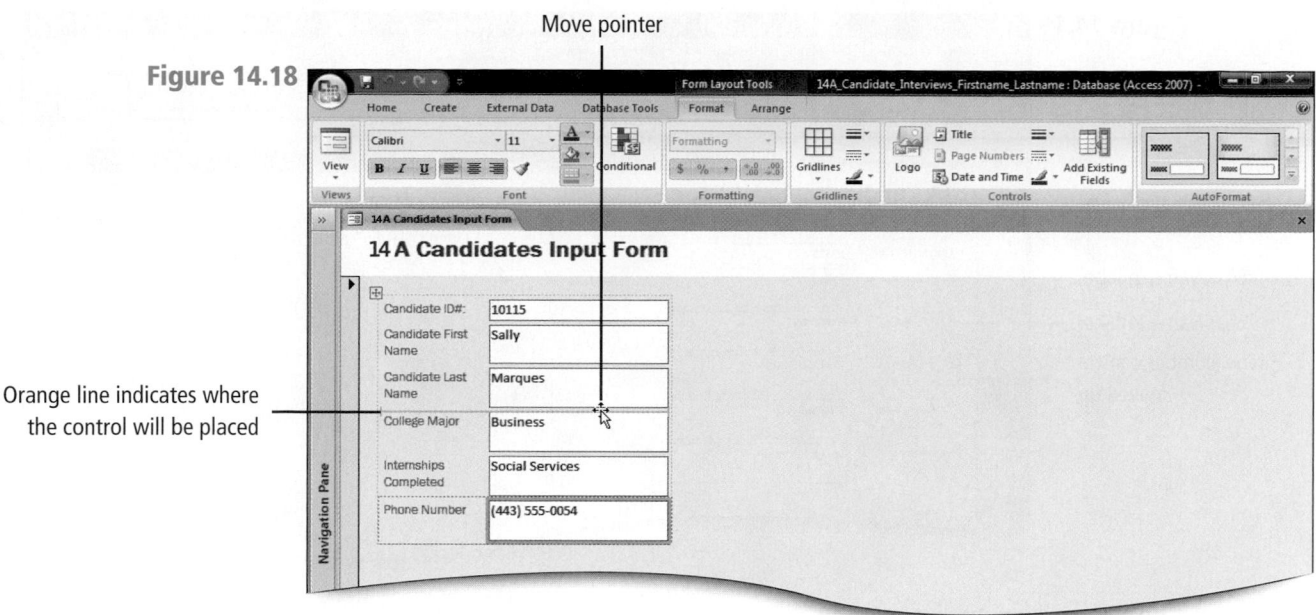

Orange line indicates where
the control will be placed

6 Release the mouse button to place the **Phone Number control** above the **College Major control**.

7 Click the **Candidate First Name label** to select it. Click to the left of the word *First* to place the insertion point in the control, and then press ←Bksp as necessary to delete the text *Candidate* so that the label indicates *First Name*.

With the insertion point placed in the label, you can edit the label. The form label text does not have to match the field name of the associated table.

8 Using the technique you just practiced, edit the **Candidate Last Name label** to indicate *Last Name*. Then, click in a shaded area of the form so that no controls are selected and compare your screen with Figure 14.19.

Figure 14.19

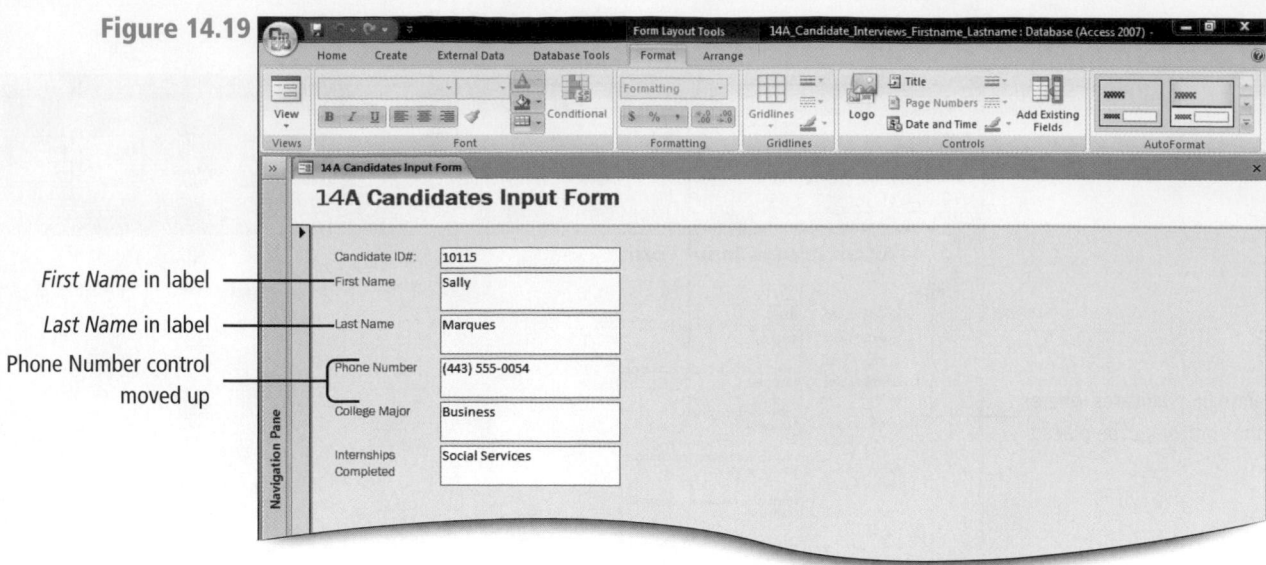

First Name in label ——

Last Name in label ——

Phone Number control
moved up ——

9 On the **Quick Access Toolbar**, click the **Save** button 🖫 to save the changes you have made to the design of your form in Layout view.

Activity 14.08 Formatting and Aligning Controls in Layout View

1 With the form still displayed in Layout view, hold down ⇧Shift, and then click each of the **white text box controls**.

Alert! | **Do your controls change order when selecting?**

If, when selecting all the controls, the controls change order, click Undo and select the controls again.

2 With the six text box controls selected, on the **Format tab**, in the **Font group**, click the **Fill/Back Color button arrow** 🖋 . Under **Access Theme Colors**, in the second row, click the fourth color—**Access Theme 4**. Click the **Font Size button arrow** 11 , and then click **12**.

3 Click in a shaded area of the screen to deselect all the **text box controls**. Hold down ⇧Shift, and then click each of the six labels to the left of the text box controls. With the six label controls selected, change the **Font Size** 11 to **12**, change the **Font Color** 🅰 to **Access Theme 9**, and then apply **Bold** **B** . Click in a shaded area to deselect, and then compare your screen with Figure 14.20.

Text box controls formatted with Font Size 12 and Access Theme 4 fill color

Figure 14.20

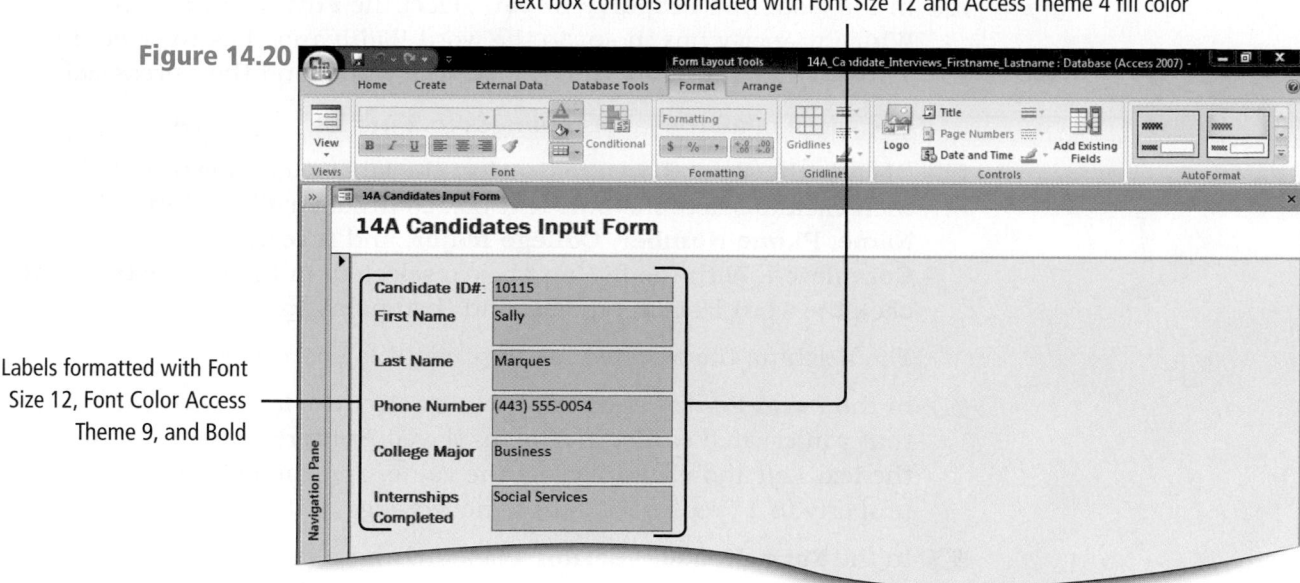

Labels formatted with Font Size 12, Font Color Access Theme 9, and Bold

4 Click the **Internships Completed** label. On the Ribbon, click the **Arrange tab**, and then in the **Tools group**, click the **Property Sheet** button. Compare your screen with Figure 14.21.

The *Property Sheet* for the selected label displays. Each control has an associated Property Sheet where you can make precision changes to the properties—characteristics—of selected controls.

Arrange tab selected

Property Sheet button in Tools group

Figure 14.21

Property Sheet for label

Label selected

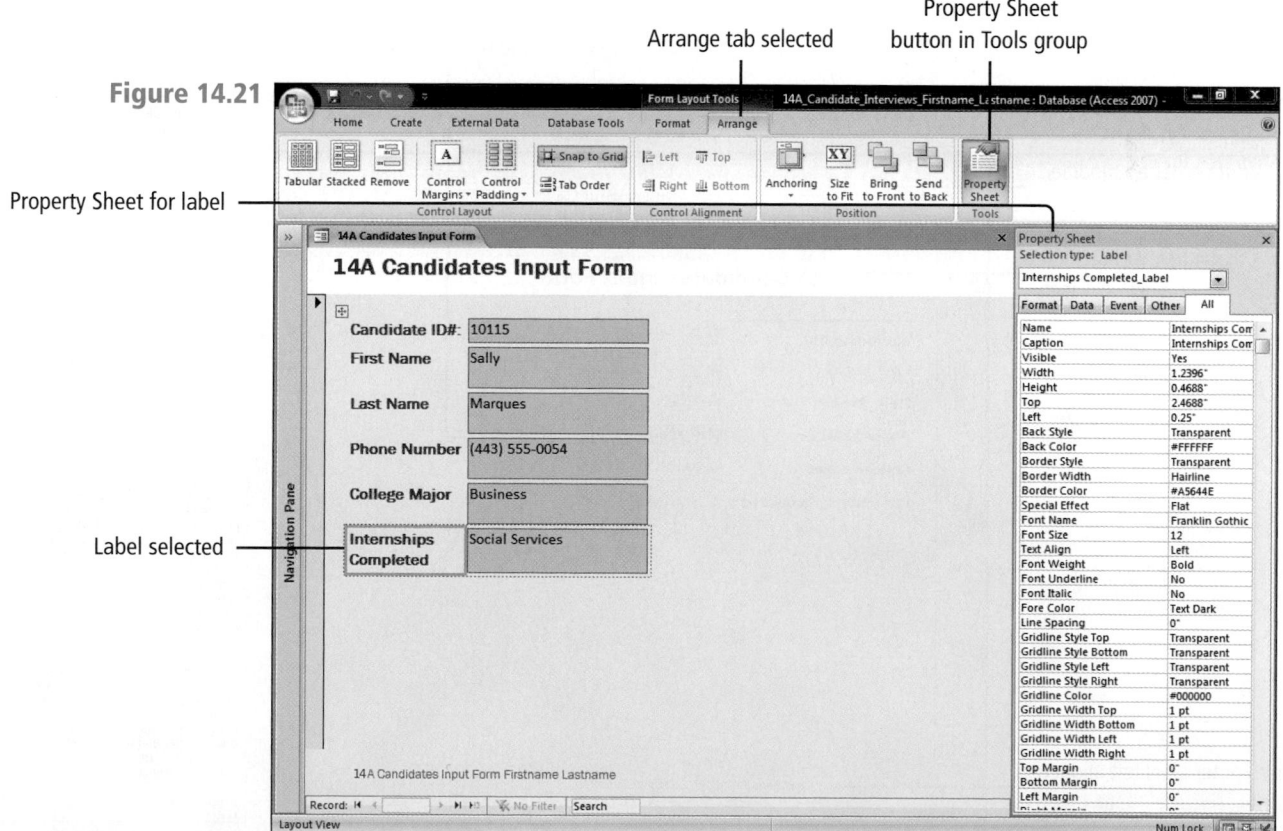

5 In the displayed **Property Sheet**, select the **Format tab**. In the **Width** property box, point to the word *Width* and click to select its value to the right. Type **2** to replace the value, and then press Enter.

The width of all the labels changes to 2 inches.

6 Click in the shaded area to deselect the label. Hold down ⬆Shift, and then click to select the blue text box controls for **First Name**, **Last Name**, **Phone Number**, **College Major**, and **Internships Completed**. With the five text boxes selected, in the **Property Sheet**, click the word *Height*, type **0.3** and then press Enter.

The height of the selected text box controls decreases.

7 In the **Form Footer section**, click to select the label with your name that you created earlier. In the displayed **Property Sheet**, point to the text *Left* and click to select the value, and then change the **Left** property to **1** Press Enter to align the left edge of the label at 1 inch.

8 In the **Form Header section**, click anywhere in the title label text *14A Candidates Input Form*. In the **Property Sheet**, on the **Format tab**, change the **Left** property to **1** and then press Enter. Compare your screen with Figure 14.22.

Recall that each control has an associated Property Sheet on which you can change the properties—characteristics—of the control. Because this is a label that was added to the form, Access assigns it a number. The number on your property sheet may differ. The left edge of the Form Header label moves so it aligns at 1 inch. In this manner, you can place a control in a specific location on the form.

Height of five controls
modified to 0.3 inch

Label number

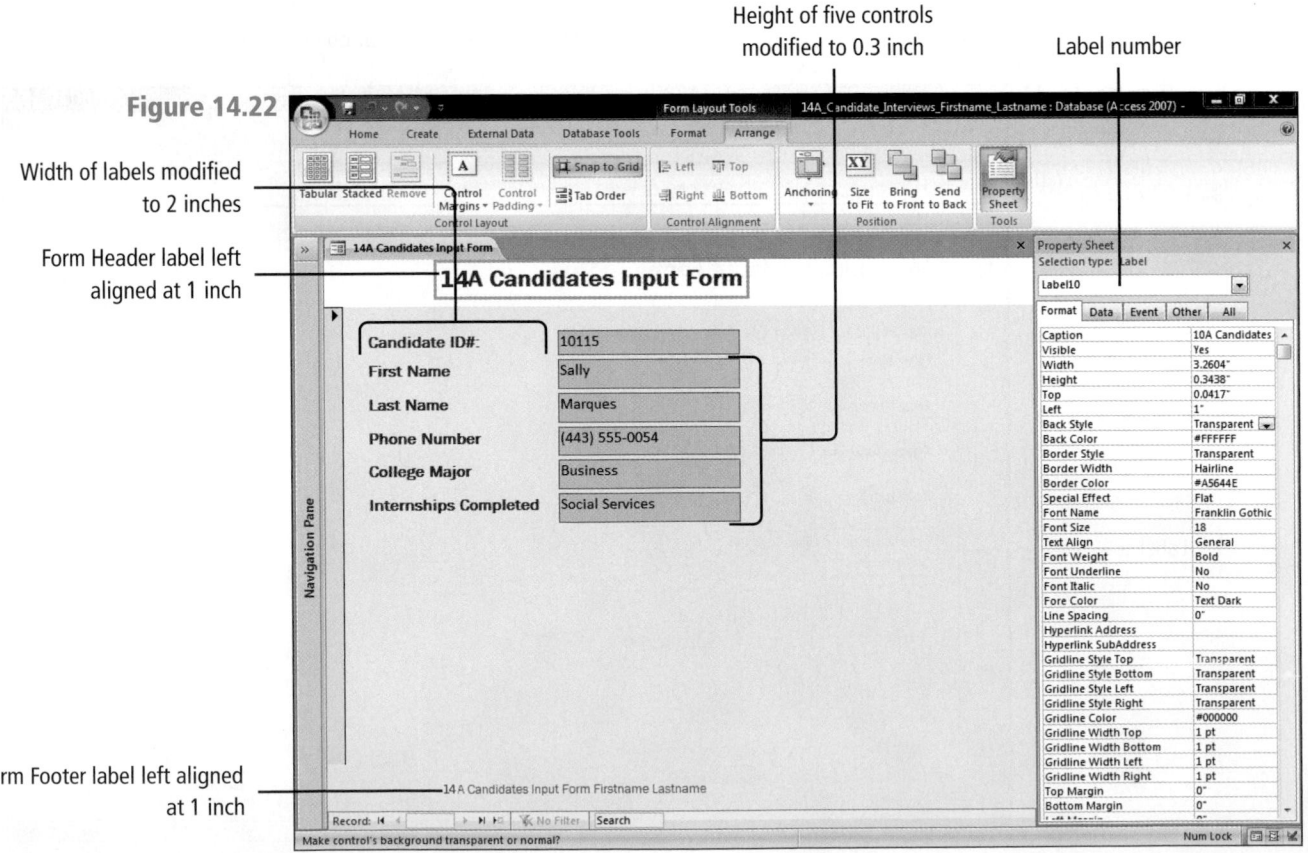

Figure 14.22

Width of labels modified
to 2 inches

Form Header label left
aligned at 1 inch

Form Footer label left aligned
at 1 inch

9 In the upper right corner of the **Property Sheet**, click the **Close** button ⊠. On the right side of the status bar, click the **Form View** button. Compare your screen with Figure 14.23.

The form displays in Form view. Using these techniques, you can make a form attractive and easy to use for those who must use the form to view and enter records on a screen.

Figure 14.23

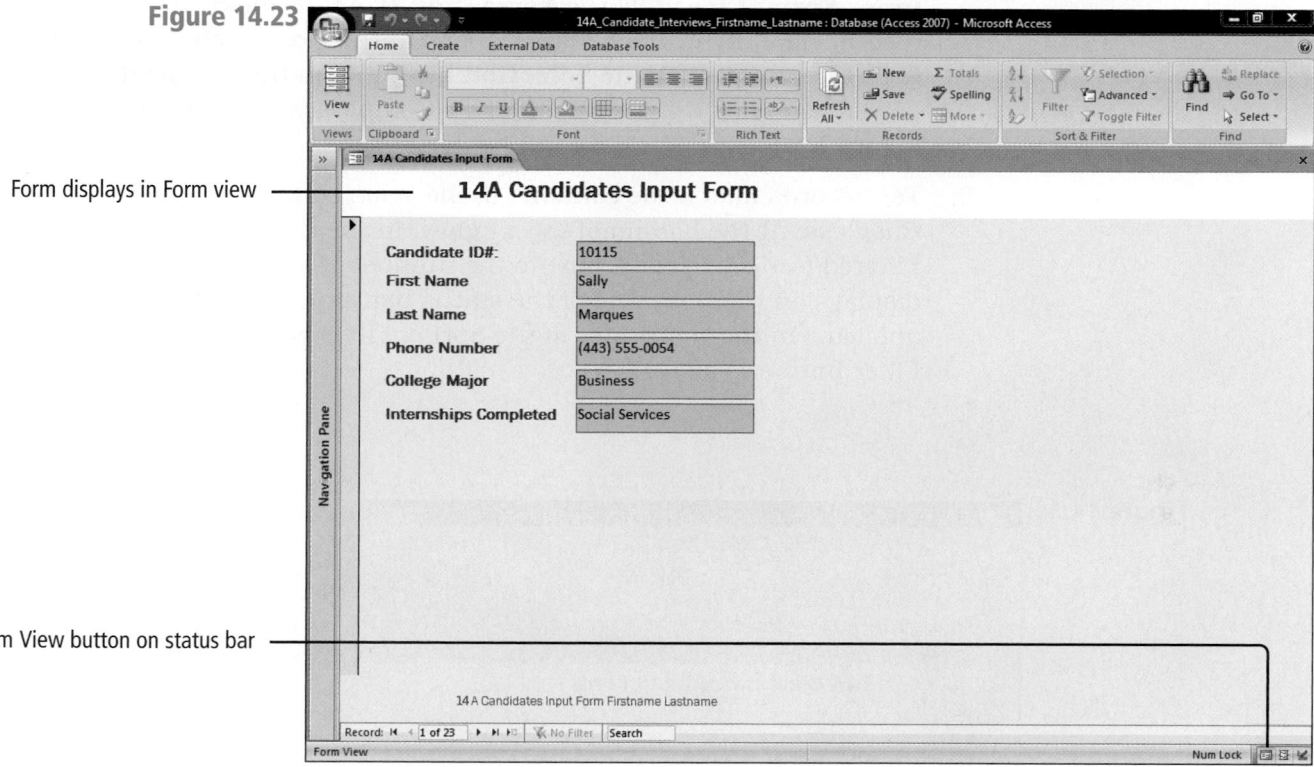

Form displays in Form view

Form View button on status bar

10 On the **Quick Access Toolbar**, click the **Save** button to save the changes you have made to your form's design. In the navigation area, click the **Last record** button to display the record containing your name. Then, from the **Office** menu , click **Print**. In the displayed **Print** dialog box, under **Print Range**, click the **Selected Record(s)** option button. Click **OK** to print, or submit electronically as directed.

11 **Close** ⊠ the form, and if necessary, click **Yes** to save the changes.

Objective 5
Filter Records

Filtering records in a form is the process of displaying only a portion of the total records—a ***subset***—based on matching specific values. Filters are commonly used to provide a quick answer, and the result is not generally saved for future use. For example, by filtering records in a form, you can quickly display a subset of records for students majoring in Business.

Activity 14.09 Filtering Data by Selection on One Field

Several interviewers at the Baltimore Job Fair would like to see records for candidates who are majoring in Business. Use the *Filter By Selection* command—which retrieves only the records that contain the value in the selected field—to temporarily remove the records that do *not* contain the value in the selected field.

1 **Open** ⟩⟩ the **Navigation Pane**, and then open the **14A Candidates Input Form**. **Close** ⟨⟨ the **Navigation Pane**. In the displayed first record, click the **College Major** label. On the **Home tab**, in the **Sort & Filter group**, click the **Selection** button, and then in the displayed list, click **Equals "Business"**. Compare your screen with Figure 14.24.

Ten records match the contents of the selected College Major field—*Business*. At the bottom of the window, in the navigation area, a Filtered button displays next to the number of records. *Filtered* also displays on the right side of the status bar to indicate that a filter is applied. On the Home tab, in the Sort & Filter group, the Toggle Filter button is active.

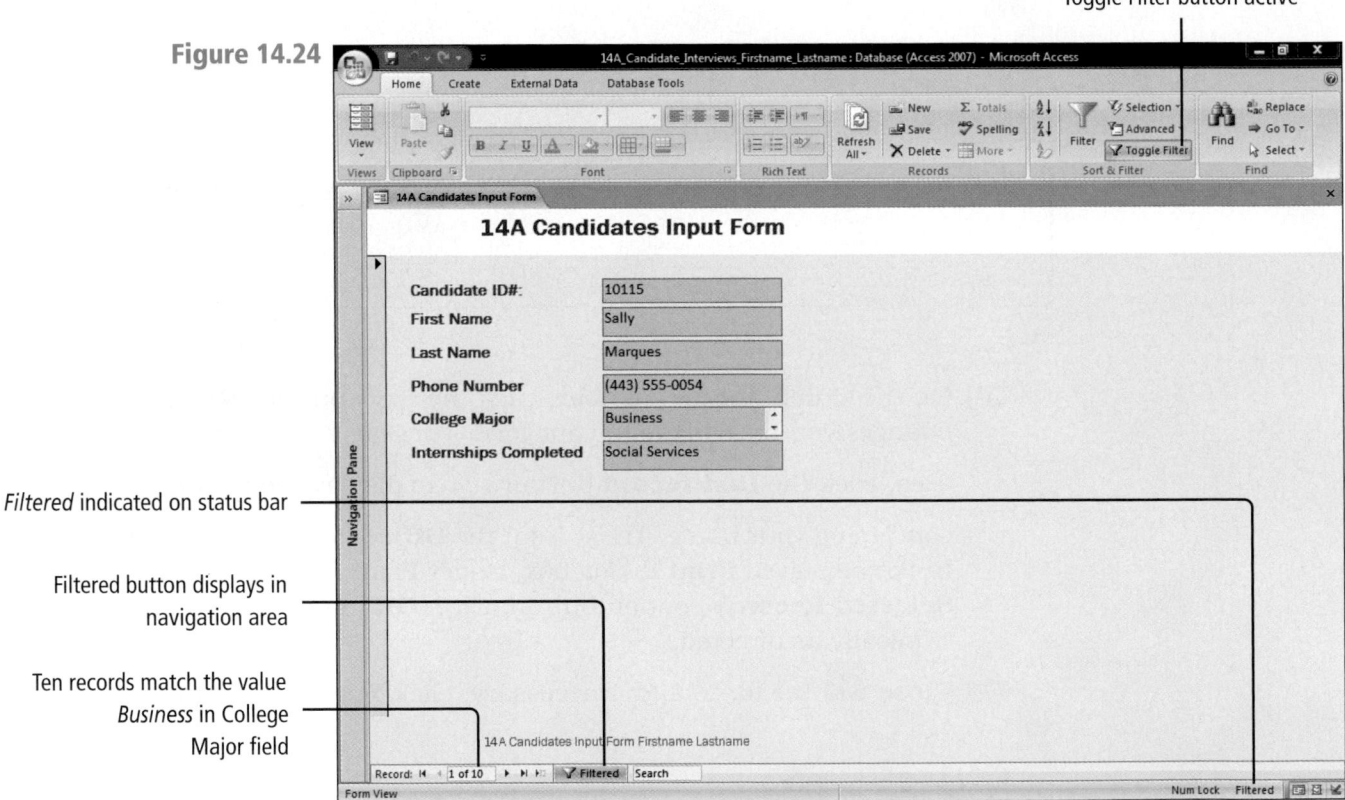

Toggle Filter button active

Figure 14.24

Filtered indicated on status bar

Filtered button displays in navigation area

Ten records match the value *Business* in College Major field

2 On the **Home tab**, in the **Sort & Filter group**, click the **Toggle Filter** button to remove the filter and activate all 23 records. Notice the **Unfiltered** button in the navigation area. Alternatively, click the Filtered button in the navigation area to remove a filter.

3 Be sure the first record—for Sally Marques—displays, and then click to place the insertion point in the blue **College Major** text box control to display up and down arrows. On the **Home tab**, in the **Sort & Filter group**, click the **Toggle Filter** button to reapply the filter, and then in the navigation area, click the **Last record** button ▶| to display the last of the ten records that match *Business*.

The record for *Candidate ID# 22155* displays—the record with your name.

4 In the **Sort & Filter group**, click the **Toggle Filter** button to remove the filter and activate all of the records. In the navigation area, click the **Next record** button ▶ one time to move to **Record 2**. In the **Phone Number** field, select the text *(410)* including the parentheses, which is the Area Code. On the **Home tab**, in the **Sort & Filter group**, click the **Selection** button, and then click **Begins with "(410)"**.

A new filter is applied that retrieves the fourteen records in which the *Phone Number* contains the (410) Area Code.

5 On the **Home tab**, in the **Sort & Filter group**, click the **Toggle Filter** button to remove the filter and activate all of the records.

Activity 14.10 Using Filter by Form

Use the *Filter By Form* command to filter the records in a form based on one or more fields, or based on more than one *value* in the same field. The Filter By Form command offers greater flexibility than the Filter by Selection command when you want an answer to a question that requires matching multiple values. In this activity, you will help Janna Sorokin determine how many candidates have a major of *Communications* or *Graphic Arts*, because several interviewers are interested in candidates with one of those two backgrounds.

1 With the **14A Candidates Input Form** still open, on the **Home tab**, in the **Sort & Filter group**, click the **Advanced** button, and then in the displayed list, click **Filter By Form**. Click the **Advanced** button again, and then click **Clear Grid**. Compare your screen with Figure 14.25.

The Filter by Form window displays; all the field names are included, but without any data. In the empty text box for each field, you can type a value or choose from a list of available values. The *Look for* and *Or* tabs display at the bottom.

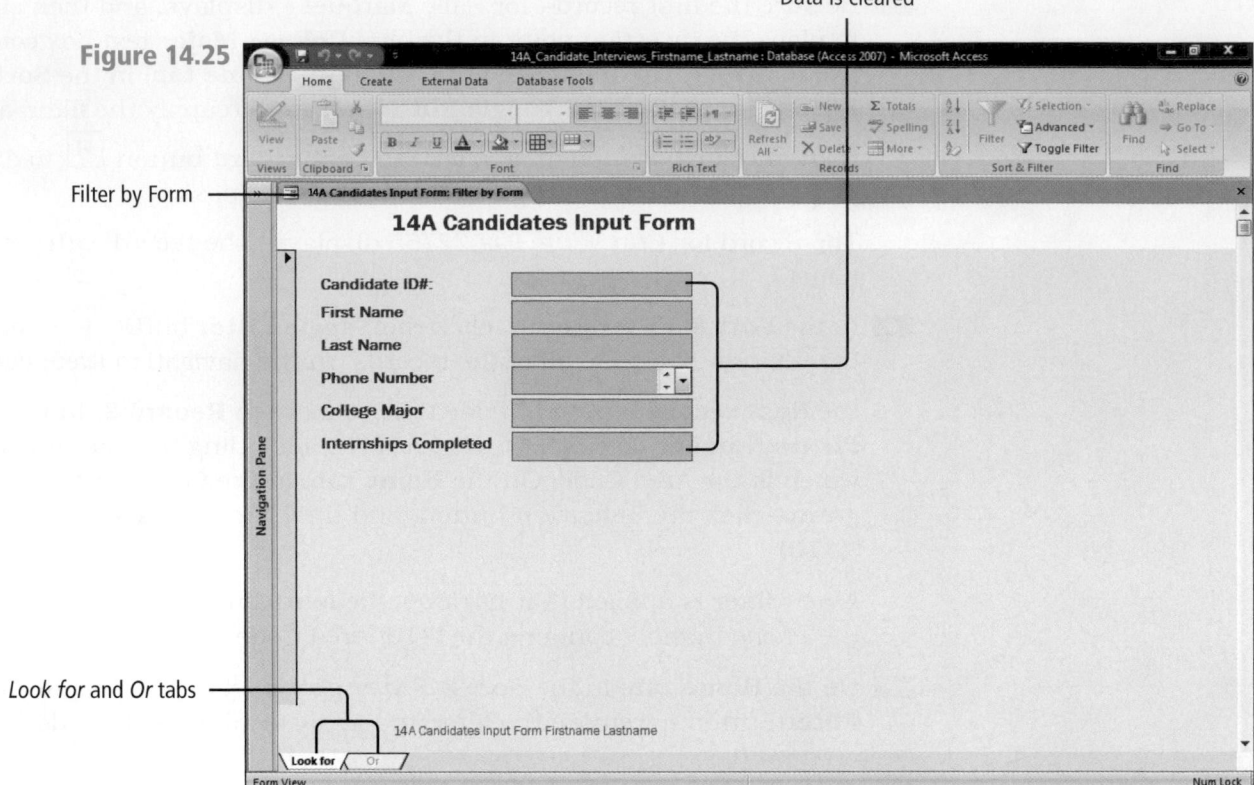

Figure 14.25

Data is cleared

Filter by Form

14A Candidates Input Form

Candidate ID#:

First Name

Last Name

Phone Number

College Major

Internships Completed

Look for and *Or* tabs

14A Candidates Input Form Firstname Lastname

2 Click the blue **College Major** text box control. At the far right edge of the text box, click the larger **down arrow**, and then in the displayed list, click **Communications**. In the **Sort & Filter group**, click the **Toggle Filter** button, and then compare your screen with Figure 14.26.

As indicated in the navigation area, six candidate records indicate a College Major of *Communications*.

Figure 14.26

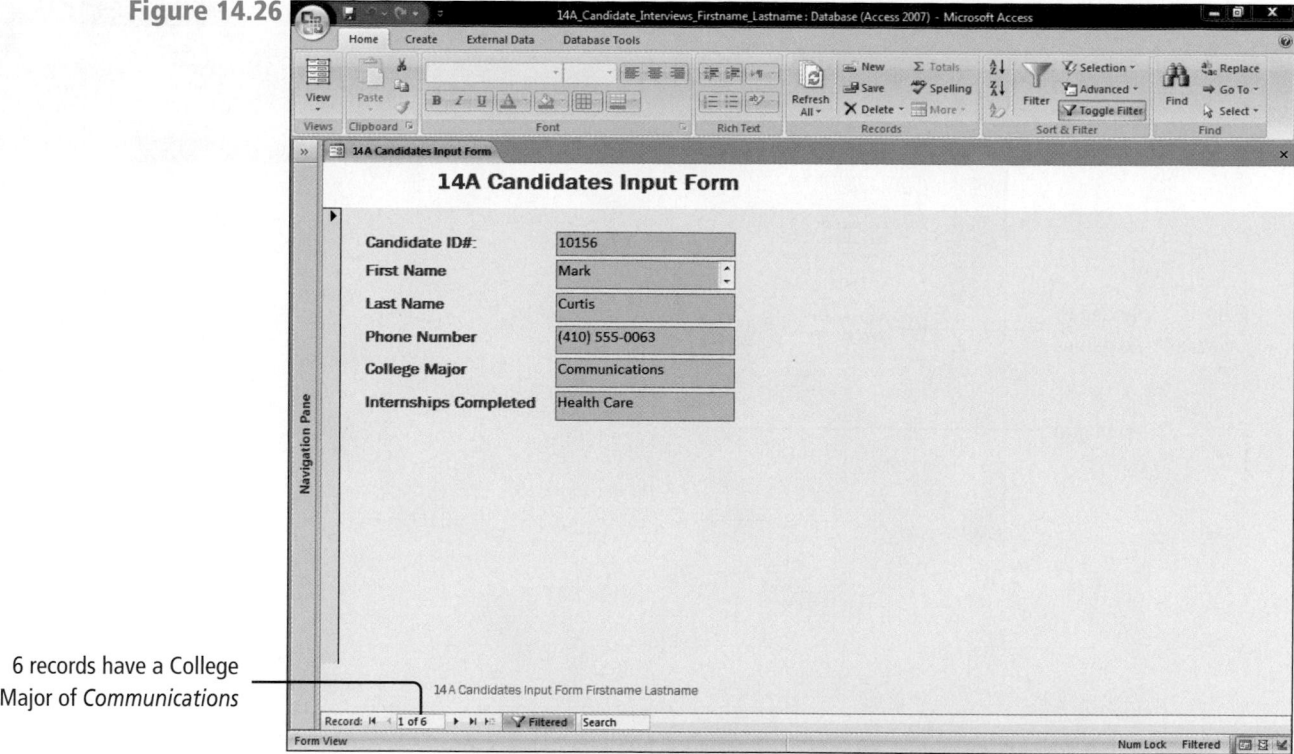

6 records have a College
Major of *Communications*

Note — Toggle Filter Button

On the Home tab, the Toggle Filter button is used to apply or remove a filter. If no filter has been created, the button is not active—it is dimmed. After a filter is created, this button becomes active. Because it is a toggle button used to apply or remove filters, the ScreenTip that displays for this button will alternate between Apply Filter—when a filter has been created but is not currently applied—and Remove Filter—when a filter has been applied.

3 Click in the blue **College Major** text box control again. In the **Sort & Filter group**, click the **Filter** button. From the displayed menu, select the **Graphic Arts** check box, and then click **OK**.

As indicated in the navigation area, eight candidate records have a College Major in either Communications *or* Graphic Arts. You have created an **OR condition**; that is, only records where one of two values—Communications *or* Graphic Arts—is present in the selected field are activated.

4 Click in the blue **College Major** text box control. In the **Sort & Filter group**, click the **Advanced** button, and then from the displayed menu, click **Clear All Filters**. Click the **Advanced** button again, and then from the displayed menu, click **Advanced Filter/Sort**. Use the pointer to expand the field list so that you can view all of the field names. Compare your screen with Figure 14.27.

The Advanced Filter design grid displays. The design grid is similar to the query design grid.

Figure 14.27

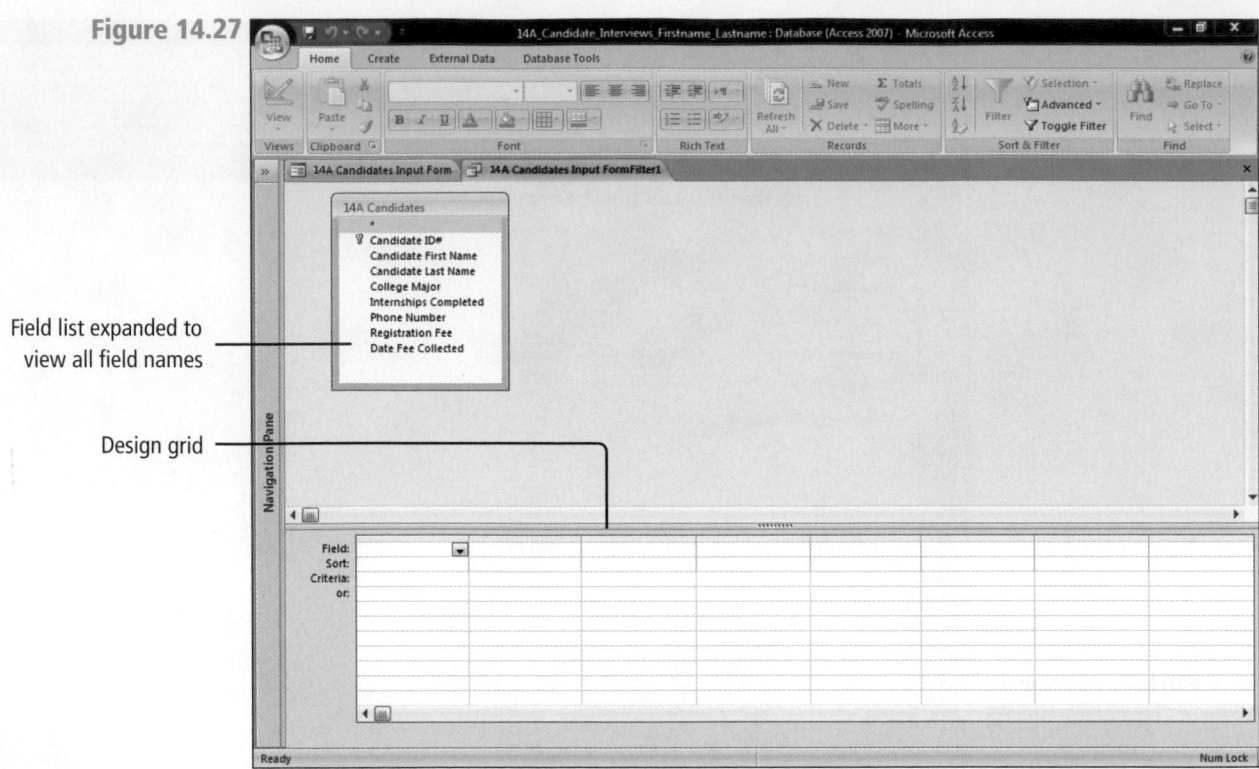

Field list expanded to view all field names

Design grid

5 From the **14A Candidates** field list, double-click the **College Major** field to add it to the design grid. Then, add the **Internships Completed** field to the design grid. In the **Criteria** row, in the **College Major** field, type **Business** In the **Criteria** row, in the **Internships Completed** field, type **Finance** and then press Enter. In the **Sort & Filter group**, click **Toggle Filter**. Compare your screen with Figure 14.28.

As indicated in the navigation area, three records match the criteria. You have created an **_AND condition_**; that is, only records where both values—Business _and_ Finance—are present in the selected fields display. There are three Business majors who have completed an internship in Finance.

Figure 14.28

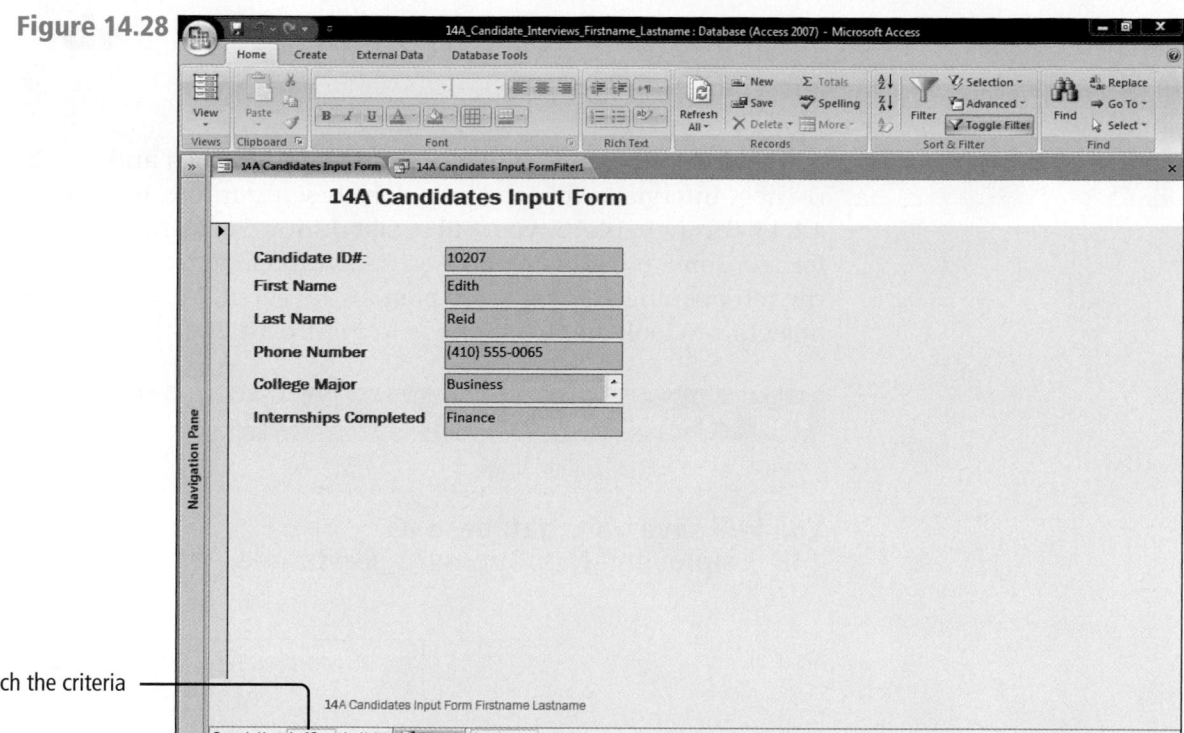

Three records match the criteria ———

In the **Sort & Filter group**, click the **Toggle Filter** button to unfilter
the records. **Close** all open objects, from the **Office** menu 🔘 , **Close**
the database, and then **Exit Access**.

End **You have completed Project 14A** ———————————

Project 14B Employers and Job Openings

At the Job Fair event, employers post job openings and candidates can request interviews for jobs in which they are interested. In Activities 14.11 through 14.16, you will assist Janna Sorokin, database manager for the Job Fair, in using an Access database to track the employers and the job openings they plan to post at the event. Your completed database objects will look similar to those in Figure 14.29.

For Project 14B, you will need the following file:

a14B_Employers_Job_Openings

You will save your database as
14B_Employers_Job_Openings_Firstname_Lastname

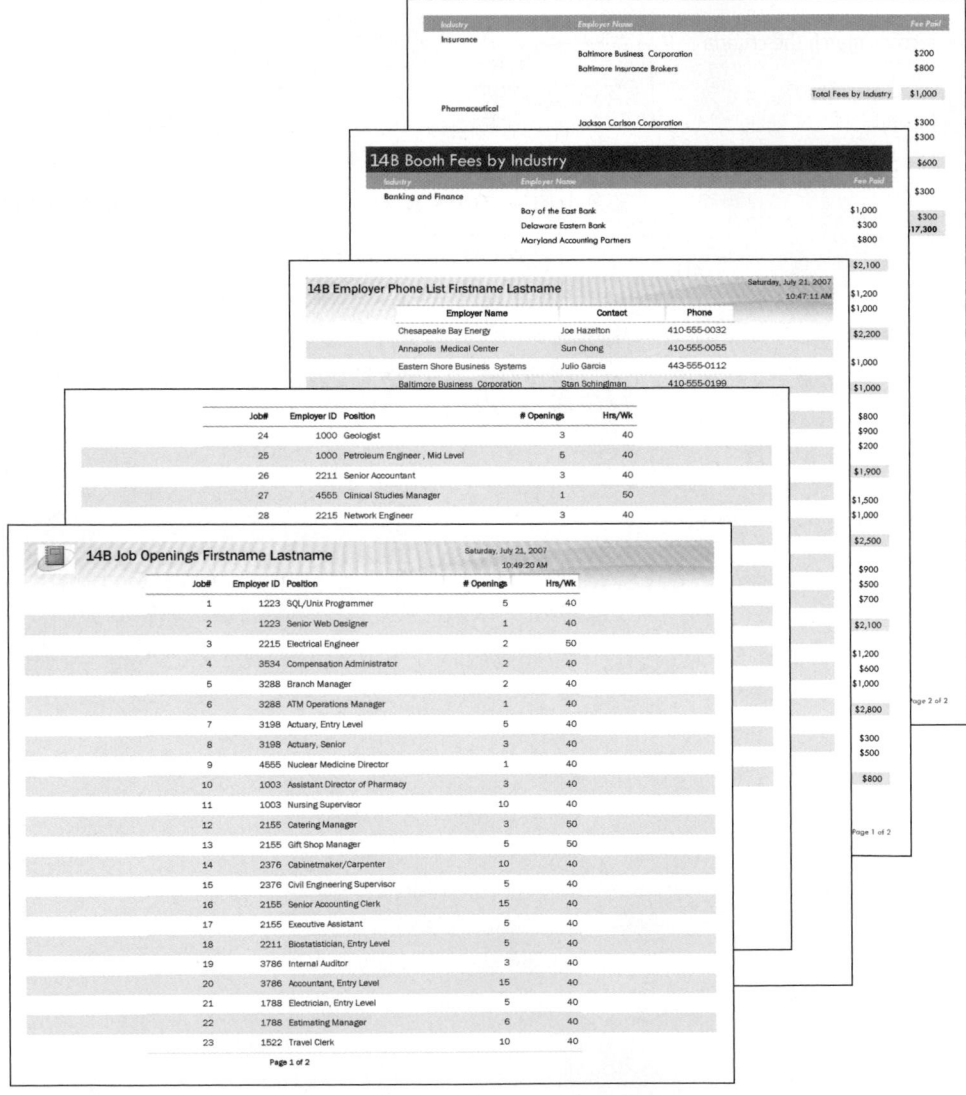

Figure 14.29
Project 14B—Employers and Job Openings

Objective 6
Create a Report Using the Report Tool

A *report* is a database object that summarizes the fields and records from a table, or from a query, in an easy-to-read format suitable for printing. The report consists of information pulled from tables or queries, as well as information that is stored with the report's design, such as labels, headings, and graphics.

The tables or queries that provide the underlying data for a report are referred to as the report's *record source*. If the fields that you want to include in your report all come from the same table, then you can use the table as the report's record source.

Access provides three ways to create a report: by using the Report tool, the Blank Report tool, or the Report Wizard. After you create a report, you can modify the report in Layout view or in Design view.

Activity 14.11 Creating and Modifying a Report Using the Report Tool and Layout View

The *Report tool*, which is the fastest way to create a report, generates a report immediately by displaying all the fields and records from the record source that you choose—the underlying table or query. This method of creating a report is useful as a way to quickly look at the underlying data in an easy-to-read format, after which you can save the report and then modify it in Layout view or in Design view.

In this activity, you will use the Report tool to create a report for Janna Sorokin that lists all of the employers who are participating in the Job Fair, modify the report in Layout view, and then print the report.

1 Open **Computer**. From the student files that accompany this text, locate the file **a14B_Employers_Job_Openings**. Copy and then paste the file to your **Access Chapter 14** folder. Rename the file as **14B_Employers_Job_Openings_Firstname_Lastname Start** Access, open your **14B_Employers_Job_Openings** database, and then if necessary, enable the content.

2 Click the **Database Tools tab**, and then in the **Show/Hide group**, click the **Relationships** button. Compare your screen with Figure 14.30. If your relationships do not display, in the Relationships group, click the **All Relationships** button.

At the Job Fair event, *one* employer can have *many* job openings. Thus, a one-to-many relationship has been established between the 14B Employers table and the 14B Job Openings table using Employer ID# as the common field—the field that displays in both tables.

Join line with symbols indicating a one-to-many relationship

Figure 14.30

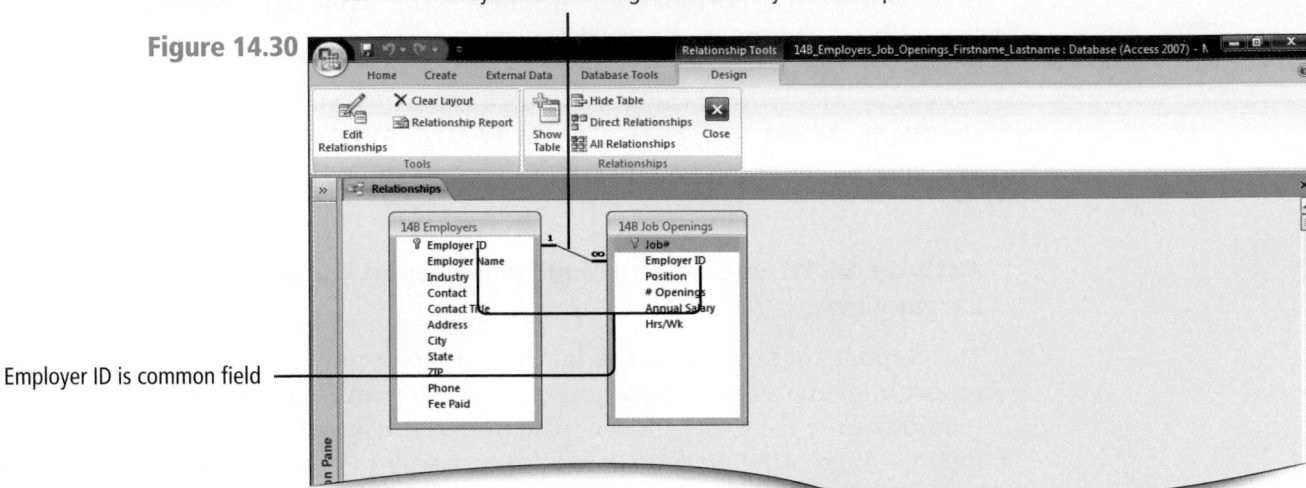

Employer ID is common field

3 In the **Relationships group**, click the **Close** button ⊠ to close the **Relationships** window. If prompted to save your changes, click No.

4 **Open** ⟩⟩ the **Navigation Pane**, click to select the **14B Job Openings table**, and then on the **Create tab**, in the **Reports group**, point to the **Report** button and read its ScreenTip. Click the **Report** button, and then **Close** ⟪ the **Navigation Pane**. Compare your screen with Figure 14.31.

Access creates the 14B Job Openings report and displays it in Layout view. The report includes all of the fields and all of the records in the table. In Layout view, you can see the margins and page breaks in the report as the pages are currently set up.

All fields from table display in report

Figure 14.31

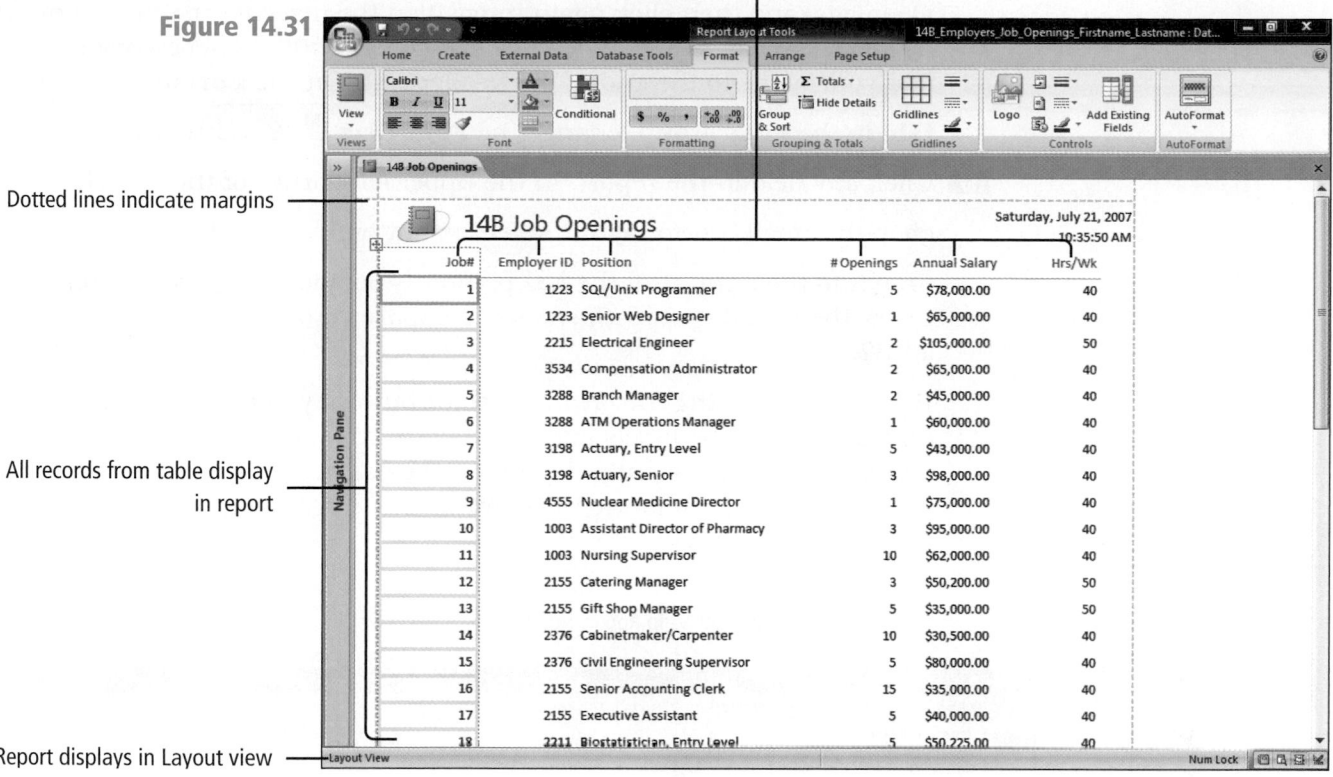

Dotted lines indicate margins

All records from table display in report

Report displays in Layout view

Saturday, July 21, 2007
10:35:50 AM

14B Job Openings

Job#	Employer ID	Position	# Openings	Annual Salary	Hrs/Wk
1	1223	SQL/Unix Programmer	5	$78,000.00	40
2	1223	Senior Web Designer	1	$65,000.00	40
3	2215	Electrical Engineer	2	$105,000.00	50
4	3534	Compensation Administrator	2	$65,000.00	40
5	3288	Branch Manager	2	$45,000.00	40
6	3288	ATM Operations Manager	1	$60,000.00	40
7	3198	Actuary, Entry Level	5	$43,000.00	40
8	3198	Actuary, Senior	3	$98,000.00	40
9	4555	Nuclear Medicine Director	1	$75,000.00	40
10	1003	Assistant Director of Pharmacy	3	$95,000.00	40
11	1003	Nursing Supervisor	10	$62,000.00	40
12	2155	Catering Manager	3	$50,200.00	50
13	2155	Gift Shop Manager	5	$35,000.00	50
14	2376	Cabinetmaker/Carpenter	10	$30,500.00	40
15	2376	Civil Engineering Supervisor	5	$80,000.00	40
16	2155	Senior Accounting Clerk	15	$35,000.00	40
17	2155	Executive Assistant	5	$40,000.00	40
18	2211	Biostatistician, Entry Level	5	$50,225.00	40

5 Click to select the field name **Annual Salary** to surround it with an orange border and to select the entire column. Right-click over the selected name, and then from the displayed shortcut menu, click **Delete**.

The Annual Salary field is deleted from the report.

6 Click to select the field name **# Openings** to surround it with an orange border and to select the entire column. On the **Format tab**, in the **Grouping & Totals group**, click the **Totals** button. In the displayed list, click **Sum**. Scroll down to view the last line of the report, and notice that Access summed the numbers in the field and that the total number of job openings is *182*.

Use Layout view in this manner to make quick changes to a report created with the Report tool. The Report tool is not intended to create a perfectly formatted formal report, but rather it is a way to quickly summarize the data in a table or query in an easy-to-read format suitable for printing and reading.

7 Click the **Page Setup tab**, and then in the **Page Layout group**, click the **Landscape** button. Click the **Format tab**, and then in the **AutoFormat group**, click the **AutoFormat** button. From the displayed gallery of formats, locate, and then click the **Trek** AutoFormat.

AutoFormat enables you to apply a predefined format to a report, which is another way to give a professional look to a report created quickly with the Report tool. Apply AutoFormat before performing other editing to the text of your report.

8 In the **Report Header** at the top of the screen, click the text *14B Job Openings*, and then click again to position the insertion point in the header. Alternatively, double-click the header. Edit as necessary to add your name to the end of the header text. On the **Format tab**, in the **Font group**, change the **Font Size** 11 to **16**.

9 Click any field in the report. In the upper left corner of the report, click the small brown **layout selector** button, and then drag it to the right until the pointer is positioned approximately below the *O* in the word *Openings*. Compare your screen with Figure 14.32.

Recall that by using the layout selector button, you can move the entire layout of the labels and text box controls. In this manner, you can easily center the entire layout on the page visually, instead of opening and manipulating the controls in Design view.

Your name displays in Report Header   *Trek* AutoFormat applied

Figure 14.32

Report Header Font Size changed to 16 pt.

Layout selector button

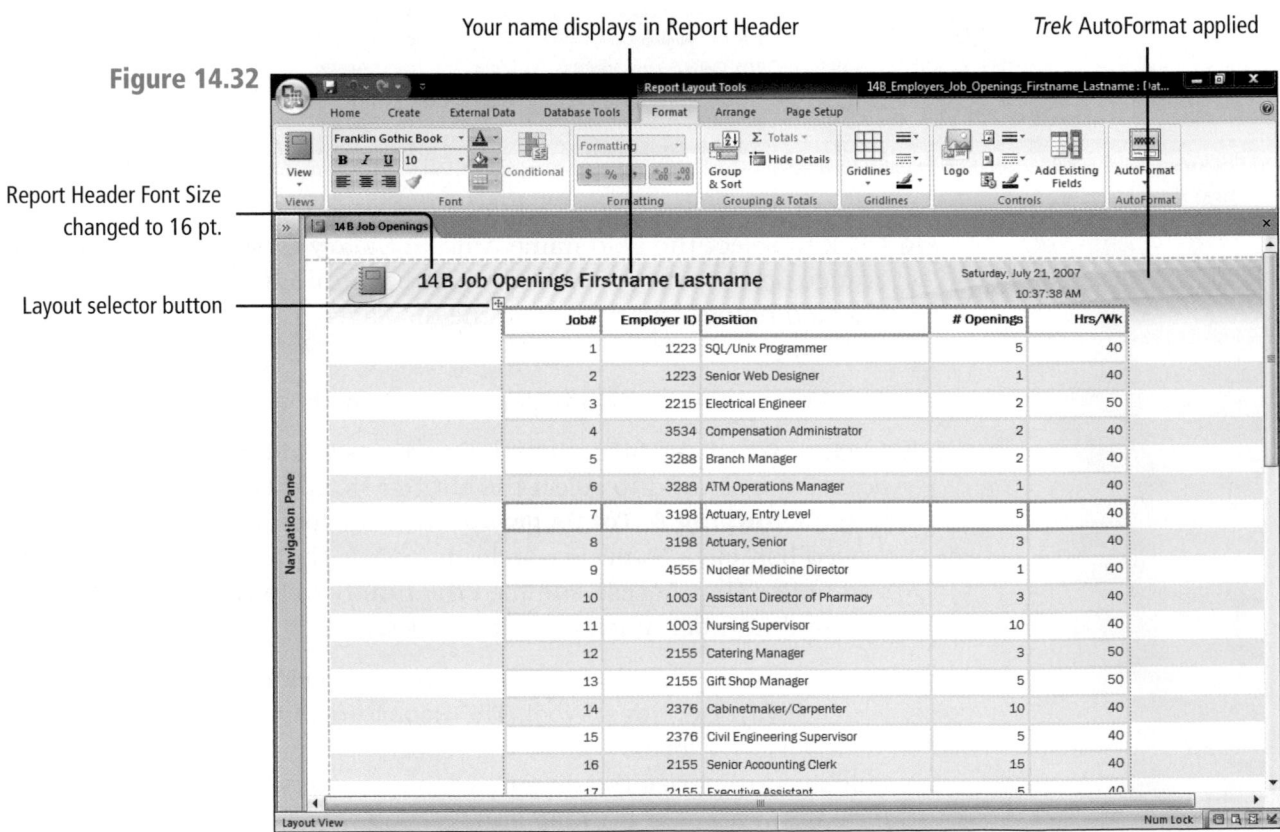

10 In the lower right corner of the screen, at the right edge of the status bar, click the **Print Preview** button. On the **Print Preview tab**, in the **Zoom group**, click the **Two Pages** button to view the two pages of your report.

11 To print your report, on the **Print Preview tab**, in the **Print group**, click **Print** to print the report. Or, submit electronically as directed.

On the **Print Preview tab**, in the **Close Preview group**, click the **Close Print Preview** button, and then **Close** ☒ the **14B Job Openings report**. In the displayed message box, click **Yes** to save changes to the design of the report. In the **Save As** dialog box, click **OK** to accept the default name—*14B Job Openings*.

Objective 7
Create a Report Using the Blank Report Tool

Activity 14.12 Creating a Report Using the Blank Report Tool

Use the ***Blank Report tool*** to create a report from scratch. This is an efficient way to create a report, especially if you plan to include only a few fields in your report.

In this activity, you will use the Blank Report tool to build a report that lists only the Employer Name, Contact, and Phone fields, which Janna will use as a quick reference for phoning various employers to verify the details of their Job Fair participation.

1 On the **Create tab**, in the **Reports group**, click the **Blank Report** button.

A blank report displays in Layout view, and the Field List pane displays.

2 In the **Field List** pane, if necessary click **Show all tables**, and then click the **plus sign (+)** next to the **14B Employers table**. Compare your screen with Figure 14.33.

The list of fields in the 14B Employers table displays.

Field List pane

Figure 14.33

Field list for the 14B Employers table expanded

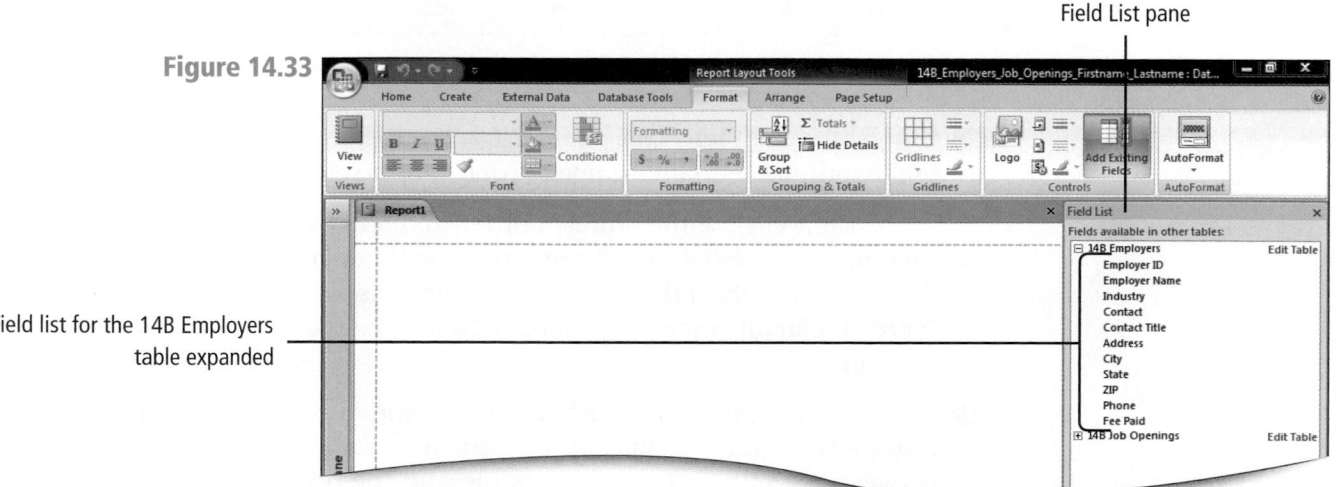

3 Point to the **Employer Name** field, right-click, and then click **Add Field to View**.

The Employer Name field and its associated records display as the first column of the report. In this manner, you build the report field by field, in the order you want the fields to display.

4 From the **Field List** pane, drag the **Contact** field into the blank report—anywhere to the right of **Employer Name**. Double-click the **Phone** field to add it as the third field in the report. Compare your screen with Figure 14.34.

You can use any of the techniques you just practiced when you want to include fields in a blank report.

Three fields added to the report

Figure 14.34

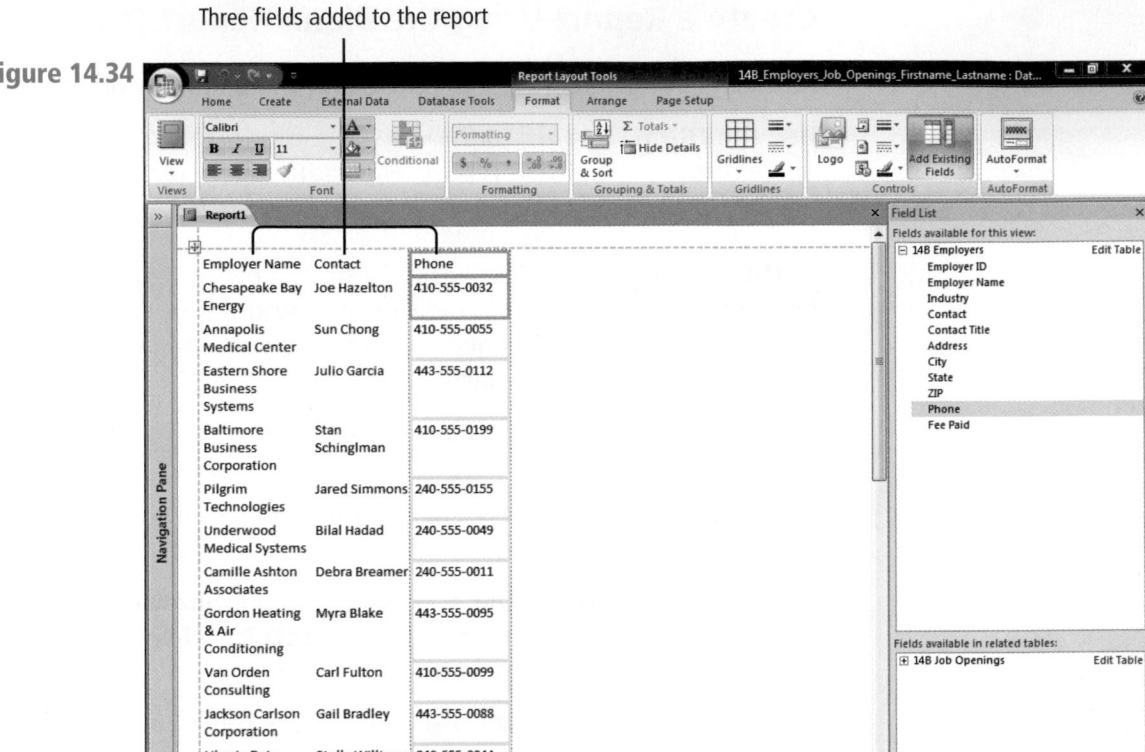

5 **Close** ☒ the **Field List** pane. Click the field name **Employer Name** to surround it with an orange border and to select the column. Point to the right edge of the orange border to display the ↔ pointer, and then drag to the right until the name for *Baltimore Management Association* (toward the bottom of the list) displays on one line and there is a small amount of space between the name and the next column.

6 Using the technique you just practiced, widen the **Contact** field so that all the names display on one line and some space is allowed between the end of the longest name and the beginning of the next column. Compare your screen with Figure 14.35.

Figure 14.35

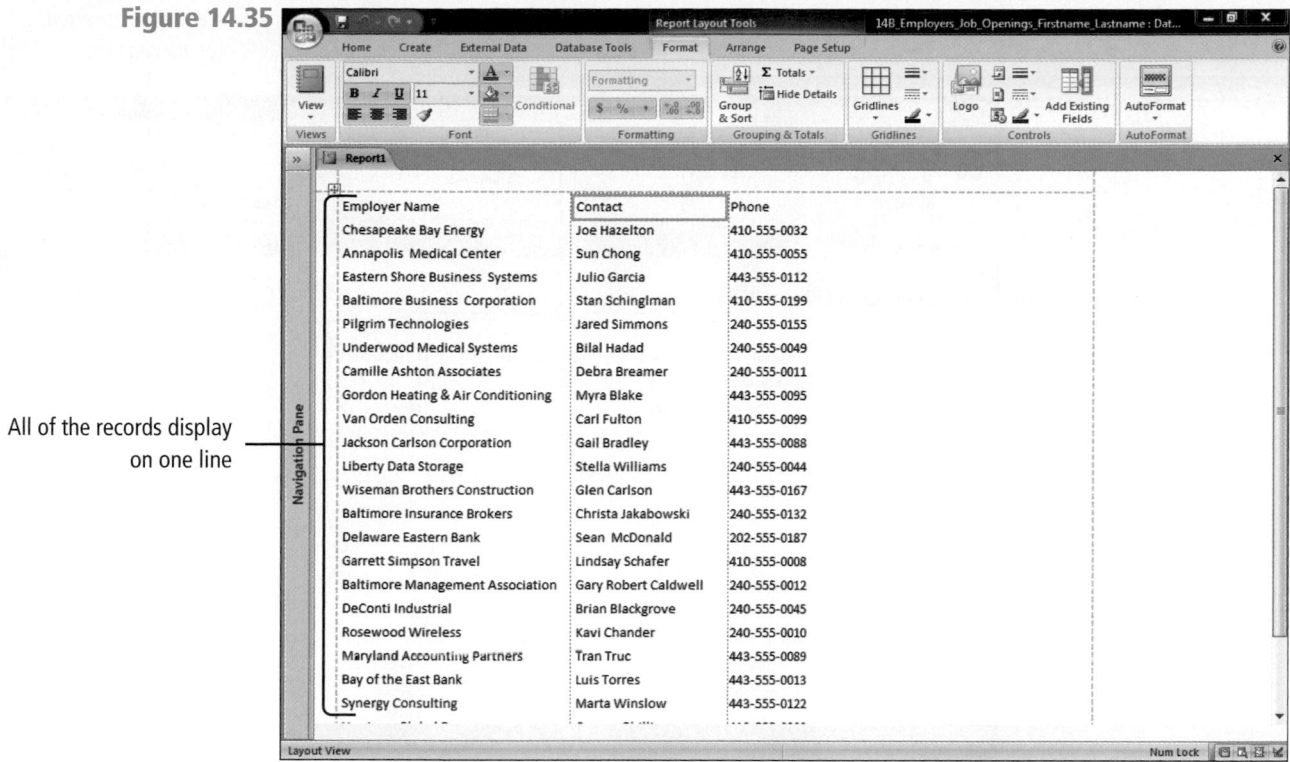

All of the records display on one line

7 On the **Format tab**, in the **Controls group**, click the **Date & Time** button 🔢. In the displayed **Date and Time** dialog box, click **OK**.

In the **Controls group**, click the **Title** button 🗐, and then using your own name, type **14B Employer Phone List Firstname Lastname** In the **AutoFormat group**, click the **AutoFormat** button, and then apply the **Trek** AutoFormat. With the title still selected, in the **Font group**, change the **Font Size** 11 ▾ to **14**.

8 Click the field name **Employer Name** to select it, hold down ⇧Shift, and then click the **Contact** field name and the **Phone** field name. On the **Format tab**, in the **Font group**, click the **Center** button ≡.

9 In the upper left corner of the report, click the small brown **layout selector** button ⊞, and then drag it to the right until the ⬚ pointer is positioned approximately below the *P* in the word *Phone*—or to whatever position appears to center the group of controls horizontally between the dotted margin lines. Compare your screen with Figure 14.36.

Apply the AutoFormat first, and then edit other formatting. Recall that by using the layout selector button, you can move the entire layout of the label and text box controls to easily center the entire layout on the page visually.

Figure 14.36

Field names formatted
and centered over data

Date and Time inserted
(yours will vary)

Report title added

Trek AutoFormat applied

Layout visually centered
horizontally on the page

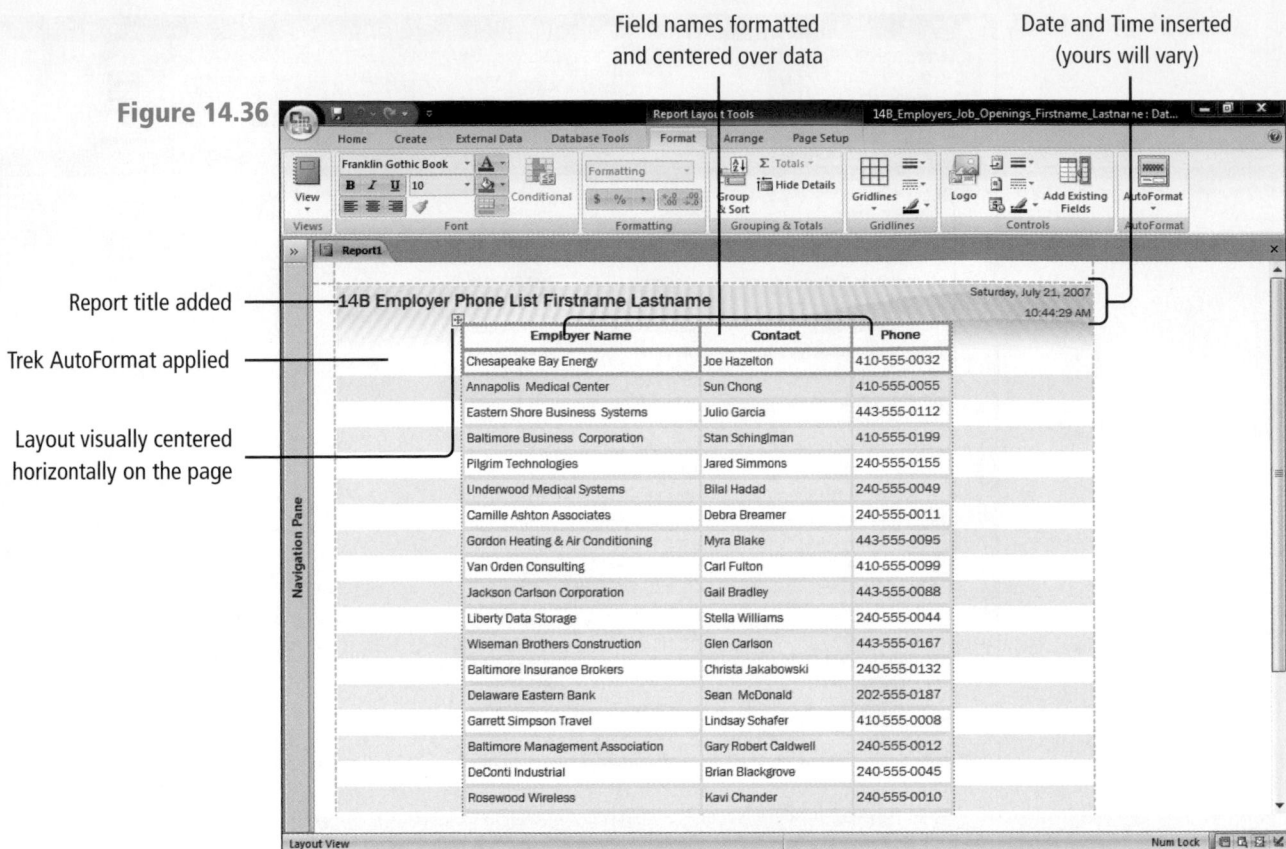

10 To print your report, on the status bar, click the **Print Preview** button
[icon] . On the **Print Preview tab**, in the **Print group**, click **Print** to
print the report. Or, submit electronically as directed.

11 On the **Print Preview tab**, in the **Close Preview group**, click the
Close Print Preview button, and then **Close** [×] the report. In the
displayed message box, click **Yes** to save the changes to the design of
the report. In the **Save As** dialog box, type **14B Employer Phone List**
and then click **OK**.

12 **Open** [»] the **Navigation Pane**. Notice that in this Navigation Pane
arrangement—Tables and Related Views—reports display below the
table with which they are associated. Notice also that report objects
display a small green notebook icon, which visually identifies
them as reports. **Close** [«] the **Navigation Pane**.

Objective 8
Create a Report by Using the Report Wizard

Use the **Report Wizard** when you need flexibility and want to control the
report content and design. The Report Wizard enables you to specify how
the data is grouped and sorted, and you can use fields from more than

one table or query, provided you have specified the relationships between the tables and queries beforehand.

The Report Wizard is similar to the Form Wizard; it creates a report by asking you a series of questions and then designs the report based on your answers.

Activity 14.13 Creating a Report by Using the Report Wizard

The Greater Baltimore Area Job Fair database includes data regarding employment information such as industry sectors, employers, job openings, and annual salaries. Based on the data that has been collected, Janna would like to have a report that shows groupings by industry, employer, and the total fees paid by employers for renting a booth at the Job Fair.

1 On the **Create tab**, in the **Reports group**, click **Report Wizard**.

The Report Wizard displays with its first question. Here you select the tables or queries from which you want to get information, and then select the fields that you want to include in the report. You can also choose from more than one table or query.

2 Click the **Tables/Queries arrow**, and then click **Table: 14B Employers**. Using either the **One Field** button ![>] or by double-clicking the field name, move the following fields to the **Selected Fields** list in the order given: **Industry**, **Employer Name**, and **Fee Paid** (scroll down as necessary to find the *Fee Paid* field). Click **Next**.

The Report Wizard displays its second question. Here you decide if you want to add any grouping levels.

3 With **Industry** selected, click the **One Field** ![>] button, and then compare your screen with Figure 14.37.

Figure 14.37

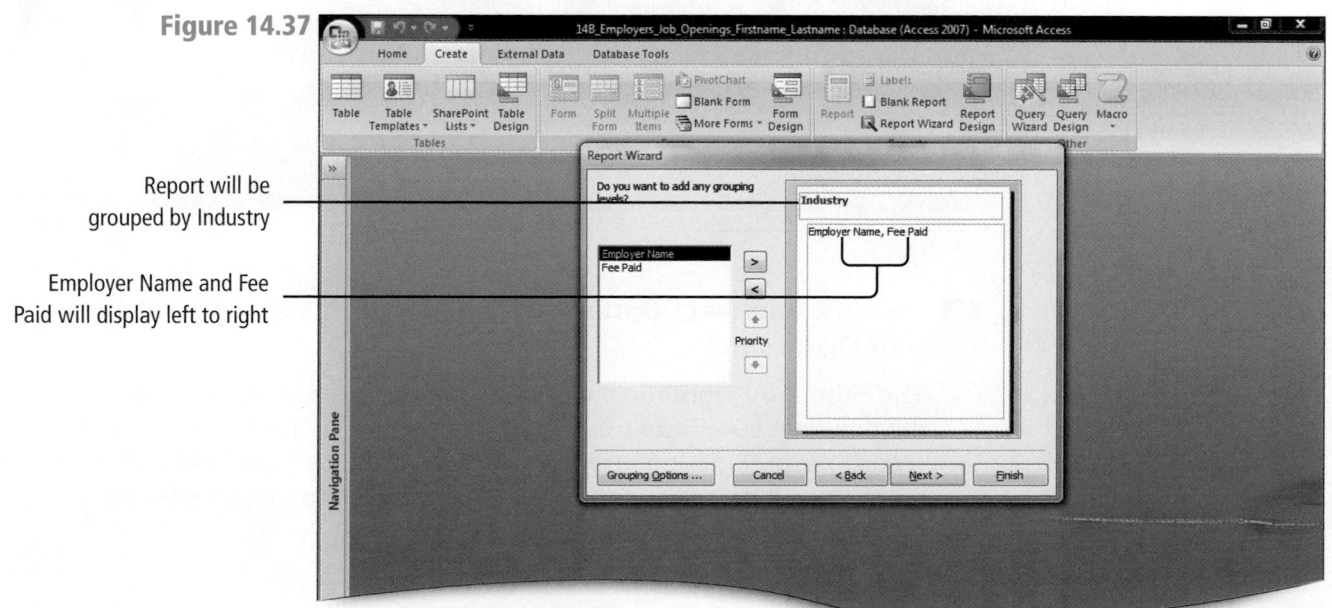

Report will be grouped by Industry

Employer Name and Fee Paid will display left to right

Grouping data helps you organize and summarize the data in your report. Grouping data in a report places all of the records that have the same data in a field together as a group—in this instance, each *Industry* will display as a group.

4 Click **Next**. In the **1** box, on the right, click the **arrow**, and then click **Employer Name**. Compare your screen with Figure 14.38.

Here you decide how you want to sort and summarize the information. You can sort on up to four fields. The Summary Options button displays because the data is grouped and contains numerical or currency data. This action will cause the records in the report to be sorted alphabetically by Employer Name within the grouping option specified, which is *Industry*. Sorting records in a report presents a more organized report.

Select the fields you want to sort by here

Use to change the sort order from Ascending to Descending

Figure 14.38

Summary Options button displays because numerical or currency fields are included

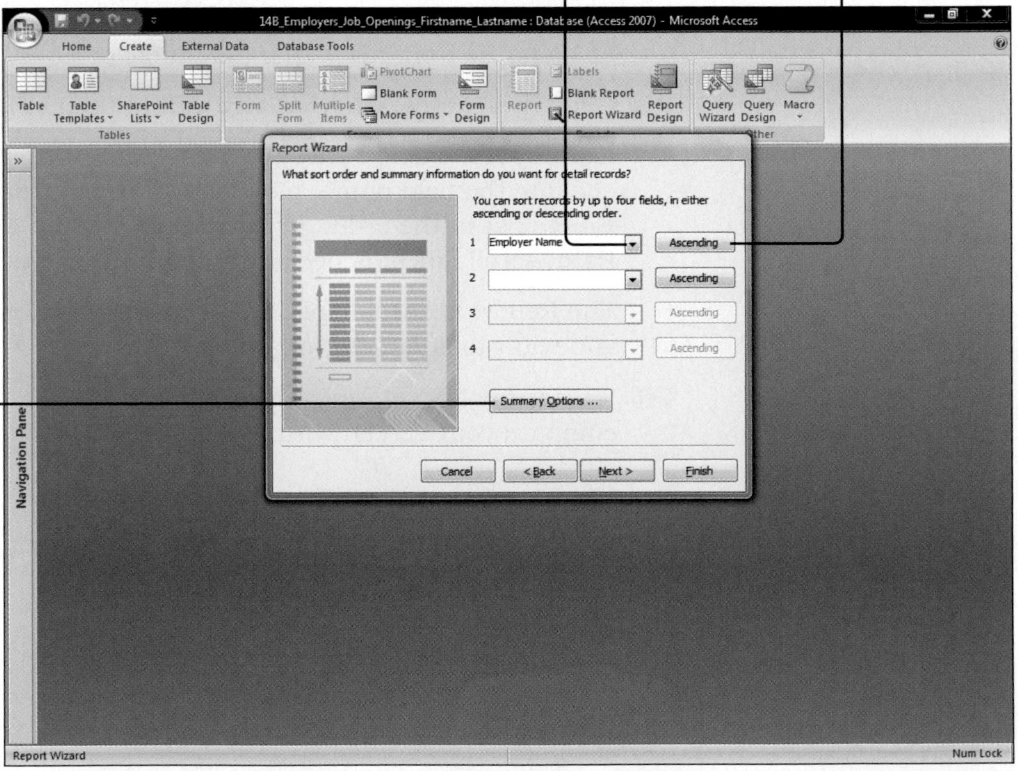

5 Click the **Summary Options** button, and then compare your screen with Figure 14.39.

The Summary Options dialog box displays. Here you can choose to display only summary information or to display both details—each record—and the summary information. The Fee Paid field can be summarized by selecting one of the four options displayed—Sum, Avg, Min, or Max.

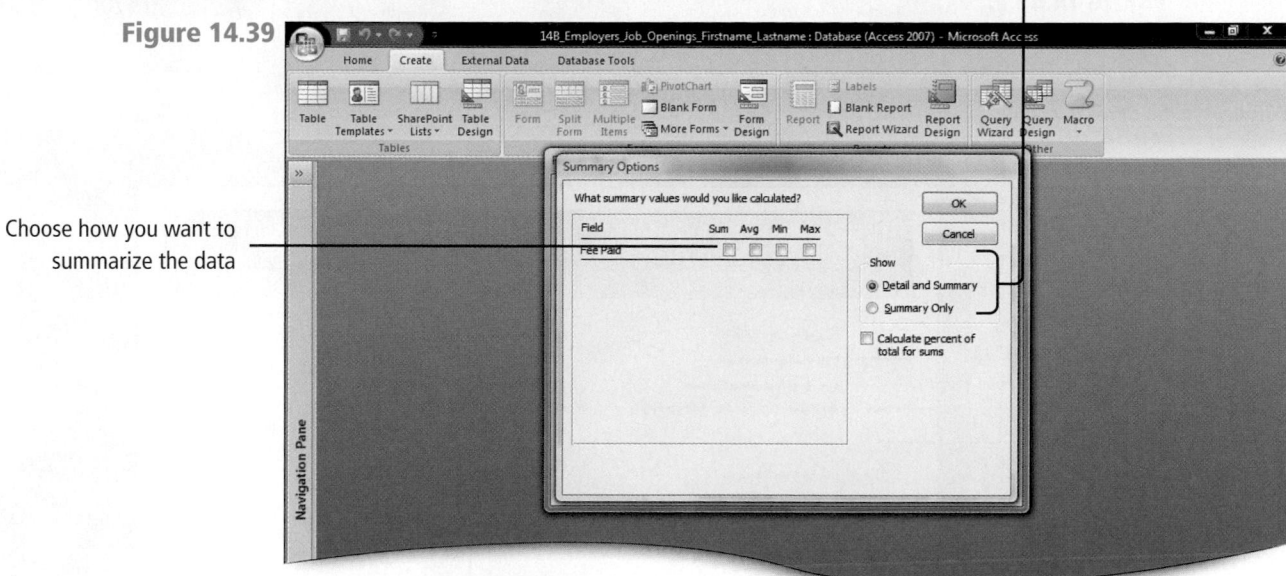

Figure 14.39

Choose to show details and
summary or only summary information

Choose how you want to
summarize the data

6 To the right of **Fee Paid**, select the **Sum** check box. Under **Show**, be
sure the **Detail and Summary** option button is selected, and then
click **OK**. Click **Next**.

Here you select the layout and the page orientation. The box on the
left displays a preview of the currently selected layout.

7 Click each **Layout** option button and view the options, and then
click the **Stepped** option button to select it as the layout for your
report. On the right side of the dialog box, under **Orientation**, be
sure **Portrait** is selected, and at the bottom be sure the **Adjust the
field width so all fields fit on a page** check box is selected.

8 Click **Next**. In the displayed list of styles, click one or more styles to
view the preview to the right.

9 Click the **Median** style, and then click the **Next** button. In the **What
title do you want for your report?** text box, name the report **14B
Booth Fees by Industry** and then click the **Finish** button. Compare
your screen with Figure 14.40.

The report is named and displays in Print Preview. This step also
saves the report with the name that you entered as the report title.

Each of the specifications you defined in the Report Wizard is
reflected in the report, although some data is not completely visible.
The records are grouped by Industry, and then within each Industry,
the Employer Names are alphabetized. In a manner similar to an
Excel spreadsheet, numeric data that does not fit into the space may
display as a series of # signs. Within each Industry grouping, the Fee
Paid is summarized—the word *Sum* displays at the end of the grouping. However, some information is not fully displayed.

indicates data too wide for field

Figure 14.40

Report displays in Print Preview

Data grouped by Industry

Records sorted by Employer Name

Summary information included

Fees summed by Industry

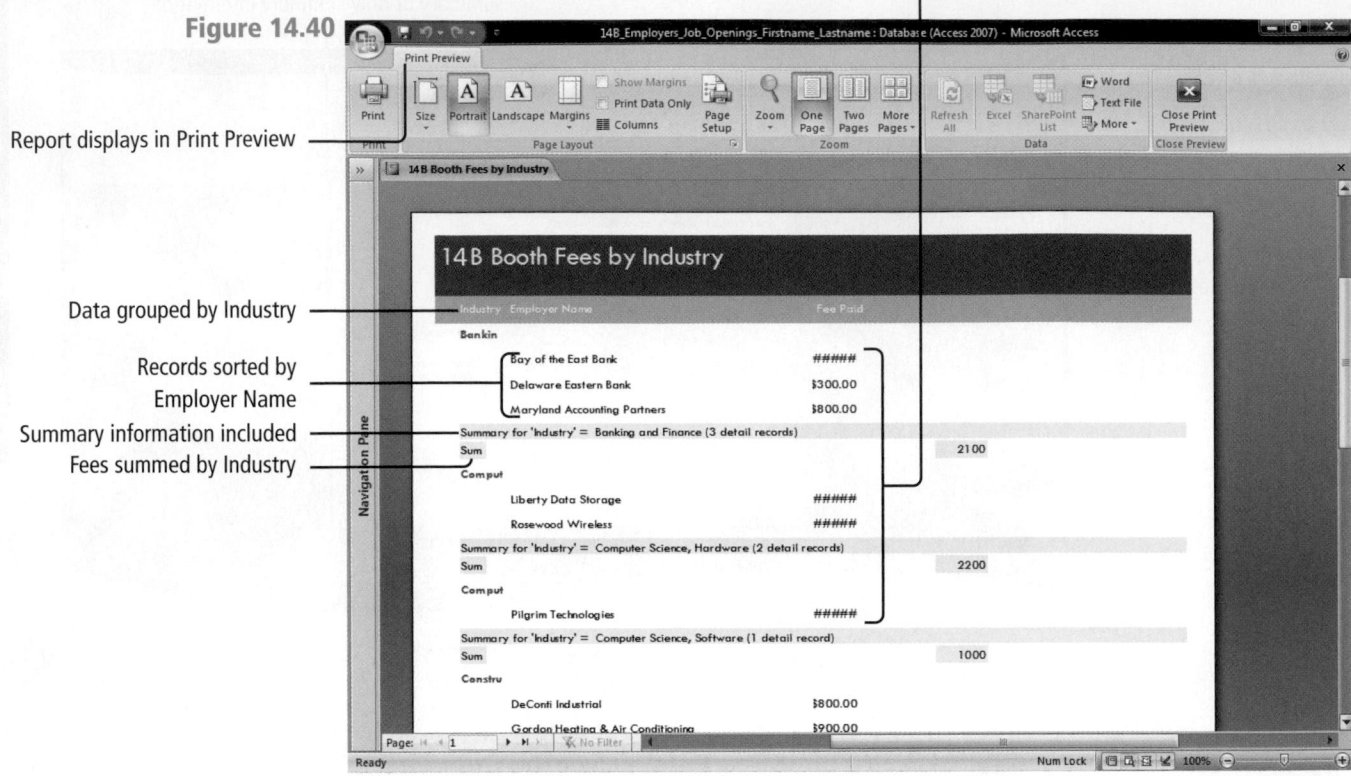

10 In the **Zoom group**, click the **Two Pages** button.

As currently formatted, the report will print on two pages.

11 In the lower right corner of your screen, on the status bar, click the

Layout View button to switch to Layout view, and leave the
report open in this view for the next activity.

Objective 9
Modify the Design of a Report

After a report is created, you can modify its design by using tools and
techniques similar to those you used to modify the design of a form. You
can change the format of controls, add controls, remove controls, or
change the placement of controls in the report. Most report modifications
can be made in Layout view.

Activity 14.14 Modifying a Report in Layout View

In your *14B Booth Fees by Industry* report, under the *Industry* heading,
several of the industry names are truncated—not fully displayed.

Likewise, some of the amounts under Fee Paid are not fully displayed and display as # signs. You can modify the controls on a report to accommodate the data that displays.

In this activity, you will adjust the size and position of the controls so that the data is visible and attractively presented.

1 Be sure that your **14B Booth Fees by Industry** report displays in Layout view; if necessary click the Layout View button 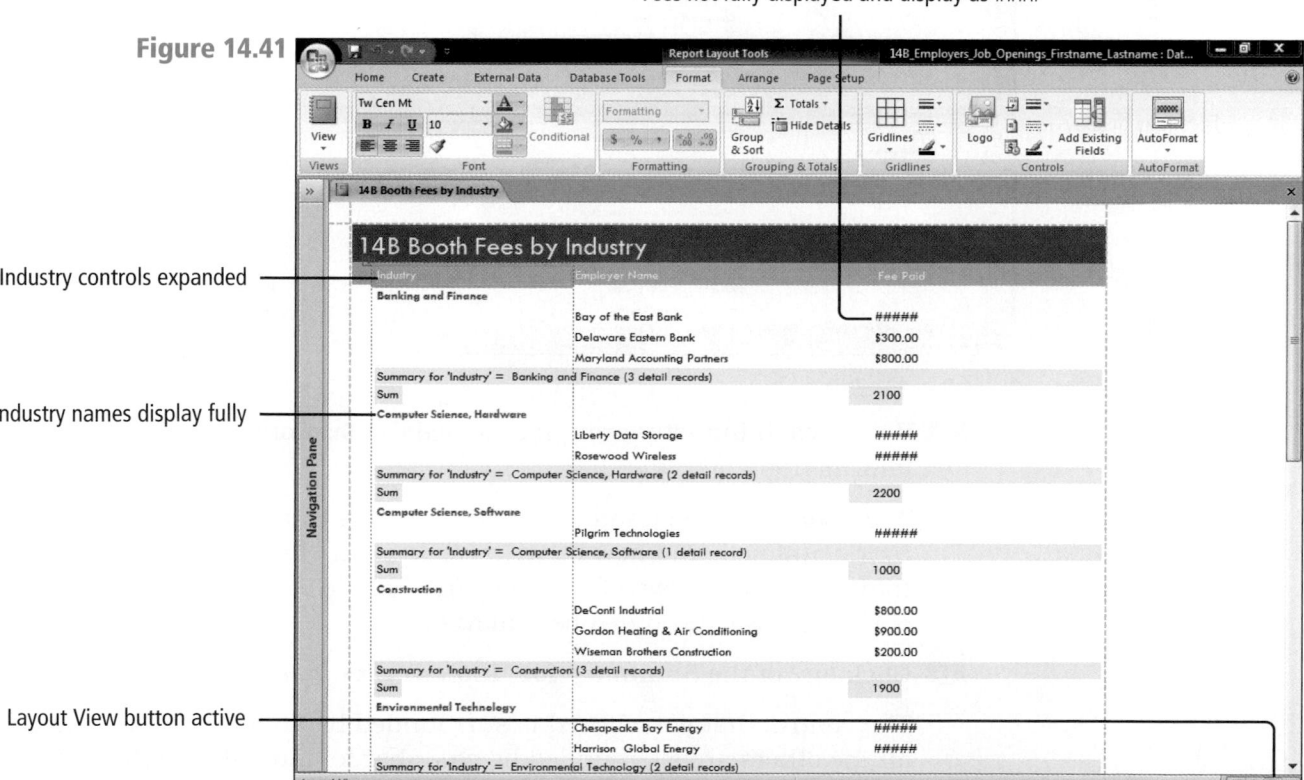 on the status bar.

2 In the upper left corner of the report, click to select the **Industry label control** to surround it with an orange border and to select the column. Point to the right side of the selected label control to display the ↔ pointer, and then drag to the right until the right edge is aligned under the *I* in *Industry* in the Report Header above. Compare your screen with Figure 14.41.

Fees not fully displayed and display as ####

Figure 14.41

Industry controls expanded

Industry names display fully

Layout View button active

3 Click to select the **Fee Paid label control**, and then drag its right edge to the right just slightly inside the dashed margin. Then drag the left side of the control to the right to shorten the control and leave a small amount of space to the left of the dollar signs ($) in the fees. Compare your screen with Figure 14.42.

The # signs are removed and the fee amounts display fully.

Left side of
control shortened

Right side of control
moved to right margin

Figure 14.42

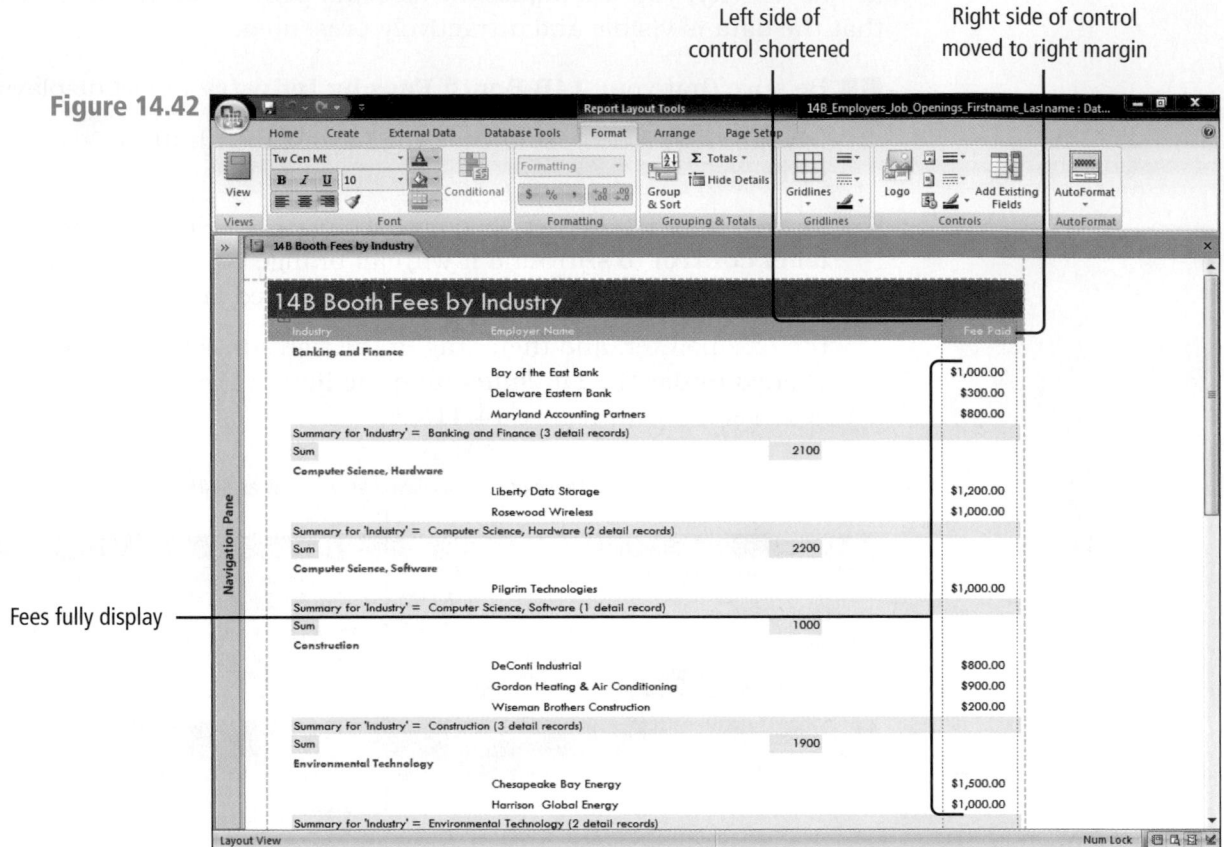

Fees fully display

4 Within each Industry grouping, notice the **Summary for 'Industry'** information.

Access includes a summary line that details what is being summarized (summed) and how many records are included in the total. Now that Janna has viewed the report, she has decided this information is not necessary and can be removed.

5 Click any of the **Summary for 'Industry' controls**.

The control that you clicked is surrounded by an orange border and all the others are surrounded by paler borders to indicate that all are selected.

6 Right-click any of the selected controls, and then from the displayed shortcut menu, click **Delete**. Alternatively, press Del.

7 In the **Fee Paid** field, click any of the fee amounts to select these controls. Right-click any of the selected controls, and then from the displayed shortcut menu, click **Properties**.

8 In the **Property Sheet**, on the **Format tab**, click the name of the second property—**Decimal Places**—and then click the **arrow** that displays. Compare your screen with Figure 14.43.

Figure 14.43

Property Sheet

Format tab

Decimal Places property box

Controls selected

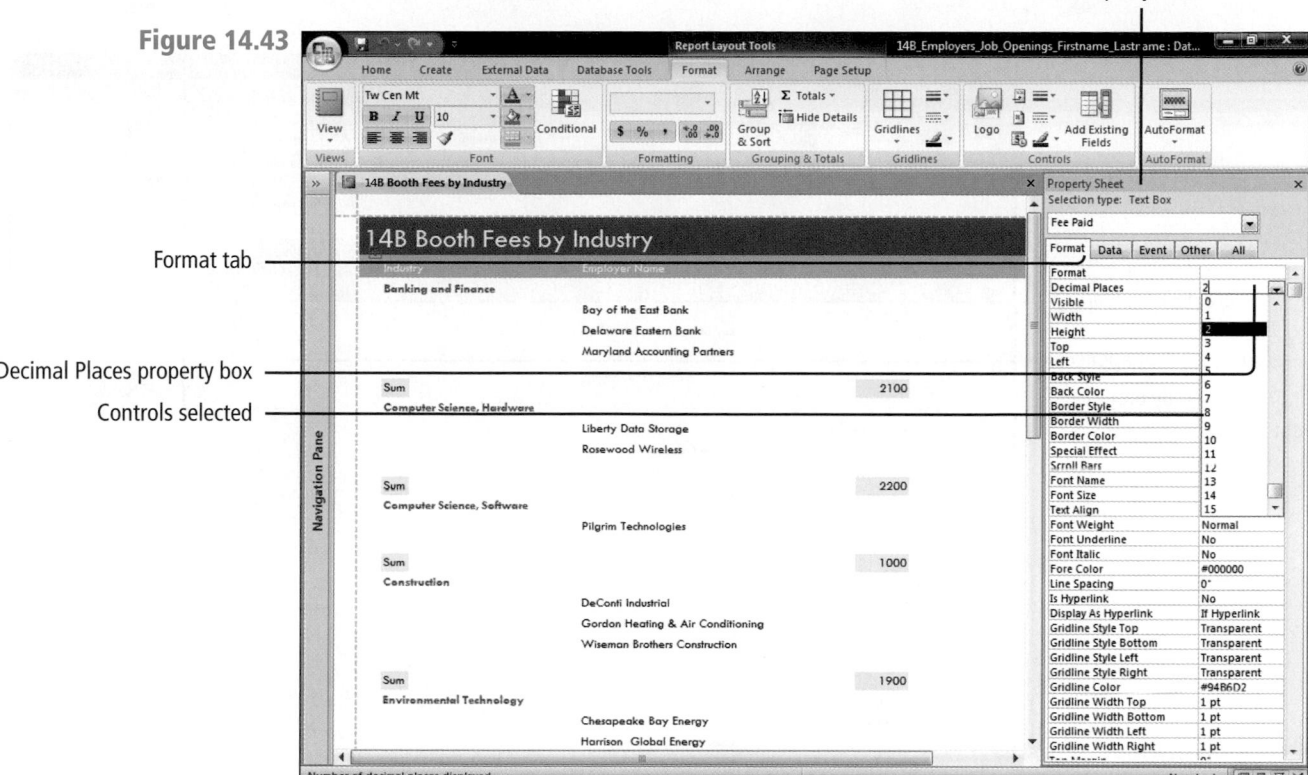

9 In the displayed list, click **0**. **Close** ✕ the **Property Sheet**.

The fees display with no decimal places.

10 In the **Banking and Finance grouping** of the report, to the right of the word *Sum*, click **2140** to select these controls. Point to any of the selected controls, right-click, and then from the displayed shortcut menu, click **Properties**.

These amounts would be more relevant if they included currency formatting to indicate that they are the sum of the fees paid within each industry grouping.

The summary controls are examples of ***calculated controls***—controls that contain an expression—often a formula—that uses one or more fields from the underlying table or query.

11 In the **Property Sheet**, on the **Format tab**, click the name of the first property—**Format**—and then click the **arrow** that displays to the right.

12 In the displayed list of formats, click **Currency**. Click the **Decimal Places** property box, click the **arrow** that displays, and then click **0**.

Close ✕ the **Property Sheet**.

13 With the ↔ pointer, drag the right side of any of the selected controls to the right, just inside the dotted margin line. After you release the mouse button adjust as necessary so that the summed amounts display directly under the fees above. Then, shorten the control by dragging the left side to the right with just enough space to accommodate the data. Compare your screen with Figure 14.44.

Figure 14.44

Controls selected

Zero decimal places

Currency format applied

Controls moved by dragging right side and then left side

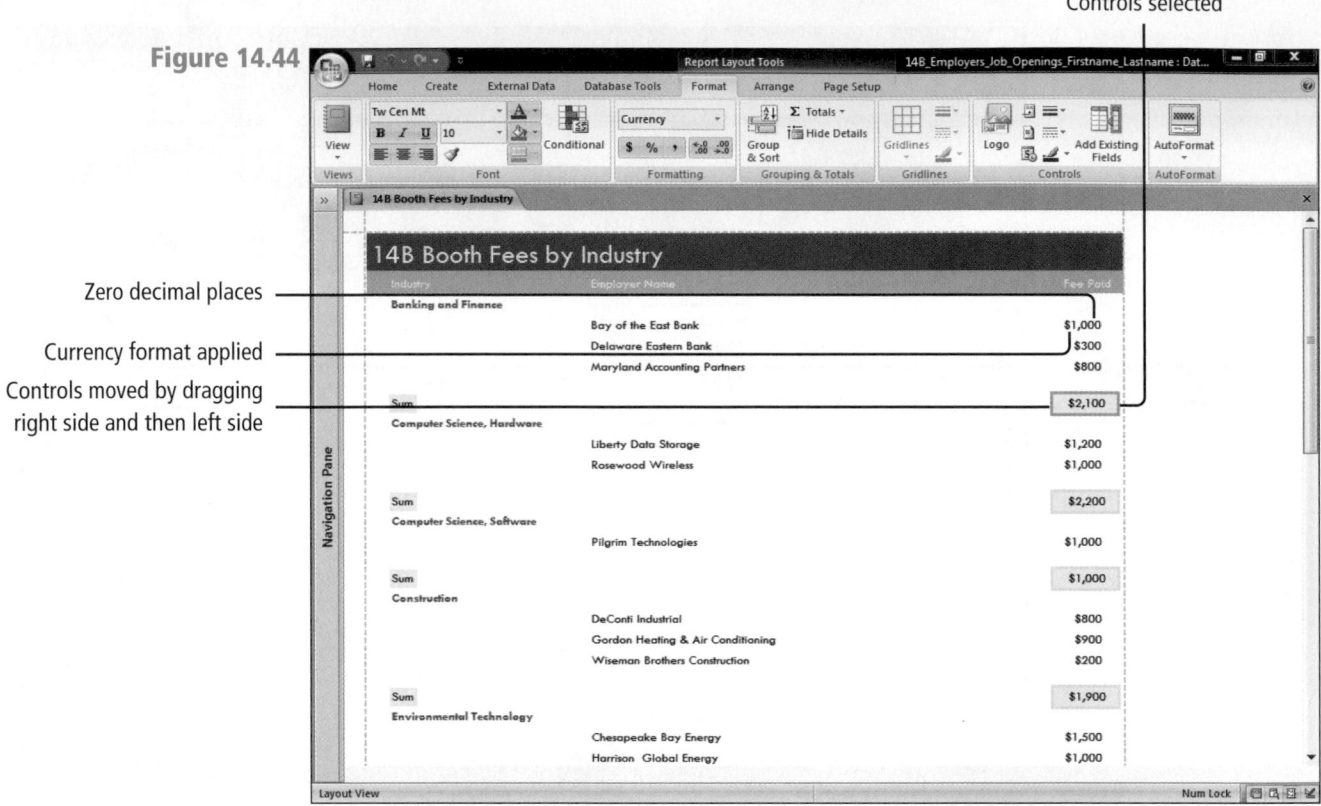

14. On the left side of the report, click one of the **Sum** controls to select these controls, and then click again to place the insertion point inside the selected control. Alternatively, double-click to place the insertion point inside the control.

15. Delete the text, type **Total Fees by Industry** and then press Enter. Notice that the label is on the left side of the page, but the Fee Paid to which it refers is on the right.

The new text more clearly states what is being summed, however, the label would be more useful positioned next to the summary value.

16. Use the ↔ pointer to lengthen the right side of the control so that it is slightly to the left of the total amount, and then shorten the left side so that the control accommodates the text with no extra space. Compare your screen with Figure 14.45.

Figure 14.45

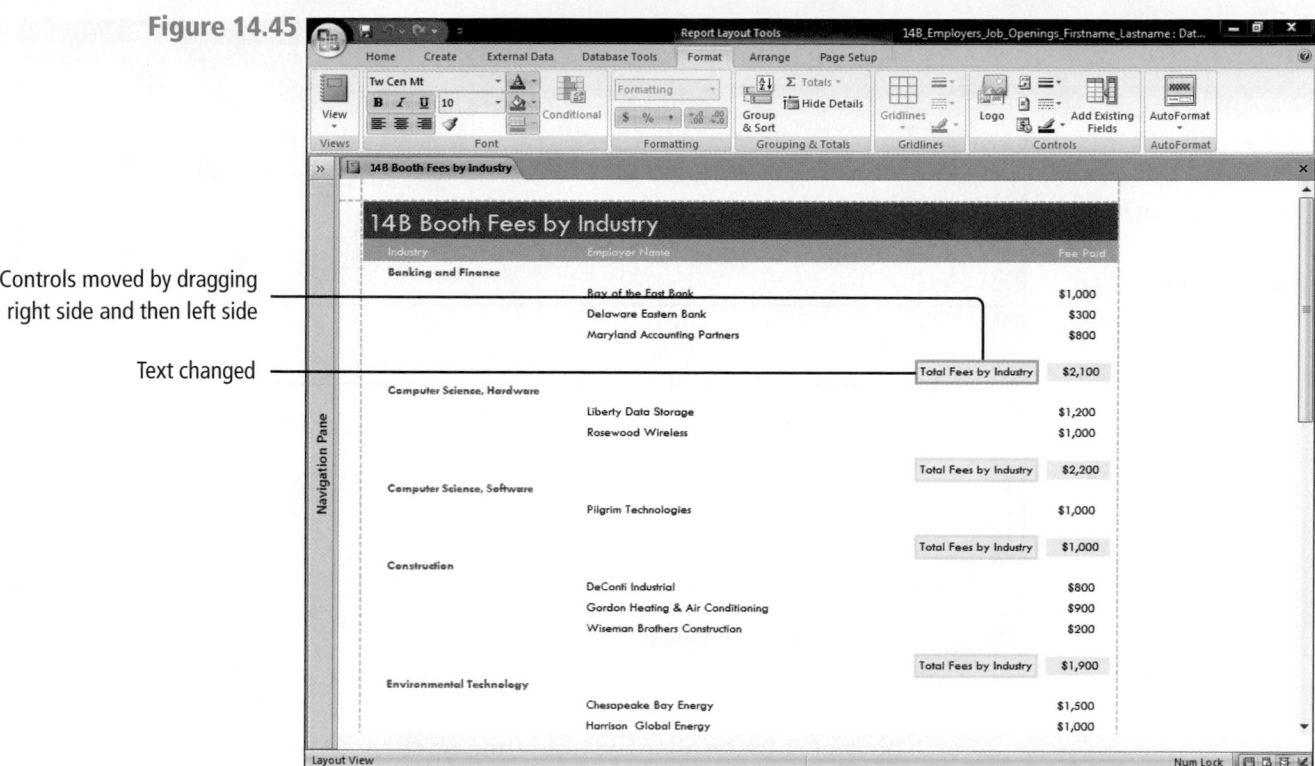

Controls moved by dragging right side and then left side

Text changed

17 At the top of your report, click to select the **Industry label control**, hold down ⇧ Shift, and then click the **Employer Name label control** and the **Fee Paid label control**. In the **Font group**, click the **Italic** button ⟦ *I* ⟧, and then click the **Bold** button ⟦ **B** ⟧.

18 Scroll downward to view the end of the report. Click to select the sum **17300**, which is the Grand Total for all fees paid. Using the techniques you have practiced, display the **Property Sheet** for this control and change its format to **Currency** with **0 Decimal Places**. **Close** ⟦ **X** ⟧ the **Property Sheet**, and then adjust each side of the control to position it below the other fees.

19 By adjusting the right and left sides of the control, move the text *Grand Total* to the immediate left of **$17,300**. Compare your screen with Figure 14.46.

The *Grand Total* amount is the **report footer** and displays at the end of the data. The current date and the page number information that display on the bottom of the page is the **page footer**.

Figure 14.46

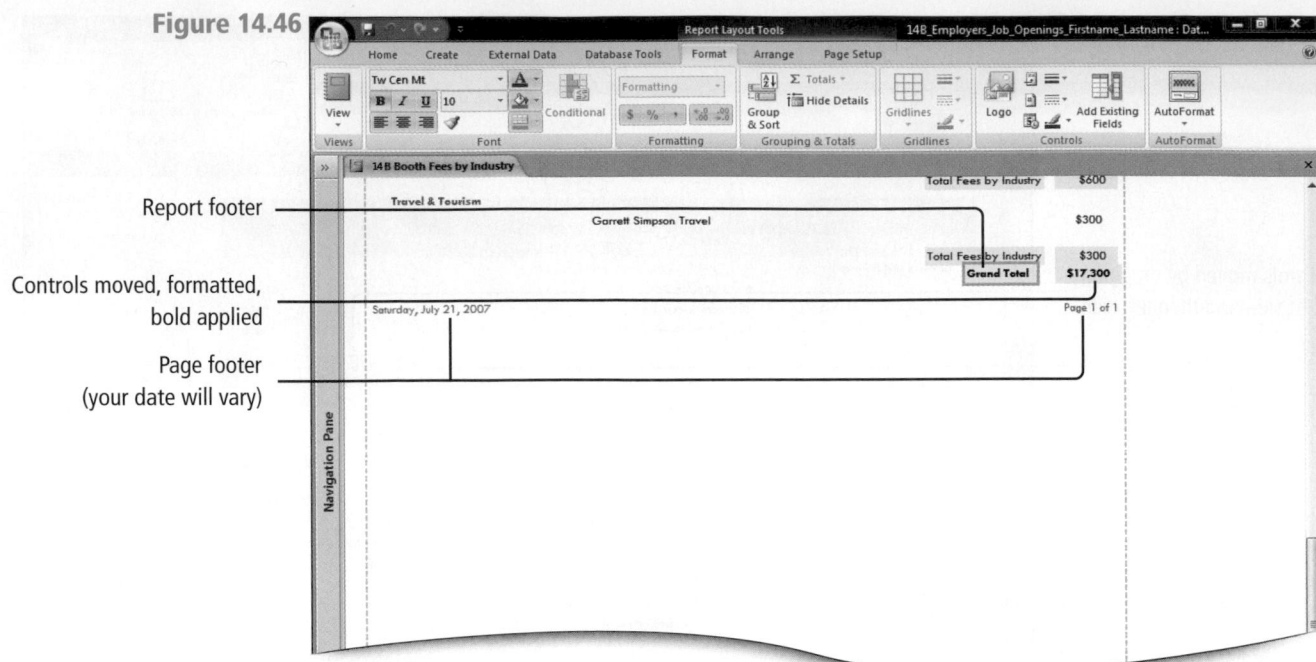

Report footer

Controls moved, formatted, bold applied

Page footer (your date will vary)

The report footer displays one time at the end of the data, and displays items such as report totals. It displays *only* if the data has been summarized. A page footer displays at the bottom of every page of the report.

20 On the **Quick Access Toolbar**, click **Save**. Leave your report open in Layout view for the next activity.

Activity 14.15 Modifying a Report in Design View

Design view gives you a more detailed view of the structure of your report. You can see the header and footer bands for the report, for the page, and for groups. In Design view, your report is not actually running, so you cannot see the underlying data while you are working. However, some tasks, such as adding labels and images, are accomplished in Design view. In this activity, you will add a label to the Page Footer section of your *14B Booth Fees by Industry* report and insert identifying information there.

1 Be sure that your **14B Booth Fees by Industry** report is displayed in Layout view. Press Ctrl + Home to display the top of the report. On

the right end of the status bar, click the **Design View** button . Compare your screen with Figure 14.47.

You can see that the Design view for a report is similar to the Design view for a form. You can also modify the layout of the report here, and use the dotted grid pattern to align controls. This report contains a **Report Header**, a **Page Header**, a **Group Header**, which in this instance is the *Industry* grouping, a Detail section that displays the data, a **Group Footer** (Industry), a Page Footer, and a Report Footer.

The Report Header displays information at the top of the *first page* of a report. The Page Header displays information at the top of *every page* of a report. The Group Header and Group Footer displays the field label by which the data has been grouped—*Industry* in this instance. If you do not group data in a report, the Group Header does not display. Similarly, if you do not summarize data, the Group Footer does not display.

Figure 14.47

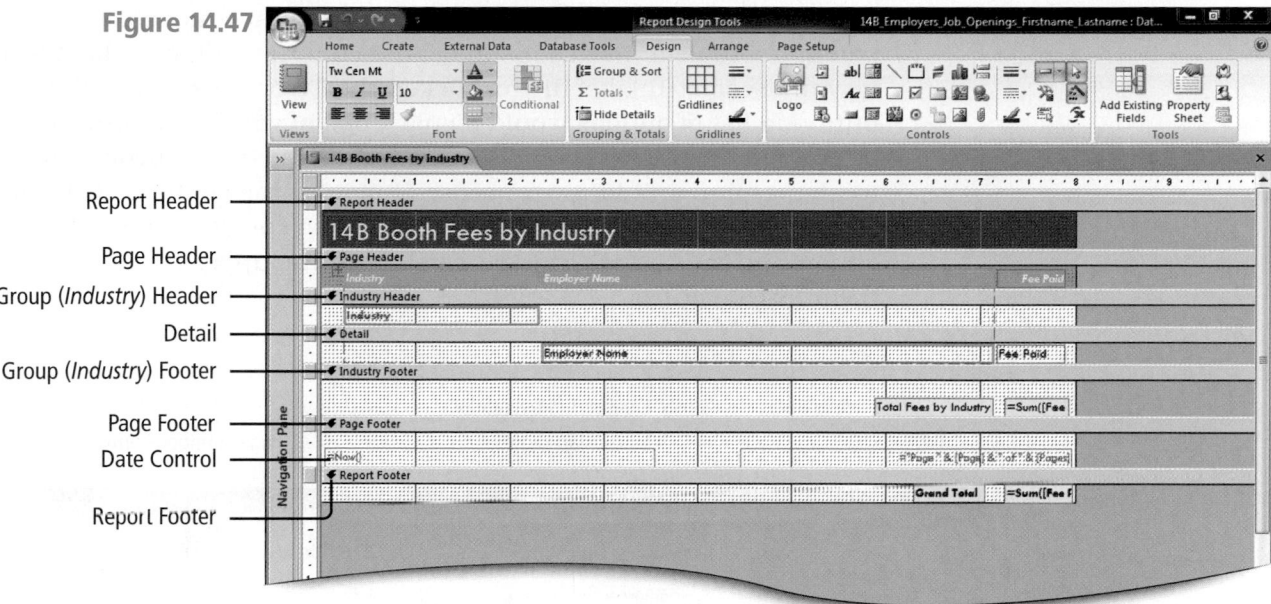

Report Header —
Page Header —
Group (*Industry*) Header —
Detail —
Group (*Industry*) Footer —
Page Footer —
Date Control —
Report Footer —

2 Locate the **Page Footer** section of the report and examine the two controls in this section.

The ***date control*** on the left, identified as *=Now( )*, inserts the current date each time the report is opened. The ***page number control*** on the right, identified as *="Page" & [Page] & " of " & [Pages]*, inserts the page number, for example Page 1 of 2, in the report when the report is displayed in Print Preview or when you print the report. Both of these are examples of programming code that is used by Access to create controls in a report.

3 In the **Page Footer** section, click to select the **date control**. Shorten this control by dragging the right sizing handle to the left to **1.75 inches on the horizontal ruler**.

The Page Footer displays information at the bottom of *every page* in the report, including the page number and the current date inserted by those controls.

4 Click the **page number control** on the right. Shorten this control by dragging the left sizing handle to the right to **5.5 inches on the horizontal ruler**.

5 On the **Design tab**, in the **Controls group**, click the **Label** button **Aa**, and then in the **Page Footer** section, position the ⊞ portion of the pointer vertically in the middle of the section and horizontally at **2 inches on the horizontal ruler**. Click one time, and then using your own name, type **14B Booth Fees by Industry Firstname Lastname** Press Enter to select the control. If necessary, hold down Ctrl, and then press ↑ to align the top edge even with the other two controls, but do not be concerned if this control overlaps the page number control. Compare your screen with Figure 14.48.

As you type, the label expands to accommodate your typing. The Error Checking Options button displays to the left of the label. The Error Checking Options button displays when Access detects a potential problem. In this instance, the control you have added is a new unassociated label. If you clicked the Error Checking Options button, a list of options would display, one of which is to associate—attach—the new label to another control so the two controls could be treated as one unit for the purpose of moving the controls. This label should not be attached to another control so you can ignore this option button. A green triangle displays in the upper left corner of the affected control.

Label control added (yours may overlap slightly)

Page Number Control

Figure 14.48

Error Checking Options button

Date Control

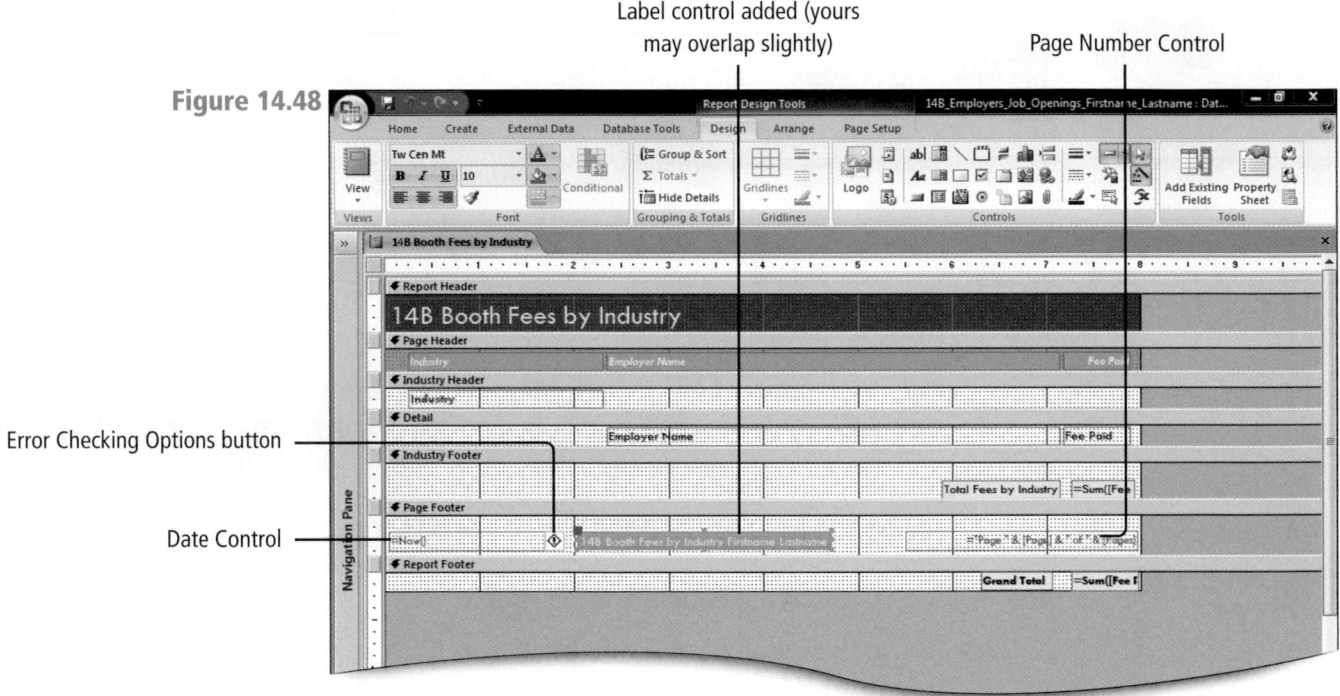

6 With the label control selected, on the **Design tab**, in the **Font group**, click the **Font Color button arrow** [A], and then under **Access Theme Colors**, click **Access Theme 1**. On the **Quick Access Toolbar**, click the **Save** button [icon]. At the right edge of the status bar, click the **Report View** button [icon]. Scroll to the bottom of the page and compare your screen with Figure 14.49.

The new label displays with your name and the font color.

Figure 14.49

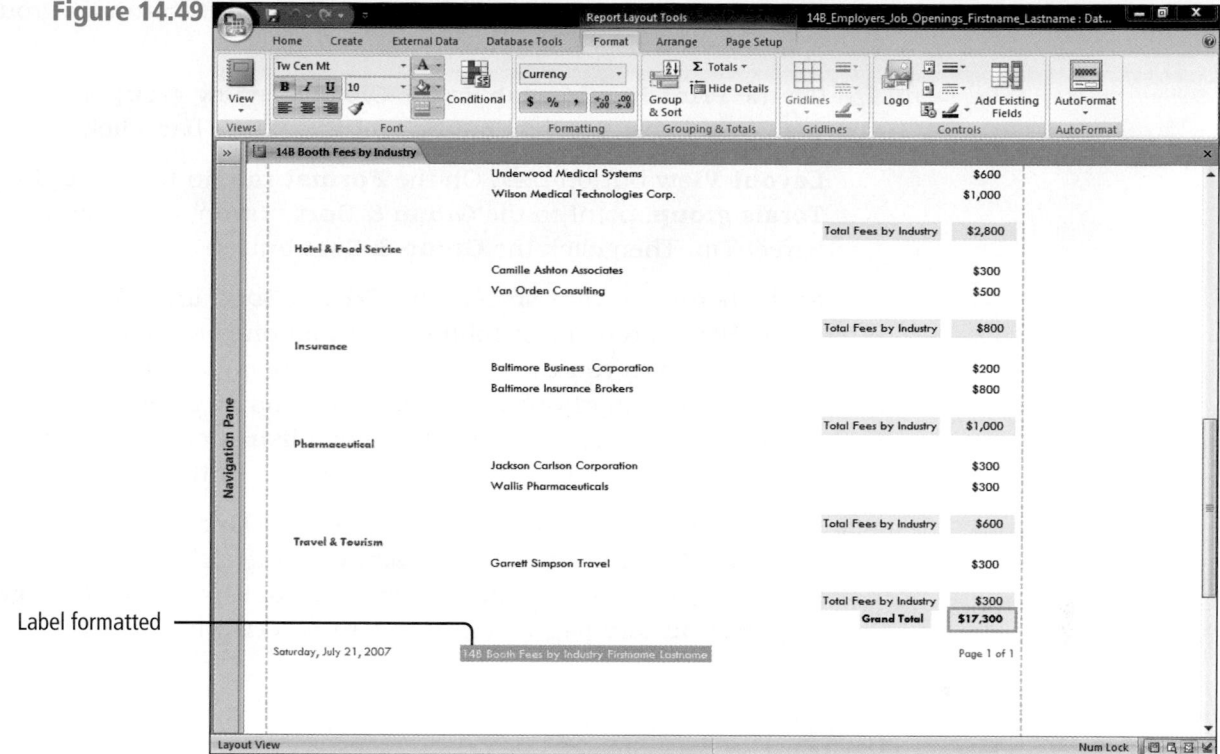

Label formatted

Objective 10
Print a Report and Keep Data Together

Before you print a report, examine the preview of the report to ensure that all of the labels and data are fully displayed, and to make sure that all of the data is properly grouped. Sometimes a page break occurs in the middle of a group of data, leaving the labels on one page and the data or totals on another page.

Activity 14.16 Keeping Data Together and Printing a Report

It is possible to keep the data in a group together so it does not break across a page unless, of course, the data itself exceeds the length of a page.

1 From the **Office** 🗔 menu, point to the **Print** button, and then click **Print Preview**. In the **Zoom group**, click the **One Page** button. Click the **Zoom button arrow**, and then click **Zoom 100%**. Scroll to the bottom of the report to see where the first page ends, and then at the bottom of the screen, click the **Next Page** button and scroll to view the top of **Page 2**. Alternatively, in the Zoom group, click the Two Pages button to see a reduced view of the pages side by side.

This report prints on two pages. The data in the *Insurance* group is split between pages 1 and 2.

2 On the **Print Preview tab**, in the **Close Preview group**, click the **Close Print Preview** button. On the status bar, click the **Layout View** button [image icon]. On the **Format tab**, in the **Grouping and Totals group**, point to the **Group & Sort** button, and then read its ScreenTip. Then click the **Group & Sort** button.

At the bottom of your screen, the *Group, Sort, and Total pane* displays. Here you can control how information is sorted and grouped. This pane gives you the most flexibility when you want to add or modify groups, sort orders, or totals options on a report. Layout view is the preferred view in which to accomplish such tasks, because you can see how your changes affect the display of the data.

3 In the **Group, Sort, and Total** pane, on the **Group on Industry bar**, click the **More** button, click the **arrow** to the right of **do not keep group together on one page**, and then point to **keep whole group together on one page**. Compare your screen with Figure 14.50.

Group, Sort, and Total
button on the Ribbon

Figure 14.50

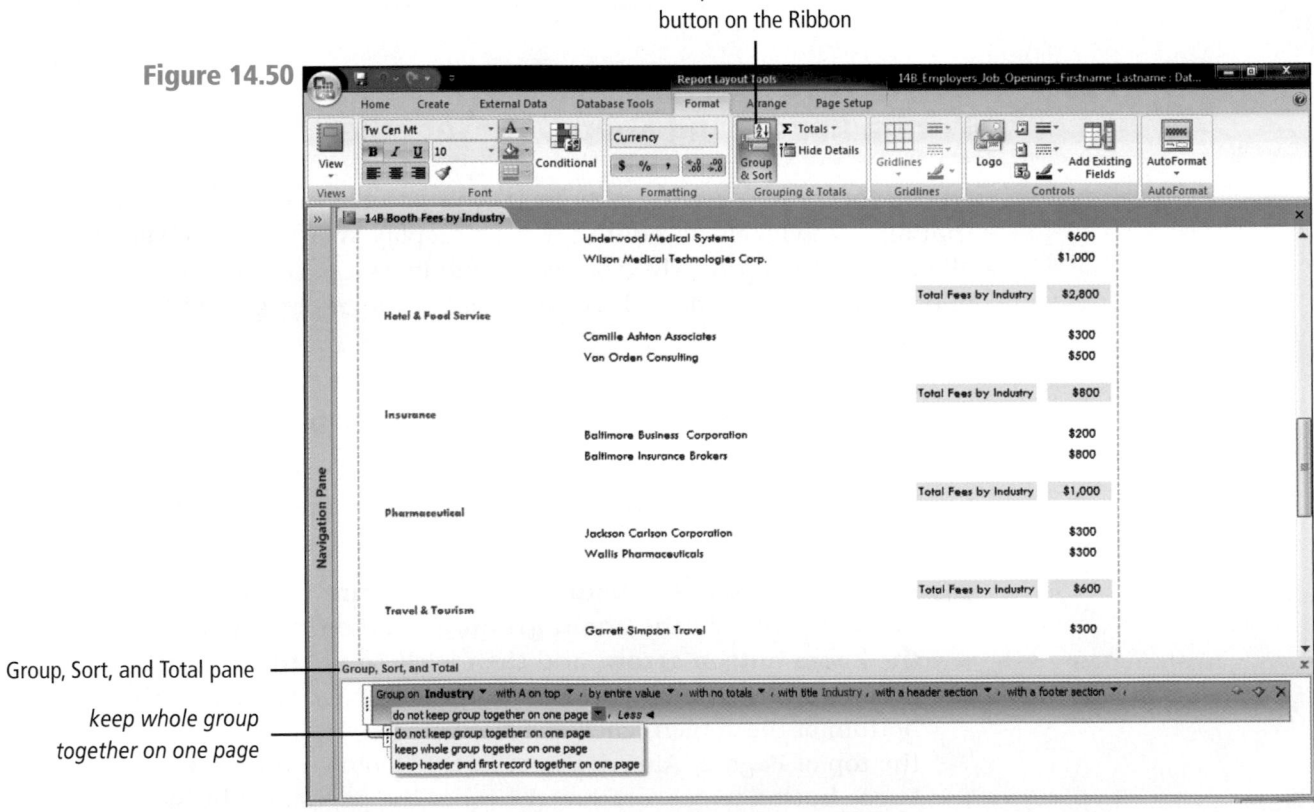

Group, Sort, and Total pane

keep whole group together on one page

4 Click **keep whole group together on one page**, and then click the **with A on top arrow**. In the displayed list, click **with A on top,** which indicates this field is sorting in ascending order. Compare your screen with Figure 14.51.

The *keep whole group together on one page* command will keep each employer together as a group, from the name in the group header, through the summary in the group footer.

Figure 14.51

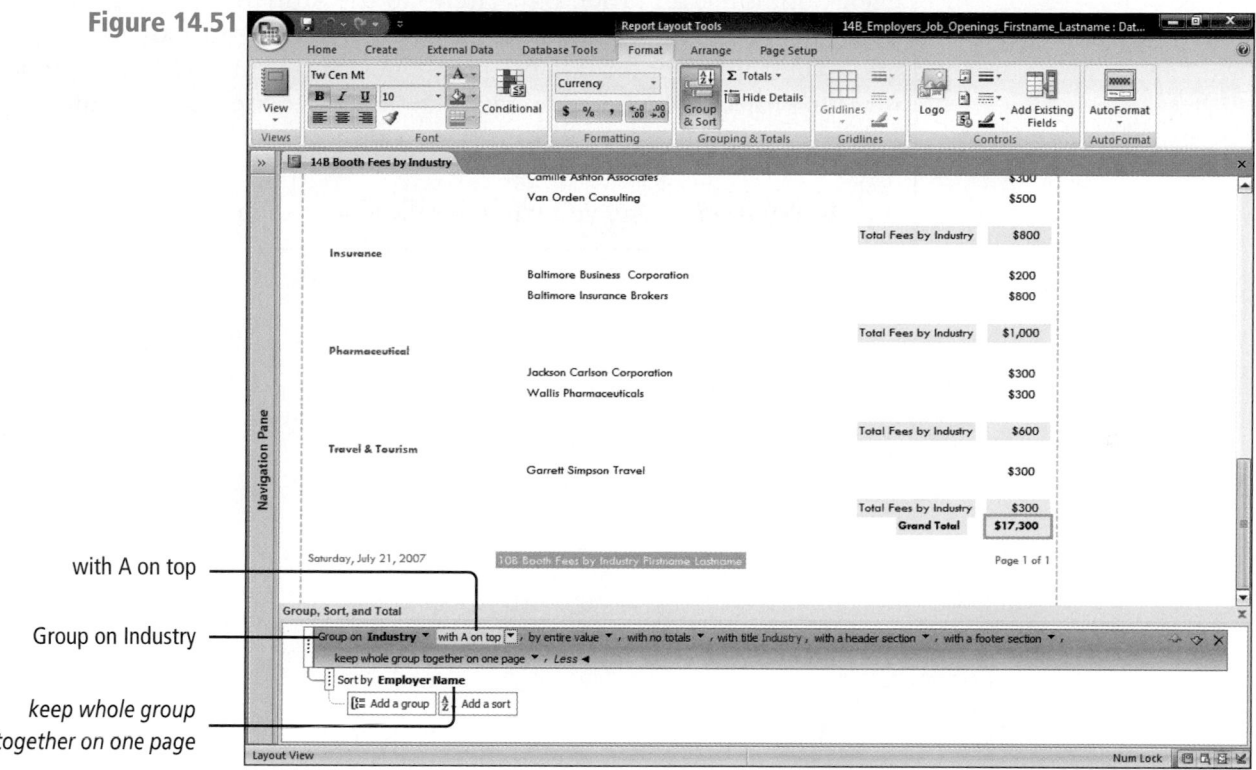

with A on top

Group on Industry

keep whole group together on one page

 5 On the Ribbon, in the **Grouping & Totals group**, click the **Group & Sort** button again to close the **Group, Sort & Total** pane. From the **Office** 🪟 menu, point to the **Print** button, and then click **Print Preview**. Display the top of **Page 2** to verify that the two records and total for the **Insurance** group display together.

6 On the **Print Preview tab**, in the **Print group**, click the **Print** button to print the report. Or, submit electronically as directed.

7 On the **Print Preview tab**, in the **Close Preview group**, click the **Close Print Preview** button. **Close** ✕ the report, and then click **Yes** to save the changes to the design of your report. **Exit Access**.

End **You have completed Project 14B** ——————

There's More You Can Do!

Close Access and any other open windows. Display the Start menu, click Computer, and then navigate to to the student files that accompany this textbook. In the folder **02_theres_more_you_can_do** locate and open the folder for this chapter. Open and print the instructions for this project, which are provided to you in Adobe PDF format.

Try IT! 1—Insert a Logo into a Form or a Report

In this Try It! exercise, you will insert a logo into an Access form.

Content-Based Assessments

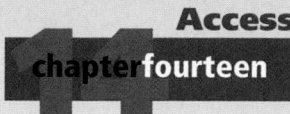

Summary

A form is a tool for either entering or viewing information in a database. Although you can both enter and view database information in the database table itself, using a form is easier because it can display one record at a time. The Form tool creates an instant form based on the fields in the table. Using the Form Wizard, you can create a customized form. Once created, a form can be modified in Layout view or in Design view.

Reports in Access summarize the data in a database in a professional-looking manner suitable for printing. The Report tool, the Blank Report tool, and the Report Wizard assist in report creation. The design of a report can be modified so that the final report is laid out in a format that is useful for the person reading it.

Key Terms

Content-Based Assessments

 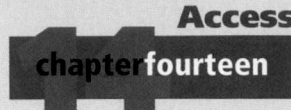
Matching

Match each term in the second column with its correct definition in the first column by writing the letter of the term on the blank line in front of the correct definition.

_____ **1.** An Access object with which you can enter, edit, or display data from a table or a query; a window for displaying and collecting information.

_____ **2.** The action of typing a record into a database.

_____ **3.** The Access tool that creates a form with a single mouse click, and that includes all the fields from the underlying data source (table or query).

_____ **4.** The Access view in which you can make changes to a form or to a report while the form is running, and in which the data from the underlying record source displays.

_____ **5.** The term used to describe objects and controls that are based on data that is stored in tables.

_____ **6.** The order in which the insertion point moves from one field to the next in a form when you press the Tab key.

_____ **7.** The bar on the left side of a form with which you can select the entire record.

_____ **8.** The detailed structured view of a form or report, and the view in which some tasks must be performed; only the controls, and not the data, are visible in this view.

_____ **9.** Information, such as a form's title, which displays at the top of the screen in Form view, and that is printed at the top of the first page when records are printed as forms.

_____ **10.** The section of a form or report that displays the records from the underlying table or query.

_____ **11.** Information at the bottom of the screen in Form view that is printed after the last Detail section on the last page.

_____ **12.** In Design view, a bar in a form or report that identifies and separates one section from another; used to select the section and to change the size of the adjacent section.

_____ **13.** Objects on a form or report that display data, perform actions, and let you view and work with information.

_____ **14.** The graphical object on a form or report that displays the data from the underlying table or query.

_____ **15.** A control on a form or report that contains descriptive information, typically a field name.

A Bound

B Controls

C Data entry

D Design view

E Detail section

F Form

G Form footer

H Form header

I Form tool

J Label

K Layout view

L Record selector

M Section bar

N Tab order

O Text box control

Content-Based Assessments

Fill in the Blank

Write the correct answer in the space provided.

1. A control that does not have a source of data is a(n) _____ control.

2. The small boxes around the edge of a control indicating the control is selected and that can be adjusted to resize the selected control are _____ handles.

3. The grouped arrangement of controls on a form or report is referred to as the _____ layout.

4. A small symbol that displays in the upper left corner of a selected control layout, and with which you can move the entire group of controls is the _____ _____.

5. A list of characteristics for controls on a form or report in which you can make precision changes to each control is the _____ Sheet.

6. The process of displaying only a portion of the total records (a subset) based on matching specific values is called _____.

7. An Access command that retrieves only the records that contain the value in the selected field is called _____ _____ _____.

8. An Access command that filters the records in a form based on one or more fields, or based on more than one value in the same field is called _____ _____ _____.

9. A condition in which only records where one of two values is present in the selected field is the _____ condition.

10. A condition in which only records where both specified values are present in the selected fields is a(n) _____ condition.

11. A database object that summarizes the fields and records from a table, or from a query, in an easy-to-read format suitable for printing is a(n) _____.

12. The tables or queries that provide the underlying data for a report are referred to as the _____ _____.

13. The Access feature that creates a report with one mouse click, and which displays all the fields and records from the record source that you choose is the _____ _____.

Content-Based Assessments

Fill in the Blank

14. An Access feature with which you can create a report from scratch by adding the fields you want in the order you want them to appear is the _____ _____ _____.

15. A control whose source of data is an expression—typically a formula—rather than a field is called a(n) _____ control.

Content-Based Assessments

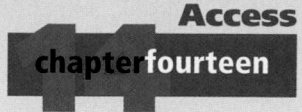

Project 14C—Counseling Sessions

In this project, you will apply the skills you practiced from the Objectives in Project 14A.

Objectives: 1. *Create a Form;* **2.** *Use a Form to Add and Delete Records;* **3.** *Create a Form by Using the Form Wizard;* **4.** *Modify a Form in Design View and in Layout View;* **5.** *Filter Records.*

At the Job Fair, various professional organizations schedule personal one-on-one counseling sessions with interested candidates to give them advice about opportunities in the fields they represent. Janna Sorokin, the database manager, has a database in which she is tracking the counseling sessions that have been scheduled thus far. Your completed database objects will look similar to those in Figure 14.52.

For Project 14C, you will need the following file:

a14C_Counseling_Sessions

You will save your database as
14C_Counseling_Sessions_Firstname_Lastname

Figure 14.52

14C Candidates Input Form	
Candidate ID#:	22155
First Name	Firstname

14C Candidates	
Candidate ID#:	22155
Candidate First Name:	Firstname
Candidate Last Name:	Lastname
Phone Number:	(443) 555-0765
Professional Interest:	Business
Registration Fee:	$15.00
Date Fee Collected:	10/10/2009

(Project 14C–Counseling Sessions continues on the next page)

Content-Based Assessments

(Project 14C–Counseling Sessions continued)

1. Open **Computer** and navigate to the location where the student files that accompany this textbook are located. Click once to select the file **a14C_Counseling_Sessions**; copy and then paste the file to your chapter folder. **Rename** the file 14C_Counseling_Sessions_Firstname_Lastname

2. **Start** Access, and then open your **14C_Counseling_Sessions** database. If necessary, enable the content. Click the **Database Tools tab**, and then in the **Show/Hide group**, click the **Relationships** button. If your relationships do not display, in the Relationships group, click the All Relationships button. Examine the one-to-many relationship, and then **Close** the Relationships window. If prompted, do not save your changes. *One* candidate can attend *many* counseling sessions.

3. **Open** the **Navigation Pane**, select the **14C Counseling Sessions table**, and then on the **Create tab**, in the **Forms group**, click **Form**. **Close** the **Navigation Pane**. Click the **Next record** button four times to display the record for *Session ID# 105*. Click the **Last record** button to display the record for *Session ID# 132*, and then click the **First record** button to display the record for *Session ID# 101*. Recall that you can view records one at a time in this manner by using a form. On the **Quick Access Toolbar**, click the **Save** button. In the displayed **Save As** dialog box, edit as necessary to name the form **14C Counseling Sessions Form** and then click **OK**. As additional candidates schedule sessions, you can use this form to enter the data into the 14C Counseling Sessions table. **Close** the form object.

4. **Open** the **Navigation Pane**, select the **14C Candidates table**, click the **Create tab**, and then in the **Forms group**, click **Form**. **Close** the **Navigation Pane**. Notice that the form displays the scheduled sessions for the first candidate's record. On the **Quick Access Toolbar**, click **Save**, name the form **14C Candidates Form** and then click **OK**. **Close** the form object. As new candidates register, you can use this form to enter the data into the Candidates table.

5. **Open** the **Navigation Pane**, and then open the **14C Counseling Sessions Form**. **Close** the **Navigation Pane**. Click the **New (blank) record** button. In the **Session ID#** field, type **133** and then press Tab. Continue entering the data as shown in the following table:

Candidate ID#	Counseling Session Host	Counselor
10776	Graphic Arts Professionals	Connie Rogers

6. **Close** the **14C Counseling Sessions Form**—the record is added to the associated table. **Open** the **Navigation Pane**, open the **14C Candidates Form**, and then **Close** the **Navigation Pane**. Click the **New (blank) record** button. Using your own first and last name, fill in the form using the information in the following table:

Candidate ID#	Candidate First Name	Candidate Last Name	Phone Number	Professional Interest	Registration Fee	Date Fee Collected
22155	Firstname	Lastname	(443) 555-0765	Business	$15.00	10/10/2009

7. **Close** the **14C Candidates form**. **Open** the **Navigation Pane**, open the **14C Candidates table**, and then verify that your record as a candidate displays as the last record in the table. **Close** the table.

(Project 14C–Counseling Sessions continues on the next page)

Content-Based Assessments

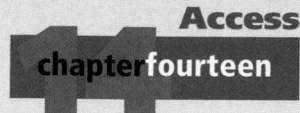
(Project 14C–Counseling Sessions continued)

8. From the **Navigation Pane**, open the **14C Counseling Sessions Form**. **Close** the **Navigation Pane**. Click in the **Session ID#** field, and then on the **Home tab**, in the **Find group**, click the **Find** button. In the **Look In** box, notice that *Session ID#* is indicated, and then in the **Find What** box, type **106** Click **Find Next**, and then confirm that the record for **Session ID# 106** displays. **Close** the **Find and Replace** dialog box.

9. On the **Home tab**, in the **Records group**, click the **Delete button arrow**, and then in the displayed list, click **Delete Record**. Click **Yes** to delete the record, and notice that the number of records in the table is *32*. **Close** the form object.

10. **Open** the **Navigation Pane**, open the **14C Counseling Sessions table**. Examine the table and verify that the record for *Session ID# 106* no longer displays. Then, verify that the new record you added for **Session ID# 133** is included in the table. **Close** the table.

11. From the **Navigation Pane**, open the **14C Candidates Form**. **Close** the **Navigation Pane**. Press Ctrl + F to display the **Find and Replace** dialog box. In the **Find What** box, type **22155** In the **Look In** box, be sure that *Candidate ID#* is indicated, and then click **Find Next** to display the record with your name. **Close** the **Find and Replace** dialog box. With this record displayed, from the **Office** menu, click **Print**. In the displayed **Print** dialog box, under **Print Range**, click the **Selected Record(s)** option button. Click the **Setup** button, click the **Columns tab**, and then under **Column Size**, in the **Width** box, delete the existing text and type **7"** Click **OK** two times to print only your record in the form layout, or submit electronically as directed. **Close** the **14C Candidates form**.

12. **Open** the **Navigation Pane**, and then select the **14C Candidates table**. On the **Create tab**, in the **Forms group**, click the **More Forms button**, and then in the displayed list, click **Form Wizard**. Click the **Tables/Queries arrow**, and then in the displayed list, click **Table: 14C Candidates**. Move the following fields to the **Selected Fields** list in the order given: **Candidate First Name**, **Candidate Last Name**, **Professional Interest**, and **Phone Number**. Click **Next**. Be sure **Columnar** is selected, and then click **Next**. Click **Solstice**, click **Next**, name the form **14C Candidates Input Form** and then click **Finish** to close the wizard and create the form.

13. **Close** the **Navigation Pane** and be sure your **14C Candidates Input Form** displays. Click the **Design View** button; if necessary close the Field List pane. Point to the upper edge of the **Detail section bar** to display the ➕ pointer, and then drag downward approximately **0.5 inch**. In the **Form Header section**, click in the title *14C Candidates Input Form* to select it. On the **Design tab**, in the **Font group**, click the **Font Size arrow**, and then click **18**. Click the **Bold** button. Click the **Font Color arrow**, and then under **Access Theme Colors**, click **Access Theme 9**.

14. Point to any **sizing handle** and double-click to fit the size of the label. Point to the upper edge of the **Detail section bar**, and then by using the ➕ pointer, drag upward until the bar is at **0.50 inch on the vertical ruler**.

(Project 14C–Counseling Sessions continues on the next page)

Content-Based Assessments

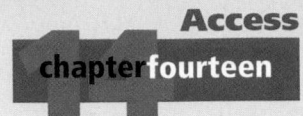

(Project 14C–Counseling Sessions continued)

15. Expand the lower edge of the **Form Footer section bar** approximately **0.50 inch**. On the **Design tab**, in the **Controls group**, click the **Label** button. Position the plus sign of the pointer in the **Form Footer** section at approximately **0.25 inch on the horizontal ruler** and even with the top edge of the section. Drag to the right to **5 inches on the horizontal ruler**, and then downward approximately **0.25 inch**. Using your own name, type **14C Candidates Input Form Firstname Lastname** and then press Enter. Double-click a sizing handle to fit the label to the text you typed. On the status bar, click the **Form View** button. On the **Quick Access Toolbar**, **Save** the changes you have made thus far.

16. On the status bar, click the **Layout View** button. In the **Controls group**, click the **Add Existing Fields** button to display the **Field List** pane. Point to **Candidate ID#**, and then drag to position the pointer in the upper portion of the white **Candidate First Name** text box control until a thick orange line displays above the control. Release the mouse button. **Close** the **Field List** pane. Click the white text box control for **Candidate ID#**, which currently displays *10115*, to surround it with an orange border. Point to the right edge of the white text box control, and then drag to the left until all of the white text box controls align under the *m* in the form title above.

17. Click the white text box control for **Phone Number**, which currently displays *(443) 555-0054*. With the control selected, drag upward with the ⬚ pointer until a thick orange line displays above **Professional Interest**. Release the mouse button to place the **Phone Number control** above the **Professional Interest control**. Click the **Candidate First Name label** to select it, and then click again to place the insertion point in the control. Edit the **Candidate First Name** and **Candidate Last Name** labels so that the labels indicate *First Name* and *Last Name*. On the **Quick Access Toolbar**, **Save** the changes you have made.

18. Click in a shaded area of the form to deselect any controls. Hold down ⇧Shift, and then click to select each of the five **white text box controls**. On the **Format tab**, in the **Font group**, click the **Fill/Back Color** button arrow. Under **Access Theme Colors**, click **Access Theme 3**. Click the **Font Size button arrow,** and then click **12**. Click in a shaded area of the screen to deselect all the controls. Using the technique you just practiced, select the five labels, change the **Font Size** to **11**, change the **Font Color** to **Access Theme 9**, and then apply **Bold**.

19. Click the **Professional Interest** label, right-click, and then click **Properties**. In the **Property Sheet**, on the **Format tab**, click **Width**, and then change the width to **1.75** Click in a shaded area to deselect. Hold down ⇧Shift, and then select the blue **First Name**, **Last Name**, **Phone Number**, and **Professional Interest** text box controls. In the **Property Sheet**, change the Height to **0.3** and then press Enter.

20. In the **Form Footer** section, click to select the label with your name. In the displayed **Property Sheet**, change the **Left** property to **1** and then press Enter. In the **Form Header** section, click anywhere in the label text *14C Candidates Input Form*. In the **Property Sheet**, change the **Left** property to **1** and then press Enter. **Close** the **Property Sheet**. On the status bar, click the **Form View** button. Click the **Last record** button to display the record containing your name. Then, from the **Office** menu, click **Print**. Under **Print Range**, click the

(Project 14C–Counseling Sessions continues on the next page)

(Project 14C–Counseling Sessions continued)

Selected Record(s) option button. Click **OK** to print, or submit electronically as directed. **Close** the form, and then click **Yes** to save the changes you have made.

21. **Open** the **Navigation Pane**, and then open the **14C Candidates Input Form**. **Close** the **Navigation Pane**. In the displayed first record, click the **Professional Interest** label. On the **Home tab**, in the **Sort & Filter group**, click the **Selection** button, and then in the displayed list, click **Equals "Business"**. Ten records indicate *Business* in the Professional Interest field. On the **Home tab**, in the **Sort & Filter group**, click **Toggle Filter** to remove the filter and activate all 22 records. Notice the **Unfiltered** button in the navigation area.

22. Be sure the first record displays, and then click to place the insertion point in the **Professional Interest** text box control. On the **Home tab**, in the **Sort & Filter group**, click the **Toggle Filter** button to reapply the filter. In the navigation area, click the **Last record** button to display the tenth record that matches *Business,* which is your record. In the **Sort & Filter group**, click the **Toggle Filter** button to reactivate all of the records. In the navigation area, click the **Next record** button one time to move to **Record 2**. In the **Phone Number** field, select the area code text *(443)* including the parentheses. On the **Home tab**, in the **Sort & Filter group**, click the **Selection** button, and then click **Begins With "(443)"**. Nine records contain this area code. On the **Home tab**, in the **Sort & Filter group**, click the **Toggle Filter** button to remove the filter and reactivate all 22 records.

23. With the **14C Candidates Input Form** still open, on the **Home tab**, in the **Sort & Filter group**, click the **Advanced** button, and then click **Filter By Form**. Click the **Advanced** button again, and then click **Clear Grid**. Click the **Professional Interest** text box control, click the **arrow** at the far right edge of the control, and then click **Nursing**. In the **Sort & Filter group**, click the **Toggle Filter** button. Click in the **Professional Interest** text box again. In the **Sort & Filter group**, click the **Filter** button. Select the **Biology** check box, and then click **OK**. Five records meet the OR condition; that is, five candidates have a Professional Interest of either Nursing *or* Biology.

24. Click the **Toggle Filter** button to remove all filters. **Close** the form object, and then **Exit Access**.

 End **You have completed Project 14C** ——————————————————

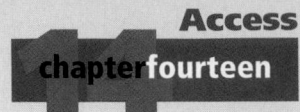
Project 14D — Workshops and Rooms

In this project, you will apply the skills you practiced from the Objectives in Project 14B.

Objectives: 6. *Create a Report by Using the Report Tool;* **7.** *Create a Report by Using the Blank Report Tool;* **8.** *Create a Report by Using the Report Wizard;* **9.** *Modify the Design of a Report;* **10.** *Print a Report and Keep Data Together.*

In the following Skills Review, you will create, modify, and print reports for Janna Sorokin regarding details about the Workshop rooms for the Job Fair. Your completed database objects will look similar to Figure 14.53.

For Project 14D, you will need the following file:

a14D_Workshops_Rooms

**You will save your database as
14D_Workshops_Rooms_Firstname_Lastname**

Figure 14.53

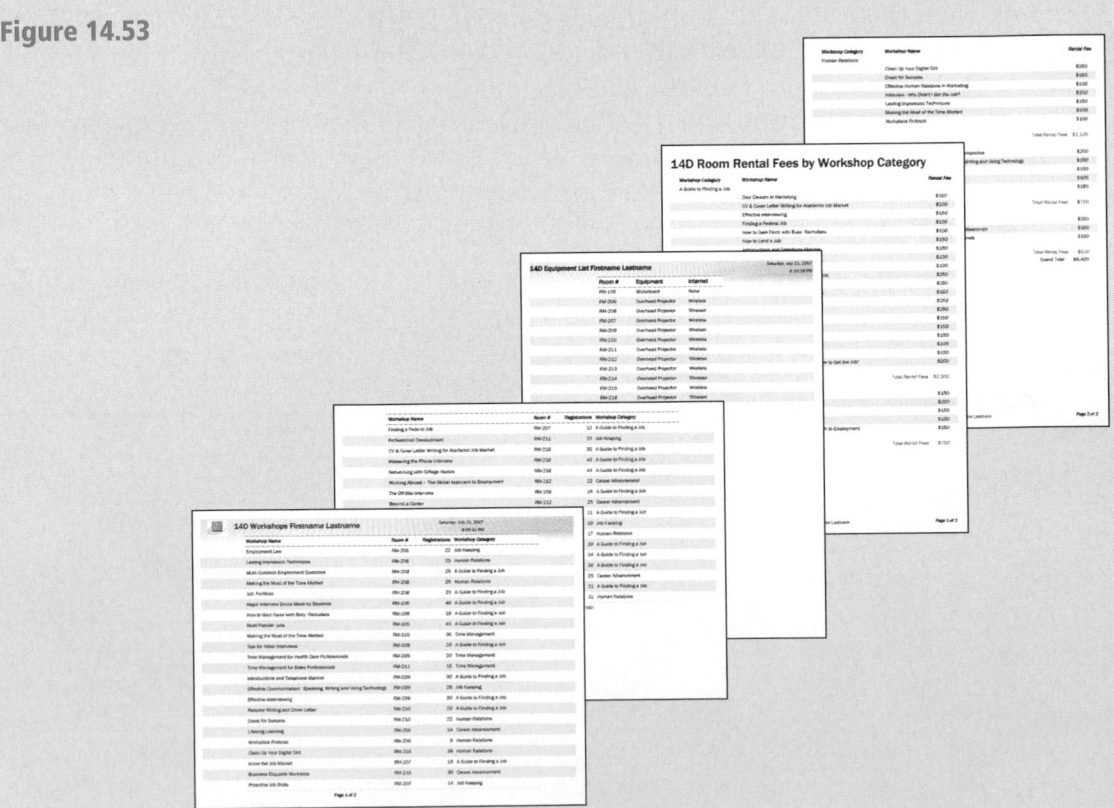

(Project 14D–Workshops and Rooms continues on the next page)

Content-Based Assessments

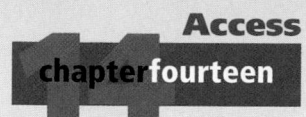
(Project 14D–Workshops and Rooms continued)

1. From the student files that accompany this text, locate the file **a14D_ Workshops_ Rooms**. Copy and then paste the file to your **Access Chapter 14** folder. Rename the file as **14D_Workshops_ Rooms_ Firstname_Lastname Start** Access and open your **14D_Workshops_Rooms** database. If necessary, enable the content. Click the **Database Tools tab**, and then in the **Show/Hide group**, click the **Relationships** button to view the relationship between the two tables; one room can have many workshops. If your relationships do not display, in the Relationships group, click the All Relationships button. **Close** the Relationships window, but do not save changes if prompted.

2. **Open** the **Navigation Pane**, and then select the **14D Workshops table**. On the **Create tab**, in the **Reports group**, click the **Report** button, and then **Close** the **Navigation Pane**. Click to select the field name **Workshop #**, right-click over the selected name, and then click **Delete**. Click the **Rental Fee** field, and then delete it. Click to select the field name **Registrations**. On the **Format tab**, in the **Grouping & Totals group**, click the **Totals** button. In the displayed list, click **Sum**. Scroll to the bottom of the report; the total registrations for the various workshops is *988*.

3. Click the **Page Setup tab**, and then in the **Page Layout group**, click **Landscape**. Click the **Format tab**, and then in the **AutoFormat group**, click the **More** button. Locate, and then click the **Trek** AutoFormat. In the **Report Header** at the top of the screen, double-click the header text *14D Workshops* to position the insertion point in the header. Edit as necessary to add your name to the end of the

header text, and then on the **Format tab**, in the **Font group**, change the **Font Size** to **16**.

4. Click the **Workshop Name** field name, point to the right edge of the orange border to display the ↔ pointer, and then drag to the right until each name displays on one line. Click the **Room #** field name, point to the right edge of the orange border to display the ↔ pointer, and then drag to the left to set the column width to accommodate the longest entry with a small amount of space to the right. Click any record in the report. In the upper left corner of the report, click the small brown **layout selector** button, and then drag it to the right until the pointer is positioned approximately below the *D* in *14D* of the report header.

5. In the lower right corner of the screen, at the right edge of the status bar, click the **Print Preview** button. On the **Print Preview tab**, in the **Zoom group**, click the **Two Pages** button to view the two pages of your report. To print your report, on the **Print Preview tab**, in the **Print group**, click **Print**. Or, submit electronically as directed. On the **Print Preview tab**, in the **Close Preview group**, click the **Close Print Preview** button, and then **Close** the **14D Workshops** report. In the displayed message box, click **Yes** to save changes to the design of the report. In the **Save As** dialog box, edit the Report Name to indicate **14D Workshop Attendance Report** and then click **OK**.

6. On the **Create tab**, in the **Reports group**, click the **Blank Report** button. In the **Field List** pane, click **Show all tables**, and then click the **plus sign (+)** next to the **14D Rooms table**. Point to the **Room #**

(Project 14D–Workshops and Rooms continues on the next page)

Content-Based Assessments

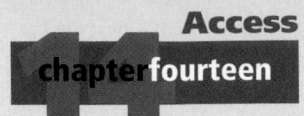
(Project 14D–Workshops and Rooms continued)

field, right-click, and then click **Add Field to View**. In the **Field List** pane, drag the **Equipment** field into the blank report—anywhere to the right of **Room #**. Double-click the **Internet** field to add it as the third field in the report. **Close** the **Field List** pane.

7. Click the **Equipment** field name, point to the right edge of the orange border to display the ↔ pointer, and then drag to the right until the text *Overhead Projector* displays on one line and there is a small amount of space between the name and the next column. On the **Format tab**, in the **Controls group**, click the **Date & Time** button. In the displayed **Date and Time** dialog box, click **OK**. In the **Controls group**, click the **Title** button, and then using your own name, type **14D Equipment List Firstname Lastname** In the **AutoFormat group**, click the **More** button, and then apply the **Trek** AutoFormat. With the title still selected, in the **Font group**, change the **Font Size** to **14**.

8. Click the field name **Room #**, hold down ⇧Shift, click the **Equipment** and **Internet** field names, and then with the three field names selected, change the **Font Size** to **12**. By using the **layout selector** button, move the group of controls until the pointer is positioned approximately below the *t* in the word *List*—or to whatever position appears to be horizontally centered between the margins. From the status bar, click **Print Preview**, and then print the report or submit electronically as directed. **Close Print Preview**, and then **Close** the report. In the displayed message box, click **Yes** to save the changes to the

design of the report. In the **Save As** dialog box, type **14D Equipment List** and then click **OK**.

9. On the **Create tab**, in the **Reports group**, click the **Report Wizard** button. Click the **Tables/Queries arrow**, and then click **Table: 14D Workshops**. Use the **One Field** button to move the following fields to the **Selected Fields** list in the order given: **Workshop Category**, **Workshop Name**, and **Rental Fee**. Click **Next**. With **Workshop Category** selected, click the **One Field** button to group the report by this field. Click **Next**. In the **1** box, on the right, click the **arrow**, and then click **Workshop Name** to sort by the name of the workshop. Click the **Summary Options** button. To the right of **Rental Fee**, select the **Sum** check box. Under **Show**, be sure the **Detail and Summary** option button is selected, and then click **OK**.

10. Click **Next**. Under **Layout**, be sure the **Stepped** option button is selected. On the right side of the dialog box, under **Orientation**, be sure **Portrait** is selected, and at the bottom be sure the **Adjust the field width so all fields fit on a page** check box is selected. Click **Next**. In the displayed list of styles, click the **Trek** style, and then click the **Next** button. In the **What title do you want for your report?** text box, name the report **14D Room Rental Fees by Workshop Category** and then click the **Finish** button. In the **Zoom group**, click the **Two Pages** button, and then examine the report as currently formatted. Then, in the lower right corner of your screen, on the status bar, click the **Layout View** button.

(Project 14D–Workshops and Rooms continues on the next page)

Content-Based Assessments

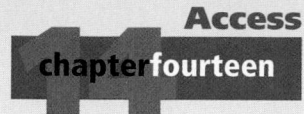

Access

Skills Review

(Project 14D–Workshops and Rooms continued)

11. Select the **Workshop Category label control**, and then widen the right side of the controls to align under the *t* in *Rental* in the Report Header above. Widen the right side of the **Rental Fee label controls** to just slightly inside the dashed margin. Then drag the left side of the control to the right to shorten the control and leave a small amount of space to accommodate the data.

12. Within each **Workshop Category group**, notice the **Summary for 'Workshop Category'** information. Click any of the **Summary for 'Workshop Category' controls**. Right-click any of the selected controls, and then from the displayed shortcut menu, click **Delete**. In the **Rental Fee** field, click any of the fee amounts to select these controls. Right-click any of the selected controls, and then from the displayed shortcut menu, click **Properties**. In the displayed **Property Sheet**, click the **Format tab**. In the **Property Sheet**, on the **Format tab**, click the name of the second property—**Decimal Places**—and then click the **arrow** that displays to the right of *Auto*. In the displayed list, click **0. Close** the **Property Sheet**. In any of the **Workshop Category groupings** of the report, to the right of the word *Sum*, click the dollar amount to select these controls. Point to any of the selected controls, right-click, and then from the displayed shortcut menu, click **Properties**. Change the number of decimal places to **0**, and then **Close** the **Property Sheet**.

13. By using the ↔ pointer, move the right and then the left border to position the summed amounts directly under the fees above with just enough space to accommodate the data. On the left side of the report, click one of the **Sum** controls to select these controls, and then click again to place the insertion point inside the selected control. Alternatively, double-click to place the insertion point inside the control. Delete the text, type **Total Rental Fees** and then press (Enter). Move the controls to the immediate left of the summed amounts.

14. At the top of your report, click to select the **Workshop Category label control**, hold down (Shift), and then click the **Workshop Name**, and the **Rental Fee label controls**. Apply **Italic**. Scroll down to view the end of the report. Click to select the sum **$6400.00**, which is the Grand Total for all the rental fees. Display the **Property Sheet** for this control and change its format to **0 Decimal Places**. **Close** the **Property Sheet**, and then adjust each side of the control to position it below the other fees. From the **Format tab**, apply **Bold** formatting. By adjusting the right and left sides of the control, move the text *Grand Total* to the immediate left of **$6,400**, and then apply **Bold**. On the **Quick Access Toolbar**, click **Save** to save the changes you have made to your report thus far.

15. Press (Ctrl) + (Home) to display the top of the report, and then on the right end of the status bar, click the **Design View** button. Drag the upper edge of the **Page Header section bar** downward approximately **0.5 inch**. Click the **Report Header** *14D Room Rental Fees by Workshop Category*, and then change the **Font Size** to **26**. Double-click a sizing handle to fit the control to the larger text. Drag the **Page Header section bar** upward slightly to approximately **0.5 inch on the vertical ruler**.

(Project 14D–Workshops and Rooms continues on the next page)

Content-Based Assessments

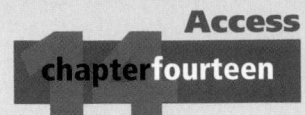

(Project 14D–Workshops and Rooms continued)

16. In the **Page Footer** section, click to select the **date control**. Shorten this control by dragging the right sizing handle to the left to **1.75 inches on the horizontal ruler**. Click the **page number control** on the right. Shorten this control by dragging the left sizing handle to the right to **5.5 inches on the horizontal ruler**. On the **Design tab**, in the **Controls group**, click the **Label** button, and then in the **Page Footer** section, position the plus sign portion of the pointer vertically in the middle of the section and horizontally at **2 inches on the horizontal ruler**. Click one time, and then using your own name, type **14D Rental Fees by Category Firstname Lastname** Press Enter to select the control. If necessary, hold down Ctrl, and then press ↑ to align the top edge even with the other two controls, but do not be concerned if this control overlaps the page number control. With the label control selected, on the **Design tab**, in the **Font group**, click the **Font Color button arrow**, and then under **Access Theme Colors**, click **Access Theme 9**. On the **Quick Access Toolbar**, click **Save**. Click the **Layout View** button.

17. On the status bar, click the **Print Preview** button. In the **Zoom group**, click the **Two Pages** button to view how your report is currently laid out. Notice that the bottom of **Page 1** does not break at the end of a category. **Close Print Preview**.

18. On the **Format tab**, in the **Grouping and Totals group**, click the **Group & Sort** button. In the **Group, Sort, and Total** pane, on the **Group on Workshop Category bar**, click the **More** button, click the arrow to the right of **do not keep group together on one page**, and then click **keep whole group together on one page**. Click the **with A on top arrow**. In the displayed list, click **with A on top**, which indicates this field is sorting in ascending order. In the **Grouping & Totals group**, click the **Group & Sort** button again to close the **Group, Sort & Total** pane.

19. On the status bar, click the **Print Preview** button. **Print** the report, or submit electronically as directed. **Close** the report, click **Yes** to save the changes to the design of your report. **Exit Access**.

End **You have completed Project 14D** ————————————————

Content-Based Assessments

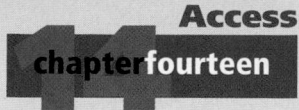

Access

chapter**fourteen**

Mastering Access

Project 14E — Booth Duty

In this project, you will apply the skills you practiced from the Objectives in Project 14A.

Objectives: 1. *Create a Form;* **2.** *Use a Form to Add and Delete Records;* **3.** *Create a Form by Using the Form Wizard;* **4.** *Modify a Form in Design View and in Layout View;* **5.** *Filter Records.*

In the following Mastering Access assessment, you will assist Janna Sorokin, database manager for the Greater Baltimore Area Job Fair, in using a database to track the staff and booth duty schedule during the fair event. Your completed database objects will look similar to Figure 14.54.

For Project 14E, you will need the following file:

a14E_Booth_Duty

**You will save your database as
14E_Booth_Duty_Firstname_Lastname**

Figure 14.54

14E Staff Input Form

First Name   Samantha

14E Staff

STAFF ID#:	STAFF-1119
Staff First Name:	Firstname
Staff Last Name:	Lastname
Phone Number:	(410) 555-0765
Title:	Assistant

(Project 14E–Booth Duty continues on the next page)

Content-Based Assessments

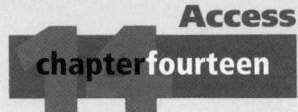
(Project 14E–Booth Duty continued)

1. From the student files that accompany this textbook, locate the file **a14E_Booth_Duty**. Copy and paste the file to your **Access Chapter 14** folder. Rename the file **14E_Booth_Duty_ Firstname_Lastname Start** Access and open your **14E_Booth_Duty** database. Enable the content. On the **Database Tools tab**, view the table relationships, and then **Close** the window. One staff member can be assigned many booth duties during the Job Fair event.

2. Based on the **14E Booth Duty** table, use the **Form** tool to create a new form. From the status bar, switch to Form view. Scroll through the records, and then after verifying that you can view the 48 records, **Save** and name the form **14E Booth Duty Form** Use the form to add the following new record:

Booth Duty ID#	BOOTH	STAFF ID#	Time Slot	Booth Location	Day
BD-49	BOOTH-I	STAFF-1109	8-12	South Hall	Day 1

3. **Close** the form, and then based on the **14E Staff table**, use the **Form** tool to create a new form. Switch to Form view, **Save** the form, name it **14E Staff Form** and then using your own first and last name, add the following new record:

STAFF ID#	Staff First Name	Staff Last Name	Phone Number	Title
STAFF-1119	Firstname	Lastname	(410) 555-0765	Assistant

4. After adding the record, display the **Print** dialog box, click the **Selected Record(s)** option button, click the **Setup** button, click the **Columns tab**, and then under **Column Size**, in the **Width** box, type **7"** Click **OK** two times to print only your record in the form layout, or submit electronically as directed. **Close** the **14E Staff Form**.

5. Open the **14E Staff table**, verify that your record as a staff member displays as the last record in the table, and then **Close** the table. Open the **14E Booth Duty Form**. Display the **Find and Replace** dialog box, locate, and delete the record for **Booth Duty ID# BD-06** and then **Close** the form. Open the **14E Booth Duty table**. Examine the table and verify that the record for **Booth Duty ID# BD-06** no longer displays. Then, look at the last record in the table, and verify that the new record that you added for **BOOTH-I** is included in the table. **Close** the table.

6. Based on the **14E Staff table**, use the **Form Wizard** to create a form. Add the following fields to the **Selected Fields** list in the order listed: **Staff First Name**, **Staff Last Name**, **Title**, and **Phone Number**. Select the **Columnar** layout and the **Trek** style for the form. Edit the title as necessary to name the form **14E Staff Input Form** and then click **Finish**.

(Project 14E–Booth Duty continues on the next page)

Content-Based Assessments

(Project 14E–Booth Duty continued)

7. Switch to Design view. Expand the lower edge of the **Form Footer section bar** approximately **0.50 inch**, and then in the expanded **Form Footer section**, create a label, beginning at approximately **0.25 inch on the horizontal ruler** and even with upper edge of the section. Drag to the right to **5 inches on the horizontal ruler**, and then downward approximately **0.25 inch**. Using your own name, type **14E Staff Input Form Firstname Lastname** and then press Enter. Double-click a sizing handle to fit the control to the text you typed.

8. Switch to Layout view. Display the **Field List** pane, and then drag the **Staff ID#** field into the form slightly below the **Phone Number control**. **Close** the **Field List** pane. Adjust the right side of the white text box controls to align under the *m* in the form title. Move the **Phone Number** control above the **Title** control. Edit the **Staff First Name** and **Staff Last Name** labels to indicate *First Name* and *Last Name*.

9. Deselect all controls. Then, hold down ⇧Shift and select all five **text box controls**. Change the **Font Size** to **12**, and if necessary, widen the controls so that the phone number displays on one line. Deselect all the controls. Select all the labels, change the **Font Size** to **12**, and then apply **Bold**.

10. Deselect all controls, and then select all of the labels. From the **Arrange tab**, display the **Property Sheet**. Change the **Width** property for all of the labels to **1.25** Select all the text box controls, and then change the **Height** property for all the text box controls to **0.35** and the **Width** property to **1.25** Select the **Form Footer label**, hold down ⇧Shift and click the **Form Header label**, and then change the **Left** property to **1** Close the **Property Sheet**. Switch to Form view. Click the **Last record** button to display the record containing your name. Display the **Print** dialog box, click the **Selected Record(s)** option button, and then click **OK** to print; or submit electronically as directed. **Close** the form and save the changes.

11. Open the **14E Staff Input Form**. In the displayed first record, click the **Title** label. In the **Sort & Filter group**, click the **Selection** button, and then in the displayed list, click **Equals "Associate"**. Six records contain the title *Associate*. In the **Sort & Filter group**, click **Toggle Filter** to remove the filter and activate all 19 records. Be sure the first record displays, and then click to place the insertion point in the **Title** text box control. Click the **Toggle Filter** to reapply the filter, and then in the navigation area, click the **Last record** button to display **Record 6**. In the **Phone Number** field, select the Area Code text *(410)*. Click the **Selection** button, and then click **Begins with "(410)"**. Four records meet the condition. Click the **Toggle Filter** button to remove the filter and reactivate all of the records. **Close** all the open objects, and then **Exit Access**.

End **You have completed Project 14E** ————————————————

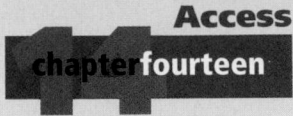

Access

chapter fourteen

Mastering Access

Project 14F—Lectures and Presenters

In this project, you will apply the skills you practiced from the Objectives in Project 14B.

Objectives: 6. *Create a Report by Using the Report Tool;* **7.** *Create a Report by Using the Blank Report Tool;* **8.** *Create a Report by Using the Report Wizard;* **9.** *Modify the Design of a Report;* **10.** *Print a Report and Keep Data Together.*

In the following Mastering Access assessment, you will create reports for Janna Sorokin regarding information about the various informational lectures and presenters that will be conducted during the Job Fair event. Your completed database objects will look similar to Figure 14.55.

> ### For Project 14F, you will need the following file:

a14F_Lectures_Presenters

**You will save your database as
14F_Lectures_Presenters_Firstname_Lastname**

Figure 14.55

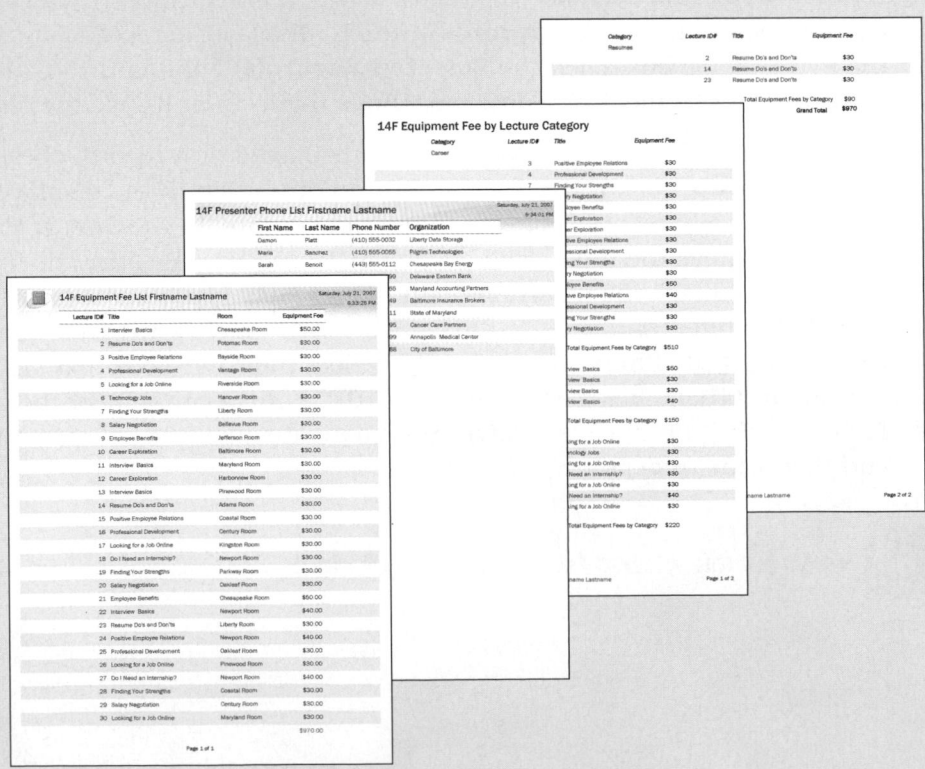

(Project 14F–Lectures and Presenters continues on the next page)

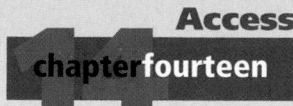
(Project 14F–Lectures and Presenters continued)

1. From the student files that accompany this textbook, locate the file **a14F_Lectures_Presenters**. Copy and then paste the file to your **Access Chapter 14** folder. Rename the file as **14F_Lectures_Presenters_Firstname_Lastname Start** Access, and then open your **14F_ Lectures_Presenters** database. Enable the content. On the **Database Tools tab**, view the table relationships, and then **Close** the window. One presenter can give many lectures during the Job Fair event.

2. Based on the **14F Lectures table**, use the **Report** tool to create a new report. Delete the following fields from the report: **Presenter ID**, **Lecture Date**, **Lecture Time**, and **Category**. At the bottom of the **Equipment Fee** column, notice that the Report tool automatically summed the column; the total is *$970.00*. Apply the **Trek** AutoFormat. Edit the Report Header text to indicate **14F Equipment Fee List Firstname Lastname** and then change the **Font Size** to **14**. Shorten the right side of the **Room** field leaving a small amount of space between the columns. Use the **layout selector** button to visually center the entire layout horizontally between the margins. Click the **Print Preview** button, click the **One Page** button, check your centering. **Print** the report, or submit electronically as directed. **Close Print Preview**, **Close** the report, save, and then name the report **14F Equipment Fee List**

3. Based on the **14F Presenters table**, create a **Blank Report**. Add the following fields: **First Name**, **Last Name**, **Phone Number**, and **Organization**. Widen the **Organization** field until all the names display on one line. Click the **Date & Time** and **Title** buttons, and type **14F Presenter Phone List Firstname Lastname** as the report title. Apply the **Trek** AutoFormat, and then with the title still selected, change the

title's **Font Size** to **16**. Select the four field names, change the **Font Size** to **12**. Center the layout horizontally on the page. Check the layout in **Print Preview**. **Print** the report, or submit electronically as directed. **Close Print Preview**, **Close** the report, save, and then name the report **14F Presenter Phone List**

4. Based on the **14F Lectures** table, create a report by using the **Report Wizard**, and then add the following fields in the order listed: **Category**, **Lecture ID#**, **Title**, and **Equipment Fee**. Group the report by **Category**, sort by **Lecture ID#** in **Ascending order**, and **Sum** the **Equipment Fee** field. Select the **Stepped** option, **Portrait** orientation, and **Trek** style. For the report title, type **14F Equipment Fee by Lecture Category** In **Print Preview**, click the **Two Pages** button, and notice that one category is split between two pages.

5. Switch to Layout view. Widen the right side of the **Category** field to accommodate the longest category name, which is *Job Search Techniques*. Shorten the right side of the **Title** field to accommodate the longest line with just a small amount of space between the columns. Click any of the **Lecture ID#** numbers, and in the **Font group**, click the **Center** button. Select the four field names, and then apply **Italic**. By using the **layout selector** button, visually center the entire layout horizontally on the page.

6. Select and delete the **Summary for 'Category'** controls. In the **Career** grouping of the report, to the right of the word *Sum*, click **$510.00** to select these controls, right-click, and then click **Properties**. Change the number of **Decimal Places** to **0**.

(Project 14F–Lectures and Presenters continues on the next page)

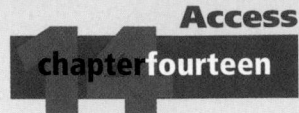

(Project 14F–Lectures and Presenters continued)

7. Select one of the amounts in the **Equipment Fee** field, display the **Property Sheet**, and then change the number of **Decimal Places** to **0**. Select the summed amount of **$510**, and then adjust as necessary so that the summed amounts display directly under the fee above with just enough space to accommodate the data. Change the font color to **Access Theme 10**. Select one of the **Sum** controls, place the insertion point inside the control, delete the text, type **Total Equipment Fees by Category** change the font color to **Access Theme 10**, and then press Enter. Position theses controls to the immediate left of the total amount.

8. At the end of the report, select the sum **$970.00**, which is the Grand Total for all equipment fees, change the number of decimal places to **0**, apply **Bold**, and then change the font color to **Access Theme 10**. Position the total directly below the other totals. Apply the same formatting to the text *Grand Total*, and then position this label to the immediate left of the total amount. **Save** the changes you have made to your report thus far.

9. Switch to Design view. In the **Page Footer** section, shorten the date control by moving its right edge to **1.75 inches on the horizontal ruler**. Shorten the **page number control** by moving its left edge to **5.5 inches on the horizontal ruler**. In the **Page Footer section**, create a label, and then position the pointer at **2 inches on the horizontal ruler** and in the vertical center of the section. Click one time, and then using your own name, type **14F Equipment Fees by Category Firstname Lastname** and then press Enter. Double-click a sizing handle to fit the control. With the label control selected, change the font color to **Access Theme 9**.

10. Display the **Print Preview** in the **Two Pages** arrangement, notice the bottom of **Page 1**, and then **Close Print Preview**. Switch to Layout view. In the **Grouping and Totals group**, click the **Group & Sort** button. From the **Group, Sort, and Total** pane, choose to **keep whole group together on one page** and **with A on top arrow**. **Close** the pane, click **Print Preview**, display **Two Pages**, and then verify that the entire *Resumes* group displays at the top of **Page 2**.

11. **Print** the report or submit electronically as directed. **Close** the report, save your changes, and then **Exit Access**.

End **You have completed Project 14F**

Content-Based Assessments

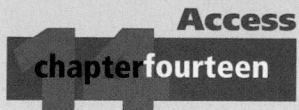

Mastering Access

Project 14G — Raffle Sponsors

In this project, you will apply skills you practiced from the Objectives in Projects 14A and 14B.

Objectives: 1. *Create a Form;* **2.** *Use a Form to Add and Delete Records;* **6.** *Create a Report by Using the Report Tool;* **7.** *Create a Report by Using the Blank Report Tool;* **10.** *Print a Report and Keep Data Together.*

In the following Mastering Access Assessment, you will assist Janna Sorokin, database manager for the Greater Baltimore Area Job Fair, in using a database to track raffle items and sponsors for the fair event. Your completed form and report will look similar to Figure 14.56.

For Project 14G, you will need the following file:

a14G_Raffle_Sponsors

You will save your database as
14G_Raffle_Sponsors_Firstname_Lastname

Figure 14.56

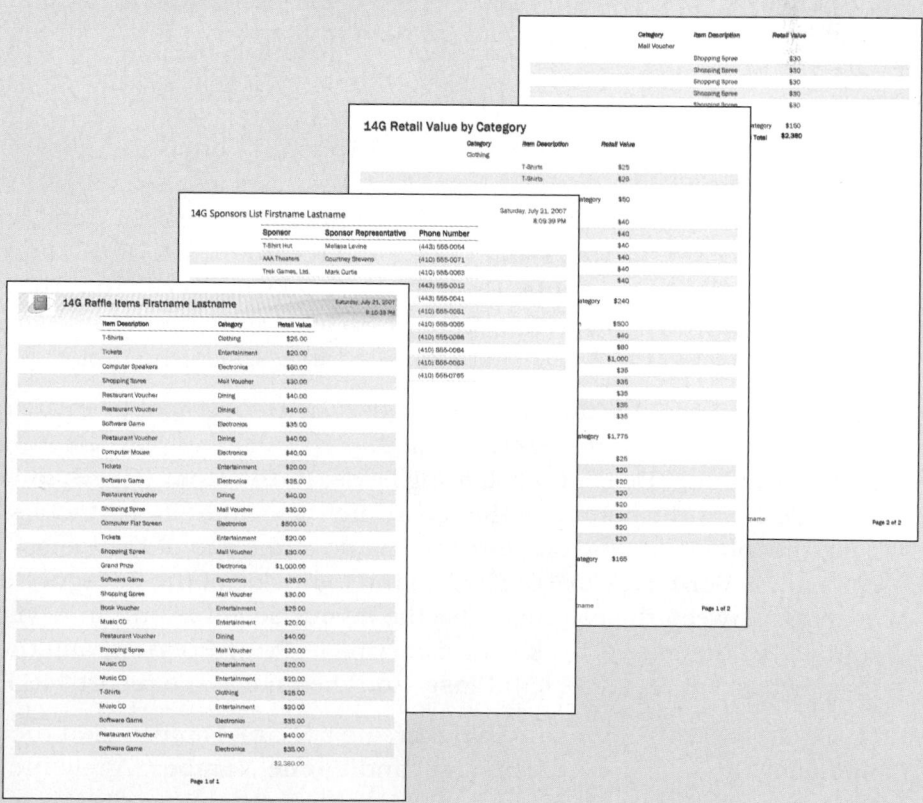

(Project 14G–Raffle Sponsors continues on the next page)

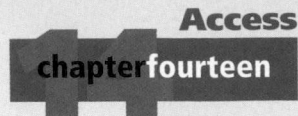
(Project 14G–Raffle Sponsors continued)

1. From the student files that accompany this textbook, locate the file **a14G_Raffle_Sponsors**. Copy and then paste the file to your **Access Chapter 14** folder. Rename the file **14G_Raffle_Sponsors_Firstname_Lastname Start** Access, and then open your **14G_Raffle_Sponsors** database. Enable the content. On the **Database Tools tab**, view the table relationships, and then **Close** the window. One sponsor can provide many raffle items during the Job Fair event.

2. Based on the **14G Raffle Items table**, use the **Form** tool to create a form. Switch to Form view and scroll through the records. Add a new record as follows:

Raffle Item ID#	Item Description	Sponsor ID#	Provider's Item Code	Category	Retail Value
RAFF-31	Software Game	SP-1203	TG-79044	Electronics	35

3. **Close** the form, and then save it as **14G Raffle Items Form** Based on the **14G Sponsors table**, use the **Form** tool to create a form. Switch to Form view, and then scroll through the records. Add a new record as follows, using your own first and last name:

Sponsor ID#	Sponsor	Phone Number	Sponsor Representative
SP-1211	Baltimore Sweets	(410) 555-0765	Firstname Lastname

4. **Close** the form, and then save it as **14G Sponsors Form** Open the **14G Sponsors table**, verify that your record as a sponsor representative displays as the last record in the table, and then **Close** the table. Open the **14G Raffle Items Form**. Use the **Find and Replace** dialog box to locate the record for **RAFF-02**, **Delete** the record for **RAFF-02**, and then **Close** the form. Open the **14G Raffle Items table**. Examine the table and verify that the record for *RAFF-02* no longer displays. Then scroll to **Record 30** and verify that the new record you added for **Sponsor ID# SP-1203** is included in the table. **Close** the table.

5. Based on the **14G Raffle Items** table, use the **Report** tool to create a new report. Apply the **Trek** AutoFormat to the report; recall that you should apply the AutoFormat first, and then edit other formatting. Delete the following fields: **Raffle Item ID#**, **Sponsor ID#**, and **Provider's Item Code**. At the bottom of the report, notice that the Report tool summed the **Retail Value** field; the total is *$2,380.00*. Add your name to the end of the Report Header text, and then change the **Font Size** to **16**. Shorten the right side of the **Category** field leaving a small amount of space between the columns. Use the **layout selector** button to visually center the layout horizontally on the page. Check your centering in **Print Preview**, and then **Print** the report, or submit electronically as directed. **Close**, and then name the report **14G Retail Value List**

6. Based on the **14G Sponsors table**, create a **Blank Report**. Add the following fields: **Sponsor**, **Sponsor Representative**, and **Phone Number**. Apply the **Trek** AutoFormat to the report. Widen the **Sponsor** field until all the names display on one line. Click

(Project 14G–Raffle Sponsors continues on the next page)

Content-Based Assessments

(Project 14G–Raffle Sponsors continued)

the **Date & Time** and **Title** buttons, and then as the report title, type **14G Sponsors List Firstname Lastname** Change the title's **Font Size** to **14**. Select the three field names, and then change the **Font Size** to **12**. Visually center the layout horizontally on the page. Check your centering in print preview, and then **Print** the report; or, submit electronically as directed. **Close**, save, and then name the report **14G Sponsors List**

7. Based on the **14G Raffle Items** table, create a report by using the **Report Wizard**, and then add the following fields in the order listed: **Category**, **Item Description**, and **Retail Value**. Group the report by **Category**, sort by **Item Description** in **Ascending order**, and **Sum** the **Retail Value** field. Select the **Stepped** option, **Portrait** orientation, and **Trek** style. As the report title, type **14G Retail Value by Category** In **Print Preview**, click the **Two Pages** button, and then examine how the records break across the two pages.

8. Switch to Layout view. Widen the right side of the **Category controls** to accommodate the longest category name. Shorten the right side of the **Item Description controls** to accommodate the longest line and leave a small amount of space between the columns. Select the three field names and apply **Italic**. Visually center the layout horizontally.

9. Select, and then delete the **Summary for 'Category'** controls. Select any value in the **Retail Value** field, and then from the **Property Sheet**, change the **Decimal Places** to **0**. In the **Clothing** grouping of the report, to the right of the word *Sum*, click **$50.00** to select these controls. Change the number of **Decimal Places** to **0**, change the **Font Color** to **Access Theme 10**, and then align the total under the values above.

10. Select one of the **Sum** controls and change the text to **Total Retail Value by Category** Align this control to the immediate left of the amount, and then change its **Font Color** to **Access Theme 10**.

11. At the end of the report, select the Grand Total **$2,380.00**, change the number of decimal places to **0**, apply **Bold**, and then change the **Font Color** to **Access Theme 10**. Position the total directly below the other totals. Apply the same formatting to the text *Grand Total*, and then position this label to the immediate left of the total amount. **Save** the changes you have made thus far.

12. Switch to Design view. In the **Page Footer** section, shorten the date control by moving its right edge to **1.75 inches on the horizontal ruler**. Shorten the **page number control** by moving its left edge to **5.5 inches on the horizontal ruler**. In the **Page Footer section**, create a label, and then position the pointer at **2 inches on the horizontal ruler** and in the vertical center of the section. Click one time, and then using your own name, type **14G Retail Values by Category Firstname Lastname** and then press Enter. Double-click a sizing handle to fit the control. With the label control selected, change the **Font Color** to **Access Theme 9**.

13. Display the **Print Preview** in the **Two Pages** arrangement, notice the bottom of **Page 1**, and then **Close Print Preview**. Switch to Layout view. In the **Grouping and Totals group**, click the **Group & Sort** button. From the **Group, Sort, and Total** pane, choose to **keep whole group together on one page** and **with A on top arrow**. **Close** the pane, display the **Print**

(Project 14G–Raffle Sponsors continues on the next page)

(Project 14G–Raffle Sponsors continued)

Preview, display **Two Pages**, and then verify that the entire *Mall Voucher* group displays at the top of **Page 2**.

14. Print the report or submit electronically as directed. **Close** the report, save your changes, and then **Exit Access**.

 You have completed Project 14G ————————————————————————

Content-Based Assessments

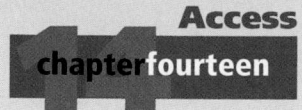

Mastering Access

Project 14H — Contractors and Facility Services

In this project, you will apply skills you practiced from the Objectives in Projects 14A and 14B.

Objectives: 1. *Create a Form;* **2.** *Use a Form to Add and Delete Records;* **6.** *Create a Report by Using Report Tool;* **7.** *Create a Report by Using the Blank Report Tool;* **8.** *Create a Report by Using the Report Wizard;* **9.** *Modify the Design of a Report;* **10.** *Print a Report and Keep Data Together.*

In the following Mastering Access assessment, you will assist Janna Sorokin, database manager for the Greater Baltimore Area Job Fair, in using a database to track facility and staff services for the fair event. Your completed objects will look similar to Figure 14.57.

> **For Project 14H, you will need the following file:**
>
> a14H_Contractors_Facility_Services

**You will save your database as
14H_Contractors_Facility_Services_Firstname_Lastname**

Figure 14.57

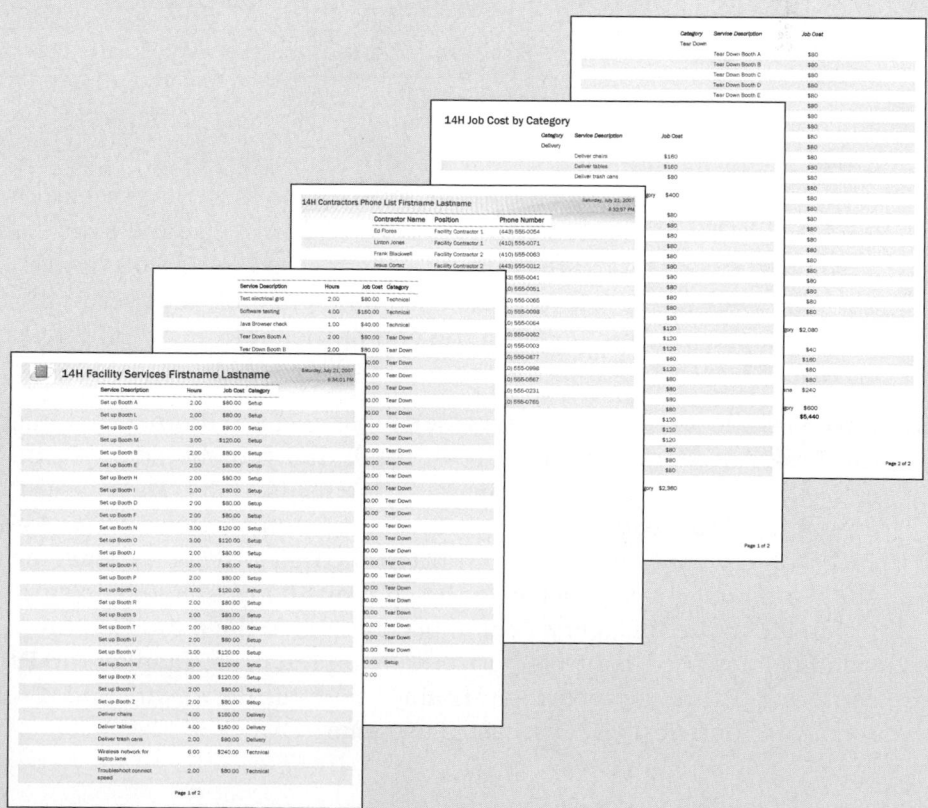

(Project 14H–Contractors and Facility Services continues on the next page)

Content-Based Assessments

Access
chapter fourteen   Mastering Access

(Project 14H–Contractors and Facility Services continued)

1. From the student files that accompany this textbook, locate the file **a14H_Contractors_Facility_Services**. Copy and then paste the file to your **Access Chapter 14** folder. Rename the file **14H_Contractors_Facility_Services_Firstname_Lastname** Start Access, and then open your **14H_Contractors_Facility_Services** database. Enable the content. On the **Database Tools tab**, view the table relationships, and then **Close** the window. One contractor can provide many facility services during the Job Fair event.

2. Based on the **14H Facility Services table**, use the **Form** tool to create a form. Switch to Form view, and then scroll through some of the 60 records. Add a new record as follows:

Job#	Date	Service Description	Contractor ID#	Hours	Job Cost	Category
JB-061	4/11/2009	Set up workroom	CO-3009	2	$80.00	Setup

3. **Close** the form, and then save it as **14H Facility Services Form** Based on the **14H Contractors table**, use the **Form** tool to create a form. Switch to Form view, and then scroll through the some of the 15 records. Add a new record as follows, using your own first and last name:

Contractor ID#	Contractor Name	Position	Phone Number
CO-3016	Firstname Lastname	Facility Contractor 1	(410) 555-0765

4. **Close** the form, and then save it as **14H Contractors Form** Open the **14H Contractors table**, verify that your record as a contractor displays as the last record in the table, and then **Close** the table. Open the **14H Facility Services Form**. Use the **Find and Replace** dialog box to locate the record for **JB-003**, **Delete** the record for **JB-003**, and then **Close** the form. Open the **14H Facility Services table**. Examine the table and verify that the record for *JB-003* no longer displays. Then, scroll to the end of the table and verify that the new record you added for **JB-061** is included in the table. **Close** the table.

5. Based on the **14H Facility Services** table, use the **Report** tool to create a new report. Apply the **Trek** AutoFormat to the report; recall that you should apply the AutoFormat first, and then edit other formatting. Delete the following fields: **Job#**, **Date**, and **Contractor ID#**. At the bottom of the **Job Cost** column, notice that the total job cost is *$5,440.00*. Add your name to the end of the Report Header text. Shorten the right side of the **Service Description** field leaving a small amount of space between the columns (longest line is toward the bottom). Shorten the right side of the **Category** field to accommodate the data. Use the **layout selector** button to visually center the controls horizontally on the page. Display the **Print Preview** to check your centering. **Print** the report, or submit electronically as directed. **Close**, and then name the report **14H Job Cost List Firstname Lastname**

(Project 14H–Contractors and Facility Services continues on the next page)

Content-Based Assessments

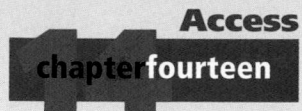
(Project 14H–Contractors and Facility Services continued)

6. Based on the **14H Contractors table**, create a **Blank Report**. Add the following fields: **Contractor Name**, **Position**, and **Phone Number**. Widen the **Position** field until all the positions display on one line. Click the **Date & Time** and **Title** buttons, and then as the title, type **14H Contractors Phone List Firstname Lastname** With the title still selected, apply the **Trek** AutoFormat, and then change the title's **Font Size** to **14**. Select the three field names, and then change the **Font Size** to **12**. Visually center the controls horizontally on the page. Display **Print Preview** to check your centering. Print the report, or submit electronically as directed. **Close**, and then name the report **14H Contractors Phone List Firstname Lastname**

7. Based on the **14H Facility Services table**, create a report by using the **Report Wizard**. Select the following fields in the order given: **Category**, **Service Description**, and **Job Cost**. Group the report by **Category**, sort by **Service Description** in **Ascending order**, and **Sum** the **Job Cost** field. Select the **Stepped** option, **Portrait** orientation, and **Trek** style. For the report title, type **14H Job Cost by Category** In **Print Preview**, click the **Two Pages** button and examine your report.

8. Switch to Layout view. Widen the right side of the **Category controls** to accommodate the longest category name, which is *Technical*. Shorten the right side of the **Service Description controls** to accommodate the longest line, and leave a small amount of space between the columns (the longest line is at the bottom of the list). Select the three field names, and then apply **Italic**. Visually center the layout horizontally.

9. Select, and then delete the **Summary for 'Category'** controls. Select any value in the **Job Cost** field, right-click, click **Properties**, and then change the number of **Decimal Places** to **0**. In the **Delivery** grouping of the report, to the right of the word *Sum*, click the value displayed as ##### to select these controls. Change the number of **Decimal Places** to **0**, change the **Font Color** to **Access Theme 10**, and then align the total under the values above.

10. Select one of the **Sum** controls, place the insertion point inside the control, delete the text, type **Total Job Cost by Category** and then press Enter. Align this control to the immediate left of the amount, and then change its **Font Color** to **Access Theme 10**. Be sure you have aligned the amount properly so that each Category's amount displays completely.

11. At the end of the report, expand if necessary, and then select the Grand Total sum that displays as #####, change the number of decimal places to **0**, apply **Bold**, and then change the **Font Color** to **Access Theme 10**. Position the total directly below the other totals. Apply the same formatting to the text *Grand Total*, and then position this label to the immediate left of the total amount. **Save** the changes you have made thus far.

12. Switch to Design view. In the **Page Footer** section, shorten the date control by moving its right edge to **1.75 inches on the horizontal ruler**. Shorten the **page number control** by moving its left edge to **5.5 inches on the horizontal ruler**. In the **Page Footer section**, create a label, and then position the pointer at **2 inches on the horizontal ruler** and in the vertical center of the section. Using your own name, type **14H Job Cost by Category Firstname Lastname** and then press Enter. Double-click a sizing handle to fit the control. With the label control selected, change the **Font Color** to **Access Theme 9**.

(Project 14H–Contractors Band Facility Services continues on the next page)

Content-Based Assessments

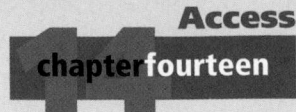
(Project 14H–Contractors and Facility Services continued)

13. Display the **Print Preview** in the **Two Pages** arrangement, notice how the groups flow from the bottom of **Page 1**, and then **Close Print Preview**. Switch to Layout view. In the **Grouping and Totals group**, click the **Group & Sort** button. From the **Group, Sort, and Total** pane, choose to **keep whole group together on one page** and **with A on top arrow**. View the Print Preview again, display **Two Pages**, and then verify that the entire *Tear Down* group displays on **Page 2**.

14. **Print** the report or submit electronically as directed. **Close Print Preview**, **Close** the report, save your changes, and then **Exit Access**.

End **You have completed Project 14H** ———————————————

Content-Based Assessments

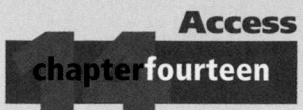

Mastering Access

Project 14I — Career Bookstore

In this project, you will apply all the skills you practiced from the Objectives in Projects 14A and 14B.

Objectives: 1. *Create a Form;* **2.** *Use a Form to Add and Delete Records;* **3.** *Create a Form by Using the Form Wizard;* **4.** *Modify a Form in Design View and in Layout View;* **5.** *Filter Records;* **6.** *Create a Report by Using the Report Tool;* **7.** *Create a Report by Using the Blank Report Tool;* **8.** *Create a Report by Using the Report Wizard;* **9.** *Modify the Design of a Report;* **10.** *Print a Report and Keep Data Together.*

In the following Mastering Access assessment, you will assist Janna Sorokin, database manager for the Greater Baltimore Area Job Fair, in using a database to track publishers and book titles for the books that are for sale at the Career Bookstore during the Job Fair event. Your completed objects will look similar to Figure 14.58.

For Project 14I, you will need the following file:

a14I_Career_Bookstore

You will save your database as
14I_Career_Bookstore_Firstname_Lastname

Figure 14.58

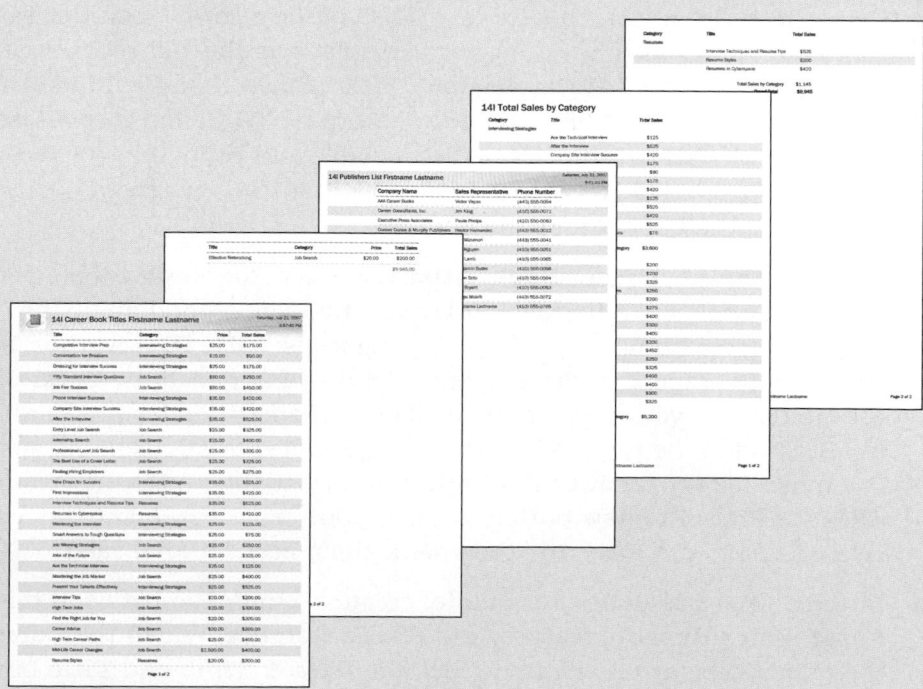

(Project 14I–Career Bookstore continues on the next page)

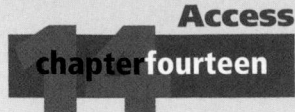
(Project 14I–Career Bookstore continued)

1. From the student files that accompany this textbook, locate the file **a14I_Career_Bookstore**. Copy and then paste the file to your **Access Chapter 14** folder. Rename the file **14I_Career_Bookstore_Firstname_Lastname Start** Access, and then open your **14I_Career_Bookstore** database. Enable the content. Examine the data in the two tables. On the **Database Tools tab**, view the table relationships, and then **Close** the window. One publisher can provide many career book titles during the Job Fair event.

2. Based on the **14I Career Book Titles table**, use the **Form** tool to create a form. Switch to Form view, and then scroll through the records. Add a new record as follows:

Title ID #	Title	Author	Publisher ID#	Category	Price	Total Sales
T-33	Effective Networking	Jean Flowers	PUB-100	Job Search	20	200

3. **Close** the form, and then save it as **14I Career Book Titles Form** Based on the **14I Publishers table**, use the **Form** tool to create a form. Switch to Form view, and then scroll through the records. Add a new record as follows, using your own first and last name:

Publisher ID#	Phone Number	Sales Representative	Company Name	Title
PUB-111	(410) 555-0765	Firstname Lastname	Associated Publishers	Sales Associate

4. **Close** the form, and then save it as **14I Publishers Form** Open the **14I Publishers table**, verify that your record as a Sales Associate displays as the last record in the table, and then **Close** the table. Open the **14I Career Book Titles Form**. Use the **Find and Replace** dialog box to locate the record for **T-05**, **Delete** the record for **T-05**, and then **Close** the form. Open the **14I Career Book Titles table**. Examine the table and verify that the record for *T-05* no longer displays. Then scroll to **Record 33** and verify that the new record you added for **Title ID# T-33** is included in the table. **Close** the table.

5. Based on the **14I Career Book Titles table**, use the **Report** tool to create a new report. Apply the **Trek** AutoFormat to the report; recall that you should apply the AutoFormat first, and then edit other formatting. Delete the following fields: **Title ID#**, **Author**, and **Publisher ID#**. At the bottom of the report, notice that the Report tool summed the **Total Sales** field, the total is *$9,945.00*. Add your name to the end of the Report Header text, and then change the **Font Size** to **16**. Shorten the right side of the **Category** field leaving a small amount of space between the columns. Use the **layout selector** button to visually center the layout horizontally on the page. Click the **Print Preview** button to check your centering. **Print** the report, or submit electronically as directed. **Close**, and then name the report **14I Total Sales**

6. Based on the **14I Publishers table**, create a **Blank Report**. Add the following fields: **Company Name**, **Sales Representative**, and **Phone Number**. Widen the **Company Name** field until all the names display on one line. Click the **Date & Time** and **Title** buttons, and then as the

(Project 14I–Career Bookstore continues on the next page)

Content-Based Assessments

(Project 14I–Career Bookstore continued)

report title, type **14I Publishers List Firstname Lastname** With the title still selected, apply the **Trek** AutoFormat, and then change the title's **Font Size** to **14**. Select the three field names, change the **Font Size** to **12**. Check your centering in print preview, and then **Print** the report; or, submit electronically as directed. **Close**, save, and then name the report **14I Publishers List**

7. Based on the **14I Career Book Titles table**, create a report by using the **Report Wizard**, and add the following fields in the order listed: **Category**, **Title,** and **Total Sales**. Group the report by **Category**, sort by **Title** in **Ascending order**, and then **Sum** the **Total Sales** field. Select the **Stepped** option, **Portrait** orientation, and **Trek** style. As the report title, type **14I Total Sales by Category** In **Print Preview**, click the **Two Pages** button, and then examine how the records break across the two pages.

8. Switch to Layout view. Widen the right side of the **Category controls** to accommodate the longest category name. Shorten the right side of the **Title controls** to accommodate the longest line and leave a small amount of space between the columns. Select the three field names and apply **Italic**. Visually center the layout horizontally.

9. Select, and then delete the **Summary for 'Category'** controls. Select any value in the **Total Sales** field, right-click, click **Properties**, and then change the **Decimal Places** to **0**. In the **Interviewing Strategies** grouping of the report, to the right of the word *Sum*, click **$3,600.00** to select these controls. Change the number of **Decimal Places** to **0**, change the **Font Color** to **Access Theme 10**, and then align the total under the values above.

10. Select one of the **Sum** controls and change the text to **Total Sales by Category** Align this control to the immediate left of the amount, and then change its **Font Color** to **Access Theme 10**.

11. At the end of the report, select the sum **$9,945.00**, which is the Grand Total, change the number of decimal places to **0**, apply **Bold**, and then change the **Font Color** to **Access Theme 10**. Position the Grand Total directly below the other totals. Apply the same formatting to the text *Grand Total*, and then position this label to the immediate left of the Grand Total amount. **Save** the changes you have made to your report thus far.

12. Switch to Design view. In the **Page Footer** section, shorten the date control by moving its right edge to **1.75 inches on the horizontal ruler**. Shorten the **page number control** by moving its left edge to **5.5 inches on the horizontal ruler**. In the **Page Footer section**, create a label, and then position the pointer at **2 inches on the horizontal ruler** and in the vertical center of the section. Click one time, and then using your own name, type **14I Total Sales by Category Firstname Lastname** and then press Enter. Double-click a sizing handle to fit the control. With the label control selected, change the **Font Color** to **Access Theme 9**.

13. Display the **Print Preview** in the **Two Pages** arrangement, notice the flow between the bottom of **Page 1** and the top of **Page 2**, and then **Close Print Preview**. Switch to Layout view. In the **Grouping and Totals group**, click the **Group & Sort** button. From the **Group, Sort, and Total** pane, choose to **keep whole group together on one page** and **with A on top arrow**. **Close** the pane, click **Print Preview**, display **Two Pages**, and then verify that the entire *Resumes* group displays at the top of **Page 2**. **Print** the report or submit electronically as directed. **Close**, and then save the report.

(Project 14I–Career Bookstore continues on the next page)

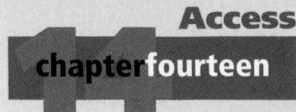

(Project 14I–Career Bookstore continued)

14. Open the **14I Publishers Form**. In the displayed first record, click the **Title** label. In the **Sort & Filter group**, click the **Selection** button, and then in the displayed list, click **Equals "Sales Representative"**. Six records contain the title *Sales Representative*. In the **Sort & Filter group**, click **Toggle Filter** to remove the filter and activate all 12 records. Be sure the first record displays, and then click to place the insertion point in the **Title** text box control. Click the **Toggle Filter** to reapply the filter, and then in the navigation area, click the **Last record** button to display the sixth record in the filtered group. In the **Phone Number** field, select the Area Code text *(443)*. Click the **Selection** button, and then click **Begins with "(443)"**. Four records meet the condition. Click the **Toggle Filter** button to remove the filter and reactivate all of the records. **Close** all the open objects, and then **Exit Access**.

 You have completed Project 14I

Content-Based Assessments

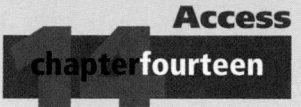

Project 14J — Business Running Case

In this project, you will apply the skills you practiced in Projects 14A and 14B.

Close Access and any other open windows. Display the Start menu, click Computer, and then navigate to to the student files that accompany this textbook. In the folder **03_business_running_case**, locate and open the folder for this chapter. Open and print the instructions for this project, which are provided to you in Adobe PDF format. Follow the instructions and use the skills you have gained thus far to assist Jennifer Nelson in meeting the challenges of owning and running her business.

End You have completed Project 14J ———————

Content-Based Assessments

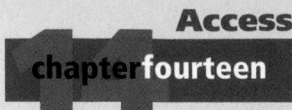
Mastering Access

Project 14K — *GO!* Fix It

In this project, you will apply the skills you practiced from the Objectives in Projects 14A and 14B.

> **For Project 14K, you will need the following file:**
>
> a14K_fixit_Resume_Workshops
>
> **You will save your workbook as**
> **14K_Resume_Workshop_Firstname_Lastname**

From the student files that accompany this textbook, open the folder **05_go_fix_it**. Locate and make a copy of the database **a14K_fixit_Resume_Workshops** in your chapter folder. Name the copy **14K_Resume_Workshops_Firstname_Lastname**

This database contains **five errors** that you must find and correct. Read and examine the database, and then edit to correct the errors that you find. Types of errors could include:

- Missing or incorrect data in tables, queries, forms, and reports such as filenames, field names, types, descriptions, properties, records, and criteria.
- Table design errors such as primary key.
- Forms design errors such as form header and footer, page header and footer, detail, and layout.
- Reports design errors such as report header and footer, page header and footer, detail, and layout.
- Page setup errors such as margins, orientation, layout, or alignment.

To complete the project you should check for the following:

- In the Workshop Schedule Report, the items in the first column should display on one line. After adjusting the report, add your first name and last name to the report title.
- In the Workshops and Participants report, the columns are not fully visible and there is no attractive format. Adjust accordingly and use the Trek AutoFormat. After adjusting the report, add your first name and last name to the report title.
- Examine the Participant Input form and adjust the field widths and heights to accommodate the data. Add your name to the title.

(Project 14K–*GO!* Fix It continues on the next page)

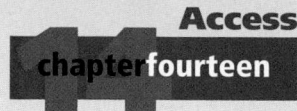

(Project 14K–*GO!* Fix It continued)

- Add a title to the Participant Fees report, include your name.
- Examine the Participant Fees table for accurate calculations; the report should indicate the total Workshop Fees.

Print each database object that you corrected, or submit your database as directed.

 End **You have completed Project 14K**——————————

Outcomes-Based Assessments

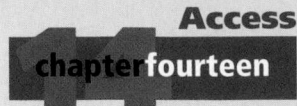

Rubric

The following outcomes-based assessments are *open-ended assessments*. That is, there is no specific correct result; your result will depend on your approach to the information provided. Make *Professional Quality* your goal. Use the following scoring rubric to guide you in *how* to approach the problem and then to evaluate *how well* your approach solves the problem.

The *criteria*—Software Mastery, Content, Format and Layout, and Process—represent the knowledge and skills you have gained that you can apply to solving the problem. The *levels of performance*—Professional Quality, Approaching Professional Quality, or Needs Quality Improvements—help you and your instructor evaluate your result.

	Your completed project is of Professional Quality if you:	**Your completed project is Approaching Professional Quality if you:**	**Your completed project Needs Quality Improvements if you:**
1-Software Mastery	Choose and apply the most appropriate skills, tools, and features and identify efficient methods to solve the problem.	Choose and apply some appropriate skills, tools, and features, but not in the most efficient manner.	Choose inappropriate skills, tools, or features, or are inefficient in solving the problem.
2-Content	Construct a solution that is clear and well organized, contains content that is accurate, appropriate to the audience and purpose, and is complete. Provide a solution that contains no errors of spelling, grammar, or style.	Construct a solution in which some components are unclear, poorly organized, inconsistent, or incomplete. Misjudge the needs of the audience. Have some errors in spelling, grammar, or style, but the errors do not detract from comprehension.	Construct a solution that is unclear, incomplete, or poorly organized, containing some inaccurate or inappropriate content; and contains many errors of spelling, grammar, or style. Do not solve the problem.
3-Format and Layout	Format and arrange all elements to communicate information and ideas, clarify function, illustrate relationships, and indicate relative importance.	Apply appropriate format and layout features to some elements, but not others. Overuse features, causing minor distraction.	Apply format and layout that does not communicate information or ideas clearly. Do not use format and layout features to clarify function, illustrate relationships, or indicate relative importance. Use available features excessively, causing distraction.
4-Process	Use an organized approach that integrates planning, development, self-assessment, revision, and reflection.	Demonstrate an organized approach in some areas, but not others; or, use an insufficient process of organization throughout.	Do not use an organized approach to solve the problem.

Outcomes-Based Assessments

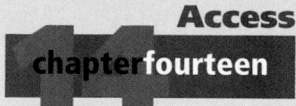
Problem Solving

Project 14L — Candidates and Offers

In this project, you will construct a solution by applying any combination of the Objectives found in Projects 14A and 14B.

> **For Project 14L, you will need the following file:**
>
> a14L_Candidates_Offers

You will save your database as
14L_Candidates_Offers_Firstname_Lastname

Copy the student file **a14L_Candidates_Offers** to your Access Chapter 14 folder and rename it **14L_Candidates_Offers_Firstname_Lastname** Michael Dawson, Executive Director of the Baltimore Area Job Fair, would like one form and two reports created from the Job Fair database. Mr. Dawson wants a report listing the Organization Name and Offer Amount of each job offered to a candidate as a result of the Job Fair.

Create and save the report as **14L Offers Firstname Lastname** Print the report or submit electronically as directed. Mr. Dawson also wants a report of the names, college majors, and phone numbers of the candidates. Save the report as **14L Candidates Firstname Lastname** Print the report or submit electronically as directed. Using the skills you have practiced in this chapter, create an attractive, easy-to-follow input form that can be used to update candidate records. Using your own information, add a new record as Candidate ID# 22102. Save the form as **14L Candidate Update Firstname Lastname** For the report that you added, print or submit electronically.

End **You have completed Project 14L**

Outcomes-Based Assessments

Access
chapter fourteen

Problem Solving

Project 14M — Applicants and Job Openings

In this project, you will construct a solution by applying any combination of the Objectives found in Projects 14A and 14B.

For Project 14M, you will need the following file:

a14M_Applicants_Job_Openings

You will save your database as
14M_Applicants_Job_Openings_Firstname_Lastname

Copy the file **a14M_Applicants_Job_Openings** to your Access Chapter 14 folder and rename it **14M_Applicants_Job_Openings_Firstname_Lastname** Janice Strickland, Employer Coordinator, wants to know which types of positions have the most openings so she can highlight them on the Job Fair Web site.

Sort the records in the table so you can provide Janice with the appropriate information, print the table in the sorted order, save the table as **14M Table Sort Firstname Lastname** or submit electronically; and save the changes to the table's design. Janice also needs an input form for Job Fair applicants so she can update the database if needed. Save the form as **14M Applicant Input Form Firstname Lastname** Print the form, or submit electronically. Create an Applicant input form, and using your own information, add a new record as Applicant ID# 4600. Janice needs a report with applicant contact information so she can send updates about new job openings. Create an attractive, easy-to-read applicant contact information report. Include a Report Header with **14M Applicant Contact Information Firstname Lastname** Save and print the report, or submit electronically.

End **You have completed Project 14M**

Outcomes-Based Assessments

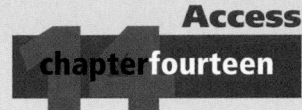

Problem Solving

Project 14N — Candidates and Activities

In this project, you will construct a solution by applying any combination of the Objectives found in Projects 14A and 14B.

For Project 14N, you will need the following file:

a14N_Candidates_Activities

**You will save your database as
14N_Candidates_Activities_Firstname_Lastname**

Copy the file **a14N_Candidates_Activities** to your Access Chapter 14 folder and rename it **14N_Candidates_Activities_Firstname_Lastname** Janice Strickland, Employer Coordinator, wants a report that shows the room where each activity is being held so that she can give the Activity Coordinators their room assignments.

Create an attractive, easy-to-read report that shows the Meeting Room for each Activity. Include your name in the report heading, save the report as **14N Activity Meeting Rooms Firstname Lastname** and then print the report or submit electronically. Then, create a Candidate Input Form for adding information for new candidates. Using your own information, add a new record as STU-2049 to the form. Save as **14N Candidate Input Form Firstname Lastname** and then print the STU-2049 record or submit electronically.

 End You have completed Project 14N ————————

Outcomes-Based Assessments

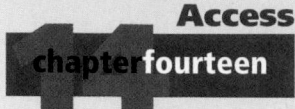

Problem Solving

Project 14O — Donors and Gifts

In this project, you will construct a solution by applying any combination of the Objectives found in Projects 14A and 14B.

> **For Project 14O, you will need the following file:**
>
> a14O_Donors_Gifts

You will save your database as
14O_Donors_Gifts_Firstname_Lastname

Copy the file **a14O_Donors_Gifts** to your Access Chapter 14 folder and rename it **14O_Donors_Gifts_Firstname_Lastname** Michael Dawson, Executive Director of the Baltimore Area Job Fair, wants a Donor Gifts Report so he can determine the total retail value of gift items distributed during the Job Fair.

Create a report grouped by Category and sorted by Item Description that includes the Retail Value totals. Include the Grand Total of the Retail Value of the gift items. Create a footer with the project name (14O Donors and Gifts) and your name in the footer. Save the report as **14O Gift Retail Value Firstname Lastname**

Mr. Dawson also needs a donor list with phone numbers so he can call the donor representatives and thank them for participating in the Job Fair. Create a report with the date and a report title that includes the project name and your name. Save the report as **14O Donor List Firstname Lastname** Print or submit the reports electronically.

End **You have completed Project 14O** _____

Outcomes-Based Assessments

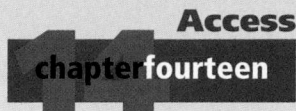

Problem Solving

Project 14P—Food Services Staffing

In this project, you will construct a solution by applying any combination of the Objectives found in Projects 14A and 14B.

For Project 14P, you will need the following file:

a14P_Food_Services_Staffing

**You will save your database as
14P_Food_Services_Staffing_Firstname_Lastname**

Copy the file **a14P_Food_Services_Staffing** to your Access Chapter 14 folder and rename it **14P_Food_Services_Staffing_Firstname_Lastname** Roy McLean, Food Services Manager for the Baltimore Area Job Fair, would like a report created with Food Service staff contact information. He needs the report for calling staff members when the schedule changes.

Create an attractive, easy-to-read staff contact report. Include the project name (14P Food Services Staffing) and your name in the report heading. Save the report as **14P Staff Contact Firstname Lastname** Print or submit electronically.

 End **You have completed Project 14P** ————————————

Outcomes-Based Assessments

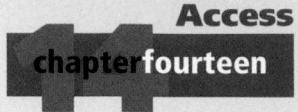
 You and *GO!*

Project 14Q — You and *GO!*

In this project, you will construct a solution by applying any combination of the skills you practiced from the Objectives in Projects 14A and 14B.

Close Access and any other open windows. Display the Start menu, click Computer, and then navigate to to the student files that accompany this textbook. In the folder **04_you_and_go**, locate and open the folder for this chapter. Open and print the instructions for this project, which are provided to you in Adobe PDF format. Follow the instructions to create forms and reports for your personal database.

 End You have completed Project 14Q ————————

GO! with Help

Project 14R — *GO!* with Help

In addition to creating single-record forms, you can create a multiple items form. Use the Access Help system to find out how to create a form that displays multiple records.

1 **Start** Access. Click the **Microsoft Office Access Help** button ⓘ. Click the **Search arrow**, and then under **Content from this computer**, click **Access Help**. In the **Search box**, type **create a form** and then press Enter. Scroll the displayed list as necessary, and then click **Create a form**. Under **What do you want to do?**, click **Create a form that displays multiple records by using the Multiple Items tool**.

2 If you would like to keep a copy of this information, click the **Print** button 🖨. Click the **Close** button ✖ in the top right corner of the Help window to close the Help window, and then **Close** Access.

 End You have completed Project 14R ————————

Outcomes-Based Assessments

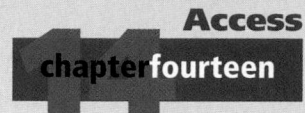

Group Business Running Case

Project 14S — Group Business Running Case

In this project, you will apply the skills you practiced from the Objectives in Projects 14A and 14B.

Your instructor may assign this group case project to your class. If your instructor assigns this project, he or she will provide you with information and instructions to work as part of a group. The group will apply the skills gained thus far to help the Bell Orchid Hotel Group achieve its business goals.

 You have completed Project 14S ——————————

chapterfifteen

Getting Started with Microsoft PowerPoint 2007

OBJECTIVES

At the end of this chapter you will be able to:

1. Open, View, and Save a Presentation
2. Edit a Presentation
3. Format a Presentation
4. Create Headers and Footers and Print a Presentation

5. Create a New Presentation
6. Use Slide Sorter View
7. Add Pictures to a Presentation
8. Use the Microsoft Help System

OUTCOMES

Mastering these objectives will enable you to:

PROJECT 15A
Open, Edit, Save, and Print a Presentation

PROJECT 15B
Create and Format a Presentation

Skyline Bakery and Cafe

Skyline Bakery and Cafe is a chain of casual dining restaurants and bakeries based in Boston. Each restaurant has its own in-house bakery, which produces a wide variety of high-quality specialty breads, breakfast sweets, and desserts. Breads and sweets are sold by counter service along with coffee drinks, gourmet teas, fresh juices, and sodas. The full-service restaurant area features a menu of sandwiches, salads, soups, and light entrees. Fresh, high-quality ingredients and a professional and courteous staff are the hallmarks of every Skyline Bakery and Cafe.

Getting Started with Microsoft Office PowerPoint 2007

Presentation skills are among the most important skills you will ever learn. Good presentation skills enhance all of your communications—written, electronic, and interpersonal. In our technology-enhanced world of e-mail and wireless phones, communicating ideas clearly and concisely is a critical personal skill. Microsoft Office PowerPoint 2007 is a presentation graphics software program used to create electronic slide presentations and black-and-white or color overhead transparencies that you can use to effectively present information to your audience.

Project 15A Expansion

In Activities 15.01 through 15.17, you will edit and format a presentation that Lucinda dePaolo, Chief Financial Officer, has created that details the Skyline Bakery and Cafe's expansion plan. Your completed presentation will look similar to Figure 15.1.

For Project 15A, you will need the following file:

p15A_Expansion

You will save your presentation as
15A_Expansion_Firstname_Lastname

Skyline Bakery and Cafe

Expansion Plans

Mission

To provide a nutritious, satisfying, and delicious meal experience for each of our customers in a relaxing and temptingly aromatic environment.

Company Information

- Founded in Boston by Samir Taheri in 1985
- Current locations in Massachusetts and Maine
- Expansion plans in 2009
  - Rhode Island
  - Virginia
- Awards received this year
  - Golden Bakery
  - Cuisine Excellence

Expansion Plans

- 2009
  - Rhode Island and Virginia
- 2010
  - New Hampshire and New Jersey
- 2011
  - West Virginia and Ohio
- 2012
  - New York and Connecticut

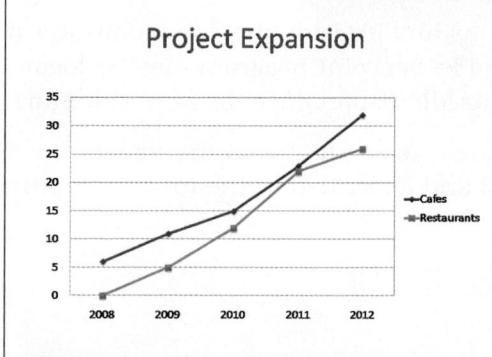

Figure 15.1
Project 15A—Expansion

Objective 1
Open, View, and Save a Presentation

Microsoft Office PowerPoint is a ***presentation graphics software*** program that you can use to effectively present information to your audience. The purpose of any presentation is to influence your audience. Whether you are presenting a new product to coworkers, making a speech at a conference, or expressing your opinion to your city council, you want to make a good impression and give your audience a reason to agree with your point of view. The way in which your audience reacts to your message depends on the information you present and how you present yourself. In the following activities, you will start Microsoft Office PowerPoint 2007, become familiar with the PowerPoint window, and then open, edit, and save an existing PowerPoint presentation.

Activity 15.01 Starting PowerPoint and Identifying Parts of the PowerPoint Window

In this activity, you will start PowerPoint and identify the parts of the PowerPoint window.

Note — Comparing Your Screen with the Figures in This Textbook

Your screen will match the figures shown in this textbook if you set your screen resolution to 1,024 × 768. At other resolutions, your screen will closely resemble, but not match, the figures shown. To view your screen's resolution, on the Windows Vista desktop, right-click in a blank area, click Personalize, and then click Display Settings.

1 On the left side of the Windows taskbar, point to, and then click, the **Start** button 🔵.

2 From the displayed **Start** menu, locate the **PowerPoint** program, and then click **Microsoft Office PowerPoint 2007**.

Organizations and individuals store computer programs in a variety of ways. The PowerPoint program may be located under All Programs, or Microsoft Office, or from the Start menu.

3 Take a moment to study the main parts of the screen as shown in Figure 15.2 and described in the table in Figure 15.3.

Figure 15.2

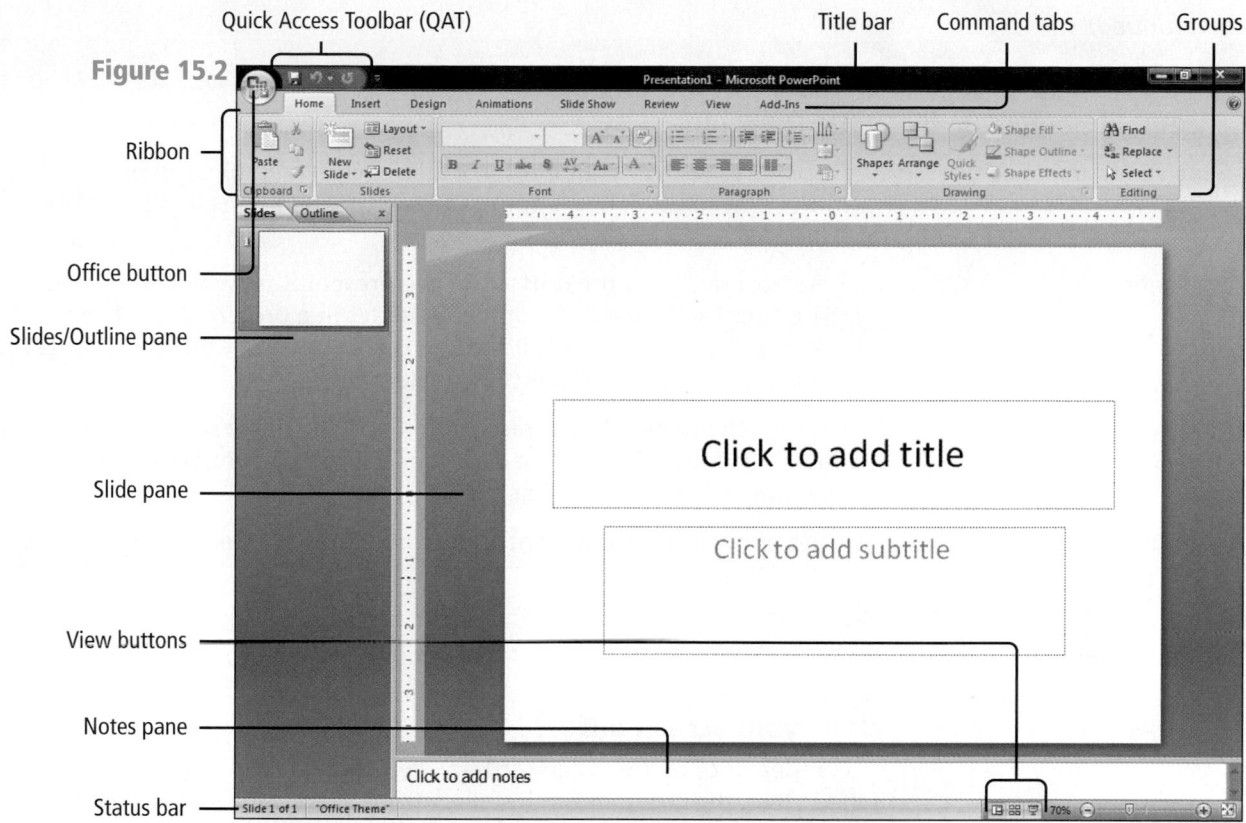

Quick Access Toolbar (QAT)

Title bar   Command tabs   Groups

Ribbon

Office button

Slides/Outline pane

Slide pane

View buttons

Notes pane

Status bar

Microsoft PowerPoint Screen Elements

Screen Element	Description
Command tab	Displays the commands most relevant for a particular task area, such as inserting, designing, and animating.
Group	Identifies related command buttons associated with the selected command tab.
Notes pane	Displays below the Slide pane and allows you to type notes regarding the active slide.
Office button	Displays a list of commands related to things you can do with a presentation, such as opening, saving, printing, or sharing.
Quick Access Toolbar (QAT)	Displays buttons to perform frequently used commands with a single click. Frequently used commands in PowerPoint include Save, Undo, and Repeat. For commands that you use frequently, you can add additional buttons to the Quick Access Toolbar.
Ribbon	Organizes commands on tabs, and then groups the commands by topic for performing related presentation tasks.
Slide pane	Displays a large image of the active slide.

(Continued)

(Continued)
Microsoft PowerPoint Screen Elements

Screen Element	Description
Slides/Outline pane	Displays either the presentation outline (Outline tab) or all of the slides in the presentation in the form of miniature images called *thumbnails* (Slides tab).
Status bar	A horizontal bar at the bottom of the presentation window that displays the current slide number, number of slides in a presentation, Theme, View buttons, Zoom slider, and Fit slide to current window button. The status bar can be customized to include other information.
Title bar	Displays the name of the presentation and the name of the program. The Minimize, Maximize/Restore Down, and Close buttons are grouped on the right side of the title bar.
View buttons	A set of commands that control the look of the presentation window.

Figure 15.3

Alert!

Does your screen differ?

The appearance of the screen can vary, depending on settings that were established when the program was installed. For example, the Add-Ins tab may or may not display on your Ribbon. Additionally, the Quick Access Toolbar can display any combination of buttons, and may occupy its own row on the Ribbon.

Activity 15.02 Opening a Presentation

To open a presentation that has already been created in PowerPoint, use the Office button. As you work on a presentation, save your changes frequently.

1 In the upper left corner of the PowerPoint window, click the **Office** button 🔲 , and then click **Open** to display the Open dialog box.

2 On the left side of the **Open** dialog box, in the **Navigation pane**, under **Favorite Links**, if necessary click **More**, and then click **Computer** to view a list of the drives available to you as shown in Figure 15.4.

Your list of available drives may differ.

Your list of available drives will differ

Figure 15.4

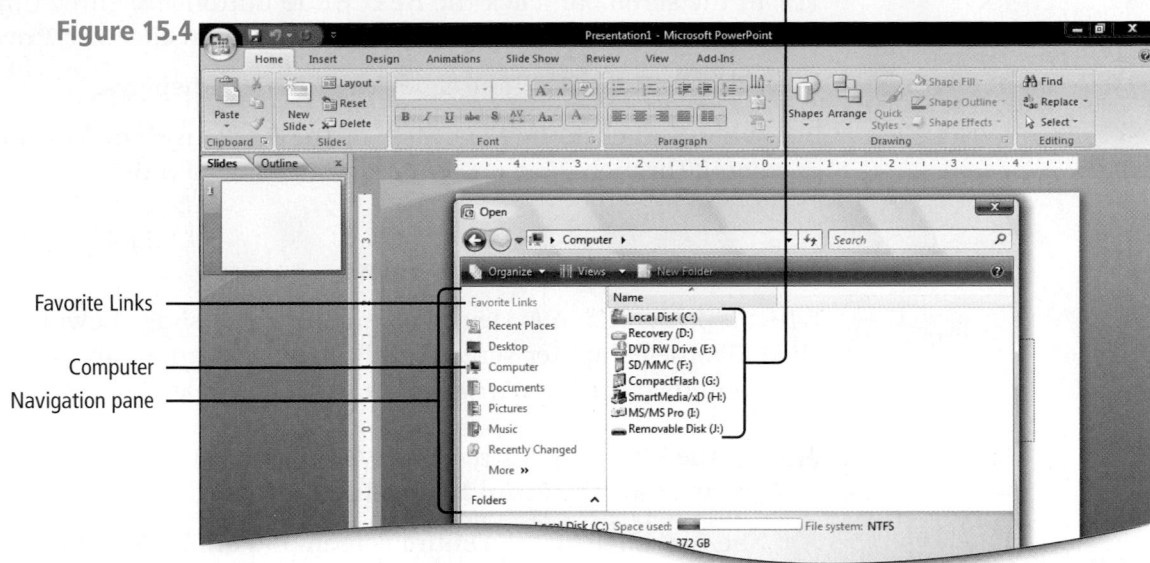

Favorite Links

Computer

Navigation pane

▢**3** Navigate to the location where the student files for this textbook are stored. Click **p15A_Expansion**, and then click the **Open** button or press Enter to display **Slide 1** of the presentation in the PowerPoint window.

PowerPoint displays the file name of the presentation in the title bar at the top of the screen.

▢**4** Look at the **Slides/Outline pane** on the left side of the window and notice that the presentation contains four slides. Additionally, at the right side of the window, a scroll bar displays a scroll box and up and down pointing arrows for navigating through your presentation.

Below the scroll bar, the Previous Slide [▲] and Next Slide [▼] buttons display. See Figure 15.5.

Figure 15.5

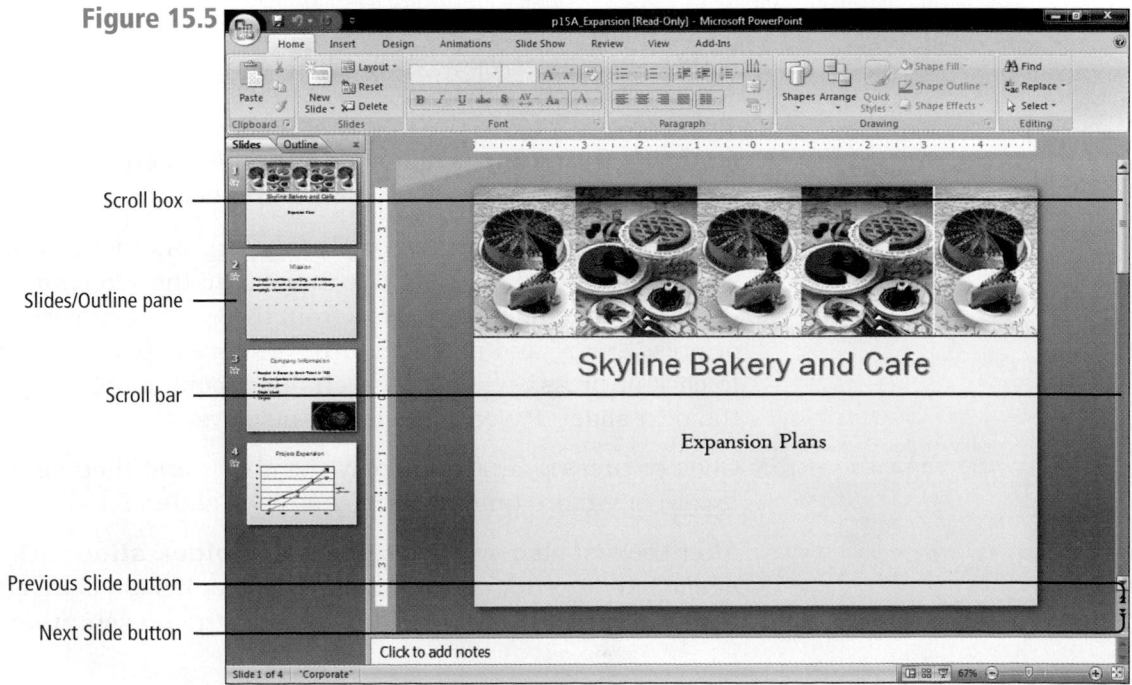

Scroll box

Slides/Outline pane

Scroll bar

Previous Slide button

Next Slide button

5 In the scroll bar, click the **Next Slide** button ⬇ three times so that each slide in the presentation displays. Then click the **Previous Slide** button ⬆ three times until Slide 1 displays.

When you click the Next Slide or the Previous Slide button, you can scroll through your presentation one slide at a time.

Activity 15.03 Viewing a Slide Show

When a presentation is viewed as an electronic slide show, the entire slide fills the computer screen, and a large audience can view your presentation if your computer is connected to a projection system.

1 On the Ribbon, click the **Slide Show tab**. In the **Start Slide Show group**, click the **From Beginning** button.

The first slide fills the entire screen and animation effects display the picture, and then the title and subtitle. *Animation effects* introduce individual slide elements one element at a time. These effects add interest to your slides and draw attention to important features.

Another Way — **To Start a Slide Show**

Press F5 to start the slide show from the beginning. You can also display the first slide you want to show, and click the Slide Show button on the lower right side of the status bar, or press Shift+F5.

2 Click the left mouse button or press Spacebar to advance to the second slide, noticing the transition as **Slide 1** moves off the screen and **Slide 2** displays. An animation effect stretches the graphic images across the screen from left to right.

Transitions refer to the way that a slide appears or disappears during an onscreen slide show. For example, when one slide leaves the screen, it may fade or dissolve into another slide.

3 Click the left mouse button or press Spacebar and notice that the third slide displays and the slide title drops onto the screen from the top of the slide and a picture appears from the lower right corner. Click again or press Spacebar and notice that the first bullet point displays. Continue to click or press Spacebar until each bullet point displays on the slide and the next slide—*Project Expansion*—displays.

4 Click or press Spacebar to display the chart, and then click or press Spacebar one more time to display a black slide.

After the last slide in a presentation, a *black slide* with the text *End of slide show, click to exit.* displays. A black slide is inserted at the end of every slide show to indicate that the presentation is over.

5 On the black slide, click the left mouse button to exit the slide show and return to **Slide 1**.

Activity 15.04 Creating Folders and Saving a Presentation

In the same way that you use file folders to organize your paper documents, Windows Vista uses a hierarchy of electronic folders to keep your electronic files organized. When you save a presentation file, the Windows Vista operating system stores your presentation permanently on a storage medium. Changes that you make to existing presentations, such as changing text or typing in new text, are not permanently saved until you perform a Save operation.

1 In the upper left corner of the PowerPoint window, click the **Office** button ⬚, and then click **Save As** to display the **Save As** dialog box.

2 In the **Save As** dialog box, in the **Navigation pane**, click **Computer** to view a list of the drives available to you, as shown in Figure 15.6. If you are saving your files on your hard drive, in the Navigation pane, click Documents.

Figure 15.6

Navigation pane ——

Click Computer ——

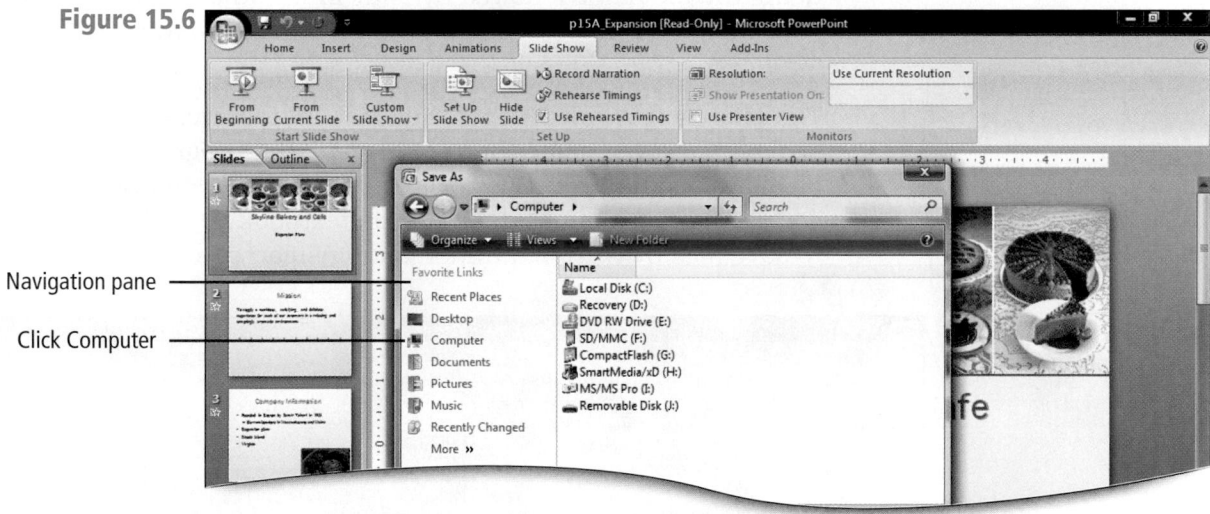

3 Navigate to the location in which you will be storing your folders and projects for this chapter—for example, a USB flash drive that you have connected, a shared drive on a network, the Documents folder on your computer's hard drive, or the drive designated by your instructor or lab coordinator.

4 In the **Save As** dialog box, on the toolbar, click the **New Folder** button. With the text *New Folder* selected, type **PowerPoint Chapter 15** as shown in Figure 15.7, and then press Enter. If the text *New Folder* is not selected, right-click the words *New Folder*, and then from the displayed shortcut menu, click Rename and type the new folder name.

The new folder name displays in the Address Bar at the top of the Save As dialog box, indicating that the folder is open and ready to store your presentation.

Figure 15.7

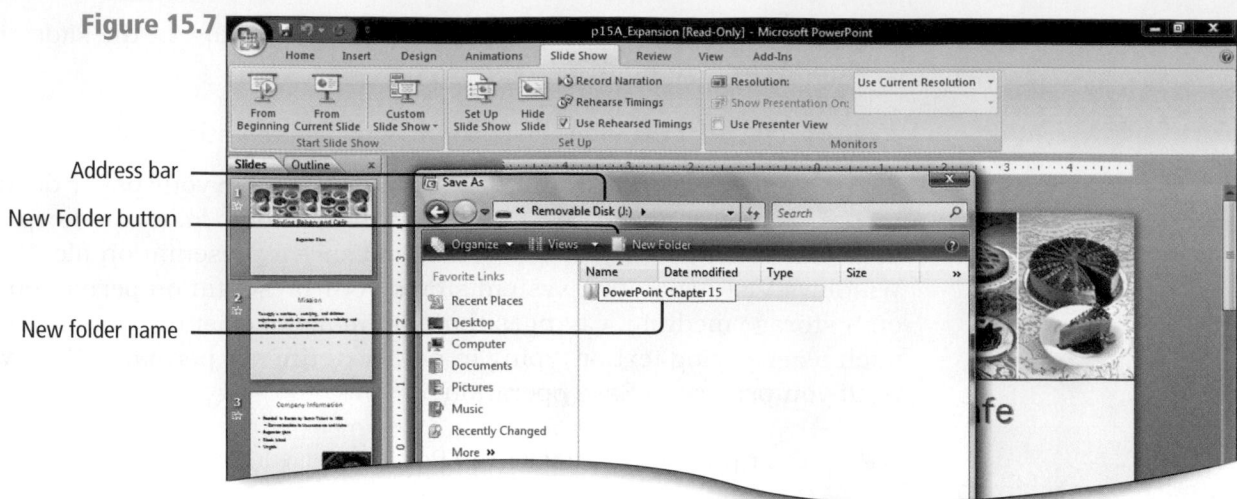

Address bar

New Folder button

New folder name

5 In the lower portion of the **Save As** dialog box, locate the **File name** box. If necessary, select or delete the existing text, and then in the **File name** box, using your own first and last names, type **15A_Expansion_Firstname_Lastname** as shown in Figure 15.8.

Throughout this textbook, you will be instructed to save your files, using the file name followed by your first and last names. Check with your instructor to see if there is some other file-naming arrangement for your course.

The Microsoft Windows operating system recognizes file names with spaces. However, some Internet file transfer programs do not. To facilitate sending your files over the Internet if you are using a course management system, in this textbook you will be instructed to save files by using an underscore instead of a space.

Figure 15.8

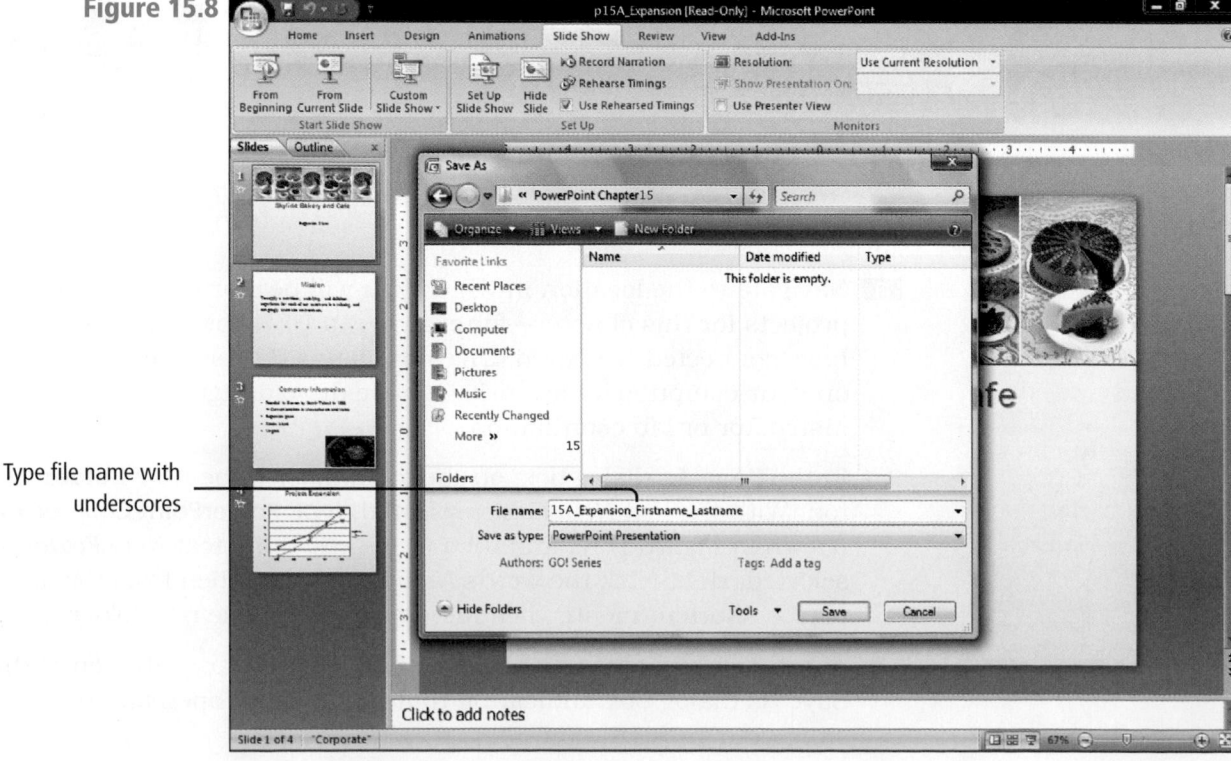

Type file name with underscores

6 In the lower portion of the **Save As** dialog box, click the **Save** button, or press Enter.

Your presentation is saved on the storage device that you selected, and it is contained in the *PowerPoint Chapter 15* folder with the new file name. The new file name also displays in the title bar.

Objective 2
Edit a Presentation

In **Normal view**, the PowerPoint window is divided into three areas—the Slide pane, the Slides/Outline pane, and the Notes pane. When you make changes to the presentation in the Slides/Outline pane, the changes are reflected immediately in the Slide pane. Likewise, when you make changes in the Slide pane, the changes are reflected in the Slides/Outline pane.

Activity 15.05 Editing Slide Text

Editing is the process of adding, deleting, or changing the contents of a slide. When you click in the middle of a word or sentence and start typing, the existing text moves to the right to make space for your new keystrokes. In this activity, you will edit text in the Slide pane.

1 In the **Slides/Outline pane**, if necessary, click the **Slides tab** to display the slide thumbnails.

You can use the slide thumbnails to navigate in your presentation. When you click on a slide thumbnail, the slide displays in the Slide pane.

2 In the **Slides/Outline pane**, on the **Slides tab**, click **Slide 2** to display the company's mission statement. Move your pointer into the paragraph that contains the company's mission statement, and then click to the left of the word *experience* as shown in Figure 15.9.

On this slide a red wavy underline indicates that there is a misspelled word. Do not be concerned at this time with the misspelling—you will correct it in a later activity.

Figure 15.9

Click here

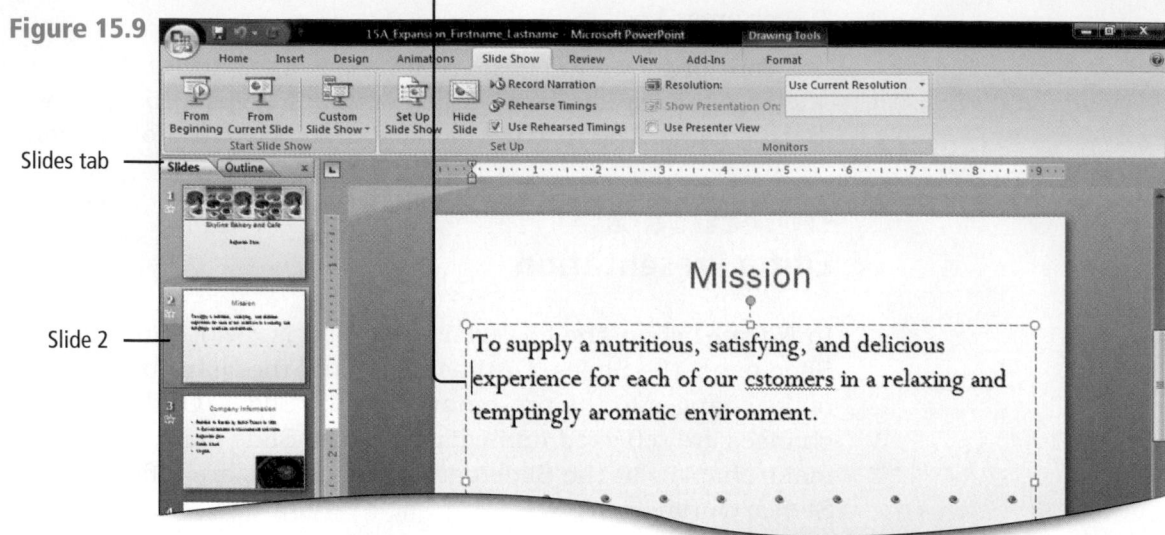

Slides tab

Slide 2

---

3 Type **meal** and notice that as you type, the existing text moves to the right to accommodate the text that you are inserting. Press Spacebar to insert a space between *meal* and *experience*.

After you type the space, the word *meal* moves to the first line of the paragraph because there is enough space in the first line to accommodate the text.

4 In the **Slides/Outline pane**, on the **Slides tab**, click **Slide 3**. In the bulleted list, in the third line, click to the right of the word *plans* and press Spacebar. Type **in 2009**

5 On the **Quick Access Toolbar**, click the **Save** button ![Save icon] to save the changes you have made to the presentation since your last save operation.

Activity 15.06 Inserting a New Slide

To insert a new slide in a presentation, display the slide that will come before the slide that you want to insert.

1 If necessary, display **Slide 3**. On the Ribbon, click the **Home tab**.

On the Home tab, the Slides group includes the New Slide button. The New Slide button is divided into two parts: the upper part contains the New Slide icon, which inserts a slide without displaying options; the lower part contains the words New Slide and a down-pointing arrow that when clicked, displays a gallery. The *gallery*—a visual representation of a command's options—displays slide layouts. *Layout* refers to the placement and arrangement of the text and graphic elements on a slide.

2 In the **Slides group**, click the lower part of the **New Slide** button to display the gallery.

Alert!

Did you insert a slide without displaying the gallery?

The New Slide button is divided into two parts. If you click the upper part, a new slide is inserted, using the layout of the previous slide. To view the gallery, you must click the lower part of the New Slide button. Do not be concerned if the gallery did not display—the correct type of slide was inserted. Read Step 3, and then continue with Step 4.

3 Point to **Title and Text** as shown in Figure 15.10, and then click to insert a slide with the Title and Text layout. Notice that the new blank slide displays in the Slide pane and in the Slides/Outline pane.

The new slide contains two *placeholders*—one for the slide title and one for content. A placeholder reserves a portion of a slide and serves as a container for text or other content, including pictures, graphics, charts, tables, and diagrams.

Title and Text layout

Figure 15.10

Click New Slide

Gallery

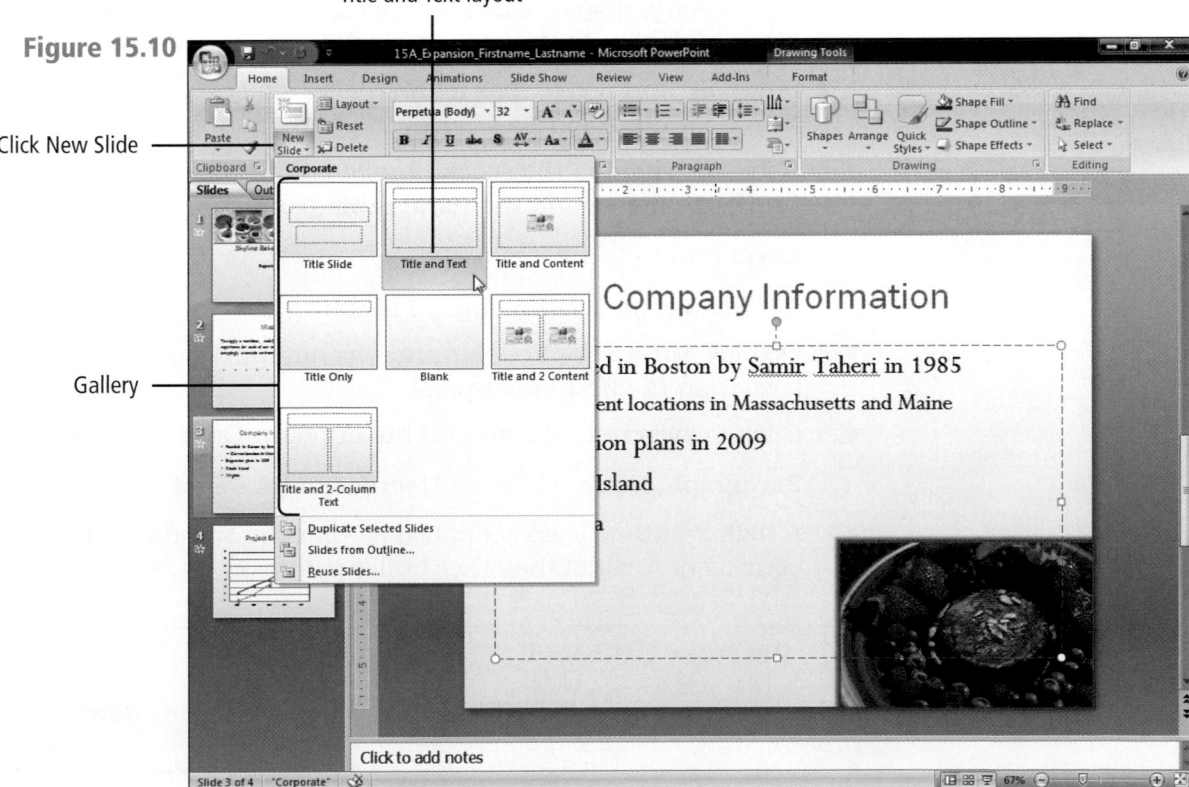

4 In the **Slide pane**, the title placeholder displays the text *Click to add title*. Click in the title placeholder. Type **Expansion Plans** and then click in the *Click to add text* content placeholder.

5 Type **2009** and then press Enter.

6 Type **Rhode Island and Virginia** and then press Enter.

7 Type **2010** and then on the **Quick Access Toolbar**, click the **Save** button 💾 to save your presentation.

Activity 15.07 Increasing and Decreasing List Levels

Text in a PowerPoint presentation is organized according to outline levels, similar to the outline levels you might make for a book report. The highest level on an individual slide is the title. ***Bulleted levels***—outline levels represented by a bullet symbol—are identified in the slides by the indentation and the size of the text. Indented text in a smaller size indicates a lower outline level. It is easy to change the outline level of text to a higher or lower level. For example, you may create a presentation with four bullets on the same level. Then you may decide that one bulleted item relates to one of the other bullets, rather than to the slide title. In this case, a lower outline level should be applied. You can increase the list or indent level of text to apply a *lower* outline level, or decrease the list or indent level of text to apply a *higher* outline level.

1 If necessary, display **Slide 4**, click at the end of the last bullet point—*2010*—and then press Enter to create a new bullet.

2 Press Tab and notice that a lower level bullet point is created. Type **New Hampshire and New Jersey**

3 Click anywhere in the second bullet point—*Rhode Island and Virginia*. On the **Home tab**, in the **Paragraph group**, click the **Increase List Level** button 🔳.

A lower outline level is applied to the text.

4 Display **Slide 3**. Notice that the second bullet point is a lower outline level than the first bullet point.

5 Click anywhere in the second bullet point. On the **Home tab**, in the **Paragraph group**, click the **Decrease List Level** button 🔳.

A higher outline level is applied so that the second bullet point is equivalent to all of the other bullet points on the slide.

Another Way ── **To Decrease List Level**

You can decrease the list level of a bullet point by holding down Shift and pressing Tab.

6 You can change the outline level of more than one bullet point by first selecting all of the text whose outline level you want to change. In the fourth bullet point, position the pointer to the left of *Rhode*, hold down the left mouse button, and then drag to the right and down to select the *Rhode Island* and the *Virginia* bullet points as shown in Figure 15.11. Release the mouse button.

Dragging is the technique of holding down the left mouse button and moving over an area of text so that it is selected. Selected text is indicated when the background changes to a different color than the slide background. When you select text, a ***Mini toolbar*** displays near the selection. The Mini toolbar displays buttons that are commonly used with the selected object, as shown in Figure 15.11. The Mini toolbar is semi-transparent unless you move the pointer over it. When you move the pointer away from the Mini toolbar, it disappears.

Figure 15.11

Mini toolbar

Both bullet points selected

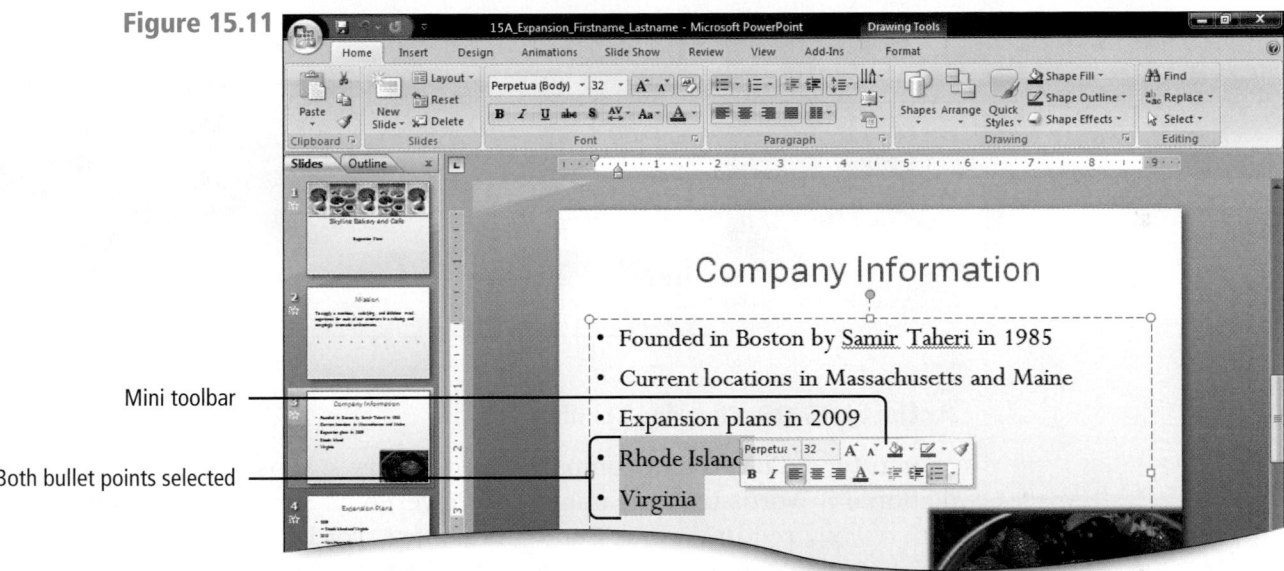

Note — Demoting and Promoting Text

Increasing and decreasing the list level of a bullet point is sometimes referred to demoting and promoting text.

7 On the **Home** tab, in the **Paragraph group**, click the **Increase List Level** button .

Both bulleted items are demoted to lower levels.

8 Click at the end of the word *Virginia*. Press Enter to create a new bullet, and notice that the new bullet is indented at the same level as *Virginia*.

9 Click the **Decrease List Level** button to promote the new bullet. Type **Awards received this year** and then press Enter.

10 Click the **Increase List Level** button . Type **Golden Bakery** and press Enter. Type **Cuisine Excellence**

11 Compare your slide to Figure 15.12. **Save** your presentation.

Figure 15.12

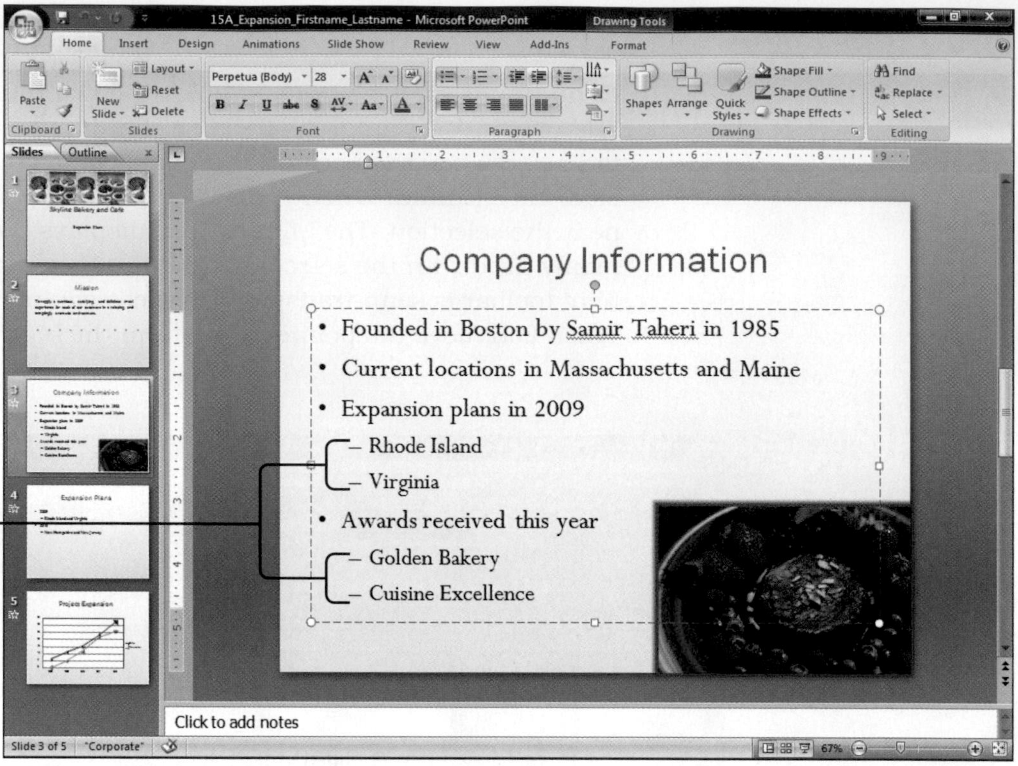

Increase list level to indent ——————————

Activity 15.08 Checking Spelling

As you type, PowerPoint compares your words to those in the PowerPoint dictionary. Words that are not in the PowerPoint dictionary are marked with a wavy red underline. Sometimes these words are correct. For example, a person's name may not be in the dictionary and may be flagged as misspelled even though it is correctly spelled. The red wavy underline does not display when the presentation is viewed as a slide show.

One way to check spelling errors flagged by PowerPoint is to right-click the flagged word or phrase and, from the displayed shortcut menu, select a suitable correction or instruction.

1 Display **Slide 2**. Notice that the word *cstomers* is flagged with a red wavy underline, indicating that it is misspelled.

2 Point to *cstomers* and right-click to display the ***shortcut menu*** with a suggested solution for correcting the misspelled word, and the Mini toolbar, as shown in Figure 15.13.

A shortcut menu is a context-sensitive menu that displays commands and options relevant to the selected object.

Figure 15.13

Mini toolbar

Misspelled word

Suggested solution

Shortcut menu

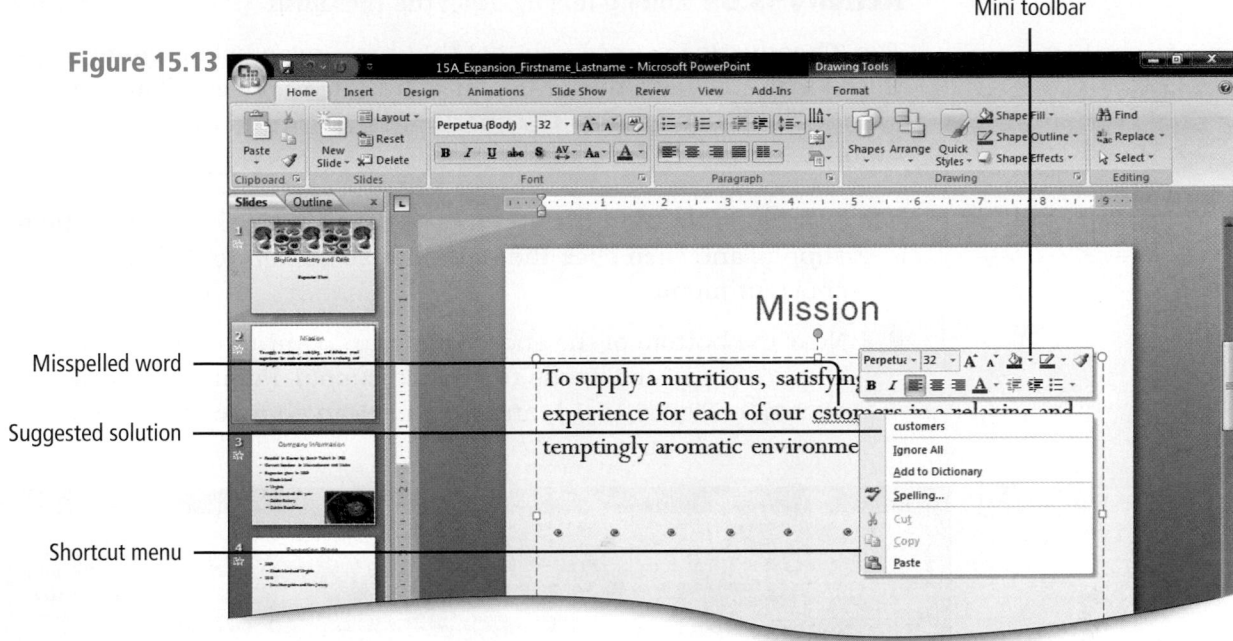

3 From the shortcut menu, click **customers** to correct the spelling of the word.

4 Display **Slide 3** and notice that the name *Samir Taheri* is flagged as misspelled, although it is spelled correctly.

5 Right-click *Samir*, and then from the shortcut menu, click **Ignore All** so that every time the name *Samir* displays in the presentation, it will not be flagged as a misspelled word. Repeat this procedure to ignore the flagged word *Taheri*.

More Knowledge

Spelling Correction Options

The Ignore All option is particularly useful when proper nouns are flagged as spelling errors even when they are spelled correctly. If you are using PowerPoint 2007 on a system that you can customize—such as your home computer—you can add frequently used names and proper nouns to the PowerPoint custom dictionary by clicking the Add to Dictionary option from the shortcut menu.

6 Display each slide in the presentation and correct any spelling errors that you may have made when editing the slides.

7 **Save** your presentation.

Another Way — **To Check Spelling**

You can check the spelling of the entire presentation at one time. On the Ribbon, click the Review tab. In the Proofing group, click the Spelling button to display a dialog box that will select each spelling error in your presentation and provide options for correcting it.

Activity 15.09 Editing Text by Using the Thesaurus

The **Thesaurus** is a research tool that provides a list of **synonyms**— words with the same meaning—for text that you select. You can access synonyms by using either the shortcut menu or the Review tab on the Ribbon.

1 Display **Slide 2**. In the first line of the paragraph, point to the word *supply*, and then click the right mouse button to display the shortcut menu.

2 Near the bottom of the shortcut menu, point to **Synonyms** to display a list of suggested words to replace *supply*. Point to **provide** as shown in Figure 15.14, and then click to change *supply* to *provide*.

Figure 15.14

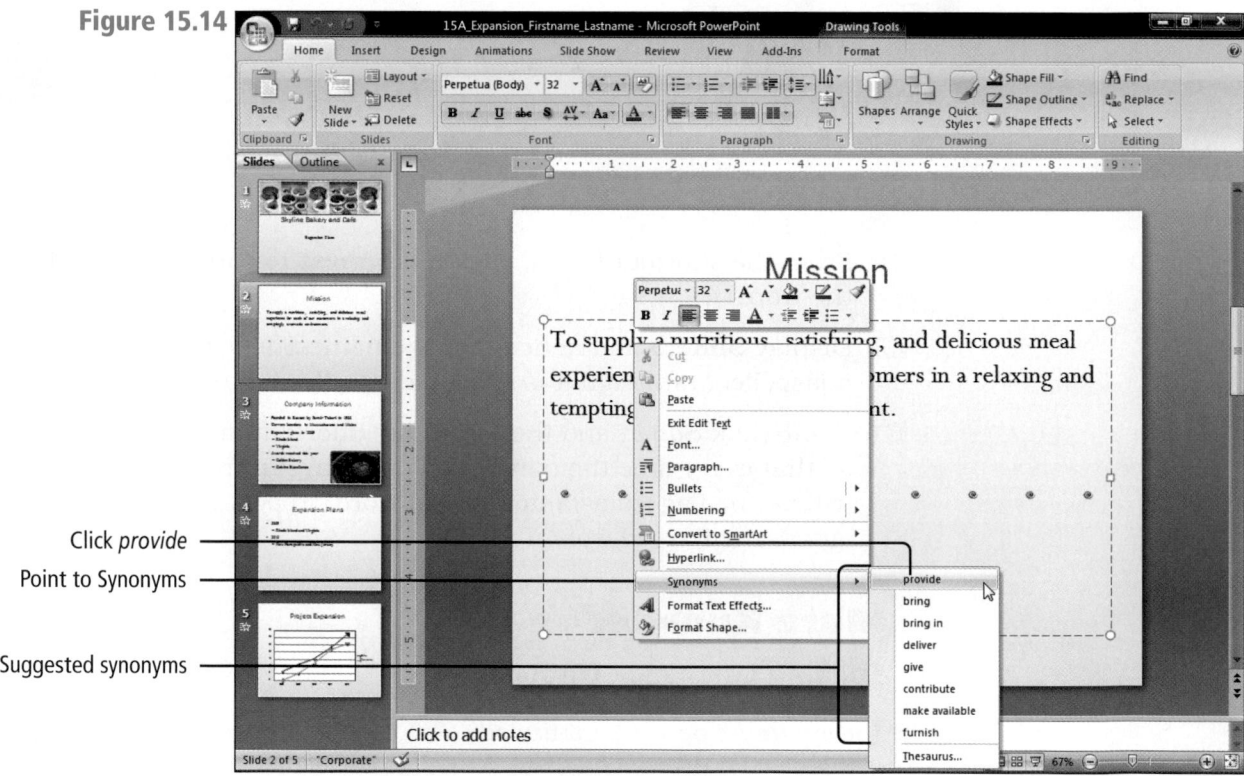

Click *provide*

Point to Synonyms

Suggested synonyms

3 **Save** the presentation.

Another Way

To Access the Thesaurus

After you select the word that you want to replace, on the Ribbon, click Review. In the Proofing group, click Thesaurus to display the Research task pane, which contains a more comprehensive list of suggested synonyms.

Activity 15.10 Adding Speaker's Notes to a Presentation

Recall that when a presentation is displayed in Normal view, the Notes pane displays below the Slide pane. The Notes pane is used to type speaker's notes that can be printed below a picture of each slide. You can refer to these printouts while making a presentation, thus reminding you of the important points that you want to make while running an electronic slide show.

1 Display **Slide 4**. Look at the PowerPoint window and notice the amount of space that is currently dedicated to each of the three panes—the Slides/Outline pane, the Slide pane, and the Notes pane. Locate the horizontal and vertical borders that separate the three panes.

These narrow borders are used to adjust the size of the panes. If you decide to type speaker notes, you may want to make the Notes pane larger.

2 Point to the border that separates the **Slide pane** from the **Notes pane**. The resize pointer displays as an equal sign with an upward-pointing and a downward-pointing arrow, as shown in Figure 15.15.

Figure 15.15

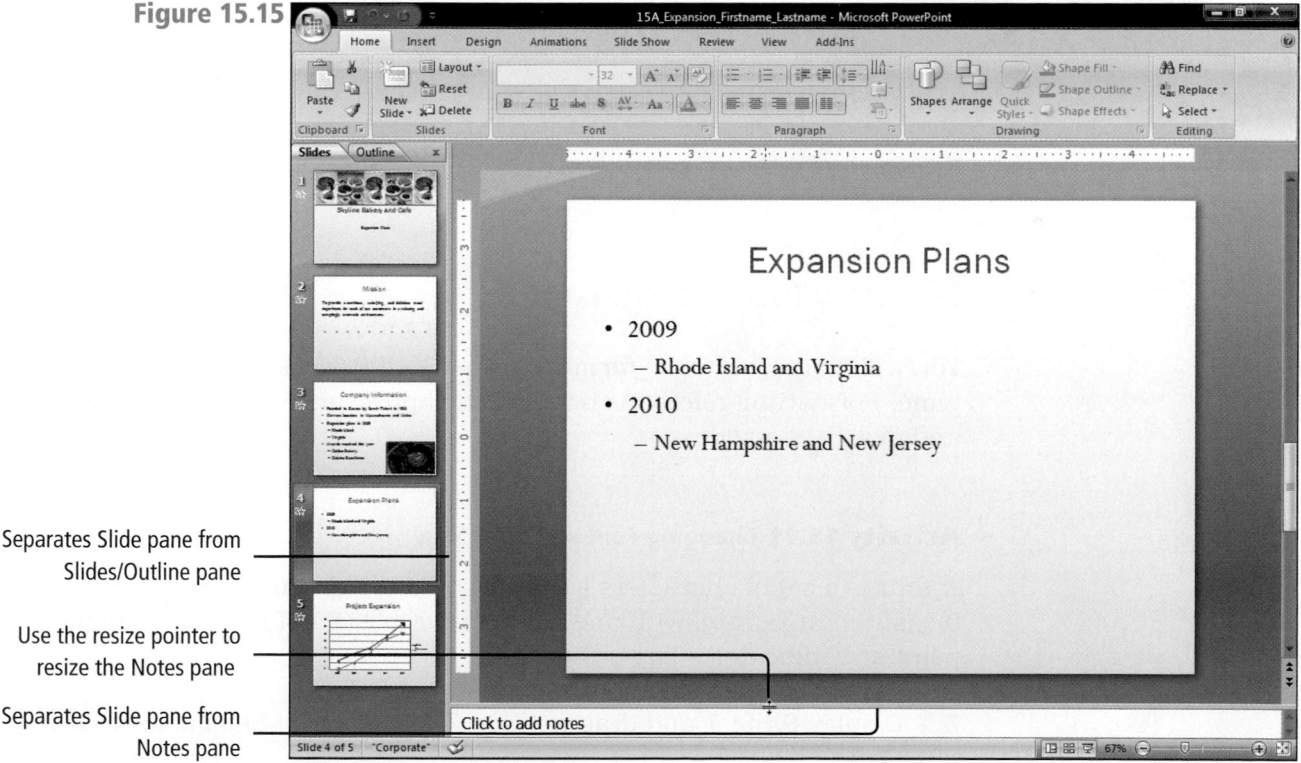

Separates Slide pane from Slides/Outline pane

Use the resize pointer to resize the Notes pane

Separates Slide pane from Notes pane

3 Press and hold down the left mouse button and drag the ⬍ pointer up approximately 1 inch, and then release the left mouse button to resize the pane.

4 With **Slide 4** displayed, click in the **Notes** pane and type **These expansion plans have been approved by the board of directors.** Compare your screen with Figure 15.16.

Figure 15.16

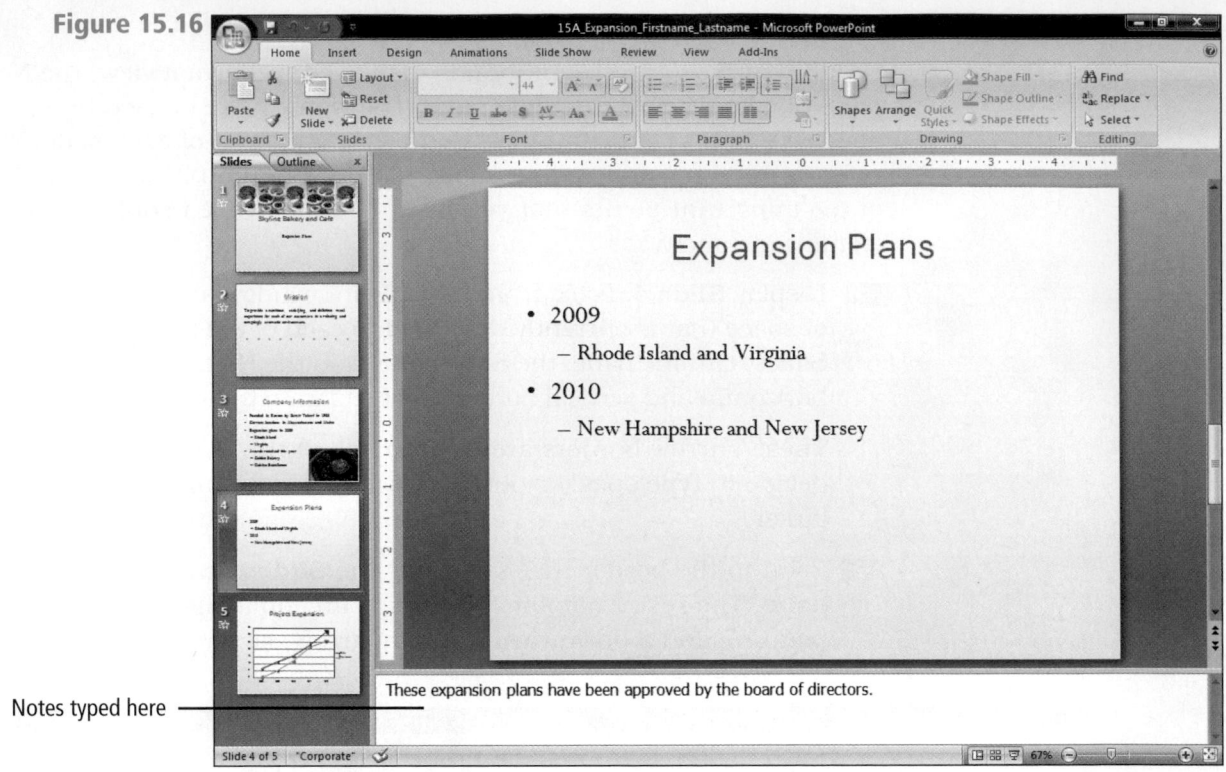

Notes typed here

5 **Save** 💾 the presentation.

Objective 3
Format a Presentation

You will do most of your *formatting* work in PowerPoint in the Slide pane. Formatting refers to changing the appearance of the text, layout, and design of a slide.

Activity 15.11 Changing Font and Font Size

A *font* is a set of characters with the same design and shape. Fonts are measured in *points*, with one point equal to 1/72 of an inch. A higher point size indicates a larger font size.

1 Display **Slide 1** and drag to select the title text—*Skyline Bakery and Cafe.*

2 Point to the Mini toolbar so that it is no longer semi-transparent, and then click the **Font button arrow** Calibri (Headings) ▼ to display the available fonts, as shown in Figure 15.17.

The two fonts that display at the top of the list are the fonts currently used in the presentation.

Did the Mini toolbar disappear?

When you select text, the Mini toolbar displays. If you move your pointer away from the selection and into the slide area without pointing to the Mini toolbar, it may no longer display. If this happened to you, select the text again, and then point to the Mini toolbar, making sure that you do not point to another area of the slide.

Figure 15.17

Mini toolbar

Font button arrow

Selected text

List of fonts

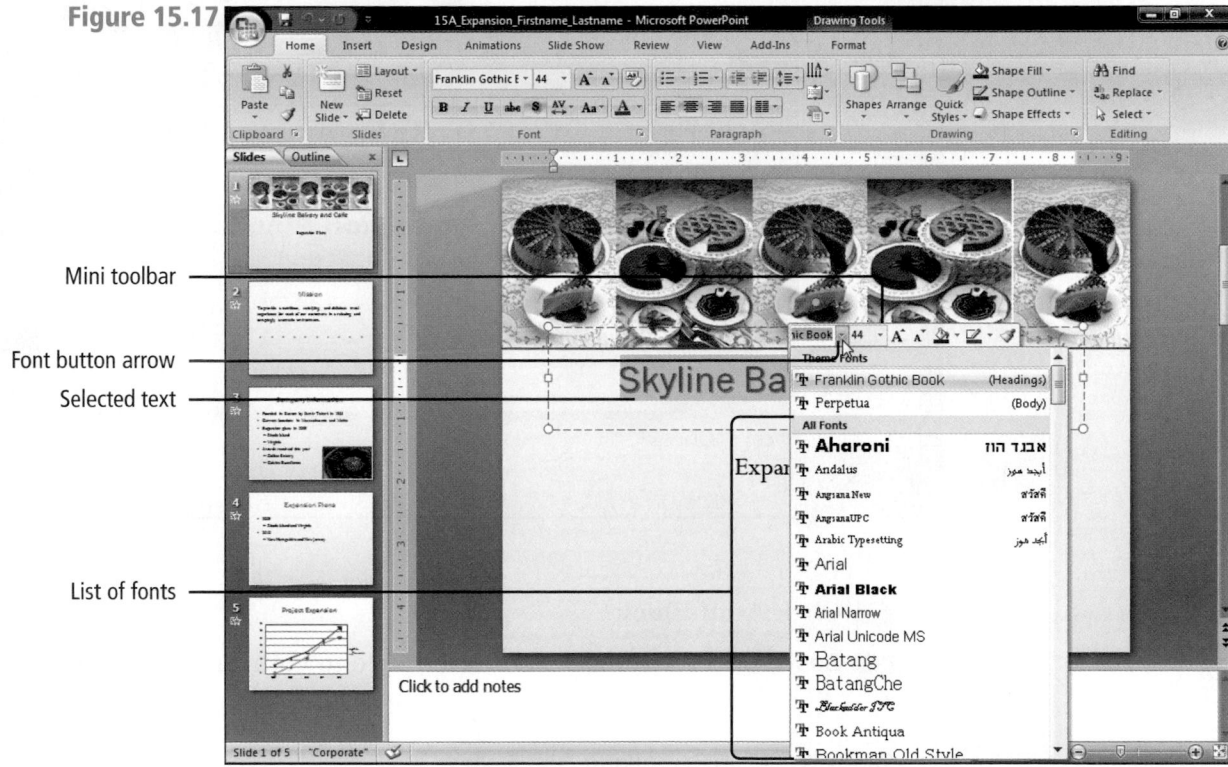

3 Scroll the displayed list as necessary, and then click **Book Antiqua**.

4 On the Ribbon, if necessary, click the **Home tab**. In the **Font group**, click the **Font Size button arrow** 44 ▾. On the displayed list, click **48**.

5 Select the subtitle text—*Expansion Plans*. On the **Home tab** in the **Font group**, click the **Font button arrow** Calibri (Headings) ▾. In the displayed list, scroll as necessary, and then point to—but do not click—**Arial Black**. Compare your screen with Figure 15.18.

Live Preview is a feature that displays formatting in your presentation so that you can decide whether or not you would like to apply the formatting. In this case, Live Preview displays the selected text in the Arial Black font, even though you did not click the font name. The font will actually change when you click the font name.

Figure 15.18

Live Preview displays the selection in the selected font

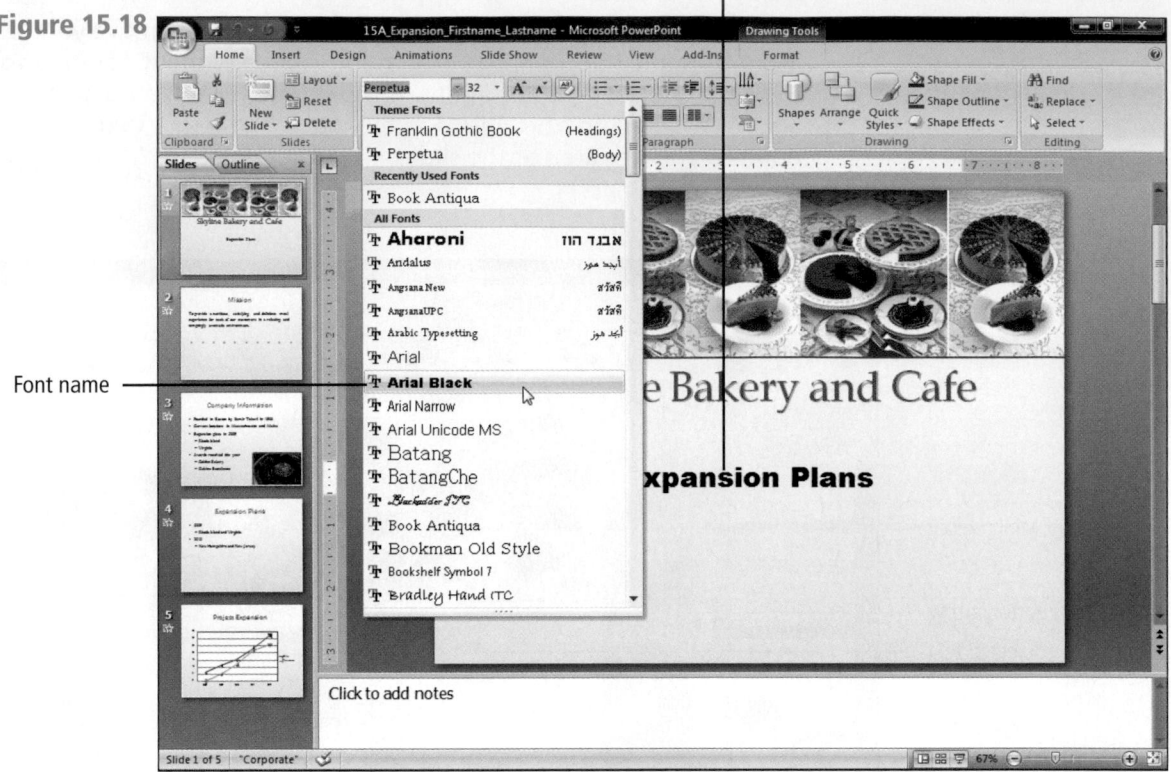

Font name

6 Click **Arial Black**.

7 **Save** 💾 the changes you have made to your presentation.

Activity 15.12 Applying Font Styles

Font styles emphasize text and are a visual cue to draw the reader's eye to important text. Font styles include bold, italic, and underline.

1 On **Slide 1**, select the title—*Skyline Bakery and Cafe*. On the **Home tab**, in the **Font group**, point to the **Bold** button **B** as shown in Figure 15.19, and then click to apply bold to the title.

Figure 15.19

Click the Bold button

Selected text

2 Select the subtitle—*Expansion Plans*. On the Mini toolbar, click the **Bold** button **B**, and then click the **Italic** button **I** to apply both bold and italic to the selection. Notice that on the **Home tab**, in the **Font group**, the **Bold** and **Italic** buttons are selected.

The Bold, Italic, and Underline buttons are *toggle buttons*; that is, you can click the button once to turn it on and click it again to turn it off.

3 With the subtitle still selected, on the **Home tab**, in the **Font group**, click the **Bold** button **B** to turn off the bold formatting.

4 **Save** 💾 your changes.

Another Way

To Apply Font Styles

There are four methods to apply font styles:

- On the Home tab, in the Font group, click the Bold, Italic, or Underline button.
- On the Mini toolbar, click the Bold or Italic button.
- From the keyboard, use the keyboard shortcuts of Ctrl + B for bold, Ctrl + I for italic, or Ctrl + U for underline.
- On the Home tab, in the Font group, click the Dialog Box Launcher to open the Font dialog box, and then click the font styles that you want to apply.

Activity 15.13 Aligning Text and Changing Line Spacing

Text alignment refers to the horizontal placement of text within a placeholder. Text can be aligned left, centered, aligned right, or justified. When text is justified, the left and right margins are even.

1 Display **Slide 2** and click in the paragraph.

2 On the **Home tab**, in the **Paragraph group**, click the **Center** button ≡ to center align the paragraph within the placeholder.

3 In the **Paragraph group**, click the **Line Spacing** button $\boxed{\downarrow\equiv\raisebox{0.3ex}{\tiny▾}}$. In the displayed list, click **1.5** to change from single-spacing between lines to one and a half spaces between lines.

4 **Save** $\boxed{🖫}$ your changes.

Activity 15.14 Modifying Slide Layout

Recall that layout refers to the placement and arrangement of the text and graphic elements on a slide. PowerPoint includes a number of pre-defined layouts that you can apply to your slide for the purpose of arranging slide elements. For example, a Title Slide contains two place-holder elements—the title and the subtitle. Additional slide layouts include Title and Text, Title and Content, Title Only, Blank, Title and 2 Content, and Title and 2-Column Text. When you design your slides, consider the content that you want to include, and then choose a layout that contains elements that best display the message that you want to convey.

1 Display **Slide 4.**

2 On the **Home tab**, in the **Slides group**, click the **Layout** button to display the **Slide Layout gallery**. The gallery displays an image of each layout and the name of each layout.

3 Point to each layout and notice that a **ScreenTip** also displays the name of the layout.

A ScreenTip is a small box, activated by holding the pointer over a button or other screen object, that displays information about a screen element.

4 Point to **Title and 2-Column Text**—as shown in Figure 15.20—and then click to change the slide layout.

The existing text displays in the placeholder on the left and a blank content placeholder is displayed on the right.

Figure 15.20

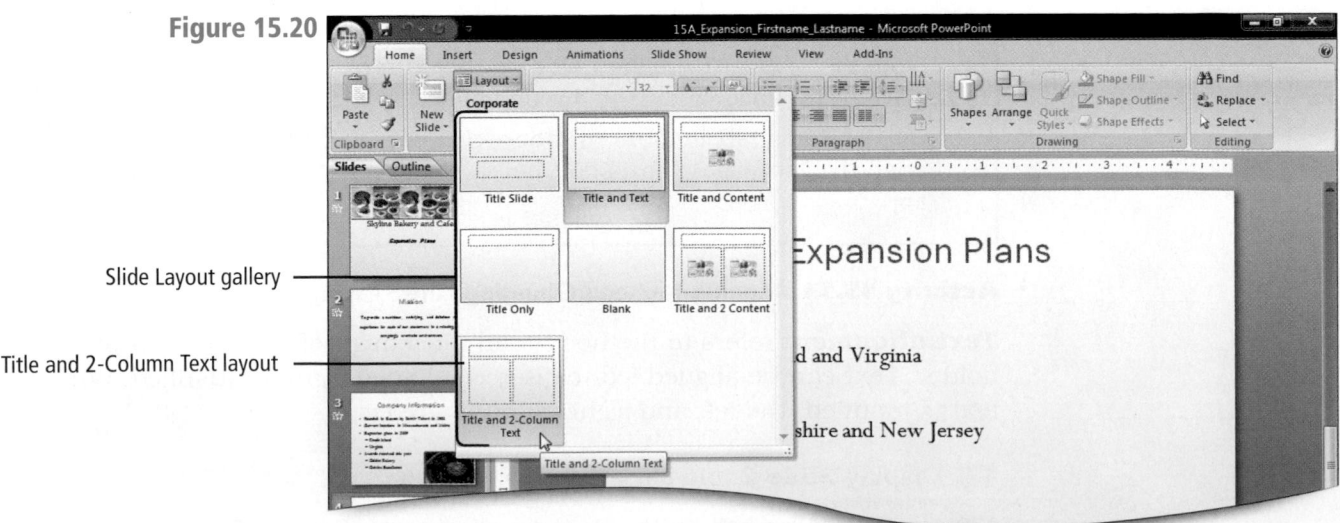

Slide Layout gallery

Title and 2-Column Text layout

5 Click in the placeholder on the right. Type **2011** and then press Enter. Press Tab to increase the list level. Type **West Virginia and Ohio** and then press Enter.

6 Press ⇧ Shift + Tab to decrease the list level. Type **2012** and then press Enter. Press Tab to increase the list level. Type **New York and Connecticut**

7 Click outside of the placeholder so that it is not selected, and then compare your slide to Figure 15.21.

8 **Save** 💾 your changes.

Figure 15.21

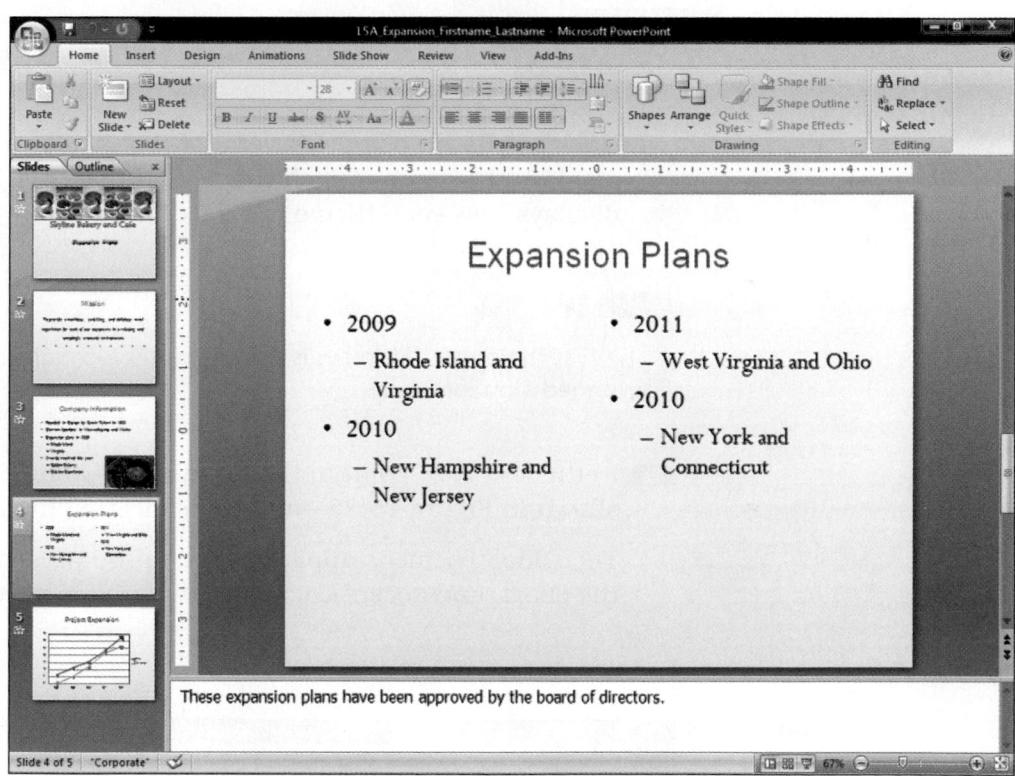

Activity 15.15 Changing the Presentation Theme

A **theme** is a set of unified design elements that provides a look for your presentation by using color, fonts, and graphics. The overall *presentation theme* may include background designs, graphics, and objects that can be customized, using one of the three additional types of themes available in PowerPoint 2007. The color themes include sets of colors; the font themes include sets of heading and body text fonts; and the effect themes include sets of effects that can be applied to lines and other objects on your slides.

1 On the Ribbon, click the **Design tab**. In the **Themes group**, to the right of the last displayed theme, point to the **More** button ▼ as shown in Figure 15.22, and then click to display the **Themes gallery**.

Figure 15.22

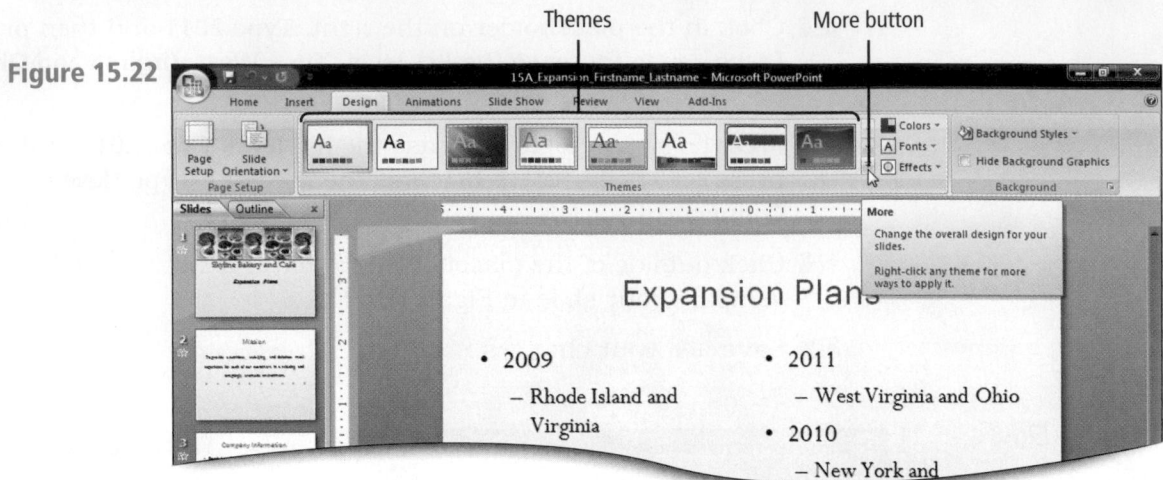

2 Under **Built-In**, *point* to several of the themes and notice a ScreenTip displays the name of each theme and that the Live Preview feature displays how each theme will look if applied to your presentation.

Note

The first theme that displays is the Office theme. Subsequent themes are arranged alphabetically.

3 In the first row, point to the first theme—the **Office Theme**, as shown in Figure 15.23—and then click to change the theme.

The Office Theme is applied to the entire presentation, and all text, the chart, and accent colors are updated to reflect the change.

Figure 15.23

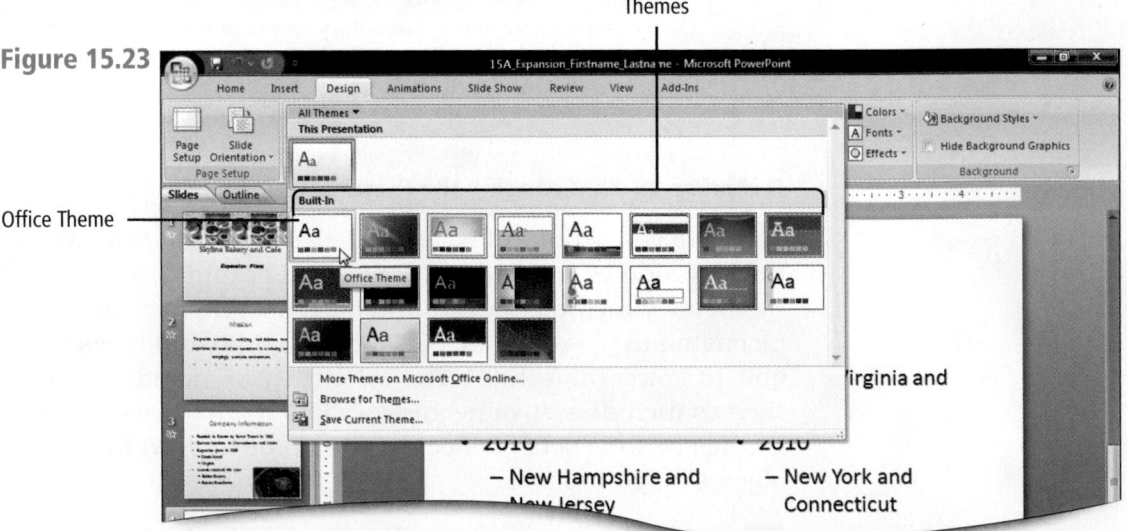

4 In the **Slides/Outline pane**, click to select **Slide 3**, and then press and hold down ⇧ Shift and click **Slide 4**. Compare your screen with Figure 15.24.

Both slides are selected as indicated by the contrasting colors that surround the slides in the Slides/Outline pane.

Figure 15.24

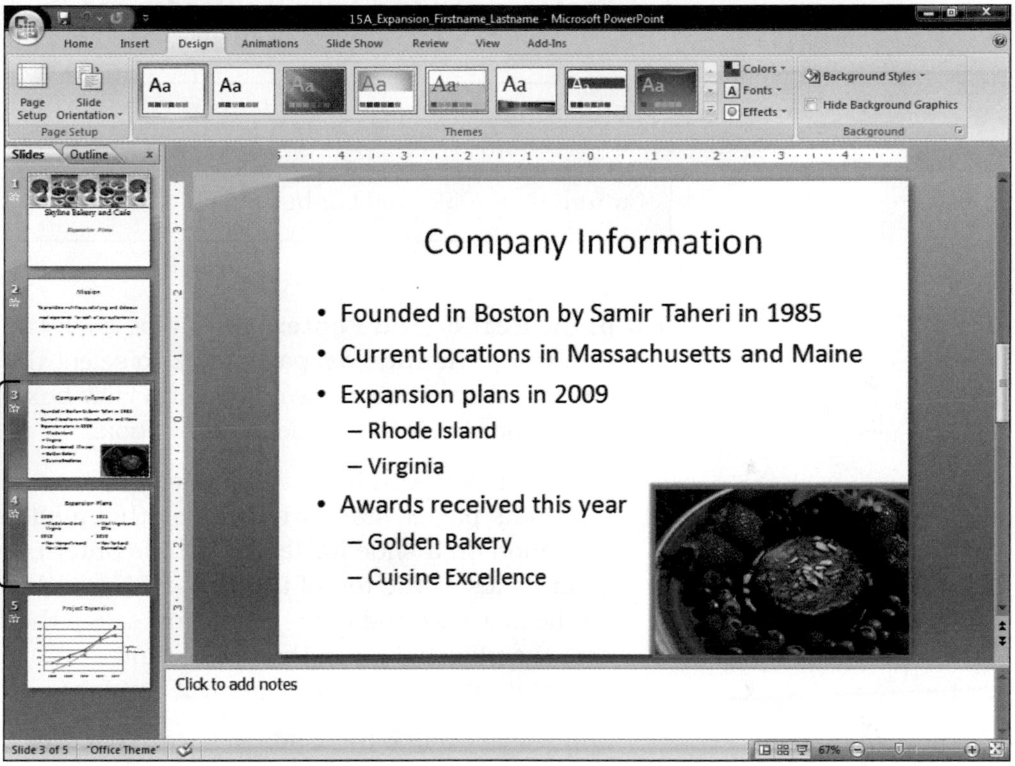

Selected slides

5 On the **Design tab**, in the **Themes group**, click the **More** button ⏷ to display the **Themes gallery**. Under **Built-In**, in the first row, *point* to the fifth theme—**Concourse**—and then click the right mouse button to display the shortcut menu. Click **Apply to Selected Slides**.

The Concourse Theme is applied to Slides 3 and 4.

6 **Save** 🖫 your presentation.

Objective 4
Create Headers and Footers and Print a Presentation

A **header** is text that prints at the top of each sheet of **slide handouts** or **notes pages**. Slide handouts are printed images of multiple slides on a sheet of paper. Notes pages are printouts that contain the slide image in the top half of the page and notes that you have created in the Notes pane in the lower half of the page.

In addition to headers, you can create **footers**—text that displays at the bottom of every slide or that prints at the bottom of a sheet of slide handouts or notes pages.

Activity 15.16 Creating Headers and Footers

In this activity, you will add a header to the handouts and notes pages that includes the current date and a footer that includes the page number and the file name.

1 Click the **Insert tab**, and then in the **Text group**, click the **Header & Footer** button to display the **Header and Footer** dialog box.

Another Way — **To Display the Header and Footer Dialog Box**

On the Insert tab, in the Text group, you can click either the Date & Time button or the Slide Number button.

2 In the **Header and Footer** dialog box, click the **Notes and Handouts tab**. Under **Include on page**, click to select the **Date and time** check box, and as you do so, watch the Preview box in the lower right corner of the Header and Footer dialog box.

The Preview box indicates the placeholders on the printed Notes and Handouts pages, similar to the way that a slide placeholder reserves a location on a slide for text or other content. The two narrow rectangular boxes at the top of the Preview box indicate placeholders for the header text and date. When you select the Date and time check box, the placeholder in the upper right corner is outlined, indicating the location in which the date will display.

3 If necessary, click the **Update automatically** button so that the current date prints on the notes and handouts each time the presentation is printed.

4 If necessary, click to *clear* the **Header** check box to omit this element. Notice that in the Preview box, the corresponding placeholder is not selected.

5 If necessary, click to select the **Page number** and **Footer** check boxes, noticing that when you do so, the insertion point displays in the Footer box. Using your own first and last names, type **15A_Expansion_Firstname_Lastname** and then compare your dialog box with Figure 15.25.

6 Click **Apply to All**. **Save** 🖫 your changes.

Figure 15.25

Notes and Handouts tab   Preview box

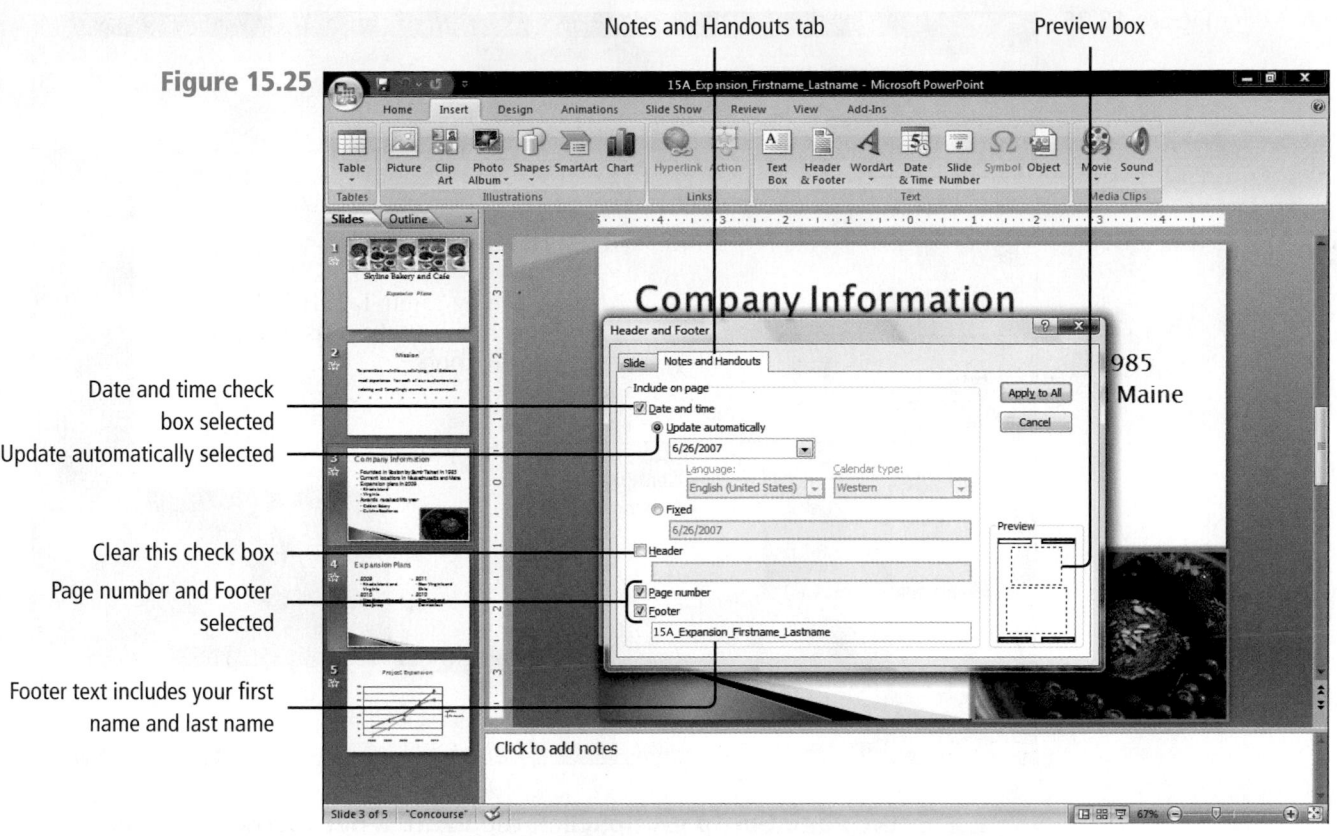

Date and time check
box selected

Update automatically selected

Clear this check box

Page number and Footer
selected

Footer text includes your first
name and last name

More Knowledge

Adding Footers to Slides

You can add footers to slides by using the Slide tab in the Header and Footer dialog box. Headers cannot be added to slides.

Activity 15.17 Previewing and Printing a Presentation and Closing PowerPoint

1 Click the **Office** button 🔘 , point to **Print** as shown in Figure 15.26, and then click **Print Preview**.

Print Preview displays your presentation as it will print, based on the options that you choose. In the Print Preview window, you can click the Orientation button to change the direction in which the paper prints—landscape or portrait. You can choose whether you will print slides, handouts, note pages, or the presentation outline by clicking the Print What button. In the Print group, the Options button enables you to print your presentation in color, grayscale, or black and white.

Figure 15.26

Office button —

Print Preview —

Point to Print —

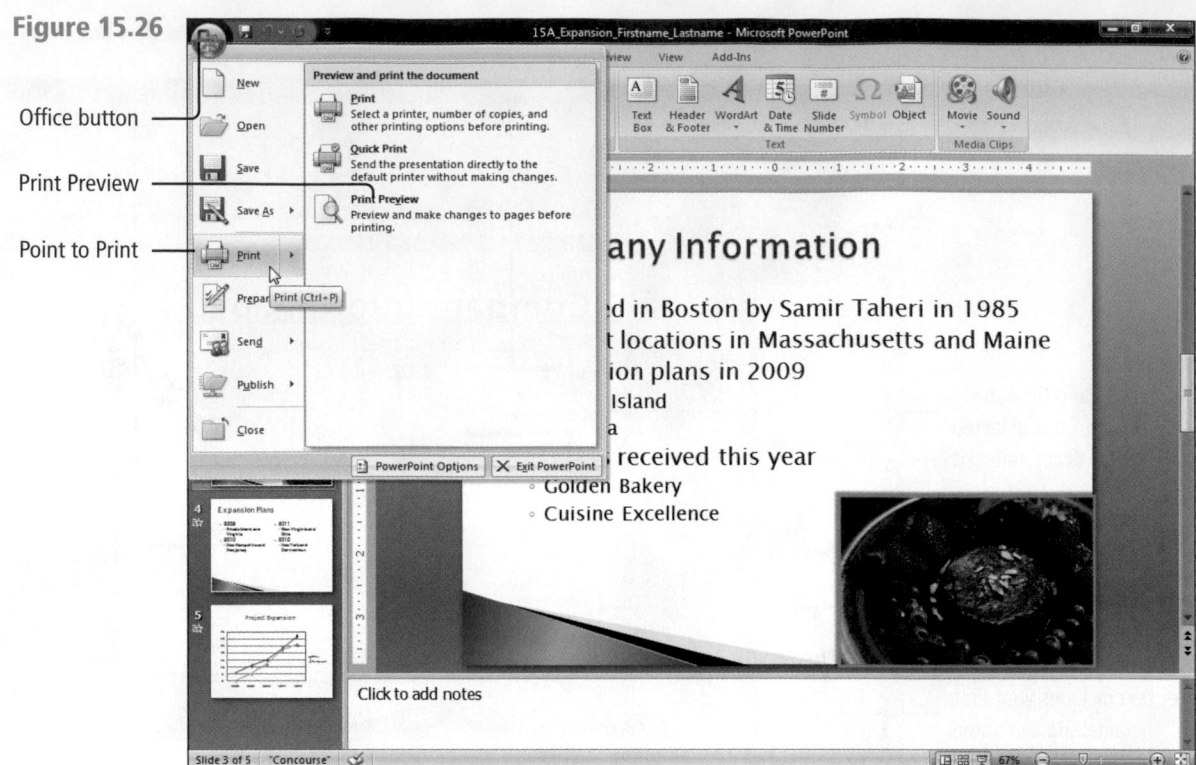

In the **Page Setup group**, click the **Print What arrow**, and then click **Handouts (6 Slides Per Page)** as shown in Figure 15.27. Notice that the preview of your printout changes to reflect your selection.

Note — Printing Slide Handouts in Grayscale

Printing a presentation as Slides uses a large amount of ink and toner. Thus, the majority of the projects in this textbook require that you print handouts, not slides. If your system is connected to a color printer, your handouts may display in color. If you want to conserve colored ink, in the Print Group, click the Options button, point to Color/Grayscale, and then click Grayscale.

Figure 15.27

Print What arrow —

Click Handouts (6 Slides Per Page) —

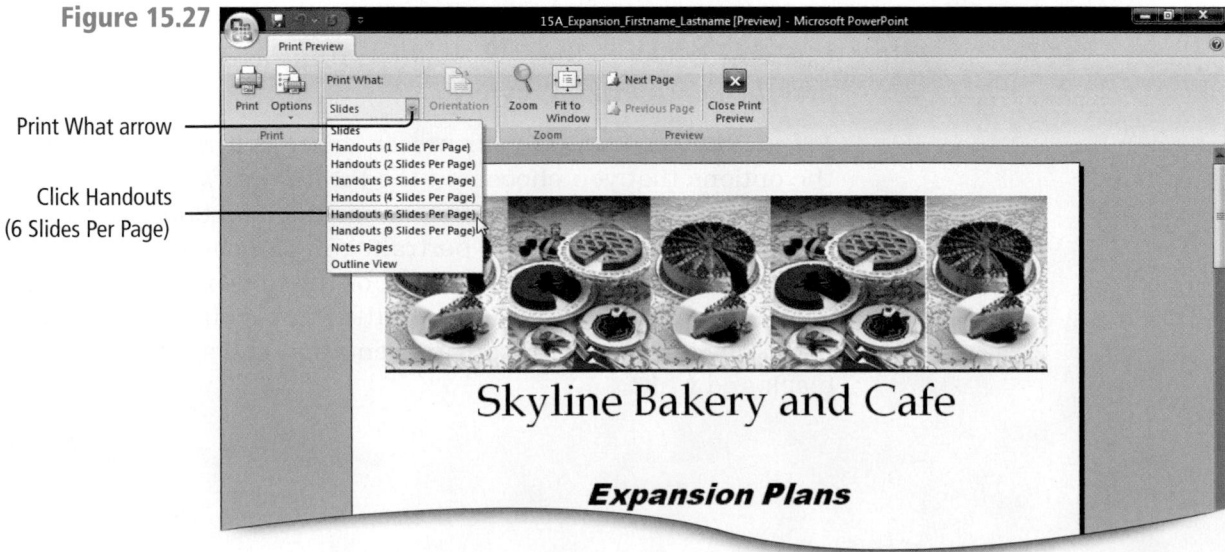

3 Check your *Chapter Assignment Sheet* or *Course Syllabus*, or consult your instructor, to determine if you are to submit your assignments on paper or electronically by using your college's course management system. To submit electronically, go to Step 8, and then follow the instructions provided by your instructor.

4 In the **Print group**, click the **Print** button, and then in the **Print** dialog box, click **OK** to print your handouts.

5 In the **Page Setup group**, click the **Print What arrow**, and then click **Notes Pages** to preview the presentation notes for **Slide 1**.

Recall that you created Notes for Slide 4.

6 At the right side of the **Print Preview** window, drag the scroll box down until **Slide 4** displays.

7 In the **Print group**, click the **Print** button. In the middle of the **Print** dialog box, under **Print range**, click **Current slide**, and then click **OK** to print the Notes pages for Slide 4.

8 Click **Close Print Preview** to close the Print Preview window and return to the presentation.

Another Way — **To Print a Presentation**

Click the Office button, and then click Print to display the Print dialog box. The options that are available in Print Preview can be accessed and modified in the Print dialog box.

9 **Save** your presentation. On the right edge of the title bar, click the **Close** button to close the presentation and **Close** PowerPoint.

Note — Changing Print Options

When you preview your presentation, check to be sure that the text displays against the slide background. If it does not, on the Print Preview tab in the Print group, click Options. Point to Color/Grayscale, and then click Color or Color (On Black and White Printer).

End **You have completed Project 15A**

Project 15B Overview

In Activities 15.18 through 15.25 you will create a presentation that provides details of the Skyline Bakery and Cafe projected expansion. You will add a graphic image to the presentation, insert slides from another PowerPoint presentation, and rearrange and delete slides. Your completed presentation will look similar to Figure 15.28.

For Project 15B, you will need the following files:

p15B_Skyline
p15B_Cake
p15B_Template

You will save your presentation as
15B_Overview_Firstname_Lastname

Figure 15.28
Project 15B—Overview

Objective 5
Create a New Presentation

Microsoft Office PowerPoint 2007 provides a variety of options for starting a new presentation. You can use a *template* that is saved on your system or that you access from Microsoft Office Online. A template is a file that contains the styles in a presentation, including the type and size of bullets and fonts, placeholder sizes and positions, background design and fill color schemes, and theme information. You can also start a blank presentation that has no text, background graphics, or colors that you can then customize yourself.

Activity 15.18 Starting a New Presentation

In this activity, you will create a new presentation based on a template from Microsoft Office Online.

1 **Start** PowerPoint. From the **Office** menu 🔵 , click **New** to display the **New Presentation** window. See Figure 15.29.

At the left of the New Presentation window is a list of the Template categories installed on your system or available from Microsoft Office Online. The center section displays either subcategories or thumbnails of the slides in the category that you select. When you click on a template, the right section displays a larger view of the selected template and in some cases, additional information about the template.

New blank presentation

Figure 15.29

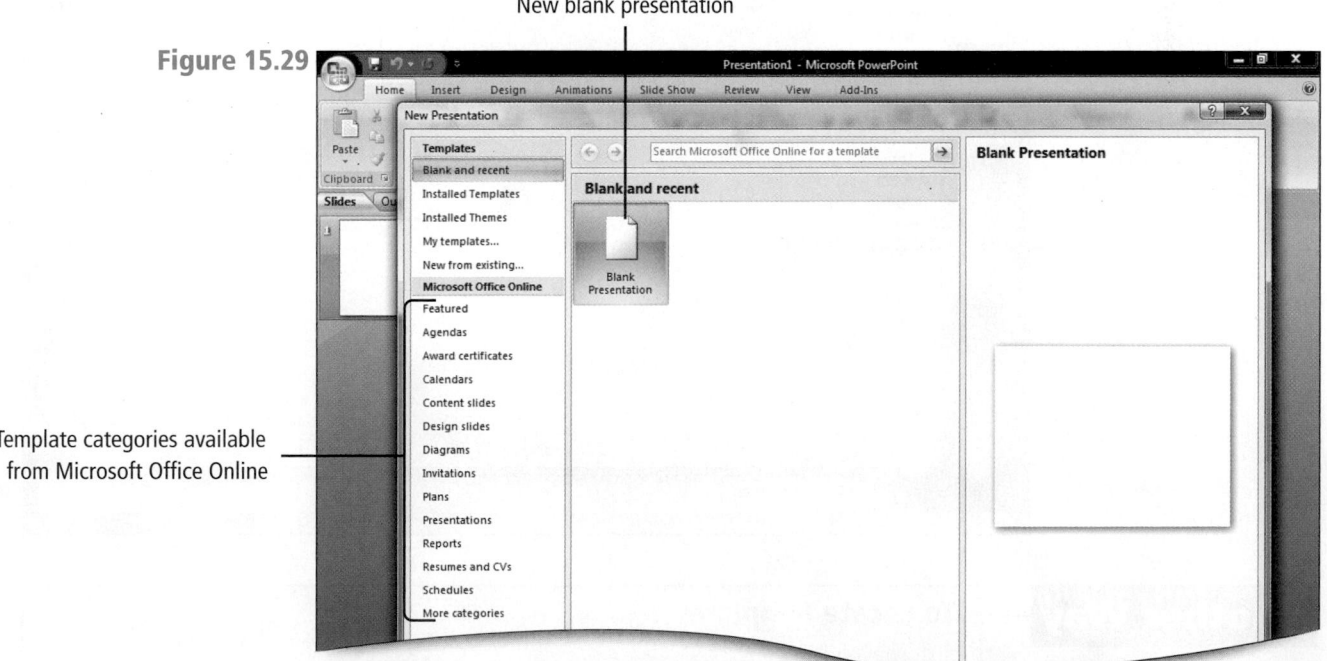

Template categories available from Microsoft Office Online

2 Under **Templates**, click **Installed Templates**, and then click each displayed template to preview it.

3 In the left panel under **Microsoft Office Online**, click several of the categories. Notice that as you do so, the title of the center panel changes to the name of the category that you have chosen, and in some instances, subcategories display.

4 Under **Microsoft Office Online**, click **Presentations**, and then in the center panel, point to **Other presentations** to display the Link Select pointer ⌐ as shown in Figure 15.30.

Figure 15.30

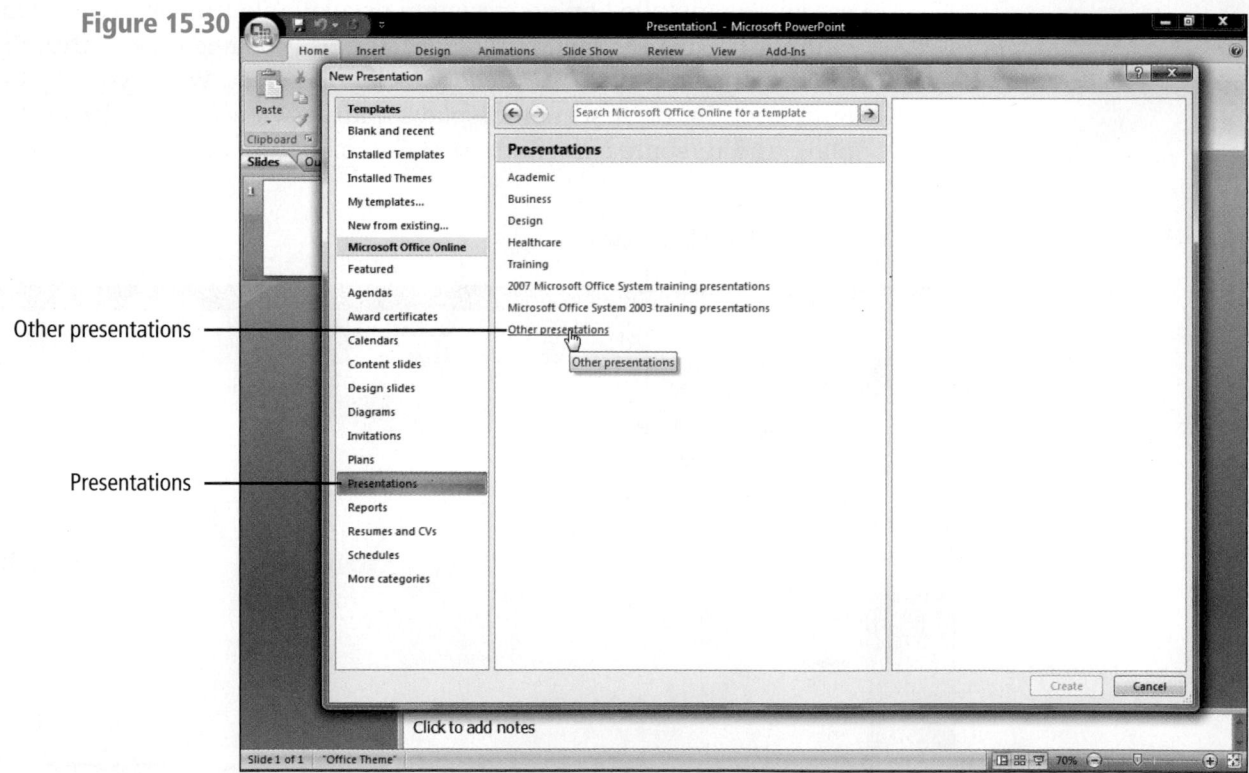

Other presentations

Presentations

5 Click **Other presentations**. In the center section of the New Presentation window, if necessary, scroll to display the **Project overview presentation** template. Click **Project overview presentation**, and then in the lower right corner of the window, click **Download** to access the template from Microsoft Office Online.

Alert!

Does a Microsoft window display?

If a window displays regarding the validation of your software, click Continue. If you are unable to download the template, close all message windows and the New Presentation window. Click the Office button, and then click Open. Navigate to your student files, open the p15B_Template file, and then continue with Step 6.

6 If necessary, close any windows that display after the template is downloaded.

The new presentation includes 11 slides with ideas for content when making a project overview presentation. Scroll through the presentation to view the suggested content. Later, you will delete slides that are not relevant to the presentation and you will modify slide text so that the content is specific to this presentation topic.

7 On **Slide 1**, select the text in the title placeholder—*Project Overview*—and then type **Skyline Bakery and Cafe** to replace it. Select the three lines of text in the subtitle placeholder, and then type **Planning for the Future**

8 Display **Slide 2**. Select the text *Ultimate goal of project*, and then type **To develop a culinary presence throughout the East Coast**

9 Select the remaining two bullet points on the slide, and then type to replace them with the text **To expand operations in a manner that maximizes profit while providing outstanding service to customers**

10 Display **Slide 4**. In the bulleted list, select the *Competitors* bullet point and its second-level bullet point—*You may want to allocate one slide per competitor*—and then press Delete. Select *Your strengths relative to competitors*, and then type **Outstanding reputation for quality service** and then press Enter. Type **Nationally recognized chefs**

11 Replace the text *Your weaknesses relative to competitors* with **Inexperience in marketing in new locations**

12 In the scroll bar, click the **Next Slide** button [↓] several times until **Slide 11** displays. Select and delete the *Post-mortem* and *Submit questions* bullet points and their subordinate bullet points. Under the *Marketing plan* bullet point, select *Location or contact name/phone*, and then type **Janet Liu/555-9012** Under the *Budget* bullet point, select *Location or contact name/phone*, and then type **Lucinda dePaolo/555-9019**

13 Click the **Office** button [icon], and then click **Save As** to display the **Save As** dialog box. Navigate to your **PowerPoint Chapter 15** folder.

14 In the **File name** box, delete any existing text, and then using your own first and last names type **15B_Overview_Firstname_Lastname** and then click **Save**.

Activity 15.19 Inserting Slides from an Existing Presentation

Teamwork is an important aspect of all organizations, and presentations are often shared among employees. Another employee may create several slides for a presentation that you are developing. Rather than re-creating the slides, you can insert slides from an existing presentation into the current presentation. In this activity, you will insert slides from an existing presentation into your 15B_Overview presentation.

1 Display **Slide 1**. Click the **Home tab**, and in the **Slides group**, click the **New Slide arrow** to display the **Slide Layout gallery** and additional options for inserting slides as shown in Figure 15.31.

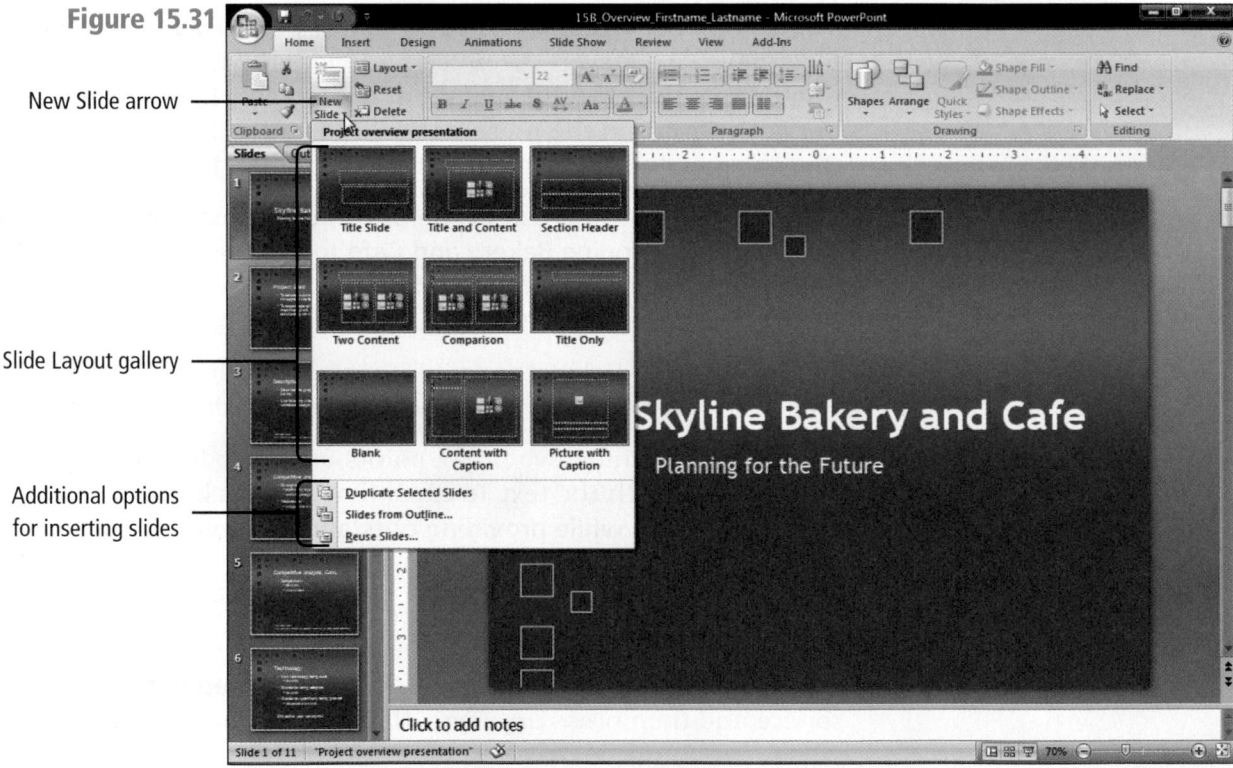

Figure 15.31

New Slide arrow

Slide Layout gallery

Additional options
for inserting slides

2 Below the gallery, click **Reuse Slides** to open the **Reuse Slides** task pane on the right side of the PowerPoint window.

A **task pane** enables you to enter options for completing a command.

3 In the **Reuse Slides** task pane, click the **Browse** button, and then click **Browse File**. In the **Browse** dialog box, navigate to where your student files are stored, and then double-click **p15B_ Skyline**.

The slides contained in the p15B_Skyline presentation display in the Reuse Slides task pane. The title of each slide displays to the right of the slide image.

4 In the **Reuse Slides** task pane, point to **Slide 2** and notice that a zoomed image displays along with a ScreenTip with the presentation title and the slide title. See Figure 15.32.

Figure 15.32

Reuse Slides task pane

Zoomed image of slide

5 Click **Slide 2—Mission**—and notice that it is inserted into the current presentation after Slide 1.

The theme of the current presentation is applied to the slide that you inserted. If you want to retain the theme and other formatting from the slide that you insert, you can click to select the *Keep source formatting* check box at the bottom of the Reuse Slides task pane.

More Knowledge
Inserting All Slides

You can insert all of the slides from an existing presentation into the current presentation at one time. In the Reuse Slides task pane, right-click one of the slides that you want to insert, and then click Insert All Slides.

6 In your **15B_Overview** presentation, in the **Slides/Outline pane**, scroll the slide thumbnails to display **Slide 11**. Click **Slide 11** to display it in the **Slide** pane. In the **Reuse Slides** task pane, click **Slide 3—Company Information**, and then click **Slide 4—Expansion Plans** to insert both slides after **Slide 11**.

Your presentation contains 14 slides.

7 In the **Reuse Slides** task pane, click the **Close** button ⊠. **Save** 🖫 your presentation.

Note — Inserting Slides

You can insert slides in any order into your presentation. Just remember to display the slide that will precede the slide that you want to insert.

Objective 6
Use Slide Sorter View

Slide Sorter view displays all of the slides in your presentation in miniature. You can use Slide Sorter view to rearrange and delete slides, to apply formatting to multiple slides, and to get an overall impression of your presentation.

Activity 15.20 Selecting and Deleting Slides

To select more than one slide, click the first slide that you want to select, press and hold down ⟨⇧ Shift⟩ or ⟨Ctrl⟩, and then click another slide. Using ⟨⇧ Shift⟩ enables you to select a group of slides that are adjacent. Using ⟨Ctrl⟩ enables you to select a group of slides that are nonadjacent (*not* next to each other). When multiple slides are selected, you can move or delete them as a group. These techniques can be used in Slide Sorter view and on the Slides tab in the Slides/Outline pane.

1 Recall that the View buttons are located on the status bar in the lower right corner of the PowerPoint window. Locate the **View** buttons, and then click the **Slide Sorter** button ⊞ to display all of the slide thumbnails. Alternatively, on the Ribbon, click the View tab, and then in the Presentation Views group, click Slide Sorter.

2 Click **Slide 4** and notice that a thick outline surrounds the slide, indicating that it is selected. On your keyboard, press ⟨Delete⟩ to delete the slide.

3 Click **Slide 5**, and then hold down ⟨⇧ Shift⟩ and click **Slide 10** so that slides 5 through 10 are selected. Compare your screen to Figure 15.33.

Selected slides

Figure 15.33

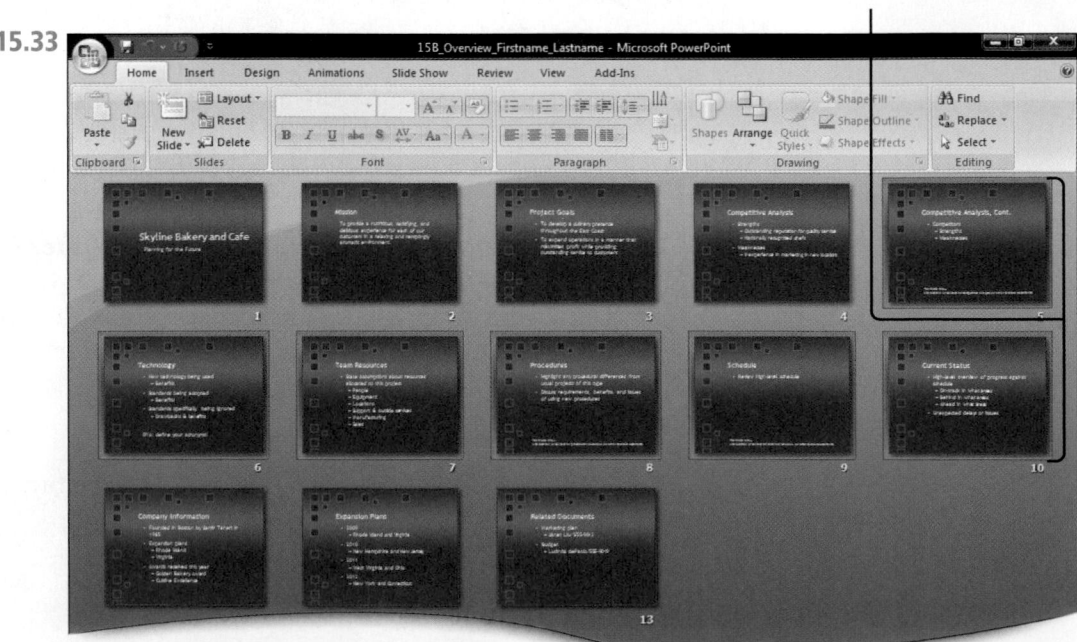

4 Press Delete to delete the selected slides.

Your presentation contains seven slides.

5 **Save** 💾 your changes.

Activity 15.21 Moving Slides

1 Click **Slide 5** to select it.

2 While pointing to **Slide 5**, press and hold down the left mouse button, and then drag the slide to the left until the displayed vertical bar is positioned to the left of **Slide 2**, as shown in Figure 15.34. Release the left mouse button.

The slide that you moved becomes Slide 2.

Selected slide

Figure 15.34

Vertical bar positioned between Slides 1 and 2 to move slide to this position

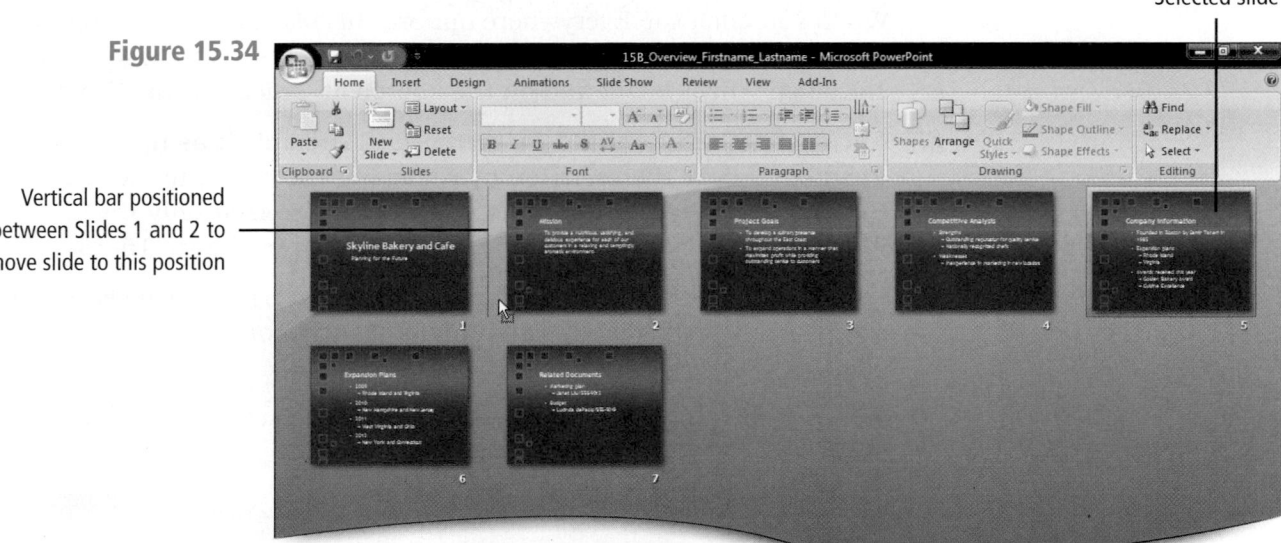

3 Select **Slide 6**. Using the same technique that you used in Step 2, drag to position the slide between **Slides 4** and **5**.

4 In the status bar, click the **Normal** button 🔲. **Save** 💾 your presentation.

Objective 7
Add Pictures to a Presentation

Images can be inserted into a presentation from many sources. One type of image that you can insert is *clip art*. Clip art can include drawings, movies, sounds, or photographic images that are included with Microsoft Office or downloaded from the Web.

Activity 15.22 Inserting Clip Art

In this activity you will access Microsoft Office Online to insert a clip art image on the title slide.

1 Display **Slide 1**. On the Ribbon, click the **Insert tab**, and then in the **Illustrations group**, click **Clip Art** to display the **Clip Art** task pane.

2 In the **Clip Art** task pane, click in the **Search for** box and type **wedding cake** so that PowerPoint 2007 can search for images that contain the keywords *wedding cake*.

A message may display asking if you would like to include additional clip art images from Microsoft Office online. If this message displays, click Yes.

3 In the **Clip Art** task pane, click the **Search in arrow**, and if necessary, click to select the **Everywhere** check box. Click the **Search in** arrow again to collapse the search list.

When you click the Everywhere option, *All collections* displays in the Search in box. This action instructs PowerPoint to search for images stored on your system and on the Microsoft Office Online Web site.

4 Click the **Results should be arrow**, and then click as necessary to *deselect*—clear the selection by removing the check mark—the **Clip Art**, **Movies**, and **Sounds** check boxes so that only the **Photographs** check box is selected as shown in Figure 15.35.

With the Photographs check box selected, PowerPoint will search for images that were created with a digital camera or a scanner.

Figure 15.35

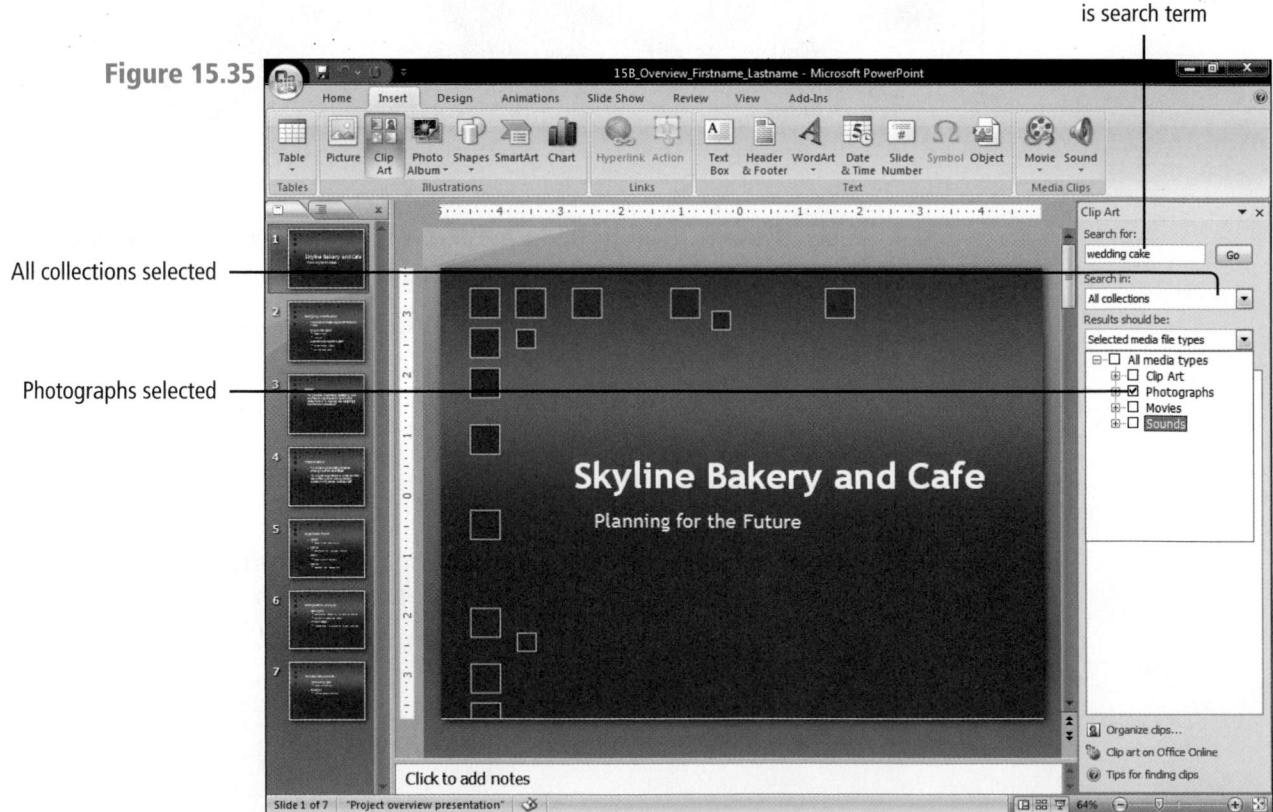

wedding cake is search term

All collections selected

Photographs selected

5 In the **Clip Art** task pane, click **Go**. After a brief delay, several images display in the Clip Art task pane. Locate the image of the wedding cake shown in Figure 15.36.

Figure 15.36

Selected image

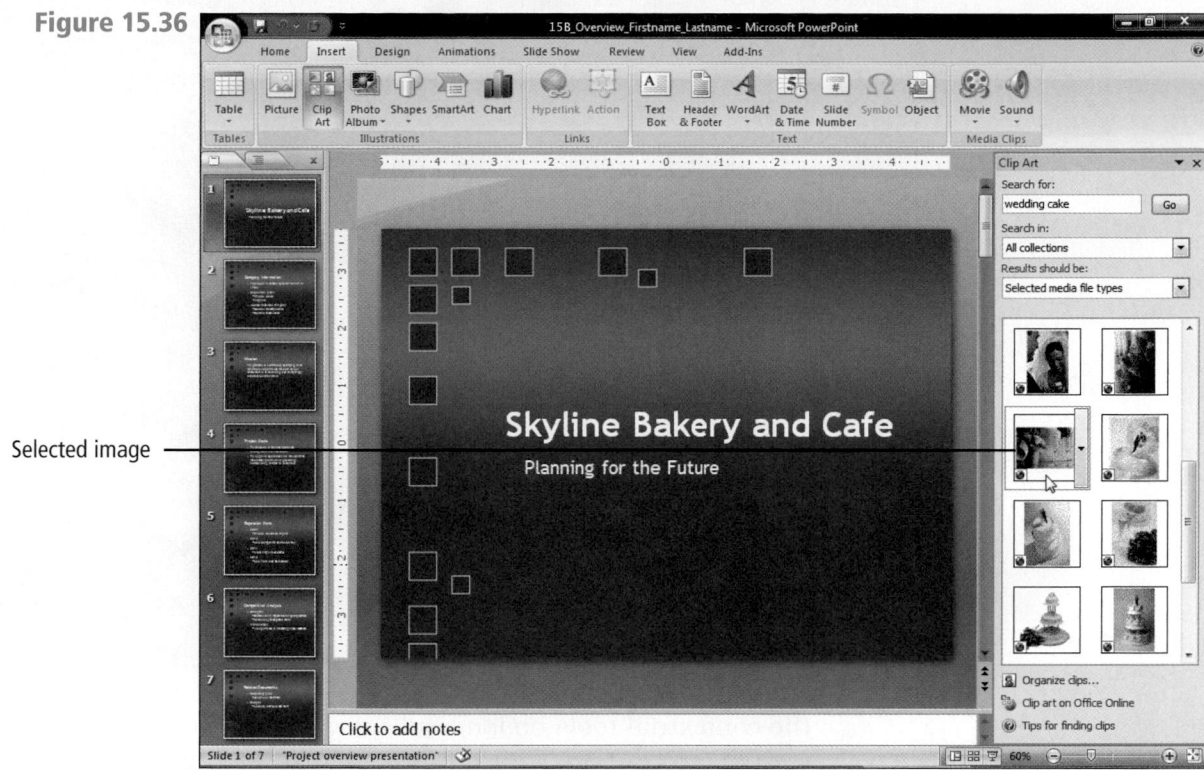

Alert!

Was the wedding cake picture unavailable?

If you are unable to locate the picture for this project, it is available from your student data files. On the Insert tab, in the Illustrations group, click Picture. Navigate to your student files, and then double-click the p15B_Cake file.

6 Click the wedding cake picture to insert it in the center of Slide 1, and then notice that the Ribbon has changed and the picture is surrounded by white square and circular handles, indicating that it is selected.

Because the picture is selected, ***contextual tools*** named *Picture Tools* display and add a ***contextual tab***—*Format*—next to the standard tabs on the Ribbon as shown in Figure 15.37.

Contextual tools enable you to perform specific commands related to the selected object, and display one or more contextual tabs that contain related groups of commands that you will need when working with the type of object that is selected. Contextual tools display only when needed for a selected object; when you deselect the object,

Figure 15.37

Contextual tool

Contextual tab

the contextual tools no longer display. In this case, the Format contextual tab contains four groups—Adjust, Picture Styles, Arrange, and Size. In a later activity, you will use the Picture Styles group to format the wedding cake picture.

7 **Close** ☒ the Clip Art task pane. **Save** 🖫 your changes.

Activity 15.23 Moving and Sizing Images

When an image is selected, it is surrounded by white **sizing handles** that are used to size the image. In the corners of the image, the handles are circular. When you point to a circular sizing handle, a diagonal pointer displays, indicating that you can resize the image by dragging up or down. In the center of each side of the selected image, the handles are square. When you point to a square handle, a left- and right-pointing arrow or an up- and down-pointing arrow displays. These arrows indicate the direction in which you can size the image. When you point to an image without positioning the pointer over a handle, a four-headed arrow displays, indicating that you can move the image.

1 If necessary, click to select the picture of the wedding cake so that the handles display.

2 Position the pointer anywhere over the image to display the Move pointer ⊕. Drag down and to the right until the lower right corner of the picture is aligned with the lower right corner of the slide as shown in Figure 15.38. Release the mouse button.

3 If necessary, select the picture, and then point to the upper left circular handle to display the Diagonal Resize pointer ⬉.

Figure 15.38

Drag to this position

4 Drag down and to the right, noticing that as you do so, a semi-transparent image displays the size of the picture. Continue to drag until the semitransparent image is approximately half the height and width of the original picture as shown in Figure 15.39. Release the mouse button to size the picture.

5 Save the presentation.

Figure 15.39

Original picture

Resized semi-transparent image

Sizing a Picture

Using one of the corner sizing handles ensures that the original proportions of the image are maintained. When a top or side sizing handle is used, the picture is stretched either taller or wider, thus distorting the image.

Activity 15.24 Applying a Style to a Picture

Recall that when a picture is selected, the Picture Tools contextual tool and the Format contextual tab display on the Ribbon. You can use the Format tab to change the color and brightness of your picture; apply a shape, border, or effect; arrange multiple images; or size your picture.

1 If necessary, click the picture of the wedding cake to select it and notice that the Picture Tools are available.

2 On the **Format tab**, in the **Picture Styles group**, click the **More** button ⬇ to display the **Picture Styles gallery**.

3 In the displayed gallery, move your pointer over several of the picture styles to display the ScreenTip and to use Live Preview to see the effect of the style on your picture. Then, in the first row, click **Simple Frame, White**.

4 Click on a blank area of the slide so that the picture is not selected, and then compare your slide to Figure 15.40. Make any necessary adjustments to the size and position of the picture.

Figure 15.40

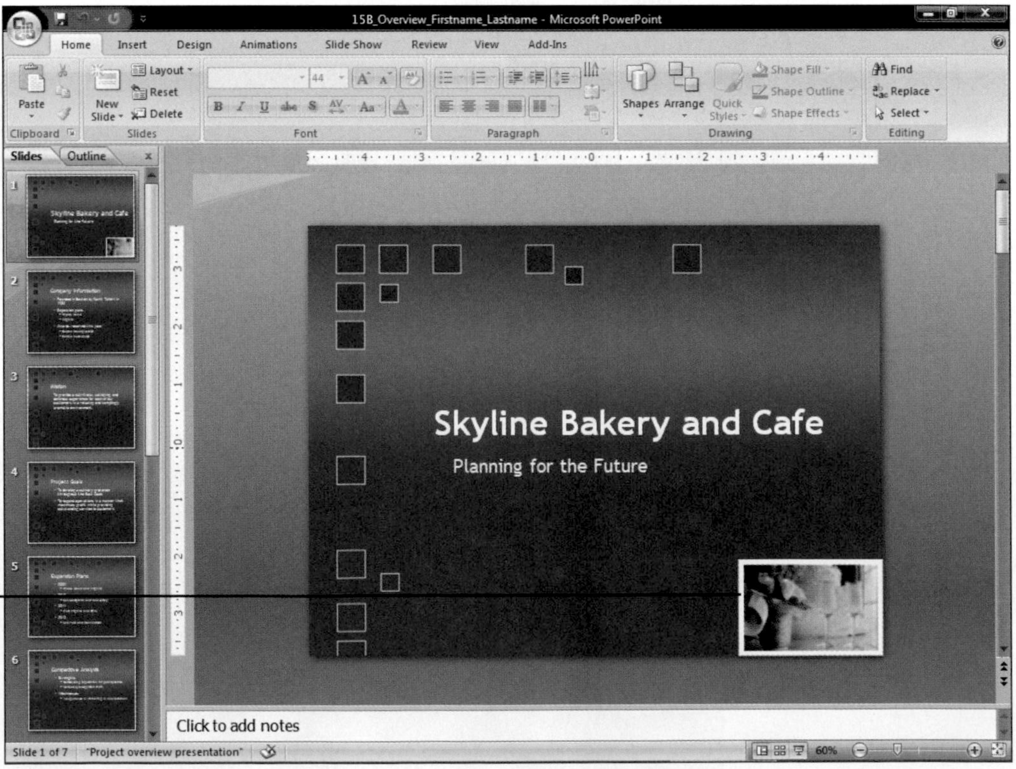

Picture size adjusted and
Simple Frame, White applied

5 Click the **Insert tab**, and then, in the **Text group**, click the **Header & Footer** button to display the **Header and Footer** dialog box. Click the **Notes and Handouts tab**. Under **Include on page**, click to select the **Date and time** check box, and if necessary, click the **Update automatically** button so that the current date prints on the notes and handouts each time the presentation is printed. If necessary, *clear* the **Header** check box to omit this element from your handouts. Click to select the **Page number** and **Footer** check boxes, noticing that when you do so, the insertion point displays in the Footer box. Using your own first and last names, type **15B_Overview_ Firstname_Lastname** and then click **Apply to All**.

6 Check your *Chapter Assignment Sheet* or *Course Syllabus* or consult your instructor to determine if you are to submit your assignments on paper or electronically. To submit electronically, go to Step 8, and then follow the instructions provided by your instructor.

7 From the **Office** menu, point to **Print**, and then click **Print Preview** to make a final check of your presentation. In the **Page Setup group**, click the **Print What arrow**, and then click **Handouts (4 Slides Per Page)**. Your presentation will print on two pages. Click the **Print** button, and then click **OK** to print the handouts. In the **Preview group**, click the **Close Print Preview** button.

8 **Save** 💾 the changes to your presentation, and then from the **Office** menu, click **Exit PowerPoint**.

Objective 8
Use the Microsoft Help System

As you work with PowerPoint 2007, you can get assistance by using the Help feature. You can ask questions and Help will provide you with information and step-by-step instructions for performing tasks.

Activity 15.25 Accessing PowerPoint Help

In this activity, you will use the Microsoft Help feature to learn more about this feature.

1 **Start** PowerPoint. In the upper right corner of your screen, click the

Microsoft Office PowerPoint Help button 📀. Alternatively, press F1.

You can browse the PowerPoint Help topics by clicking any of the listed items; or, near the top of the Help window, you can click in the search box and type a keyword to search for a specific item. If you have access to the Internet, PowerPoint will search Office Online for your help topic.

2 Near the upper left corner of the Help window, in the **Search** box, type **Printing Slides** as shown in Figure 15.41.

Figure 15.41

Search box

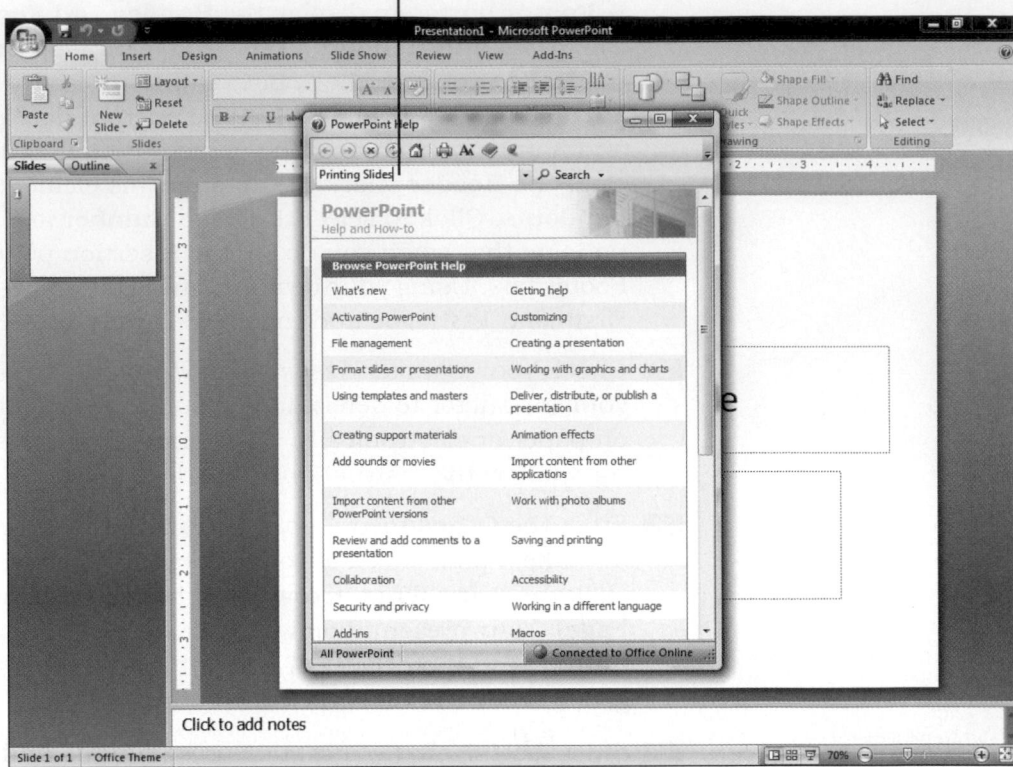

3 Press Enter or click **Search**. On the list of results, click **Print your slides** and then read the information that displays.

4 On the PowerPoint Help title bar, click the **Close** button . On the right side of the title bar, click the **Close** button  to close PowerPoint.

End **You have completed Project 15B** ————————————

There's More You Can Do!

Close PowerPoint and any other open windows. Display the Start menu, click Computer, and then navigate to the student files that accompany this textbook. In the folder **02_theres_more_you_can_do**. Locate and open the folder for this chapter. Open and print the instructions for this project, which are provided to you in Adobe PDF format.

Try IT!—Set Slide Orientation and Size

In this Try It! exercise, you will change the size and orientation of a slide.

Content-Based Assessments

PowerPoint
chapterfifteen

Summary

In this chapter, you started PowerPoint and opened a PowerPoint presentation. You entered, edited, and formatted text in Normal view and worked with slides in Slide Sorter view; you added speaker notes; and you viewed the presentation as a slide show. The spelling checker tool was demonstrated, and you practiced how to change font style and size and add emphasis to text.

You created a new presentation, added content and clip art, and moved and deleted slides. You also added a footer to the notes and handouts pages and created a chapter folder to help organize your files. Each presentation was saved, previewed, printed, and closed. Finally, the Help program was introduced as a tool that can assist you in using PowerPoint.

Key Terms

Content-Based Assessments

Matching

Match each term in the second column with its correct definition in the first column. Write the letter of the term on the blank line in front of the correct definition.

_____ **1.** A feature that introduces individual slide elements one element at a time.

_____ **2.** The PowerPoint view in which the window is divided into three panes—the Slide pane, the Slides/Outline pane, and the Notes pane.

_____ **3.** Outline levels represented by a symbol that are identified in the slides by the indentation and the size of the text.

_____ **4.** A feature that displays buttons that are commonly used with the selected object.

_____ **5.** A context-sensitive menu that displays commands and options relevant to the selected object.

_____ **6.** The action of holding down the left mouse button and moving the mouse pointer over text to select it.

_____ **7.** A set of characters (letters and numbers) with the same design and shape.

_____ **8.** A unit of measure to describe the size of a font.

_____ **9.** A container that reserves a portion of a slide for text, graphics, and other slide elements.

_____ **10.** A slide that is inserted at the end of every slide show to indicate that the presentation is over.

_____ **11.** The changing of the appearance of the text, layout, and design of a slide.

_____ **12.** A feature that displays formatting in your presentation so that you can decide whether or not you would like to apply the formatting.

_____ **13.** A feature that changes the horizontal placement of text within a placeholder.

_____ **14.** Printouts that contain the slide image in the top half of the page and notes that you have created in the Notes pane in the lower half of the page.

_____ **15.** A feature that displays your presentation as it will print, based on the options that you select.

A Animation

B Black slide

C Bulleted levels

D Dragging

E Font

F Formatting

G Live Preview

H Mini toolbar

I Normal view

J Notes pages

K Placeholder

L Point

M Print Preview

N Shortcut menu

O Text alignment

Content-Based Assessments

Fill in the Blank

Write the correct word in the space provided.

1. Microsoft Office PowerPoint 2007 is a presentation _____ program that you can use to effectively present information to your audience.

2. Miniature images of slides are known as _____.

3. A slide _____ controls the way in which a slide appears or disappears during an onscreen slide show.

4. The process of adding, deleting, or changing the contents of a slide is known as _____.

5. A _____ is a visual representation of a command's options.

6. The placement and arrangement of the text and graphic elements on a slide refer to its _____.

7. Tools that enable you to perform specific commands related to the selected object are _____ tools.

8. A file that contains the styles in a presentation, including the type and size of bullets and fonts, placeholder sizes and positions, background design and fill color schemes, and theme information, is known as a _____.

9. The _____ is a research tool that provides a list of synonyms for a selection.

10. Words with the same meaning are known as _____.

11. Font _____ add emphasis to text, and may include bold, italic, and underline.

12. A _____ button is one in which you can click the button once to turn it on and click it again to turn it off.

13. Text that prints at the top of a sheet of slide handouts or notes pages is known as a _____.

14. Text that displays at the bottom of every slide or that prints at the bottom of a sheet of slide handouts or notes is known as a _____.

15. The view in which all of the slides in your presentation display in miniature is _____ _____ view.

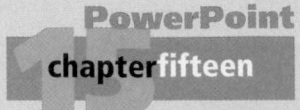
Skills Review

Project 15C — Hospitality

In this project, you will apply the skills you practiced from the Objectives in Project 15A.

Objectives: 1. *Open, View, and Save a Presentation;* **2.** *Edit a Presentation;* **3.** *Format a Presentation;* **4.** *Create Headers and Footers and Print a Presentation.*

In the following Skills Review, you will edit a presentation created by Shawna Andreasyan, the Human Resources Director, for new Skyline Bakery and Cafe employees. Your completed presentation will look similar to the one shown in Figure 15.42.

For Project 15C, you will need the following file:

p15C_Hospitality

You will save your presentation as 15C_Hospitality_Firstname_Lastname

Figure 15.42

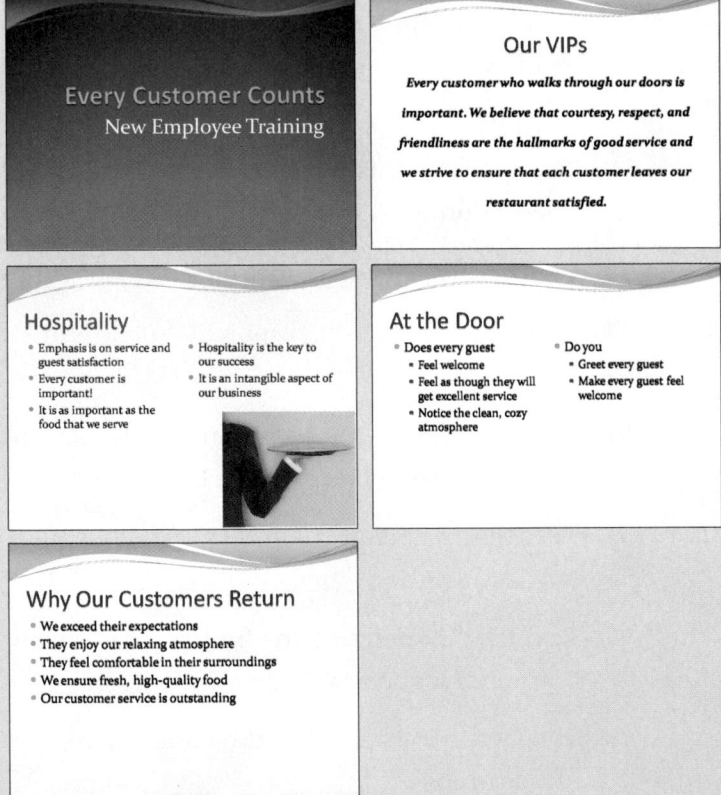

(Project 15C–Hospitality continues on the next page)

Content-Based Assessments

(Project 15C–Hospitality continued)

1. **Start** PowerPoint. Click the **Office** button, and then click **Open.** Navigate to the location where your student files are stored and open the file **p15C_Hospitality**. Click the **Office** button, and then click **Save As.** Navigate to your **PowerPoint Chapter 15** folder, and then using your own first and last name, save the file as **15C_Hospitality_Firstname_Lastname**

2. Click the **Design tab**. In the **Themes group**, to the right of the last displayed theme, click the **More** button to display the **Themes gallery**. Recall that after the first theme—Office—the remaining themes display alphabetically. Under **Built-In**, locate and click the **Flow** theme to apply the theme to the entire presentation.

3. Display **Slide 2**, and then click in the paragraph. Click the **Home tab**, and then, in the **Paragraph group**, click the **Center** button to center align the paragraph within the placeholder. In the **Paragraph group**, click the **Line Spacing** button, and then click **2.0** to apply double-spacing to the paragraph. Then, click in the slide title, and click the **Center** button to center align the title.

4. On **Slide 2**, select all of the text in the paragraph. Point to the Mini toolbar, and then click **Bold** and **Italic** to apply both font styles to the paragraph.

5. Display **Slide 4** and notice the red wavy underline under the last word of the last bullet. Point to *atmoshere*, and then click the right mouse button to display the shortcut menu. Click **atmosphere** to correct the spelling of the word.

6. On **Slide 4**, in the third bullet point, right-click the word *good* to display the shortcut menu. Near the bottom of the menu, point to **Synonyms**, and then in the synonyms

list, click **excellent** to use the Thesaurus to change *good* to *excellent.*

7. With **Slide 4** still displayed, on the **Home tab**, in the **Slides group**, click **Layout** to display the **Slide Layout gallery**. Click the **Two Content** layout.

8. Click in the placeholder on the right. Type **Do you** and then press Enter. Press Tab to increase the list level. Type **Greet every guest** and then press Enter. Type **Make every guest feel welcome**

9. In the placeholder at the left of **Slide 4**, select the last three bulleted items. On the **Home tab**, in the **Paragraph group**, click the **Increase List Level** button to demote the three bulleted items one level below the first bulleted item.

10. With **Slide 4** still displayed, on the **Home tab**, in the **Slides group**, click the **New Slide arrow**, and then in the gallery, click **Title and Content** to create a new Slide 5.

11. On **Slide 5**, click in the title placeholder, type **Why Our Customers Return** and then click in the content placeholder. Type the following five bulleted items, pressing Enter at the end of each line to create a new bullet. Do not press Enter after the last item.

   We exceed their expectations

   They enjoy our relaxing atmosphere

   They feel comfortable in their surroundings

   We ensure fresh, high-quality food

   Our customer service is outstanding

12. With **Slide 5** displayed, click in the **Notes** pane and type **Remember that every single one of our customers is a VIP!** Make spelling corrections as necessary on the slide and in the notes.

(Project 15C–Hospitality continues on the next page)

Content-Based Assessments

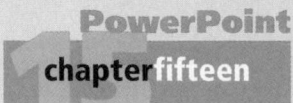
(Project 15C–Hospitality continued)

13. Display **Slide 1** and select the subtitle text—*New Employee Training*. On the Mini toolbar, click the **Font size button arrow**, and then change the font size to **44**.

14. Click the **Insert tab**, and then, in the **Text group**, click **Header & Footer** to display the **Header and Footer** dialog box.

15. Click the **Notes and Handouts tab**. Under **Include on page**, select the **Date and time** check box and, if necessary, click the **Update automatically** button so that the current date prints on the notes and handouts each time the presentation is printed. If necessary, clear the **Header** check box to omit this element. If necessary, select the **Page number** and **Footer** check boxes, noticing that when you do so, the insertion point displays in the Footer box. Using your own first and last names, in the **Footer** box type **15C_Hospitality_ Firstname_Lastname** and then click **Apply to All**.

16. On the Ribbon, click the **Slide Show tab**, and then in the **Start Slide Show group**, click **From Beginning**. Press Spacebar or click the left mouse button to advance

through the presentation and view the slide show.

17. Check your *Chapter Assignment Sheet* or *Course Syllabus* or consult your instructor to determine if you are to submit your assignments on paper or electronically. To submit electronically, go to Step 20, and then follow the instructions provided by your instructor.

18. From the **Office** menu, point to **Print**, and then click **Print Preview** to make a final check of your presentation. In the **Page Setup group**, click the **Print What arrow**, and then click **Handouts (6 Slides Per Page)**. Click the **Print** button, and then click **OK** to print the handouts.

19. In the **Page Setup group**, click the **Print What arrow**, and then click **Notes Pages**. Click the **Print** button, and in the **Print** dialog box, under **Print range**, click the **Slides** option button. In the **Slides** box, type **5** to instruct PowerPoint to print the notes pages for Slide 5. Click **OK**, and then close Print Preview.

20. **Save** changes to your presentation, and then from the **Office** menu, click **Exit PowerPoint**.

End **You have completed Project 15C**

Content-Based Assessments

Project 15D — Funding

In this project, you will apply the skills you practiced from the Objectives in Project 15B.

Objectives: 5. *Create a New Presentation;* **6.** *Use Slide Sorter View;* **7.** *Add Pictures to a Presentation.*

In the following Skills Review, you will create the preliminary slides for a presentation that Lucinda dePaolo, Chief Financial Officer for Skyline Bakery and Cafe, will use to provide an overview of financial plans to a group of investors. Your completed presentation will look similar to the one shown in Figure 15.43.

For Project 15D, you will need the following files:

p15D_Background
p15D_Proposal_Template
p15D_Calculator

You will save your presentation as
15D_Funding_Firstname_Lastname

Figure 15.43

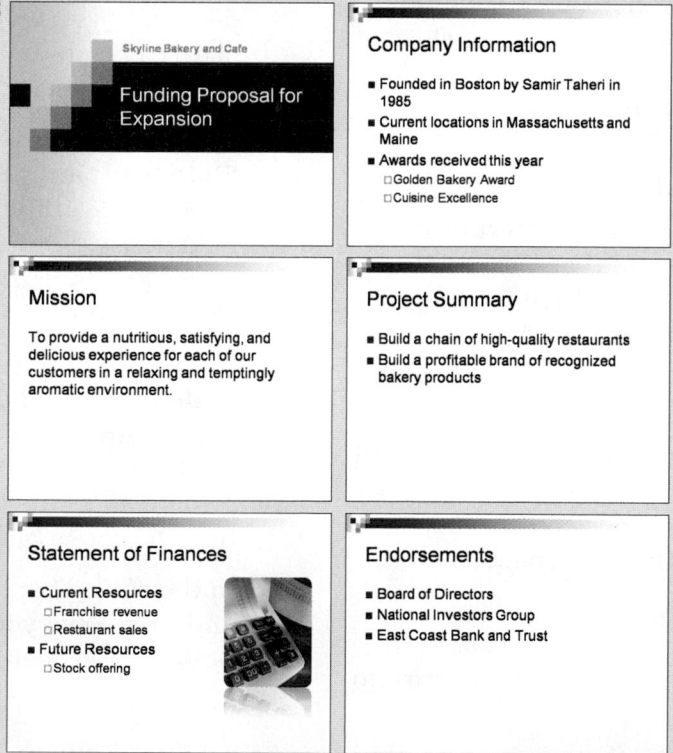

(Project 15D–Funding continues on the next page)

(Project 15D–Funding continued)

1. **Start** PowerPoint. From the **Office** menu, click **New** to display the **New Presentation** window. Under **Microsoft Office Online**, click **More categories** and then under **More categories**, click **Proposals**. Click the **Grant proposal** template, and then in the lower right corner of the **New Presentation** window, click **Download** to access the template from Microsoft Office Online. If a Microsoft Office window displays, click Continue. Alternatively, if you are unable to access the templates from Microsoft Office Online, the template for this project is available from your student data files. Click the Office button, and then click Open. Navigate to your student files and open the p15D_Proposal_Template presentation.

2. On **Slide 1**, select the text *Organization Name*, and type **Skyline Bakery and Cafe** to replace it. Select the text that you just typed, and on the Mini toolbar, click the **Font Size button arrow**, and then click **24**. Select the text in the title placeholder, and then type **Funding Proposal for Expansion**

3. Click the **Office** button, and then click **Save As**. Navigate to your **PowerPoint Chapter 15** folder, and then using your own first and last name, **Save** the file as **15D_Funding_Firstname_Lastname**

4. Scroll through the presentation to view the content suggested for a funding proposal. Notice that in **Slide 2**, an introduction and mission statement are suggested. This content exists in another presentation and can be inserted without retyping the slides.

5. Display **Slide 1**. On the **Home tab**, in the **Slides group**, click the **New Slide arrow** to display the **Slide Layout gallery** and additional options for inserting slides. At the bottom of the gallery, click **Reuse Slides** to open the **Reuse Slides** task pane.

6. In the **Reuse Slides** task pane, click the **Browse** button, and then click **Browse File**. In the **Browse** dialog box, navigate to where your student files are stored and double-click **p15D_Background**. In the **Reuse Slides** task pane, point to either of the two slides that display and right-click. From the shortcut menu, click **Insert All Slides** to insert both slides into the presentation. **Close** the **Reuse Slides** task pane.

7. On the status bar, locate the **View** buttons, and then click the **Slide Sorter** button to display the 15 slides in the presentation. Click **Slide 4**, and then press Delete to delete the slide. Click **Slide 5**, hold down ⇧ Shift and click **Slide 7** so that slides 5 through 7 are selected. Press Delete to delete the selected slides.

8. Click **Slide 6**, hold down ⇧ Shift and click **Slide 9** so that slides 6 through 9 are selected. With the four slides still selected, hold down Ctrl, and then click **Slide 11**. Press Delete to delete the selected slides. Six slides remain in the presentation.

9. Click **Slide 3** to select it. While pointing to **Slide 3**, press and hold down the left mouse button, and then drag the slide to the left until the displayed vertical bar is positioned to the left of **Slide 2**. Release the left mouse button to move the slide.

10. In the status bar, click the **Normal** button, and then **Save** your presentation. Display **Slide 4**, and then select the text in the

(Project 15D–Funding continues on the next page)

(Project 15D–Funding continued)

content placeholder. Replace the selected text with the following two bullets:

Build a chain of high-quality restaurants

Build a profitable brand of recognized bakery products

11. Display **Slide 5,** change the title to **Statement of Finances** and then select the text in the content placeholder. Replace the selected text with the following bullet points, increasing and decreasing the list level as indicated:

Current Resources

　Franchise revenue

　Restaurant sales

Future Resources

　Stock offering

12. Click the **Insert tab**, and then in the **Illustrations group**, click **Clip Art** to display the **Clip Art** task pane. In the **Clip Art** task pane, click in the **Search for** box, delete the existing text, and then type **calculator**

13. In the **Clip Art** task pane, click the **Search in arrow**, and if necessary, click the **Everywhere** check box so that it is selected. Click the **Results should be arrow**, and then click as necessary to *clear* the **Clip Art**, **Movies**, and **Sounds** check boxes so that only **Photographs** is selected. Click **Go** to display the photographs of calculators. Click the picture of the white calculator with an adding machine tape on a blue background. Check Figure 15.43 at the beginning of this project if you are unsure of the picture that you should insert. **Close** the **Clip Art** task pane. (Note: If you cannot locate the picture, on the Insert tab, in the Illustrations group, click Picture. Navigate to your student files and then double-click p15D_Calculator.)

14. Position the pointer anywhere over the picture to display the  pointer. Drag to the right so that the picture is positioned approximately one-half inch from the right edge of the slide.

15. If necessary, click the picture of the calculator to select it and to activate the Picture Tools. On the Ribbon, click the **Format tab**, and then in the **Picture Styles group**, in the first row, click **Reflected Rounded Rectangle**.

16. Display **Slide 6**. Select the bulleted list text, and then replace it with the following bulleted items:

Board of Directors

National Investors Group

East Coast Bank and Trust

17. Click the **Insert tab**, and then in the **Text group**, click **Header & Footer** to display the **Header and Footer** dialog box.

18. Click the **Notes and Handouts tab**. Under **Include on page**, select the **Date and time** check box and, if necessary, click the **Update automatically** button so that the current date prints on the notes and handouts each time the presentation is printed. If necessary, clear the **Header** check box to omit this element. Select the **Page number** and **Footer** check boxes. Using your own first and last names, in the **Footer** box, type **15D_Funding_Firstname_Lastname** and then click **Apply to All**.

19. Check your *Chapter Assignment Sheet* or *Course Syllabus* or consult your instructor to determine if you are to submit your assignments on paper or electronically. To submit electronically, go to Step 21, and then follow the instructions provided by your instructor.

(Project 15D–Funding continues on the next page)

Content-Based Assessments

(Project 15D–Funding continued)

20. From the **Office** menu, point to **Print**, and then click **Print Preview** to make a final check of your presentation. In the **Page Setup group**, click the **Print What arrow**, and then click **Handouts (6 Slides Per Page)**. Click the **Print** button, and then click **OK** to print the handouts. **Close** Print Preview.

21. **Save** the changes to your presentation, and then from the **Office** menu, click **Exit PowerPoint**.

 End **You have completed Project 15D**

PowerPoint
chapter fifteen

Mastering PowerPoint

Project 15E — Recruitment

In this project, you will apply the skills you practiced from the Objectives in Project 15A.

Objectives: 1. *Open, View, and Save a Presentation;* **2.** *Edit a Presentation;* **3.** *Format a Presentation;* **4.** *Create Headers and Footers and Print a Presentation.*

In the following Mastering PowerPoint project, you will edit a presentation created by Shawna Andreasyan regarding the new online recruiting program at Skyline Bakery and Cafe. Your completed presentation will look similar to Figure 15.44.

For Project 15E, you will need the following file:

p15E_Recruitment

You will save your presentation as
15E_Recruitment_Firstname_Lastname

Figure 15.44

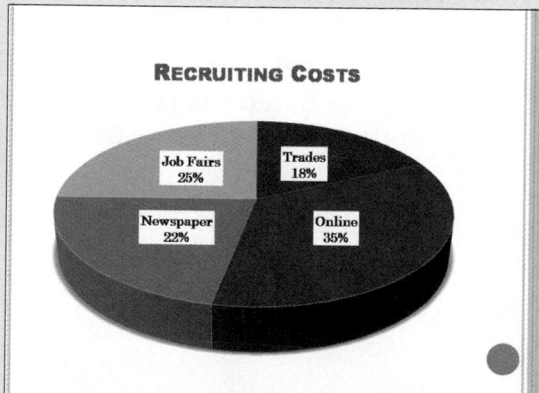

(Project 15E–Recruitment continues on the next page)

Content-Based Assessments

PowerPoint

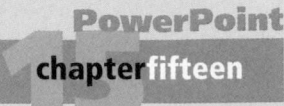

chapterfifteen   **Mastering PowerPoint**

(Project 15E–Recruitment continued)

1. **Start** PowerPoint and from your student data files, **Open** the file **p15E_Recruitment**. **Save** the presentation in your **PowerPoint Chapter 15** folder as **15E_Recruitment_Firstname_Lastname**

2. On **Slide 1**, change the **Font Size** for the title to **48** so that the entire title fits on one line. Add the subtitle **Online Recruiting Plan** and then apply **Italic** to the subtitle.

3. Add a **New Slide** to the presentation with the **Title and Content** layout. The slide title is **Need for Online Recruiting** In the content placeholder, type the following bullet points and correct any spelling errors that you make while typing:

   Expansion into new geographic locations

   Cost savings over traditional methods

   New graduates search online for jobs

   Reach a more diverse applicant pool

4. On **Slide 3**, **Center** the slide title, and then change the **Font** to **Arial Black**. Add the following speaker's notes, correcting spelling errors as necessary. **We currently use three major recruiting methods. This chart indicates the amount that will be spent on each method once online recruiting is established.**

5. Add a **New Slide** to the presentation with the **Title and Content** layout. The slide title is **Online Recruiting Advantages** In the content placeholder, type the following bullet points, and then correct any spelling errors that you make while typing. After you type the text, increase the list level of the fourth bullet point—*Automated database.*

Access to more qualified applicants

Streamlined application process

Improved manageability

Automated database

Easily maintained and updated

6. Display **Slide 3**, and then on the Ribbon, click the **Design tab**. Using the **More** button, display the **Themes gallery**. Under **Built-In**, apply the **Oriel** theme to **Slide 3** only. (Hint: Right-click the theme, and then click **Apply to Selected Slides.**)

7. Display **Slide 1** and view the slide show, pressing Spacebar to advance through the presentation. When the black slide displays, press Spacebar one more time to return to the presentation.

8. Insert a **Header and Footer** for the **Notes and Handouts**. Include only the **Date and time updated automatically**, the **Page number**, and a **Footer** with the file name **15E_Recruitment_Firstname_Lastname** using your own first and last names.

9. Check your *Chapter Assignment Sheet* or *Course Syllabus* or consult your instructor to determine if you are to submit your assignments on paper or electronically. To submit electronically, go to Step 11, and then follow the instructions provided by your instructor.

10. **Print Preview** your presentation, and then print **Handouts (4 Slides Per Page)** and the **Notes Pages** for **Slide 3**.

11. **Save** the changes to your presentation, and then **Close** the presentation.

 You have completed Project 15E

Content-Based Assessments

Mastering PowerPoint

Project 15F—Kitchen

In this project, you will apply the skills you practiced from the Objectives in Project 15B.

Objectives: 5. *Create a New Presentation;* **6.** *Use Slide Sorter View;* **7.** *Add Pictures to a Presentation.*

In the following Mastering PowerPoint project, you will create a presentation that Peter Wing, Executive Chef for Skyline Bakery and Cafe, will use to describe the different types of chefs employed by the restaurant. Your completed presentation will look similar to Figure 15.45.

> ### For Project 15F, you will need the following files:
>
> p15F_Chefs
> p15F_Tools
> p15F_Nutrition_Template
>
> **You will save your presentation as**
> **15F_Kitchen_Firstname_Lastname**

Figure 15.45

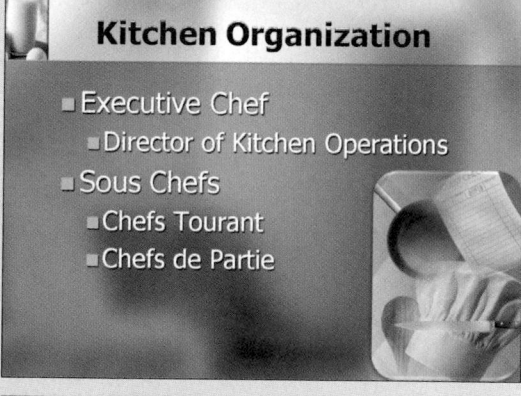

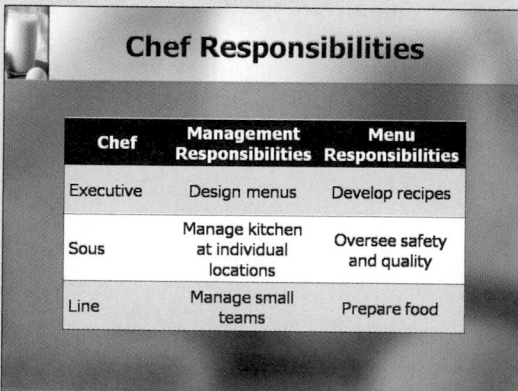

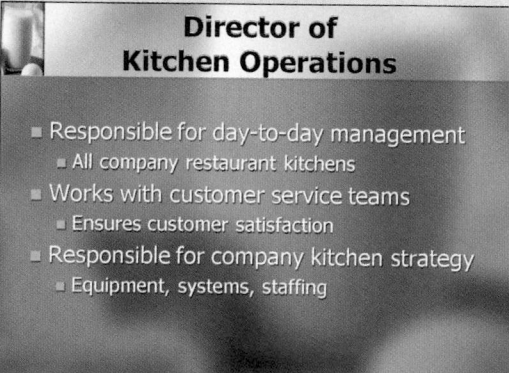

(Project 15F– Kitchen continues on the next page)

Content-Based Assessments

(Project 15F–Kitchen continued)

1. **Start** PowerPoint and begin a new presentation based on the **Nutrition** design template. You may search by using the keyword *Nutrition* or you can find the template in the **Design slides, Academic** category. If you do not have access to the online templates, open **p15F_Nutrition_ Template** from your student files. **Save** the presentation in your **PowerPoint Chapter 15** folder as 15F_Kitchen_ Firstname_ Lastname

2. The title for the first slide is **The Kitchen is Open!** and the subtitle is **Skyline Bakery and Cafe**

3. From your student files, add all of the slides in the **p15F_Chefs** presentation into the current presentation. Then, display the presentation in **Slide Sorter view** and rearrange the slides so that the *Kitchen Organization* slide is the second slide, and the *Director of Kitchen Operations* slide is the fourth slide.

4. Display **Slide 2** in **Normal** view and insert a clip art image by searching for **Photographs** in **All collections**, using the keyword **skillet** Insert the picture that con-

tains a chef's hat, skillet, wooden spoon, knife, and guest check. If you cannot find the picture, insert the picture found in your student files, p15F_Tools.

5. Drag the picture to the lower right corner of the slide, and then apply a **Picture Style—Bevel Rectangle**. (Hint: Picture Styles are found in the Format tab of the Picture Tools contextual tool.)

6. Insert a **Header and Footer** for the **Notes and Handouts**. Include only the **Date and time updated automatically**, the **Page number**, and a **Footer** with the file name **15F_Kitchen_Firstname_Lastname** using your own first and last names.

7. Check your *Chapter Assignment Sheet* or *Course Syllabus* or consult your instructor to determine if you are to submit your assignments on paper or electronically. To submit electronically, go to Step 9, and then follow the instructions provided by your instructor.

8. **Print Preview** your presentation, and then print **Handouts (4 Slides Per Page)**.

9. **Save** the changes to your presentation, and then **Close** the file.

End **You have completed Project 15F**

Content-Based Assessments

Mastering PowerPoint

Project 15G — Flyer

In this project, you will apply the skills you practiced from the Objectives in Projects 15A and 15B.

Objectives: 2. *Edit a Presentation;* **3.** *Format a Presentation;* **4.** *Create Headers and Footers and Print a Presentation;* **5.** *Create a New Presentation;* **7.** *Add Pictures to a Presentation.*

In the following Mastering PowerPoint project, you will create a single slide to be used as a flyer for the annual employee baking contest. Your completed presentation will look similar to Figure 15.46.

For Project 15G, you will need the following files:

New blank PowerPoint presentation
p15G_Cookies

You will save your presentation as
15G_Flyer_Firstname_Lastname

Figure 15.46

(Project 15G–Flyer continues on the next page)

Content-Based Assessments

(Project 15G–Flyer continued)

1. **Start** PowerPoint and begin a new blank presentation. Change the **Layout** of the title slide to the **Comparison** layout. Change the **Design** of the presentation by applying the **Oriel** theme. **Save** your presentation as **15G_Flyer_Firstname_Lastname**

2. The title of the slide is **Annual Employee Baking Contest** Change the **Font** to **Bradley Hand ITC** and the **Font Size** to **36**. Apply **Bold**, and then **Center** the title.

3. In the orange box on the left side of the slide, type **How do you participate and join the fun?** In the orange box on the right side of the slide, type **Bring your favorite yummy dessert! Center** the text in both boxes.

4. In the content placeholder on the left side of the slide, type the following bullet points:

   Bake your favorite secret recipe!

   Bring it to work on December 15!

   Our chefs will be judging all day!

   Great prizes in lots of different categories!

5. Click in the content placeholder on the right side of the slide and insert a clip art by using the keyword **cookies** Search for **Photographs** in **All collections**. Click the picture with the star-shaped cookie on the brown background. If you cannot find the picture, insert the picture found in your student files, p15G_Cookies.

6. If necessary, move the picture so that it is centered below the *Bring your favorite yummy dessert!* text. Then, apply **Picture Style—Drop Shadow Rectangle**.

7. Insert a **Footer** on the **Slide** (*not* the Notes and Handouts), that includes the file name **15G_Flyer_Firstname_Lastname** Because of the layout of this slide, the footer will display vertically on the right side of the slide.

8. Check your *Chapter Assignment Sheet* or *Course Syllabus* or consult your instructor to determine if you are to submit your assignments on paper or electronically. To submit electronically, go to Step 10, and then follow the instructions provided by your instructor.

9. **Print Preview** your presentation. There is only one slide in the presentation, so print **Slides**.

10. **Save** and **Close** your presentation.

 You have completed Project 15G ——————————

Content-Based Assessments

Mastering PowerPoint

Project 15H — Fresh

In this project, you will apply the skills you practiced from the Objectives in Projects 15A and 15B.

Objectives: 2. *Edit a Presentation;* **3.** *Format a Presentation;* **4.** *Create Headers and Footers and Print a Presentation;* **5.** *Create a New Presentation;* **6.** *Use Slide Sorter View;* **7.** *Add Pictures to a Presentation.*

In the following Mastering PowerPoint project, you will create a presentation that describes some of the steps taken by Skyline Bakery and Cafe to ensure that their food is fresh. Your completed presentation will look similar to Figure 15.47.

For Project 15H, you will need the following files:

New blank PowerPoint presentation
p15H_Text
p15H_Apple_Template
p15H_Vegetables
p15H_Tomato

You will save your presentation as 15H_Fresh_Firstname_Lastname

Figure 15.47

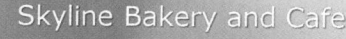

(Project 15H–Fresh continues on the next page)

(Project 15H–Fresh continued)

1. **Start** PowerPoint and begin a new presentation by searching for a template with the keyword **Apple** Click the template with the three green apples. If the template is not available, from your student files, open **p15H_Apple_Template**.

2. The title of this presentation is **Keeping It Fresh!** and the subtitle is **Skyline Bakery and Cafe Save** the presentation as **15H_Fresh_Firstname_Lastname**

3. Add the two slides from the **p15H_Text** presentation. Display **Slide 3**, and then in the left bulleted list placeholder, increase the list level of the *Patisserie chef*, *Executive chef*, and *Line chef* bullet points. In the right bulleted list placeholder, increase the list level of the *Federally regulated* bullet point.

4. Add a **New Slide** with the **Title and Content** layout, and in the title placeholder, type **Our Commitment** In the bulleted list placeholder, type the following bullet points:

   Fresh food, unforgettable taste, served in a clean and cozy setting

   Quality ingredients picked by our discerning staff of chefs

   Cooked to perfection at all times

5. In **Slide Sorter** view, switch **Slides 2 and 4** so that **Slide 2** becomes the last slide and the **Our Commitment** slide becomes the second slide. Return the presentation to **Normal** view.

6. On **Slide 2**, in the second bullet point, use the shortcut menu to view **Synonyms** for the word *picked*. Change the word *picked* to **selected**.

7. Display **Slide 4**. Insert a clip art image by using the keyword **cabbage** Search for

Photographs in **All collections**. Click the picture with many different types and colors of vegetables. Move the picture down and to the left so that it covers the apples and is positioned in the lower left corner of the slide. If you cannot locate the picture, it is available in your student files. The file name is p15H_Vegetables.

8. Insert the vegetable picture again so that there are two copies of the same picture on the slide. Move the picture down and to the right so that it is positioned in the lower right corner of the slide.

9. Insert another clip art image, this time by using the keywords **cherry tomato** Search for **Photographs** in **All collections**. Click the picture with tomatoes that look like they are spilling out of a bowl as shown in the figure at the beginning of this project. If you cannot locate the picture, it is available in your student files. The file name is p15H_Tomato. Drag the tomato picture straight down so that it overlaps the two vegetable pictures and its bottom edge aligns with the bottom edge of the slide. Apply **Picture Style—Simple Frame, Black**.

10. Insert a **Header and Footer** for the **Notes and Handouts**. Include only the **Date and time updated automatically**, the **Page number**, and a **Footer** with the file name **15H_Fresh_Firstname_Lastname** and then view the slide show.

11. Check your *Chapter Assignment Sheet* or *Course Syllabus* or consult your instructor to determine if you are to submit your assignments on paper or electronically. To submit electronically, go to Step 13, and then follow the instructions provided by your instructor.

(Project 15H–Fresh continues on the next page)

Content-Based Assessments

(Project 15H–Fresh continued)

12. **Print Preview** your presentation, and then print **Handouts (4 Slides Per Page)**. If the text or pictures do not display, on the Print Preview tab, in the Print group, click Options, point to Color/Grayscale, and then click Color or Color (On Black and White Printer).

13. **Save** the changes to your presentation. **Close** the presentation.

 You have completed Project 15H

Mastering PowerPoint

Project 15I — Holiday

In this project, you will apply the skills you practiced from the Objectives in Projects 15A and 15B.

Objectives: 1. *Open, View, and Save a Presentation;* **2.** *Edit a Presentation;* **3.** *Format a Presentation;* **4.** *Create Headers and Footers and Print a Presentation;* **5.** *Create a New Presentation;* **6.** *Use Slide Sorter View;* **7.** *Add Pictures to a Presentation.*

In the following Mastering PowerPoint project, you will create a presentation that details the holiday activities at Skyline Bakery and Cafe. Your completed presentation will look similar to Figure 15.48.

For Project 15I, you will need the following files:

New blank PowerPoint presentation
p15I_December
p15I_Green_Template
p15I_Coffee
p15I_Ornaments

You will save your presentation as 15I_Holiday_ Firstname_Lastname

Figure 15.48

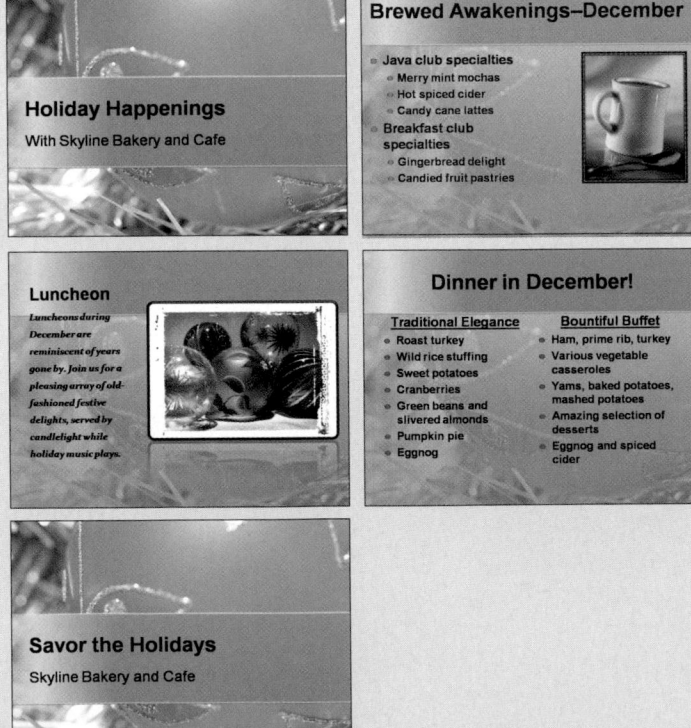

(Project 15I–Holiday continues on the next page)

(Project 15I–Holiday continued)

1. **Start** PowerPoint and begin a new presentation by searching for the green and gold holiday template. If the template is not available, from your student files, open **p15I_Green_Template**. The title of the presentation is **Holiday Happenings** and the subtitle is **With Skyline Bakery and Cafe** Insert all of the slides from the presentation **p15I_December**. **Save** the presentation as **15I_Holiday_Firstname_Lastname**

2. On **Slide 2**, increase the list level for bullet points 2, 3, and 4 and for the last two bullet points. Change the **Layout** to **Two Content**, and then in the right placeholder insert a clip art photograph of a white coffee mug—search for **coffee**—on a green background. If you cannot find the image, it is located with your student files— **p15I_Coffee**. Size the picture so that it is approximately as wide as the word *December* and as tall as the text in the left placeholder. Apply **Picture Style— Compound Frame, Black** and position the picture, using Figure 15.48 at the beginning of this project as your guide.

3. Display **Slide 3** and change the **Layout** to **Comparison**. In the *Click to add text* box on the left side of the slide, type **Traditional Elegance** and then in the box on the right side of the slide type **Bountiful Buffet Center** and **Underline** the text in both boxes, and then change the **Font Size** to **28**.

4. Insert a **New Slide** with the **Content with Caption** layout. In the *Click to add title* box, type **Luncheon** and then change the **Font Size** to **36**. In the text placeholder on the left side of the slide, type the following paragraph:

Luncheons during December are reminiscent of years gone by. Join us for a pleasing array of old-fashioned festive delights, served by candlelight while holiday music plays.

5. Select the paragraph, and then change the **Font** to **Constantia** and the **Font Size** to **20**. Apply **Bold** and **Italic**, and then change the **Line Spacing** to **1.5**.

6. In the content placeholder on the right side of the slide, insert a clip art of five brightly colored glass **ornaments** Apply **Picture Style—Reflected Bevel, Black** and use Figure 15.48 at the beginning of this project as your guide for sizing and positioning the picture. If you cannot locate the picture, the file name in your student files is p15I_Ornaments.

7. Insert a **New Slide** with the **Title Slide** layout. In the title placeholder, type **Savor the Holidays** and in the subtitle placeholder type **Skyline Bakery and Cafe**

8. Move **Slide 4** so that it is between **Slides 2** and **3**. Insert a **Header and Footer** for the **Notes and Handouts** that includes the **Date and time updated automatically**, the **Page number**, and the file name **15I_Holiday_Firstname_Lastname** Check the presentation for spelling errors, and then view the slide show from the beginning.

9. Check your *Chapter Assignment Sheet* or *Course Syllabus* or consult your instructor to determine if you are to submit your assignments on paper or electronically. To submit electronically, go to Step 11, and then follow the instructions provided by your instructor.

10. **Print Preview** your presentation, and then print **Handouts (6 Slides Per Page)**.

11. **Save** the changes to your presentation, and then **close** the file.

 You have completed Project 15I

Content-Based Assessments

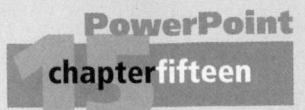 

Business Running Case

Project 15J—Business Running Case

In this project, you will apply the skills you practiced in Projects 15A and 15B.

Close PowerPoint and any other open windows. Display the Start menu, click Computer, and then navigate to the student files that accompany this textbook. In the folder **03_business_running_case**, locate and open the folder for this chapter. Open and print the instructions for this project, which are provided to you in Adobe PDF format. Follow the instructions and use the skills you have gained thus far to assist Jennifer Nelson in meeting the challenges of owning and running her business.

End **You have completed Project 15J**

Content-Based Assessments

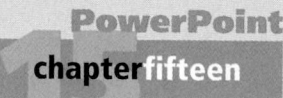
Project 15K — *GO!* Fix It

In this project, you will apply the skills you practiced from the Objectives in Projects 15A and 15B.

For Project 15K, you will need the following file

p15K_fixit_Fundraiser

You will save your presentation as
15K_Fundraiser_Firstname_Lastname

In this project, you will edit a draft slide presentation by Sandra Lee, Director of Marketing for Skyline Bakery and Cafe in Springfield, Massachusetts. She is requesting approval from corporate head-quarters for Skyline to become the business sponsor of the Springfield Firefighters Barbecue and Auction. From the student files that accompany this textbook, open the folder **05_go_fix_it**. Locate and open the file **p15K_fixit_Fundraiser**, and then save the file in your chapter folder as **15K_Fundraiser_Firstname_Lastname**

This presentation contains **five errors** that you must find and correct. Read and examine the presentation, and then edit to correct the errors that you find. Types of errors could include:

- Content errors such as misspellings, missing or incorrect text, pictures, hyperlinks, or other objects.
- Font and paragraph formatting and positioning errors such as fonts, font styles, font sizing, alignment, text color, indent levels, and bullet features.
- Slide layout, orientation, design themes, backgrounds, animation and transition errors.
- Page setup errors on slides, handouts, notes and outlines such as margins, orientation, layout, alignment, headers and footers, date and time, color, grayscale, black and white, and sizing.

To complete the project you should know:

- There are two spelling errors.
- Ms. Lee prefers the Civic presentation theme for the presentation.
- Slide 4 is missing a picture; use 15K_Firefighter.
- Slide 5 topics should be all the same level.
- On slide 8, Ms. Lee prefers the Two Content layout.

Create a footer for the Notes and Handouts. Include only the date and time updated automatically, the page number, and a footer with your name included. Submit as directed, using 4 slides per page.

End You have completed Project 15K

Outcomes-Based Assessments

Rubric

The following outcomes-based assessments are *open-ended assessments*. That is, there is no specific correct result; your result will depend on your approach to the information provided. Make *Professional Quality* your goal. Use the following scoring rubric to guide you in *how* to approach the problem, and then to evaluate *how well* your approach solves the problem.

The *criteria*—Software Mastery, Content, Format and Layout, and Process—represent the knowledge and skills you have gained that you can apply to solving the problem. The *levels of performance*—Professional Quality, Approaching Professional Quality, or Needs Quality Improvements—help you and your instructor evaluate your result.

	Your completed project is of Professional Quality if you:	Your completed project is Approaching Professional Quality if you:	Your completed project Needs Quality Improvements if you:
1-Software Mastery	Choose and apply the most appropriate skills, tools, and features and identify efficient methods to solve the problem.	Choose and apply some appropriate skills, tools, and features, but not in the most efficient manner.	Choose inappropriate skills, tools, or features, or are inefficient in solving the problem.
2-Content	Construct a solution that is clear and well organized, contains content that is accurate, appropriate to the audience and purpose, and is complete. Provide a solution that contains no errors of spelling, grammar, or style.	Construct a solution in which some components are unclear, poorly organized, inconsistent, or incomplete. Misjudge the needs of the audience. Have some errors in spelling, grammar, or style, but the errors do not detract from comprehension.	Construct a solution that is unclear, incomplete, or poorly organized, containing some inaccurate or inappropriate content; and contains many errors of spelling, grammar, or style. Do not solve the problem.
3-Format and Layout	Format and arrange all elements to communicate information and ideas, clarify function, illustrate relationships, and indicate relative importance.	Apply appropriate format and layout features to some elements, but not others. Overuse features, causing minor distraction.	Apply format and layout that does not communicate information or ideas clearly. Do not use format and layout features to clarify function, illustrate relationships, or indicate relative importance. Use available features excessively, causing distraction.
4-Process	Use an organized approach that integrates planning, development, self-assessment, revision, and reflection.	Demonstrate an organized approach in some areas, but not others; or, use an insufficient process of organization throughout.	Do not use an organized approach to solve the problem.

Outcomes-Based Assessments

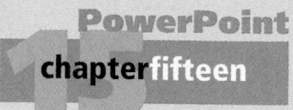

Problem Solving

Project 15L — Catering

In this project, you will construct a solution by applying any combination of the skills you practiced from the Objectives in Projects 15A and 15B.

For Project 15L, you will need the following file:

New blank PowerPoint presentation

**You will save your presentation as
15L_Catering_Firstname_Lastname**

Using the information provided, create a presentation that contains four to six slides that Nancy Goldman, Chief Baker, can use to describe the catering services offered by Skyline Bakery and Cafe. The presentation will be used at a business expo attended by representatives of many companies that frequently host business luncheons and dinners for their clients. The presentation should include a title slide, a slide that describes why customers would be interested in Skyline Bakery and Cafe's catering services, at least two slides with sample menus, and an ending slide that summarizes the presentation. The tone of the presentation should be positive and sales oriented so that the audience is encouraged to try Skyline's catering service.

The presentation should include a theme or template that is creative and is appropriate to the upbeat tone of the presentation. Use at least two different slide layouts to vary the way in which the presentation text is displayed. Search for clip art that visually represents the types of menu items described. Add the file name to the Notes and Handouts footer and check the presentation for spelling errors. Save the presentation as **15L_Catering_Firstname_Lastname** and submit it as directed.

End **You have completed Project 15L** —————————

Outcomes-Based Assessments

Problem Solving

Project 15M — Picnic

In this project, you will construct a solution by applying any combination of the skills you practiced from the Objectives in Projects 15A and 15B.

For Project 15M, you will need the following file:

New blank PowerPoint presentation

You will save your presentation as
15M_Picnic_Firstname_Lastname

In this project, you will create a one-slide flyer to be distributed to employees of Skyline Bakery and Cafe advertising the upcoming employee picnic. The picnic is held every summer at a large, regional park. The tone of the flyer is fun! Use two fonts that are informal and inviting and large enough to easily read if the flyer were posted on a bulletin board. Include in the flyer a slide title that will make the employees feel welcome and excited about attending. Choose a content layout that includes multiple placeholders for the information that you need to provide. The flyer should include information on location, date, time, and types of activities. Include a picture that is reminiscent of a picnic or large outdoor gathering. Refer to Project 15G for ideas on how to lay out the flyer.

Add the file name to the footer and check the presentation for spelling errors. Save the presentation as **15M_Picnic_Firstname_Lastname** and submit it as directed.

 End **You have completed Project 15M** _____

Outcomes-Based Assessments

PowerPoint
chapterfifteen

Problem Solving

Project 15N — Customer Service

In this project, you will construct a solution by applying any combination of the skills you practiced from the Objectives in Projects 15A and 15B.

For Project 15N, you will need the following files:

New blank PowerPoint presentation
p15N_Mission_Statement

You will save your presentation as
15N_Customer_Service_Firstname_Lastname

In this project, you will create a six-slide customer service presentation to be used by Shawna Andreasyan, Director of Human Resources for Skyline Bakery and Cafe. All employees will be attending customer service training seminars and this presentation is a brief introduction to the overall topic of customer service.

Good customer service is grounded in the Skyline Bakery and Cafe's mission statement. The mission statement has been provided for you in presentation p15N_Mission_Statement and should be inserted early in the presentation. Think about the mission statement, and then in the next slide, use a title slide layout to make a brief statement that summarizes how the mission statement is tied to customer service. Then consider some of the following principles of good customer service. A company should make a commitment to customer service so that every employee believes in it and is rewarded by it. Employees should also understand that everyone is involved in good customer service. The company is not just about the product; people are critically important to the success of any business and good customer service ensures that success. Furthermore, employees who are rewarded for good customer service will likely continue to work with good practices, perhaps leading to increased sales.

Using the information in the previous paragraph and other information that you may gather by researching the topic of "restaurant customer service," create at least two additional slides that Shawna Andreasyan can use to describe the importance of good customer service and how it is rewarded at Skyline Bakery and Cafe. When creating the design template, search Microsoft Office Online for customer service or training templates; there are several available. The tone of this presentation is informative and serious. Keep this in mind when choosing a template, theme, fonts, and clip art. Add the date and file name to the Notes and Handouts footer and check the presentation for spelling errors. Save the presentation as **15N_Customer_Service_Firstname_Lastname** and submit it as directed.

End **You have completed Project 15N**

Outcomes-Based Assessments

Problem Solving

Project 15O — Menus

In this project, you will construct a solution by applying any combination of the skills you practiced from the Objectives in Projects 15A and 15B.

For Project 15O, you will need the following file:

New blank PowerPoint presentation

You will save your presentation as
15O_Menus_Firstname_Lastname

In this exercise, you will create a presentation that contains special menus that are used for different holidays. Recognizing that holiday menus are frequently used in a number of presentations throughout the year, Peter Wang, Executive Chef, has decided to create sample menus in one presentation so that the menus are available when the marketing staff need to insert them into PowerPoint presentations.

Choose five holidays and create slides that include one holiday menu per slide. You can research holiday menus on the Internet, visit local restaurants to find out if they have special holiday menus, or you can use your own experience with family traditions in creating these menus. The slide title should identify the holiday and every slide should include a picture that portrays the holiday meal or represents the holiday in some way. Alternatively, consider using a Two Content layout in which the menu is in one column and a quote describing why the menu is special is in the other column. Keep your theme simple so that it does not interfere with the pictures that you have selected. Because these slides will likely be used in different presentations throughout the year, you may choose different fonts and font styles that characterize each holiday.

Add the date and file name to the Notes and Handouts footer and check the presentation for spelling errors. Save the presentation as **15O_Menus_Firstname_Lastname** and submit it as directed.

End **You have completed Project 15O** ——————————

Outcomes-Based Assessments

Problem Solving

Project 15P — Opening

In this project, you will construct a solution by applying any combination of the skills you practiced from the Objectives in Projects 15A and 15B.

For Project 15P, you will need the following file:

New blank PowerPoint presentation

**You will save your presentation as
15P_Opening_Firstname_Lastname**

In this project, you will create a presentation to be shown by Skyline Bakery and Cafe's Chief Executive Officer, Samir Taheri, at a Chamber of Commerce meeting. The presentation will explain the details of the company's grand opening of two new locations in Rhode Island taking place in June. The presentation should contain six to eight slides and the first two to three slides should include background information that may be taken from the following paragraph that describes the company and the new restaurant's location.

Skyline Bakery and Cafe is a chain of casual dining restaurants and bakeries based in Boston. Each restaurant has its own in-house bakery, which produces a wide variety of high-quality specialty breads, breakfast sweets, and desserts. Breads and sweets are sold by counter service along with coffee drinks, gourmet teas, fresh juices, and sodas. The full-service restaurant area features a menu of sandwiches, salads, soups, and light entrees. Fresh, high-quality ingredients and a professional and courteous staff are the hallmarks of every Skyline Bakery and Cafe.

The new restaurant is located in an outdoor lifestyle center where many residents gather in the evening to socialize. The restaurants are opening in June, so consider a summer theme as you develop ideas about the kinds of events that the owners may host during the grand opening. Include in the presentation four slides representing four different days of events—two at each of the new locations. The Comparison and Two Content slide layouts may be very effective for these four slides. Use fonts and clip art to enhance your presentation but do not clutter the presentation with excess images or many different types of fonts. Add the date and file name to the Notes and Handouts footer and check the presentation for spelling errors. Save the presentation as **15P_Opening_Firstname_Lastname** and submit it as directed.

End **You have completed Project 15P** ———————

Outcomes-Based Assessments

 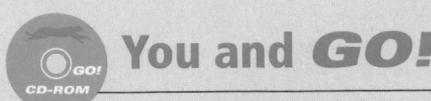

Project 15Q — You and *GO!*

In this project, you will construct a solution by applying any combination of the skills you practiced from the Objectives in Projects 15A and 15B.

Close PowerPoint and any other open windows. Display the Start menu, click Computer, and then navigate to the student files that accompany this textbook. In the folder **04_you_and_go**, locate and open the folder for this chapter. Open and print the instructions for this project, which are provided to you in Adobe PDF format. Follow the instructions to create a presentation about a place to which you have traveled or would like to travel.

 End You have completed Project 15Q ――――――――――――――

GO! with Help

Project 15R — *GO!* with Help

The PowerPoint Help system is extensive and can help you as you work. In this project, you will view information about getting help as you work in PowerPoint.

1 **Start** PowerPoint. At the right end of the Ribbon, click the **Microsoft Office PowerPoint Help** button to display the **PowerPoint Help** dialog box. In the **Search** box, type **keyboard shortcuts** and then press Enter.

2 In the displayed search results, click **Keyboard shortcuts for PowerPoint 2007**. Maximize the displayed window and read how you can use keyboard shortcuts in PowerPoint.

3 If you want to do so, print a copy of the information by clicking the **Print** button at the top of the Microsoft Office PowerPoint Help window.

4 **Close** the Help window, and then **Close** PowerPoint.

 End You have completed Project 15R ――――――――――――――

Outcomes-Based Assessments

Group Business Running Case

Project 15S — Group Business Running Case

In this project, you will apply the skills you practiced from the Objectives in Projects 15A and 15B.

Your instructor may assign this group case project to your class. If your instructor assigns this project, he or she will provide you with information and instructions to work as part of a group. The group will apply the skills gained thus far to help the Bell Orchid Hotel Group achieve its business goals.

End **You have completed Project 15S** —————————

chaptersixteen

Designing a PowerPoint Presentation

OBJECTIVES

At the end of this chapter you will be able to:

1. Format Slide Elements
2. Insert and Format Pictures and Shapes
3. Apply Slide Transitions

OUTCOMES

Mastering these objectives will enable you to:

PROJECT 16A
Format a Presentation

4. Reorganize Presentation Text and Clear Formats
5. Create and Format a SmartArt Graphic

PROJECT 16B
Enhance a Presentation with SmartArt Graphics

Montagna del Pattino

Montagna del Pattino was founded and built by the Blardone family in the 1950s. It has grown from one ski run and a small lodge to 50 trails, 6 lifts, a 300-room lodge, and a renowned ski and snowboard school. Luxurious condominiums on the property have ski in/ski out access. A resort store offers rental and sale of gear for enthusiasts who want the latest advances in ski and snowboard technology. A variety of quick service, casually elegant, and fine dining restaurants complete the scene for a perfect ski-enthusiast getaway.

Designing a PowerPoint Presentation

A PowerPoint presentation is a visual aid in which well-designed slides help the audience understand complex information, while keeping them focused on the message. Color is an important element that provides uniformity and visual interest. When used correctly, color enhances your slides and draws the audience's interest by creating focus. When designing the background and element colors for your presentation, use a consistent look throughout the presentation and be sure that the colors you use provide contrast so that the text is visible on the background.

Project 16A Welcome

In Activities 16.01 through 16.13, you will edit and format a presentation that Kirsten McCarty, Director of Marketing, has created for a travel fair that introduces potential resort visitors to the types of activities available at Montagna del Pattino. Your completed presentation will look similar to Figure 16.1.

For Project 16A, you will need the following files:

p16A_Snow
p16A_Snowboard
p16A_Welcome
p16A_Winter

You will save your presentation as
16A_Welcome_Firstname_Lastname

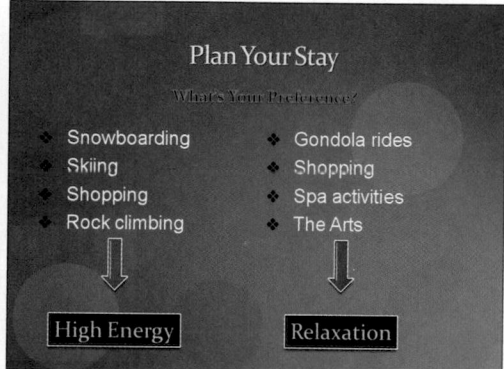

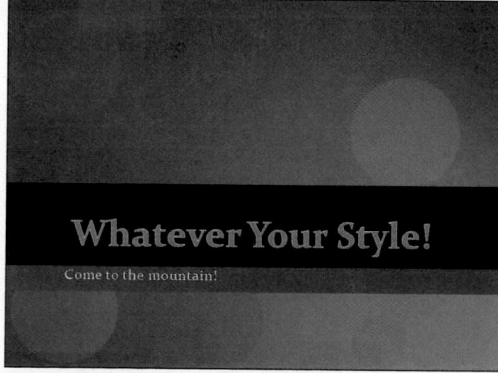

Figure 16.1
Project 16A—Welcome

Objective 1
Format Slide Elements

Recall that formatting is the process of changing the appearance of the text, layout, and design of a slide. You have practiced formatting text by changing the font and font size, and by applying bold and italic text styles. Other slide elements can be formatted, such as bulleted and numbered lists, and there are other methods that you can use to enhance text, including WordArt and the Format Painter.

> ## Note — Comparing Your Screen With the Figures in This Textbook
>
> Your screen will match the figures shown in this textbook if you set your screen resolution to 1024 × 768. At other resolutions, your screen will closely resemble, but not match, the figures shown. To view your screen's resolution, on the Windows Vista desktop, right-click in a blank area, click Personalize, and then click Display Settings.

Activity 16.01 Selecting Placeholder Text and Using the Repeat Key

1 **Start** PowerPoint. From your student files, **Open** the file **p16A_Welcome**. From the **Office** menu 🔘, click **Save As**, and then click the **New Folder** button. Navigate to the location where you are saving your files, create a folder with the name **PowerPoint Chapter 16** and then click **OK**. In the **File name** box, type **16A_Welcome_Firstname_Lastname** and then click **Save** to save your file.

2 Display **Slide 2**. Click anywhere in the bulleted list on the left side of the slide and notice that the placeholder is surrounded by a dashed border, as shown in Figure 16.2.

The dashed border indicates that you can make editing changes to the placeholder text.

Figure 16.2

PowerPoint | chapter 16

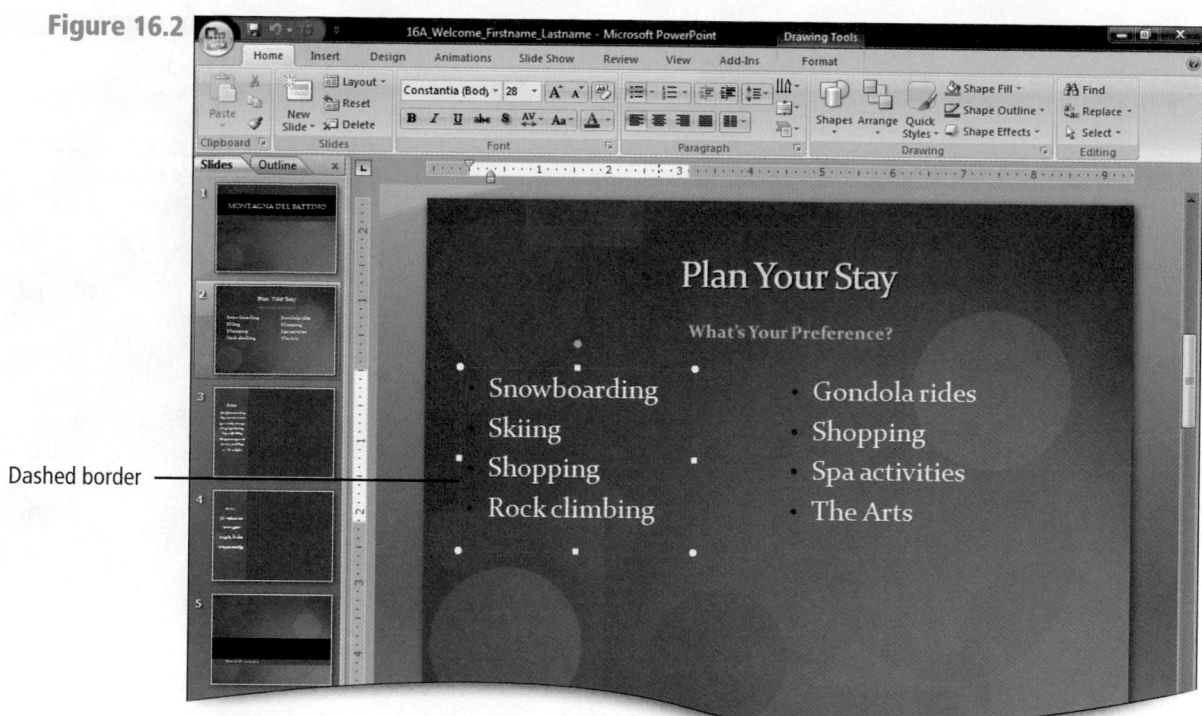

Dashed border

3 Point to the dashed border to display the ⊕ pointer, as shown in Figure 16.3.

Figure 16.3

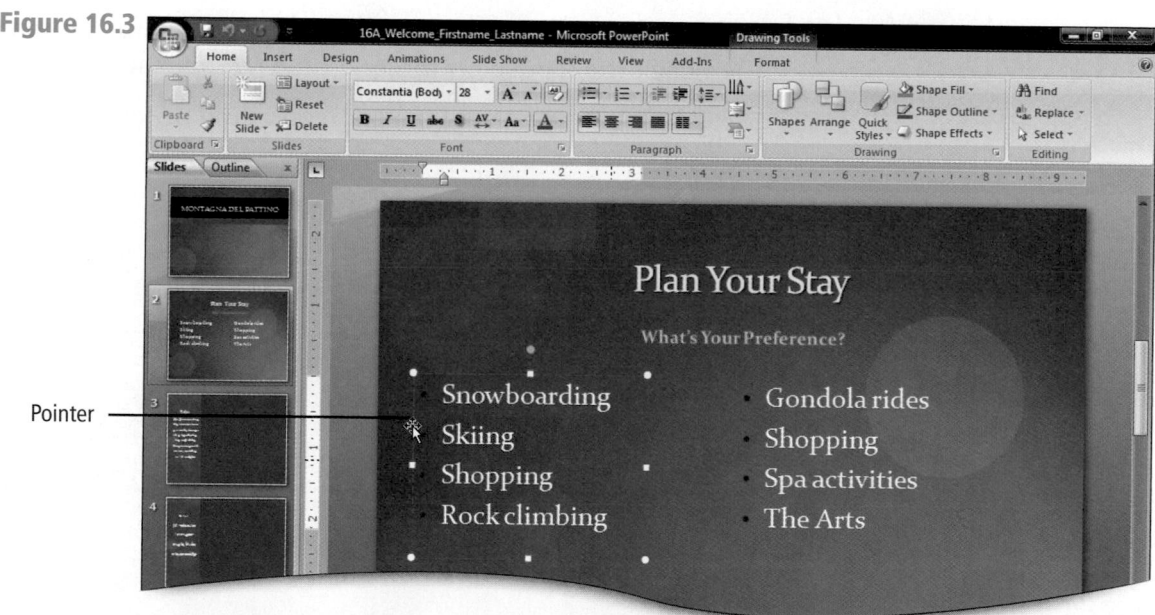

Pointer

4 With the ⊕ pointer displayed, click the mouse button one time to display the border as a solid line as shown in Figure 16.4.

When a placeholder's border displays as a solid line, all of the text in the placeholder is selected and can be formatted at one time. Thus, any formatting changes that you make will be applied to all of the text in the placeholder.

Figure 16.4

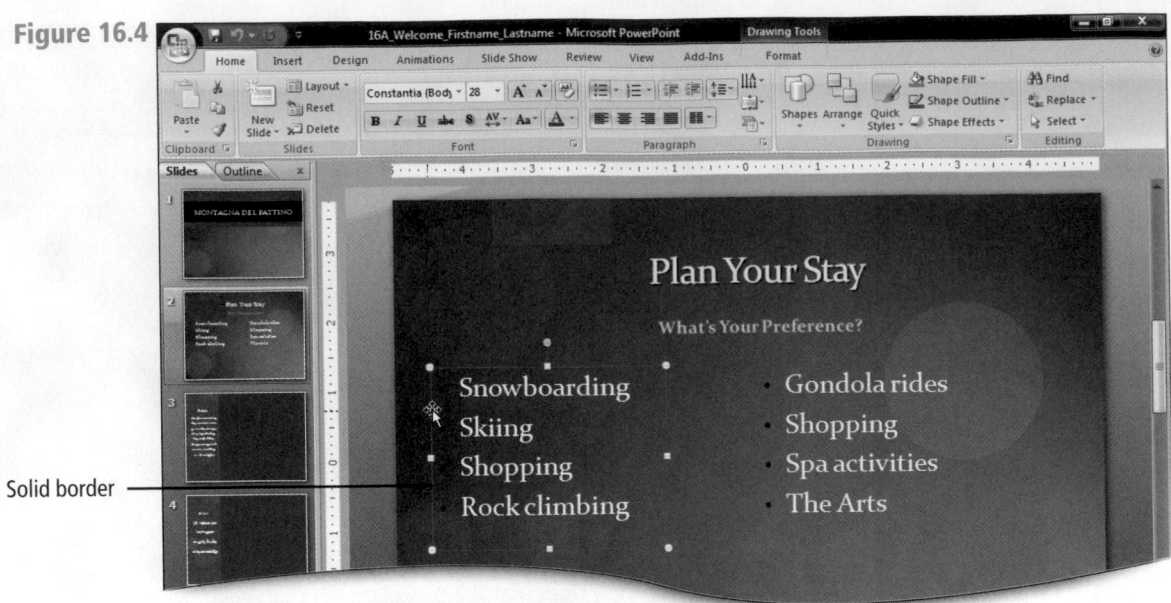

Solid border

5 With the border of the placeholder displaying as a solid line, on the **Home tab**, in the **Font group**, click the **Font button arrow**, and then click **Arial**.

All of the text in the placeholder is changed to Arial.

6 Click in the text in the bulleted list placeholder on the right side of the slide. Point to the dashed border to display the [pointer icon] pointer, and then click the mouse button one time so that the border is solid.

7 Press F4, which repeats the last command or keystroke that you entered.

All of the text in the placeholder on the right is formatted in Arial.

8 **Save** [save icon] your changes.

Another Way

To Repeat a Command

On the Quick Access Toolbar, click the Repeat button [repeat icon] to repeat the last command or keystroke that you entered.

Activity 16.02 Changing a Bulleted List to a Numbered List

1 With **Slide 2** still displayed, click anywhere in the bulleted list on the left side of the slide, and then point to its dashed border to display the ⬚ pointer. Click the dashed border so that it displays as a solid line, indicating that all of the text is selected.

2 On the **Home tab**, in the **Paragraph group**, click the **Numbering** button ⬚.

All of the bullets are converted to numbers. The color of the numbers is determined by the presentation theme.

Alert!

Did you display the Numbering gallery?

If you clicked the Numbering button arrow instead of the Numbering button, the Numbering gallery displays. Click the Numbering button arrow again to close the gallery, and then click the Numbering button to convert the bullets to numbers.

3 Select the bulleted list placeholder on the right side of the slide so that the border displays as a solid line. In the **Paragraph group**, click the **Numbering** button ⬚.

4 **Save** ⬚ the presentation.

Activity 16.03 Modifying the Bulleted List Style

The theme that is applied to your presentation includes default styles for the bulleted points in content placeholders. In this presentation, the default bullet is a blue circle. You can customize a bullet by changing its style, color, and size.

1 With **Slide 2** still displayed, click anywhere in the numbered list on the left side of the slide, and then point to its dashed border. Click the dashed border so that it displays as a solid line, indicating that all of the text is selected.

2 On the **Home tab**, in the **Paragraph group**, click the **Bullets button arrow** ⬚ to display the **Bullets gallery**, as shown in Figure 16.5.

The gallery displays several bullet characters that you can apply to the selection.

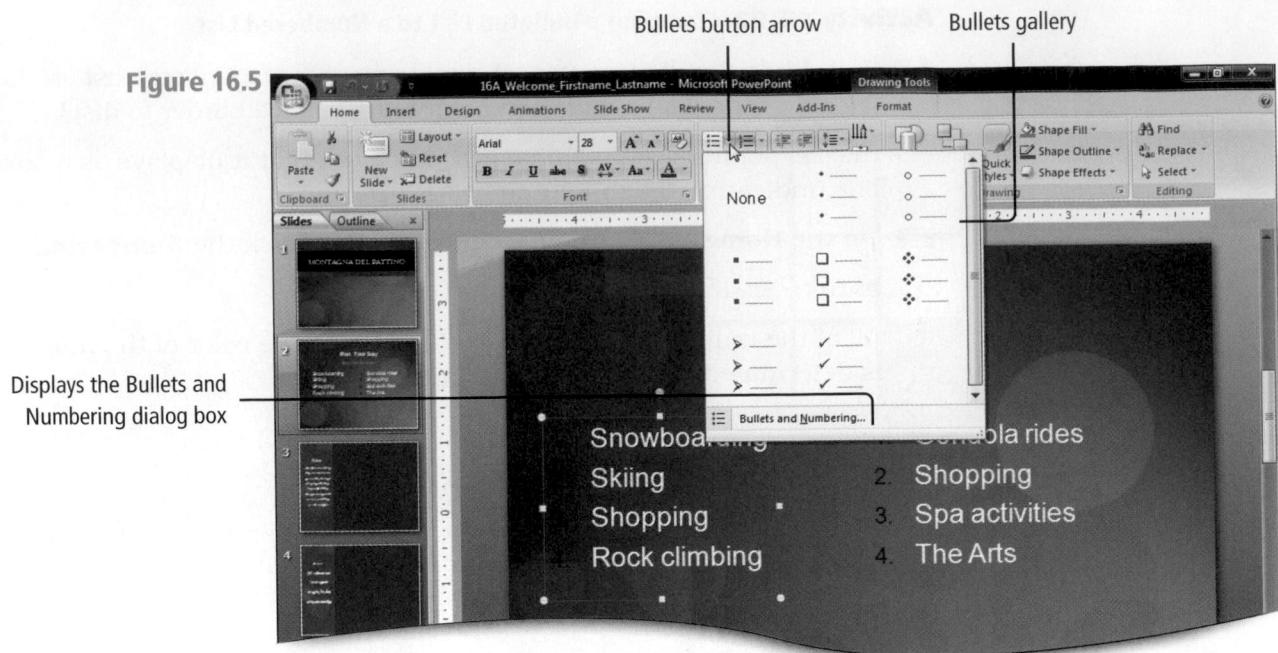

Figure 16.5

Bullets button arrow

Bullets gallery

Displays the Bullets and
Numbering dialog box

Alert!

Did you replace the numbers with bullets?

If you replaced the numbers with bullets, then you clicked the Bullets *button* instead of the Bullets *arrow*. Click the Bullets arrow, and then continue with Step 3.

3 At the bottom of the **Bullets gallery**, click **Bullets and Numbering**. In the displayed **Bullets and Numbering** dialog box, point to each bullet style to display its ScreenTip. Then, in the second row, click **Star Bullets**. If the Star Bullets do not display, in the second row of bullets, click the second bullet style. At the bottom of the Bullets and Numbering dialog box, click Reset.

4 Below the gallery, click the **Color** button. Under **Theme Colors**, in the first row, click the first color—**Black, Background 1**. Click **OK** to apply the bullet style.

5 Click in the text in the numbered list placeholder on the right side of the slide. Point to the dashed border to display the ⬚ pointer, and then click the mouse button so that the placeholder border is solid, indicating that all of the text in the placeholder can be formatted at one time.

6 Press F4 to repeat the bullet formatting, and then compare your slide with Figure 16.6.

Figure 16.6

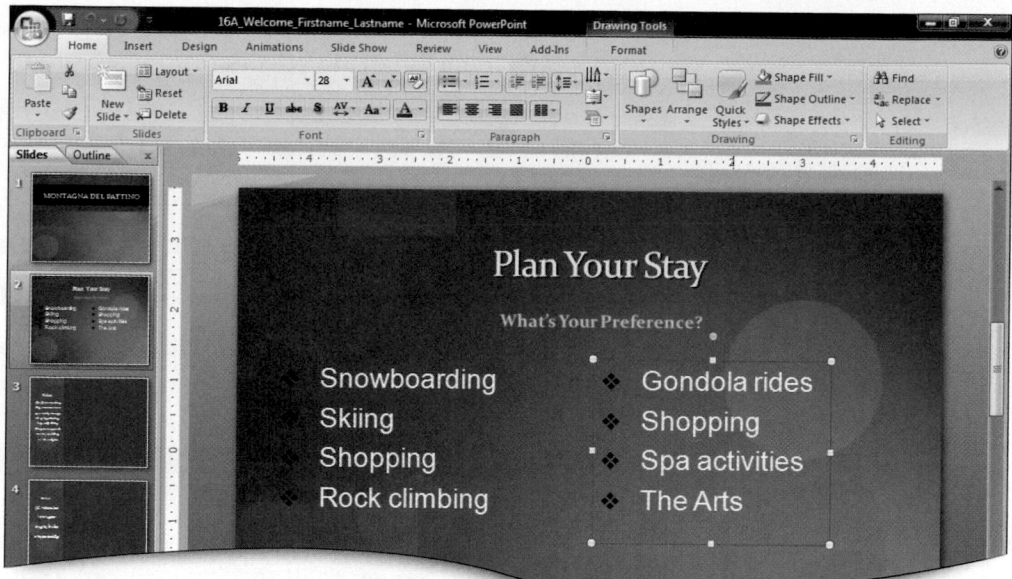

7 **Save** 💾 your changes.

More Knowledge

Using Other Symbols as Bullet Characters

Many bullets styles are available for you to insert in your presentation. In the Bullets and Numbering dialog box, click the Customize button to view additional bullet styles.

Activity 16.04 Applying WordArt Styles to Text

WordArt is a feature that applies combinations of decorative formatting to text, including shadows, reflections, and 3-D effects, as well as changing the line and *fill color* of text. A fill color is the inside color of text or of an object. You can choose from a gallery of WordArt styles to insert a new WordArt object or you can customize existing text by applying WordArt formatting.

1 Display **Slide 3**, and then select the word *Relax*. On the **Format tab**, in the **WordArt Styles group**, click the **More** button ▼ to display the **WordArt Styles gallery**.

The WordArt gallery is divided into two sections. If you choose a WordArt style in the *Applies to Selected Text* section, you must first select all of the text to which you want to apply the WordArt. If you choose a WordArt style in the *Applies to All Text in the Shape* section, the WordArt style is applied to all of the text in the placeholder or shape.

2 Point to several of the WordArt styles and notice that Live Preview displays the formatting effects on the selected word.

3 Under **Applies to Selected Text**, in the first row, click the second style—**Fill – None, Outline – Accent 2**.

The word *Relax* displays outlined in blue.

4 With the word *Relax* still selected, in the **Word Art Styles group**, click the **Text Fill button arrow** ![A]. Under **Theme Colors**, in the first row, click the first color—**Black, Background 1**, and then compare your slide with Figure 16.7.

Figure 16.7

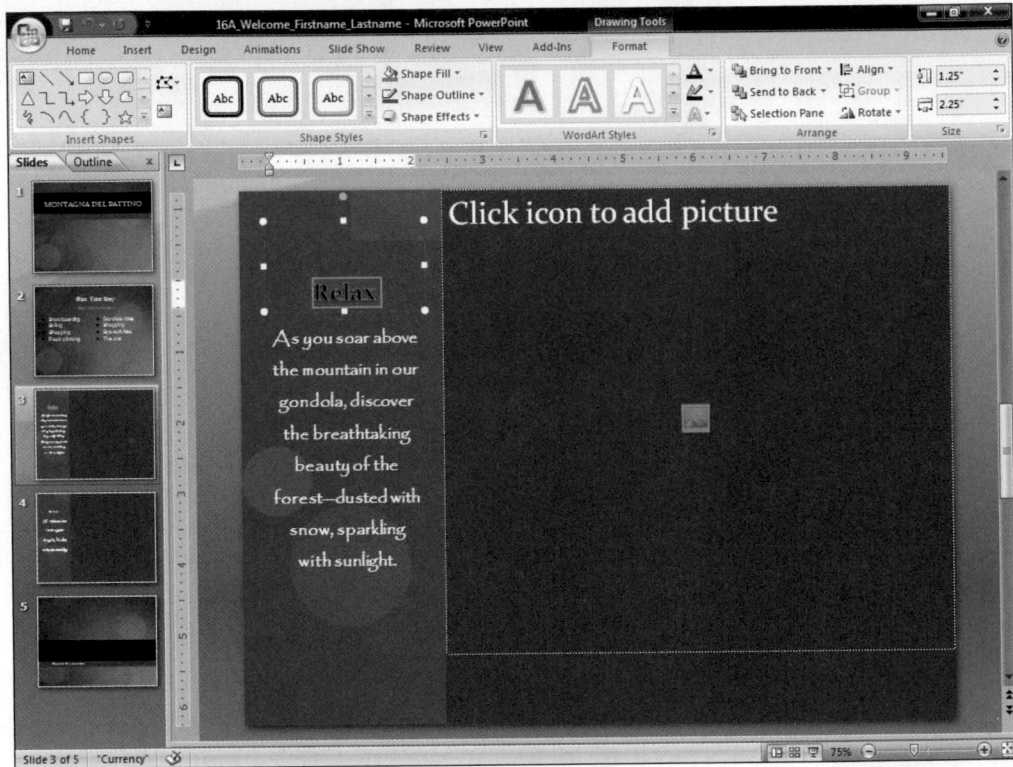

5 Display **Slide 5**. Click the **Insert tab**, and then in the **Text group**, click the **WordArt** button. In the gallery, click the first WordArt style in the first row—**Fill – Text 2, Outline – Background 2**.

In the center of your slide, a WordArt placeholder displays *Your Text Here*. When you type, your keystrokes will replace this text and fill the placeholder with wide letters. The placeholder will expand to accommodate the text. The WordArt is surrounded by sizing handles with which you can adjust its size by using the same technique that you practiced when sizing clip art.

6 Type **Whatever Your Style!** to replace the WordArt placeholder text.

7 Look at the Slide pane and verify that the horizontal ruler displays above the slide and that the vertical ruler displays to the left of the slide. If the rulers do not display, on the Ribbon, click the View tab, and then in the Show/Hide group, click to select the Ruler check box.

8 Point to the WordArt border to display the ⟨pointer⟩ pointer. Using Figure 16.8 as a guide, drag down and to the left approximately 1 inch to move the WordArt.

Figure 16.8

Position WordArt here

9 **Save** 🖫 the presentation.

Activity 16.05 Using Format Painter

Format Painter copies *formatting* from one selection of text to another, thus ensuring formatting consistency in your presentation.

1 Display **Slide 3**, and then select the word *Relax*. On the **Home tab**, in the **Clipboard group**, *double-click* the **Format Painter** button 🖌️, and then move your pointer anywhere into the Slide pane. Compare the pointer on your screen with the one shown in Figure 16.9.

The pointer displays with a small paintbrush attached to it, indicating that Format Painter is active.

Figure 16.9

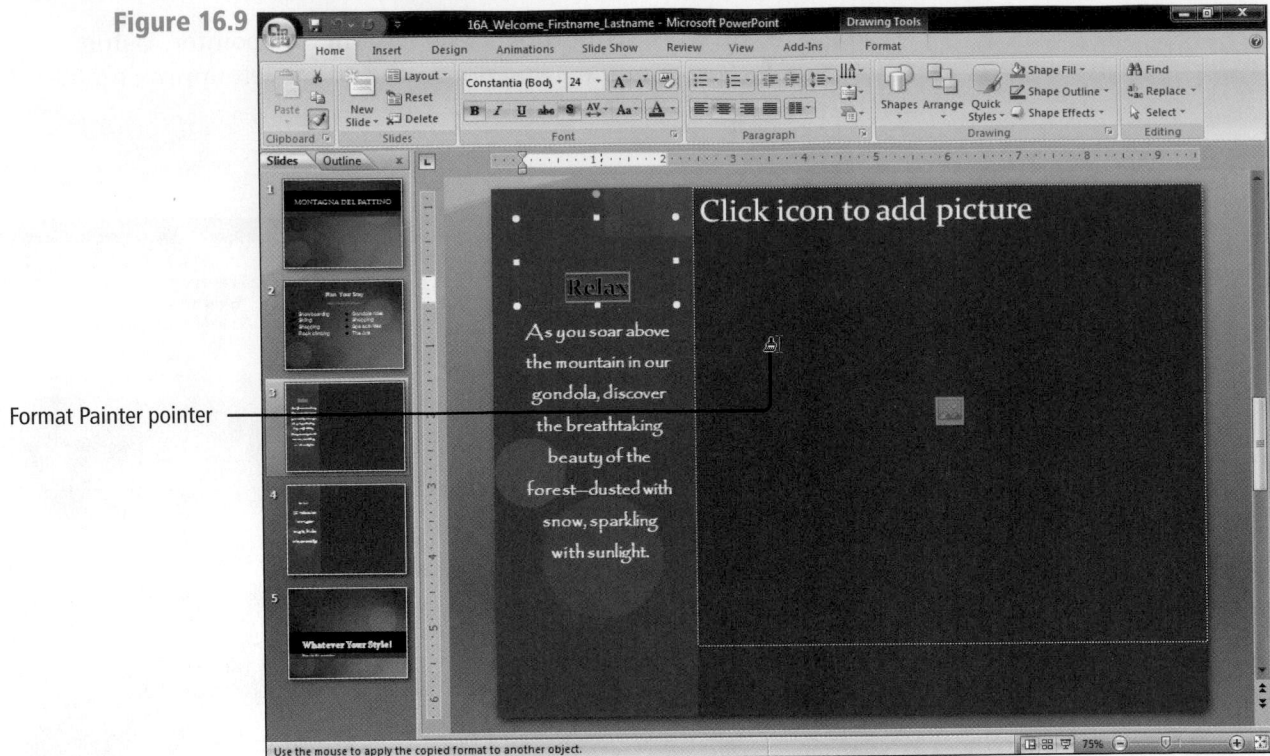

Format Painter pointer

2 In the **Slides/Outline** pane, click **Slide 4** to display it. Drag the [icon] pointer over the slide title—**Or Not!**

The WordArt formatting is applied to the title on Slide 4.

3 Display **Slide 2**. Drag the Format Painter pointer over the text **What's Your Preference?**, and then click the **Format Painter** button [icon] one time to turn off the Format Painter.

4 **Save** [icon] the presentation.

Alert!   **Were you unable to use Format Painter more than one time?**

When the Format Painter button is clicked one time instead of double-clicked, you can only use it to apply formatting to one selection. If you were only able to use Format Painter once, repeat Steps 1, 3, and 4.

Objective 2
Insert and Format Pictures and Shapes

PowerPoint 2007 provides a number of options for adding pictures and shapes to your presentation. You can draw lines, arrows, stars and banners, and a number of other basic shapes including ovals and rectangles. You can add text to a shape that you create and position it anywhere on a slide, and you can fill a shape with a picture. After you create a shape, you can add 3-D, glow, bevel effects, and shadows, or you can apply a predefined *Shape Style* that includes a combination of formatting effects.

Activity 16.06 Inserting a Picture Using a Content Layout

Many of the slide layouts in PowerPoint 2007 are designed to accommodate digital pictures that you have stored on your system or on a portable storage device.

1 Display **Slide 3**, which is formatted with the Content and Caption layout.

In the center of the large Content placeholder on the right side of the slide, the *Insert Picture from File* button displays.

2 In the center of the content placeholder, click the **Insert Picture from File** button to open the **Insert Picture** dialog box. Navigate to the location in which your student files are stored, and then double-click **p16A_Winter**. Alternatively, click p16A_Winter, and then click Insert.

The picture fills the entire placeholder.

3 Display **Slide 4**. Using the technique that you practiced in **Step 2**, insert the picture **p16A_Snowboard**, and then compare your slide with Figure 16.10.

Figure 16.10

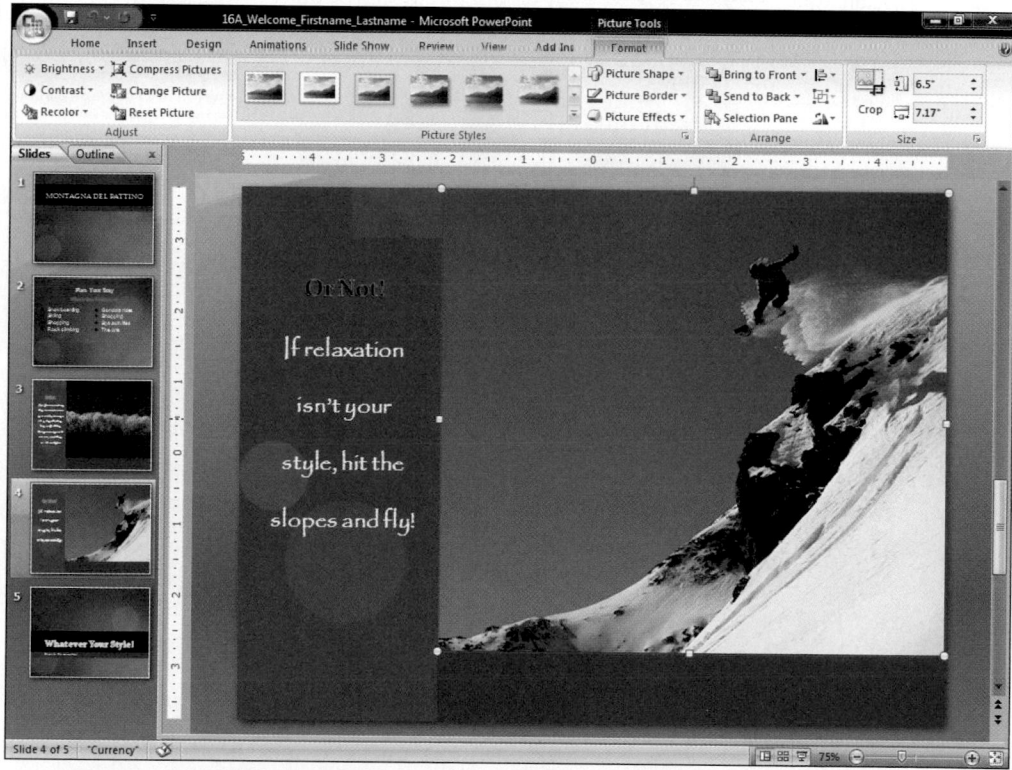

4 **Save** the presentation.

Workshop

Using Pictures Effectively in a Presentation

Large photographic images add impact to a presentation and help the audience visualize the message that you are trying to convey.

Activity 16.07 Changing the Size and Shape of a Picture

Recall that you can resize a picture by dragging the sizing handles. Alternatively, you can use the Picture contextual tools to specify a picture's height and width. You can also modify a picture by changing its shape.

1 Display **Slide 1**. Click the **Insert tab**, and then in the **Illustrations group**, click **Picture**. Navigate to the location where your student files are stored, and then double-click **p16A_Snow**.

The picture is inserted in the center of your slide and the Picture Tools contextual tab displays on the Ribbon.

2 On the **Format tab**, in the **Size group**, notice that the height of the picture is 5.34 inches and the width of the picture is 6.68 inches, as shown in Figure 16.11.

Figure 16.11

Picture height

Picture width

Inserted picture

3 On the **Format tab**, in the **Size group**, click in the **Shape Height box** so that 5.34 is selected. Type **3** and then press Enter. Notice that the height of the picture is resized to 3 inches and the width is also resized. When you change the height of a picture, the width is adjusted proportionately unless you type a new size in the Width box.

4 If necessary, select the picture. On the **Format tab**, in the **Picture Styles group**, click the **Picture Shape** button to display a gallery of shapes that you can apply to the picture. Under **Basic Shapes**, in the third row, click the third to last shape—**Cloud**.

5 Point to the picture to display the ⬚ pointer and then drag straight down so that the bottom edge of the cloud touches the bottom of the slide. Compare your slide with Figure 16.12.

Figure 16.12

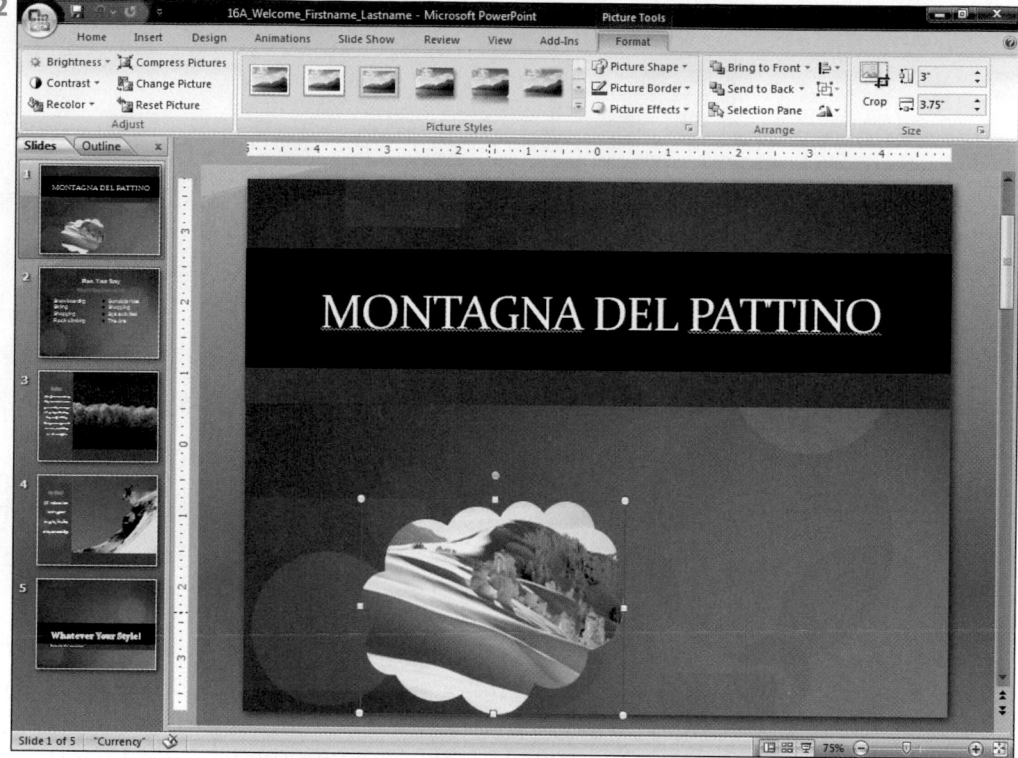

6 Save 💾 your presentation.

More Knowledge

Moving an Object by Using the Arrow Keys

You can use the directional arrow keys on your keyboard to move a picture, shape, or other object in small increments. Select the object so that its outside border displays as a solid line. Then, on your keyboard, hold down the Ctrl key and press the directional arrow keys to precisely move the selected object.

Activity 16.08 Inserting and Positioning a Text Box

The slide layouts in PowerPoint 2007 are versatile and provide a variety of options for positioning text and objects on the slide. One way that you can customize a slide layout is by adding a **text box**. A text box is an object that is used to position text anywhere on the slide. When you create a text box, the **insertion point**—a blinking vertical line that indicates where text will be inserted—displays inside the text box, indicating that you can begin to type.

1 Display **Slide 4**. Click the **Insert tab**, and then in the **Text group**, click the **Text Box** button. Move the pointer into the slide to position the pointer below the picture as shown in Figure 16.13.

Figure 16.13

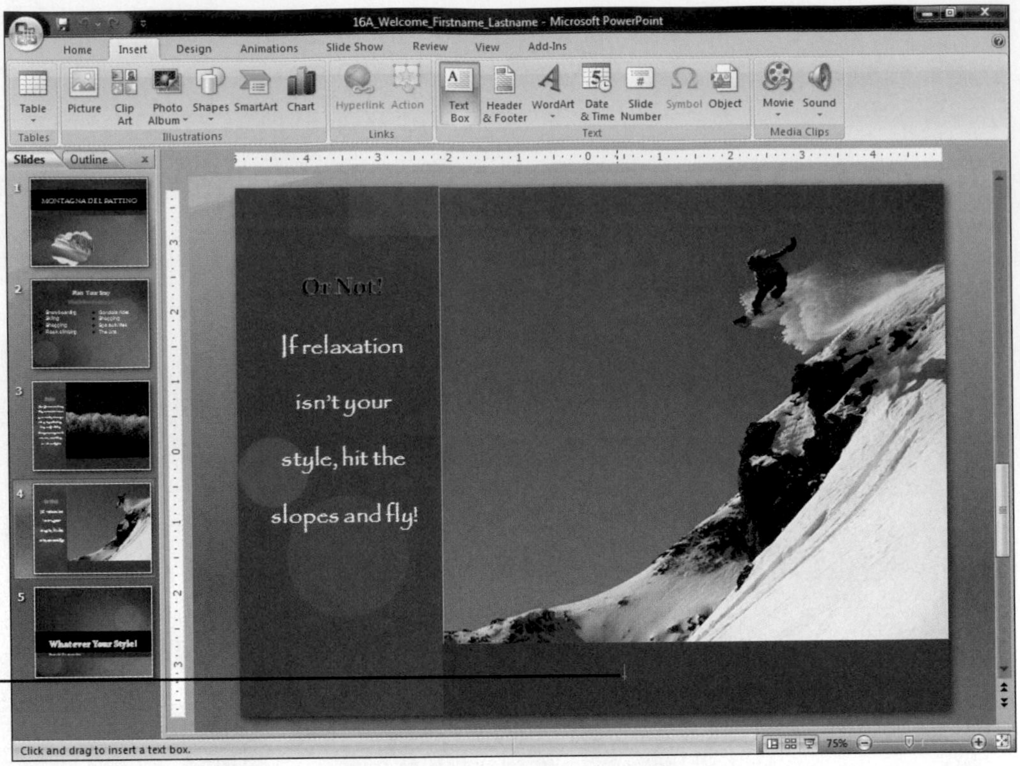

Position pointer here

2 Click to create a narrow rectangular text box. Type **Another View From Above** and notice that as you type, the width of the text box expands to accommodate the text.

Alert! **Does the text that you type in the text box display vertically, one character at a time?**

If you move the pointer when you click to create the text box, PowerPoint sets the width of the text box and does not widen to accommodate the text. If this happened to you, your text may display vertically instead of horizontally or it may display on two lines. Point to the center right sizing handle and drag to the right so that the text box is approximately 3 inches wide. When you finish typing the text, adjust the width of the text box as necessary so that all of the text displays on one line.

3 Compare your slide with Figure 16.14 and if necessary, use the pointer to adjust the size and position of the text box.

Do not be concerned if your text box does not match Figure 16.14 exactly. In a later Activity, you will practice using the Align tools to position slide elements precisely.

4 Display **Slide 3**. On the **Insert tab**, in the **Text group**, click the **Text Box** button. Click to create a text box in approximately the same position as the one that you created on Slide 4. Type **Spectacular Morning Vistas** and then click in a blank area of the slide.

Figure 16.14

Position text box here

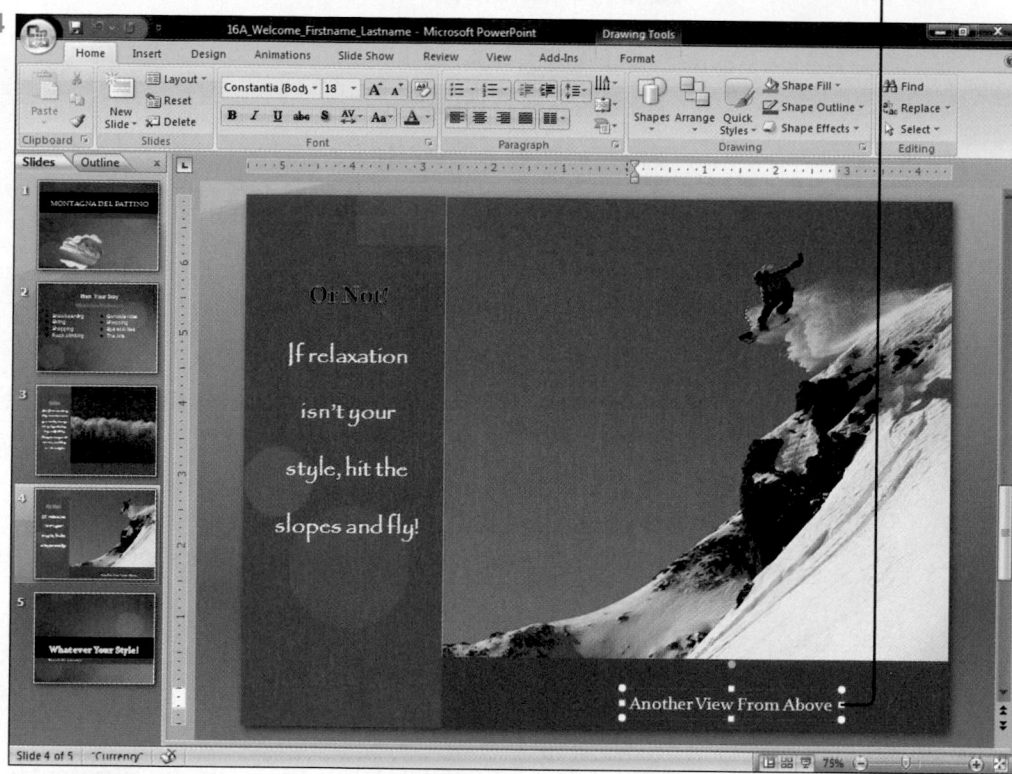

5 Compare your slide with Figure 16.15, and if necessary, re-select the text box, and use the pointer or Ctrl + any arrow key to adjust the position of the text box.

Figure 16.15

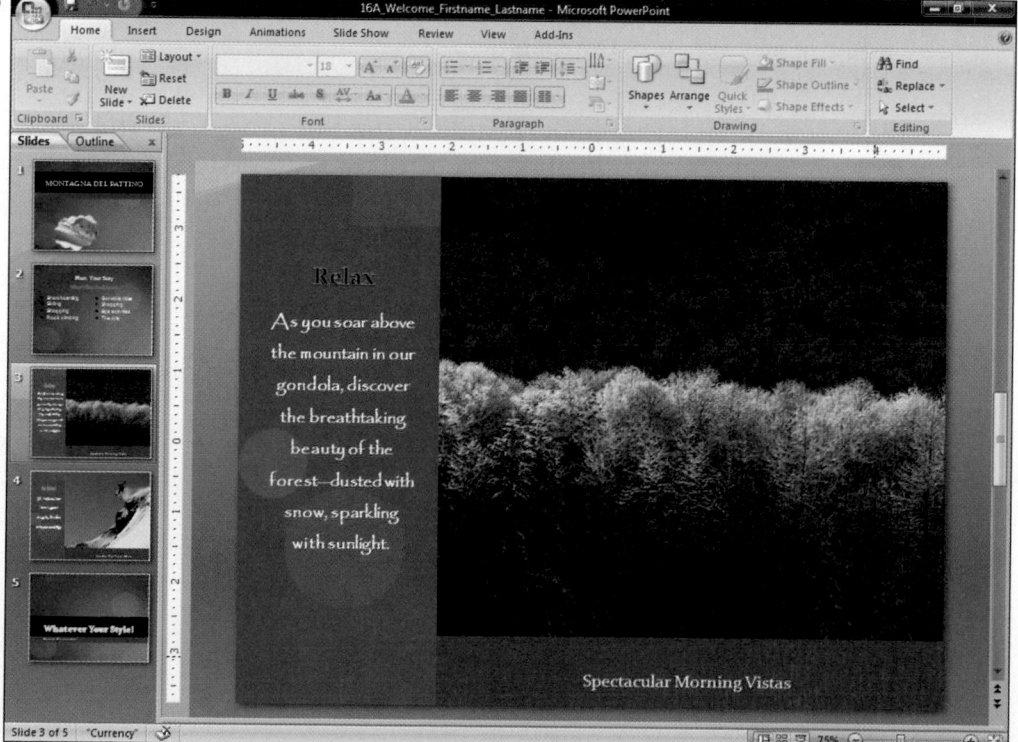

6 **Save** 💾 the presentation.

More Knowledge

Formatting a Text Box

You can format the text in a text box by using the same techniques that you use to format text in any other placeholder. For example, you can change fonts, font styles, and font sizes, and you can apply WordArt styles to the text in a text box.

Activity 16.09 Inserting, Sizing, and Positioning Shapes

Shapes can help convey your message by illustrating an idea, a process, or a workflow. You can draw lines, arrows, stars and banners, and a number of other basic shapes including ovals and rectangles. Shapes can be sized and moved by using the same techniques that you use to size and move clip art images.

1 Display **Slide 1**, and then verify that the rulers display. If the rulers do not display, on the View tab, in the Show/Hide group, select the Ruler check box.

2 Click the **Insert tab**, and then in the **Illustrations group**, click the **Shapes** button to display the **Shapes gallery**. Under **Basic Shapes**, in the first row, click the seventh shape—**Diamond**.

3 Move the pointer into the slide until the ⊞ pointer—called the *crosshair pointer*—displays, indicating that you can draw a shape.

Notice that when you move the ⊞ pointer into the slide, *guides*—vertical and horizontal lines—display in the rulers to give you a visual indication of where the pointer is positioned so that you can draw a shape.

4 Move the ⊞ pointer so that the guides are positioned at approximately **1 inch to the left of zero on the horizontal ruler** and **1 inch above zero on the vertical ruler**, as shown in Figure 16.16.

Figure 16.16

Guide on horizontal ruler

Guide on vertical ruler

Crosshair pointer

5 Hold down the left mouse button, and then drag down and to the right so that the guide displays at **1 inch to the right of zero on the horizontal ruler** and at **zero on the vertical ruler**. Release the mouse button to draw the diamond.

The Drawing Tools contextual tab displays on the Ribbon.

6 On the **Format tab**, in the **Size group**, look at the **Shape Height** ▸ 2" ◂ and **Shape Width** ▸ 2.67" ◂ boxes. If necessary, change the **Height** to **1** and the **Width** to **2** and then click on the diamond to change its size and to keep the diamond selected. Compare your slide with Figure 16.17. If necessary, use Ctrl + any arrow key to position the diamond correctly.

Figure 16.17

Shape Width is 2″

7 **Save** 💾 your presentation.

Another Way

To Insert a Shape

On the Home tab, in the Drawing group, click the Shapes button.

Activity 16.10 Adding Text to Shapes

Shapes can serve as a container for text. After you add text to a shape, you can change the font and font size, apply font styles, and change text alignment.

1 On **Slide 1**, if necessary, click the diamond so that it is selected.

Text can be typed in a shape when the shape is selected.

2 Type **Visit Today!** Notice that the text wraps to two lines and is centered.

3 Point to the left of the word *Today*, and then click so that the insertion point displays to the left of the word. Type **Us** and press Spacebar, and then click outside of the shape.

The text wraps to three lines and extends slightly outside of the diamond. The diamond shape is not large enough to accommodate the amount of text that you have typed.

4 Select the text *Visit Us Today!* On the **Home tab**, in the **Font group**, click the **Decrease Font Size** button [A▾] to change the font size to **16**. Click outside of the shape.

The text displays on two lines and fits within the diamond shape.

5 Compare your slide with Figure 16.18. **Save** [💾] the presentation.

Figure 16.18

Text displays on two lines

Activity 16.11 Applying Shape and Picture Styles and Effects

Shapes and pictures can be formatted using a variety of effects, including 3-D, glow, bevel, and shadows. These effects soften the outer edges of a shape or image. Shapes can also be formatted by changing the inside fill color and the outside line color. Predefined combinations of these styles are available in the Shape Styles, Quick Styles, and Picture Styles galleries.

1 On **Slide 1**, click to select the diamond, and then click the **Format tab**. In the **Shape Styles group**, click the **Shape Fill** button, and then point to several of the theme colors and watch as Live Preview changes the inside color of the diamond.

2 Point to **Gradient** to display the **Gradient Fill** gallery. A *gradient fill* is a color combination in which one color fades into another. Under **Dark Variations**, in the second row, click the second variant—**From Center**.

The diamond is filled with a blue gradient in which the outer points of the diamond are light and the center of the diamond is a darker color.

3 In the **Shape Styles group**, click the **Shape Outline** button, and then point to **Weight**. Click **6 pt** and notice that a thick outline surrounds the diamond.

4 With the diamond still selected, in the **Shape Styles group**, click the **Shape Effects** button. Point to **Bevel**, and then under **Bevel**, in the first row, click the last bevel—**Cool Slant**.

The Cool Slant bevel applies a 3-dimensional effect to the diamond.

5 Select the snow picture in the shape of a cloud. Click the **Format tab**, and then in the **Picture Styles group**, click **Picture Effects**. Point to **Soft Edges**, and then click the second to last effect—**25 Point** to blur and soften the edges of the picture, giving it a more cloudlike effect.

6 Click on a blank part of the slide so that none of the objects are selected, and then compare your slide with Figure 16.19.

Figure 16.19

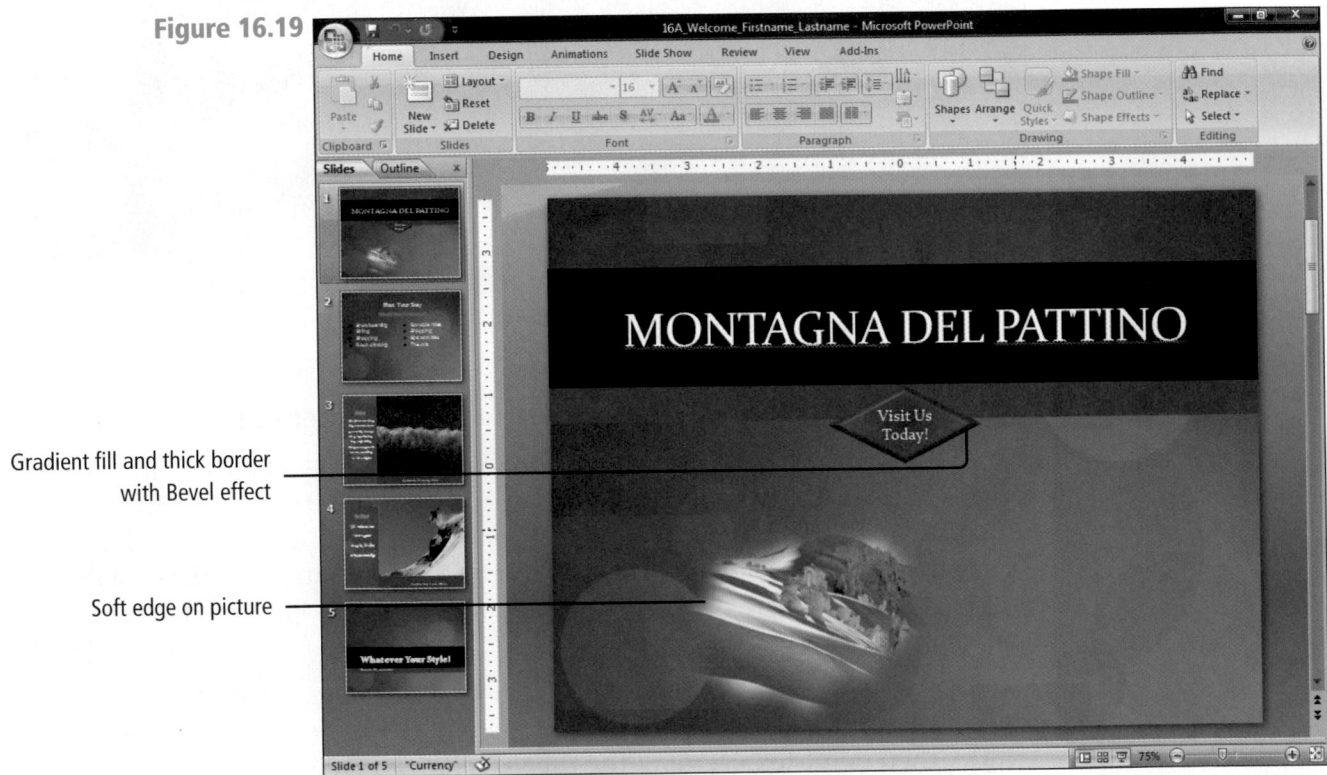

Gradient fill and thick border with Bevel effect

Soft edge on picture

7 **Save** your presentation.

More Knowledge

Applying a Quick Style or Shape Style to a Shape or Placeholder

You can format an object such as a shape, text box, or placeholder quickly by using one of the predefined Quick Styles or Shape Styles. Quick Styles and Shape Styles apply combinations of edges, shadows, line styles, gradients, and 3-D effects to the selected object. To apply a Quick Style, select the object, and then on the Home tab, click Quick Styles to display the gallery. To apply a Shape Style, select the object, and then on the Format Tab, in the Shape Styles group, click the More button to display the gallery.

Activity 16.12 Duplicating and Aligning Objects

You can duplicate an object by using a keyboard shortcut. You can align objects by dragging the object to another position on the slide or by using the Ribbon.

1 On **Slide 1**, click to select the picture. Press and hold down Ctrl, and then press D one time. Release Ctrl.

A duplicate of the picture overlaps the original picture and the duplicated image is selected.

2 Point to the duplicated image to display the pointer. Drag the duplicated image up and to the right so that its left edge overlaps the right edge of the picture, using Figure 16.20 as a guide.

Figure 16.20

Duplicated picture overlaps original picture

3 Display **Slide 2**. Click the **Insert tab**, and then in the **Illustrations group**, click the **Shapes** button to display the **Shapes gallery**.

4 Under **Block Arrows**, in the first row, click the fourth arrow—**Down Arrow**. Position the ⊞ pointer at approximately **3 inches to the left of zero on the horizontal ruler** and at **1 inch below zero on the vertical ruler**, as shown in Figure 16.21.

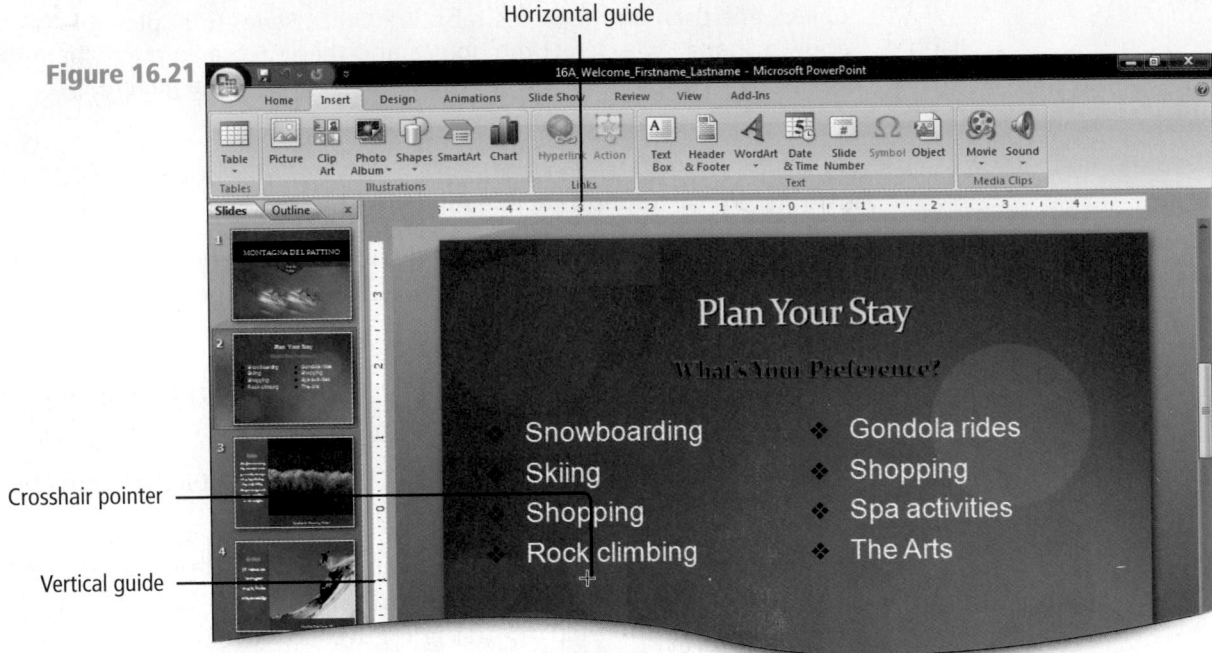

Horizontal guide

Figure 16.21

Crosshair pointer

Vertical guide

5 Drag approximately **1/2 inch to the right** and **1 inch down** to create the arrow and to display the **Drawing Tools** contextual tab. Check the size of the shape by looking at the **Format tab** in the **Size group**. If necessary, adjust the size of the arrow to a Height of 1 inch and a Width of 0.5 inch.

6 With the arrow selected, on the **Format tab**, in the **Shape Styles group**, click the **More** button ▼. In the last row, click the second effect—**Intense Effect – Accent 1**.

7 With the arrow still selected, hold down Ctrl, and then press D to duplicate the arrow. Drag the new duplicate arrow to the right so that the arrow is positioned below the text on the right of the slide at approximately **2 inches to the right of zero on the horizontal ruler**.

8 With the arrow on the right selected, hold down ⇧ Shift, and then click the arrow on the left so that both arrows are selected. Release ⇧ Shift, click the **Format tab**, and then in the **Arrange group**, click the **Align** button. Click **Align Selected Objects**.

The Align Selected Objects option aligns the objects that you select relative to each other. The Align to Slide option aligns objects with the edges of the slide determining placement.

9 On the **Format tab**, in the **Arrange group**, click the **Align** button , and then click **Align Top**.

With the two arrows selected, the lower arrow moves up so that its top edge is aligned with the top edge of the higher arrow. Thus, the tops of the two arrows are positioned at the same location on the vertical ruler. Compare your slide with Figure 16.22.

Figure 16.22

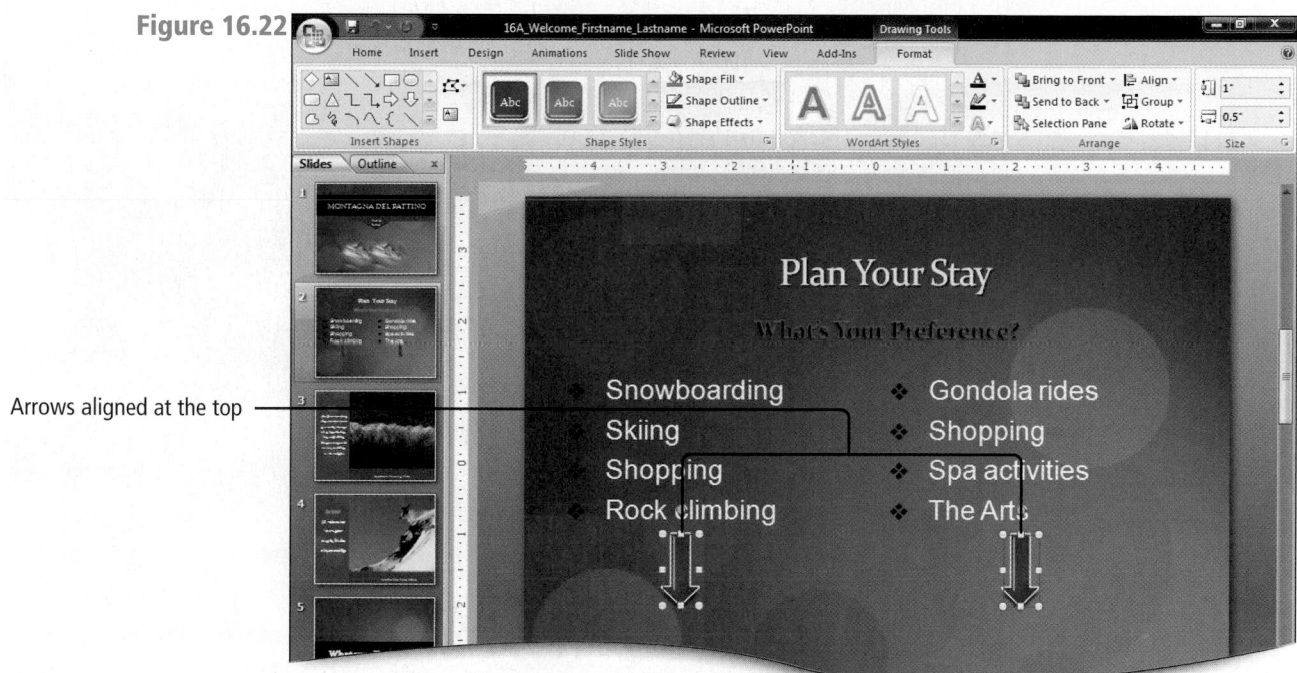

Arrows aligned at the top

10 Click the **Insert tab**, and then in the **Text group**, click **Text Box**. Position the pointer at approximately **4 inches to the left of zero on the horizontal ruler** and at **2.5 inches below zero on the vertical ruler**. Click to create a text box, type **High Energy** and then select the text that you typed. On the Mini toolbar, click the **Font Size button arrow** , and then click **32**. Click the **Center** button . If the text box does not expand to accommodate the text, use the center right sizing handle to widen the text box.

11 Click the **Format tab**, and then in the **Shape Styles group**, click the **More** button . In the last row, click the first style—**Intense Effect – Dark 1**.

12 Point to the outer edge of the text box to display the pointer and then click to select the text box. Hold down Ctrl, and then press D to duplicate the text box. Drag the duplicated textbox to the right so that it is positioned below the arrow on the right side of the slide. Select the text **High Energy**, and then type **Relaxation** to replace the text.

13 Use the ⇧Shift key to select the two text boxes—**High Energy** and **Relaxation**. On the **Format tab**, in the **Arrange group**, click the **Align** button. Click **Align Top** to align the top edges of the two text boxes, and then click anywhere on the slide so that none of the objects are selected.

14 Click the bulleted list placeholder on the left side of the slide. Press ⇧Shift and click the arrow on the left and the **High Energy** text box so that all three objects are selected, as shown in Figure 16.23.

Figure 16.23

Selected objects ————

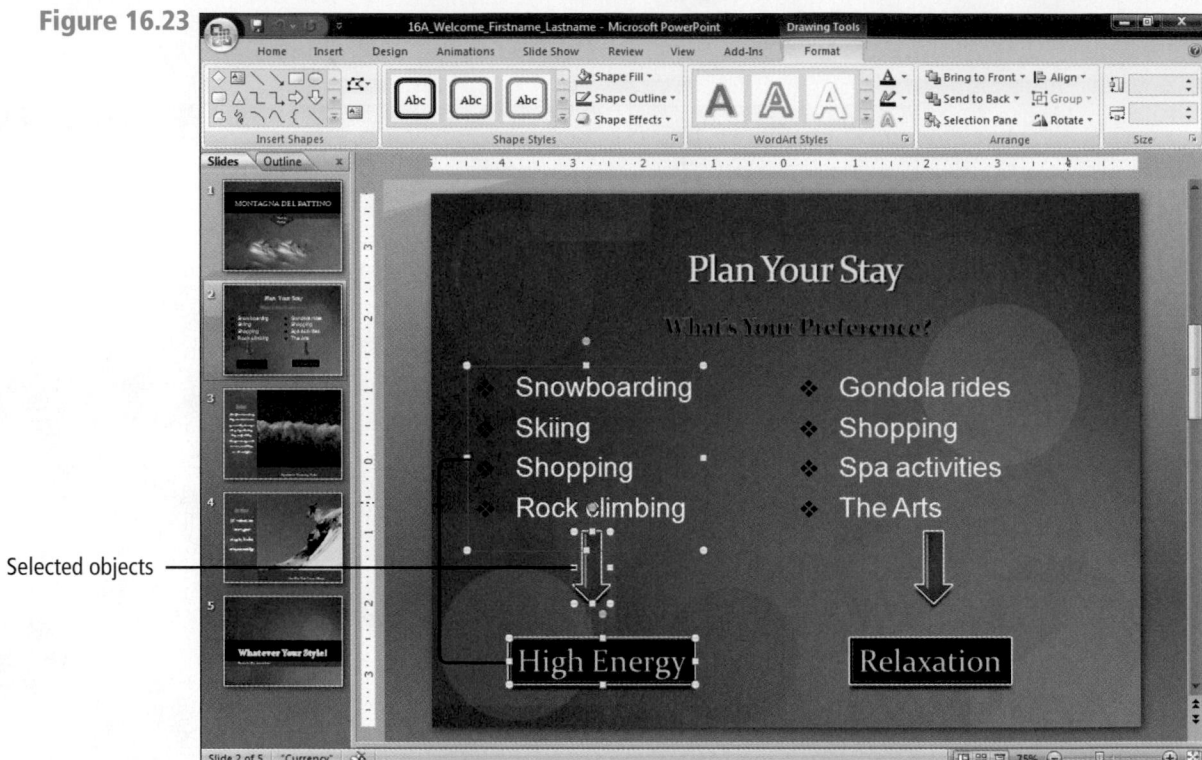

15 Release the ⇧Shift key. On the **Format tab**, in the **Arrange group**, click the **Align** button. Click **Align Selected Objects**. Click the **Align** button again, and then click **Align Center**.

The three objects are aligned at their center points.

16 Using the same procedure that you used in Steps 14 and 15, **Align Center** the placeholder, arrow, and text box on the right side of the slide.

17 **Save** 📇 the presentation.

Objective 3
Apply Slide Transitions

Recall that a slide transition controls the way that a slide appears or disappears during an onscreen slide show. For example, when one slide leaves the screen, it may fade or dissolve into another slide. You can choose from a variety of transitions, and you can control the speed and method with which the slides advance during a presentation.

Activity 16.13 Applying Slide Transitions to a Presentation

In this activity, you will add slide transitions to all of the slides in the presentation.

1 If necessary, in the **Slides/Outline pane**, click the **Slides tab** so that the slide thumbnails display. Display **Slide 1**.

2 Click the **Animations tab**. In the **Transition to This Slide group**, click the **More** button ▼ to display the **Transitions gallery** as shown in Figure 16.24.

The slide transitions are categorized in six groups—No Transition, Fades and Dissolves, Wipes, Push and Cover, Stripes and Bars, and Random. You may need to scroll the gallery in order to view all of the transitions. The pictures illustrate the type of transition and the arrows indicate the direction in which the slide moves.

Figure 16.24

Transitions gallery

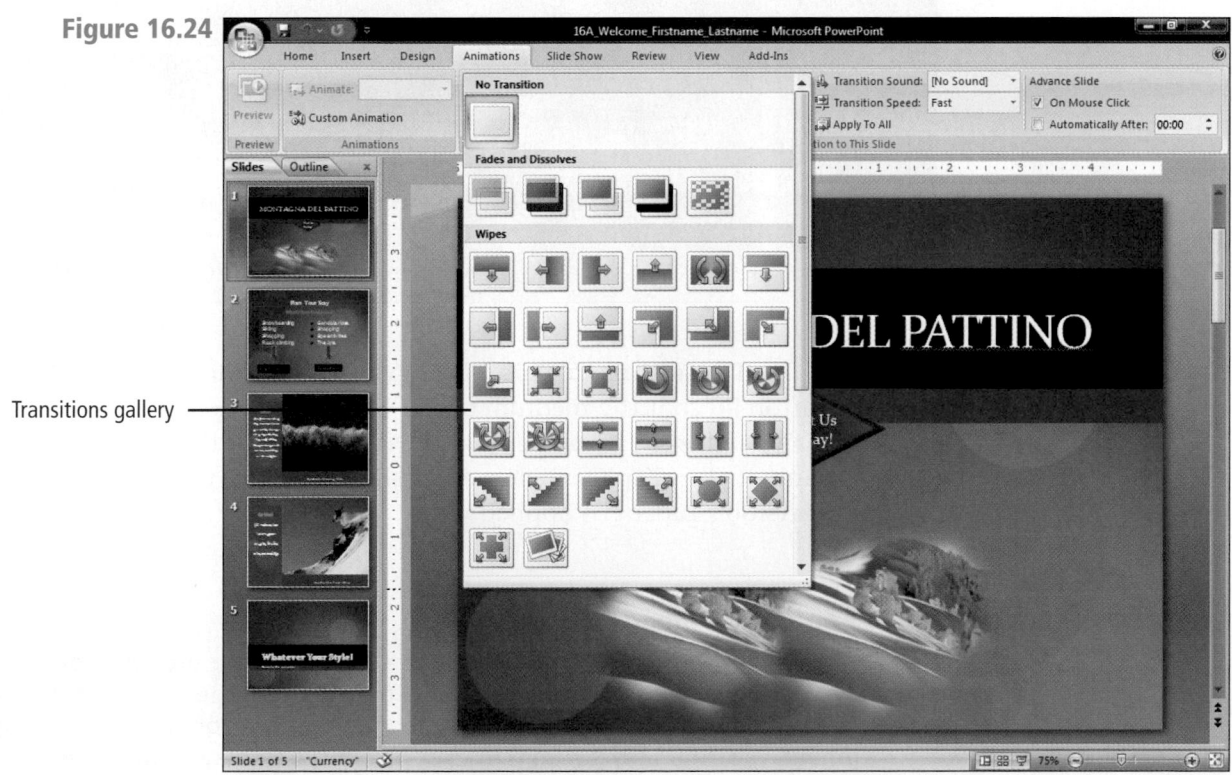

3 Point to several of the transitions to view the Live Preview of the transition effects and to display the ScreenTip with the transition name. Under **Wipes**, locate and then click the **Box Out** transition.

4 In the **Transition to This Slide group**, click the **Transition Speed arrow**, and then click **Medium**.

5 In the **Transition to This Slide group** verify that under **Advance Slide**, **On Mouse Click** is selected. If it is not, click the On Mouse Click check box, as shown in Figure 16.25.

The On Mouse Click option enables you to control when the slide will advance to the next slide. During the slide show, you can click the mouse button or press Spacebar to advance the presentation.

Figure 16.25

Medium speed

On Mouse Click selected

6 In the **Transition to This Slide group**, click the **Apply To All** button so that the medium speed Box Out transition is applied to all of the slides in the presentation. Notice that in the Slides/Outline pane, a star displays below each slide number, indicating that a transition has been applied.

Workshop

Applying Transitions

You can apply more than one type of transition in your presentation by displaying the slides one at a time, and then clicking the transition that you want to apply instead of clicking the Apply To All button. However, using too many different transitions in your presentation may distract the audience. Choose one basic transition to use on most of the slides in your presentation, and use one or two additional transitions if you feel that a particular slide would display effectively with a different transition.

7 Click the **Slide Show tab**. In the **Start Slide Show group**, click the **From Beginning** button, and then view your presentation, clicking the mouse button to advance through the slides. When the black slide displays, click the mouse button one more time to display the presentation in Normal view.

8 Create a **Header and Footer** for the **Notes and Handouts**. Include only the **Date and time updated automatically**, the **Page number**, and a **Footer** with the file name **16A_Welcome_Firstname_Lastname**

9 Check your *Chapter Assignment Sheet* or *Course Syllabus* or consult your instructor to determine if you are to submit your assignments on paper or electronically. To submit electronically, go to Step 11, and then follow the instructions provided by your instructor.

10 Display your presentation in **Print Preview**, and then print **Handouts (6 Slides Per Page)**.

11 **Save** the changes to your presentation. **Close** the presentation.

End **You have completed Project 16A** ——————————

Project 16B Itinerary

In Activities 16.14 through 16.22, you will edit a presentation that Kirstin McCarty, Director of Marketing, has created that includes itineraries and contact information for resort guests. You will move and copy text, and you will create diagrams that will illustrate different types of itineraries. Your completed presentation will look similar to Figure 16.26.

For Project 16B, you will need the following files:

p16B_Itinerary
p16B_Reservations_Director
p16B_Ski_Lodge_Director
p16B_Spa_Director
p16B_Tour_Director

You will save your presentation as
16B_Itinerary_Firstname_Lastname

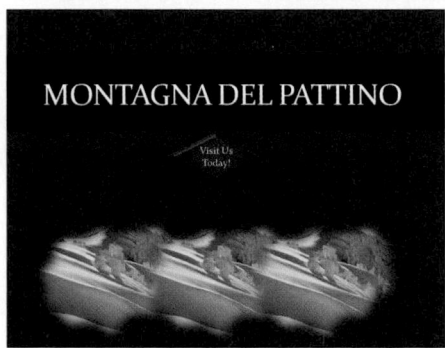

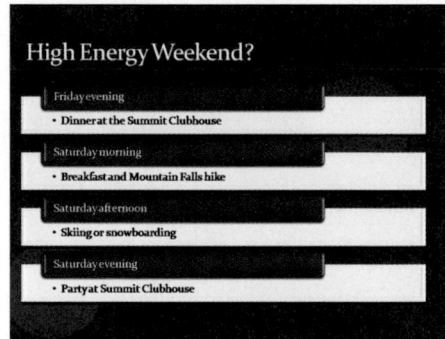

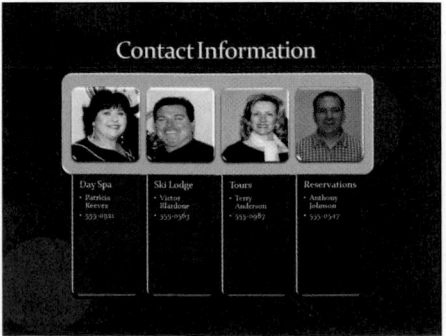

Figure 16.26
Project 16B—Itinerary

Objective 4
Reorganize Presentation Text and Clear Formats

When you select text or objects and then perform the Copy command or the Cut command, the selection is placed on the **Office Clipboard**—a temporary storage area maintained by your Microsoft Office program. From the Office Clipboard storage area, the object is available to **paste** into other locations, including other Office programs.

Activity 16.14 Moving and Copying Text

The **Cut** command removes selected text or graphics from your presentation and moves the selection to the Office Clipboard. From the Office Clipboard, the selection can be pasted to a new location. The **Copy** command duplicates a selection and places it on the Office Clipboard.

1 **Start** PowerPoint and from your student files, open **p16B_Itinerary**. **Save** the file in your **PowerPoint Chapter 16** folder as 16B_Itinerary_Firstname_Lastname

2 Display **Slide 2**, and then on the **Home tab**, in the **Slides group**, click the **New Slide arrow**. In the displayed gallery, click **Title and Content**. If you inserted a slide without displaying the gallery, on the Home tab, in the Slides group, click Layout, and then click Title and Content. In the title placeholder, type **High Energy Weekend?**

3 Display **Slide 4,** and then select all of the text in the bulleted list placeholder. On the **Home tab**, in the **Clipboard group**, click the **Copy** button 🖺. Alternatively, hold down Ctrl, and then press C.

4 Display **Slide 3**, and then click in the content placeholder. In the **Clipboard group**, click the **Paste** button to copy the selection to **Slide 3**. Alternatively, hold down Ctrl, and then press V.

Below the pasted text an additional bullet may display and notice that a button displays, as shown in Figure 16.27. This is the Paste Options button that provides three options for formatting pasted text.

Figure 16.27

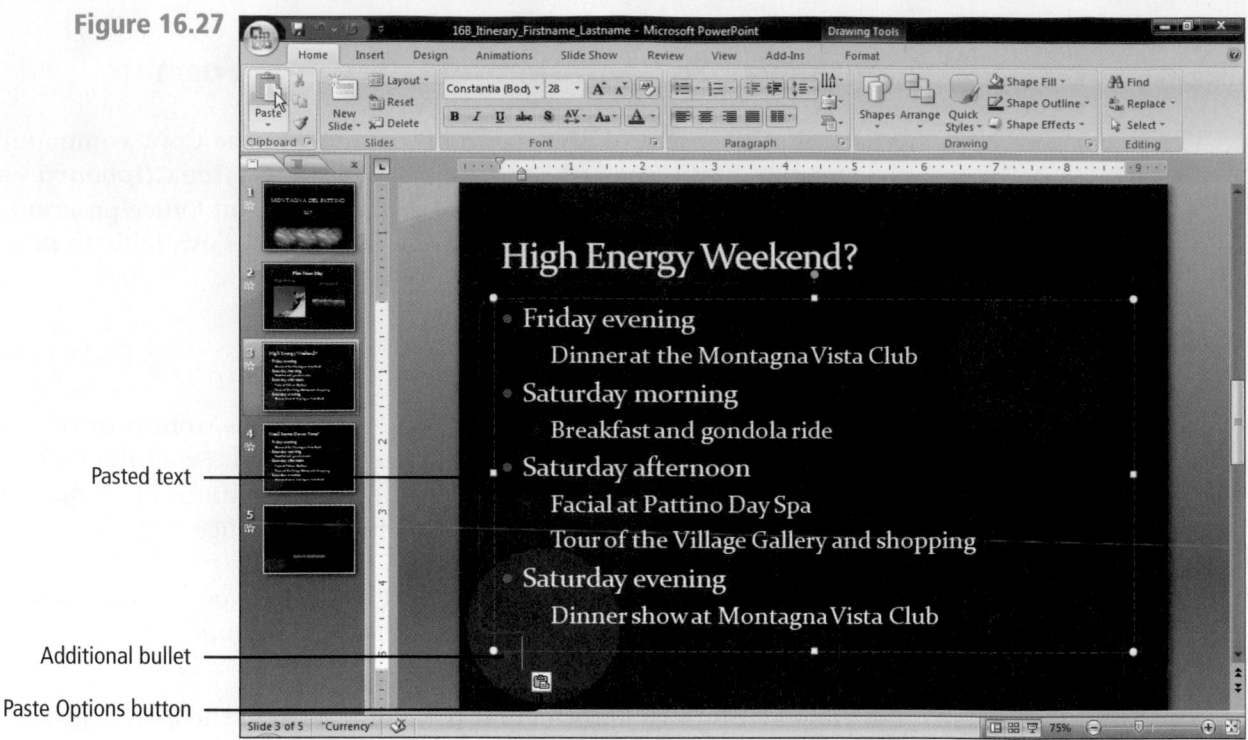

Pasted text

Additional bullet

Paste Options button

5 Point to the **Paste Options** button so that an arrow displays to its right, and then click the arrow to display the formatting options. Be sure that **Use Destination Theme** is selected so that the formatting of Slide 3 is applied to the pasted text.

Use Destination Theme applies the format of the slide to which you pasted the text to the selection, and *Keep Text Only* removes all formatting from the selection.

Note — Removing the Paste Options Button

You do not need to click the Paste Options button arrow every time you paste a selection. The default setting is *Use Destination Theme*. Thus, you need only click the arrow if you want to apply a different option. The Paste Options button will remain on the screen until you perform another action.

6 Click outside of the button menu to close it. If necessary, use ⌫Bksp or Delete to delete any extra bullets at the bottom of the pasted text. In the second bullet point, replace the text *Montagna Vista Club* with **Summit Clubhouse** In the fourth bullet point, replace *gondola ride* with **2-mile hike** Under *Saturday afternoon*, select both of the subordinate level bullet points, and then type **Skiing or snowboarding** to replace both of the selected bullet points. Select the last bullet point on the slide, and then replace it with **Party at Summit Clubhouse**

7 Click outside the content placeholder, and then compare your slide with Figure 16.28. Make spelling and layout corrections as necessary.

Figure 16.28

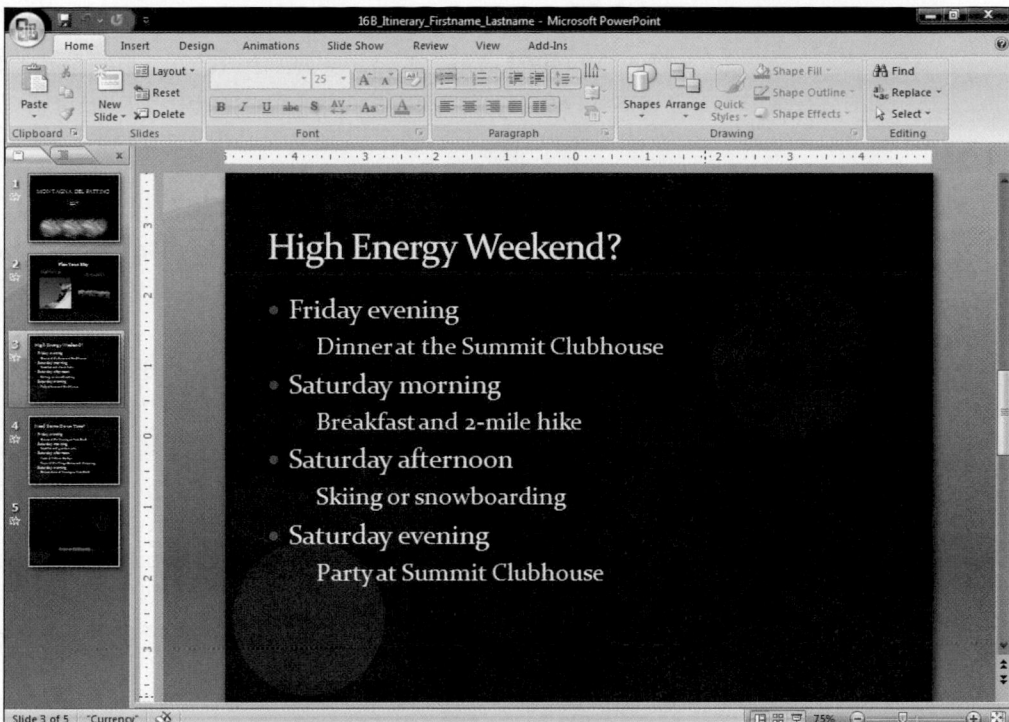

---

8 Display **Slide 2**. Click the WordArt text at the bottom of the slide—*Whatever Your Style*, and then click its dashed boundary box so that it displays as a solid line, indicating that all of the text is selected.

9 In the **Clipboard group**, click the **Cut** button ✂. Alternatively, hold down Ctrl, and then press X.

The text is removed from the slide and is stored on the Clipboard.

10 Display **Slide 5**. In the **Clipboard group**, click the **Paste** button to move the selection to the bottom of the last slide. Point to the edge of the pasted text to display the ✣ pointer, and then drag up to position the text in the center of the black rectangle.

11 **Save** 💾 the presentation.

More Knowledge

Using Drag-and-Drop Text Editing

Another method to move text is the ***drag-and-drop*** technique, which uses the mouse to drag selected text from one location to another. To use drag-and-drop text editing, select the text you want to move, and then position the pointer over the selected text to display the 🔲 pointer. Drag the text to the new location. A vertical line attached to the pointer enables you to see exactly where the text will be pasted.

Activity 16.15 Copying Multiple Selections by Using the Office Clipboard

The Office Clipboard can store up to 24 selections that you have cut or copied, and each one can be pasted multiple times. Additionally, groups of items on the Office Clipboard can be pasted all at one time.

1 Display **Slide 1**. On the **Home tab**, in the lower right corner of the **Clipboard group**, click the **Dialog Box Launcher** to display the Clipboard task pane on the left side of the PowerPoint window.

2 In the **Clipboard** task pane, check to see if any items display. Compare your screen with Figure 16.29.

When the Office Clipboard is empty, *Clipboard empty* displays in the task pane. If items have been cut or copied, they will display on the Office Clipboard. In Figure 16.29, the WordArt text that was cut in the previous Activity displays. You may or may not have items displayed on the Office Clipboard, depending upon its last use.

Figure 16.29

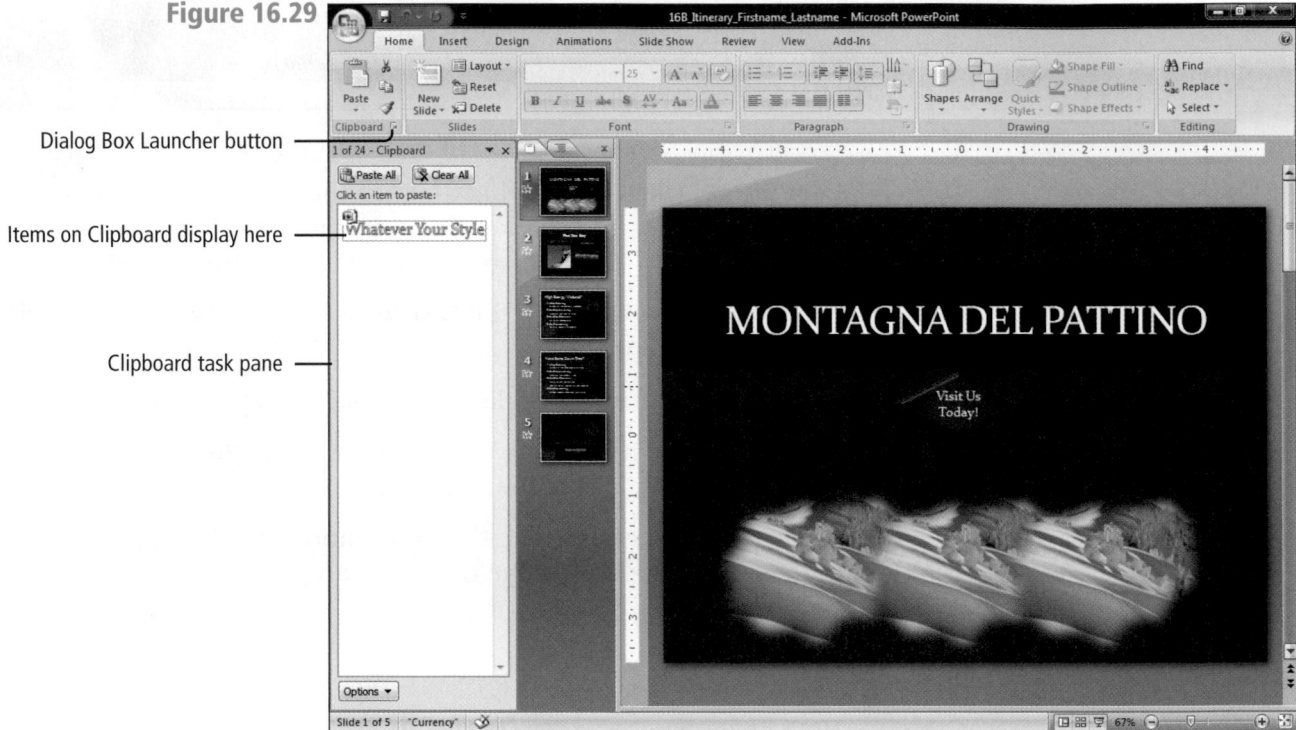

Dialog Box Launcher button

Items on Clipboard display here

Clipboard task pane

3 At the top of the **Clipboard** task pane, click the **Clear All** button to delete any items that are stored on the Office Clipboard.

4 Click in the slide title, and then click its dashed border so that it displays as a solid line. In the **Clipboard group**, click the **Copy** button, and then notice that a boxed object displays in the Clipboard task pane.

The box appears to be empty, because the text is white, and the Clipboard task pane uses a white background. Even though the letters are not visible, they are still there.

5 At the bottom of the slide, three copies of the same picture display. Click any one of the three pictures to select it. In the **Clipboard**

group, click the **Copy** button 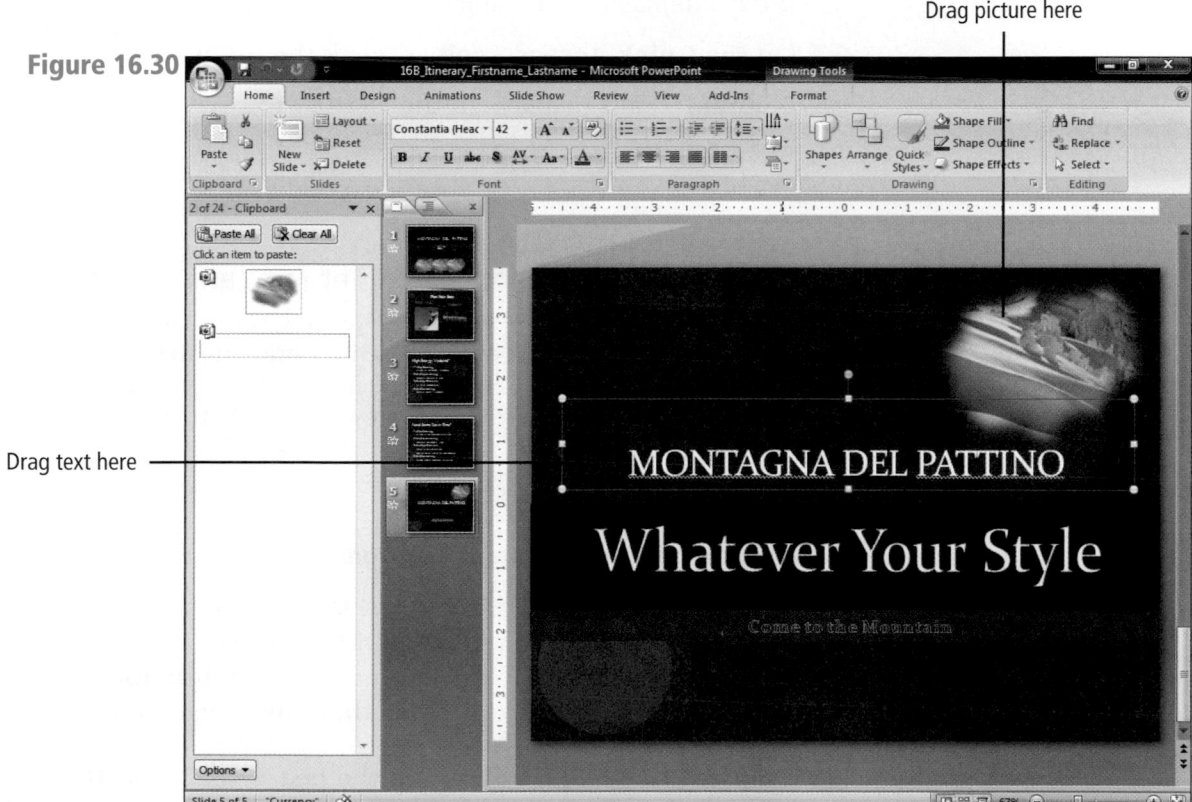, and then notice that the object displays in the Office Clipboard as the first item, and the previous item that you copied moves down.

You have collected two objects for copying.

6 Display **Slide 5**. In the **Clipboard** task pane, click **Paste All** to paste both objects to Slide 5.

The objects are pasted in the same location from which they were copied.

7 Drag the picture to the upper right corner of the slide.

8 Click the pasted text so that its dashed border displays. Point to the dashed border to display the pointer. Using Figure 16.30 as a guide, hold down ⇧ Shift, and then drag the pasted text down approximately one inch.

Pressing ⇧ Shift while dragging constrains the textbox so that it does not move off center, thus allowing for precision placement.

Drag picture here

Figure 16.30

Drag text here

9 In the **Clipboard** task pane, click the **Clear All** button to delete the two selections from the Office Clipboard. **Close** X the task pane.

10 **Save** the presentation.

More Knowledge

Pasting and Deleting Single Items from the Office Clipboard

When you point to an item on the Office Clipboard, a down arrow displays to its right. Click the arrow to display a menu with two options—Paste and Delete. You can paste and delete individual items from the Office Clipboard using this menu.

Activity 16.16 Undoing and Redoing Changes

PowerPoint remembers each change that you make so that you can undo them if you change your mind or perform an action by mistake. You can change your mind again and reverse an undo by using the Redo command.

1 Display **Slide 3**. In the fourth bullet point, select the words *2-mile*, and then type **Mountain Falls** to replace the selected words.

2 On the **Quick Access toolbar**, click the **Undo** button.

2-mile displays on the slide.

3 On the **Quick Access Toolbar**, click the **Redo** button.

Mountain Falls displays in the slide.

4 **Save** the presentation.

Alert!

Did you repeat an action instead of redo an action?

The Redo button is context-sensitive—it changes depending upon the action that you have performed. Before you click Undo, the Redo button displays as the Repeat button. Recall that the Repeat button repeats the last command or keystroke. In order to activate the Redo button, you must first Undo a command.

Activity 16.17 Clearing Formatting from a Selection

After applying multiple formats to a selection of text, you may decide that the selection is best displayed without the formats that you applied. You can clear formatting from a selection and return it to its default font and font size, and you can remove styles that have been applied.

1 Display **Slide 5** and notice that the text *Come to the Mountain* does not display well against the background.

2 Select *Come to the Mountain*, and then on the **Home tab**, in the **Font group**, click the **Clear All Formatting** button, and then click in a blank area of the slide.

The text is restored to its original formatting and contrasts with the background, making it easier to read.

3 **Save** the presentation.

Creating Contrast on a Slide

Contrast is an important element of slide design because it helps in distinguishing text and objects from the slide background. Be sure that the font color that you choose contrasts with the background so that your audience can easily read the text. For example, if your background is dark, choose a light-colored font. If your background is light, choose a dark-colored font.

Objective 5
Create and Format a SmartArt Graphic

A *SmartArt graphic* is a designer-quality visual representation of information that you can create by choosing from among many different layouts to communicate your message or ideas effectively. SmartArt graphics can illustrate processes, hierarchies, cycles, lists, and relationships. You can include text and pictures in a SmartArt graphic, and you can apply colors, effects, and styles that coordinate with the presentation theme.

Activity 16.18 Creating a SmartArt Diagram by Using a Content Layout

When you create a SmartArt graphic, it is a good idea when choosing a layout to consider the message that you are trying to convey. Large amounts of text can make some types of SmartArt graphics difficult to read so keep that in mind when choosing a layout. The table in Figure 16.31 describes types of SmartArt layouts and suggested purposes.

Microsoft PowerPoint SmartArt Graphic Types

Graphic Type	Purpose of Graphic
List	Show nonsequential information.
Process	Show steps in a process or timeline.
Cycle	Show a continual process.
Hierarchy	Show a decision tree or display an organization chart.
Relationship	Illustrate connections.
Matrix	Show how parts relate to a whole.
Pyramid	Show proportional relationships with the largest component on the top or bottom.

Figure 16.31

1 Display **Slide 4**, and then on the **Home tab**, in the **Slides group**, click the **New Slide** button to add a slide with the **Title and Content** layout. In the title placeholder, type **Contact Information** and then **Center** ⬛ the title. Notice that in addition to adding text to this slide, you can insert a SmartArt graphic by clicking the Insert SmartArt Graphic button ⬛ in the center of the slide, as shown in Figure 16.32.

Figure 16.32

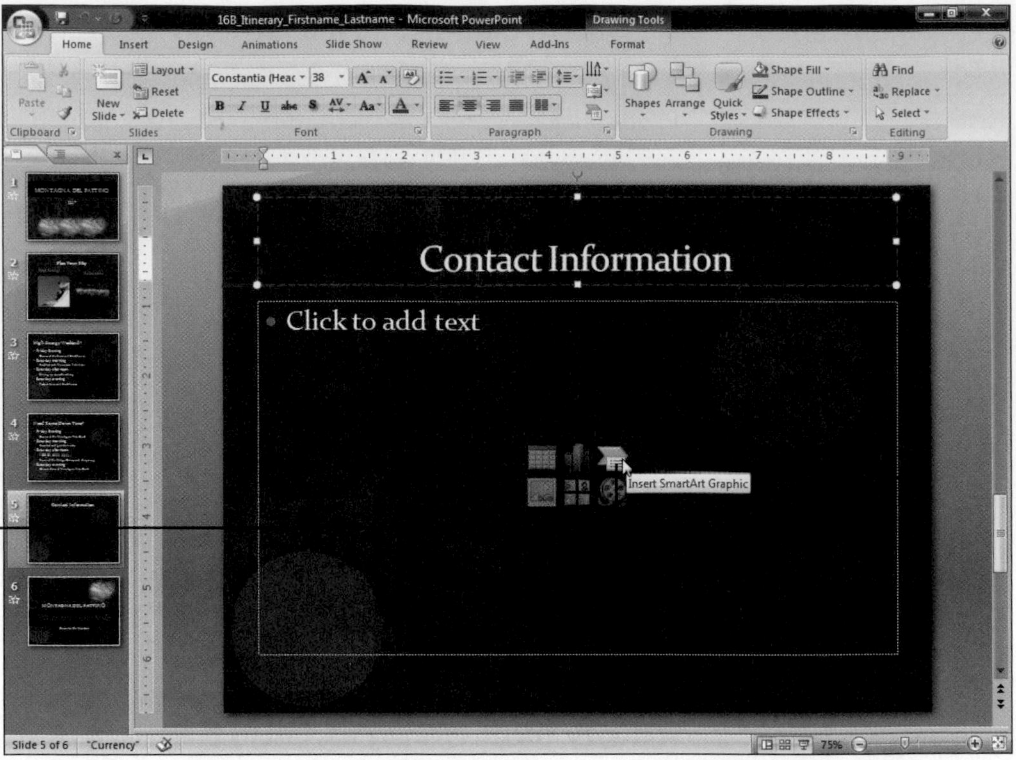

Insert SmartArt Graphic button

2 In the center of the slide, click the **Insert SmartArt Graphic**

button ⊞ to open the **Choose a SmartArt Graphic** dialog box.

The dialog box is divided into three sections. The left section lists the diagram types. The center section displays the diagrams according to type. The third section displays the selected diagram, its name, and a description of its purpose and how text displays.

Another Way

To Insert a SmartArt Graphic

On the Insert tab, in the Illustrations group, click the SmartArt button.

3 Explore the types of diagrams available by clicking on several and reading their descriptions. Then, on the left side of the **Choose a SmartArt Graphic** dialog box, click **Hierarchy**. In the center section in the second row, click the last diagram—**Hierarchy List**—and then click **OK** to create a hierarchical diagram surrounded by a thick border, indicating the area that the diagram will cover on the slide. Notice that on the Ribbon, the SmartArt contextual tools display two tabs—Design and Format, as shown in Figure 16.33.

The hierarchical diagram displays with two upper level shapes and two subordinate level shapes under each upper level shape. You will use the upper level shapes to enter the resort areas that customers frequently call, and the lower level shapes to enter the contact person's name and phone number. You can type text directly into the shapes or you can type text in the Text pane. The Text pane is displayed by clicking the Text pane tab on the left side of the SmartArt graphic border. Depending on your software settings, the Text pane may be displayed.

SmartArt
Design and Format tabs

Figure 16.33

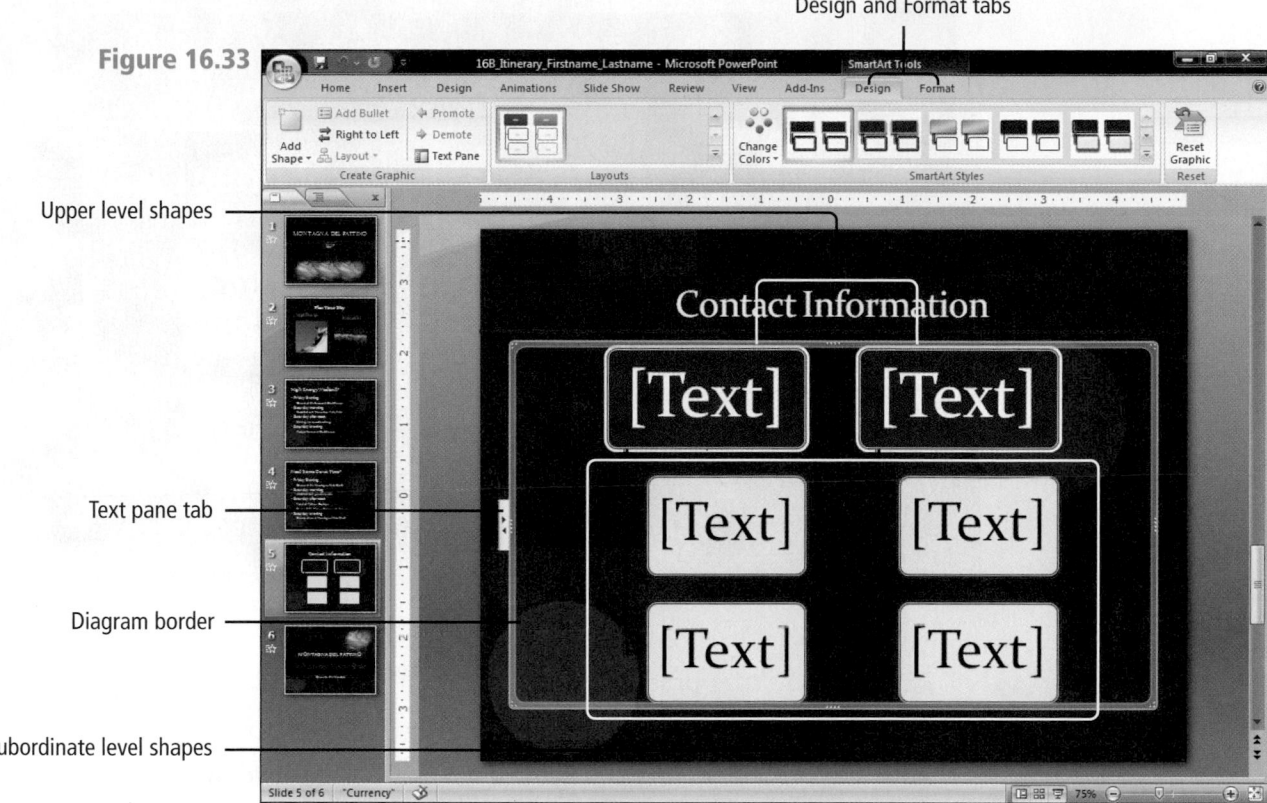

Upper level shapes

Text pane tab

Diagram border

Subordinate level shapes

Note — Displaying and Closing the Text Pane

On the Ribbon, in the SmartArt Tools group, click the Design tab. In the Create Graphic group, click the Text pane button to toggle the Text pane on and off.

4 In the diagram, click in the dark red box on the left, and then type **Day Spa** Click in the box below it, and then type **Patricia Reeves** Click in the box below Patricia's name, and then type **555-0921**

The text is resized and when necessary, wraps to two lines in order to fit into each shape. When text is typed into additional shapes, the text in all shapes at the same level adjusts to the same size.

5 On the right side of the diagram, enter the following information in the boxes, and then click in a blank area of the slide. Compare your slide with Figure 16.34.

Ski Lodge

Victor Blardone

555-0563

Figure 16.34

[6] **Save** 💾 the presentation.

Activity 16.19 Adding and Removing Shapes in a Diagram

If a diagram does not have enough shapes to illustrate a concept or display the relationships, you can add more shapes.

[1] Click in the shape that contains the text *Ski Lodge*. In the SmartArt Tools, click the **Design tab**. In the **Create Graphic group**, click the **Add Shape arrow**, and then click **Add Shape After** to insert an upper level shape to the right of the *Ski Lodge* shape. Type **Tours**

Alert! | **Did you add a shape below the Ski Lodge shape?**

If you clicked the Add Shape button instead of the arrow, the new shape displays below the phone number shape. Click Undo to delete the shape, and then repeat Step 1, being sure to click the Add Shape arrow.

[2] On the **Design tab**, in the **Create Graphic group**, click the **Add Shape** button.

When an upper level shape is selected and the Add Shape button is clicked, a lower level shape is added.

[3] Type **Terry Anderson** and then click the **Add Shape** button. Type **555-0987** and then click the **Add Shape** button.

An additional shape is added below the phone number. You can promote the shape so that it is at the same level as the Day Spa, Ski lodge, and Tours shapes.

4 On the **Design tab**, in the **Create Graphic group**, click the **Promote** button to create a fourth, upper level shape. Type **Reservations** and notice that the text in all of the upper level shapes is resized. Add a shape, type **Anthony Johnson** and then add one more shape, and then type **555-0547**

5 On the **Design tab**, in the **Create Graphic group**, click the **Add Shape** button to create an extra shape below Anthony Johnson's phone number.

6 Press Delete to delete the shape, and then click on a blank area of the slide. Compare your slide with Figure 16.35.

Figure 16.35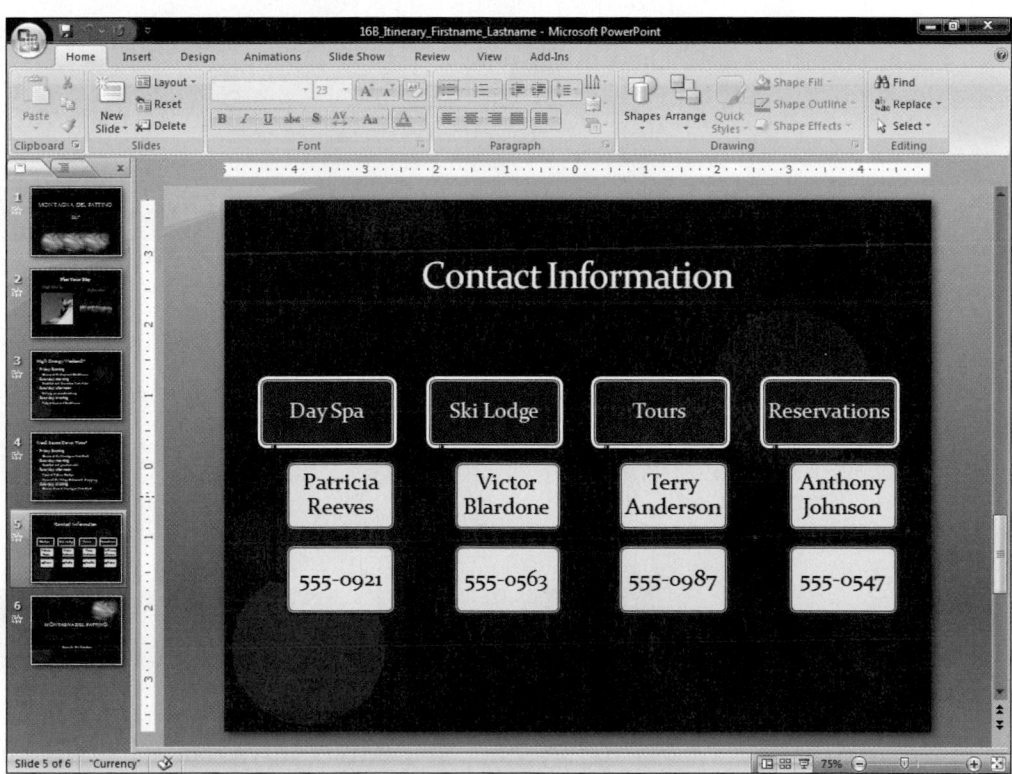

7 **Save** the presentation.

More Knowledge

Deleting Shapes that Contain Text

To delete a shape that contains text, you must click its border. If you click the shape without clicking the border, you will delete text instead of the shape. When you delete an upper level shape that has subordinate shapes with text, the first subordinate shape is promoted to an upper level shape.

Activity 16.20 Changing the Diagram Type and Size

When you are creating a diagram, remember that it is important to choose the layout and type that provides the best visual representation of your information. In this Activity, you will change the diagram type to one that includes placeholders for pictures of each contact person.

1 Click anywhere in the diagram. In the SmartArt Tools, click the **Design tab**. In the **Layouts group**, click the **More** button ⬇, and then click **More Layouts** to display the **Choose a SmartArt Graphic** dialog box.

2 On the left side of the dialog box, click **List**, and then click **Horizontal Picture List**, as shown in Figure 16.36. Click **OK**.

The diagram is converted and contains shapes at the top of each group to insert pictures.

Figure 16.36

Horizontal Picture List

3 In the shape above the *Day Spa* information, click the **Insert Picture From File** button 🖼. Navigate to the location where your student files are stored, and then double-click **p16B_Spa_Director** to insert the picture of Patricia Reeves. Repeat this process in each of the three remaining shapes by inserting the files **p16B_Ski_Lodge_Director**, **p16B_Tour_Director**, and **p16B_Reservations_Director**.

Alert! | **Did you move a shape when inserting a picture?**

If you move the mouse when you click the Insert Picture from File button in one of the diagram shapes, the shape may move. If this happens, click the Undo button to reposition the shape. Then, click the Picture button, making sure that you hold the mouse steady.

4 Notice that the shapes of that contain the pictures are wider than they are long, and thus distort the pictures. You can adjust the size of all of the pictures at one time by sizing the SmartArt graphic.

5 The border surrounding a diagram contains sizing handles in the shape of three small circles in the corners and at the center of each side. You can use these sizing handles to size the diagram. Point to the center-right sizing handle to display the ⟷ pointer, as shown in Figure 16.37.

Figure 16.37

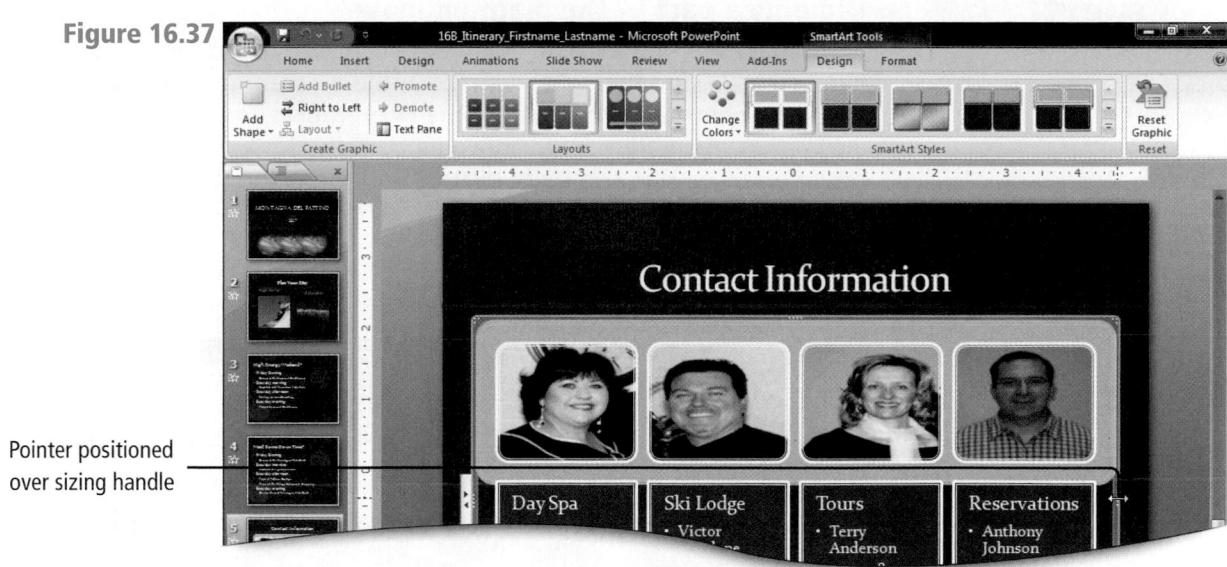

Pointer positioned over sizing handle

6 Hold down the mouse button and drag to the left, noticing that as you do so the ➕ pointer displays, as does a semi-transparent rectangle that indicates the size of the SmartArt graphic. Continue to drag to the left until the pointer and semi-transparent rectangle display between the Tours and Reservations shapes, as shown in Figure 16.38. Release the mouse button to size the diagram.

Figure 16.38

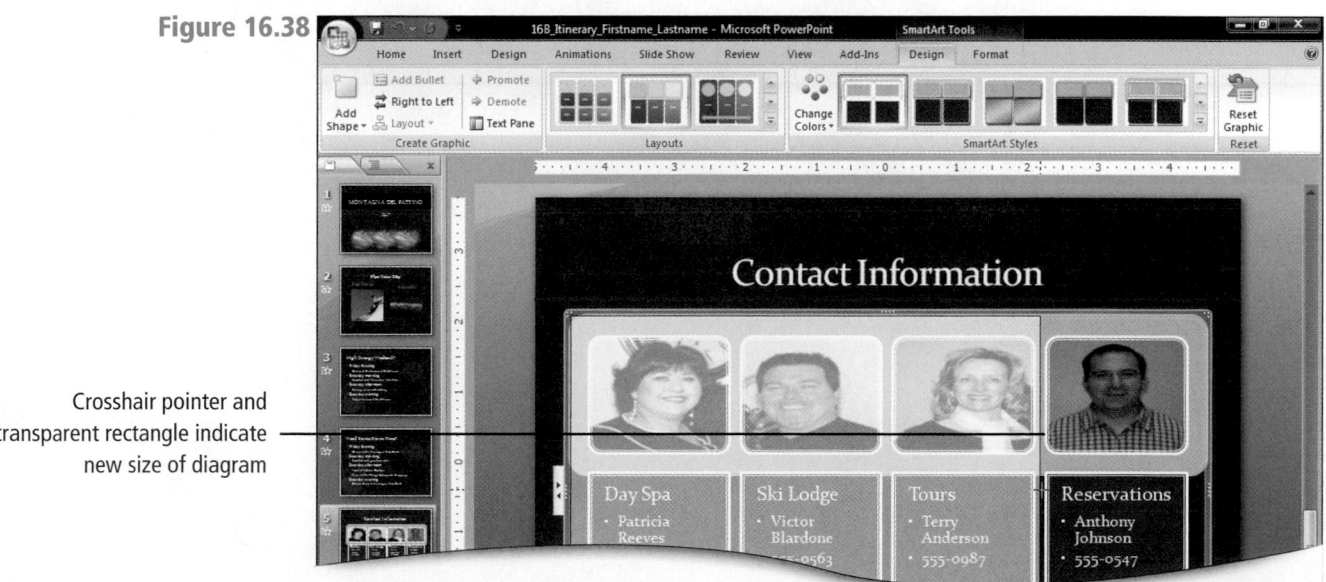

Crosshair pointer and transparent rectangle indicate new size of diagram

7 Point to the border surrounding the diagram to display the ⬚ pointer, and then drag to the right to center the diagram.

8 Compare your slide with Figure 16.39, and then **Save** 💾 your presentation.

Alert!

Did only a part of the diagram move?

Individual parts of a SmartArt diagram, such as text and picture shapes, can be moved. Be sure that when you move the diagram that you are pointing to the border that surrounds the SmartArt graphic and not to an individual element. If you inadvertently moved a portion of the diagram instead of the entire diagram, click the Undo button, and then repeat step 7.

Figure 16.39

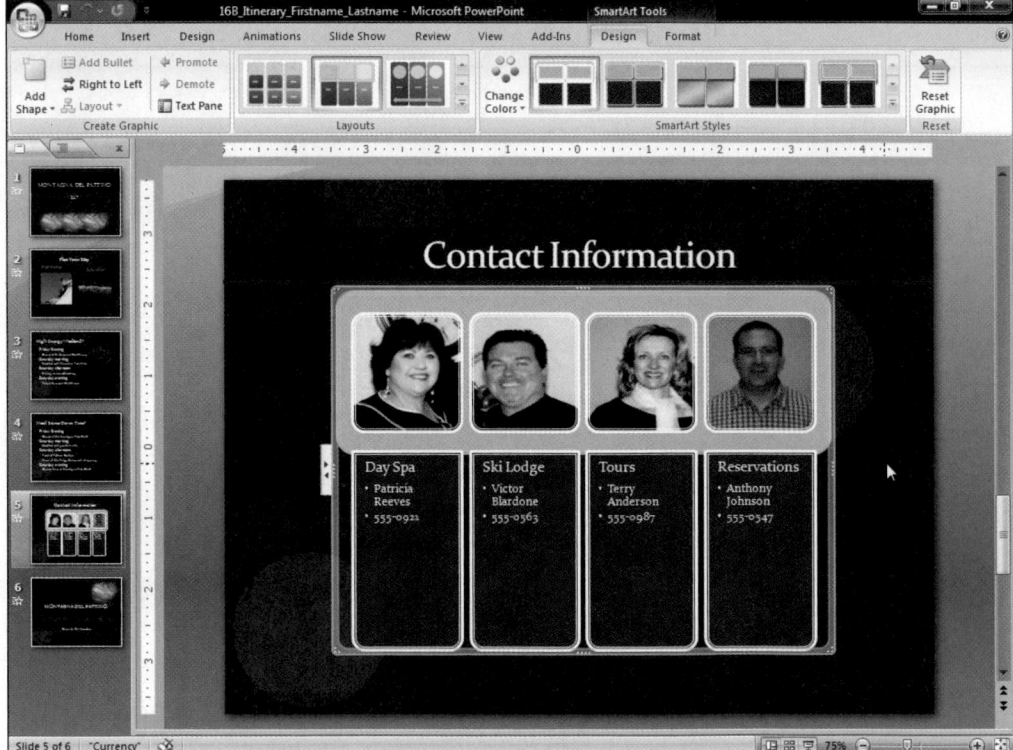

Activity 16.21 Creating a SmartArt Diagram from Bullet Points

You can convert an existing bulleted list into a SmartArt diagram. In this Activity, you will convert the bulleted lists on Slides 3 and 4 to list diagrams.

1 Display **Slide 3**. Right-click anywhere in the bulleted list placeholder to display the shortcut menu. Point to **Convert to SmartArt**, and at the bottom of the gallery, click **More SmartArt Graphics**.

2 In the **Choose a SmartArt Graphic** dialog box, click **List**, and then in the first row, point to each SmartArt graphic so that the ScreenTips display, and then click **Vertical Box List**. Click **OK**.

The entire bulleted list is converted to a diagram. It is not necessary to select all of the text in the bulleted list. By clicking in the list, PowerPoint converts all of the bullet points to the selected diagram.

3 Display **Slide 4**, and then click anywhere in the bulleted list placeholder. On the **Home tab**, in the **Paragraph group**, click the **Convert to SmartArt Graphic** button. At the bottom of the gallery, click **More SmartArt Graphics**. In the **Choose a SmartArt Graphic** dialog box, click **List**, and then use the ScreenTips to locate **Vertical Block List**. Click **Vertical Block List**, and then click **OK** to convert the bulleted list to a SmartArt graphic.

4 **Save** the presentation.

Activity 16.22 Changing the Color and Style of a Diagram

SmartArt Styles are combinations of formatting effects that you can apply to diagrams. If you change the layout of a diagram, the SmartArt Style is applied to the new layout, as are any color changes that you have made.

1 Display **Slide 5** and click on the diagram. Click the **Design tab**. In the **SmartArt Styles group**, click the **Change Colors** button to display the color gallery.

The colors that display are coordinated with the presentation theme.

2 Under **Accent 1**, click the last style—**Transparent Gradient Range - Accent 1**—to change the color scheme of the diagram.

3 On the **Design tab**, in the **SmartArt Styles group**, click the **More** button to display the **SmartArt Styles gallery**. Point to several of the styles to display the Live Preview of their effects on the diagram. Then, under **3-D**, in the first row, click the first style—**Polished**. Click in a blank area of the slide, and then compare your slide with Figure 16.40.

Figure 16.40

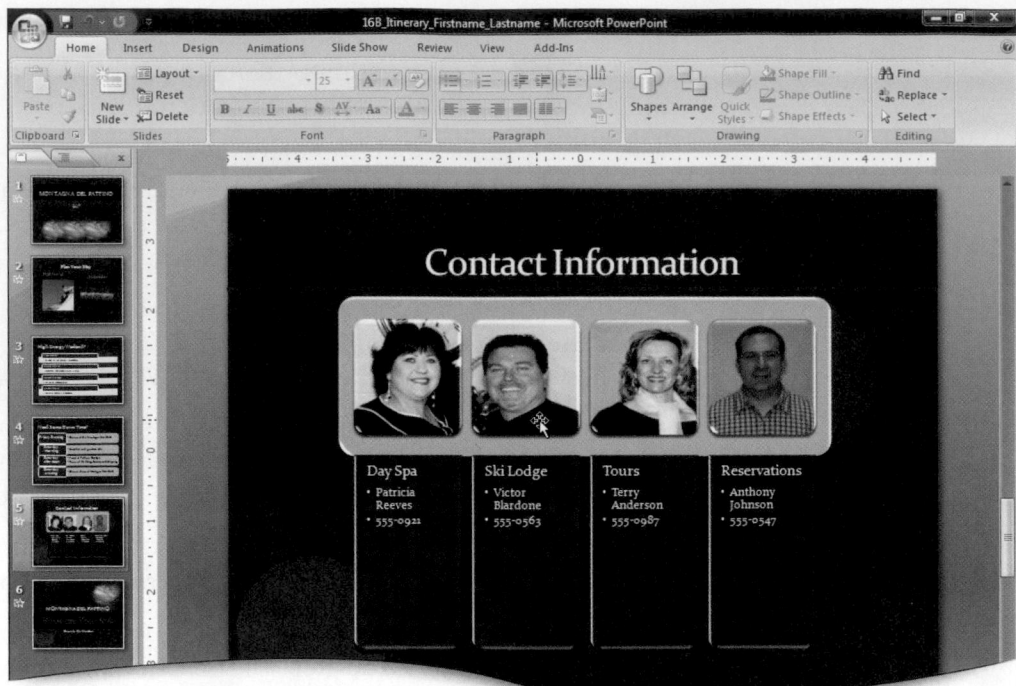

4 Display **Slide 3** and click on the diagram. Click the **Design tab**.

In the **SmartArt Styles group**, click the **More** button ▼ to display the **SmartArt Styles gallery**. Under **3-D**, in the first row, click the second style—**Inset**.

5 Display **Slide 4**. Using the same technique that you used in Step 4, under **Best Match for Document** apply the last style—**Intense Effect**.

6 Click the **Slide Show tab**. In the **Start Slide Show group**, click **From Beginning**, and then view your presentation, clicking the mouse button to advance through the slides. When the black slide displays, click the mouse button one more time to display the presentation in Normal view.

7 Create a **Header and Footer** for the **Notes and Handouts**. Include only the **Date and time updated automatically**, the **Page number**, and a **Footer** with the file name **16B_Itinerary_Firstname_Lastname**

8 Check your *Chapter Assignment Sheet* or *Course Syllabus* or consult your instructor to determine if you are to submit your assignments on paper or electronically. To submit electronically, go to Step 10, and then follow the instructions provided by your instructor.

9 Display your presentation in **Print Preview**, and then print **Handouts (6 Slides Per Page)**.

10 **Save** the changes to your presentation, and then **Close** the presentation.

 **You have completed Project 16B**

 **There's More You Can Do!**

Close PowerPoint and any other open windows. Display the Start menu, click Computer, and then navigate to the student files that accompany this textbook. In the folder **02_theres_more_you_can_do**, locate and open the folder for this chapter. Open and print the instructions for this project, which are provided to you in Adobe PDF format.

Try IT! 1—Prepare a Presentation for Remote Delivery

In this Try It! exercise, you will prepare a presentation for remote delivery by compressing images and packaging the presentation for CD.

Content-Based Assessments

Summary

In this chapter, you formatted a presentation by changing the bullet style and by applying WordArt styles to text. You copied formatting by using Format Painter and you also copied text and objects using the Office Clipboard. You enhanced your presentations by inserting, sizing, and formatting shapes, pictures, and SmartArt diagrams. You gave your presentation a finished look by applying transitions to your slides, resulting in a professional-looking presentation.

Key Terms

Copy 1023	**Gradient fill** 1013	**Shape Style** 1004
Crosshair pointer ..1010	**Guides** 1010	**SmartArt graphic** ..1029
Cut 1023	**Insertion point** 1007	**SmartArt Styles** 1037
Drag-and-drop 1025	**Office Clipboard** 1023	**Text box** 1007
Fill color 1001	**Paste** 1023	**WordArt** 1001
Format Painter 1003	**Shapes** 1010	

Content-Based Assessments

chapter sixteen

Matching

Match each term in the second column with its correct definition in the first column. Write the letter of the term on the blank line in front of the correct definition.

_____ **1.** A feature that applies combinations of decorative formatting to text, including shadows, reflections, and 3-D effects, and that changes the line and fill color of text.

_____ **2.** The inside color of text or an object.

_____ **3.** A feature that copies formatting from one selection of text to another, ensuring formatting consistency in your presentation.

_____ **4.** A combination of formatting effects that includes 3-D, glow, and bevel effects and shadows that can be applied to shapes.

_____ **5.** An object that is used to position text anywhere on the slide.

_____ **6.** The pointer that indicates that you can draw a shape.

_____ **7.** Vertical and horizontal lines that display in the rulers to give you a visual indication of the pointer position so that you can draw a shape.

_____ **8.** A blinking vertical line that indicates where text will be inserted.

_____ **9.** A color combination in which one color fades into another.

_____ **10.** The way a slide appears or disappears during an onscreen slide show.

_____ **11.** The action of placing text or objects that have been copied or moved from one location to another location.

_____ **12.** A temporary storage area maintained by your Microsoft Office program.

_____ **13.** The action of moving a selection by dragging it to a new location.

_____ **14.** A designer-quality visual representation of your information that you can create by choosing from among many different layouts to effectively communicate your message or ideas.

_____ **15.** Combinations of formatting effects that are applied to diagrams.

A Crosshair pointer

B Drag-and-drop

C Fill color

D Format Painter

E Gradient fill

F Guides

G Insertion point

H Office Clipboard

I Paste

J Shape Styles

K SmartArt graphic

L SmartArt Styles

M Text box

N Transition

O WordArt

Content-Based Assessments

Fill in the Blank

Write the correct word in the space provided.

1. When you click the dashed border of a placeholder, it displays as a(n) _____ line.

2. To repeat the last command or text that you entered, press the _____ function key.

3. To copy formatting to multiple selections, _____-_____ Format Painter.

4. To horizontally or vertically position selected objects on a slide relative to each other, use the _____ tools.

5. When you apply slide transitions, you can control the _____ and the method with which the slides advance during the presentation.

6. The Clipboard can store up to _____ selections that you have cut or copied.

7. You can reverse an Undo by using the _____ command.

8. To show nonsequential information, use a(n) _____ diagram.

9. To show steps in a process or timeline, use a(n) _____ diagram.

10. To show a continual process, use a(n) _____ diagram.

11. To show a decision tree or create an organization chart, use a(n) _____ diagram.

12. To illustrate connections, use a(n) _____ diagram.

13. To show how parts relate to a whole, use a(n) _____ diagram.

14. To show proportional relationships with the largest component on the top or bottom, use a(n) _____ diagram.

15. When you are creating a diagram, choose the layout and type that provides the best _____ representation of your information.

Content-Based Assessments

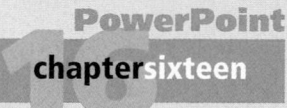
Skills Review

Project 16C—Snowboarding

In this project, you will apply the skills you practiced from the Objectives in Project 16A.

Objectives: 1. *Format Slide Elements;* **2.** *Insert and Format Pictures and Shapes;* **3.** *Apply Slide Transitions.*

In the following Skills Review, you will edit a presentation created by Dane Richardson, the Director of Ski and Snowboarding Instruction, that describes the snowboarding events and services available at Montagna del Pattino. Your completed presentation will look similar to the one shown in Figure 16.41.

For Project 16C, you will need the following files:

p16C_Board
p16C_Hillside
p16C_Silhouette
p16C_Snowboarding

You will save your presentation as
16C_Snowboarding_Firstname_Lastname

Figure 16.41

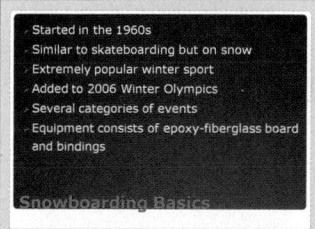
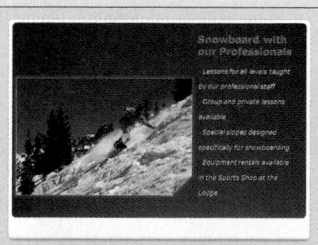

(Project 16C–Snowboarding continues on the next page)

(Project 16C–Snowboarding continued)

1. **Start** PowerPoint, and then from your student data files, open **p16C_Snowboarding**. Click the **Office** button, and then click **Save As**. Navigate to your **PowerPoint Chapter 16** folder and using your own first and last name, save the file as **16C_Snowboarding_Firstname_Lastname**

2. Display **Slide 1** and select the title text. On the **Format tab**, in the **WordArt Styles group**, click the **More** button to display the **WordArt gallery**. Under **Applies to All Text in the Shape**, in the last row, click the last style—**Fill – Accent 1, Metal Bevel, Reflection**.

3. Click the **Insert tab**, and then in the **Illustrations group**, click **Picture**. Navigate to the location where your student files are stored, and then double-click **p16C_Silhouette** to insert the picture in the middle of the slide.

4. With the picture selected, click the **Format tab**. In the **Size group**, click in the **Height** box, and then type **4** Click on the picture to change its size, and then point to the picture to display the ⬚ pointer. Drag the picture up and to the left so that its upper left corner aligns with the upper left corner of the white rounded rectangle.

5. With the picture still selected, in the **Picture Styles group**, click **Picture Effects**. Point to **Soft Edges**, and then click **50 Point** to blur the edges of the image.

6. Display **Slide 2**, and then click in the bulleted list placeholder. Point to the dashed border so that the ⬚ pointer displays, and then click so that the border displays as a solid line, indicating that all of the text in the placeholder is selected. On the **Home tab**, in the **Paragraph group**, click the

Bullets button arrow to display the **Bullets gallery**, and then click **Arrow Bullets**.

7. Display **Slide 3**, and then select the bulleted list placeholder on the right side of the slide so that its solid border displays. Press [F4] to repeat the bullet formatting that you applied in the previous step. If you have entered another action before pressing [F4] and the bullet formatting does not repeat, click the Bullets button arrow, and then apply the Arrow Bullets style.

8. On **Slide 3**, in the placeholder on the left of the slide, in the second row of buttons, click the first button—**Insert Picture from File**. From your student files, double-click **p16C_Hillside**. In the **Picture Styles group**, click the **Picture Shape** button. Under **Basic Shapes**, in the third row, click the fourth shape —**Folded Corner**. In the **Picture Styles group**, click the **Picture Effects** button, point to **Glow**, and then under **Glow Variations**, in the third row, click the first effect—**Accent color 1, 11 pt glow**.

9. Click in the bulleted list placeholder on the right, and then click its border so that it displays as a solid line, indicating that all of the text is selected. On the **Home tab**, in the **Font group**, apply **Italic**, and then, in the **Paragraph group**, click the **Line Spacing** button. Click **2.0**. **Save** your presentation.

10. Display **Slide 4** and verify that the rulers display. If the rulers do not display, on the View tab, in the Show/Hide group, select the Ruler check box. Click the **Insert tab**, and then in the **Illustrations group**, click the **Shapes** button to display the **Shapes gallery**.

(Project 16C–Snowboarding continues on the next page)

(Project 16C–Snowboarding continued)

11. Under **Block Arrows**, in the first row, click the fourth arrow—**Down Arrow**. Position the crosshair pointer at approximately **2.5 inches to the left of zero on the horizontal ruler** and at **2 inches above zero on the vertical ruler**.

12. Drag approximately 0.5 inch to the right and 1 inch down to create the arrow. Check the size of the shape by looking at the **Format tab** in the **Size group**. If necessary, adjust the size of the arrow to a Height of **1** and a Width of **0.5**.

13. With the arrow selected, on the **Format tab**, in the **Shape Styles group**, click the **More** button. In the last row, click the second style—**Intense Effect – Accent 1**.

14. With the arrow still selected, hold down Ctrl, and then press D to duplicate the arrow. Point to the new arrow, and then drag to the right so that the arrow is positioned above the text on the right of the slide at approximately **2 inches to the right of zero on the horizontal ruler**.

15. With the arrow on the right selected, press ⇧ Shift, and then click the arrow on the left so that both arrows are selected. On the **Format tab**, in the **Arrange group**, click the **Align** button. Click **Align Selected Objects** to align the objects that you selected relative to each other. On the **Format tab**, in the **Arrange group**, click the **Align** button, and then click **Align Top**.

16. Click the **Insert tab**, and then in the **Text group**, click **Text Box**. Position the pointer at approximately **3 inches to the left of zero on the horizontal ruler** and at **3 inches above zero on the vertical ruler**. Click to create a text box, and then type **Gear** Select the text that you typed, and then on the **Home tab**, in the **Font group**,

click the **Font Color arrow** and then click **White, Background 1**. Change the **Font Size** to **24**, and then click on a blank area of the slide.

17. Click the **Insert tab**, and then in the **Text group**, click **Text Box**. Position the pointer at approximately **1 inch to the right of zero on the horizontal ruler** and at **3 inches above zero on the vertical ruler**. Click to create a text box, and then type **Accessories** Select the text that you typed, and then on the **Home tab**, in the **Font group**, click the **Font Color button arrow**, and then click **White, Background 1**. Change the **Font Size** to **24**.

18. Use the ⇧ Shift key to select the two text boxes—*Gear* and *Accessories*. Click the **Format tab**, and then in the **Arrange group**, click the **Align** button. Click **Align Top** to align the top edges of the two text boxes, and then click anywhere on the slide so that none of the objects are selected. **Save** your presentation.

19. Click the bulleted list placeholder on the left side of the slide. Hold down ⇧ Shift and then click the arrow on the left and the *Gear* text box so that all three objects are selected. On the **Format tab**, in the **Arrange group**, click the **Align** button. Click **Align Selected Objects**. Click the **Align** button again, and then click **Align Center**.

20. Using the same process that you used in Step 19, align center the placeholder, arrow, and text box on the right side of the slide. **Save** your presentation.

21. Display **Slide 5**. In the placeholder on the left side of the slide, click the **Insert Picture from File** button, and then navigate to your student files. Double-click **p16C_Board**. On the **Format tab**, in the

(Project 16C–Snowboarding continues on the next page)

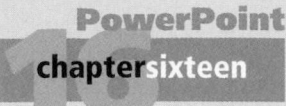

(Project 16C–Snowboarding continued)

Picture Styles group, click the **Picture Effects** button, and then point to **Glow**. In the last row, click the first glow effect—**Accent color 1, 18 pt glow**.

22. On **Slide 5**, select the slide title. On the **Home tab**, in the **Clipboard group**, click the **Format Painter** button. Display **Slide 3**, and then drag the ⬛ pointer over the title to apply the font, font size, and shadow effects from the title on **Slide 5** to the title on **Slide 3**.

23. Click the **Animations tab**. In the **Transition to This Slide group**, click the **More** button, and then under **Wipes**, in the first row, click the third transition—**Wipe Right**. In the **Transition to This Slide group**, click the **Apply To All** button. Click the **Slide Show tab**. In the **Start Slide Show group**, click **From Beginning**, and then view your presentation, clicking the mouse button to advance from slide to slide.

24. Create a **Header and Footer** for the **Notes and Handouts**. Include only the **Date and time updated automatically**, the **Page number**, and a **Footer** with the file name 16C_Snowboarding_Firstname_Lastname

25. Check your *Chapter Assignment Sheet* or *Course Syllabus* or consult your instructor to determine if you are to submit your assignments on paper or electronically. To submit electronically, go to Step 27, and then follow the instructions provided by your instructor.

26. From the **Office** menu, point to the **Print arrow**, and then click **Print Preview** to make a final check of your presentation. In the **Page Setup group**, click the **Print What arrow**, and then click **Handouts (6 Slides Per Page)**. Click the **Print** button, and then click **OK** to print the handouts.

27. **Save** the changes to your presentation, and then close the file.

End **You have completed Project 16C** ─────────

Skills Review

Project 16D — Lessons

In this project, you will apply the skills you practiced from the Objectives in Project 16B.

Objectives: 4. *Reorganize Presentation Text and Clear Formats;* **5.** *Create and Format a SmartArt Graphic.*

In the following Skills Review, you will edit a presentation created by Dane Richardson, the Director of Ski and Snowboarding Instruction, that describes the ski and snowboarding lessons for children at Montagna del Pattino. Your completed presentation will look similar to the one shown in Figure 16.42.

For Project 16D, you will need the following files:

p16D_Cara
p16D_Dane
p16D_Lessons
p16D_Marty

You will save your presentation as
16D_Lessons_Firstname_Lastname

Figure 16.42

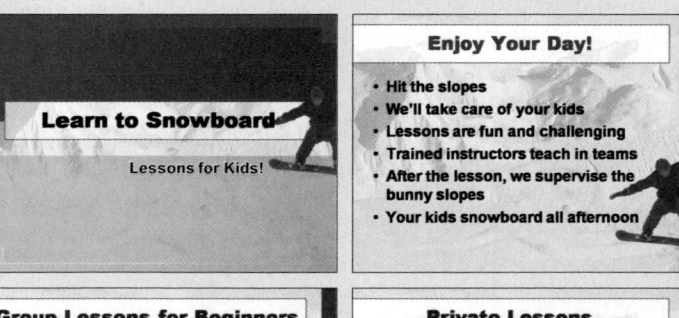

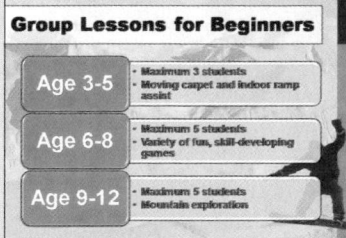

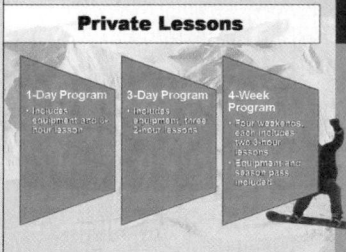

(Project 16D–Lessons continues on the next page)

Content-Based Assessments

(Project 16D–Lessons continued)

1. **Start** PowerPoint, and then from your student files, open **p16D_Lessons**. Click the **Office** button, and then click **Save As**. Navigate to your **PowerPoint Chapter 16** folder, and then using your own first and last name, save the file as **16D_Lessons_Firstname_Lastname**

2. Display **Slide 3**. On the **Home tab**, in the **Clipboard group**, click the **Dialog Box Launcher** to display the Clipboard task pane. In the **Clipboard** task pane, click the **Clear All** button. Select the slide title—**Private Lessons**. In the **Clipboard group**, click the **Cut** button to move the title to the Office Clipboard.

3. Display **Slide 4**. Select the title, and then on the **Home tab**, in the **Clipboard group**, click the **Cut** button to move the title to the Office Clipboard.

4. With **Slide 4** still displayed and the insertion point blinking in the title placeholder, in the **Clipboard** task pane, click **Private Lessons** to paste the item to the title placeholder.

5. Display **Slide 3**, and then click in the title placeholder. In the **Clipboard** task pane, click **Group Lesson for Beginners** to paste the item to the title placeholder. In the **Clipboard** task pane, click **Clear All**, and then **Close** the Clipboard task pane.

6. On **Slide 3**, right-click in the bulleted list placeholder to display the shortcut menu, and then point to **Convert to SmartArt**. In the first row, click the second graphic—**Vertical Block List**.

7. Click in the blank, fourth shape, and then press [Delete] to delete the extra shape. **Save** your presentation.

8. Click the **Design tab**. In the **SmartArt Styles group**, click the **Change Colors** button. Under **Primary Theme Colors**,

click the third color set—**Dark 2 Fill**. In the **SmartArt Styles group**, click the **More** button. Under **3-D**, in the first row, click the third style—**Cartoon**.

9. Display **Slide 4**, and then click in the bulleted list placeholder. On the **Home tab**, in the **Paragraph group**, click the **Convert to SmartArt Graphic** button, and then click **More SmartArt Graphics**. Click **List**, and then in the fifth row, click **Trapezoid List**. Click **OK** to create a diagram with four shapes. Click in the blank, fourth shape, and then press [Delete] to delete the extra shape. In the **SmartArt tools Design tab**, click the **Change Colors** button, and then under **Primary Theme Colors**, click the third color—**Dark 2 Fill**.

10. Click the **Home tab**. In the **Slides group**, click the **New Slide** button to insert a slide with the **Title and Content** layout. Click in the title placeholder, and then type **Meet the Team Leaders**

11. In the content placeholder, click the **Insert SmartArt Graphic** button. In the fourth row, click the second graphic—**Vertical Picture Accent List**, and then click **OK**. Click in the first **Text** shape, type **Cara Nielsen** and then press [Enter]. Type **Specializes in 3–5 year olds**

12. In the second shape, type **Dane Richardson** and then press [Enter]. Type **Specializes in 6-9 year olds**

13. In the third shape, type **Marty Blair** and then press [Enter]. Type **Specializes in 10-15 year olds** and then **Save** your presentation.

14. Click the **Design tab**. In the **SmartArt Styles group**, click the **Change Colors** button. Scroll the color list, and then under **Accent 4**, click the second color set—**Colored Fill - Accent 4**. In the **SmartArt Styles group**, click the **More**

(Project 16D–Lessons continues on the next page)

(Project 16D–Lessons continued)

button. Under **Best Match for Document**, click the last style—**Intense Effect**.

15. To the left of Cara Nielsen's information, in the circle shape, click the **Insert Picture From File** button. Navigate to your student files, and then double-click **p16D_Cara** to insert the picture. Repeat this process for the remaining two circles, inserting the files **p16D_Dane** and **p16D_Marty**.

16. Click the **Slide Show tab**. In the **Start Slide Show group**, click **From Beginning**, and then view your presentation, clicking the mouse button to advance from slide to slide. Create a **Header and Footer** for the **Notes and Handouts**. Include only the **Date and time updated automatically**, the **Page number**, and a **Footer** with the file name **16D_Lessons_Firstname_Lastname**

17. Check your *Chapter Assignment Sheet* or *Course Syllabus* or consult your instructor to determine if you are to submit your assignments on paper or electronically. To submit electronically, go to Step 19, and then follow the instructions provided by your instructor.

18. From the **Office** menu, point to the **Print arrow**, and then click **Print Preview** to make a final check of your presentation. In the **Page Setup group**, click the **Print What arrow**, and then click **Handouts (6 Slides Per Page)**. Click the **Print** button, and then click **OK** to print the handouts. **Close** Print Preview.

19. **Save** the changes to your presentation, and then from the **Office** menu, click **Exit PowerPoint**.

End **You have completed Project 16D** ⸻⸻⸻

Content-Based Assessments

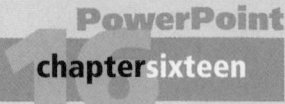
Mastering PowerPoint

Project 16E — Condos

In this project, you will apply the skills you practiced from the Objectives in Project 16A.

Objectives: 1. *Format Slide Elements;* **2.** *Insert and Format Pictures and Shapes;* **3.** *Apply Slide Transitions.*

In the following Mastering PowerPoint project, you will create a presentation that Kirsten McCarty, Director of Marketing will use to showcase the new timeshare condos at Montagna del Pattino. Your completed presentation will look similar to Figure 16.43.

For Project 16E, you will need the following files:

New blank PowerPoint presentation
p16E_Condominiums
p16E_Timeshare

**You will save your presentation as
16E_Condos_Firstname_Lastname**

Figure 16.43

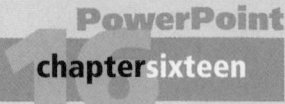

(Project 16E–Condos continues on the next page)

Content-Based Assessments

(Project 16E–Condos continued)

1. **Start** PowerPoint, and then begin a new blank presentation. On the **Design tab**, display the **Themes gallery**, and then under **Built-In**, apply the **Median** theme. The title of the presentation is **Montagna del Pattino Vacation Club** and the subtitle is **Luxurious Timeshare Condos Save** the presentation as **16E_Condos_Firstname_ Lastname**

2. On the **Insert tab**, display the **Shapes gallery**. Under **Stars and Banners**, in the second row, click the second shape— **Down Ribbon**. Position the crosshair pointer at **1 inch above zero on the vertical ruler** and aligned with the **M** in *Montagna*. Drag down approximately 1 inch and to the right so that the ribbon shape extends to the **o** in *Pattino*. On the **Format tab**, verify the **Size** of the shape and if necessary, change the **Height** to **1** and the **Width** to **7**

3. With the ribbon shape selected, type **A Blue Ribbon Resort** and then apply a **Shadow Shape Effect**, using **Inner** style—**Inside Center**. Select the text, and then change the **Font Size** to **24**.

4. Add a new slide to the presentation with the **Title and Content** layout. The slide title is **Why Buy?** Type the following bullet points, increasing and decreasing the list levels as indicated. Correct any spelling errors that you make while typing.

Great investment

> **More affordable than buying a vacation home**

Vacation prices are increasing

> **Buying a timeshare guarantees future vacation opportunities at today's prices**

Year-round availability

> **The resort does not shut down during summer**

(Project 16E–Condos continues on the next page)

5. Add a **New Slide** to the presentation with the **Picture with Caption** layout. The slide title is **A Place to Call Home** Select the title text. On the **Format tab**, display the **WordArt Styles gallery**, and then apply the **Fill – White, Warm Matte Bevel** style—the first style under **Applies to All Text in the Shape**. In the text placeholder, type the following two bullet points, increase the **Font Size** to **18**, and then apply the **Star Bullets** bullet style.

1-, 2-, and 3-bedroom units available with balconies and fireplaces

Fully furnished including TV, DVD, washer and dryer, and telephone

6. From your student files, insert the picture **p16E_Condominiums** in the picture placeholder.

7. Add a **New Slide** to the presentation with the **Two Content** layout. The slide title is **Common Areas and Features** Type the following bullet points in the placeholder on the left, and then correct any spelling errors that you make while typing.

Welcome center lounge for use by all owners

Weekly cleaning service available for a fee

Exercise room and indoor swimming pool

Ski-in and ski-out access

8. Apply **Numbering** to the list. On the right side of the slide, from your student files, insert the picture **p16E_Timeshare**. On the **Format tab**, display the **Picture Shape** gallery, and then under **Rectangles**, apply the second shape—**Rounded Rectangle**. Apply a **5 Point**, **Soft Edges Picture Effect**.

9. Insert a **Text Box** approximately 0.5 inch below the picture, and then type **The Summit Lodge** Use ⇧Shift to select the picture and the text box. Using the **Drawing Tools Format tab** (Note: Be sure to use

Content-Based Assessments

Mastering PowerPoint

(Project 16E–Condos continued)

the *Drawing Tools*, not the Picture Tools), **Align Center** the picture and the text box.

10. Add a **New Slide** to the presentation with the **Section Header** layout. The title of the slide is **Contact Information** and the subtitle is **Timeshare Division: 555-0965**

11. Display **Slide 2** and change the title font to **Bodoni MT**. Use **Format Painter** to copy the formatting to the slide title on **Slide 4**. Apply the **Wipe Down Transition**, and then change the **Transition Speed** to **Medium** for all of the slides in the presentation. View the slide show from the beginning.

12. Create a **Header and Footer** for the **Notes and Handouts**. Include only the **Date and time updated automatically**, the **Page**

number, and a **Footer** with the file name **12E_Condos_Firstname_Lastname** using your own first and last name.

13. Check your *Chapter Assignment Sheet* or *Course Syllabus* or consult your instructor to determine if you are to submit your assignments on paper or electronically. To submit electronically, go to Step 15, and then follow the instructions provided by your instructor.

14. Display your presentation in **Print Preview**, and then print **Handouts (6 Slides Per Page)**.

15. **Save** the changes to your presentation, and then close the presentation.

End **You have completed Project 16E**

Content-Based Assessments

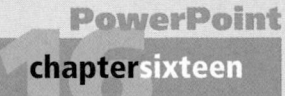
Mastering PowerPoint

Project 16F — Job Listings

In this project, you will apply the skills you practiced from the Objectives in Project 16B.

Objectives: 4. *Reorganize Presentation Text and Clear Formats;* **5.** *Create and Format a SmartArt Graphic.*

In the following Mastering PowerPoint Assessment, you will create a presentation that Leah Huynh, Director of Human Resources will use to describe some of the seasonal employment opportunities available at Montagna del Pattino. Your completed presentation will look similar to Figure 16.44.

> ### For Project 16F, you will need the following files:
>
> New blank PowerPoint presentation
> p16F_Employment
> p16F_Snowflake_Template

**You will save your presentation as
16F_Job_Listings_Firstname_Lastname**

Figure 16.44

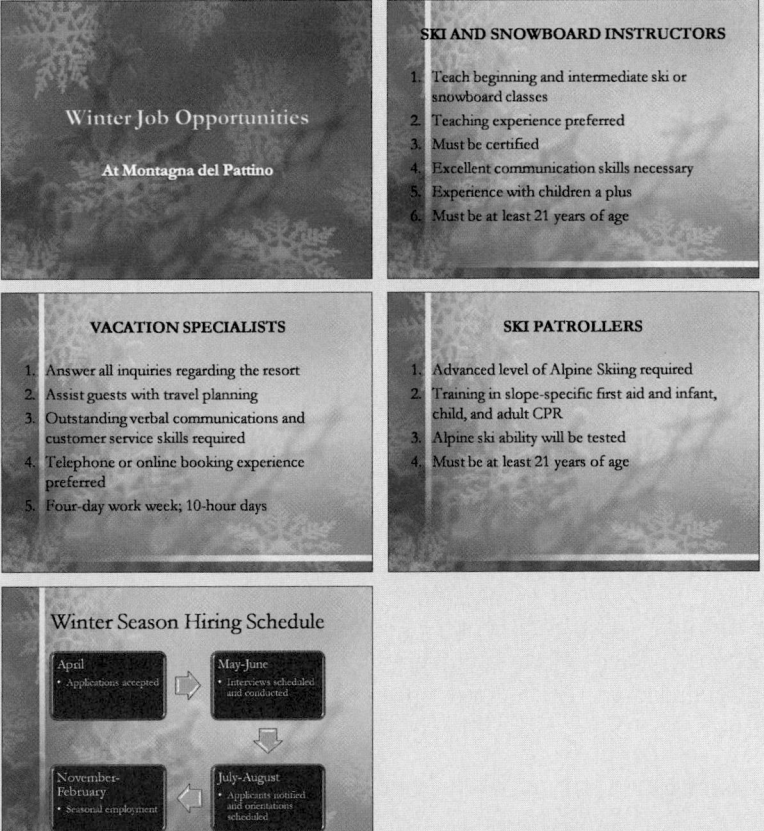

(Project 16F–Job Listings continues on the next page)

Content-Based Assessments

(Project 16F—Job Listings continued)

1. **Start** PowerPoint, and then open **p16F_Snowflake_Template** from your student files. **Save** the file as **16F_Job_Listings_Firstname_Lastname**

2. The title for the first slide is **Winter Job Opportunities** The subtitle is **At Montagna del Pattino**

3. Several slides for this presentation are contained in a file that lists summer and winter seasonal employment opportunities. From the file **p16F_Employment**, reuse **Slides 2—Ski and Snowboard Instructors**; **3—Vacation Specialists**; and **4—Ski Patroller**. (Hint: In the New Slide gallery, click Reuse Slides).

4. Display **Slide 2**, and then select and **Copy** the last bullet point—*Must be at least 21 years of age.* **Paste** the selection to **Slide 4** so that it is the fifth bullet point. On **Slide 4**, **Cut** the second to last bullet point— *Four-day work week; 10-hour days*, and then paste it to **Slide 3** so that it is the fifth bullet point.

5. Display **Slide 2**, and then select the bullet list placeholder so that its border displays as a solid line. Apply **Numbering** to the list and then use F4 to repeat the numbering for the bulleted lists on **Slides 3 and 4**.

6. Display **Slide 4**, and then add a new slide with the **Title and Content** layout. The title of the new slide is **Winter Season Hiring Schedule**

7. In the content placeholder, insert the second **Process** type **SmartArt Graphic —Accent Process**. In the first blue box, type **April** and then in its attached white box, type **Applications accepted** In the second blue

box, type **May-June** and then in its attached white box, type **Interviews scheduled and conducted** In the third blue box, type **July-August** and then in its attached white box, type **Applicants notified and orientations scheduled**

8. Click in the third blue box, and then in the **SmartArt Tools** click the **Design tab**. Add a shape at the same level, and then in the blue box, type **November-February** In its attached white box, type **Seasonal employment** Notice that this diagram does not use the slide space efficiently and the font size of the text is small and difficult to read. Change the **Layout** of the **SmartArt** to a **Process** layout—**Basic Bending Process** and its color to the second **Accent 2** scheme—**Colored Fill - Accent 2**. Apply **3-D Style Cartoon**.

9. Create a **Header and Footer** for the **Notes and Handouts**. Include only the **Date and time updated automatically**, the **Page number**, and a **Footer** with the file name **16F_Job_Listings_Firstname_Lastname** using your own first and last name.

10. Check your *Chapter Assignment Sheet* or *Course Syllabus* or consult your instructor to determine if you are to submit your assignments on paper or electronically. To submit electronically, go to Step 12, and then follow the instructions provided by your instructor.

11. Display your presentation in **Print Preview**, and then print **Handouts (6 Slides Per Page)**.

12. **Save** the changes to your presentation, and then close the presentation.

End **You have completed Project 16F**

Content-Based Assessments

Mastering PowerPoint

Project 16G — Packages

In this project, you will apply the skills you practiced from the Objectives in Projects 16A and 16B.

Objectives: 1. *Format Slide Elements;* **2.** *Insert and Format Pictures and Shapes;* **3.** *Apply Slide Transitions;* **5.** *Create and Format a SmartArt Graphic.*

In the following Mastering PowerPoint project, you will edit a presentation that Kirsten McCarty, Director of Marketing, will be showing at a travel fair to highlight the vacation packages offered at Montagna del Pattino. Your completed presentation will look similar to Figure 16.45.

For Project 16G, you will need the following files:

p16G_Fireworks
p16G_Mountain
p16G_Packages
p16G_Ski_Lift
p16G_Sunset

You will save your presentation as
16G_Packages_Firstname_Lastname

Figure 16.45

(Project 16G–Packages continues on the next page)

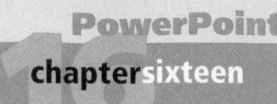
(Project 16G–Packages continued)

1. **Start** PowerPoint, and then from your student files, open **p16G_Packages**. **Save** your presentation as **16G_Packages_Firstname_Lastname**

2. Display **Slide 2**, and then change the bulleted list to **Numbering**. Insert a **Basic Shape Bevel** at **1 inch to the right of zero on the horizontal ruler** and at **0.5 inch below zero on the vertical ruler**. Size the bevel so that its **Height** is **1.3** inches and its **Width** is **3** inches. In the bevel, type **We'll customize your package; just call for reservations! Center** the text.

3. Select the shape so that its outer border is solid, and then duplicate the shape by using Ctrl + D. Drag the new shape down so that it almost touches the bottom of the slide. Replace the text with **Book two packages in one year; get a free weekend stay!**

4. Select both shapes, and then **Arrange** the shapes, using **Align Left** so that the left edge of the two shapes align. Apply a **Shape Style** found in the third row, **Light 1 Outline, Colored Fill – Accent 1** to both shapes.

5. Display **Slide 3**. In the placeholder on the left side of the slide, use the **Insert Picture from File** button in the placeholder to insert from your student files **p16G_Ski_Lift**. Change the **Picture Shape** under **Basic Shapes** to **Parallelogram**, and then apply the first **Reflection** effect—**Tight Reflection, touching.**

6. Display **Slide 4**, and then add a **New Slide** with the **Comparison** layout. Type and **Center** the title **Fifth Night Free Package** In the caption box on the left, type **Stay an extra day** and then in the caption box on the right, type **Enjoy the evening view**

(Project 16G–Packages continues on the next page)

Center both captions, and then in the content placeholder on the left, type the following bullet points:

Accommodations at the Summit Lodge

Book four nights, stay for free on the fifth

Complimentary breakfast every morning

7. Select the placeholder so that its outer edge displays as a solid line, and then change the **Line Spacing** to **1.5** and the **Font Size** to **20**. With the placeholder border displayed as a solid line, the change is applied to all of the text.

8. In the placeholder on the right side of the slide, use the **Insert Picture from File** button in the placeholder to insert from your student files **p16G_Sunset**. Apply the second **Glow Picture Effect** in the second row—**Accent color 2, 8 pt. glow**. **Save** the presentation.

9. Add a **New Slide** to the presentation with the **Content with Caption** layout. The slide title is **Fourth of July Celebration Package Center** the title and increase the **Font Size** to **24**. Remove the **Bold** formatting. In the text placeholder on the left of the slide, type **Stay Fourth of July weekend at the Summit Lodge and receive preferred seating at the evening fireworks show and complimentary tickets for four to our barbecue**

10. Change the **Font Size** of the text that you typed to **16**, and then change the **Line Spacing** to **2.5**. **Center** the text and apply **Italic**. In the placeholder on the right side of the slide, use the **Insert Picture from File** button to insert **p16G_Fireworks** from your student files.

11. Add a **New Slide** with the **Title and Content** layout. The slide title is **Summer Festivals** In the content placeholder, use the **SmartArt Graphic** button to insert a **List** graphic found in the fifth row—**Table List**. Apply the **3-D Powder SmartArt Style**

Content-Based Assessments

(Project 16G–Packages continued)

to the graphic. In the long rectangular box at the top of the SmartArt graphic, type **Stay For Any Weekend Festival** and then select the text. In the Format tab, display the **WordArt Styles** gallery. In the first row of WordArt styles, apply **Fill – White, Outline – Accent 1** to the selection. In the three remaining boxes, type the following points, one in each box from left to right.

Free admission to festival

Complimentary lunch

Free parking or free trolley ride to event

12. Display **Slide 8**. Click the **Insert Picture from File** button in the placeholder and insert from your student files **p16G_Mountain**. Apply the second **Reflection** effect in the first row—**Half Reflection, touching**.

13. Display **Slide 2**, and then select the title. Change the **Font** to **Tahoma**. Use the **Format Painter** to apply the formatting to the titles on **Slides 3**, **4**, and **7**. (Hint: Double-click Format Painter so that you can apply the formatting multiple times).

14. In the **Transitions** gallery, under **Wipes**, apply the **Uncover Left-Up** transition, and then change the **Transition Speed** to **Medium** for all of the slides. View the **Slide Show** from the beginning.

15. Create a **Header and Footer** for the **Notes and Handouts**. Include only the **Date and time updated automatically**, the **Page number**, and a **Footer** with the file name **16G_Packages_Firstname_Lastname** using your own first and last name.

16. Check your *Chapter Assignment Sheet* or *Course Syllabus* or consult your instructor to determine if you are to submit your assignments on paper or electronically. To submit electronically, go to Step 18, and then follow the instructions provided by your instructor.

17. Display your presentation in **Print Preview**, and then print **Handouts (4 Slides Per Page)**.

18. **Save** your presentation, and then close the file.

End **You have completed Project 16G**

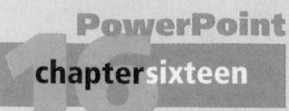

PowerPoint
chaptersixteen

Mastering PowerPoint

Project 16H—Family

In this project, you will apply the skills you practiced from the Objectives in Projects 16A and 16B.

Objectives: 2. *Insert and Format Pictures and Shapes;* **3.** *Apply Slide Transitions;* **4.** *Reorganize Presentation Text and Clear Formats;* **5.** *Create and Format a SmartArt Graphic.*

In the following Mastering PowerPoint project, you will create a presentation based on the activities that the Gillis family enjoyed while spending a day at Montagna del Pattino. Your completed presentation will look similar to Figure 16.46.

For Project 16H, you will need the following files:

New blank PowerPoint presentation
p16H_Baby
p16H_Group
p16H_Memories
p16H_Snowflake
p16H_Winner

You will save your presentation as
16H_Family_Firstname_Lastname

Figure 16.46

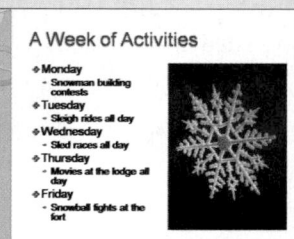

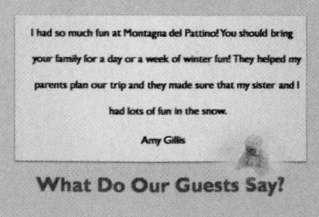

(Project 16H–Family continues on the next page)

Content-Based Assessments

(Project 16H–Family continued)

1. **Start** PowerPoint, and then begin a new blank presentation. On the **Design tab**, display the **Themes** gallery, and then under **Built-In**, apply the **Solstice** theme. In the **Themes group**, click the **Theme Colors** button, and then click the fifth color theme under **Built-In—Civic**. **Save** the file as **16H_Family_Firstname_Lastname**

2. The title of this presentation is **Family Friendly Activities** and the subtitle is **At Montagna del Pattino** From your student files, insert the **p16H_Group** picture. Adjust the picture **Height** to **4.5** and the **Width** to **3**. Drag the picture to the lower right corner of the slide. Change the picture shape to **Bevel**, and then apply a **Soft Edges Picture Effect** of **10 Point**.

3. Add a **New Slide** with the **Two Content** layout, and then in the title placeholder, type **A Week of Activities** In the content placeholder on the left, type the following bullet points, increasing and decreasing the list level as necessary:

    Monday

     Snowman building contests

    Tuesday

     Sleigh rides all day

    Wednesday

     Sled races

    Thursday

     Movies at the lodge

    Friday

     Snowball fights at the fort

4. On the right, click the **Insert Picture from File** button in the placeholder and from your student files, insert **p16H_Snowflake**.

5. Add a **New Slide** with the **Picture with Caption** layout. In the title placeholder, type **Family Memories** and then apply **WordArt Style Gradient Fill – Black, Outline – White, Outer Shadow**. Increase the **Font Size** to **32** and **Center** the title. In the Picture placeholder, from your student files insert **p16H_Winner**. In the caption box below the picture, type **One of our sled race winners!** In the slide title, select the word *Family*, and then use **Format Painter** to apply the WordArt style to the caption. **Center** the caption and change the **Line Spacing** to **1.0**.

6. On the **Insert tab**, display the **Shapes** gallery. Under **Stars and Banners**, in the first row, click the second shape—**Explosion 2**. Draw a shape that extends from **zero on the horizontal** and **vertical rulers** to **4 1/2 inches to the right of zero on the horizontal ruler** and **3 inches below zero on the vertical ruler**. Type **First Place!** in the shape, and then change the **Font Size** to **28**. Display the **Shape Styles gallery**, and then in the fourth row apply **Subtle Effect – Accent 1**. Apply the **Bevel Shape Effect Soft Round**—the second effect in the second row.

7. Add a **New Slide** with the **Two Content** layout, and then in the title placeholder, type **A Great Place to Vacation!** In the content placeholder on the left, insert the **Vertical Process SmartArt** graphic. In the first box, type **Family!** In the second box, type **Snow!** In the last box, type **Fun!** Apply **SmartArt Style 3-D Polished** to the graphic.

8. In the placeholder on the right of the slide, from your student files, insert the picture **p16H_Memories**. Apply **Picture Style Rotated, White**, and then apply the **Glow Picture Effect—Accent color 1, 5 pt glow**.

(Project 16H–Family continues on the next page)

(Project 16H–Family continued)

9. Add a **New Slide** with the **Comparison** layout, and then in the title placeholder at the bottom of the slide, type **What Do Our Guests Say?** Click in the white placeholder at the top left of the slide, hold down ⇧Shift and click the white placeholder at the top right to select both placeholders. **Delete** both placeholders.

10. Click in the placeholder on the left, and then type **I had so much fun at Montagna del Pattino! You should bring your family for a day or a week of winter fun! They helped my parents plan our trip and they made sure that my sister and I had lots of fun in the snow.** Press Enter, and then type **Amy Gillis**

11. In the placeholder on the right, use the **Insert Picture from File** button to insert from your student files **p16H_Baby**. Change the shape of the picture to the **32-Point Star**, and then apply the **Soft Edges 50 Point Picture Effect** so that the baby almost appears to be crawling on the slide. Drag the picture to the right so that the points of the stars and its border box aligns with the right edge of the slide.

12. With the picture selected, press ⇧Shift, and then click the slide title to select both the picture and the title. On the **Drawing Tools Format tab**, in the **Arrange group**, click **Align**, and then click **Align Bottom** to align the bottom edges of the two objects. The baby displays slightly above the word *Say*.

13. Select the text in the bulleted list placeholder, and then on the **Home tab**, click the **Bullets** button to toggle the bullets off. **Center** all of the text in the placeholder.

Point to the placeholder's right-center sizing handle and drag to the right to **4.5 inches to the right of zero on the horizontal ruler** to resize the placeholder. Apply the **Shape Style** found in the fourth row— **Subtle Effect – Accent 3**, and then change the **Line Spacing** of the text to **2.0**.

14. Display **Slide 2**, and then click in the first bullet point—**Monday**. Change the Bullet style to **Star Bullets**. Use F4 or Format Painter to apply the same bullet style to each bullet point that includes a day of the week. In the fourth bullet point, **Copy** the words *all day* to the end of the sixth and eighth bullet points after the words *races*, and *lodge*.

15. Apply the **Box In** transition and change the **Transition Speed** to **Medium**. Click **Apply To All**, and then view the slide show from the beginning.

16. Create a **Header and Footer** for the **Notes and Handouts**. Include only the **Date and time updated automatically**, the **Page number**, and a **Footer** with the file name **16H_Family_Firstname_Lastname**

17. Check your *Chapter Assignment Sheet* or *Course Syllabus* or consult your instructor to determine if you are to submit your assignments on paper or electronically. To submit electronically, go to Step 19, and then follow the instructions provided by your instructor.

18. Display your presentation in **Print Preview**, and then print **Handouts (6 Slides Per Page)**.

19. **Save** changes to your presentation, and then close the file.

 You have completed Project 16H

Content-Based Assessments

Mastering PowerPoint

Project 16I — Summer

In this project, you will apply the skills you practiced from all the Objectives in Projects 16A and 16B.

Objectives: 1. *Format Slide Elements;* **2.** *Insert and Format Pictures and Shapes;* **3.** *Apply Slide Transitions;* **4.** *Reorganize Presentation Text and Clear Formats;* **5.** *Create and Format a SmartArt Graphic.*

In the following Mastering PowerPoint Assessment, you will edit a presentation that Kirsten McCarty, Director of Marketing, will be showing at a travel fair describing the summer activities at Montagna del Pattino. Your completed presentation will look similar to Figure 16.47.

For Project 16I, you will need the following files:

p16I_Art
p16I_Balloons
p16I_Fireworks
p16I_Summer

You will save your presentation as
16I_Summer_Firstname_Lastname

Figure 16.47

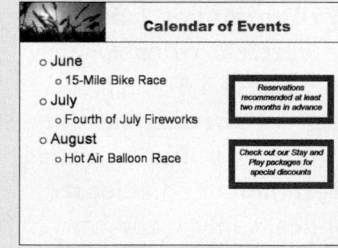

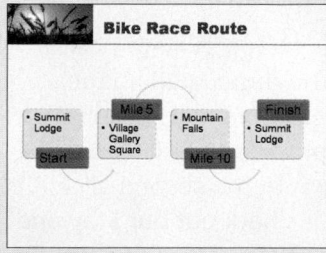

(Project 16I–Summer continues on the next page)

(Project 16I–Summer continued)

1. **Start** PowerPoint, and then from your student files open the file **p16I_Summer**. **Save** the presentation as 16I_Summer_Firstname_Lastname

2. On **Slide 2**, apply a **WordArt Style—Gradient Fill – Accent 6, Inner Shadow** found in the fourth row—to the title, and then decrease the **Font Size** to **32**. Select the bulleted list placeholder so that its border displays as a solid line, and then display the **Bullets and Numbering** dialog box. Change the bullet style to the third style in the first row of the Bullets gallery—**Hollow Round Bullets**. Change the bullet **Color** to the first color under **Standard Colors—Dark Red**.

3. On **Slide 2**, display the **Shapes** gallery. Under **Basic Shapes**, insert the fifth shape in the second row—**Frame**. Position the pointer at **1.5 inches to the right of zero on the horizontal ruler** and at **1.5 inches above zero on the vertical ruler**. Draw the shape with a **Height** of **1.5** and a **Width** of **3.25**, using the **Format Tab** to adjust the size as necessary. In the frame, type **Reservations recommended at least two months in advance** Apply **Italic** and **Center** the text.

4. Duplicate the frame shape by using Ctrl + D, and then drag the duplicated shape down so that it is approximately 0.5 inch below the first shape. Align the left edges of the shapes, and then in the second shape, replace the text with **Check out our Stay and Play packages for special discounts** On the **Format tab**, click the **Shape Fill arrow**, and then under **Standard Colors**, click the first color—**Dark Red**. Use F4 to repeat the fill color formatting to the other frame shape.

5. Display **Slide 3**. In the placeholder on the right, use the **Insert Picture from File**

button to insert from your student files, **p16I_Art**. Change the **Picture Shape** to a **Rounded Rectangle**. Apply the fourth **Glow Effect** in the first row—**Accent color 4, 5 pt glow**.

6. Display **Slide 4**. Select the title, and then in the **Font group**, click the **Clear All Formatting** button to remove the WordArt formatting from the selection.

7. On **Slide 4**, right-click in the content placeholder text, and then point to **Convert to SmartArt**. Click **More SmartArt** Graphics to display the **Choose a SmartArt Graphics** dialog box. Click **Process**, and then in the first row, double-click the last graphic—**Alternating Flow** to convert the text to a diagram. Click in the **Mile 10** shape, and then in the **Create Graphic group**, click **Add Shape**. In the gray box, type **Finish** and then in the brown box, type **Summit Lodge**

8. Change the color of the SmartArt to the first **Accent 1** color—**Colored Outline - Accent 1**, and then apply **3-D Style Powder**.

9. Display **Slide 5**. Select the *Fireworks Display* text, and then apply the second **Word Art Style** in the first row. Change the **Text Fill** color to **Dark Red**. Use the **Format Painter** to apply the same formatting to the *Hot Air Balloon Race* text. In the placeholder on the left, use the **Insert Picture from File** button to insert the picture **p16I_Fireworks**. Apply the **Glow Picture Effect Accent color 2, 8 pt glow**.

10. In the placeholder on the right, use the **Insert Picture from File** button to insert the picture **p16I_Balloons**. Apply the **Soft Edges Picture Effect 5 Point**. Size the picture to a **Height** of **2.5** and a **Width** of

(Project 16I–Summer continues on the next page)

Content-Based Assessments

(Project 16I–Summer continued)

3.75 and then drag the picture up so that its top edge is positioned at **1 inch above zero on the vertical ruler**. It should *not* align with the fireworks picture.

11. Insert a 4-inch-wide **Text Box** positioned at **zero on the horizontal ruler** and at **2 inches below zero on the vertical ruler**. Type **Color lights up the sky in July and August. Join us for both events and enjoy a barbecue, carnival rides, and music.** Apply the second **WordArt Style—Fill – None, Outline – Accent 2**, and then change the **Text Fill** to **Dark Red**. Apply **Italic**, and then change the **Font Size** to **16**. **Center** the text.

12. Use [⇧Shift] to select the text box that you created in Step 11, the balloon picture, and the *Hot Air Balloon Race* text box. **Align Center** the three objects. (Hint: Use the Drawing Tools Format tab).

13. In the first row of the **Wipes** transitions, apply the **Wedge Transition** to all of the slides in the presentation, and then view the slide show.

14. Create a **Header and Footer** for the **Notes and Handouts**. Include only the **Date and time updated automatically**, the **Page number**, and a **Footer** with the file name **16I_Summer_Firstname_Lastname** using your own first and last name.

15. Check your *Chapter Assignment Sheet* or *Course Syllabus* or consult your instructor to determine if you are to submit your assignments on paper or electronically. To submit electronically, go to Step 17, and then follow the instructions provided by your instructor.

16. Display your presentation in **Print Preview**, and then print **Handouts (6 Slides Per Page)**.

17. **Save** any changes to your presentation, and then close the presentation.

End **You have completed Project 16I** _____

Content-Based Assessments

Project 16J—Business Running Case

In this project, you will apply the skills you practiced in Projects 16A and 16B.

Close PowerPoint and any other open windows. Display the Start menu, click Computer, and then navigate to the student files that accompany this textbook. In the folder **03_business_running_case**, locate and open the folder for this chapter. Open and print the instructions for this project, which are provided to you in Adobe PDF format. Follow the instructions and use the skills you have gained thus far to assist Jennifer Nelson in meeting the challenges of owning and running her business.

End **You have completed Project 16J** _____

Content-Based Assessments

Mastering PowerPoint

Project 16K — *GO!* Fix It

In this project, you will apply the skills you practiced from the Objectives in Projects 16A and 16B.

For Project 16K, you will need the following file:

p16K_fixit_SkiFest

**You will save your document as
16K_SkiFest_Firstname_Lastname**

In this project, you will edit a draft slide presentation being prepared for Dane Richardson, Director of Ski and Snowboard Instruction at Montagna del Pattino, to advertise their Monster Mogul SkiFest to skiers. From the student files that accompany this textbook, open the folder **05_go_fix_it**. Locate and open the file **p16K_fixit_SkiFest**, and then save the file in your chapter folder as **16K_SkiFest_Firstname_Lastname**

This presentation contains **five errors** that you must find and correct. Read and examine the document, and then edit to correct the errors that you find. Types of errors could include:

- Spelling, grammar, punctuation, and usage errors such as text case, subject-verb agreement, and meaning.
- Content errors such as missing or incorrect data, text, pictures, hyperlinks, or other objects.
- Font and paragraph formatting and positioning errors such fonts, font styles, font sizing, alignment, text color, indent levels, and bullet features.
- Slide layout, orientation, design themes, backgrounds, animation and transition errors.
- Image or object formatting and positioning errors on tables, illustrations, links, text, and media clips relating to color, lines, size, scale, styles, layout, positioning, and control.
- Page setup errors on slides, handouts, notes and outlines such as margins, orientation, layout, alignment, headers and footers, date and time, color, grayscale, black and white, and sizing.

To complete the project, you should know that:

- Mr. Richardson wants an additional photo on Slide 1, resized to 3.75" high x 5" wide, and positioned in the upper right section of the slide. Use the p16K_Skier photo from your student files.
- On all of the slides with time periods, correct as necessary to use a consistent format for the times; for example *4:00 pm*.
- There are some errors in bullet styles.

(Project 16K–*GO!* Fix It continues on the next page)

Mastering PowerPoint

(Project 16K–*GO!* Fix It continued)

- On Slide 7, Mr. Richardson wants a duplicate picture, moved to the right side of the slide.
- On Slide 7, Mr. Richardson wants the phrase *Don't Miss It!* in the slide using the WordArt Gallery Fill - Accent 2, Bevel format, positioned at the top edge of the text box below the date, and aligned Center.

Create a footer for the Notes and Handouts. Include only the date and time updated automatically, the page number, and a footer with your name included. Submit as directed, using 4 slides per page.

 End **You have completed Project 16K** —————————————

Outcomes-Based Assessments

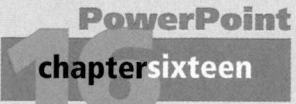
Rubric

The following outcomes-based assessments are *open-ended assessments*. That is, there is no specific correct result; your result will depend on your approach to the information provided. Make *Professional Quality* your goal. Use the following scoring rubric to guide you in *how* to approach the problem and then to evaluate *how well* your approach solves the problem.

The *criteria*—Software Mastery, Content, Format and Layout, and Process—represent the knowledge and skills you have gained that you can apply to solving the problem. The *levels of performance*—Professional Quality, Approaching Professional Quality, or Needs Quality Improvements—help you and your instructor evaluate your result.

	Your completed project is of Professional Quality if you:	Your completed project is Approaching Professional Quality if you:	Your completed project Needs Quality Improvements if you:
1-Software Mastery	Choose and apply the most appropriate skills, tools, and features and identify efficient methods to solve the problem.	Choose and apply some appropriate skills, tools, and features, but not in the most efficient manner.	Choose inappropriate skills, tools, or features, or are inefficient in solving the problem.
2-Content	Construct a solution that is clear and well organized, contains content that is accurate, appropriate to the audience and purpose, and is complete. Provide a solution that contains no errors of spelling, grammar, or style.	Construct a solution in which some components are unclear, poorly organized, inconsistent, or incomplete. Misjudge the needs of the audience. Have some errors in spelling, grammar, or style, but the errors do not detract from comprehension.	Construct a solution that is unclear, incomplete, or poorly organized, containing some inaccurate or inappropriate content; and contains many errors of spelling, grammar, or style. Do not solve the problem.
3-Format and Layout	Format and arrange all elements to communicate information and ideas, clarify function, illustrate relationships, and indicate relative importance.	Apply appropriate format and layout features to some elements, but not others. Overuse features, causing minor distraction.	Apply format and layout that does not communicate information or ideas clearly. Do not use format and layout features to clarify function, illustrate relationships, or indicate relative importance. Use available features excessively, causing distraction.
4-Process	Use an organized approach that integrates planning, development, self-assessment, revision, and reflection.	Demonstrate an organized approach in some areas, but not others; or, use an insufficient process of organization throughout.	Do not use an organized approach to solve the problem.

Outcomes-Based Assessments

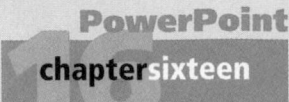

Problem Solving

Project 16L — Adult Lessons

In this project, you will construct a solution by applying any combination of the skills you practiced from the Objectives in Projects 16A and 16B.

For Project 16L, you will need the following file:

New blank PowerPoint presentation

You will save your presentation as
16L_Adult_Lessons_Firstname_Lastname

Using the information provided, create a presentation that contains four to six slides that Dane Richardson, Director of Ski and Snowboard Instruction, can use to describe the adult ski and snowboard lessons offered at Montagna del Pattino. The presentation will be used as a part of a larger presentation on resort activities to be shown to an audience of varying skiing abilities at a regional ski and snowboard convention.

The resort offers Adult Group Lessons that are comprised of individuals with similar skill levels. Two-hour group lessons include equipment. Private lessons, which are one-on-one instruction geared toward an individual's skill level and preferences, are also available. The resort offers 8-week programs, which are group lessons for those who prefer more in-depth, ongoing instruction. The resort also offers several specialty lessons. The Ladies Only group lessons are geared specifically toward women and participants are encouraged to bring a friend. The Backcountry Adventure is a chance for advanced skiers to explore lesser-known areas of the resort. Finally, the Racing Camps are for recreational skiers seeking to fine-tune their skills, and feature gate running and on-hill training.

Use the techniques that you learned in this chapter to insert and format graphics to visually enhance your presentation. The tone of the presentation should be positive and encouraging so that the audience—regardless of skill level—will be interested in visiting the resort and attending the Ski and Snowboard School. Add the file name to the Notes and Handouts footer and check the presentation for spelling errors. Save the presentation as **16L_Adult_Lessons_Firstname_Lastname** and submit it as directed.

Note: You can find many appropriate images available to Office users. To access these images, click the Insert tab, and then from the Illustrations group, click the Clip Art button. In the Clip Art task pane, type a key word—such as *ski*—in the *Search for* box. You can specify the image type (clip art or photographs) and where to search. The largest variety of photographs can be found by including Web Collections in the *Search in* box. You can also use images from earlier projects in this chapter, or images from your personal collection.

End You have completed Project 16L

Outcomes-Based Assessments

PowerPoint

chaptersixteen

Problem Solving

Project 16M — Festivals

In this project, you will construct a solution by applying any combination of the skills you practiced from the Objectives in Projects 16A and 16B.

For Project 16M, you will need the following file:

New blank PowerPoint presentation

You will save your presentation as
16M_Festivals_Firstname_Lastname

In this project, you will create a presentation that Justin Mitrani, Hotel Manager, is creating as part of a collection of presentations given to guests on CDs. The presentation describes the seasonal festivals and events held at Montagna del Pattino. The events that are sponsored at the resort include a Celtic Festival, a Chili Cook-Off, and a Country Music Festival. The tone of the presentation should be fun and interesting so that guests will be encouraged to return to the resort during the events. Research these types of events on the Internet to develop content and use a SmartArt graphic to highlight the dates of the festivals. Include pictures and shapes that are relevant to the events, and format the pictures using the techniques that you learned in this chapter. (See the note at the end of Project 16L for hints about locating images.) Add the file name to the Notes and Handouts footer and check the presentation for spelling errors. Save the presentation as **16M_Festivals_Firstname_Lastname** and submit it as directed.

End You have completed Project 16M ——————

Outcomes-Based Assessments

Problem Solving

Project 16N — Orientation

In this project, you will construct a solution by applying any combination of the skills you practiced from the Objectives in Projects 16A and 16B.

For Project 16N, you will need the following file:

New blank PowerPoint presentation

**You will save your presentation as
16N_Orientation_Firstname_Lastname**

In this project, you will create an orientation presentation consisting of four to six slides to be used by Justin Mitrani, Hotel Director for Montagna del Pattino. This presentation will be used to introduce new employees to the resort and to the importance of customer service. Begin the presentation with slides that include information about the resort. You can summarize from the following information, and you can expand upon this information by researching mountain ski resorts.

Montagna del Pattino was founded and built by the Blardone family in the 1950s. It has grown from one ski run and a small lodge to 50 trails, 6 lifts, a 300-room lodge, and a renowned ski and snowboard school. Luxurious condominiums on the property have ski in/ski out access. A resort store offers rental and sale of gear for enthusiasts who want the latest advances in ski and snowboard technology. A variety of quick service, casually elegant, and fine dining restaurants complete the scene for a perfect ski-enthusiast getaway.

Include at least two slides that describe why customer service and hospitality are important at the resort. Guests who return year after year are impressed by the friendly attitude and helpfulness of the staff and the cleanliness of the facilities. Stress the importance of greeting guests and making them feel at home, thus exemplifying the family-friendly atmosphere that is a hallmark of the resort. Use a process SmartArt graphic to illustrate how hospitality and customer service lead to satisfied guests.

The tone of this presentation is informative and should include examples of how customer service is provided on a daily basis. Keep this in mind when choosing a theme, diagrams, bullet styles, and pictures. (See the note at the end of Project 16L for hints about locating images.) Add the date and file name to the Notes and Handouts footer and check the presentation for spelling errors. Save the presentation as **16N_Orientation_Firstname_Lastname** and submit it as directed.

End **You have completed Project 16N** ——————————

Outcomes-Based Assessments

Problem Solving

Project 16O — Restaurants

In this project, you will construct a solution by applying any combination of the skills you practiced from the Objectives in Projects 16A and 16B.

For Project 16O, you will need the following file:

New blank PowerPoint presentation

You will save your presentation as
16O_Restaurants_Firstname_Lastname

In this project, you will create a presentation that contains information about the restaurants that are onsite at Montagna del Pattino resort. This presentation is being used by Justin Mitrani, Hotel Director, at a Chamber of Commerce meeting. Mr. Mitrani's purpose is to inform Chamber members of the restaurant and catering services available at the resort in an effort to expand catering, conference, and business meeting operations. Create a presentation about the restaurant services, using the following information.

The resort offers a variety of quick service, casually elegant, and fine dining restaurants. The Summit Clubhouse and the Montagna Vista Club are fine dining restaurants known for their superb buffets and desserts. The Mediterranean buffet includes Whole Chicken, slow-roasted and quartered, Rice Pilaf with Pine Nuts and Raisins, Classic Greek Salad with Vinaigrette, Hummus, and Baklava. The Italian buffet includes Lasagna, Italian Vegetable Sauté, Classic Caesar salad, Garlic Bread and Bread Sticks, and Cheesecake. Other buffets include the All American Barbecue, the Cajun Cookout, and the Heartland buffet. The Summit Clubhouse can accommodate large groups of up to 150 guests and the Montagna Vista Club is best suited for more intimate gatherings of no more than 65 guests. The restaurants offer full beverage service, event-planning services, and coordination with hotel operations to accommodate conference guests who plan to stay overnight. The Summit Clubhouse includes three conference rooms off of the main banquet room that can be used for smaller group meetings. The resort recently hired a full-time conference and catering director who will act as a liaison with business representatives to coordinate event planning.

Using the preceding information, create a presentation with a minimum of six slides that describes the resort restaurants, menus, banquet and conference facilities, and services. Create a SmartArt graphic that demonstrates the catering and event-planning process. The process may include an initial meeting with the catering director, a meeting to choose

(Project 16O–Restaurants continues on the next page)

Outcomes-Based Assessments

Problem Solving

(Project 16O–Restaurants continued)

the date and location, and other meetings to choose menus and finalize reservations. Illustrate your presentation with pictures that will entice the intended audience to use the Montagna del Pattino resort for their catering and business meeting needs. (See the note at the end of Project 16L for hints about locating images.) Add the date and file name to the Notes and Handouts footer and check the presentation for spelling errors. Save the presentation as **16O_Restaurants_Firstname_Lastname** and submit it as directed.

 End **You have completed Project 16O** ————————————

Outcomes-Based Assessments

Problem Solving

Project 16P — Triathlon

In this project, you will construct a solution by applying any combination of the skills you practiced from the Objectives in Projects 16A and 16B.

For Project 16P, you will need the following file:

New blank PowerPoint presentation

You will save your presentation as
16P_Triathlon_Firstname_Lastname

In this project, you will create a presentation to be shown by Montagna del Pattino's President, Albert Blardone, at a company meeting that details the Annual Triathlon sponsored by the resort. The presentation will explain the details of the triathlon including the events, the routes, major sponsors, prizes, and medical and security measures. The triathlon takes place in July and is attended by international competitors who excel in three sporting events—swimming, cycling, and running. The triathlon is open to men and women of all ages. Men and women compete concurrently but in separate categories. In addition to gender, the athletes are further categorized according to the following age brackets: 18 to 24; 25 to 35; 36 to 45; and over 45.

Conduct research on triathlon events and begin the presentation with at least two slides that describe traditional triathlon competitions. The next two slides should include the categories in which competitors are separated and a diagram that illustrates the race route. The 1600-meter swimming event takes place in Lake Hennessy, which adjoins Montagna del Pattino. The 50-mile cycling event begins at the lake and finishes at the Brownsville Town Square. The 26-mile marathon finishes at Montagna del Pattino Summit Lodge. Refer to Project 16I_Summer, Slide 4 to see an example of how this information can be included in a SmartArt graphic.

As you conduct your research, explore the types of sponsors involved in triathlon events and the prizes awarded to winners. Include this information on two slides and conclude the presentation with one slide that discusses the mobile medical facilities that will be available to competitors and bystanders as heat exhaustion can affect both athletes and fans. The event draws a large number of spectators, with rooms at the Summit Lodge typically reserved two months in advance. Use the techniques that you learned in this chapter to illustrate the presentation. (See the note at the end of Project 16L for hints about locating images.) Add the date and file name to the Notes and Handouts footer and check the presentation for spelling errors. Save the presentation as **16P_Triathlon_Firstname_Lastname** and submit it as directed.

End **You have completed Project 16P** _____

Outcomes-Based Assessments

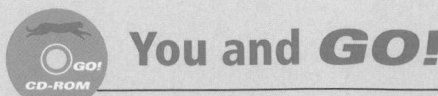

You and *GO!*

Project 16Q — You and *GO!*

In this project, you will construct a solution by applying any combination of the skills you practiced from the Objectives in Projects 16A and 16B.

Close PowerPoint and any other open windows. Display the Start menu, click Computer, and then navigate to the student files that accompany this textbook. In the folder **04_you_and_go**, locate and open the folder for this chapter. Open and print the instructions for this project, which are provided to you in Adobe PDF format. Follow the instructions to create a presentation about a place to which you have traveled or would like to travel.

 End You have completed Project 16Q —————————

GO! with Help

Project 16R — *GO!* with Help

The PowerPoint Help system is extensive and can help you as you work. In this project, you will view information about creating a photo album in PowerPoint.

1 **Start** PowerPoint. On the right side of the Ribbon, click the **Microsoft Office PowerPoint Help** button to open the PowerPoint Help window. In the **Search** box, type **Create a Photo Album** and then press ⏎.

2 In the displayed search results, click **Create a photo album**. Maximize the displayed window, and then read about photo albums and how you can create them in PowerPoint.

3 If you want to do so, print a copy of the information by clicking the printer button at the top of Microsoft Office PowerPoint Help window.

4 Close the **Help** window, and then close PowerPoint.

 End You have completed Project 16R —————————

Outcomes-Based Assessments

PowerPoint
chaptersixteen

Group Business Running Case

Project 16S — Group Business Running Case

In this project, you will apply the skills you practiced from the Objectives in Projects 16A and 16B.

Your instructor may assign this group case project to your class. If your instructor assigns this project, he or she will provide you with information and instructions to work as part of a group. The group will apply the skills gained thus far to help the Bell Orchid Hotel Group achieve its business goals.

End **You have completed Project 16S** —————————————

chapter seventeen

17

Enhancing a Presentation with Animation, Tables, and Charts

OBJECTIVES

At the end of this chapter you will be able to:

OUTCOMES

Mastering these objectives will enable you to:

---

1. Customize Slide Backgrounds and Themes
2. Animate a Slide Show

PROJECT 17A
Customize a Presentation

---

3. Create and Modify Tables
4. Create and Modify Charts

PROJECT 17B
Present Data with Tables and Charts

Select National Properties

Select National Properties is a diversified real estate company that develops, builds, manages, and acquires a wide variety of properties nationwide. Among the company's portfolio of properties are shopping malls, mixed-use town center developments, high-rise office buildings, office parks, industrial buildings and warehouses, multifamily housing developments, educational facilities, and hospitals. Residential developments are mainly located in and around the company's hometown, Chicago; commercial and public buildings in the portfolio are located nationwide. The company is well respected for its focus on quality and commitment to the environment and economic development of the areas where it operates.

Enhancing a Presentation with Animation, Tables, and Charts

Recall that the presentation theme applies a consistent look to a presentation. You can customize a presentation by modifying the theme and by applying animation to slide elements, and you can enhance your presentations by creating tables and charts that help your audience understand numeric data and trends just as pictures and diagrams help illustrate a concept. The data that you present should determine whether a table or a chart would most appropriately display your information. The charts most commonly used in PowerPoint presentations are bar, column, line, and pie. Styles applied to your tables and charts unify these slide elements by complementing your presentation theme.

Project 17A New Homes

In Activities 17.01 through 17.8, you will edit and format a presentation that Shaun Walker, President of Select National Properties, has created for a City Council meeting that describes a proposed residential development. Your completed presentation will look similar to Figure 17.1.

For Project 17A, you will need the following files:

p17A_Bedroom

p17A_Community

p17A_Family_Room

p17A_New_Homes

You will save your presentation as
17A_New_Homes_Firstname_Lastname

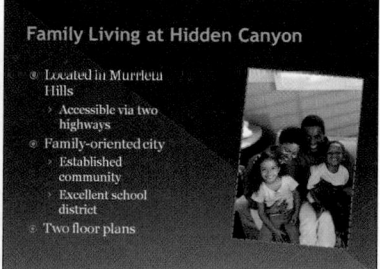

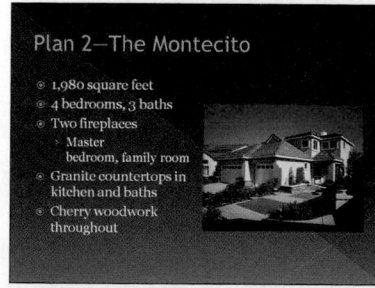

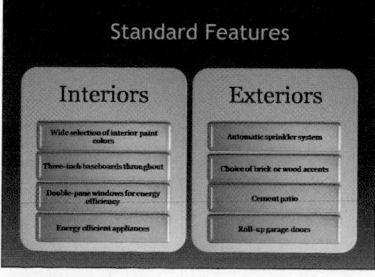

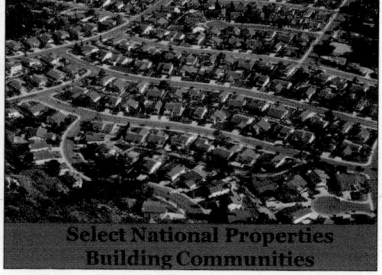

Figure 17.1

Project 17A—New Homes

Objective 1
Customize Slide Backgrounds and Themes

You have practiced customizing presentations by applying themes with unified design elements, backgrounds, and colors that provide a consistent look in your presentation. You can further customize a slide by changing the background color, applying a background style, or by inserting a picture on the slide background.

Activity 17.01 Applying a Background Style

Recall that the presentation theme is a coordinated, predefined set of colors, fonts, lines, and fill effects. In this activity, you will open a presentation in which the Verve theme is applied, and then you will change the theme colors for the entire presentation and the background style for the first slide.

Note — Comparing Your Screen With the Figures in This Textbook

Your screen will match the figures shown in this textbook if you set your screen resolution to 1024 x 768. At other resolutions, your screen will closely resemble, but not match, the figures shown. To view your screen's resolution, on the Windows desktop, right-click in a blank area, click Personalize, and then click Display Settings.

---

1 **Start** PowerPoint. From your student files, **Open** the file

p17A_New_Homes. From the **Office** menu 🗐 , click **Save As**, and then click the **New Folder** button. Navigate to the location where you are saving your solution files, create a folder with the name **PowerPoint Chapter 17** and then click **OK**. In the **File name** box, type **17A_New_Homes_Firstname_Lastname** and then click **Save** to save your file.

2 Click the **Design tab**, and then in the **Themes group**, click the **Colors** button. Click **Trek** to change the theme color for the entire presentation.

3 With **Slide 1** displayed, on the **Design tab**, in the **Background group**, click the **Background Styles** button to display the Background Styles gallery, as shown in Figure 17.2.

A **background style** is a slide background fill variation that combines theme colors in different intensities.

Figure 17.2

Background Styles gallery

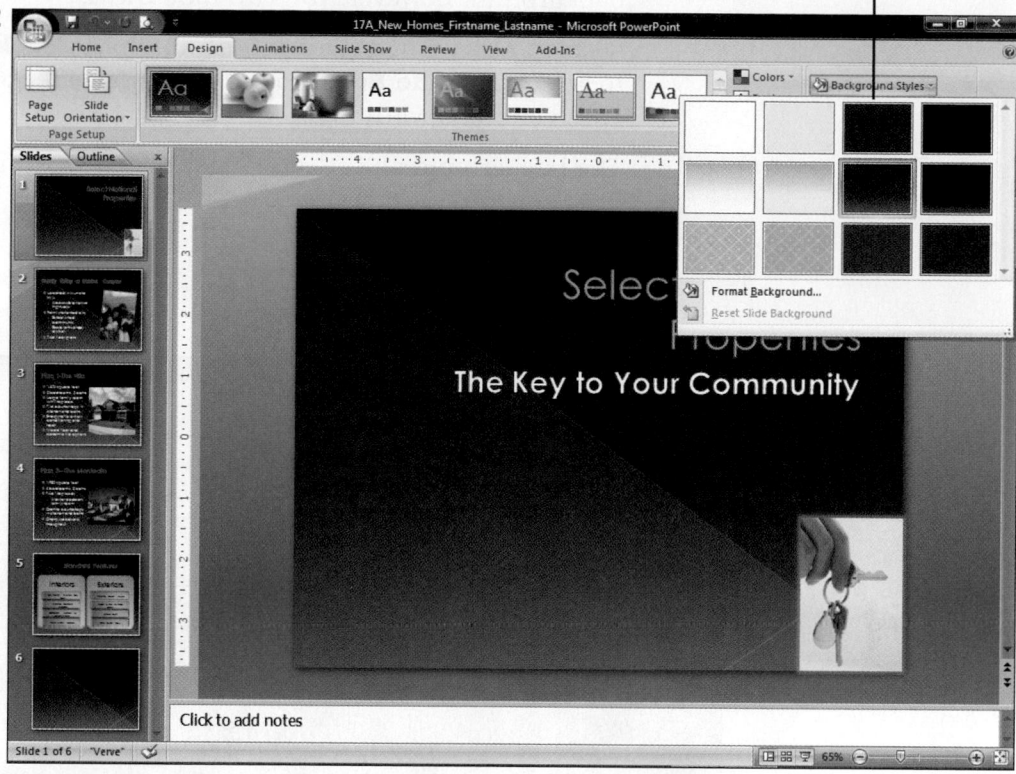

4 Point to each of the background styles to use Live Preview to view the style on **Slide 1**. Then, in the first row, *right-click* **Style 2** to display the shortcut menu. Click **Apply to Selected Slides**.

The background style is applied to Slide 1.

5 **Save** your presentation.

More Knowledge

Applying Background Styles to All Slides in a Presentation

You do not need to display the shortcut menu to apply a background style to all of the slides in a presentation. Click the background style that you want to apply and the style will be applied to all of the slides in the presentation.

Activity 17.02 Hiding Background Graphics

Slide themes and backgrounds often contain graphic elements that display on slides with various layouts. In the Verve theme applied to this presentation, the background includes a triangle and a line that intersect near the lower right corner of the slide. Sometimes the background graphics interfere with the slide content. When this happens, you can hide the background graphics.

1 Display **Slide 6** and notice that on this slide, you can clearly see the triangle and line on the slide background.

You cannot *delete* these objects because they are a part of the slide background; however, you can hide them.

2 Display **Slide 5**. On the **Design tab**, in the **Background group**, click to select the **Hide Background Graphics** check box, and then compare your slide with Figure 17.3.

The background objects no longer display behind the SmartArt diagram.

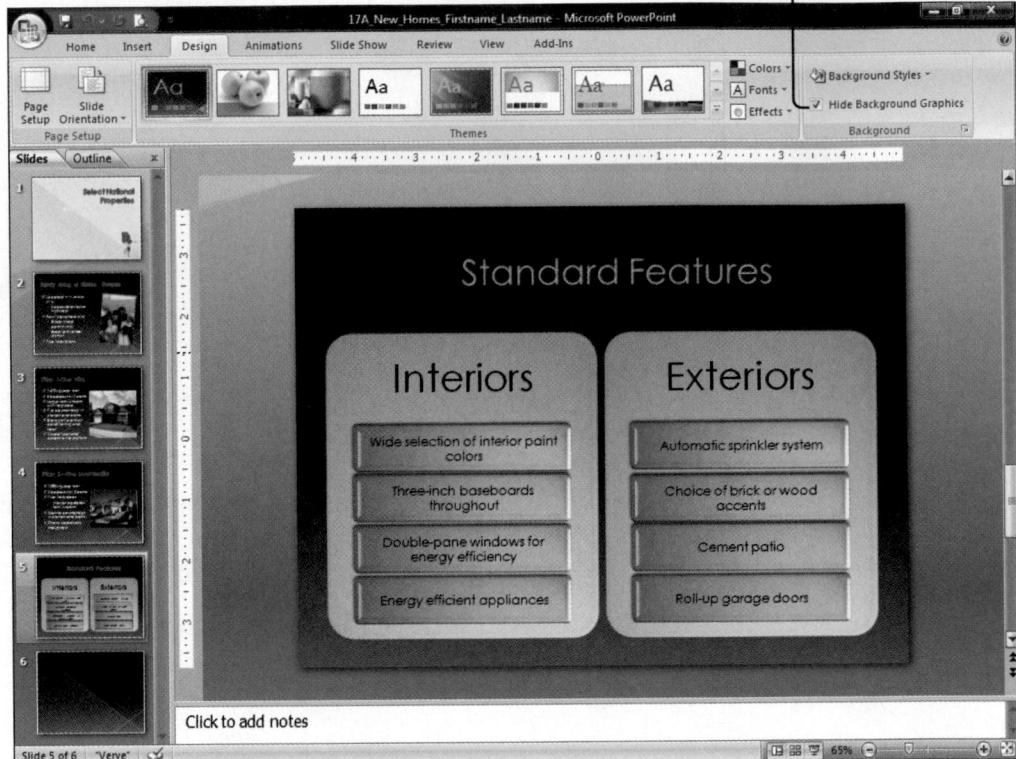

Figure 17.3

Hide Background Graphics check box selected

3 Display **Slide 1**. On the **Design tab**, in the **Background group**, select the **Hide Background Graphics** check box to toggle the graphics off.

4 Click the **Hide Background Graphics** check box again to toggle the graphics on.

5 **Save** the presentation.

Activity 17.03 Formatting a Slide Background with a Picture

You can insert a picture on a slide background so the image fills the entire slide.

1 Display **Slide 3**, and then click the **Home tab**. In the **Slides group**, click the **New Slide arrow**, and then click the **Title Only** layout.

2 Click the **Design tab**. In the **Background group**, click the **Hide Background Graphics** check box, and then click the **Background Styles** button. Below the displayed gallery, click **Format Background**.

The Format Background dialog box displays, providing options for customizing slide backgrounds.

3 If necessary, on the left side of the dialog box, click Fill. On the right side of the dialog box, under **Fill**, click the **Picture or texture fill** option button as shown in Figure 17.4, and then notice that on the slide background, a textured fill displays.

Your background may differ

Figure 17.4

Fill selected

Picture or texture fill option button selected

4 Under **Insert from**, click the **File** button to display the **Insert Picture** dialog box. Navigate to the location where your student files are located, and then click **p17A_Bedroom**. Click **Insert**.

Notice that the picture displays on the background of Slide 4.

5 In the **Format Background** dialog box, under **Stretch options**, verify that the **Left**, **Right**, **Top**, and **Bottom Offsets** are set to **0%** and make changes as necessary. Compare your dialog box with Figure 17.5.

The Stretch options enable you to control the way in which the picture displays on the slide background by cropping portions of the picture and then stretching it to fit on the background. Setting the Offsets to 0% ensures that the slide background is formatted with the original picture in its entirety.

Figure 17.5

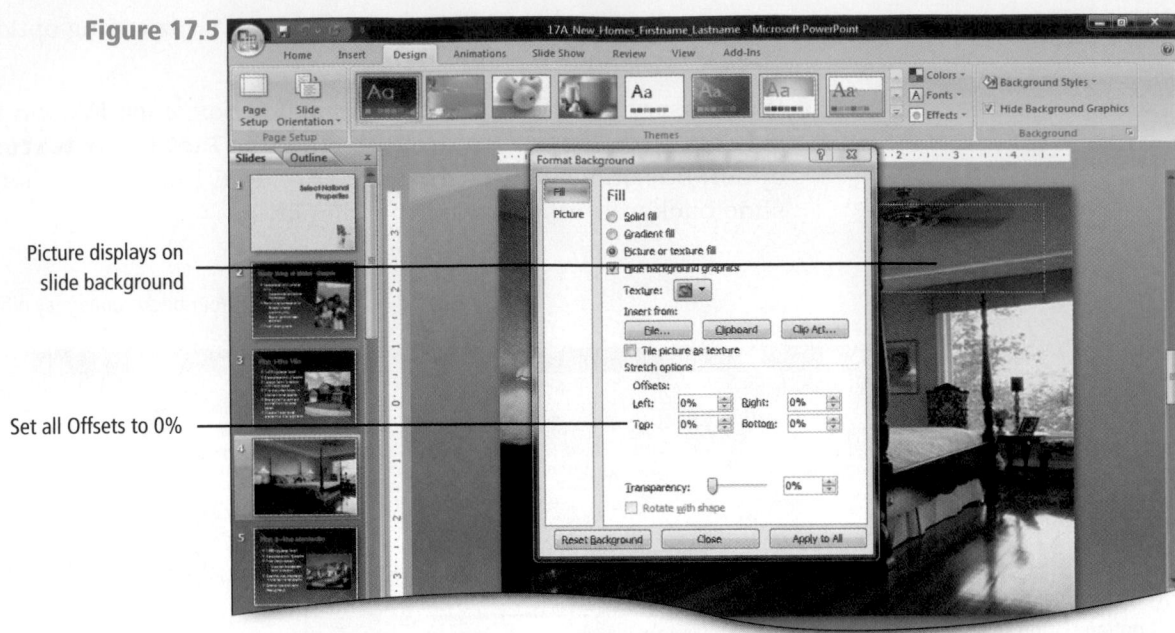

Picture displays on
slide background

Set all Offsets to 0%

6 Click **Close** and notice that the picture has been applied to the slide
background.

When a picture is applied to the slide background using the Format
Background option, the picture is not treated as an object. Thus,
you cannot move it or size it.

7 Click in the title placeholder, type **Master Bedroom** and then notice
that the background picture does not provide sufficient contrast with
the text to display the title effectively.

8 Point to the outer edge of the title placeholder so that the 🔀 pointer
displays. Drag the title placeholder down and to the left so that its
lower left corner aligns with the lower left corner of the slide. Release
the mouse button, and then compare your slide with Figure 17.6.

The brown background of the floor provides good contrast for the
title text.

Figure 17.6

Workshop

Overlaying Text on a Picture

When you insert a picture on a slide background, it is a good idea to choose a picture that has a solid area in which you can overlay a text box or title. For example, in the picture that you inserted on Slide 4, the lower left corner has a brown area that provides good contrast for light-colored text. When the picture that you choose does not contain a solid area, you can create one by filling the text box with color.

9 Display **Slide 5**, and then insert a **New Slide** with the **Title Only** layout.

10 On the **Design tab**, in the **Background group**, select the **Hide Background Graphics** check box, and then click the **Background Styles** button. Click **Format Background**. Under **Fill**, click the **Picture or texture fill** option button. Under **Insert from**, click **File**. Navigate to your student files, click **p17A_Family_Room**, and then click **Insert**. Under **Stretch options**, change as necessary the **Left**, **Right**, **Top**, and **Bottom Offsets** to **0%**. **Close** the **Format Background** dialog box to format the slide background with the picture.

11 In the title placeholder, type **Family Room** Select the text, and then on the Mini toolbar, click the **Font Color button arrow**  to display the **Theme Colors gallery**. In the first row, click the first color, **Black, Background 1**. On the Mini toolbar, click the **Align Text Right** button ▤ .

12 Point to the outer edge of the placeholder to display the 🔾 pointer, and then drag the placeholder up and to the right so that its upper right corner aligns with the upper right corner of the slide. Compare your slide with Figure 17.7.

Figure 17.7

13 Display **Slide 8**. Using the process that you practiced in **Step 10**, insert the picture **p17A_Community** on the background of **Slide 8**.

Notice that the background does not provide sufficient contrast for the slide title to be easily read. You can apply a Shape Style to the title placeholder so that the text is visible.

14 Click in the title placeholder, and then click the **Format tab**. In the **Shape Styles group**, click the **More** button . In the second row of the **Shape Styles gallery**, click the third style—**Colored Fill – Accent 2**.

15 Point to the outer edge of the placeholder to display the ⊕ pointer, and then drag the placeholder down so that its bottom edge aligns with the bottom of the slide. Click outside of the placeholder, and then compare your slide with Figure 17.8.

Figure 17.8

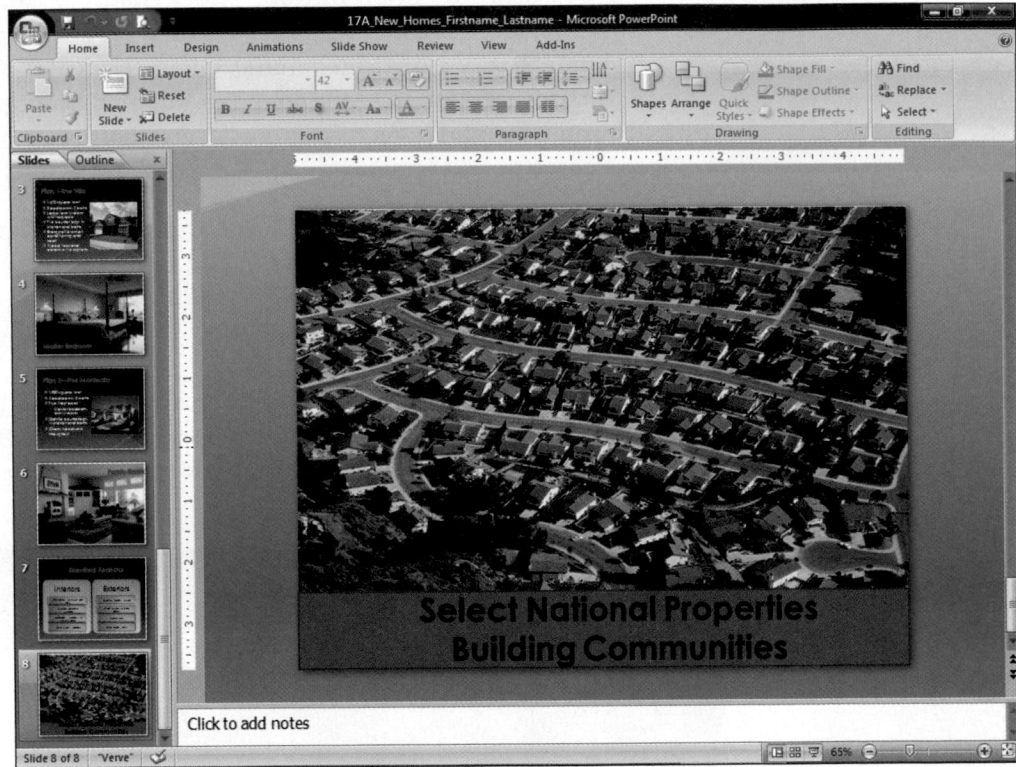

16 **Save** 🖫 your presentation.

Activity 17.04 Applying a Background Fill Color and Resetting a Slide Background

1 Display **Slide 1**, and then click the **Design tab**. In the **Background group**, click the **Background Styles** button, and then click **Format Background**. In the **Format Background** dialog box, if necessary, click the Solid fill option button, and then click the **Color** button 🎨▾. Under **Theme Colors**, in the last row, click the second color—**Black, Text 1, Lighter 5%**. Click **Close**.

The solid fill color is applied to the slide background.

2 On the **Design tab**, in the **Background group**, click the **Background Styles** button. Below the gallery, click **Reset Slide Background**.

After making many changes to a slide background, you may decide that the original theme formatting is the best choice to display the text and graphics on a slide. The Reset Slide Background feature restores the original theme formatting to a slide.

3 **Save** 🖫 the presentation.

Activity 17.05 Modifying Font Themes

Every presentation theme includes a ***font theme*** that determines the font applied to two types of slide text—headings and body. The ***headings font*** is applied to slide titles and the ***body font*** is applied to all other text. Sometimes the heading and body fonts are the same, but are different sizes. In other font themes, the heading and body fonts are different. When you apply a new font theme to the presentation, the text on every slide is updated with the new heading and body fonts.

1 If necessary, display **Slide 1**. Click anywhere in the title placeholder. Click the **Home tab**, and then in the **Font group**, click the **Font button arrow** `Calibri (Headings)  ▾`. Notice that at the top of the Font list, under **Theme Fonts**, *Century Gothic (Headings)* and *Century Gothic (Body)* display as shown in Figure 17.9.

Figure 17.9

Theme fonts ————

2 Click anywhere on the slide to close the Font list.

3 Click the **Design tab**, and then in the **Themes group**, click the **Fonts** button.

This list displays the name of each font theme and the pair of fonts in the theme. The first and larger font in each pair is the Headings font and the second and smaller font in each pair is the Body font.

4 Scroll the **Theme Fonts** list and notice that the last theme—*Verve*—is selected as shown in Figure 17.10.

Current font theme

Figure 17.10

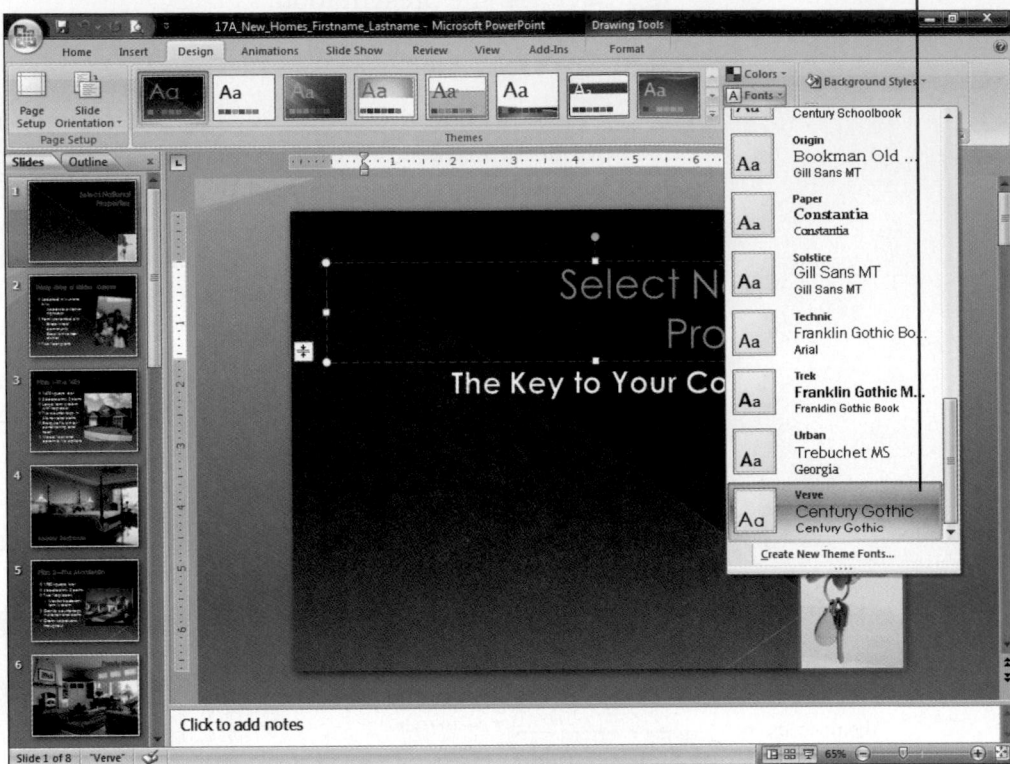

5 Point to several of the themes and watch as Live Preview changes the title and subtitle text. Click the **Urban** theme, and then scroll through the slides in the presentation, noticing that the font changes have been applied to every slide.

6 **Save** the presentation.

Objective 2
Animate a Slide Show

Animation effects are used to introduce individual slide elements so that the slide can progress one element at a time. When used correctly, animation effects focus the audience's attention, providing the speaker with an opportunity to emphasize important points using the slide element as an effective visual aid.

Activity 17.06 Applying Entrance Effects

Entrance effects are animations that bring a slide element onto the screen.

1 Display **Slide 1**. Click the **Animations tab**, and then in the

Transition to This Slide group, click the **More** button. Under **Wipes**, click the transition that contains four arrows pointing inward toward a center box—**Box In**. Click the **Transition Speed arrow**, and then click **Medium**. Click the **Apply To All** button.

2 Display **Slide 2**, and then click the bulleted list placeholder. In the **Animations group**, click the **Custom Animation** button. At the top of the displayed **Custom Animation** task pane, click the **Add Effect** button, and then point to **Entrance**. Compare your screen with Figure 17.11.

A list of the most recently used animation effects displays. At the bottom of the list, the *More Effects* option displays.

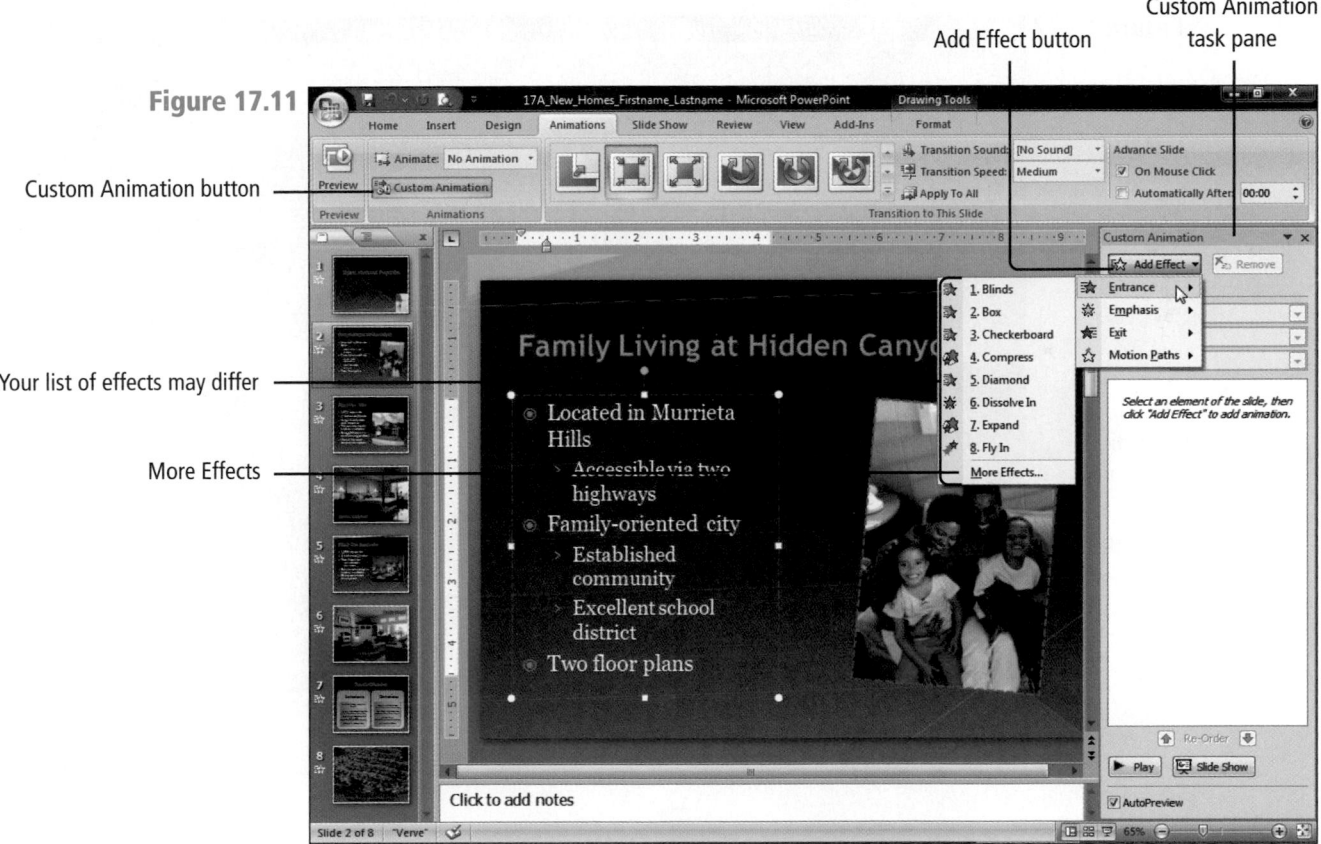

Figure 17.11

Custom Animation button

Your list of effects may differ

More Effects

Add Effect button

Custom Animation task pane

3 Click **More Effects** to display the **Add Entrance Effect** dialog box. Scroll through the list to view the *Basic*, *Subtle*, *Moderate*, and *Exciting* entrance effects.

4 At the bottom of the **Add Entrance Effect** dialog box, if necessary, click to select the Preview Effect check box. Click several of the effects in each of the four categories to view the animation.

5 Under **Basic**, click **Blinds**, and then click **OK**. Compare your screen with Figure 17.12.

On the slide, notice that the numbers *1*, *2*, and *3* display to the left of the bulleted list placeholder, indicating the order in which the bullet points will display. For example, the first bullet point and its subordinate bullet are both numbered *1*. Thus, both will display at the same time.

In the task pane, the *custom animation list* indicates that an animation effect has been applied to the selected item. The custom animation list displays the animation sequences for a slide. The mouse image next to item 1 in the custom animation list indicates that the animation will display the bulleted list placeholder text when the left mouse button is clicked or when the Spacebar is pressed. Below item 1, a button with two downward-pointing arrows displays. This is the *Click to expand contents* button, which when clicked, displays the animation for bullet points 1, 2, and 3.

Click to expand contents button   Custom animation list

Figure 17.12

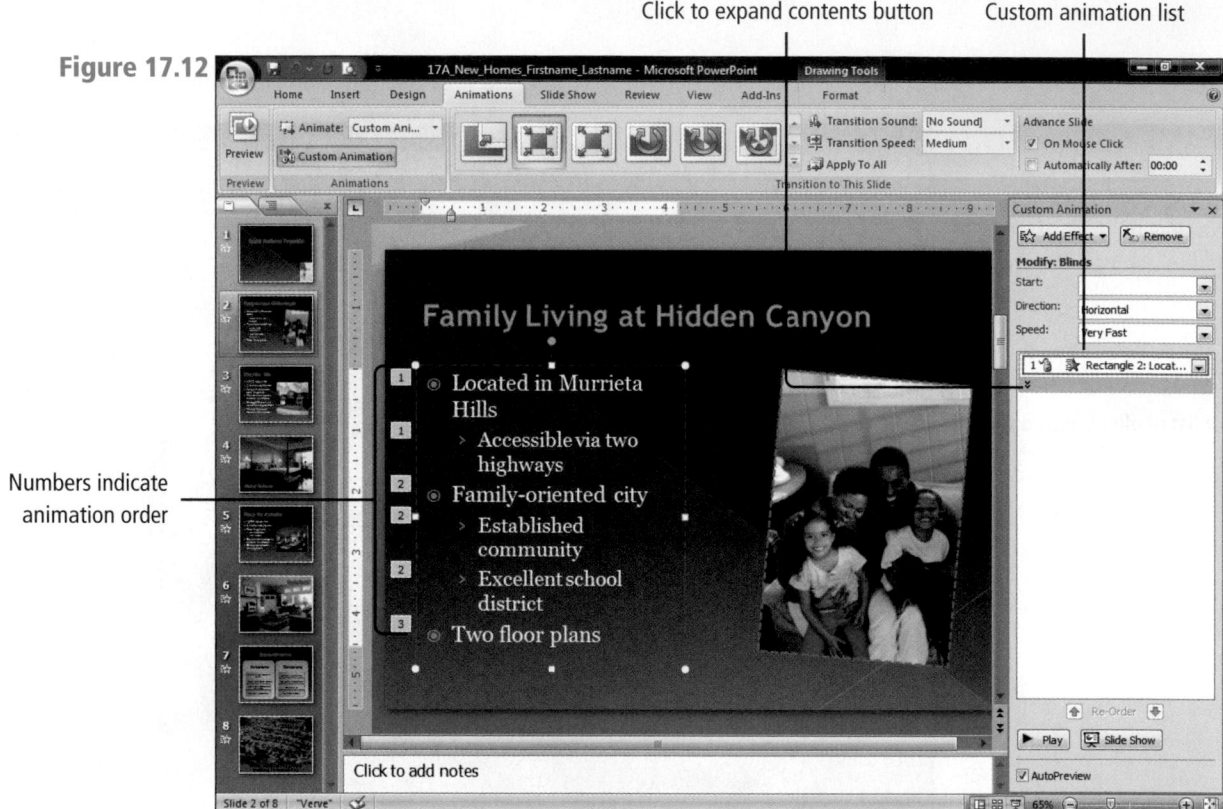

Numbers indicate
animation order

6 Click to select the picture. In the **Custom Animation** task pane, click the **Add Effect** button, point to **Entrance**, and then click **More Effects**. In the displayed **Add Entrance Effect** dialog box, under **Basic**, click **Dissolve In**, and then click **OK**.

The task pane displays item number 4 in the custom animation list, and the number 4 also displays on the slide next to the picture. These numbers display only when the Custom Animation task pane is open.

7 At the bottom of the task pane, click the **Play** button.

For the active slide only, the slide transition and each animation display. Additionally, the task pane indicates the number of seconds that elapse with each animation. This is a good way to test the animations you have applied to a single slide, without switching to Slide Show view.

8 **Save** 🖫 the presentation.

More Knowledge

Removing Animation Effects

You can remove animation that you have applied to a slide element by clicking the element in the Custom Animation task pane, and then clicking the Remove button. If you have applied an animation effect to a slide element, and then change your mind and decide to apply a different one, be sure to remove the animation that you do not want to use. Otherwise, when you view your slide show, all of the animation effects will display one after another.

Activity 17.07 Setting Effect and Timing Options

After animation is applied, you can set *effect options*. By using effect options, you can change the direction of the effect and play a sound when an animation takes place. Effect options also enable you to control the levels of text that display. For example, you can animate text by first-level paragraphs, so that first-level bullet points and their subordinate text display all at once. Or, you can animate text by second-, third-, fourth-, or fifth-level paragraphs so that each bullet on the slide, regardless of level, displays individually. Finally, you can use the effect options to control how text displays when the next animation sequence occurs. For example, after you have discussed a bullet point, you can click the mouse button to display the next point and dim the previous point, thus keeping the audience focused on the new bullet point.

1 With **Slide 2** displayed, click in the bulleted list placeholder. If necessary, display the Custom Animation task pane by clicking the Custom Animation button, in the Animations group.

2 In the **custom animation list**, notice that item 1 is selected and a downward-pointing arrow displays to the right of the item. In the **custom animation list**, click the **item 1 arrow**, and then point to **Effect Options**, as shown in Figure 17.13.

Figure 17.13

Effect Options

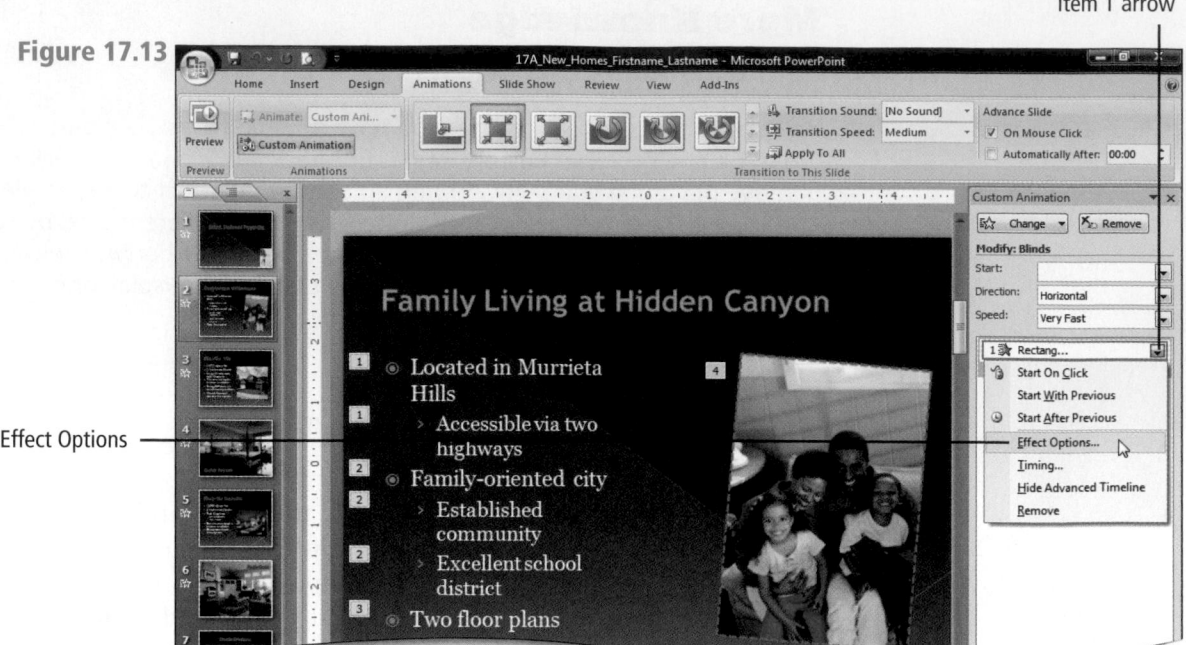

3 Click **Effect Options** to display the **Blinds** dialog box.

When you click the Effect Options command, the dialog box that displays is named according to the applied animation.

4 In the **Blinds dialog box**, if necessary, click the **Effect tab**. Under **Enhancements**, click the **After animation arrow**.

Use the After animation options to choose how the text will display after it is animated and you click the mouse button. The default—*Don't Dim*—keeps the text onscreen without any changes. You can dim the text by choosing a color that blends with the slide background, or you can hide the text so that it does not display at all.

5 In the row of colors, click the **fifth color**, as shown in Figure 17.14, and then click **OK** to apply the effect option.

Figure 17.14

After animation arrow

Click this color

6 Click to select the picture. Near the top of the **Custom Animation** task pane, under **Modify: Dissolve In**, click the **Start arrow** to display three options—On Click, With Previous, and After Previous.

The *On Click* option begins the animation sequence for the selected slide element when the mouse button is clicked or the Spacebar is pressed. The *With Previous* option begins the animation sequence at the same time as the item preceding it in the custom animation list. The *After Previous* option begins the animation sequence for the selected slide element immediately after the completion of the previous animation or transition.

7 Click **After Previous**. In the **Custom Animation** task pane, under **Modify: Dissolve In**, click the **Speed arrow**, and then click **Fast**. Compare your task pane with Figure 17.15.

Figure 17.15

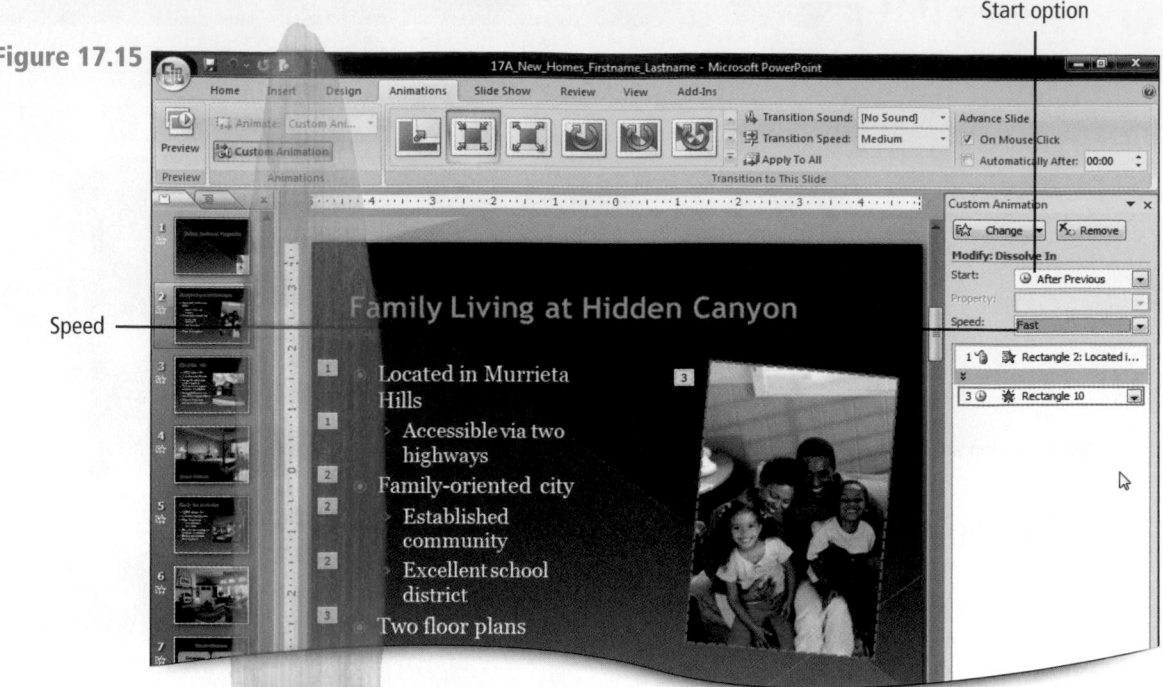

Start option

Speed

8 At the bottom of the **Custom Animation** task pane, click **Play** to view the animation applied to the slide.

9 Display **Slide 4**, and then click in the title placeholder. In the **Custom Animation** task pane, click **Add Effect**, and then point to **Entrance**. Click **More Effects**. Under **Basic**, click **Fly In**, and then click **OK**.

10 In the **Custom Animation task pane**, click the **Start arrow**, and then click **After Previous** so that the title displays immediately after the slide transition. If necessary, click the **Direction arrow**, and then click **From Bottom**. In the **Custom Animation** task pane, click **Play** to view the animation applied to the slide.

11 Display **Slide 6**, and then click in the title placeholder. In the **Custom Animation** task pane, click **Add Effect**, and then point to **Entrance**.

Recall that the Animation Effects list displays the most recently applied animations.

12 In the **Animation Effects list**, click **Fly In**. Click the **Start arrow**, and then click **After Previous**. Click the **Direction arrow**, and then click **From Top**. In the **Custom Animation** task pane, click **Play** to view the animation applied to the slide.

13 **Close** ☒ the **Custom Animation** task pane, and then **Save** 🖫 the presentation.

Workshop

Applying Animation Effectively

It is not necessary to animate every item on every slide in your presentation. Too much animation can distract your audience by focusing their attention on what the presentation is going to do instead of the message that you are trying to convey. Remember, the purpose of animation is to draw attention to important text and graphics!

Activity 17.08 Applying Animation to a SmartArt Graphic

The most efficient way to animate a SmartArt graphic is to use one of the choices in the Animate list. Your animation choice can be modified using the Custom Animation task pane.

1 Display **Slide 7**, and then click anywhere in the *Interiors/Exteriors* SmartArt graphic to select it.

2 On the **Animations tab**, in the **Animations group**, click the **Animate arrow** to display the Animate list, as shown in Figure 17.16.

Animate arrow

Figure 17.16

Animate list

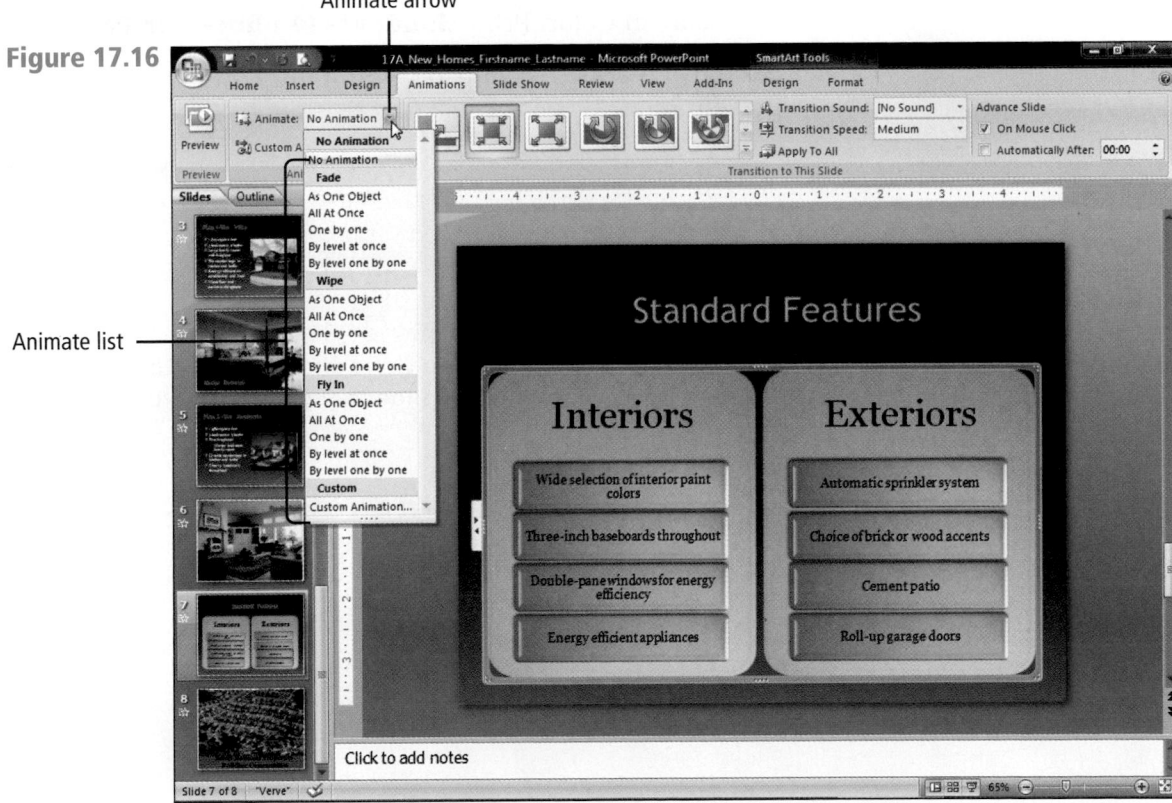

3 Point to several of the **Animate** options and watch as Live Preview displays the animation effects.

4 Under **Wipe**, click **By level at once**.

By level at once animates all shapes at the same level at the same time. In this case, the light-colored Interiors and Exteriors boxes will display at the same time, and then all of the gold boxes will display.

5 Click the **Slide Show tab**. In the **Start Slide Show group**, click **From Current Slide** to view the animation on Slide 7. Press Spacebar to advance through the SmartArt graphic animation effects. After the animations for Slide 7 are complete, press Esc to end the slide show and return to the presentation.

6 In the **Start Slide Show group**, click **From Beginning**, and then view your presentation, clicking the mouse button to advance through the slides. Notice the animation that is applied to each slide, and then when the black slide displays, click the mouse button one more time to display the presentation in Normal view.

7 Insert a **Header and Footer** for the **Notes and Handouts**. Include the **Date and time updated automatically**, the **Page number**, and a **Footer** with the file name **17A_New_Homes_Firstname_Lastname**

8 Check your *Chapter Assignment Sheet* or *Course Syllabus* or consult your instructor to determine if you are to submit your assignments on paper or electronically. To submit electronically, go to Step 10, and then follow the instructions provided by your instructor.

9 Display your presentation in **Print Preview**. If the pictures on the background of Slides 4, 6, and 8 do not display, set the Print Preview to display in Color. Print **Handouts (4 Slides Per Page)**.

10 **Save** the changes to your presentation, and then close the presentation.

More Knowledge

Showing Selected Slides During a Slide Show

When you are delivering a presentation, you can right-click to display the shortcut menu, and then point to Go to Slide to view a list of the slides in the presentation. Then, click the slide that you want to display.

End **You have completed Project 17A** —————————————

Project 17B **Developments**

In Activities 17.09 through 17.14, you will add a table and two charts to a presentation that Shaun Walker, President of Select National Properties, is creating to apprise investors of the status of several new residential developments. Your completed presentation will look similar to Figure 17.17.

You will save your presentation as
17B_Developments_Firstname_Lastname

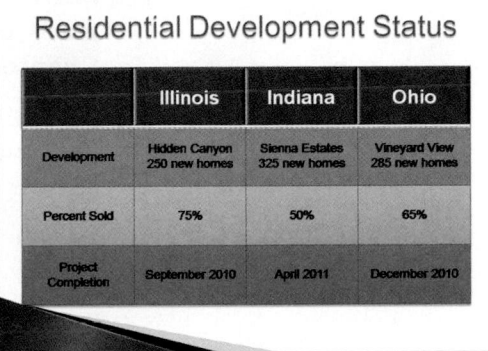

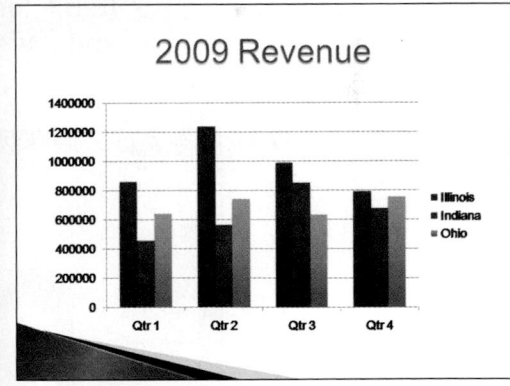

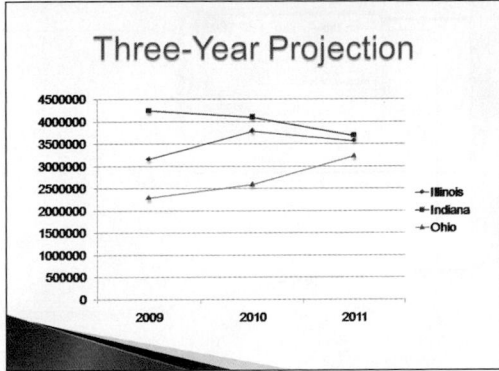

Figure 17.17
Project 17B—Developments

Objective 3
Create and Modify Tables

A *table* is a format for information that organizes and presents text and data in columns and rows. The intersection of a column and row is a *cell* and is the location in which you type text in a table.

Activity 17.09 Creating a Table

There are several ways to insert a table. You can create a table in Microsoft Office Word or Excel, and then paste and edit it in PowerPoint. You can also draw a table using the Draw Table pointer—a feature that is useful when the rows and columns contain cells of different sizes. You can insert a slide with a Content Layout and then click the Insert Table button, or you can click the Insert tab and then click Table. In this Activity, you will use a Content Layout to create a table.

1 **Start** PowerPoint, and then from your student files, open **p17B_Developments**. **Save** the presentation in your **PowerPoint Chapter 17** folder as **17B_Developments_Firstname_Lastname**

2 With **Slide 1** displayed, on the **Home tab**, in the **Slides group**, click the **New Slide** button to insert a slide with the **Title and Content** layout. In the title placeholder, type **Residential Development Status** and then **Center** [≡] the title.

3 In the content placeholder, click the **Insert Table** button [⊞] to display the Insert Table dialog box, as shown in Figure 17.18.

In the Insert Table dialog box, you can enter the number of columns and rows that you want the table to contain.

Figure 17.18

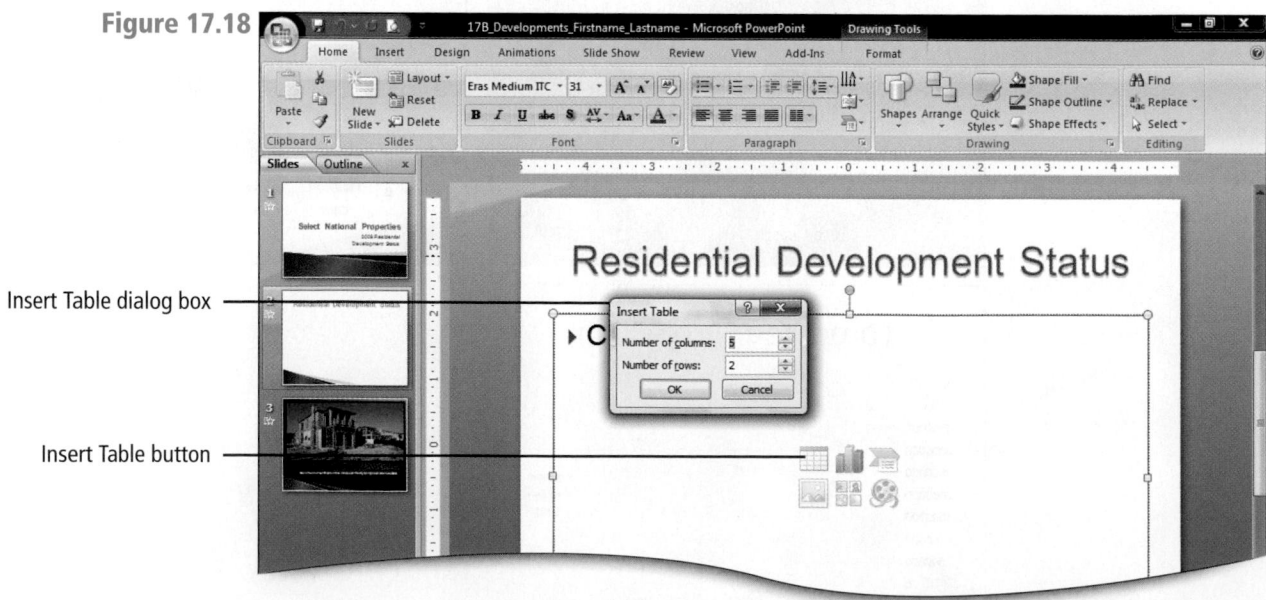

Insert Table dialog box

Insert Table button

4 In the **Insert Table** dialog box, in the **Number of columns** box, type **3** and then press Tab. In the **Number of rows** box, type **2** and then compare your dialog box with Figure 17.19.

Figure 17.19

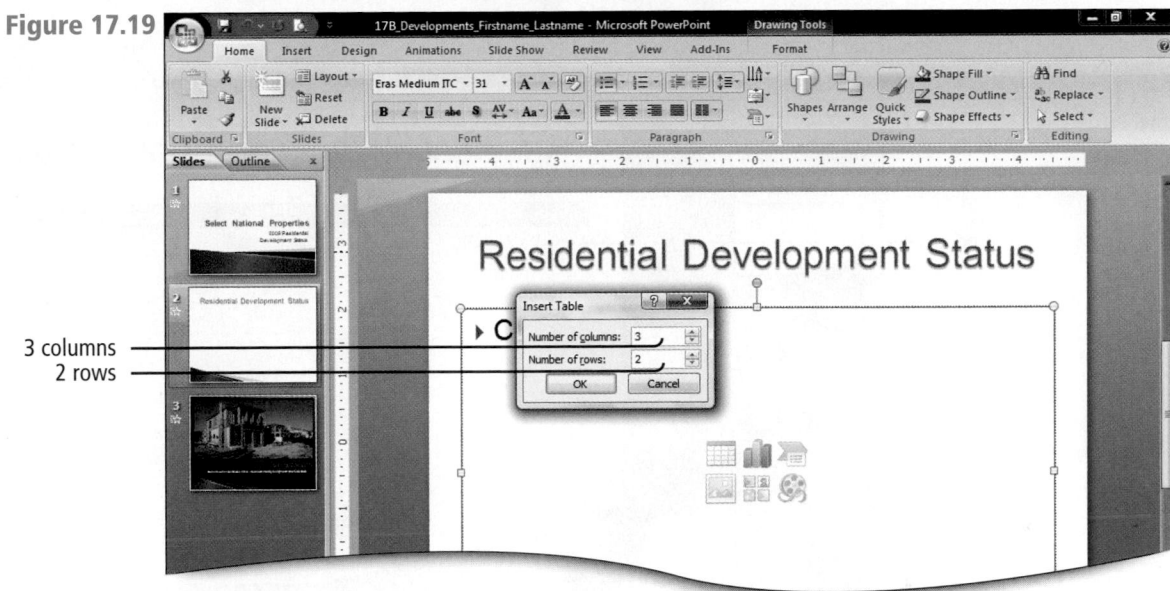

3 columns
2 rows

5 Click **OK** to create a table with three columns and two rows. Notice that the insertion point is blinking in the upper left cell of the table.

The table extends from the left side of the content placeholder to the right side and the three columns are equal in width. By default, a style is applied to the table.

6 With the insertion positioned in the first cell of the table, type **Illinois** and then press Tab.

Pressing Tab moves the insertion point to the next cell in the same row. If the insertion point is positioned in the last cell of a row, pressing Tab moves the insertion point to the first cell of the next row.

Alert!   **Did you press Enter instead of Tab?**

In a table, pressing Enter creates another line in the same cell, similar to the way you add a new bullet point in a content placeholder. If you press Enter by mistake, you can remove the extra line by pressing ←Bksp.

7 With the insertion point positioned in the second cell of the first row, type **Indiana** and then press Tab. Type **Ohio** and then press Tab to move the insertion point to the first cell in the second row. Compare your table with Figure 17.20.

Text inserted in table

Figure 17.20

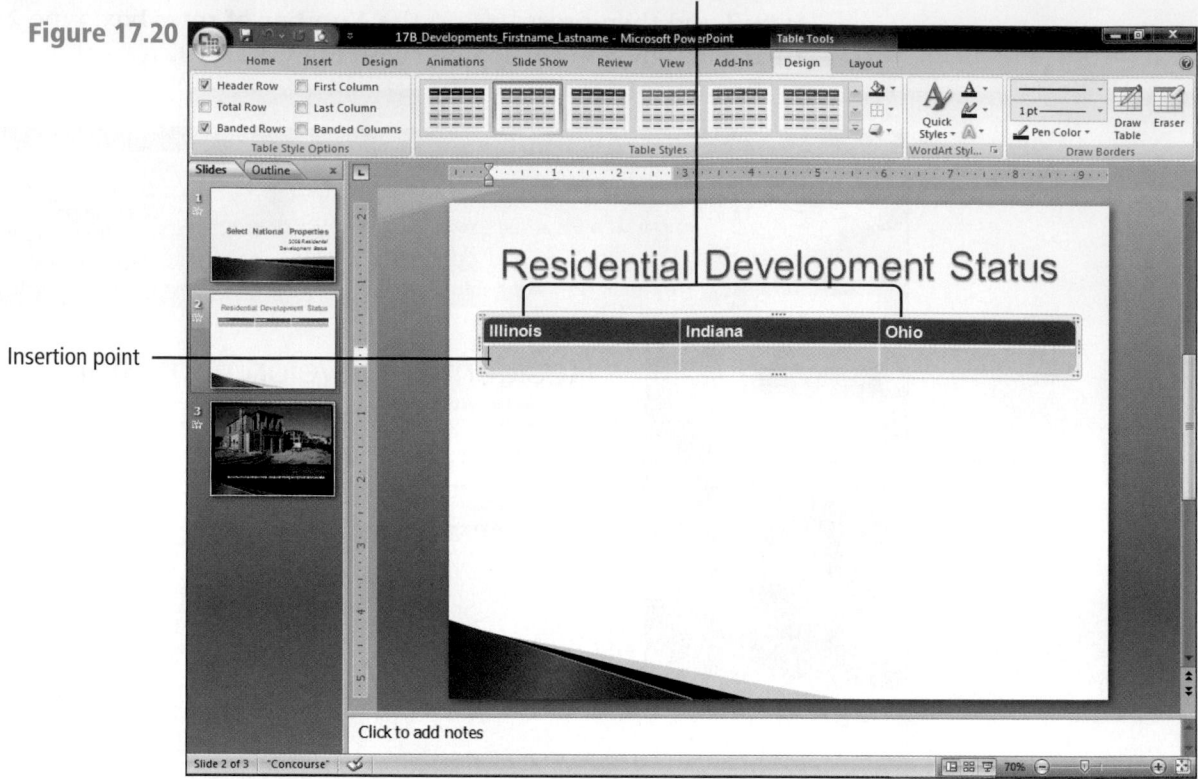

Insertion point

Residential Development Status

Illinois	Indiana	Ohio

Click to add notes

Slide 2 of 3   "Concourse"   70%

8 With the insertion positioned in the first cell of the second row, type **Hidden Canyon** and then press Enter to create a second line in the cell. Type **250 new homes** and then press Tab. Type **Sienna Estates** and then press Enter to create a second line in the cell. Type **325 new homes** and then press Tab. Type **Vineyard View** and then press Enter. Type **285 new homes** and then press Tab to insert a new blank row.

When the insertion point is positioned in the last cell of a table, pressing Tab inserts a new blank row at the bottom of the table.

9 In the first cell of the third row, type **September 2010** and then press Tab. Type **April 2011** and then press Tab Type **December 2010** and then compare your table with Figure 17.21.

Figure 17.21

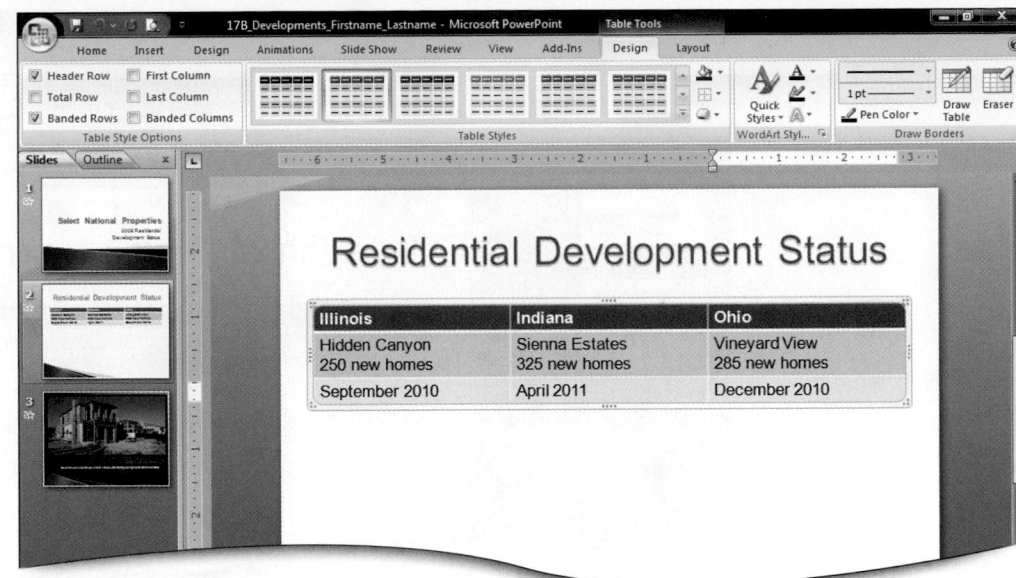

Alert! Did you add an extra row to the table?

Recall that when the insertion point is positioned in the last cell of the table, pressing ⟨Tab⟩ inserts a new blank row. If you inadvertently inserted a blank row in the table, on the Quick Access Toolbar, click Undo.

10 Save 💾 the presentation.

Activity 17.10 Modifying the Layout of a Table

You can modify the layout of a table by inserting or deleting rows and columns, changing the alignment of the text in a cell, adjusting the height and width of the entire table or selected rows and columns, and by merging multiple cells into one cell.

1 Click in any cell in the first column, and then click the **Layout tab**. In the **Rows & Columns group**, click the **Insert Left** button.

A new first column is inserted and the width of the columns is adjusted so that all four columns are the same width.

2 Click in the first cell in the *second row*, and then type **Development** Click in the first cell in the third row, type **Projected Completion** and then compare your table with Figure 17.22.

Figure 17.22

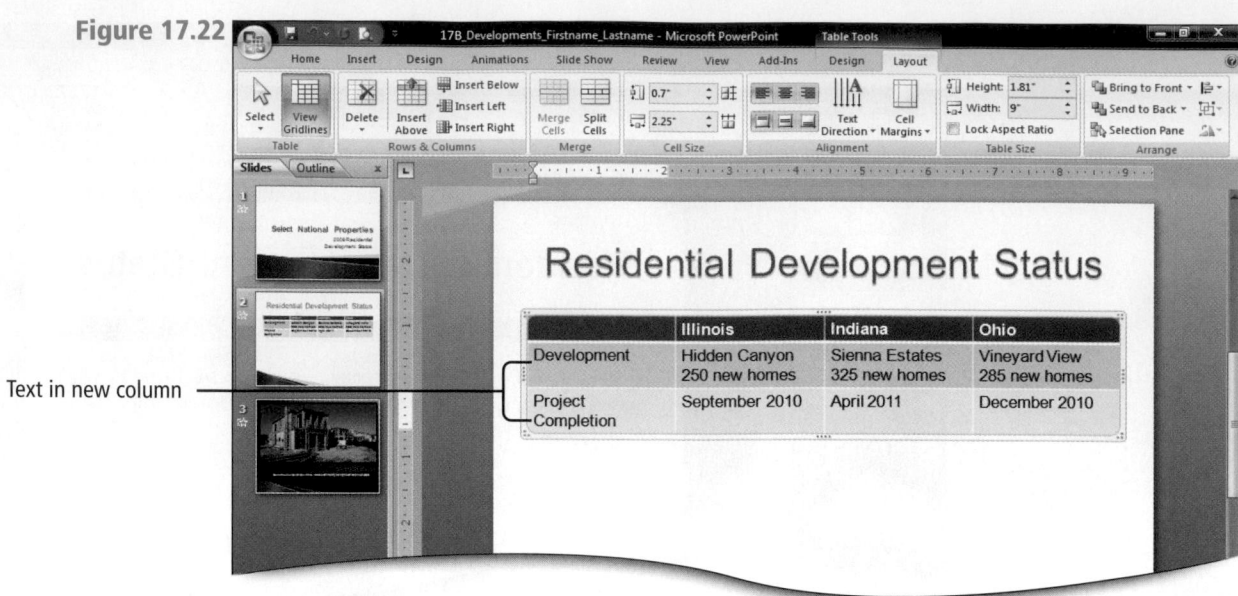

Text in new column ——

3 With the insertion point positioned in the third row, on the **Layout tab**, in the **Rows & Columns group**, click the **Insert Above** button to insert a new third row. In the first cell type **Percent Sold** and then press Tab. Type the remaining three entries, pressing Tab to move from cell to cell: **75% 50%** and **65%**

More Knowledge

Deleting Rows and Columns

To delete a row or column from a table, click in the row or column that you want to delete. Click the Layout tab, and then in the Rows & Columns group, click Delete. In the displayed list, click Delete Columns or Delete Rows.

4 At the center of the lower border surrounding the table, point to the four dots—the sizing handle—to display the [↕] pointer, as shown in Figure 17.23.

Sizing handle

Figure 17.23

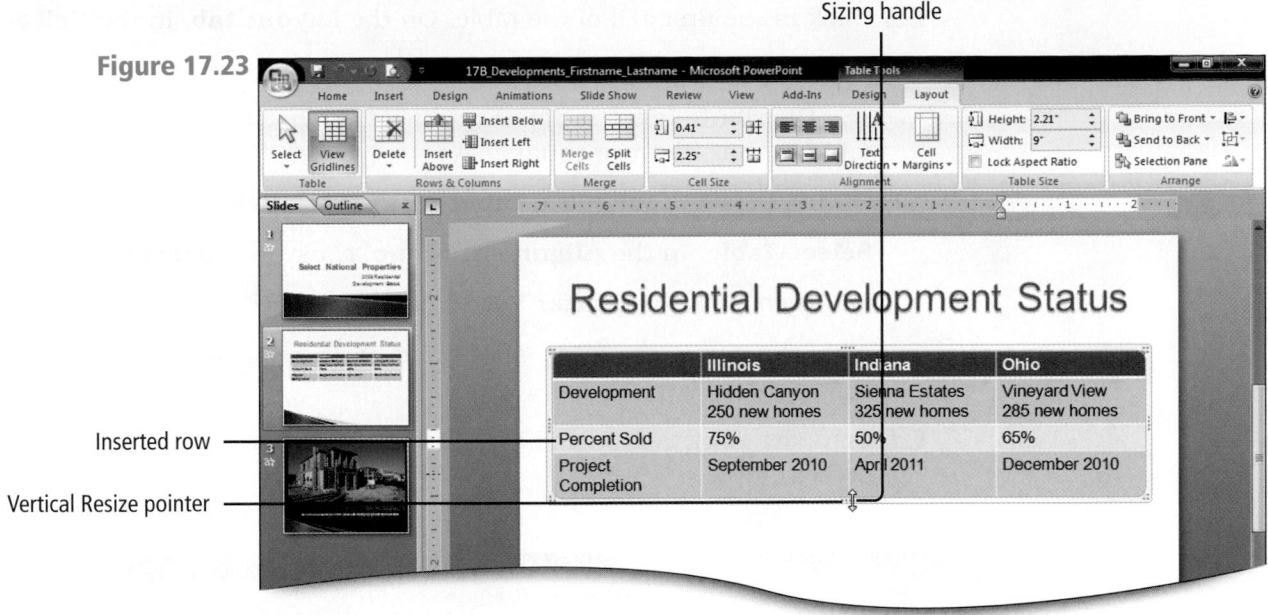

Inserted row

Vertical Resize pointer

5 Drag down until the lower left corner of the table outline touches the graphic in the lower left corner of the slide as shown in Figure 17.24, and then release the mouse button to size the table.

When you drag the pointer down, an outline of the table displays, indicating the new size of the table.

Figure 17.24

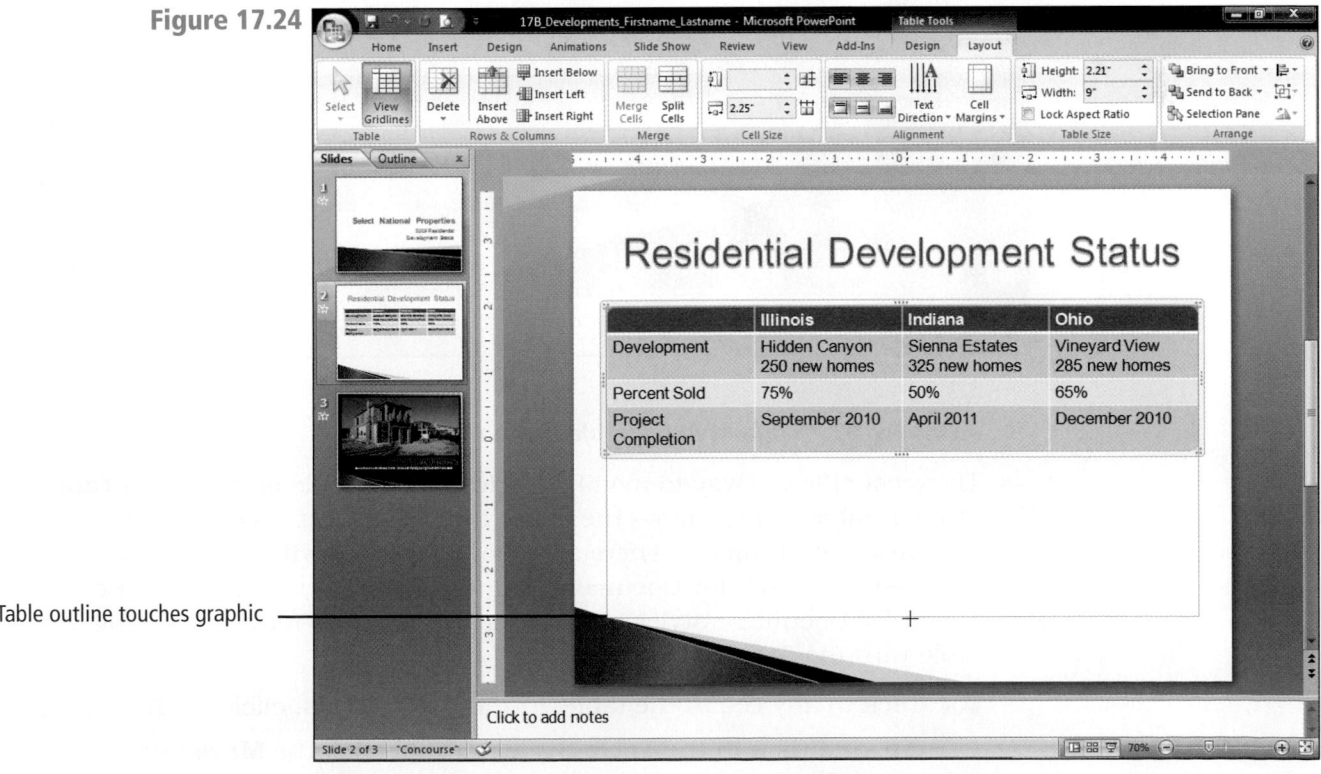

Table outline touches graphic

6 Click in the first cell of the table. On the **Layout tab**, in the **Cell Size group**, click the **Distribute Rows** ⊞ button.

The Distribute Rows command adjusts the height of the rows in the table so that they are equal.

7 On the **Layout tab**, in the **Table group**, click **Select**, and then click **Select Table**. In the **Alignment group**, click the **Center** button ≡, and then click the **Center Vertically** button ⊟.

All of the text in the table is centered horizontally and vertically within the cells.

8 Compare your table with Figure 17.25, and then **Save** 🖫 your presentation.

Figure 17.25

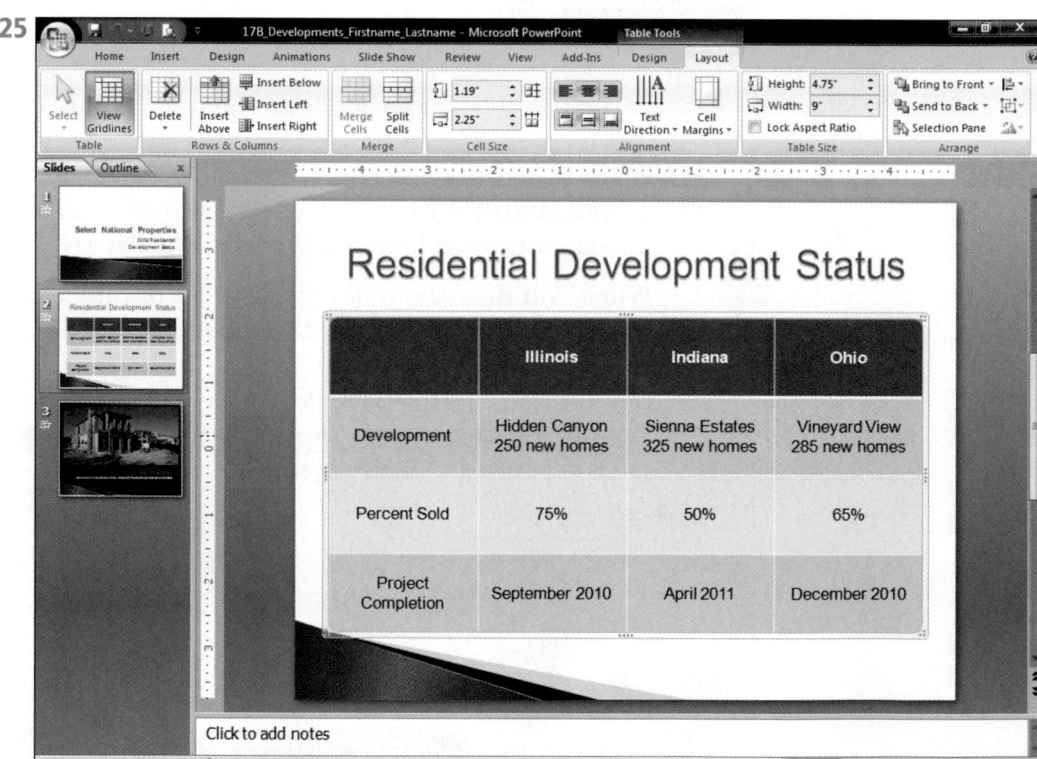

Activity 17.11 Modifying a Table Design

The most efficient way to modify the design of a table is to apply a *table style*. A table style formats the entire table so that it is consistent with the presentation theme. There are color categories within the table styles—Best Match for Document, Light, Medium, and Dark. The Best Match for Document styles provide the best choices for coordinating the table with the document theme.

1 Click in any cell in the table. In the **Table Tools**, click the **Design tab**, and then in the **Table Styles group**, click the **More** button ⊽. In the displayed **Table Styles gallery**, point to several of the styles to view the Live Preview of the style.

2 Under **Best Match for Document**, click the second button—**Themed Style 1 – Accent 1**—to apply the style to the table.

3 On the **Design tab**, in the **Table Style Options group**, click to clear the **Banded Rows** check box. Notice that each row except the header row displays in the same color.

The check boxes in the Table Style Options group control where Table Style formatting is applied.

4 Click again to select the **Banded Rows** check box.

5 Move the pointer outside of the table so that is positioned to the left of the first row in the table to display the ➡ pointer, as shown in Figure 17.26.

Figure 17.26

Right-pointing Row Select arrow

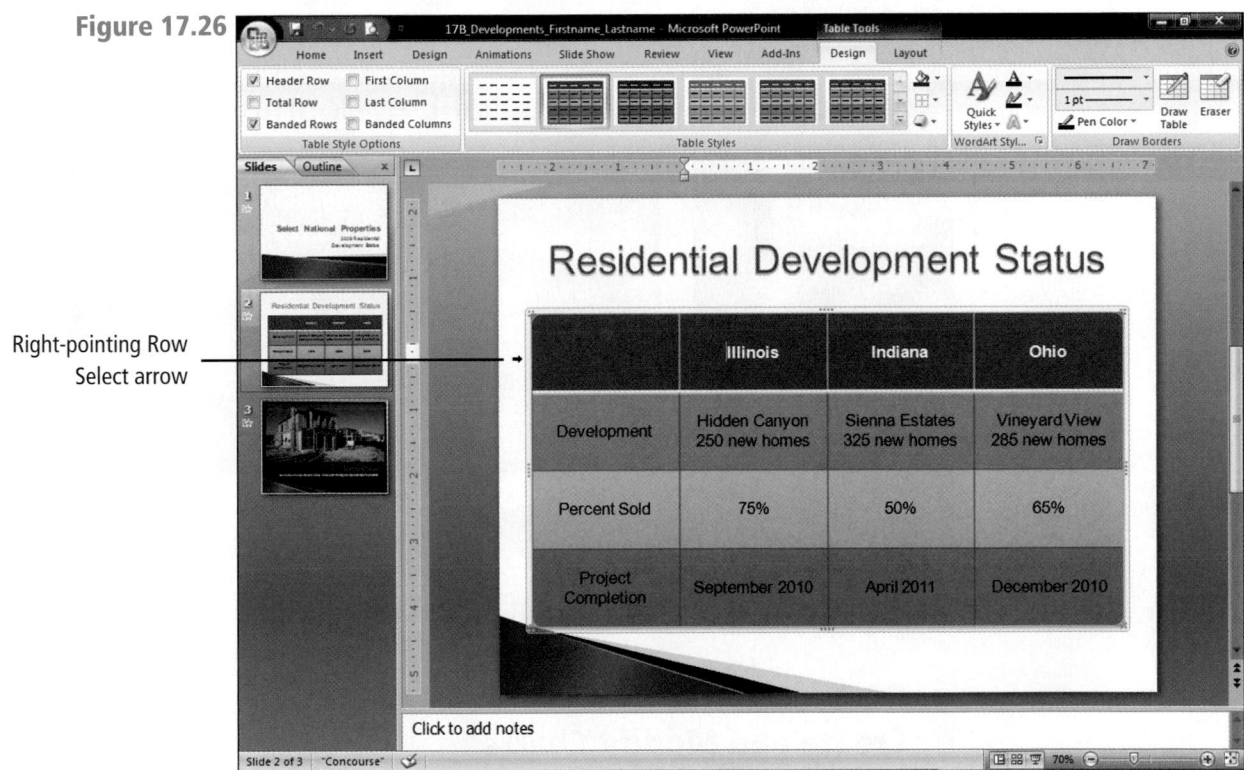

6 With the ➡ pointer pointing to the first row in the table, click the mouse button to select the entire row so that you can apply formatting to the selection. Move the pointer into the selected row, and then right-click to display the Mini toolbar and shortcut menu. On the Mini toolbar, change the **Font Size** to **28**.

More Knowledge

Selecting Columns

To select an entire column, position the pointer above the column that you want to select to display the ⬇ pointer, and then click to select the column.

7 Verify that the first row is still selected. Click the **Design tab**, and then in the **Table Styles group**, click the **Effects** button. Point to **Cell Bevel**, and then under **Bevel**, click the first bevel— **Circle**.

The Bevel effect is applied to the first row in the table.

8 Click in a blank area of the slide, and then compare your slide with Figure 17.27. **Save** the presentation.

Figure 17.27

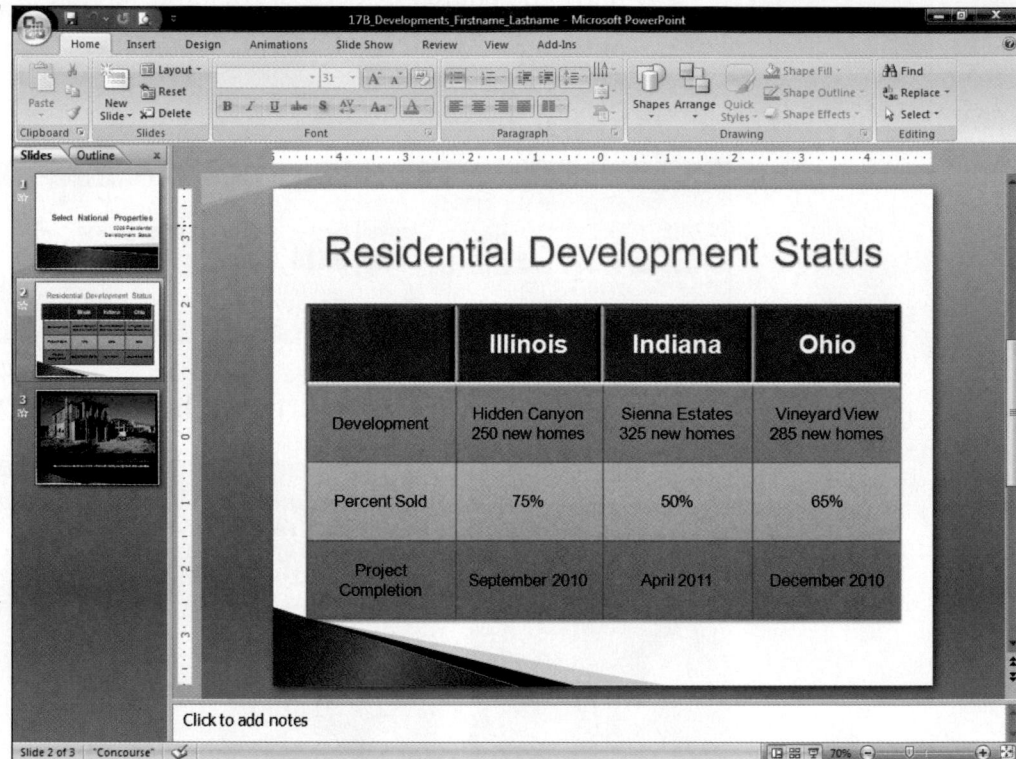

Objective 4
Create and Modify Charts

A **chart** is a graphic representation of numeric data and is often easier to understand than a table of numbers. Chart types frequently used in presentations include bar and column charts, pie charts, and line charts. When you create a chart in PowerPoint, the chart data is stored in an Excel worksheet that is incorporated in the PowerPoint file.

Activity 17.12 Creating a Column Chart and Applying a Chart Style

A **column chart** is useful for illustrating comparisons among related numbers. In this activity you will create a column chart that compares the quarterly 2009 revenue generated by the Residential Development Sector of Select National Properties.

1 Display **Slide 3**, and then add a **New Slide** with the **Title and Content** layout. In the title placeholder, type **2009 Revenue** and then **Center** the title.

2 In the content placeholder, click the **Insert Chart** button 🔳 to display the **Insert Chart** dialog box. In the dialog box, scroll down to view the types of charts that you can insert in your presentation, and then on the left side of the dialog box, if necessary, click Column.

3 Point to the first chart to display the ScreenTip *Clustered Column*, and then if necessary, click to select it. Compare your screen with Figure 17.28.

Figure 17.28

Clustered Column chart

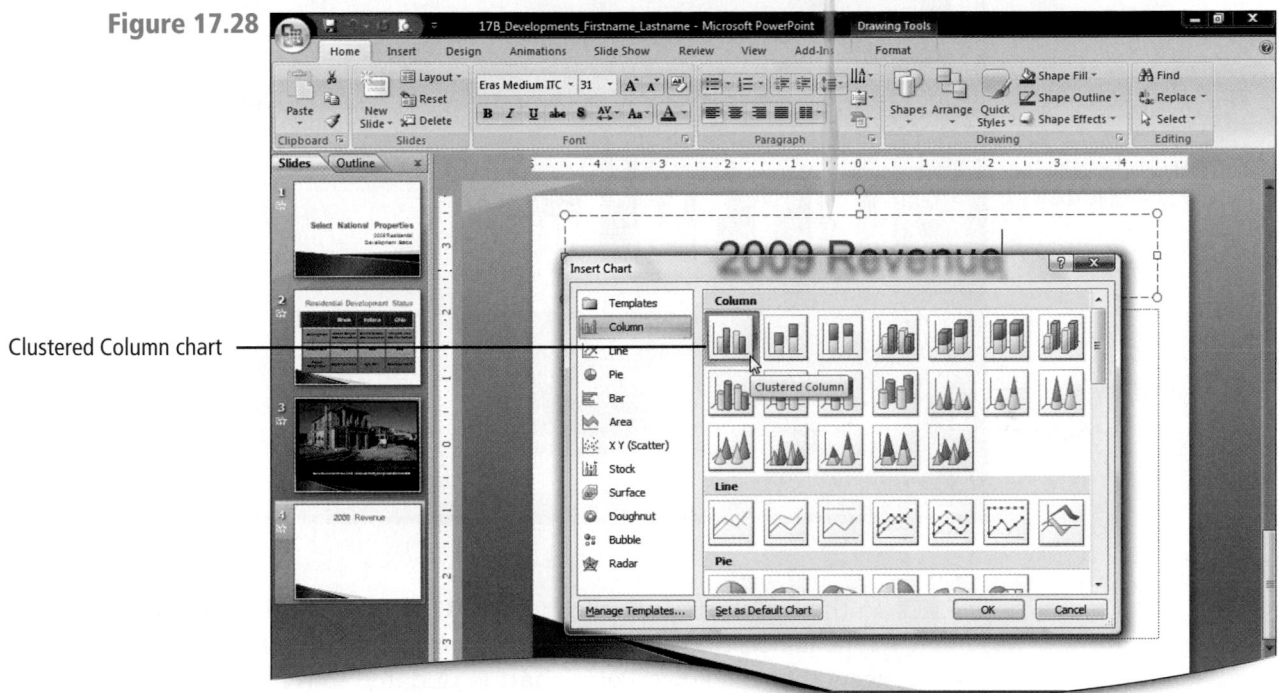

4 Click **OK**, and then compare your screen with Figure 17.29.

On the left side of your screen, the PowerPoint window displays a column chart. On the right side of your screen, a Microsoft Office Excel worksheet displays containing vertical columns and horizontal rows. Recall that the intersection of a column and a row forms a small rectangular box referred to as a cell. A cell is identified by the intersecting column letter and row number, which forms the ***cell reference***.

The worksheet contains sample data in a data range outlined in blue, from which the chart in the PowerPoint window is generated. You can include additional data by dragging the lower right corner of the data range, and you can replace the sample data to update the chart. The column headings—*Series 1*, *Series 2*, and *Series 3* display in the chart ***legend*** and the row headings—*Category 1*, *Category 2*, *Category 3*, and *Category 4*—display as ***category labels***. The legend identifies the patterns or colors that are assigned to the categories in the chart. The category labels display along the bottom of the chart to identify the categories of data.

Figure 17.29

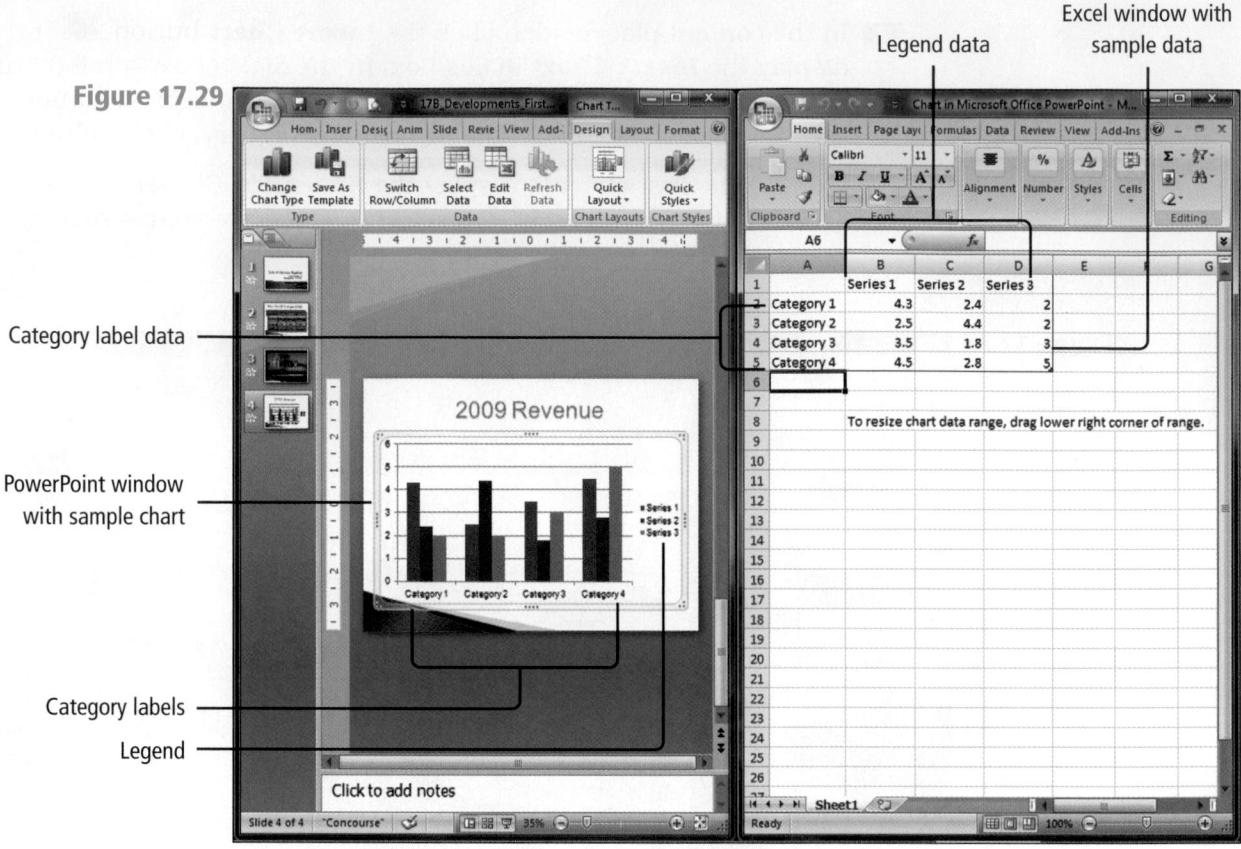

Legend data

Excel window with sample data

Category label data

PowerPoint window with sample chart

2009 Revenue

Category labels

Legend

⑤ In the Excel window, click in cell **B1**, which contains the text *Series 1*. Type **Illinois** and then press Tab to move to cell **C1**. Notice that the legend in the PowerPoint chart is updated to reflect the change in the Excel worksheet.

⑥ In cell **C1**, which contains the text *Series 2*, type **Indiana** and then press Tab to move to cell **D1**, which contains the text *Series 3*. Type **Ohio** and then press Tab. Notice that cell **A2**, which contains the text *Category 1*, is selected.

The blue box outlining the range of cells defines the area in which you are entering data. When you press tab in the rightmost cell, the first cell in the next row becomes the active cell. Compare your screen with Figure 17.30.

Figure 17.30

Column headings

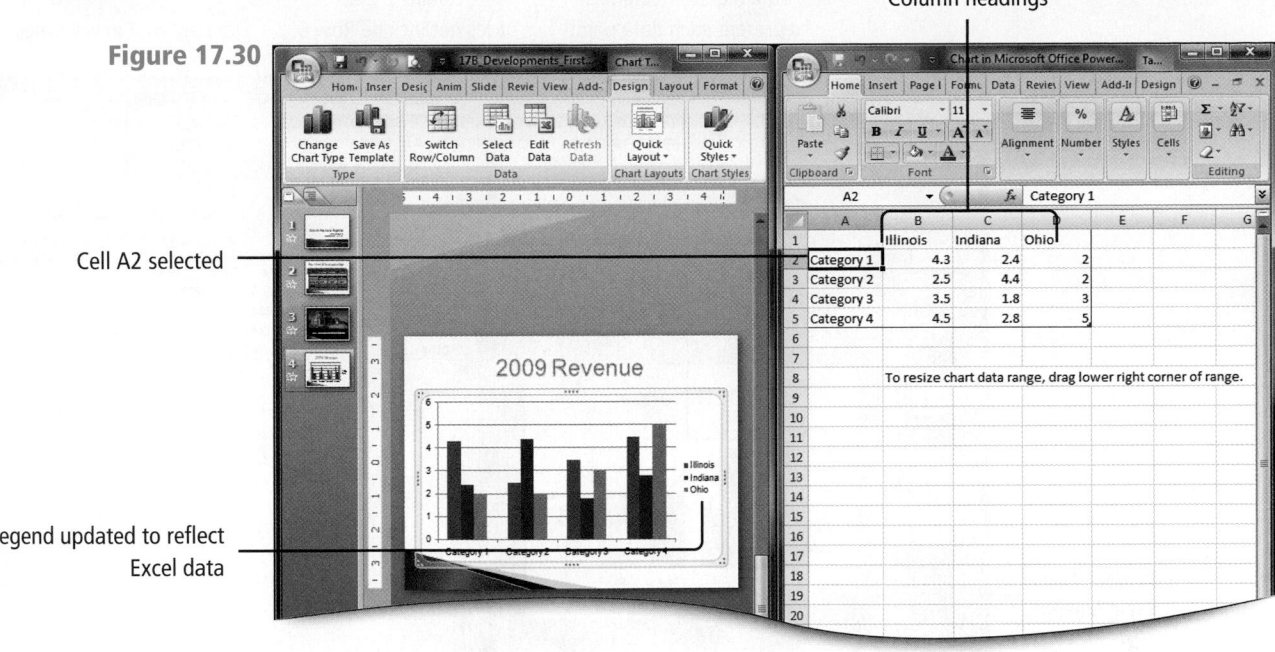

Cell A2 selected

Legend updated to reflect Excel data

7 Beginning in cell **A2**, type the following data, pressing Tab to move from cell to cell.

	Illinois	**Indiana**	**Ohio**
Qtr 1	857300	453228	639852
Qtr 2	1235750	563214	741258
Qtr 3	987653	852147	632145
Qtr 4	789000	674982	

8 In cell **D5**, which contains the value 5, type **753951** and then press Enter.

Pressing Enter in the last cell of the blue outlined area maintains the existing data range. Pressing Tab expands the chart data range by including the next row.

9 Compare your worksheet and your chart with Figure 17.31. If you have made any typing errors, click in the cell that you want to change, and then retype the data.

Alert!

Did you press Tab after the last entry?

If you pressed Tab after entering the data in cell D5, you expanded the chart range. In the Excel window, click Undo.

Each of the twelve cells containing the numeric data that you entered is a **data point**—a value that originates in a worksheet cell. Each data point is represented in the chart by a **data marker**—a column, bar, area, dot, pie slice, or other symbol in a chart that represents a single data point. Related data points form a **data series**; for example, there is a data series for *Illinois*, *Indiana*, and *Ohio*. Each data series has a unique color or pattern represented in the chart legend.

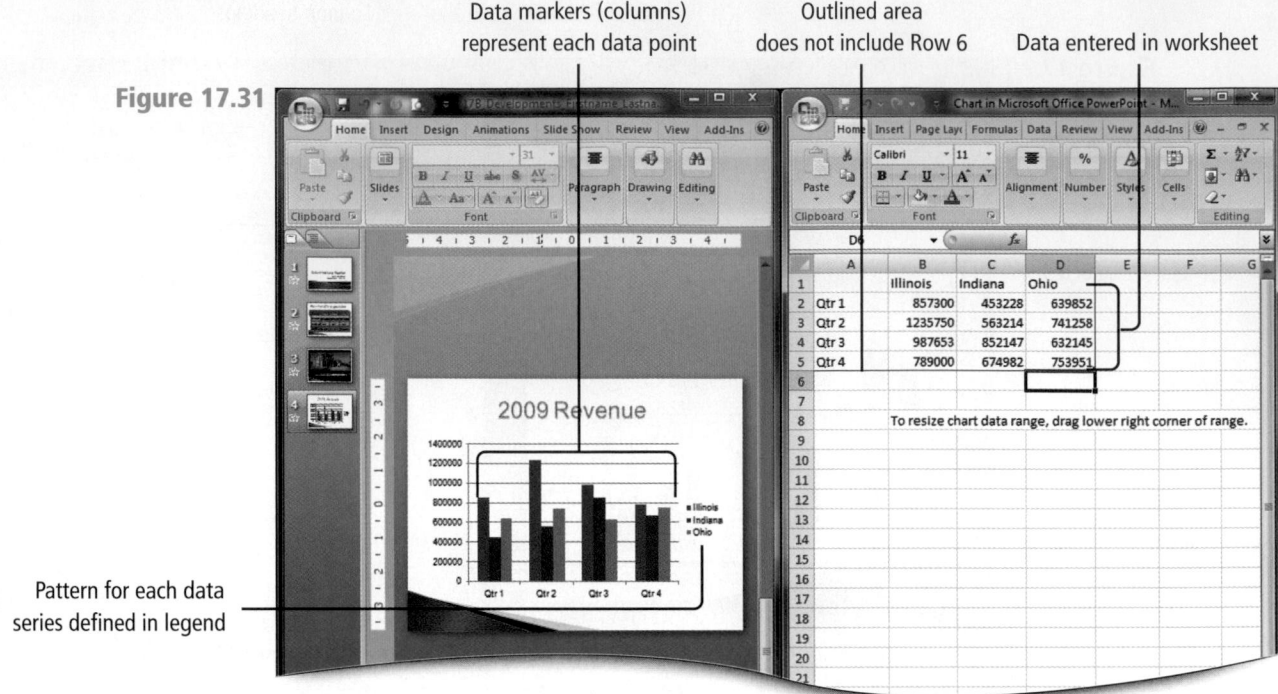

Data markers (columns) represent each data point

Outlined area does not include Row 6

Data entered in worksheet

Figure 17.31

Pattern for each data series defined in legend

10 In the **Excel window**, click the **Office** button 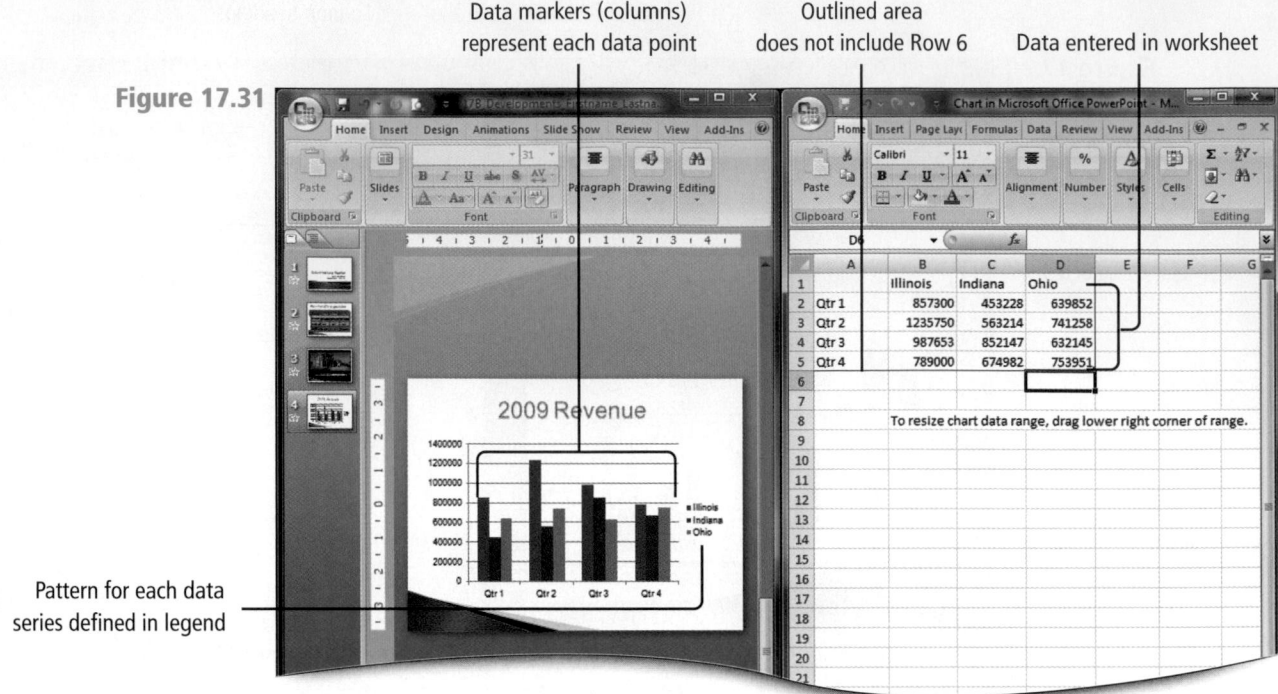, and then click **Close**.

You are not prompted to save the Excel worksheet because the worksheet data is a part of the PowerPoint presentation. When you save the presentation, the Excel data is saved with it.

More Knowledge

Editing the Chart Data After Closing Excel

You can redisplay the Excel worksheet and make changes to the data after you have closed Excel. In PowerPoint, click the chart to select it, and then on the Design tab in the Data group, click Edit Data to redisplay the Excel worksheet.

11 If necessary, click on the chart so that it is selected. In the **Chart Tools**, click the **Design tab**, and then in the **Chart Styles group**, click the **More** button.

12 In the displayed **Chart Styles gallery**, notice that the chart styles are numbered sequentially and ScreenTips display the style numbers. Click **Style 20** to apply the style to the chart.

13 **Save** the presentation.

Activity 17.13 Deleting Chart Data and Changing the Chart Type

To analyze and compare annual data over a three-year period, an additional chart must be inserted. Recall that there are a number of different types of charts that you can insert in a PowerPoint presentation. After a chart has been created, you can easily change the chart type. In this activity, you will create a column chart and then change it to a line chart.

1 With **Slide 4** displayed, add a **New Slide** with the **Title and Content** layout. In the title placeholder, type **Three-Year Projection** and then **Center** ☰ the title.

2 In the content placeholder, click the **Insert Chart** button 📊. In the displayed **Insert Chart** dialog box, click the first **Column** chart—**Clustered Column**—and then click **OK**.

3 In the displayed Excel worksheet, click in cell **B1**, which contains the text *Series 1*. Type **Illinois** and then press Tab. Type **Indiana** and then press Tab. Type **Ohio** and then press Tab.

4 Beginning in cell **A2**, type the following data, pressing Tab to move from cell to cell. If you make any typing errors, click in the cell that you want to change, and then retype the data.

	Illinois	Indiana	Ohio
2009	3156951	4238714	2289746
2010	3786521	4095372	2589674
2011	3569782	3679850	3226915

5 In the Excel window, position the pointer over **row heading 5** so that the ➡ pointer displays as shown in Figure 17.32.

Column headings

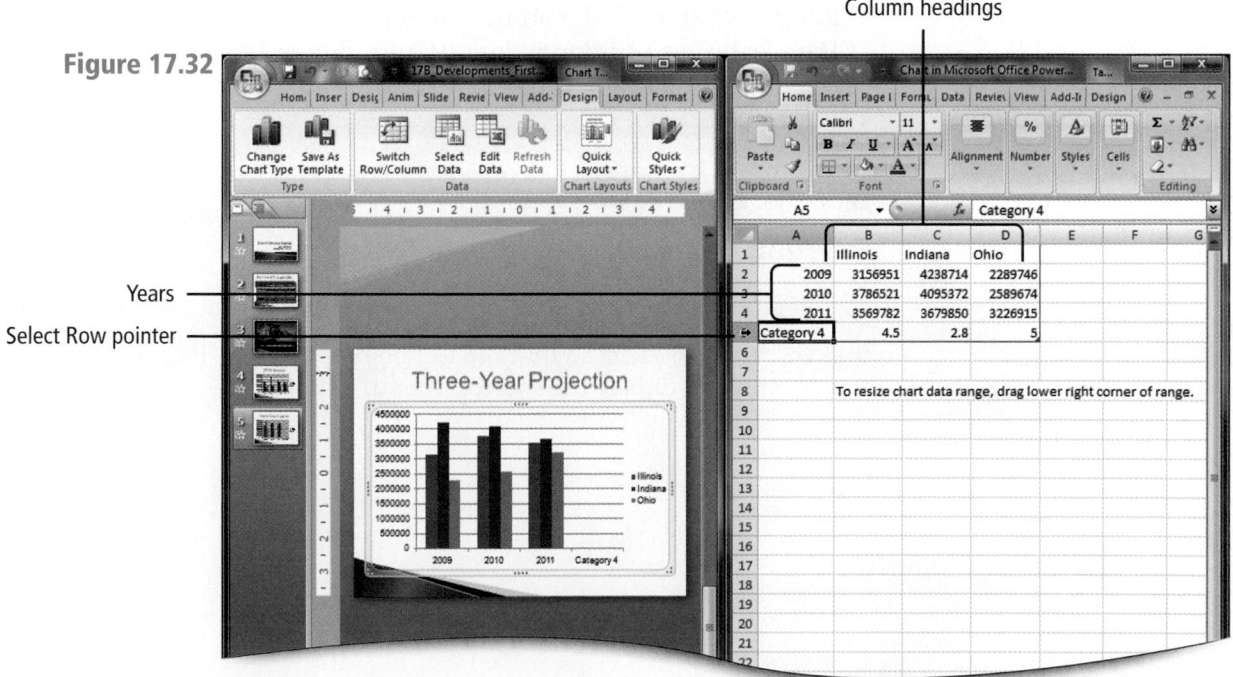

Figure 17.32

Years

Select Row pointer

6 With the ➡ pointer displayed, click the *right* mouse button to select the row and display the shortcut menu as shown in Figure 17.33.

Figure 17.33

Selected row

Shortcut menu

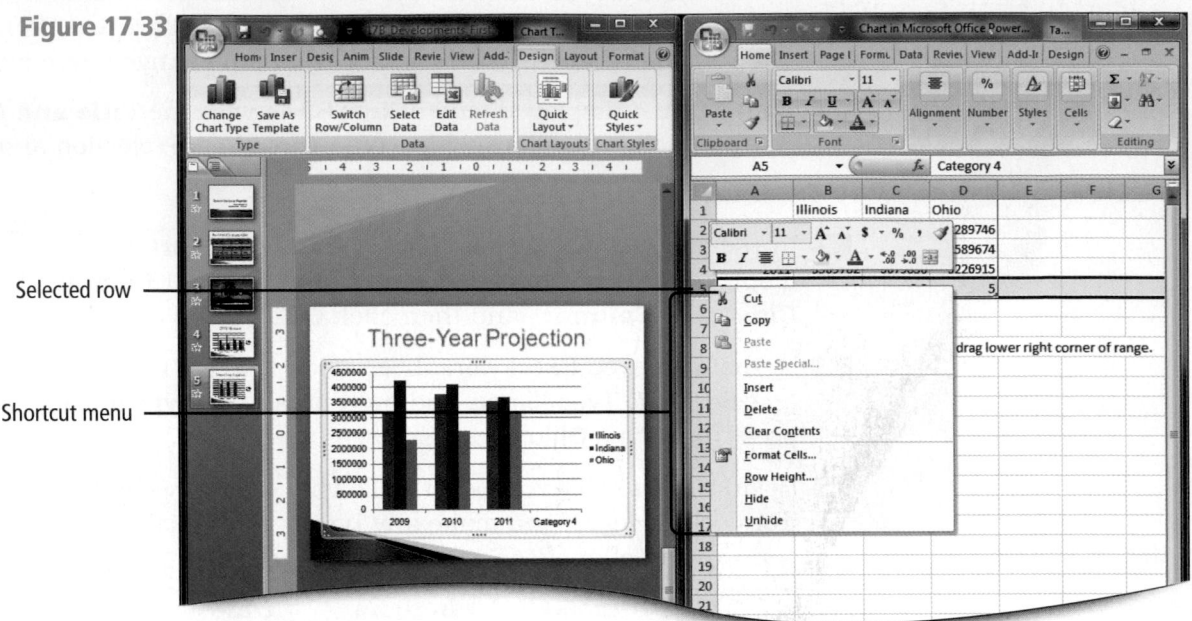

7 From the shortcut menu, click **Delete** to delete the extra row from the worksheet.

The sample data in the worksheet contains four columns and four rows and the blue outline defining the chart data range is resized. You must delete columns and rows that you do not want to include in the chart. Alternatively, you can resize the data range. You can add additional rows and columns by typing column and row headings and then entering additional data. When data is typed in cells adjacent to the chart range, the range is resized to include the new data.

More Knowledge

Deleting Columns

To delete a worksheet column, position the pointer over the column letter that you want to select so that the ⬇ pointer displays. Right-click to select the column and display the shortcut menu. Click Delete.

8 **Close** ![X] the Excel window.

9 If necessary, click the chart to select it, and then in the **Chart Tools**, click the **Design tab**. In the **Type group**, click **Change Chart Type**. Under **Line**, click the fourth chart type—**Line with Markers**—and then click **OK**.

The column chart is converted to a ***line chart***. A line chart is ideal for this data because line charts show trends over time.

10 In the **Chart Styles group**, click the **More** button ![More]. In the displayed **Chart Styles gallery**, click **Style 26**, and then compare your slide with Figure 17.34.

Figure 17.34

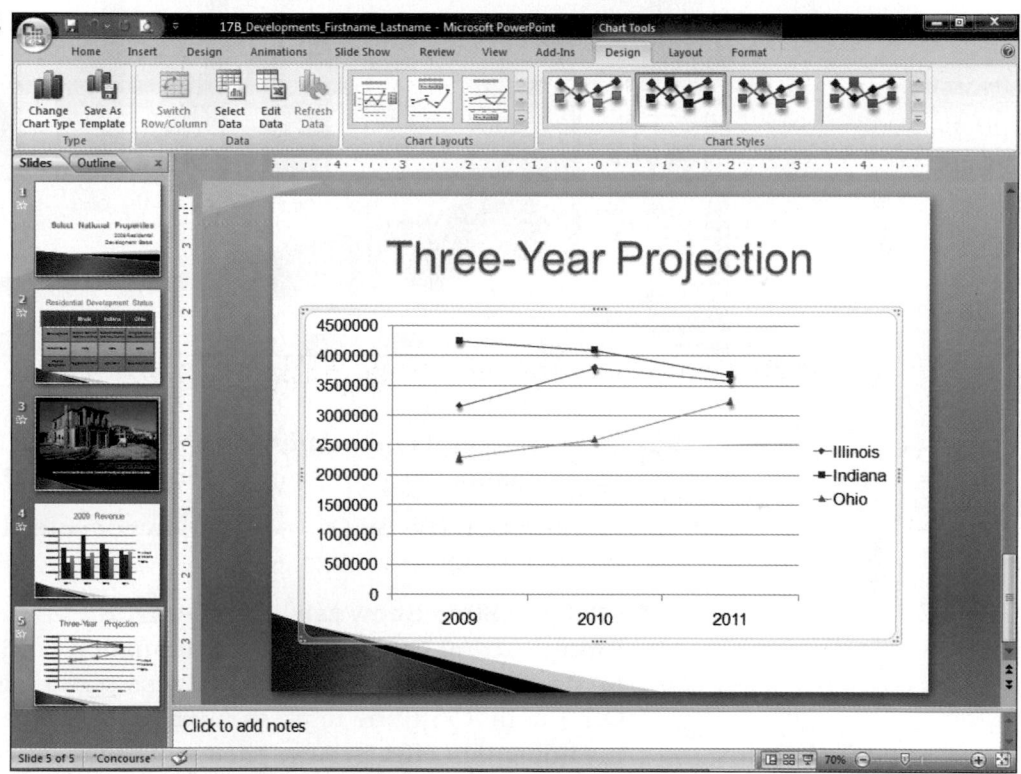

11 **Save** ![Save] the presentation.

Activity 17.14 Animating a Chart

1 Display **Slide 4**, and then click the column chart to select it.

2 Click the **Animations tab**, and then in the **Animations group**, click the **Animate arrow** to display the Animate list as shown in Figure 17.35.

Animate arrow

Figure 17.35

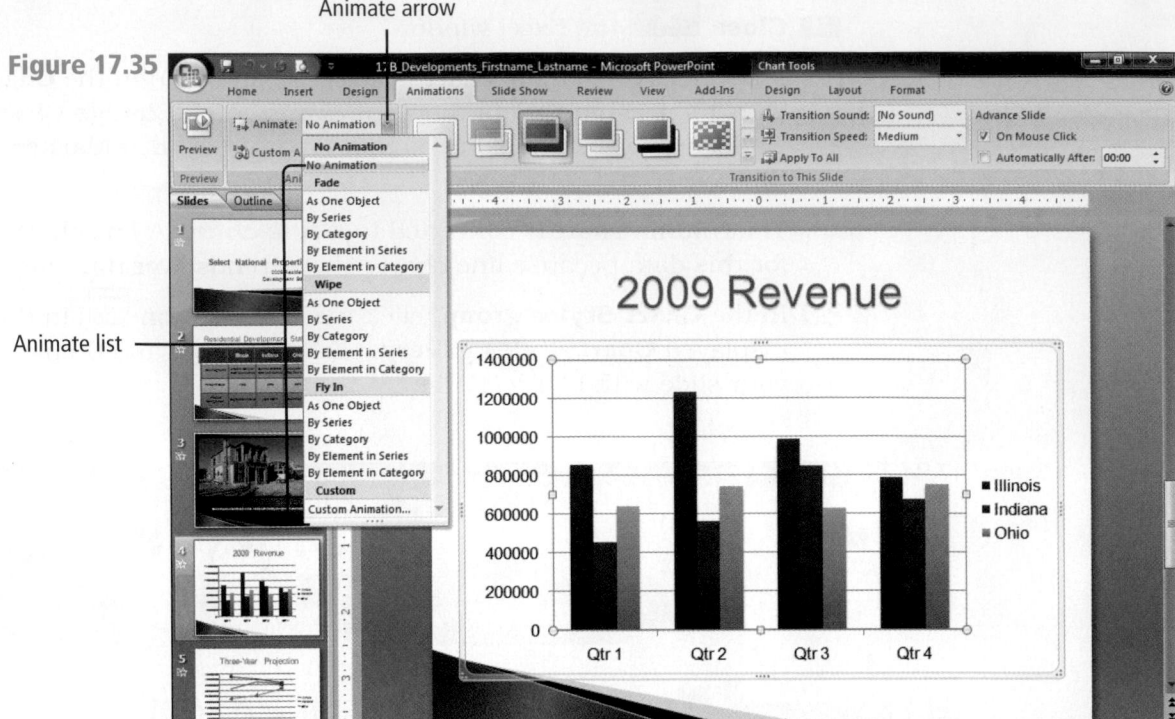

3 Point to several of the **Animate** options to view the Live Preview of the animation effects. Then, under **Wipe**, click **By Category**.

In this chart, the *By Category* option animates the column data markers by Qtr.

4 Click the **Slide Show tab**. In the **Start Slide Show group**, click **From Current Slide** to view the animation on Slide 4. Press Spacebar to display the legend and labels. Press Spacebar again to display the Qtr 1 data. Continue to press Spacebar to advance through the remaining animation effects. After the animations for Slide 4 are complete, press Esc to end the slide show and return to the presentation.

5 Create a **Header and Footer** for the **Notes and Handouts**. Include the **Date and time updated automatically**, the **Page number**, and a **Footer** with the file name **17B_Developments_Firstname_Lastname**

6 Check your *Chapter Assignment Sheet* or *Course Syllabus* or consult your instructor to determine if you are to submit your assignments on paper or electronically. To submit electronically, go to Step 8, and then follow the instructions provided by your instructor.

7 Display your presentation in **Print Preview**, and then print **Handouts (6 Slides Per Page)**.

8 **Save** the changes to your presentation, and then close the presentation.

End You have completed Project 17B ⸻

There's More You Can Do!

Close PowerPoint and any other open windows. Display the Start menu, click Computer, and then navigate to the student files that accompany this textbook. In the folder **02_theres_more_you_can_do**, locate and open the folder for this chapter. Open and print the instructions for this project, which are provided to you in Adobe PDF format.

Try IT!—Compress Pictures

In this Try It! exercise, you will compress pictures in a presentation in order to reduce file size.

Content-Based Assessments

PowerPoint
chapterseventeen

Summary

In this chapter, you formatted a presentation by applying background styles, inserting pictures on slide backgrounds, and by changing the theme fonts. You enhanced your presentation by applying animation effects and by changing effect and timing options. You practiced creating tables to present information in an organized manner and you used charts to visually represent data.

Key Terms

Content-Based Assessments

Matching

Match each term in the second column with its correct definition in the first column. Write the letter of the term on the blank line in front of the correct definition.

_____ **1.** A slide background fill variation that combines theme colors in different intensities.

_____ **2.** A theme that determines the font applied to two types of slide text—headings and body.

_____ **3.** The font applied to slide titles.

_____ **4.** The font applied to all slide text except titles.

_____ **5.** Effects used to introduce individual slide elements so that the slide can progress one element at a time.

_____ **6.** Animations that bring a slide element onto the screen.

_____ **7.** A list that indicates the animation effects applied to slide items.

_____ **8.** Animation options that include changing the direction of an effect and playing a sound when an animation takes place.

_____ **9.** A format for information that organizes and presents text and data in columns and rows.

_____ **10.** The intersection of a column and row.

_____ **11.** Formatting applied to an entire table so that it is consistent with the presentation theme.

_____ **12.** A graphic representation of numeric data.

_____ **13.** A type of chart used to compare data.

_____ **14.** A combination of the column letter and row number identifying a cell.

_____ **15.** A chart element that identifies the patterns or colors that are assigned to the categories in the chart.

A Animation effects

B Background style

C Body font

D Cell

E Cell reference

F Chart

G Column chart

H Custom animation list

I Effect options

J Entrance effects

K Font theme

L Headings font

M Legend

N Table

O Table style

Content-Based Assessments

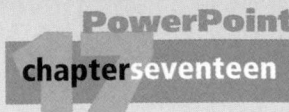
Fill in the Blank

Write the correct word in the space provided.

1. To help an audience understand numeric data and trends, insert a(n) _____ or a(n) _____ on a slide.

2. The charts most commonly used in PowerPoint presentations are _____, _____, _____, and _____.

3. When the background graphics interfere with slide content, you can _____ the background graphics.

4. When you insert a picture on a slide background, it is a good idea to choose a picture that has a(n) _____ area in which you can overlay a text box or title.

5. When you apply a new font theme to the presentation, the text on every slide is updated with the new _____ and _____ fonts.

6. Animation effects focus the audience's attention, providing the speaker with an opportunity to emphasize an important point using the slide element as an effective _____ _____.

7. The most efficient method of animating a SmartArt graphic is to use one of the choices in the _____ _____.

8. When you are delivering a presentation, to view a list of the slides in the presentation, display the shortcut menu, and then point to _____ _____ _____.

9. You can modify the layout of a table by inserting or deleting _____ and _____.

10. The document matching styles provide the best choices for coordinating the table with the presentation _____.

11. When you create a chart in PowerPoint, the chart data is stored in a(n) _____ worksheet.

12. In a chart, categories of data are identified by _____ _____.

13. A chart value that originates in a worksheet cell is a(n) _____ _____.

14. A group of related data points is a(n) _____ _____.

15. A column, bar, area, dot, pie slice, or other symbol in a chart that represents a single data point is a(n) _____ _____.

Content-Based Assessments

Skills Review

Project 17C—Seniors

In this project, you will apply the skills you practiced from the Objectives in Project 17A.

Objectives: 1. *Customize Slide Backgrounds and Themes;* **2.** *Animate a Slide Show.*

In the following Skills Review, you will edit a presentation created by Marla Rodriguez, the Marketing Director for Select National Properties, which describes a new real estate development in Illinois. Your completed presentation will look similar to the one shown in Figure 17.36.

For Project 17C, you will need the following files:

p17C_Seniors
p17C_Walkway

You will save your presentation as
17C_Seniors_Firstname_Lastname

Figure 17.36

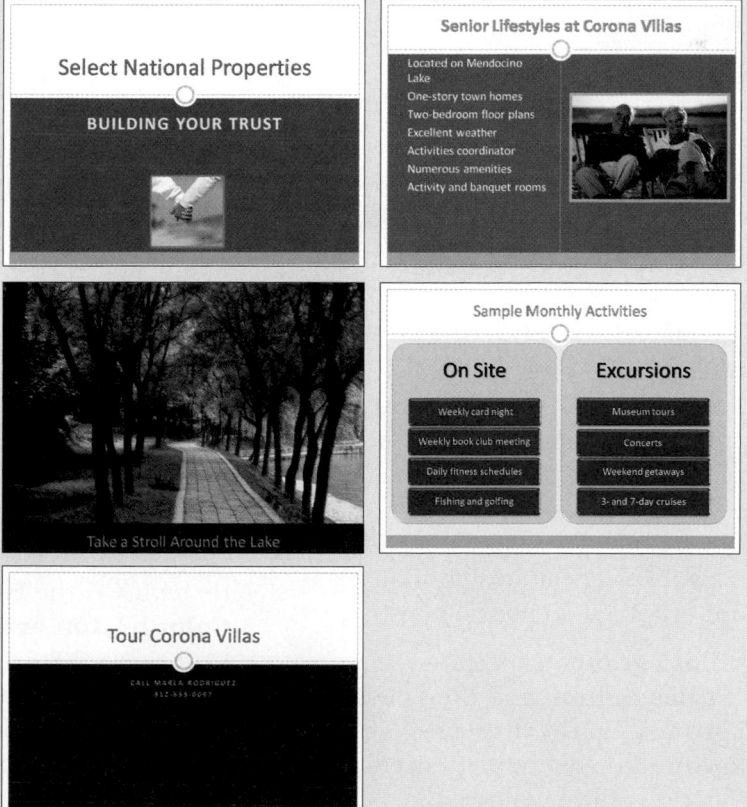

(Project 17C–Seniors continues on the next page)

Content-Based Assessments

(Project 17C–Seniors continued)

1. **Start** PowerPoint. From your student files, **Open** the file **p17C_Seniors**. From the **Office** menu, click **Save As**, and then navigate to your **PowerPoint Chapter 17** folder. In the **File name** box, type **17C_Seniors_ Firstname_Lastname** and then click **Save** to save your presentation.

2. Click the **Design tab**, and then in the **Themes group**, click the **More** button to display the Themes gallery. Under **Built-In**, in the first row, click **Civic**. In the **Themes group**, click the **Colors** button, and then click **Office** to change the theme color for the entire presentation. In the **Background group**, click the **Background Styles** button to display the Background Styles gallery. In the second row, right-click **Style 7**. From the displayed shortcut menu, click **Apply to Selected Slides** to apply the style to **Slide 1**.

3. Display **Slide 2**. On the **Design tab**, in the **Background group**, click the **Background Styles** button to display the Background Styles gallery. In the last row, right-click **Style 11**, and then click **Apply to Selected Slides** to apply the style to **Slide 2**.

4. With **Slide 2** displayed, click the **Home tab**. In the **Slides group**, click the **New Slide arrow**, and then click the **Title Only** layout to create a new Slide 3. In the title placeholder, type **Take a Stroll Around the Lake** Click the **Design tab**, and then in the **Background group**, click to select the **Hide Background Graphics** check box so that the background graphics do not display.

5. In the **Background group**, click the **Background Styles** button, and then click **Format Background**. In the displayed **Format Background** dialog box, if necessary, on the left side of the dialog box,

click **Fill**. On the right side of the dialog box, under **Fill**, click the **Picture or texture fill** option button.

6. Under **Insert from**, click the **File** button. In the displayed **Insert Picture** dialog box, navigate to the location where your student files are located, and then click **p17C_Walkway**. Click **Insert**, and then under **Stretch options**, if necessary, change the **Left**, **Right**, **Top** and **Bottom Offsets** to **0%** and then click **Close** to close the **Format Background** dialog box.

7. If necessary, click in the title placeholder. Click the **Format tab**, and then in the **Shape Styles group**, click the **Shape Fill** button. In the last row, click the fourth color—**Dark Blue, Text 2, Darker 50%** so that the text displays against the background.

8. Point to the outer edge of the placeholder to display the ⬚ pointer, and then drag the placeholder down so that its bottom edge aligns with the bottom of the slide. Point to the center, right sizing handle to display the ↔ pointer. Drag to the right so that the right side of the placeholder touches the right edge of the slide. Point to the center, left sizing handle to display the ↔ pointer. Drag to the left so that the left side of the placeholder touches the left edge of the slide.

9. Display **Slide 5**, and then select the subtitle text. On the **Home tab**, click the **Font Color button arrow**. Under **Theme Colors**, in the first row, click the seventh color—**Olive Green, Accent 3**. Click the **Design tab**. In the **Background group**, click the **Background Styles** button, and then click **Format Background**. In

(Project 17C–Seniors continues on the next page)

Content-Based Assessments

(Project 17C–Seniors continued)

the **Format Background** dialog box, if necessary, click the **Solid fill** option button, and then click the **Color** button. Under **Theme Colors**, in the last row, click the fourth color—**Dark Blue, Text 2, Darker 50%**. Click **Close**.

10. Display **Slide 1**. On the **Design tab**, in the **Themes group**, click the **Fonts** button. Click the first font theme—**Office**—and then scroll through the slides in the presentation, noticing that the font changes have been applied to every slide.

11. Click the **Animations tab**, and then in the **Transition to This Slide group**, click the **More** button. Under **Wipes**, click **Box Out**. Click the **Transition Speed arrow**, and then click **Medium**. Click the **Apply To All** button.

12. Display **Slide 2**, and then click the bulleted list placeholder. In the **Animations group**, click the **Custom Animation** button. At the top of the displayed **Custom Animation** task pane, click the **Add Effect** button, and then point to **Entrance**. Click **More Effects** to display the **Add Entrance Effect** dialog box.

13. At the bottom of the **Add Entrance Effect** dialog box, if necessary, click to select the **Preview Effect** check box. Under **Basic**, click **Blinds**, and then click **OK**. In the **Custom Animation** list, click the **item 1 arrow**, and then click **Effect Options** to display the **Blinds** dialog box.

14. In the **Blinds dialog box**, if necessary, click the **Effect tab**. Under **Enhancements**, click the **After animation arrow**. In the row of colors, click the **fifth color**, and then click **OK** to apply the effect option.

15. Click to select the picture. In the **Custom Animation** task pane, click the **Add Effect**

button, point to **Entrance**, and then click **More Effects**. In the displayed **Add Entrance Effect** dialog box, under **Basic**, click **Dissolve In**, and then click **OK**.

16. Near the top of the **Custom Animation** task pane, under **Modify: Dissolve In**, click the **Start arrow**, and then click **After Previous** to display the picture immediately after the last bulleted item displays. In the **Custom Animation task pane**, under **Modify: Dissolve In**, click the **Speed arrow**, and then click **Fast**.

17. Display **Slide 3**, and then click in the title placeholder. In the **Custom Animation** task pane, click **Add Effect**, and then point to **Entrance**. Click **More Effects**. Under **Basic**, click **Fly In**, and then click **OK**. In the **Custom Animation task pane**, click the **Start arrow**, and then click **After Previous** to display the title immediately after the slide transition. If necessary, click the **Direction arrow**, and then click **From Bottom**. **Close** the task pane.

18. Display **Slide 4**, and then select the **SmartArt graphic**. On the **Animations tab**, in the **Animations group**, click the **Animate arrow** to display the Animate list. Under **Wipe**, click **By level at once**.

19. Click the **Slide Show tab**. In the **Start Slide Show group**, click **From Beginning**, and then view your presentation, clicking the mouse button to advance through the slides. Notice the animation that is applied to each slide, and then when the black slide displays, click the mouse button one more time to display the presentation in Normal view.

20. Create a **Header and Footer** for the **Notes and Handouts**. Include only the **Date and time updated automatically**, the **Page**

(Project 17C–Seniors continues on the next page)

Content-Based Assessments

(Project 17C–Seniors continued)

number, and a **Footer** with the file name 17C_Seniors_Firstname_Lastname

21. Check your *Chapter Assignment Sheet* or *Course Syllabus* or consult your instructor to determine if you are to submit your assignments on paper or electronically. To submit electronically, go to Step 23, and

then follow the instructions provided by your instructor.

22. Display your presentation in **Print Preview**, and then print **Handouts (6 Slides Per Page)**.

23. **Save** the changes to your presentation, and then close the presentation.

 End You have completed Project 17C _____

Content-Based Assessments

Skills Review

Project 17D — Commercial Developments

In this project, you will apply the skills you practiced from the Objectives in Project 17B.

Objectives: 3. *Create and Modify Tables;* **4.** *Create and Modify Charts.*

In the following Skills Review, you will add a table and two charts to a presentation that Shaun Walker, President of Select National Properties, is creating to apprise investors of the status of several new commercial developments. Your completed presentation will look similar to the one shown in Figure 17.37.

For Project 17D, you will need the following file:

p17D_Commercial_Developments

You will save your presentation as
17D_Commercial_Developments_Firstname_Lastname

Figure 17.37

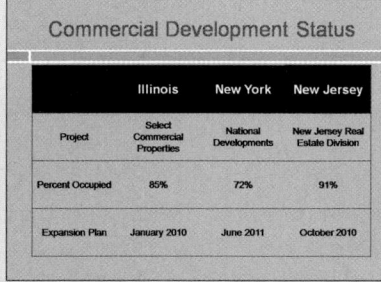

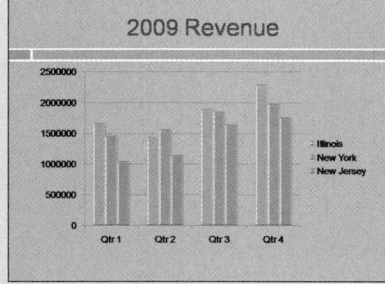

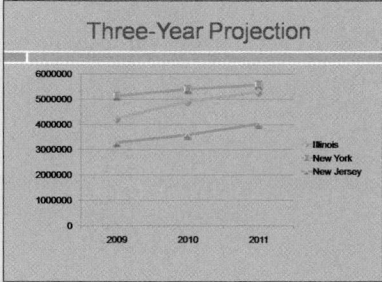

(Project 17D–Commercial Developments continues on the next page)

(Project 17D–Commercial Developments continued)

1. **Start** PowerPoint and from your student files, open **p17D_Commercial_ Developments**. **Save** the presentation in your **PowerPoint Chapter 17** folder as 17D_Commercial_Developments_ Firstname_Lastname

2. With **Slide 1** displayed, on the **Home tab**, in the **Slides group**, click the **New Slide** button to insert a slide with the **Title and Content** layout. In the title placeholder, type **Commercial Development Status** and then **Center** the title.

3. In the content placeholder, click the **Insert Table** button. In the displayed **Insert Table** dialog box, in the **Number of columns** box, type **4** and then press Tab. In the **Number of rows** box, type **2**. Click **OK** to create a table with four columns and two rows.

4. Click in the second cell of the first row— the first cell will remain blank. Type **Illinois** and then press Tab. With the insertion point positioned in the third cell of the first row, type **New York** and then press Tab. Type **New Jersey** and then press Tab to move the insertion point to the first cell in the second row.

5. With the insertion point positioned in the first cell of the second row, type **Project** and then press Tab. Type **Select Commercial Properties** and then press Tab. Type **National Developments** and then press Tab. Type **New Jersey Real Estate Division** and then press Tab to insert a new blank row.

6. In the first cell of the third row, type **Expansion Plan** and then press Tab. Type **January 2010** and then press Tab. Type **June 2011** and then press Tab. Type **October 2010**

7. With the insertion point positioned in the third row, click the **Layout tab**. In the **Rows & Columns group**, click the **Insert Above** button to insert a new third row. In the first cell of the newly inserted row, type **Percent Occupied** and then press Tab. Type the remaining three entries, pressing Tab to move from cell to cell: **85% 72%** and **91%**

8. If necessary, on the View tab, in the Show/Hide group, click to select the Ruler check box so that the Ruler displays. At the center of the lower border surrounding the table, point to the four dots—the sizing handle—to display the ⬍ pointer. Drag down so that the bottom edge of the table is aligned at approximately **3 inches below zero on the vertical ruler**.

9. Click in the first cell of the table. On the **Layout tab**, in the **Cell Size group**, click the **Distribute Rows** button so that the four rows are equal in height. In the **Table group**, click **Select**, and then click **Select Table**. In the **Alignment group**, click the **Center** button, and then click the **Center Vertically** button.

10. In the **Table Tools**, click the **Design tab**, and then in the **Table Styles group**, click the **More** button. Under **Light**, in the second row, click the first style—**Light Style 2**.

11. Move the pointer outside of the table so that is positioned to the left of the first row to display the ➡ pointer. Click to select the entire row. Move the pointer into the selected row, and then right-click to display the Mini toolbar and shortcut menu. On the Mini toolbar, change the **Font Size** to **24**.

(Project 17D–Commercial Developments continues on the next page)

Content-Based Assessments

(Project 17D–Commercial Developments continued)

12. With the first row still selected, in the **Table Tools** click the **Design tab**. In the **Table Styles group**, click the **Effects** button. Point to **Cell Bevel**, and then under **Bevel**, click the first bevel—**Circle**.

13. Display **Slide 3**, and then insert a **New Slide** with the **Title and Content Layout**. In the title placeholder type **2009 Revenue** and then **Center** the title. In the content placeholder, click the **Insert Chart** button. In the displayed **Insert Chart** dialog box, point to the first chart to display the ScreenTip *Clustered Column*, and then if necessary, click to select it. Click **OK**.

14. In the **Excel** window, click in cell **B1**, which contains the text *Series 1*. Type **Illinois** and then press ⎀Tab⎀ to move to cell **C1** containing the text *Series 2*. Type **New York** and then press ⎀Tab⎀ to move to cell **D1**. Type **New Jersey**

15. Click in cell **A2**, and then type the data from the following table, pressing ⎀Tab⎀ to move from cell to cell. Be sure that you press ⎀Enter⎀ after the last entry— 1753840—not ⎀Tab⎀.

	Illinois	**New York**	**New Jersey**
Qtr 1	1657305	1453230	1039855
Qtr 2	1434850	1563360	1141290
Qtr 3	1887640	1852175	1632785
Qtr 4	2286730	1974930	1753840

16. **Close** the Excel window. If necessary, click to select the chart. In the **Chart Tools**, click the **Design tab**, and then in the **Chart Styles group**, click the **More** button. In the displayed **Chart Styles gallery**, click **Style 26**. On the **Animations tab**, in the **Animations group**, click the **Animate**

arrow to display the Animate list. Under **Wipe**, click **As One Object**.

17. With **Slide 4** displayed, insert a **New Slide** with the **Title and Content Layout**. In the title placeholder type **Three-Year Projection** and then **Center** the title. In the content placeholder, click the **Insert Chart** button. In the displayed **Create Chart** dialog box, under **Line**, click **Line with Markers**, and then click **OK**.

18. In the displayed **Excel** worksheet, click in cell **B1**. Type **Illinois** and then press ⎀Tab⎀. Type **New York** and then press ⎀Tab⎀. Type **New Jersey** and then press ⎀Tab⎀.

19. Beginning in cell **A2**, enter the projected revenue for each state and each year as shown in the following table. If you make any typing errors, click in the cell that you want to change, and then retype the data.

	Illinois	**New York**	**New Jersey**
2009	4236950	5138726	3289728
2010	4896525	5395318	3589622
2011	5289862	5569857	4026935

20. Position the pointer over **row heading 5** to display the ➡ pointer. Click the right mouse button to select the row. From the displayed shortcut menu, click **Delete** to delete the extra row from the worksheet.

21. **Close** the Excel window. In the **Chart Tools**, click the **Design tab**. In the **Chart Styles group**, click the **More** button. In the displayed **Chart Styles gallery**, click **Style 26**.

22. Create a **Header and Footer** for the **Notes and Handouts**. Include only the **Date and**

(Project 17D–Commercial Developments continues on the next page)

Content-Based Assessments

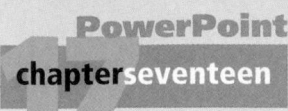

Skills Review

(Project 17D–Commercial Developments continued)

> **time updated automatically**, the **Page number**, and a **Footer** with the file name 17D_Commercial_Developments_Firstname_Lastname

23. Check your *Chapter Assignment Sheet* or *Course Syllabus* or consult your instructor to determine if you are to submit your assignments on paper or electronically. To submit electronically, go to Step 25, and then follow the instructions provided by your instructor.

24. Display your presentation in **Print Preview**, and then print **Handouts (6 Slides Per Page)**.

25. **Save** the changes to your presentation, and then close the presentation.

End **You have completed Project 17D**

Content-Based Assessments

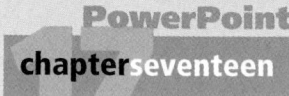

chapterseventeen Mastering PowerPoint

Project 17E — Civic Center

In this project, you will apply the skills you practiced from the Objectives in Project 17A.

Objectives: 1. *Customize Slide Backgrounds and Themes;* **2.** *Animate a Slide Show.*

In the following Mastering PowerPoint project, you will edit a presentation that Shaun Walker, President of Select National Properties plans to show at a Farrington City Council meeting regarding the renovation of City Hall. Your completed presentation will look similar to Figure 17.38.

For Project 17E, you will need the following files:

p17E_Civic_Center
p17E_City_Hall

You will save your presentation as
17E_Civic_Center_Firstname_Lastname

Figure 17.38

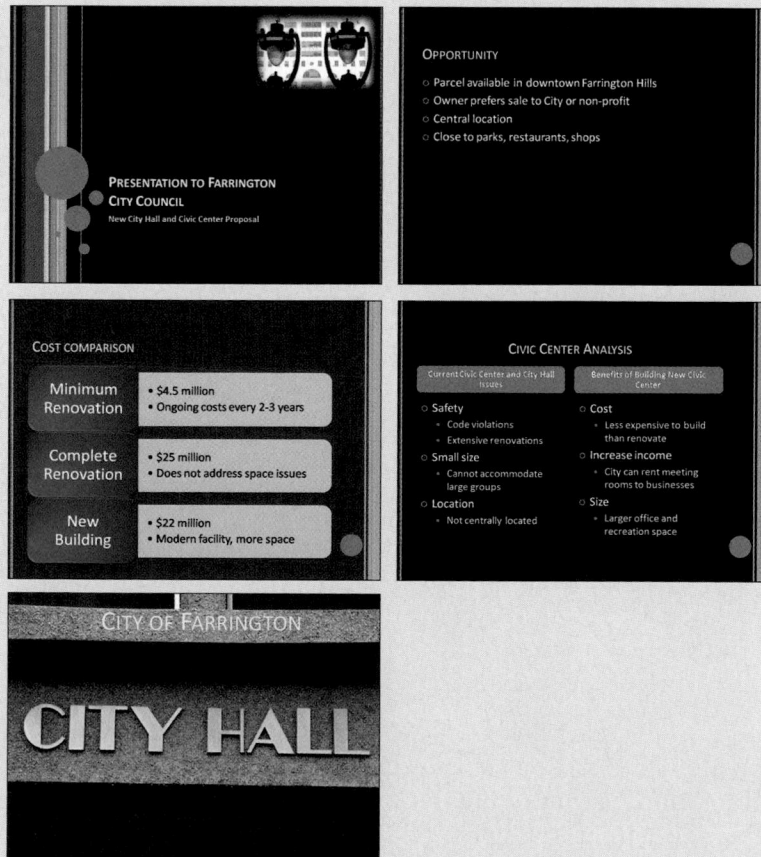

(Project 17E–Civic Center continues on the next page)

Content-Based Assessments

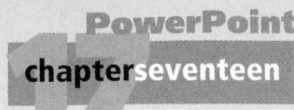
(Project 17E–Civic Center continued)

1. **Start** PowerPoint. From your student files, **Open** the file **p17E_Civic_Center**. **Save** the presentation in your **PowerPoint Chapter 17** folder as **17E_Civic_Center_Firstname_Lastname**

2. Apply the **Oriel Theme** to the presentation, and then change the presentation **Background** to the solid black **Style 4** for all of the slides in the presentation. Change the **Fonts** theme to the **Office** theme, which includes the *Cambria* and *Calibri* fonts. Display **Slide 3**, and then change the **Background** to **Style 12** using the **Apply to Selected Slides** option.

3. Display **Slide 4**, and then insert a **New Slide** with the **Title Only** layout. In the title placeholder, type **City of Farrington** and then **Center** the title. On the **Design tab**, in the **Background group**, click to select the **Hide Background Graphics** check box so that the background graphics do not display.

4. Change the **Background Style** by inserting a picture on the background using the **Format Background** dialog box. Under **Fill**, click the **Picture or texture fill** option button. From your student files, insert the file **p17E_City_Hall**, and then verify that the **Stretch options Offsets** are set to **0%**. **Close** the **Format Background** dialog box.

5. Select the title text, and then change the **Font Size** to **54**. Drag the title placeholder up and slightly to the right so that the top of the placeholder aligns with the top edge of the slide and the words *City of Farrington* are centered over *City Hall*.

6. Display **Slide 2**, and then click the bulleted list placeholder. Display the **Custom Animation** task pane, and then display the **Add Entrance Effect** dialog box.

Under **Subtle**, click **Expand**, and then click **OK** to apply the animation to the bulleted list.

7. In the **Custom Animation** list, click the **item 1 arrow**, and then click **Effect Options** to display the **Expand** dialog box. In the **Effect tab** of the **Expand dialog box**, under **Enhancements**, click the **After animation arrow**. In the row of colors, click the **third color**, and then click **OK** to apply the effect option.

8. Display **Slide 3**, and then select the **SmartArt graphic**. Display the **Animate** list, and then under **Fade**, click **As One Object**.

9. Display **Slide 5**, and then click in the title placeholder. In the **Custom Animation** task pane, click **Add Effect**, and then point to **Entrance**. Click **More Effects**. Under **Basic**, apply the **Fly In** effect. In the **Custom Animation task pane**, click the **Start arrow**, and then click **After Previous** so that the title displays immediately after the slide transition. Click the **Direction arrow**, and then click **From Top**. **Close** the task pane.

10. For the transition, under **Wipes**, apply the **Split Horizontal In** transition to all the slides in the presentation. View the slide show from the beginning, clicking the mouse button to advance through the slides. Notice the animation that is applied to each slide, and then when the black slide displays, click the mouse button one more time to display the presentation in Normal view.

11. Create a **Header and Footer** for the **Notes and Handouts**. Include only the **Date and time updated automatically**, the **Page number**, and a **Footer** with the file name **17E_Civic_Center_ Firstname_Lastname**

(Project 17E–Civic Center continues on the next page)

Content-Based Assessments

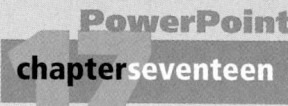
(Project 17E–Civic Center continued)

12. Check your *Chapter Assignment Sheet* or *Course Syllabus* or consult your instructor to determine if you are to submit your assignments on paper or electronically. To submit electronically, go to Step 14, and then follow the instructions provided by your instructor.

13. Display your presentation in **Print Preview**, and then print **Handouts (6 Slides Per Page)**.

14. **Save** the changes to your presentation, and then close the presentation.

End You have completed Project 17E —————————————————

PowerPoint
chapter seventeen

Mastering PowerPoint

Project 17F — Forest Glen

In this project, you will apply the skills you practiced from the Objectives in Project 17B.

Objectives: 3. *Create and Modify Tables;* **4.** *Create and Modify Charts.*

In the following Mastering PowerPoint project, you will edit a presentation that the Marketing Department will use to showcase the Forest Glen Lifestyle Center. Your completed presentation will look similar to Figure 17.39.

For Project 17F, you will need the following file:

p17F_Forest_Glen

You will save your presentation as
17F_Forest_Glen_Firstname_Lastname

Figure 17.39

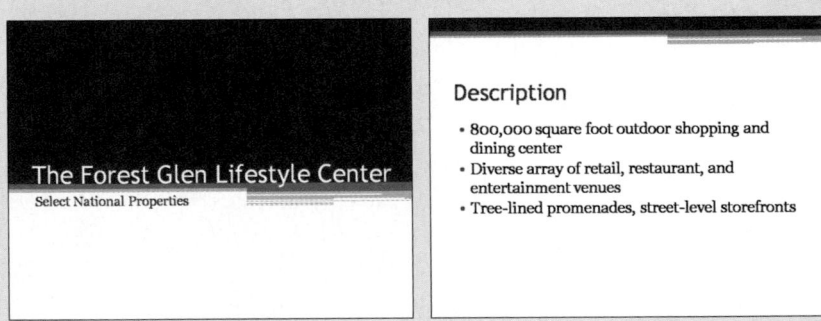

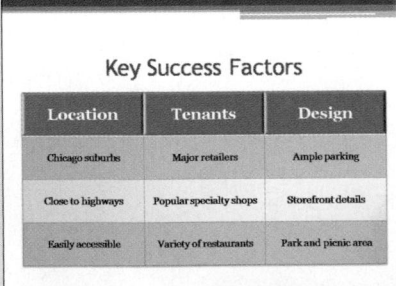

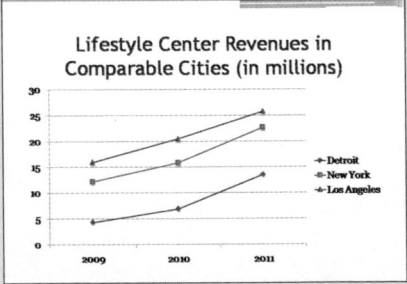

(Project 17F—Forest Glen continues on the next page)

Content-Based Assessments

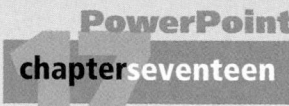

Mastering PowerPoint

(Project 17F–Forest Glen continued)

1. **Start** PowerPoint. From your student files, **Open** the file **p17F_Forest_Glen**. **Save** the file in your **PowerPoint Chapter 17** folder as 17F_Forest_Glen_Firstname_Lastname

2. Display **Slide 2**, and then insert a **New Slide** with the **Title and Content** layout. In the title placeholder, type **Key Success Factors** and then **Center** the title. In the content placeholder, insert a table with **3 columns** and **4 rows**. Type the following information in the table:

Location	Tenants	Design
Chicago suburbs	Major retailers	Ample parking
Close to highways	Popular specialty shops	Storefront details
Easily accessible	Variety of restaurants	Park and picnic area

3. If necessary, display the Ruler. Size the table so that the bottom edge of the table is aligned at approximately **3 inches below zero on the vertical ruler**. On the **Layout tab**, in the **Cell Size group**, click the **Distribute Rows** button so that the four rows are equal in height. Select the table, and then **Center** the text horizontally and vertically in the cells.

4. Apply a **Best Match for Document** table style—**Themed Style 1 – Accent 2**—and in the **Table Style Options**, apply the **Header Row** and **Banded Row** options.

5. Select the first row of the table, change the **Font Size** to **28**, and then apply a **Cell Bevel** effect to the first row—**Circle**.

6. Insert a new slide with the **Title and Content Layout**. In the title placeholder, type **Lifestyle Center Revenues in Comparable Cities (in millions)** and then **Center** the title.

7. In the content placeholder, insert a **Clustered Column** chart, and then replace the data in the Excel window with the data below. Be sure to delete the extra row of data in **Row 5** in the Excel window.

	Detroit	New York	Los Angeles
2009	4.3	12.2	15.9
2010	6.9	15.8	20.4
2011	13.5	22.6	25.7

8. **Close** the Excel window. Select the chart, and then on the **Design tab**, in the **Type group**, click the **Change Chart Type** button. Under **Line**, click **Line with Markers**, and then apply chart **Style 26**.

9. Create a **Header and Footer** for the **Notes and Handouts**. Include only the **Date and time updated automatically**, the **Page number**, and a **Footer** with the file name **17F_Forest_Glen_ Firstname_Lastname**

10. Check your *Chapter Assignment Sheet* or *Course Syllabus* or consult your instructor to determine if you are to submit your assignments on paper or electronically. To submit electronically, go to Step 12, and then follow the instructions provided by your instructor.

11. Display your presentation in **Print Preview**, and then print **Handouts (6 Slides Per Page)**.

12. **Save** the changes to your presentation, and then **Close** the presentation.

 You have completed Project 17F _____

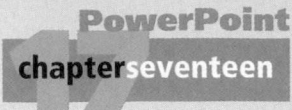

Mastering PowerPoint

Project 17G — Restaurants

In this project, you will apply the skills you practiced from the Objectives in Projects 17A and 17B.

Objectives: 1. *Customize Slide Backgrounds and Themes;* **2.** *Animate a Slide Show;* **3.** *Create and Modify Tables;* **4.** *Create and Modify Charts.*

In the following Mastering PowerPoint project, you will edit a presentation that the president of Select National Properties will make to the National Restaurant Owners Association proposing new restaurant construction in the city of Monroe Heights. Your completed presentation will look similar to Figure 17.40.

For Project 17G, you will need the following files:

New blank PowerPoint presentation
p17G_Tables

You will save your presentation as
17G_Restaurants_Firstname_Lastname

Figure 17.40

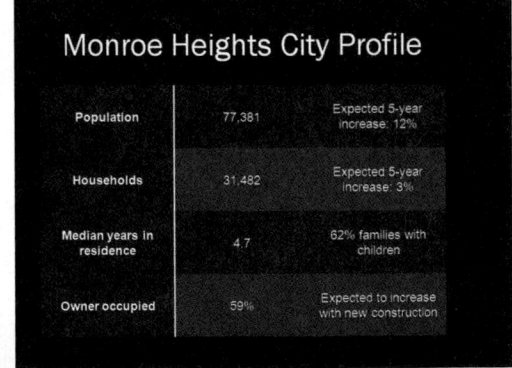

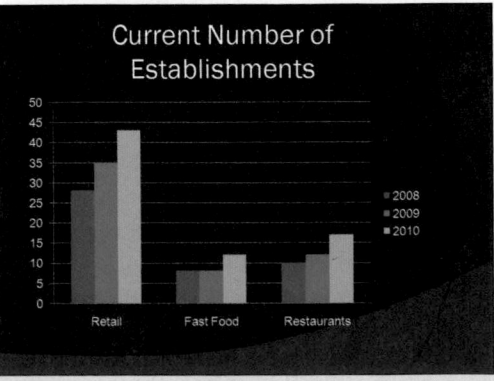

(Project 17G–Restaurants continues on the next page)

Content-Based Assessments

(Project 17G–Restaurants continued)

1. **Start** PowerPoint and begin a new blank presentation. In the title placeholder, type **Presentation to the National Restaurant Owners Association** and then in the subtitle placeholder, type **Select National Properties Save** the presentation in your **PowerPoint Chapter 17** folder as 17G_Restaurants_Firstname_Lastname

2. Apply the **Technic** theme to the presentation, and then change the **Theme Colors** to **Solstice**. Hide the background graphics, and then display the **Format Background** dialog box. Use the **Picture or texture fill option** to insert the **p17G_Tables** picture on the slide background. Verify that the **Stretch options Offsets** are set to **0%**.

3. Click in the title placeholder, and then on the **Format tab**, click the **Shape Fill** button, and then in the first row of colors, apply the **Brown, Background 2** fill to the title placeholder. In the **Size group**, change the **Height** to **1.5** and the **Width** to **10** and then **Center** the text. Move the title placeholder so that its lower edge aligns with the lower edge of the slide and the left and right edges of the slide and placeholder also align.

4. Click in the subtitle placeholder, and then change the **Shape Fill** color to **Black, Background 1**. Adjust the **Height** to **1.0** and the **Width** to **10** and then **Center** the text and change the **Font Size** to **28**. Drag the subtitle placeholder down so that its lower edge aligns with the top edge of the title placeholder and the left and right edges of the slide and placeholder also align.

5. Insert a **New Slide** with the **Title and Content** layout. Hide the background graphics on this slide.

6. In the title placeholder, type **Monroe Heights City Profile** and then **Center** the title. In the content placeholder, insert a table with **3 columns** and **4 rows**. Type the following table text:

Population	77,381	Expected 5-year increase: 12%
Households	31,482	Expected 5-year increase: 3%
Median years in residence	4.7	62% families with children
Owner occupied	59%	Expected to increase with new construction

7. If necessary, display the Ruler, and then adjust the size of the table so that its lower edge aligns at approximately **3 inches below zero on the vertical ruler**. Select the table, and then **Center** the text horizontally and vertically in the cells. Click **Distribute Rows** so that all of the rows are the same height.

8. Change the table **Design** by changing the **Table Style Options** so that only the **Banded Rows** and **First Column** check boxes are selected. In the **Tables Styles gallery**, under **Dark**, apply **Dark Style 1 – Accent 5**.

9. Add a slide with the **Two Content** layout. In the title placeholder, type **Increased Demand for New Restaurants in Monroe Heights** and then **Center** the title.

10. On **Slide 3**, hide the background graphics. In the placeholder on the left, insert a **SmartArt** graphic. In the **Choose a Smart Graphic** dialog box, click **Pyramid**, click the last pyramid graphic—**Segmented Pyramid**—and then click **OK**.

(Project 17G–Restaurants continues on the next page)

(Project 17G–Restaurants continued)

11. In the top triangle shape, type **Large family base** and then click in the center triangle. Type **Clientele from nearby cities** and then click in the lower left triangle. Type **New theaters** and then click in the lower right triangle. Type **New retail outlets**

12. On the **SmartArt Tools**, click the **Design tab**, and then click **Change Colors**. Under **Colorful**, click the last color set—**Colorful Range – Accent Colors 5 to 6**. In the **SmartArt Styles group**, under **3-D**, apply the fourth effect—**Powder**.

13. In the placeholder on the right, type the following bullet points.

Vibrant economic climate

Growing population

Community loyal to local merchants

Close to major suburbs

Small number of restaurants relative to population

14. Insert a **New Slide** with the **Title and Content** layout. In the title placeholder, type **Current Number of Establishments** and then **Center** the title.

15. In the content placeholder, insert a **Clustered Column** chart. In the **Excel** worksheet, type the following data, deleting extra columns and rows as necessary:

	2008	2009	2010
Retail	28	35	43
Fast Food	8	8	12
Restaurants	10	12	17

16. **Close** Excel, and then apply **Style 3** to the chart. Use the **Animate** list to apply the **Wipe By Category** animation.

17. Apply the **Wipe Down** transition, and then change the **Transition Speed** to **Medium**. Apply the transition setting to all of the slides in the presentation.

18. Display **Slide 3**, and then select the **SmartArt graphic**. Use the **Animate list** to apply the **Fade As One Object** animation. Click the bulleted list placeholder, and then use the **Custom Animation** task pane to apply the **Blinds Entrance Effect**. View the slide show from the beginning.

19. Create a **Header and Footer** for the **Notes and Handouts**. Include only the **Date and time updated automatically**, the **Page number**, and a **Footer** with the file name 17G_Restaurants_ Firstname_Lastname

20. Check your *Chapter Assignment Sheet* or *Course Syllabus* or consult your instructor to determine if you are to submit your assignments on paper or electronically. To submit electronically, go to Step 22, and then follow the instructions provided by your instructor.

21. Display your presentation in **Print Preview**, and then print **Handouts (4 Slides Per Page)**.

22. **Save** the changes to your presentation, and then **Close** the presentation.

 You have completed Project 17G ⏤⏤⏤⏤⏤⏤⏤⏤⏤

Content-Based Assessments

Project 17H — Town Centers

In this project, you will apply the skills you practiced from the Objectives in Projects 17A and 17B.

Objectives: 1. *Customize Slide Backgrounds and Themes;* **2.** *Animate a Slide Show;* **4.** *Create and Modify Charts.*

In the following Mastering PowerPoint Assessment, you will edit a presentation that Randall Thomas, Select National Properties Chief Executive Officer, has created to explain the growth of mixed-use town centers in large cities. Your completed presentation will look similar to Figure 17.41.

For Project 17H, you will need the following files:

New blank PowerPoint presentation
p17H_Definition

You will save your presentation as
17H_Town_Centers_Firstname_Lastname

Figure 17.41

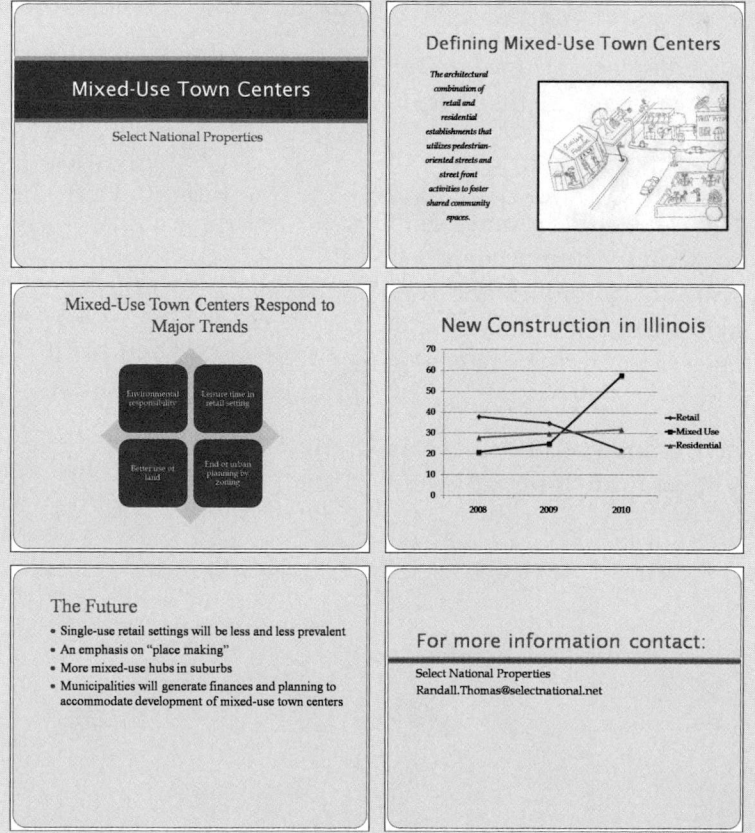

(Project 17H–Town Centers continues on the next page)

(Project 17H–Town Centers continued)

1. **Start** PowerPoint and begin a new blank presentation. In the title placeholder, type **Mixed-Use Town Centers** In the subtitle placeholder, type **Select National Properties** and then **Save** the file in your **PowerPoint Chapter 17** folder as **17H_Town_Centers_ Firstname_ Lastname**

2. Apply the **Equity** theme to the presentation, and then apply **Background Style 2**. Apply the **Apex Fonts Theme** which consists of the *Lucida Sans* and *Book Antiqua* fonts.

3. From your student files, insert all of the slides from the **p17H_Definition** file. (**Hint**: click the **New Slide arrow**, and then click **Reuse Slides**). Display **Slide 2**, and then click in the text on the left side of the slide. Apply the **Compress Entrance Effect**. **Start** the effect **After Previous**, and change the **Speed** to **Medium**.

4. With **Slide 2** still displayed, move the picture so that its lower edge aligns at **2.5 inches below zero**.

5. Display **Slide 3**. Select the SmartArt graphic, and then use the **Animate** list to apply the **Wipe**, **One by one** animation. Apply the **Wipe Left** transition, and then set the **Transition Speed** to **Fast**. Apply the transition settings to all of the slides in the presentation.

6. With **Slide 3** still displayed, insert a **New Slide** with the **Title and Content** layout.

In the title placeholder, type **New Construction in Illinois** and then **Center** the title. In the content placeholder, insert a **Line with Markers** chart, and then enter the following data in the **Excel** worksheet:

	Retail	Mixed Use	Residential
2008	38	21	28
2009	35	25	30
2010	22	58	32

7. Delete the unused row, and then **Close** Excel. Apply **Chart Style 18**, and then view the slide show from the beginning of the presentation.

8. Create a **Header and Footer** for the **Notes and Handouts**. Include only the **Date and time updated automatically**, the **Page number**, and a **Footer** with the file name **17H_Town_Centers_Firstname_Lastname**

9. Check your *Chapter Assignment Sheet* or *Course Syllabus* or consult your instructor to determine if you are to submit your assignments on paper or electronically. To submit electronically, go to Step 11, and then follow the instructions provided by your instructor.

10. Display your presentation in **Print Preview**, and then print **Handouts (6 Slides Per Page)**.

11. **Save** the changes to your presentation, and then close the presentation.

 End **You have completed Project 17H**

Content-Based Assessments

Mastering PowerPoint

Project 17I — Clients

In this project, you will apply the skills you practiced from all the Objectives in Projects 17A and 17B.

Objectives: 1. *Customize Slide Backgrounds and Themes;* **2.** *Animate a Slide Show;* **3.** *Create and Modify Tables;* **4.** *Create and Modify Charts.*

In the following Mastering PowerPoint Assessment, you will edit a presentation that Randall Thomas, Select National Properties Chief Executive Officer will present to a group of prospective clients. Your completed presentation will look similar to Figure 17.42.

For Project 17I, you will need the following files:

p17I_Clients
p17I_Building

You will save your presentation as
17I_Clients_Firstname_Lastname

Figure 17.42

Mastering PowerPoint

(Project 17I–Clients continued)

1. **Start** PowerPoint. From your student files, **Open** the file **p17I_Clients**. **Save** the file in your **PowerPoint Chapter 17** folder as **17I_Clients_Firstname_Lastname**

2. Apply **Background Style 8** to all of the slides in the presentation, and then change the **Fonts Theme** to **Equity**. Apply the **Split Vertical Out** transition to all of the slides in the presentation.

3. Display **Slide 3**, and then in the content placeholder, insert a **SmartArt** graphic. In the **Choose a SmartArt Graphic** dialog box, insert the **Process** type graphic—**Funnel**. On the **Design tab**, in the **Create Graphic group**, click the **Text Pane** button to display the text pane. Type the following text in each of the four bullet points:

   Integrity

   Trust

   Loyalty

   Success

4. **Close** the text pane. Apply the **Fade As one object** animation to the SmartArt graphic.

5. With **Slide 3** displayed, insert a **New Slide** with the **Title Slide** layout. In the title placeholder, type **Quality** and then in the subtitle placeholder, type **Large enough to meet all your needs; small enough to give your project the attention it deserves. Center** the title and subtitle text.

6. With **Slide 4** still displayed, hide the background graphics, and then on the **Background**, insert a picture from your student files—**p17I_Building**. Before closing the **Format Background** dialog box, verify that the **Stretch options Offsets** are set to **0%**.

7. Drag the title placeholder up so that the top edge of the placeholder aligns with the top edge of the slide and the word *Quality* is centered at the intersection of the two buildings. Select **Quality**, and then change the **Font Color** to **Black, Background 1**.

8. Select the subtitle placeholder, and then change the **Shape Fill** color to **Black, Background 1**. Size the placeholder so that it extends from the left edge to the right edge of the slide, and then drag the placeholder down so that its lower edge aligns with the lower edge of the slide.

9. Display **Slide 6**, and then in the content placeholder, insert a **Clustered Column** chart. In the **Excel** worksheet, enter the following data:

	2009	2010	2011
Commercial	318	402	435
Housing	122	257	305
Non-profit	216	268	322

10. Delete the unused row in the worksheet, and then **Close** Excel. Apply chart **Style 42**, and then from the **Animate** list, apply the **Fade By Category** animation.

(Project 17I–Clients continues on the next page)

Content-Based Assessments

(Project 17I–Clients continued)

11. Display **Slide 7**, and then in the content placeholder, insert a **Table** with **3 columns** and **4 rows**. Type the following text in the table:

Service	Number	Location
Development	Over 15 million square feet	Throughout Midwest
Property Management	Over 40 properties	Illinois and Indiana
Current Construction	5 million square feet	Illinois and Maine

12. If necessary, display the Ruler. Size the table so that its lower edge aligns at approximately **1 inch below zero on the vertical ruler**. Distribute the rows, and then **Center** the text horizontally and vertically. In the **Tables Styles gallery**, apply **Dark Style 1 – Accent 1**. Select the entire table, and then change the **Font Size** to **28**. With the table still selected, apply the **Circle, Cell Bevel** effect.

13. Display **Slide 8**, and then select the title placeholder. Display the **Custom Animation** task pane, and then apply the **Blinds Entrance Effect**. **Start** the animation **After Previous**, and then change the **Speed** to **Fast**. Apply the same animation effect and settings to the subtitle, and then view the slide show from the beginning.

14. Create a **Header and Footer** for the **Notes and Handouts**. Include only the **Date and time updated automatically**, the **Page number**, and a **Footer** with the file name 17I_Clients_Firstname_Lastname

15. Check your *Chapter Assignment Sheet* or *Course Syllabus* or consult your instructor to determine if you are to submit your assignments on paper or electronically. To submit electronically, go to Step 17, and then follow the instructions provided by your instructor.

16. Display your presentation in **Print Preview**, and then print **Handouts (4 Slides Per Page)**.

17. **Save** the changes to your presentation, and then close the presentation.

 End **You have completed Project 17I** ——————————————

Content-Based Assessments

Project 17J—Business Running Case

In this project, you will apply the skills you practiced in Projects 17A and 17B.

Close PowerPoint and any other open windows. Display the Start menu, click Computer, and then navigate to the student files that accompany this textbook. In the folder **03_business_running_case**, locate and open the folder for this chapter. Open and print the instructions for this project, which are provided to you in Adobe PDF format. Follow the instructions and use the skills you have gained thus far to assist Jennifer Nelson in meeting the challenges of owning and running her business.

 You have completed Project 17J ———————————

Content-Based Assessments

Project 17K — *GO!* Fix It

In this project, you will apply the skills you practiced from the Objectives in Projects 17A and 17B.

> ### For Project 17K, you will need the following files:
>
> p17K_fixit_Kid_Fun_Nursery_School
> p17K_fixit_Vacant_Lot

You will save your document as
17K_Kid_Fun_Nursery_School_Firstname_Lastname

In this project, you will edit a presentation that is being made to the Kid Fun Nursery School board of directors. Select National Properties is bidding on the development and construction of a new nursery school and two sites are under consideration. SNP had its architects develop energy-efficient buildings. From the student files that accompany this textbook, open the folder **05_go_fix_it**. Locate and open the file **p17K_fixit_Kid_Fun_Nursery_School**, and then save the file in your chapter folder as **17K_Kid_Fun_Nursery_School_Firstname_Lastname**

This presentation contains **five errors** that you must find and correct. Read and examine the document, and then edit to correct the errors that you find. Types of errors could include:

- Spelling, grammar, punctuation, and usage errors such as text case, subject-verb agreement, and meaning.
- Content errors such as missing or incorrect data, text, pictures, hyperlinks, or other objects.
- Font and paragraph formatting and positioning errors such fonts, font styles, font sizing, alignment, text color, indent levels, and bullet features.
- Slide layout, orientation, design themes, backgrounds, animation and transition errors.
- Image or object formatting and positioning errors on tables, illustrations, links, text, and media clips relating to color, lines, size, scale, styles, layout, positioning, and control.
- Page setup errors on slides, handouts, notes and outlines such as margins, orientation, layout, alignment, headers and footers, date and time, color, grayscale, black and white, and sizing.

(Project 17K–*GO!* Fix It continues on the next page)

Content-Based Assessments

(Project 17K–*GO!* Fix It continued)

To complete the project, you should:

- Change the theme from **Concourse** to **Oriel**.
- On **Slide 1**, on the photo of the boy and girl painting, add the animated picture effect **Moderate Grow & Turn, Fast speed, After Previous**.
- On **Slide 1**, add slide transition **Newsflash, Medium speed**.
- On **Slide 2**, add and format the background with the picture **p17K_fixit_Vacant_Lot** from your student files, hide the background graphics, and set all of the **Stretch option offsets** to **0**. In the bulleted lists, change the **Font Color** to **Light Yellow, Background 2, Darker 25%**.
- On **Slide 6**, format the sun graphic with **Orange, Accent 1** fill. Animate the graphic using the entrance effect **Exciting Swivel** with **Very Slow speed**.

Create a footer for the Notes and Handouts. Include only the date and time updated automatically, the page number, and a footer with your name included. Submit as directed, using 6 slides per page.

End **You have completed Project 17K** ⎯⎯⎯⎯⎯⎯⎯⎯

Outcomes-Based Assessments

PowerPoint
chapter seventeen

Rubric

The following outcomes-based assessments are *open-ended assessments*. That is, there is no specific correct result; your result will depend on your approach to the information provided. Make *professional quality* your goal. Use the following scoring rubric to guide you in *how* to approach the problem and then to evaluate *how well* your approach solves the problem.

The *criteria*—Software Mastery, Content, Format and Layout, and Process—represent the knowledge and skills you have gained that you can apply to solving the problem. The *levels of performance*—Professional Quality, Approaching Professional Quality, or Needs Quality Improvements—help you and your instructor evaluate your result.

	Your completed project is of Professional Quality if you:	Your completed project is Approaching Professional Quality if you:	Your completed project Needs Quality Improvements if you:
1-Software Mastery	Choose and apply the most appropriate skills, tools, and features and identify efficient methods to solve the problem.	Choose and apply some appropriate skills, tools, and features, but not in the most efficient manner.	Choose inappropriate skills, tools, or features, or are inefficient in solving the problem.
2-Content	Construct a solution that is clear and well organized, contains content that is accurate, appropriate to the audience and purpose, and is complete. Provide a solution that contains no errors of spelling, grammar, or style.	Construct a solution in which some components are unclear, poorly organized, inconsistent, or incomplete. Misjudge the needs of the audience. Have some errors in spelling, grammar, or style, but the errors do not detract from comprehension.	Construct a solution that is unclear, incomplete, or poorly organized, containing some inaccurate or inappropriate content; and contains many errors of spelling, grammar, or style. Do not solve the problem.
3-Format and Layout	Format and arrange all elements to communicate information and ideas, clarify function, illustrate relationships, and indicate relative importance.	Apply appropriate format and layout features to some elements, but not others. Overuse features, causing minor distraction.	Apply format and layout that does not communicate information or ideas clearly. Do not use format and layout features to clarify function, illustrate relationships, or indicate relative importance. Use available features excessively, causing distraction.
4-Process	Use an organized approach that integrates planning, development, self-assessment, revision, and reflection.	Demonstrate an organized approach in some areas, but not others; or, use an insufficient process of organization throughout.	Do not use an organized approach to solve the problem.

Outcomes-Based Assessments

Problem Solving

Project 17L — Coral Ridge

In this project, you will construct a solution by applying any combination of the Objectives found in Projects 17A and 17B.

For Project 17L, you will need the following file:

New blank PowerPoint presentation

You will save your presentation as
17L_Coral_Ridge_Firstname_Lastname

Select National Properties has developed a new housing development in the suburbs of Chicago. Randall Thomas, CEO, will be making a presentation on the new community to prospective home buyers. The development—Coral Ridge—consists of 55 homes with two different floor plans. The first floor plan—The Oakmont—includes 1,700 square feet and has 3 bedrooms and 2 baths. There is a fireplace in the family room and the kitchen and bathrooms have tile countertops. The second floor plan—The Seneca—has 1,925 square feet with 4 bedrooms and 2 baths. There are fireplaces in the master bedroom and in the family room, and the bathrooms and kitchens have granite countertops. The community has an excellent school district and is accessible by major highways.

Create a presentation with six slides that describes the community and the development. Apply a design template of your choice, change the background style on at least one slide, and include a picture on the background of one slide. Using the information in the preceding paragraph, insert a slide with a table that compares the two floor plans. Apply slide transitions and animation. Add the file name to the Notes and Handouts footer and check the presentation for spelling errors. Save the presentation as **17L_Coral_Ridge_Firstname_Lastname** and submit it as directed.

Note: You can find many appropriate images available to Office users. To access these images, click the Insert tab, and then from the Illustrations group, click the Clip Art button. In the Clip Art task pane, type a key word—such as *construction*—in the *Search for* box. You can specify the image type (clip art or photographs) and where to search. The largest variety of photographs can be found by including Web Collections in the *Search in* box. You can also use images from earlier projects in this chapter, or images from your personal collection.

 You have completed Project 17L ⎯⎯⎯⎯

Outcomes-Based Assessments

Problem Solving

Project 17M — Land Development

In this project, you will construct a solution by applying any combination of the Objectives found in Projects 17A and 17B.

> **For Project 17M, you will need the following file:**
>
> New blank PowerPoint presentation

**You will save your presentation as
17M_Land_Development_Firstname_Lastname**

Select National Properties owns several land parcels in the growing community of Lake Monahan. The Chief Financial Officer, Morgan Bannon-Navarre, is creating a presentation for the members of the Lake Monahan Real Estate Association that describes the available parcels located in three areas of the city: North, South, and Central. Create a presentation with four to six slides describing the community and the parcels using the following information.

The City of Lake Monahan is a vacation destination for many out-of-state families. The lake provides opportunities for water sports, fishing, and boating. Select National Properties invested in the city by purchasing several land parcels approximately 15 years ago and is now ready to develop and sell the parcels.

In your presentation, insert one slide with a picture on the slide background that depicts the lake. (See the note at the end of project 17L for ideas on locating images.) Insert a slide titled **Available Parcels** and use the data below to create a table describing the parcels.

	North	South	Central
Parcels	10	15	18
Size	.75 acres	1.2 acres	1.05 acres
Price	$45,000	$68,000	$52,000

Insert a slide with the title **Average Parcel Price** and then insert an appropriate chart using the following data:

	North	South	Central
2008	$22,300	$55,675	$41,375
2009	$32,500	$62,420	$45,850
2010	$45,000	$68,000	$52,000

Use formatting and animation techniques that you learned in this chapter to create a professional presentation. Add the file name to the Notes and Handouts footer and check for spelling errors. Save the presentation as **17M_Land_Development_Firstname_Lastname** and submit it as directed.

End You have completed Project 17M —————————

Outcomes-Based Assessments

Problem Solving

Project 17N—Renovation

In this project, you will construct a solution by applying any combination of the Objectives found in Projects 17A and 17B.

For Project 17N, you will need the following files:

New blank PowerPoint presentation
p17N_Scaffold
p17N_Scaffold2

**You will save your presentation as
17N_Renovation_Firstname_Lastname**

Select National Properties' Vice President of Construction, Michael Wentworth, is presenting the status of The Lincoln Plaza—a large renovation project—to the project investors. Use the following information to create a presentation with at least four slides, including a table and a chart.

The Lincoln Plaza consists of three 10-story buildings on the perimeter of a large courtyard. The renovation is taking place in three overlapping phases: Exteriors that are 75 percent complete with an expected completion date of September 2009; Interior Infrastructure that is 55 percent complete with an expected completion date of June 2010; and Courtyard Enhancements that is 35 percent complete with an expected completion date of December 2010. The cost of each phase in millions is estimated as follows:

	Exterior	Interior	Courtyard
Labor	22.6	33.8	5.25
Materials	36.9	48.7	12.6

Apply an appropriate design and background style, and change the Fonts Theme. Format the background of one slide using one of the pictures provided with your student files—p17N_Scaffold or p17M_Scaffold2. Apply chart and table styles and slide transitions and animation. Add the file name to the Notes and Handouts footer and check for spelling errors. Save the presentation as **17N_Renovation_Firstname_Lastname** and submit it as directed.

 End **You have completed Project 17N** ————————

Outcomes-Based Assessments

Problem Solving

Project 17O — High School

In this project, you will construct a solution by applying any combination of the Objectives found in Projects 17A and 17B.

For Project 17O, you will need the following file:

New blank PowerPoint presentation

You will save your presentation as
17O_High_School_Firstname_Lastname

Select National Properties has been chosen as one of three contractors bidding on the construction of a new high school in Monroe Heights. Company President Shaun Walker is making a presentation to the Monroe Heights School Board regarding the company's proposal. Create a presentation that includes one or two slides with information about the company, one slide with a table, one slide with a chart, and two slides that include slide backgrounds with pictures of school facilities. (See the note at the end of project 17L for ideas on locating images). Use the following information for your presentation.

Select National Properties is a diversified real estate company that develops, builds, manages, and acquires a wide variety of properties nationwide. Among the company's portfolio of properties are shopping malls, mixed-use town center developments, high-rise office buildings, office parks, industrial buildings and warehouses, multifamily housing developments, educational facilities, and hospitals. Residential developments are mainly located in and around the company's hometown, Chicago; commercial and public buildings in the portfolio are located nationwide. The company is well respected for its focus on quality and commitment to the environment and economic development of the areas where it operates. Use the information below to create a slide with a table using columns 1, 2, and 3 and a slide with a chart using columns 1 and 4.

	Description	Completion	Estimate
Buildings	45 classrooms	January 2010	$18.0 million
Network	Wireless access	July 2010	$0.5 million
Pool	Outdoor Olympic size with bleachers	December 2010	$1.5 million
Exteriors	Parking, landscape	July 2010	$5.0 million

Apply an appropriate design and background style and change the Fonts Theme. Apply chart and table styles and slide transitions and animation. Add the the file name to the Notes and Handouts footer and check for spelling errors. Save the presentation as **17O_High_School_Firstname_Lastname** and submit it as directed.

End **You have completed Project 17O** _____

Outcomes-Based Assessments

Problem Solving

Project 17P — Recruiting

In this project, you will construct a solution by applying any combination of the Objectives found in Projects 17A and 17B.

For Project 17P, you will need the following file:

New blank PowerPoint presentation

You will save your presentation as
17P_Recruiting_Firstname_Lastname

To serve the growing national needs of the company, the Board of Directors for Select National Properties has decided to open an office in Austin, Texas. Nancy Chung, Human Resources Director, will be recruiting college graduates for professional opportunities in the new location. Use the following information to create a presentation that she can show at several colleges she is visiting.

Select National Properties is a diversified real estate company that develops, builds, manages, and acquires a wide variety of properties nationwide. The mission of Select National Properties is to be a leader in the real estate development business through a commitment to integrity, high ethical standards, and operational expertise. Among the company's portfolio of properties are shopping malls, mixed-use town center developments, high-rise office buildings, office parks, industrial buildings and warehouses, multifamily housing developments, educational facilities, and hospitals. Residential developments are mainly located in and around the company's hometown, Chicago; commercial and public buildings in the portfolio are located nationwide. The company is well respected for its focus on quality and commitment to the environment and economic development of the areas where it operates.

The following table includes information about the sales growth of Select National Properties in millions over the past 10 years.

Sector	2000	2005	2010
Residential	125	158	209
Commercial	167	219	282
Land	95	132	191

(Project 17P–Recruiting continues on the next page)

Outcomes-Based Assessments

Problem Solving

(Project 17P—Recruiting continued)

The following table summarizes the types of positions for which Nancy is recruiting.

Position	Description	Starting Salary
Civil Engineer	**Applies knowledge of design, construction procedures, zoning and building codes, and building materials to render structural designs.**	**$45,000**
Project Manager	**Prepares and reviews facilities plans, construction contract bid documents, and specifications for projects. Monitors project progress and costs.**	**$53,000**
Accountant	**Performs professional accounting work, including auditing, analyzing, and verifying fiscal records and reports.**	**$38,000**

Create a presentation that includes at least six slides, including background information on the company, and a table and a chart using the preceding information. Apply an appropriate design and background style and change the Fonts Theme. Apply chart and table styles, and slide transitions and animation. Add the file name to the Notes and Handouts footer and check for spelling errors. Save the presentation as **17P_Recruiting_Firstname_Lastname** and submit it as directed.

 End You have completed Project 17P ————————————

Outcomes-Based Assessments

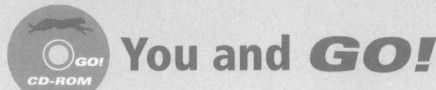 You and *GO!*

Project 17Q — You and *GO!*

In this project, you will construct a solution by applying any combination of the skills you practiced from the Objectives in Projects 17A and 17B.

Close PowerPoint and any other open windows. Display the Start menu, click Computer, and then navigate to the student files that accompany this textbook. In the folder **04_you_and_go**, locate and open the folder for this chapter. Open and print the instructions for this project, which are provided to you in Adobe PDF format. Follow the instructions to create a presentation about the registration process at your school.

End You have completed Project 17Q

GO! with Help

Project 17R — *GO!* with Help

There are a number of different types of charts that you can create in PowerPoint. Use Microsoft Office PowerPoint Help to learn about the different types of charts in PowerPoint.

1 **Start** PowerPoint. At the far right end of the Ribbon, click the **Microsoft Office PowerPoint Help** button.

2 In the **Type words to search for** box, type **Chart Types** and then press Enter.

3 Click the **Available chart types** link, and then read the information on each type of chart. When you are through, close the Help window, and then close PowerPoint.

End You have completed Project 17R

Outcomes-Based Assessments

Group Business Running Case

Project 17S — Group Business Running Case

In this project, you will apply all the Objectives found in Projects 17A and 17B.

Your instructor may assign this group case project to your class. If your instructor assigns this project, he or she will provide you with information and instructions to work as part of a group. The group will apply the skills gained thus far to help the Bell Orchid Hotel Group achieve its business goals.

 You have completed Project 17S ——————————

chaptereighteen

Using Access Data with Other Office Programs

OBJECTIVES

At the end of this project you will be able to:

1. Export Access Data to Excel
2. Create a Formula in Excel
3. Create a Chart in Excel
4. Copy Access Data into a Word Document
5. Copy Excel Data into a Word Document
6. Insert an Excel Chart into a PowerPoint Presentation

OUTCOMES

Mastering these objectives will enable you to:

PROJECT 18A

Use Access Data with Other Office Programs

Introduction

An Access database may be the source of information you want to use to create content for a variety of other kinds of documents. For example, you may want to create an Excel worksheet to show numerical information, create a table within a Word document to list information, or create an Excel chart to include as part of a PowerPoint presentation.

You are preparing information in a Word document and in a PowerPoint presentation for a meeting. You will complete your materials for the meeting with some additional data from an Access database and an Excel worksheet.

Project 18A **Meeting Slides**

In Activities 18.01 through 18.6, you will prepare for a meeting by updating a Word document and creating a PowerPoint presentation using information gathered from Excel and Access. Your completed project will look similar to Figure 18.1.

For Project 18A, you will need the following files:

Ip18A_Dept_Data
Ip18A_Meeting_Topics
Ip18A_Meeting_Slides

You will save your workbook as
18A_Meeting_Data_Firstname_Lastname
You will save your document as
18A_Meeting_Topics_Firstname_Lastname
You will save your presentation as
18A_Meeting_Slides_Firstname_Lastname

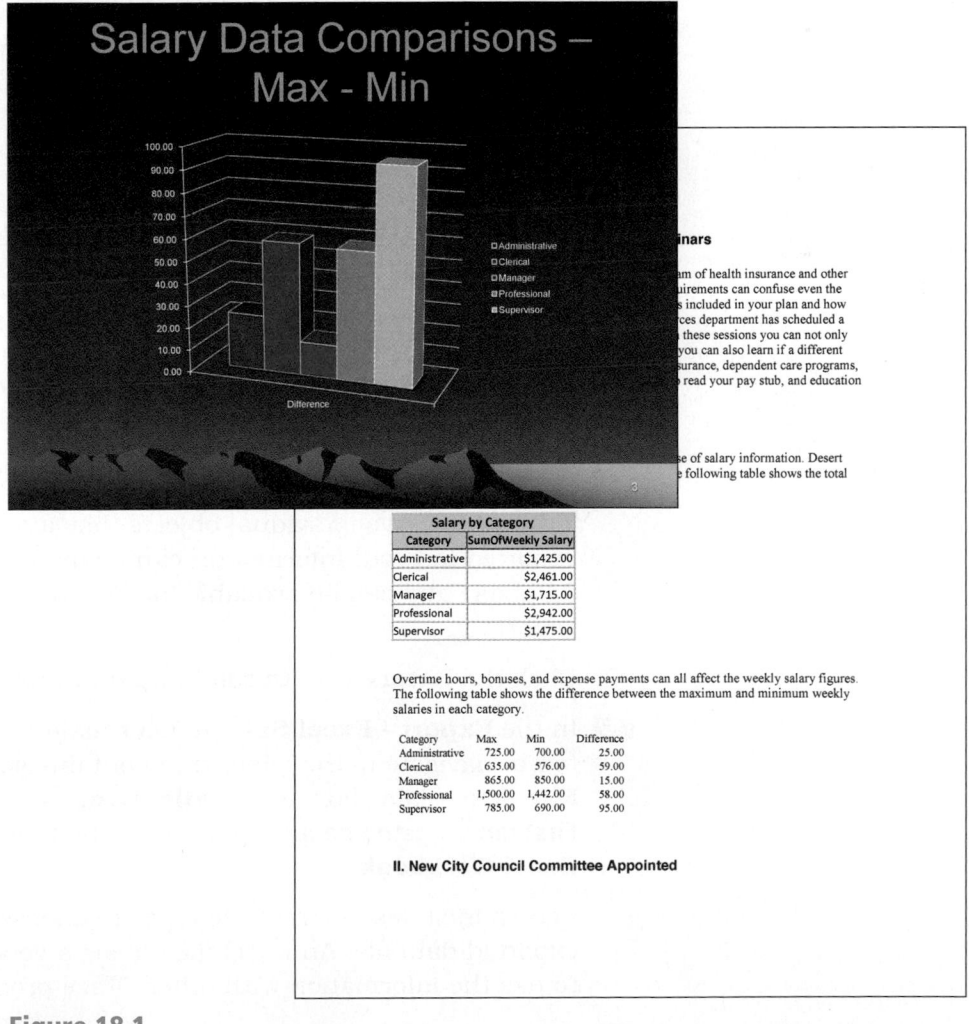

Figure 18.1
Project 18A—Meeting Information

Objective 1
Export Access Data to Excel

Activity 18.01 Exporting Access Data to Excel

Access includes a tool to export data from an Access database to an Excel workbook.

1 **Start** Access. From the folder that contains your project files, open the Access database **ip18A_Dept_Data**.

An Access database can have many different objects that organize the database information and that output data for different uses. The different types of Access objects are available in the Navigation Pane on the left side of the screen. Clicking the down arrow on the Navigation Pane changes what is displayed or selects a different object type. Selecting an object type from the list displays the objects of that type in the Navigation Pane.

Alert!	**Did you get a security alert?**
	If you see a Security Alert Warning at the top of the screen, click the Options button. In the Microsoft Office Security Options dialog box, click the Enable this content option button and click OK.

2 In the **Navigation Pane**, if necessary, click **Queries** to review the list of query objects.

A query uses criteria to select, sort, or manipulate only those records in the database that meet the criteria. Queries are useful for reports and for searching for data to meet specific conditions, such as a date or a value.

3 Double-click the **Weekly Salary Query** to display the selected data.

You cannot save individual objects, like a query, as a file. Data is exported instead. Information can be maintained in an Access database and can be available for use by other programs through exporting.

4 Click the **External Data tab**, and in the **Export group**, click **Excel**.

5 In the **Export - Excel Spreadsheet** dialog box, use the **Browse** button to navigate to the folder that contains your project files. In the **File Save** dialog box, in the **File name** box, type **18A_Meeting_Data_Firstname_Lastname** and make sure the **Save as type** box displays **Excel Workbook**.

Access includes different file types to choose from to create the exported data file. An Excel file type is a good choice when you plan to use the information with other Office programs.

6 Click the **Save** button, and then in the **Export - Excel Spreadsheet** dialog box, click **OK**. At the next prompt to

Save Export Steps, leave the Save export steps check box unchecked, and then click **Close**.

This saves the data from the Access query as a new Excel workbook.

7 **Close** the Query window, and leave Access open.

Objective 2
Create a Formula in Excel

Activity 18.02 Creating a Formula for Calculation in Excel

One of Excel's most powerful and valuable features is the ability to perform mathematical calculations. Although Excel has many automatic functions for calculating, you may need to create your own formulas. In this activity, you will create a formula to calculate the difference between numbers.

1 **Start** Excel. From the folder that contains your project files, open the Excel workbook **18A_Meeting_Data_Firstname_Lastname** that you saved in the previous export activity.

Excel refers to columns by letters and to rows by numbers. The intersection of a row and a column—a cell—is always named using the column letter first and then the row number, for example, A2. Clicking in a cell location enables you to enter or edit information in that cell.

2 Click cell **B1**, and then type **Max** to change the column heading. Press Tab to complete the entry. In cell **C1**, type **Min** to change the column heading. Press Tab. In cell **D1**, type **Difference** as a new column heading. Press Enter to complete the last cell entry.

You want Excel to calculate the difference between the Max and Min salary values in columns B and C. Excel formulas always begin with an = sign and use the cell reference (such as A2), not the actual value displayed in a cell.

3 In cell **D2**, type the formula **=B2-C2** and then press Enter.

Cell D2 displays the calculated value. You want to use the same calculation for the other items. The Auto Fill feature in Excel lets you duplicate the difference formula for the rest of the rows. The cell references will change relative to the new cell location for the formula, using the cells in the new row.

The Fill handle is a solid box at the lower right corner of a selected cell. When the mouse pointer is on the fill handle, it changes to a ⊞.

4 Click cell **D2**, and drag the **fill handle** at the lower right corner of the cell to cell **D6**, and then release the mouse button.

This copies the formula to the other selected cells in the Difference column and changes the cell references for each row's calculation. The calculated value is displayed in each cell.

 Select columns **A:D**. On the **Home tab**, in the **Cells group**, click **Format**, and then in the displayed gallery, click **AutoFit Column Width**. Click outside the selection to cancel the selection. Compare your screen with Figure 18.2.

Figure 18.2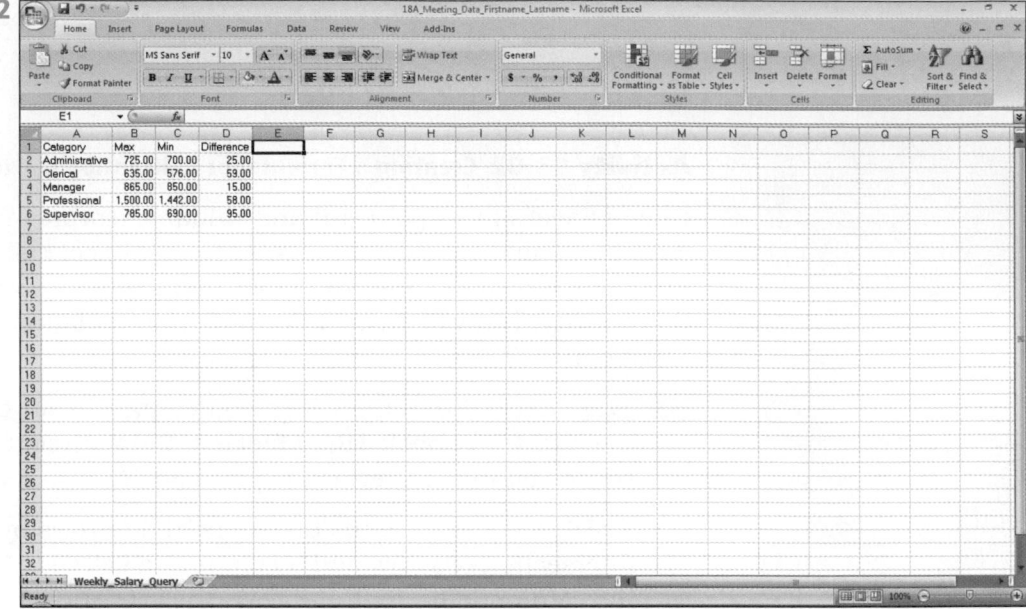

 **Save** your workbook and leave it open for the next activity.

Objective 3
Create a Chart in Excel

Activity 18.03 Creating a Chart in Excel

To create a chart quickly, you can use the default settings in Excel. You can also select specific cells of data from the worksheet to include in the chart. Press and hold the Ctrl key when selecting multiple nonadjacent ranges.

1 Select cells **A1:A6**. Press and hold the Ctrl key, and then select cells **D1:D6**. You should have two nonadjacent areas of shaded selected cells.

Because you include the cells showing column headings in your selection, these labels will also display on your chart.

2 Click the **Insert tab**, and then in the **Charts group**, click **Column**. In the displayed gallery, click the first choice in the gallery.

This creates a chart with the default choices, a column chart on the current sheet, with a legend, and adds the Design contextual tab to the Ribbon. The Chart Area is the background area of the chart object that has no other chart content. When you use the mouse to point to the Chart Area, a ScreenTip displays that shows the name *Chart Area*.

3 Move the insertion point into the **Chart Area**, right-click, and then click **Select Data**. In the **Select Data Source** dialog box, click the **Switch Row/Column** button, and then click **OK**.

This creates a data set and legend items based on each row instead of each column. When you create charts, you will select rows or columns based on how you need to present the data.

Excel displays the chart along with the other information on the worksheet. You can move and position the chart on the sheet by clicking on the colored outer border on the chart, and then dragging the chart to a new position. You can also resize the chart using its sizing handles.

4 At the lower right corner of the chart object, drag the sizing handle to the right and down a bit, making the chart larger and easier to read. Point to the top border of the chart to display the ⊕ pointer, hold down the left mouse button, and then drag the upper left corner of the chart just inside the upper left corner of cell **A8** so it is under the cells containing the data.

5 On the **Design contextual tab**, in the **Chart Styles group**, click the **More** button. In the displayed gallery, move your mouse pointer over the chart styles and click **Style 11** to format the chart. Compare your screen with Figure 18.3.

Figure 18.3

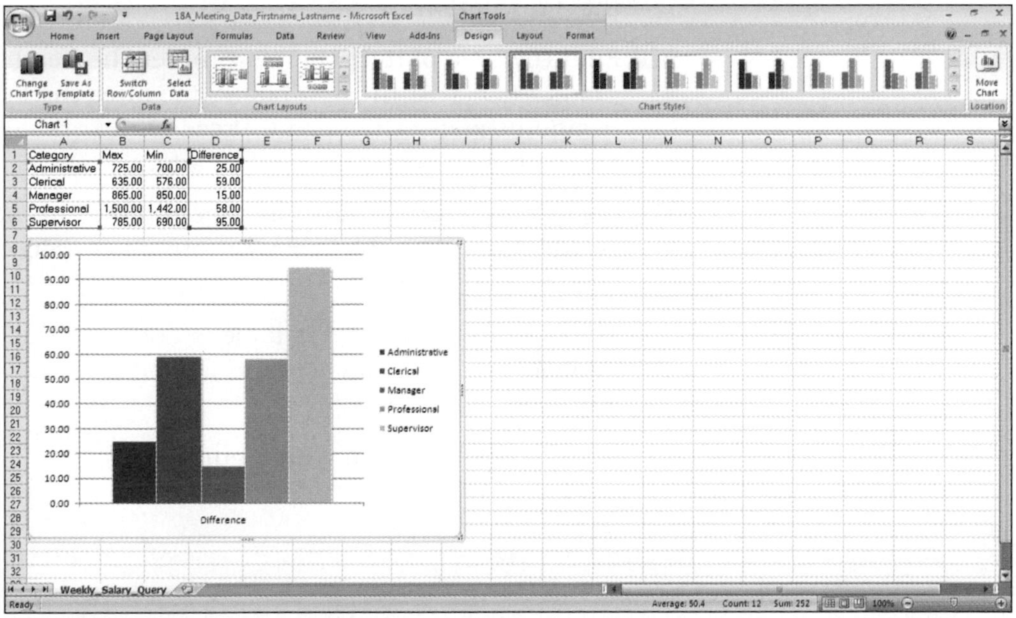

6 **Save** your workbook and leave it open.

Objective 4
Copy Access Data into a Word Document

Activity 18.04 Copying Access Data to a Word Document

Copy and paste are Windows tools. In this activity, you will use them to add data from an Access database to a Word document.

1 **Start** Word. Open the Word document **ip18A_Meeting_Topics** from the folder that contains your project files. **Save** the document as **18A_Meeting_Topics_Firstname_Lastname**

2 On the taskbar, click the button to return to the Access database **ip18A_Dept_Data**, or open the file from the folder that contains your project files if you have closed it.

3 In the **Navigation Pane** in the **Queries** list, double-click to open the **Salary by Category** query.

You can copy data from Access, and then use it in another Office program.

4 Click the **Home tab**. In the **Find group**, click the **Select arrow**, and then click **Select All**. In the **Clipboard group**, click **Copy**, and then on the Windows taskbar, click the button to return to your open Word document.

Be sure to locate the correct position in the document before pasting the information.

5 Find the area of the document under the heading *II. Salary Data Comparisons*. At the first blank line after the first paragraph, click to position the insertion point. Press Enter to create another blank line for the information you want to add.

6 In the **Clipboard group**, click the top part of the **Paste** button. If you accidentally click the Paste button arrow, you will need to click Paste again.

The data from the Access table is added to the Word document in a table format. You can edit and format it in the same way as you can any other Word table.

Compare your screen with Figure 18.4.

Figure 18.4

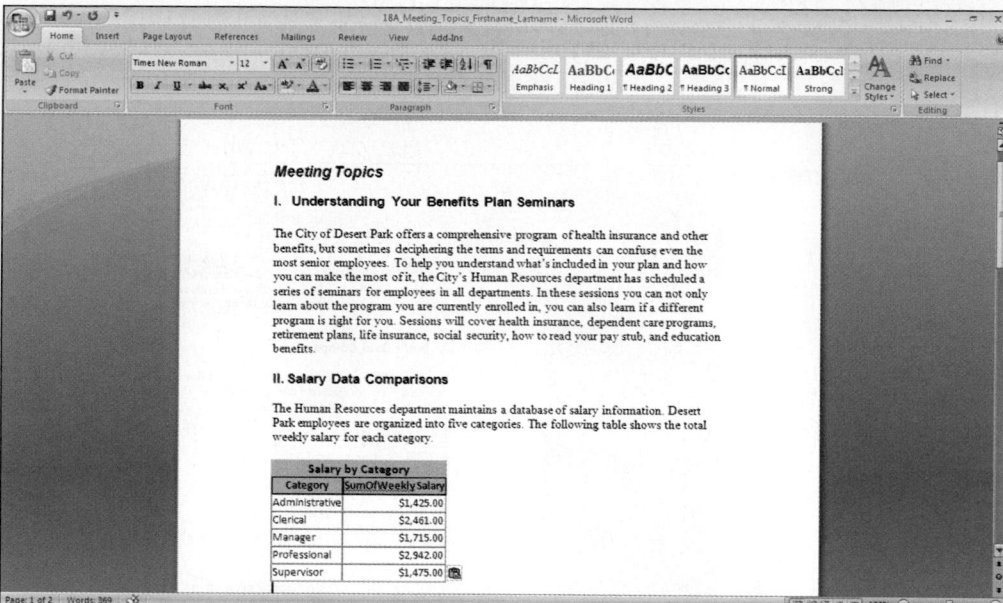

7 **Save** the document and leave it open for the next activity. **Close** Access.

Your Windows taskbar should now show buttons for your Excel workbook and your Word document.

Objective 5
Copy Excel Data into a Word Document

Activity 18.05 Copying Excel Data to a Word Document

You can also use copy and paste with Excel to get information to use in other Office programs. You can select only the cells that contain the information you want to use.

1 On the Windows taskbar, click the button to return to your Excel workbook **18A_Meeting_Data_Firstname_Lastname**.

2 Click and drag, starting in cell **A1** and ending with cell **D6**. In the **Clipboard group**, click **Copy**, and then on the Windows taskbar, click the button to return to your Word document.

3 Find the text paragraph after the *Salary by Category* table. Click in the first blank line after the paragraph to position the insertion point. Press [Enter] to create a new blank line for the data you will add.

4 In the **Clipboard group**, click the top part of the **Paste** button. The information from the cells in Excel is added to the Word document as a table. Compare your screen with Figure 18.5.

Tables in Word are easy to format and work with in your document. You can use Excel for performing any calculations, and then copy your results to paste as a table into your Word document.

Figure 18.5

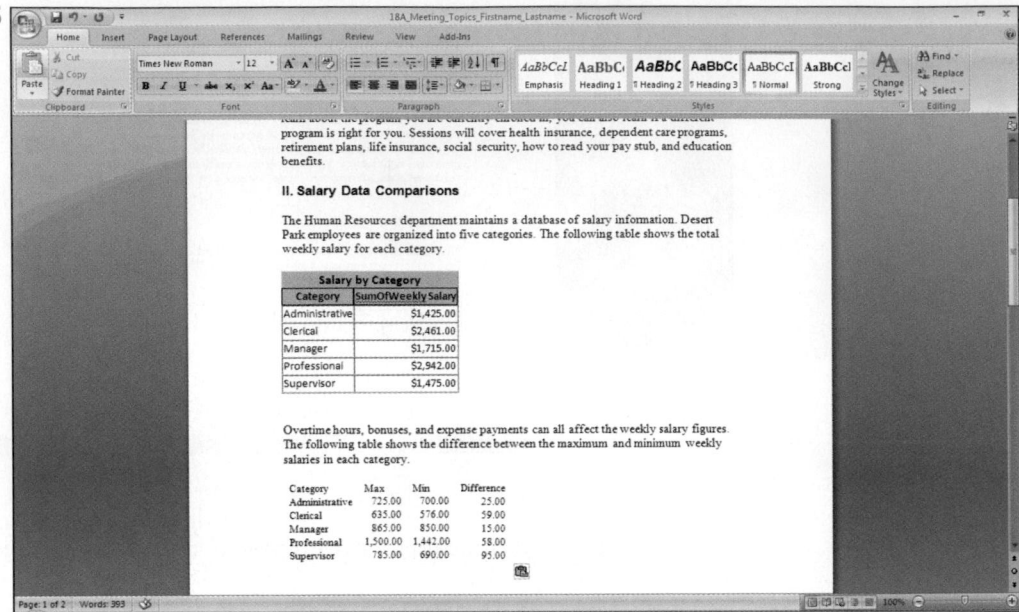

5 **Save** your document and **Close** Word. Leave the Excel workbook open to use in the next activity.

Objective 6
Insert an Excel Chart into a PowerPoint Presentation

Activity 18.06 Adding an Excel Chart to a PowerPoint Presentation

The last step in your preparation for the meeting is to add the chart you created in Excel to your PowerPoint slides.

1 **Start** PowerPoint. **Open** the file **ip18A_Meeting_Slides** from the folder that contains your project files. **Save** the file as **18A_Meeting_Slides_Firstname_Lastname**

PowerPoint presentations can convey ideas with visual impact. The Excel chart created from the Access data will add more visual content to the presentation. Because each of the Office programs has tools that are more specialized for the ideas you want to convey, you may need to create the information in one program and then copy it into another program.

2 Click **Slide 3**, where you will add your chart.

3 On the Windows taskbar, click the button to return to your Excel workbook **18A_Meeting_Data_Firstname_Lastname**. In the **Chart Area**, click to select the chart.

In the Office programs, a chart is a graphic object. When you want to select a chart, click the Chart Area to display the sizing handles on the corners and borders of the chart object.

4 In the **Clipboard group**, click **Copy**, and then on the Windows taskbar, click the button to return to your PowerPoint presentation.

5 In the **Clipboard group**, click the top of the **Paste** button.

The chart will be placed on the slide, but it may be sized and positioned differently than you want it to be in your presentation. You can size and position the chart on the slide just as you did in the Excel workbook.

6 Use the sizing handle in the lower right corner of the chart to make the chart about .75 inches wider and .75 inches longer. Point to the top border of the chart to display the $\boxed{\oplus}$ pointer, hold down the left mouse button, and then position the chart on the slide so that it is centered on the slide and below the title.

You may decide to edit the appearance of the chart. An Excel chart pasted into another Office program will have Excel contextual tabs available for editing the chart. The ribbon will change to show these contextual tabs when editing the chart.

7 On the **PowerPoint** slide, if necessary, click in the **Chart Area**. The Ribbon will show the Chart Tools contextual tabs. Click the **Design tab**, and in the **Type group**, click **Change Chart Type**. The **Change Chart Type** dialog box displays.

Chart types display to the left, and subtypes of these categories display to the right.

8 In the **Change Chart Type** dialog box, click the **3-D Clustered Column** subtype—the fourth item in the first row—and then click **OK**. The chart columns now have a different look to them.

9 Click outside of the chart to cancel the chart selection and remove the Excel contextual tabs.

Compare your screen with Figure 18.6.

Figure 18.6

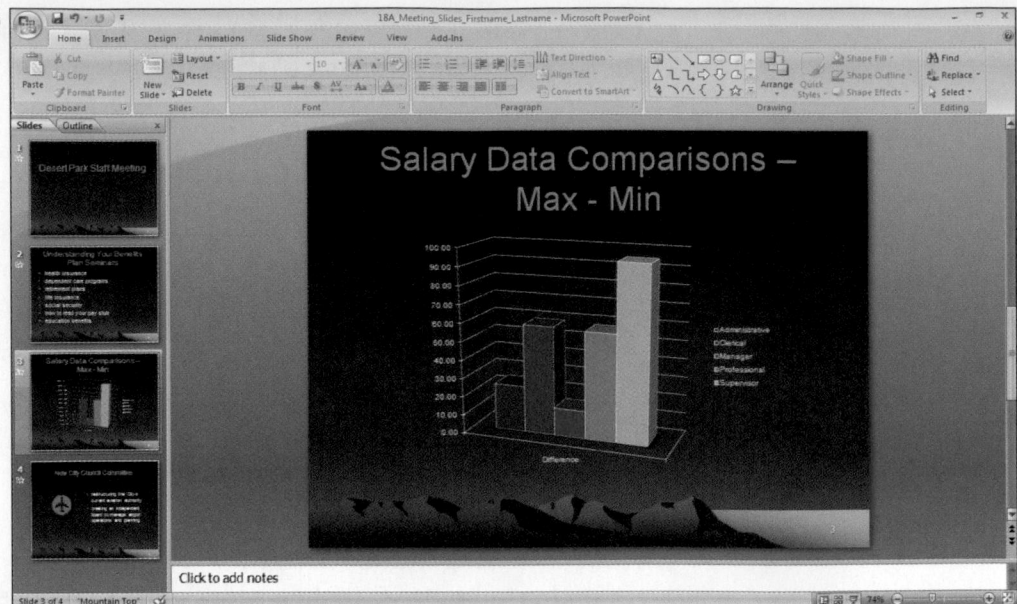

10 **Save** and **Close** the PowerPoint presentation and **Exit** PowerPoint, and then **Close** the Excel workbook and **Exit** Excel.

End **You have completed this integration project** ——

chapternineteen

Using Tables in Word and Excel

OBJECTIVES

At the end of this project you will be able to:

OUTCOMES

Mastering these objectives will enable you to:

1. Plan a Table in Word
2. Enter Data and Format a Table in Word
3. Create a Table in Word from Excel Data
4. Create an Excel Worksheet from a Word Table

PROJECT 19A

Use Tables in Word and Excel

Introduction

You are preparing information in a Word document for a meeting. You will complete your information for the meeting by adding two tables to the Word document.

Tables are an efficient way to organize information using rows and columns. Excel also uses rows and columns in its worksheet structure. This makes it easy to use Excel data in Word to create a table and to use a Word table to add information to an Excel worksheet.

Project 19A Meeting Notes

In Activities 19.1 through 19.5, you will create a meeting notes document in Word 2007 by adding and formatting a Word table, and then creating another table using data from Excel. You will also create an Excel worksheet using data from a Word table. Your completed project will look similar to Figure 19.1.

For Project 19A, you will need the following files:

Ip19A_Meeting_Notes
Ip19A_Campus_List

You will save your document as
19A_Meeting_Notes_Firstname_Lastname
You will save your workbook as
19A_Campus_List_Firstname_Lastname

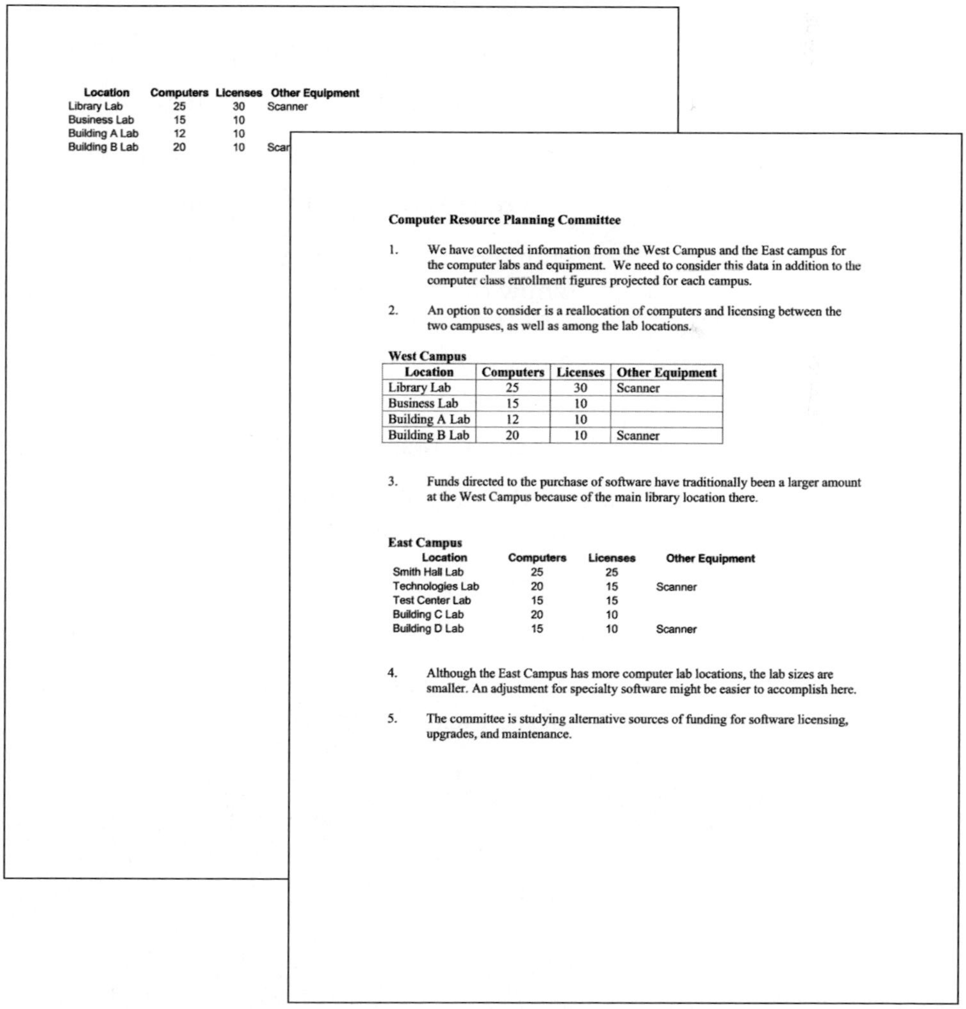

Figure 19.1
Project 19A—Meeting Notes

Objective 1
Plan a Table in Word

Activity 19.01 Starting Word and Planning the Table

Creating a table in Word requires that you specify the number of columns and rows for the table. In this activity you will plan the structure for organizing your information before inserting the table.

1 **Start** Word. From the folder that contains your project files, open the Word document **ip19A_Meeting_Notes**. **Save** the document as **19A_Meeting_Notes_Firstname_Lastname**

2 In the document, scroll down (if necessary) to see the heading *West Campus*. After the heading, on the first blank line, position the insertion point.

You will create a blank table in which to enter the information. You need to review the information to determine how to structure the table. You will complete the table later in this activity. Look at the list that follows:

Library Lab	25 Computers	30 Software licenses	Scanner
Business Lab	15 Computers	10 Software licenses	
Building A Lab	12 Computers	10 Software licenses	
Building B Lab	20 Computers	10 Software licenses	Scanner

For this information, you can create a table that has four columns to show the information for lab location, number of computers, number of software licenses, and other equipment. Creating four rows in the table will show the information for each lab location. You also want to add another row to display headings for the columns.

3 Click the **Insert tab**, and then in the **Tables group**, click **Table**.

4 In the displayed gallery, move the mouse pointer across four columns and five rows.

At the top of the displayed gallery, a *4x5 Table* displays.

5 Click the mouse while the 4x5 Table is displayed.

You have added the table structure to the document. Compare your screen with Figure 19.2.

Figure 19.2

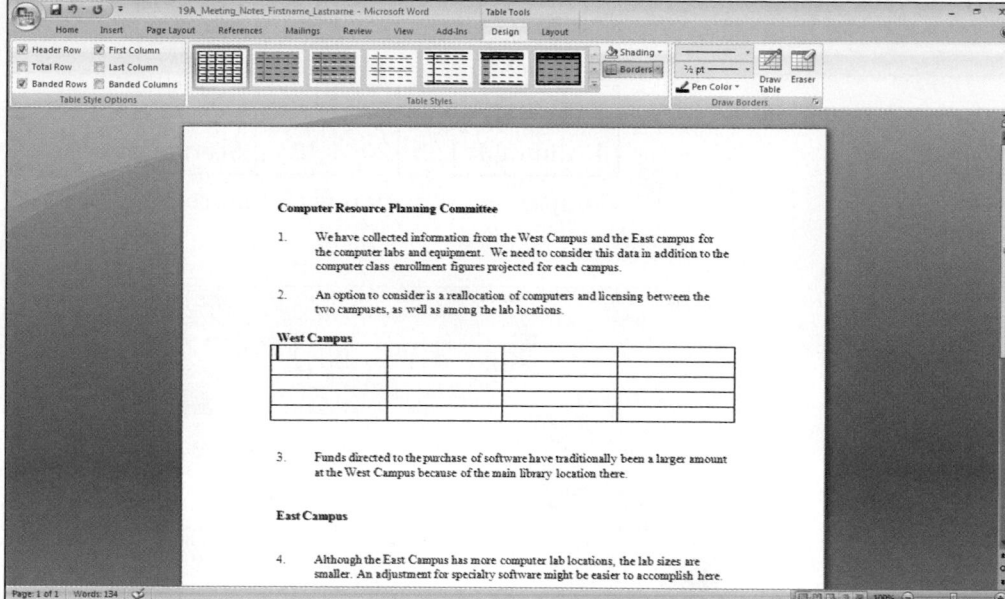

6 **Save** your document and leave it open for the next activity.

Objective 2
Enter Data and Format a Table in Word

Activity 19.02 Entering Data

In a table, the intersection of a column and a row is a cell. Use the ⎡Tab⎤ key to move to each cell, from left to right, as you enter data. Pressing ⎡Tab⎤ in the last cell of a row moves the insertion point to the next row. Pressing ⎡Enter⎤ in a cell creates a new paragraph and blank line in the cell.

The first row of the table will have headings to label each of the columns.

1 In the first row of the table, position the insertion point in the first cell. Type **Location** as the heading for this column, and then press ⎡Tab⎤.

2 Type **Computers** and then press ⎡Tab⎤.

3 Type **Licenses** and then press ⎡Tab⎤.

4 Type **Other Equipment** and then press ⎡Tab⎤.

5 Use the following list to complete the table and enter the information. In each row, type the information for each lab in the appropriately labeled columns. Do not press ⎡Tab⎤ or ⎡Enter⎤ after the last *Scanner* entry. Just enter the numbers in the Computers and Licenses columns.

Library Lab	**25**	**30**	**Scanner**
Business Lab	**15**	**10**	
Building A Lab	**12**	**10**	
Building B Lab	**20**	**10**	**Scanner**

Compare your screen with Figure 19.3.

Figure 19.3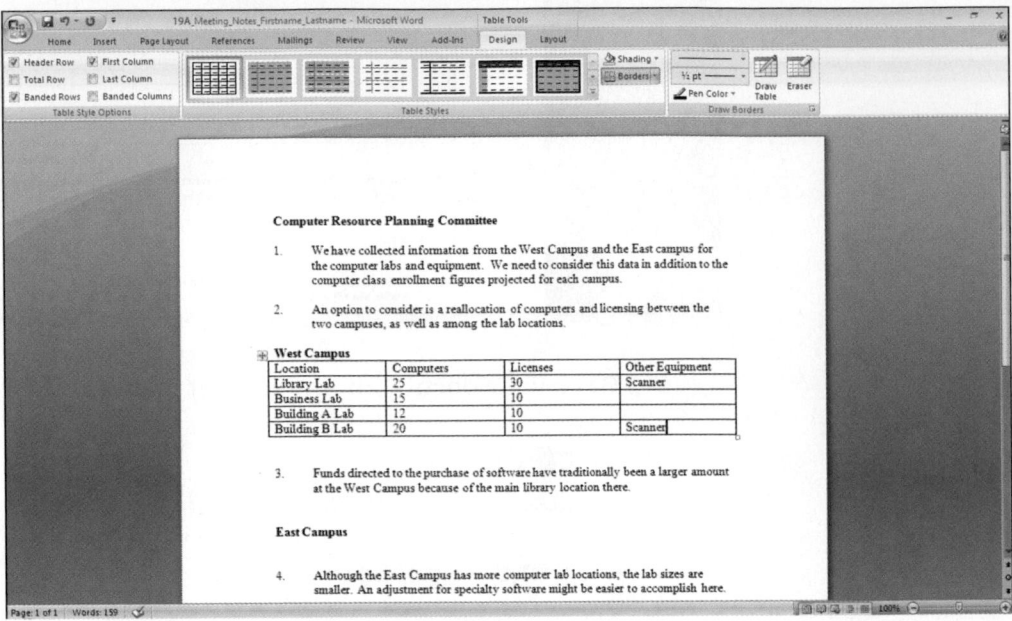

Alert!

Did you press [Tab] in the last cell?

If you press [Tab] in the last cell of the last row, you will create a new blank row. The insertion point will be in the first cell of the new row. To delete the row, on the Layout contextual tab, in the Rows & Columns group, click Delete, and then click Delete Rows.

Activity 19.03 Formatting a Table

Formatting the table will make the information easier to read. You can apply formatting to a table by first selecting text, rows, columns, or the entire table. Next, choose the formats you want to apply to that selection.

1 Move the mouse pointer to the left of the first row in the table to display the ⬓ pointer. Click to select the first row. Click the **Home tab**, and in the **Font group**, click the **Bold** button. In the **Paragraph group**, click the **Center** button.

2 Click and drag over the remaining cells in the second and third columns to select them. In the **Paragraph group**, click the **Center** button.

3 Click anywhere in the table. Click the **Layout contextual tab**. In the **Cell Size group**, click **AutoFit**, and then click **AutoFit Contents**.

The bold headings now stand out, center alignment is applied, and the column sizes are adjusted. Compare your screen with Figure 19.4.

Figure 19.4

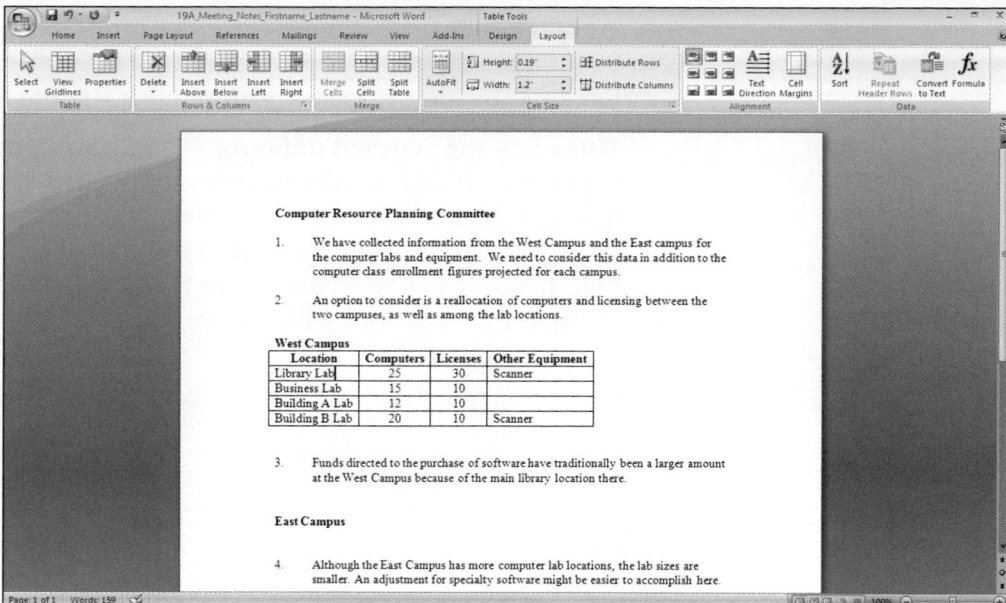

> **Computer Resource Planning Committee**
>
> 1. We have collected information from the West Campus and the East campus for the computer labs and equipment. We need to consider this data in addition to the computer class enrollment figures projected for each campus.
>
> 2. An option to consider is a reallocation of computers and licensing between the two campuses, as well as among the lab locations.
>
> **West Campus**
>
> | Location | Computers | Licenses | Other Equipment |
> |---|---|---|---|
> | Library Lab | 25 | 30 | Scanner |
> | Business Lab | 15 | 10 | |
> | Building A Lab | 12 | 10 | |
> | Building B Lab | 20 | 10 | Scanner |
>
> 3. Funds directed to the purchase of software have traditionally been a larger amount at the West Campus because of the main library location there.
>
> **East Campus**
>
> 4. Although the East Campus has more computer lab locations, the lab sizes are smaller. An adjustment for specialty software might be easier to accomplish here.

4 **Save** your document and leave Word open for the next activity.

Objective 3
Create a Table in Word from Excel Data

Activity 19.04 Creating a Table in Word from Excel Data

You can copy and paste data from an Excel worksheet into Word. Word will create a table from the information. You can format this table as you would any other table you create in Word.

1 In the document, if necessary, scroll down to see the heading *East Campus*. After the heading, on the first blank line, position the insertion point.

The information from the Excel worksheet will be pasted here.

2 **Start** Excel. From the folder that contains your project files, open the workbook **ip19A_Campus_List**. **Save** the workbook as **19A_Campus_List_Firstname_Lastname**

When you select data in the rows and columns in Excel, select only the cells, not the row numbers that display to the left of the rows or the column letters above the columns.

3 Select cells **A1:D6**. In the **Home tab**, in the **Clipboard group**, click **Copy**.

Excel displays a moving border around the selected cells to verify your copy selection.

4 On the Windows taskbar, click the button to return to your Word document. The insertion point should be under the *East Campus* heading. In the **Clipboard group**, click the **Paste** button.

This adds the selected data from the Excel worksheet to your Word document. It will be similar to the table structure you created and developed in the previous activities; however, there will not be visible borders on the table imported from Excel. The column sizing and bold headings were formatted in Excel and are copied into Word. Compare your screen with Figure 19.5.

Figure 19.5

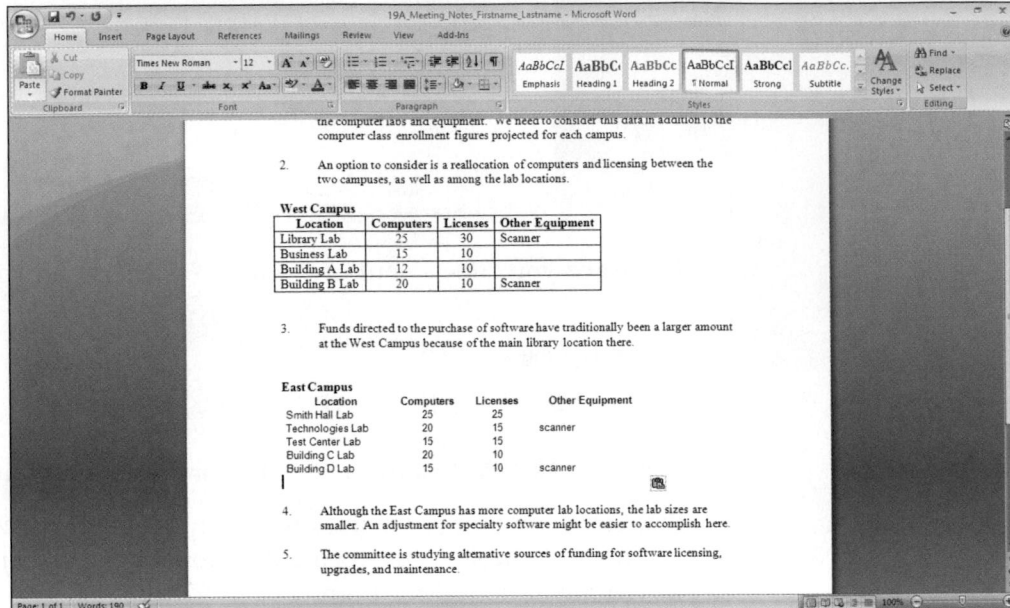

5 In the **East Campus** table, under the **Other Equipment** column, click in each cell that contains the word *scanner* and capitalize the word for each instance.

6 **Save** your Word document and leave it open for the next activity.

Objective 4
Create an Excel Worksheet from a Word Table

Activity 19.05 Creating an Excel Worksheet from a Word Table

If you want to copy or format a Word table, you need to select the table first. There are various ways to select an entire table in a Word document:

- Click anywhere in the table. On the Layout contextual tab, in the Table group, click Select, and then click Select Table.

- Click and drag across the table to select all the table rows and columns.

- Move the mouse pointer over the table, and then click the four-headed arrow at the upper left corner of the table.

- Move the mouse pointer to the left of the table to display the 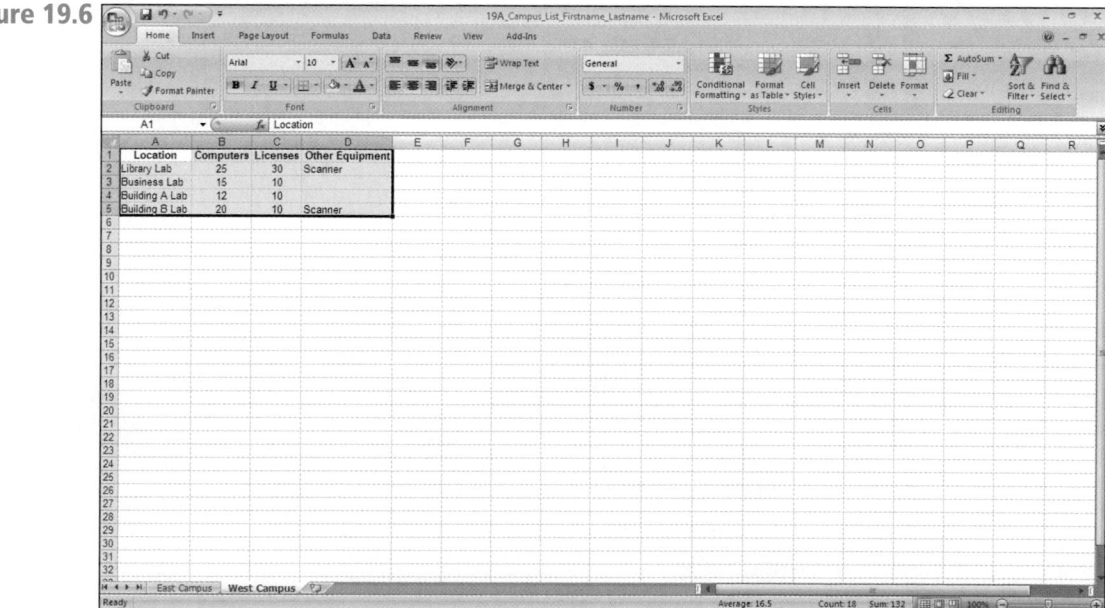 pointer. Click and drag down the left side of all rows of the table.

1 In your Word document, select the entire table that shows the data for the West Campus. On the **Home tab**, in the **Clipboard group**, click **Copy**.

2 On the Windows taskbar, click the button to return to your Excel workbook. Click the **West Campus sheet tab**.

3 Click cell **A1**. In the **Clipboard group**, click the **Paste** button.

The information from the Word table is copied to the rows and columns in the Excel worksheet. Column sizes are not copied from Word into Excel, so additional formatting is necessary to make it consistent with the East Campus worksheet.

4 Click the **Paste Options down arrow**, and then click the **Match Destination Formatting** button.

5 Select cells **A1:D1**. On the **Home tab**, in the **Font group**, click the **Bold** button, and then in the **Alignment group**, click the **Center** button.

6 Select cells **B2:C5**. On the **Home tab**, in the **Alignment group**, click the **Center** button.

7 Select cells **A1:D5**. On the **Home tab**, in the **Cells group**, click the **Format** button, and then click **AutoFit Column Width**. Compare your screen with Figure 19.6.

Figure 19.6

8 **Save** and then **Close** your Excel workbook. **Close** the Word document and then **Exit** both Word and Excel.

End You have completed this integration project. ——

chapter**twenty**

Using Excel as a Data Source in a Mail Merge

OBJECTIVES

At the end of this project you will be able to:

1. Prepare a Mail Merge Document for Mailing Labels
2. Choose an Excel Worksheet as a Data Source
3. Produce and Save Merged Mailing Labels
4. Open a Saved Main Document for Mail Merge

OUTCOMES

Mastering these objectives will enable you to:

PROJECT 20A
Use Excel as a Data Source in a Mail Merge

Introduction

You are preparing a flyer for a mailing. Your coworker has created a mailing list in an Excel worksheet that you want to use to create the address labels for the flyers.

You can create a data source by entering names and addresses in the Mail Merge Wizard in Word. However, if you already have names and addresses in an existing Excel worksheet, you do not need to enter them again in the Mail Merge process.

Project 20A Mailing Labels

Microsoft Office 2007 programs can work together to quickly automate tasks such as creating mailing labels from various data sources.

In Activities 20.01 through 20.5, you will create mailing labels in Word from data in Excel. Your completed project will look similar to Figure 20.1.

For Project 20A, you will need the following files:

New blank Word document
Ip20A_Address_List_1

**You will save your document as
20A_Mailing_Labels_Firstname_Lastname
You will save your labels document as
20A_Labels1_Firstname_Lastname**

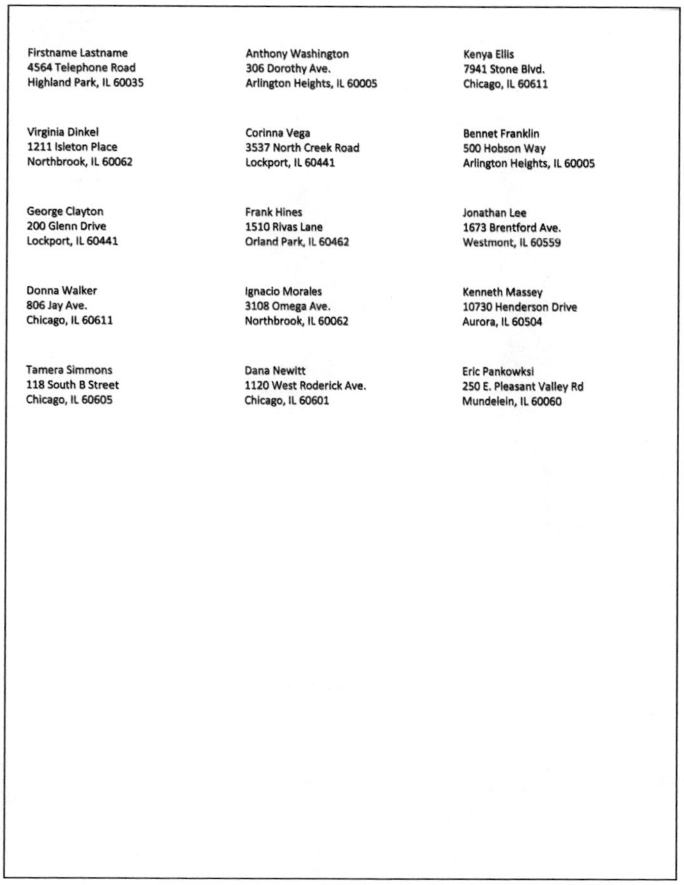

Firstname Lastname 4564 Telephone Road Highland Park, IL 60035	Anthony Washington 306 Dorothy Ave. Arlington Heights, IL 60005	Kenya Ellis 7941 Stone Blvd. Chicago, IL 60611
Virginia Dinkel 1211 Isleton Place Northbrook, IL 60062	Corinna Vega 3537 North Creek Road Lockport, IL 60441	Bennet Franklin 500 Hobson Way Arlington Heights, IL 60005
George Clayton 200 Glenn Drive Lockport, IL 60441	Frank Hines 1510 Rivas Lane Orland Park, IL 60462	Jonathan Lee 1673 Brentford Ave. Westmont, IL 60559
Donna Walker 806 Jay Ave. Chicago, IL 60611	Ignacio Morales 3108 Omega Ave. Northbrook, IL 60062	Kenneth Massey 10730 Henderson Drive Aurora, IL 60504
Tamera Simmons 118 South B Street Chicago, IL 60605	Dana Newitt 1120 West Roderick Ave. Chicago, IL 60601	Eric Pankowksi 250 E. Pleasant Valley Rd Mundelein, IL 60060

Figure 20.1
Project 20A—Mailing Labels

Objective 1
Prepare a Mail Merge Document for Mailing Labels

Activity 20.01 Setting up Mailing Labels Using the Mailings Tab

In this activity, you will create a new document for mailing labels by using the Mailings tab. You will select a layout for the type of mailing labels.

1 **Start** Word and display a new blank document. **Save** the document as **20A_Mailing_Labels_Firstname_Lastname**

2 On the **Mailings tab** in the **Start Mail Merge group**, click **Start Mail Merge**, and then click **Labels**.

The Label Options dialog box displays.

3 In the **Label Options** dialog box, in the **Product number** list, click the second **30 Per Page**. Compare your screen with Figure 20.2, and then click **OK**.

Figure 20.2

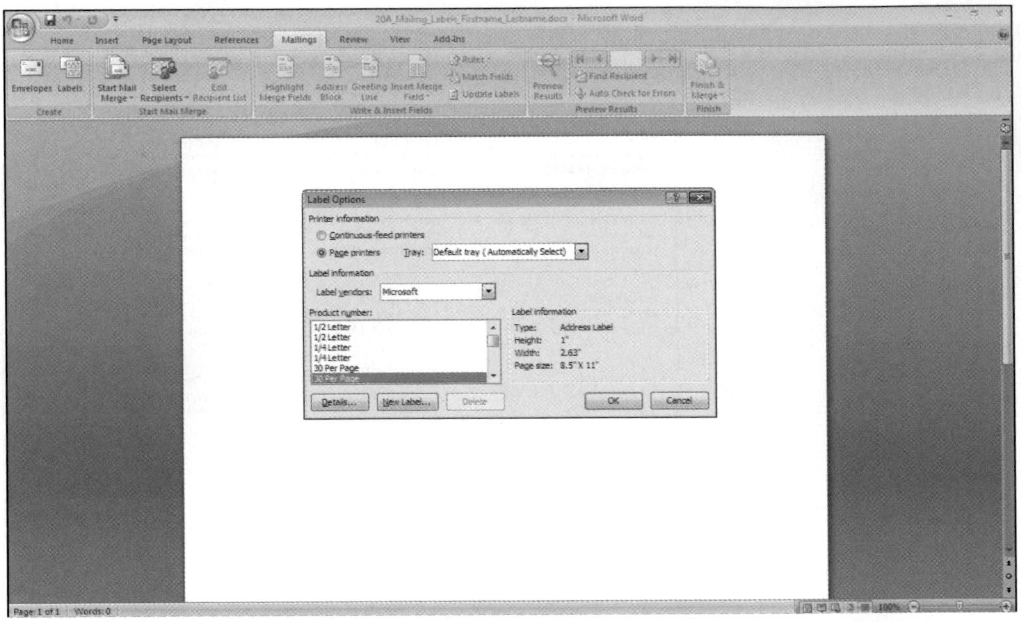

4 **Save** your document and leave it open for the next activity.

Objective 2
Choose an Excel Worksheet as a Data Source

Activity 20.02 Selecting the Data Source for the Mailing Labels

The data source contains the name and address information for the mailing labels. The data source you will use is an Excel worksheet.

1 On the **Mailings tab**, in the **Start Mail Merge group**, click **Select Recipients**, and then click **Use Existing List**.

The Select Data Source dialog box opens and displays the default folder All Data Sources. You want to use an Excel worksheet that was not created as a data source in a Mail Merge process. You are familiar with the Excel worksheet that you want to use, and you know that it has a header row to label last name, first name, and so on.

2 From the **Favorites Link**, select **Computer list**, select the drive, directory, and the folder that contains your project files. Click on the workbook **Ip20A_Address_List_1**, and then click **Open**.

The Select Table dialog box displays, the sheet name *Address List$* is highlighted, and at the bottom of the dialog box the First row of data contains column headers check box is selected.

3 Click **OK**. Your document should show all the labels, except the first one, with *Next Record* in each label space. Compare your screen with Figure 20.3.

Figure 20.3

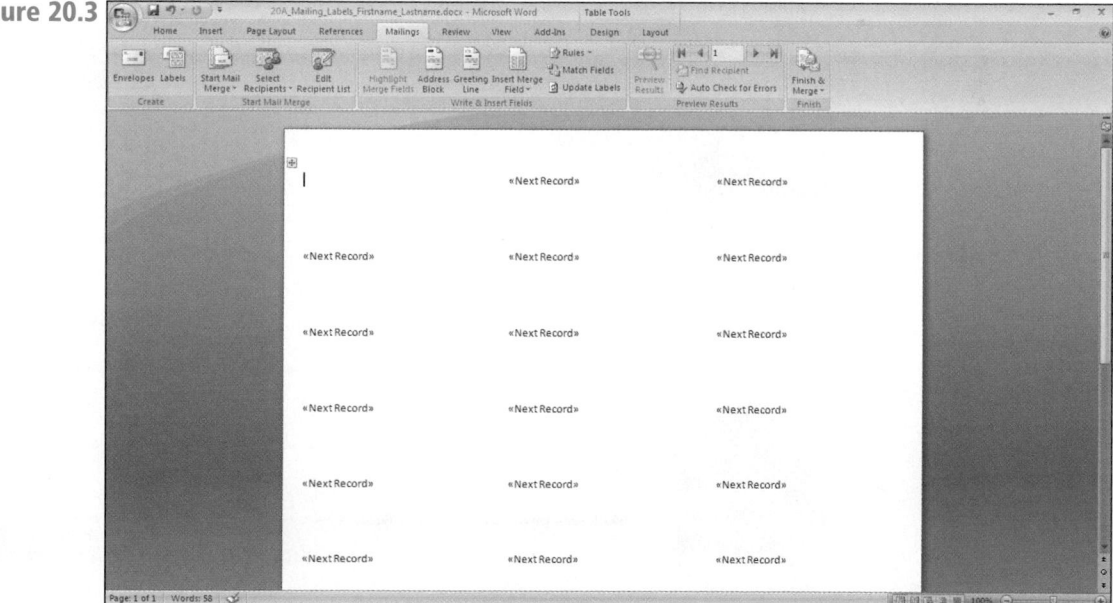

4 **Save** your document and leave it open for the next activity.

Information about the Excel worksheet as the data source is also saved with the Word document. This creates a main document for a mail merge. When you use the main document again, you can make revisions and additions to the data source before completing the mail merge.

Objective 3
Produce and Save Merged Mailing Labels

Activity 20.03 Adding Merge Fields to the Mailing Labels

Next, you will add merge fields as placeholders for the information that will be inserted from the data source.

1 The insertion point should be in the first label. In the **Write & Insert Fields group**, click **Address Block** to display the **Insert Address Block** dialog box. Click **OK** to accept the default address layout.

The first label shows the merge field <<*AddressBlock*>>.

2 In the **Write & Insert Fields group**, click **Update Labels**. All the remaining labels should now show the merge field for the address block in addition to the next record field. The first label still displays only the address block. Compare your screen with Figure 20.4.

Figure 20.4

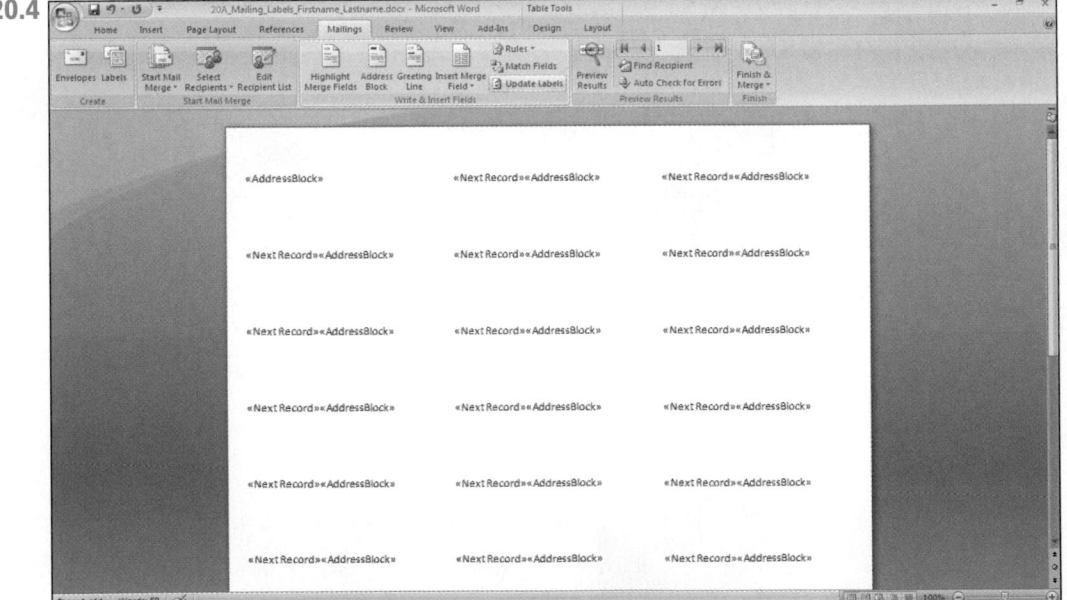

3 **Save** your document.

You are saving the main document, including the merge fields that you have arranged on the labels for the inserted data.

Activity 20.04 Producing the Mailing Labels

The Mail Merge process includes the data source and the main document with which you have been working so far. Now you will produce a completed new document that contains the finished labels.

1 In the **Finish group**, click **Finish & Merge**, and then click **Edit Individual Documents**. The **Merge to New Document** dialog box displays. Under **Merge records**, be sure the **All** option button is selected, and then click **OK**.

A new Word window opens with the mailing labels as the document. The title bar displays *Labels1 - Microsoft Word*. You will save this as a completed merged document.

2 In the first label, edit the name, and change it to your own name.

3 Click anywhere in the document. Click the **Layout** contextual tab. In the **Table** group, click **Select** and then click **Select Table**.

4 On the **Home** tab, in the **Paragraph group**, click the **Line spacing** button and click **Remove Space Before Paragraph** to single space the labels. Click anywhere in the labels to cancel the selection.

5 **Save** the document as **20A_Labels1_Firstname_Lastname** The saved document has only the finished labels showing names and addresses.

6 **Close** all Word documents, saving if prompted, and **Exit** Word.

Objective 4
Open a Saved Main Document for Mail Merge

Activity 20.05 Opening a Main Document for Mail Merge

You can open the main document you created in the Mail Merge process to edit and produce the mailing labels again at any time.

1 Open **Word** and open the document **20A_Mailing_Labels_Firstname_Lastname** that you completed earlier in this chapter. An information box displays, referring to the linked data source used in the merge and asking whether you want to continue. Click **Yes**.

2 Click the **Mailings tab**.

From here you can make changes to the merge fields, add recipients, and perform other editing tasks. Only the main document allows you to do this—the saved merged document does not.

3 **Close** the document without saving it and **Exit** Word.

End **You have completed this integration project.** ———

chapter twenty-one

21

Linking Data in Office Documents

OBJECTIVES

At the end of this project you will be able to:

1. Insert and Link an Excel Object in Word
2. Revise a Linked Excel Worksheet and Update Links in Word
3. Open a Word Document That Includes a Linked Object and Update Links

OUTCOMES

Mastering these objectives will enable you to:

PROJECT 21A
Link Data in Office Documents

Introduction

You are responsible for preparing information for a weekly meeting, and you want to include a chart showing the weekly sales figures. The sales data is entered and updated in an Excel worksheet by a coworker.

By using the linking tools in Office, you can create a connection to the Excel data within a Word document. Changes in the Excel data will also be updated in Word. Your Word document for the meeting will update each week with any changes from the Excel data.

Project 21A **Weekly Sales**

In previous projects, you practiced how to work with several Microsoft Office 2007 programs at once and share data among them.

In Activities 21.01 through 21.4, you will create a document summarizing weekly sales. The document will use information that is automatically updated by linking to an Excel worksheet. Your completed project will look similar to Figure 21.1.

For Project 21A, you will need the following files:

Ip21A_Weekly_Sales_Chart
Ip21A_Sales_Totals

You will save your document as
21A_Weekly_Sales_Chart_Firstname_Lastname

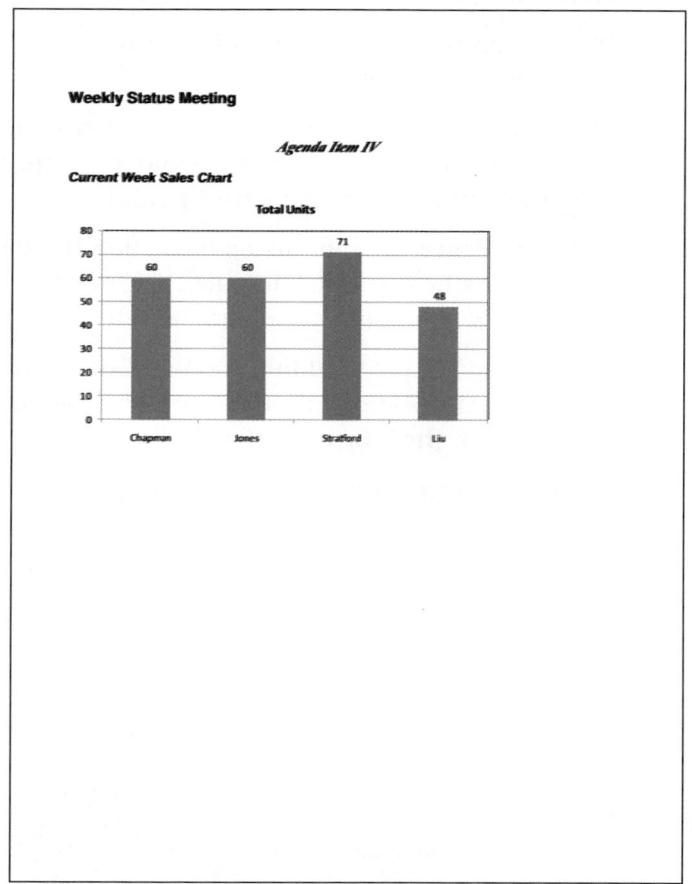

Figure 21.1
Project 21A—Weekly Sales

Objective 1
Insert and Link an Excel Object in Word

Activity 21.01 Inserting and Linking an Excel Object

In this activity, you will add the Excel chart to the agenda page for the meeting. By selecting options in the Paste Special dialog box, you can link your Word document to the Excel chart in another file.

1 **Start** Word, and then open the document **Ip21A_Weekly_Sales_ Chart** from the folder that contains your project files. **Save** the document as **21A_Weekly_Sales_Chart_Firstname_Lastname**

2 In the document, position the insertion point below the heading **Current Week Sales Chart**.

3 **Start** Excel, and then open the workbook **Ip21A_Sales_Totals**. **Save** the workbook as **21A_Sales_Totals_Firstname_Lastname**

The Excel workbook that contains the sales information you want to use includes a chart that shows the totals for the salespeople.

4 Click on the chart to select it and then on the **Home tab**, in the **Clipboard group**, click **Copy**.

5 On the taskbar, click the button to return to your Word document. On the **Home tab**, in the **Clipboard group**, click the **Paste button arrow**, and then click **Paste Special**.

6 In the **Paste Special** dialog box, click the **Paste link** option button, in the **As** box, select **Microsoft Office Excel Chart Object**, and then click **OK**. Compare your screen with Figure 21.2.

The chart is inserted into the Word document and a link is created to the Excel workbook that enables changes from the Excel workbook to update the Word document.

7 **Save** your document and leave it open for the next activity.

Figure 21.2

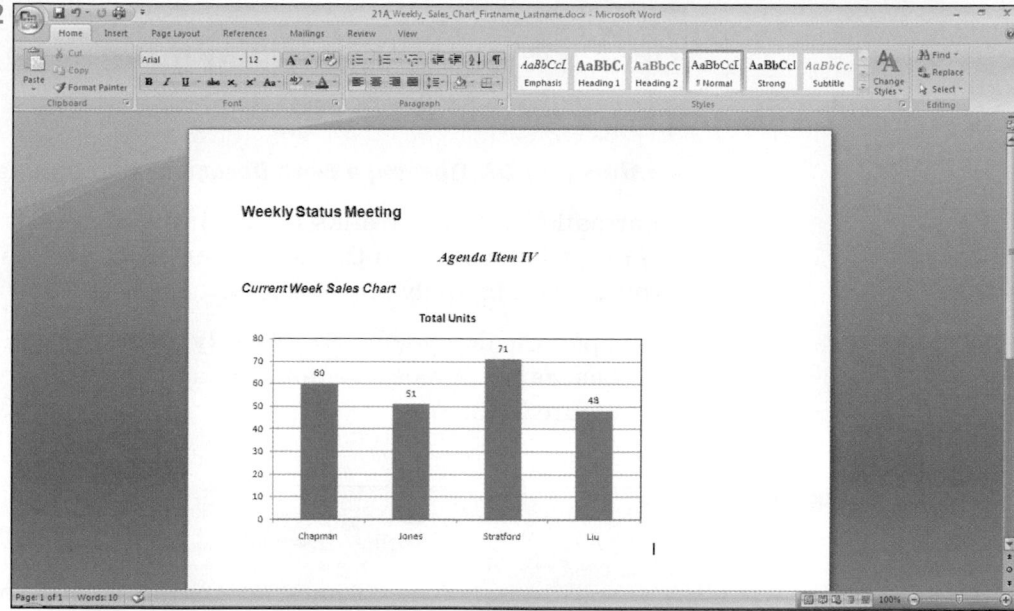

Objective 2
Revise a Linked Excel Worksheet and Update Links in Word

Activity 21.02 Revising a Linked Worksheet and Updating Links in a Document

In this activity, you will make a correction to the sales information in Excel and then update the chart object in the agenda page for the meeting.

1 On the task bar, click on the button to return to your Excel workbook, **21A_Sales_Totals_Firstname_Lastname**. Click cell **C2**, change the sales units to **21**, and then press Enter.

In the Totals Unit chart, the data label for Jones changed from 51 to 60 and the bar height increased to 60 units, making it the same height as the Chapman bar.

2 On the taskbar, click the button to return to your Word document, **21A_Weekly_Sales_Chart_Firstname_Lastname**.

Notice that the chart object has not yet changed to match the changes in Excel.

3 Right-click on the chart, and click **Update Link**.

The chart object in the agenda document is now updated to the Excel workbook.

4 **Close** the Word document, saving changes when prompted, and leave Word open for the next activity.

5 On the taskbar, click on the button to return to your Excel workbook. **Close** the Excel workbook, saving changes when prompted and **Exit** Excel.

Objective 3
Open a Word Document That Includes a Linked Object and Update Links

Activity 21.03 Opening a Word Document That Includes a Linked Object

Information about any links is saved with the Word document. By default, when you open the document, Word checks the linked files and prompts you to apply any changes.

1 Open the document **21A_Weekly_Sales_Chart_Firstname_Lastname**. A message box displays. Compare your screen with Figure 21.3.

Figure 21.3

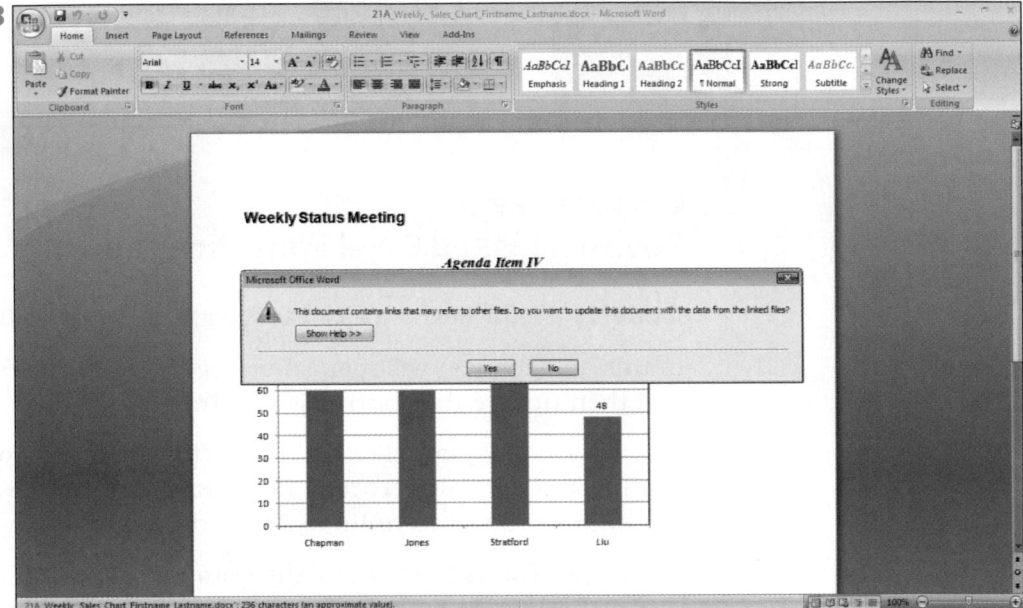

2 The message box asks whether you want to update the data in the document. Click **Yes**.

Any changes made to the Excel workbook are changed in the Word document as well. This is an automatic update.

Activity 21.04 Updating a Linked Object

When you pasted the Excel chart in the Word document, you selected the Paste link option that created a shortcut to the source file. Now you can select other options for how the link to the Excel workbook will update the Word document.

1 Right-click on the chart and point to **Linked Worksheet Object**, and then click **Links**. Compare your screen with Figure 21.4.

The Links dialog box displays.

In the Source information for selected link section, the file path for the linked Excel workbook displays beside Source file.

The option button for Automatic update is selected by default. When you opened the Word document, it automatically looked at the Excel workbook for any changes and then updated the data in Word.

Figure 21.4

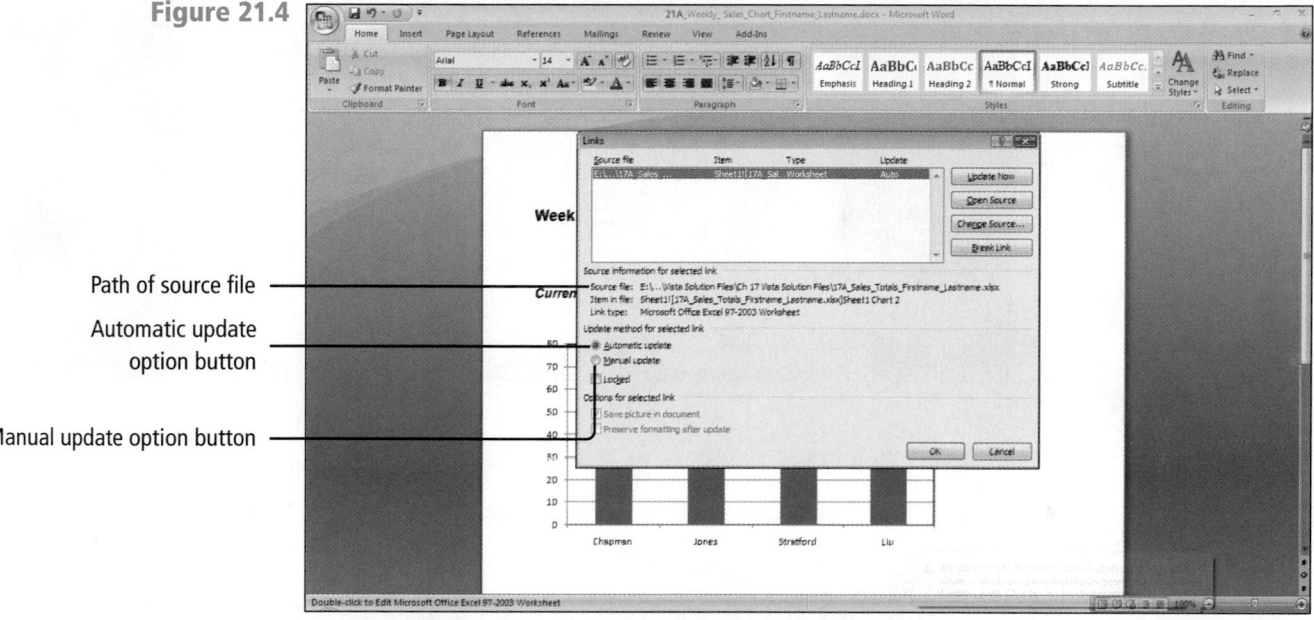

Path of source file

Automatic update option button

Manual update option button

More Knowledge
Using Manual Update Instead

If you want to use Manual update instead, you can control which file links you want to update and when to update them. You will not see the update message box when the document opens.

2 Click **Cancel** to leave Automatic update as the update method. Next, in the Word Options, you will check that automatic update for links is also selected.

3 To check update for links options in Word, click the **Office** button, and then click the **Word Options button**. In the **Word Options** dialog box, click the **Advanced** command, scroll down to the **General** section, and confirm that the **Update automatic links at open** check box is selected. Compare your screen with Figure 21.5.

Figure 21.5

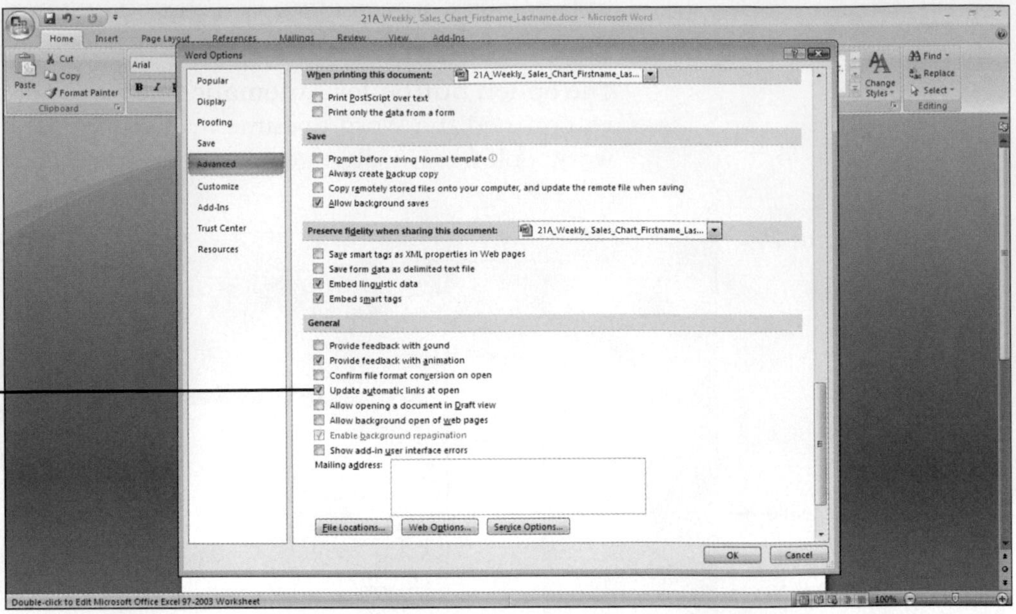

Update automatic links
at open option

4 Click **OK**.

5 **Save** and **Close** your document, and then **Exit** Word.

End **You have completed this integration project.** ——

chapter twenty-two

Creating Presentation Content from Office Documents

OBJECTIVES

At the end of this project you will be able to:

1. Insert a Word Outline into PowerPoint
2. Import Excel Data into a PowerPoint Chart
3. Insert a Hyperlink into a PowerPoint Slide

OUTCOMES

Mastering these objectives will enable you to:

PROJECT 22A
Create Presentation Content from Office Documents

Introduction

You are preparing a PowerPoint presentation for new employees and want to include a variety of content from existing Word and Excel files.

Project 22A New Employees

PowerPoint 2007 lends itself well to using data from Word and Excel files.

In Activities 22.01 through 22.3, you will create a PowerPoint presentation for new employees, using data from Word and Excel. Your completed project will look similar to Figure 22.1.

For Project 22A, you will need the following files:

Ip22A_New_Employees_List
Ip22A_Salary_Levels
Ip22A_Benefits_Seminars

You will save your document as
22A_New_Employees_List_Firstname_Lastname
You will save your presentation as
22A_New_Employees_Firstname_Lastname

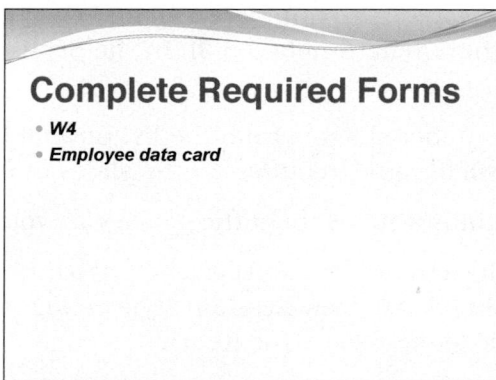

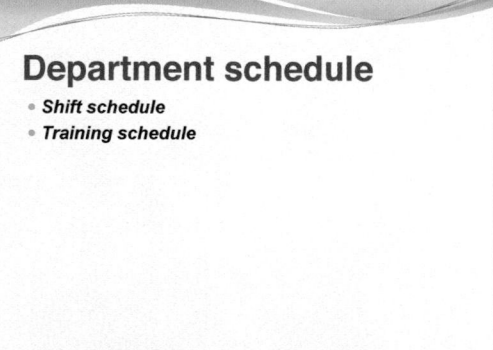

Figure 22.1
Project 22A—New Employees

Objective 1
Insert a Word Outline into PowerPoint

Activity 22.01 Inserting a Word Outline into PowerPoint

You can apply heading styles to Word content and then insert the Word outline in PowerPoint to create the presentation's content. This process will create multiple slides at one time. The slides will have titles and bullets.

1 **Start** Word, and then open the document **Ip22A_New_Employees_ List** from the folder that contains your project files. **Save** the document as **22A_New_Employees_List_Firstname_Lastname**

2 Select the first item, numbered 1) in the list, **Complete Required Forms**. On the **Home tab** in the **Styles group**, click **Heading 1**. The Heading 1 style changes the format and removes the numbering.

Text formatted as Heading 1 style will become the title on a new slide in PowerPoint. Text formatted as Heading 2 will become the first bulleted level on a slide. Text formatted as Heading 3 will indent below the first bulleted level.

3 Select the second item, numbered 2). and then hold the ⌈Ctrl⌋ key and select the third item, numbered 3). In the **Styles group**, click **Heading 1**.

The three numbered items from the list now all have a Heading 1 style and will become the titles on the slides in PowerPoint.

To select multiple items, hold the ⌈Ctrl⌋ key as you select the text.

4 Select all the lettered items below each heading. In the **Styles group**, click **Heading 2**. The new heading style changes the format and removes the letters before the items.

5 Click in the document to deselect the text.

These items will become bullet items on each slide. Compare your screen with Figure 22.2.

Figure 22.2

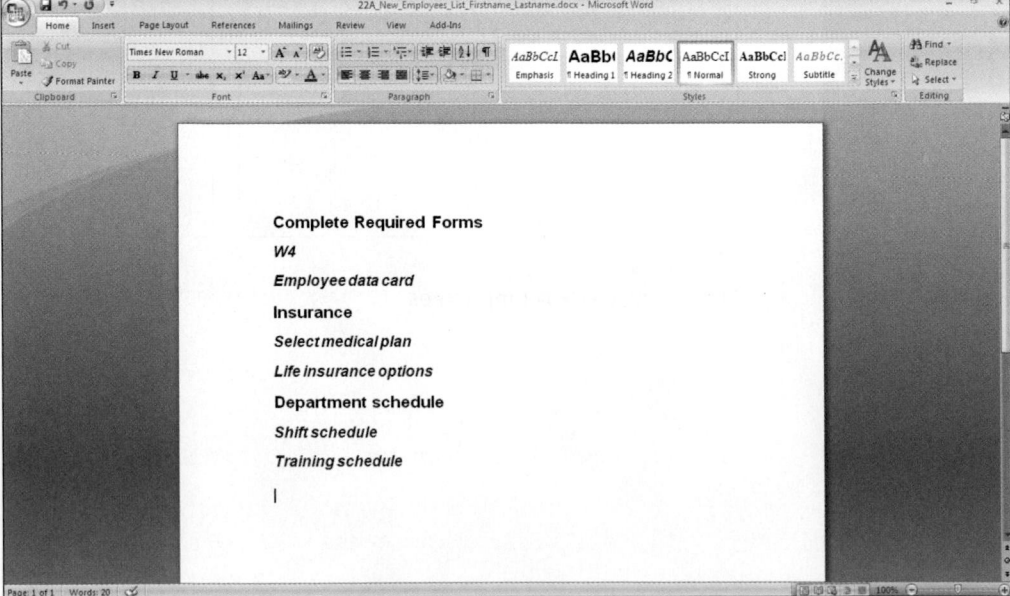

6 **Save** and **Close** your document and then **Close** Word.

7 **Start** PowerPoint. On the **Slides tab** at the left of the screen, click **Slide 1**, and press the ⌈Delete⌋ key.

8 On the **Home tab,** in the **Slides group**, click the **New Slide arrow**, and then click **Slides from Outline**.

The Insert Outline dialog box displays.

9 In the **Insert Outline** dialog box, in the **Look in** list, select the folder that contains your project files, click the **22A_New_ Employees_List_Firstname_Lastname** file, and then click **Insert**.

The Slides tab shows three slides created from the Word content. Compare your screen with Figure 22.3.

Figure 22.3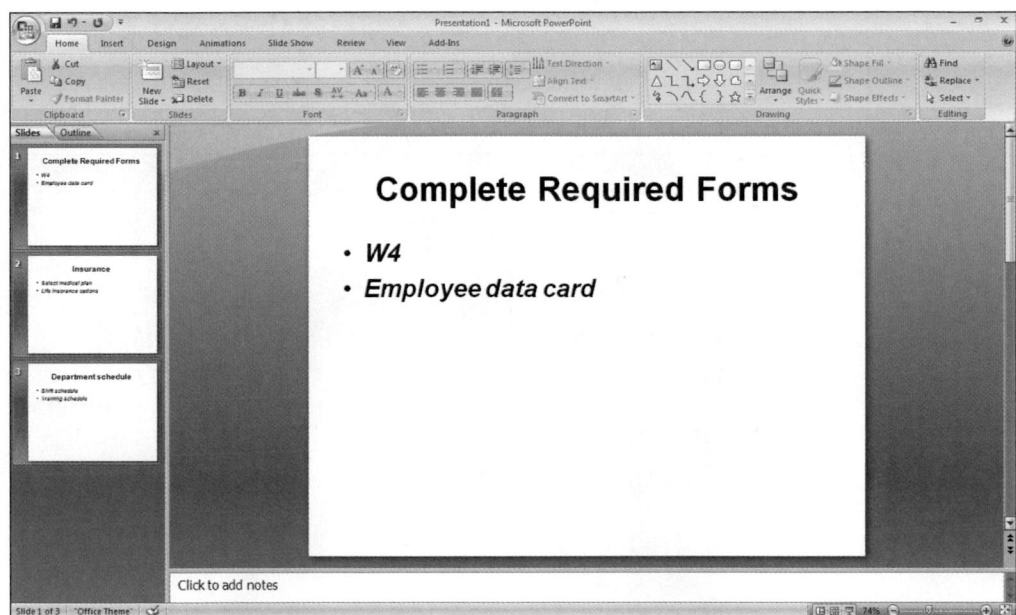

10 **Save** the PowerPoint presentation as **22A_New_Employees_ Firstname_Lastname** Leave the presentation open for the next activity.

Objective 2
Import Excel Data into a PowerPoint Chart

Activity 22.02 Importing Excel Data into a Chart in PowerPoint

In this activity, you continue to work with the PowerPoint slides created in the previous activity. You will add a chart as another slide and get data from an Excel workbook.

1 Click the **Design tab,** and in the **Themes group**, click the **More arrow**.

The All Themes gallery displays. You can drag the mouse over each thumbnail, without clicking, to see the name of each theme.

2 In the **Built-In** section, click the **Flow** theme. If the Flow theme does not display in the list, choose another design. The Flow theme adds background, graphics, and bullets to your slide's appearance.

3 On the **Slides tab**, click **Slide1**. On the Ribbon, click the **Home tab**, and in the **Slides group**, click the top of the **New Slide** button.

A new slide is inserted into the presentation after Slide1.

4 On the **Insert tab**, in the **Illustrations group**, click **Chart**.

The Insert Chart dialog box displays.

5 In the **Insert Chart** dialog box, click **OK** to accept the default Clustered Column chart.

PowerPoint adds a default chart to the new slide and opens a worksheet with default data in a new Excel window. Compare your screen with Figure 22.4.

PowerPoint presentation window   New data window

Figure 22.4

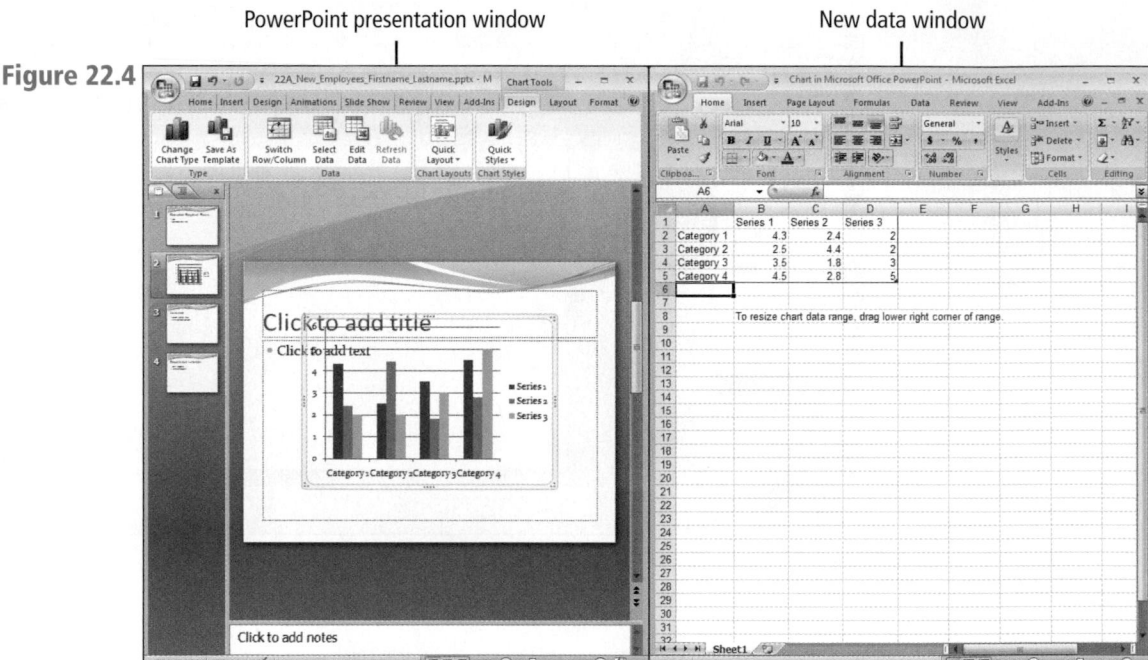

6 In the new Excel window, on the Ribbon, click the **Data tab.** Click the **Get External Data** button, click **Existing Connections**, and then click the **Browse for More button**.

The Select Data Source dialog box opens.

7 In the **Select Data Source** dialog box, in the **Favorites Links** list, select **Computer**, and then locate the folder that contains your project files, and then double-click on the file **Ip22A_Salary_Levels**.

The Select Table dialog box opens.

8 In the **Select Table** dialog box, click on the sheet named **Salary$**, and then click **OK**.

9 In the **Import Data** dialog box, click the **New worksheet** option button, and then click **OK**.

10 In the **PowerPoint** window, with the chart selected, on the **Design contextual tab** of the **Chart Tools,** in the **Data group**, click **Select Data**.

The Select Data Source dialog box opens.

11 In the **Select Data Source** dialog box, in the **Chart data range** box, Sheet1!$A$1:$D$5 should be displayed. Click the **Sheet2 tab**, and the **Chart data range** box should change to **=Table_Ip22A_ Salary_Levels[#All]**. If it does not change, select cells **A1:D5** in **Sheet2**. In the **Select Data Source** dialog box, click the **Switch Row/Column** button. Compare your screen with Figure 22.5.

Chart data range changed   Switch Row/ Column button

Figure 22.5

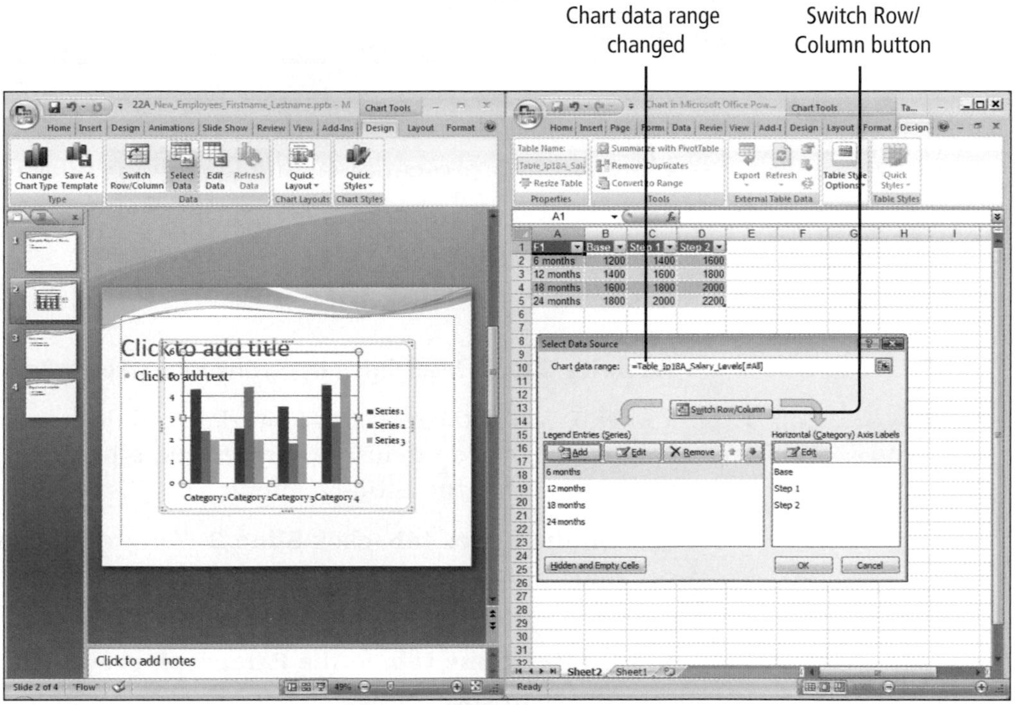

12 Click **OK**, and then **Close** Excel.

13 On the slide, click in the **Click to add title** text box. Type **Salary Levels** Click on the border of the **Click to add text** box, and press Delete. If necessary, click on the chart and drag it down so it is below the title, and then click outside the chart to cancel selection. Also, if necessary, drag the title down so that it is below the blue flow design. Compare your screen with Figure 22.6.

Figure 22.6

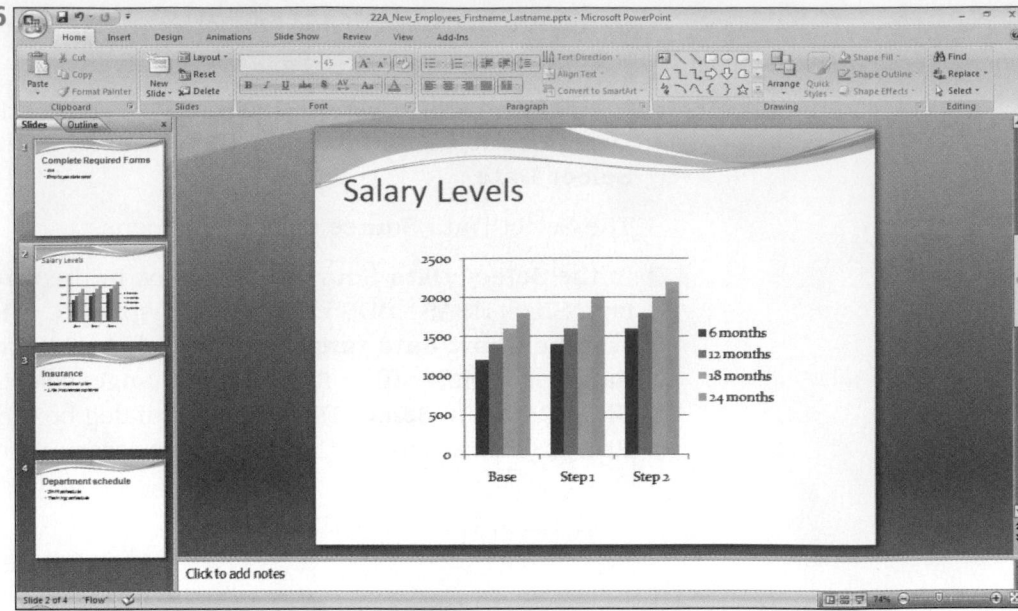

14 **Save** your presentation, and leave it open for the next activity.

Objective 3
Insert a Hyperlink into a PowerPoint Slide

Activity 22.03 Inserting a Hyperlink into a PowerPoint Slide

You can also add content to PowerPoint slides using Copy and Paste. If you use the option to insert a hyperlink, a link is inserted in the document instead of the actual content.

1 On the **Slides tab**, click **Slide 3**. You want to add the link to this slide. Click at the end of *Life insurance options* and press Enter two times.

2 On the **Home tab**, in the **Paragraph group**, click the **Bullets arrow**, and then click **None**.

3 Click on the **Insert tab**, and in the **Links group**, click **Hyperlink**.

The Insert Hyperlink dialog box opens.

4 In the **Insert Hyperlink** dialog box, in the **Text to display** box, type **Seminars** In the **Look in** box, scroll to where your data files are stored and click the **Ip22A_Benefits_Seminars** HTML file, and then click **OK**.

5 Click to the left of *Seminars*, and on the **Home tab**, in the **Paragraph group**, click the **Center** button. Compare your screen with Figure 22.7.

Figure 22.7

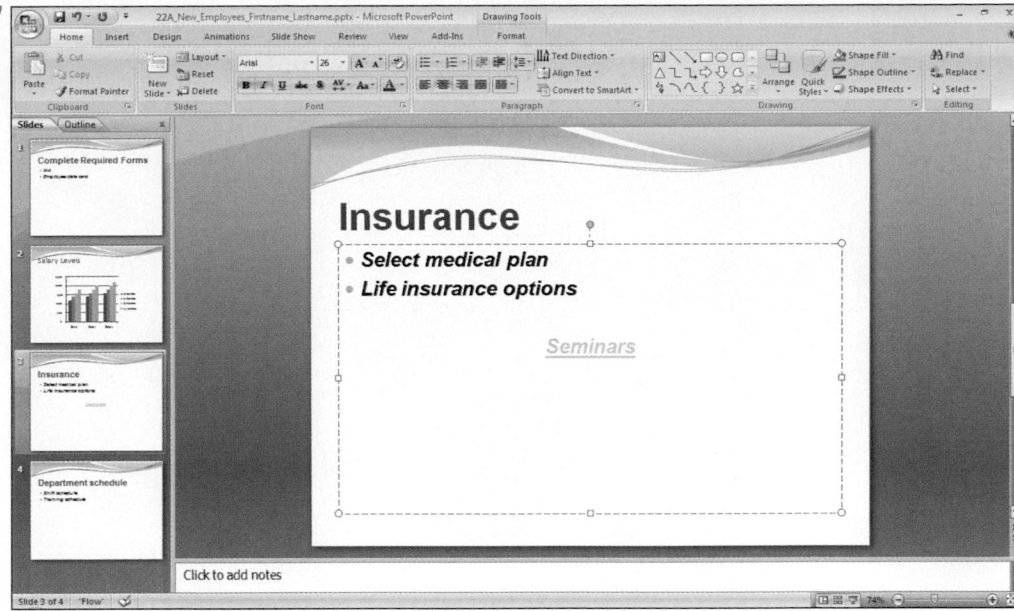

6 On the **Slide Show tab**, in the **Start Slide Show group**, click **From Beginning**. Click to advance to **Slide 2** and then to **Slide 3**.

7 On **Slide 3**, click the link for **Seminars**.

The Ip22A_Benefits_Seminars HTML file is saved as a Web page and opens in a browser window.

You might link to a document like this on a company intranet. Documents do not have to be in a Web format to use a hyperlink in PowerPoint.

8 Click the **Close** button on the browser window to return to the PowerPoint slides, and then view the rest of the slides.

9 **Save** and **Close** your presentation, and then **Close** PowerPoint.

End You have completed this integration project. ——

Glossary

Absolute cell reference A cell reference that refers to cells by their fixed position in a worksheet; an absolute cell reference remains the same when the formula is copied.

Accounting Number format The Excel number format that applies a thousand comma separator where appropriate, inserts a fixed U.S. dollar sign aligned at the left edge of the cell, applies two decimal places, and leaves a small amount of space at the right edge of the cell to accommodate a parenthesis for negative numbers.

Active cell The cell, surrounded by a black border, ready to receive data or be affected by the next Excel command.

Active window The window in which the mouse pointer movements, commands, or text entry occur when two or more windows are open.

Adaptive A feature where menus adapt to the way you work by displaying the commands you most frequently use.

Address bar Displays the path of the current file or folder; also, in Internet Explorer, displays the address of the active Web page.

Adjacent ranges Cell ranges that are next to each other.

Adjustment handle A handle on a selected object that can be used to drag parts of an object into various positions.

Adware Spyware that tracks a user's Internet browsing and installs malicious cookies.

Aggregate functions Calculations that are performed on a group of records.

Alignment The placement of paragraph text relative to the left and right margins

American Psychological Association (APA) style One of two commonly used styles for formatting research papers.

Anchor A symbol that indicates to which paragraph an object is attached.

AND condition A condition in which only records where both specified values are present in the selected fields.

Animated banner A series of rotating or changing text and images embedded within the Web page.

Animation effects Effects used to introduce individual slide elements so that the slide can progress one element at a time.

Antispyware software A program that protects a computer from malicious software designed to threaten privacy and confidentiality.

Antivirus software A program that protects a computer from malicious codes such as viruses, worms, and Trojan horses.

Application software Programs with which you accomplish tasks such as word processing, photo editing, or sending email, and use the computer in a productive manner.

Appointment A calendar activity occurring at a specific time and day that does not require inviting other people.

Appointment area A one-day view of the current day's calendar entries.

Archive To back up files and store them somewhere other than the main hard drive.

Arguments The values that an Excel function uses to perform calculations or operations.

Arithmetic logic unit (ALU) Part of the CPU that performs all the arithmetic and logic functions for the computer; handles addition, subtraction, multiplication, and division, and also makes logical and comparison decisions.

Arithmetic operator The symbols +, −, *, /, %, and ^ used to denote addition, subtraction (negation), multiplication, division, percentage, and exponentiation in an Excel formula.

Arrow keys The keys at the lower right section of the keyboard, used to move the insertion point within the program window.

Ascending order A sorting order that arranges text in alphabetical order (A to Z) or numbers from the lowest to highest number.

Aspect ratio The relationship of an object's height to its width; if locked, changing either the height or width will resize the object proportionally.

Audio port A port that connects audio equipment to the sound card of a computer to facilitate the exchange of data.

Auto fill An Excel feature that extends values into adjacent cells based on the values of selected cells.

AutoComplete (Excel) A feature that speeds your typing and lessens the likelihood of errors; if the first few characters you type in a cell match an existing entry in the column, Excel fills in the remaining characters for you.

AutoComplete (Word) A feature that assists in your typing by suggesting words or phrases.

AutoCorrect (Excel) A feature that assists in your typing by automatically correcting and formatting some text as you type; for example Excel compares your typing to a list of commonly mistyped words and when it finds a match, it substitutes the correct word.

AutoCorrect (Word) A feature that corrects common typing and spelling errors as you type, for example changing *teh* to *the*.

AutoFormat As You Type A Word feature that anticipates formatting based on what you type.

AutoNumber An Access feature that sequentially numbers entered records creating a unique number for each record; useful for data that has no distinct field that could be considered unique.

AutoSum Another term for the Sum function.

AutoText A Word feature with which you can create shortcuts to quickly insert long phrases with just a few keystrokes.

AVERAGE function A pre-written formula that adds a group of values and then divides the result by the number of values in the group.

Background style A slide background fill variation that combines theme colors in different intensities.

Backup tape drive A storage device used to save data to tapes resembling audiocassettes.

Banner area The screen area that displays important calendar information including *Day*, *Week*, and *Month* view buttons.

Base The starting point when you divide the amount of increase by it to calculate the rate of increase.

Between. . . And operator A comparison operator that looks for values within a range.

Bibliography A term used to describe a list of referenced works in a report or research paper, also referred to as Works Cited, Sources, or References, depending upon the report style.

Black slide A slide that displays at the end of a slide presentation indicating the end of the slide show.

Blank database A database that has no data and has no database tools; you create the data and the tools as you need them.

Blank form In Outlook, a lined page added to the printout of the Card print style that you can use to manually list new contacts.

Blank Report tool An Access feature with which you can create a report from scratch by adding the fields you want in the order you want them to appear.

Bluetooth Wireless technology that uses radio waves to transmit data over short distances, and often used with mobile devices.

Body font A font that is applied to all slide text except titles.

Boot The process of starting up a computer.

Boot process See Boot.

Bound The term used to describe objects and controls that are based on data that is stored in tables.

Building block Pre-formatted content that you can add to your document, such as cover pages, pull quotes, and letterheads.

Bulleted levels Outline levels identified by a symbol.

Bulleted list A list of items with each item introduced by a symbol such as a small circle or check mark—useful when the items in the list can be displayed in any order.

Bullets Text symbols such as small circles or check marks used to introduce items in a list.

Burn The process of recording data to optical media such as a CD or DVD.

Bus topology A networking configuration in which all devices are connected to a central high-speed cable called the bus or backbone.

Calculated controls Controls whose source of data is an expression—typically a formula—rather than a field.

Card Style In Outlook, a print style which displays the name and address information alphabetically by last name.

Category axis The area along the bottom of a chart that identifies the categories of data; also referred to as the x-axis.

Category labels The labels that display along the bottom of a chart to identify the categories of data; Excel uses the row titles as the category names.

Cathode-ray tube (CRT) A picture tube device used in a monitor, similar to a television.

CD burner An optical storage device capable of reading data from and writing data to a CD.

CD drive A storage device used to read and, possibly, write data to CD.

CD-R Another name for a CD-ROM disc.

CD-ROM The acronym for Compact Disc-Read Only Memory; an optical storage device used to permanently store data and from which you can read and open files.

CD-RW A compact disc that can be reused to read and save files.

Cell (Access) The box formed by the intersection of a row and a column in a datasheet.

Cell (Excel) The small box formed by the intersection of a column and a row.

Cell address Another name for a cell reference.

Cell content Anything typed into a cell.

Cell reference The identification of a specific cell by its intersecting column letter and row number.

Center alignment Text centered between the left and right margin.

Central processing unit (CPU) The part of the computer responsible for controlling all the commands and tasks the computer performs, acting as the brain of the computer.

Chart (Excel) The graphic representation of data in a worksheet; data presented as a chart is usually easier to understand than a table of numbers.

Chart A graphic representation of numeric data.

Chart layout The combination of chart elements that can be displayed in a chart such as a title, legend, labels for the columns, and the table of charted cells.

Chart Layouts gallery A group of predesigned chart layouts that you can apply to an Excel chart.

Chart sheet A workbook sheet that contains only a chart and is useful when you want to view a chart separately from the worksheet data.

Chart style The overall visual look of a chart in terms of its graphic effects, colors, and backgrounds; for example, you can have flat or beveled columns, colors that are solid or transparent, and backgrounds that are dark or light.

Chart Styles gallery A group of predesigned chart styles that you can apply to an Excel chart.

Chart types Various chart formats used in a way that is meaningful to the reader; common examples are column charts, pie charts, and line charts.

Citation A list of information about a reference source, usually including the name of the author, the full title of the work, the year of publication, Web address, and other publication information.

Click To press the left (or primary) mouse button once.

Click and type pointer The text select (I-beam) pointer with various attached shapes that indicate which formatting will be applied when you double-click—such as a left-aligned, centered, or right-aligned.

Client In a client/server network, this is the computer most people interact with to request information from the server and to perform many of the tasks that can be accomplished with a computer.

Client/server network A network consisting of client and server computers; often used in businesses.

Clip art Graphic images included with the Microsoft Office program or obtained from other sources.

Clip art (PowerPoint) Images included with Microsoft Office or downloaded from the Web that can make your presentation more interesting and visually appealing; drawings, movies, sounds, or photographic images that are included with Microsoft Office or downloaded from the Web.

Clipboard A temporary storage area in Windows that stores the most recently copied item.

Clock speed A measurement of how quickly a CPU processes data, an indication of a CPU's processing power.

Close button The button in a title bar that closes a window or a program.

Collapse button A small minus (−) button to the left of a folder that you click to hide the items in that folder.

Collect and paste The process of collecting a group of graphics or selected text blocks, and then pasting them into a document at any time; the Office Clipboard holds up to 24 items, and the Office Clipboard task pane displays a preview of each item.

Color scales Visual guides that help you understand data distribution and variation.

Column A vertical group of cells in a worksheet.

Column chart A chart in which the data is arranged in columns and which is useful for showing data changes over a period of time or for illustrating comparisons among items.

Column heading The letter that displays at the top of a vertical group of cells in a worksheet; beginning with the first letter of the alphabet, a unique letter or combination of letters identifies each column.

Comma style The Excel number format that inserts thousand comma separators where appropriate, applies two decimal places, and leaves space at the right to accommodate a parenthesis for negative numbers.

Comment A note that can be added to a Word document from the Review tab; comments are not generally printed.

Comments area In Outlook, the area in the lower half of the Appointments form and Task form where you can enter information not otherwise specified in the form.

Common fields Fields that contain the same data in more than one table.

Communication or organizational software A program such as Microsoft Outlook, used to send and retrieve email and manage day-to-day tasks.

Comparison operators Symbols that evaluate each field value to determine if it is the same (=), greater than (>), less than (<), or in between a range of values as specified by the criteria.

Complimentary closing A parting farewell in a business letter.

Compound criteria Multiple conditions in a query or filter.

Compress A process to reduce the size of a file.

Computer A programmable electronic device that can input, process, output, and store data.

Computer fluent The term used to describe a person who understands the capabilities and limitations of computers and knows how to use computer technology to accomplish tasks.

Conditional format A format that changes the appearance of a cell range—for example by adding cell shading or font color—based on a condition; if the condition is true the cell range is formatted based on that condition, and if the condition is false the cell range is *not* formatted based on the condition.

Connectivity port A port that enables a computer to be connected to other devices or systems, such as networks, modems, and the Internet.

Constant value Numbers, text, dates, or times of day that you type into a cell.

Contact A person or organization about whom you can save information such as street and e-mail addresses, telephone and fax numbers, Web page addresses, birthdays, and pictures.

Context-sensitive command A command associated with activities in which you are engaged; often activated by right-clicking a screen item.

Contextual tabs Tabs that are added to the Ribbon when a specific object, such as a chart, is selected, and that contain commands relevant to the selected object.

Contextual tools Sets of commands added to the Ribbon when a specific object is selected and which enable you to perform specific commands related to the selected object; contextual tools display only when needed and no longer display after the object is deselected.

Control Objects on a form or report that display data, perform actions, and let you view and work with information.

Control keys Special keys, such as Ctrl, Alt, or Esc, used to increase keyboard functionality or provide shortcuts.

Control layout The grouped arrangement of controls on a form or report.

Control unit The part of the CPU responsible for obtaining instructions from the computer's memory; the control unit interprets the instructions and executes them, thereby coordinating the activities of all the other computer components.

Cookie A small text file containing information that identifies a visitor to a Web site.

Copy A command that duplicates a selection and places it on the Clipboard.

Copyright Laws that protect the rights of authors of original works, including text, art, photographs, and music.

COUNTIF function A statistical function that counts the number of cells within a range that meet the given condition—the criteria that you provide.

CPU See Central processing unit.

Criteria (Access) Conditions that identify the specific records you are looking for.

Criteria (Excel) Conditions that you specify in a logical function.

Crosshair pointer The pointer that indicates that you can draw a shape.

CRT See Cathode-ray tube.

Curly quote A decorative quotation mark, with curved lines instead of the straight lines found in straight quotes.

Custom animation list A list that indicates the animation effect applied to slide items.

Cut (PowerPoint) A command that removes selected text or graphics from your presentation and moves the selection to the Clipboard.

Cut (Word) The command to remove selected text from a document and move it to the Office Clipboard.

Daily Style In Outlook, a print style that prints the appointments for the currently displayed day.

Daily Task List In Outlook, an abbreviated list of current tasks stored in the Tasks folder.

Data Words, numbers, sounds, or pictures that represent facts about people, events, things, or ideas.

Data (Access) Facts about people, events, things, or ideas.

Data (Excel) Text or numbers in a cell.

Data bar A cell format consisting of a shaded bar that provides a visual cue to the reader about the value of a cell relative to other cells; the length of the bar represents the value in the cell—a longer bar represents a higher value and a shorter bar represents a lower value.

Data entry The action of typing the record data into a database.

Data marker A column, bar, area, dot, pie slice, or other symbol in a chart that represents a single data point; related data points form a data series.

Data point A value that originates in a worksheet cell and that is represented in a chart by a data marker.

Data series Related data points represented by data markers; each data series has a unique color or pattern represented in the chart legend.

Data source (Word) A list of variable information, such as names and addresses, that is merged with a main document to create customized form letters or labels.

Data source The table or tables from which a query selects its data.

Data table A range of cells that shows how changing certain values in your formulas affects the results of those formulas, and which makes it easy to calculate multiple versions in one operation.

Data type The characteristic that defines the kind of data that can be entered into a field, such as numbers, text, or dates.

Database An organized collection of facts about people, events, things, or ideas related to a particular topic or purpose.

Database software Programs, such as Microsoft Access, used to store and organize large amounts of data and perform complex tasks such as sorting and querying to generate specialized reports.

Datasheet view The Access view that displays an object organized in a format of columns and rows similar to an Excel spreadsheet.

Date control A control on a form or report that inserts the current date each time the form or report is opened.

Date line The first line in a business letter.

Date Navigator In Outlook, a one-month view of the calendar that you can use to display specific days in a month.

DBMS An acronym for database management system.

Dedicated server A computer that is assigned to handle one specific task on a network.

Denial of service (DoS) An attack caused when a large number of computers attempt to access a Web site at the same time, effectively overloading it and causing it to shut down.

Descending order A sorting order that arranges text in reverse alphabetical (Z to A) order or numbers from the highest to the lowest number.

Deselect The action of canceling a selection.

Design grid The lower pane of the Query window, which displays the design of the query.

Design view The detailed structured view of a form or report, and the view in which some tasks must be performed; only the controls, and not the data, are visible in this view.

Desktop The basic screen from which Windows and programs are run, and which consists of program icons, a taskbar, a Start button, and a mouse pointer.

Desktop computer A class of microcomputer, such as a PC or a Mac.

Detail section The section of a form or report that displays the records from the underlying table or query.

Dialog box A box that asks you to make a decision about an individual object or topic.

Dialog Box Launcher A small icon that displays to the right of some group names on the Ribbon, and which opens a related dialog box or task pane providing additional options and commands related to that group.

Digital camera A type of camera that saves photographs in a digital format rather than on film.

Digital Video Interface (DVI) port A port used to connect an LCD monitor to a computer in order to use a pure digital signal.

Digital video recorder A device used to record video in digital format directly to a hard drive, without the need for videotape.

Display screen See Monitor.

Displayed value The data that displays in a cell.

Document Information Panel The area of the screen just below the Ribbon that displays document properties.

Document properties The detailed information about a document that can help you identify or organize your files, including author name, title, and keywords.

Document window The Word window that displays the active document.

Dot leader A series of dots preceding a tab.

Dot matrix An impact printer, useful for printing multi-page forms.

Dot pitch The diagonal distance between adjacent pixels, measured in millimeters and that is used to determine image quality for monitors.

Dots per inch (dpi) A measurement of printer resolution.

Double-click The action of clicking the left mouse button twice in rapid succession while keeping the mouse still.

Downloading The action of requesting and copying a file or program from a remote server, such as a Web server, and saving it on your local computer or storage device.

Draft view A simplified view of a document that does not show graphics, margins, headers, or footers.

Drag The action of moving something from one location on the screen to another; the action of dragging includes releasing the mouse button at the desired time or location.

Drag and drop The action of moving a selection by dragging it to a new location.

Drag and drop (Excel) A method of moving or copying the content of selected cells in which you point to the selection and then drag it to a new location.

Drag and drop (Word) A technique by which you can move selected text from one location in a document to another—best used with text that will be moved a short distance, such as on the same screen.

Dragging The technique of holding down the left mouse button and moving over an area of text in order to select it.

Drawing canvas A work area for creating and editing complex figures created using the drawing tools.

Drawing object A graphic object, including shapes, diagrams, lines, and circles.

Drive An area of storage that is formatted with the Windows file system and that has a drive letter such as C.

Dual-boot A system with two different operating systems installed, giving the user the option to boot the computer using either one.

Dual-core A CPU that includes two microprocessors on a single integrated circuit. See also Multicore.

DVD drive A storage device used to read and, possibly, write data to DVD.

DVI port See Digital Video Interface (DVI) port.

E-Mail Account A unique address that you can use to receive and send e-mail.

Edit (Word) The action of making changes to the text or format of a document.

Edit (Excel) The action of making changes in a worksheet or workbook.

Edit mode A Windows mode that enables you to change the name of a file or folder, and works the same in all Windows programs.

Editing (PowerPoint) The process of adding, deleting, or changing the contents of a slide.

Effect options Animation options that include changing the direction of an effect and playing a sound when an animation takes place.

Em dash The word processing name for a long dash in a sentence, and which marks a break in thought, similar to a comma but stronger.

Embedded chart A chart that displays as an object within a worksheet.

Embedded computers Components of larger products, devices that perform pre-defined tasks using specially programmed processors.

Enclosure An additional document included with a letter.

Endnotes In a report or research paper, references placed at the end of the chapter containing the reference.

Enhanced ScreenTip A ScreenTip for a button that has more information than just the name, sometimes including a link to the topic in the Help system.

Entrance effects Animations that bring a slide element onto the screen.

Ethernet port A port, slightly larger than a telephone jack, that can transmit data at speeds up to 1,000 megabits per second (Mbps) and is usually used to connect to a cable modem or a network.

Excel table A series of rows and columns in a worksheet that contains related data, and that is managed independently from the data in other rows and columns in the worksheet.

Expand button A small plus (+) button to the left of a folder that you click to display the items in that folder.

Expand Formula Bar button An Excel window element with which you can increases the height of the Formula Bar for the purpose of displaying lengthy cell content.

Expand horizontal scroll bar button A button with which you can increase the width of the horizontal scroll bar.

Favorites Center An area in Internet Explorer that lets you manage your favorites list, the history list, and the feeds list.

Field A category that describes each piece of data stored in a table.

Field list A list of the field names in a table.

Field properties Characteristics of a field that control how the field will display and how the data can be entered in the field.

File Data that you save and store on a drive, such as a Word document or a PowerPoint presentation.

File extension The characters to the right of the period in a file name, and that tell the computer the program to use to open the file; extensions can be displayed or hidden.

Fill color (Excel) The background color a cell.

Fill color The inside color of text or an object.

Fill handle The small black square in the lower right corner of a selected cell.

Filter By Form An Access command that filters the records in a form based on one or more fields, or based on more than one value in the same field.

Filter By Selection An Access command that retrieves only the records that contain the value in the selected field.

Filtering The process of displaying only a portion of the total records (a subset) based on matching a specific value.

Financial functions Prewritten formulas that perform common business calculations such as calculating a loan payment on a vehicle or calculating how much to save each month to buy something; financial functions commonly involve a period of time such as months or years.

Find and Replace (Excel) A command that searches the cells in a worksheet—or in a selected range—for matches and then replaces each match with a replacement value of your choice.

Firewall See Personal firewall.

FireWire port A port used to send data at rates up to 800 megabits per second (Mbps), frequently used for digital cameras or digital video recorders.

Flash drive A small, portable, digital storage device that connects to a computer's USB port; also called a thumb drive, jump drive, or USB drive.

Flash memory Portable, nonvolatile memory, that uses electronic, solid-state circuitry.

Flat panel See Liquid crystal display.

Flat screen A type of screen used in CRT monitors, and which differs from flat panel monitors.

Floating object An object or graphic that can be moved independently of the surrounding text.

Floppy disk drive (or floppy drive) The original storage device for a microcomputer, which enables portable, permanent storage on floppy disks.

Folder A storage area, represented on the screen by a picture of a paper file folder, used to store files or other folders.

Font A set of characters with the same design and shape.

Font size The size of characters in a font measured in points; there are 72 points in an inch, with 10 or 11 points being a typical font size.

Font style Formatting emphasis such as bold, italic, and underline.

Font theme A theme that determines the font applied to two types of slide text—headings and body.

Footer (PowerPoint) Text that displays at the bottom of every slide or that prints at the bottom of a sheet of slide handouts or notes pages.

Footer (Word) A reserved area for text and graphics that displays at the bottom of each page in a document or section of a document.

Footers (Excel) Text, graphics, or page numbers that print at the bottom of every page of a worksheet.

Footnotes In a report or research paper, references placed at the bottom of a report page containing the source of the reference.

Foreign key The field that is included in the related table so that it can be joined to the primary key in another table for the purpose of creating a relationship.

Form A window for displaying and collecting information.

Form (Access) An Access object with which you can enter new records into a table, edit existing records in a table, or display existing records from a table.

Form footer Information at the bottom of the screen in Form view that is printed after the last detail section on the last page.

Form header Information, such as a form's title, which displays at the top of the screen in Form view, and that is printed at the top of the first page when records are printed as forms

Form tool The Access tool that creates a form with a single mouse click, and that includes all the fields from the underlying data source (table or query).

Format as you type The Excel feature by which a cell takes on the formatting of the number typed into the cell.

Format Painter (Excel) An Excel feature with which you can copy the formatting of a specific cell to other cells.

Format Painter (PowerPoint) A feature that copies formatting from one selection of text to another, thus ensuring formatting consistency in your presentation.

Format Painter (Word) A Word tool with which you can copy the formatting of specific text, or of a paragraph, to text in another location in the document.

Formatting (Excel) The process of specifying the appearance of cells and the overall layout of a worksheet; accomplished through various commands on the Ribbon, many of which are also available using shortcut menus or keyboard shortcuts.

Formatting (PowerPoint) Changing the appearance of the text, layout, and design of a slide.

Formatting marks Characters that display on the screen, but do not print, indicating where the Enter key, the Spacebar, and the Tab key were pressed; also called nonprinting characters.

Formatting text The process of establishing the overall appearance of text in a document.

Formula An equation that performs mathematical calculations on values in a worksheet.

Formula AutoComplete An Excel feature which, after typing an = (equal sign) and the beginning letter or letters of a function name, displays a list of function names that match the typed letter(s), and from which you can insert the function by pointing to its name and pressing the Tab key or double-clicking.

Formula Bar An element in the Excel window that displays the value or formula contained in the active cell; here you can also enter or edit values or formulas.

Frames Separate areas of content placed closely together so they will display as one unified Web page with or without any visible demarcation lines between them.

Freeze Panes A command that enables you to select one or more rows or columns and freeze (lock) them into place; the locked rows and columns become separate panes.

Full Screen Reading view A view that displays easy-to-read pages that fit on the screen.

Function A predefined formula—a formula that Excel has already built for you—that performs calculations by using specific values in a particular order.

Function key The keys, numbered F1 through F12, located above the numeric keys on a keyboard that have different functions depending upon the software program in use.

Future value The value at the end of time periods in an Excel function; the cash balance you want to attain after the last payment is made—usually zero for loans.

Fv The abbreviation for *future value* in various Excel functions.

Gallery An Office 2007 feature that displays a list of potential results; it shows the results of commands rather than just the command name.

General format The default format that Excel applies to numbers; the general format has no specific characteristics—whatever you type in the cell will display, with the exception that trailing zeros to the right of a decimal point will not display.

Gigabyte (GB) Approximately one billion bytes; a unit of measure for memory and storage space.

Gigahertz (GHz) One billion hertz; hertz is the unit of measure for processor speed.

Goal Seek One of Excel's What-If Analysis tools that provides a method to find a specific value for a cell by adjusting the value of one other cell.

Gradient fill A color combination in which one color fades into another.

Graphic A picture, clip art image, chart, or drawing object.

Graphical user interface (GUI) A computer interface with which you interact with the computer through the use of graphics and point-and-click technology; GUIs show documents as they will look in their final form.

Group A set of command buttons related to the Ribbon tab that is currently selected.

Group footer Displays the field label by which the summarized data has been grouped.

Group header Information printed at the beginning of each new group of records, for example the group name.

Group, Sort, and Total pane A pane that opens at the bottom of your screen in which you can control how information is sorted and grouped in a report; provides the most flexibility for adding or modifying groups, sort orders, or totals options on a report.

GUI See Graphical user interface.

Guides Vertical and horizontal lines that display in the rulers to give you a visual indication of where the crosshair pointer is positioned so that you can draw a shape.

Handheld computers See Personal digital assistant.

Hanging indent An indent style in which the first line of a paragraph extends to the left of the remaining lines, and that is commonly used for bibliographic entries.

Hard copy Data or information retrieved from a computer and printed.

Hard drive A large disk drive inside your computer, also referred to as a Local Disk.

Hardware The physical components of the computer and any equipment connected to it.

Header (PowerPoint) Text that displays at the top of every slide or that prints at the top of a sheet of slide handouts or notes pages.

Header (Word) A reserved area for text and graphics that displays at the top of each page in a document or section of a document.

Headers (Excel) Text, graphics, or page numbers that print at the top of every page of a worksheet.

Headings font The font that is applied to slide titles.

Help button A button at the far right of the Ribbon tabs that you click to display the program's Help window.

History A feature of Internet Explorer that tracks recently visited Web pages and sites.

Home page The Web page that displays every time you start Internet Explorer.

Horizontal scroll bar The bar at the bottom of a window that enables you to move left and right to view information that extends beyond the left and right edges of the screen.

Horizontal window split box A small box with which you can split the document into two horizontal views of the same document.

Hyperlink Text that you click to go to another location in a document, another document, or a Web site; the text is a different color (usually blue) than the surrounding text, and commonly underlined.

Hyperlinks Text, buttons, pictures, or other objects displayed on Web pages that, when clicked, access other Web pages or display other sections of the active page.

Hyperthreading Technology that allows a CPU to emulate multiple processors, improving processing power and speed.

Icon A graphic representation of an object that you can click to open that object.

Icon set A collection of icons such as arrows, flags, bars, or circles that annotate and classify data into three to five categories separated by a threshold value.

IF function A logical function that uses a logical test to check whether a condition is met, and then returns one value if true, and another value if false.

Impact A type of printer that resembles a typewriter; a key and ink ribbon are used to imprint a character on paper.

Inbox In Outlook, the folder that stores e-mail.

Indenting A format for text in which lines of text are moved relative to the left and right margins, for example, moving the beginning of the first line of a paragraph to the right or left of the rest of the paragraph.

Information Data that has been organized in a useful manner.

Information processing cycle The cycle composed of the four basic computer functions: input, process, output, and storage.

Ink-jet Type of printer that uses a special nozzle and ink cartridges to distribute liquid ink on the surface of the paper.

Inline object An object or graphic inserted in a document that acts like a character in a sentence.

Innermost sort field When sorting on multiple fields in datasheet view, the field that will be used for the second level of sorting.

Input The act of entering data into a computer.

Input devices Computer hardware used to enter data and instructions into a computer; examples include the keyboard, mouse, stylus, scanner, microphone, and digital camera.

Insert mode The mode in which text moves to the right to make space for new keystrokes.

Insert Worksheet button Located on the row of sheet tabs, a sheet tab that, when clicked, inserts an additional worksheet into the workbook.

Insertion point A blinking vertical line that indicates where text or graphics will be inserted.

Inside address The address block under the date in a business letter.

Interest The amount charged for the use of borrowed money.

Internet control key Usually found at the top of a keyboard, this type of key can be used for various Internet-related activities including opening a Web browser and sending email.

Internet Explorer 7.0 A software program that allows you to view the contents of the World Wide Web.

Internet Service Provider (ISP) A company that provides an Internet connection through a regular telephone line, a special high-speed telephone line, or a cable.

IrDA port A port enabling data transmission through the use of infrared light waves; the devices sharing data require a clear line of site with no visual obstructions.

Is Not Null A criteria that searches for fields that are not empty.

Is Null A criteria that searches for fields that are empty.

Items An element of information in Outlook, such as a message, a contact name, a task, or an appointment.

Join line In the Relationships window, the line joining two tables that visually indicates the related field and the type of relationship.

Joysticks Input devices used to control actions and movement within computer games.

Justified alignment Text aligned on both the left and right margins.

Key logger A software program or hardware device that records every keystroke made on the computer.

Keyboard The hardware device used to input typed data and commands into a computer.

Keyboard shortcut A combination of keys on the keyboard that perform a command.

Label control A control on a form or report that contains descriptive information, typically a field name.

LAN See Local area network.

Landscape orientation A page orientation in which the printed page is wider than it is tall.

Laser A type of printer that uses a drum, static electricity, and a laser to distribute dry ink or toner on the surface of the paper.

Layout (PowerPoint) The placement and arrangement of the text and graphic elements on a slide.

Layout selector A small symbol that displays in the upper left corner of a selected control layout, and with which you can move the entire group of controls.

Layout view The Access view in which you can make changes to a form or to a report while the form is running—the data from the underlying record source displays.

LCD See Liquid crystal display.

Leader characters Characters that form a solid, dotted, or dashed line that fills the space preceding a tab stop.

Left aligned The cell format in which characters align at the left edge of the cell; this is the default for text entries and is an example of formatting information stored in a cell.

Left alignment Text aligned at the left margin, leaving the right margin uneven.

Left pane In the My Computer window, a pane at the left that displays information and commonly used tools.

Legend A chart element that identifies the patterns or colors that are assigned to the categories in the chart.

Line chart A chart type that displays trends over time; time displays along the bottom axis and the data point values are connected with a line.

Line spacing The distance between lines of text in a paragraph.

Link Select pointer The mouse pointer displaying as a pointing hand as you point to an item that links to another Web page.

Linux An open-source operating system based on the UNIX operating system developed for mainframe computers.

Liquid crystal display (LCD) Technology used in flat panel monitors, resulting in thinner and lighter monitors.

Live Preview A technology that shows the result of applying an editing or formatting change as you move your pointer over the results presented in a gallery.

Local area network (LAN) A network in which the nodes are located within a small geographic area.

Local Disk A large disk drive inside your computer, also referred to as a hard disk.

Logical functions Pre-written formulas that test for specific conditions, and which typically use conditional tests to determine whether specified conditions, referred to as criteria, are true or false.

Logical operators (Access) The criteria of AND and OR used to enter criteria for the same field or different fields; AND requires that both conditions be met and OR requires that either condition be met.

Logical test Any value or expression that can be evaluated as being true or false.

Mac OS The operating system designed specifically for Apple's Mac computers.

Magnetic A type of storage process using magnetized film to store data; used by media such as floppy disks or Zip disks.

Mail merge A Word feature that joins a main document and a data source to create customized letters or labels.

Main document The document that contains the text or formatting that remains constant in a mail merge.

Mainframe A large computer capable of performing more than one task at the same time and supporting many users simultaneously.

Manual column break An artificial end to a column to balance columns or to provide space for the insertion of other objects.

Manual line break The action of ending a line, before the normal end of the line, without creating a new paragraph; this is useful, for example, if your paragraph style includes space before or after paragraphs and you want to begin a new line without the space.

Margins The space between the text and the top, bottom, left, and right edges of the paper.

MAX function A statistical function that determines the largest value in a group of values.

Maximize To increase the size of a window to fill the screen.

MEDIAN function A statistical function commonly used to describe a group of data, and which finds the middle value in a group of values that has as many values above it in the group as are below it.

Megabyte (MB) Approximately one million bytes; a unit of measure for memory and storage space.

Megahertz (MHz) One million hertz; hertz is the unit of measure for processor speed.

Memo Style In Outlook, a print style that prints a single item on a single page and provides detailed information about that item.

Menu A list of commands within a category.

Menu bar The bar beneath the title bar that lists the names of menu categories.

Message Bar The area directly below the Ribbon that displays information such as security alerts when there is potentially unsafe, active content in an Office 2007 document that you open.

Message header In Outlook, the basic information about an e-mail message such as the sender's name, the date sent, and the subject.

MFD See Multifunction device.

Microcomputer The computer most users are familiar with, ranging in size from large desktop systems to handheld devices.

Microphones Input devices used to digitally record sound.

Microprocessor chip See Central processing unit.

Microsoft Exchange Server An e-mail based communications server for businesses and organizations.

Microsoft Windows The operating system found on most microcomputers.

MIDI port Musical Instrument Digital Interface port used to connect electronic musical instruments to a system.

MIN function A statistical function that determines the smallest value in a group of values.

Mini toolbar A small toolbar containing frequently used formatting commands, and sometimes accompanied by a shortcut menu of other frequently used commands, which displays as a result of right-clicking a selection or of selecting text.

Mini toolbar (Excel) A small toolbar containing frequently used formatting commands and which displays as a result of right-clicking or selecting cells; the toolbar fades when you move the mouse away and dismisses itself when you click outside of the toolbar.

Minimize Removing the window from the screen without closing it; minimized windows can be reopened by clicking the associated button in the taskbar.

Mobile devices Lightweight, portable computing devices such as PDAs, smartphones, and handheld computers.

Modem port A port that connects to a standard telephone line, usually used to connect to the Internet or a local network, with a maximum speed of 56 kilobits per second (Kbps).

Modern Language Association (MLA) style One of two commonly used styles for formatting research papers.

Monitor (or display screen) A common output device that displays text, graphics, and video.

Monitor port A port used to connect a monitor to a computer's graphic processing unit, located on the motherboard or video card.

Motherboard A large printed circuit board located in the system unit to which all other boards are connected; the motherboard contains the central processing unit (CPU), the memory (RAM) chips, and expansion card slots.

Mouse An input device used to enter commands and user responses into a computer.

Mouse pointer The arrow, I-beam, or other symbol that shows the location or position of the mouse on your screen; also called the pointer.

Multicore A CPU that includes more than two microprocessors on a single integrated circuit. See also Dual-core.

Multifunction device (MFD) A device that has more than one purpose, often combining input and output capabilities.

Multimedia control key Usually found at the top of a keyboard, this type of key can be used to control or mute speaker volume.

Multimedia projectors Output devices used to display information on a screen for viewing by an audience.

Multiple items form A form in which multiple records can be entered into or displayed from a table.

Multitask The action of performing more than one task at the same time.

Name Box An element of the Excel window that displays the name of the selected cell, table, chart, or object.

Navigate To move within a document or workbook.

Navigation Pane (Access) The area of the Access window that displays and organizes the names of the objects in a database; from here you open objects for use.

Navigation Pane (Outlook) The area on the left side of the Outlook window that provides quick access to Outlook's components.

Network A group of two or more computers (or nodes) connected to share information and resources.

Network topology The layout and structure of a computer network.

Node Any object connected to a network—may be a computer or a peripheral device.

Non-breaking hyphen A special type of hyphen that will not break at the end of a line and is useful for telephone numbers in which you normally do not want the number to be placed on two separate lines by the word wrap feature.

Non-breaking space A special type of space inserted between two words that results in treating the two words as one, and thus forcing both words to wrap even if the second word would normally wrap to the next line.

Nonadjacent ranges Cell ranges that are not next to each other.

Nonimpact A type of printer that does not actually touch the paper.

Nonprinting characters Characters that display on the screen, but do not print, indicating where the Enter key, the Spacebar, and the Tab key were pressed; also called formatting marks.

Nonvolatile Permanent storage, as in read only memory (ROM); data remains even when power is shut down.

Normal view (PowerPoint) The view in which the PowerPoint window is divided into three areas: the Slides/Outline pane, the Slide pane, and the Notes pane.

Normal view (Excel) A screen view that maximizes the number of cells visible on your screen and keeps the column letters and row numbers close to the columns and rows.

Notebook computer Also known as a laptop, this microcomputer is smaller than a desktop and designed to be portable.

Notes area In Outlook, a blank area of the Contact form that can be used for any information about the contact that is not otherwise specified in the form.

Notes pages Printouts that contain the slide image in the top half of the page and speaker's notes in the lower half of the page.

Notification area The area on the right side of the taskbar that keeps you informed about processes that are occurring in the background, such as antivirus software, network connections, and other utility programs; also displays the time.

NOW function A function within the *Date & Time* category that retrieves the date and time from your computer's calendar and clock and inserts the information into the selected cell.

Nper The abbreviation for *number of time periods* in various Excel functions.

Number format A specific way in which Excel displays numbers in a cell.

Numbered lists A list of items with each item introduced by a consecutive number to indicate definite steps, a sequence of actions, or chronological order.

Numeric keypad A bank of keys on a keyboard with which you can input numbers, it is located on the right side of a keyboard and is similar to an adding machine or calculator.

Object window The portion of the Access window that displays open objects.

Objects The basic parts of a database, which includes tables, forms, queries, reports, and macros.

Office button The large button to the left of the Quick Access Toolbar that displays a list of commands related to things you can do *with* a workbook, such as opening, saving, printing, or sharing.

Office Clipboard A temporary storage area maintained by your Microsoft Office program.

Office Clipboard (Word) A temporary storage area that holds text or graphics that has been cut or copied, and that can subsequently be placed in another location in the document or in another Office program.

Offline Your status when you are not connected to a network or to the public Internet.

OLE An abbreviation for *object linking and embedding*, a technology for transferring and sharing information among applications.

One-to-many relationship A relationship between two tables where one record in the first table corresponds to many records in the second table—the most common type of relationship in Access.

One-variable data table A data table that changes the value in only one cell.

Online Your status when you are connected to your organization's network or to the public Internet.

Open-source Software whose code is made available for developers to modify and use as they wish, usually available at no cost.

Operating system A set of instructions that coordinates the activities of your computer; Microsoft Windows XP is an operating system.

Operating system (OS) System software that controls the way in which a computer system functions, including the management of hardware, peripherals, and software; Microsoft Windows XP is an operating system.

Operators The symbols with which you can specify the type of calculation you want to perform in an Excel formula.

Optical A type of storage process using a laser to read and write data; used by media such as CDs and DVDs.

OR condition A condition in which only records where one of two values is present in the selected field.

Order of operations The mathematical rules for performing multiple calculations within a formula.

OS See Operating system.

Outermost sort field When sorting on multiple fields in datasheet view, the field that will be used for the first level of sorting.

Outline view A document view that shows headings and subheadings, which can be expanded or collapsed.

Outlook Today In Outlook, a summary view of your schedule, tasks, and e-mail for the current day.

Output To retrieve data or information from a computer.

Output devices Computer hardware used to retrieve processed data and information from a computer; examples include the monitor, printer, and speakers.

P2P network See Peer-to-peer network.

Page footer Information printed at the end of every page in a report; used to print page numbers or other information that you want to appear at the bottom of every report page.

Page header (Access) Information printed at the top of every page of a report.

Page Layout view A screen view in which you can use the rulers to measure the width and height of data, set margins for printing, hide or display the numbered row headings and the lettered column headings, and change the page orientation; this view is useful for preparing your worksheet for printing.

Page number control A control on a form or report that inserts the page numbers of the pages when displayed in Print Preview or when printed.

Page orientation (Excel) The position of your printed worksheet on paper—either portrait or landscape.

Paint A Windows program in which graphics are created or edited.

Pane A portion of a worksheet window bounded by and separated from other portions by vertical and horizontal bars.

Parallel port A port used to connect a printer to a computer, and which sends data in groups of bits at speeds of up to 500 kilobits per second (Kbps).

Parenthetical reference In the MLA report style, references placed in parenthesis within the report text that include the last name of the author or authors, and the page number in the referenced source.

Paste The action of placing text or objects that have been copied or moved from one location to another location.

Paste (Excel) The action of placing cell contents that have been copied or moved to the Office Clipboard to another location.

Paste area The target destination for data that has been cut or copied using the Office Clipboard.

Paste Options button (Excel) A button that displays in the lower right corner of a pasted selection and that displays a list of options that lets you determine how the information is pasted into your worksheet; the list varies depending on the type of content you are pasting and the program you are pasting from.

Paste Special A dialog box that offers various options for the manner in which you can paste the contents of the Office Clipboard into one or more cells; for example, you can paste the calculated result of a formula rather than the actual formula.

PDA See Personal digital assistant.

Peer-to-peer (P2P) network A network in which each node can communicate directly with every other node, and which is often used for home and small business networks.

Percent for new value = base percent + percent of increase The formula for calculating a percentage by which a value increases by adding the base percentage—usually 100%—to the percent increase.

Percent rate of increase The percent by which one number increases over another.

Peripheral A hardware device connected to a computer, but not located within the system unit, such as a monitor, printer, or mouse.

Permanent memory Memory used by storage devices to retain data and information.

Personal digital assistant (PDA) Also known as a hand-held computer, a small device that enables a user to carry digital information.

Personal firewall A software program or hardware device designed to prevent unauthorized access to a computer.

Personal information manager In Outlook, a feature that enables you to electronically store and manage information about contacts, appointments, and tasks.

Phishing Email that masquerades as an authentic entity such as a bank or credit card company, requesting confidential information.

Picture element A point of light measured in dots per square inch on a screen; sixty-four pixels equals 8.43 characters, which is the average number of digits that will fit in a cell using the default font.

Pie chart A type of chart that shows the relationship of each part to a whole.

Pixel An abbreviated name for picture element.

Placeholder A slide element that reserves a portion of a slide and serves as a container for text, graphics, and other slide elements.

PMT function An Excel function that calculates the payment for a loan based on constant payments and at a constant rate of interest.

Point (noun) A measurement of the size of a font; there are 72 points in an inch, with 10–12 points being the most commonly used font size.

Point (verb) The action of moving the mouse pointer over something on the screen.

Point and click method The technique of constructing a formula by pointing to and then clicking cells; this method is convenient when the referenced cells are not adjacent to one another.

Pointer See mouse pointer.

Pointing Positioning the tip of the pointer in the center of an icon or other screen object.

Pop-up blocker A command on the Tools menu that stops or allows pop-ups to display as you browse the Internet.

Pop-ups Small windows that display on your screen without you actually requesting them as your browse the Internet.

Populate The action of filling a database table with records.

Port An interface through which external devices are connected to the computer.

Portals Home pages that act as launching sites to other Web pages, for example containing links to access frequently visited sites, up-to-the-minute news, weather reports, and maps and directories.

Portrait orientation A page orientation in which the printed page is taller than it is wide.

Present value The total amount that a series of future payments is worth now; also known as the principal.

Presentation graphics software A program used to effectively present information to an audience.

Presentation software A program used to create dynamic slideshows and generate speaker notes and audience handouts.

Primary key The field that uniquely identifies a record in a table—for example, a Student ID number at a college.

Principal Another term for present value.

Print Layout view A view of a document that looks like a sheet of paper, and which displays margins, headers, footers, and graphics.

Print Preview A feature that displays information as it will print based on the options that you select.

Print styles A combination of paper and page settings that determines the way items print.

Printer An output device used to generate hard copy.

Process The term used to describe the action of a computer when it converts data into information.

Program A set of instructions used by a computer to perform certain tasks.

Program tab A tab on the Ribbon that replaces the standard set of tabs when you switch to certain authoring modes or views, such as Print Preview.

Program-level buttons Buttons at the far right of the title bar that minimize, restore, or close the program.

Property sheet A list of characteristics—properties —for controls on a form or report in which you can make precision changes to each property associated with the control.

Protocol A set of rules for transferring data over the Internet.

Pt. An abbreviation for point.

Pv The abbreviation for *present value* in various Excel functions.

Query A database object that retrieves specific data from one or more tables and then displays the specified data in datasheet view.

Quick Access Toolbar A small toolbar in the upper left corner of the program window that displays buttons to perform frequently used commands with a single click.

Quick Launch toolbar An area to the right of the Start button that contains shortcut icons for commonly used programs.

RAM See Random access memory.

Random Access Memory (RAM) A computer's temporary storage space or short-term memory and stored on chips located on the motherboard; measured in megabytes (MB) and gigabytes (GB).

Range Two or more selected cells on a worksheet that are adjacent or nonadjacent; because the range is treated as a single unit, you can make the same change, or combination of changes, to more than one cell at a time.

Range finder An Excel feature that outlines cells in color to indicate which cells are used in a formula; useful for verifying which cells are referenced in a formula or for quickly positioning the insertion point within the cell to perform editing directly in the cell.

Rate In the Excel PMT function, the term used to indicate the interest rate for a loan.

Rate = amount of increase/base The mathematical formula to calculate a rate of increase.

RE Commonly used to mean *in regard to* or *regarding*.

Read Only Memory (ROM) A set of memory chips located on the motherboard that stores data and instructions that cannot be changed or erased; it holds all the instructions the computer needs to start up.

Reading Pane In Outlook, a window in which you can preview an e-mail message without actually opening it.

Recognizer A purple dotted underscore beneath a date or address indicating that the information could be placed into another Microsoft Office application program such as Outlook.

Record All of the categories of data pertaining to one person, place, thing, event, or idea.

Record selector The bar on the left side of a form with which you can select the entire record.

Record selector box The small box at the left of a record in datasheet view which, when clicked, selects the entire record.

Record source The tables or queries that provide the underlying data for a report.

Recycle Bin A storage area for files that have been deleted; files can be recovered from the Recycle Bin or permanently removed.

References Within a report or research paper, a notation to indicate information that has been taken from another source; also in APA style, the title on the page that lists the sources used in the document.

Referential integrity A set of rules that Access uses to ensure that the data between related tables is valid.

Refresh rate The speed at which the pixels are reilluminated, measured in cycles per second and expressed as hertz (Hz).

Relational database A type of database in which the tables in the database can relate or connect to other tables through common fields.

Relationship An association that is established between two tables using common fields.

Relative cell reference In a formula, the address of a cell based on the relative position of the cell that contains the formula and the cell referred to.

Reminder A small dialog box that displays in the middle of the Outlook screen that is used to remind you of a pending appointment or task.

Report A database object that summarizes the fields and records from a table, or from a query, in an easy-to-read format suitable for printing.

Report footer Information printed once at the end of a report; use to print report totals or other summary information for the entire report.

Report header Information printed once at the beginning of a report; used for logos, titles, and dates.

Report tool The Access feature that creates a report with one mouse click, and which displays all the fields and records from the record source that you choose—a quick way to look at the underlying data.

Report Wizard An Access feature with which you can create a report by answering a series of questions; Access designs the report based on your answers.

Resolution The measurement used to assess the clarity of an image on a monitor; determined by pixel density.

Restore Using the Restore Down button to return a window to the size it was before it was maximized.

Restore point A record created by Windows XP for all of a computer's system settings.

Ribbon (Outlook) The area along the top of an Outlook form that contains frequently needed commands.

Ribbon The user interface in Office 2007 that groups the commands for performing related tasks on tabs across the upper portion of the program window.

Rich Text Format A universal document format that can be read by nearly all word processing programs, and that retains most text and paragraph formatting.

Right alignment Text aligned on the right margin, leaving the left margin uneven.

Right-click The action of clicking the right mouse button.

Ring (or token-ring) topology A networking configuration in which all devices are set up in a circular layout; data flows in a circular fashion, in one direction only.

ROM See Read only memory.

Root folder The first folder from which all other folders branch.

Rotate handle A handle on a selected image that can be dragged to rotate the image to any angle.

Rounding A procedure in which you determine which digit at the right of the number will be the last digit displayed and then increase it by one if the next digit to its right is 5, 6, 7, 8, or 9.

Row A horizontal group of cells in a worksheet.

Row headings The numbers along the left side of an Excel worksheet that designate the row numbers.

Ruler (Word) Displays the location of paragraph margins, indents, and tab stops for the selected paragraph.

Run The process in which Access searches the records in the table(s) included in a query design, finds the records that match the specified criteria, and then displays those records in a datasheet; only the fields that have been included in the query design display.

S-video port A port used to connect ancillary video equipment, such as a television or projector to a computer.

Salutation The greeting line of a business letter.

Sans serif font A font with no lines or extensions on the ends of characters.

Scanners Input devices used to convert hard copy documents or images into digital files.

Screen (or window) In a graphical user interface, the rectangular box that contains the program displayed on the monitor.

ScreenTip A small box that displays useful information when you perform various mouse actions such as pointing to screen elements or dragging.

Scroll box The box in the vertical and horizontal scroll bars that can be dragged to reposition the document on the screen.

Scroll box (Excel) The box in the vertical and horizontal scroll bars that can be dragged to reposition the worksheet on the screen.

Scroll wheel A feature on some mouse pointing devices; rolling the wheel enables you to quickly move a page up or down within a window.

Scrolling The action of moving a pane or window vertically (up or down) or horizontally (side to side) to bring unseen areas into view.

Search Engines Software programs that search for keywords in files and documents or other Web sites found on the Internet.

Section bar A gray bar in a form or report that identifies and separates one section from another; used to select the section and to change the size of the adjacent section.

Sectors Wedge-shaped sections of a hard disk drive, each measured from the center point to the outer edge.

Select (Excel) Highlighting, by clicking or dragging with your mouse, one or more cells so that the selected cells can be edited, formatted, copied, or moved; selected cells are indicated by a dark border.

Select All box A box in the upper left corner of the worksheet grid that selects all the cells in a worksheet.

Select Query A database object that retrieves (selects) specific data from one or more tables and then displays the specified data in datasheet view.

Selecting text Highlighting text so that it can be formatted, deleted, copied, or moved.

Separator character A character used to identify column placement in text; usually a tab or a comma.

Serial port A type of port that sends data one bit at a time at speeds of up to 115 kilobits per second (Kbps).

Series A group of things that come one after another in succession; for example, January, February, March, and so on.

Serif A font design that includes small line extensions on the ends of the letters to guide the eye in reading from left to right.

Server In a client/server network, the computer that manages shared network resources and provides access to the client computer when requested.

Shape Style A combination of formatting effects that includes 3-D, glow, and bevel effects and shadows.

Shapes Drawing objects including lines, arrows, stars and banners, and ovals and rectangles that are used to help convey a message by showing process and by containing text.

Sheet tab The labels along the lower border of the workbook window that identify each worksheet.

Sheet tab scrolling buttons Buttons to the left of the sheet tabs used to display Excel sheet tabs that are not in view; used when there are more sheet tabs than will display in the space provided.

Shortcut menu A context-sensitive menu that displays commands and options relevant to the selected object.

Simple select query Another name for a select query.

Sizing handle A small square or circle in the corners and the middle of the sides of a graphic that can be used to increase or decrease the size of the graphic.

Sizing handles (Access) The small boxes around the edge of a control indicating the control is selected and that can be adjusted to resize the selected control.

Slide handouts Printed images of more than one slide on a sheet of paper.

Slide Sorter View A view useful for rearranging slides in which all of the slides in the presentation display as thumbnails.

Small caps A font effect, usually used in titles, that changes lowercase text into capital (uppercase) letters using a reduced font size.

SmartArt graphic A designer-quality visual representation of your information that you can create by choosing from among many different layouts to effectively community your message or ideas.

SmartArt Styles Combinations of formatting effects that are applied to diagrams.

Smartphones Cell phones with additional computing capabilities or the ability to access the Internet.

Soft copy Data or information displayed on a monitor.

Software patches Quick software fixes provided to resolve an error found in program code until a software update can be issued.

Software updates Small, downloadable software modules that repair errors identified in commercial program code.

Sorting The process of arranging data in a specific order based on the value in each field.

Sources A term used to describe a list of referenced works in a report or research paper, also referred to as Works Cited, Bibliography, or References, depending upon the report style.

Spam Junk or unsolicited email.

Speakers Output devices that allow the user to hear any auditory signals the computer sends.

Spin box A small box with an upward- and downward-pointing arrow that lets you move rapidly through a set of values by clicking.

Spin box arrows The upward- and downward-pointing arrows in a spin box.

Split bar The gray bar that indicates the location of the border between two Word windows.

Sponsored links Web sites that pay to be prominently displayed as results at a search engine site.

Spotlight The area in the opening Access program screen that displays content from Microsoft's Web site.

Spreadsheet Another name for a worksheet.

Spreadsheet software A program with which you perform calculations and numerical analyses.

Spyware Software designed to capture personal and confidential information that resides on a computer and then send it elsewhere.

Star topology A flexible and frequently used network configuration for businesses, in which nodes connect to a central communication device known as a switch.

Start button The button on the left side of the taskbar that is used to start programs, change system settings, find Windows help, or shut down the computer.

Statistical functions Pre-written formulas that analyze a group of measurements.

Status area Another name for the notification area on the right side of the taskbar.

Status bar The area along the lower edge of the program window that displays, on the left side, the current mode, page number, and document information, and on the right side, displays buttons to control how the window looks.

Status bar (Word) A horizontal bar at the bottom of the document window that displays, on the left side, the page and line number, word count, and the Proof button. On the right side, displays buttons to control the look of the window. The status bar can be customized to include other information.

Storage To retain data or information for future use.

Straight quote A quotation mark that uses straight, rather than curved, lines.

Style A set of formatting characteristics—such as line spacing, space after paragraphs, font, and font style—that can be applied to text, paragraphs, tables, or lists.

Styles Formats for paragraphs stored in one shortcut command.

Stylus An input device used to write on a tablet computer or PDA.

Subject line The line following the subject line in a business letter that states the purpose of the letter.

Submenu A second-level menu activated by selecting a menu option.

Subpoint Secondary-level information in a SmartArt graphic.

Subset A portion of the total records available.

Suite A collection of application software programs developed by the same manufacturer, bundled together and sold at a price that is usually less than the cost of purchasing each program individually.

SUM function A predefined formula that adds all the numbers in a selected range of cells.

Supercomputer A large, powerful computer typically devoted to specialized tasks.

Synonyms Words with the same meaning as a selected word.

System software The set of programs that enables a computer's hardware devices and program software to work together; it includes the operating system and utility programs.

System tray Another name for the notification area on the right side of the taskbar.

System unit The tower, box, or console that contains the critical hardware and electrical components of a computer.

Tab order The order in which the insertion point moves from one field to the next in a form when you press the Tab key.

Tab stop Specific locations on a line of text, marked on the Word ruler, to which you can move the insertion point by pressing the ⌜Tab⌟ key; used to align and indent text.

Table A format for information that organizes and presents text and data in columns and rows.

Table (Access) The Access object that stores your data organized in an arrangement of columns and rows.

Table area The upper pane of the Query window, which displays the field lists for tables that are used in the query.

Table design The number of fields, and the type of content within each field, in an Access table.

Table Style In Outlook, a format that lists the contents of a folder on a single page and provides limited information about each item.

Table style (Excel) A predefined set of formatting characteristics, including font, alignment, and cell shading.

Table style (PowerPoint) Formatting applied to an entire table so that it is consistent with the presentation theme.

Table template A pre-built table format for common topics such as contacts, issues, and tasks.

Tables and Views category An arrangement of objects in the Navigation Pane in which the objects are grouped by the table to which they are related.

Tablet computer A portable computer that features a screen that swivels and can be written on using advanced handwriting recognition software.

Tabs A feature of Internet Explorer 7.0 that allows multiple Web pages to be displayed at the same time without opening multiple browsers.

Task A personal or work-related activity that you want to track until it is complete.

Task Pane In Outlook, a pane, usually below the appointment area, that can be used to schedule tasks.

Task pane A window within a Microsoft Office application that allows you to enter options for completing a command.

Taskbar The area of the screen that displays the Start button and the name of any open documents.

Template The horizontal placement of text within a placeholder.

Template (Access) A pre-formatted database designed for a specific purpose.

Text box A movable, resizable container for text or graphics.

Text box control The graphical object on a form or report that displays the data from the underlying table or query; a text box control is known as a bound control because its source data comes from a table or a query.

Text format A universal document format that retains text and paragraph marks, but does not support any text or paragraph formatting.

Text string A sequence of characters, which when used in query criteria, much be matched.

Text wrapping The manner in which text displays around an object.

Theme A predefined set of colors, fonts, lines, and fill effects that look good together and that can be applied to your entire document or to specific items

Theme (Excel) A predefined set of colors, fonts, lines, and fill effects that look good together and that can be applied to your entire workbook or to specific items—for example to a chart or table.

Thesaurus A research tool that provides a list of synonyms.

Three-color scale Compares a range of cells by using a gradation of three colors; the shades represent higher, middle, or lower values.

Thumb drive A small storage device that plugs into a computer USB port; also called a USB drive or a flash drive.

Thumbnail A miniature representation of the contents of a picture file.

Thumbnails (PowerPoint) Miniature images of each slide.

Title bar The bar at the top edge of the program window that indicates the name of the current workbook and the program name.

To-Do Bar A pane, usually along the right edge of the Outlook window, which provides quick access to daily tasks.

To-Do List pane In Outlook, a pane that displays an area to type a new task and a flag for each task.

Toggle button A button that can be turned on by clicking it once, and then turned off by clicking it again.

Toggle key A keyboard key that switches on or off each time it is pressed.

Token-ring topology See Ring topology.

Toolbars Rows of buttons, usually located under a menu bar, from which you can perform commands using a single click.

Top-level point The main text points in a SmartArt graphic.

Top/Bottom Rules A set of rules that enable you to apply conditional formatting to the highest and lowest values in a range of cells; for example, you can identify the top 5 selling products or the top 25 salaries in a personnel analysis.

Topology See Network topology.

Track Changes A Word tool that provides a visual indication of deletions, insertions, and formatting changes in a document.

Tracks Concentric circles on a hard disk drive.

Transitions The manner in which a slide appears or disappears during an onscreen slide show.

Trojan horse A program that appears to be useful or desirable, but acts maliciously in the background after installation.

Trust Center (Access) An area of the Access program where you can view the security and privacy settings for your Access installation.

Two-color scale Compares a range of cells by using a gradation of two colors.

Two-variable data table A data table that changes the values in two cells.

Type argument An optional argument in the PMT function that assumes that the payment will be made at the end of each time period.

Unbound control A term used to describe a control that does not have a source of data.

Underlying formula The formula entered in a cell and visible only on the Formula Bar.

Underlying value The data that displays in the Formula Bar.

Uniform Resource Locator (URL) The unique address used to locate a Web page or Web site.

Universal serial bus (USB) port A versatile port used to connect a wide array of peripheral devices to a computer.

USB drive A small storage device that plugs into a computer USB port; also called a thumb drive or a flash drive.

User interface The features of a computer operating system that enable you to interact with the computer.

Utility program A component of system software, typically a small program used to perform routine maintenance and housekeeping tasks for the computer.

Value Another name for constant value.

Value after increase = base x percent for new value Formula for calculating the value after an increase by multiplying the original value—the base—by the percent for new value (see the *Percent for new value* formula).

Value axis A numerical scale on the left side of a chart that shows the range of numbers for the data points; also referred to as the Y-axis.

Vertical scroll bar The bar at the right side of a window that enables you to move up and down to view information that extends beyond the top and bottom of the screen.

Vertical window split box A small box on the vertical scroll bar with which you can split the window into two vertical views of the same document.

View options (Word) Area on the right side of the status bar that contains buttons for viewing the document in Print Layout, Full Screen Reading, Web Layout, Master Document Tools, or Draft views, and also displays controls to Zoom Out and Zoom In.

View options Buttons on the right side of the status bar for viewing in normal, page layout view, or page break preview; also displays controls for zoom out and zoom in.

Views Ways to look at similar information in different formats and arrangements

Virus Malicious code or program, usually installed on a computer without the user's knowledge or permission.

Volatile Temporary storage, as in random access memory (RAM); data is erased when power is shut down.

Volatile (Excel) A term used to describe an Excel function that is subject to change each time the workbook is reopened; for example, the NOW function updates itself to the current date and time each time the workbook is opened.

WAN See Wide area network.

Web browser Software that enables you to use the Web and navigate from page to page and site to site.

Web Layout view A document view that shows how the document would look if viewed with a Web browser.

Web page A document on the World Wide Web that displays as a screen with associated links, frames, pictures, and other features of interest.

Web site A group of related Web pages published to a specific location on the World Wide Web.

What-if analysis The process of changing the values in cells to see how those changes affect the outcome of formulas in your worksheet.

Wide area network (WAN) A network composed of local area networks connected over long distances.

Wildcard A character, such as an asterisk, that can be used to match any number of characters in a file search.

Wildcard character In a query, a character that serves as a placeholder for one or more unknown characters in your criteria.

Window A box or screen that displays information or a program.

Windows See Microsoft Windows.

Wireless network A network that connects using radio waves instead of wires or cable.

Wizard A feature in Microsoft Office programs that walks you step by step through a process.

Word document window Displays the active document.

Word processing software A program used to create and edit written documents such as papers, letters, and resumes.

WordArt A feature that applies combinations of decorative formatting to text, including shadows, reflections, and 3-D effects, as well as changing the line and fill color of text.

Wordpad A simple word processing program that comes with Windows XP.

Wordwrap The feature that moves text from the right edge of a paragraph to the beginning of the next line as necessary to fit within the margins.

Work week A calendar option that shows only the weekdays, Monday through Friday.

Workbook An Excel file that contains one or more worksheets.

Workbook-level buttons Buttons at the far right of the Ribbon tabs used to minimize or restore a displayed workbook.

Works Cited A term used to describe a list of referenced works placed at the end of a research paper or report when using the MLA Style.

Worksheet The primary document that you use in Excel to store and work with data, and which is formatted as a pattern of uniformly spaced horizontal and vertical lines.

Worksheet grid The area of the Excel window that displays the columns and rows that intersect to form the cells of the worksheet.

Worm A program that is able to replicate and spread from computer to computer without human interaction.

Writer's identification The name and title of the author of a letter, placed near the bottom of the letter, under the complimentary closing.

X-axis Another name for the category axis.

Y-axis Another name for the value axis.

Zip drive A magnetic storage device used to save and retrieve data on Zip disks.

Zombie A computer that is controlled remotely and can be used to help spread viruses, spyware, and spam.

Zoom The action of increasing or decreasing the viewing area of the screen.

Index

The CD symbol represents Index entries found on the CD (See CD file name for page numbers).

animation effects *(continued)*
   in slide shows, 1088–1096
      chart animation, 1113–1114
      exercises, 1119, 1127, 1132, 1135, 1137
      SmartArt animation, 1095–1096
animation list, custom, 1090
APA style. *See* American Psychological Association style
arguments, 533. *See also* functions
   Fv, 565
   optional in PMT function, 565
   Type, 565
arithmetic operators, 393–394
Arrange button, 293, 314
arrow keys, moving objects with, 1007
ascending order (sort), 724–725, 752
aspect ratio, 42–44, 270
asterisk [*] wildcard, 766
attachments, 630
Auto Fill, 347–348
   Options button, 347, 364, 396, 479
AutoComplete
   Excel, 346
   Word, 7
AutoCorrect
   Excel, 350
   Word, 123–126, 147
      button, 46
      shortcuts, 126
AutoCorrect Options button, 111–112
AutoFit Column Width, 367, 391, 476, 1148, 1173
AutoFormat, 849
AutoFormat As You Type, 110–113, 208, 221
AutoNumber, 630
AutoSum button, 361, 532, 582
AutoText, ❷ 140
AVERAGE function, 534–535
AVG function, 772–774. *See also* queries
Axes group, 380, 412
Axis Label dialog box, 489, 502

B

backgrounds, slides, 1080–1087.
   fill color, 1086–1087
   hiding graphics, 1081–1082
   pictures in, 1082–1086
   resetting, 1086–1087
   style, 1080–1081
Backspace command, 101
Backspace key, 15
Baltimore Area Job Fair, 816
bar charts, ❷ 403
bar tab, 188
base, 477
Bell Orchid Hotel Group
   Access project, 710
   Excel projects, 443, 528, 617
   PowerPoint projects, 991, 1075, 1161
   Word projects, 83, 172, 258, 332
Between. . . And comparison operator, 757–759
Bibliography, 128, 137
black slides, 922
Blank Database button, 619
blank databases, 618
Blank document button, 31
blank lines, insertion of, 7–8

Blank Report tool, 851–854
blue wavy lines, 43
body font, 1087
bold font style, 23–24, 371
bold italic font style, 371
book citations, 133, 135, 148, 152, 162
Border button, 274
borders
   page, 186–187
   paragraph, 273–275
   Top and Double Bottom, 369, 400, 412, 416, 425, 431, 466, 470, 498, 505
   Word table, 215–216
Borders and Shading dialog box, 186, 215, 226, 231, 240, 273–275, 305, 316, 320
Borders arrow, 369
bound, 821
bound control, 828
Breaks gallery, 269
browsers, Web, 294
Building block, ❷ 140
bullet character symbols, 115, 1001
bulleted levels, 928
bulleted lists, 109–110, 145
   in slides, 997
      changing to numbered lists, 999
      SmartArt in, 1037
      style modification, 999–1001
Bullets gallery, 115–117, 1000
Business Communication Process and Product, Fourth Edition (Guffey), 8
Business Running Cases, ❷ *See also* Group Business Running Cases
   Access, 701, 805, 903
   Excel, 433, 518, 607
   PowerPoint, 982, 1064, 1151
   Word, 73, 163, 247, 322
buttons. *See* specific names of *buttons*

C

calculated controls, 861
calculated fields in queries, 768–772
calculations
   on Excel status bar, 362
   Excel worksheets, 354, 357
   of payment options in data tables, 572–575
   percent increase or decrease, 483
   of percentages, 395, 481
   value after increase, 481–483
Cambria font, 370
caret, 471, 499
category axis, 375
category labels, 374, 1107
cell references, 342, 1107
   absolute, 394–397
   relative, 364, 384–385
cells (Excel), 336
   active, 342
   addresses, 342
   Clear Formats in, 453, 496, 504, 511, 513, 515
   clearing, 453–454
   content, 345, 453–457
   dates in, 451–453
   formats, 453, 479–481
   numbers edited in, 361–362
   ranges, 342

Q

themes *(continued)*
  PowerPoint presentation, 939
  Word, 21
There's More You Can Do!. *See* **Try It! exercises**
Thesaurus (PowerPoint), 932. *See also* **dictionary**
three-color scales, ● 577
thumbnails, 920
time. *See* **date/time**
time number format, 366
timing options, slide show, 1091–1095
Title and Text, 927
title bar
  Access, 620
  Excel, 337
  PowerPoint, 920
  Word, 4–5
titles, for worksheet columns/rows, 390–391
toggle buttons, 6, 113, 371, 937
Toggle Filter button, 840, 843
Top and Double Bottom Border, 369, 400, 412, 416,
  425, 431, 466, 471, 498, 505
Top/Bottom Rules, ● 576
top-level points, 292
tracking changes in Word documents, 299
transitions, slide, 922, 1019–1021, 1043, 1050, 1055,
  1058, 1061
Trust Center, 715
Try It! exercises ●
  charts in Word documents, 221
  charts type changing, 404
  comments/tracking changes in documents, 299
  Quick Part gallery entry, 139
  Rich Text Format, 53
  text format, 53
turning off/ending lists, 113
two-color scales, ● 577
two-variable data tables, 570–572
Type argument, 565
Type your text here **box, 291, 294, 308**

U

unbound control, 828
underline font style, 23
underlying
  formulas, 359
  values, 353–354
underscore characters, 11–12, 339, 621, 924
undo action, 99, 105–106, 145, 355, 1028
unfreezing/freezing panes, 550–551

V

value after increase = base × percent for new value,
  481
value after increase calculations, 481–483
value axis, 374
values, 344
  constant, 345
  displayed, 353, 387
  underlying, 353–354
Var function, 772
Vertical Arrow List, 291
vertical scroll bar, 4–5, 33
vertical window split box, 340
View buttons, 920
View Ruler button, 89
View Side by Side button, 39

viewing reports, 669–670
views
  Access, 634
    Datasheet, 624, 634
    Design, 624, 634–635, 828–832
    Layout, 819, 832–836, 847–851
  Excel
    Normal, 385
    options, 337
    Page Layout, 382
  Full Screen Reading, 36
  PowerPoint
    Normal, 925
    Slide Sorter, 952–953, 967, 973, 977, 980
  Word, 35–36
    Draft, 36
    Full Screen Reading, 36
    of keyboard shortcuts, 24
    options, 5
    Outline, 36
    Print Layout, 4, 36
    Web Layout, 36
volatile, 549

W

Web browsers, 294
Web Layout
  button, 295, 308, 314
  view, 36
Web pages
  documents as, 294–298, 309, 314, 316, 318, 321
  Single File, 296, 309, 314, 316, 318, 321, 328
  Zoom slider for, 295–296
Web sites
  citations, 135, 148, 154, 161
  Gardening Web Sites project 4N, 328
Weekly Sales integration project-17A, 1185–1190
What-If Analysis, 476–486, 497. *See also*
  Goal Seek
  exercises, 500, 507, 513, 515
  tools, 566
Where function, 773
wildcard characters, 766
  asterisk [*], 766, ● , 813
  in queries, 766–767
  question mark [?], 767
window elements
  Access, 619–620, 623
  Excel/Excel workbook, 336–338, 340
  PowerPoint, 919–920
  Word/Word document, 4–5
Wizards, 648
  Form, 826–828
  Import Spreadsheet, 751
  Lookup, 630
  Mail Merge, 275–283
  Report, 854–858
  Simple Query, 648–651
Word 2007
  Business Running Cases, ● 73, 163, 247, 322
  dictionary, 9
  fill in blanks, 56, 142, 224, 302
  GO! Fix It, 74, 164, 248–249, 323–324
  GO! with Help, 82, 171, 257, 331
  Group Business Running Cases, 83, 172, 258, 332
  Help feature, 51–53
  key terms, 54, 140, 222, 300

SINGLE PC LICENSE AGREEMENT AND LIMITED WARRANTY

READ THIS LICENSE CAREFULLY BEFORE OPENING THIS PACKAGE. BY OPENING THIS PACKAGE, YOU ARE AGREEING TO THE TERMS AND CONDITIONS OF THIS LICENSE. IF YOU DO NOT AGREE, DO NOT OPEN THE PACKAGE. PROMPTLY RETURN THE UNOPENED PACKAGE AND ALL ACCOMPANYING ITEMS TO THE PLACE YOU OBTAINED THEM. *THESE TERMS APPLY TO ALL LICENSED SOFTWARE ON THE DISK EXCEPT THAT THE TERMS FOR USE OF ANY SHAREWARE OR FREEWARE ON TH E DISKETTES ARE AS SET FORTH IN THE ELECTRONIC LICENSE LOCATED ON THE DISK:*

1. GRANT OF LICENSE and OWNERSHIP: The enclosed computer programs ("Software") are licensed, not sold, to you by Prentice-Hall, Inc. ("We" or the "Company") and in consideration of your purchase or adoption of the accompanying Company textbooks and/or other materials, and your agreement to these terms. We reserve any rights not granted to you. You own only the disk(s) but we and/or our licensors own the Software itself. This license allows you to use and display your copy of the Software on a single computer (i.e., with a single CPU) at a single location for academic use only, so long as you comply with the terms of this Agreement. You may make one copy for back up, or transfer your copy to another CPU, provided that the Software is usable on only one computer.

2. RESTRICTIONS: You may not transfer or distribute the Software or documentation to anyone else. Except for backup, you may not copy the documentation or the Software. You may not network the Software or otherwise use it on more than one computer or computer terminal at the same time. You may not reverse engineer, disassemble, decompile, modify, adapt, translate, or create derivative works based on the Software or the Documentation. You may be held legally responsible for any copying or copyright infringement which is caused by your failure to abide by the terms of these restrictions.

3. TERMINATION: This license is effective until terminated. This license will terminate automatically without notice from the Company if you fail to comply with any provisions or limitations of this license. Upon termination, you shall destroy the Documentation and all copies of the Software. All provisions of this Agreement as to limitation and disclaimer of warranties, limitation of liability, remedies or damages, and our ownership rights shall survive termination.

4. DISCLAIMER OF WARRANTY: THE COMPANY AND ITS LICENSORS MAKE NO WARRANTIES ABOUT THE SOFTWARE, WHICH IS PROVIDED "AS-IS." IF THE DISK IS DEFECTIVE IN MATERIALS OR WORKMANSHIP, YOUR ONLY REMEDY IS TO RETURN IT TO THE COMPANY WITHIN 30 DAYS FOR REPLACEMENT UNLESS THE COMPANY DETERMINES IN GOOD FAITH THAT THE DISK HAS BEEN MISUSED OR IMPROPERLY INSTALLED, REPAIRED, ALTERED OR DAMAGED. THE COMPANY DISCLAIMS ALL WARRANTIES, EXPRESS OR IMPLIED, INCLUDING WITHOUT LIMITATION, THE IMPLIED WARRANTIES OF MERCHANTABILITY AND FITNESS FOR A PARTICULAR PURPOSE. THE COMPANY DOES NOT WARRANT, GUARANTEE OR MAKE ANY REPRESENTATION REGARDING THE ACCURACY, RELIABILITY, CURRENTNESS, USE, OR RESULTS OF USE, OF THE SOFTWARE.

5. LIMITATION OF REMEDIES AND DAMAGES: IN NO EVENT, SHALL THE COMPANY OR ITS EMPLOYEES, AGENTS, LICENSORS OR CONTRACTORS BE LIABLE FOR ANY INCIDENTAL, INDIRECT, SPECIAL OR CONSEQUENTIAL DAMAGES ARISING OUT OF OR IN CONNECTION WITH THIS LICENSE OR THE SOFTWARE, INCLUDING, WITHOUT LIMITATION, LOSS OF USE, LOSS OF DATA, LOSS OF INCOME OR PROFIT, OR OTHER LOSSES SUSTAINED AS A RESULT OF INJURY TO ANY PERSON, OR LOSS OF OR DAMAGE TO PROPERTY, OR CLAIMS OF THIRD PARTIES, EVEN IF THE COMPANY OR AN AUTHORIZED REPRESENTATIVE OF THE COMPANY HAS BEEN ADVISED OF THE POSSIBILITY OF SUCH DAMAGES. SOME JURISDICTIONS DO NOT ALLOW THE LIMITATION OF DAMAGES IN CERTAIN CIRCUMSTANCES, SO THE ABOVE LIMITATIONS MAY NOT ALWAYS APPLY.

6. GENERAL: THIS AGREEMENT SHALL BE CONSTRUED IN ACCORDANCE WITH THE LAWS OF THE UNITED STATES OF AMERICA AND THE STATE OF NEW YORK, APPLICABLE TO CONTRACTS MADE IN NEW YORK, AND SHALL BENEFIT THE COMPANY, ITS AFFILIATES AND ASSIGNEES. This Agreement is the complete and exclusive statement of the agreement between you and the Company and supersedes all proposals, prior agreements, oral or written, and any other communications between you and the company or any of its representatives relating to the subject matter. If you are a U.S. Government user, this Software is licensed with "restricted rights" as set forth in subparagraphs (a)-(d) of the Commercial Computer-Restricted Rights clause at FAR 52.227-19 or in subparagraphs (c)(1)(ii) of the Rights in Technical Data and Computer Software clause at DFARS 252.227-7013, and similar clauses, as applicable.

Should you have any questions concerning this agreement or if you wish to contact the Company for any reason, please contact in writing:

Multimedia Production
Higher Education Division
Prentice-Hall, Inc.
1 Lake Street
Upper Saddle River NJ 07458